Poetry
Criticism

Guide to Gale Literary Criticism Series

For criticism on	Consult these Gale series
Authors now living or who died after December 31, 1959	*CONTEMPORARY LITERARY CRITICISM (CLC)*
Authors who died between 1900 and 1959	*TWENTIETH-CENTURY LITERARY CRITICISM (TCLC)*
Authors who died between 1800 and 1899	*NINETEENTH-CENTURY LITERATURE CRITICISM (NCLC)*
Authors who died between 1400 and 1799	*LITERATURE CRITICISM FROM 1400 TO 1800 (LC)* *SHAKESPEAREAN CRITICISM (SC)*
Authors who died before 1400	*CLASSICAL AND MEDIEVAL LITERATURE CRITICISM (CMLC)*
Black writers of the past two hundred years	*BLACK LITERATURE CRITICISM (BLC)*
Authors of books for children and young adults	*CHILDREN'S LITERATURE REVIEW (CLR)*
Dramatists	*DRAMA CRITICISM (DC)*
Hispanic writers of the late nineteenth and twentieth centuries	*HISPANIC LITERATURE CRITICISM (HLC)*
Native North American writers and orators of the eighteenth, nineteenth, and twentieth centuries	*NATIVE NORTH AMERICAN LITERATURE (NNAL)*
Poets	*POETRY CRITICISM (PC)*
Short story writers	*SHORT STORY CRITICISM (SSC)*
Major authors from the Renaissance to the present	*WORLD LITERATURE CRITICISM, 1500 TO THE PRESENT (WLC)*

Poetry Criticism

*Excerpts from Criticism of the Works
of the Most Significant and Widely
Studied Poets of World Literature*

VOLUME 14

Nancy Dziedzic
Christine Slovey

Editors

GALE

STAFF

Nancy Dziedzic, Christine Slovey, *Editors*

Laurie DiMauro, Jennifer Gariepy, Margaret Haerens, Jeff Hill, Drew Kalasky,
Julie K. Karmazin, Thomas Ligotti, Marie Rose Napierkowski, Mary K. Ruby
Associate Editors

Marlene S. Hurst, *Permissions Manager*
Margaret A. Chamberlain, Maria Franklin, *Permissions Specialists*

Susan Brohman, Diane Cooper, Michele Lonoconus, Maureen Puhl,
Shalice Shah, Kimberly F. Smilay, Barbara A. Wallace,
Permissions Associates

Sarah Chesney, Edna Hedblad, Margaret McAvoy-Amato,
Tyra Y. Phillips, Lori Schoenenberger, Rita Valazquez,
Permissions Assistants

Victoria B. Cariappa, *Research Manager*

Julie C. Daniel, Tamara C. Nott, Michele P. Pica,
Norma Sawaya, Cheryl L. Warnock, *Research Associates*

Mary Beth Trimper, *Production Director*
Deborah Milliken, *Production Assistant*

Sherrell Hobbs, *Macintosh Artist*
Randy Bassett, *Image Database Supervisor*
Robert Duncan, *Scanner Operator*
Pamela Hayes, *Photography Coordinator*

Library of Congress Catalog Card Number 91-118494
ISBN 0-7876-0473-9
ISSN 1052-4851

Printed in the United States of America

10 9 8 7 6 5 4 3 2 1

Contents

Preface vii

Acknowledgments xi

Preface

A Comprehensive Information Source on World Poetry

P *oetry Criticism (PC)* provides substantial critical excerpts and biographical information on poets throughout the world who are most frequently studied in high school and undergraduate college courses. Each *PC* entry is supplemented by biographical and bibliographical material to help guide the user to a fuller understanding of the genre and its creators. Although major poets and literary movements are covered in such Gale Literary Criticism Series as *Contemporary Literary Criticism (CLC)*, *Twentieth-Century Literary Criticism (TCLC)*, *Nineteenth-Century Literature Criticism (NCLC)*, *Literature Criticism from 1400 to 1800 (LC)*, and *Classical and Medieval Literature Criticism (CMLC)*, *PC* offers more focused attention on poetry than is possible in the broader, survey-oriented entries on writers in these Gale series. Students, teachers, librarians, and researchers will find that the generous excerpts and supplementary material provided by *PC* supply them with vital information needed to write a term paper on poetic technique, examine a poet's most prominent themes, or lead a poetry discussion group.

Coverage

In order to reflect the influence of tradition as well as innovation, poets of various nationalities, eras, and movements are represented in every volume of *PC*. Each author entry presents a historical survey of the critical response to that author's work; the length of an entry reflects the amount of critical attention that the author has received from critics writing in English and from foreign critics in translation. Since many poets have inspired a prodigious amount of critical explication, *PC* is necessarily selective, and the editors have chosen the most significant published criticism to aid readers and students in their research. In order to provide these important critical pieces, the editors will sometimes reprint essays that have appeared in previous volumes of Gale's Literary Criticism Series. Such duplication, however, never exceeds fifteen percent of a *PC* volume.

Organization

Each *PC* author entry consists of the following components:

- **Author Heading:** the name under which the author wrote appears at the beginning of the entry, followed by birth and death dates. If the author wrote consistently under a pseudonym, the pseudonym will be listed in the author heading and his or her legal name given in parentheses in the lines immediately preceding the Introduction. Uncertainty as to birth or death dates is indicated by question marks.

- **Introduction:** a biographical and critical essay introduces readers to the author and the critical discussions surrounding his or her work.

- **Author Portrait:** a photograph or illustration of the author is included when available. Most entries also feature illustrations of people and places pertinent to an author's career, as well as holographs of manuscript pages and dust jackets.

- **Principal Works:** the author's most important works are identified in a list ordered chronologically by first publication dates. The first section comprises poetry collections and book-length poems. The second section gives information on other major works by the author. For foreign authors, original foreign-language publication information is provided, as well as the best and most complete English-language editions of their works.

- **Criticism:** critical excerpts chronologically arranged in each author entry provide perspective on changes in critical evaluation over the years. All individual titles of poems and poetry collections by the author featured in the entry are printed in boldface type to enable a reader to ascertain without difficulty the works under discussion. For purposes of easy identification, the critic's name and the publication date of the essay are given at the beginning of each piece of criticism. Unsigned criticism is preceded by the title of the journal in which it originally appeared. Publication information (such as publisher names and book prices) and parenthetical numerical references (such as footnotes or page and line references to specific editions of a work) have been deleted at the editor's discretion to enable smoother reading of the text.

- **Explanatory Notes:** introductory comments preface each critical excerpt, providing several types of useful information, including: the reputation of a critic, the importance of a work of criticism, and the specific type of criticism (biographical, psychoanalytic, historical, etc.).

- **Author Commentary:** insightful comments from the authors themselves and excerpts from author interviews are included when available.

- **Bibliographical Citations:** information preceding each piece of criticism guides the interested reader to the original essay or book.

- **Further Reading:** bibliographic references accompanied by descriptive notes at the end of each entry suggest additional materials for study of the author. Boxed material following the Further Reading provides references to other biographical and critical series published by Gale.

Other Features

Cumulative Author Index: comprises all authors who have appeared in Gale's Literary Criticism Series, along with cross-references to such Gale biographical series as *Contemporary Authors* and *Dictionary of Literary Biography*. This cumulated index enables the user to locate an author within the various series.

Cumulative Nationality Index: includes all authors featured in *PC*, arranged alphabetically under their respective nationalities.

Cumulative Title Index: lists in alphabetical order all individual poems, book-length poems, and collection titles contained in the *PC* series. Titles of poetry collections and separately published poems are printed in italics, while titles of individual poems are printed in roman type with quotation marks. Each title is followed by the author's name and the volume and page number corresponding to the location of commentary on specific works. English-language translations of original foreign-language titles are cross-referenced to the foreign titles so that all references to discussion of a work are combined in one listing.

Citing *Poetry Criticism*

When writing papers, students who quote directly from any volume in the Literary Criticism Series may use the following general formats to footnote reprinted criticism. The first example pertains to material drawn from periodicals, the second to material reprinted from books:

[1]David Daiches, "W. H. Auden: The Search for a Public," *Poetry* LIV (June 1939), 148-56; excerpted and reprinted in *Poetry Criticism*, Vol. 1, ed. Robyn V. Young (Detroit: Gale Rescarch, 1990), pp. 7-9.

[2]Pamela J. Annas, *A Disturbance in Mirrors: The Poetry of Sylvia Plath* (Greenwood Press, 1988); excerpted and reprinted in *Poetry Criticism*, Vol. 1, ed. Robyn V. Young (Detroit: Gale Research, 1990), pp. 410-14.

Comments Are Welcome

Readers who wish to suggest authors to appear in future volumes, or who have other suggestions, are cordially invited to contact the editors.

Acknowledgments

The editors wish to thank the copyright holders of the excerpted criticism included in this volume and the permissions managers of many book and magazine publishing companies for assisting us in securing reprint rights. We are also grateful to the staffs of the Detroit Public Library, the Library of Congress, the University of Detroit Mercy Library, Wayne State University Purdy/Kresge Library Complex, and the University of Michigan Libraries for making their resources available to us. Following is a list of the copyright holders who have granted us permission to reprint material in this volume of *PC*. Every effort has been made to trace copyright, but if omissions have been made, please let us know.

COPYRIGHTED EXCERPTS IN *PC*, VOLUME 14, WERE REPRINTED FROM THE FOLLOWING PERIODICALS:

The American Book Review, v. 9, September-October, 1987. © 1987 by The American Book Review. Reprinted by permission of the publisher.—*The American Poetry Review*, v. 7, March-April, 1978, for "May Swenson and the Shapes of Speculation" by Alicia Ostriker. Copyright © 1978 by World Poetry, Inc.; v. 23, September-October, 1994, for "Life's Miracles: The Poetry of May Swenson" by Grace Schulman. Copyright © 1994 by World Poetry, Inc. Both reprinted by permission of the respective authors.—*The Atlantic Monthly*, v. 221, February, 1968, for "New Poetry: The Generation of the Twenties" by Peter Davison. Copyright 1968 by The Atlantic Monthly Company Boston, MA. Reprinted by permission of the author.—*Australian Literary Studies*, v. 3, May, 1968, for "Some Poems of Judith Wright" by James McAuley. Reprinted by permission of the publisher and the author.—*Brick: A Journal of Reviews*, n. 23, Winter, 1985, for "Not in Time" by bp Nichol. Reprinted by permission of the Literary Estate of bp Nichol.—*Canadian Literature*, n. 56, Spring, 1973, for "A Dash for the Border" by Stephen Scobie; n. 60, Spring, 1974, for "Bissett's Best" by Stephen Scobie; n. 66, Autumn, 1975, for "Animate Imaginings" by Mike Doyle; n. 101, Summer, 1984 for "Free Subject" by Ann Mandel. All reprinted by permission of the respective authors.—*Canadian Poetry*, n. 34, Spring-Summer, 1994, for "Self Selected/Selected Self: Bill Bissett's 'Beyond Even Faithful Legends'" by Don Precosky. © 1994 by the author. Reprinted by permission of the publisher and the author.—*Commentary*, v. 57, June, 1974 for "Mandelstam's Witness" by Robert Alter. Copyright © 1974 by the American Jewish Committee. All rights reserved. Reprinted by permission of the author.—*Concerning Poetry*, v. 16, Fall, 1983. Copyright © 1983, Western Washington University. Reprinted by permission of the publisher.—*The Dalhousie Review*, v. 50, Spring, 1970, for "The Young Poets and the Little Presses" by Douglas Barbour. Reprinted by permission of the publisher and the author.—*ELH*, v. 35, December, 1968 for "The Figure of the Poet in Shelley" by Judith S. Chernaik. Copyright © 1968 by The Johns Hopkins University Press. All rights reserved. Reprinted by permission of the publisher and the author.—*Essays on Canadian Writing*, n. 5, Fall, 1976. © 1976 Essays on Canadian Writing Ltd. Reprinted by permission of the publisher.—*The Hollins Critic*, v. XVIII, December, 1981. Copyright 1981 by Hollins College. Reprinted by permission of the publisher.—*The Journal of Commonwealth Literature*, v. VI, June, 1971, for "The Crystal Glance of Love: Judith Wright as a Love Poet" by Devindra Kohli. Copyright by the author. Reprinted by permission of Hans Zell Publishers, an imprint of Bowker-Saur Ltd.—*The Kenyon Review*, n.s. v. XVI, Summer, 1994, for "A Mysterious and Lavish Power: How Things Continue to Take Place in the Work of May Swenson" by Sue Russell. Copyright 1994 by Kenyon College. All rights reserved. Reprinted by permission of the author.—*Melbourne Slavonic Studies*, n. 5-6, 1971. Reprinted by permission of the publisher.—*Modern Language Review*, v. 77, July, 1982, for "Two Poems by Marina Tsvetayeva from 'Posle Rossii'" by Barbara Heldt. © Modern Humanities Research Association, 1982. Reprinted by permission of the publisher and the author.—*New Letters*, v. 52, Winter-Spring, 1986, for an interview with Etheridge Knight by Ron Price. © Copyright 1986, The Curators of the University of Missouri. Reprinted by permission of the publisher, Etheridge Knight, and Ron Price.—*The New York Review of Books*, v. XXIX, April 15, 1982. Copyright © 1982, Nyrev Inc. Reprinted with permission from The New York Review of Books.—*The New York Times Book Review*, November 26, 1978; June 12, 1988; January 19, 1992. Copyright © 1978, 1988, 1992 by The New York Times Company. All reprinted by permission of the publisher.—*Nottingham French Studies*, v. 15, November, 1976. Reprinted by permission of the publisher.—*Obsidian*, v. VII, Summer-Winter, 1981, for "The Poet, the Poem, the People: Etheridge Knight's Aesthetic" by Craig Werner. Copyright © 1981 by Alvin Aubert. All rights reserved. Reprinted by permission of the author.—*Orbis Litterarum*, v. 46, 1991. Reprinted by permission of the

Bill Bissett
1939-

Canadian poet and performance artist.

INTRODUCTION

A prolific and innovative poet, Bissett has been a vital force in Canadian literature since the mid-1960s. In addition to penning numerous volumes of poetry, many of which he has illustrated and printed himself, he has performed his poetry for audiences internationally. Bissett is best known as a romantic, visionary poet whose disregard for rules of spelling, grammar, and syntax follows from his belief that institutions hamper human freedom and communal vitality.

Biographical Information

Bissett, who spells his name entirely in lowercase letters, was born in Halifax, Nova Scotia. He attended Dalhousie University for one year, then moved to Vancouver, British Columbia. There he briefly attended the University of British Columbia and held a variety of jobs before his marriage and the birth of his daughter. In 1966, Bissett published his first volume of poetry, *we sleep inside each other all,* and soon afterward cofounded his own publishing house, the blewointmentpress. *NOBODY OWNS TH EARTH* (1971), his first work with a major small press, was edited by the esteemed Canadian author Margaret Atwood. In the late 1970s, Bissett received attention in the mainstream press when his poetry became the subject of a controversy regarding the merit of certain works produced with the assistance of the Canada Council, a government body that distributes funding for the arts. The Bissett anthology *SELECTED POEMS: BEYOND EVEN FAITHFUL LEGENDS* was published in 1980. Since that time he has continued publishing and performing his works at festivals in North America and Europe.

concrete or "sound-vizual" pieces. *SELECTED POEMS,* which Bissett edited and arranged, offers a sampling from the first decade of his career. Prominent among his literary subjects is the search for religious experience through sexual connection, communal life, and natural surroundings. Of Bissett's publications since 1980, *Northern Birds in Color* (1981), *Seagull on Yonge Street* (1983), and *Canada Gees Mate for Life* (1985) are among the most admired.

Major Works

Bissett first gained attention with his collections *lebanon voices* (1967) and *awake in th red desert* (1968); the latter was accompanied by a recording of Bissett reading his work. These and other early works drew praise for their incorporation of chant and rejection of conventions of grammar and spelling. *NOBODY OWNS TH EARTH* contains some of his most celebrated poems against authoritarianism, while 1972's *pomes for yoshi* comprises a volume-length narrative about a troubled relationship. *MEDICINE my mouths on fire* (1974) includes an audio recording and contains several of his

Critical Reception

Throughout his career, Bissett has earned praise for his romantic vision and stylistic experiments, though even his most ardent admirers admit that his output has been uneven. During the Canada Council scandal, Bissett was scorned by some as an illiterate hippie getting a free ride from national arts funding. Yet many literary commentators find Bissett's idiosyncratic, fiercely individual style a continuation of the English Romantic tradition of William Blake, William Wordsworth, and W. B. Yeats—an inspiring effort to imagine humanity unconstrained by convention and authority.

PRINCIPAL WORKS

Poetry

we sleep inside each other all 1966
fires in th tempul OR th jinx shp nd othr trips 1966
The Gossamer Bedpan 1967; revised edition, 1974
lebanon voices 1967
what poetiks 1967
where is miss florence riddle? 1967
awake in th red desert 1968
OF TH LAND DIVINE SERVICE 1968
liberating skies 1969
lost angel mining company 1969
sunday work (?) 1969
s th story i to 1970
tuff shit 1970
blew trewz 1971
dragon fly 1971
drifting into war 1971
IBM 1971
NOBODY OWNS TH EARTH 1971
TH ICE BAG 1972
pomes for yoshi 1972
RUSH/WHAT FUCKAN THEORY 1972
th first sufi line 1973
pass th food release th spirit book 1973
living with th vishyun 1974
MEDICINE my mouths on fire 1974
space travl 1974
what 1974
yu can eat it at the opening 1974
th fifth sun 1975
image being 1975
stardust 1975
Venus 1975
an allusyun to macbeth 1976
plutonium missing 1976
th wind up tongue 1976
Sailor 1978
th first snow 1979
*SELECTED POEMS: BEYOND EVEN FAITHFUL LEG-
   ENDS* 1980
soul arrow 1980
Northern Birds in Color 1981
Seagull on Yonge Street 1983
Canada Gees Mate for Life 1985
ANIMAL UPROAR 1987
The Last Photo Uv the Human Soul 1993

CRITICISM

Douglas Barbour (essay date 1970)

SOURCE: "The Young Poets and the Little Presses," in *The Dalhousie Review,* Vol. 50, No. 1, Spring, 1970, pp. 112-16.

[*Barbour is a Canadian author and educator. In the following excerpt, he favorably reviews* OF TH LAND DIVINE SERVICE *and* lebanon voices.]

Nelson Ball has . . . published two recent volumes by Bill Bissett, a true West Coast hippie poet, if such a being exists. Bissett breaks all the rules and does not care. When he fails, which is often, there is nothing to say. But his successes are always worth while, and often very powerful. Bissett has been experimenting for a long time in what he, and a number of other young poets call the "borderblur" area of literature. *Of th [sic] Land Divine Service* contains some results of one area of that experimentation: chants, meant to be heard, rather than read on the page. Nevertheless, Ball has performed a real service here to anyone interested in poem-chants who might not have the chance to hear Bissett perform. They are the equivalent to a score for a symphony, but even that is useful. Besides, the ideas these poems reveal and the religious attitudes they contain are very interesting. *Lebanon Voices* is a long poem in three parts dedicated to the moon-goddess in whatever contemporary form she deigns to assume for the poet. It is an intriguing poem, despite the many difficulties inherent in Bissett's style and approach.

bp Nichol (essay date 1971)

SOURCE: "Not in Time," in *Brick: A Journal of Reviews,* No. 23, Winter, 1985, pp. 5-18.

[*Nichol is a Canadian poet. In the following excerpt from an essay that was written in 1971, he examines Bissett's attempt to evoke human breath in poetry, points out the influence of Gertrude Stein on his work, and discusses his resistance to conventional grammar and spelling.*]

in the early sixties out of the creative writing programme at ubc the tish group emerged with their insistence upon a poetry whose visual notation on the page was linked to & inseparable from the poets breath   how you see it on the page is as score for how it should be read   here they have brought the poem back to the music of the human body its breathing & reunited it with music from which for so long it seemed to have strayed

at the same time out of the painters studios & homes in the 4th & yew area in vancouver a different approach to the same concern was emerging in th work of most notably bill bissett but also lance farrell & martina clinton   in order to appreciate what bissett has accomplished in the years since his emergence it is necessary to take this concern with breath in a poetry which is an extension of the body & put it into a very broad perspective

the modern composer norman dello joio has said "notation is a primitive guide to music. The unimaginative are slaves to it, others see behind it" & the composer david behrman "a perfect notation is not one which documents exactly. If it were, today's technology would finally have provided the ideal notation—a tape recording or film of a correct performance. Notation is lively when it calls for a temporal result that can only be hinted at by its spatial systems, requiring more than an automaton to bring it to life."   & john cage commenting on a particular composers work in his *Notations* "He erased his own music but it remains visible, paler than what he later superimposed. Suggestion: the concert of his various decisions. In this case, greater carelessness would automatically produce a music of greater complexity."   now i have put these three quotes here to give you an introduction into an entirely different way of looking at the same area of concern we have already been talking about namely a poetry of breath and some way to notate it on the page

> when lance farrel martina nd i were disregarding the boxd margins back in the early 60's nd bein considerd hopeless by our friends nd fellow poets we didint know th word concrete or any *kind* of poetry we were writing into, that this is what we were expressing, that what we were experiencing was outside of the narrow margins so we carried that to where th poem was too nd it was tough and no one understood ovr th years thru blew ointment ganglia tlaloc marajuana papers labris approches etc we began to see all ovr th world that othrs were into it too get a poem from japan nd yu got to understand it cause it wasint basd on grammar or sentence type thot so yu were there too which is what you want to be there
>
> we fear the darkness but its cummin nd always turns into light
>
> writing what s now calld concrete sound borderblur poetry etc is why we enjoyd so much malnutrition etc for so many years so i feel a special fondness for it
>
> (bissett—undated letter)

> sort of groovy about this concrete thing 'cause *sort of* what i've been doing all along to little avail around here th others sum of them to see it, what it is, that distant fuzz, an then here it breaks of its own, guess there were others screaming loving telling of how they were seeing it all ovr the world, that we are not to be bound, nor is any audience, cum & go, free to as they wish in & out of th poem, fill it with what they will— spaces for *them*
>
> (undated letter)

what has from the first distinguished much canadian & american concrete [particularly the vancouver toronto niagara cleveland grouping (bissett, copithorne, levy, kryss, nichol, aylward, wagner, uu etc)] from the rest of the world movement has been a fascination with the primitive   by this i mean a fascination with chant   another way of looking at chant is as insistence the use of which term brings up the lady who is probably bissett's biggest influence & certainly his starting point gertrude stein   stein always made that distinction that tho in *the making of americans* she said everyone had repeating in them all the time she was to say later that in her way of writing about

it her writing was not so much repeating as insistent or rather   since here is the important distinction & why she used the word insistence   that rather everyone should realize that it was not repetition it was repeating & that of course behind repeating there is that something which is insisting itself   all of bissett's published works to date are illuminated with this insisting of certain things over & over again certain concerns & within that insistence an evolution of content concern context & conception   "gertrude stein went into what do i carry inside me so much of the time of her went over within myself working thru it ever since saw to yur letter" (undated letter)

in an unpublished essay titled "Joyce, Stein and the Single Vision" steve mccaffery has written

> gertrude stein showed us that imagery is a matter of syntax   james joyce showed us imagery is an event of mental association stein showed us that the image is of language and not showed us that the image is through language that is she did not think   the image as beyond the word but that images are a part of imagery and that imagery is a relationship of words to other words she knew that grammatical subordination prevents the single vision she knew that such subordination trapped the word in function and evil relationship   she saw that this could be wrong

bill bissett in a section of *S The Story I To* writes

> saying it
> ovr and ovr again, moving out, stepping out
> (in 200 words or less) & th endless night magic
> sound it yrself. yu can shout it. out
> correct spelling and grammar have nothing to do
> with clouds or mountains or thunder or th animals
> yu are and th glory of th musculd heart or all
> of the planets and eyes breathing in yr spine.
>
> & chant.

& a little later

> correct grammar   subject verb object   imperialism,
> th subject, king bullshit acts *on* victims   screw that

lets go back for a moment to looking at what stein meant by insistence

> If you think anything over and over and eventually in connection with it you are going to succeed or fail, succeeding and failing is repetition because you are always either succeeding or failing but any two moments of thinking it over is not repetition. Now you see that is where I differ from a great many people who say I repeat and they do not. They do not think their succeeding or failing is what makes repetition, in other words they do not think that what happens makes repetition but that it is the moment to moment emphasizing that makes repetition. Now I think the succeeding and failing is what makes the repetition not the moment to moment emphasizing that makes repetition. . . . There was the period of The Making of

Americans portraiture, when by listening and talking I conceived at every moment the existence of some one, and I put down each moment that I had the existence of that one inside me until I had completely emptied myself of this that I had had as a portrait of that one. This as I say made what has been called repetition but, and you will see, each sentence is just the difference in emphasis that inevitably exists in the successive moment of my containing within me the existence of that other one achieved by talking and listening inside in me and inside in that one. . . . As I said it was if you like, it was like a cinema picture made up of succession and each moment having its own emphasis that is its own difference and so there was the moving and the existence of each moment as it was in time.

(gertrude stein *Lectures in America*)

lets pause for a moment to refind bearings   shooting out a barrage of information to present the context in which bissetts work moves   stein said that for her her work was not repetitive that she was following the successive shifts in emphasis from moment to moment the longer she contained a thing inside her   mccaffery points out that imagery is a relationship of words to other words   "words appear to be names for things that arent there" (bissett—undated letter)   what bissett is saying then is that the rules that have governed language & hence the people who live within that language for the last 1000 years are no longer good enough

william carlos williams stated once in an article on james joyce

If to achieve truth we work with words purely, as a writer must, and all the words are dead or beautiful, how then shall we succeed any better than might a philosopher with dead abstractions? or their configurations? . . . There must be something new done with the words. Leave beauty out or, conceivably, one might begin again, one might break them up to let the staleness out of them.

bissett is expressing exactly the same concern when he says in a letter "what else can yu do with goddesses except (screw) make love to them i ask yew" & in **"The Caruso Poem"**

we have called
  so much
      sentimental
that we have
  very little
left
  perhaps nothing

but here is where bissett veers off from stein   stein was very concerned with keeping in control of what was happening

In the portraits that I did in that period of which I have just been speaking the later period considerably after the war the strictness of not letting remembering

mix itself with looking and listening and talking . . . this strictness perhaps weakened a little weakened a little because and that in a way was an astonishment to me, I found that I was for a little while very much taken with the beauty of the sounds as they came from me as I made them. This is a thing that may be at any time a temptation. . . . The strict discipline that I had given myself, the absolute refusal of never using a word that was not an exact word . . . resulted . . . in an extraordinary melody of words and a melody of excitement in knowing that I had done this thing. . . . This melody for a little while after rather got the better of me . . . But as I say I did begin to think that I was rather drunk with what I had done. And I am always one to prefer being sober. I must be sober. It is so much more exciting to be sober, to be exact and concentrated and sober.

(gertrude stein *Lectures in America*)

bissett's position is made very clear in **"The Caruso Poem"** where he states

you have a voice
      the galleries go clear
to the sky
      you must use it

& then after a cautionary note to the reader

listen closely
  to the dialogue / you
will know an aspect
  of what is

he goes on to say

the truth is
  the man does not
have the voice
  the voice has him

for bissett then that intoxication with sound is what he chose to follow   stein made the conscious decision to veer away to return to the concerns which had informed the writing of *The Making of Americans*   bissett plunges into the maelstrom   & there is a fatalism involved   as he has said the voice owns the man

no
one voice
can sing
  forever

the myth
has him
die
  when his voice
    dies
  and that
is the end

("The Caruso Poem")

so what we are seeing here is bissett's concern with sound for it is very important to understand this   it is very important to understand that out of his concerns with sound grew his assessment of the page as a visual field in the sense that the optophonetic poets such as raoul hausmann have defined it

> The optophonetic poem must create an absolute unity of noises, sounds, and typographical forms which, when printed on the page, give a strange, exceptional space and a complex concretized abstraction.

> It is no longer a grouping of vowels and consonants semantically arranged according to the rules of syntax, but rather a polarity of complements from a new spiritual world.

> (Hausmann—"The Optophonetic Dawn")

this involvement with sound has been the basic one for the majority of the canadian "concrete" poets. . . . bissett has never been concerned with a literal transmission of sense   he is concerned with ecstasy

> we are not only images
> cumming together, within
> this permission we suspend
> doubt, are flesh, are
> material, are meat filld
> of air, of blood, fire, of
> what matters is our waters
> meet, again, we found time

> (bissett—**"The Sun Does Not Move"**)

he is concerned with getting across the instant of experience in whatever way necessary convinced that the only way to actually communicate with someone is to place them into your perceptual system

> in especially th worst of th jail pomes th rhetorik spills ovr into undead for altho sum of ths pomes arent ordinarily worth publishing or writing and ium no critic seems like most convincing way to demonstrate that for me at least life th living of it its tensions energy needed to write in lively way, where only sittin' is waitin' for meal call or bissett bag nd baggage transfer to nother wing, th pomes tend to be downbeat a bit sorry bout that nd not in themselves very eventful: iron bars may be do not a prison make but wud yu believe this cardboard replica, tho with all life removd so were all distractions, nd such good opportunity for meditating is met: what is never ends: this is well, and perhaps also well it is for th element of choice to be

> (bisett—introduction to **Sunday Work (?)**)

the use of chant of insistence in the form of repeating phrases over and over again with the change being that of emphasis or intonation shows his roots in & debt to stein   at the same time his losing of himself in the ecstasy that accompanies the chant experience his losing of himself in sound his giving himself up into that mys-

tery is where he steps away from stein into the unknown into that region which is both primitive & uncharted tied in us as it is to deeper racial memory and the awareness of the universe as one organic entity within which sound is the key that sets the mechanism that balances things in motion   this involvement with chant has been the central experience for all canadian poets working in this area   even in the pure non-linear morpheme & sub-morpheme pieces you will find in all canadian work an underlying basis of chant   it is the identifying characteristic of canadian sound poetry

---

bissett has never been concerned with a literal transmission of sense   he is concerned with ecstasy

—bp Nichol

---

equally characteristic of canadian sound poetry is the importance of improvisation   none of the poets extensively involved in sound use the text as anything more than a point of departure   thus notation becomes something to simply suggest the phonetic space the poem should or could occupy   mccaffery insists his visual texts are acoustic pieces in themselves heard with the eye rather than the ear   the same is true of bissett's work   which brings us to a consideration of bissetts visual approach to aural notation

> I gazed at Arabic letters today & saw the pictures.
> Ium trying that with English now, getting nowhere.
> So David sd that is, I am th picture. Why.
> (bissett—*Blew Ointment,* Vol 2 No 4)

the man is inside his own language   he is in there in the sense that he takes over the sound and claims it for himself takes language back to himself   in *S The Story I To* bissett says "concrete   only a categorie so yu can label it out of yr depth, not *feel it change yu*"   and a few years back in a letter to me when i was referring to the things i was writing then as ideopomes

> does it help to name yur pomes at all, bp, theyre there grown, the name is possibly for the filers, th staff cards, like "sweet william", or hollyhock, whether theyre ideopomes or whatever, they are still being there, and it doesnt become an ideopome rather than a cap poetry poem just because theyre called one or th other, they surely always become what they are

it has always been one of bissetts concerns & indeed the concern of all the poets involved in what ive already referred to elsewhere as the vancouver toronto niagara cleveland grouping it has always been their concern to present the perceptual system the way it wants to present itself   what this means is no manifesto declaring certain items as no longer fit for inclusion as poetry but rather a sensitivity to the moving spirit which manifests itself as language & allowing it to show itself thru you in what ever way seems natural to it   thus the broad scope of bissetts work   the wide variation in terms of how the poem that is inside him ends up outside him

bissetts visual notation encompasses six different approaches

    1) visual organization
    2) spelling
    3) run-ons & combinations
    4) atomization
    5) overlays
    6) hand drawn or written pieces

i would like to look at this first of all from a purely visual point of view that is to say the poem as an ideogramme since this too is part of bissetts concern but keeping always in mind its basis for bissett in sound

the beginning of written language is the sign a symbol agreed upon by everybody to mean the same thing   the first signs were pictorial & representative   the ox was symbolized by the drawing of an ox and then gradually thru constant usage by only its head the drawing of which soon became simplified & stylized. . . . bissett begins at the point where language has become abstract symbol & attempts to move backwards . . . to arrive at his conclusions. . . .

all art has moved toward a reexamination of basic materials   what too many people have seen as a disintegrative tendency in art BECAUSE THEY SEE MAKING PRETTY PICTURES OR TELLING NICE STORIES OR THINKING BIG THOTS AS THE END PRODUCT is in fact an attempt to regain the magic   to rediscover the basic tools. . . .

visual organization like we have been discussing often leads directly into word combinations & the running together of words & phrases   this sets up areas within the poem that lack logical connections areas of stress in which the brain strains to make the imaginative jump & fill in the gaps bissett has left   the effect is similar to that obtained by sitting in a room where dozens of people carry on as many conversations   the message (if you wish it) is the lack of real communication in the way we use language   that this is a concern of bissett's is obvious from such poems as **"Nuclear Circular"** where he writes

    reach those peopul
    who printed this circular
    which robs me of my peace
    which carries to those few
    i have with me i love
    to this typewriter / breaking
            down on me

clearly stating his own fear that he will be unable to communicate to those people it is most important he communicate with   he has made it even clearer in two

subsequent pieces   at one point in *Lost Angel Mining Company* in a moment of anger he writes

    yr friends tryin to bring yu down, always putting yu
    on trips, their jive comments. meddling in where yr
    aiming to be. that it strengthens the species all th gossip
    and bullshit. if yu can survive it yu can go further.
    what might strengthen th species etc is for peopul to
    mind their own business. for what appears to be is
    only misdirection, boring data.

& in a poem published in *Tamarack* 56

    spookd by how i dont really
    care anyway nor do my
    friends i mean how

    can yu particularly
    care, after all this hand
    waving's gone down, done
    nothing, except beg for

    what is necessary

but for bissett in his particular quest the moments of despair & anger alternate with the moments of ecstasy   in two poems written almost five years apart bissett shows us the problem as he sees it   in the first from his first book *We Sleep Inside Each Other All* he says

                i have slain the
    albatross he thought with my bow of guilt
    and my arrow of fear

the albatross here is language & the i man for man has tied language to him & killed it thru divorcing it from sound thru fear of his own voice the real use of his own voice guilt over the use of the power that is there   if this interpretation seems far fetched then listen to what bissett says here in **"Beyond Even Faithful Legends"** a poem written years later

    Patterns, geometries, don't step on th cracks, yul
    break whose back, there it is, mothr or who, those
       choices to
    me child, help, help th children children destroy even
    those patterns yu place upon their undrstandings, i
    once thot . . . , or my childish attempt to see
    a suggested pattern, tho i probably that way got it all
    wrong, o, if theres any way

    out of th programmd albatross take it loves

for bissett the way out of this intolerable situation is the perception of the organic totality the path of chant & magic. . . .

    no reason to believe any one else's version of where
    yu are. what is constant. th radically changing flow
    yu are a tiny part of mysteriously a small polishd
    stone sumtimes a croaking frog sumtimes evolvd
    spirit. what are we. we are on this earth to love each

other. it is a garden. let us play. fighting janguls the
antennae.

patience and love bring yu thru th peaceful opening to
harmony. it isn't peaceful just cause you want it to be.
be where there is already peace. this conveys moving
around sum.

             (*Lost Angel Mining Company*)

sumtimes it seems yu just hav only to find yur place
in the wheel, and then everything is allright, an' that
yur place is anywhere that yu can accept it being there
what yu are anyways doing

everything alive part of the same energy but sum get
cut off guess everyone is cut off sumtime where how
we have to only spread the energy to all, but like sum
whun who is hungry just wants to eat, to do any thing
fancy like spreading energy

             (undated letter)

here bissett states that social conditions interfere with our
perception of this totality   constantly he is torn between what he sees as the need for violent social action
to help the starving homeless oppressed people he sees
around him & the perception that violence breeds more
violence & distracts from the pursual of magic   in a
poem published in an issue of *Blew Ointment* titled **"Nerve
Gas part II"** he states   "for th journey is both higher
nd lower than we may think and widr nd hardr when its
even easy than evr"

and in **"Arrows of Flowers"**

so hard to speak, as th changes do not occur
in words only but in th flesh, and its annointing
is confused with th admixtures of words
and society, striking imperfect balances

the two have not come together for him "yeah, if it wer-
ent for life, i wudint need a witchdoctor" (**"Our Friends
In Jail"**) the two streams are there   the american takeover of canadian resources   surrounded by violence to
respond with violence

how duz it work

me ium gonna start carrying a gun
all th time i dont get that one at all
                 ("th Earth Lantern")

the duality is constant   bissett's recognition that you
have to "believe in th positive energy sumtimes" (**"th
Earth Lantern"**) & too the recognition that there are
forces around you working to distract you from what may
be the major work

      fuck theyre crazy. theres a
cactus growin in yr veins the moon rising
in yr forehead along th blood path
remembering no history no programmes whats

going down half asleep as yu try
to make out th letters
it aint easy thers peopul
who dont want to see
yu and peopul who yu
dont want to see the thing
is of thundr th opening
light th secret tunnel
by th sea wall who dusint
know th mountain side
glares at yr
ambition

                 ("th Earth Lantern")

and in **"Looking for th Lammas"** which follows **"th
Earth Lantern"** in *S The Story I To* the opening line
states "th ancient lord of th universe asks yu to be" &
then

yeah
i want to hear th soul of th world
     opening to itself

the order & type of bissetts most recent publications is in
itself significant here for what i am saying   *Lost Angel
Mining Company* was followed by *Liberating Skies* the
purest concrete poetry bissett had yet done   page after
page of chant overlays   this was followed by *S The
Story I To* which ends with these lines

                watch out for the invadrs
who take over yr wires yr media yr schools who
announce whats next / as th black top is rolld out all
ovr yr earth all th way to th concentration / camp the
robot ville ofth mind, th drive-in, th newstand, even
tellin yu its good / for yu poets too sure / know thr th
steam roller on yr face

     ("Love of Life, th 49th Parallel")

this was followed by *Blew Trewz* another book of pure
concrete   bissett is alternating the moments of ecstasy
of magic with the screams of rage against what is going
down around him   nowhere is the dilemma so clearly
stated as in **"Hey Yu"**

           an th times belong

       to yur
       grasp
       disappear
       keep
       eternity
       warm

       in th mind
       only parallel
       lines also
       meet

       words words
       th holy spider
       is yr heart

the parallel lines are the two areas of concern   the social revolution & the magical awareness   & yet they meet   they meet in his poetry   & the centre of poetry is the spinning of words   the nets cast out to catch the moment   "words words / the holy spider / is yr heart"   they meet in his poetry & yet do not meet since they are parallel   bissett speaks again & again from the heart of this dilemma

> what it smells like th burning fire
> of yr soul tunnels thru th mountains
> like meat like yolk
> as precious thots
> birthd by th union
> of th lightning
> flashes that blind
> yr will
>
> and th children sleep
> soft til dawn all
> around them th jackals creep
>
> o love past play past memory
> let th children be
> let th children be

("Circles in th Sun")

what i have been trying to show here is bissetts immense concern with addressing a people & being heard   within this concern is his constant awareness that old uses of language are part of what have trapped us & thus he seeks new exits new ways of using language   "So David sd that is, I am th picture. Why."   when those lines were written bissett had perceived that man was the ideogramme   that at the heart of language is or should be a human concern   yet it puzzled him   the further he moves into magic into perceiving language as part of the totality the less he needs somebody outside of him to answer that question   *S The Story I To* is his way of saying that the single letter is the story   s is the story   that this is what he does   that he is the story he is the alphabet   & with the shock of recognition goes the despair & anger about the way the world has been played with   used for selfish ends   as language has again & again   as all parts of the totality have

it is to regain this sense of the totality that bissett has gone into the primitive elements of language into chant into insistence into the approaches he uses to putting the poem on the page

his use of word combinations & the running together of phrases that I discussed earlier leads into another area of bissett's approach to visual organization   his interest in atomization   by breaking up words so that they lose their recognizable surface & throwing the emphasis on to the elements of the word bissett causes areas of tension to be set up inside the poem that are the reverse of those created by his run-ons & combinations   in the latter one attempts to separate the recognizable words from the mass he has created & in the former to piece them togeth-

er from the fragments presented   there is nothing new in any of these methods   breaking up words &/or combining them is the way we gain new words & enrich our language   by doing this within the body of his poems bissett is working in the way william carlos williams suggested would be necessary in order to rid the language of staleness

it is in spelling that bissett makes the language most his own   bissett is one of the few modern poets consistently & systematically to change the spelling of a large number of words to suit his own purposes   the difference between "come" & "cum" is not in the meaning of the word or in the sound but in the reaction of the reader who gains an entirely different aura of sense reading it   reading it we recognize the word "come" but recognize it also as being different from the word we are familiar with   the difference is interpreted by the eye in terms of the sound   in fact bissett has altered the sonic space that the word occupies visually   he has put his own interpretation on the word & made the language come alive for both himself & the reader   we can see here how the visual & the aural concerns are really one & the same. . . .

the advantage for the poet of hand written texts is direct contact with the page   typewritten poems involve direct contact with the keys & secondarily the imprinting of your poems on paper   in that sense a typed poem is almost published already   you have the experience of type right there   in bissetts conception of an organic universe the hand drawn poems which sometimes pass over into drawings or paintings & the hand written chants like **"Windows in th Straw"** which appears at the end of *Liberating Skies* come closest to direct transmission   in the drawn poems there is the central concern of the ideogramme & the mandala both objects which contain the poet   "i am th picture"   he creates a sign which is meaningless in terms of our language which has a visual meaning rather than a verbal or auditory one & is able to work at a level of communication where each encounter is fresh & exciting & forces us to come forth with new unstereotyped responses   here as in his overlays he comes close to a pure iconography   & tho the link to chant is more obvious in the overlays the link to magic in terms of the sign is most obvious in his hand drawn pieces

the hand written chants are direct muscular transmission of the chant instinct   the same phrase written over and over and over the emphasis shifting from line to line in terms of the rise & fall of the letter the slight shifts in shape & thickness of lines   in the typewritten overlays (most notable in *Liberating Skies* & *Blew Trewz*) bissett translates into visual terms the sonic space the poem occupies   by heavily overlaying line after line of a chant the shifts in emphases occur in terms of a blurring out of the previous line by the line being typed over it not perfectly but slightly down from it so that part of the previous line appears above the next line building up in some areas into a total blurring of the line & then its gradual reemergence into legibility   it is a visual equivalent of a sonic space now what i have been doing here is looking at the devices bissett uses to notate the poem   i have been looking at the visual devices & seeing them in terms of their visuality keeping in mind always that for bissett there is this underlying concern of the ideogram of the man at the centre of language & this mans presence in terms of the sound of his voice in language   every device bissett uses bends towards an understanding of language & its uses a seeking for exits from the death it has so long carried with it by merging it again with the totality

in an unpublished essay titled "The New Geomancers" steve mccaffery places bissetts work in a clear line of historical succession

> bissett in a context
>   william blake: every–
> thing that lives is holy   the grammatically contained
> word can do no justice to these living things   the
> word must be the object to survive   the object must
> be the word in order to survive
>
>   william collins:
> ode to evening via palgrave a perceptual experience
> through language becomes a totally bodily experience
>   vocabulary syntax as muscle   collins words
> are collins sinews
>
>   christopher smart: penetration
> through the word behind it into word events   the
> ultimate fusion of language and the body   repetition
> as this determination to get it back there   smart
> seeing poetry as adoration trapped in merely verbalistic
> praise   poetry becoming bodily action   physical
> nakedity inseparable from verbal perspicacity   read
> his biography as a truly symbolic document and a
> perfect critical analogy
>
>   henri chopin: la poème c'est
> moi   instance of the single vision. . . .

symons in his book *Man's Presumptious Brain* refers to the fact that man is evolving towards a point of totally denying the emotional life   bissett outlined this trap a long time ago in a poem called **"The Body"** in which he pointed out that any system eventually grows more powerful than the people using it and takes on an independent life of its own,

> The largeness of THE BODY would increase
> and diffuse hopelessly the initial self-
> betrayals invited aroused to sustain it.
> As a consequence, the belief in self,
> in character would drop away behind
> the larger movement of the General Body.

this is not a finding of the self in a larger community but rather the surrender of self thru despair to a less obvious conformity   the traps here are subtle   as we have already seen the language itself carries the death inside it   in this same poem bissett outlines an avenue of escape he chose to use and the reasons for his attempt to return to the root elements of both the written and aural language

> to attempt our retreat from
> the General Body, to let it go on without
> us, to no longer allow truth to include
> ourselves. Doing this we have found
> is still to live without hope. Our sense
> of hope has been permanently altered or
> damaged through our involvements with
> THE BODY. We are not the same as we
> were inside THE BODY, or as we were
> coming to it or taking our departure.
> We have become outside remembrance
> and forgettings, its illusions and skills
> outside time.

and yet bissett continues   it is not an easy quest. . . . bissett is aware the path he has chosen thru language is not always easy for the very people he wants to reach "he complained there was no plot nd went out slamming th door befor he got to it."   this is in *The Lost Angel Mining Company* and it is followed by

>   close yr eyes
> and see a procession of holy grateful spirits weaving
> thru th illusions of light and shadow seeking places to
> make offering loves as green as rich golden fires within
> th one heart spinning th gathring stories thru th floating
> grain

& a little later

>   who knows what it means, theres no
> time like th future, but yu hear the notes sound th
> beat, yuve herd it ovr nd ovr again, in yr heart, th
> furnace at th centre boiling lava, th stars measurd
> radiance, th tempo of th changes, this person cums to
> see yu, what th exchange might be, yu go now without
> reason, but th time is for it, an invisible move but
> changing tides yu don't initiate yu are air earth fire
> water th fabric and vessel who expresses being
>
>   th
> obscurity forces were kept busy how close th light
> house came was. also found alive and well. words
> can't tell. generous and brave. none of us knows what
> is to come. ive seen this picture already and there
> appears not to be any othr.

the role of prophet or seer sits uneasy on him & yet he feels he has something to say

there is nothing	the wind	there is much
to know, please		to know,
don't listen to	a cloud	please
me		listen to me
	sun	

("Concerto to a Runaway")

thru it all he does continue   and thru it all the continuing re-examination of language of the forms of being   the page as a visual sonic field   the poem as an extension of the body   the insistence of what is inside you and how it changes from moment to moment thru chant

And for th word offering
remember me
according to th language
of every peopul

("Of Th Land Divine Service")

bissett is seeking for some new footing in the void of
falling & not without hope for as he says somewhat to his
own surprise in **"We Need The Setting"**

    someone else
   might want to experience
   this suffocation
   shadow held back
   dense cancerous quiet

   were it oddly enough
   that we can make love well
   or that we
   stagger into poems

Margaret Atwood (essay date 1972)

SOURCE: "Jail-Breaks and Re-Creations," in *Survival: A
Thematic Guide to Canadian Literature,* Anansi Toronto,
1972, pp. 233-47.

[*Atwood is an acclaimed Canadian-born writer. In the
following excerpt, she outlines Bissett's political vision as
articulated in* NOBODY OWNS TH EARTH.]

The amazing thing about [*Nobody Owns th Earth*] is that
it juxtaposes visions of Edenic happiness and peace with
angry political poems like **"Th Canadian"** and **"Love of
Life, th 49th Parallel,"** the latter being probably the most
all-inclusive poem on American takeover to appear so
far. And yet it isn't, finally, amazing: anger and the desire
for change depend on the assumption that change will be
for the better, that it is in fact possible to achieve not only
individual but social freedom. The title, *Nobody Owns th
Earth,* predicts a world that will be not "international"
but post-national, in which people will live on the earth
with love both for it and for each other, and some of the
individual poems give us glimpses of this world. The angry
"political" poems, however, recognize the fact that we do
not yet live in this world, and if we assume too soon that
the millennium has arrived we will simply end up as victims again, owned by people who do not even admit the
possibility of a non-"owned" Earth. These Bissett identifies as "th Americans." A lot of the energy in the poems
comes from the frustration experienced by someone who
lives in the freedom of Position Four, communes with the
mysticism of Position Five, but is forced to witness the
effects of Position Two on himself and those around him.
Like [English poet William] Blake, Bissett is a kind of
social visionary, and for such a visionary there must always be Songs of Experience as well as Songs of Innocence. Paradise here and now is individual and sexual, Hell
here and now is social and mechanical; but the potential

for social redemption is present, as witness the strength of
the image at the beginning of **"Nobody Owns th Earth,"**
in which "a whole peopul" is seen "moving / together."

Stephen Scobie (essay date 1973)

SOURCE: "A Dash for the Border," in *Canadian Literature,* No. 56, Spring, 1973, pp. 89-92.

[*Scobie is a Scottish-born Canadian poet, author, and
educator. In the following review of* drifting into war, *he
discusses the strengths and weaknesses of Bissett's poetic
method.*]

In Bill Bissett, we continue to find a tremendous energy
of form, directed almost against itself. Bissett reaches to
the edges of language and destroys it, yet keeps returning.
The visual forms on the page (and how curious to see the
determined untidiness of Bissett's gestetnered productions
faithfully reproduced in the normally immaculate Talon
format) always tend towards the destruction of any form
they set up, while in sound Bissett returns to the strict and
revivifying form of the chant. One tends to think of Bissett as a romantic artist, with a strong innate capacity for
self-destruction, but he is also (at what I think is his best)
capable of the strong control of his chants, or of the almost classical under-statement of poems like **"Killer
Whale"** and **"Th Emergency Ward."** Thus, for me the
best things in *Drifting Into War* are the simple, controlled
typestracts, produced by overtyping certain spaces within
squares and rectangles of letters, which present clean,
abstract visual designs. At other times, as in **"A warm
place to shit,"** Bissett proves that he is better than anybody else at parodying the worst of Bill Bissett.

Drifting Into War is not a book which will produce any
converts to Bissett, nor is it really a good introduction to
his work: both these functions are best served by Anansi's *Nobody Owns Th Earth*. It ranges widely in quality,
some of it being rather awful, some of it splendid; as
always, Bissett needs a good editor, though it has to be
admitted that a good editor might take away from the
total impact of his work, which perhaps depends as much
on the bad as the good.

Whatever "inadequacies" language may have, it is still the
material of poetry: there is no other. For a poet working
clearly and gracefully in the centre of a tradition, like [Gary]
Geddes, the resources of the word are still amply sufficient;
for those like [B. P.] Nichol and Bissett, working at the
limits, there are always new discoveries, new routes leading
simultaneously back into language and on into silence.

Stephen Scobie (essay date 1974)

SOURCE: "Bissett's Best," in *Canadian Literature,* Vol.
60, Spring, 1974, pp. 120-22.

[In the following review of pomes for yoshi, *Scobie argues that, despite appearances, Bissett's work is the result of careful stylistic control.]*

In her selection of Bill Bissett's poetry for the volume *Nobody Owns Th Earth,* Margaret Atwood provided Bissett with what many of his readers had long felt he needed: a good editor. While Bissett has seldom published anything totally without interest, or without flashes of his own very individual brilliance, far too many of the books and pamphlets which pour out of the Blew Ointment Press have been random and haphazard collections of whatever he had to hand, with the good poems inextricably mixed up among the bad.

Indeed, it might be argued that this randomness, this deliberate abdication of selectivity and control, are so central to Bissett's aesthetic and life-style that it would seem like a distortion of his vision for him to present a tightly edited, carefully chosen selection. Certainly Bissett is best when read at some length, but Atwood's selection goes some way towards proving that the better poems can be successfully separated from the mass.

Nor is it absolutely clear that Bissett at his best *does* depend on uncontrolled haphazardness. On the contrary, his chants depend on a very strict manipulation of rhythmical effects, and anyone who has heard him perform can testify to the extraordinary control he has over his voice. Moreover, in some of his longer satirical poems—I'm thinking especially of **"Th' Emergency Ward"** and **"Killer Whale"**—the pretence of the poem's being an unadulterated recital of facts *is* surely just a pretence. These poems practice a kind of reticence, an ironic understatement, a refusal to comment which is in the end far more effective than any actual comment could have been (especially the rather frenzied political rhetoric that Bissett often indulges in). These poems, with their very studied naivety in accepting all the strange things that happen to him, show Bissett as a master of narrative and ironic tone.

These considerations are very important when approaching **Pomes for Yoshi,** which I think is Bissett's best collection to date (excluding Atwood's selection.) In the first place, it is a book with a unified theme: in effect, it is one long sequence of poems in which every piece bears directly on the central concerns. The major concern is with the poet's love for a girl called Yoshi, who has left him (he hopes temporarily) because she wants to be alone for a while. Juxtaposed to the poet's expressions of longing, as a kind of contrapuntal minor concern, are accounts of Bissett's attempts to move out of the house he's living in. The increasingly hectic disorder of that house may be taken as an image of the disorder of the poet's emotions, and his final escape to a saner, more human environment hints at a resolution of the major theme as well.

In the love poems, Bissett tackles head on the oldest poetic theme in the world, and he succeeds in giving it a remarkable freshness by the very naivety, directness, and openness with which he treats it. In simple, colloquial language he speaks of how he misses her, and of how he accepts her need to be away from him for a while, even if she's with some other man. Love is not possession, Bissett says, and seldom has this ideal been realised more fully and more convincingly. The poems take the emotional warmth and idealistic romanticism of Bissett's earlier work and manage to focus them on a particular situation, a particular relationship.

The sub-theme, the housemoving, reaches its climax in a long poem at the end of the book which fully deserves to stand alongside **"Th' Emergency Ward"** and **"Killer Whale"**. As with these poems, the ostensible form is that of a purely factual narrative of an increasingly fantastic sequence of events. (Bissett appears to be the kind of person that the wildest things just naturally happen to.) But again, the tone is perfectly judged, and the absence of comment becomes a comment in itself. It also produces a hilarious kind of straight-faced humour.

None of this, I think, is accidental. It is a product of Bissett's life-style and aesthetic (the two are almost the same), an openness which seems naive but isn't, an innocence which has gone through experience and out the other side, a purity of outlook which brings freshness to the most outrageously clichéd situations and phrases. Nothing but this consistency of tone could account for the way in which Bissett is able to use such terrible clichés of counter-culture jargon as "Far out", "I can dig it", "Heavy", and "Got to get my shit together" with such complete honesty that the reader accepts them as being meaningful (accurate descriptions of a certain state of mind), amusing (in slyly self-mocking, understated asides), and even deeply moving (see especially the final page of the book)

Such sophisticated manipulations of language may be accidental, or unconscious, but I rather doubt it. *Pomes for Yoshi* strikes me as a very carefully crafted book, as well as a deeply personal one. It is surely the mark of a good poet that very strong personal emotions intensify rather than decrease his sensitivity to language. Such is certainly the case with this book.

Frank Davey (essay date 1974)

SOURCE: "Bill Bissett," in *From There to Here,* Press Porcepic, 1974, pp. 49-54.

[Davey is a Canadian poet, author, and educator. In the following essay, he considers the mystical and political ideas informing Bissett's work.]

For the past fifteen years Vancouver has contained the largest and most cohesive left-wing artistic subculture in Canada. Throughout all of these years Bill Bissett has been one of its most outspoken and iconoclastic poets. Bissett's rejection of the conventional or "straight" world has been vigourous expressed not only in lifestyle but in ruthless alterations to conventional syntax and spelling. His contempt for orthodox society has caused him to be ejected from cross-Canada trains, evicted by countless landlords, beaten, harrassed by police, and arrested and sentenced to prison. His contempt for the orthodoxies of the printed word caused him for at least a decade to be regarded by the bourgeois world of literary criticism as little more than a wild man or a freak.

Bissett published more than fifteen books in the sixties, and so far in the seventies has published ten more. His first significant recognition outside of the underground literary world in which he works and lives, however, was the publication in 1972 by the House of Anansi Press of a selected Bissett, *Nobody Owns th Earth*. This was followed quickly by his inclusion in Eli Mandel's certifying anthology, *Poets of Contemporary Canada* (1972). Neither book, however, recognizes Bissett on his own anarchic terms. The Anansi selected poems, edited by Margaret Atwood and Dennis Lee, is a "Bissett methodized"— Bissett represented by his most tractable and accessible material. Much of the flavour of a real Bissett publication—that created by his use of smudged and broken typefaces, varying page sizes, one-of-a-kind crayon sketches and collages, and consciously obscure or sentimental material is absent.

Bissett has been a one-man literary happening, almost impossible to contain in a single book. He is an exciting sound poet—particularly in his chants based on west coast Indian material; this part of his work can be sampled through his record *Awake in th Red Desert*. He is an innovator in concrete or visual poetry. His most interesting work here has been his use of the dimensions of the page as a principal element, and his occasional transformation of the page into a single alphabetic and orthographic tapestry. Bissett is also an accomplished graphic artist, with a recognizably unique style in both collage and pen-and-ink sketching. In addition, he has been an important west coast editor, working through his cavalierly named Blew Ointment Press and *Blew Ointment* magazine to preserve and advance the careers of numerous Vancouver writers including Judith Copithorne, Maxine Gadd, Gerry Gilbert, and Bertrand Lachance. In all of these activities, as well as in his day-to-day life, he has been politically active, attempting to disturb the complacent, enrage the dogmatic, and obstruct the mechanical and the unjust whether in literature or in the streets.

Informing all of Bissett's action has been a mystical and religious view of the world. Behind our own unreliable world of death, war, and persecution, Bissett sees a transcendent and immutable one in which pure joy, energy, and spontaneous form exclude the petty boundaries and restrictions of our philistine and puritanical culture. More Blakean than Emersonian, this other world of "th endless sun, the rose in th forhead", can become visible to us during incantation, prayer, or dream. At moments of extreme intensity—drug experience, sexual orgasm—a person can enter completely into this world of eternal condition. Many of Bissett's poems celebrate physical love in which the body becomes a "tempul burning" and opens the way to complete escape from materiality and temporality. Many other poems are religious chants—

"holy day is due holy / day is due . . ."—ostensibly designed to induce mystic feeling.

Because of the Platonic overtones of these poems, their diction superficially appears extremely limited. The dominant part of speech is the noun; most nouns are from a narrow elemental range—*tree, earth, fire, wind, water, sky, sun, moon, blood, heart* (in some books by Bissett such a list would comprise 80% of the nouns). They are nearly always unmodified. But these limitations are deliberately chosen by Bissett in his attempt to write of an unqualified, elemental, and pure visionary world—a world distinct from ours in its lack of categories, pluralities, divergencies, in its consisting only of elemental substance. Bissett's idiosyncratic quasi-phonetic spelling—*yu* for *you*, *th* for *the*, *tempul* for *temple*—is both a similar kind of simplification and a symbolic act of social rebellion. It is meant to indicate a sensibility that prefers cosmic clarity to the vagaries and stupidities of earthly convention, and is successful in doing this. To Bissett, the rules of grammar, church, academy, and state are all equally pernicious conspiracies to imprison the human spirit.

To Bissett, the rules of grammar, church, academy, and state are all equally pernicious conspiracies to imprison the human spirit.

—Frank Davey

A major part of Bissett's work is his poetry of political and social castigation. This poetry is more accessible to the conventionally pragmatic reader than is the mystical verse, but most clearly has its origin in Bissett's mystic vision. The poet who yearns for heaven lives in hell—a hell not only of corporeality and plurality but of human deceit, brutality, exploitation, and petty distinction, a hell in which the poet must cynically inquire "were yu normal today did yu screw society". In these poems Bissett presents himself persecuted by police narcotic squads, incarcerated in a provincial prison, or mortally endangered by power-hungry doctors, psychiatrists, and bureaucrats. All of such poems have the rare quality in contemporary poetry of total authenticity. Bissett is no detached middle-class social critic; he has lived and continues to live on the streets of hell, and has the artistic power to convey this experience in its fullness to the reader.

The two sides to Bissett's poetry cannot be fully understood in separation. One is the mystic's hope, the other is his horror at what still surrounds him. Together they make him one of the major voices in new Canadian writing. Despite the slowness of his recognition, it is clear that of all the new poets of the past two decades Bissett is definitely one of the most stubbornly and self-confidently unique talents. Although the idea must be repugnant to him, he has already assured himself an important place in Canada's literary history.

Mike Doyle (essay date 1975)

SOURCE: "Animate Imaginings," in *Canadian Literature*, No. 66, Autumn, 1975, pp. 94-7.

[*In the following excerpt, Doyle discusses the connection between Bissett's formal approach and his poetic vision.*]

Bill bissett's . . . mixture of chant-poems, visual concretes, and commitment poems, always offered with engaging energy, is very familiar. The *shapes* of the poems (in the mouth, in the eye) fix one's attention, the personal phonetics and typo-orthography and the absence of "careful libran". Again one notes the absence of venturesome syntax (a strong preference for the declarative sentence) but perceives it in a different universe, not of thought, but meditation, here in many instances on the soul, "yr soul twind around th orange ths time".

Many of the "soul" pieces are shape poems, based on the single word, apparently exploring the soul's (physical?) dimensions. Others ("soul", and other) are based on a mantra-like line repetition, which is often also visual. Still others shape as a repeated line which gradually modulates into either an exploration of the *meaning* ("what does mean mean?") of that line, or takes a direction (or variety of directions) the frame-line opens the way to (such are "a forest in the shell and water" and "into the open lips of th sun"). Others again are discursive, though these too commonly offer arresting individual visual shapes. For obvious reasons these are the easiest to talk about at length, but they often have the least impact. One here offers a poetic, "a pome dusint have to be about anything often it can be abt nothing". His best poems are not "about", but are meditation-objects. Approximately, the one critical note in the book, struck several times, is anti-government, anti-political. Though perhaps the weakest of the poetry, these add a dimension and to some extent *earth* the book, which is a welcome addition to the canon of a distinctive poet.

Len Early (essay date 1976)

SOURCE: "Bill Bissett: Poetics, Politics & Vision," in *Essays on Canadian Writing*, No. 5, Fall, 1976, pp. 4-24.

[*In the following essay, Early provides an overview of Bissett's work and emphasizes the political meaning of his idiosyncratic style.*]

> "Frivolity and ecstasy are the twin poles between which play moves."
>
> —Johan Huizinga, *Homo Ludens*

In some three dozen books of poetry published since 1966, bill bissett has often seemed intent on making a virtue of disorder. If the redundancy of much of his work is undeniable, so is its great variety. Challenging all manner of authority, literary and otherwise, he has mounted an at-

tack on convention that at times appears nihilistic to the point of stunting his considerable artistry. Nevertheless, there is a vital consistency in his theories, forms and themes. The most idiosyncratic and the most ideological of his poems reflect a visionary writer whose achievement is already an impressive one.

While bissett's poetic is fairly obvious in many of his volumes, two are expressly addressed to questions of language and style: *Rush / What Fuckan Theory* (1971) and *Words in th Fire* (1972). The first of these is a book subverted by its own attitudes. As an assertion of bissett's idea that relationships such as hierarchy, cause-effect sequences, and linear writing are repressive, *Rush* proclaims its defiance by remaining determinedly incoherent. The verbal chaos is extreme; only occasionally are there passages of striking intellectual or lyrical interest. Almost all the important points in bissett's aesthetic view which are diffused, obscured and repeated elsewhere in the book, are tellingly concentrated in one poem, **"Poetry dusint have to be,"** which presents some of his most persistent themes. He declares that poetry should be free from any prescriptions of subject; indeed, like the most elementary child's play, it can do "nothing well." Nevertheless, as the bulk of this manifesto demonstrates, poetry can very well be about political and social issues of the utmost consequence—and much of bissett's own work is. The idea that there is a close connection between rules of language and political oppression (one of bissett's central convictions) occurs in the third part of the poem, and in the fourth he touches on another of his main themes: life in a primitive, natural terrain. In conclusion he suggests that the poet may be a medium for the utterance of perceptions which elude his conscious understanding:

> writing pomes can be abt many things
> can be abt nothing but what it itself is
> writing pomes in a way is longr than we are
> and what we can know writing pomes
> is also th voice uv ths things speaking thru us

"Poetry dusint have to be" is typical in form of those of bissett's poems which develop as predominantly discursive works, as distinguished from the visceral chants and visual designs at which he also excels. While he eschews conventional grammar and punctuation in such poems, they give an impression of copious vitality, of perceptions rendered articulate through the rhythms of phrase, line and section—or as bissett would have it, through the rhythms of breathing.

Words in th Fire (1972) uses this discursive mode to develop "anothr / study uv langwage" with much greater lucidity than *Rush*. In this series of semi-continuous meditations, bissett sees himself as participating in a "langwage revolution" which, however, appears to him to be faltering at the time he writes this poem. One aspect of this revolution, he suggests, is the wide availability of typewriters, copiers, small presses a cultural phenomenon which subverts authority systems. Among bissett's ideals is that of an organic principle in poetic structures:

                    each pome has within its

happening its own ordering it own rule sumtimes
                evn takes thru a lot uv
trubul to make it have it look like what it is
                its energy
        transmitted without any forcing that
                isint in th pome
            itself how it shapes its parts how it
                holds
                together

This notion is hardly revolutionary, unless we extend the history of the revolution back at least as far as [William] Wordsworth and [Samuel] Coleridge. However, the radical practices of bissett and some of his contemporaries are almost unprecedented. While the history of twentieth-century poetry is in large part an account of the revolt against nineteenth-century stanzas, rhythm and rhyme schemes, concrete poets in our time have carried the revolt further, in their suspicion of basic semantic conventions like grammar, spelling and linear printing, which they regard as repressive systems. Bissett stresses the importance in his kind of poetry, of *sound,* especially of language as spoken, as opposed to language as it is taught in schools. He seeks to present:

        that vois ther on th page moving along into that
    nd it skips yes it stops yes it pauses cheks yu out
                to see if yr

                                gettin it right
                        all that so it dont
                    on th page vizually stay
            in square bloks

Bissett's "revolutionary" spelling is conceived as a political act, intended to embody the values of phonetic simplification and vocal authenticity. "Correct" expression is in his view elitist, one more self-perpetuating device of the privileged classes, and one more restriction on the creative spirit. The anatomy of his books reflects this attitude: variations in the size of pages, inserts of advertisements and items clipped from magazines and newspapers, crayon drawings, inverted pages, pages of different colors—chiefly pastels in green, pink, grey, and blue, print that ranges from pica type to Olde English lettering, handwritten poems—his methods of defying standardization seem inexhaustible.

Bissett praises the potential of poetry to stir our faculties and involve readers in something akin to the act of poetic creation, an experience directly in contrast to the chief "recreation" of our age, television, which is generally manipulative rather than stimulating. Or as bissett himself says with more point, in "radiashun collaps":

    cant watch tv no mor man
    ths tv's gotta go or me go
    cant watch it baby how cum
    it needs to be watchd
    all th time cant lord

    cant no way lord ths tv
    just a pile of shit

                    (in *Th High Green Hill*)

This is not to say that bissett is unaware of the power of words to deceive and subjugate. His enthusiasm for language as delight, as freedom, as discovery, is equalled by his suspicion of language as an instrument of tyranny. As early as *Th Jinx Ship nd Othr Trips* (1966), he is quite clear about the power of language to constrict and damage our lives. Fundamental to bissett's work is his conviction that because poetry issues from minds which are continually conditioned by their environment, and view of poetry must take account of the social, the political, indeed the *physical* milieu in which it emerges. Hence *Words in th Fire* includes passages on the urbanization of modern consciousness, on discrimination against Canadian poets, the inequities of book distribution, Canadian complicity in the war in Vietnam, and on the Americanization of Canada. For bissett, political empire is intimately associated with language and thought control. Similarly, literary criticism is a form of power politics: "tastes get stratified nd start to stand for / what is permitted to get thru."

In the interest of "liberating" language from traditional poetic forms, bissett has explored its visual and aural qualities: the former is the route to concrete poetry, the latter leads to sound poetry. An extremely protean phenomenon, concrete poetry is hard to define with any precision: generally, it exploits the strictly visual properties of words while making more or less use of their semantic content. I think that bissett's **"am or,"** from *Awake in th Red Desert* (1968), is a paradigm of concrete. Semantically, "am" expresses the fundamental human condition of isolated subjectivity, and "or" raises the question of an alternative state: can one's loneliness be eased? Yes, in fact the solution to human isolation is love: "amor." And the culmination of love is reached at the end of the poem in the form of sexual communion popularly known as "sixty-nine." Visually, the stark columns of "ams" and "ors" may suggest the monotonous isolation of two individuals. The fact that these columns merge into the cluster of "69's" and the fact that in contrast to the columns, most of the "69's" are linked, reinforces my "semantic" reading. The 69's are also a clue to another visual dimension of the poem. If one inverts the page, the phallic shape becomes instantly apparent, accounting for the notch at the top of the figure. Righting the page, we now perceive the figure as a female emblem as well. (The fact that the shape of the poem is male upside down and female rightside up, corresponds to the physical positions of the lovers as they engage in "sixty-nine.") This is at once a love poem and an erotic sketch, altogether a work of considerable cleverness and perhaps of some emotional value, as far as it touches our own sense of loneliness and our knowledge or our hope of love.

The variety of bissett's concrete poems continually challenges his readers' abilities to respond to the unusual. In **"am or,"** the visual and semantic elements are almost in balance. As the proportion of semantic content in concrete poetry diminishes, the form approaches that of the purely visual arts—indeed, bissett is a graphic artist of considerable talent. One of his favorite methods is collage. Towards the end of the *Pass th Food Release th Spirit Book* (1973), we come upon a page on which a panel evidently clipped from a comic book is placed amid four snapshots arranged to form a frame and background. The cartoon depicts two girls fleeing on horseback from a looming tyrannosaurus which has just emerged from the jungle. Each of the photographs shows a modern high-rise office or apartment building. The only words in the collage are those of one of the girls, whose speech-balloon says, "Go, Samiel" (We can't be sure whether she's addressing her horse or the other girl.) Commentary: the collage invites a comparison of the tyrannosaurus with the rampant high-rises of our concrete jungles, modern monsters which threaten to devour us. The monstrous qualities of the high-rises—their dehumanized geometry and the standardized compartments (apart/ments) into which they separate people—are suggested by contrast. In the photographs only a solitary human figure appears, so tiny as to be nearly imperceptible, dwarfed at the entrance to his building; the comic strip, however, is vivid with creatures and companions as well as with terror. The whole effect is deliberately hokey, but nevertheless makes a point about the tyranny wrought by technologized environments. Such work can also remind us that the conceptual content of concrete poetry is not contingent on its semantic content. The pictorial symbols and many of the figures in bissett's drawings are full of meaning, and often enrich and complement the themes of his more traditional poems.

One obvious way to reduce the semantic content of a concrete poem is to keep the words to a minimum. Another way is to repeat a particular word or group of words until our sense of their conceptual meaning disappears. This is a primary technique of sound poetry but it also has a function in printed works. In a poem from *What* (1974), as the semantic import of the word evaporates, our attention is attracted by its concrete properties—the shapes and patterns of letters:

what

what what

what

what what

what

what what

what

what what

what

what what

what

Traditional writing tends to abstract us from the phenomenal world; a number of bissett's concrete poems seek to reverse this tendency by insisting on the shapes and spaces of print and of calligraphy.

Like conventional poetry, concrete ranges from the utterly simple to the highly complex, from merely formal designs which can be appreciated at a glance, to collages of words and shapes which yield sophisticated meanings. And like conventional poetry, it ranges from the lightest, most sportive poems, to works of profound moral import. The former seems to be more generally the case: more often concrete poetry amuses and delights than it informs and instructs. It would be more faithful to the spirit of the genre to dispense with the critical term "work" and to speak of art*play*. Bissett's *What Poetiks* (1967) is a series of childish scrawls, bad jokes, elementary puns—a treatment of language as simple visual and semantic counters. *IBM / Saga uv th Relees uv Human Spirit from Compuewterr Funckshuns* (no date) plays concrete games with the alphabet, chiefly through discerning pictures in the shapes of letters, and through word-association. *What* (1974) is a brown envelope containing loose pages which can be shuffled into any sequence. Among the poems is **"vowl man,"** a human figure constructed of a's, e's, i's, o's and u's. Other pages present more or less recognizable shapes built out of numerous "what's"—there are a building, a table, a barbecue and I *think* a handsaw. There are a couple of dim photographs of what appears to be lovemaking, and there is an introductory poem which needn't, naturally, appear at the beginning of the sequence. The title word is a brilliant stroke. As a query, "what" expresses precisely our attitude as we encounter each poem; as an assertion, it quite rightly indicates that each poem is no more nor less than itself. What? what. That's what.

Often the puzzling forms which bissett's work takes have the effect of slowing down our experience of the poetry. Perhaps this is one of the fundamental virtues of his technique: it forces us to assume a more leisurely pace, to enter into the spirit of play, of reverence, of creation itself.

—Len Early

As does concrete, sound poetry moves from relatively familiar uses of language (recitation, song), to works devoid of conceptual meaning: wails, hums and chants in which the voice is used strictly as an instrument of sound, speaking only to our emotions, not at all to our intellect. The most satisfactory experience of bissett's sound poetry is, of course, a live performance by the man himself. Listening to bissett on a record player or tape deck is similar to watching a rock concert on television: one feels that the performance is unnaturally packaged and controlled, and misses a vital sense of immediacy and of communal experience. Very little of bissett's sound poetry eschews the semantic element altogether, though most of his auditors will respond to only sound qualities in those chants ("shun da kalensha ta da lee") which are, according to Frank Davey, "based on west coast Indian material." "Take th river into yr heart," is a typical section of bissett's chant, **"The water falls in yr mind nd yu get wet tooo,"** which is printed in *Liberating Skies* (1969), and recorded on the LP that accompanies *Medicine My Mouth's on Fire* (1974). Perhaps the line can be understood in several ways, but it is certainly an exhortation to transcend oneself. The repetition which characterizes bissett's chanting frequently acquires ritual and sacramental overtones; indeed, much of his sound poetry ultimately amounts to a religious use of language and is closely related to the sacred vision which surges through such volumes as *Polar Bear Hunt* (1972) and *Th High Green Hill* (1972). As it is chanted, the line undergoes a variety of spontaneous vocal modulations. Its printed version can illustrate another facet of bissett's sound poetry: the typewritten "notation" for the work renders a concrete poem of considerable visual beauty. Such "tapestries" of words approach another of bissett's art forms: designs created by the typewriter which have no cognitive meaning, and whose charms are purely visual.

Often the puzzling forms which bissett's work takes have the effect of slowing down our experience of the poetry. Perhaps this is one of the fundamental virtues of his technique: it forces us to assume a more leisurely pace, to enter into the spirit of play, of reverence, of creation itself; it resists the "expert" response of programmed analysis and cataloguing. Indeed a number of concrete poets have stated that a primary aim of their work is involvement of the reader in completing or contributing to the poem's meaning in much greater measure than conventional poetry demands. Thus Claus Bremer, in an explanation of one of his poems: "this arrangement is intended to arouse curiosity, to reveal something, and then again to become obscure; to arouse the reader's curiosity, to reveal something to him, and then again confront him with himself. . . . Concrete poetry gives us no results. It yields a process of discovery. It is motion. Its motion ends in different readers in different ways." Much of bissett's work is intriguing in this way and gratifies our efforts to appreciate it.

There are, however, numerous poems and passages throughout the spate of volumes by bissett, which for me lack any aesthetic merit. In poems such as **"run tonight"** from *Pass th Food Release th Spirit Book* (1973), I can find neither the exuberance nor the beauty which are outstanding qualities elsewhere in his work. I remarked that as a revolutionary writer, bissett seeks to shatter the conventional orders of language, and that some of his most vital work is a consequence of this enterprise. Poems like **"run tonight,"** though, strike me as applications of his theories about language rather than explorations of the medium itself.

```
run tonight and i ull
use yur assa im poemd well
lots of wanta sure have they
look            like
yu              th
cud             white one in
have            our stomachs
a               i im just yank
```

```
pressed       it du yu
book                  hees gone to
isint                 jiggul him self
that                  must have atnos
xcitin                hair he married
                              all those flowers
yu see        all kinds f things  thats what togo r
it            for i cin smell   going    stop
  wud         hasint                    nd
very be                    swept         one
    good       this room              heel
for            it even he sat on        south
  blind      that where i cud have found  nd
   peopul   mail nd                    mirrors
     its here this time it well there was no in th back
                              one  as
                                 these webs
                              ahaaha
                              these nd
                              th bay
                           pardon
                              belonged
                                    to
                                       us
                                          wild
                        fuckan things
```

This self-conscious effect is reminiscent of Dada and surrealist art; indeed many of bissett's poems which baffle attempts to "read" them, echo the Dada interest, noted by Nahma Sandrow, in "dissociation and negation, in mocking with obscene gestures society and intellect and art, all illusions of an era too pigheaded to confront its chaos." In **"run tonight,"** disordered structure and violation of coherence are themselves the point. While such work may have a purpose of sorts, it fails to realize the aesthetic possibilities of either concrete or "trad" poetry. It has neither formal nor intellectual appeal, and seems to me essentially the printed equivalent of noise. Too often one feels that bissett is merely giving the raspberry to an especially pedantic fifth-rate English teacher he may have encountered in grammar school. It's worth noting that bissett himself is quite willing to make judgements about the quality of his poetry. Though he frequently urges us to let things, and poems, "be themselves," he acknowledges in a preface to *Sunday Work* (1969) that "sum uv ths pomes aren't ordinarily worth publishing or writing," and the volume *Living with th Vishyun* (1974) begins with this invitation:

```
       ar
  sum   uv ths
 pomes  bull
 shit     see if
 yu can tell
    wch ar
    wch ar
            sum
        timez i
       dont
     know
```

Alternatively, perhaps works such as **"run tonight"** can be regarded as raw material, the soupy verbal matrix from which moments of startling lyrical clarity emerge as we read through a bissett volume. By his own account, poetry is an abandonment of repressive rationality and ego distortions, an utterance of the "true" discoveries of untrammelled perception. He produces great wordfloods, evidently on the assumption that undirected consciousness will issue in something worthy of print. But it may also issue in the banal and the unintelligible, poems equally as bad as those "made up" by the excessively self-conscious poet. Voyagers through strange seas of thought and language risk shipwreck as they seek new worlds, and numerous of bissett's poems seem to me debris. Even so, the voyage is often worth the risk.

Though much of bissett's art is innovative, much is also fairly traditional in form, once one looks past superficial novelties of spelling and grammar. His versatility and vision overflow the forms of concrete and often issue in poetry that is both fluent and cogent. Notwithstanding his misgivings about doctrines and his diatribes against the tyranny of rational meaning, much of his work is full of meaning, and much is "message" poetry of a distinctly didactic orientation. He has produced many fine poems of a traditional sort: long meditations, brief lyrics, satiric narratives. These are more accessible than much of his experimental work, and it is probably no coincidence that one of his more conventional volumes has been praised as one of his best. In his review of *Pomes for Yoshi* (1972), Stephen Scobie confronts the question of the nebulous relation between spontaneity and order in bissett's poetic, and he makes a strong case for bissett's ability as a craftsman of poetry, in the traditional sense. As Scobie points out, "in some of his longer satirical poems—I'm thinking especially of **'Th' Emergency Ward'** and **'Killer Whale'** the pretence of the poem's being an unadulterated recital of facts *is* surely just a pretence. These poems practice a kind of reticence, an ironic understatement, a refusal to comment which is in the end far more effective than any actual comment could have been . . .". Scobie rightly singles out for admiration a genre in which bissett excels, the "realistic" personal anecdote which becomes an avenue of social criticism. Bissett's narrative versatility extends also to visionary romance and fantasy in poems such as **"let me tell yu a story of how they met"** in *Polar Bear Hunt* (1972), but I wish to follow up Scobie's judgement of **"Killer Whale,"** from *Lost Angel Mining Company* (1969), as a particularly fine example of the realistic narratives. . . .

[This] is a personal anecdote that implies a sweeping view of the impersonal present, together with a sense of fundamental values. The poet recounts a hitch-hiking episode with his lady, martina, during which they look at some captive whales. Their bad day becomes an indictment of our culture's bad times. The prevalent causes of tyranny and constriction in our lives dominate the environment the poem describes: corporate and bureaucratic institutions like MacMillan-Blodell, like the legal system which has "busted" the speaker—presumably for a marijuana offence, like the official policy which precludes charity in

government employees (an attitude echoed in the indifference of the attendants to the suffering whales). Similarly, details such as bus schedules, phone booths and plastic bags, suggest the technologizing of our lives which threatens on occasion to overturn our sense of freedom. The whales are a magnificent embodiment of the vitality and beauty which our civilization assaults, and they also represent a natural community of creatures which contrasts with the social isolation of the human figures in the poem. Contrary to the generally spirited character of bissett's writing, **"Killer Whale"** is stamped by an almost Arnoldian despondency about psychic exhaustion inflicted by the contingencies and shocks of modern life:

> after th preliminary hearing, martina
> and me and th hot sun, arguing
> our way thru th raspberry bushes
> onto a bus headin for Van, on th ferry
> analyzing th hearing and th bust, how
> th whole insane trip cuts at our life
> giving us suspicions and knowledge
> stead of innocence and th bus takes
> off without us from th bloody B.C.
> government ferry—I can't walk too good
> with a hole in my ankle and all why
> we didn't stay with our friends back
> at th farm—destined for more places
> changes to go thru can feel th pull
> of that heavy in our hearts and in th air

At least bissett and martina muddle through the disorder and anguish here, and reach their immediate goal, Vancouver, for what it's worth. Bissett's skill at relating idiom, circumstantial detail, and an implicit vision of our world, is obvious in works such as **"Killer Whale."**

These works can also demonstrate that poetry need not be formally radical to undertake inquiries or discoveries. In *Pomes for Yoshi* (1972), we observe the speaker assessing and reassessing his thoughts and behavior, measuring his feelings against his principles—doing, in short, what good poets have always done in exploring the paradoxes of sexual love. This book is so clearly the issue of an articulate consciousness seeking a realization of its experience in language. And this is the point at which bissett's "trad" poems intersect with his experimental writing. A number of his more homogeneous volumes also illustrate the questing attitude—perhaps "groping" would be more precise—which informs his work. Volumes such as *Pomes for Yoshi, Th First Sufi Line* (1973), and *Yu Can Eat It at th Opening* (1974), are serially arranged: they are flowing congeries of ideas, perceptions, moods, which taken individually may well form satisfactory brief poems, but which also body forth a larger meditative context. *Living with th Vishyun* (1974) is similar, and different: a collection of relatively spare and cryptic poems which often give the impression of memoranda from the poet to himself.

I have used the term "realistic" in speaking of those poems by bissett which reflect, and reflect upon, his experience in a world which we recognize as the familiar context of our daily lives. Such realism, especially in its comic and satirical perspectives, is one way bissett controls, amplifies, and makes compelling the visionary intervals in his work. Here I would suggest that bissett has affinities with those writers over the past two centuries whose work is impelled by a dialectic of irony and lyricism. Writers such as [William] Blake, [Thomas] Carlyle, [Herman] Melville and—closer to bissett's own time and space—Leonard Cohen, have sustained the most profound lyrical visions through an equally powerful sense of the comic. Their work testifies to a peculiar feature of modern history: that glimpses of sublimity can be achieved only within a frame of irony. With these writers bissett shares, variously: a wish to exhort and inspire; an undertaking to express and interpret a whole epoch and culture; a distrust of reductive interpretation and a subversion of linear conventions; a taste for both epigrammatic brilliance and verbal luxuriance; and certainly not least, a delight in *playing* with language, an obsession with word-coining, puns, jests, and a relish for sound and rhythm. Some of these qualities, especially the lyrical genius which complements bissett's realism, are concentrated in a poem from *Awake in th Red Desert* (1968):

> song composed just after the alarm clock
> before going to social assistance
>
> who was that in th red boat
> riding down sugar lane
>
> who was that in th red boat
> riding down sugar lane
>
> who did yu see in th red boat
> riding down sugar lane
>
> who cud yu hear in th red boat
> never to hear again
>
> who cud yu hear in th red boat
> never to hear again

Commentaries on poems like this one inevitably risk the appearance of millstones appended to ponies. I think, nevertheless, that "song" illustrates precisely my point about an ecstatic vision within an ironic frame. Some of the most crucial Romantic perspectives are here: the discovery of primordial glories in dreams and childlike imagination, and the loss of this magic upon awakening to the world of experience. The rhythms are those of children's chanting games or ritual incantation, qualities which permeate many of the visionary poems in *Th High Green Hill* (1972). But before looking further at the world conjured up in the course of bissett's song, I want to consider the world referred to in its title.

Bissett's criticism of social and political structures is as radical as his subversion of literary conventions. Indeed, he believes they are fundamentally related. As a social critic he is representative of the counter-culture, that conspicuous if nebulous rebellion which blossomed in the sixties against traditional North American mores and in-

stitutions. Bissett locates the center of social corruption in the United States and identifies "Amerika" as the source and symbol of heartless, devouring modernism, the Moloch against which [Allen] Ginsberg raised his howl in the fifties. Bissett's treatments of this theme range from relatively ironic, dramatic works like **"Killer Whale"** to jeremiads like **"LOVE OF LIFE, th 49th PARALLELL,"** in *Nobody Owns th Earth* (1971), in which sides are quickly chosen up and a torrent of accusation is loosed against the invasion by "plastik" American culture which (bissett believes) is destroying some kind of tutelary spiritual presence in the Canadian landscape. The outrage that vibrates through the long lines of this poem seems to quicken its tempo as the indictment surges forward. The repulsive imagery of American "power / sadism" is brilliantly chosen. Though the rhetorical violence of the poem makes me suspect the strict accuracy of the historical view proposed, it is clearly intended, like "Howl," as a rallying cry for rebels, not as a scholarly investigation.

The political affinities of the counter-culture are with socialism, in the priority it gives to collective values, and anarchism, in its loathing of centralized government and bureaucracies. Hence its members are frequently interested in primitive societies, especially the Amerindian culture which they regard as both a victim of and a saving alternative to the infernal structures of modernity. A facet of the Canadian counter-culture, as we can see in **"LOVE OF LIFE,"** is an espousal of nationalism as a way of resisting "American" values, especially individualism, in the interest of evolving communal societies. The pervasive problems of "identity" in modern life are met by a renunciation of ego, an abandonment of the contingencies of our individual identities in favor of a sense of tribal relationship. For the present, survivors of the counter-culture generally share a sense of underground solidarity as victims of persecution by the "straight" world of corporate interests, power politics, parental authority and police harrassment. They shun careers in the service of the technological state, preferring the kind of lifestyle bissett aptly calls "gypsy."

One token of solidarity among the widely dispersed counter-culture nomads and their fellow travellers has been a lingo of stock phrases upon which bissett draws heavily in his work. It is a measure of bissett's talent that he can use this sublanguage so effectively, as Stephen Scobie pointed out in his review of *Pomes for Yoshi*: "nothing but this consistency of tone could account for the way in which Bissett is able to use such terrible cliches of counter-culture jargon as 'Far out', 'I can dig it', 'Heavy', and 'Got to get my shit together' with such complete honesty that the reader accepts them as being meaningful . . .". The same courage with which bissett resorts to popular slang is evident in those numerous poems which risk a plunge into the maudlin. Simple feelings of love, delight, tenderness and wonder are the motives of many poems so direct and childlike that they are apt to baffle the hard-earned worldliness of literary critics:

> In th mushroom village
> all th littul children

brightly smiling
in th mushroom village
all th littul children
brightly be

        (from **"Circles in th Sun,"** in *Lost
Angel Mining Company*)

One of bissett's great gifts is his ability to make compelling poetry of feelings which may embarrass our tortuous sophistications or superficial notions of masculinity. As he says elsewhere, much to the point:

We have called
   so much
     sentimental
that we have
   very little

left
   perhaps nothing.

        (from **"The Caruso Poem,"** in
Awake in th Red Desert)

Paramount among counter-culture attitudes is a revulsion from technological mentalities oblivious to simple human values. In **Th High Green Hill** bissett deplores our practice of "trying so hard to build we cant / help but destroy." A distrust of systems, analysis and judgement may express a crucial insight into our contemporary malaise, but it may also provide an excuse for intellectual mediocrity, puerile behavior, or bad poems. Sophisticated spokesmen of the counter-culture frequently attack the idea of progress as one of the principal motives in the development of our civilization. Against the technician's view of time as linear, with a past to be studied and a future to be engineered, the counter-culture values moments of ecstasy achieved through drugs, music, sex and mysticism. And against the modernist view of nature as raw material to be exploited, the counter-culture perceives intrinsic value in natural things. This attitude is reflected in a preference for spontaneous over calculated behavior, a respect for ecological values, a recoil from urban living, a regard for the wilderness as a source of spiritual nourishment and a reverence for the human body. Bissett's poetry teems with references to biological functions and rhythms: vision, breath, heartbeat, blood circulation, excretion, copulation. Many of his poems present grim interludes of city-dwelling and images of desolation row. In others, seeking a liberation from the oppressions of history, he celebrates a paradisal relation of man with the natural world. His commitment to these values is not, however, without certain paradoxes: the general denunciation of order, but the systematic precision of some of his designs; the devaluation of ego, but the production of an enormous *oeuvre* under his name. And in his recourse to stereo recording to disseminate his sound poetry, there is perhaps a trivial clue to an important principle: that technology rightly employed may after all be the best way for the general population toward that condition of freedom and pleasure sought by the counter-culture.

But the implications of bissett's poetics and politics are apt to divert our attention from the first things we notice about his books: the quirks of format and content, the visual whimsey, the ingenuous lyrical beauty, and the rhapsodic power. This last quality I consider the sign of his most important work, the visionary poetry in his longest volume, **Th High Green Hill**. Though it includes a few collages, wordgames and concrete experiments, this book is largely made up of brief visionary lyrics and long visionary meditations. I suggested earlier that bissett's sound poetry has a religious dimension. His performance on the LP which accompanies **Medicine My Mouth's on Fire** expresses the attitudes which inform traditional hymns, prayers and sermons. These attitudes are also implicit in **Th High Green Hill,** which offers a vision of spiritual redemption and fulfilment. Many passages delineate grimmer realities: the damage to nature and to people wrought by corporate exploitation and technological processing. The irony and rage which we observed in bissett's political poems provide the minor theme of the book. "America" appears again as the exemplar of all that is destructive in the exaltation of egotism as a personal and political philosophy. But the major theme is a transformation of vision and a recovery of those blessings of joy, beauty and mystery, of which modern culture deprives us:

late 1971 distance, when thr is
no dawn, too many dumb side trips, i wanna go

      home, is home ths night. wher ar th birds th flowrs
   th changing earth th real cold th hard togerhr work in
all ths enslaving comfort

The idea that the transformed vision involves a change in our relation to the natural world, indicates bissett's affinities with the great Romantic visionaries. Though the concern with vision exists throughout **Th High Green Hill,** the most explicit development of the theme occurs in a similar though much shorter volume, *Polar Bear Hunt* (1972). Here bissett insists that we need only cultivate "th eye uv th soul" to end the spiritual exile suffered through our habitual way of seeing the world. (We may recall Blake's distinction between imaginative and corporeal sight.) We suffer from our conviction that we see most clearly when we divorce ourselves "objectively" from the world around us. Objectivity is for bissett a life-denying stance, the hallmark of egotism and the rationale for destruction; he urges our *participation* as whole creatures in the glories of our world, whether through dreams, imagination, love or celebration. As expressed in one of the chants in **Th High Green Hill**: "yr heart is th eye uv th universe." He urges an opening up of our responses to the world we inhabit. Abandoning the ego, we become fit for revelation and enter into ecstasies.

Many of the poems in **Th High Green Hill** evoke these ecstasies. Their language and structures reflect the awareness of plenitude, beauty, and mystery which is their main theme. If the style often becomes opaque, it seems less a reflection of vagueness in the experience than of the inadequacy of language to describe it. **"Th breath"** is perhaps the most splendid of bissett's visionary poems. The poet's sense of union with the world around him is conveyed through sharply realistic images of wood-chopping, cooking, and a vivid evocation of a winter camp in a forest by the sea. We understand that the palpable measure of things is our own body and its rhythms, not the abstract criteria by which we generally mark the passing of time or the extent of space—these are merely "veils / to pass thru," as bissett puts it elsewhere. Images of steaming breath, of smoke rising from a woodfire, and of mist rising from a river, affirm the spiritual identity of natural things. Perhaps the harmony of visionary experience and physical realities in bissett's poetry can best be illustrated by one of his brief lyrics, **"snow cummin"**:

> it takes just about
> one tree fr a weeks
> fire wood
>
> our arms thru th branches
>
> ther was a moose out
> ther last three nights
> calling
>
>   nd one night last
> week pack a wolves howling
> ther cries cummin from back
> a ways ovr th pond sum funny
> clouds passin ovr th moon
> a strange charge nd th blood
> was up high thru th dreams
>
> yu can see th frost in th air
>
> th original plan
>
> yu put on yr shirt in
> th early morning nd its a
> sheet uv ice ovr yr skin
>
> yr blanket uv hair kiss th
> blew tits rise in yr mouth
> th white snow flyin all aroun
> th warmth th trees green
>
> fingr th sky

Notice the rich asociations between the images of this extraordinary poem—the iconic unity of man and tree suggested in the lines on getting in the firewood; and the way the erotic images bend our attention back to the title, **"snow cummin,"** which then becomes a metaphor for the onrushing seed that seals the union of man and woman in the greater unity of earth, sky and forest. And what is "th original plan"? Merely the poet's morning routine? perhaps the breathtakingly beautiful communion with the land, which our race has somehow forsaken?

The "return to nature" is such a popular cliche and a persistent theme in our literature that there can be no question of its psychic pressure in our lives. Throughout *Th High Green Hill* bissett recharges the most common

images of nature with mystery and radiance: birds, flowers, hills, ice, snow, grass, animals, stars, sun, moon, earth, air, fire, water—all recover their primal power as kindred presences in our lives. Two images especially seem to acquire a crucial symbolic meaning: waves, as a trope for breath, continuity, duration; and fire, as the spiritual incandescence in natural things. The long meditations— **"WILD FLOWRS ABOVE TH TREE LINE," "th high green hill," "MEDICINE," "th mountain," "lettrs (for a passing comet," and "PRAYRS FOR TH ONE HABITATION"**—variously develop bissett's visionary themes: desire for the eclipse of the established order and the rise of an ecstatic community, the quest for a faith to endure and discover primitive ways, the prophesying of ancestral voices. Some of them share a common pattern: beyond the doubts and anger they express, they close with a rising crescendo of affirmation, a sense of homecoming to the land, to the present, to the blessings of the green world.

"PRAYRS FOR TH ONE HABITATION" begins by considering the treacheries and possibilities in words. Like so much of bissett's work, it merges comic realism with lyrical vision. The poet leaps out of bed, urged by a sense of imminent revelation, and runs smack into the wall. The admission to the poem of this level of human experience makes us the more willing to take its higher vision seriously. And of course, "higher" is the wrong word to use. Bissett envisions not a transcendence of "th one habitation," but a revelation of its beauty and fullness through our departure from personal obsessions and a tremendous intensification of our powers of apprehension. The poem implies a reverence for the elemental forms of life. "Animal" is no more a pejorative term for bissett than for the North American Indians with whom he shares a sense of affinity with other creatures, a respect for the powers of nature, and a desire to participate in rather than master the natural world. The meditation turns toward the question of evil—the destitution wrought by our social and political systems on the creative core of our beings. . . .

> mind creatures trying to influence nature
> telling th tree its beautiful then cutting it down
>   pouring concrete on its roots, more parking lots
>   For anothr thousand years, more gasoline
>
>   more amerikan controlled middul east crises
> for th oil rights, more parks and zoos, museums of
>   th last exampuls of ths life forms, befor
>   fossilized professors take ovr sayin class once
>
>   ther was a planet.

The poem ends with a mighty song celebrating the earth and all of its natural forms as *home,* reminiscent of apocalyptic passages in Romantic and modern poetry from *The Prelude* to "Sunday Morning."

Though the motif of pilgrimage in some of bissett's meditations, and his emphasis on achieving bliss through a kind of self-renunciation, suggest parallels with the great world religions, his work reflects more closely the values of primitive religion. . . .

[In] performing his sound poetry, bissett often passes over completely from art to ritual. And the willingness with which he has suffered deprivation and persecution for the sake of living a life consistent with his vision, is not unlike the shaman's arduous discipline for the sake of cultivating his powers.

Many of bissett's drawings and paintings also reflect the primitive sympathies in his vision. Numerous designs in his volumes resemble the petroglyphs which continue to be discovered in the Canadian wilderness, remnants of the sacred arts of various Amerindian tribes. As though expressing the spiritual energy which (the Indians believed) pervades nature, bissett's favorite designs are peculiarly fluid, suggesting the shapes of flames, or sunbursts, or flowers, or wings, sometimes simultaneously. His drawings have a primordial quality: ample space, simple lines, a curious brilliance. Perhaps their most significant motif is the interpenetration of tapucuman havtomy with elemental images of the world's body: waves, sun, mountains, hills, trees. The human or semi-human figures often suggest primitive people and their priests, or gods. . . .

A final point I'd like to make about bissett is beautifully illustrated in a concrete poem near the end of *Th High Green Hill*. This **"rattle poem"** is a delightful visual pun: there is no need for me to comment on the appropriateness of its shape and "sound." But I think it's important to ask, who uses rattles? And of course the answer is, two sorts of people: babies and shamans. "I wanta rattul" could be merely a peremptory demand for the toy, but it can also mean, for the baby, "I want to play," and for the shaman, "I want to perform a ritual." Nor are these last two meanings very distinct from one another. As Johan Huizinga has suggested, ritual and play are intrinsically related, and express impulses which may also issue in poetry—especially lyric poetry, which comes "closest to supreme wisdom but also to inanity." Such an insight can illuminate the main features of bill bissett's art: its affinity to the primitive; its frequently enigmatic quality; its heavy use of repetition; its subversive intent; its exuberance, its capriciousness, its moments of astounding beauty and power. It may also give us some understanding of one of the most marvellous of his achievements: the demeanour of perfect seriousness and perfect non-seriousness, simultaneously. Perhaps this is one of the rich dimensions missing from our lives—at least, since we grew up.

Jack David (essay date 1977)

SOURCE: "Visual Poetry in Canada: Birney, Bissett, and bp," in *Studies in Canadian Literature,* Vol. 2, No. 2, 1977, pp. 252-66.

[*David is a Canadian editor and writer. In the following excerpt, he analyzes several of Bissett's concrete poems.*]

For Bill Bissett, 1962 was the year that he first "allowed the words to act visually on the page." Most noticeable, initially, about Bissett's poetry is his peculiar orthography, described by Frank Davey as "idiosyncratic quasi-phonetic spelling" which is part of his "attempt to write of an unqualified, elemental, and pure visionary world" as well as "a symbolic act of social rebellion." For example, Bissett spells "the" as "th", "and" as "nd", and "some" as "sum". Bissett defends his way of spelling by observing that "as recently as 17th century," there was "no consistency in spelling rules." He wonders why poetry has "to be / lockd in th structure of 17th c. / bourgeousie stuffd / chair art forms." It is hard to know where to begin talking about Bissett's visual poetry; perhaps I should begin with a poem that uses only two typewritten letters, *u* and *o*. A first glance shows that this poem, "uo," has a black/white image created by the typing of the *o* over the *u*; a light-coloured bird is visible, wings outspread. Furthermore, the bird is encased within a square, like a cage. However, "uo" can be viewed from different angles with different results. By concentrating on the darker image, one can see the outline of a building, maybe the Parliament Buildings in Ottawa. Still viewing the darker image, but from the opposite direction, one can make out a schematic version of a phallus. The whiter image can also be seen as a profile of a human face. Bissett says of the "visual form" of his poetry that it is the "apprehension of th spirit shape of th pome rather than stanzaic nd rectangular."

The letters themselves carry content; *ou* might be read as "oh, you!" or "oh! you?" or some variation thereof. The letters could also be read in the other direction; "you, oh." or "you owe!" The *u*'s, read upside down, look much like *n*'s, and the word "no" is a possibility, may be advising "you," the reader, to avoid seeing too much in the poem. . . .

Bill Bissett's **"quebec bombers"** is very complex because of its unusual shape and its overlapping typographies and because of the tremendous concentration of meaning into small bits of language. Each of the three typographies has a separate function, both decorative and functional.

The graphically designed borders provide vertical stability and the *fleur-de-lis* recall Quebec. The big letters are cracking, like the insecurity of the province of Quebec itself (P.Q.), and the letters *P* and *Q* are not immediately followed by *R* and *S*, leaving the impression that Bissett has chosen the letters for reasons other than simply alphabetic. The next letters, *T* and *U*, have two translations: first, *tu* means "you" in French; and *tu* also is part of the verb *tuer*, to kill. The *tu tu* means "you kill," and refers to either the killing of the ruling class of Quebec by the FLQ or the killing of the working class by the ruling class. The rest of the big letters could indicate the end of the alphabet as we know it, and symbolically the end of the English language as the language of business in Quebec. Their very largeness denotes them as the dominant power on the page (and in the province), but as a power which is splitting apart under pressure. The third layer of typography is typewritten words—solid, direct, and simple. They represent the new radical citizen of Quebec who moves against the old power-base from a humble, yet secure foundation. These typewritten letters contain the heart of the poem's message. The fragment at the top of the page, "wer only human too wer," describes the effect of the non-Quebec ruling class who change Quebeckers from human to sub-human. What was once human (wer is a contraction of we're, we are) has now lost its humanity (were or we were). Just beneath this opening phrase is a large section of typewritten words, partly obscured by the larger letters. "what can we say" is repeated for the first two lines and signifies not only a rhetorical question suggesting both resignation and action, but also a locale where words no longer have any ability to change things. A large block of typewritten and partially superimposed *y*'s follows, asking repeatedly "why?" In the centre of the page, a clear unequivocal "keep yr cell clen" (keep your cell clean) refers to the small revolutionary FLQ cadres and urges them to remain true to their idealistic purposes.

The final block of typewriting is the largest in the poem. It begins with the phrase "dirty concrete poet" repeated twice, then changes to "the concrete is dirty dirty," "sum like it clean what dew they ooo." The distinction between "clean" and "dirty" concrete poetry is that "in clean concrete . . . the visual shape of the work is primary, linguistic signs secondary." Dirty concrete poems have "amorphous physical shape and complex and involute arrangements of the linguistic elements." As related to **"quebec bombers,"** the comparison presents the clean ordered life of a capitalist system and the dirty chaotic life of the lower classes. "dirt" fills the next five lines from margin to margin in an even pattern, an empty line follows, and then "dirt" returns in some of its anagrammatical forms: "ddt" (a permanent insecticide) and "dt's" (delirium tremens). These latter variations of the word "dirt" describe the results (dt's) of poor living conditions, where ddt is necessary. Lastly, the word "spray" is printed, and its anagrams underscore the thrust of the whole poem: the "spray" of ddt; the religious "prey" of the Catholic church in Quebec; the "spas" of the captialists; the occasional "rays" of hope; the lack of "pay"; and the ultimate sterilization of the people—"spays." This line is followed by a row of "augh" and "agh," the sounds of deep distress and pain.

Bill Bissett often writes anti-establishment poetry. In **"quebec bombers,"** by manipulating three different typographies, Bissett sets up a complex group of graphic and semantical correspondences which result in overwhelming "praise" for those "quebec bombers" who dare to shatter the forms of political and social repression. The poem represents a kind of culmination of visual poetry that depends predominantly on typography. . . .

Bill Bissett is both an artist and a poet; it is not uncommon for him to combine his graphics with his linguistic creations.

In **"th pull,"** he superimposes his own printing over a page from a book about Indians of the west coast, begin-

ning with the Pueblos of the American Southwest and ending on the line "Northward up the coast, a different breed could be." Bissett's printing describes "the pull tord th / north" and leaves the implication that, unlike the south where "each tribe remained in its own snug," in the north the "different breed" was now flourishing. This is a vision of unity, not of "Babel," which is emphasized by the final lines: "at night th / northern star / so clear." Handwriting leaves no question about the persona of the poem; in a collage poem, like Bissett's, it is important to know which point of view is the poet's.

Len Early   (essay date 1980)

SOURCE: An introduction to *SELECTED POEMS: BEYOND EVEN FAITHFUL LEGENDS,* by Bill Bissett, Talonbooks, 1980, pp. 11-18.

[*In the following excerpt, Early discusses Bissett's visionary politics and places his work in the context of contemporary Canadian poetry.*]

Writing on bill bissett in 1980 is a rather different venture than responding to his books as they appeared ten or even five years ago. Bissett's poetry was so closely identified with the political/cultural convulsion of the 1960's that even its admirers were bound to wonder how many of its features would retain interest as the years passed. This selection should reassure them. In the first place, it will remind us that his poetry had deeper sources than topical issues and literary fashion. In the second, it shows that his best work has always been charged with the energy and formal ingenuity of enduring art.

As a radical presence on the Canadian literary scene, bissett has been a controversial figure for some fifteen years. He emerged in the early 1960's in Vancouver as a pioneer in mixed-media, an innovator in concrete and sound poetry, a founder of blewointmentpress, and a frequent target of the local reaction against counterculture styles and values. He has been one of the most supportive of his own generation of Canadian writers and artists. He has also been subject to police harassment, and with fellow experimental poet, bp Nichol, has been denounced as a pornographer in the House of Commons. He has been attacked by reviewers in critical journals and praised by some of the most accomplished Canadian writers among both his elders and his peers.

Resistance to bissett's work has been so far largely conservative in tone. It is a resistance which most readers probably feel initially in the face of his startlingly unconventional writing and drawing. Objections to avant-garde poetry in the name of "the tradition," however, usually imply either an undeveloped or a fixated aesthetic sense. Whatever its critics may fear or its practitioners wish, the avant garde is unlikely to imperil the classics. What it can do is nourish and extend our aesthetic capacity through transforming our assumptions about art. Those who dismiss bissett's work out of hand and who, like Mr. Mustart, the unsympathetic bank manager in one of his poems, swing away

> toward th
> blank wall or a typical Canadian
> landscape

will miss one of the most exhilarating voices in our recent poetry. By now, the number and stature of bissett's admirers ought to guarantee his reputation against literary traditionalists, outraged parliamentarians, and other institutional agents. Conventional resistance may be replaced, however, by resentment among some of his more polemical contemporaries that his work crosses boundaries rather than closing them down, for an experimental poetics has never prevented his simultaneous and often skillful use of more traditional lyric and narrative forms.

An aversion to all doctrine, conservative or avant garde, fuels bissett's creativity, and a sense of wholeness is what distinguishes his work from much modern poetry. This wholeness is manifest in his central concern—the quest for "yunyun" (psychic, sexual, communal or cosmic), in his inclusive technique as poet and painter and in the personality which we come to recognize in his work. If at times his sympathies take him treacherously close to ideology or cliché, a leaven of irony, often self-directed, is apt to appear. In **"the tomato conspiracy aint worth a whol pome,"** he parodies one of the obsessions of his own constituency; plotting by entrenched powers against the people. While he is quite clear about what he hates, he is too aware of his own complexity to make his hatred an icon or a dogma to close off the new insight or the next poem. In general, he has made his self-consciousness a condition of growth and strength rather than a fetish—or what amounts to the same thing, the spectre of an enervating malaise.

To read bissett carefully and at length is to be successively confounded, provoked, harrowed and delighted. It is also to become familiar with a variety of techniques explored by bissett, bp Nichol, and others, and introduced into Canadian writing in the 1960's. For bissett, the discovery of an art appropriate to his vision meant the questioning of every stylistic and formal assumption inherited from poets of the past, as well as prolonged experimentation with the visual and vocal aspects of language. His suspicion of convention led him to reject standard spelling and grammar. It also inspired a rebuke to the very notion of "meaning," if that is what we impose upon works of art to avoid the disturbing stimulus that a full experience of them may demand. Hence, certain pieces by bissett confront us with sheer disorder, defying interpretation and inviting us to reconsider our comfortable conceptions of reality.

The political significance of bissett's style can hardly be overestimated. From the beginning, he has maintained that "correct" spelling and prescribed grammar are instruments of class oppression and insidious restrictions upon imagination and its expression. His own peculiar composition and spelling (often phonetic) amounts to a personal dec-laration of independence from linguistic authority in general and traditional poetic practice in particular. He may well be the purest type in Canadian poetry of the visionary artist who, in William Blake's famous statement, must create a system or be enslaved by another man's. As a radical visionary, bissett resembles Blake, Shelley and certain other Romantic writers in his uncompromising advocacy of personal and intellectual freedom against power-seekers and claimants of privileged knowledge. "Knowledge" is in fact a negative term for bissett, signifying our division from the world and its creatures, or our abstraction from the artist's word or image. It is contrary to the primary values of participation, relationship and love. His work is intended neither to mystify nor to compel deference in its readers, but to enrich their imaginative life and evoke their own creative powers.

> **The political significance of bissett's style can hardly be overestimated. From the beginning, he has maintained that "correct" spelling and prescribed grammar are instruments of class oppression and insidious restrictions upon imagination and its expression.**
>
> *—Len Early*

Among his most intriguing poems are those which stress the visual properties of words and letters, singly or in combination, beyond their strictly semantic value. His concrete poems tease us out of thought and challenge our imaginations. We are confronted, in one example, by a solid rectangle composed of alternating W's and M's. It is merely a typographical design to please the eye? A closer look discovers that it's not quite solid after all: a single "O" in the upper right corner breaks the pattern to suggest a number of words (if read vertically and diagonally as well as horizontally): "womb" "mom" "woe" "ow" "mow" "om" "wow". These terms form sets which can be related, with and without irony. Similarly, the "O" itself has diverse connotations: surprise and understanding, perfection and nothingness. Contrary nuances are also registered in the strong contrast between the angular shapes of the two consonants and the rounder contour of the vowel. The design indicates that even a slight swerve from uniform patterning can eventuate in the profundities of birth, suffering and consciousness. Light out of darkness. Or so I see it. While it may not be profound in itself, like many of bissett's concrete poems, this one has the deft suggestiveness of successful art.

Bissett's concrete pieces, like his more traditional poems, range from the playful and one-dimensional through the complex and satiric to visionary work informed with beauty and intensity. Akin to his concrete poems in their primarily visual technique are his paintings (abstract/representational), found art (cartoons, newspaper clippings, commercial graphics), photographs, and collages of any of the above. A number of these collages combine fragments of the alphabet with pictures of primitive or tribal figures, often in moments of violence or suspense. Each of these should be considered on its own, but cumulatively, they invite a meditation on the role of language in human experience. They seem to me to approach in a more detached perspective the primitivism of some of bissett's most distinctive creations, his line drawings of human or godlike beings, and his chants. The latter, of course, take us directly into the aural dimension of his poetry.

Like most of his generation of Canadian poets, bissett has been much concerned with the vocal aspect of his writing. His interest in "sound" goes far beyond the struggle for an authentic personal voice, however. While many of his poems invite reading in a conversational tone, others demand a more heavily stressed, even rhetorical intonation, and others still move into the realms of chant and incantations. One of the first steps necessary to appreciate bissett's poems is an awareness of his vocal patterns. It helps a good deal to have heard him live or on record; without that advantage it helps to read him aloud. A sense of his characteristic rhythms and attention to his spacing, line breaks and the larger shapes of poems clarifies much that at first perplexes in his disregard of normal syntax and punctuation. Amost all his traditional and much of his experimental poetry attests that "our desire moves / thru our lungs."

While bissett's sound poems have affinities with Oriental and Amerindian chanting, they are more than imitations. Remarkably, they combine with their reverence or praise the playful quality we often sense in uncodified ritual. While their power is limited in print, they are evidently designed to "release th spirit" from its accustomed prisons of belief and unbelief, boredom and distraction, anxiety and regret. In their "pure" form as sound without conceptual substance, they reach universal levels of feeling beneath the diverse vocabularies and idioms which distance us even within a common language. What force bissett's chants lose in print is partially compensated in their visual appeal as concrete poetry or as typographical abstracts.

Bissett's chants take to an extreme the repetition which is fundamental in his poetry. While he has developed various styles appropriate to his personal, political and visionary themes, certain features remain constant: elementary diction, a distinctive use of the copula, structural sequences of participles and conjunctions. To some extent he shares with other important poets of the 1960's and 1970's a sense of flux, an assumption that the poem only registers a condition or perception to be dissolved in the next moment or the next poem; however, his poetry as a whole also implies a powerful vision of enduring spiritual forces associated with sexuality and with the radiance of nature. At its best, his visionary poetry reflects certain timeless recognitions, largely through the recurrence which pervades its rhythms and imagery.

Like most visionaries, bissett is convinced that dreams are the source of poetry and that the greatest of dreams is the dream of paradise. This idea is most explicit in brief lyrics such as: **"TH GOLDEN DAWN," "canoe,"** and **"treez,"** but is also the essential impulse in much longer and more complex works marked by a fascinating constellation of images. Just as bissett's poems surge into extraordinary passages of sound, they generate motifs which seem extravagant compared to the scrupulously commonplace imagery of many of his contemporaries. The elements of wind, fire and water combine with more exotic images of jewels, dragons and chariots to suggest his affinities with traditional visionary art. One of his major poems here is **"th breath,"** which opens a previous selection of his work, *pass th food release th spirit book* (1973), and which closes the present one:

> th fire burning its song thru yr blood
>
> of all th peopul animal plant creatures
> dancing along th flames of all th colors
> shapes expressions fierce loving and nameless
>
> th one blood stream

Where bissett's writing differs from traditional visionary poetry and most resembles his contemporaries' work is in the fluid quality of his lines. If his evocations of paradise imply ultimate realities, his forms tend to avoid ordered delineation. He is much like other poets of his generation in his suspicion of the definitive or the conclusive. His work conveys the impression of an emerging vision, a revelation in process rather than the closure of achievement; hence, many of his poems approximate dreams in form as well as in content. **"th missyun"** and **"rainbow music,"** for example, have the rich associative patterning and reverberatino of dreams. [**"beyond even faithful legends"**] is slightly different. While its fluidity may confuse us upon first reading, confusion is the problem it addresses. Readers who take time to give it a second or third reading will discover an exceptionally moving statement emerging from the text, a sense of emotional desolation surprised by a strength to endure and to seek a way out. The question is: how "to go on living" when conventional wisdom has failed. Do we "cease to care"? Align ourselves with political power? Find solace in the praxis love? The poem finally affirms the last course, while simultaneously challenging the popular notion of romantic love ("say who built this valentine"). Bissett urges us to look "beyond even faithful legends" for what will nourish our spirits and our relations with one another. For his own part as a writer, he must look beyond the legends of traditional art for a form faithful to his own vision.

Clearer in their delineations and more traditional in their use of language are a number of poems concerned not with harmonious states but with the contingencies of bissett's universe: personal and public circumstances which baffle or divert or menace. "Art is all use," bissett maintains, and we would be wrong to regard his concrete or visionary pieces as less political in implication than **"NUCLEAR CIRCULAR"** or **"chile."** The latter, however, deal more directly with the enormities of our destructive ingenuity in the late twentieth century and with the "power intrigue" which corrupts our institutions. The more successful political poems seem rooted in bissett's personal experience, setting very particular details—the preposterous and violent facts—in an ironic context. Generally, they affirm the curious dignity of most victims and the one-dimensional nature of their oppressors and exploiters. The "authorities" bissett encounters are always potentially human, though often dehumanized in their function. Bissett's own humanity appears in his range of tone, from the comic through the impassioned to the verge of despair. Until our collective visionary powers become more vigorous, a sense of irony may be our best aid to individual survival. Bissett's irony is seldom bleak, closer to humour and to the playful impulse which informs so much of his work. His blewointmentpress, wryly named after a treatment for body lice, since 1963, has tendered fantastic medicine for our rampaging social dis-ease.

The issues of integrity and exploitation are central to bissett's reflections on Canada, which increase the small number of good national medications in our poetry. To a degree, these create the same effect as his other political poems in identifying personal circumstances within larger problems. In **"th north aint easy to grow food in"** and **"Th Canadian,"** bissett relates his life as a writer to a question of a national consciousness; in both circumstances, he urges the need for continuity between our material and spiritual resources, through the metaphor of "food." What will inspire our common health? In **"canada,"** he probes our recalcitrant climate and history for qualities which might free myth from our reality and he articulates our contradictions and wholeness, our pettiness and strength. How can we realize the possibilities of this place in its largest sense? Bissett's best poems demonstrate the imagination's ability to break out of traps, even of its own making. . . .

Living with the vision does mean distress as well as glory, in those intervals when the vision clouds or weakens or undergoes eclipse, and a survey of bissett's previous books (some forty of them) might well map out those intervals. But it would be of minor relevance in the end. His poetry springs not from a random or relative sense of his experience, but from an imagination which forms and reforms its intuitions of a vision potent in us all.

Ann Mandel   (essay date 1984)

SOURCE: "Free Subject," in *Canadian Literature,* No. 101, Summer, 1984, pp. 149-53.

[*In the following excerpt, Mandel reviews Bissett's* Northern Birds in Color *and praises the vitality of his writing.*]

[Bissett] is certainly Canada's poet of "the tribal dream." *Northern Birds,* his forty-seventh book of poetry, is a continuation of his constant prayer for the world to be a home for everyone, a vision to be realized by "th heeling vibraysyun uv th trust," a tribal caring of one for another. His poems articulate the grace of acknowledging and yield-

ing to cycles of nature, rage against political and nuclear madness, wittily criticize the pope, dentists, ecological destruction (he has a wonderful plan for cleaning up English Bay involving diving cows), and his own eccentric inconsistencies. Like a rare northern bird, his imagination ranges from vast constellations and cataclysmic visions to minute worlds in grains of sand where

> ther ar cities whol undr th sand
> uv a diffrent molecular ordr
> yu b cum th wish uv hevn to go to.

Bissett's remarkable ability to keep his vision moving and fresh over the years comes largely from a linguistic energy which creates visible sound and aural shapes. We can see and hear him like the birds in his poems

> xplooring   th   colors   uv auras
>   n   secret   treez   singing
> spinning   letting   out   brite
>   cones   uv   sound   thru
>   th air. . . .

Between the migratory poles of his winged vision, there's an essentially domestic area, a place of friendships and gentle humour. In my favourite poem in the book, **"we live in a hundrid yeer old house,"** the house is both the reality of and metaphor for what the world can and could be:

> ths house is groundid in
>   all th original
> ways uv love n hurt . . .
>
>   an opn being
>   uv what is possibul . . .
>
>   no building is old enuff to house
> us aftr
>   wev livd heer
>
>   partees that wer
> whol lives changes that stop analysis
> so many desires realizd
>
>   generasyuns
> heer previous
>
>   ther lives permit ours.

Karl Jirgens   (essay date 1992)

SOURCE: "Bill Bissett," in *Canadian Writers and Their Works, Vol. 8,* edited by Robert Lecker, Jack David, and Ellen Quigley, ECW Press, 1992, pp. 17-109.

[*In the following excerpt, Jirgens places Bissett's work in the tradition of English Romantic poetry.*]

bissett can be thought of as a late Romantic maverick. In many ways, his writing seems anachronistic. On the one hand, it displays structural manipulations that are typical of the twentieth century. On the other hand, it embraces a timeless transcendental philosophy.

From a philosophical viewpoint, it could be argued that bissett is working in the tradition of Romantic writers such as Blake, Shelley, and perhaps Yeats. Like his Romantic predecessors, bissett values individualism and original imagination. On one level, the distinctive variety of approaches in bissett's writing can be seen as an affirmation of his will as an individual.

David Perkins, in his *English Romantic Writers,* discusses the qualities of Romanticism and the contributions made by German critics Friedrich and August Wilhelm von Schlegel in 1798:

The "Romantic" refuses to recognize restraints in subject matter or form and so is free to represent the abnormal, grotesque, and monstrous and to mingle standpoints, *genres,* modes of expression (such as philosophy and poetry), and even the separate arts in a single work. Ultimately it mirrors the struggle of genius against all limitation, and it leads to a glorification of yearning, striving, and becoming and of the personality of the artist as larger and more significant than the necessarily incomplete expression of it in his work.

The parallels between this tradition and bissett's own writing are obvious. Like the Romantics, bissett refuses to be limited by either structure or subject. His representation of social ills is often grotesque or bizarre. The yearning or striving for self-growth in his writing parallels a self-actualization in real life.

As several critics have already pointed out, it is possible to trace a number of Romantic influences in bissett's poetry. While an understanding of the Romantic aspect of bissett's poetry is quite useful, I believe that we must go further in order to gain a deeper appreciation of his writing. The relationship between bissett's transcendentalism and his poetic structure is significant, particularly if one considers his lyric poems.

bissett's poetry serves a bridge-like function linking the real or actual world with a transcendental ideal world. For bissett, the transcendental world represents an ideal Other and bissett's lyric poetry is characterized by the desire to become one with this Other. bissett continually returns to the matter of "yunyun" (i.e., union). The process by which this union happens is what bissett himself calls a molecular dissolve. The breakdown of the ego is accompanied by the structural fragmentation of the text. The dissolve begins with a type of propulsion. The aggressive psychic drives inspired by desire and death are initially used to propel the protagonist towards the ideal or the Other. However, upon transcending the physical world, notions of desire and death become irrelevant. Instead, the subject enters into a spiritual union with the cosmos. At this point, the ego has dissolved and merged with the cosmic environment.

bissett uses the language of poetry to create a bridge between the depths of his unconscious and the ineffable limits of the external world. Poetry is the bridge between the individual unconscious and a collective cosmic consciousness, between actual and ideal. bissett's earthly world is like Plato's, an inferior mirror of the idyllic astral plane. However, unlike Plato's, bissett's ideal or spiritual world is accessible here and now, if only for brief moments. Aspects of the natural world such as forests, lakes, birds, and so on are already invested with the essence of the ideal. It is only a question of recognizing this essence. It is as though the real and the ideal are parallel universes. One can be standing in a forest and suddenly be transported to an alternate world provided one is able to transcend the limits of conventional perception. Much of bissett's poetry deals with the effort to transcend the quotidian in order to reach the ideal plane which is characterized by grace, beauty, and love. Frequently, his poems deal with binary relationships, surfaces which must be penetrated, reflections, mirror doubles, and so on. These binary pairs establish the two aspects of the self that bissett is concerned with in his writing. Similarly, images of doorways, passages, and journeys frequently recur in his writing. bissett's poems, and especially his lyric poems, often feature an earth-bound self and an Other self which transcends this reality. The Other self and the Other reality become synonymous because within the idylic world there is no differentiation between the individual and the rest of creation. The dissolution of differentiation is in keeping with bissett's molecular view of the universe. For bissett, the dissolve of the ego that is necessary in order to achieve a transcendental state is complemented by a dissolve of language:

> evreething goez in th molecular dissolv
> i leev the room th room leevs evreething bcums
> goldn i heer angels
> singing thers a highr vibraysyun seems an eternitee
> i was singing

(Canada Gees Mate For Life)

bissett's linguistic form transcends literary convention in a way that echoes his protagonist's transcendence of the physical dimension. While the fragmentation or dissolve is not as extreme in the lyric poems as in some of the concrete poems, it is still significant. The absence of punctuation, the frequent chant-like quality, and the dissolution of conventional form all serve to suggest a state of being that goes beyond our linear conceptions of time and space.

There is also a dissolution of the more conventional signifying function of the language of the text. The various signifiers ultimately refer to a single cosmic union. A unique set of conditions distinguishes things on the transcendental level. Waves, intervals, and densities are conditions that describe the properties of the ideal plane. Images of lakes, birds, and mountains serve a purely symbolic function representing the pulse, the freedom, and the sense of timelessness that is experienced by the journeying soul. The dissolution of a difference between self and Other is frequently celebrated in bissett's more ecstatic lyrics. Within this state, the subject enters into a communion with the sacred living things of the ideal world. The features of the landscape in bissett's lyric poems are perceived to be alive. Like the birds and trees, the sky and the water are invested with a kind of sentient energy. The earth itself is often depicted as being alive or breathing. Further, this ideal astral world is illuminated by colourful auras of the type that are depicted in bissett's paintings. But, only those who can transcend the conscious barriers of the material world are able to become one with the idyllic metaphysical plane.

There is something primal about the journey of the soul to the ideal plane. In a way the journey can be thought of as a return. The protagonist as a child of the earth-mother seeks to return to the comforts and nourishments of the paradise that existed before "civilization" deteriorated the earthly plane. The cosmic plane can be understood in terms of a spiritual rather than physical fulfilment. bissett's lyric poetry features brief flights in a timeless realm of being beyond the shifting, sensory world of earth-bound experience:

> i remembr us riding th bird in our
> dreems past attachments thru a series uv veils
>
> to anothr place

On the transcendental plane spatio-temporal laws are suspended infinity appears to lie within a single idyllic moment.

The desire to return to an ideal world or a type of paradise can be explained in terms of neo-Platonic transcendentalism and Amerindian shamanism. Scott Watson, in his introduction to *fires in the tempul,* explains: "The ecstatic outward movement of the artist/shaman is an attempt at return." Watson discusses Mircea Eliade's theories as expressed in *Shamanism: Archaic Techniques of Ecstasy,* and explains that the shaman is interested in abolishing the present human condition and recovering the situation as it was at the beginning of time. Friendship with animals and knowledge of their language can be read as signs that the shaman has re-established the "paradisal" situation that was lost at the dawn of time. Generally speaking, bissett's lyric poems are marked by an attempt to return to the paradise which, it could be argued, has a paternal aspect. In bissett's poems, the protagonist unites with a kind of universal father and mother figure upon reaching cosmic consciousness. Sometimes these figures are represented as gods, at other times in the guise of a living and breathing earth. The figures are identified in poems such as **"sonik prayr"** as **"th ancient lord laydee uv th univers."** It is significant that the god and goddess are omnipresent. An awareness of their presence is dependent upon the protagonist's level of consciousness.

In bissett's poetry a union between the spiritual self and spirit of the cosmos can only happen by becoming unconscious of the physical world. Theoretically, in bissett's poetry a completely transcendental state of beauty and goodness is simultaneous with the moment of death.

Only with death can the physical plane be completely abandoned. This view may have something to do with bissett's own out-of-body and near-death experiences. He has explained in the past that his brief visions during moments of physical crisis have given him glimpses of what he believes to be a paradisal world on the spiritual plane.

I mentioned above that for bissett, modes of expression such as poetry can form temporary bridges between the physical real and the spiritual ideal. However, it is important to keep in mind that bissett is engaged with painting and writing as process rather than product. Poetry not only can form a bridge, it can be the impetus by which the link between the physical and spiritual is formed. By being fully engaged in the act of painting or writing, the body, mind, and spirit become in tune with the cosmos. If we confine ourselves to linguistic expression, then, for bissett each act of writing can be seen as having the potential of becoming a transcendental experience. bissett appears to be aware of the bridging power of writing. The following excerpt from **"poetry dusint have to be"** serves to illustrate this premise:

> writing poems can be abt many things
> can be abt nothing but what it itself is
> writing pomes in a way is longr than we are
> and what we can know writing pomes
> is also th voice uv ths things speaking thru us
> (*MEDICINE MY MOUTH'S ON FIRE*)

For bissett, poetry can form a bridge between self and Other; it can also be the thing that opens up the channels between the two worlds. . . .

While poetry serves as a link or bridge between the material and spiritual worlds, physical activities do play an important role in bissett's lyric poetry. Activities such as breathing, chanting, taking drugs, working, meditating, copulating, and praying are used in order to abandon the restrictions of the conscious mind in order to achieve transcendental psychic states. With sexual encounters the figure of the Other is especially significant. On the physical plane the paradisal world finds an earthly counterpart in the sexual partner. The poem **"in ths forest"** in *Beyond Even Faithful Legends,* which originally appeared in *MEDICINE MY MOUTH'S ON FIRE,* is a good example. In that poem a transcendental awareness is simultaneous with the sexual experience:

> with our touch n th treez moov thru us
> th earth moov thru us watr sky cum thru our
> limbs our flesh nd th skin is nd th skin is opn to our
> touch thru our belly th spine uv th univers all is
> opn th skin is opn thru our soul
>
> thats mor like it
> thn ths changes cum
> aiii anjee yukee uuuuuuauuuauuuaye
> kunjanaihaiyee ajakukalikunjakaleeee
> chunakahaneeeeeeeeeeeeeeeeee
> (*Beyond Even Faithful Legends*)

A profound sexual relationship with a physical Other can potentially establish a transcendental channel or bridge to the spiritual Other. The ejaculation simultaneously becomes the release from the physical and the entrance to the astral plane.

The poem **"rose th night nd th green flowr"** is an especially good example of the interrelationship between sexuality and the transcendental state. In this poem bissett uses a great deal of personification:

> nd the legs uv th great trees bow down take
> ea othrs warmth to join wrappd round
> ea limb nd th blood runs thru th flowr
> (*Beyond Even Faithful Legends*)

This is not the vegetation of the physical world. It exists on an alternate and ideal plane of existence. The living plants and trees become an extension of the protagonist and his lover/Other. The sexual union between the two lovers is complemented by their union with the immediate environment. Later in the poem the connection is emphasized:

> lie down in here with th branches around
> yu yr legs on th moss th fire between us nd
> th evening star climbing ovr th far mountain
> (*Beyond Even Faithful Legends*)

Where earlier the trees and plants embraced each other, here they embrace the lover. The connection between natural environment and lover is further emphasized by the fact that there is a "rose" in the lover's "forehead." The relationship is discussed in terms of floral images. When the speaker says "ths flowr opening takes yu," he is referring to the growth of feeling between the two. Later, he describes their love as a "bright green flowr." The floral imagery throughout the poem serves to reinforce the union between the lovers and the union between lovers and environment. At least on a symbolic level, the environment and the lovers are one.

The unity of the lovers is further symbolized by images of smoke and fire:

> what we beleev is what we reaching thru th
> flame for th smoke   yr lungs full is that
> th place is smoke again th hot coals n th
> rising smoke is passing it back ovr th
> flame we see by is taking hold uv
> th smoke again is what we are
> passing thru
> (*Beyond Even Faithful Legends*)

The smoke and the fire between them become gateway images that open the door between the conventional physical world and a heightened awareness of the spiritual plane. The act of smoking unites the two individuals and prepares them for the transcendental journey. Related to the images of fire are sexual images:

> only th shade along th neck th rose in yr forhead th
> rose th univers btween yr legs

> and th endless rope yu swing on high aint like
> anything els above th mist th jewl opns n
> th flower
> (*Beyond Even Faithful Legends*)

The fact that the "univers" can be found between the lover's legs is a strong indication of the transcendental quality of the sexual experience. Further, there is a confluence of vegetable and sexual images in this passage. This confluence is characteristic of bissett's molecular dissolve. That is, the various image sets start sharing the same signifying function. Everything enters into the transcendental union:

> and th watrs nd flame pour fall thru
> us as our hands n toes meet becum
> each othr th grass grow
> (*Beyond Even Faithful Legends*)

The transcendental quality of this plane of experience is emphasized by the suspension of conventional physical laws. For example, the lover is not subject to the laws of gravity: "thn as yu walk ovr th cliff nevr falling n all / is light n tendrness" (*Beyond Even Faithful Legends*).

Not only are physical laws suspended, but so are temporal ones. Near the opening of the poem, time is measured by the lover's "nevr ending heart / beat" (*Beyond Even Faithful Legends*). The poem itself can be thought of as a type of return to an original paradise which can only be perceived by those who can transcend the physical plane. The narrator/protagonist points out that he

> saw th bird ovr th rock
> saw th legs opn saw th tree rise
> th earth moov . . .

but that

> . . . sum didint
> see much els only th skies opning
> n th fur along yr hand . . .
> (*Beyond Even Faithful Legends*)

Unlike the others, the two lovers are able to transcend the limits of conventional perception. The notion of a return to a primal origin is emphasized in the final line: "glad to cum home" (*Beyond Even Faithful Legends*). In **"rose th night nd th green flowr,"** sexuality becomes a means by which a transcendental state can be reached.

A related transcendental bridge in bissett's poetry is built by breath and breathing. Perhaps the most subtle as well as most important image in bissett's shorter lyric poems is breath. In bissett's work, breath is perceived as evidence of spiritual energies unified with the physical body. Through breath comes vocal expression, and in vocal expression the physical and spiritual are united, resulting in a temporary transcendence of this plane. The rhythm of breathing often suggests an ecstatic coupling with the spiritual plane as this passage from **"th breath"** suggests:

th breath

             is continuous
    is how we move holds th seas within
                   of our moshun
    is th same as th eyee
           opening

(Beyond Even Faithful Legends)

Just as the image of the spirit ship becomes a metaphor for the journeys of the soul, so breathing becomes a metaphor for the sea of all life through which the body as vessel travels through:

    th breath
           cums to yu is yu for a

    while
        is evry part of yr moving flesh

    goes thru yu a long way

    no way at all th distance is nevr

    measured, . . .

(Beyond Even Faithful Legends)

The sea of life is limitless; therefore, it goes "a long way" and yet it is all around us hence "no way at all." For bissett the journey of the soul occurs on this sea of living breath.

A kind of enlightenment occurs in the poem. The protagonist arrives at a point where he realizes that he is in a union with the things that he experiences:

    even inside th light and darkness th
    same as my extended hand i did not know
        what i touchd on

            was so part of

    th boat great sea rolling rolling rolling
    ovr and ovr nd again

(Beyond Even Faithful Legends)

The boat can be understood as the physical self. Initially, the speaker is unaware of the connections between things. But a kind of molecular dissolve is accompanied by a dissolution of the ego. The protagonist in the poem realizes that he is part of a kind of rhythmic concatenation. His breathing keeps time with the strokes of his axe as he cuts wood. The image of his breath is echoed by the fire and by the vapour of the snow melting and then boiling in the pot. The metamorphosis of the snow from solid to liquid to vapour marks various levels of being which align themselves with the speaker's state of mind. He realizes that he is both an active agent and a part of much larger metamorphosis when he says earlier that, "at th first breath

of life we stir and rise" (*Beyond Even Faithful Legends*). He becomes aware that he is included in a larger cycle of birth, death, and rebirth. The cycles echo the images of waves and breath that come earlier in the poem. Schematically, the smaller cycles of breath are part of the larger cycles of day and night, which are part of the still larger cycles of life and death and so on. A mantric pattern emerges in the poem and the cycles within larger cycles could be described as being akin to a sinusoidal wave which pulses rhythmically.

Finally there is an awareness that all living things, whether sentient or not, are part of the same rhythmic song of life:

        th sun cuts its way thru

    th fire burning its song thru yr blood
           of all th peopul animal plant creatures
         dancing along th flames of all th colors
    shapes expressions fierce loving and nameless

            th one blood stream

(Beyond Even Faithful Legends)

The poem as lyric becomes a type of metasong. It is a song about universal rhythm. The sun becomes an image of enlightenment. It dawns on the protagonist and on the reader that all life is part of the same cosmic cycle. Since one is part of the universal whole, to destroy or lose any part of life, however insignificant, is to diminish the whole as well as the self. The notion is an ancient one, and perhaps finds its most eloquent expression well before the Romantics in Donne's *Meditation xvii*. If for Donne, "No man is an island, entire of itself," then for bissett, we are all united in a transcendental sense by being part of "th one blood stream" which is the cosmic all. It could be said that the rhythms and intervals in bissett's lyric poetry are an echo of the pulse of this universal blood stream.

Don Precosky (essay date 1994)

SOURCE: "Self Selected/Selected Self: Bill Bissett's *BEYOND EVEN FAITHFUL LEGENDS*," in *Canadian Poetry*, No. 34, Spring-Summer, 1994, pp. 57-78.

[*In the following excerpt, Precosky discusses the significance of the order of poems in* BEYOND EVEN FAITHFUL LEGENDS.]

When a poet selects and arranges his poetry for a retrospective collection we must pay special attention, because he is probably telling us something about the way in which he views his work. While the revisions performed on certain individual poems are an interesting subject of study and conjecture, bissett's ultimate act of revision in *Beyond Even Faithful Legends* lies in his selection and arrangement of the poems for the book. In this book, the poems are not arranged in order according to publication or composition date. And, in those rare instances when consecutive poems in the *Selected* are from the same book, they were not in the same order in the original. The new arrangement that bissett creates is based upon opposites. To put it in very simple terms, he alternates poems about good things with poems about bad things. One group of poems about things he values can be followed by poems about forces that threaten them. Pieces about social evils are followed by works that suggest solutions. The poems, especially the non-concrete ones, have been very carefully chosen and arranged by bissett in order to create a desired flow of topics, moods, and images. bissett has reread himself, and has partially discovered, partially created, an order and pattern.

In one notable instance the rearrangement of original book order creates a new poetic situation with new meanings and significances. **"back in th city,"** a "written" poem, is followed by a concrete visual. The concrete poem is not given its own listing in the table of contents—the only full page visual in the book to be so treated. The arrangement and lack of table of contents reference suggests that together they form a single work. Both are from *stardust,* but in that book they are not on consecutive pages. The poem talks about loneliness, and the visual contains details which support the message of the poem. bissett has cut out lines from the original of **"back in th city"** that disparage movies. He now wants to see in a movie a reflection of his own life, so he cannot undercut the medium.

The concrete visual is a collage made largely from images (most likely taken from a promotional poster) from the film *Royal Wedding*. In the poem, bissett tells us that he has been watching the film on television while nervously brooding over a difficult love affair. As the poem ends, its lines change from moderately long ones to a trail of one word lines: a narrow look that reflects bissett's "strung out" feeling:

> evry
> time
> yr
> not
> heer
>
> a
> lite
> burns
> out

The collage shows Fred Astaire and Jane Powell dancing in a drawing room before an audience of well-dressed people. The "wall" of the room is made up of rows of densely packed typewriter "x's". In this wall of "x's" are white circles that look like holes made with a paper punch. The holes are the burnt out lights of the poem. They are flaws in the safe fantasy world of the movie, and are evocative of the anxiety of the poem. Furthermore, the holes are arranged to form long lines snaking down the wall. They are reminiscent of the shape of the poem and its anxious petering out (into the word "out"). They are

also sinister, suggesting advancing tentacles or lightning bolts aimed at the unsuspecting dancers and their audience. . . . The poem highlights the contrast between the escapist world of *Royal Wedding,* where the course of true love runs smoothly, and the real world of bissett's nervousness, where it does not. The collage, with its disintegrating background, makes the same statement. This deliberate act of re-arrangement by bissett is a miniature version of what he does in the *Selected* as a whole.

The poems begin—one concrete visual on the title page and another facing the table of contents—before the table of contents. The unorthodox placement of the two initial pieces suggests the exuberance and fecundity of bissett's imagination. It is as if he cannot wait to get started. The collection is bursting with poems; they are spilling out of the regular book into the prefatory matter.

The first five poems after Len Early's Introduction serve as an introduction and invitation to the book. **"yu sing"** is an imagined address by an audience to a poet. Such an eager and appreciative audience is the sort any writer would wish to have:

> yu sing
>
> of th time
> when th story
> wud amaze, nd
>
> . . . . .
>
> yu write about
> th cumming dawn
>
> th dragon,
> dreeming,

In the course of the poem bissett lays claim to the ancient roles of singer and storyteller, and to the capacity to teach and delight. Though we do not yet know it, bissett is laying out the plan for the book: to teach, to entertain, to tell a story. And in the *Selected* he moves back and forth among these functions, balancing the serious with the comic, the didactic with the entertaining. Singing, telling stories, making pictures—it is a varied and engrossing show.

The next poem, **"may / all thes blessings,"** is a call for blessings for the reader: "may all / thes blessings shine on yu." Like the first poem, this one mentions dreams and has a religious quality to it. It serves as an answer to the initial poem. First the audience has called upon the poet, asking him to sing, and now the poet responds to this audience. It also illustrates bissett's serious attitude toward the writer's vocation. It is a priestlike, quasi-religious calling.

"OF TH LAND DIVINE SERVICE" continues to build the feeling that there is something divine about poetry. It presents a figure, possibly the archetypal poet, in images reminiscent of Coleridge's inspired poet in "Kubla Khan":

and because of such strength well we wait

and th soul's light
and th body's light
and eye's light

and there is nothing
in his hand
but light

and th chorus
of th tempul jewels
flashing

This build up, we must remember, is of poetry and "the poet" as a type and is not in any way an egotistical self-promotion by bissett. When he finally introduces himself as a person, in **"i come from halifax,"** bissett does not present himself as anything particularly wonderful. The detail is very spare. He tells us that he comes from two cities, Halifax and Vancouver. Both have many churches, but both "have trouble / with their visions and the world" and bissett admits to fear. This poem is our introduction to the two opposites between which most of the book moves: the ecstatic, visionary, holy and positive ideal that poetry aspires to and the fallen, cruel, frightening world in which the poet lives.

"speaking speaking," the last of the introductory poems, is a chant about inspiration. Everything is speaking to him; all of existence is a source for poetry. It introduces a favourite theme—oneness with nature ("th eagle / talks")—and a favourite method synaesthesia ("th eye is / speaking").

This introductory movement then ends abruptly when we come to **"tarzan collage." "tarzan collage"** plunges the reader into a world of violence. It depicts Tarzan fighting with two alien looking creatures, one of whom is apparently screaming, and moves the reader into the next group of poems, one that continues to **"POST RESURRECTION CITY BLUES."** They deal with violence, oppression, social problems, and the ideological contradictions hinted at in **"i come from halifax."**

bissett identifies with the oppressed, and asks time and again why oppression exists. **"OUT ON TH TOWN JOY RIDIN"** focuses on police violence toward prisoners in the Vancouver city lock up, and probably grows out of personal experience. It poses, but does not answer, the question "do most peopul live in such fear"? The question implies a caring that goes beyond concern for just himself. This concern for others carries on into the next poem, **"BEYOND EVEN FAITHFUL LEGENDS."** In it, bissett rhetorically suggests that "we cud cease to care so much," but the suggestion is meant to be rejected because, he says, we would have to "give / to go on living . . . to go on living / with our broken hearts, batterd heads." In other words, if we were to "cease to care" we would still have to "give" (i.e. pay) for the right to go on suffering. Surrender will only make oppressors bolder.

"anodetodalevy" is dedicated to one such victim of oppression. Darryl Allen Levy (1942-1968) was an American poet with whom bissett could identify on many levels. Like bissett, Levy used only lower-case letters to spell his name, was arrested on drug charges, and was harassed for publishing allegedly obscene poems. He described himself as a "passive anarchist". In 1968, at the age of twenty-six, he killed himself with a .22-calibre rifle. Like any good elegy, the poem is both mournful and triumphant as its subject transcends the mortal world to acquire a power and significance that he never held in life:

he moves out from th librarie into yr sleep
into th night into th secret known alla over th
world high worlds within worlds light on
. . . . .

da levy praise him stay with
him we are all with him ther is much to
laugh about we are much to laugh about we
are th nights eyes th bright eyes d a
levys eyes are everywhere ya better
believe it now laughter is so sweet
clapping yr hands is so sweet
praising d a levy is so
sweet . . .

bissett follows this ode up with **"POST RESURRECTION CITY BLUES,"** which contains an example of oppression from his own life. Like Leacock's little man in "My Financial Career," bissett feels "rattled" by a banker:

(i cud see him thinking,
my god, what if peopul like this
were able to buy houses, th whole
structure of society wud change)

Mister Mustard, the bank official, typifies the middle class's mistrusting and dismissive attitude toward artists. bissett's voice suddenly hardens and what seemed to be a simple personal anecdote becomes an indictment of society's undervaluation of its creative people:

. . . be romantik, in
the tradition of good chocolate box
covr designs, dont get anything,
lose everything, tell us, th ownrs
about loss, Aunt Jemima, Louis Armstrong,
Bessie Smith, be religious nd hungry
to ease our consciences on our way
to th Bank

The poem's ending, with bissett reminding Mister Mustard that he too could die, suggests an important change from the helplessness of the prisoner in **"OUT ON TH TOWN JOY RIDIN"** whom the "big bull" can force to crawl across the lockup floor, to the defiance of one who can remind an authority figure of his mortality. Throughout the body of his writing there is an implied refusal to give in to or be intimidated by people with power.

The next several poems, from **"TH GOLDEN DAWN"** to "dawn," turn from the bureaucratic impersonality of Mister Mustard to more intimate and personal experiences. **"TH GOLDEN DAWN," "HEAt MAkes TH HEARts wINDOw,"** and **"SHE CALLS ME ADONIS"** are all upbeat poems focusing on private moments of love, security, and, in the last, joyful kidding around. The happiness is shortlived as forces from the greater world menace the fragile security of his little world.

The mood changes in **"WHATS HAPPINING/OZONE CUM BACK WE STILL LOV YU"** when his private happiness is threatened from without by industrial pollution. In **"why dew magazines lie"** the threat is a kind of pollution of the intellect: "ther attempt to frustrate us." Finally, in **"NUCLEAR CIRCULAR"** there comes the ultimate threat—destruction of himself and all that he loves. He asks

> can my precious littul love
>
> . . . . .
>
> reach those peopul
> who printed this circular
> which robs me ofmy peace
> which carries to those few
> i have with me i love

These poems illustrate the preciousness of private life and the impossibility of separating it from the bigger world.

From such examples, it is a small step to a realization that political involvement is an inevitable part of being a poet. The next several poems, from **"th konkreet pome is on its hed"** to **"how we avoid prayr"** touch on poetics and politics.

In **"tell me what attacked yu"** bissett makes his attitude clear

> most peopul have been led to believe
> by th emergd middul class, that art
> and politikal involvment greet each othr
> only across sum imponderabul chasm,
>   th middul class sz yeah its a good pome
>   but what use is it, th professors
> lift up our hearts, in repudiation of that,
> to th credo that art transcends use, either
> view is nowhere, art is all use; only
> th technicians of a fragmented society,
>   interested in propagating such a nightmare
>   encourage us to believe in realities
>   that split our breath into filing cards, p
> for politiks, a for art—th full breath
> is what knowledge is, is human, is
> wholly real, includes what is
>   in all things

Politics and poetry are connected. To separate them would be to fragment the creative process—to allow it the traditional role of delighting through the verbal creation of beauty "in," as he says in **"POST RESURRECTION CITY BLUES,"** "the tradition of good chocolate box / covr designs." But to deny its teaching (analytical) function is to remove from the poet the ability to alter his world through his vision. The act of separating art from politics is a grab for power by "th emerged middul class" and "th professors." Both groups are among "th technicians of a fragmented society" who would chop life (symbolised by bissett as "breath") up "into filing cards." But for bissett "breath" cannot be subdivided into categories. Wholeness of being is what makes one human: "th full breath / is what knowledge is, is human." The attempt to separate art from politics is an attempt by a few to gain control by fragmenting human experience. bissett is a poet of wholeness and will not allow his poetry to be defused by having its political function removed.

Having explained the political nature of his poetics, bissett continues in the political vein. The mood turns darker as he focuses on what it is like to be marginalized. In **"whilst waiting for"** he identifies with the villains of horror movies. He does not see them as evil monsters, but as the victims of the intolerance of "normal" society. Vampires suffer at the hands of religious bigots: "to / have to put up / with those / christians / impoverished phony / symbolism how they / use our existence to / keep their pockets / full." **"Hand"** is a song of the marginalized and a plea to be allowed to pursue happiness without harassment. Material comfort, or even mere acceptance by society, seem too much to hope for:

> . . . let
> all th mad creatures freely love what
> cums to them without success but
> being
>
>   let us dance entwine our
> thighs round our dreams

His speakers even find an internal, though muted, triumph in the midst of an uncaring society: "we cum out uv th richness / uv our poor dreems." Once again, bissett refuses to be defeated.

"LEBANON VOICES" continues the thread of spiritual or subjective triumph, speaking of "the mysteries of th night" and the "green hope" of dreams, culminating in a vision of a dance of triumph:

> . . . in
> bliss to th stars they were dancing, th
> creatures n flesh, of one mind n body

Just as quickly as the mood rises to triumph in the magical night of dreams, it falls to the pain of real life. **"feed th prisoners now baby"** is a chant of suffering and defiance, while **"in nova scotia th peopul"** heaps contempt upon the political institution for exploitation, poverty, and selling out to foreign-owned big business:

> nd th peopul cant b unified if
> we dont own what we do our own

resources food cultur ideas
media

But real life is not all gloom. With **"rose th night nd th green flowr"** the book enters into what may be the longest stretch of beautiful, peaceful, and joyful writing in modern Canadian poetry. There is not a trace of false sentimentality in it. The predominant theme is harmony—with self, others, and nature. **"rose th night nd th green flowr"** presents an Edenic setting with two lovers at one with each other and with nature: "what yu hold / what engulfs yu frees yu / ths flowr opening takes yu." bissett explores sexual relations as a road to harmony in "aint no words for th tast uv yu"—the pairs of right- and wrong-side up lines suggesting sexual congress, and **"konkreet vizual"** from *drifting into war* with shapes suggesting an erect penis and a dove of peace.

Several joyful chants give voice to his sense of oneness with nature. They include **"what we dew if thrs anything," "i herd ya laffin in th water," "and th green wind is mooving thru th summr trees,"** and **"vaalee daancers."**

Perhaps the most beautiful of this group of poems are those concerning children, in particular his daughter Ooljah. His **"SONG FOR OOLJAH"** is a wonderfully pure-hearted and gentle poem that expresses his love in such a way that every child's purity is captured:

into an emerald dream tree
th littul girl ot gold sang
of love so strong nd free
th flowers unfold to hear

In **"Circles in th Sun"** he realizes the fragility of this innocence:

o love past play past memory
let th children be
let th children be

And in **"SOLACE IN WORDS"** he finds what every parent knows: that some moments are so perfect that they cannot be analyzed; they can only be described:

watching
our baby
daughter sleep,

undr th blue
eiderdown, her
features,

th eye
lids curve, th
curve of her nose,

her mouth, her
fingers curving
into her hand
curvd above th

blue blanket, perfect
angelically
transformed
in sleep

The optimism of this group of poems culminates in **"i have evn herd uv thee"**:

th spirit uv th godes is in th
beet uv our blending in is in us in our
love.

Like Donne, bissett can see a mystical significance growing out of the act of making love.

Just as we are, perhaps, falling into complacency because of the warm glow of all this happiness, bissett suddenly jerks the book back into the oppressive world of jails, contracts, and law courts, beginning with **"THE / INDIANS / WERE / WELCOMED / AS BRIDGEBUILDERS."** The bleakness is somewhat tempered in the next poem, **"treez,"** which talks about harmony and peace, but only as things dreamed of and not as states already achieved.

The idea of a dream continues in the following three poems, but the dream is really a nightmare in disguise, for it is the false "dream" of what life should be as it is fed to the populace by the mass media. In **"th tarot match covr uv th lovrs"** bissett says that "all th / music cumming thru th / speekrs bleed[s] us" and adds that the endless watching of television "had to / altr his / view / uv any / world." Television is the subject of **"keep on th grass."** The title suggests support for marijuana use as an alternative to television viewing, and the poem itself focuses in on the illusory world being served up by the tube:

telvishyun is so much brain washing xcept for
th in concert show tonite with anne murray cumming
from saratoga springs new york   th spinnrs
with her   shes weering tite   white lethr
rhinestones sparkling   10,000
peopul raging with her   following
her song

In **"evry whun at 2 oclock"** it is newspapers that are attacked for spreading a false view of things—specifically about nuclear weapons: "th vancouvr / sun newspaper sz N-blast / successful and safe only it / isnt an all th peopul know." The net effect of the mass media is to substitute an illusion for reality in order to keep the citizenry pacified and unaware of the dangers and evils that the politicians have created.

From the specific social problem of the mass media bissett moves on to other, somewhat more abstract concerns. In **"th north aint easy to grow food in"** the problem is basic survival in a harsh climate: "yu got a coupul / cans a food only nd th canyun closd / th big mamadaddy transport trucks / cant cum in." In **"the water falls in yr mind nd yu get wet tooo"** it is more a case of emotional survival in a post-Fall world where Adam is apt to find himself "sittin cryin undr a tree." Alienation plays an important part in several of the poems in the next dozen pages, including **"ode to frank silvera," "th lonliness of literacy," "KILLER WHALE"** (in which bissett is, like the whales, trapped inside someone elsés system), **"yu know th creaturs are ourselvs"** and, possibly his finest narrative, **"TH EMERGENCY WARD"** in which the forces of caring and gentleness embodied by the "beautiful neurologist chick" and the forces of alienating, impersonal bureaucracy represented by "th shrink" battle for control of bissett's body and his mind. Luckily for him it was "an intr / cerebral bleed" and he escapes electroshock treatment at the hands of "th shrink," who seems to want to punish him for being an artist.

The political theme takes an odd, and at first baffling, twist as the book goes through a series of poems that allude to conspiracy or mystery or spying. **"ther may have been a tunnul thru which my train rolld"** mentions spy activity at a railroad station, involving high tech gimmicks, false identities, and violence. **"th / missyun"** also has spyish intrigue, including diamonds, camels, and a mysterious "trading stashun." On a more comic note there is **"th tomato conspiracy aint / worth a whole poem"** which mocks paranoia and conspiracy theories, but which is based upon a commercial fact—that chemicals *are* used to enhance the colour (and sales value) of fruits and vegetables. The secret agent/spy/conspiracy motif serves as thematic reference to bissett's theme of political marginalization and alienation. The "spy" poems dramatize the state of being on the outside and not able to live as oneself, while the political poems show the causes and conditions of the alienation. There is, in fact, a rhythm to the *Selected* of always moving back to the political theme from other subjects, as if political marginalization were the one constant factor, while joy or love or dreams or harmony with nature are only temporary releases.

Over the next several pages bissett presents us with a number of "cum" poems. "Cum" is one of bissett's power words. Orgasmic ecstasy is presented as a means of overcoming alienation and achieving oneness, not only with another person, but with all creation. Playfully, he includes poems such as **"TH DAY MAY CUM"** and **"i was just cummin"** which have "cum" in the title, but which are not about sex, but are, instead, about oneness. Other of these "cum" poems are **"jed bi kor benskt trik," "cum cum cum cumly witchcraft i know you care,"** and most blatantly the **"konkreet vizual"** from *space travl,* which features a representation of a man with a prominently erect penis.

bissett also explores attainment of a type of oneness beyond social cohesion between physical and spiritual through mystic vision. **"wer they angels i didnt know"** talks about trumpet-blowing angels "lifting th sun up ovr th horizon." Puckishly, he chides the reader for his naivité: "yu think th sun cums up [by itself?]." **"th lifting hands"** is a chant about lifting up hands, eyes, and fingers to hail the sunrise.

Like a Donne or a Leonard Cohen, bissett forges a link between sex and mystical experience, as is evident in po-

ems such as **"eet me alive," "LIVING WITH TH VISHYUN"** and **"yu want th music."** In the last of these he writes

> . . . yu want th lafftr th sun in
> yr hand yu want th earth turning watr thrut th eye yu
> ar grace cum flesh hair uv jeweld bird thru th watr

He also arranges a group of poems about his relationship with the land. Again, the ideal goal is a self-transcending oneness. The poems include **"canada," "i / belong with th wind," "bringing home th bacon,"** and **"TH MAGIC LURE OF SEA SHELLS." "bringing home th bacon"** expresses his theme most succinctly: "horse nd rider along th rivers bank merge / with th revolving suns."

Then, after all of these poems about various aspects of merging and oneness and coming together, he reverses his line of thought in **"THE BODY."** The title could more accurately have been "THE BODY POLITIC". The poem is a political allegory (always back to politics) about the development of individualism and about how people came to be parts of the larger social body, with each part having its own specialized function. The development of such individualized roles is associated with corruption and discord:

> Out of THE BODY was to
> be artist to steal the dreams of each of
> the rest to make his to make believe
> that only he dreamt

and

> A stream of THE BODY was
> to be famly, that the self-betrayal of each
> of its members might be absorbed in
> a general rancour.

and

> . . . Our sense
> of hope has been permanently altered or
> damaged through our involvements with
> THE BODY

This idea of oneness between people and nature is answer to the fragmentation that he sees as both a spiritual and political malady in our society. Loss of oneness causes the unhappiness of individuals and creates the state of individual vulnerability that allows unjust political systems to wield power.

The last ten pages of the book consist of mostly individual, unrelated poems with **"th breath"** providing an upbeat envoi to the collection, a celebration of the wonder of being:

> yr spirit being dancing in th fire each petal of th flowr
>   opening to th light th warmth
>   for th opening seed th ice all
>   around th breath moves
>   . . . . .

of all the peopul animal plant creatures
dancing along th flames of all th colors
shapes expressions fierce loving and nameless

th one blood stream

Beyond Even Faithful Legends is bill bissett's self-edited retrospective presentation of himself, and constitutes a summation of his career up to that point. It is an opportunity for him to update some of his older writing and bring it into line with his more mature abilities. In the ordering of the poems bissett has created a unified work with a newly created flow of thematic statements. Although the general pattern is one of alternating opposites, with a group of poems about positive things being followed by another group about negative things, bissett does not merely describe the eternal battle of good and evil. Running through all of the poems is a tremendous life affirming energy. bissett writes about good in order to support it and about evil in order to defy and undermine it.

The **Selected** also marks a major turning point in bissett's career. Beginning with this book and continuing to the present he is no longer a self publishing poet whose works appear in basement printed booklets, but a member of the stable of a nationally distributed commercial publisher. Although there is the observably negative effect of the infringement of mainstream publishing methods upon the exuberant style of some of the concrete poems, bissett's association with Talonbooks is a good one for him because it leaves him free to concentrate upon the writing of poetry, and leaves the tasks of production and distribution to others.

FURTHER READING

Criticism

Davey, Frank. Review of *NOBODY OWNS TH EARTH. The Canadian Forum* LII, Nos. 618-19 (July-August 1972): 44-5.

Asserts that this collection establishes Bissett as "specifically a religious poet," and notes Romantic, transcendentalist tendencies in certain poems.

Hopkins, Thomas. "Tempest in the West." *Maclean's* 91, No. 24 (23 October 1978): 66.

Covers the Canada Council scandal that thrust Bissett into the public eye.

McCaffery, Steve. "Bill Bissett: A Writing Outside Writing." *Open Letter* III (Fall 1978): 7-23.

Draws on the work of such theorists as Roland Barthes, Jacques Derrida, and Julia Kristeva in discussing Bissett's poetic style.

McCarthy, Dermot. "Shit from Musturd." *Essays on Canadian Writing,* No. 6 (Spring 1977): 86-9.

Negative appraisal of works by Bissett and "the blewointment coterie." According to McCarthy, "Reading bissett and his gang is like sitting down to a meal of Coke and corn-chips."

Precosky, Don. "Bill Bissett: Controversies and Definitions." *Canadian Poetry,* No. 27 (Fall/Winter 1990): 15-29.

Provides an overview of critical response to Bissett's work, discussing the Canada Council controversy in detail.

Interview

Hilmo, Maidie. "Interview with Bill Bissett." *Essays on Canadian Writing,* No. 32 (Summer 1986): 134-46.

Discusses Bissett's life and work, including his travels, his approach to writing, and the political controversy surrounding his works in the late 1970s.

Additional coverage of Bissett's life and career is contained in the following sources published by Gale Research: *Contemporary Authors,* Vols. 69-72; *Contemporary Authors Autobiography Series,* Vol. 19; *Contemporary Authors New Revision Series,* Vol. 15; *Contemporary Literary Criticism,* Vol. 18; *Dictionary of Literary Biography,* Vol. 53; and *Major 20th-Century Writers.*

Etheridge Knight
1931-1991

American poet, essayist, editor, and short story writer.

INTRODUCTION

Knight was one of the most popular poets of the Black Arts Movement, a period during the 1960s of literary and cultural revival for black writers and artists. His work often protested the oppression of blacks and the underprivileged and reflected his experience as an inmate at the Indiana State Prison. He strove for a balance between "the poet, the poem, and the people," deliberately using direct language, slang, and simple poetic techniques to make his work accessible to the greatest possible number of readers.

Biographical Information

Born in Corinth, Mississippi, in 1931, Knight dropped out of school after the eighth grade and began frequenting bars and poolrooms. At the age of sixteen Knight joined the United States Army; he served in Korea as a medical technician. During the war he began to use drugs, and by his discharge in 1957 he had become a drug addict, committing crimes to support his habit. In 1960 he was found guilty of armed robbery and sentenced to ten to twenty-five years in prison. While incarcerated, he published his first volume of poetry, *Poems from Prison*. After his release, he published two other volumes, *Belly Song and Other Poems* and *Born of a Woman: New and Selected Poems*. Knight died of lung cancer in 1991 at the age of fifty-nine.

Major Works

Born of a Woman is considered Knight's most popular and well-received collection. The volume is divided into three sections: "Inside-Out," "Outside-In," and "All About—And Back Again." The poems in the first section convey different aspects of prison life: "For Freckle-Faced Gerald" concerns a young boy who is raped and brutalized by older convicts—an act that also symbolically represents society's oppression of the innocent and defenseless; "Hard Rock" depicts a strong and rebellious hero who defies the system's attempts to break his spirit until a lobotomy forcibly changes his character; and "The Idea of Ancestry" reveals the loneliness and isolation of a prisoner who reflects upon his crime, his family, and his heritage while looking at photographs of his relatives on his cell wall. The second section contains poems about love, and the final section includes more recent poetry that develops a greater scope of themes and subjects.

Critical Reception

Although some commentators derided his verse for its unpoetic language and strident political rhetoric, Knight's works were generally well received by critics, who most often commended their vitality of language and personal subject matter. His poetry, which detailed his personal struggles with drugs and prison life, as well as his encounters with war and prejudice, was considered courageous and evocative of the African-American experience. He is frequently compared with such African-American poets as Langston Hughes, Gwendolyn Brooks, and Sonia Sanchez.

PRINCIPAL WORKS

Poetry

Poems from Prison 1968
Belly Song and Other Poems 1973
Born of a Woman: New and Selected Poems 1980
The Essential Etheridge Knight 1986

CRITICISM

Craig Werner (essay date 1981)

SOURCE: "The Poet, the Poem, the People: Etheridge Knight's Aesthetic," in *Obsidian*, Vol. VII, Nos. 2 & 3, Summer-Winter, 1981, pp. 7-17.

[*In the following essay, Werner examines Knight's work in light of contemporary African-American poetry, focusing in particular on the populist roots of his verse.*]

In the "Preface" to **Born of a Woman: New and Selected Poems,** Etheridge Knight endorses an aesthetic which balances the demands of "The Poet, the Poem, and the People." The third term is crucial. While numerous influential poets and critics, among them Michael Harper and Robert B. Stepto in their recent anthology *Chant of Saints,* [1979] turn to the relatively elitist transatlantic and academic traditions of Afro-American poetry, Knight's theory and practice provide a necessary reminder of the equally important populist roots of black expression. A polished craftsman, capable of exploiting both traditional Euro-American and experimental Afro-American (frequently musical) forms, Knight has emerged as a major voice in the tradition of Langston Hughes and Gwendolyn Brooks.

This emergence is particularly significant in the light of recent trends in Afro-American literary criticism. While it would be fallacious to suggest that either editor, or *Chant of Saints* as a whole, rejects the relationship of the artist and his community, Stepto's identification of Harper, Robert Hayden (in his last poems) and Jay Wright as the major contemporary poets raises serious questions concerning the mode and direction of that interaction. Expressing their concern for the Afro-American tradition through what Stepto calls a "synthesis of process, vocation, myth and language," all three work primarily in the modernist tradition pioneered by Euro-American writers such as Pound and Stevens and fused with the Afro-American tradition by Jean Toomer and Melvin B. Tolson. This is, of course, a legitimate aesthetic tradition and does not necessarily entail the isolation of the poet from his audience, though such isolation remains a danger. Harper, Hayden and Wright all seem aware of this danger and choose their historical materials to emphasize their link with Afro-American culture. Nonetheless, the tradition elevates the poet; his sensibility fuses the fragments of history, philosophy and whatever else touches his experience into a coherent statement. At its most effective, this aesthetic transforms the poet into a teacher in the tradition of Frederick Douglass or Walt Whitman. At its least effective, it leaves him talking to himself in a crumbling cathedral.

To a large extent, the current critical emphasis on this tradition reflects the changed social and political currents of the late 1970s which were marked by a protracted retreat from the positions of the "Black Aesthetic" movement. *Chant of Saints* in many ways signals the start of a new phase in Afro-American letters. Nonetheless, if the volume is to be seriously advanced as the best "yardstick

by which to measure the evolution of Afro-American literature and culture" since Alain Locke's *The New Negro,* it should be complemented by a recognition of current works with roots in the Black Aesthetic movement which, whatever its excesses, was an important evolutionary phase. Taking its primary impulse from the populist tradition, arguably the dominant tradition of Afro-American literature from David Walker through Langston Hughes to Amiri Baraka, the Black Aesthetic movement has not totally died out, but has evolved into new forms visible in the works of poets such as Knight. However much obscured by the social and critical currents of the 1970s, the presence of the People remains a central fact of Afro-American culture. Their voices, with or without formal recognition, provide the ground base for the evolutionary chant.

Knight's personal voice sounds a melody which interacts intricately with the pulse of the chant. The publication of **Born of a Woman,** which includes most of the work from Knight's two previous volumes, furnishes the occasion for an assessment of the ways in which this voice expresses both the political and cultural currents of black nationalism and readjusts the position of the Black Aesthetic movement in the populist tradition. Technically, Knight merges musical rhythms with traditional metrical devices, reflecting the assertion of an Afro-American cultural identity within a Euro-American context. Thematically, he denies that the figures of the singer, central to the aesthetic of *Chant of Saints,* and the warrior, central to the Black Aesthetic movement, are or can be separate.

One of the most recent in a long line of black writers to have discovered his vocation while in prison Knight began writing under the encouragement of Gwendolyn Brooks. His artistic awakening coincided both with the critical dominance of the Black Aestheticians and with Brooks' evolution from a "universalist" to a black nationalist perspective. Black Aesthetic spokesmen such as Addison Gayle, Jr., insisted that the historical oppression of black people in the United States had created a situation in which the Afro-American writer must commit himself to the freedom of his people and reject Euro-American cultural traditions and forms as a mark of his independence. In its most extreme forms, the Black Aesthetic demanded that the Afro-American writer serve as another tool of the revolution, creating works which would inspire the masses of black people to commmit themselves anew to political action. The artist must be a warrior first, a singer only second.

Reflecting this political and aesthetic climate, Knight's early work, while employing numerous poetic devices associated with Euro-American traditions, insists on a specifically black poetry. **"On Universalism"** dismisses the concept of encompassing human brotherhood as a response to the oppression of the people:

> No universal laws
> Of human misery
> Create a common cause
> Or common history
> That ease black people's pains
> Nor break black people's chains.

This, of course, echoes the Black Aesthetic's insistence upon the primacy of the People in all artistic endeavour.

Knight's aesthetic as reflected both in his metrics and his imagery, however, always balanced the demands of Poet, Poem, and People, granting equal attention to the aesthetic demands of the language and to the impulse toward self-expression. This synthetic approach raised questions from the beginning of Knight's career. Even while identifying *Poems from Prison* as a "major announcement," Haki R. Madhubuti (then writing as Don L. Lee [in *Dynamite Voices,* 1971]) questioned the propriety of Knight's allusions to Euro-American culture. Rather than abandoning such allusions, Knight soon relinquished the emphasis on a separate black aesthetic. Even while altering his stance, however, he maintained a strong sense of the black populist heritage: "Our poetry will always speak mainly to black people, but I don't see it being as narrow in the 70s as it was in the 60s." Extending this argument, Knight proposed a version of universalism based on shared emotional experience, rather than of specific images or forms: "My poetry is also important to white people because it invokes feelings. . . . The feelings are common, whether or not the situations that create the feelings are common . . . I might feel fear in a small town in Iowa. You might be afraid if you get off the subway in Harlem. It's the same fear, but the situations are different." This widening of the definition of the People to include any reader capable of responding to his emotional impulse in no way entails a movement away from populism. The lasting contribution of the Black Aesthetic to Knight's poetics lies precisely in his continuing commitment to the People: "I pay attention only to the people in the audience. If they don't dig it, then it ain't nothing no way."

This commitment to the People, even when "it is lonely . . . and sometimes/ THE PEOPLES can be a bitch" (**"A Poem to Galway Kinnell"**), defines Knight's poetic achievement throughtout his career. As the structure of *Born of a Woman* indicates, Knight has approached this commitment from a variety of perspectives. Part I, titled "Inside-Out," focuses on Knight's awakening in prison and his dawning awareness of his relationship with an outside world. Part II, "Outside-In," concentrates on his self-exploration—the Poet is one-third of Knight's aesthetic trinity—once released. Part III, "All About—And Back Again," reemphasizes that, whatever his explorations, the Poet Knight ultimately returns to the base he finds in the People and expresses in the Poems.

The political poetry written concurrently with **"On Universalism"** attests to the complexity of Knight's practice. His eulogy **"For Malcolm, A Year After,"** originally published in *Poems from Prison,* carefully manipulates metrical tensions and rhyme schemes to make its statement of support for the nationalist warrior. Knight begins with a bitter statement that he will stay within the Euro-American tradition for fear that any formal departure might bring in its wake a self-destructive emotional explosion:

> Compose for Red a proper verse;
> Adhere to foot and strict iamb;

> Control the burst of angry words
> Or they might boil and break the dam.
> Or they might boil and overflow
> And drench, drown me, drive me mad.

Rhyme connects the form in the "iamb" and the anger in "dam" which he then inverts in "mad" to complete the conceptual sight-oriented off-rhyme. He concludes the opening section by at once embracing and rejecting the very language, the white man's language, in which he writes:

> Make empty anglo tea lace words—
> Make them dead white and dry bone bare.

The very words he molds into the "proper verse" embody the values of a literally murderous culture.

A polished craftsman, capable of exploiting both traditional Euro-American and experimental Afro-American (frequently musical) forms, Knight has emerged as a major voice in the tradition of Langston Hughes and Gwendolyn Brooks.

—*Craig Werner*

The second stanza emphasizes that while Knight uses the Euro-American culture's form, he uses it to advance the political cause of black nationalism. Inverting the traditional conceit of the poem living eternally despite the death of the man, Knight writes that his poem, an artifact of the oppressive culture, will die, but its message, the message of Malcolm X, will live:

> Compose a verse for Malcolm man,
> And make it rime and make it prim.
> The verse will die—as all men do—
> But not the memory of him.

The concluding triplet of the poem, implicitly parodying the standard couplet form, further emphasizes the revolutionary emotion inspired by both the life and death of Malcolm X:

> Death might come singing sweet like C
> Or knocking like the old folk say,
> The moon and stars may pass away,
> But not the anger of that day.

While Knight the singer works within traditional forms, his vision is insistently that of the nationalist warrior.

Most of the poems in "Inside-Out" echo this intensity of anger. Knight portrays Hard Rock, lobotomized, serving as a symbol of contemporary "slavery:"

> The fears of the years, like a biting whip
> Had cut deep bloody grooves
> Across our backs.

He writes of his own isolation from his family in **"The Idea of Ancestry,"** an isolation which leads him back to prison. And, ironically juxtaposing his statement with the largely traditional forms in the first section, he concludes in **"A Poem for Black Relocation Centers"** with the portrait of Flukum who "couldn't stand the strain. Flukum/ who wanted inner and outer order" and who meets an uncomprehending death in Vietnam. Clearly, the poems in "Inside-Out" point to the necessity of a vision of the world going beyond the simple recognition of victimization.

"Outside-In" reflects both Knight's concern with the Poet's personal struggles to attain this vision and his determination to generate forms, many of them reflecting the Afro-American musical tradition, which adequately express this vision. Both a cry of personal agony and a demonstration of Knight's ability to shape his poem out of the materials of both Euro- and Afro-American culture, **"The Violent Space"** stands among the most powerful lyrics and recent decades. Mingling allusions to the Garden of Eden and the folklore of black Mississippi, Knight begins:

> Exchange in greed the ungraceful signs. Thrust
> The thick notes between green apple breasts.
> Then the shadow of the devil descends,
>
> The violent space cries and angel eyes,
> Large and dark, retreat in innocence and in ice.
> (Run sister run—the Bugga man comes!)

The intricate interplay of sound (large-dark; the repeated "in" sound which stresses the feeling of entrapment of innocence) and rhyme (cries-eyes-ice which implies the freezing of the emotions and tears) is set against the fear of the inchoate "Bugga man." The Bugga man image recurs throughout the poem; even the Poet's mystic chant is an insufficient response:

> Well, shit, lil sis, here we are:
> You and I and this poem.
> And what should I do? should I squat
> In the dust and make strange markings on the
>   ground?
> Shall I cant a spell to drive the demon away?
> (Run sister run—the Bugga man comes).

Finally the Poet invokes the authority and strength of the black spiritual tradition, but that too fails to repulse the demon:

> *"O Mary don't you weep don't you moan"*
> O Mary shake your butt to the violent juke,
> Absorb the demon puke and watch the white eyes
>   pop,
> (Run sister run—the Bugga man comes).

The demon, now clearly associated with the white culture which passively supports the agony, undercuts the black source of strength. The Poet, unable to make his connection with the Person he loves, is isolated:

> I am not bold. I cannot yet take hold of the demon
> And lift his weight from your black belly.
> So I grab the air and sing my song.
> (But the air cannot hold my singing long).

Clearly, isolated singing is an insufficient response to the situation of individuals victimized by an oppressive culture. Knight once again implies the need for the warrior to act when the song fades or erupts.

Not all of Knight's explorations in "Outside-In" lead to such stark confrontations. He has never been simply the Poet of the victim. Knight's musical experiments with toasts (**"Dark Prophecy: I Sing of Shine"**), blues (**"A Poem for Myself"**), and African percusive rhythms (**"Ilu the Talking Drum"**) involve a wide range of emotional experiences, including that of remembered and discovered love in the jazz poem **"For Eric Dolphy."** He returns most insistently to jazz in poems which employ irregular but insistent rhythmical patterns and repetitions in the place of a basic Euro-American meter. **"Another Poem for Me"** typifies this practice:

> what now
> what now dumb nigger damn near dead
> what now
> now that you won't dance
> behind the pale white doors of death
> what now is to be
> to be what you wanna be
> what you spozed to be
> or what white / america wants you to be.

The tension between the "what now" and the "to be" phrases moves the poem rhythmically and thematically, insisting that the Poet must not remain a victim but must shape his own being. Jazz, ultimately, aids the Poet in the necessary journey back into himself.

In the poems of "All About—And Back Again," most of which are collected for the first time in *Born of a Woman,* these explorations and experiments merge in Knight's mature poetic voice. **"I and Your Eyes"** exemplifies the music and the concerns of this voice. The "And I . . . your eyes" pattern forms a rhythmic base, derived more from jazz than from traditional metrics:

> And I   your eyes
> draw round about a ring of gold
> and shout their sparks of fire
> And I   your eyes
> hold untold tales and conspire
> with the stars. And stirs my soul.

Using the pause between the two repeated phrases, Knight creates a tension, a sense of separation leading toward the connection embodied by the imagery. As he expresses the separation and pain of love, he departs from the ground rhythm, leaving an emptiness in the sound of the poem:

> Then I
> could stand alone the pain

of flesh alone the time and space
and stone.   but I am shaken.
It has taken

                    your eyes
to move this stone.

The traditional use of rhyme to emphasize crucial thematic points reenforces the jazz devices. This is the voice of an accomplished singer.

Along with this technical maturity, the poems in "All About—And Back Again" reveal that Knight has attained a commensurate maturity of vision. Just as **"I and Your Eyes"** combines the control of traditional devices with jazz techniques, **"We Free Singers Be"** insists on the importance of both the warrior embodying the values of the Black Aesthetic movement and the singer, reflecting the evolutionary emphasis of *Chant of Saints*. The poem's title implies this. "We" gives the sense of group identity, the nationalist perspective, the People. "Free" provides an internal rhyme, demonstrating Knight's continuing willingness to work with the Euro-American tradition in a way which renders it indistinguishable from the authenticity of his individual, clearly black, voice, and establishes the political emphasis on liberation. "Singers" invokes the emphasis on the artist, the *Chant of Saints* orientation, the Poet. "Be," the third rhyme word invoking the verbal play, the mock-excess of black oral tradition, provides the fulcrum for both the thematic and rhythmic movement of the poem.

Knight opens the poem with contrasting pastoral and military images of the "free singers":

    We free singers be
    sometimes swimming in the music
    like porpoises playing in the sea.
    We free singers be
    come agitators at times, be
    come eagles circling the sun
    hurling stones at hunters.

They are at once porpoises swimming in music and eagles challenging the predators. "Be," which ends four lines, serves both as a statement of what they are and as the first term of what they will become. The rhythmic tension between the "we free singers be" phrase and the "become" phrases mirrors the tension between their essence—their total being which connects the singer and the warrior—and their specific circumstance in which they must become one or the other.

Throughout the poem Knight alternates the warrior and the singer images. He intersperses a number of memories: of days "of the raging fires when I clenched my teeth in my sleep and refused to speak"—the days of the warriors; and of days "when children held our hands and danced around us in circles"—the days of the singers. The circle imagery connected with the children echoes the circle imagery connected with the warrior eagles. No matter what the momentary manifestation, both the singer and the warrior coexist in the individual at all times. The function of the singer is in large part to be a visionary:

    We free singers be
    voyagers
    and sing of cities
    with straight streets
    and mountains piercing the moon—
    and rivers that never run dry.

But even the visionary cannot afford to forget the reality of conflict:

    Remember, oh, do you remember
    the snow
    falling
    on broadway
    and the soldiers marching
    thru the icy streets
    with blood on their coat sleeves.

The fact, one with which Knight began the poem, and with which he ends it, is simply that each individual must be both: "We Free singers be, baby, / We free singers be." Ultimately, Knight says, the warriors of the Black Aesthetic and the singers of the *Chant* merge in the individual striving for the freedom of the Poet and the People.

Howard Nelson (essay date 1981)

SOURCE: "Belly Songs: The Poetry of Etheridge Knight," in *The Hollins Critic,* Vol. XVIII, No. 5, December, 1981, pp. 1-11.

[*Nelson is an American poet and critic. In the following essay, he provides a thematic and stylistic analysis of Knight's poetry.*]

"Cell Song"

    Night Music Slanted
    Light strike the cave
    of sleep. I alone
    tread the red circle
    and twist the space
    with speech.

    Come now, etheridge, don't
    be a savior; take
    your words and scrape
    the sky, shake rain

    on the desert, sprinkle
    salt on the tail
    of a girl,

    can there anything
    good come out of
    prison

While doing eight years (1960-68) in Indiana State Prison on a drug-related armed robbery charge, Etheridge Knight turned to poetry. Within the bleakness of steel bars and

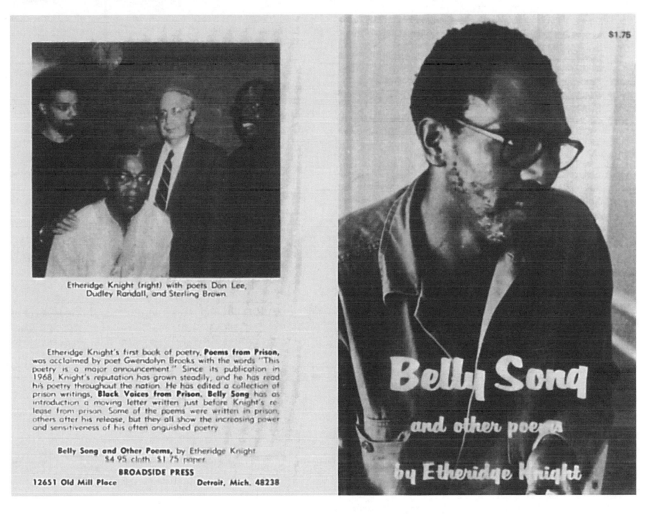

Etheridge Knight (right) with poets Don Lee, Dudley Randall, and Sterling Brown.

Etheridge Knight's first book of poetry, **Poems from Prison**, was acclaimed by poet Gwendolyn Brooks with the words "This poetry is a major announcement." Since its publication in 1968, Knight's reputation has grown steadily, and he has read his poetry throughout the nation. He has edited a collection of prison writings, **Black Voices from Prison. Belly Song** has as introduction a moving letter written just before Knight's release from prison. Some of the poems were written in prison, others after his release, but they all show the increasing power and sensitiveness of his often anguished poetry.

Belly Song and Other Poems, by Etheridge Knight
$4.95 cloth $1.75 paper
BROADSIDE PRESS
12651 Old Mill Place   Detroit, Mich. 48238

Front and back covers for Knight's 1973 poetry collection.

concrete walls, the frustration, immobility, rage, fear, and loneliness of prison life, and the long stretches of prison time, Knight twisted the space and created poems of remarkable force and clarity. This work was published in 1968, while Knight was still incarcerated, by Dudley Randall's Broadside Press as a chapbook titled simply, *Poems from Prison*. This slender book was one of several important additions to the tradition of prison writing to come out of the sixties. (Another, overlapping contribution was an anthology Knight edited, published by Pathfinder Press, called *Black Voices from Prison,* which contained in addition to Knight's poems a number of valuable prose pieces, by himself and others.) Beyond that, *Poems from Prison* was, as Gwendolyn Brooks said in her extremely concise and penetrating preface, "a major announcement." In terms of poetry, both in the context of the black poetic explosion of those years and of American poetry as a whole, an important new voice was making itself known. It was poetry that came out of painful experience, but instead of any shrillness or self-pity, there was a boldness, a solidness, that suggested deep reservoirs of strength.

In 1973 Broadside brought out a second collection by Knight, *Belly Song*. The title was well-chosen, because it identified precisely the two outstanding qualities of Knight's art: powerful feeling, which centers in the belly, the gut; and music, a vital, full-breathed music that demonstrates steadily that the poet is in touch with old, elemental sources of poetic energy.

Now Houghton Mifflin has brought out *Born of a Woman,* which brings together virtually all of the poems from the earlier books and a good deal of more recent material. It isn't a thick book for nearly twenty years' work, and it is no doubt uneven. But it contains a number of poems—**"The Idea of Ancestry," "The Violent Space," "For Freckle-Faced Gerald," "As You Leave Me,"** and **"Ilu, the Talking Drum"**—would certainly be among them—which should become permanent entries in the ledger of American poetry, should "lodge themselves in a place where they will be hard to get rid of." As a total volume, too, *Born of a Woman* is a moving and life-enhancing book, recording the motions of a spirit that is torn and frayed but resilient and persistently loving.

Through the qualities of life it contains and the qualities of its art, it describes a victory over desolation, against the odds.

. . . . .

What keeps us alive? In or out of prison, one answer is other people. "We must love one another or die," as Auden put it. Knight has always been sure to acknowledge this. In the preface to the *Black Voices from Prison* anthology, he acknowledged "Gwendolyn Brooks, Sonia Sanchez, Dudley Randall, and Don L. Lee: black poets whose love and words cracked these walls." In *Born of a Woman,* he gives a list that has grown to over forty people he feels indebted to.

In a way, Knight's poetry itself is another form of acknowledgement. People, relationships between and among people, are his compelling theme; it is present in nearly all his work in one form or another. I want to follow this thread in talking about Knight's poetry.

In *Belly Song* Knight had a nice existential individualist blues fragment, dated 8/72, called **"Evolutionary Poem No. 1"**:

> I ain't got nobody
> that i can depend on
> 'cept myself

In *Born of a Woman* he has followed this piece immediately with **"Evolutionary Poem No. 2,"** in which a switch to the plural pronoun points in a different direction:

> We ain't got nobody
> that we can depend on
> 'cept ourselves.

"No. 2" is dated September 1979, the same date as that of the book's preface, nine months before its publication. Very likely Knight noticed, as he was rereading and reorganizing his work for the new collection, that his earlier statement, though in large ways true for himself and everyone, was counter to the fundamental current running through his poems: the impulse to celebrate nourishing human relationships, to lament their various breakdowns, to protest their betrayals.

On the broadest scale, this impulse appears in a sense of racial solidarity, as in **"Poem for 3rd World Brothers"** and **"For Black Poets Who Think of Suicide,"** both exhortations to blacks to give themselves deeply to the energies and causes of their people. Elsewhere on the spectrum, the same basic theme emerges out of such a small, unexpected incident as the one in **"A WASP Woman Visits a Black Junkie in Prison."** At first outraged by the absurdity of this unasked-for visit from a "prim blue and proper-blooded" stranger, he soon recognizes that it is a situation of one loneliness reaching out toward another, and ultimately he finds himself strangely moved and quieted by the simple exchange they manage to construct.

The theme often appears in the form of celebrations of "heroes" of various kinds. There are poems honoring artists—Langston Hughes, Max Roach, Otis Redding—, and three strong elegies to Malcolm X. There are also other sorts of heroic characters, from Pooky Dee, whose "great 'two 'n' a half' gainer" from a railroad trestle one summer afternoon long ago ended with the sickening "sound of his capped/Skull as it struck the block," and left a permanent scar in his watchers' memories; to Shine, the black stoker on the Titanic in Knight's marvelous version of the folk poem, who rejected the pleas and bribes of various white establishment figures who couldn't stay afloat by themselves, and "swam on"; to Hard Rock, a black convict who refuses to cooperate in his own imprisonment and performs exploits of resistance which end in his lobotomy but also confront the other inmates with an unsettling example of courage and integrity. Each of these people, real or legendary (often both), from Langston Hughes to Hard Rock, has in some form or other given a gift, left a mark, that turns mere existence into reality.

In the last three poems mentioned, there is a blend of vivid lyric and narrative impulses which is typical of Knight. "Hard Rock," for example, is a character sketch and an elegy, a compressed short story and a meditation on moments of intense feeling and realization. Another poem that contains the matter of a story and the music and intensity of a lyric is **"For Freckle-Faced Gerald."** While most of Knight's poems are in one way or another expressions of admiration or gratitude or love—are in one way or another affirmations—in the case of Gerald the most the poet can do is offer grief and outrage in the form of clear-eyed description of his subject's hopeless situation. Truly written and felt, this turns out to be an expression of a kind of love too.

The poem deals with a sixteen-year-old boy who has been sent to prison. In addition to his youth and inexperience, Gerald has going against him his inability even to strike a pose of self-assurance and toughness. Instead, he has "precise speech and an innocent grin." For him, being put in prison amounts, as the poem tersely puts it, to being "thrown in as 'pigmeat'/for the buzzards to eat." The buzzards in prison are the men who exploit Gerald sexually and otherwise. But they are only part of a much larger scenario of exploitation and dehumanization, which the poem opens out upon in its last stanza:

> Gerald, sun-kissed ten thousand times on the nose
> and cheeks, didn't stand a chance,
> didn't even know that the loss of his balls
> had been plotted years in advance
> by wiser and bigger buzzards than those
> who now hover above his track
> and at night light upon his back.

Such writing is a tough-minded song of protest and mourning. It is powerful because it is direct and firmly crafted, and also because of its sense of controlled rage. Knight is as aware of the violations human beings commit against one another, on all levels, in endless forms, as he is of the bonds that help to sustain us.

Another strong character sketch is **"He Sees Through Stone."** It is a portait of an old black convict, apparently long imprisoned, who has taken on a wisdom that gives him a kind of mythic significance. "Pressed by the sun/ against the western wall/his pipe between purple gums," the old man is surrounded by young inmates. Possibly they gather around him to hear stories he has to tell, but the poem does not tell us this. Instead, it describes a more subtle attraction. The poet says, "I have known him/in a time gone by," and goes on to describe a sense in the old man's presence of a timeless guide or initiator who has somehow been with him through all the rites of passage of his life:

> he led me trembling cold
> into the dark forest
> taught me the secret rites
> to make it with a woman
> to be true to my brothers
> to make my spear drink
> the blood of my enemies

Apparently the other younger men sense this in him also. It is this recognition that sets up the old man's ability to "see through stone."

In the work of most poets there are certain words or images that recur regularly, in some cases obsessively. Not surprisingly in a poet who spent years in prison, one of Knight's persistent images is stone. It represents not just physical walls and imprisonment, of course; more importantly it stands for emotional barriers, insensitivity, the dead weight in the spirit that needs to be pushed away or penetrated or transformed in order for caring energies to flow again.

Knight is as aware of the violations human beings commit against one another, on all levels, in endless forms, as he is of the bonds that help to sustain us.

—Howard Nelson

There are two kinds of stone in the poem: the stone walls of the prison, and the stone wall each person sets up himself. Knight picks up the slang metaphor "cats" and elaborates its suggestions: the "black cats" "circle," "flash white teeth," "snarl," have "shining muscles." But all this fierceness is a pose, a mask, ultimately another kind of stone wall erected in the name of defense. The old man leaning in the sun against actual stone is not impressed by the posturing. He understands and penetrates it: "he smiles/he knows"—knows the vulnerability that lives behind it. And somehow, the poem suggests, he is consequently a reassuring force, an outer presence who is also an inner presence, a kind of steady witness and companion to the hidden life the self lives within walls within walls.

In a broad sense, about ninety per cent of Knight's work could be called love poetry. And naturally, poems that fit that term in the conventional sense make up an important part of his book. My personal favorites in this category are **"As You Leave Me,"** which creates haunting currents of emotion through imagery of great precision and dramatic effect, and **"Feeling Fucked Up,"** marvelous in its use of sound, a profane litany, a down-to-earth lament, written wonderfully at gut level all the way through to its culminating repetitions:

> . . . fuck joseph fuck mary fuck
> god jesus and all the disciples fuck fanon nixon
> and malcolm fuck the revolution fuck freedom fuck
> the whole muthafucking thing
> all i want now is my woman back
> so my soul can sing

Another strong group is the poems that deal with family. Some of these take a sort of ritual form—words spoken for important events, such as a birth (**"On the Birth of a Black/Baby/Boy"**) or an escape from death (**"Another Poem for Me—after Recovering from an O.D."**). There are straight-forward elegies, such as **"The Bones of My Father,"** and anecdotes, as in the warm, low-key **"Talking in the Woods with Karl Amorelli."** Also within this group are two poems which, rightfully, have usually been among those representing Knight in anthologies: **"The Idea of Ancestry"** and **"The Violent Space."**

"The Idea of Ancestry" is a poem about what it means to belong to a family—not just a nuclear family, but a large weaving of people that spreads out to include several branches and generations—and what it feels like to be isolated from it. The poem is in two parts. It begins with the poet lying on his prison bunk gazing at the forty-seven photographs of relatives he has taped to his wall. Looking at them, he gives a series of small catalogues of connectedness: "I know/their dark eyes, they know mine. I know their style, they know mine . . . /I have at one time or another been in love with my mother,/ 1 grandmother, 2 sisters, 2 aunts (1 went to the asylum) . . . /I have the same name as 1 grandfather, 3 cousins, 3 nephews,/and 1 uncle. . . ." The pictures and his thoughts make him feel part of a vital human flow—the ongoing, complex, living thing a family that has a sense of itself can be—but at the same time sharpens his loneliness. This is particularly so because the uncle at the end of the last list, it turns out, has long since vanished: "disappeared when he was 15, just took/off and caught a freight (they say)." He is at once a part of the family and "an empty space." Year after year he has been discussed by the family, especially by the ninety-three-year-old matriarch of the clan who is the keeper of the family Bible and the symbol of family roots and tradition. "There is no/ place in her Bible for 'whereabouts unknown.'" The uncle's absence is a presence when the family gathers, and the poet, alone in his cell, ripped out of the fabric by a prison sentence, is haunted by the feeling that he has more in common with his uncle than a name.

The second section of the poem is a flashback to a family reunion which took place a year earlier. Both parts of the poem are set in fall, the season when the poet's yearning to get back to the family is always strongest—appropriate because of Thanksgiving as well as more subtle mortal reasons. With his characteristic vivid conciseness, Knight describes the longing to get back among family and family places—as basic as the instinctual drive of a migrating salmon—and the pleasure and ease of finally being on home ground again. But this time too he was pulled away from the family, in this case by a narcotics habit which forced him to leave and in turn led to his imprisonment. Then the poem returns to the present and the cell with its silent "47 black faces." The poet's thoughts have made him very restless: he paces, flops down on his bed—torn by his double sense of connectedness and isolation. He repeats a sort of invocation of the lone individual to the family spirit, spoken earlier as well—"I am all of them,/they are all of me, I am me, they are thee"—, then closes with another specter of loneliness and the breakdown of his life-lines within the family: ". . . . and I have no children/to float in the space between." In these last two statements the poem follows its fundamental curve, away from abstract formulation of an "idea of ancestry" into definition in terms of a field of emotions grounded in concrete situations and images. The idea may remain unparaphrasable, but when Knight has finished his poem it has become a solid, subtle, moving thing.

"The Violent Space (or When Your Sister Sleeps Around for Money)" is another extraordinary poem. (When Knight reads this poem to an audience, he makes a point of reminding them that the "I" in a poem, even with a poet as autobiographical as himself, cannot be assumed to be the author. In reality the poem grew out of talks with a fellow inmate whose sister had been a prostitute. Knight's own sisters, he explains, confronted him in not very good humor after having first seen the poem, and out of courtesy to them he gives a brief lecture on persona and negative capability, though he doesn't use those terms. Knight often has a way of bringing matters of literary technique and theory down to a practical, common sense level.) The poem's subject has the potential for a great deal of emotion built into it, but that emotion is only realized and communicated through Knight's masterful dramatization and use of language.

The speaker's sister is "all of seventeen." He is a heroin addict; quite likely some of his sister's earnings go to support his habit. In an agonizing present, the brother makes a poem for his sister that has woven within it memories and feelings of their childhood: the far different, simpler pain she felt once when stung by a wasp; the refrain from a children's rhyme. The juxtaposition of these memories and associations against the present situation is skillfully handled, as is the rendering of the brother's protective impulses, then and now, toward his sister. When she was stung by the wasp, they "flew home" together. But now, rather than coming to her aid, he is only the outraged, ineffectual observer—perhaps even beneficiary of her suffering.

The poem's imagery is worth noting. Typical of Knight, it favors directness over ingenuity. The images—e.g., "green apple breasts," "red wasp," "twisted spoon"—are clear and sharp but do not call attention to themselves; their purpose is to convey scenes and feelings in a vivid, imme-

diate way. In this quality they are reminiscent of the imagery one finds often in folk ballads. Also working through the poem is a powerful motif of religious references. More important still, however, is sound. Throughout the poem there are musical effects that are at once elemental and sophisticated. Alliteration, assonance, rhymes and slant rhymes within and at the ends of lines, refrains, parallelisms, fragments of actual songs—all are used to great effect. One could go through the poem and point out instances of these musical devices, but a better way to present these superb rhythms and repetitions is to set down the poetry itself so its total music can be heard. Here are the last three stanzas of **"The Violent Space."**

> Well, hell, lil sis, wasps still sting.
> You are all of seventeen and as alone now
> In your pain as you were with the sting
> On your brow.
> Well, shit, lil sis, here we are:
> You and I and this poem.
> And what should I do? should I squat
> In the dust and make strange markings on the
>   ground?
> Shall I chant a spell to drive the demon away?
> (Run sister run—the Bugga man comes!)
>
> In the beginning you were the Virgin Mary,
> And you are the Virgin Mary now.
> But somewhere between Nazareth and Bethlehem
> You lost your name in the nameless void.
> *"O Mary don't you weep don't you moan"*
> O Mary shake your butt to the violent juke,
> Absorb the demon puke and watch the white eyes
>   pop,
> (Run sister run—the Bugga man comes!)
>
> And what do I do. I boil my tears in a twisted
>   spoon
> And dance like an angel on the point of a needle.
> I sit counting syllables like Midas gold.
> I am not bold. I cannot yet take hold of the demon
> And lift his weight from your black belly,
> So I grab the air and sing my song.
> (But the air cannot stand my singing long.)

The speaker feels a terrible anguish at the fact that all he is able to do in the face of this situation is to "grab the air and sing [a] song." Yet for the rest of us, readers, listeners, brought into wider, more intense feeling and awareness by the song, it makes a tremendous difference—the difference great poetry makes in life. One thing that helps to heal our alienations is relationships, bonds of feeling and concern; another, not separate thing is poetry. Galway Kinnell has written a poem to Etheridge Knight, the final lines of which are worth quoting here. The painfully beautiful **"The Idea of Ancestry"** and **"The Violent Space"** must have been among the poems he was thinking of when he wrote them: "broken heart brother, sing to us/here, in this place that loses its brothers,/ in this emptiness only the singing sometimes almost fills."

. . . . .

Shifting away from the theme of relationships which I've been following, I want to say more now about the key element in Knight's work that I've already begun discussing: sound. The entire book is laced together by Knight's unabashed sense of verbal music, right down to the titles of its three sections: "Inside-Out," "Outside-In," "All About—And Back Again." But I want to talk about sound not just in terms of poetic devices within poems, but also in terms of the actual spoken voice, the whole question of how we read and appreciate poetry.

I know that many people don't consider it quite legitimate to talk in criticism about poetry as a spoken, performed thing. There are various reasons for this. In America, most people who read poetry have been conditioned to think that the poem on the page is what really matters. (It is—but not exclusively.) Contributing to this is a training that leads us to think of poetry as a set of ideas and techniques rather than as an experience that includes them, the notion that there is an equation between greatness in poetry and how much explication it will sustain, and a condescension toward poetry whose strength lies in direct oral communication of emotion. We're suspicious of poetry which doesn't seem to have the impact on the page that it did when we heard it read well aloud. This is sometimes valid, but one needs to be careful here. Just as the poem must do its work well, so must the reader. I have often seen poems undervalued or misunderstood because of failures of aural (i.e., oral) imagination on the part of readers.

Ironically, the proliferation of poetry readings in recent years has also fed the prejudice against poetry in its oral incarnation. I certainly wouldn't deny that poetry readings can be creepy and tedious occasions, or that some poets are such poor readers that they do their audience and poetry a disservice when they give a reading. On the other hand, there is a cranky, reactionary attitude that is blind to the fact that it is fundamentally proper and healthy that poetry is being read aloud to audiences across the country. The prejudice can be observed in a segment of almost any college English department, but also in a statement by no less than the editor of *Poetry* magazine, John F. Nims, in a letter to another poet reported in *The Chowder Review*:

> I probably won't be able to make your reading.
> Mostly because I don't like poetry readings, or
> other kinds of show-biz. My eyes glaze and I
> have to gag a lot to keep from vomiting. Better
> a week-end in a leprosarium than a poetry reading.

In the years since his release from prison Etheridge Knight has earned his living principally by giving poetry readings. He is an excellent reader. His deep, resonant voice is a gift. He is sensitive to the rhythms and inflections of poetry and "ordinary" speech, and he is sensitive to his audiences and knows how to reach them. As a black poet he stands in a living tradition of toast-tellers, rhymers, and singers. He believes that poetry is most fully itself when it is spoken aloud to other people; and as I've said, his poems have an immediacy and music that lend themselves to that kind of presentation. So I suppose he has all the qualifications to be called an oral poet. But the term is not

a very precise or useful one, and too often it is used to put poems in a category without granting them full status as poems.

> I think that poetry can be made accessible to the
> so-called general reader if it can be heard—and
> I've written almost everything I've done to be heard.
> Once that occurs, there's usually understanding.

The author of this statement is Theodore Roethke. Was he an oral poet, or just a poet? What I'm suggesting is that, generally, drawing this line is misleading rather than clarifying.

There is of course poetry that strains violently against the printed page in an effort at what Larry Neal has called "the destruction of the text," in which the text becomes roughly suggestive, a rudimentary score for improvisational performance. This is a good ways further out on the spectrum that what I am discussing here. My point is simply that reading poetry aloud is fundamental to the art, and that oral presentation draws forces out of the words which otherwise lie in them to some degree lost or wasted. Some poems lose more than others in a reading that doesn't do justice to their oral aspects, but whether one is reading *The Waste Land* or "After Apple-Picking" or "The Windhover" or "The Sea Elephant" or "The Navajo Night Chant," one needs really to hear the sounds, the tones, the voices, to truly receive the poem. Poetry readings—good ones, such as Etheridge Knight or Allen Ginsberg or Donald Hall or Gwendolyn Brooks or Galway Kinnell or William Heyen, for example, are capable of giving—become therefore not only heartening public performances but lessons we might learn in trying to become better readers ourselves—of all poetry, not just that of the poets we've heard reading.

In relation to these ideas, consider Knight's **"Ilu, the Talking Drum."** The best way to learn to read this poem is to hear Knight's extraordinary rendering of it, but this is not essential. While it's true that probably no one else could speak the poem as well as he does, it has its power within its words and will have still a hundred years from now.

The theme is again a human relationship, and in this case the poem describes how sound and rhythm themselves can create a bond among people. The poet is with a group of fifteen Nigerians. The setting is somewhat ambiguous, except for the fact that it is alien. A mood of torpor and restlessness hangs over them, and is communicated largely through the sounds of the words. We begin in a chafing silence: "The stillness was skinny and brittle and wrinkled." Those stingy, shallow i sounds are soon picked up again, joined by sharp p's, t's, and s's and bald long a's: "We twisted, turned, shifted positions, picked our noses,/stared at our bare toes, hissed air through our teeth . . ." The stifling tedium is also conveyed through a series of monosyllabic phrases using doubled, very ordinary adjectives: "wide green lawn," "wide white porch," "big white house."

A breakthrough occurs, however, when one of the Nigerians rises and begins to play a rhythm on **"Ilu, the talk-**

ing drum." The emotional change is announced before it begins to happen, through sound—the entrance of long, open o's and u's: "Then Tunji, green robes flowing as he rose, strapped on Ilu, the talking drum." It is in what follows that the poem becomes either boring or marvelous, depending on how we read. The drum speaks, and Knight lets us hear it:

> kah doom / kah doom-doom / kah doom / kah
> doom-doom-doom
> kah doom / kah doom-doom / kah doom / kah
> doom-doom-doom
> kah doom / kah doom-doom / kah doom / kah
> doom-doom-doom
> kah doom / kah doom-doom / kah doom / kah
> doom-doom-doom

If one follows habits learned from reading newspapers and most other prose, and skims over this as if it were so much filler, the point of the poem is missed. But if one reads the words carefully, actually sensing the reverberations, one is pulled inside a rhythmic flow that stands for life itself. In the next stanza Knight does in fact identify the drum beat with the heart beat. Much repetition; generous sound; a profound theme:

> the heart, the heart beats, the heart, the heart beats
> slow
> the heart beats slowly, the heart beats
> the blood flows slowly, the blood flows
> the blood, the blood flows, the blood, the blood
> flows slow
> kah doom / kah doom-doom / kah doom / kah
> doom-doom-doom

At the end of the poem Knight suggests the great human distances that can be spanned within such sound, the freshened consciousness and sense of liberation it can create. Then he closes with the drum beat. When the poem ends there is an amazing silence, in which we seem to hear the echoes of the drum, or possibly it is the buried sound of our own blood beating—a very different silence from that which the opening of the poem described. **"Ilu, the Talking Drum"** is a marvelous poem, with rich veins of music and meaning and feeling. But it needs to be read truly.

There are other chant-like poems in *Born of a Woman*, such as **"We Free Singers Be"** and, especially, **"Belly Song."** But the book as a whole, from the incantatory effects of **"Ilu"** and **"Belly Song,"** to the fine unsolemn repetitions of **"Feeling Fucked Up"** and **"Welcome Back, Mr. Knight: Love of My Life,"** to the simple refrains of **"It Was a Funky Deal"** and **"I and Your Eyes,"** to the small, tight rhymes of **"A Shakespearean Sonnet: To a Woman Liberationist,"** to notations like **"Cop-Out Session,"** where the music is just the live music of black speech itself (working everywhere in Knight's poems): the whole book is wound around sound—vigorous, invigorating sound.

. . . . .

"The warmth of this poet is abruptly robust. The music that seems effortless is exquisitely carved." These are further words from Gwendolyn Brooks' preface to *Poems from Prison*. The two aspects Brooks put her finger on are the basic ones I've tried to deal with; and Knight has carried them on in the continuing creation that has now become *Born of a Woman*.

Here is another of the notation-like poems that are scattered through the book, making something like a gloss:

> **"MY LIFE, THE QUALITY OF WHICH"**
> My Life, the quality of which
> From the moment
> My Father grunted and comed
> Until now
> As the sounds of my words
> Bruise your ears
> IS
> And can be felt
> In the one word: DESPERATION
>
> But you have to *feel* for it

We do have to feel for it, just as we may have to retune our reading to the potencies of Knight's music. But doing these things shouldn't be too hard, because the desperation—which in Knight's case is entirely bound up in and a part of tenacity and loving concern—as well as the music are ample and made fully accessible through the skill of Knight's art. *Born of a Woman* contains a harsh, generous, beautiful poetry. It is breath of life.

Fifteen years ago, when Knight began writing while in prison, the angry black racist rhetoric may have had impact; but, however valid the reasons behind these cries against exploitation, oppression, and desperate existence remain, the rhetoric has worn rather thin.

—J. P., in a review of Born of a Woman, *in* Booklist, *September 1, 1980*.

Ashby Bland Crowder (essay date 1983)

SOURCE: "Etheridge Knight: Two Fields of Combat," in *Concerning Poetry*, Vol. 16, No. 2, Fall, 1983, pp. 23-5.

[*In the following essay, Crowder discusses the theme of racism in Knight's "2 Poems for Black Relocation Centers."*]

Etheridge Knight's **"2 Poems for Black Relocation Centers"** have the standard ingredients of social protest poetry. Knight presents two case histories of black men victimized by white racist America: the first concerns a worker

Dust jacket for Knight's 1980 book of poems, which takes its title from the Book of Job:
"Man that is born of a woman is of few days and full of troubles."

in the military field of combat; the second is about an industrial worker in Detroit. Both die prematurely and senselessly, following bouts of neglect, betrayal, and defeat. If taken at face value, these companion poems might be seen as variations on the it's-tough-to-be-black-in-America theme. Yet I believe that in them Knight is going beyond the victim pose. He understands and uses the vocabulary of victimization not simply to issue a complaint but to investigate the irony of the concept of relocation.

The idea of black relocation, Knight's central metaphor, is older than the War Between the States, and the term "relocation" carries with it far-ranging associations. It brings to mind the relocation of Africans to southern plantations. It recalls the freed slaves who were relocated in Liberia in 1847. It suggests the Nazi relocation centers for Jews; the U.S. relocation centers for Japanese Americans during World War II; the centers in cities all over the country provided for the down-and-out, the transient, the homeless, the dislocated; and even Urban Renewal's relocations of entire ghettos. In our recent social history, concepts of relocation, refuge, and elimination have become merged and confused, a phenomenon that Knight uses to advantage in these two poems.

The first of Knight's **"2 Poems"** concerns the black man Flukum (his name suggestive of his uncertain existence) who seeks "inner and outer order" and so joins the army. The army has a remedy for Flukum's uncertainty, a system for attending to all of his needs and for ordering all aspects of his life. Like Cummings' Olaf, Flukum must adapt his own conscience to the unconscionable demands of the system; in return he is taught "how to button his shirt, / and how to kill the yellow men." If he experiences doubt about genocide, there is a "Troop Information Officer" and an official overseas newspaper, the "Stars / and Stripes," to set him straight. A "good Chaplain" will absolve him of residual guilt, and Flukum will be paid for his services. For awhile, on the other side of racism, he feels acceptance. And in war he feels safety.

Back from the war, Flukum distributes the spoils he has won ("presents for all"), but he is "surprised" to find that nothing at home has changed. He "had thought / the enemy far away on the other side of the sea." But the enemy at home, his real enemy, shoots him in "his great wide chest." When his effects are distributed to his family, U.S. officialdom withholds his dagger, the only item on the list that might conceivably symbolize power. The black war veteran finds, then, that his homecoming is more dislocating than the battlefield.

In the second of the **"Poems for Black Relocation,"** Knight presents another black man, this one unnamed and unmourned, who has died on the home front, in Detroit. He has died with lice in his beard, surrounded by filth, in a slumlord's firetrap flat. This gruesome image of charred beams and splintered glass is heightened by the stench of "roasted rats / and fat baby rumps."

Here the relocation theme takes a different turn, for Knight sees the second man as a phoenix figure ("And he arose out of his own ashes. Stripped.") whose "halo glowed / and his white robe flowed magnificiently / over the charred beams." This resurrection figure is a more powerfully imagined character than Flukum, perhaps even a Christ figure; but the point still seems to be that the only possible relocation center for the poor black man in America is a traditional afterlife, the kind of other-worldly redemption that Blake implies for his blackened chimney sweeps in *The Songs of Innocence*.

The poem's final line is a packed image, in which the dead man is summed up as "A faggot in steel boots." The term "faggot" carries the obvious reference to homosexuality and suggests that the dead man experienced in life a double liability, according to the orthodoxy of the society in which he lived. The word "faggot" brings together several suggestions made earlier in the poem. The faggot (a bundle of twigs for fuel) is linked to the Holy Inquisition, during which unorthodox persons (including homosexuals) were eliminated in great autos-da-fé. A faggot is also a bundle of iron rods to be worked into something, suggestive of the industrial worker; and there is an obsolete sense of the word, apt here, that ties the industrial worker to the soldier of poem one: "a person temporarily hired to supply a deficiency at the muster, or on the roll of a company or regiment." In addition, "faggot" also evokes the expression "fag end," the remnant or "last part . . . of anything, after the best has been used . . .". And the simple verb "fag" means to work hard, strain, and toil. Thus the poem's final line condenses the references to the fire that charred the room and the phoenix soul arising. Knight thus argues that the black man has been the human fuel for society's building and productivity, a drudge used temporarily in the industrial workplace. His fate is to be reduced to a part of the material of building, to be consumed in the act of fueling, yet in the end to transcend the "shouting [of] impieties and betrayals."

The steel boots are presumably the protective footwear required of an industrial worker in Detroit, but they also imply an alloy in the black character and experience that is not combustible, and that will survive in some form. Thus the phrase "faggot in steel boots" combines implications of toughness and vulnerability.

The individual ironies of **"2 Poems for Black Relocation Centers"** add up to an overall ironic intention. The title itself turns out to be ironic, for the poems do not advocate relocation centers; instead, they negatively suggest that what are needed are alternatives to displacement of all kinds—institutional, psychological, racial, religious. Throughout **"2 Poems"** Knight has pointed out the kinds of reversals of justice and expectation that lead to a world lacking "inner and outer order"; his observations lead to an ironic reversal of the usual prescription to solve social problems.

Etheridge Knight with Ron Price (interview date 1986)

SOURCE: "The Physicality of Poetry: An Interview with Etheridge Knight," in *New Letters*, Vol. 52, Nos. 2-3, Winter-Spring, 1986, pp. 167-76.

[*In the following interview, Knight discusses major themes of and influences on his poetry, as well as his relationship with his audience.*]

[New Letters]: *Etheridge, you often speak of an "inverted sensibility" characteristic of prisoners, the way they are shaped by the cages that keep them. In **"To Make A Poem In Prison"** you write:*

> It is hard
> to make a poem in prison.
> The air lends itself not
> to the singer.
> *(Poems From Prison)*

*And with **"Belly Song"** you develop this theme into a kind of leitmotif:*

> this poem
> this poem/is
> for me/and the nights
>   when I
>   wrapped my feelings
>   in a sheet of ice
>   and stared
>   at the stars
>   through iron bars
>   and cried
> in the middle of my eyes . . .
>   *(Belly Song And Other Poems)*

*In a letter you subsequently used as the introduction to **Belly Song And Other Poems**, you write of your upcoming parole: "I'll soon be with my woman and children in the larger outside prison." What begins in a specific place in your first book of poems, generalizes in the second into the condition of life in America, if not the world.*

[Etheridge Knight]: My major metaphor is prison. I think art is ultimately about freedom, the celebration of that freedom—whether it's individual or general. One of the major themes of art is aloneness: You're constantly reaching out for community, for communication. Art is a reaching out. When you're in prison you become extremely aware of your aloneness, or any place where you're isolated and you've got that introspection going on. When you become involved in the creative process, you become extremely aware. In prison, when you're pregnant with creativity, you're extremely aware of the outside world. You tend to not want to deal with that outside world. There's so much pain and brutality and oppression that you want to encapsulate yourself. You just want to pull covers and covers and covers over yourself. Just to be aware of your existence when you're in prison, man, is painful. Sports: You can wrap yourself around that and not be aware of all the other levels. You get in such a deep rut you can't get out of it. You won't be aware of who is elected governor. It doesn't make any difference what food is put on the table. You just read the sport's page and that's all.

In the introduction to **Born Of A Woman,** *you write:*

> I see the Art of Poetry as the logos ("In the beginning was the Word") as a Trinity: the Poet, the Poem and the People. When the three come together, the communion, the communication, the Art happens.

If you get into just I, I, I, I, I—the first person, the poet as strictly personal—you don't get a revolving going on. Art is revolutionary. The language—the written word and the spoken word, but especially the spoken word—is so evocative that there's a constant recreation going on.

My birthday was last Monday. It's funny . . . My mamma told me again how I was born. She's walking down this country road and she's complaining how hot it was and wasn't no shade trees along this road and she wanted to sit down and I was born before the midwife got there. Well, that's recreating.

When you get these three things revolving, a communion takes place: It's ritualistic. Saying a poem or telling a story, you have got to evoke. Each one in the audience will use his or her imagination and identification. You send out a line to each one. It ain't like you was throwing out a big net and catching all the fish. What you're saying is one straight line from you to each person. And some you miss. Generally, if you try to reach "universality" by just throwing out a net of abstractions, you ain't going to get it. That ain't the way people operate. That's why it's so important to know your poems.

Now, I remember when I first started reading. I'd be nervous. A lot of people don't understand what's going on at a poetry reading. It's damn near like going to church: everyone all uptight and proper. I'll pick out the friendly faces and make eye contact with them first, until I get over my nervousness, and then I move on. But at some point you get caught up; you're aware. You can look out there and tell. It's not like the form you get in public speaking: raise your eyes up every now and then from the page. I have seen people do that. And when they be looking at the audience, they'll be looking over the audience, looking off into left field or right field. Like Ronald Reagan. Yea. He'll turn to the audience and at the precise

moment: blah, blah, blah, blah, blah to the left; blah, blah, blah, blah, blah to the right. It's performance.

In addition to public speaking, then, you make a distinction between a poetry reading and a performance?

Yea, because performance is, simply, prescribed. The whole thing is drama. There are certain ways you start off making contact. There's a greeting, an exchange. "Hello. How ya doing?" There are these same ground rules in drama, but to follow a script is what I see as performance.

There ain't no exact course. You're moving in a general direction, but you can't just follow what's written. When we started the Free People's [Poetry Workshop], one of the things was to get out of the controlled environment of a campus, to be public. There are variables that are going to come in that you have to deal with: A drunk might stagger up; a baby might start crying. And you have to deal with it. You can't just keep on with what's prescribed. In the first place, you aren't being aware. You're depending more on what's written than on what is happening right now.

The texts for most of the toasts and anecdotes you use— **"The Signifying Monkey," "Shine," "Eulogy For Slick," "Fight Him Fair Nigger"**—*were developed inside jails and barracks and bars, but you have also given a lot of readings in college communities. Does that have an influence on what you're saying now? And how much does your audience affect the dynamic interaction you are describing?*

A lot. If I'm saying a toast in a pool room or a jail, I'm going to get feedback that's different than if I say it on a college campus to a mixed audience. The emphasis, the connotation of the words, the rhythm and march and cadence, it changes. In the first place, you'll be breathing differently than if you're at your mother's house. The way you walk and talk, everything is going to be different. If you're in the company of children you're going to breathe differently. It's the same wine, you're just putting it in a different jug.

During a poetry reading, then, this expanded sense of what comprises the text is part of what facilitates the communication, the communion?

Yea. The main difference is the word, the spoken word. You're going to use your body, if it ain't no more than a few hand gestures. Understand: The spoken word is the main vehicle. For me, drama is the total art: You've got visual and you've got movement; but it's the dialogue that's going on; that's the center. If there's a point of departure, that's it. That's why it's hard for me to stand behind a podium. Most good preachers and politicians, when they get caught up, they are going to move. It's a motion. You get a rhythm going. In the Baptist churches the choir and preacher will start rocking. It's a very primal thing. When you get everybody into this, that's the universe. One verse.

Could you say a little more about "getting caught up?"

I think it happens on two levels. One is a physical level. When the poet and the audience start coming together in some kind of ritual—the part in a poem that might happen with cataloging or a litany or intoning. A change takes place, the words become familiar, the audience relaxes, they can anticipate. This has to do with mechanics, the poetics, the sound and rhythm. Once you recognize this intoning, you can feel what will come next before it is said.

One of the major themes of art is aloneness: You're constantly reaching out for community, for communication. Art is a reaching out. When you're in prison you become extremely aware of your aloneness, or any place where you're isolated and you've got that introspection going on.

—Etheridge Knight

When I think of trance, I think of non-concentration. That's not it. It's also not like concentrating on a flame or on a point. It's an extreme awareness, a common motion. If I say "1, 2, 3, 4, 5, 6, 7, 8, 9," you're going to expect "10." The audience and the poet latch onto something shared, a common movement. There's a line from the poet out to one person and back to the poet, and then out to another person. Then individual lines in the audience crisscross and some come back to the poet and others don't.

So you're not changing your mind about the kind of give and take that goes on between you and your audience so much as your description of that event, decentralizing your position in the event?

Yea, yea. A physical change takes place. I've seen it in preachers . . . just people, when they get angry: There's a physical thing. You see it in the audience. They may just sit back and let the poems come, but when a poet starts to sing, when that leap takes place, you can see the audience shifting. It's the same way with a congregation: They start to breathe together, they start to lean forward, they start rocking.

The other thing, besides the physical, is the audience expecting something familiar, the abstraction. Sometimes this getting caught up happens quickly, sometimes more slowly. The main thing is what the poet addresses, what he's dealing with, the audience will have to be in general agreement with to sustain that community. It doesn't have to be political; it could be a passion. Community is determined in part by physical closeness, and in part by history and common ideas. The intoning has got to be in the language of the people and the rhythm of the audience, or else they won't know what is happening.

You have written:

> No universal laws
> Of human misery
> Create a common cause
> Or common history.

How are these lines qualified by what you are saying now?

I made that poem up in response to a lot of poets and scholars, especially academics, who said Black poets weren't addressing "universal" themes. You know, "Black poets shouldn't talk about politics or their particular pains. They should address themselves to abstract and universal ideas." That's bullshit.

Art has to address specific things—one's own. It is always subjective. If I talk about my loneliness, it has more authority and validity. Loneliness is probably the same for a Tibetan monk as it is for an Irish potato farmer. Loneliness is loneliness. There are feelings and ideas common to all people. The poet addresses these generalizations by being specific. You have to move from the subject to the object. To discuss war in the abstract is different than discussing war with your brother whose leg was blown off in Vietnam.

How do you understand the relationship between poetry and religion?

They are close. The main vehicle for the poet and the preacher is the spoken word. And they both deal with intangibles, the spiritual and the aesthetic aspect of people. So a poet has to be familiar with his or her audience. An audience might not be familiar with poetics; but when a good reading happens, the audience is aware of the poet as a person, the same way a congregation is aware of the preacher's presence above the mechanics of the sermon or even the message of the sermon.

One reason the church failed and one of the main reasons that art has failed is because the language of the church and the language of the arts (the authority of the church and the authority of Western European art) never adequately dealt with the contemporary side of the language. The use of the historical authority was not tied in with now. Anytime you depend on history to determine your outlook without taking into consideration what is happening right now—without giving that equal authority—you become institutionalized, and you're going to get inertia. It's going to die out.

The Word is a living thing. Its life depends upon constant renewal. The life of the Word does not depend entirely on history; it also depends on what is going on right now. The word that comes into the language now is as important as a word that has been in the language a thousand years.

Again, there have been other influences recently, but it's still a Western European orientation, and that nullifies a lot of sensibility. When you consider the geography and the history of America, it's very different from Europe. Most of the countries of Europe are tribes. They speak different languages. Our states are as big as most of their countries, and we've got one language spread all over America. America is like the top of a table. Instead of four legs, some try making it rest on one European leg. Our consciousness, our sensibility has been informed by the Indians, by Africans, by Hispanics, as well as by Europeans. History is important: world history. When I was in high school, and we were supposed to be studying world history, we were studying Western European history. That's world view, but it isn't world history. Europe is not irrelevant to the life of America, but it is no more important than Nicaragua.

If you don't want a center—Rome or Paris or New York City or Moscow—how do you see this community, this uni-verse, existing?

Constantly moving, constantly whirling: spheres of influence and confluence, like currents in the ocean. Power shifts. Civilizations shift around this planet, and the reason they are constantly shifting has more influence or certainly as much of an influence as what men do. Biology is a part of this shifting, along with the movement of the oceans and volcanos and the movement of the stars. The way the world is determines the way power shifts. Since there are so many variables, so many determinants, I think the best name for this shifting is Chance. We can't put our finger on a single thing, or even a small group of things, to explain why people are like they are, why power shifts. We know that language is informed and, in part, determined by history and by what is happening right now. But there are also dreams and hopes and fears about the future. Language grows out of so many different things. We can't get down in words exactly what happens that causes wars, causes peace, causes ecstatic experiences, causes tears and pain and love. We can't pin it down because language grows out of these things.

Between the introduction to **Born Of A Woman** *and your current analogies with Christianity, it's as if the relationship you understand to be so close is different, primarily, because it emphasizes immanence instead of transcendance. It's as if you would drag Paradise down from some "elsewhere" and into this world: as if the condition of this world is a prison without that sense of communion; as if freedom is the process of such a community.*

Yea, it's the activity. We can theorize and talk about freedom in prison: that's all subjective. You get into the activity, you move to the verb, and a lot of theory will be thrown by the wayside, or revised.

Somehow we are all moving toward this uni-verse, this great song and dance. It's like boogying in a dance hall: Everybody might be moving differently, individually, but the big beat, the great rhythm, everybody's into the same. . . .

You move from the "I" to the "We" through the Verb. It goes back and forth. It's not a polarity. It's a trinity. It keeps going around.

You know, there's this debate in Arkansas about whether children ought to be taught the biblical idea of the beginning or the scientific idea of the beginning. Ain't nobody seriously considered the third alternative: We always were; we always will be. Here are all these Ph.D.s talking about, "This is how it all began." Each one starts with the same assumption: There was a beginning. No. We are: We always were; we always will be.

That eternal quality is the part that is set free through the communion of the poet, the poem, and the people?

Yea, yea! You draw on memory (the past) and imagination (the future)—you tie them to right now. Your address has got to be now. You can exploit memory, the status quo. "Back in the good ole days . . ." There wasn't any "good ole days." That's the Garden of Eden. "I remember when things were cool." Or, "Twenty years from now when I retire. . . ." That's Heaven. "I'm just passing through this world. Heaven's going to be my home." You can exploit that in people. Now: That's where the freedom is.

That breaking out? Not being locked into the past or the future?

Yea. When you make contact, the communion, the community happens. It's a celebration. The whole thing is a celebration, always. Then you move to the universe. It's not static. There ain't no one big long come; we know that. You move in and out. You're always moving; that's the thing. Otherwise, you fall asleep. You're always in motion, constantly moving. That's why it takes three. Otherwise, you've got a beginning and an end. You've got polarity: plus and minus, black and white, rich and poor, young and old. You don't have a verb. You've got a subject and an object. Now, what's going on between them is as important. The two things by themselves—there ain't a fucking thing going on. So what?

Do you think such dynamic interaction is possible outside the context of a poetry reading? When someone is privately reading a poem in a book?

Yea, if the reader is approaching the poem right . . . in the same way my mother approaches the Bible: looking for something. There's an actual physical thing going on. Even when we're trying to read silently, there'll be little things moving in your throat and ear. That's the thing I'm talking about—the physicality of poetry. It's in the breath.

Raymond R. Patterson (essay date 1987)

SOURCE: A review of *The Essential Etheridge Knight,* in *The American Book Review,* Vol. 9, No. 4, September-October, 1987, p. 1.

[*Patterson is an American critic. In the following review of* The Essential Etheridge Knight, *he explores the defining characteristics of Knight's poetry.*]

Whose idea was it to call this collection *The Essential Etheridge Knight,* the word *Essential* laying the poet to rest while at the same time granting him eternal life? A paradox? Certainly a provocation (the *essence* of Etheridge Knight, the *indispensable* Etheridge Knight), but also an interesting idea—to have captured the poet's essence and to have found him indispensable.

A photograph on the back cover of *The Essential Etheridge Knight* shows the mature author looking into the smiling face of a child. Recall the 1968 Broadside Press chapbook *Poems from Prison,* Knight's first collection. The back cover shows the author seated on a cot in an attitude of willed composure, his right leg across his left, his hands clasping the right knee, the fingers interlocked, ridged, echoing the grid of cell bars at his back. "I died in Korea from a shrapnel wound and narcotics resurrected me," the author tells us. "I died in 1960 from a prison sentence and poetry brought me back to life." The essence of Etheridge Knight?

Many of the twenty-eight poems first published in *Poems from Prison*—"a major announcement," declared Gwendolyn Brooks—appear in *The Esential Etheridge Knight.* They are placed among work drawn from two later collections, *Belly Songs and Other Poems* (1973) and *Born of a Woman* (1980), followed by a section of recent poems. While *Poems from Prison* opens with "Cell Song," a grim statement of alienation ("I alone / tread the red circle / and twist the space / with speech") softened by earthy humor ("Come . . . sprinkle / salt on the tail / of a girl"), *The Essential Etheridge Knight* opens with a bit of flim-flam: "Split my skin / with the rock / of love old / as the rock / of Moses / my poems / love you" ("Genesis"). But once inside the book, we encounter the familiar gallery of doomed prison inmates: Hard Rock, "known not to take no shit," until "the doctors . . . bored a hole in his head, / Cut out part of his brain, and shot electricity / Through the rest"; the aged convict who "sees through stone," "who under prison skies / sits pressed by the sun / against the western wall"; the raped Freckled-Faced Gerald, "sun-kissed ten thousand times on the nose / and cheeks . . . Pigmeat / for the buzzards to eat." We meet again the doomed of society's larger prison: the streetwalker and her impotent lover in "As You Leave Me"; the ineffectual brother in "The Violent Space"; the almost-saved prodigal in "The Idea of Ancestry"; the patriotic Flukum, the soldier home from war, "shot in his great wide chest, bedecked with good / conduct ribbons" ("A Poem for Black Relocation Centers"). Here, too, are the elegies for Langston Hughes and Dinah Washington, and four poems for Malcolm X, one addressed to Gwendolyn Brooks: "The Sun came, Miss Brooks. / And we goofed the whole thing." So much doom, frustration, and failure redeemed by poetic feats of visual and psychic accuracy, such poignant detailing of loss: "In the August grass / Struck by the last rays of sun / The cracked teacup screams." The essence of Etheridge Knight?

Reading *The Essential Etheridge Knight,* one notices sun images recurring almost too frequently, as if designed to

tempt speculation: Let's see—the sun/son is father to the man, but the father hasn't been much help, and neither has the son, for that matter. "Social workers say I miss my Daddy too much," admits the poet in **"Various Protestations from Various People."** Something Freudian? And how vulnerable and sensitive a personality, so full of love and self-confessed flaws that beg forgiveness: "I been confused, fucked-up, scared, phony / and jive / to a whole / lot of people . . . / Haven't you?" (**"Cop-Out Session"**).

The book also contains the stuff of myth: the ignoring of chronology in the ordering of poems; the wanderings of a hero; his initiations through loss; his homecoming announced in **"The Bones of My Father,"** completing a cycle; then the hero's setting out again, filled with disappointment: "O Mother don't send me / To the Father to fix / it— / He will blow it / He fails / and kills / His sons—"(**"Report to the Mother"**). The essence of Etheridge Knight? More like the work of an experienced escape artist covering his tracks.

of America's Major Black Poets" by the sburgh Press, Knight is quoted in a news jor metaphor is prison. . . . I think art is freedom. . . ." Freedom? The essence of t? Perhaps? But what strikes this reader is the poet s ivist aesthetic, the periodic turning to the always invincible instrumentalities of oppression, initially identified as prison, but subsequently translated into other forms.

By bringing together poems that for two decades have gained Knight well-deserved attention, *The Essential Etheridge Knight* will attract comment on the poet's personal and political life. It will reveal his undeniable empathy for children. It will draw attention to his achievements with forms such as the haiku, the blues, and the toast (a rhymed narrative of a traditionally oppressed street/ prison folk hero who for the moment is in control of his life). It will also show that Knight's place in an Afro-American literary tradition cannot be described simply. The characteristic themes of family and black identity addressed in **"The Idea of Ancestry"** ("I am all of them, they are all of me") are treated with an irony in **"Another Poem for Me (after Recovering from an O.D.)"** that is illuminated by a reading of **"A Wasp Woman Visits a Black Junkie in Prison."** "I made / up / the poem," Knight says about **"The Idea of Ancestry"** (see Stephen Berg's *Singular Voices: American Poetry Today,* 1985). "The initial creative/impulse for the poem occurred . . . during one of my many stays in Solitary Confinement."

Dedicated to members of the poet's family, *The Essential Etheridge Knight* closes with **"Rehabilitation & Treatment in the Prisons of America,"** a parable that casts prison administration as a mechanism for destroying blacks, based on their acknowledgment of identity: "He was black, so he rushed—*ran*—through that door—and fell nine sto-

ries to the street." It is significant that Knight dedicated *Poems from Prison,* his first book, to "all the other black cats everywhere." Black cats, folk belief has it, have nine lives and always land on their feet. Indispensable Etheridge Knight? "Can there anything / good come out of / prison" asks the poet of **"Cell Song."** To read *The Essential Etheridge Knight* leaves no doubt.

FURTHER READING

Criticism

Gibbons, Reginald. Review of *The Esssential Etheridge Knight* by Etheridge Knight. *TriQuarterly* 71, (Winter 1988): 222-23.
> Positive assessment of Knight's poetry.

Hill, Patricia Liggins. "'Blues for a Mississippi Black Boy': Etheridge Knight's Craft in the Black Oral Tradition." *Mississippi Quarterly* XXXVI, No. 1 (Winter 1982-83): 21-33.
> Explores the influence of the black oral tradition on Knight's work.

Pinsker, Sanford. "A Conversation with Etheridge Knight." *Black American Literature Forum* 18, No. 1 (Spring 1984): 11-14.
> Interview in which Knight discusses the concepts of black aesthetics and "poeting."

Tracy, Steven C. "A MELUS Interview: Etheridge Knight." *MELUS* 12, No. 2 (Summer 1985): 7-23.
> Explores the work of several African-American writers, including Knight.

Additional coverage of Knight's life and career is contained in the following sources published by Gale Research: *Black Literature Criticism*; *Black Writers*, Vol. 1; *Contemporary Authors*, Vol. 133; *Contemporary Authors*, Vol. 21-24 (rev. ed.); *Contemporary Authors New Revision Series*, Vol. 23; *Contemporary Literarary Criticism*, Vol. 40; and *Dictionary of Literary Biography*, Vol. 41.

Jules Laforgue
1860-1887

French poet, short story writer, essayist, and dramatist.

INTRODUCTION

Laforgue was an early experimenter in *vers libre* (free verse). A member of the French Symbolist movement, he advocated abandoning popular literary conventions and maintained that art should be the expression of the subconscious mind. Laforgue's earliest writings, particularly the posthumously published *Le sanglot de la terre* (1901-03), resemble the poetry of Charles Baudelaire and Walt Whitman. The impressionistic language, fluid metric construction, and vivid imagery of his later works influenced such twentieth-century authors as T. S. Eliot, Ezra Pound, and Hart Crane. While widely recognized for his *Moralités légendaires* (1887; *Moral Tales*), a collection of short stories which parody famous literary works, including William Shakespeare's *Hamlet*, Laforgue is perhaps best known for his final poems, published posthumously as *Les derniers vers de Jules Laforgue* (1890). The experimental rhythmic patterns, psychological realism, and evocative language of these poems provided the Symbolists with a dynamic model for their later, more refined free verse.

Biographical Information

Laforgue was born in Montevideo, Uruguay. His father was an indigent teacher from Gascony, who in 1866 sent his family to Tarbes, France, where Jules and his brother Emile attended school. Although exceptionally intelligent, Laforgue was a mediocre student at the Lycée Tarbes. While there he made his first attempt at prose, writing a melodramatic account of his experiences entitled "Stéphane Vassiliew." In 1876, he enrolled at the Lycée Fontanes in Paris, and, although he liked the school, his work did not improve; he failed his baccalaureate exams twice and never received a diploma. In 1880, while studying art and working as a part-time journalist in Paris, Laforgue met Gustave Kahn, a poet and editor of the periodical *Le vogue et le symboliste*, who later became his mentor. With the encouragement of Kahn and Paul Bourget, a noted literary critic, Laforgue wrote his first significant poetic work, *Le sanglot de la terre*, a collection that evinces the influence of Arthur Schopenhauer's pessimistic philosophy and Edward von Hartmann's concept of the unconscious mind. In 1881, Laforgue accepted the position of French reader and secretary to Empress Augusta of Germany. For five years he traveled with the Empress, leading a leisurely life that kept him estranged from Parisian literary circles. *Les complaintes* (1885), his first poetry to employ the image of Pierrot—a white-faced mime that symbolizes humor, fate, and humanity, and personifies themes of uncertain-

ty and anguish—was published during his stay at the Berlin court, as were *L'imitation de notre-dame la lune* (1886) and *Le concile féerique* (1886), a verse drama that remained unperformed until four years after Laforgue's death. Leaving Berlin in 1886 after his marriage to Leah Lee, an English tutor, Laforgue moved to Paris, where a particularly harsh winter severely affected his health. Supported by loans, he wrote for Kahn's periodical *Le vogue* and tried unsuccessfully to find a publisher for *Moral Tales* until the opiates given him for his illness left him too weak to eat or work. He died, at the age of twenty-seven, virtually unknown. His *Moral Tales,* published within weeks of his death, were immediately acclaimed.

Major Works

Laforgue's earliest poetic work is reflected in the thirty-one poems entitled *Le sanglot de la terre*. Laforgue himself denied the consequence of these pieces during his lifetime, but the poems themselves dramatize some of the themes that were to occupy him throughout his literary career. The subjects of these and other early works is decidedly existential in character, containing a young man's musings on cosmic despair and the lack of meaning in the universe. Laforgue abandoned these works by about 1882 in favor of a more innovative form of the *complainte*. *Les complaintes* (1885), Laforgue's first published volume of poetry, reveals a thematic affinity with the poems of *sanglot* along with the additional exploration of love, a topic unbroached in the earlier collection. This later volume, however, demonstrates a broad technical development and a move toward a new poetic sensibility. Laforgue's varied and innovative experiments with language began in *Les complaintes*, especially with the use of invented words and slang adopted from everyday speech. This work was also strongly informed by a philosophical system, specifically Edward von Hartmann's *Philosophy of the Unconscious*, and exhibits Laforgue's interest in the poetic personae, particularly in that of Pierrot, a stylized projection of the author as a *fin de siècle* Decadent in clown-face. Pierrot is also one of the binding aspects of Laforgue's next volume, *L'imitation de notre-dame la lune*. The figure of the clown and images of the moon give the collection a sense of ironic detachment from nature, and pervade the work with a tone of modern sterility. In terms of technical skill, *L'imitation* is said to be transitional between the early experimentalism of *Les complaintes* and the free verse of *Les denier vers*. In the latter, which consists of twelve sections or monologues, Laforgue dramatized the anxieties and tensions prevalent in the modern world, including those of alienation, disillusionment, and fragmentation.

Critical Reception

According to many critics the overall strength of Laforgue's poetry lies in his sustained use of self-ridiculing irony. His works consistently display individuals and forces locked in the drama of conflict, but undercut by a pervasive sense of parody and humor. Several critics, however, have disapproved of the dissonance in tone and theme found in many of Laforgue's poems. Some, for instance, have argued that *Les dernier vers* lacks unity and is marred by its ambivalence. While early critics called *Les complaintes* incomprehensible and decried its excessive "modernness," more recently, Laforgue has been hailed as a brilliant technical innovator and as one of the creators of modern free verse. His motto of "originality at any cost" and his outright rejection of old forms, such as his abandonment of syntax in *Les dernier vers* and his experimentation with language and form in *Les complaintes*, have added to his reputation as an iconoclast. Overall, scholars have accorded him attention in terms of his ironic wit and bold originality, even though he is often remembered more for his technical virtuosity than his intellectual depth, and for his influence on succeeding generations of poets than the quality of his own writings.

PRINCIPAL WORKS

Poetry

Les complaintes 1885
L'imitation de Notre Dame la lune 1886

Les derniers vers de Jules Laforgue 1890
Poems of Jules Laforgue 1958

Other Major Works

Le concile féerique (verse drama) 1886
Moralités légendaires (short stories) 1887
    [*Moral Tales,* 1928]
*Oeuvres complètes. 3 vols. (poetry, verse drama, short stories, essays, and letters) 1901-03
Lettres à un ami: 1880-1886 (letters) 1941
Selected Writings of Jules Laforgue (poetry, short stories, essays, letters, and sketches) 1956

**This work includes *Le sanglot de la terre, Pierrot fumiste,* and *Mélanges posthumes.*

CRITICISM

Benjamin De Casseres (essay date 1926)

SOURCE: "Jules Laforgue," in *Forty Immortals,* Joseph Lawren, 1926, pp. 159-62.

[*In the following essay, De Casseres records his impressions of Laforgue as an artist.*]

Jules Laforgue, Frenchman, who died at twenty-seven, left three volumes—a book of poems, a book of legendary moralities and a book of epigrams and meditations.

Three great poets of modern times have left for us in their work mirrors of the beauty that is ghastly—Edgar Allan Poe, Charles Baudelaire and Jules Laforgue. The beauty of the ghastly—whence comes it? In the poems of Laforgue one is in the midst of death and in the midst of life at once. The ghastly, the cynical, the Ideal and Absolute make up the monstrous arabesque of his nature. Moored to the wharf of the flesh, the sails of his spirit strain with breezes from the Open. What Open? The cimmerian Open of the Néant or the light-blasting Open of a boreal Absolute?

Down the spine of the gods themselves there runs a chill at the reading of his poems and satires. And yet from them drifts a beauty, nameless and unconsecrated, ethereal and super-Chopinesque.

This unshriven Dante, whose moods were the rungs to his secret hell, was touched with moonmadness. He was an immigrant from the moon. He was moon-botanist. He tells us of its flora, its fauna, its metaphysical opalescence, its incandescent and stalactitic marvels, its bloodless arteries, its arcanum of nothing and its sadic chastity.

All speculation, all thought, all of life with its utter wisdom are in these poems, satires and thoughts. Laforgue was one of those strange beings born at the ends of time. He was one of the predestined, a nomad of metaphysical countries, the unfaithful lover of Isis, Astoreth and Astarte. He was a voluptuary of contrarieties. He volplaned with his metaphor-machine from the highest altitudes to the bogs and gutters. His anticlimaxes were more tremendous than Heine's and his flights were to the very ridge of Nirvana—where he played Pierrot!

But he came back sometimes from those heights with a fistful of stars and in tears composed a requiem for the living. His heartlessness was mystical and literary. The chastity of his satanism made him at once a Joseph and a Don Juan. Exotic to earth, sentenced to eternity, commanded by his demon to engrave a Z on all he saw and touched, yet rammed into a sack of flesh and blood: Do we wonder that in Jules Laforgue the adulterous relations of Sneer and Sob broke the bed of his brain?

To such minds, dowered with the wit of eternity, to whom all todays are ancient and all tomorrows coffins in the making, there is one escape: cosmophobia. Wing the soul with poetry and metaphysics. That flight into the azure is the magnificent eloquence of fatigue. And then there is the rapturous delight of an eternal sabotage against the instincts and manners of the average man and woman.

Cruel? Yes, divinely cruel. It is the revenge on the race, on the species, for the birth of the seraphic demon that we call the great poet. Pierrot-Fumiste? Pierrot-Parabrahma, rather! Even Time, with its suckers of the Hours, is spat upon in the miracle of art.

Laforgue was always trying to puncture the carapace of the relative with the stiletto of his absolutism. He was supremely a bovaryst, as Jules de Gaultier would say. "Chevalier of the Holy Grail," another great French writer has called Jules Laforgue. His aspiration to be nothing was his aspiration for absorption in the All. He put into poetry and satire what Hegel put into unreadable prose. At the last nothing could satisfy that soul but God, and yet he would have ventured into the Presence dressed as Harlequin—with a crown of thorns on his head.

Imprisoned in the aura of his metaphysical passion, rolling from boreal hell to boreal hell, the carapace of Reality stood against the battering of that mighty soul. He stanched the flow of thought and drove it back into the arteries of the subconscious. Still no answer.

The moon, that floating pole, was silent. Silent the brain, silent the heart; and so his dreams congealed in death, as happens to all of us.

And now the soul of Jules Laforgue is become a magnificent butterfly imprisoned in the center of an iceberg on the Moon.

G. M. Turnell (essay date 1936)

SOURCE: "The Poetry of Jules Laforgue," in *Scrutiny*, Vol. V, No. 2, September, 1936, pp. 128-49.

[*In the following essay, Turnell examines Laforgue poetic method, primarily through an analysis of his* Dernier vers *and a comparison of his poetry to that of Charles Baudelaire.*]

Je songe à une poésie qui serait de la psychologie dans une forme de rêve, avec des fleurs, du vent, des senteurs, d'inextricables symphonies avec une phrase (un sujet) mélodique dont le dessin reparaît de temps en temps.

J.L. in a letter to Charles Henry, December, 1881.

I.

The influence of Laforgue on modern poetry has been decisive. In the ordinary way it is a mistake to distinguish too sharply between the influence of a writer's outlook and the influence of his style or, as I should prefer to call it, his *method*. In the case of Laforgue, however, some sort of distinction between the two is necessary. I think the point can be illustrated by a comparison between Mr. Pound and Mr. Eliot. It seems to me that Laforgue's influence on Mr. Pound has been almost exclusively of the first, and his most lasting influence on Mr. Eliot of the second kind. It is Mr. Pound's limitation that his best work is sometimes no more than the mature expression of Laforgue's outlook—the mature expression of an outlook that was essentially immature in the sense of *uncompleted,* a term to which I shall try to give precision later. Now one of the most indubitable signs of Mr. Eliot's originality is that his development since "Prufrock" and "Portrait of a Lady" has always been *away* from the outlook of his master. In *The Waste Land* he has clearly learnt all there was to learn technically from the **Derniers vers** and used it to express something infinitely richer and more complex.

For this reason I wish to concentrate in this paper on the method of Laforgue. I may as well begin by recording my own opinion that, from a technical point of view and to a critic writing with Mr. Eliot's work before him, the **Derniers vers** is the most important single poem published in Europe since the seventeenth century, though its intrinsic merits fall far short of the best work of Baudelaire, Corbière and Rimbaud.

II.

'When we get to Laforgue,' wrote Mr. Eliot in one of his illuminating asides, 'we find a poet who seems to express even more clearly even than Baudelaire the difficulties of his own age: he speaks to us, or spoke to my generation, more intimately than Baudelaire. Only later we conclude that Laforgue's "present" is a narrower "present" than Baudelaire's, and that Baudelaire's present extends to more of the past and more of the future.'

The 'intimacy' with which Laforgue speaks to us and the 'narrowness' of his outlook are factors of the first importance and need to be carefully investigated—investigated, as Mr. Eliot points out, in relation to Baudelaire. For Baudelaire dominates his age to such a degree that his contemporaries and successors can only be placed in relation to him. There are lines in the *Sanglot de la terre*, Laforgue's earliest collection of verse, which an intelligent candidate in a practical criticism paper at Cambridge might pardonably attribute to the author of the *Fleurs du mal*. For instance:

> O convoi solennel des soleils magnifiques,
> Nouez et dénouez vos vastes masses d'or,
> Doucement, tristement, sur de graves musiques,
> Menez le deuil très lent de votre soeur qui dort.

But though the mistake might be made with a short extract, it would scarcely happen with a whole poem.

> Le blanc soleil de juin amollit les trottoirs.
> Sur mon lit, seul, prostré comme en ma sépulture
> (Close de rideaux blancs, Æuvre d'une main pure),
> Je râle doucement aux extases des soirs.
>
> Un relent énervant expire d'un mouchoir
> Et promène sur mes lèvres sa chevelure
> Et, comme un piano voisin rêve en mesure,
> Je tournoie au concert rythmé des encensoirs.
>
> Tout est un songe. Oh! viens, corps soyeux que
>   j'adore,
> Fondons-nous, et sans but, plus oublieux encore;
> Et tiédis longuement ainsi mes yeux fermés.
>
> Depuis l'éternité, croyez-le bien, Madame,
> L'Archet qui sur nos nerfs pince ces tristes
>   gammes
> Appelait pour ce jour nos atomes charmés.

There is a good deal of Baudelaire here. The rhythm of some of the lines is his. *Amollit* is one of the soft, voluptuous words that he loved; and the *sépulture,* the *extases des soirs* and the *encensoirs* are all part of the furniture of the *Fleurs du mal*. But often when Laforgue is being most imitative, he will suddenly become most himself. The prostrate young man is a glimpse of the peculiar spiritual defeatism which contributes so largely to the sense of 'intimacy' we get from his work. We shall meet the curtained windows and the pianos again and again—they are an important part of Laforgue's symbolism. We shall also meet the adolescent hunger not simply for love, but for chaste love which is so different both from the weary satiety of Baudelaire and the healthy animality of Corbière. The *main pure* looks forward to the

> Jeunes Filles inviolables et frêles

of the *Derniers vers*. It is significant that Laforgue's 'chastity' is essentially negative. Indeed, his half-heartedness about sexual love and his recoil from the physical contribute more than anything to the impression of immaturity that his verse creates. The last three lines of the poem are the most characteristic of all. They point to the *Complaintes* and indicate the direction his development was to take.

Although the fact that Laforgue's development after the *Sanglot de la terre* was always *away* from Baudelaire is one of the clearest signs of his originality, it is also one of the clearest signs of his limitation—not merely a personal limitation, but a limitation inherent in the age. In placing Laforgue we have to remember that his 'intimacy' and his 'narrowness' are inseparable. In other words, his limitations are peculiarly a function of his genius. With this reservation, it can be said that his practice is a radical and thorough-going criticism of the work of Baudelaire. It can be seen in his language and imagery, in his versification, and in his wit. I propose to consider them in that order.

Laforgue tried, as Corbière before him had tried, to get rid of the old worn out 'poetic' words; but both his aim and his procedure were different from Corbière's and far more like Donne's. Corbière's work represents the restoration of an old language rather than the invention of a new one. He tried to purge words of their romantic associations and restore their natural properties in order to express an elemental, and in a sense a primitive experience. Thus where Corbière's language is simple Laforgue's is extremely sophisticated, but it marks a definite extension of the field of poetry. He had to forge a language which would express the new feelings that were emerging with the progress of urban civilization and which would also express his peculiar and, it seems to me, very limited disillusion. His third group of poems, *L'Imitation de Notre-Dame de la lune,* is the product of a period of the wildest experiments with language; and the results of these experiments can be seen all through his work. It is completely successful in

> La rouille ronge en leurs *spleens kilométriques*
> Les fils télégraphiques des grandes routes où nul
>   ne passe

which admirably express his own particular *ennui,* but is unsuccessful and forced in

> *Armorial d'anémie!*
> Psautiers d'automne!

As with his imagery, so with his language. He did not merely use words which had been considered unpoetic, he invented new ones. The sort of words he invented and the way he invented are curiously reminiscent of Donne when faced with a similar situation. He has, for instance, *ennuiversel, éternullité, sexiproque, enflaquer, féminiculture, kilométrique, lunalogue, ritourneller, spleenuosite.*

Contemporary critics have stressed the 'counter-romantic' tendency of Baudelaire's poetry, but it is generally recognized that it retained certain romantic traits. Superficially Laforgue's experiments with language seem to complete Baudelaire's work by making a clean sweep of those romantic elements from which he had failed to free himself. This view strikes me as frankly mistaken. There were certainly romantic elements in Baudelaire, but they were accidentals and not essentials. They were his macabre sensationalism and a love of the theatrical and not, as is commonly supposed, his use of the grand style or of words (apparently) borrowed from the vocabulary of the Romantics like *beauté, tristesse, solitaire, splendeur*— the words which, in Laforgue's admirable phrase, *enchasublent* the subject. His use of them has little in common with that of the Romantics—a point of capital importance in discussing his relations with Laforgue.

What makes Baudelaire a very great figure indeed is that he explored the potentialities of human experience far more thoroughly than any of his contemporaries, and was capable of regarding the human situation from a greater number of different angles than they. The deepest thing in his poetry is his awareness of the contrast between the potential splendour of human life and its actual squalor. This perpetual contrast could not have been adequately expressed in the style and language of Laforgue, which have a sort of thinness—excellent no doubt for Laforgue's purpose, but useless for Baudelaire's. What Baudelaire had to say could only have been said in the ample measure of the alexandrine and in a language that described the present and at the same time suggested what had been lost.

The difference between the two poets can be seen most clearly in their presentation of Paris. The Paris of Baudelaire has the universality and the impersonality of great poetry which we do not find in Laforgue's. There is nothing absurd in the parallels that French critics are fond of drawing between Baudelaire's Paris and the *Inferno,* but no one could possibly make the same claim for Laforgue. In comparison his Paris is local and personal. But if Laforgue seems narrow and pedestrian in comparison with Baudelaire, if he can only offer one point of view, it is not altogether his fault. With Baudelaire something went out of French poetry and, except for a fugitive reappearance in Rimbaud, went out for good.

III.

The origins of free verse have been the source of a good deal of speculation in France, mostly of a somewhat fruitless nature. Gourmont's chapter in the *Esthétique de la langue française* contains one or two suggestive remarks, but on the whole it is disappointing, and in one particular thoroughly misleading. Gourmont was too good a critic not to realize that the free verse of a writer like Laforgue was something completely new; but when he goes on to trace parallels between nineteenth-century free verse and free verse in Latin compositions of the eighth century—he had a maddening strain of pedantry which comes out to the full in this book -he is simply confusing the issues. He is not the only person who has done it. 'The *vers libre* of Jules Laforgue . . .' wrote Mr. Eliot, 'is free verse in much the same way that the later verse of Shakespeare, Webster, Tourneur, is free verse: that is to say, it stretches, contracts, and distorts the traditional French measure as later Elizabethan and Jacobean poetry stretches, contracts and distorts the blank verse measure.'

It is interesting to learn, as we do from Mr. Eliot's Introduction, that his own versification was based on a study of Laforgue and the later Elizabethans; but the connection is a personal one and the suggestion that there is some objective relation between the two strikes me as hopelessly misleading. And to speak of Laforgue as one who 'stretches, contracts and distorts' the alexandrine is to minimize his technical brilliance unnecessarily.

Mr. Edouard Dujardin, Laforgue's editor and the reputed inventor of the 'silent monologue,' is a more satisfactory guide. In an article published in the *Mercure de France* he argues that free verse was not the invention of a single poet, but the spontaneous result of a collective movement. That is the main point. A vital art-form must be the spontaneous outcome of the conditions in which the artist is living. Free verse appeared when it did because it was the only medium capable of expressing the modern poet's experience. It is essentially a nineteenth-century phenomenon. It has nothing to do with the versification of any other period. Its real affinities are with similar movements in the other arts—with impressionism in painting, the silent monologue in the novel and— most striking of all—with the cinema.

This is not the place to discuss the relations between the different arts in detail, but it is only when we see modern poetry in relation to painting, the novel and the cinema that we are in a position to appreciate the importance of free verse and 'place' the poets of the movement. The simultaneous appearance of free verse and impressionism was due to changes that had been going on in the European sensibility. They were the outcome of the same impulse and as literary critics it is our business to isolate that impulse.

Free verse and impressionism were both movements of liberation, simultaneous reactions against romanticism and a decadent classicism. It was Laforgue's achievement to have realized that the grand style was all over and done with and that the poet's experience could no longer be forced into the *cadre* of the alexandrine. He saw that traditional verse-forms were incapable of expressing the subtleties of the modern sensibility and in particular the *movement* of the contemporary mind. And the impressionist realized that the classical painter's angle of vision had become stereotyped and distorted the artist's experience. Thus there appears to me to be a connection between the disuse of the alexandrine and the disuse of the classical line of David and Ingres. Baudelaire, as usual, puts his finger on the point when he says *La phrase poétique peut imiter la ligne horizontale, la ligne droite ascendante, la ligne droite descendante.* What is striking about poetry is the disappearance of line, of the sculptural element that we find in Vigny, Leconte de Lisle and in Baudelaire's own *La Beauté.* As a final comment there is Baudelaire's criticism of Ingres. *Le grand défaut de M. Ingres,* he wrote, *est de vouloir imposer à chaque type qui pose sous son oeil un perfectionnement plus ou moins despotique emprunté au répertoire des idées classiques.*

It is necessary to carry the analysis a stage further, to go behind art to changes that were taking place in the mind of Europe. Classical theories of art are based ultimately on classical metaphysics, on the assumption that reality is independent of the perceiving mind and that the function of the artist is to represent it. The origins of modern art go back to the period when the classical metaphysic was challenged by the rise of the idealist philosophies. It is a change, in other words, from a philosophy of *being* to a philosophy of *knowing*. It no longer matters what a thing *is*—what matters is my experience of it. Thus the idealist's assertion that the real was not independent of mind, but a synthesis of the perceiving subject and the thing perceived, meant that the artist was no longer occupied with things but with his reactions to them. It means that instead of the mind conforming to the real, the real is made to conform to the mind which imposes its own pattern on everything.

The implications of these theories are patent. Classical metaphysics, by insisting that the real was the same for all and that everyone had a similar experience of it, guaranteed the social basis of art. The art produced under its influence tended to express what was common to all—to be the consummate expression of a social experience. In departing from this assumption the artist rejects the social basis of art, but he reveals human nature to itself in a way that would otherwise have been unthinkable.

Le vrai vers libre, wrote Gourmont, *est conçu comme tel, c'est-à-dire comme fragment dessiné sur le modèle de son idée émotive, et non plus déterminé par la loi fixe du nombre.*

In short, anything that was likely to fetter the artist's experience, to interfere with the *idée émotive,* was removed. Laforgue gave to poetry an instrument that was capable of reflecting the rapidly shifting vision of our time. The **Derniers vers** is a poem of 816 lines which registers the constant shift and change of feeling, the play of feeling within a prevailing mood, that a sensitive person experiences in modern urban conditions. Its great virtues are the fidelity and insight with which the changes are recorded, its great fault the absence of any unity but the poet's personality. It contains astonishing passages, but is not completely successful as a criticism of the human situation. It does not possess the same finality in this respect as *The Waste Land* because of the absence of any intellectual structure. But this in no way alters its technical importance. Take the beginning of the fourth section:

C'est l'automne, l'automne, l'automne,
Le grand vent et toute sa séquelle
De représailles! et de musiques! . . .
Rideaux tirés, clôture annuelle,
Chute des feuilles, des Antigones, des Philomèles:
Mon fossoyeur, *Alas poor Yorick*!
Les remue à la pelle! . . .

'Autumn'—symbol of a definite emotional state in this poem -restates the principal theme of the poem, the dominant mood. The repetition shows the poet's growing despair. The next two lines refer back to the storm in the previous section. The wind that roars and thunders all through the **Derniers vers** is no romantic accompaniment, but a symbol of the tumult going on in the poet's mind. The drawn curtains, tattered notices on the hoardings and falling leaves are familiar symbols of *ennui* and despair. The precise images and exact noting of the names on the play bills fix the particular scene in the mind. I take Antigone and Philomel to stand for certain human values which are in the process of disappearing. They may also be symbols of the departed glamour of 'the Season' and suggest the poet's sense of exile from the gay and prosperous world. The mingling of the falling leaves and the fragments of the play bills is deliberate: the general mood is related to the loss of particular values (spiritual and material). The reference to *Hamlet—Hamlet* played a role of capital importance in Laforgue's development—is the focal point of the passage. It deftly continues the literary allusion and at the same time provides an ironical comment on the whole situation—on the futility of certain virtues in a civilization like our own. The image of the comic grave-digger disrespectfully turning up the bones of the dead suggests the crossing-sweeper whisking away the relics of past splendour. The suddenness of the gesture is an admirable instance of Laforgue's technical dexterity. The whole passage is a good illustration of the way in which the pliancy of Laforgue's medium and his method of allusion enable him to evoke the mood of the entire poem whenever he likes and to bring it into relation with a particular situation. This alone is a technical innovation of the first importance.

'Words, images and entire friezes of imagery recur, not once or twice but constantly,' wrote Mr. Quennell of Laforgue. The implication that Laforgue's range of feeling is limited is true, but this does not mean that his use of stock-imagery is a short-coming. Indeed, part of his achievement was to have worked out an elaborate system of reference and association, a sort of poetic short-hand. The recurring image, which has been brilliantly developed in *The Waste Land,* is an important part of the system.

One of the results of the change of sensibility already discussed was that the emotional life of Europe was suddenly divided, forming new combinations of feeling. A verse-form was needed which would not only express the rapid change from one feeling to its opposite, but would also show the mind simultaneously possessed by diverse and even conflicting feelings. Thus instead of describing emotion, Laforgue translates it into precise, visual images which recur again and again. They are symbols in the strict sense, or as he himself described them, *phrases mélodiques.* In his latest work they are used with kaleidoscopic effect and constantly shifted so as to form new patterns of feeling. The 'meaning' of his poetry, indeed, often consists in the relations between the symbols, in the sudden transitions from one emotion to its opposite. The most important symbols are the processions of school girls going two by two to Mass which stand for innocence and faith in contrast to the poet's sophistication and unbelief; Paris streets on Sunday afternoons and the mingling of the out-of-tune piano with the vespers bell suggesting the receding tide of faith; the curtained windows suggesting boredom and bourgeois degradation of life; and the storm discussed above.

The symbol of autumn, which plays the same part in the *Derniers vers* as spring in *The Waste Land,* is so important that it needs some elucidation. The poem begins:

> Blocus sentimental! Messageries du Levant! . . .
> Oh, tombée de la pluie! Oh! tombée de la nuit,
> Oh! le vent! . . .
> La Toussaint, la Noël et la Nouvelle Année,
> Oh, dans les bruines, toutes mes cheminées! . . .
> D'usines . . .

Laforgue seldom used the device of omitting his main verbs more skilfully than he does in this remarkable passage. It suggests a state of complete instability—an instability that could only be represented by the poet's powerlessness to make any *statement* about his feelings at all. The halting rhythms and broken lines give the impression of some one floundering helplessly in the dark, struggling pathetically against the storm without making any headway; and, by implication, of the poet's powerlessness to dominate his own emotions.

The sudden impact of *Blocus sentimental* on the reader is tremendous. It gives a physical sense of emotional inhibition which is heightened by the succession of short, abrupt phrases that seem to beat down on one like the rain and the gusts of wind. *Messageries du Levant* means a biting east wind—the sort of wind that numbs. In this way *emotional numbness* and *physical numbness* become associated. The description of the rain and the dark emphasizes the feeling of helplessness. The names of the principal winter feasts suggest a long, dreary expanse of time. *Bruines* refers back to the second line: the image is the obliteration of the landscape by the rain and the dark, and is clearly intended to express the poet's sense of personal obliteration. *Toutes mes cheminées* suggests a total loss of direction. The fading of the factories in the mist may refer to the world of practical activity from which the poet is cut off. The sudden break at *usines* gives the sensation of collapse which is emphasized a few lines later by

> Il bruine;
> Dans la forêt mouillée, les toiles d'araignées
> Ploient sous les gouttes d'eau, et c'est leur ruine.

The bending of the spiders' webs reinforces the image of the man bending under the storm. This is clinched by *ruine* which is the theme of the *Derniers vers* as death is the theme of *The Waste Land.*

The expression of the mood of the poem is so complete in these lines that the merest reference—as, for instance, in the passage from the fourth section analysed above—is sufficient to evoke the whole.

The opening of the third section is one of the finest passages in the *Derniers vers*:

> Ainsi donc, pauvre, pâle et piètre individu
> Qui ne croit à son Moi qu'à ses moments perdus,
> Je vis s'effacer ma fiancée
> Emportée par le cours des choses,
> Telle l'épine voit s'effeuiller,
> Sous prétexte de soir sa meilleure rose.
> Or, cette nuit anniversaire, toutes les Walkyries du vent
> Sont revenues beugler par les fentes de ma porte:
> *Vae soli!*
> Mais, ah! qu'importe?
> Il fallait m'en étourdir avant!
> Trop tard! ma petite folie est morte!
> Qu'importe *Vae soli!*
> Je ne trouverai plus ma petite folie.
>
> Le grand vent bâillonné,
> S'endimanche enfin le ciel du matin.
> Et alors, eh! allez donc, carillonnez,
> Toutes cloches des bons dimanches!
> Et passez layettes et collerettes et robes blanches
> Dans un frou-frou de lavandes et de thym
> Vers l'encens et les brioches!
> Tout pour la famille, quoi! *Vae soli!* C'est certain.

These lines are a perfect example of Laforgue's peculiarly delicate sensibility. They are also an admirable example of his transition from one set of feelings to another.

The *pauvre, pâle et piètre individu* re-emphasizes the poet's devastating sense of his own helplessness which is characteristic of all Laforgue's work. The *Moi* contrasts the poet's real helplessness with his assumed bravado and attempts to pass it off as a joke. *S'effacer* re-introduces the obliteration motif. The woman is snatched away and becomes part of the world from which the poet is cut off. *Emportée . . .* suggests movement, suggests someone irresistibly carried away and lost, which is one of the themes of the poem. *L'épine*—the desolate, despoiled thorn goes back to *pauvre, pâle et piètre.* The short, broken lines which follow suggest the short, violent gusts of the storm and, at the same time, the feverish workings of the mind.

The change from the short line to the long and gradually lengthening line in the second part indicates the calm which follows the storm. The transition is superbly managed. The calm of nature reflects the calm of the poet, though we must not overlook the implication that it is a calm born of exhaustion. *Bâillonné,* 'gagged,' is another instance of the word that pulls us up short. *S'endimanche* is the pivotal word of the passage and links two sets of images—the calm of nature and spiritual calm. This is reinforced by the troop of girls going to Mass. The sound of the storm merges into the carolling of church bells. The whistling of the wind (blowing away the rose leaves) is replaced by the delicate *frou-frou* of the dresses; the smell of the rose, with its romantic associations, by the scent of lavender suggesting domestic peace, clean clothes and neat drawers. The reference to *brioches* (bread that is blessed and given to the faithful to take home) is apparently used to contrast the families united in the Faith with the outcast poet. (Hence the repeated *Vae soli!*)

There is a passage in the seventh section which calls for comment:

> Où est-elle à cette heure?
> Peut-être qu'elle pleure . . .
> Où est-elle à cette heure?
> Oh! du moins, soigne-toi, je t'en conjure!
>
> O fraîcheur des bois le long de la route,
> O châle de mélancolie, toute âme est un peu aux
> écoutes,
> Que ma vie
> Fait envie!
> Cette impériale de diligence tient de la magie.

I have chosen this as an example of cinema technique. It is a common cinematic device—very much used by Pudovkin—to show a perfectly calm landscape after a scene of great emotional intensity. In this passage feeling is worked up to its maximum by the use of short, abrupt lines (paralleled by the short staccato Russian cutting), the agonized self-questioning and the hysterical *Soigne-toi,* then there is a sudden change to landscape. The word *fraîcheur* comes with a shock of inexpressible relief. (It should be noted that Mr. Eliot has made use of this device—the opening of *The Waste Land* is a good instance—by his references to flowers and the sea which provide the same form of release as this passage).

The importance of Laforgue's work should now be apparent. The result of his experiments was that the contemporary poet found an instrument at hand which was capable of expressing the full complexity of his outlook. This is a different thing from saying that Laforgue's own poetry is complex or mature. In spite of the fact that his feelings are often complicated, his outlook is neither complex nor mature. His poetry is a little deceptive. When one first comes to it, it appears far more complex than it really is. It is only later that one sees that it has a surface-complexity which is sometimes little more than a peculiar kind of verbiage. His symbolism depends for its success on a close correspondence between the symbol and the emotion symbolized; but Laforgue was sometimes inclined to throw unusual words and images together in the hope that something astonishing would come of it. It is a fault that we find repeatedly in the *Imitation de Notre-Dame de la lune* (*e.g.* the piece called **"La lune est stérile"**), but there are also instances in the *Derniers vers.* I wish to examine in detail a passage from the tenth section.

> O géraniums diaphanes, guerroyeurs sortilèges,
> Sacrilèges monomanes!
> Emballages, dévergondages, douches! O pressoirs
> Des vendanges des grands soirs!
> Layettes aux abois,
> Thyrses au fond des bois!

> Transfusions, représailles,
> Relevailles, compresses et l'éternelle potion,
> *Angelus!* n'en pouvoir plus
> De débâcles nuptiales! de débâcles nuptiales! . . .

This passage has been singled out by Mr. Eliot as an example of 'something which looks very like the [metaphysical] conceit' in French poetry. I cannot help feeling that there is a strange confusion here. It is an example of Laforgue's impressionist psychological notation, and though it certainly has the surface-complexity noted above, it has nothing of the genuine complexity of the metaphysical conceit. There are words suggesting violent attacks and counter-attacks like *guerroyeurs, sortilèges, représailles.* There is another group suggesting compression—*emballages, pressoirs, compresses*—which is set off against words suggesting outburst or overflow—*dévergondages, douches, transfusions.* A further group is less obscure—words like *layettes, relevailles, Angelus,* meaning baby-clothing, churchings, religion, apparently signify happy married life as opposed to the *débâcles nuptiales.* They may also be contrasted with the violence and confusion suggested by the first two lines.

The feelings are certainly 'tangled,' but I find nothing that can be called 'a whole of tangled feelings'—though clearly there ought to be. If the poet's aim was to suggest mental conflict, a tug of war between opposing feelings, what he tried to do is very imperfectly realized. What I wish to contrast is the internal disconnection of the passage with the internal coherence of Donne's conceits. There seems to me to be one essential difference between the metaphysical conceit and Laforgue's method of psychological association. A conceit like 'On a round ball' or the compasses is a unity in which the parts are rigorously subordinated to a central purpose. It is an *intellectual* process, and it is the intellectual element that distinguishes it from the apparent conceits in Laforgue's poetry. The metaphysical conceit is used to relate a particular experience—one might almost call it a thought-experience—to a general *body of principles* and not, as with Laforgue, simply to relate a particular feeling to a general *body of feelings.* Thus the structure of Donne's work is intellectual in a way that Laforgue's is not. It is also apparent from the internal disconnection of this passage that Laforgue's attitude was necessarily fragmentary and disconnected too.

This difference between Laforgue and the Metaphysical Poets is so vital that I must be forgiven for underlining it. 'Donne, Corbière, Laforgue,' wrote Mr. Eliot in another place, 'begin with their own feelings, and their limitation is that they do not always get much outside or beyond; Shakespeare, one feels, arrives at an objective world by a process from himself, whoever he was, as the centre and starting point. . . . With the Donne and the French poets the pattern is given by what goes on in the mind, rather than by the exterior events which provoke the mental activity and play of thought and feeling.'

This is an acute criticism of Laforgue; but it is only partly true of Corbière and scarcely true at all of Donne.

It is not true of Donne because Donne was after all a Christian; and however personal his religion may have been, it did provide a point of reference *outside* his immediate feelings. His mind and outlook show the impress of a training in scholastic philosophy, and the *tension* we find in his work comes precisely from the endeavour to integrate new experiences into a system of traditional philosophy. The weakness of Laforgue's poetry, as we have it, is largely due to the fact that he had no system—his preoccupation with German philosophy is decisive on this point—and that his only point of reference was his own *personality*. Thus one feels obliged to dissent when Mr. Eliot remarks that 'A poet like Donne, or like Baudelaire or Laforgue, may almost be considered the inventor of an attitude, a system of feeling or of morals.' This confuses the issues by attributing to Laforgue precisely that quality which Donne and Baudelaire possessed and which he was without. What makes Donne and Baudelaire 'bigger' men than their contemporaries is the fact that in their work the mood of the moment—the personal mood—is subordinated to something lasting and impersonal which can be described as an 'outlook' in the fullest sense of the term. For Donne and for Baudelaire the problem was never merely a personal one: there was a complete correspondence between the personal problem and the problem of the age. With Laforgue, one feels, the problem was largely a personal one, far more personal than critics have realized.

IV.

Laforgue's wit has had a considerable influence on later poets and has also attracted a great deal of attention from critics. It must be confessed, however, that the influence has not been wholly for the good and that the critical attention has not always been of the right kind. The criticism has been on the whole too indulgent, and it has not discriminated sufficiently between the use to which his wit ought to have been put and the uses to which it was put. It has never been pointed out that it sometimes degenerates into a trick or that it is far too limited an instrument to serve as the basis of an outlook. There is an immense difference in this respect between the wit of Corbière and the wit of Laforgue. Corbière's wit is essentially positive and is used in the service of an aggressive attitude, while Laforgue's is negative and is often used not to affirm a position, but to avoid taking up a position at all.

The proper use of Laforgue's wit is as an ironic commentary on experience—a use which is well illustrated by the opening of the fifth section of the *Derniers vers*:

> Amour absolu, carrefour sans fontaine;
> Mais, à tous les bouts, d'étourdissantes fêtes
>   foraines.
>
> Jamais franches,
> Ou le poing sur la hanche:
> Avec toutes, l'amour s'échange
> Simple et sans foi comme un bonjour.

There is a deliberate contrast between the solemn opening in the romantic style and the brisk movement of the next four lines, suggesting the bustle and the crude tunes of the fair. *Le poing sur la hanche* probably refers to the gesture of the hardboiled prostitute and provides further comment of the opening line. *Simple et sans foi comme un bonjour* is a cynical and startling final comment which is entirely successful.

There is a better known, but less successful example in the tenth section:

> J'aurai passé ma vie le long des quais
> A faillir m'embarquer
> Dans de bien funestes histoires,
> Tout cela pour l'amour
> De mon coeur fou de la gloire d'amour.
>
> Oh, qu'ils sont pittoresques les trains manqués! . .
> .

The procedure is the same as in the last passage. The wit consists largely in the tone, in the 'levity' of the treatment. The suspended image at the close performs the same function as before—the sudden concentration of the whole feeling of the passage into a single image raises it to a fresh level of intensity and seriousness. The passage as a whole, however, is unconvincing. It leaves us with the same feeling of uneasiness that we get from the **"Autre complainte de Lord Pierrot,"** in spite of the undeniable brilliance of that poem, and from a good deal that Laforgue wrote besides. For the poet is not as detached or as single-minded as he tries to appear. There is something specious about the jaunty, man-of-the-world attitude which is used to conceal the underlying sentimentality. A comparison between these lines and Corbière's "Poète contumance," where the same method is used to express a genuinely mature attitude, should be decisive.

The truth is that Laforgue's wit is often an attempt to solve his own emotional problems. Thus in the **"Autre complainte de Lord Pierrot"** his criticism of romantic love in ineffectual *as criticism* because it is perfectly clear that he is ridiculing an attitude from which he is trying to free himself, but has not yet managed to do so. The fact that he uses irony as a means to something else makes disasters inevitable. One nearly always has the feeling that his wit may collapse at any moment into sentimentality, and this sometimes happens even in the *Derniers vers*:

> Bref, j'allais me donner d'un 'Je vous aime '
> Quand je m'avisai non sans peine
> Que d'abord je ne me possédais pas bien moi-
>   même.

This is a palpable attempt to pass off one's confusion as a joke.

I can make my point best in considering an important but neglected side of Laforgue's poetry—his religious symbolism. We might begin by comparing some lines from Baudelaire's "Franciscae meae laudes" with a passage from a poem in the *Fleurs de bonne volonté:*

> Esto sertis implicata
> O femina delicata,
> Per quam solvuntur peccata
>
> . . . . .
>
> Quum vitiorum tempestas
> Turbabat omnes semitas
> Apparuisti, Deitas,
> Velut stella salutaris
> In naufragiis amaris . . .

Laforgue has:

> J'aime, j'aime de tout mon siècle! cette hostie
> Féminine en si vierge et destructible chair
> Qu'on voit, au point du jour, altièrement sertie
> Dans de cendreuses toilettes déjà d'hiver,
> Se fuir le long des cris surhumains de la mer!

Superficially the procedure is the same—an ironic contrast between the sacredness of the subject and the levity of the poet's tone—but the result is entirely different. Baudelaire combines two opposing feelings in order to form a new and perverse one. By an ingenious twist *solvuntur peccata* is made to suggest liberation from sin by salvation and liberation from desire through satisfaction, and this is emphasized by the play on *salutaris.* Laforgue compares a successful seduction with the reception of the Sacrament. The woman is described as *cette hostie féminine* and *hostie* is given its double sense of Sacrament and Victim.

The difference between the two passages is primarily a difference of tone. It is clear that for Baudelaire the religious emotion was at least as real as the sexual, and his words could be accurately described as blasphemous. The allusions in Laforgue, on the other hand, are those of a man who has consciously and deliberately detached himself from the Faith. The words have lost something of their former meaning and become convenient counters, and there is an instinctive lack of reverence which prevents them from being blasphemous in the way in which Baudelaire's undoubtedly are. What is strikingly new is the note of spiritual apathy. It is very marked in the little known **"Petite prière sans prétentions"**:

> Et laissez-nous en paix, morts aux mondes
>   meilleurs,
> Paître, dans notre coin, et forniquer, et rire! . . .
>
> Paître, dans notre coin, et forniquer et rire! . . .

where the last line appears to be a mocking imitation of an invisible congregation repeating the prayer after the priest.

Laforgue's peculiar state of mind is revealed most strikingly, however, in a passage from the *Derniers vers*:

> Ah! moi, je demeure l'Ours Blanc!
> Je suis venu par ces banquises
> Plus pures que les communiantes en blanc . . .
> Moi, je ne vais pas à l'église,
> Moi, je suis le Grand Chancelier de l'Analyse,
> Qu'on se le dise.

This passage is clearly intended as a contrast between the poet's sophistication and unbelief and the innocence and faith of the children going to Mass. The important point is the use of capitals for *Ours Blanc* and *Grand Chancelier de l'Analyse.* The bear represents the outcast poet, but is deliberately turned into a comic bear. It is the trick—familiar in the later work of Mr. Aldous Huxley—of a writer who wishes to express a point of view without committing himself definitely to any one position, and takes refuge in caricature. The poet chooses to present himself as the nineteenth-century sceptic, but is careful not to identify himself too closely with the tradition of Renan and Taine. The passage is not altogether successful—it is obviously the voice of the romantic young man and not that of the convinced sceptic—but it illustrates the way in which Laforgue was using poetry in an attempt to solve his personal problems.

The passage is important for another reason. It shows that in spite of his curious intellectual timidity, Laforgue did recognize the necessity of taking up a definite position and that at bottom he was not content with the evasion he practised. There seems to me to be a marked tendecy in his later work to free himself from all accepted attitudes—from traditional religion and traditional (romantic) love—as he had freed himself from traditional verse-forms. At the time of his death the process was incomplete and it is impossible to say how much further it would have gone. He seemed to be moving towards a position of spiritual neutrality and was very far from formulating anything resembling a positive outlook at all. His detachment was still incomplete, and his interest in German philosophy shows that he felt the need of a substitute for the thing he had abandoned. All this makes him a bad master as far as the content of his work is concerned and explains why the influence of his very seductive spiritual defeatism on later poets has been unfortunate. It is possible that he might have become 'the inventor of an attitude,' but we cannot be certain. The disparity between his technical maturity and his emotional immaturity tells heavily against him; and his extreme spiritual defeatism makes one wonder whether he had it in him to develop a positive attitude towards anything.

What would have happened can only be a matter of conjecture. It is important to stress the fact that Laforgue was trying to work out a position. He therefore belongs to Baudelaire and his school and not to Mallarmé and his descendants. The significance of Mallarmé and Valéry is that they make a definite attempt to dispense with a positive outlook of any sort. This explains the negative element, the constant preoccupation with sterility, that we find in Mallarmé. And I cannot help feeling that 'pure poetry,' for which he was ultimately responsible, is a subtle form of escapism. It is an attempt to make the worship of form a substitute for an outlook, and it therefore becomes a means of avoiding the necessity of committing oneself to a position at all.

William Jay Smith   (essay date 1956)

SOURCE: "A Record of Many Voices: The Complaintes of Jules Laforgue," in *The Western Review,* Vol. 20, No. 3, Spring, 1956, pp. 219-27.

[*In the following essay, Smith comments on* Les complaintes, *Laforgue's first published collection of poetry, highlighting the poet's innovative use of language in the work.*]

Les complaintes, the first volume published by Jules Laforgue during his brief life, expressed immediately and firmly a poetic personality with which succeeding generations would have to deal. The poems in the **Complaintes** are so very different from those of **Le Sanglot de la Terre** that one would think at first that they were the work of another poet. But the change is not so extraordinary as it seems; it is merely a shift in tone. The poet treats the same major themes but in a minor key, the macrocosm is reduced to microcosm: the instrument is smaller, but capable nevertheless of vibrant echoes. The pale, serious young organist in the loft is replaced by the nimble, playful, sentimental organ-grinder on the street corner. The cosmic is dealt with in terms of the ordinary and everyday. When the volume was virtually complete, Laforgue wrote to his sister that he had given up his ideal of philosophical poetry: "I find it stupid to speak in a booming voice and adopt a platform manner. Today when I am more sceptical and don't get so easily carried away and moreover control my language in more minute clown-like fashion, I write little whimsical poems with only one aim in view: to be original at any cost." Lofty poetic diction gives way to popular speech; no subject is either too grand or too trivial to be treated. The romantic dirges of the early unpublished volume are replaced by *complaintes,* popular laments patterned after ballads of the sort people had sung for centuries. The words of the two titles are significant—*sanglot* and *complainte*—for they suggest the fact that Laforgue thought of the earth as a living and suffering thing:

> O terre, ô terre, ô race humaine,
> Vous me faites bien de la peine.

The lines are said in mockery, but they are meant.

Here is the Laforgue we have come to know. Here more than anywhere else in his work the poet has put down the world of the *quartier,* the hotel room, the café, the gas-lit street with all the people who frequent it. He has recorded for all time the twilit atmosphere of the suburbs with the little girl playing the piano somewhere in the distance, the sadness of Sunday. One could list the titles of hundreds of books, plays, and songs that go right back

to this Parisian universe that Laforgue made his own. Here are the "one-night cheap hotels" and "sawdust restaurants" that caught the imagination of T. S. Eliot and have continued to fascinate his readers:

> La nuit bruine sur les villes;
> Se raser le masque, s'orner
> D'un frac deuil, avec art diner,
> Puis, parmi des vierges débiles,
>   Prendre un air imbécile.

The whole of "Prufrock" is there.

No one has been more successful than Laforgue in bringing the machinery, the shabby and sordid décor of modern life into poetry, right down to the "marbre banal du lavabo." One feels that he was compelled to make poetry out of everything, omitting, as Arthur Symons pointed out, no hour of the day or night. He does not always succeed, of course, but the attempt is impressive. Everything animate or inanimate, has its rhythm and its song, clocks and foetuses, pine trees and bells, wind and stars, space and time. He attempts throughout to record a world that is living, moving, breathing, ticking, grinding. In **"Complainte des débats mélancoliques et littéraires"** he writes

> Deux frictions de vie courante
> T'auront bien vite exorcisé.

It is the sounds of *vie courante,* "running life," like running water, that he catches in the rhythms of popular songs, nursery tunes, old refrains. The instrument, the reed-pipe, on which the poet plays these melodies is the "chalumeau de ses nerfs"; and Laforgue uses the word *calamus* of Walt Whitman, whom he admired and translated.

Laforgue stated that the reader of the **Complaintes** would be absolutely overcome by a glance at the table of contents; the list of titles is indeed staggering. Among them are: Complaint of the Voices under the Buddhistic Fig Tree, Complaint of pianos heard in the suburbs, Complaint of a certain Sunday, Complaint of another Sunday, Complaint of the poet's foetus, Complaint of difficult puberties, Complaint of the moon in the provinces, Complaint of the incurable angel, Complaint of prehistoric nostalgias, Complaint of the blackballed, Complaint of the wind that is bored at night, Complaint of the tall pines around an abandoned villa, Complaint of time and her lady friend, space, Complaint on the Complaints, Complaint-Epitaph. One of the most amusing and typical of the poems is the **"Complaint of the Poor Knight Errant,"** which begins with the Knight Errant asking:

> Jupes des quinze ans, aurores de femmes,
> Qui veut, enfin, des palais de mon âme?

But the young ladies will have none of the "palaces of his soul" and the pilgrimage of the poor knight concludes thus:

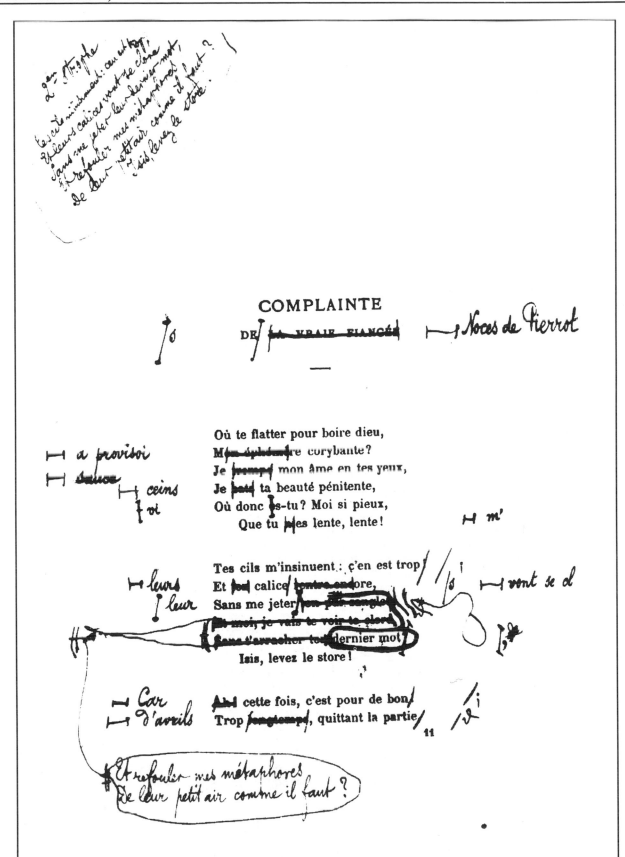

COMPLAINTE

DE LA VRAIE FIANCÉE — Noces de Pierrot

Où te flatter pour boire dieu,
Mon ... corybante?
Je ... mon âme en tes yeux,
Je ... ta beauté pénitente,
Où donc es-tu? Moi si pieux,
Que tu mes lente, lente!

Tes cils m'insinuent : ç'en est trop,
Et ... calice ...,
Sans me jeter ...
... je vais te voir ...
... dernier mot
Isis, levez le store!

... cette fois, c'est pour de bon,
Trop ..., quittant la partie

11

Proof of Les complaintes *corrected by Laforgue.*

—Mais j'ai beau parader, toutes s'en fichent!
Et je repars avec ma folle affiche,
Boniment incompris, piteux *sandwiche*:
  Au Bon Chevalier-Errant,
    Restaurant,
Hôtel meublé, Cabinets de lecture, prix courants.

The Knight-Errant is reduced to base reality: he is the man between the sandwich-boards wandering up and down the sidewalk, and the "palaces of the soul" are the rooms at The Knight-Errant, the hotel-restaurant he advertises. Laforgue's genius is verbal, everything exists on the surface, but always for the sake of what lies below it. Here we have the inner man, the introvert, buttressed against the external world, but held and contained within it: the man who is literally a *sandwich.*

The *Complaintes* is the record of many voices seeking to become one. In the **"Complainte propitiatoire à l'inconscient,"** which opens the volume after the **"Préludes autobiographiques,"** Laforgue addresses the Unconscious:

  Que votre inconsciente Volonté
  Soit faite dans l'Eternité!

And he means what he says. The Unconscious is what the poet saw as "the law of the world, which is the great melodic voice resulting from the symphony of the consciousness of races and individuals." Laforgue gives to Hartmann's metaphysical concept a psychological and imaginative extension. Poetry for him was no longer the romantic outpourings of the individual, as it had been in his early poems, but rather the expression of the many individuals that go to make up the one. The strength of the *Complaintes* lies in Laforgue's realization of the complex nature of the subconscious mind. Although he affected the air of a *dilettante,* he was a psychologist in poetry long before the advent of modern psychology. The discoveries of Freud and Jung, which lie behind so much of the writing of the twentieth century, owe a great deal to Hartmann. Laforgue's interest in the Unconscious and his interpretation of it prepared the way, in a very real sense, for Eliot and Joyce.

Behind all the rhythms of these poems there is one fundamental, immediate rhythm which Laforgue strives to set down: it is the human heart-beat. This is made clear in what was probably the first *complainte* that he composed, the **"Chanson du petit hypertrophique:"**

  C'est d'un' maladie d' coeur
  Qu'est mort', m'a dit l'docteur,
    Tir-lan-laire!
    Ma pauv' mère;
  Et que j'irai là-bas,
  Fair' dodo z'avec elle.
  J'entends mon coeur qui bat,
  C'est maman qui m'appelle!

The poet is too close to his subject for this to be a successful poem, but it strikes the keynote of the work. The reader hears in the lines—in the dropping of the mute

e's and the linking of the vowels with the *z* sound as would popular street-singers—exactly what the boy hears, the thumping heart and the voice of the mother calling from beyond the grave. Death is always somewhere between the lines of the poems, and accounts for their effect of urgency, their hurried manner, their staccato beat.

The idea of writing *complaintes* came to Laforgue, he tells us, during the carnival which followed the dedication of the Lion de Belfort in the Place Denfert-Rochereau on 20 September 1880. In November 1882 he had composed only five *complaintes;* by August 1883 he had written forty (ten were to be added later). He began immediately to look for a publisher, and finally agreed to pay Léon Vanier, who had published Verlaine's poems, to bring out the book. Vanier was so long, however, in getting around to it that the work did not appear until July 1885, by which time the author had already embarked on other important projects.

What impressed, surprised, and confounded Laforgue's contemporaries was not only his innovations in rhythms and rhyme, but the freedom of his vocabulary, his appropriation of popular speech and his invention of words. He introduced words from every branch of human activity, mixing them together as if they naturally belonged side by side and came as readily to the tongue as the simplest child's phrase. Terms from philosophy, biology, medicine, phrases from aesthetics, sentimental song titles, words from billboards and advertisements all mingle in such a fashion that one has the impression at times that the poems are *collages* made up from the pages of a daily newspaper. Not content with giving existing words new meanings, the poet invents new ones whenever it serves his purpose. He combines two words of very different sense which bear some orthographical resemblance; he makes nouns of adjectives and adjectives of nouns:

  Dans les soirs,
Feu d'artificeront envers vous mes sens encensoirs.

which might be translated:

  My censer-y senses
Will firework toward you through the evenings.

Much of the punning and verbal invention is, of course, quite untranslatable into English: "cloches exilescentes des *dies iraemissibles,*" "s'in-Pan-filtrer," "sangsuelles," "crucifiger." Nor does it always go so well in French; far from it. Marcel Raymond remarks that the "marriages biscornus" of some of these verbal associations have the appearance of laboratory products. Laforgue himself was later to realize that he had overdone these extravagances, and yet, in his campaign against the cliché and the hackneyed phrase, he was trying for, and at times achieved, a kind of verbal freedom that had not existed in France since Rabelais.

English, because of its double Anglo-Saxon and Latin roots, lends itself more readily than French to verbal dislocation and invention. And if we cannot translate many of the phrases of Laforgue, we can point to a contemporary English parallel. It exists where one would least expect to find it—in the nonsense poems and prose of Edward Lear and Lewis Carroll. It is doubtful that Jules Laforgue ever read Lear, but as an admirer of Kate Greenaway and Caldecott, he would certainly have approved of Lear's drawings for children; and he would surely have delighted in such words as "runcible," "plumdomphious," "sponge-taneously," and "scroobious." Lear and Laforgue, in their different ways, were revolting against the poetic eloquence of their day, an eloquence of which at the same time they had great appreciation. Laforgue admired the poems of Hugo, Lear wept on hearing the lyrics of Tennyson. Like Lear, Laforgue was unique in poetry, and like him he was an innovator: they both sang "warbling songs with a silvery voice and in a minor key." Laforgue is perhaps elsewhere more poignant and moving, but with this book he gave modern poetry, French and English, a new direction and a new life.

Russell S. King (essay date 1976)

SOURCE: "Jules Laforgue's Symbolist Language: Stylistic Anarchy and Aesthetic Coherence," in *Nottingham French Studies,* Vol. 15, No. 2, November, 1976, pp. 1-11.

[*In the following essay, King examines Laforgue's attempt to make a new language for poetic expression.*]

Of the three principal poetic "movements" of nineteenth-century French literature romanticism, parnassianism and symbolism—the last was the most revolutionary in its exploration of the possibilities of language. Whereas romanticism inaugurated a new poetic sensibility, symbolism produced a new form of poetic expression. Though Mallarmé is most identified with the symbolist revolution, other poets, and most notably Laforgue, exemplified the contradictory and multi-directional nature of a venture which created a language alternating between acceptance and rejection of traditional norms, and between a language of transparent communication and anarchic obscurity.

No contemporary critic of symbolist writing in general, and Laforgue in particular, whether sympathetic or hostile, was able to ignore the problem presented by the deviant use of language. Laforgue's friend, Léo Trézenik, declared in a review that "Laforgue est un sphinx . . . pour les énigmes duquel peu d'Oedipes sont nés encore." Another critic insisted that "le livre de M. Laforgue demeure parfaitement inintelligible," whilst another more sympathetic reviewer of the *Moralités légendaires* wrote: "Si l'on ne s'arrête point aux imprévues abracadabrances d'images, aux multicolores et inusités vêtements de phrases, aux sauts de carpe des dialogues, bientôt voici de la profonde psychologie et de la philosophie nette." Incomprehension and incoherence are words which characterize the majority of responses to Laforgue: "M. Jules

Laforgue . . . fut de toute la pléiade décadente celui qui sut le mieux allier le décousu des mots de la phrase à l'incohérence des idées." In modern criticism of symbolist writing obscurity of expression and the reader's difficulty in deciphering the poem's "message" are seen less as negative values than as defining characteristics.

Ezra Pound was perhaps the first critic to attempt some more sympathetic definition—albeit brief and questionable—of Laforgue's use of language. In an essay, "How to read," Pound divided poetry into three kinds: *melopoeia* ("wherein the words are charged, over and above their plain meaning, with some musical property"); *phanopoeia* ("which is the casting of images upon the visual imagination"); and *logopoeia* which he defined as "the dance of the intellect among words, that is to say, it employs words not only for their direct meaning, but it takes count in a special way of usage, of the context we expect to find with a word, its usual concomitants of its known acceptances, and of ironical play." According to Pound "Laforgue found or refound logopoeia." In another essay, "Irony, Laforgue, and some satire," Pound again emphasised the "verbal" quality of Laforgue's poetry: "Bad verbalism is rhetoric, or the use of *cliché* unconsciously, or a mere playing with phrases. But there is good verbalism, distinct from lyricism or imagism, and in this Laforgue is a master. He writes not the popular language of any country but an international tongue common to the excessively cultivated, and to those more or less familiar with French literature of the first three-fourths of the nineteenth century." Thus Pound clearly identified the primary value of Laforgue's poetry, both intrinsically and in the history of French poetry, with his language and style.

However much Laforgue's verbalism may be explained in terms of a particular sensibility, it nonetheless represented a desire to create a "new poetic language", as editors and critics have been quick to point out. A more recent critic of Laforgue, Pierre Reboul, has written, with special reference to the prose "nouvelles" of *Moralités légendaires*: "Les *Moralités* sont à la fois des mythes, une 'expression' et des mots. En guerre déclarée avec le dictionnaire, ce prosateur-poète se moque de la syntaxe et du bon goût. Les compléments s'entassent et s'imbriquent, les adjectifs se multiplient, comme en surcharge, les parenthèses ruinent les exposés qu'elles coupent, les constructions pendent interruptae. Laforgue n'emploie pas une langue: il crée la sienne." Another critic, D. J. Abraham, examining Laforgue's "heritage", considered that Laforgue tended "vers la simplicité d'une nouvelle langue," with his neologisms anticipating the stylistic peculiarities of the Dadaists, Jarry and the Surrealists.

Laforgue's attempt to create a new poetic expression and his obsession with linguistic experimentation are, at a most obvious level, related to his quest for originality. In the notes and essays which make up the *Mélanges posthumes* the poet constantly insisted on the value of novelty and "interest", in a manner reminiscent of Baudelaire's association of beauty and surprise: "En art il s'agit d'être intéressant . . . Il s'agit de n'être pas médiocre. Il faut être un nouveau." Not surprisingly his claim to verbal originality depends on his occasional use of Joycian portmanteau words (sexciproque, volupté, éléphantaisiste) and his conspicuous deviations in syntax. For other critics however his originality resides rather in his use of cosmic imagery in his first collection of poems, *Le Sanglot de la Terre* (published posthumously in 1902), in his special sensibility which mingled pathos and burlesque in a manner which appealed so much to T. S. Eliot, and his use of popular ballad forms in *Les Complaintes* (1885), and in his early use of *vers libres*.

It is not my present intention to describe and analyse the stylo-linguistic devices characterising Laforgue's poetry, but rather to explore the "styloæsthetic" dimension of his hesitant attempt to create a new language.

Like Laforgue's contemporary critics, any modern reader of *Moralités légendaires* or *Derniers vers* is immediately aware that Laforgue was attempting something new. On the one hand there is in his poetry a tendency to simplicity and a conversational style apparent even in his earliest writing. On the other hand however this tendency is counter-balanced by another towards concision and obscurity. François Ruchon, who wrote the first major study of Laforgue [*Jules Laforgue: Sa Vie, Son Oeuvre*, 1924], has most clearly drawn attention to the complexity of the poet's "styles": "Il s'en faut de beaucoup que le style de Laforgue soit un. Il n'y a rien de plus complexe au contraire. Il serait plus juste de dire: ses styles. Laforgue module sur tous les tons. On rencontre chez lui des notations analytiques, concentrées, claires, dures et taillées comme des diamants, puis d'autres du plus pur impressionnisme."

Like Laforgue's contemporary critics, any modern reader of *Moralités légendaires* or *Derniers vers* is immediately aware that Laforgue was attempting something new. On the one hand there is in his poetry a tendency to simplicity and a conversational style apparent even in his earliest writing. On the other hand however this tendency is counter-balanced by another towards concision and obscurity.

—*Russell S. King*

The stylistic variations in Laforgue's writing in part reflect a rapid evolution which is apparent in any thematic, formal or stylistic comparison between the early *Sanglot de la Terre* and *Derniers Vers*. However the first major step towards the creation of a new form of poetic expression had already been made by the end of 1881 when he wrote in a letter to his friend, Charles Henry: "C'est vous

dire que je fais pas mal de vers. Mes idées en poésie changent. Après avoir aimé les développements éloquents, puis Coppée, puis la *Justice* de Sully, puis baudelairien, je deviens (comme forme) kahnesque et mallarméen . . . Je tâtonne beaucoup les albums anglais de Kate Greenaway, Swerby, Emmerson." By the time of the composition (1883-86) of the *Moralités légendaires* his idiosyncratic style (or styles) was largely and distinctively formed. He described in a note, published under the heading "Rêve d'écriture" in the *Mélanges posthumes,* the complexity of his "ideal" style: "Ecrire une prose très claire, très simple (mais gardant toutes ses richesses), contournée non péniblement mais naïvement, du français d'Africaine géniale, du français de Christ. Et y ajouter par des images hors de notre répertoire français, tout en restant directement humaines." Already the key qualities are apparent: on the one hand those qualities which tend towards easy comprehension like clarity, simplicity, naïvety and obvious human relevance; and those which tend to difficulty: complexity of construction and unusual, novel images.

Laforgue was conscious of the difficulty of reconciling the "what one says" of naturalist writing with the "how one says it" of decadent and symbolist æsthetics:

> La vie est grossière, c'est vrai—mais, pour Dieu! quand il s'agit de poésie, soyons distingués comme des œillets; disons tout, tout (ce sont en effet surtout les saletés de la vie qui doivent mettre une mélancolie humoristique dans nos vers), mais disons les choses d'une façon raffinée. Une poésie ne doit pas être une description exacte (comme une page de roman), mais noyée de rêve.

The "coarseness" and "saletés de la vie" which one more readily associates with the transitive discourse and æsthetics of naturalist prose writing are to be expressed in the self-conscious refined style of decadent-symbolism: "soyons distingués comme des œillets . . . disons les choses d'une façon raffinée . . . description noyée de rêve." The fusion of naturalism in subject matter, the frequent use of colloquial language and popular art forms, with decadent æsthetics provides one key to Laforgue's poetic universe.

This refinement of expression must not be associated with notions of eloquent communication, for eloquence would undermine the impression of dreamlike naïvety which Laforgue sought to convey. Like Verlaine who urged in "Art Poétique": "Prends l'éloquence et tords-lui son cou," Laforgue condemned his early *Le Sanglot de la Terre* for its excessive eloquence: "J'en suis dégoûté: à cette époque je voulais être éloquent, et cela me donne aujourd'hui sur les nerfs. Faire de l'éloquence me semble si mauvais goût, si jobard." Eloquence belongs rather to the committed, passionate poet for whom poetry is primarily a vehicle of communication. "Je trouve stupide de faire la grosse voix et de jouer de l'éloquence. Aujourd'hui que je suis plus sceptique et que je m'emballe moins aisément et que, d'autre part, je possède ma langue d'une façon plus minutieuse, plus clownesque, j'écris de petits poèmes de fantaisie, n'ayant qu'un but: faire de l'original à tout prix . . ." This rejection of eloquent expression in favour of neglect of form and an appearance of childlike naïvety brings Laforgue close to Verlaine, as the poet himself recognized: "La 'Sagesse' de Verlaine -Quel vrai poète -C'est bien celui dont je me rapproche le plus - négligence absolue de la forme, plaintes d'enfant." Laforgue's identification with Verlaine is to be explained in a large measure by the two poets' partial adoption of impressionist æsthetics: the artistic reflection of impressions of relatively insignificant life and scenes resulting from direct confrontation with, and apprehension of, ephemeral reality, unformed by the intellect and expressed with a sense of directness and immediacy rather than in elaborate diction and traditional forms. In a sense their impressionism explains their appearance of naturalism in content and symbolism in expression. The purest literary impressionist poems are the "Paysages belges" in Verlaine's *Romances sans paroles* (1874) and the landscape-poems of the final section of *Sagesse* (1881).

Laforgue's preoccupation with trivial reality is therefore not in contradiction with the main direction(s) of his æsthetic: "La vie, la vie et encore rien que la vie, c'est-à-dire le nouveau. Faites de la vie, vivant telle quelle, et laissez le reste, vous êtes sûrs de ne pas vous tromper." In a sense therefore Laforgue's impressionism accounts for the language which at times appears colloquial and banal rather than "literary". Nowhere is this more obvious than in the many long passages of dialogue in *Moralités légendaires* -the most original part according to Ruchon -which invite the reader to suppose that Laforgue is simply aiming at parody and burlesque. In fact the poet is attempting to recreate heroes and heroines (Hamlet, Lohengrin, Pan, Perseus and Andromeda, and Salome) as real, living people:

> Moi, créature éphémère, un éphémère m'intéresse plus qu'un héros absolu . . . jamais, Dieu en est témoin, la pauvre humanité n'a produit un héros pur, et . . . tous ceux qu'on nous cite dans l'antiquité sont des créatures comme nous, cristallisées en légendes, ni Bouddha, ni Socrate, ni Marc-Aurèle,—je voudrais bien connaître leur vie quotidienne.

This concept of a modern hero whose daily existence is recreated, almost in terms of parody, sets itself in opposition to the moral, universal art formulated by Taine whom Laforgue vigorously condemned in his critical writings.

By the time Laforgue wrote the *Moralités légendaires* which portray these impressionist heroes his theory of prose writing had evolved in such a manner that the underlying principles governing prose and poetry largely coincided. Before 1883, however, Laforgue's poetic ideal centred around verse forms and was distinctly separate from "functional" prose: "Je rêve de la poésie qui ne dise rien, mais soit des bouts de rêverie sans suite. Quand on veut dire, exposer, démontrer quelque chose, il y a la prose." By the time he wrote **"Salomé"** he became preoccupied with the difficulties of adapting prose to literary purposes: "Tu connais l'*Hérodias* de Flaubert. Je viens de finir une petite **"Salome"** de moi. Ah! mon cher, qu'il est plus facile de tailler des strophes que d'établier de la prose! Je ne m'en étais jamais douté." The poet's difficulty in working in poetic prose partly results from the absence of any real tradition before Baudelaire's *Le Spleen de Paris* (1869), for the poet to accept or reject. In a sense, therefore, in adapting his own stylistic and æsthetic principles to the *nouvelles* he was exploring an area of poetic expression more novel than the ballad forms of **Les Complaintes** (1885) and perhaps almost as novel as the free verse of **Derniers Vers** (published in 1890). Indeed, as Pierre Reboul suggests, the poetic prose of the *Moralités* may well have influenced his subsequent practice of free verse.

The adoption of free verse is not an isolated phenomenon, but must be understood with reference to Laforgue's æsthetic as a whole. Without doubt the two principal stylo-linguistic features of his writing comprise his frequent rejection of standard norms of syntax and his lexical inventions. All his poetry after **Le Sanglot de la Terre** reflects an increasingly daring rejection of conventionally accepted syntax. As one contemporary critic declared, "les membres de phrase paraissent avoir été tirés au sort et assemblés au hasard." This supposedly hostile comment would not have displeased Laforgue whose poetic ideal was a "poésie qui ne dise rien, mais soit des bouts de rêverie sans suite." This devaluation of subject matter and the simple construction or juxtaposition of "bouts de rêverie sans suite" could never adequately be adapted to the language of logical realism.

Logical realism, positivism, analysis are totally inconsistent with Laforgue's adoption of von Hartmann's *Philosophy of the Unconscious* which largely informed or reinforced the poet's intellectual and metaphysical thinking. The unconscious, both in a Freudian sense, and as a universal life force, was in a large measure the unifying factor, but not the organizing principle, of the poet's writing. The "bouts de rêverie", preconscious day dreaming, a tendency to childlike naïvety, an absence of interest in causality, insignificant "bits" of individual experience of daily existence rather than rational generalizations about universal experience, are all to be expressed in a language of "broken", incomplete syntax reflecting the non-intellectual, pre-conscious progression of the mind. Long ago Ferdinand Brunot summed up this aspect of syntax which characterises almost all symbolist writing: "Pourquoi l'école symboliste fait-elle si peu de cas de la syntaxe? La syntaxe n'est qu'un instrument logique. Les rapports qu'elle établit ont pour effet d'enchaîner les sens des éléments grammaticaux, de manière à les coordonner en propositions rigoureuses. Or, cela, c'est la langue de ceux qui cherchent à définir. L'évocation n'a que faire de ces liens." Laforgue's rejection of syntax as a "logical instrument" anticipates the Dadaists' obsession with instinct and their refusal to be concerned with any explicit explanation, motive and conscious ordering.

The absence of explanation and coordination, the transformation of normally dependent grammatical structures into independent units juxtaposed with others, the abandonment in *Derniers Vers* of traditional verse forms, a fusion of naturalist triviality with decadent refinement, all tend to create an impression of anarchy of expression and obscurity of content. However this appearance of anarchy and obscurity needed to be orientated towards some counterbalancing artistic coherence. There is an obvious thematic unity in the earlier collections: cosmology in *Le Sanglot de la Terre* and the moon in *L'Imitation de Notre-Dame La Lune* (1885). In a letter to Léo Trézenik in which he compared himself with Tristan Corbière he insisted: "Je vis d'une philosophie absolue et non de tics." Yet the structuring of his poetry with its thematic and grammatical discontinuity gives precisely the impression of "tics", however much there may be an underlying "philosophie absolue". This is the "philosophy of the unconscious" which evocatively and suggestively translates itself into a language of discontinuity and apparent disassociation. Only the intellectual analyst, as opposed to the symbolist, dadaist or surrealist poet, can retranslate the apparent anarchy into patterns of logic, which of course would destroy the poetry as poetry.

The Laforguian "sentence" often seems to be in a state of decomposition, a state particularly associated with social and cultural attitudes of "decadent" writing in the 1880's.

—Russell S. King

The Laforguian "sentence" often seems to be in a state of decomposition, a state particularly associated with social and cultural attitudes of "decadent" writing in the 1880's. Bourget, in an essay on Baudelaire, described this state in which "l'unité du livre se décompose pour laisser la place à l'indépendance de la page, où la page se décompose pour laisser la place à l'indépendance de la phrase, et la phrase pour laisser la place à l'indépendance du mot." Thus the decomposition of unity between poems - as in Baudelaire's *Le Spleen de Paris* and all Laforgue's collections -is related to the decomposition of the sentence, and, in its turn, to lexical decomposition, which provides an important link between Laforgue's syntactic experimentation and his lexical peculiarities. However it would perhaps be more accurate to say that, in respect of poetry as a reflection of mental processes, Laforgue's language is intended to suggest a state of pre-composition. Psychology is still in a state of dream, and has not yet reached the stage of consciousness and intellectual analysis: "Je songe à une poésie qui serait de la psychologie dans une forme de rêve, avec des fleurs, du vent, des senteurs, d'inextricables symphonies avec une phrase (un sujet) mélodique, dont le dessin reparaît de temps en temps." A comparison of manuscript first drafts of poems and the final draft reveals that this reflexion of pre-conscious thinking has been carefully and consciously

achieved: Laforgue revised his poems by "deconstructing" and "degrammaticalizing" the conventional, comprehensible sentences into concise, deviant, juxtaposed structures.

The difficulty in achieving some sense of unity was one which Laforgue constantly sought to overcome. He wrote about *Le Sanglot de la Terre*: "Je me suis aperçu que mon volume de vers était un ramassis de petites saletés banales et je le refais avec rage." The *Moralités* too seemed to be a "ramassis": "A quoi bon, je veux travailler, faire de mon volume de nouvelles quelque chose de plus qu'un médiocre bouquet de fleurs disparates. Ce sera de l'Art. D'ailleurs -hélas! je sais qu'en quatre ans je pourrais faire fortune si je voulais écrire des romans à la Guy de Maupassant. *Bel-Ami* est d'un maître, mais ce n'est pas de l'art pur. Peut-être ce désir de créer de l'art pur est-il un louable mais pauvre désir de nos vingt-cinq ans? Et tout n'est-il pas égal devant la face de la Mort?" Laforgue's æsthetic necessitated a reconciliation of some notion of "pure art" which at first seems restrictive with an inclusive evocation of life in all its trivial experiences and with the meanderings of the pre-conscious and unconscious mind. In a letter he suggested the image of the kaleidoscope—Verlaine too composed a poem entitled "Kaleidoscope"—which would provide a theoretical reconciliation of coherence and anarchy: "Heureusement j'aime les vers, les livres, les vrais tableaux, les bonnes eaux-fortes, des coins de nature, des toilettes de femmes, des types imprévus. Bref tout le kaléidoscope de la vie. Mais on est fini et bien misérable au fond quand la vie n'a pour vous que l'intérêt d'un kaléidoscope, n'est-ce pas?" The image of a kaleidoscope transforms the chaos -thematic and syntactic -into relatively harmonious patterns through multiplication and repetition. Within the late Laforguian poem patterning is not provided in any formal way through verse or stanza forms but through refrains and the repetition of certain lines or words at regular or irregular intervals. Similarly there is abundant parallelism and tripling of syntactic structures, particularly in vocative forms and lists of nouns. This multiplication, which often appears gratuitous, of lexical and grammatical elements within the poem parallels the patterning of thematic elements -the kaleidoscope of life - with images of the dying universe, autumn, wind, rain, boring Sundays, absence of love etc.

It is difficult to determine whether Laforgue's particular sensibility resulted from, or lead to, the æsthetic of a new poetic expression. Those critics who seek to define and describe the poet's new sensibility tend to fall into a possible psychological fallacy: the dislocations in sensibility and linguistic expression are to be explained against a background portrait of Laforgue's own psychology. Martin Turnell, in his essay in *Scrutiny*, interprets the movements from high to low styles in purely psychological terms: Laforgue is "ridiculing an attitude from which he is trying to free himself, but has not yet managed to do so." Guy Michaud, in *Message du Symbolisme*, entitles his study of Laforgue "la parodie de l'angoisse." Ruchon too follows the psychological tradition in reading Laforgue: "Laforgue est la victime d'un trouble douloureux produit par le tourment de la méditation, par l'intrusion de l'analyse dans le moindre acte de sa vie, et cet esprit, fatigué de son éternelle analyse et dissociation de lui-même, n'a aucun désir: se dépasser, se nier, s'absorber en une sorte de Nirvana." Ruchon closely equates the sensibility of Laforgue with his portrayal of Hamlet: "Tout Laforgue est dans cette étroite union d'ironie et de pensée grave, nulle part mieux réalisée que dans Hamlet." It must of course be accepted that there must exist some reciprocal relationship (of cause and effect) between the poet's particular sensibility and his writing. In the case of Laforgue, after the more philosophic-prophetic poems of *Le Sanglot de la Terre,* stylistic and æsthetic considerations play a more dynamic function in the moulding of words and images into poems. In a letter written in 1882, Laforgue described himself as a dilettante, and seemed to shift emphasis away from the value of poetry as an act of philosophic communication to a more playful thing-in-itself: "Sachez, cher poète, qu'avant d'avoir des ambitions littéraires, j'ai eu des enthousiasmes de prophète, et qu'à une époque je rêvais toutes les nuits que j'allais consoler Savonarole dans sa prison. Maintenant, je suis dilettante en tout, avec parfois de petits accès de nausée universelle." This humorous but certainly sincere self-portrayal as a "dilettante en tout" combines with his kaleidoscopic image of life as it is to be reflected or recreated in art.

Laforgue's admission of dilettantism underlines the multidirectional nature of almost all aspects of his writing. For Laforgue vacillated, abruptly and unexpectedly, between an intellectual's desire to use language as a medium of clear and even eloquent communication and an anti-intellectual artist's rejection of "transitive discourse". Though his basic subject matter ("la vie, vivant telle quelle") may have coincided in a large measure with that of naturalist writing (Maupassant rather than Zola), his perception of reality and the verbal means of communicating this perception reflect rather a fusion of impressionist and decadent principles and techniques. All Laforgue's writing in fact is based on polarized tensions: between colloquial language and refined ornamentation; between banality and vulgarity, and decadent artifice; between coherence and anarchy; and between an appeal to a special coterie of initiated readers and a desire to create living heroes accessible to the general public. In this manner the poet's "stylo-æsthetic" novelty with its clever juggling -logopoeia -of themes and words requires a very considerable mental agility on the part of the reader. Neologisms and unusual technical terms along with syntactic innovations reflect not only a particular sensibility but also a new form of poetic expression which is a composite of realism, naturalism, impressionism, Tainian and anti-Tainian methodologies, and which anticipates æsthetic principles associated with, for example, the language and style of the Dadaists, T. S. Eliot and James Joyce.

Michael Collie   (essay date 1977)

SOURCE: *"Dernier vers,"* in *Jules Laforgue,* The Athlone Press, 1977, pp. 57-74.

[*In the following essay, Collie studies the stylistic and thematic aspects of Laforgue's* Dernier vers.]

DERNIERS VERS

Having published the boldly inventive volume *Les Complaintes* in 1885 and the modish *L'Imitation de Notre-Dame la Lune* in 1886, Laforgue remarkably went on, the next year, to fashion for himself an entirely new type of poem which appeared posthumously as *Derniers Vers*. Laforgue was the first poet to write free-verse in France. By this it is not meant that he was *literally* the first person to write unmetrical poems with lines of varying lengths, but that he was the first poet to do so successfully. The *Derniers Vers* can be seen either as a natural part of Laforgue's development, as the poems to which his experimental writing of the years in Germany was naturally leading, or they can be seen as neither superior nor inferior to *Les Complaintes,* but just very different both from a technical and a thematic point of view. In either case, they represent a considerable achievement and constitute a landmark in the history of French poetry, inasmuch as, from this point on, writers and readers were progressively less disturbed and alarmed by the idea of unmetrical verse.

During the spring of 1886, while still a member of the Empress Augusta's household, Laforgue once again wrote a great deal, perhaps with greater determination than in earlier years. A number of things occurred to give him confidence -or, if 'confidence' is too heavily a moral word for a decadent, to increase his interest in existence. The publication of his earlier poetry had helped: it did not in the least matter that the volumes did not sell. He was involved, from December 1885, in a new love affair -with Leah Lee, whom he was to marry within the twelve-month. He was more and more determined to leave Germany, where he knew he could only stagnate imaginatively, and to live in Paris where, with any luck, he would be able to make his way as a writer. Since he was not in the least a practical person and had spent his savings on the publication of his books, he did not have a coherent plan of action. He just had the increasingly strong feeling that a French poet ought to live in Paris. This feeling was reinforced by his strengthened friendship with Gustave Kahn and by Kahn's creation of the literary magazine *La Vogue*. The magazine, together with the two friends' talk about it, seems to have been the catalyst which stimulated Laforgue's imagination during a twelve-month period of work in which he produced the stories that came to be called *Moralités légendaires . . .* and the poems which were for a while called *Des Fleurs de Bonne Volonté*.

Des Fleurs de Bonne Volonté is the composite title for *all* the poems written during 1886. Various opinions are current about the status these poems, taken as a total group, enjoy. When Dujardin and Fénéon published *Les Derniers Vers de Jules Laforgue* in 1890, which was the first time the poems appeared in book form, they divided the volume into three sections: Des Fleurs de Bonne Volonté, Le Concile féerique, and Derniers Vers. They did this because the little dialogue called *Le Concile féerique* had already been extracted from the mass of poems written in 1886 and published separately as a chapbook by *La Vogue* and because they knew that Laforgue had prepared the twelve poems that now constitute *Derniers Vers* for publication as a book. In other words, *Le Concile féerique* and *Derniers Vers* are the volumes Laforgue himself made from all that he had written since the beginning of 1886. Unclear is the question of whether Laforgue would have published other poems from *Des Fleurs de Bonne Volonté* had he lived. The existence of a titlepage for such a volume in one of the surviving manuscripts has made some people think that Laforgue did intend such a publication. Thus Pia prints the poems as a volume in his *Poésies complètes.* It seems more likely, however, that this intention was abandoned when Laforgue began to write *Derniers Vers* during the summer of 1886. This view will be assumed to be the correct one in the account which follows; that is, that when Laforgue found himself writing vigorously in the early part of 1886 he at first had in mind a volume to be called *Des Fleurs de Bonne Volonté* but that this idea was abandoned when his previous thoughts about the writing of an entirely new kind of poem were suddenly realized in **'L'Hiver qui vient'**. Once embarked upon **Derniers Vers,** he raided his own collection for material, as in the poems called **'Dimanches'**. This means that the two sets of poems have a different status. What we now have as *Des Fleurs de Bonne Volonté* is no more than a writer's notebook, 'un répertoire pour de nouveaux poèmes'. This is emphasized because some critics have been incapable of distinguishing critically, or indeed in any way, between the poems which Laforgue wanted to have published and those which he suppressed.

To return to the spring of 1886, Laforgue as usual found that he had more time when the court moved to Baden-Baden. It may turn out to be the case that it was in Baden over the years that he did most of his work. During this period he corresponded with Kahn. In May he announced that he had thirty-five poems for a new book; by June the number had increased to sixty. Only part of what must have been an exceptionally interesting correspondence has survived, but that it existed is clear from the frequency of Laforgue's contributions to *La Vogue.* The first number of *La Vogue* had appeared on 11 April; Laforgue had received a copy from Kahn shortly afterwards; he had contributed four poems to the fourth issue, in May, and to the fifth a prose poem, **'L'Aquarium'**, which is in fact a few paragraphs from one of the *nouvelles,* -**'Salomé'**. The magazine lasted for less than a year, but between May and December 1886 Laforgue contributed to twenty of its thirty issues. It has already been seen that the publication of a few of the *Complaintes* had a considerable effect upon Laforgue: the importance to him of this continuous publication in *La Vogue* could hardly be overestimated. It covered the whole period between the spring of 1886 and the Christmas of the same year, the continuous activity of writing and publishing giving some point to his otherwise chaotic existence. The first number of *La Vogue* had included work by Verlaine, Mallarmé, Villiers de l'Isle-Adam, and Rimbaud, as well as by the 'Hydropathes' themselves, Henry, Bourget and Kahn. This issue, even by itself, had an impact in that it immediately made Laforgue wish to join forces with this illustrious company. In fact, he may have visited Paris briefly in May to discuss the possibility of his contributing to the magazine.

Whether he went to Paris or not, the activity associated with *La Vogue* had three immediate consequences. The first was that he read and thought about Rimbaud, whose work he had scarcely known until then. Kahn probably showed him the manuscript of *Les Illuminations.* At all events, he realized that Rimbaud was a poet whose strong imagination brought together the disparate facts of experience in the creative act of the making of a poem and that the kaleidoscope of life, whose separate, fragmented effects Laforgue had celebrated in *Les Complaintes,* could also render a modern art which was not merely fragmented, but which expressed the modern sensibility in unique, newly-invented configurations of words and metaphors that established their own integrity. 'Ce Rimbaud fut bien un *cas.* C'est un des rares qui m'étonnent. Comme il est entier! presque sans rhétorique et sans attaches.' Secondly, Laforgue and Kahn in discussion made explicit the possibility of a free-verse poem. These discussions went unrecorded for the most part, though they were later recollected by Kahn who, of course, must share the honours of having 'invented' the new type of poem. When Laforgue came to write **Derniers Vers** it obviously made a difference that he knew in advance that Kahn would publish them. Few other editors would even have considered doing so. Thirdly, Kahn asked Laforgue to translate Whitman. In a letter which should be dated June, not July, 1886, Laforgue tells Kahn that he has translated at least one poem: 'Je t'envoie—au moins pour boucher des trous de Moncanys—un Whitman. Lis-le, c'est un des plus Whitman du volume. Je crois l'avoir très heureusement traduit.' The translations were published in two issues of *La Vogue,* those for 25 June-5 July and for 5-12 July 1886. While there is no record of what Laforgue thought about Whitman, nor even any evidence that he chose these poems for a particular reason, it seems fair to speculate that Laforgue's encounter with an American poet who had already written a type of free-verse reinforced his notion that the same could be done in French. (Incidentally, when these Whitman translations were published in book form for the first time in *Walt Whitman Œuvres choisies,* Paris, 1918, the editor silently tidied them up, correcting Laforgue's errors and making a few other changes that would perhaps be difficult to justify.)

For the first time in his life, then, Laforgue was in touch with literary Paris, at least a part of it. His correspondence with Kahn is full of references to other little magazines -*La Revue politique et littéraire, La Nouvelle revue, La Revue moderne naturaliste, La Revue contemporaine, La Revue Wagnérienne, La Revue Indépendante* and several others. The friends were excited by the real possibility of *avant-garde* publishing. Furthermore, Laforgue had already met at a concert in Berlin at the beginning of April two of his future editors, Dujardin and Wyzewa, both of whom were also editors of journals. Wyzewa already knew Kahn, having met him first at one of Mallarmé's Tuesday evenings in 1885. It made a difference to Laforgue that this enlarged circle of friends was already sensitive to the latest developments in art and literature and was sympathetic to innovation.

Yet, whatever Laforgue may have felt about his status as a writer, and whatever view he took, theoretically, of his development as a poet, in July 1886 he consciously began to write a new type of poem. He announced this fact to Kahn and sent him **'L'Hiver qui vient'**. Eleven more poems, or what were to become eleven poems in the first edition (making a total of twelve), followed during the summer and autumn of 1886 and were published in *La Vogue* and, in the case of the last two, in *La Revue Indépendante*. Back in Paris, he revised the poems for book publication. The revised text consisted of a fair copy made by Laforgue during the winter of 1886-7 when he attempted to interest Léon Vanier, and perhaps other publishers, in the possibility of book publication -this time not at the author's expense. When Vanier failed to respond positively, Laforgue sent his fair copy, by that time with both additional autograph corrections and an accretion of doodle, to Dujardin, who used it as the basis for his edition of 1890. Clearly this corrected autograph MS, now in the Jacques Doucet Library, should have replaced the magazine version for all subsequent editions of the **Derniers Vers**. Laforgue thoroughly revised the poems (so that the first edition is significantly different from that of *La Vogue*), clearly divided the poems into the twelve poems of the **Derniers Vers** as we now have them, and altered the epigraph. With this revision in mind and the physical evidence still available for inspection, some readers have decided that the twelve poems of the **Derniers Vers** are separate or, at least, separable from each other and that Laforgue rather emphasized this by the way he marked the work copy for Dujardin. On the basis of the same evidence, other readers feel that the poems have a thematic and metaphorical consistency which allows or even requires them to be regarded as a single work. There is no way to settle this question. The strongest of the poems can be read out of context and indeed they are the anthology poems of nineteenth-century free-verse. On the other hand, even the strongest poems must gain in imaginative coherence by being seen in context. It seems worth considering this possibility first.

One can think of the **Derniers Vers** as a whole by considering the way in which the author's own thoughts and preoccupations are gradually introduced into the complex of visual impression and mood. The first poem, **'L'Hiver qui vient'**, is almost entirely evocative. So is the second, **'Le Mystère des trois cors'**. In these two poems, Nature is imagined as a compelling but automatic system (random fertilization, a meaningless life, death) and the cause of all this, the sun, is now itself dead, having been hunted to death across the autumn landscape, its previous splendour nothing but a mockery. After the sound of the hunting horns, there is winter, the poet's season. In the third poem, **'Dimanches'**, the person-

al element becomes more strong. The poet, though he wishes to believe in love, sees himself as a 'pauvre, pâle et piètre individu' who cannot even believe in himself. He engages perhaps in the fantasy that real engagements and real marriages are possible, but what he actually sees are the symbols of an alien world, Sundays, pianos, genteel dresses, and the young girl returning home after church whose body, one observes, knows 'qu'il appartient / A un tout autre passé que le mien!' He also fears lust, for marriage would lead him to: 'adorer d'incurables organes'. Because of the hopelessness of this, the girl should not accommodate herself to life; there should be the same rupture as between Hamlet and Ophelia; and the poet should go for a little walk to get rid of his spleen. In the next poem, also called **'Dimanches'**, the balance is redressed. He plays ironically with a view of the same symbol, the convent girl. He himself he imagines as a Polar Bear, a remote Arctic creature uninvolved apparently in the comings and goings of ordinary existence.

> Les Jeunes Filles inviolables et frêles
> Descendent vers la petite chapelle
> Dont les chimériques cloches
> Du joli joli dimanche
> Hygiéniquement et élégamment les appellent.
>
>   . . .
>
> Je suis venu par ces banquises
> Plus pures que les communiantes en blanc . . .
> Moi, je ne vais pas à l'église,
> Moi, je suis le Grand Chancelier de l'Analyse,
> Qu'on se le dise.

The fifth poem, **'Pétition'**, sustains the same balance. The absolute, pure love for which the poet has been craving is unobtainable. The imaginative location of the poem is an empty square, without a fountain in it, from which, at the ends of the streets which lead away in different directions, the life that other people lead is seen and heard distantly. 'Mais, à tous les bouts, d'étourdissantes fêtes foraines.' There are no absolutes, only compromise. 'Tout est pas plus, tout est permis.' That is to say, in the old determinist *impasse*, only what is permitted is permitted, and the individual can conceive of no life for himself outside the rigid scheme of things he sees more and more clearly the more he thinks. Despite this knowledge, however, there is still a desire for a genuine existence and this is the subject of the sixth poem, **'Simple Agonie'**. The sensibility which makes the poet a pariah and sets him away from the world also inclines him to 'les sympathies de mai', the seductive allurement of rebirth, the provocative pleasures of a springtime almost irresistible to a Nihilist, so that his poems are ambiguous, insubstantial things, like the life of an insect. Laforgue in these poems is, in other words, that very modern figure who lets the weaknesses of his own personality be the lens through which a faithful, credible view is given definition. In moral art, where there is an emphasis upon the possibility of things being better than they are observed to be, limitations of personality are thought to weaken the impact of the work; in art which is taking care not to be moral but has a different ambition, in this case impressionistic, a character who is sensitive even in an anaemic way is taken to be a greater guarantee of authenticity than his more heroic predecessors.

The next poem, **'Solo de Lune'**, which is discussed in greater detail below, is the recapitulation, as in music. In **'Légende'**, the seventh of the twelve poems, it is the woman who argues with the man to make him or let him feel that there is something more than exile, at least 'the sweetness of legend'. The ninth and tenth poems were published together in *La Vogue* as **'Les Amours'**. In the first, there is another masculine-feminine dramatic situation, again from the point of view of the woman who, as sure of love as 'du vide insensé de mon cœur', might come, 'évadée, demi-morte, / Se rouler sur le paillasson que j'ai mis à cet effet devant ma porte'. Once again there is the ambivalent male detachment of the poet who desires yet desires not to desire the craving for affection confused with a haughty disdain for it, in a formulation in which disdain expresses love and love is the expression of disdain. In the next poem, more or less a continuation emotionally, the poet laments the fact that his life has been spent on the quayside of existence from which he never departs on a journey of any significance. No Odysseys for him.

> J'aurai passé ma vie le long des quais
> A faillir m'embarquer
> Dans de bien funestes histoires.

Finally, the twelfth of the **Derniers Vers** has as epigraph Hamlet's speech to Ophelia beginning with the words: 'Get thee to a nunnery: why wouldst thou be a breeder of sinners?' In this context the poet recalls his home town:

> Un couvent dans ma ville natale
> Douce de vingt mille âmes à peine,
> Entre le lycée et la préfecture
> Et vis à vis la cathédrale . . .

and, rather than consign his lover to such a fate, prefers to be 'two in the chimney corner', resigned to the 'fatalistic hymn' of existence and still seeing it, existence, as 'a deafening fairground'. So it must always be, if it depends upon men and women: 'Frailty thy name is woman: everything's routine.' The poem then ends with lines which, despite the reference to Baudelaire, would be hollow indeed without the substance of twelve poems behind them:

> O Nature, donne-moi la force et le courage
> De me croire en âge,
> O Nature, relève-moi le front!
> Puisque, tôt ou tard, nous mourrons . . .

Theoretically, then, the poems are a single, well sustained, tone poem in which the *fin-de-siècle* atmosphere of pessimism and disbelief is the world also of psychological tension, of psychological disaccord, of tension between man and woman, of desires that are never fulfilled, and of fears and anxieties which are never com-pletely understood but are expressible only in negatives. The predicaments, situations, insights of the poems, as well as their half-statements and ambivalences are metaphors for existence itself, psychological metaphors which predicate the fractured world of misunderstanding and personal alienation. In this sense, the poems are not *about* a situation, anecdotally; rather they are the situation -the world of disillusion now given an artistic not a doctrinaire treatment. Thematically, the poems protect each other, as it were, from over particular exegesis and by their unity of language and metaphor insist upon the qualities of the tone poem, like something in Whistler or Debussy.

> **Theoretically, the poems in *Dernier vers* are a single, well sustained, tone poem in which the *fin-de-siècle* atmosphere of pessimism and disbelief is the world also of psychological tension, of psychological disaccord, of tension between man and woman, of desires that are never fulfilled, and of fears and anxieties which are never completely understood but are expressible only in negatives.**
>
> —*Michael Collie*

Quite clearly, Laforgue had achieved something a good deal more substantial than the previous 'kaleidoscope' poems. He has given the twelve poems an imaginative unity and turned away from, and left behind, the naïveté of plain statement.

Even the reader who is impressed by the symphonic variation of the **Derniers Vers** as a whole will be necessarily affected also by the exceptional originality of individual poems. Laforgue's innovation was to write a longer poem than any in *Des Fleurs de Bonne Volonté*—a poem whose length was not predetermined by logic of thought or metaphor. If Valéry's 'Le Cimetière Marin' is at one end of the scale of tight, poetic discipline and organization, poems like **'L'Hiver qui vient'** are at the other. There is a kind of poem where the pattern of thought or metaphor takes the reader naturally to a 'conclusion' which satisfies because of the feeling that the imaginative implications of the poem have been thoroughly worked out and 'realized'. This is the opposite of what Laforgue does in **Derniers Vers**. In fact, the reader is denied the satisfactions of form and logical consistency. These are replaced by a psychological consistency which is expressed in sets of complementary and conflicting image patterns. By psychological consistency one means that the images and metaphors of a particular poem taken together constituted the world of the poem's fictive poet, whose view may be arbitrary, perverse, sentimental, without being invalid for that reason, since nothing of a general nature is being asserted. The philosophical attitudinizing of **Le Sanglot de la Terre** has been overcome. Lofty or grandly pessimistic ideas about humanity are not proposed. Nothing is proposed. Rather, an interwoven pattern of poetic ideas is made to represent the inner world of an imagined poet who is not Laforgue. The best way to demonstrate this is to discuss a poem in some detail, and since the author of the present book has already written about the **Derniers Vers** in two other places and since space is limited, a examination of a single poem, '**Solo de Lune**', must suffice.

Even Laforgue's friend, Bourget, refused to comment on '**Solo de Lune**' and the other poems in the volume because they were 'si peu traditionnels'. Part of the effect of the poem is obviously its deliberate 'anti-literature' character; for that period it was extremely unusual, almost aggressively different, iconoclastic, provocative. Even when the poem is made familiar by re-reading, its fragmented, poetic world still has this disturbing effect, at least on the surface.

The superficial qualities of the poem that contributed to its initial impact were its apparent incoherence, its rather sensational phrasing, and the negative attitudes to life that it seemed to imply. The poem lacks logical structure or development: there are time shifts, shifts of tense, without explanation. The occasion of the poem and its imaginative direction must be deduced, if they can be grasped at all, from incomplete dialogue, ellipses, and statements made out of context. At first it seems an occasional poem whose occasion is almost completely concealed. Secondly, the language of the poem is aggressive and startling. The man and woman of the poem, who desired but failed to achieve love and understanding, are 'maniaques de bonheur' because happiness is not to be expected in the world, a sentiment not everyone was prepared to accept in 1886. The juxtaposition of 'marriage' and 'bonheur' seems forced, merely for effect. At first reading the poem seems frustratingly evasive when it might have been explicit and overly explicit when it might have been discreet. With the unexpressed love that eluded both man and woman the poet associates a bitter sexuality:

Oh! que de soirs je vais me rendre infâme
En ton honneur!

while in the same compulsively ironical vein, and almost immediately, he takes away from the seriousness of the poem with a brilliant image, which is also a pun, in which the moon is seen as a 'croissant' in the 'confiserie' of the cloudy night sky. In these two examples, one sees easily enough the 'decadence' of which early readers complained. Thirdly, the poem, though a type of love poem, seemed to deny the normally understood human verities in as much as the poet adopts a cynical, detached, nihilistic attitude to the possibility of a real relation between man and woman. Married or unmarried their life would lack meaning: 'On s'endurcira chacun pour soi'. What does it matter? the poem appears to say. 'Tout n'en va pas moins à la Mort'.

What seemed difficult in 1886 is easily accessible, in retrospect, since the poem is a period-piece but, though a period-piece, a modern poem. It is an example, an excellent one, of *fin-de-siècle* or Nihilist literary art, a 'solo' performance because the poet is solitary, knows no absolutes and has only his own unsatisfactory experiences to live by, and a 'solo de lune' because the sun, with implications of fecundity and meaning, is denied and because the poet's song asserts not the romantic feelings associated with moon-light but the opposite, the lack of love and fulfilment. Therefore: 'ô nulle musique'. Much of the phrasing derives from and belongs to the period, particularly lines like: 'Un spleen me tenait exilé', where 'spleen' is being used in its Baudelairian sense of disgust or nausea caused by the world from which the poet is alienated, and where 'exilé', denoting the individual intellect or 'déraciné' (that is, not a literal exile but one in which the individual is cut off imaginatively from the normal processes of life), would out of the poem be a mere cliché but here is not. In the next line: 'Et ce spleen me venait de tout', one sees the way in which the decadent poet replaced the social values and social absolutes in which he could not believe with equally vast, but negative generalities of his own. Every aspect of life engenders this nausea, a nausea which is associated, in this group of lines, with 'foolish' love and inarticulate parting.

To the extent that the poem is about a relationship between man and woman it is informed by the pessimism of the age. The lovers fail to communicate their desires: 'Pourquoi ne comprenez vous pas?' Having failed, the poet is resigned to the loss: 'Accumulons l'irréparable!' Conscious of age-old sexual compulsions—'O vieillissante pécheresse'—he is not able to respond to her unspoken desire, although he imagines, ironically, 'un beau couple d'amants' who act out their love freely, that is 'hors la loi'. Fulfilment is denied or, rather, genuine, human love is denied: 'Je n'ai que l'amitié des chambres d'hôtel.' This overriding pessimism is a type of despair but one which is expressed with such persistent irony that the poem can assert itself at the very time the experience behind it is eluding the reader. He *would* have been a model husband. 'J'eusse été le modèle des époux!' but, such is the implication, only by accepting the charade of nature and sacrificing individuality for the sake of playing a rôle: 'Comme le frou-frou de ta robe est le modèle des frou-frou.' A brilliantly laconic conclusion.

'**Solo de Lune**' only seems incoherent. Its organizing principle is not logic but it has an internal poetic integrity nonetheless. First the free verse is used with complete control. As mentioned already, Laforgue was the first poet to master the 'form'. Though metre has been abandoned and though the poem is in not stanzas but 'paragraphs' made of lines of different length, it is held together by a firm, rhythmical movement, by rhyme (sometimes of a preposterous kind), by internal rhyme and assonance, and more generally by a tonal assurance that holds in place detail that, by itself, would be quite alarming. It is a tone-poem: a poem aspiring to musical not rational coherence. Reading it aloud reveals this perfectly well. Second, the poem reflects a new interest in the poetry of the unconscious. The poet is Ariel, detached from the workaday world. Sensations, presentiments, fleeting insights, ephemeral experiences, make up the fabric of life, not ordered thought or organized social habits. It is a stream of consciousness poem asserting the validity of personal experience however incoherent, as against the 'meanings' of normal life. Thus, to the poet lying on the roof of a diligence or coach, smoking, alone, reflecting on what might have been, longing for love and sympathy though not believing in either, and going over in his mind ('récapitulons') his feelings about a relationship which did not mature, everything that is perceived or thought takes a place in the total impression, which is entirely located in and indeed created by the poet's mind. He travels a 'route en grand rêve'. The physical and the metaphysical come together in momentary associations as the coach travels through the night. In the moment which is the poem ('O fugacité de cette heure') everything is recalled ('Dans ces inondations du fleuve du Léthé') and everything is lost.

Third, the poem is a sustained piece of poetic irony in a recognizably modern mode. It has a deliberately anti-romantic vein. A marriage will not take place. Indeed, Laforgue pokes fun at matrimonial expectations partly by making mock use of stilted, romantic language, as in

> Mais nul n'a fait le premier pas
> Pour tomber ensemble à genoux. Ah! . . .

partly by imagining a colourless wedding by moonlight, not a wedding in the light of the sun which would signify fecundity and a belief in life but rather a celebration of the poet's essential loneliness: 'Noce de feux de Bengale noyant mon infortune'. The irony is sustained and habitual, a style, a way of thought, something more deeply ingrained than a mere striving after effect. To take only one example, Laforgue is the type of poet who enjoys the play on words in lines like

> Mais *nul* n'a fait le premier *pas*

where 'nul' is a key, tonal word in the poem, where 'pas' is a pun, where the pun is combined with an ancient resonant word (for lovers), i.e. 'tomber', but where, though they fall, they do not fall far enough, but only, like puppets, to their knees. Yet this sort of thing is in passing. It is a detail absorbed within the highly wrought fabric of the poem as a whole.

The new sounds, the new imaginative patterns of **'Solo de Lune'** have for some readers proved as impenetrable or as unpalatable as the new effects of Wagner for Laforgue's contemporaries. English readers will have in mind perhaps the resistance of the old guard brought up on metre when the issue became crucial at the turn of the century: the way Bridges edited Hopkins so that he would be accessible to the reader accustomed to mid-Victorian metrical poems; or those chillingly conservative discussions by Siegfried Sassoon, Robert Graves and Wilfred Owen about the state of English poetry just before the first world war, talk which showed only too well how they felt obliged to search for a modern poem *within* the traditional received forms; or the letters of Rupert Brooke,

dating from the same period, which express his nostalgia for ancient forms and his dependence upon the correct English of the educated. As everyone knows, the break only happened in the second decade of the twentieth century with Pound and T. S. Eliot, which is a measure of the popular resistance to the unmetrical. In France, one might mention the comparable but bizarre reluctance of generations of readers to accept Saint-John Perse who was 'si peu traditionnel'. Even when he was at last recognized, in France, as a major poet there were still critics prepared to show us orthodox Racinian lines embedded in his verse paragraphs. No wonder that there were readers who literally could not hear a Laforgue poem. Laforgue's genius was clearly not of the traditional kind, or at least not in this sense. His world was that of Manet and Toulouse-Lautrec, of Huysmans and Proust, of Rimbaud and Apollinaire, of Debussy and Stravinsky. A poem like **'Solo de Lune'** was a highly crafted tone poem whose quite daring internal modulations were analogous to their novel harmonies and dissonances. That Laforgue had achieved in poetry what others had achieved in painting and music is much easier to see now than then. **'Solo de lune',** and the other strong poems in *Derniers Vers,* constituted an artistic breakthrough. After them it needed a poet of exceptional ability to resort to conventional metres and forms.

Evidence of conscious care and craftsmanship can also be seen in the third of the *Derniers Vers,* **'Dimanches',** though in a different way. This is one of those with ancestors in earlier collections and in particular in *Des Fleurs de Bonne Volonté.* Poems with thematic or tonal relations to the *Derniers Vers* poem include **'Le vrai de la chose', 'Célibat, Célibat, tout n'est que Célibat', 'Gare au bord de le mer',** and poems XXVIII and XXX in *Des Fleurs de Bonne Volonté,* which are also called **'Dimanches'.** A reader new to Laforgue may well wish to check for himself the relationship between the published poems and the rejected ones. By comparison with the finished poem, these earlier poems are more like improvisations on a theme played by some artist whose imagination is stalking the form by which his sustained but vague sense of a subject may be realized. Not only are these thematic preoccupations seen to have greater significance when they are absorbed into the substance of the longer poem, but the play of words is also no longer there for the sake of the exercise, but now contributes in an artistically consistent way to the counterpoint of the tone-poem. Though it is not possible here to compare these poems in detail, an example will show the kind of change that Laforgue makes.

The **'Dimanches'** in the *Derniers Vers* begins with the lines:

> Bref, j'allais me donner d'un 'Je vous aime'
> Quand je m'avisai non sans peine
> Que d'aboard je ne me possédais pas bien moi-même.
>
> (Mon Moi, c'est Galathée aveuglant Pygmalion!
> Impossible de modifier cette situation.)

Unpublished poem "Un ciel du soir pluvieux," which Laforgue composed in 1886.

The 'I' of the poem sees himself as the equivalent of the Pygmalion of Moreau, or the pre-Raphaelite Pygmalion who spurns the world, disregards the women of his home town, dreams of an ideal love, is inspired to create the ideal form in art, and is rewarded by a statue so perfect that it comes to life, so that he is after all confronted by a real Galatea. The irony of this would be very congenial to Laforgue. Since, at more or less the same time, Laforgue (in his letter to Kahn of June 1886) was considering an article on Ruskin, and since there are many references to English painters like Burne-Jones and Madox-Brown, both in the letters and in *Mélanges posthumes,* it is tempting to suppose that Laforgue's interest had increased since his meeting with Leah Lee, and that he in fact knew of Burne-Jones' four paintings on the theme of Pygmalion and Galatea. Though there are other pre-Raphaelite passages in the *Derniers Vers* which substantiate his general interest, the precise point is of course hypothetical. The reference to Pygmalion has the same effect as the reference to Watteau in 'L'Hiver qui vient': very economically it throws the first lines into a new perspective. It does this in the same way as in a painting a tension is produced by the juxtaposition of objects not immediately expected together. It is also a more than usually oblique way of speaking about himself, the self-knowledge implied here being at least more forceful than the open confessions of the earlier poems.

The 'Dimanches' xxx of *Des Fleurs de Bonne Volonté* is at any rate a much cruder piece of work. In it the poet plays with a conceit. Marriage is a dancing, colourful life-buoy; he a morose Corsair, who knows he has been shipwrecked for ever. Immediately after this, the last lines of the poem:

> Un soir, je crus en Moi! J'en faillis me fiancer!
> Est-ce possible . . . Où donc tout ça est-il passé! . . .
>
> Chez moi, c'est Galathée aveuglant Pygmalion!
> Ah! faudrait modifier cette situation . . .

In the *Derniers Vers* version a good part of the bathos of this has been omitted, the essential metaphor retained. Laforgue was aware of the weakness of his distinction between the Ideal and the Real, though for him it was 'impossible to alter this situation'. 'Dimanches' xxviii in *Des Fleurs de Bonne Volonté* also makes it clear that this same distinction is behind his interest in Hamlet, since the epigraph of the poem is Hamlet's conversation with Ophelia in the play scene. The poem in the *Derniers Vers* is the expression of the dilemma of the fatalist. Either he chooses to compromise himself by accepting the world on terms he knows to be unsatisfactory or, alternatively, he remains aloof without any consolation at all, and certainly without the satisfaction of believing in his own judgment. But, despite the thematic similarity between the two poems, and the similarity is so close that the first can be used to elucidate the second, it is immediately obvious that it is the 'Dimanches' of the *Derniers Vers* that is the more mature work, with a greater internal integrity.

These examples are not isolated ones. The eighth and ninth poems in the *Derniers Vers,* for instance, are quite heavily dependent upon *Des Fleurs de Bonne Volonté.* Drawing upon his earlier poems at will, he achieves the poem that in a sense had been haunting him for many years: 'une poésie qui serait de la psychologie dans une forme de rêve . . . d'inextricables symphonies avec une phrase (un sujet) mélodique, dont le dessin reparaît de temps en temps.'

The single example that space permits will be the last half of the *Derniers Vers* iii 'Dimanches':

> Oh! voilà que ton piano
> Me recommence, si natal maintenant!
> Et ton cœur qui s'ignore s'y ânonne
> En ritournelles de bastringues à tout venant,
> Et ta pauvre chair s'y fait mal! . . .
> A moi, Walkyries!
> Walkyries des hypocondries et des tueries!
>
> Ah! que je te les tordrais avec plaisir,
> Ce corps bijou, ce cœur à ténor,
> Et te dirais leur fait, et puis encore
> La manière de s'en servir
> De s'en servir à deux,
> Si tu voulais seulement m'approfondir ensuite un
>   peu!
>
> Non, non! C'est sucer la chair d'un cœur élu,
> Adorer d'incurables organes
> S'entrevoir avant que les tissus se fanent
> En monomanes, en reclus!
>
> Et ce n'est pas sa chair qui me serait tout,
> Et je ne serais pas qu'un grand cœur pour elle,
> Mais quoi s'en aller faire les fous
> Dans des histoires fraternelles!
> L'âme et la chair, la chair et l'âme,
> C'est l'Esprit édénique et fier
> D'être un peu l'Homme avec la Femme.
>
> En attendant, oh! garde-toi des coups de tête,
> Oh! file ton rouet et prie et reste honnête.
>
> —Allons, dernier des poètes,
> Toujours enfermé tu te rendras malade!
> Vois, il fait beau temps tout le monde est dehors,
> Va donc acheter deux sous d'ellébore,
> Ça te fera une petite promenade.

Again there is the balance or counterpoint of the last lines, anticipating for example passages in Joyce. Disgust is weighed against charity, then dissolved into a final irony. He will tolerate neither a bluntly sexual union nor an anaemic brotherly affair, a Platonic friendship. Rather, he will go for a little walk: 'Go out and buy a pennyworth of hellebore.' This hellebore, with its highly pertinent and delightful reference back to the tortoise and the hare of La Fontaine, is both the realist's laxative that will purge the poet of the neuroticism of the poem and the traditional remedy for madness. The irony that at the earlier date was expressed in ostentatiously violent and shocking contrasts is now achieved economically with the pointing of a single word.

Laforgue died without having the satisfaction of seeing *Derniers Vers* published in book form. Dujardin's important editions of 1890 and 1894 did not achieve wide circulation. Not until the Mercure de France edition of 1902-3 were the poems published in the normal sense, and even then it took T. S. Eliot to understand their significance for the modern poet.

Elisabeth A. Howe (essay date 1990)

SOURCE: "Self-mockery: Laforgue," in *Stages of Self: The Dramatic Monologues of Laforgue, Valéry & Mallarmé,* Ohio University Press, 1990, pp. 51-91.

[*In the following excerpt, Howe undertakes a stylistic analysis of Laforgue's poetry that focuses on its dramatic qualities.*]

i) From unicity to multiplicity

> Quand j'organise une descente en Moi,
> J'en conviens, je trouve là, attablée,
> Une société un peu bien mêlée,
> Et que je n'ai point vue à mes octrois.

Such is the experience of the speaker of Laforgue's poem "Ballade." "JE est un autre," Rimbaud had written some fifteen years earlier, in the context of his critical remarks about Romantic poetry; Laforgue shares this sense of the "otherness" of the self, insisting indeed on the presence of a multiplicity of "others." According to Warren Ramsey, Laforgue had learned from the philosopher Hartmann "to think of the human individual as an aggregate, a sum of many individuals." Such a viewpoint must clearly affect the nature of the poetic "I," tending to invalidate the notion of the single, unified persona typical of Browning's early dramatic monologues, and of the lyric "I" associated with Romantic poetry. Yet Laforgue had begun writing in a highly Romantic vein: the speaker of the poems collected under the title *Le Sanglot de la terre,* but never published, dwells constantly on his own personal preoccupations: his awe at the vastness of the universe; his shocked awareness of the insignificance and transience of man's life; his horror of death. "Je puis mourir demain" is an oft-repeated phrase, and he hates to think that after death "Tout se fera sans moi!" ("L'Impossible"). These poems are of a philosophical cast, inspired by Laforgue's reading of Hartmann and his knowledge of Schopenhauer; the tone is for the most part one of high seriousness. Meditations on the fate of mankind produce a sense of cosmic despair:

> Eternité, pardon. Je le vois, notre terre
> N'est, dans l'universel hosannah des splendeurs,
> Qu'un atome où se se joue une farce éphémère.
>
>   ("Farce éphémère")

The speaker of these poems pontificates about Man and Life in verse reminiscent of both Hugo and Baudelaire:

> Enfin paraît un jour, grêle, blême d'effroi,
> L'Homme au front vers l'azur, le grand maudit, le roi.
>
>   . . . . .
>
> La femme hurle aux nuits, se tord et mord ses draps
> Pour pondre des enfants vils, malheureux, ingrats.
>
>   ("Litanies de misère")

Already in February 1881 Laforgue expressed "disgust" with this early verse; by 1882 he was more emphatic: "Je me suis aperçu que mon volume de vers était un ramassis de petites saletés banales et je le refais avec rage." The result of this burst of activity in 1883 was the *Complaintes,* published in 1885.

[Warren Ramsey notes in *Jules Laforgue and the Ironic Inheritance,* 1953, that there exists] in the majority of the *Complaintes,* "a movement towards dramatization, a tendency, having its origin in self-awareness and self-defence, to exteriorize the lyric emotion." This exteriorization is achieved largely through the use of different voices, leading away from the straightforward expression of the personal feeling of a single "I." The disgust Laforgue later felt for the *Sanglot* poems was undoubtedly partly inspired by their self-centred mode of writing: in the "Préludes autobiographiques," a long poem which he insisted on including as a prologue to the *Complaintes* in order to show what his literary "autobiography" had been and how his poetic aims had changed, he mocks his former tendency to see himself as the centre of the universe:

> J'espérais
> Qu'à ma mort, tout frémirait, du cèdre à l'hysope;
> Que ce Temps, déraillant, tomberait en syncope,
> Que, pour venir jeter sur mes lèvres des fleurs,
> Les Soleils très navrés détraqueraient leurs choeurs.

The themes of the *Complaintes* are often similar to those of the *Sanglot* poems, but they are treated differently. Instead of the first-person diction of *Le Sanglot de la terre,* thoughts and feelings are distributed among many voices belonging to different personae and expressed indirectly, resulting in a much lighter, less morbid type of verse, even when the subject is still death. In the poem "Guitare," from the *Sanglot* collection, a solemn narrating (or sermonizing) voice predicts, in alternating alexandrines and octosyllables, the death of a beautiful Parisienne and how soon she will be forgotten by her contemporaries. No "I" speaks in this poem, but the address to the lady in the second person presupposes a first-person "shifter," a lyric "I," as the serious-minded speaker of these lines. In the *Complaintes,* however, the very different "Complainte de l'oubli des morts" also treats the theme of the dead being forgotten by the living, but the identity of the poem's speaker radically alters the tone of the poem. Rather than a heavily moralistic accent we hear the more light-hearted, if wistful, voice of the grave-digger, a man with plenty of experience of death, which explains his familiar, almost flippant remarks:

> Les morts
> C'est sous terre;
> Ça n'en sort
> Guère.

He has considerable sympathy for the dead ("Pauvres morts hors des villes!") and his attitude to the living is not without sympathy, though the very nature of his employment represents a threat to them, as he gently points out:

> Mesdames et Messieurs,
> Vous dont la soeur est morte,
> Ouvrez au fossoyeux
> Qui claque à votre porte;
>
> Si vous n'avez pitié,
> Il viendra (sans rancune)
> Vous tirer par les pieds,
> Une nuit de grand'lune!

The introduction of the grave-digger's voice, the shorter lines and choppier rhythms, together with the removal of the Baudelairean emphasis on *pourriture* that we find in **"Guitare,"** transform a slow-moving, trite poem-sermon into a much more original and effective one.

The question of love arises less often than one might expect in the *Sanglot* collection, the "I" of these poems being preoccupied with his own destiny to the exclusion of all else. In one poem, however, **"Pour le livre d'amour,"** he complains that

> Je puis mourir demain et je n'ai pas aimé.
> Mes lèvres n'ont jamais touché lèvres de femme,
> Nulle ne m'a donné dans un regard son âme,
> Nulle ne m'a tenu contre son coeur pâmé.
>
> Je n'ai fait que souffrir. . . .

This expression of personal distress can easily be read as that of the poet himself. At one point in the *Complaintes* we hear virtually the same phrase, "Nulle ne songe à m'aimer un peu," but the whole tone of this poem, the **"Complainte de l'automne monotone,"** suggests an ironical attitude on the part of the speaker towards himself, a self-awareness which tends, as Ramsey says, to "exteriorize the lyric emotion":

> Automne, automne, adieu de l'Adieu!
> La tisane bout, noyant mon feu;
> Le vent s'époumonne
> A reverdir la bûche où mon grand coeur tisonne.
> Est-il de vrais yeux?
> Nulle ne songe à m'aimer un peu.

The words "nulle ne veut m'aimer" recur again in the *Complaintes* but this time in the mouth of a third person, the "lui" of the **"Complaintes des pubertés difficiles"**—a thin disguise for Laforgue himself perhaps, but a disguise nevertheless, once more indicating a desire to disclaim direct responsibility for the utterance:

> Mais lui, cabré devant ces soirs accoutumés,
> Où montait la gaîté des enfants de son âge,
> Seul au balcon, disait, les yeux brûlés de rages:
> "J'ai du génie, enfin: nulle ne veut m'aimer!"

Laforgue uses various disguises, or masks, throughout the *Complaintes*: the "ange incurable" and the "Chevalier errant," the "roi de Thulé," the "Sage de Paris" and, most of all, Pierrot. Each disguise makes possible the utterance of a new voice. In subsequent collections also, *L'Imitation de Notre-Dame la lune* and the *Derniers vers,* different voices can be heard, speaking, in David Arkell's words [*Looking for Laforgue,* 1979], for the "multiple selves of Laforgue and others." It is significant that this move from a unified to a multiple self accompanies Laforgue's choice of a more popular, collective form, since the *complainte* was originally a type of folksong. Henri Davenson, in his *Livre des chansons,* distinguishes two categories of oral folk-song, "les *rondes* ou chansons à danser que caractérise la présence d'un refrain," and "les *complaintes* ou récits continus" which have affinities with English "complaints" and ballads. Ballads are a form without an author not only because they are often anonymous, but because they specifically aim at objectivity: the "I" of the poet is never mentioned, only that of the various characters. Laforgue seems to be seeking a similar kind of anonymity by attributing his poems to different speakers.

According to Laforgue himself, he first thought of writing poems based on *complaintes* on September 20, 1880, during a celebration in the Place Danfert-Rochereau, when he heard—not of course for the first time—popular songs sung in the street. By the late nineteenth century, the style of the *complainte* had lost the freshness and vigour of the original folk-songs. Davenson is reluctant even to mention the "compositions auxquelles avait fini par se restreindre le nom de complainte," namely "chansons volontairement composées à l'intention du public populaire . . . qui prétendaient descendre du peuple, et qui en fait étaient descendues bien bas." They had become "récits détaillés . . . d'un prosaïsme écoeurant et . . . d'une intolérable tristesse"; their sentimentality can be seen reflected in the work of poets such as Richepin. Nevertheless, Laforgue seizes on those aspects of the *complaintes* which suit his purposes. He frequently imitates the popular diction of the *complainte,* for the phrasing, syntax and vocabulary of his second volume of poetry are far removed from the more literary tone of *Le Sanglot.* The songs sung by organ-grinders and other street musicians employed, not the traditional versification of poetry but the rhythms of popular speech, in which mute "e's" did not count as syllables and the hiatus between vowels was filled with a "z" or a "t" sound. Laforgue sometimes adopts these features, as if to emphasize that what we hear is not his voice but the anonymous speech of the "folk," as in:

> Je suis-t-il malhûreux!
>> ("**Autre complainte de l'orgue de barbarie**")
>
> C'est l'printemps qui s'amène
>> ("**Complainte des printemps**")
>
> Voyez l'homme, voyez!
> Si ça n'fait pas pitié!
>> ("**Complainte du pauvre corps humain**")

and in the two poems which he indicates as being variations on actual songs, the "**Complainte du pauvre jeune homme**" and the "**Complainte de l'époux outragé.**"

Davenson defines *complaintes* as "récits continus," in opposition to the "chanson" or "ronde." Like the ballad, the *complainte* implies narrative, which is, to some extent, a feature of Laforgue's *Complaintes*. Almost all his speakers have a story to tell, usually involving a loss they have sustained and which forms the subject of their lament: a lost love in the "**Complainte de la bonne défunte**" or the "**Complainte des blackboulés**," lost innocence in the "**Complainte du roi de Thulé**," lost wealth and health in the "**Complainte des grands pins dans une villa abandonnée**." However, the affinity of the *Complaintes* to the ballad is limited, since the latter is essentially a third-person form, whereas the *Complaintes,* as well as Laforgue's later poetry, are written in the first person: they are monologues and many of them, specifically, dramatic monologues.

ii) Dramatic monologue and interior monologue

It is significant that, like Browning, though in a much more modest fashion, Laforgue began his career by attempting to write plays, as well as poetry. In 1882—the year he abandoned the *Sanglot de la terre* poems—he wrote, but did not complete, *Pierrot fumiste,* in which the hero puts on "the same ironic and poignant comic mask" as Lord Pierrot in the *Complaintes*. According to Haskell Block, Laforgue "planned several plays . . . and worked on at least some of them," in 1882-83, as his correspondence shows. Apart from the unfinished *Pierrot fumiste,* however, his only published play, or playlet, is *Le Concile féérique* (1886), a verse drama composed of five poems from the *Fleurs de bonne volonté,* which Laforgue had decided not to publish.

Various critics have noted the basically dramatic impulse of Laforgue's poetry, though few refer to his poems as dramatic monologues. Block talks of the "intrinsically dramatic character of Laforgue's poetry with its complex interplay of several voices," and Ramsey mentions the "dramatic form of the most characteristic *Complaintes,*" with their dialogues of "many voices." Not surprisingly, the "many voices" heard in Laforgue's *Complaintes* and later collections often engage one another in dialogue, and dialogue is inherently dramatic, since it constitutes the distinctive form of stage drama. Again it represents a move away from the authoritative discourse of a central

"I," allowing room for the speech of others or for internal debate. In some of Laforgue's earlier poems, opposing voices are channelled into an actual dialogue between two speakers like the "LUI" and "ELLE" of the "**Complainte des formalités nuptiales.**" The "**Complainte sous le figuier boudhique**" boasts four sets of speakers, all named; but more commonly speakers are not designated in this way, the alternations in their speech being indicated by the use of quotation marks, as in the "**Complainte des grands pins dans une villa abandonnée.**" Sometimes the main speaker's words are not enclosed in quotation marks, only those of his imaginary interlocutor, for example in the "**Complainte des printemps,**" the "**Complainte des pianos . . .**" and *Derniers vers* VIII and IX. Finally, the voices of the dialogue can reflect opposing views solely within the mind of one speaker—the conflicting attitudes of the "société un peu bien mêlée" making up the self:

> Mais, Tout va la reprendre!—Alors Tout m'en absout.
> Mais, Elle est ton bonheur!—Non, je suis trop immense
> Trop chose.
>> ("**Complainte des Consolations**")

The frequent suggestion of a dialogue within the mind of one speaker, as in this poem and especially in the *Derniers vers,* reflects the fact that many of Laforgue's speakers are engaged in some form of conflict with themselves, which again contributes an element of drama to his poems, since conflict is in itself essentially dramatic. Indeed, Laforgue's personae are nearly always torn between two opposite impulses: between the desire for love and a mocking rejection of it, as in *Derniers vers* IX; between a feeling of sympathy for women and an instinctive suspicion of their motives (e.g., in *Dv* V and VIII); between a sensual and an ideal love (*Dv* III and "**Complainte de Lord Pierrot**"); between patient devotion and impatient desire ("**Locutions des Pierrots, I**"). Whereas the speakers of Browning's early dramatic monologues are not engaged in any conflict with themselves, only with the outside world, their freedom from inner division confirming their status as characters with well-defined personalities and views, Laforgue's protagonists, on the contrary, suffer from inner conflicts, doubts and hesitations, and from a general lack of confidence that makes it hard for them to establish their own identity. The speaker of *Dv* III confides:

> . . . j'allais me donner d'un "Je vous aime"
> Quand je m'avisai non sans peine
> Que d'abord je ne me possédais pas bien moi-même.

The dramatic irony in Browning's poems, arising from the discrepancy between the speaker's apprehension of his situation and the reader's understanding of it, leads to collusion between author and reader behind the speaker's back; the factor causing the speaker to distort reality is, very often, simply his own personality, with its prejudices and blind spots. In Laforgue's work there is still enough emphasis on character traits for the reader (and the poet) similarly to judge the speakers—but not behind their backs, because they forestall criticism by judging themselves, too. Thus the speaker of *Dv* IX avoids being labelled as incurably romantic in his desire to "Faire naître un 'Je t'aime!'" by the irony implicit in the sheer exaggeration of his wishes:

> Qu'il vienne, comme à l'aimant la foudre,
> Et dans mon ciel d'orage qui craque et qui s'ouvre,
> Et alors, les averses lustrales jusqu'au matin,
> Le grand clapissement des averses toute la nuit!
>   Enfin!

Again, in *Dv* XII, the patent irony of the speaker's exclamation "Oh! arrose, arrose / Mon coeur si brûlant, ma chair si intéressante!" shows that although he feels desperate and melancholy, he is also the sort of sophisticated person who—like the reader and the poet—finds desperate melancholy ludicrous. The drama in Laforgue's poems derives more from the internal conflict within the speaker and from the irony that discloses it, than from any discrepancy between his view of himself and our own.

The presence of dialogue in Laforgue's poetry disguises, paradoxically, another essential difference between his monologues and those of Browning. In the majority of Browning's dramatic monologues, the speaker directly addresses a listener, with the poem as a whole representing one side of a dialogue. In most of Laforgue's poems, however, the speakers are alone; any dialogue is purely imaginary, consisting either of comments which the speaker mentally attributes to someone else or words which one side of his personality addresses to another, within the privacy of his own mind. In other words these monologues present, not the speech of a given character to an interlocutor, but his private thoughts, his inner language. For this reason, Laforgue's poems are sometimes referred to as "interior" rather than "dramatic" monologues. J. P. Houston, for example, suggests [in *French Symbolism and the Modernist Movement*, 1980] that the "monologue created by Laforgue is largely an inner one, and if the analogy with drama is appropriate to the monologue invented by Browning, that with the stream-of-consciousness novel is more so in this case." Interior monologue, as practised by Joyce and by Dujardin before him, strives to transcribe in writing the random, fragmentary nature of the "stream of consciousness," of thought as it is formed in the mind. Dujardin asserts that interior monologue represents "un discours antérieur à toute organisation logique"; its form is therefore very simple: "il se réalise en phrases directes réduites au minimum syntaxial." He admits, however, that interior monologue cannot claim to reproduce man's barely-conscious thought-processes verbatim, but can only give the impression of doing so: "Le monologue intérieur ne doit pas donner la pensée 'tout venat,' mais en donner l'impression." This impression is conveyed partly by the use of short "direct sentences" with very loose and abbreviated syntax, and partly by the way the thoughts expressed jump from one subject to another, by a process of free association, often

without any apparent logical connection: "Notre pensée court d'un plan à l'autre avec une rapidité qui après coup peut sembler mais n'est pas de la simultanéité; et c'est précisément cette course" à bâtons rompus' dont le monologue intérieur donne l'impression."

Laforgue's *Derniers vers,* in particular, answer to some of these criteria. Written in *vers libres,* where each line represents a unit of meaning, they adopt a loose, elliptical syntax impossible in regular verse:

> Noire bise, averse glapissante,
> Et fleuve noire, et maisons closes,
> Et quartiers sinistres comme des Morgues,
> Et l'Attardé qui à la remorque traîne
> Toute la misère des coeurs et des choses,
> Et la souillure des innocentes qui traînent. . . .
>
>   (*Derniers vers* XII)

The paratactic arrangement of this passage, with juxtaposition replacing logical subordination, is typical of the *Derniers vers,* and of the interior monologue, since the barely-formulated thoughts which spring from the stream of consciousness have not yet been ordered by logic. They tend to be linked together by a process of free-association, also found in certain passages of the *Derniers vers,* for example the opening of *Dv* X, where the basic themes—of love-making and marriage—conjure up a variety of unexpected but related images:

> O géraniums diaphanes, guerroyeurs sortilèges,
> Sacrilèges monomanes!
> Emballages, dévergondages, douches! O pressoirs
> Des vendanges des grands soirs!
> Layettes aux abois,
> Thyrses au fond des bois!
> Transfusions, représailles,
> Relevailles, compresses et l'éternelle potion,
> Angélus! n'en pouvoir plus
> De débâcles nuptiales! de débâcles nuptiales! . . .

These characteristics of Laforgue's poetry have led Scarfe to claim not only that he wrote interior monologues, but that he invented the form; in an essay on Eliot [in *Eliot in Perspective,* edited by Graham Martin, 1970], he asserts that Laforgue "invented a new kind of dramatic monologue, usually known as the interior or internal monologue, close to common speech," and implies that Dujardin developed the technique of *Les Lauriers sont coupés* from Laforgue "without acknowledgement." It is true that many lines in Laforgue resemble "common speech' in rhythm, vocabulary and syntax, but at the same time the abundance of scientific, erudite, foreign and archaic words in his poetry destroys the illusion of oral speech, and with it the impression of spontaneity appropriate to interior monologue. In any case, the all-pervading irony of his poetry (to which these verbal juxtapositions contribute) suggests a fully-conscious, deliberate type of writing, irony being the opposite of spontaneous. Furthermore, it is difficult to see how the acoustic effects Laforgue achieves through alliteration, assonance and rhyme can be associated with the supposedly barely-formulated thoughts of the stream of consciousness; or indeed how poetry, which always involves organisational principles of one kind or another, could ever seriously attempt to imitate the disorderly ramblings of the inner monologue.

Though it may be true, then, that certain features of Laforgue's poetry, such as the use of parataxis and of free association, influenced his friend Dujardin to some extent, the claim that Laforgue "invented the internal monologue" is exaggerated. Both interior monologue and poems like Laforgue's *Derniers vers* present a character's thoughts rather than his speech, but there is another important difference between the two, besides the issue of spontaneity. The thoughts of Laforgue's monologues are concentrated on a specific problem or event, unlike the loosely-connected discourse of interior monologue which supposedly records a character's stream of consciousness over a period of time and is not directed solely at a particular topic. Wayne Booth makes this point regarding Stephen's interior monologue in *A Portrait of the Artist as a Young Man,* which "unlike speech in a dramatic scene," does not "lead us to suspect that the thoughts have been in any way aimed at an effect." The discourse of a Laforguian monologue, however, like "speech in a dramatic scene," *is* aimed at an effect. Apart from the poem's effect on the reader, obtained by the deliberate manipulation of rhythms, sounds, or images, and dramatic effects achieved through irony, the speakers themselves have an aim, namely to come to terms with a specific problem or event around which the whole poem revolves. Such problems are, for example, in *Dv* **VII**—regret for a lost love; in **XI** the faithlessness of women, and how to deal with it; in **X**—the conflict between the speaker's need for independence and his nostalgia for a "petit intérieur" to share with his "petite quotidienne"; in **V**—a call for a change from love as practised by men and women of the time to the type of love-relationship the speaker advocates, in which the woman would no longer be regarded as an "angel," but as man's equal. In these poems, all the thoughts expressed are in some way relevant to those themes, whereas in interior monologue the thought "court d'un plan à l'autre," as Dujardin says, reflecting the "course à bâtons rompus" of the stream of consciousness. The content of a Joycean interior monologue is often very much affected by the subject's surroundings, which impinge on his thoughts, but in Laforgue's *Derniers vers* the speaker's present position is not necessarily mentioned at all; if so, then it is directly relevant to the problem in hand, as in *Dv* **III**:

> Or, cette nuit anniversaire, toutes les Walkyries du vent
> Sont revenues beugler par les fentes de ma porte:
> *Vae soli!*

or in *Dv* **VII**:

> Voici qu'il fait très très-frais
> Oh! si à la même heure,
> Elle va de même le long des forêts. . . .

Laforgue's monologues, then, though they may have some stylistic similarities with interior monologue, are "aimed at an effect—that of examining and attempting to solve a problem which worries the speaker, or of resolving a conflict within him—and to this extent they are dramatic.

John McCann (essay date 1991)

SOURCE: "Jules Laforgue: Constructing the Text," in *Orbis Litterarum,* Vol. 46, No. 5, 1991, pp. 276-93.

[*In the following essay, McCann explains the creation of meaning in Laforgue's poetry as a process characterized by intertextuality and the changeable nature of language.*]

Many readers may share James Hiddleston's bafflement when faced with Laforgue's writing:

> Calembours, jeux de mots, barbarismes, anacoluthes, non-sens, babil, intertextes saccagés, comment sortir de ce tournoiement chaotique de signifiants apparemment coupés pour toujours de leurs signifiés?

Hiddleston here outlines the main difficulties confronting the reader who tries to establish the meaning of Laforgue's verse. But there is a problem with what Hiddleston proposes as the central principle underlying these semantic difficulties: what are 'signifiants apparemment coupés . . . de leurs signifiés? Surely a 'signifiant' presupposes a linkage to a 'signifié' or 'signifiés'? This point seems to be conceded by Hiddleston when he uses 'apparemment', which implies that the 'signifiants' are only apparently cut off from their 'signifiés'—as though in reality they are still safely attached.

This permits Hiddleston to argue [in *Laforgue aujourd'hui,* 1988, edited by James Hiddleston] that sense is still possible. For him, Laforgue's language is ultimately revelatory:

> Pourtant les mots sont là pour (comme on disait) révéler les obsessions: feuilles, vent, sang, dimanches, couchants, pianos, vendanges . . . , et l'on ne saurait nier l'effect cathartique que produit la lecture. Le miracle, c'est que Laforgue ait réussi à faire de tant de fragments éphémères et du disparate de son expérience un univers unique, entièrement "sui generis", et qui compte parmi les plus émouvants et peut être parmi les plus durables du dix-neuvième siècle.

Laforgue's poetic world is a collage, made up of 'fragments éphémères.' Yet it is constructed in such a way as to be meaningful. It is 'émouvant' for it touches a nerve of understanding within us.

However, Hiddleston is dealing with two different types of meaning. In the first extract quoted above, he is concerned with the semantic content of language. It is this which is so difficult to pin down. In the second quotation, he is interested in the context to which language refers, Laforgue's obsessions, and in the context which it shapes, the 'univers unique.' The question that arises is how it is possible to have a meaningful text that tells the reader something about the world to which it refers when the words in the text are 'signifiants apparemment coupés pour toujours de leurs signifiés.'

There is a third type of meaning that needs to be considered: the significance of our lives, our feeling that it is for some purpose that we live in the universe. Laforgue is in constant search for such meaningfulness in the world:

> Manger, rire, changer—pourtant tout est mystère!
> Dans quel but venons-nous sur ce vieux monde
> et d'où?

Throughout the early poems, his thinking is dominated by a world whose meaning is denied to mankind. It produces in him a variety of reactions including the numbing despair found in **'Spleen.'** This poem creates an enclosed world in which Laforgue is trapped between 'Tout m'ennuie ajourd'hui' and 'je m'ennuie encor.' Physical displacement is no solution since there is in the streets nothing to excite his interest.

The second quatrain is particularly interesting:

> Je regarde sans voir fouillant mon vieux cerveau,
> Et machinalement sur la vitre ternie
> Je fais du bout du doigt de la calligraphie.
> Bah! sortons, je verrai peut-être du nouveau.

The word 'machinalement' is significant for it indicates that the mind is not fully engaged in what is being done. This is important for it is the mind that distinguishes us from the machine and allows us to make meaning. So, what Laforgue is writing is not the bearer of any intended meaning. It has no signified. In other words, this would be an example of what would happen if 'signifiants' were really rather than apparently 'coupés de leurs signifiés.' What would be left would be, not a signifier on its own, but something different—what Laforgue calls 'calligraphie.' What we have is a simulacrum of language, a non-functioning model. There is substance—the marks on the window—without any meaningful content. Consequently, there is neither signifier nor signified.

Laforgue's 'calligraphie' is an object and no more. It has no spiritual, intellectual or emotional charge to convey. Hiddleston would find here no 'tournoiement' nor would he find it 'émouvant.' The letters on the window are meaningless and random in their order. In this respect they are to be distinguished from the fully functioning language of the poem which is the meaningful arrangement of letters into a text.

Walter Ong argues [in *Oralicy and Literacy: The Technologising of the Word,* 1982] that dealing with language in its written form affects our experience of it:

> Sound, as has earlier been explained, exists only when it is going out of existence. I cannot have all the word present at once: when I say 'existence,' by the time I get to the '-tence,' the 'exis-' is gone. The alphabet implies that matters are otherwise, that a word is a thing, not an event, that it is present all at once, and that it can be cut up into little pieces, which can even be written forwards and pronounced backwards: 'p-a-r-t' can be pronounced 'trap.' If you put the word 'part' on a sound tape and reverse the tape, you do not get 'trap,' but a completely different sound, neither 'part' nor 'trap.'

Words, then, may be considered not just as signs composed of signifiers and signifieds but as being composed of letters, the irreducible building-blocks of written script just as atoms are the building blocks of the world. In other words, it is not only Laforgue's poetic world which is made up of 'fragments éphémères,' but words themselves—the fragments in this case being letters which can be brought together into various combinations which may or may not be signs belonging to a signifying system.

This may appear to be an empirical view of language but is in fact as analytical and abstract as the Saussurean division into signifiers and signifieds. In this case the division is into the letters of the alphabet, or as Ong would put it: language is 'cut up into little pieces.' Our alphabet, which is a variant of the one invented by the Greeks, does not attempt to depict objects as do pictograms. Nor does it try to transcribe actual sound units as do syllabaries. The latter, as their name suggests, treat the syllable as the smallest possible sound unit—a reasonable procedure since that is the least that we can pronounce. The alphabet, on the other hand goes beyond the syllable, analysing the subsounds that compose it, as Eric Havelock explains [in *The Literate Revolution in Greece and Its Cultural Consequences,* 1982]:

> Whereas all syllabic systems, including the Semitic shorthand, aim to reproduce the actual spoken units on a one-for-one basis, the Greek produces an atomic system which breaks all units into at least two abstract components and possibly more.

These abstract components which from the basis of our writing are consonants and vowels. It is the former which makes abstraction necessary and useful. A 'consonant' as its name suggests cannot be pronounced in isolation but must always be attached to a vowel. Consequently, a 'b' can be isolated as an abstract idea in writing but when enunciated there will always be a vowel attached to it. A pure 'b' can never be pronounced and, even when we seek to isolate it in speech, as when we spell aloud, the 'b' is always followed by the sound 'i,' thereby becoming a syllable. It is only in alphabetic writing that a 'b' can exist other than as part of a syllable. This ability to divide a sound unit into constituent elements allows the writer to use a limited number of symbols in a variety of permutations so that any sound unit can be conveyed. One result of this is that we also start to consider the spoken language as being capable of similar division. For example, the word 'part' may be thought of as being made up of the sounds 'p-a-r-t' whereas Ong's example of the tape shows that this is not the case. We rarely think of the spoken language as a continuum but rather as an sequence of objects made of smaller basic sound-units or phonemes.

Such an atomistic view of language accords with Laforgue's vision of the structure of the world:

> Puisque le Temps dévore
> Des siècles de soleils, où serez-vous alors,
> Atomes qu'aujourd'hui j'ose appeler mon corps?
> Non, mon corps est à tout, et la nature entière
> N'est qu'un perpétuel échange de matière.
>
> ('Suis-je')

The world of which he is a part is, as he has put it earlier, an 'incessant va et vient / D'atomes éternels.' In short the same bits are shuffled around eternally, just as a basic stock of letters or phonemes is shuffled around to make new bits of language.

The whole world and even the very language used to describe it is made up of Hiddleston's 'fragments éphémères.' Such a view helps us understand better how Laforgue's writing functions. Take the case of words like 'éternullité.' What sort of a signifier are we dealing with here? Does describing language atomistically, as a series of marks help? It does—provided we extend the sense of 'mark' to include that which strikes the ear as well as the eye.

Daniel Grojnowski explains Laforgue's neologisms as follows [in *Jules Laforgue et l'originalité*, 1988]:

> Le plus souvent c'est en effet la sexualité qui met Laforgue en verve de néologie. Au moment où ils sont énoncés, les vocables se chargent d'un sens second. La contiguïté phonique produit un signifiant parasitaire qui démystifie le premier, à moins qu'il ne lui confère sa plénitude signifiante. Les mots font l'amour et s'engrossent les uns les autres:

volupté	*devient* violupté
nuptial	voluptial
réciproque	sexciproque
sensuelles	sangsuelles.

Grojnowski's description of words making love is a witty one but it is limited—a fact acknowledged by the expression 'le plus souvent.' Yet, Grojnowski points us in the right direction. Time becomes space and the 'moment où ils sont énoncés' becomes 'la contiguïté phonique.' Language becomes a spatial phenomenon and this spatialization, this turning of language into a thing, is a prerequisite for the neologisms. It permits us to perceive them as collages. These, furthermore, are not haphazard but are at the service of meaning. They modify it by stripping away romantic accretions—as in 'violupté,' made up of fragments of 'violence' and 'volupté'—a neologism which also brings out the element of cruelty in the voluptuous, thereby restoring to the word its 'plénitude signifiante.' Sometimes the collage is apparent to the

ear, but in others, notably 'sangsuelles,' the effect is more perceptible in the written form. In both cases language is treated as thing—either an acoustic or visual object capable of being broken into fragments which can then be used to form new and interesting words.

Indeed, such an argument would be supported by the following claim by Grojnowski:

> Plus de trente fois répété, le mot LUNE incante par anagramme l'entité NULE, de même que RIEN recèle et dissémine NIER.

In the first example there is a collage of the written and spoken forms with the inclusion of the 'e,' silent in both cases and so perceptible only to the eye, and the use of a single 'l' instead of the double 'l' the eye expects, the justification being that there is no difference in sound. In the second case, the anagram is visual: it is not the sounds of 'rien' that are rearranged but its letters. This is a slightly more complex version of the expressive possibilities hinted at by Ong's example of 't-r-a-p' and 'p a r-t.'

The process can be carried a stage further, as Grojnowski argues:

> Le jeu des mots transforme les virtualités de la compétence en performance de fait. Si l'"Eternullité" comprend également l' "Ether-nullité," elle produit également l'"Ether-nue-litée" dans sons sens érotique et cosmique. Alors que l'univers est agi par un seul et même tropisme, "omniversel" produit fatalement "omni-vers-celle," et ainsi de suite.

Thus the reader is invited to read beyond the level of the word, to scrutinize its component atoms and see that they too have logic and sense. Meaning is present in abundance. Yet, if all this is made possible through points of resemblance between language and 'calligraphie,' why is it that 'calligraphie' is devoid of meaning? What is it that allows language to function as a means of communication while 'calligraphie' does not?

That something is missing is clear. Language is calligraphie combined with something else. Remove this vital element and all that is left is the nonfunctioning model found above in **'Spleen.'** A parallel may be drawn here between language and man. In many traditions, the latter is held to be an amalgam of body and spirit. The body is the physical substance while the spirit animates it. When the spirit is separated from the body as in death, then the body ceases to function:

> Le long des marbriers (Encore un beau commerce!)
> Patauge aux défoncés un convoi, sous l'averse.
>
> Un trou, qu'asperge un prêtre âgé qui se morfond,
> Bâille à ce libéré de l'être; et voici qu'on
>
>   Le déverse
>   Au fond.
>   **'Complainte de l'ange incurable'**

The corpse is unable to move under its own power. Rather, it has movement imposed upon it. Furthermore, it is impelled into an area where the living cannot follow. Thus the mourners accompany the body to the graveside. The 'prêtre âgé' whose sounds are echoed by 'ce libéré de l'être' is a threshold figure but one who remains firmly on this side of the grave. The separation of the living and the dead is brought out by the rupture between 'on,' the anonymous source of the corpse's movement, and the 'Le,' the corpse itself. In addition the break is over a stanza and the suddenly shortened lines, whose endings are clearly marked by rhyme, convey the impression of an object receding from view.

The description of the body as 'ce libéré de l'être' suggests that the living being is made up of two parts, one of which is the 'être' and the other of which is the remains thrown into the grave. The idea is a striking, and perhaps even perverse, inversion of the traditional notion of the spirit being liberated from the body. In this case the liberation is ironic since without its spiritual essence, its 'être,' the body ceases to function and becomes a mere simulacrum of a human being. A parallel may be drawn here with the split between signified and signifier which turns normal 'écriture' into 'calligraphie,' so that the latter may be said to be the cadaver of writing.

Language is like human beings, or for that matter the world—a collection of atoms, which in this case are letters, animated by some force which gives them meaning and purpose. The question then arises of whether or not the world is like a piece of writing and so capable of decipherment like any written text:

> Je songe à notre Terre, atome d'un moment,
> Dans l'Infini criblé d'étoiles éternelles,
> Au peu qu'ont déchiffré nos débiles prunelles,
> Au Tout qui nous est clos inexorablement.
>
> ('**Triste, triste**')

Hence, we constantly see Laforgue questioning the stars, seeking the meaning and purpose of the universe. Yet the only reply is silence as in '**Sanglot perdu**' which concludes:

> "Quelqu'un veille-t-il aux nuits solennelles?
> Qu'on parle! Est-ce oubli, hasard ou courroux?
> Pourquoi notre sort? C'est à rendre fous!" . . .
> —Les étoiles d'or rêvaient éternelles . . .

The last line is a repetition of the first line of the poem but with a slightly different function a pattern repeated elsewhere in these early poems. However, the meaning in context of each line, its referential as opposed to semantic meaning, is different. When the line first appears it suggests the possibility that the stars may be aroused to give a response whereas its second appearance indicates the unchanging indifference of the heavens to humanity.

It is important to distinguish here between what changes and what does not. The stars do not change. They are in the same pattern as before and these patterns to not re-

spond to the probing by humanity. The words and letters used are the same in the first line and in the last. Semantically there is no difference. What changes is the situation they describe. The reality to which an utterance refers, therefore, is detachable. It can be replaced by a different one. If it is not replaced, if the words do not refer, then they become truly dead, as uncommunicative as the letters Laforgue draws on the windowpane. On the other hand, meaning can only make itself manifest through the material of language—it cannot be apprehended otherwise. If it exists outside language, then it is cut off from our apprehension of it.

This is what lies at the heart of the story told in the '**Complainte du Roi de Thulé**':

> "Soleil! Soleil! moi je descends
> Vers vos navrants palais polaires,
> Dorloter dans ce Saint-Suaire
>   Votre cœur bien en sang,
>   En le bêrçant!"
>
> Il dit, et, le Voile étendu,
>   Tout éperdu,
> Vers les coraux et les naufrages,
> Le roi raillé des doux corsages,
>   Beau comme un Mage
>   Est descendu!

The king is a man obsessed by change and yet unable to come to terms with it. He is himself 'Immaculé,' insulated from sin and the corruption that it brings but deeply hurt by the nature of the changing world: '[il] Pleurait sur la métempsychose / Des lys en roses.' At last, he follows the dying sun as it withdraws from the world, beyond the coral reefs and shipwrecks.

The poem, however, does not follow the king all the way. It goes as far as the edge of the known world and then watches the king as he descends out of view. When the king returns, he is transformed:

> Braves amants! aux nuits de lait,
>   Tournez vos clés!
> Une ombre d'amour pur transie,
> Viendrait vous gémir cette scie:
> "Il était un roi de Thulé
>   Immaculé . . ."

Not only has the masculine become feminine in the change from 'roi' to 'ombre,' but the physical has been changed into the spiritual. The king is a spirit of pure and absolute love. He contrasts with the particular and physical 'amants,' whose plural suggests a dependence on each other. Yet, how does this spirit make itself felt in the world? The answer is through language—but not perhaps as we normally understand it. The shade's language is described as a 'scie,' that is, language which exists in a pre-fixed form. In fact, as in '**Sanglot perdu**,' the poem ends with a reprise of the opening. These words, which even on their initial appearance recall a popular song, Gounod's *Faust,* a poem by Goethe and a song by

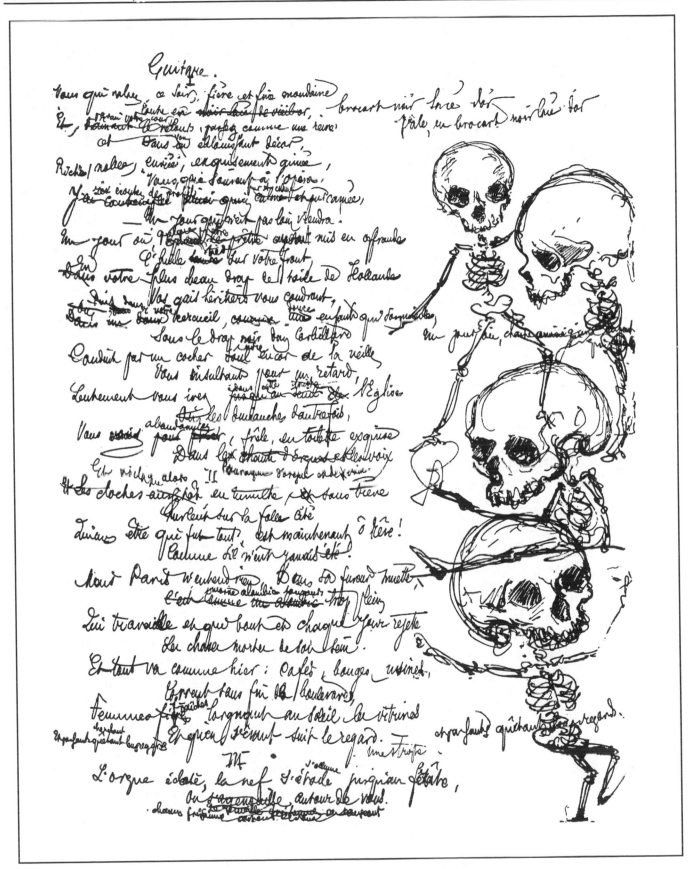

Early verse and sketches by Laforgue.

Schubert, are quoted as a bloc but, as in **'Sanglot perdu,'** their significance is different from that of their first appearance. We are less tempted to look through them than at them. Their nature as artefact—or as part of an artefact—is more obvious. They are not about the king but are the king in so far as they are the only means by which we can apprehend him.

It is thus possible to say that for Laforgue, language is like matter. It is made of a limited number of letters just as matter is made of the atoms of the elements listed in the periodic table. Moreover, the combinations that we call words can themselves be combined into bigger groupings which are sentences or phrases just as substances such as clay can be made into bricks or iron into rods. It is possible furthermore to take phrases and sentences, bits of language, and use them to build other structures just as bricks make houses or rods are used to create a piece of machinery. Morover, just as it is possible to re-use bricks or rods in other structures of which they were not originally a part, so it is possible to use bits of language from other sources to make up a text. Sometimes as has been seen this will be simply reprises within poems. On other occasions there will be re-use of elements from one poem to another as in:

> Dans l'Infini criblé d'étoiles éternelles
> > ('**Triste, triste**')
> Dans l'Infini criblé d'éternelles splendeurs
> > ('**Médiocrité**')

Another clear example of this is the re-using of elements from *Les Fleurs de Bonne Volonté* in the composition of the **Derniers Vers**. Yet it is clear from the above example and from a study of the parallels between the two collections mentioned above that Laforgue is capable of varying existing elements when he uses them again.

Using old material in new ways enables Laforgue to exploit the clich—something normally avoided in poetry. **'Autre complainte de lord Pierrot'** demonstrates how the cliché may be successfully used:

> Celle qui doit me mettre au courant de la Femme!
> Nous lui dirons d'abord, de mon air le moins froid:
> "La somme des angles d'un triangle, chère âme,
> > "Est égale à deux droits."
>
> Et si ce cri lui part: "Dieu de Dieu! que je
> t'aime!"
> —"Dieu reconnaîtra les siens." Ou piquée au vif:
> —"Mes claviers ont du coeur, tu seras mon seul
> thème."
> > Moi: "Tout est relatif."

The literal meaning of each item of speech is clear and poses no difficulties. Each in fact is a cliché, whose meaning in most contexts is accepted without reflection. A conversation built up of clichés is one where the speakers assemble ready-made elements so as to speed to a conclusion without having to stop for thought along the way. In fact, the way they are normally combined is also ruled by cliché so that when the expression 'que je t'aime' is met it is not hard to predict a likely response. No real meaning, nothing of any significance, is communicated. What happens in this poem is that the literal meanings of each of the elements do not fit into a coherent whole. This is because Pierrot's speech, although just as cliché-ridden as the woman's and therefore just as pointless, uses clichés inappropriate to the situation. There is no predictability. He is breaking the conventions, providing new combinations rather like those in 'violupté,' except that these are at the level of the sentence. In so doing, he forces the reader to look at the words and try to work out a way of proceeding from one utterance to the next. The cliché'd ways of relating one to another do not work and so new relationships are sought that will allow the various utterances to form a coherent dialogue. As was the case with the neologisms, this can bring out shades of meaning that were potentially there in the original but which habit had obscured. Thus when the penultimate line of the above quotation claims that the bond between the lovers is unique, the reply claims that everything is relative to everything else. Such a denial of exclusivity can be seen to be relevant to what has preceded it so that Pierrot's side of the dialogue is an oblique and ironic commentary on the woman's. Behind the literal meaning of the words lies hidden another meaning that can only be discovered by considering the way the various utterances relate to each other. The context of an atterance, determined by its relationship to other utterances, thus determines its meaning, changing it into something new.

This element of change is very important. It is change that is the basis of all life—which is as Laforgue has put it above a 'perpétuelle échange de matière' or a 'métempsychose.' The dead body has lost its power to change just as the king has lost his power to say anything new in words new-minted for the occasion. Yet that limitation does not apply to Laforgue when writing his poetry. Unlike the occasion when he writes on the window, Laforgue is dealing with a language that is capable of change and where change is significant. Altering a meaningless letter in a meaningless sequence makes no difference—and difference is what lies at the heart of meaning. Thus the words of the king repeated unchangingly by him, have, as we have seen, a different meaning for the reader on each appearance because the latter takes into account the context as well as semantics.

Once again we are confronted with the phenomenon whereby meaning is not indissolubly linked to a particular form of words or a particular form of words tied down to just one meaning even though meaning cannot make itself manifest except through these words. Language is a medium for meaning. Without language there would be no meaning and without meaning there would be no language. However, the link between the two is subject to flux. As we have seen, meaning may change even though the language may be the same but, by the same token, language itself may be subject to alteration.

It no less than human beings is subject to the rearrangement of living matter described in '**Triste, triste**':

> Puis nous allons fleurir les beaux pissenlits d'or.

This is what distinguishes living matter from what is inert: the possibility of absorbing other matter into the organism and making it part of itself.

Transformation is a part of both life and language. Laforgue's starting point for this process is below the level of the word. His building blocks are smaller and this is what allows him to create neologisms such as 'violupté' or 'éternullité.' Furthermore, the reader understands what is being said—he grasps the compositional principles that lie behind such new words. This is because he accepts that words are made up of sub-units which are combined in a meaningful way.

However, if change is an essential part of life, then the question of its being a source of anguish must be tackled. As was seen in the '**Complainte du Roi de Thulé**,' it was 'métempsychose' that caused his weeping. The purity of the lily was being changed into the rose with its intimations of passion, blood and mortality. Change is presented as a change for the worse. This is true elsewhere in Laforgue's poetry as, for example, '**Locutions des Pierrots xiv**':

> Retroussant d'un air de défi
> Mes manches de mandarin pâle,
> J'arrondis ma bouche et—j'exhale
> Des conseils doux de Crucifix.

Christ is reborn as Pierrot. His miracles and teachings become a magician's tricks and patter. The world is gradually winding down and what exists now is a lesser version of what happened in the past. The grandeur of Christ finds its modern counterpart in Pierrot. Yet, even in the very heart of Pierrot's ridiculousness, there is still preserved some of the grandeur that was Christ's. The comparison is double-edged. It presents Pierrot as a figure of both tragedy and farce.

Thus change is diminution but it is not total loss. Something of value is preserved as life is recycled, as can be seen in the following example from the '**Complainte de l'ange incurable**':

> Où vont les gants d'avril et les rames d'antan?

which echoes Villon's refrain:

> Mais ou sont les neiges d'antan?

The re-use of Villon is more than just decorative. It is more than a learned allusion that allows Laforgue to show off the extent of his reading. Instead it is there to express meaning. Villon's language is dislocated in the 'tournoiement chaotique' that is Laforgue's poetic practice so that it expresses Laforgue's meaning rather than Villon's. Laforgue is not quoting Villon but rather using words similar to his but with a meaning that is the

former's alone. Thus the imagery is changed to fit the poem's evocation of a lakeside in Spring while at the same time 'rames' which belongs to the literary register underscores the point made by the reference to Villon—that this is a linguistic artefact. Change is vital to meaning and it is the difference between Laforgue and Villon rather than literal quotation that is of interest to the reader. Thus the change from Villon's 'sont' to Laforgue's 'vont' is atomistic, a mere letter's difference, but that one change alters the meaning considerably. The semantic gap between the two words is indicative of the different perceptions each poet is conveying. Villon is lamenting irrevocable loss. It is a state which is incapable of change. Laforgue, on the other hand, is lamenting the process of loss. Unlike Villon's snows, Laforgue's gloves are still here even though they are under threat. The latter is thus aware of losing something but is equally conscious that something is still left.

A parallel may be drawn here with the situations of the mourners and the corpse later in the poem. The corpse cannot move of its own volition and so is dead. The mourners on the other hand may be moving towards the grave, an intimation of their own mortality, but as long as they are moving they are still alive. The paradox is that life is a process of movement towards death. Once we stop moving towards death, we die. Change may be a sign of decay but it is also a sign of vitality. Villon's words are changed and in the process become less noble. However, Laforgue's version of them gives them a new meaning: he revitalizes them. This is the 'du nouveau' denied the writer of 'calligraphie' in '**Spleen**.' It is found not in objects—whether they be things or words—but rather in the meanings they convey to us.

Consequently, intertextuality, the use of other authors' texts, is of a piece with what we have seen of Laforgue's thought. The world is made up of atoms and in a similar fashion language is made up of letters. Whatever is in the world is constructed by nature or man just as a text is constructed by its author. The laws of science mean that nothing is truly destroyed, nothing truly created—matter is endlessly recycled albeit in new forms. This applies to man as well as to what he creates. He has a repertoire of letters with which he can compose. He also has a stock of letters already assembled into words. In addition, there is at his disposal a set of pre-fabricated texts from other authors or even his own works. Laforgue's achievement is to realize that all this is part of a continuum, a single process. He understands how language is built up into a poetic text and exploits that knowledge to create 'du nouveau'—strange forms and structures that nevertheless signify. He changes and adapts the raw material that is in front of him. He dismantles language so as to build anew, using only the elements that he needs and discarding the rest. It is the same poetic process that produces both 'violupté' and:

> Où vont les gants d'avril, et les rames d'antan?

Hiddleston, however, takes a more negative view of Laforgue's intertextuality:

Grâce à l'envoûtement de ces multiples échos on croit d'abord éprouver la même ouverture de notre mémoire et de notre espace culturels que dans "Les Phares", mais on a vite fait de se rendre compte que l'effet en est beaucoup plus nuancé et ambigu. Le procédé, qu'emploie Laforgue est en fin de compte assez analogue à l'ironie de la répétition, mais là encore il s'agit d'une ironie qui démolit non seulement les textes auxquels elle renvoie, mais qui est elle aussi démolie du même coup. Le texte laforguien semble en effet se défaire sous nos yeux pour se déclarer tout aussi gratuit et éphémère que les intertextes dont il s'est nourri.

For him Laforgue's poetry shows a tendency to self-destruct and at times is reduced to 'un simple exercice de style, ou pis encore à un jeu de mots.' Indeed, he speaks of Laforgue's poetry in terms which betoken failure:

> Ce qui manque à la parole laforguienne c'est la capacité d'établir des vérités stables et permanentes, ou d'affirmer quoi que ce soit, et d'organiser le disparate des énoncés en un ensemble cohérent de significations.

Yet just a few lines later Hiddleston makes the claim (quoted above) about the value of Laforgue's work:

> Le miracle, c'est que Laforgue ait réussi à faire de tant de fragments éphémères et du disparate de son expérience un univers unique, entièrement "sui generis", et qui compte parmi les plus émouvants et peut-être parmi les plus durables du dix-neuvième siècle.

While not explaining how this comes about—it is a 'miracle'—the above does seem to point to some constructive process or other within Laforgue's poetry. The verb 'faire' echoes and reverses the earlier use of 'se défaire' and 'univers' implies some sort of coherence or fitting together of parts into a whole. Consequently, though Hiddleston lays great stress on the negative aspects of Laforgue's poetic practice, there is also a recognition that his poetry is itself a positive achievement. What Laforgue has done is create a fictional universe out of fragments of text, just as the King of Thule's veil is woven from threads. It is important to make this point in view of Hiddleston's earlier remark about Laforgue's poetry being at times reduced to the level of word play. What Laforgue is working with is language and ultimately that is what his poems are—verbal creations.

However, these exist in time and are affected by it. Hiddleston's phrase 'tournoiement chaotique' shows not just spatial movement but also implies movement in time (for without time there cannot be movement) and that this movement is no more than going round in meaningless circles. Yet, time is also essential to life and creativity. Without movement in time, there is only death. The corpse in the **'Complainte de l'ange incurable'** is displaced in space but as a corpse he is no longer free to move in the dimension of time. Similarly, the unchanging calligraphy on the window conveys no meaning either to Laforgue or the reader—unlike the shifting, protean language forms

found elsewhere in the poems. The true enemy of the meaningful is stability, lack of movement or change.

Movement may lead to the break down of order and passing time erode language as **'L'Hiver qui vient'** makes clear:

> C'est la saison, c'est la saison, la rouille envahit les masses,
> La rouille ronge en leurs spleens kilométriques
> Les fils télégraphiques des grandes routes où nul ne passe.

Yet this is not such a clear case as may at first appear. Rust does indeed do its work over time but it is particularly associated with disuse—as though an object in constant movement is kept clean of rust. This suggestion is reinforced by the reference to the unused roads along which no-one travels. The lack of movement contributes to their air of decay.

Later in the poem there is further evidence for the ambiguous nature of time:

> Non, non! C'est la saison et la planète falote!
> Que l'autan, que l'autan
> Effiloche les savates que le Temps se tricote!
> C'est la saison, oh déchirements! c'est la saison!
> Tous les ans, tous les ans,
> J'essaierai en chœur d'en donner la note.

In the midst of this unravelling and tearing of the fabric of the world—a process which is cyclic and thus involves time—we find that time itself is fighting a battle against decay. It creates while the wind destroys. However, what it makes is already old ('savates') but this is to be expected in a universe where matter is endlessly recycled. Nothing can be new but rather everything is posterior to and hence older than that which preceded it. The verbs in the third line are also significant. They are positioned at either end of the verse and there is an aural echo of the vowels 'i' and 'o' and a visual echo that is even more extended—'e,' 'i,' 'o' and 'e.' They are like two evenly matched fighters squaring up to each other. Furthermore, both verbs are in the present tense so that this is a continuous state of affairs—neither gets the upper hand. Compare the difference were 'se tricote' to be put into the perfect tense. In that case it would precede and be vanquished by 'Effiloche.' Here, however, the 'Effiloche' precedes 'se tricote' thus setting up in the reader's mind the possibility that first the old slippers are unravelled and then they are knitted again using the same thread. Consequently dismantling is a prerequisite of construction.

Not only that, but the re-use of the thread is a form of conservation. It is not completely destroyed but is given a new form. This also applies to the bits and pieces of language that Laforgue uses. At its most basic and indeed obvious level, the use of language prevents it rusting. Language forms die through lack of use. The same applies, however, to larger language units—the intertexts. As we have seen, Hiddleston claims that Laforgue's

use of other texts is 'une ironie qui démolit non seule
ment les textes auxquels elle renvoie, mais qui est elle
aussi démolie du même coup.' If we look at the example
from Villon quoted above in the light of the relationship
between 'Effiloche' and 'se tricote,' we will see that Hiddleston is only half right. The Villon original is fragmented but it is also re-used. It is brought into a nineteenth-century poem. This is not so much a 'renvoi' as
a 'rappel.' Villon is preserved by the allusion—he is not
destroyed by it. His relevance for Laforgue is proclaimed.
In a similar way, Pierrot restores the memory of Christ
albeit in different form from what we normally expect.
Whatever we may think of this, there can be no denying
that, for Laforgue, Christ is a part of Pierrot and so is
preserved through him. The alternative is oblivion.
Laforgue, like the King of Thule, weaves his text and
preserves the past.

To let things stand is to let them rot, fall into oblivion
and meaninglessness. This is the fate of the corpse in the
grave while the calligraphy on the window has never had
any place in the significant order of things. It is quite
unlike the written language whose physical form it shares.
As Eric Havelock points out, the primary function of
writing is to preserve:

> The function of the original model [i.e. writing as
> developed by the Greeks] was not to replace a prior
> knowledge of spoken speech but to trigger a recall of
> that knowledge. Its effective use depended upon the
> requirement that the oral vocabulary of the reader
> first be fluent and educated. The alphabet was and is
> an instrument of acoustic recognition, and only that.

J. Hillis Miller [in *The Future of Literary Theory*, 1989,
edited by Ralph Cohen] would agree:

> What rationale for the study of the humanities should
> be put in place of the old consensus? I think there can
> be only one answer. Preservation, conversation (*sic*),
> the keeping of the archives, the whole work of memory
> remembering, and memorialization: yes, this remains
> an indispensable task of humanistic study. But our
> past is remembered differently now and some different
> things are now recalled into memory, for example,
> black literature or the history of women and writing
> by women. Memory and the storing and interpretation
> of what is remembered is not a passive but a vital and
> passionate act, an act each generation does anew and
> differently as it appropriates history for its own
> purposes.

This is what Laforgue does. He stores experience in the
patterns of his texts—but it is an active not a passive
process. He reinterprets and updates. The past is not a
mummified past but one that is incorporated into the
present. Change, both in its positive and negative aspects, is embraced and incorporated into the preservation
of our past and present. The 'tournoiement' of the poetry
is not ultimately 'chaotique.' The language is not a bab-
bling or gratuitous word-play. If we are baffled it is
because our fixed ideas are being broken down so that
something new and memorable can be built up from the

fragments. It is this that makes for what Hiddleston recognizes as the durability of Laforgue's writing. Yet this is
a durability that incorporates the flexible, the protean. It
is in constant movement so that it may always move us.

Anne Holmes (essay date 1993)

SOURCE: "*Les Complaints*: 'Les refrains des rues'," in
Jules Laforgue and Poetic Innovation, Clarendon Press,
1993, pp. 30-49.

[*In the following essay, Holmes investigates the interplay of style, theme, and poetic technique in Laforgue's*
Les complaintes.]

THE IDEA OF THE *COMPLAINTE*

'Les vers pompeux sont embêtants', wrote André Gill,
and by 1882 Laforgue agreed with him. Having distanced
himself from the poets whom he had at first imitated, he
found for his [second] volume a quite different model. It
was surprisingly remote: the plaintive and burlesque
complainte of the sixteenth century, but Laforgue coupled this with later folk-songs, down to the doggerel
jingles of his day, a combination of traditional popular
proverb and 'refrains des rues' of the contemporary world.
The model was useful to him chiefly in two ways. Since
the *complainte* was a popular genre, intended to be spoken or sung, Laforgue was released from traditional elevated verse, and solemn self-absorption became technically impossible. The tone adopted by the *complainte*,
although it was an antiquated form, established a 'modern' down-to-earth familiarity and realism, which forced
him to attempt to implant the immediacy of the oral into
the written. Secondly, his *complainte* was a 'rewriting',
a variant on an earlier text. He was forced also to deviate
from his model: that is, to write indirectly and ironically.
Laforgue's *parlando* style and his irony both develop
therefore from this inspired move.

Variations on a recognizable model create a variety of
effects. They invite us to re-examine the human 'truth'
behind the familiar but discarded model: they offer us a
new view; they offer it in such a way that it is clear that
it also is relative and likely to be superseded. If the new
view is itself undercut by irony, we cannot escape the
realization that we inhabit a world that offers nothing
more substantial than subjective and shifting impressions.
Laforgue's talent for responsiveness, his floating sensibility, his wit and intellectual acuteness were all called
into play by this approach, without his having the possibility of making a direct comment on the world. He
could now cultivate the enigmatic and the elusive, the
qualities that had no place in philosophical verse, but
which were central to his artistic personality and, by
now, to his credo.

His new aesthetic emphasized the perfume rather than
the flower—an analogy he drew directly from Bourget.
'Je rêve de la poésie qui ne dise rien', he wrote, 'mais

soit des bouts de rêverie sans suite.' He also spoke, as we have seen, of 'de la psychologie dans une forme de rêve', and of 'd'inextricables symphonies avec une phrase (un sujet) mélodique, dont le dessin reparaît de temps en temps'. In the copy of the *Complaintes* that he sent to his sister Marie, conscious that she would find the poems strange and probably incomprehensible, he insisted that he had not changed at heart: 'Il n'a pas changé, ce cœur. Il est toujours aussi gros. Il est devenu un peu plus littéraire, voilà tout.' By many of the poems he noted particular dates and events to show that they sprang from his personal life. It was the distancing from these origins that was now aesthetically important, however, because, in Laforgue's words, 'Une poésie ne doit pas être une description exacte, (comme une page de roman), mais noyée de rêve.' The subjects could be mundane—the barrel-organ, for example—their poetic value would depend on the poet's inner world or his 'fantaisie'. So, simultaneously, in Baudelaire's famous definition, the reader is offered object and subject: 'le monde extérieur à l'artiste et l'artiste lui-même'. The genre of the Laforguian *complainte* depends on this fusion, unexpectedly creating an interior monologue from the most trivial elements of the external world. Not the least of the effects frequently created in the *Complaintes* is that of the pathos of objects: pianos and barrel-organs, an abandoned villa or an empty casino, hospital beds or old photographs; less obviously, but equally poignantly, such things as a Sèvres vase illustrating a pastoral idyll, or a lopsided window-blind on which hangs a forgotten pair of gaiters.

In 'Plainte d'automne', a prose poem that . . . Laforgue admired, Mallarmé had asked why the vulgar music of the barrel-organ, which can, of course, be seen as the musical equivalent of the folk-song, should have the power to move him deeply: 'Maintenant qu'il murmurait un air joyeusement vulgaire et qui mit la gaîté au cœur des faubourgs, un air suranné, banal: d'où vient que sa ritournelle m'allait à l'âme et me faisait pleurer comme une ballade romantique?' What has been described as 'une esthétique de la platitude', is based on the paradox of the banality that gives rise to deep emotion, and fittingly, it owed its origin to an event similar to that referred to by Mallarmé.

It was the celebration of the inauguration of the lion of Belfort, the statute in the place Denfert Rochereau, on 20 September 1880, and Laforgue recorded it vividly in a fragment that reveals the triviality of the occasion, as well as his own sense of alienated desolation.

> —Fête de nuit. Inaugurat. du lion de Belfort— pauvre—triste—temps triste. place d'Enfer, Observatoire, fête foraine. Des chevaux [de] bois tourant. des balançoires. des marchands de ferrailles. des faiseurs de caramels. des somnambules, des tourniquets où des étudiants ont gagné un vase de nuit au fond duquel un œil en émail peint regardait. Un cirque avec des toiles grossièrement peintes éclairées par des quinquets fumeux et fétides. deux femmes en maillot fané se promenant sur les planches, gueulant. Des musiciens faisant rage dans des cuivres bosselés dominés par la grosse caisse. boum! boum!

> Un paillasse avec un large pantalon, montant jusqu'au cou et serrant les chevilles, au dos une horloge brodée, perruque d'étoupe rouge, chapeau pointu blanc, masque de farine qui se plissait, se ridait quand il se pâmait sans conviction (ce monsieur, ce frère a ses soucis comme vous et moi—Drôle!).

> Une noce entière occupait un manège de chevaux de bois. la mariée en jupon sali dans tous les gargots graisseux de l'arrondissement, se disputait avec le loueur, lui mettait ses deux poings sous le nez. Le marié bêtement s'esclaffait. Une femme de la noce vomissait des flaques de vin, où un chien lappait. Une autre lui tapait maternellement dans le dos pour exciter, faciliter; bougonnant—il n'y avait pas de bon sens après avoir bu et mangé toute la journée à aller tourner sur des chevaux de bois.

> Des ménages d'ivrognes. Un souteneur faisant sortir une bande de filles dont l'une adorable et triste avait un bleu sous l'oeil, elles buvaient du vin—odeurs de quinquets, glapissement des montreurs, mélancolie des orgues jouant des airs de carrefours d'automne. en haut les étoiles vierges et éternelles—Drôle de planète!

In this passage Laforgue observes the human pathos of the failed festivity. Dissonances prevail: the crude student humour, the hints of dingy poverty, the clowns' unconvincing gestures, the vulgar arguments of bride and groom, the bride's soiled dress, the pretty young prostitute with a black eye. An outsider, Laforgue could have written with Charles Cros: 'Moi je vis la vie à côté, | Pleurant alors que c'est la fête.' He was to relive even these memories 'à côté', as he revived them for the *Complaintes* amid the luxury of the German court, which, while it suited his innate yearning for elegance, contributed a further sense of exile. Already in these 1880 notes he registered an ironic distance from the scene, with his concluding 'Drôle de planète'. The *complainte* emerged specifically from the singing of the two women, an unaccompanied singing that Laforgue described unromantically as 'gueulant'. That and other refrains, of course: 'Pour goûter cette chose', he wrote later to Kahn, 'il faudrait chanter les refrains sur un air de cor de chasse que j'ai entendu dans mon enfance en province.' But it took time for him to see that he must in a sense *be* these women, and that he must impersonate not only them, but the many voices at the festivity. The truth that the 'sincere' tone was inevitably insincere, that only oblique methods could hope to capture the actual complexity of his response to life had still to be fully assimilated. He continued, at first, simply to record his personal lament:

> Oh! la vie est trop triste, incurablement triste!
> Aux fêtes d'ici-bas j'ai toujours sangloté.
> ('**Soir de carnaval**')

or to describe such scenes objectively:

> J'errais par la banlieue en fête, un soir d'été.
> Et, triste d'avoir vu cette femelle enceinte

Glapissant aux quinquets devant sa toilc peinte,
Près des chevaux de bois je m'étais arrêté.

('**Hue, carcan!**')

Two early *complaintes*, '**Complainte de l'organiste de Nice**' and '**La Chanson du petit hypertrophique**', which Laforgue rejected for his volume, prefigure his later style. In both of them the main character is a double, on whom the poet projects his suffering. He probably rejected them because of the strong emotional element that they both contain, allowing into his volume rewritings of early poems with a more obviously satirical slant, but this now seems a mistake. Both are subtle poems that show how cliché can be rejuvenated to serve effects of pathos. In the first Laforgue describes the artist's exaggerated sorrow at the imagined death of a girl he does not know, and the final irony is directed at the poet for trying to compose a poem from so 'fictional' a subject. The idea is one that Laforgue did not abandon: he developed it in a later *complainte* and in the eleventh of the *Derniers Vers*. The irony of '**La Chanson du petit hypertrophique**' is of a similar kind. There is no attempt to mock the sufferings of the child narrator, but childish slang and metrical abbreviations ridicule the kind of poetry that might be expected to result from such a theme.

The simplest form of *complainte* used by Laforgue is that based on a popular song. The well-known words and tune form a background to the revised version. The method—if we consider the '**Complainte du pauvre jeune homme**', based on 'Quand le bonhomm' revint du bois'—takes a tragic narrative, here the suicide of a young man whose wife has abandoned him, and treats it with the anonymity and detachment of a newspaper item. As with Mallarmé's barrel-organ, the insistently cheerful rhythm drives home the pathos of the banal but tragic plot. The simplicity is deceptive, and must be so if the poem is not to be merely trivial itself. The young man is a persona of the poet, sensitive, lonely, given to ennui. His wife's desertion causes the tragedy, but the scene has already been well prepared. His is a 'belle âme', ill at ease in the modern world. While nostalgia for the nobility of soul of former happier times pervades the poem, it is simultaneously mocked: a *belle âme* is not merely something not 'found' in modern times: it is something, apparently man-made, that is no longer 'produced'. Laforgue's 'rewritings' complicate and fuse worlds, as do the neologisms that he invented most successfully at this period, and which he described as 'cet accouplement de mots qui n'ont qu'une harmonie de rêve mais font dans la réalité des couples impossibles (et qui ont pour moi le charme insoluble, obsédant, entêtant des antinomies en métaphysique . . .)'. In the '**Complainte de l'époux outragé**', the rewriting of the little tale of adultery that is the subject of the song 'Qu'allais-tu faire à la fontaine?', Laforgue mixes religion and the erotic, parodying the solemn treatment often given to this combination in contemporary verse. In the '**Complainte de Lord Pierrot**' the folk-song 'Au clair de la lune', a common-place rhyme about the ruses of physical seduction, is the prelude to the most melancholy, idealistic, and rambling of *divagations* on the subject of sexual

desire. 'Mon ami Pierrot' becomes the enigmatic 'Lord Pierrot', half English reticence, half *commedia dell'arte* mask. It is his 'cervelle' not his 'chandelle' that is dead, and the shared assonance ironically drives home the distance between the worlds that the two versions inhabit. As the later *moralité* '**Persée et Andromède**' moves from one legend, that of Perseus and Andromeda, to a second, that of Beauty and the Beast, so here one folk-song, 'Au clair de la lune', gives way to another, 'Il pleut, il pleut bergère', appropriate to the poem's final plunge into melancholy.

In the '**Complainte de cette bonne lune**' the folk-song 'Sur le pont d'Avignon' serves to introduce a celestial dance in 'l'giron du Patron' (God), in which the moon, a Cinderella-figure among the dazzling stars, far from finding her Prince Charming, rejects all invitations to the dance, because of her concern for her poor sister, the earth. So, instead of a picture in which 'all's right with the world'—and with heaven, too—which the original owed to the magical and religious associations of ritual dances on bridges, we are offered a humorous debunking of all such 'certainties', as the dialogue between the two parties degenerates into a vulgar brawl between celestial bodies. 'Est-ce assez idiot?', Laforgue wrote to [Gustave] Kahn when he sent him the preposterously inventive '**Complainte du fœtus de Poète**', and one might ask the same of this poem.

There are rewritings that are less frivolous but equally transform their 'model'. Goethe's poem 'Es war ein König in Thule', the model for the '**Complainte du roi de Thulé**', is a lyric celebrating marital fidelity, symbolized by the golden goblet bequeathed to the king by his wife on her death, which he hurls into the waves as his own death approaches. Against this uplifting example, Laforgue sets one that he places even higher. His king substitutes renunciation for fidelity. Instead of the devoted couple, we have a solitary figure, described in a cosmic landscape of great splendour, descending to mysterious polar regions to console a dying sun. In the final stanza the image of the absolute, to which the 'real' is sacrificed, is offered to young lovers as a more elevated and inspiring goal than theirs—a vision of 'amour pur'. Goethe's romantic depiction of conjugal love in the face of age and death lingers behind a poem that offers a more modern and ambiguous image, the power of which depends on the beauty of exalted negation:

Braves amants! aux nuits de lait,
  Tournez vos clés!
Une ombre, d'amour pur transie,
Viendrait vous gémir cette scie:
'Il était un roi de Thulé
  Immaculé . . . '

This poem, like the '**Complainte de Lord Pierrot**', might well be described as 'de la psychologie dans une forme de rêve', but poems where the model is woven into the text, itself forming part of the dream, best fit this description. The '**Complainte des pianos qu'on entend dans les quartiers aisés**' is an example. Here the *com-*

plainte, 'Tu t'en vas et tu nous laisses | Tu nous laiss's et tu t'en vas', is introduced as the words that accompany the piano notes that the narrator, a solitary *flâneur,* hears as he wanders through the streets in the town's well-to-do suburbs. The poem is composed of four regularly repeated strains, each set in counterpoint to the others. Differing line- and stanza-lengths make the pattern perfectly clear: two belong essentially to the narrator, and are followed by two that represent the thoughts of the girls whom he imagines playing the piano in the seclusion of their homes or convent schools. The poem moves from present to future as the narrator envisages the loveless *mariages de convenance* for which the girls are destined in place of the romantic love to which they aspire and which is the subject of the *ritournelles* they practise on the piano. The whole poem—both the image of the narrator, similarly lost in an inner world that aspires to the romantic, and the image of the present desert and future emotional death reserved for the girls—has sprung from the overheard piano tune, itself inseparable from the words of a popular song. Two lines from the song, repeated five times, are subtly modulated by the lines that complete the quatrain, in each case offering a glimpse of a different aspect of the girls' lives, and moving in an imaginative progression that leads to the final brutal glimpse of a future, the reverse of their aspirations, from which they will look back to their bored piano-playing days with longing:

> 'Tu t'en vas et tu nous laisses,
> Tu nous laiss's et tu t'en vas.
> Que ne suis-je morte à la messe!
> O mois, ô linges, ô repas!'

The *complainte* is not impenetrable, as has been suggested, but it is built on an elliptical technique that asks the reader to juxtapose and reconstruct its contrasting and mobile elements. The elements are themselves elliptical, and this is appropriate since the barely conscious world towards which the poem is directed speaks most convincingly in brief, intense ejaculations. The poem represents a journey inwards from the deceptively urbane and leisurely opening stanza, with its undercurrents of obsession and its reference to nerves where the heart would be more natural:

> Menez l'âme que les Lettres ont bien nourrie,
> Les pianos, les pianos, dans les quartiers aisés!
> Premiers soirs, sans pardessus, chaste flânerie,
> Aux complaintes des nerfs incompris ou brisés.

Laforgue's volume of *Complaintes* was found incomprehensible by most reviewers, and this despite the fact that the 'modern' and the burlesque were fashionable at the time, with the supposed Adoré Floupette's *Les Déliquescences,* which appeared in May 1885, being an example of a more frivolous excursion into parody. The tradition by now included Charles Cros's *Le Coffret de Santal* (1873), Corbière's *Les Amours jaunes* (1873), and Richepin's *La Chanson des gueux* (1876). But the *Complaintes* were just too baffling, too 'modern'—'de l'ultra-moderne', as one perceptive reviewer put it: 'Si vous aimez la vraie modernité, pas celle d'hier ni d'aujourd'hui, mais celle de demain, je vous conseillerai . . . *Les Complaintes* de M. Jules Laforgue. C'est de l'ultra-moderne.' The majority of reviewers felt that they were being fooled. 'Si ça continue', one wrote, 'il suffira dans six ans . . . d'écrire comme un Javanais: pour être un poète de génie.' Laforgue wrote one review himself, made emendations to another, written by Charles Henry, and was amazed at the perspicacity of one critic, Léo d'Orfer. His review stressed the remarkable range of the *Complaintes,* the aspect that we shall consider next. But it also described what has been the present subject: how 'des lambeaux de refrains populaires, des demicouplets de vieilles romances criaillées dans les cours, . . . toutes les chansons et chansonnettes des rues, des bois, de l'alcôve, de l'église, de la causerie bourgeoise, des grands discours, du peuple et de la solitude' could be accommodated to 'la sauce de la complainte'. 'Pour ma part', d'Orfer wrote, 'j'avais rêvé un genre de poèmes où tous les prosaïsmes et les vulgarités de la vie réelle trouveraient place à côté d'envolées superbes, les uns étant l'intelligence des autres.' This combination was what he had found in Laforgue's *Complaintes,* and it is one that the twentieth century, schooled to an aesthetic that finds dissonance indispensable, is prepared to take seriously.

MULTIPLE VOICES

J.-P. Richard points out the variety and ambiguity to be found in even the titles of the *Complaintes.* Some are votive laments, pleas dedicated to an external power (**'Complainte propitiatoire à l'Inconscient', 'Complainte à Notre-Dame des soirs'**); some are laments whose theme is an aspect of the insufficiency of life (**'Complainte sur certains ennuis', 'Complainte sur certains temps déplacés'**); most use the genitive form (*de, du, des*), but, since they employ both subjective and objective genitives, even this does not confer unity on them. The reader is, as Richard suggests, disorientated:

> Il arrive pourtant que l'ambiguïté, toujours grammaticalement possible, de la préposition s'actualise peu ou prou dans l'énoncé de tel ou tel titre, et que le lecteur ne sache plus dès lors, au cœur d'un petit trouble signifiant, si l'être nommé dans la seconde partie de la séquence titre est celui qui porte la parole ou celui que la parole vise.

As we have seen in the case of the **'Complainte des pianos',** the poem cannot be read simply as the lament of the pianos. It is dependent on a range of agents, and illustrates a number of subjectivities: on the one hand, the notes of music, the popular song, the Catholic bourgeois setting; on the other, the 'psychologies' of the girls, the narrator, and the poet. The result, in the laments of musical instruments, is a situation in which the discourse (again in Richard's words) 'tout à la fois s'adresse à eux [musical instruments], traite d'eux et constitue une transposition (phrasée) de ce qu'ils sont censés prononcer (directement) ou connoter (indirectement) sur le mode musical', and the final effect is 'un certain flou de l'énonciation qui répond, on le sait, à l'un des effets les plus vivement recherchés par la poétique laforguienne: la délocalisation du moi, la confusion discursive du sujet et de l'objet, le demi-naufrage (joué) du sens.' This effect is further increased by the fact that the representation of a multiplicity of voices is a deliberate aim; voices that are merely overheard, that emerge from a void, mobile voices representing moments in a changing narrative, and whose mobility matches that of the equally variable moods and personae of the narrator. Laforgue had learnt from Hartmann, as Warren Ramsey points out [in *Jules Laforgue and the Ironic Inheritance*, 1953], 'to think of the human individual as an aggregate, a sum of many individuals'.

In this climate of ambiguity and uncertainty what order and consistency do we find? Y.-A. Favre argues that we have a 'livre' rather than an 'album'; that is, a highly structured whole, and there is evidence that this is the case with all Laforgue's volumes, with the exception of the *Derniers Vers,* about whose intended final structure we know almost nothing. Plans were not rigid, however. The original *Complaintes,* significantly called simply **'Quelques Complaintes de la vie',** first numbered twenty poems, then grew to forty and to fifty with the help of Laforgue's publisher Léon Vanier, 'Fabius Cunctator', as Laforgue named him. The new poems were interpolated casually, and when Laforgue sent Vanier a fiftieth poem, he told him to place it 'n'importe où' in the volume. He insisted on the placing of two key poems, however: the opening **'Préludes autobiographiques',** which was to be 'answered' by the late **'Complainte du Sage de Paris':** 'Cette préface explique la dernière et longue litanie qui ferme le volume.' But, with characteristic flexibility, he added two short poems to this litany, closing his volume in a more oblique and light-hearted fashion. One is the **'Complainte des complaintes',** which serves as an apology for, and defence of, the volume: the other, the **'Complainte-épitaphe'** uses disyllabic quatrains and tercets in a parody of the sonnet form. Pointing forward to future exercises in ellipticism, such as **'Avant-dernier Mot',** and taking a leaf from various contemporary *fumiste* productions, it sums up the themes and the method of the volume, the latter by reference to other art-forms, in a supreme distancing act:

> La Femme,
> Mon âme:
> Ah! quels
> Appels!
> Pastels
> Mortels,
> Qu'on blâme
> Mes gammes!
> Un fou
> S'avance,
> Et danse.
>
> Silence . . .
> Lui, où?
> Coucou.

'La Femme', 'mon âme' are, of course, seen through a dedication to the unconscious, which, deliberately blurred

with an ascetic Buddhism, is the subject of the early votive poems. Even the **'Complainte-Placet *de* Faust fils'** is, as Favre points out, a plea *to* nature. (It is simultaneously a parody of Sully Prudhomme's sentimental poem 'Prière' and of Goethe's Faust's intellectual and guilt-ridden universe.) The volume represents a personal and moral journey from rejection and disillusionment to some kind of acceptance or resignation, a *schema* surprisingly parallel to Laforgue's plans for the *Sanglot,* a fact that might easily be overlooked because of the new volume's contrasting register and because love, which was largely absent from the *Sanglot* poems, has now become a central theme.

The second poem of the volume, **'Complainte propitiatoire à l'Inconscient',** already sets up the technique of parallel discourses that we saw in the **'Complainte des pianos'.** Here, more simply, the leading couplet takes the form of a prayer addressed to the unconscious, while the following quatrain develops an interior monologue in which 'la Pensée', from which the unconscious should deliver man, is, all too obviously, failing to find a solution to his distress. Both discourses follow a linear progression: the couplets offer ordered parodic echoes of the Lord's Prayer ('Votre Nom', 'Volonté', 'quotidienne', 'Pardonnez-nous nos offenses', 'délivrez-nous'), while the quatrains move through the obvious range of possible human ideals: love as an absolute, the Christianity of the mystic, that of the missionary, the 'religion' of art. The intellect from which man is to be delivered is both a 'lèpre originelle' and an 'ivresse insensée', since it has created these false and impossible ideals. The advance in technique over such a *Sanglot* poem as **'Marche funèbre pour la mort de la terre',** which also functions by ordered antithesis, is striking. In **'Marche funèbre'** the refrain is unchanging and the monologue explicit. Here we inhabit immediately a puzzling, elliptical, and challenging world, with parody at its centre.

Fifteen of the *Complaintes* are composed on this model, which can, as we saw in the **'Complainte des pianos',** become more intricate. In that poem each voice was subdivided. In other *complaintes* the dialogue is extended by a third voice, frequently that of a narrator, who either introduces the poem, encloses it in a first and final stanza, or develops a contrasting point of view in its conclusion. The two opposed but interrelating main voices usually contrast a general with a particular view. In the **'Complainte de l'orgue de barbarie',** for example, the barrel-organ regurgitates the commonplaces of life in disabused and cynical five-syllable quatrains. These alternate with couplets—a stanza not commonly employed for the nerve-centre of a poem—expressing individual emotion: here that of a woman, and moving from ecstasy to fear and despair. These ordered snatches of an individual's life, which nevertheless illustrate the *idées reçues* of the street organ, progress, as in the **'Complainte des pianos',** from romantic dreams to desolation, and emphasize here also that 'la vie est vraie et criminelle'. The poem thus conveys a sense of passing time by means of narrative, and of simultaneity by means of its parallel discourses.

In the **'Complainte des grands pins dans une villa abandonnée'** the personified street organ is replaced by the pines, and the personal lament of a disinherited and lonely young man provides the human narrative. The personification of objects that act as witnesses to the human situation is one way of diversifying the *moi,* since Laforgue's voice, already lent to the introductory narrator and to the young man (or girl) who is the main character, has 'become' also the voice of the pines (or street organ). The poem is an amalgam of voices, functioning in relation to each other. It is an amalgam or 'fugue' of moods also, since wit constantly breaks through, tempering the evident pathos. The sun is sulking, the clouds are 'paquets de bitume', the young man will go to Montmartre 'en cinquième classe'. And yet the lament, carried by the moaning of the pines in the wind, has the ability to inspire what Mallarmé, speaking of the street organ, called 'desperate reverie': 'l'orgue de Barbarie, dans le crépuscule du souvenir, m'a fait désespérément rêver. . . . Je la [its crude music] savourai lentement et je ne lançai pas un sou par la fenêtre de peur de me déranger et de m'apercevoir que l'instrument ne chantait pas seul.'

A *complainte* of which we happen, quite exceptionally, to have an early draft, **'Complainte du fœtus de poète',** introduces the contrasting strain only in the later version, illustrating Laforgue's inclination to complicate and to 'blur' his original texts. 'Je les retoucherai, je les *noierai* un peu plus', he wrote to his sister: 'La poésie doit être à la vie ce qu'un concert de parfums est à un parterre de fleurs.' As he did this, he was drawing poetry closer to the related art-forms of music and painting, establishing the 'pont mystérieux' of which Delacroix wrote: 'L'écrivain écrit presque tout pour être compris. Dans la peinture il s'établit comme un pont mystérieux entre l'âme des personnages et celle du spectateur.'

The techniques of theatre were useful to Laforgue in this attempt. Two *complaintes* (**'Complainte des voix sous le figuier bouddhique',** and **'Complainte des formalités nuptiales'**) employ named characters and, consequently, display considerable formal variety. The former, expanding mingled Buddhist and Hartmannian sentiments, was one that Laforgue considered important, writing to his publisher: 'Une erreur dans cette pièce me désolerait.' Both point forward in their form to *Le Concile féerique,* a drama composed of unpublished poems taken from *Des Fleurs de bonne volonté.*

Techniques drawn from the monologue form developed in the theatre of Coquelin the Younger abound: colloquialisms, the direct address to a supposed spectator, the apostrophe, the aside. One remembers that Mallarmé had originally hoped that 'L'Après-midi d'un faune' might be recited at the Théâtre-Français, and that its second title, after he rejected 'Improvisation d'un faune', was 'Monologue d'un faune'. A number of the personae that Laforgue employs for the self are . . . connected with legend or folk-song: the Pierrot, the King of Thule, the knight errant, the poor young man, the betrayed husband, the 'blackboulé', or more fantastic versions of the self: the son of Faust, the foetus of the poet, the incurable angel, the poor human body. They are 'characters' who, however strange, are lent familiarity by the definite article that always introduces them. But this familiarity is also belied by the twist that Laforgue gives to the expected personage. We have a knight errant whose only concern appears to be his inability to inspire love, an angel who regrets nothing so much as his purity, a poet-foetus in place of Baudelaire's infant-poet. Antecedents are not necessarily literary. Bizet's *Carmen,* an opera much in vogue throughout Western Europe in 1885, provides the twist in the **'Complainte des blackboulés'.** By quoting the opening words of the famous Escamillo/Carmen duet, 'Si tu m'aimes', Laforgue places behind the 'blackboulé', who is nursing a sadistic revenge, the dramatic figure of the betrayed Don José, and thus behind the harsh introspection of an apparently morbid psyche the normalization provided by the legitimate passions of a tragic narrative.

Sometimes the stylized persona is abandoned, and we are given monologues more directly attributable to the poet. The result is not simplification—rather the reverse. The more successful and substantial of these poems illustrate the divisions in the self that will be further developed in the *Derniers Vers.* **'Complainte d'une convalescence en mai',** for example, is an occasional poem with a mock-philosophical theme. The tedium of convalescence leads to meditation on life's fundamental problems and to a recognition that the narrator's 'grandes angoisses métaphysiques | Sont passées à l'état de chagrins domestiques'. The fragility of the narrator's affirmations is stressed in a dialogue with the self that employs mobile pronouns, a technique that Laforgue uses elsewhere. A 'je' takes issue with a self-addressed 'tu' in free Apollinairean fashion ('Et toi, cerveau confit dans l'alcool de l'Orgueil'), and the two add up to an internal 'nous' ('Nous savons ce qu'il nous reste à faire'). This 'nous' echoes the external 'nous' of the poem's epigraph, the well-known statement referring to Pascal's barbed iron belt: 'Nous n'avons su toutes ces choses qu'après sa mort', an epigraph that, while it indicates that the subject of the poem will be concealed pain, emphasizes also the distance between the Pascalian world and the mundane region inhabited by this poem. The *complainte* employs the alexandrine couplet to combine the presentation of suffering with its subversion ('Convalescence bien folle, comme on peut voir'), while offering on the way a number of bold elliptical formulations: 'Si la Mort, de son van, avait *chosé* mon être', for example, or 'Qui *m'a* jamais rêvé?' [emphasis added].

'Complainte d'un certain dimanche', another interior monologue, is an occasional poem whose occasion, the departure of the loved woman, becomes clear only in the third stanza. Before this we have aphorisms about the relations between the sexes, strongly coloured by the end-of-the-affair moment of which we are as yet unaware. Employing the discontinuous technique that Laforgue was to develop further in free verse, it again evokes the disunity of the self. The stanza that introduces the love theme displays three stances towards love in only four lines. We move from apparently bewildered self-questioning to an expression of overstated devotion, and from this to a stock romantic description, the cliché element in which leaves the emotion (such as it is) intact:

> Elle est partie hier. Suis-je pas triste d'elle?
> Mais c'est vrai! Voilà donc le fond de mon
>   chagrin!
> Oh! ma vie est aux plis de ta jupe fidèle!
> Son mouchoir me flottait sur le Rhin . . .

Shifting stances, again emphasized by a mobile narrative method (the girl is both 'elle' and 'tu'), reflect the frightening inner lack of centre, which is set against the equally alarming anonymity of the external world. Loss of a sense of identity does not imply any absence of feeling, however. Philosophical generalizations and pseudo-conclusions are interrupted by shock expressions of fear or horror:

> Que d'yeux, en éventail, en ogive, ou d'inceste,
> Depuis que l'Être espère, ont réclamé leurs droits!
> O ciels, les yeux pourrissent-ils comme le reste?

When the narrator finally confesses his fear of solitude, which was the theme of many *Sanglot* poems, we find that we have now been offered a landscape in which to situate it, and that it is a nuanced landscape, created from a series of fleeting perceptions—snapshots, as it were, necessarily surrounded by unbridgeable gaps between the pictures, which nevertheless inhabit a recognizable and all too human psychological terrain.

Frequently, the narrator surfaces from these explorations of inner turmoil in a final neat reversal or disclaimer, a technique that we find in the *Derniers Vers*. In this poem it is the shift in the last line from 'Faudra-t-il vivre monotone?' to 'Tâchons de vivre monotone'; in the **'Complainte d'une convalescence en mai'** we have the (already quoted) dismissive 'Convalescence bien folle, comme on peut voir'; it is the 'C'était donc sérieux?' of **'Autre Complainte de Lord Pierrot';** the unexpected throw-away, 'Ces êtres-là sont adorables', of **'Complainte sur certains ennuis';** or the Eliotesque ending of **'Complainte des débats mélancoliques et littéraires':**

> O Hélène, j'erre en ma chambre;
> Et tandis que tu prends le thé,
> Là-bas, dans l'or d'un fier septembre,
> Je frissonne de tous mes membres,
> En m'inquiétant de ta santé.
> Tandis que, d'un autre côté . . .

The reversals and disclaimers, like the use of the refrain, illustrate the centrality to the volume of techniques of counterpoint. They can be found almost buried in stylistic devices. **'Grande Complainte de la ville de Paris'**— a poem that hurls discord and fragmentation at the reader, and is, correspondingly, the only poem in the volume to be written in prose—contains units recuperable as octo-

syllables and alexandrines, as well as many rhyming effects that set up disturbing echoes of the traditionally rhythmical at the heart of the poem's prose modernity. **'Complainte d'un autre dimanche'** uses internal crossed rhyme, as Grojnowksi has convincingly shown [in *Jules Laforgue et l'originalité*, 1988], to create the *en abyme* effect of a poem within a poem. Contrapuntal links are formed between poems; this poem, for example, stands in apposition to its predecessor, **'Complainte d'un certain dimanche'**, confronting and reflecting it. The same can be said of the two Lord Pierrot poems. But chiefly, of course, systems of opposition and relationship function between the parts of the poem. The narrator's personal lament in **'Complainte d'un autre dimanche'** is set against the apparent objectivity of a precisely observed pictorial setting that turns out to be an accurate reflection of the narrator's internal landscape. The transience of the former, emphasized by first and last lines (*C'était* un très-au vent d'octobre paysage'; 'Ce *fut* un bien au vent d'octobre paysage . . . '), echoes the human instability that, as we have seen, is the true subject of the poem.

Ultimately, despite the scope it offered for the portrayal of a range of different and changing voices, Laforgue began to find the *complainte* form limiting rather than liberating. It had enabled him to discover and explore a number of ironic distancing techniques, but the many voices had become, self-confessedly, 'gerbes . . . d'un défunt moi'. He moved on, at first to the still greater artifice of *L'Imitation de Notre-Dame la lune,* and finally, in the *Derniers Vers,* to an abandonment of formal stylization—and even of versification—in his constant attempt to record the impact of reality, or, in Gide's later words, to present 'la rivalité du monde réel et de la représentation que nous nous en faisons'.

The aim pursued in the *Complaintes* necessarily involved breaking some of the venerated rules of French versification and, therefore, adopting a *vers libéré*. This might be thought natural in any case in a volume that derived its inspiration from folk-song. But the same critics who found the work intolerably obscure no doubt considered that Laforgue, like Donne before him, 'for not keeping of accent deserved hanging'. Laforgue's handling of rhyme came in for particularly vehement treatment. One critic had the wit at least to realize that the transgressions were intended: 'Il est évident qu'on dira des *Complaintes* que ce n'est pas rimé suivant les règles données par le maître Banville. Mais cette indépendance prosodique a au moins cela pour elle, qu'elle n'est pas le résultat de l'impuissance. C'est voulu.'

Laforgue insisted that his poems were 'rimées à la diable', and by this he meant that he had sought out bold and interesting rhymes and had neglected convention. Instead of alternating masculine and feminine rhymes, **'Complainte d'un autre dimanche'** uses feminine rhymes throughout, a technique that Verlaine had pioneered for effects of delicate evocation. Laforgue rhymes for the ear and not the eye. He seems actually to cultivate the juxtaposition of singular and plural rhyming words that he had recommended to Mme Mültzer already in 1882. *Rimes pauvres* are common, but so are intensive rhyming effects, created by repeating a rhyme three or more times, often in complex patterns related to the formal structure of the poem. (**'Complainte de la bonne défunte'** uses the same two feminine rhymes throughout the entire poem; **'Complainte des printemps'** uses the same feminine rhyme in the poem's quatrains only; **'Autre Complainte de l'orgue de barbarie'** uses each rhyme in its main stanzas three times, the refrain rhyme six times.) Experimentation is constantly in evidence. In **'Complainte des pubertés difficiles'** one rhyme is regularly carried over from one stanza to the next, reducing the separateness of stanzas. In **'Complainte de la fin des journées'** the refrain uses the same rhymes throughout, and is thus set apart from the main stream of the poem. In **'Complainte de l'ange incurable'** the rhymes of the first two couplets are regularly repeated in the poem's short refrain, and act as wan echoes of the main text. Dissonances occur in place of, and in addition to, rhymes, as in the complex patterning of **'Complainte du roi de Thulé,'** and can result, as here, in a sense of subtle musicality, caused by the combination of rhyme and the related dissonance, of repetition and a variation on it. Rhyming on proper names or on words drawn from foreign vocabularies (and sometimes on both at once) lends the rhyme exoticism or humour; as in 'Missouri' and 'Paris' (**'Complainte de la lune en province'**), 'draps' and 'Léda' (**'Complainte de Lord Pierrot'**), or 'affiche' and 'sandwiche' (**'Complainte du pauvre chevalier-errant'**). The 'sans-gêne' of Laforgue's rhymes, the quality he twice praised in Kahn's, is one of their most engaging characteristics, as can be seen in the following:

> Les fiords bleus de la Norwège
> Les pôles, les mers, que sais-je?
>   (**'Complainte de la lune en province'**)

> Si tu savais, maman Nature,
> Comme Je m'aime en tes ennuis,
> Tu m'enverrais une enfant pure,
> Chaste aux *"et puis?"*
>   (**'Complainte-Placet de Faust fils'**)

or in the more provocative lines of **'Complainte d'une convalescence en mai'**, with their humorous hesitancy:

> Je ne veux accuser personne, bien qu'on eût
> Pu, ce me semble, mon bon cœur étant connu . . .

Laforgue's sensitivity to the weighting of syllables and to relative degrees of stress leads to a range of novel rhythmical effects, which we can be sure were calculated. Short lines, like stanzas, are contrasted with long, the caesura is eradicated or the line disrupted by unexpected or frequent breaks, the *impair* is used for effects of disharmony and ambivalence, notably in the hendecasyllable of **'Complainte du fœtus de poète'**, with its constantly shifting main stress. In **'Complainte du pauvre chevalier-errant'** Laforgue created what he called a 'strophe absolument inédite à vers de 14 pieds', which he asked Henry to emphasize in the review that he wrote of the

Complaintes. These experimental rhyming and syllabic combinations formed part of Laforgue's attempt to make details of technique relate to meaning. 'Que pensez-vous du vers de onze pieds?', he wrote to Kahn, 'et par la même occasion, que pensez-vous aussi de l'infini?' As a result, even his experimental lines have an integrity such as might be expected from more predetermined forms. A more rigid approach towards prosody would have seemed to him, paradoxical as this may appear, a betrayal of the artistic purity to which he aspired. He set out the position most directly when he defended himself against accusations of imitating Corbière: 'Corbière ne s'occupe ni de la strophe ni des rimes (sauf comme un tremplin à concetti) et jamais de rythmes, et je m'en suis préoccupé au point d'en apporter de nouvelles et de nouveaux. J'ai voulu faire de la symphonie et de la mélodie.' The 'melody' involved using a vocabulary that frequently appeared unpoetic—familiar and tongue-in-cheek—when this contributed to the particular poetic effect that he desired. It involved shocking his critics by rhyming 'Saint-Malo' with 'sanglots', and 'bocks' with 'coq'. It involved using varied and eccentric syllabic lengths and intricate contrapuntal patterning, so that the poetic line, far from being a mechanical unit, became the base for a series of live combinations. Being concerned with 'stanzas and rhymes' meant the creation of new effects, rather than adherence to the formulations of the past, offering the reader a constant interplay between the traditional and the original, the expected and the novel. Laforgue was no doubt in agreement with (and perhaps behind) these sentences from Henry's review of the *Complainte*: 'M. Jules Laforgue fut ainsi conduit à un genre de composition où la tenue prosodique conventionnelle n'est pas de rigueur. De là ces complaintes . . . entrelacis de notes perpétuelles, échos d'humour de belle race, trouvailles de formules, bouquet de rythmes et de rimes dont la variété réjouit le savant parfois inquiet du nombre.'

FURTHER READING

Biography

Arkell, David. *Looking for Laforgue: An Informal Biography*. Manchester: Carcanet Press, 1979, 248 p.
    Anecdotal approach to Laforgue's life and literary accomplishments.

Ramsey, Warren. *Jules Laforgue and the Ironic Inheritance*. New York: Oxford University Press, 1953, 302 p.
    The first critical biography of Laforgue in English.

Criticism

Benamou, Michel. "Jules Laforgue." In *Wallace Stevens and the Symbolist Imagination*, pp. 25-44. Princeton: Princeton University Press, 1972.
    Traces affinities between the poetry of Laforgue and that of Wallace Stevens.

Collie, Michael. *Laforgue.* Edinburgh: Oliver and Boyd, 1963, 120 p.

Critical biography of Laforgue that emphasizes his literary development within social and psychological contexts.

Cowley, Malcolm. "Laforgue in America: A Testimony." *The Sewanee Review* LXXI, No. 1 (Winter 1963): 62-74.

Investigates Laforgue's influence on early twentieth-century American writers, especially Hart Crane, T. S. Eliot, and Ezra Pound.

Cutler, Maxine G. "Prosaic Language in the Poetic Text." *Teaching Language Through Literature* XVIII, No. 1 (December 1978): 3-16.

Explores Laforgue's use of irony and contradiction in his poem "Autre complainte de Lord Pierrot."

Fenollosa, Ernest. "Jules Laforgue." In *Instigations of Ezra Pound*, pp. 7-19. Freeport, N.Y.: Books for Libraries Press, 1920.

Selection of six poems by Laforgue followed by an account of his significance in French literature.

Franklin, Ursula. "Laforgue and His Philosophers: The 'Paratext' in the Intertextual Maze." *Nineteenth-Century French Studies* 14, Nos. 3-4 (Spring-Summer 1986): 324-40.

Discusses the influence on Laforgue's poetry of the philosophies of Buddhism, Heinrich Heine, Edward von Hartmann, and Arthur Schopenhauer.

Golffing, Francis C. "Jules Laforgue." *Quarterly Review of Literature* III, No. 1 (1946): 55-67.

Examines the intellectual framework surrounding Laforgue's aesthetic of poetry.

Hannoosh, Michele. "Metaphysicality and Belief: Eliot on Laforgue." *Comparative Literature* 39, No. 4 (Fall 1987): 340-51.

Considers T. S. Eliot's perceptions of Laforgue, his poetry, and his philosophy.

Lehmann, A. G. "The Unconscious and Art." In *The Symbolist Aesthetic in France, 1885-1895*, pp. 114-24. Oxford: Basil Blackwell, 1950.

Contains an analysis of Laforgue's aesthetic, especially as it is informed by Edward von Hartmann's theory of the unconscious.

Morgan, Edwin. "Notes on the Metaphysics of Jules Laforgue." *Poetry* LXIX, No. V (February 1947): 266-72.

Outlines Laforgue's philosophical outlook as implied in his poetry.

Pound, Ezra. "Irony, Laforgue, and Some Satire." *Poetry* XI, No. II (November 1917): 93-8.

Marks Laforgue's importance as a transitional figure in French letters.

Quennel, Peter. "Jules Laforgue." In *Baudelaire and the Symbolists*, pp. 97-111. London: Weidenfeld and Nicolson, 1954.

Surveys Laforgue's development as a poet while highlighting characteristic themes in his works.

Ramsey, Warren. "Crane and Laforgue." *The Sewanee Review* LVIII, No. 3 (July-September 1950): 439-49.

Studies the influence of Laforgue on the poetry of Hart Crane.

Shanahan, C. M. "Irony in Laforgue, Corbière, and Eliot." *Modern Philology* LIII, No. 2 (November 1955): 117-28.

Traces the influence of Laforgue's self-ridiculing irony on the poetry of T. S. Eliot.

"L'Art sans Poitrine." *Spectator* No. 6785 (11 July 1958): 63.

Review of the *Poems of Jules Laforgue* that discusses his influence on English-language poets.

Symons, Arthur. "Jules Laforgue." In *The Symbolist Movement in Literature*, pp. 101-11. New York: E. P. Dutton and Company, 1908.

Stylistic assessment of Laforgue's writings.

Turnell, Martin. "Jules Laforgue: Observations on the Theory and Practice of Free Verse." *Cornhill Magazine* 163, No. 973 (Winter 1947-48): 74-90.

Explores Laforgue's role as a technical innovator in versification.

Additional coverage of Laforgue's life and career is contained in the following source published by Gale Research: *Nineteenth Century Literature Criticism*, Vol. 5.

Osip Mandelstam
1891-1938

(Full name Osip Emilievich Mandelstam) Russian poet, novelist, essayist, critic, and translator.

INTRODUCTION

Considered one of the most important and influential Russian poets of his time, Mandelstam is known for his association with the Acmeist school, a movement which rejected the mysticism and stylistic obscurity of Symbolism and attempted to restore clarity to poetic language. His most characteristic poems display the acmeist emphasis on a neoclassic formalism combined with contemplation of the nature of art itself. Mandelstam's work has undergone a steady revival since the death of Stalin in 1953 and, according to Joseph Brodsky, "what he did will last as long as the Russian language exists. It will certainly outlast the present and any subsequent regime in that country, because of both its lyricism and its profundity."

Biographical Information

Born to middle-class Jewish parents in Warsaw, Mandelstam soon afterward moved with his family to St. Petersburg. Because his parents did little to make Mandelstam aware of the vibrance and relevance of Judaism, the influences of his home life and ethnicity were often overpowered by the appeal of Western European culture. He was especially attracted to the gothic spirit of the Middle Ages; to him, Notre Dame cathedral represented the ideal creative act which gives human life meaning. After graduating from the prestigious Tenishev Commercial School in St. Petersburg in 1907, he travelled extensively in Europe and the Mediterranean region, and he developed an admiration for the historic lands of Christianity. In 1911 he enrolled in Petersburg University, and in order to avoid anti-Semitic sentiment, he converted to Lutheranism. In his work Mandelstam derived much of his inspiration from sources foreign to his cultural background, including Dickens, Poe, the French Symbolists, the medieval Italian poetry of Petrarch, and the classical mythology of the Hellenic world. In 1912 he became associated with the Acmeists, especially Nikolay Gumilyov and Anna Akhmatova. His estrangement from the political scene in his homeland after the Russian Revolution led to a five year period of silence after the publication of his second book of poetry. In 1934 he was exiled for three years to the city of Voronezh for criticizing Stalin in a line of verse. Later, Mandelstam was arrested and sent to a camp for political prisoners, where he died under brutal conditions in 1938.

Major Works

Mandelstam began his literary career with a series of poems published in the journal *Apollon*. His first collection of poetry, *Kamen'* (1913; *Stone*), exhibits the transition from an early Symbolist aesthetic to the new tenets of Acmeism. The poems of this and the second collection, *Trista* (1922; *Tristia*), are architectural in style and occasionally in subject: the poet aimed for carefully constructed elegance in these works, and some of the most famous lyrics celebrate the historical buildings of Paris, Moscow, and Constantinople. His third and last collection, *Stikhotvoreniya* (1928; *Poems*), incorporated both the previous volumes and added twenty new poems that reflect a more complex, intimate style.

Critical Reception

Some commentators have derided Mandelstam's poetry as dispassionate and detached from the concerns outside art. Other critics have demonstrated, however, that Mandelstam was sensitive to and often reacted to the events of the rapidly changing world around him. The poem "Vek" ("The Age"), for example, expresses his hopes and apprehensions for the future of postrevolutionary Russia. Generally the poems in *Stone* and *Tristia* are judged superior to those Mandelstam produced in the 1930s; recent studies of his later poetry take issue with this view. Since his death Mandelstam has been recognized as one of the most important Russian writers of the twentieth century, most significantly in his homeland, where he was once reduced to the status of literary "nonperson." A Russian encyclopedia succinctly summarizes Mandelstam's predicament during the Stalin era and the subsequent revival of the poet's reputation: "Illegally repressed during the period of the cult of the individual. Rehabilitated posthumously."

PRINCIPAL WORKS

Poetry

Kamen' [*Stone*] 1913
Trista [*Tristia*] 1922
Stikhotvoreniya [*Poems*] 1928
Sobranie sochinenni. 3 vols. (poetry, autobiographical essays, novella, and letters) 1967, 1971
Complete Poetry of Osip Emilevich Mandelstam (poetry) 1973
Osip Mandelstam: Selected Poems [translated by Clarence Brown and W. S. Merwin] 1973
Osip Mandelstam. Selected Poems [translated by David McDuff] 1973

Other Major Works

Shum vremeni [*The Noise of Time*] (autobiographical essays) 1925
Egipetskaya marka [*The Egyptian Stamp*] (novella) 1928
O poezii (criticism) 1928
The Prose of Osip Mandelstam: The Noise of Time, Theodosia, The Egyptian Stamp (autobiographical essays, novella) 1965
Osip Mandelstam: Selected Essays (essays) 1977
Mandelstam: The Complete Critical Prose and Letters (criticism and letters) 1979

CRITICISM

Osip Mandelstam   (essay date 1913)

SOURCE: "On the Addressee," in *Modern Russian Poets on Poetry*, edited by Carl R. Proffer, translated by Jane Gary Harris, Ardis, 1976, pp. 52-9.

[*In the following essay, which was first published in a Russian periodical in 1913, Mandelstam describes the relationship between poet and reader.*]

I would like to know what it is about a madman which creates that most terrifying impression of madness. It must be his dilated pupils, because they are blank and stare at you so absently, focusing on nothing in particular. It must be his mad speech, because in speaking to you the madman never takes you into account, nor even recognizes your existence as if wishing to ignore your presence, to show absolutely no interest in you. What we fear most in a madman is that absolute and terrifying indifference which he displays toward us. Nothing strikes terror in a man more than another man who shows no concern for him whatsoever. Cultural pretense, the politeness by which we constantly affirm our interest in one another, thus contains a profound meaning for us all.

Normally, when a man has something to say, he goes to people, he seeks out an audience. A poet does just the opposite: he runs "to the shores of desert waves, to broad and resonant oaks." His abnormality is obvious . . . Suspicion of madness descends upon the poet. And people are right when they call a man mad whose speech is addressed to inanimate objects, to nature, but never to his living brethren. And they would be within their rights to stand back terrified of the poet, as of a madman, if, indeed, his words were actually addressed to no one. However, such is not the case.

The view of the poet as "God's bird" is very dangerous and fundamentally false. There is no reason to believe that Pushkin had the poet in mind when he composed his song about the bird. But even insofar as Pushkin's bird is concerned, the matter is not all that simple. Before he commences singing, the bird "hearkens the voice of God." Obviously, the one who orders the bird to sing, listens to its song. The bird "flaps its wings and sings," because a "natural harmony" unites the bird with God, an honor even the greatest poetic genius does not dare to dream of . . . Then to whom does the poet speak? This is a question which still plagues us, which is still extremely pertinent, because the Symbolists always avoided it, and never formulated it succinctly. By ignoring the concomitant juridical, so to speak, relationship which attends the act of speaking (for example: I am speaking: this means people are listening to me and listening to me for a reason, not out of politeness, but because they are committed to hear me out), Symbolism turned its attention exclusively to acoustics. It relinquished sound to the architecture of the spirit, but with its characteristic egoism, followed its meanderings under the arches of an alien psyche. Symbolism calculated the increase in fidelity produced by fine acoustics, and called it magic. In this respect, Symbolism brings to mind the French medieval proverb about "Prêtre Martin," who simultaneously performed and attended mass. The Symbolist poet is not only a musician, he is Stradivarius himself, the great violin-maker, fastidiously calculating the proportions of the "sound box," the psyche of the audience. Depending on these proportions, a stroke of the bow may produce a sound truly splendid in its richness or an impoverished and unsure sound. But, my friends, a musical piece has its own independent existence regardless of the performer, the concert hall, or the violin. Why then should the poet be so prudent and solicitous? And more significant, where is that supplier of poet's needs, the supplier of living violins—the audience whose psyche is equivalent to the "shell" of Stradivarius' products? We do not know, nor will we ever know, where this audience is . . . François Villon wrote for the Parisian mob of the mid-fifteenth century, but the charm of his poetry lives on today . . .

Every man has his friends. Why shouldn't the poet turn to his friends, turn to those who are naturally close to him? At the critical moment, the seafarer tosses into the ocean waves a bottle containing a message: his name and the details of his fate. Wandering along the dunes many years later, I happen upon it in the sand. I read the message, recognize the date of the event, the last will and testament of someone who has passed on. I have the right to do so. I haven't opened someone else's mail. The message in the bottle was addressed to its finder. I found it. Hence, I have become its secret addressee.

> My gift is poor, my voice is not loud,
> But I am alive. And on this earth
> My presence is a friend to someone:
> My distant heir shall find it
> In my verse; how do I know? my soul
> And his soul shall find a common ground,
> As I have found a friend in my generation,
> I will find a reader in posterity.

Reading this poem of Baratynsky, I experience the same feeling I would if such a bottle came into my possession. The ocean, in all the enormity of its element, came to its aid, helped it to fulfill its destiny. And that feeling of providence overwhelms the finder. Two equally lucid facts emerge from the tossing of the seafarer's bottle to the waves and from the dispatching of Baratynsky's poem. The message, just like the poem, was addressed to no one in particular. And yet both have addresses: the message is addressed to the person who happened across the bottle in the sand; the poem is addressed to "the reader in posterity." I would like to know who, among the readers of Baratynsky's poem, did not feel that joyous and awesome excitement experienced when someone is unexpectedly hailed by name.

Balmont asserted:

> I know no wisdom suitable for others,
> Moments only do I enclose in my verse.
> In each fleeting moment I see worlds
> Brimming with inconstant, iridescent games.
> Don't curse, wisemen, what am I to you?
> I'm but a cloud brimming o'er with flame,
> I'm but a cloud, and I shall float on
> And hail all dreamers. But you I shall not hail.

What a contrast between the unpleasant, ingratiating tone of these lines and the profound and modest dignity of

Baratysnky's verse! Balmont seeks to vindicate himself, as if he were offering an apology. Unforgivable! Intolerable for a poet! The only thing which is impossible to forgive. After all, isn't poetry the consciousness of being right? Balmont expresses no such consciousness here. He has clearly lost his bearings. His opening line murders the entire poem. From the very outset the poet declares definitively that we hold no interest for him:

> I know no wisdom suitable for others.

He does not suspect that we may pay him back in kind: if we hold no interest for you, you hold no interest for us. What do I care about his cloud when there are so many floating about . . . At least genuine clouds don't scorn people. Balmont's rejection of the "addressee" is like a red line drawn through all his poetry, severely depreciating its value. In his verse, Balmont is constantly treating someone with disrespect, brusquely, superciliously. This "someone" is the secret addressee of whom we have been talking. Unperceived and unrecognized by Balmont, he cruelly avenges him. When we converse with someone, we search his face for sanctions, for a confirmation of our sense of rightness. Even more so the poet. But the poet's invaluable consciousness of being right is frequently missing from Balmont's poetry because he lacks a constant addressee. Hence, those two unpleasant, yet antithetical, traits in Balmont's poetry: sycophancy and insolence. Balmont's insolence is artifical, contrived. His drive to vindicate himself is downright sick. He is incapable of uttering the word "I" softly. He must shout "I":

> I am a sudden outburst
> I am a thunderclap breaking.

On the scales of Balmont's poetry, the pan containing the "I" dips decisively and unjustly below the "Not-I." The latter is far too light. Balmont's blatant individualism is very unpleasant. As opposed to the calm solipsism of Sologub, which never insults anyone, Balmont's individualism emerges at the expense of an alien "I." Note how Balmont enjoys stunning his readers by turning abruptly to the intimate form of address. In this he resembles a nasty, evil hypnotist. Balmont's intimate "thou" never reaches the addressee, for it shoots past its mark like an arrow released from a bow pulled too taut.

> As I have found a friend in my generation
> I will find a reader in posterity . . .

Baratynsky's piercing eye darts beyond generations (but in each generation there are friends) to halt in front of an as yet unknown, but well-defined "reader." Thus, each person who comes to know Baratynsky's poetry feels himself to be that "reader," to be that chosen one, the one who is hailed by name . . . Why then should there not be a concrete, living addressee, a "representative of the age," a "friend in this generation"? I will answer that: because appealing to a concrete addressee dismembers poetry, removes its wings, deprives it of air, of the freedom of flight. The fresh air of poetry is the element of surprise. In addressing a known quantity, we can speak only of what is already known. This is an absolute, inflexible psychological law. Its significance for poetry cannot be underestimated.

The fear of facing a concrete addressee, of facing an audience of our "age," or that "friend in this generation," has doggedly pursued poets of all ages. And the greater the poet's genius, the more severely he has suffered from this fear. Hence, the notorious hostility between the artist and society. What may be meaningful to the prose writer or essayist, the poet finds absolutely meaningless. The difference between prose and poetry may be defined as follows. The prose writer always addresses himself to a concrete audience, to the dynamic representatives of his age. Even when making prophecies, he bears his future contemporaries in mind. His subject matter brims over into the present, in keeping with the physical law of unequal levels. Consequently, the prose writer is compelled to stand "higher" than, to be "superior" to, society. Since instruction is the nerve of prose, the prose writer requires a pedestal. Poetry, however, is quite another matter. The poet is bound only to a providential contemporary. He is not compelled to tower over his age, to appear superior to his society. Indeed, François Villon stood far below the median moral and intellectual levels of the culture of the fifteenth century.

There is only one thing that pushes poets into the addressee's embrace: the desire to be astonished by our own words, to be enchanted by their originality and unexpectedness.

—Osip Mandelstam

Pushkin's quarrel with the common people, with the "mob," may be viewed as an example of that hostility between the poet and a concrete audience which I am trying to elucidate. Pushkin, with incredible impartiality, appealed to the mob to try to justify itself. And, as it turned out, the mob was not so wild and unlightened. But then how did this very considerate "mob," imbued with the best intentions, wrong the poet? In the process of vindicating itself, one tactless phrase slipped from its tongue, overflowed the poet's cup of patience and kindled his enmity:

Here we are, all ears.

What a tactless phrase! The stupid vulgarity of these seemingly harmless words is obvious. Not without reason did the poet indignantly interrupt the mob right at this juncture . . . The sight of a hand begging for alms is repulsive, but the sight of ears pricked up, ready to listen, may provide a source of inspiration to anyone, an orator, a politician, a prose writer, to anyone, that is, except a poet . . . Concrete people, the "philistines of poetry," those who comprise the mob, will permit anyone "to offer them bold lessons." They are generally prepared to listen to anyone, but if he is a poet, he must designate a proper address: "to

such and such a mob." So it is that simple people, like children, feel flattered when they can read their names on the envelope of a letter. And there have been entire epochs when the charm and essence of poetry were sacrificed to this far from inoffensive demand. Such verse included the pseudo-civic poetry and the tedious lyrics of the 1880s. Nevertheless, the civic and the tendentious may contain a beauty of its own, for example:

A great poet, perhaps, you'll never be,
But to be a citizen is your obligation—

These lines are remarkable, flapping their powerful wings, flying toward a providential addressee. But if that addressee were a once famous Russian philistine of a particular decade, familiar to us all, the lines would simply bore us.

Yes, when I address someone, I do not know whom I am addressing; furthermore, I do not care to know, nor can I want to know, him. Without dialogue, lyric poetry cannot exist. But there is only one thing that pushes us into the addressee's embrace: the desire to be astonished by our own words, to be enchanted by their originality and unexpectedness. Logic is pitiless. Thus, if I know the person I am addressing, I know in advance how he will react to my words, whatever I say, and consequently, I will not succeed in being astonished in his astonishment, in rejoicing in his joy, in loving in his love. The distance of separation blots out the features of the loved one. Only from a distance do I feel the desire to tell him something important, something I could not utter seeing his face before me as a known quantity. Allow me to formulate this observation more succinctly: our taste for communication is in inverse proportion to our real knowledge of the addressee and in direct proportion to our active attempt to interest him in himself. Acoustics can take care of itself, hence we need not be concerned about it. Distance, however, is another matter. Whispering to a neighbor is boring. But it is downright maddening to bore one's own soul (Nadson). On the other hand, exchanging signals with the planet Mars (not merely in the realm of fantasy) is a task worthy of a lyric poet. Here we come upon Fyodor Sologub in the flesh. In many ways, Sologub is a most interesting antipode to Balmont. Certain qualities missing in Balmont's work abound in Sologub's poetry. For instance, love and admiration of the addressee, and the poet's consciousness of being right. These two remarkable characteristics of Sologub's poetry are closely related to that "enormous distance" which he presumes lies between himself and his ideal "friend"-addressee:

My mysterious friend, my distant friend,
Behold.
I am the cold and mournful
Light at dawn . . .
And so cold and mournful
In the morning,
My mysterious friend, my distant friend,
I shall die.

In order that these lines reach their destination, perhaps hundreds of years are necessary, as many as a planet needs to send its light to another planet. Consequently, Sologub's lines continue to live long after they were written, as an event, not merely as a sign of an experience which has passed.

And so, although separate poems (in the form of epistles, or dedications) may be addressed to concrete persons, poetry as a whole is always addressed to a more or less distant, unknown addressee, but in whose existence the poet does not doubt, not doubting in himself. Metaphysics has nothing to do with this. Only reality can bring to life a new reality. The poet is no homunculus, and there is absolutely no basis for ascribing to him characteristics of spontaneous generation.

The point is very simply this: if we had no friends, we would not write letters to them, and we would not gain satisfaction from the psychological freshness and novelty peculiar to this occupation.

Osip Mandelstam   (essay date 1919)

SOURCE: "The Morning of Acmeism," in *The Russian Review,* Vol. XXIV, No. 1, January, 1965, pp. 47-51.

[*In the following essay, which was first published in a Russian periodical in 1919, Mandelstam describes his poetic philosophy and defines the Acmeist movement in Russian literature.*]

In view of the enormous emotional excitement connected with works of art it is desirable that talk about art be distinguished by the greatest restraint. For the great majority of people, a work of art is seductive only to the extent that it reveals the artist's world view. For the artist himself, however, a world view is a weapon and a means, like a hammer in the hands of a stonemason, and the only reality is the work of art itself.

The artist's greatest pride is to exist. He desires no other paradise than existence, and when people talk to him about reality he only smiles ironically, for he knows the endlessly more convincing reality of art. The spectacle of a mathematician who, without reflecting on what he is about, produces the square of a ten-figure number, fills us with a sort of astonishment. But we too often fail to see that a poet raises a phenomenon to its tenth power, and the modest exterior of a work of art often deceives us with regard to the monstrously condensed reality of which it disposes. This reality in poetry is—the word as such. Just now, for instance, while I am expressing my thought in the most exact way that I can, but certainly not in a poetic way, I am speaking essentially with the consciousness, not with the word. Deaf mutes understand each other perfectly and railroad signals perform their extremely complicated function without any recourse to the word. If one is thus to regard the sense as the content, then one must consider everything else in the word as a simple mechanical appendage that only impedes the swift transmission of the thought. "The word as such" was slow aborning. Gradu-

ally, one after the other, all the elements of the word were drawn into the concept of form; up to now only the conscious sense, the Logos, has been erroneously and arbitrarily regarded as the content. There is nothing but detriment for Logos in this needless honor. Logos requires only to be on an equal footing with the other elements of the word. The Futurist, having failed to cope with the conscious sense as creative material, frivolously threw it overboard and in essence repeated the crude error of his predecessors.

For the Acmeists the conscious sense of the word, the Logos, is just as splendid a form as is music for the Symbolists.

And if for the Futurists the word as such is still creeping on all fours, in Acmeism it has for the first time assumed a more adequate vertical position and has entered upon the stone age of its existence.

The sharp edge of Acmeism is not the stiletto nor the sting of Decadence. Acmeism is for those who, seized with the spirit of building, do not cravenly refuse to bear its heavy weight, but joyously accept it, in order to awaken and use the forces architecturally sleeping in it. The architect says: I build, therefore I am right. For us the consciousness of our rightness is dearer than all else in poetry; and, casting aside the trifles of the Futurists, for whom there is no higher pleasure than hooking a difficult word on the tip of a knitting needle, we are introducing the Gothic into the relationships of words, just as Sebastian Bach established it in music.

What sort of idiot would agree to build if he did not believe in the reality of his material, the resistance of which he must overcome? A cobblestone in the hands of an architect is transformed into substance, and he for whom the sound of a chisel splitting rock is not a metaphysical proof was not born to build. Vladimir Soloviev experienced prophetic horror before gray Finnish boulders. The mute eloquence of the granite mass shook him like an evil enchantment. But Tiutchev's stone, which "having rolled down from the mountain, lay in the valley, torn loose of its own accord or thrown down by a sentient hand," is the word. The voice of the material in this unexpected fall has the sound of articulate speech. Such a challenge can be answered only with architecture. Reverently the Acmeists pick up this secret Tiutchevian stone and make it the foundation of their knowledge.

The stone thirsted, as it were, for another existence. It discovered hidden within itself its dynamic potential—as if it were asking to be let into the "groined arch" to participate in the joyous cooperative action of its fellows.

The Symbolists were not good at staying at home, they liked to travel; but they did not feel well, did not feel quite themselves in the cage of their own organisms and in that world cage which Kant built with the aid of his categories.

In order to build successfully the first condition is a genuine piety before the three dimensions of space—to look at the world not as a burden and unfortunate accident but as a palace given by God. Really, what is one to say about an ungrateful guest who lives off his host, uses his hospitality, and all the while despises him in his soul and thinks only of how to deceive him? It is possible to build only in the name of the "three dimensions," since they are the condition of all architecture. That is why an architect has to be a good stay-at-home, and the Symbolists were poor architects. To build means to fight against emptiness, to hypnotize space. The fine arrow of the Gothic belltower is angry, because the whole sense of it is to stab heaven, to reproach it with its emptiness.

The particularity of a man, that which makes him an individual, is sensed by us and forms part of the far more significant concept of the organism. Acmeists share their love for the organism and organization with the physiologically brilliant Middle Ages. In its chasing after refinement the nineteenth century lost the secret of genuine complexity. That which in the thirteenth century seemed the logical development of the concept of organism—the Gothic cathedral—now has the aesthetic effect of something monstrous: Notre Dame is a celebration of physiology, its Dionysian debauch. We do not wish to divert ourselves with a stroll in the "forest of symbols," because we have a more virgin, a denser forest—divine physiology, the boundless complexity of our dark organism.

The Middle Ages, defining in its own way the specific weight of a man, felt and acknowledged it for each man completely regardless of his merits. The title of master was applied readily and with no wavering. The humblest artisan, the very least clerk possessed the secret of impressive grandness, of the devout dignity so characteristic of that age. Yes, Europe has passed through a labyrinth of delicate open-work culture, when abstract being, totally unornamented personal existence, was treasured as a sort of heroic accomplishment. Hence the aristocratic intimacy which united all people and which is so alien in spirit to the "equality and fraternity" of the French Revolution. There is no equality, no competition—there is the complicity of those united in a conspiracy against emptiness and non-existence.

Love the existence of the thing more than the thing itself and your own existence more than yourself: that is the highest commandment of Acmeism.

A = A: what a splendid theme for poetry! Symbolism languished and was bored by the law of identity; Acmeism makes a slogan of it and offers it instead of the dubious *a realibus ad realiora*.

The ability to feel surprise is the poet's greatest virtue. But how then is one not to be surprised by that most fruitful of all laws, the law of identity? Whoever has been seized with reverential surprise before this law is undoubtedly a poet. Having thus acknowledged the sovereignty of the law of identity, poetry receives, without condition or limitation, life-long feudal possession of all existance. Logic is the kingdom of the unexpected. To think logically means to be continually amazed. We have begun to love the music of proof. For us logical connection is not some ditty about a siskin but a choral symphony with organ, so difficult and inspired that the director must exert all his powers to keep the performers under his control.

How convincing is the music of Bach! What power of proof! One must prove and prove endlessly: to accept something in art on faith alone is not worthy of an artist, it is easy and tiresome. We do not fly, we ascend only such towers as we ourselves are able to build.

The Middle Ages are dear to us because they possessed in the highest degree the felling of boundary and partition. They never mixed various levels, and they treated the beyond with huge restraint. A noble mingling of rationality and mysticism and the perception of the world as a living equilibrium makes us kin to this epoch and impels us to derive strength from works which arose on Romance soil around the year 1200. And we shall prove our rightness in such a way that the whole chain of causes and consequences from alpha to omega will shudder in response; we shall learn to carry "more easily and freely the mobile fetters of existence."

Renato Poggioli   (essay date 1960)

SOURCE: "The Poets of Yesterday," in *The Poets of Russia: 1890-1930*, Cambridge, Mass: Harvard University Press, 1960, pp. 276-316.

[*Poggioli was an Italian-born American critic and translator. Much of his critical writing treats Russian literature, including* The Poets of Russia: 1890-1930 *(1960), which is considered one of the most important examinations of that era. In the following excerpt from that study, he identifies and explores central themes in Mandelstam's poetry.*]

Osip Mandel'shtam was born in the Jewish quarter of Warsaw, in 1892, and spent his mature years in the two capitals. He died still relatively young, in faraway banishment; we do not know exactly when and where. It is rumored that in 1932 he was denounced for having imprudently recited a lampoon against Stalin in the house of a friend; that he was jailed and punished for this; that several years later he was released and then rearrested; and that in 1938 (other authorities give far different dates) he died in Vladivostok, in, or on his way to, a forced labor camp. The memory of his personality is vividly engraved in Viktor Shklovskij's *Sentimental Journey,* in the brilliant pages re-evoking the living conditions of a few young Russian writers during the early revolutionary years in Petrograd. Indifferent to both hunger and cold, oblivious of his bleak surroundings, Mandel'shtam is portrayed there while working at his poems, like a splendid "fly of marble," as Shklovskij puts it. It was also by taking such a stance toward life that Mandel'shtam fulfilled the literary ideals of the Acmeist movement, of which he had been an active and brilliant exponent in his youth.

Mandel'shtam's literary output is a small treasure, which originally was contained in four little books. The major part of his poetic production appeared at first in two slender volumes, the earlier of which, **Stone,** was issued before the First World War (1913). The other one was published in Berlin in 1922, under the Ovidian title **Tristia** (which is also that of its opening piece), but was reprinted the following year in Russia and renamed *A Second Book.* Both volumes were included in **Poems** (1928), the only full collection of Mandel'shtam's verse to appear in his lifetime. His prose, too, was originally contained in two volumes, partly containing the same materials, *The Noise of Time* of 1925, and *The Egyptian Stamp* of 1928. No line of Mandel'shtam, either old or new, ever appeared in print in Soviet Russia after the poet's political disgrace and subsequent death: and it is only thanks to the labors of two *émigré* scholars (Gleb Struve and Boris Filippov) and to the care of an *émigré* concern (Chekhov Publishing House) that we possess what up to now is the only edition of his **Complete Works** (1952) in both verse and prose. Yet it seems that the poet left important manuscripts which were not lost, and which all the friends of Russian letters hope to see some time in print. . . .

If Mandel'shtam's prose amounts to a limited number of pieces, in the main quite short, and all belonging to a short-lived phase of his career, the whole of his published poetry amounts to about two hundred lyrics, most of which were composed within a ten-year span, from 1910 to 1920. And, in contrast to his prose, it is a novel and strange sense of history which seems to have given inspiration to many of his lyrics. As had been the case with many older masters, either Decadent or Symbolist, such as Brjusov and Ivanov, and as was still the case with such younger craftsmen as the Acmeists Kuzmin and Gumilev, Mandel'shtam seems to have chosen historical erudition and literary learning as a mainspring of his poetic work. As a matter of fact, in his ability to recognize and to fulfill the imaginative potential of a cultural or scholarly subject, Mandel'shtam has, with the exception of Vjacheslav Ivanov, no rival among his peers. And like Ivanov, who was a classical philologist by trade, Mandel'shtam prefers in history the themes still offered to us by the glories which were Greece and Rome. Truly enough, Ivanov tends to translate classical and Hellenic myths in mystical terms, rendering them almost medieval or Byzantine in character, while trying at the same time to give an ancient, pagan dignity even to his poems on Christian or modern themes. In brief, the classical strain remains a permanent aspect of Ivanov's historical and religious syncretism.

Mandel'shtam's preoccupation with the classical and the Hellenic is not as exclusive and as serious as Ivanov's: generally he prefers to project his philological and archaeological reconstructions into an ironic atmosphere, as if he would place them in the cold and abstract light of a museum. All his learned poems are conversation rather than period pieces, and yet they typically convey the static and abstract quality of Mandel'shtam's vision. Hence the significance of the title of the poet's first collection, **Stone**; hence his predilection, rare in Russian poetry, for composition and architecture, for the "frozen music" of pure design. Thus, even when minuscule in scope, Mandel'shtam's art is monumental in quality, and it tries to transform the historical and the temporary into the untimely and the timeless. The poet once affirmed, paradoxically, that the poetry of the Russian Revolution should be classical in temper, and he saluted its advent with a neo-Pindaric ode, not devoid of an elegiac strain, which he entitled **"Liberty's Twilight."** Yet, as we already know and as T. S. Eliot averred, a modern poet can be classical only in tendency. That Mandel'shtam must have been aware of the same truth is shown by his splendid poem on Racine, expressing the poet's impossible longing for an art really able to separate, like a stage curtain, the opposite worlds of imagination and reality, of creation and experience. Beyond that curtain, Racine's heroes and heroines are frozen forever in their inflexible stage attitudes. Mandel'shtam yearns likewise for the absolute perfection of a vibrant, and yet motionless, pose, for the fixing of passion in a gesture both conventional and unique. For Hegel, the task of Greek art, especially of Greek sculpture, was to express life in the moment of habit, rather than in its instant of tension, or in its exceptional phases. Mandel'shtam's neoclassicism is a similar, all-too-modern, attempt to treat stasis as if it were no less a state of grace than ecstasis itself.

> Mandel'shtam recalls the Picasso of the classical period with his ability to reduce human flesh to the heavy rigidity of inorganic matter, making it both plastic and lifeless. His figures are less huge and solid, and they are molded in plaster, although they look as if they were made of alabaster.
>
> —*Renato Poggioli*

Mandel'shtam also likes to treat themes other than purely classical ones. Many of his poems deal with such divergent and extravagant topics as the poetry of Ossian and the architecture of Saint Sophia, or with such topical or fashionable subjects as Dickens' fiction, a game of tennis, or the projection of a moving picture. In general, he handles modern themes with caricatural mockery; or, when approaching such subjects in a more serious mood, he reinterprets them in classical or mythological key. This is what he does in the poem **"Tristia,"** written in 1918, to convey the peculiar fate of modern man, which is to die or to kill. The scene of the poem is Petersburg, which the poet calls Petropolis and transforms into a mythical city, where he finds again the footprints of Proserpine. The central scene evokes the Russian popular, superstitious rite of fortune-telling according to the figures shaped by melting wax. The girl performing that rite assumes the proportion and likeness of a Sibyl. As for the men going to war, for whom the horoscope is read, they will meet

Mandelstam's last days:

Everything suggested that the end was near, and M. was trying to take full advantage of his remaining days. He was possessed by the feeling that he must hurry or he would be cut short and not allowed to say what he still wanted to say. Sometimes I begged him to rest, to go out for a walk or have a nap, but he dismissed the idea: there was so little time left, and he must hurry. . . .

The poems poured out of him, one after another. He worked on several at once, and he often asked me to take down at one sitting two or three which he had already completed in his head. I could not stop him: "You must understand that I shan't have time otherwise."

Of course, he was just taking a sober view of his approaching end, but I could not yet see it as clearly as he. He never spoke about it to me in so many words, but in letters to people in Moscow (where I went a couple of times during the winter to get money) he once or twice hinted at what was in store for us—but then immediately changed the subject in mid-sentence, as though he had been talking only about our usual difficulties. Perhaps he really was trying to put such thoughts out of his mind, but the greater likelihood is that he wanted to spare my feelings and not darken the last days of our life together.

He drove himself so hard during the whole of that year that he became even more painfully short of breath: his pulse was irregular and his lips were blue. He generally had his attacks of angina on the street, and in our last year in Voronezh he could no longer go out alone. Even at home he was calm only when I was there. We sat opposite each other and I watched his moving lips as he tried to make up for lost time and hastened to record his last words.

Nadezhda Mandelstam, in her Hope Against Hope: A Memoir, *Collins & Harvill Press, 1971.*

their destiny in battle, without guessing, as the poet says, about "the Erebus of the Greeks."

The artists to whom Mandel'shtam may be likened are to be found in fields other than that of the verbal arts. He recalls Giorgio de Chirico, at least in the latter's attempt to represent classical landscapes or old Italian squares as both tragic and melodramatic décors. He recalls also the Picasso of the classical period with his ability to reduce human flesh to the heavy rigidity of inorganic matter, making it both plastic and lifeless. Mandel'shtam's figures are less huge and solid, and they are molded in plaster, although they look as if they were made of alabaster. In one of his most magnificent lyrics the poet offers to a friend the image and the gift of a chunk of honey which changes itself into sunlight after the creatures which produced it are turned into a necklace of dead bees. Yet the sense of his art is more genuinely conveyed by a far different metaphor or process: by this artist's attempt to embalm forever the worm of life within that amberlike matter which is the very substance of his poetry.

Clarence Brown   (essay date 1967)

SOURCE: "On Reading Mandelstam," in *Major Soviet Writers: Essays in Criticism,* edited by Edward J. Brown, Oxford University Press, 1973, pp. 146-63.

[*In the following essay, which was first published as an introduction to Mandelstam's collected works, Brown examines linguistic and thematic aspects of Mandelstam's poetry, and offers a close reading of "Soliminka, The Straw".*]

In his imaginative and interesting article "On Freedom in Poetry" [published in *Vozdušnye Puti,* 1961] Vladimir Markov wittily constructs the following scale of values for contemporary Russian poetry. At the bottom is Esenin "for wide, general consumption"; in the middle are Gumilyev and, since recent times, Pasternak; and at the top, where he is available only to those who aspire to membership in a poetic elite, is Osip Mandelstam. Whether this "unshakeable scale of values". . . is likely to prove permanent in all its parts need not concern us now. But few would dispute that Mandelstam's position at the summit is an accurate image of the esteem in which he is held at this moment, and not only in the West. One could go further. Are there not signs here and there—see the reference to an "elite" above—that there is *in statu nascendi* a true cult of Mandelstam?

It is perhaps a natural and even an unavoidable development, and certainly it springs from impulses that are sympathetic and right. He has been these many years an underground, forbidden poet. He is both far from us and close to us in time: there are those who actually knew him, heard him read his poetry, walked the streets of Petersburg and Theodosia with him, and retain on the retina of their memory an image of the man in life. But their number grows smaller. Mandelstam met a fate of such savage injustice that its lightest word can harrow up the soul, and in the Soviet Union he has been waiting for nearly a decade in the anteroom of posthumous rehabilitation. There is therefore a distinct cachet that attaches to knowing anything at all about him or about his difficult, demanding poetry. There is a natural outrage at what was done to him and this multiplies one's determination to see just homage paid to his legacy.

But a cult disadvantages no one so much as its own object. It requires its ikon and its vita, and these have already begun to take shape—final shape—and to freeze the living lineaments of a man into the standard image of an object of contemplation. The memoirists have begun to rely heavily on each other, and there can be little doubt that there are now certain itinerant motifs in the word-image of him that wander from one set of reminiscences to the other. When Vsevolod Roždestvenskij's memoirs began to appear in *Zvezda* there was little doubt that the unnamed poet described in the following phrases was Mandelstam: "quite short, rather puny, not much to look at . . . a huge head, grand, rather theatrical gestures . . . an almost childish naïveté . . . the bright, sharp eye of a bird." (Any remaining doubt was removed when, in 1962,

Roždestvenskij published his memoirs in book form and named Mandelstam—a hopeful sign). Virtually every one of these words can be found in several other notes on his appearance and character. One émigré writer, who never laid eyes on Mandelstam, furnishes more or less the same picture of him, citing as his authority a brother-in-law who had once (at the age of ten) heard the poet in Xarkov.

As a young man Mandelstam took frank pleasure in the evidence that his name had spread beyond the narrow limits of the literary circles of Petersburg. In Kiev he positively basked in the unexpected adulation with which he was met, and observed that many poets there knew his verse by heart. This reaction is so normal that only its absence would be remarkable. But the maturer poet had other and more complicated ideas about his audience. Some of these he put into one of the most brilliant of his critical essays, "O sobesednike." When I asked the poet N. [Akhmatova] about this work and about Mandelstam's attitude toward his readers in general, I was told, "He was unhappy about the kind of people who read him. He thought them too refined, overly subtle in their reactions to poetry. He wanted to be read by simple people, by Komsomol youngsters, and not by poets alone." For him, poetry was at the center of life, not an ornament of its rarer and more sequestered moments, and he desired that it should be so for everyone. As he did not wish to be the exclusive property of a few, he could hardly have desired for himself a worse fate than to become the center of a cult.

But he will, I think, be spared this, for a cult derives all its seductive power from the distance and inaccessibility of the object. The publication by Gleb Struve and Boris Filippov of all of the known writings of Mandelstam will make him available to a wide audience of Russian readers both in the emigration and (though less conveniently) at home. Whether Mandelstam will achieve exactly the audience he desired—does any writer?—may be doubted, but he is, at least, now removed from the category of poets whose unpublished work is sedulously concealed by some, clandestinely circulated by others, and read by few.

As a glance at the bibliography in Volume III will disclose, the publication by the same editors of a sizable collection of Mandelstam's work in 1955 had as one of its more important consequences the introduction of his poetry to readers of Russian literature in the West. The translations made by poets of the stature of the American Robert Lowell and the German Paul Celan testify to the impact that Mandelstam has had outside of the bounds of his own literature. The great growth of Russian studies in recent years, particularly in England and America, has provided a very large audience for the brilliant poets and writers of Russia's "Silver Age." Among these Mandelstam has a reputation, exaggerated but not altogether groundless, for being extraordinarily difficult and opaque. The present brief introductory note aspires to nothing more than the function of a convenient English bridge by which, it is hoped, a good part of Mandelstam's audience will find an approach to the poetry and prose which await their more concentrated attention.

Mandelstam's earliest poetry is marked by an extraordinarily low temperature and a lack of movement that sometimes amounts to virtual stasis. It is characterized by quietude of manner, whiteness of color, elegance of form. The emotions are chaste, and there is a solemn ceremoniousness in the tones and attitudes of the speaker of the poems, whose presence is seldom felt. It is remarkable how often Mandelstam's diction is colored by negative words. Here are a few examples: nežiloj ("uninhabited") . . . nezvučnyj ("soundless") . . . nebogatyj ("poor") . . . nebyvalyj ("unprecedented") . . . nebytie ("non-existence") . . . nevidimyj ("invisible") . . . neživoj ("lifeless") . . . nepodvičnyj ("motionless") . . . And so on. The list of such words could be a very long one, but these can serve to illustrate a frequent tendency of Mandelstam's: to summon up a quality or attribute only to deny it.

He was a master at describing emptiness, absence, vacancy, silence. I know of no equal to him in this regard, at least not in literature. In painting Andrew Wyeth often achieves a Mandelstamian feeling of emptiness, and I think the comparison is doubly apt since both Wyeth and Mandelstam lend poignancy to their "desert places" by including some reminder of human life. Both artists show us not the vacancies of the sea or the ininhabited steppe but the emptiness of rooms. I like to imagine to myself an illustration by Wyeth of a line that would seem peculiarly suited to his mood and talent:

> Silence, like a spinning-wheel, stood there in the
> white room.

This blankness is not altogether dead, as it never is in Mandelstam. It has a human nerve in it. The more we perceive that remarkable figure of the spinning wheel to betoken a now ended human activity, the more we sense the peculiar stillness of a thing whose function is to move, the more densely does that image gather the silence around it.

Here is a poem which has been published in different variants. I take the version that appeared in Mandelstam's first book of poetry **Kamen** (**Stone**) in 1913.

> Hearing stretches its sensitive sail,
> The widened gaze grows empty
> And through the silence floats
> A soundless chorus of midnight birds.

I think it is easy to appreciate, even across the years that separate us from this poem, the shock that was felt in the literary world of St. Petersburg when it made its appearance. The late Georgij Ivanov testified in his reminiscences of Mandelstam that his reaction on reading such poems as this was a sudden stabbing envy: "Why didn't I write that!" And he quotes Gumilyev as having said that this poetic envy was far more accurate than any rational analysis to determine the true "weight" of someone else's poetry.

How extraordinary and how daring these images are! And not merely daring, but permanently daring. Time has not effaced their originality, and one recalls Ezra Pound's having defined literature as "news that *stays* news."

Nor have they anything to fear from analysis, which is durability of a sort that again argues the genius of their author. What is their effect? In the first line

> Hearing stretches its sensitive sail

one is provided with a visual image which jolts the imagination through its equation of an abstraction (the sense of hearing) with a piece of maritime equipment. But the image is far more than visual. There is something tactile in our perception of the tautness of a sail stretched tight against the wind, and this sense is enhanced by the addition of the epithet *čutkij,* which means "delicately sensitive" in both the basic physical sense and in the transferred sense for which "tactful" is a common though not very satisfactory equivalent. And there is yet a third way in which this image strikes us, though I am not sure that I can find the words to express it (and I take such disability as the final proof that one is in the presence of poetic art of the highest calibre). "Auditory" is hardly the adequate description for a quality of sense perception which is not that of sound but of *silence* (it is later in the poem that one learns this particular aspect of the first image: the poem is about emptiness and silence). And the function of the sail metaphor is to make that silence almost palpable. This third way of perceiving the image is perhaps best expressed by calling it an intense, almost painful, *awareness* of the sense of hearing, but not of anything conveyed to the consciousness by that sense.

He was a master at describing emptiness, absence, vacancy, silence. I know of no equal to him in this regard, at least not in literature.

—*Clarence Brown*

In the next image the sense of sight is treated in much the same way, and it has much the same sort of effect:

> The widened gaze grows empty.

Here one finds not the word for sight itself (zrenie) but the word *vzor* "gaze," which is a sort of buried hypostatic image: a piece of sight, an instance of sight. This hypostatized sight is made more material by the epithet that is applied to it: *rasširennyj* "broadened, widened." And by the verb: it "becomes empty," which implies the condition of having been full, of having contained something.

This is a poem about emptiness so complete that it is hardly expressible, but obviously images and sounds must be found to convey the emptiness. That the dilemma can decidedly *not* be resolved by simple, declarative state-

ment can be learned by looking at Milton's attempt to do something similar. In *Paradise Lost* (I/62-64) his purpose is to convey the absence of light, as Mandelstam's was to convey the absence of sound and vision:

> . . . . yet from those flames
> No light, but rather darkness visible
> Served only to discover sights of woe.

The phrase "darkness visible" appeals uniquely to the intelligence, to purely rational perception and to no other.

And so it is an inevitable contradiction that after the two images which transmit the emptiness of hearing and sight, one is presented with an image that is visual and auditory:

> And through the silence sails
> A soundless chorus of midnight birds.

Silence itself is materialized as a medium through which these midnight birds fly, and the fundamental contradiction is emphasized by a device which is frequent in Mandelstam: the *contradictio in adjecto—nezvučnyj xor*: soundless chorus.

The tenaciousness of early reputations is well known. The poems that I have been talking about—the cool, quiet, laconic poetry bathed in the pale radiance of other worlds— is the poetry of Mandelstam's earliest youth. It is regarded by many as his best work (there are those who regularly prefer a poet's first poems and regard the changes wrought by maturity as a sort of betrayal), but it would be a great mistake to regard it as his only work.

In a poem of 1912 Mandelstam had exclaimed of some ball "thrown from a dim planet"

> So there it is, a genuine
> link with a mysterious world!

But one year later this Symbolist link with other worlds had been abruptly transformed into a tennis ball, batted about in a real tennis game between a "sportive girl" and an "ever-young Englishman." The pervading gloom of the Symbolist manner was replaced for a while by the Acmeist gaiety and delight in the things of this world. Mandelstam had written many poems filled with a longing for muteness—perhaps a remnant of the decadent *amor fati*— and this scheme was to return later in such superlatively moving poems as **"To the German Language"** but for the time being there was some delightfully witty poems to be written—poems about the cinema, about Carskoe Selo— perfectly empty little poems that reveal the poet disporting himself in his language and taking nonchalant delight in its consonants and vowels.

. . . . .

[Mandelstam's] themes range over the whole world of art and all of Western culture. There are the famous poems in which the poet's vision caresses the immense perspectives and the classical architecture of his beloved Petersburg (to which he gave the Deržavinian and Hellenic name of Petropol), and the architecture of Paris (Notre Dame), of Moscow, where all the gentle churches lend their voices to a maidenly choir, and where Mandelstam was attracted as always by whatever seemed to him classical and Mediterranean in Russian culture:

> And the five-domed Moscow Cathedrals
> with their Italian and Russian soul
> remind me of the coming of Aurora
> but with a Russian name and in a coat of fur.

His poem about the Hagia Sophia in Istanbul is one of his most beautiful and beloved.

Other themes come from literature—all the way from the epic poems of Homer through the classical tragedies of Racine to the Victorian novels of Dickens and the weird tales of Edgar Allan Poe. Whatever one may think of the Soviet critic Selivanovskij's other opinions about Mandelstam, there is much truth in his remark that Mandelstam's poetry is not a reflection of life, but a reflection of its reflection in art. And a critic who is far more well disposed toward Mandelstam, Viktor Žirmunskij, has applied to his work Schlegel's tag "die Poesie der Poesie."

This brings us to two remarks that are perhaps repeated more often than others about the poetry of Osip Mandelstam: that it is impersonal and that it is impenetrable.

Certainly there is enough on the surface of his poetry, and especially of the early and better known poetry, that would seem to many people impersonal. Those who call it so generally have in mind the little *thing* poems with their nearly Japanese laconism (the nameless fruit falling from the tree in four brief lines) or the architectural poems, or the meditative poems. In other poems, though a *persona* may be present, it seems to matter so little, it seems to be so much a part of the patterned movement that it becomes lost, as in a trick picture, in the general composition. In the body of his work—by which I mean those of his poems that have been heretofore published and are known to the general reader—there are so few poems that concern themselves with anything outside of poetry and the other arts, there are so few that seem, for example, to point a moral, or advance a cause, or tell an entertaining story, or in fact to solicit our attention on any ground at all that is not in the strictest sense poetic ground, that there seems to be a certain lack of warmth, of humanness, about them. Hence the recurrent phrases: pure poetry, a poet's poet, rarefied atmosphere, museum-like, etc.

As for the charge of impenetrability, this is made by people who fail to understand Mandelstam because they are looking for the meaning in a place where he did not put it. This is the more to be regretted since Mandelstam himself, who had one of the clearest and most elevated conceptions of poetry of any Russian writer of his time, left in his critical writings explicit directions for reading his poetry. Those who use the word *meaningless* against him generally have in mind the notion that few of his poems can be paraphrased. The poet himself, meanwhile, regard-

ed whatever is susceptible of paraphrase as belonging outside of poetry proper. It was not his concern to cough a prose meaning in the outward form of metered language.

Ultimately, of course, such charges are irrefutable because the terms "impersonal" and "impenetrable" are unspecifiable, relative, and subjective. But it has seemed to me that some light might be thrown on this matter by selecting a single poem of moderate length, one that already has a clear reputation for being a difficult, typically Mandelstamian poem, and examining it minutely with the aid of all that recent research into the life and work of this poet has unearthed. Such a poem is **"Solominka, The Straw."**

You will doubtless not require the citation of authorities to know that this is a difficult, refractory work. Nevertheless, it is interesting to note that Georgij Adamovič has written of **"Solominka"**: "This poem really represents a 'lofty muteness,' in the phrase of Gumilev. But can one illuminate this muteness? Hardly" [*Vozdusnye Pati,* 1961].

Adamovič, a former Acmeist and a personal acquaintance of the poet, is a warm and generous admirer of Mandelstam. His remark is not a "charge"—far from it. Yet it is true that Adamovič's question, and his answer, can be found, *mutatis mutandis,* in all the standard attacks on Mandelstam's opacity.

I do not propose to assert that this is an easy poem or that it has a vividly recognizable personal element in it. It is, however, not so difficult that it cannot be made to yield a good deal of complexly articulated meaning. And it is by no means entirely divorced from the central concerns of the author's life. If we read it as closely as we can, if we follow all the clues to the end, and relate it to as much of Mandelstam's life as we can discover, I think we will conclude that it is more than a loose organization of hints and obliquities, clothed in gorgeous sound. If it proves to be more, perhaps it will appear that we must change our notions of how it is necessary to read him.

Our first impression is that we have here some of that mere *akustika* of which Mandelstam had accused the Symbolists. By the second stanza we are enmeshed in a dense web of phonic repetitions:

> Solómka zvónkaja, solomínka sukhája,
> Vsjú smért' ty výpila i sdélalas' nezhnéj,
> Slomálas' mílaja solómka nezhivája,
> Ne Saloméja, net, solomínka skoréj.

It does not require very intense investigation to see that two names are of primary importance. One is Solominka, the title, which means "a straw" but which is here sometimes capitalized and directly addressed as a person. The other is the name Salomeja. These two words, which closely resemble each other in sound, also provide the sound pattern for much of the poem. We see the near relatives of Solominka and Salomeja turning up everywhere: bessonnaja, bessonnicy, v ogromnoj spal'ne, solomka zvonkaja, v kruglom omute, v ogromnoj komnate, the verb slomalas, etc. Certainly, there is a good deal of obsessive toying with the basic phonic material.

What, in the plainest sense, is the poem about? It pictures a huge bedchamber in a house on the bank of the Neva in Petersburg. It is night in the month of December. The day is dead, the year is dying, and the subject of the poem seems to be death and the transformation that death brings. Throughout the poem, the speaker seems uneasy about a question of identity: Solominka or Salomeja? Toward the end of the first part, a new name enters, and there is a new question of identity:

No, not Solominka—Ligeja, the dying—

Not Solominka (or Salomeja) but Ligeja, a name with the same ending as Salomeja. In the last line of the first part, the speaker himself enters with a line that reads like the happy conclusion of an effort—the blessed words have been found:

I learned you, blessed words

These blessed words are names, the new one, Ligeja, and others:

Lenore, Solominka, Ligeja, Serafita.

The identity of Solominka-Salomeja is left unclear to the end. But it can hardly matter now, since she is dead, whoever she is, and will return no more. Her place has been taken by the Decemberish Ligeja.

This name, repeated three times in the poem, has assumed an importance that cannot be ignored. Was Mandelstam using this and the other blessed words for sound effects alone, or do they have some further significance?

Ligeja is one of the pale ladies of Edgar Allan Poe. She appears in a weird tale, which bears her name as the title, published in 1838. I will not go into detail here but will describe only those features of the story that bear on Mandelstam's poem.

Ligeja is an incredibly wise, ethereal creature. She is married to the narrator of Poe's tale, but she dies of some wasting disease and leaves her husband in an agony of remorse. He goes away, marries another woman, whom he cannot love since he is forever comparing her to the lost Ligeja. They live in a ruined abbey somewhere in England. The narrator begins to depend on opium, and finally his second wife falls ill and seems to be dying. Her bedchamber is in a turret of the abbey, and Poe lavishes his weirdest touches on the description of this dismal room. It is huge in size, the ceilings are immensely high, the walls are hung in some material covered with strange arabesque designs which assume fantastic shapes as the constant wind blows behind the hangings and causes them to shift about. There are sarcophagi with carved lids standing about in corners of the room. When the second wife of the narrator dies she is wrapped in her shroud and laid on the bed in this strange room. The narrator watches by

her bed, where he is horrified to see her return to life. When the shroud is unwound, it turns out that the body of the narrator's second wife has been replaced by the resurrected Ligeja.

Limitations of space will prevent a step by step comparison of Mandelstam's poem with this story by Poe. But a close comparison would reveal how much of the tone, the atmosphere—and more importantly the specific details such as the sarcophagus, the high ceiling, the peculiar animation of the room—Mandelstam did derive from "Ligeja." The central moment of Poe's work involves the changed identity of the two female figures, the metamorphosis of one into the other, and the gradual revelation of this to the narrator, and this, as we have seen, is also the fundamental concern of **"Solominka."**

The suggestiveness of the line of "blessed words" does not stop here. The name Lenore recalls an even better known heroine of Poe, but it is the name Serafita which sheds more light on the creative processes at work in this poem.

Séraphita is the title of one of the philosophical novels of Balzac, published in 1835. Practically devoid of any novelistic events whatever, *Séraphita* is devoted mainly to an exposition of the mystical philosophy of Swedenborg. The character from whose name the title is derived is related to this philosophy by birth—she is the daughter of a disciple of the master—and also by being a veritable incarnation of Swedenborgian doctrine. The great interest which *Séraphita* presents for an interpretation of **"Solominka"** is to be seen in the fact of her disputed identity. To Minna, a young girl, she appears as a youth Séraphitus, but to Wilfrid and to Pastor Becker she appears in female form as Séraphita. Ultimately, the character is neither and both, for its essence is ethereal and angelic, but as one of the blessed names, it makes its contribution to the unified effect of Mandelstam's poem.

The poem is about death, the death of a beautiful, loved woman. The names from Poe—Lenore and Ligeja—are of two of his famous dead ladies. The name Séraphita is that of a love-ideal, a creature who in Balzac's novel is finally transfigured and taken into heaven.

But the death of the central character in Mandelstam's poem—whose name, Salomeja, deliberately left unexplained till now, engendered so much of the sound texture of this work—is happily only metaphorical. For the subject of the poem is still alive. Princess Salomeja Nikolaevna Andronikova, a famous Georgian beauty who was the toast of St. Petersburg and the object of more than one poet's attentions, left Russia after the Revolution. Her married name is Halpern, and she now resides in London. I am very grateful to her for the generous interest she has taken in my studies of Mandelstam, and for the memories of him which she has so kindly shared with me. It appears that the picture of the enormous bedchamber looking out on the black Neva derives not only from literature but also from life.

It is incidentally interesting to note that this reading of the poem **"Solominka"** by Mandel'štam serves to illuminate a much more recent poem by the last of the great trio of Acmeists, Anna Axmatova. The poem is entitled "Ten'" ("Shadow"), and it is clearly addressed to Axmatova's old friend, Princess Andronikova, for it contains the line

>   A poet called you "Solominka."

Most modern poetry demands much of its readers, but there are few modern Russian poets whose demands are so heavy as those of Mandelstam. "If you would read me, you must have my culture." He was proud to link himself to Dante and to require, as Dante did, that his reader possess that highest quality of the truly educated man: "dogadlivost," which means quickness of apprehension, the ability to take a hint.

Lidija Ginzburg   (essay date 1972)

SOURCE: "The Poetics of Osip Mandelstam," in *Twentieth-Century Russian Literary Criticism,* edited by Victor Erlich, Yale University Press, 1975, pp. 284-312.

[*In the following essay, which was first published in a Russian periodical in 1972, Ginzburg distinguishes three stages in the development of Mandelstam's poetry and determines the influence of Hellenistic and Symbolist imagery on his work.*]

Mandelstam began as an heir to the Russian symbolists. Yet he did so at the moment when the disintegration of the symbolist movement was obvious to everyone, when Blok, its erstwhile standard-bearer, was seeking different answers to the disquieting questions of the era. The poems in Mandelstam's first collection **Stone** (1913) are free from symbolism's "other-worldliness," from its positive ideology and philosophy.

In 1912 Mandelstam joined the acmeists. These widely differing disciples of the symbolists were united by a common aspiration—the desire to return to an earthly source of poetic values, to a portrayal of the tridimensional world. The principal acmeist poets differed in their interpretation of this *tridimensionality*. Gumilëv's neoromanticism and exoticism are a far cry from the concrete, everyday world of Akhmatova's early verse. As for Man-

delstam, he was attracted to various facets of "tridimensionality," including the literal sense of the word—architectural proportions and building materials.

>   Be lace, stone
>   and a spiderweb.
>   Stab the sky's empty breast
>   With a fine needle.

"Gothic dynamics" are important to Mandelstam not because they symbolize a striving toward the infinite—this is the romantic interpretation of the Gothic—but because they mark the triumph of construction over material, the transformation of stone into needle and lace.

The architectural emphasis of Mandelstam's early poems should be broadly interpreted. In general, Mandelstam tended to conceive reality—from everyday occurrences to major cultural developments—in architectural terms, that is, as completed structures. [In his *Voprosy teorii literatury,* 1928] Viktor Zhirmunskij was the first to draw attention to this salient characteristic of Mandelstam's poetry in a 1916 article entitled "Those Who Have Overcome Symbolism." Observing that Mandelstam finds inspiration in "the images . . . of life in the cultural and artistic creations of the past ages," Zhirmunskij examines a series of such "synthetic images" in Mandelstam's poetry: aging Venice, the musical élan of German romanticism, the Kremlin cathedrals, Homer.

Making his debut in the 1910s when stylization reigned supreme—and stylization is always unhistorical—Mandelstam was struggling toward a historical grasp of cultures and styles.

The personality of the poet is not the focal point of the early Mandelstam's poetic world. Later, in *The Noise of Time* Mandelstam wrote: "My desire is to speak not about myself, but to track down the age, the noise, and the germination of time. My memory is inimical to all that is personal." Yet, while constructing in **Stone** a world of objectified cultural phenomena Mandelstam did not doubt that in fact he was creating *lyric* poetry.

An epic work not only unfolds in time, but also constructs an objective space, apprehended by the reader, within which objects are located and events occur. A lyric event is quite a different matter. Whether the poem deals with personal emotions or with the outside world, it is the poet's consciousness, his inner experience that provides here the encompassing framework. Within the lyric space concepts circulate freely, remote semantic categories crisscross as the abstract encounters the concrete, as subjectivity mingles with actuality, the literal meaning with the symbolic. This is clearly the case with the poems of **Stone** where inner experience is conveyed in mediated fashion and the personal is rarely mentioned.

To the young Mandelstam "overcoming of Symbolism" meant a repudiation not merely of "other-worldliness," but also of flimsy subjectivism. Hence the author hidden behind the world both historical and concrete, hence the

---

Mandelstam's resourcefulness during hard times:

Each time I copied out a new poem, M. would count up the lines and decide how much he had "earned" at the highest current rates of payment. (He would not 'settle' for less unless, as occasionally happened, he was very unhappy about a poem, in which case he agreed to a "reduced rate." It was reminiscent of Sologub, who used to sort his verse by quality and price it accordingly!) When we had thus added up his "earnings" for the day, we would go out to borrow money for our supper on the strength of them. We got money like this from some of the actors, the compositors at the local printing works, and sometimes from two professors we knew. . .We generally arranged to meet them in some deserted side street, where, like conspirators, we walked slowly past each other while they slipped us an envelope with their offering of money. If we had not managed to arrange to meet someone (it had to be done the day before), we would look in on the compositors, M. had got to know them it the summer of 1935 when we were living in the "agent's" house, which was next to the printing works and the offices of the local newspaper M. used to go in to read them poems as he finished them—particularly if this was late at night when nobody else was awake. They were always very pleased to see him, though the younger would sometimes stagger him by spouting opinions straight out of *Literary Gazette*—to the indignation of the older ones. In the bad times that were now upon us, these same older ones listened silently as M. read his new poems and then talked to him for a while about this and that while one of their number went out to buy food for him. They were miserably paid and could hardly make ends meet themselves, but they felt that "you can't let a comrade down in times like these."

Nadezhda Mandelstam, in her Hope Against Hope: A Memoir, *Collins & Harvill, 1971.*

---

structural firmness of his poetic universe. Art itself is conceived here as an architectural principle superimposed by the artist upon life's natural disorder.

The chief among the historical and artistic cultures reflected in the early Mandelstam is the synthetic, Greco-Roman culture. Mandelstam perceives it through the prism of the Russian tradition, of eighteenth-century classicism, of Batjushkov, Pushkin, and Russian architecture. "And the architect was no Italian, / but a Russian in Rome." This reference is to Voronikhin, architect of Kazan Cathedral.

It was not propensity for stylization that led Mandelstam to travel down the paths of world culture. It was rather the need to understand these cultures historically and to locate them in the context of Russia's cultural consciousness. This urge may well be traced back to Dostoevsky's notion of *universality* or *all-embracing humanity* as an inherent characteristic of Russian national consciousness. In Mandelstam, however, the problem is transposed to the linguistic plane, the most essential one, he feels, for a poet.

In his 1922 essay, "On the Nature of the Word" [which was published in *Sobranie Sochinenij*] Mandelstam writes: "Russian is a Hellenistic language. Thanks to historical circumstances, the vital forces of Hellenic culture, having yielded to Latin influences and, having tarried for a while in childless Byzantium, rushed to the bosom of Russian speech, imparting to it the original secret of the Hellenistic world view, the secret of free incarnation. *That is why Russian became a sounding and speaking flesh.*" The point here is not how well Mandelstam's linguistic notions correspond to scientific fact, but rather the role they play in his understanding of historical cultures and cultural styles.

In *Tristia* as in *Stone* Mandelstam steers clear of the poetic language of early nineteenth-century Russian classicism with its mythological bent and its conventional formulas. His aim is to create a Hellenic poetic "dialect" of his own. Mandelstam's poetic language is synthetic and broad; it ranges from the solemn archaisms to the most ordinary words, from learned allusions to plain colloquialisms. What is at issue here is merely the classical "coloring" of Mandelstam's vocabulary, the impact of some particularly dynamic words, capable of "infecting" the entire context. Mandelstam and his contemporaries learned the use of such words from the poets of the Pushkin era: "I have studied the science of saying goodbye / in bareheaded laments at night."

In a 1924 essay, "The Interlude" [which was published in *Arkhaisty i novatory,* 1929], Jurij Tynjanov commented: "In so receptive a poetic culture the grafting of a simple foreign word is enough to make 'saying goodbye,' 'bare-headed,' and 'waiting' as Latin-sounding as the 'vigils' [*vigilij*] and to assimilate 'sciences' and 'a pair of pants' to 'chebureki'" [the latter observation is a reference to the poem **"Feodosija"**].

For Mandelstam Hellenism is not only a source that fed Russian culture. In his poetic system of the 1910s and 1920s it is also the fountainhead of beauty. During those two decades Mandelstam, it seems, could not tear himself away from the beautiful.

Classicist aesthetics of the eighteenth and the nineteenth centuries frequently equated the beautiful with the artistic. At times, however, the former was interpreted more narrowly and distinguished from the merely characteristic or expressive in art. Since there is no room here for an extended discussion of the nature of the beautiful, this must remain a moot point. Suffice it to say that the experience of beauty is, indubitably, a distinctive psychological and aesthetic fact. The artistic systems of various ages invariably lay claim to this marvelous quality. Both classicism in all its variants and romanticism, in quite a different way, were such systems, even though the latter also provided a rationale for an aesthetic of the ugly.

Symbolist aesthetics was heavily indebted to the romantic tradition, and more specifically, to the romantic concept of the beautiful. The futurists tried to refute the very principle of beauty in art, though, in actual fact the beautiful is present in the works of both Khlebnikov and Majakovskij. Among the other poets who followed in the wake of the symbolists, there was no agreement on this issue. Each in his own way sought to discover the source of beauty and of the poetic. The Roman-Italian motifs of *Stone,* the Hellenism of *Tristia* are Mandelstam's appeal to the sphere of the beautiful, consecrated by tradition, to be exact, by the Russian poetic tradition. No wonder Mandelstam loved Batjushkov so much. In Batjushkov's poetry he found the continuity of beautiful formulas rooted in tradition but transformed by a great poet's genius.

To Mandelstam of the 1910s beauty bequeathed by classical antiquity leaves its imprint on every mode of experience, be it the lofty civic-mindedness ("Let us celebrate, brothers, the twilight of freedom"), or everyday life. Thus, the tennis player plays against the girl "like Attica's soldier in love with his enemy." Thus, the street urchin staring at the ice-cream peddler's "itinerate icebox" partakes of classical splendor.

> But even the Gods do not know what he'll take—
> A diamond cream? A wafer filled with jam?
> But glittering under the sun's thin ray
> The divine ice will quickly melt.

In his programmatic essay "On the Nature of the Word," Mandelstam contends that the Russian literary tradition knew *heroic* Hellenism and *domestic* Hellenism. He elaborates: "Hellenism—that is a cooking pot, an oven fork, a milk jug. It is household utensils, dishes, everything that surrounds the body. Hellenism is the conscious encirclement of man with the untensils instead of impersonal objects, the transformation of these objects into the utensils, the humanization of the surrounding world, heating it with the most delicate teleological warmth."

These reflections are closely related to Mandelstam's own poetics as well as to that Russian literary tradition in which Mandelstam, as a zealous reader of *The Iliad* in Gnedich's translation, was well versed. In the period of 1810-30 Gnedich elaborated what has been called the Russian "Homeric style." This style departs from the French neoclassical concept of antiquity, combining solemn archaisms with vernacular expressions, workaday concreteness, and at times, elements of folklore. The Russian version of *The Iliad* is a good example of what Mandelstam meant by the domestic Hellenistic tradition. Among Mandelstam's more recent models were the translations of ancient authors done by Vjacheslav Ivanov.

In her reminiscences about Mandelstam, Marina Tsvetaeva calls him a "Petersburgite and a Crimean." Mandelstam passionately loved the Crimea and the sea. The Crimea became for him a *sui generis* native variant of antiquity. Crimean motifs permeate the Hellenism of *Tristia* and lend the cycle a certain intimacy. "In rock-strewn Taurida Hellenic science lives," writes Mandelstam.

> And in the white room silence stands like
>   a spinning wheel,
> It smells of vinegar, paint, and new wine
>   from the cellar.

> Do you remember, in the Greek house, the
>   wife everyone loved?
> Not Helen. The other one—how long she
>   could work at embroidering?

Thus Mandelstam's "household-utensil" concept of Hellenism is brought forth and the boundaries between the Crimean and classical motifs obliterated.

In Mandelstam flocks of sheep are emblematic of the Crimea. A system of images that keeps recurring in his verse of the 1910s includes flocks, shepherds, dogs, wool, sheeps' warmth. This cluster, grounded in a domestic locale, can be propelled into a Roman theme of a broad historical scope:

> The old ewes, the black Chaldeans,
> The spawn of night, cowled in darkness,
> Go off grumbling to the hills
> Like plebs annoyed at Rome.

In *Tristia* Mandelstam uses Hellenism as a mode of the beautiful to talk of the lyric poet's enduring subjects—the creative process ("I have forgotten the word I wanted to say"), the passage of time, death, and love. There are many poems about love in *Tristia.* But for the most part the direct, traditionally lyrical expression of the love theme is absent here. It enters the collection in a covert, to be exact, semicovert fashion.

"Because I Was Not Able to Restrain Your Hands" is one of the finest love lyrics in twentieth-century Russian poetry. The poet finds himself a participant in an ancient *agon;* the besieged Troy, the Achaian warriors, and Helen, not named but alluded to, are all "objective correlatives" for a throbbing, pent-up lyricism. But Mandelstam's semantics are so sensitive to lexical coloring that at times one name suffices to bring this lyricism to the fore. Why for instance, "Not Helen. The other?" Why is Penelope not named, but introduced in a roundabout, periphrastic manner? Because the beautiful Helen's name brings to the surface the personal theme, reinforced by "do you remember?" Though never fully articulated, it sends a current of lyrical uneasiness across the poem.

In the collection *Tristia* (1922) the function of the Hellenist style has changed. No longer employed to project the image of a historical culture, it now becomes authorial style, the language that encompasses Mandelstam's poetic universe, an embodiment of the beauty he seeks.

The reviewers of the 1920s contrasted the precision and concreteness of *Stone* with *Tristia*'s associative poetics. The shift from *Stone* to *Tristia* show how substantial was the evolution Mandelstam had undergone. It is, however, the evolution of a single creative personality whose continuity is evident at all stages. The two collections are held together by a certain structuring thrust that characterizes Mandelstam's perception of the world. Therefore, his associative semantics [*assotsiativnost'*], though dynamic, is not at all diffuse.

The artistic context that determines the meaning of a word may well extend far beyond the limits of a given work. Such a context can be provided by an entire literary movement or an individual poetic system. Blok's poetry, for example, cannot be understood apart from his large cycles, which ultimately merge into a single context, a "trilogy of incarnation" [literally "humanization"], to use Blok's own phrase. In Pasternak's early poems, the verses rush along impetuously, breaking out of their boundaries to form a single lyrical torrent. Mandelstam, on the other hand, is a poet of delimited, though interrelated, contexts.

Mandelstam's poetic language is synthetic and broad; it ranges from the solemn archaisms to the most ordinary words, from learned allusions to plain colloquialisms.

—Lidija Ginzburg

In a much quoted letter to Strakhov [23 April 1876], Tolstoy said that "art is a huge labyrinth of linkages" and that, as a writer, "[I am] guided by a need to gather thoughts that were linked together in order to express myself. Each thought, however, expressed separately loses its meaning and suffers terribly when it is taken out of the linkage to which it belongs." The decisive aesthetic role of the context and intensity of semantic interaction are inherent in all verbal art, not to mention lyric poetry, where interaction is especially dynamic. I keep referring to Mandelstam's associativeness, to poetics of linkages, since these characteristics acquire maximum intensity in his poetic system. There are historical reasons for this. The pupils of the symbolists repudiated their predecessors' "other-worldliness" but held firm to their discovery that in poetry the word has a heightened capacity for evoking unnamed notions, for filling the gaps with associations. This widened range of association is, perhaps, the most vital element of the symbolist legacy.

Mandelstam's taut contexts permit remote meanings to meet, crisscross, or come into conflict with one another. In his poems an epithet often refers to the context rather than to the object with which it is formally, or grammatically, linked. "I have studied the science of saying goodbye / In bare-headed laments at night."

Why are these laments "bare-headed"? The explanation is found in the last three lines of the same eight-line stanza:

When, lifting their load of sorrow for the journey,
Eyes red from weeping have peered into the distance
And the crying of women mingled with the Muses'
    singing.

These are tears and laments of bare-headed women (that is, women with uncovered heads), seeing their men off to battle.

The last collection of Mandelstam's poetry published in his lifetime (1928) includes *Stone, Tristia,* and a section labeled *1921-1925.* The poems of these latter years, although akin in many ways to the *Tristia* collection, for the most part lack the stylistic coloring suggestive of classical antiquity. Hence, the principle that underlies the Mandelstam imagery emerges even more clearly. The section opens with the 1921 poem, **"Concert at the Railway Station"** (later in *The Noise of Time* Mandelstam transferred the salient images of this poem from a poetic plane to the plane of everyday life). The architectonics of the poem are complex. The present mingles with childhood recollections of famous symphonic concerts held at the Pavlovsk train station. Within this all-embracing antithesis, three worlds collide: the *world of music* (like Blok, Mandelstam considers music not only an art form, but also a higher symbol both of the historical life of peoples and of the spiritual life of individual man), the *glass world* of the station's concert hall, and the *iron world* of the nearby railroad—a harsh, antimusical world. One should not, however, interpret such images allegorically and assign to them a single meaning; to do so would be to violate Mandelstam's poetic system.

The Aeonian maids, at whose song the station
    trembles,
And again the violin-laden air is sundered
And fused together by the whistles of trains.

Immense park. The station in a glass sphere.
A spell cast again on the iron world.
The train carriage is borne away in state
to the echoing feast in misty Elysium.

The three worlds are tightly interwoven into a single whole: the railway station with the "Aeonian maids" [muses], the whistles of trains with the violin-laden air. The iron world is drawn into the world of music. The very word *torzhestvenno* [in state] with its classical ambiance and stately sound does much to lend the train carriage a semblance of a musical "Elysium." The station trembles with music ("at the song of the Aeonian maids")—this traditional metaphor reappears in the last stanza in a new and complex guise: "And I think, how like a beggar the iron world / shivers, covered with music and lather."

The iron world shivers. It is now bewitched, overcome by music. Therefore, it is covered with music, but also with lather, because the shiver has drawn into the semantic circle the notion of a winded, lathery horse. The unusual combination of music and lather lends a material quality to music and symbolic significance to the lather.

On no account should Mandelstam's associative resonance be confused with the "trans-sense," undifferentiated semantics and kindred phenomena that Mandelstam opposed vigorously. He pitted against the symbolist verbal music the poetically transformed meaning of the word, against the signs of the "unknowable" the image as an expression of the sometimes elusive, but essentially knowable, intellectual connection between phenomena.

In the essay "The Morning of Acmeism," written about 1913, Mandelstam protests the "trans-sense" [*zaumnyj*] language of the futurists, arguing that logos, "the conscious sense of the word," is the very cornerstone of poetry: "For us a logical relationship is not some ditty about a siskin, but a choral symphony with organ, so difficult and inspired that the director must exert all his powers to keep the performers under his control." That is how Mandelstam viewed the semantic instrumentation in verse. A younger contemporary of Andrej Belyj and Khlebnikov, a peer of Tsvetaeva, Mandelstam is fully alive to phonic affinities between words, but he cherishes the auditory image chiefly as a generator of a new meaning.

Many years later Mandelstam returns to the problem of poetic logos in "Talking about Dante" [*Doles,* 1933]. In this essay he not only talks about the Italian poet, but also discusses at length both poetry in general and his own poetics in particular. "When, for example, we pronounce the word 'sun,' we do not expel a ready-made meaning—this would be a form of semantic abortion—but rather experience a *sui generis* cycle. Every word is a bundle from which meaning radiates in different directions, rather than converging on one official point. When we say 'sun,' we embark upon an enormous journey, one to which we have become so accustomed that we 'sleepwalk.' What distinguishes poetry from automatic speech is that it rouses us and shakes us awake in the middle of a word."

In his memoirs Vsevolod Rozhdestvenskij recalls Mandelstam's early pronouncement: "Ideas should blaze up now here, now there like little marsh lights. They only appear to be disconnected. Everything is subject to reason, to sound rules of logic, yet they are buried deep down and are not readily accessible" [*Pages from Life,* 1965].

Although the reader does not actually reconstruct the omitted semantic links, he nonetheless is aware of this "difficult and inspired" inner logic. With few exceptions, Mandelstam's poems can be explained; their author is not a poet who strings together "blissful and senseless" words. One should not misconstrue this formula as Mandelstam's poetic creed; it occurs in **"We Shall Gather Again in Petersburg"** (1920) and refers to the words of love. Many Mandelstam poems are effective because of their euphony or their lexical coloring. For him, however, this is always an auxiliary, secondary factor. It has been assumed that the poem **"I Have Forgotten the Word I Wanted to Say"** lacked a definable subject. Actually it has a theme—notably, creativity, the fear of muteness that haunts the poet. The young Mandelstam wrote about the delights of silence, beseeching the word to return to music. The mature Mandelstam knows that thought embodied in words is a necessity, that it is the poet's highest obligation. "More than anything else," Akhmatova recalls, "he feared his own muteness, calling it asphyxia. When it gripped him, he rushed about in terror":

> I have forgotten the word I wanted to say.
> A blind Swallow returns to the palace of shadows

> on clipped wings to flicker among the Transparent
> Ones.
> In oblivion they are singing the night song.

The blind swallow with clipped wings stands for the unspoken word. It returns to the kingdom of the dead, to the palace of shadows where everything is incorporeal and thus transparent, mute, and arid:

> No sounds from the birds. No flowers on the
> immortelles.
> The horses of night have transparent manes.
> A little boat drifts on the dry river.
> Among the crickets the word fades into oblivion.

Unembodied, the poetic word loses its bearings. Tormented, like the poet himself, it fights for life:

> And it rises slowly, like a pavilion or a temple,
> performs the madness of Antigone,
> or falls at one's feet, a dead swallow,
> with Stygian tenderness and a green branch.

The word grows, bearing a green branch like the dove released from Noah's ark. Further on there is a fear of the opening void, and the muses (Aeonian maids) weep over the poet who has lapsed into silence.

> But I have forgotten what I wanted to say
> and a bodiless thought returns to the palace
> of shadows.

Another poem also dated 1920 deals, on the other hand, with the realization of a poetic vision. The same Hellenic imagery is used simultaneously with the themes of poetry and love, death and creative immortality, and thus of time.

> Take from my palms, to soothe your heart,
> a little honey, a little sun,
> in obedience to Persephone's bees.

> You can't untie a boat that was never moored,
> nor hear a shadow in its furs,
> nor move through thick life without fear.

> For us, all that's left is kisses
> tattered as the little bees
> that die when they leave the hive.

> Deep in the transparent night they're still humming,
> at home in the dark wood on the mountain,
> in the mint and lungwort and the past.

> But lay to your heart my rough gift,
> this unlovely dry necklace of dead bees
> that once made a sun out of honey.

The poem is constructed around two fundamental—and interrelated—symbols: bees and kisses. Kisses are the symbol of love; bees traditionally have been associated with poetry. The poets of classical antiquity (Horace, in particular) compared themselves to bees. Mandelstam had employed the images of the bee as poet and honey as poetry in one of his early poems, **"On a Rocky Spur of Peoria."** In **"Take from My Palms"** the image of the bee is more polysemous. Bees are an attribute of Persephone, queen of the underground kingdom of the dead, and goddess of fertility and germination. Persephone is a symbol of the eternal cycle of death and rebirth in nature, of sprouting grain that has been dropped into the earth's womb. In the second tercet Mandelstam speaks of the subterranean, shadowy kingdom of Persephone, the ruler of the bees, and of the fear this kingdom inspires in mortals. In the third tercet kisses appear and immediately are identified with bees through the medium of Mandelstam's favorite device—the transfer of an attribute from one object to another. The kisses are "tattered [furry] as the little bees." These are the bees of poetry and love, and at the same time of the eternal cycle of death and renewal in nature. It is thus that they feed on the past as well as on lungwort. The bees, the kisses, and the feelings of the poet die. But the honey of creation and love is immortal, like the sun.

To understand this poem one need not have an extensive knowledge of mythology, but simply a general idea of the Persephone myth (much less than a reading of Pushkin's early poems and of other Russian poets of the period frequently requires). But one also needs to grasp the basic principle of Mandelstam semantics.

Poetry is a special mode of artistic cognition, of knowing things in their uniqueness, in their aspect at once generalized and individual, thus inaccessible to scientific logical cognition. This uniqueness or individuality of the percept is more essential to the modern lyric poet than the sense of the author's or the hero's individuality. That is why poetic word is always a word transformed by the context, and qualitatively different from its prose equivalent.

In "Talking about Dante," Mandelstam speaks at length about the poetic transformation of the world "with the aid of instruments commonly labeled images." Mandelstam expresses himself metaphorically: this is an organic trait of his thinking. In 1933 Mandelstam came to Leningrad. Several people, among them myself, gathered at Anna Akhmatov's to listen to him read his just completed "Talking about Dante." Mandelstam read the essay, read his poems, and talked copiously about poetry and about painting. We were struck by the remarkable affinities between the essay, the poems, and the table talk. Here was a single semantic system, a single stream of similes and juxtapositions. The image-bearing matrix from which Mandelstam's poems emerged became strangely tangible.

The same semantic principles are operative in Mandelstam's prose, including his essays. Paradoxical though it may seem, Mandelstam's prose is often more metaphorical than his poetry. This is true, at any rate, of *The Egyptian Stamp*. A metaphor brings together notions so as to form a completely new and indivisible semantic whole. This is not always the case with Mandelstam's "linkages." What matters most here are changes in meaning occa-

sioned by the words' presence in the total context of the work where they can interact at a distance, often without a syntactic contiguity.

Within this overall pattern pivotal or key words acquire special impact. Mandelstam's insight into the nature of these words owes a great deal to Annenskij's poetry with its psychological symbolism. Mandelstam accepts the notion of life refracted through poetic symbols, but he cannot accept the abstractness of "professional symbolism." In the essay "On the Nature of the Word," (1922) Mandelstam writes:

> Images are disemboweled like stuffed animals and packed with foreign content. . . . That's what happens with professional symbolism. The result is a terrible quadrille of "correspondences" nodding to one another. Eternal winking. . . . Rose motions to girl, girl to rose. No one wants to be himself. . . . The Russian symbolists . . . sealed every word and every image, having earmarked them in advance for liturgical use alone. Something extremely awkward resulted; one could neither move, stand up, nor sit down. . . . All the utensils had risen in rebellion, the broom requested a day off, the pot no longer wanted to cook, but demanded instead absolute significance (as if cooking were not an absolute significance).

In an early essay on Villon, Mandelstam says approvingly that medieval allegories are "not disembodied." The same idea is also found in the essay "Remarks on Chénier": "Very broad allegories, including such concepts as 'Liberty, Equality, and Fraternity,' are not at all incorporeal. For a poet and his epoch they are almost living persons, interlocutors. He discerns their features, feels their warm breath" [*Sobranie sochinenij*]. In an allegory or a simile Mandelstam wanted to preserve the sensual warmth of objects.

Mandelstam's key words are inherently symbolic: they were not drawn, however, from any symbolist stockpile. His symbols are original, the system his own. It is not surprising that his system took shape in the 1910s, when poets nurtured by symbolism were repudiating its philosophy. In the 1924 essay "Thrust" [which was published in *Sobranie sochinenij*] Mandelstam calls symbolism "generic [*rodovoja*] poetry," contending that after its collapse "the kingdom . . . of the poetic individual came into being," a kingdom in which "every individual stood separately, with his head bared."

In *Tristia* and in the poems written during the first half of the 1920s emphasis on the objective and the narrative tenor of *Stone* recedes; to a large degree, the poet's experience is now an inner one. It is the experience of a man who loves life in all its beauty and significance, but finds it an inordinate burden because its harsh laws bear down on him and because he carries within himself elements of weakness and inadequacy that sap his creative powers and that creativity alone might be able to overcome.

This is also true of the later period. In Mandelstam's poems written in the 1930s there is fear, confusion, and despair, and at the same time an amazing, indestructible love of life. Tragedy coexists here with an ever-increasing delight in the phenomena of existence. The poet is in love with history, art, and life. Such is the cycle **"Armenia"** (1930), which marks the beginning of Mandelstam's final creative period.

> Oh, Erivan, Erivan! Did a bird draw you,
> or, like a child, a lion paint you out of a
> colored pencilcase?

The bird and lion are heraldic animals protrayed as a rule colorfully and archetypally. The lion suggests beauty and strength, but here the lion also has a childlike quality—a marvelous schoolboy with a pencilcase in its paw.

"Batjushkov" (1932) is a poem about the triumph of poetry.

> He brought us, tongue-tied,
> Our anguish, and our wealth,
> the noise of poetry-making, the bell of
> brotherhood
> and the soft downpour of tears.

"Impressionism" is about our response to painting. Sensual concreteness of perception approaches here a visual illusion.

> But the shadow, the shadow's getting ever
> more violet—
> A bow or a whip, it goes out like a match
> You may say: in the kitchen
> The cooks are cooking fat pigeons.

Mandelstam's poetry always has its origin at the point where fear of life and love of life meet. And so it is until the very end. In one of the last Voronezh poems, Mandelstam with unprecedented directness writes about his desire to possess the earth's vital force, "to hear the axis of the earth."

> I do not draw or sing
> or ply the dark-varied bow.
> I simply drink life in and love to envy
> The strength and cunning of the wasps!
>
> Oh if only once the sting of the air and
> the heat
> of summer could make me hear
> beyond sleep and death
> the earth's axis, the earth's axis.

If in *Stone* problems of the world's cultures and of poetic styles are predominant, in *Tristia* and the poems *1921-1925* adjoining it "eternal themes" of life and death, creation and love are paramount. Here the love theme is partially concealed by imagery, now classical, now old-Russian. The poet has moved into a different dimension; in *Tristia* structural ties appear to lose their external objective and narrative outlines, becoming instead an inner logic of assocaitions.

The cluster of symbols that originally embodied Mandelstam's concept of man, of his strengths and weaknesses, gave rise to a number of secondary images. In 1915 he announced a change in his materials. He wrote:

> Fire destroys
> My *dry* life
> and I sing now
> not stones, but *tree*.

But at that time he was still speaking about "the wooden paradise where things are so light." Eventually the theme of dryness and the correlative one of wood becomes increasingly important to Mandelstam. Dryness acquires the connotation of sapped vitality, of inadequacy. In the poem **"Because I Was not Able to Restrain Your Hands"** man is imprisoned in a wooden world peopled by timbers, saws, wood, an ax, resin-oozing walls, the wooden ribs of a city, a wooden rain of arrows like a grove of nut trees, and all this is a retribution for man's powerlessness, for dryness.

> Because I was not able to restrain your hands,
> Because I betrayed your salty, tender lips,
> I must wait for dawn in this dense acropolis.
> How I despise these ancient reeking timbers.

Another key word here is *blood*. Blood is a vital force: "But blood has rushed to the stairs and started climbing . . ." Yet blood too is threatened by dryness: "Nothing quiets the blood's dry fever." The extraordinary coupling of dryness with blood is thus justified.

The meaning of Mandelstam's images is determined by the context. Sometimes, however, their meaning is quite stable and is transmitted from one poem to another. Dryness is failure—an "exchanged blood." This is fully explained by another poem of 1920 in which the love theme appears without any classical coloring:

> I want to serve you
> equally with others,
> to mumble fortunes
> with lips dry from jealousy.
> The word does not slake
> my parched mouth,
> and without you the dense air
> is empty again for me.
> I do not call you
> either joy or love,
> my blood has been exchanged
> for another, savage blood.

In two poems of 1922, **"No Way of Knowing When This Song Began,"** and **"I Climbed into the Tousled Hayloft,"** both variations on the same theme, we are no longer confronted by the dryness of wood, but rather by the stifling dryness of hay and the hayloft. Hence, a whole series of secondary images *smothering hayrick, rustling, sack of* *caraway seeds, dry grass, hay-dust, matted scurf,* and finally *squabble.* Significantly, the image of blood is present here also. The poet must free it from dryness: "So that the pink link of blood / and the one-armed ringing of the grass may pronounce / their last goodbyes." As one can see, these poems share a single semantic key. Each of them is a whole; at the same time they are linked by the symbolism that runs through Mandelstam's poetry.

Critics have noted the presence of recurrent images in Mandelstam's poetry such as *salt* and *star.* Such images, however, occur not by themselves but in specific contexts. In "Talking about Dante," salt and blood are tied in one semantic "bundle:" "This is a song about the composition of human blood, which contains oceanic salt. The origin of the journey lies in the system of blood vessels. Blood is planetary, solar, salty." If blood is always perceived as a vital force, the image of salt in Mandelstam's poetry acquires various meanings. Sometimes salt means hurt, sometimes it too is a vital force—the salt of the earth.

In the poems of the 1920s, as in *Stone,* stars inspire in the poet feelings of distrust, hostility, and fear. As in the earlier verse, they represent the inscrutable and overwhelmingly vast universe from which one must seek protection in domesticity, in utensils, in the warmth of the earth: "There are seven stars in the Great Bear's dipper, / five good senses on the earth."

In the 1925 poem **"I'll Run Wild in the Dark Streets Gypsy Camp"** the image of "prickly starry untruth" arises. Why are the stars "prickly?" Because they are cold, indifferent to man. Of course, the star's form, its slender rays, and sharp facets are also significant. Because of their sharp planes, stars resemble salt crystals. Thus salt, associated with stars through form, glitter, and milky dispersion, becomes a hostile force. And here something else comes into play—the corrosive power of salt.

I was washing outside in the darkness,
the sky burning with rough stars,
and the starlight, salt on an ax-blade.
The cold overflows the barrel.

The gate's locked,
The land's grim—as its conscience—
I don't think there is a finer warp
than the truth of a fresh canvas.

Star, like salt, is melting the barrel
Icy water is turning blacker,
Death's growing purer, misfortune saltier
The earth more truthful and dreadful.

Rough stars, salt, an ax, icy water, the stern earth, unbleached canvas are all merciless to man, demanding from him an ultimate sobriety and truth and requiring him to look death and salty misfortune in the face.

The following poem also dates from the first half of the 1920s:

To some winter is nut-stains and blue-eyed punch
to some, wine fragrant with cinnamon, and to some
it's a salt of commands from the cruel stars
to carry into a smoky hut.
The warm droppings of a few hens
and a tepid muddle of sheep.
For life, for life and care, I'll give up everything
A kitchen match could keep me warm.

Here Mandelstam's key symbols combine with a terribly direct, unvarnished conversation about the agonizing desire to live, to find warmth. And "A salt of command from cruel stars" is a new variant on the 1912 theme:

And
    in the sky gold is dancing
And bids me to sing.

The cold abstractness, the "cruelty" of vast spaces is juxtaposed with the warmth of sheep, chicken manure, smoke, wool, utensils; all these help sustain life, however frail.

Look, all I have with me is a clay pot
To smoothe out fur and turn straw in silence.

In the final stanzas, cruel stars once again are coupled with the acidity of salt, with the bitter taste of smoke and wormwood.

Since persistently recurring images wander through Mandelstam's poems, they may be said to explain one another. But sometimes the key to the poem's interpretation is found outside the confines of Mandelstam's poetry. Thus, on occasions, the meaning of an entire poem or of individual images can be fully grasped only by consulting the memoirs of a contemporary.

In her reminiscences about Mandelstam, Marina Tsvetaeva recalls that three of his 1916 poems were addressed to her, though there were no formal dedications. In 1916 Tsvetaeva in her own words, "made Mandelstam a present of Moscow," that is, showed him the city. It was her "tiger fur coat," we learn, that got intertwined with the Russo-Italian motif of Kremlin cathedrals:

And Moscow's five-domed cathedrals
With their Italian and Russian souls
Remind me of Aurora, Goddess of dawn
but with a Russian name, and in a fur coat.

The following poem in the cycle is **"On a Sledge, Overlaid with Straw."** In this multilevel poem Tsarevich Dmitrij, murdered in Uglich, blends with the False Dmitrij, who, in turn, merges with the author and assumes independent existence: "I am conveyed about the streets bare-headed," but later "They are bringing the Tsarevich, the body's numb with terror."

Let us imagine that this poem is preceded by a dedication to Marina Tsvetaeva: immediately it ceases to be enigmatic. The name Marina, bringing to mind Pushkin's *Boris Godunov,* is the key to the latent love theme in the poem.

She is Marina, and he, therefore, is Dmitrij; at the same time he is the poet who is writing about Dmitrij and Marina.

At times the poem's plot overlaps with history. For example, the line "And in Uglich the children play at knucklebones" alludes to an actual historical fact. The boyars, sent to Uglich by Godunov, declared that the Tsarevich was not murdered, but had accidentally stabbed himself with a knife while playing *svajka* (a game similar to knucklebones) with other children. The Pretender's ties with Rome and the Pope's futile attempt to use him as a means of introducing Catholicism into Russia are also historical facts. At times the poet moves away from history. The Pretender was not bound and carried around the city. He was murdered near the palace, and later his body was burned. This, perhaps, accounts for the line "And now the amber straw was set on fire." The False Dmitrij was red-haired. The chain of associations thus grows longer. Missing, however, is the final link, the name Marina Tsvetaeva, which would elucidate the poem once and for all. To find the link we must have recourse to material outside the text.

Recounting the story of the third poem dedicated to her, **"No Believers in the Resurrection,"** Tsvetaeva observes: "I do not know whether it is necessary to footnote the everyday material used in poems. Poems grind up life and then discard it." This is true, but not entirely true. One should not confuse the origin of lyric material with its artistic function. A "real-life" source sometimes is incorporated into a poem's artistic structure in the form of its principal theme or semantic key or serves as a basis for associations essential to a total response. At times, however, the realia that set the poet's thought in motion prove to be aesthetically neutral. They have indeed been milled by the verses and then discarded.

Mandelstam was clearly the kind of poet who reacted strongly to the most diverse stimuli, including the mundane, the everyday. It is this concreteness of impulse, whenever the letter is unknown to the reader, that sometimes renders a poem unintelligible.

> The clock-cricket singing,
> that's the fever rustling,
> the dry stove hissing
> that's the fire in red silk.

Speaking about this poem Akhmatova observed: "This is about how we heated the stove together. I have a fever and I take my temperature."

Most likely Mandelstam really "was washing outside in the darkness" (the opening line of a poem written in Tbilisi in 1921), or climbed the ladder ("I climbed into the tousled hayloft"). A locked gate, a barrel with icy water, the tousled hay, all these are real objects, transformed into elements of a poetic conversation about truth, death, and misfortune or about the universe and creativity. In instances such as these information about the actual sources of a poetic experience is pertinent only to the psychology of creation, remaining beyond the threshold of the work's aesthetic structure.

A similar fate befalls sometimes even the aesthetically effective realia that are essential to the interpretation of a given context. More exactly, their meaning is revealed elsewhere, notably in Mandelstam's prose or essays. One of his favorite images is the swallow. Its significance differs from one context to another. Swallows are bonded together into legions in one place and serve as a symbol of poetic language in another. The swallow is an image found in ancient Greek folksongs. But this is not all. The meaning of bird imagery is elucidated in "Talking about Dante:" "The quill is a tiny piece of bird flesh. Certainly Dante, who never forgets the origin of things, keeps this in mind. The technique of writing with all its twists and flourishes develops into a figured flight of birds in flock. . . . Old Italian grammar, not unlike our Russian grammar, is the same agitated flock of birds." Thus, for Mandelstam bird symbolism is associated with writing, with language (in *The Egyptian Stamp* there is an expression, "the swallow's flourish"). Later, while in Voronezh, Mandelstam wrote a radio essay on Goethe. In it the "technique of writing," to be exact, the handwriting of a great poet, is associated with the swallow. Goethe's "handwriting is characterized at once by the wildest swings and by harmony. His letters resemble fishermen's hooks that slant diagonally as though a whole flock of swallows were skimming smoothly and powerfully slantwise across the page." The swallow's flight is the poet's handwriting; it is letters and letters are a word. The chain of associations extend thus to blind swallow, symbol of the unembodied poetic word. But the links of these chains are buried in later essays.

For Mandelstam this was a natural process. So absorbed was he in the single thrust of his poetic thought which he realized in his verse, artistic prose, essays, and conversation, moving freely from genre to genre, that he himself did not fully appreciate its range.

The problem of the reader, the social existence of the work of art, was a matter of major concern to Mandelstam. He advocated intellectuality in poetry and inner logic in poetic thought. In "Talking about Dante" he labeled the expectation that the reader would grasp the cultural, historical, political, and technical notions introduced by the poet the poem's "reference keyboard." We have seen, nonetheless, that he himself more than once pressed a key that could not evoke the requisite response even in an experienced reader. This was so not because his verse defied sense or lacked a subject, but because in those instances the key to his poetic logic was misplaced.

Mandelstam had great faith in the power of poetic linkages, so characteristic of this system, in the dynamics of the context. (Whenever this faith was not justified, failure would ensue.) Mandelstam was confident that even where crucial poetic associations were not available to the reader, because he was not familiar with some aspect of the realia, the context would compensate by suggesting some other kindred associations. This held true for individual poetic images and occasionally also for poems constructed entirely around plots concealed from the reader.

An example of such a poem is **"On the Stage of Ghosts a Pale Gleaming."** In the last stanza we are confronted by Petrograd at night in the year 1920. "Smoke hangs in the ragged sheepskins. The street's black with drifted snow," while at the theater magnificent opera performances are taking place. We find the same theme in **"We Shall Gather Again in Petersburg."** The first two stanzas are a recollection of old Petersburg, with its grand theater exits, an illusory image of the nineteenth-century opera stage. The third stanza seems to stand at the juncture of these two planes. The name of Eurydice and the legend of Orpheus, who found Eurydice in the kingdom of shadows and lost her again thanks to a blunder, introduces a personal, lyric theme. The poem's two motifs—love and music—have been brought together.

> **The problem of the reader, the social existence of the work of art, was a matter of major concern to Mandelstam. He advocated intellectuality in poetry and inner logic in poetic thought.**
>
> *—Lidija Ginzburg*

But how is one to understand the last two lines: "The living swallow fell / On hot snow."?

What is this? A diffuse, irrational motif? No, once again the factual link is missing, and we find it in Mandelstam's prose. In *The Egyptian Stamp* Mandelstam twice talks about the circumstances surrounding the death of the Italian singer, Angiolina Bosio. Bosio sang in St. Petersburg during the years 1856-59; in 1859, at the age of thirty-five, she caught a cold and died of pneumonia. Her death made an extraordinary impression on St. Petersburg society. In the poem "On the Weather" (1865) Nekrasov recalls the event:

> Let us recall Bosio. Arrogant Petropolis
> Went all out for her.
> But in vain did you wrap up in sable
> Your nightingale throat,
> Italy's daughter! Southern roses
> Cannot cope with Russian frost.

"The stage of ghosts" of the first stanzas is the stage of the 1850s. Mandelstam's line "There's a rose under the furs," offers a variation on the above. In the next stanza he appears to take notice of Nekrasov: "Ours is a cold winter, dear Eurydice. / Never mind . . ."

The narrative core of the poem is thus encoded in the same way as the love theme. The reader's perception nevertheless moves along the track laid out, though not visible to him. What he perceives is the collision of two planes, one temporal, Petrograd of the 1920s and St. Petersburg of the nineteenth century, the other national, the

Russo-Italian motif, crowned by the image of the singer-swallow lying in the St. Petersburg snows.

In Mandelstam's poetry of 1921-25 Hellenism has been cast aside along with other stylistic conventions. It is a major step toward his works of the 1930s where the poet was to confront reality in a different, new way. A group of poems of 1923 and early 1924 help define this transition. One of the themes in *Tristia,* that of time, of alternating death and rebirth, is transferred from a philosophical domain, from the sphere of "eternal" lyric themes, to a historical one, becoming the theme of the age. This shift occurs in the poems **"The Age," "He Who Finds a Horseshoe," "The Slate Ode,"** and **"1 January 1924."**

To seek a clear political program in Mandelstam's works of the 1920s would be futile. Mandelstam did accept the October Revolution, though not without hesitation and contradictions that characterized the initial response of many intellectuals formed before the Revolution. The burden of history, however, is heavy:

> Could I ever betray to gossip-mongers
> the great vow to the Fourth Estate
> and oaths solemn enough for tears?

Dry blood of *Tristia* gives way to blood mixed with lime. The persona now experiences directly the pressure of history. He still very much wants to live. Once again the imagery moves from impoverishment and extinction ("Breath growing weaker by the day"), to bursts of indestructible vitality.

> And in the sick son's blood the deposit of lime
> Will melt, and there'll be sudden blessed laughter.

But the age itself seems to be the speaker's double; it too is frightened and hungry for life. At times it becomes difficult to distinguish the age from the lyrical "I" of this cycle. The latter is about the atrophy of the past, in particular, of the nineteenth century and "its survivors, those emigrants shipwrecked and cast by the will of fate onto a new historical continent," to use the words of Mandelstam's essay "The nineteenth century." Mandelstam is speaking of the essence of the nineteenth century, an age of reflection and "relativism" ("my splendid derelict, my age") that continues to live in the consciousness of the old intelligentsia hesitatingly accepting the Revolution. All this emerges clearly from the poetic texts themselves. In addition, we can find theoretical corroboration of such a reading in Mandelstam's essays "The Word and Culture," "The Badger's Burrow," and, especially the 1922 one entitled "The Nineteenth Century."

On the threshold of the nineteenth century Derzhavin scratched on slate several lines of poetry that may serve as a leitmotif for the entire coming century.

> The river of time in its onrush
> Carries away the affairs of men
> And drowns in the abyss of oblivion

Peoples, kingdoms, and kings.
And if anything survives
In the sounds of the lyre and the trumpet,
It shall be swallowed by the crater of eternity
And shall not escape the common fate.

The rusty tongue of an aged century serves here to express with power and penetration the latent thought of the century yet to come. A moral is drawn, a keynote is sounded. This moral is relativism or relativity, "and if anything survives". . .

The above passage provides a clue to **"The Slate Ode,"** seemingly one of Mandelstam's most difficult works. What Mandelstam cites is the first and only stanza of Derzhavin's ode "On Mortality," written down on slate several days before the poet's death (the slate is preserved in the Leningrad Public Library). **"The Slate Ode"** is also about the "river of time." It is, however, about a real river as well that cascades down, carrying an inverted reflection of its green banks.

> Like rubble from icy heights,
> from the backs of green icons,
> the famished water flows, eddying,
> playing like the young of an animal.

Mountain villages envelop the river, and Mandelstam's Caucasian and Crimean motifs again appear:

> Steep goat cities
> The massive layering of flint . . .
> In the water their lesson, time
>   wears them fine.

The theme of flint, "a student of running water," represents a new bundle of meanings. It is also, however, Mandelstam's initial theme of stone, the medium of architects and poets.

Derzhavin, one of Mandelstam's favorite poets, is the hidden motivating force of the poem, written in imitation of Derzhavin's eight-line stanza, and celebrating a singularly significant creative act. Slate, the "lead stick" becomes its symbol.

> Terror and Split write with the same little
>   stick of milk.
> Here, taking form, is the first draft
> of the students of running water
>   . . . . .
> I hear the slate screech
> On the startled
>   crag.

In the complex semantic instrumentation of **"The Slate Ode"** *water* is an emblem of time. Water-time erodes *flint,* which resists time, while *slate* is the vehicle of creativity that interprets time.

Unless the reader has read **"The Slate Ode"** with "The Nineteenth Century" in mind, he will not recognize the Derzhavin theme—that of the dying poet's writing on slate a poem about the river of time. However, the semantic current that emanates from this hidden source runs through all the poem's links. The reader is aware that the poem is about the lofty and the magnificent, about a rough draft written by a genius. In Mandelstam's poem, however, the river of time is, also, a mountain river. Mandelstam does not want his metaphors to be "incorporeal." Most likely, **"The Slate Ode"** originated at the confluence of two sets of impressions: the sight of a slate in the Public Library with the half-effaced Derzhavin autograph and the roar of a mountain river, rushing down a siliceous bed.

The 1923-24 cycle of poems about the age and time signals the appearance in Mandelstam of new tendencies. The hayloft in the poem **"I Climbed into the Tousled Hayloft,"** the ax and the icy water in the poem, **"I Was Washing Outside in the Darkness"** are actualities that set the poet's thought in motion. Within the system of these poems, however, such objects have symbolic meaning, not at all "other-worldly," but expressive of the poet's inner experience.

In 1931 Mandelstam wrote a cycle of poems associated with Moscow (**"Midnight in Moscow,"** **"I'm Still not Patriarch"**) in which the themes of the age and of time, sounded in the 1923-24 poems, are again taken up. Yet we find ourselves now in a different world. Objects remain objects here, even if they acquire a new, vastly expanded meaning. The 1931 cycle is an attempt to define the relationship between the author and his era; its language is contemporary and workaday.

This is how Mandelstam now writes about the "great vow" to the revolutionary tradition and about the passage of time. Instead of searching for domesticity in the cold expanses of the age, the poet wanders along the streets and the embankments of Moscow.

> I love the starling streetcars starting off,
> And the asphalt's Astrakhan caviar,
> Covered with straw matting,
> Reminding me of a basket of Asti
> And steel ostrich-feathers
> On the scaffolding of the Lenin Housing
>   Project.

The young Mandelstam maintained that the poet ought to grasp the tridimensional. *Stone* abounds in objects, but these are objects of a special sort. First and foremost, they are indicators of cultural structures, of historical styles, be they the exedrae of a temple or the checkered trousers of a Dickens character, the lawyer's overcoat or the "sesquipedalian parts" of a musical composition by Bach. In *Tristia* and in those poems of the early 1920s that followed in its wake, Mandelstam's is still a tridimensional world, both accessible to the senses ("five good senses on the earth") and intelligible. But the predominance of the "Hellenic" stylistic pattern dematerializes this world. For the late Mandelstam history is the immediate present. The conventional styles had to recede; they were ill equipped to tackle contemporary life, to deal the the fluid, the incomplete, the as yet unnamed. By now the very themes of poems emerge from unexpected impressions, thoughts, recollections, from any inner experience. They bring in tow everyday, prosaic words, signifying the diversity of contemporary reality and essential to the poet because they provide direct contact with it.

Mandelstam's late works point toward a new relationship between poetic symbolism and reality.

Sidney Monas   (essay date 1973)

SOURCE: An introduction to *Complete Poetry of Osip Emilevich Mandelstam,* translated by Burton Raffel and Alla Burago, State University of New York Press, 1973, pp. 1-28.

[*Monas is an American educator and critic with a special interest in Russian literature. In the following essay, he explores the defining characteristics of Mandelstam's work.*]

"Just as a person does not choose his parents," Mandelstam wrote in 1921, "a people does not choose its poets." Russia would certainly have avoided him if it could. Even today, long after his posthumous rehabilitation, most of his poems are unpublished in the USSR. A collected volume announced in 1959 has still not appeared.

Abroad he has fared better. There is now the full, if not complete, three-volume Russian collection of his works, edited by Gleb Struve and Boris Filippoff [entitled *Sobranie sochinenii*]. There have been numerous translations, including a small volume in German by a poet close to his sensibility, Paul Celan. There is a growing realization that not only was he an important poet of the twentieth century, but perhaps as much as Rilke or Pound or Yeats or Eliot, *the* poet. Yet it is astonishing how reluctantly he has been accepted even by Russians abroad.

He was not, after all, shot by the Bolsheviks in the last days of the Civil War, like his friend Gumilev. He was even rumored to have had some enthusiasm for the regime in its early days. His first three volumes always had their admirers, as did of course the unpublished poem on Stalin for which he was exiled to Voronezh. But the *Voronezh Notebooks,* heroically preserved by his remarkable widow, and by Akhmatova, with the help of a few brave friends—"late Mandelstam," difficult, obscure, obsessive—that was more problematic.

In much of Russian literature and literary criticism in the years between 1907 and 1917 there is a sense of impending catastrophe, and a certain longing for it. Expectations were apocalyptic, and both Esenin and Mayakovsky at somewhat different angles on the edge of their seats predicted the coming Revolution. In Mandelstam's poems, however, there was a *stillness,* the sense of an ominous interval, like the unease of a Chirico shadow among geometrically balanced traditional shapes, like a sailboat that has come about, and before its sails quite catch the wind on the new tack.

This nervous little man, schlemiel, luftmensch, Christian and Jew, with a sweet tooth and a dread of dentist's drills, prophet at war with linear time, artiodactyllic inhabitant of near-arctic Saint Petersburg longing for the *mezzogiorno*—he could feel the encroachment on his chosen city of the new "Assyrian," the new "Egyptian" age, for which man would not be the measure but the raw material. Like a true Joseph, he moved into Egypt. He was a "Holy Fool," a *iurodivyi* of seventeenth-century Russia, a "bird of God" (he loved swallows and identified himself with the goldfinch); he was one of those imitators of Christ, God's fools, who were during Russia's times of troubles alone privileged to criticize the State. Like Ovid, he was an exile dreaming of Rome; like Dante, he wrote poems to "the measure and rhythm of walking." All poets were exiles, "for to speak means to be forever on the road." But Mandelstam thought of himself also as a *colonizer.*

It is in his essay on Chaadaev, this push for exploration and settlement—in that essay where he portrays so brilliantly the basic inner impulse of the lonely, austere, brilliant nineteenth-century figure from whom almost all of modern Russian thought descends. In Mandelstam's portrait: Chaadaev was the first Russian to go to Europe and *return.* Mandelstam read Chaadaev's *Philosophical Letters* in the context of the work of Kliuchevsky, a history professor at Moscow University, who wrote eloquently of Russia's historic colonization of the steppe and forest lands of the vast Eurasian spaces. In the *Philosophical Letters,* Chaadaev had written bleakly of Russia's separateness, an orphan among nations, belonging neither to East nor to West; a country without a history, whose sole historical attainment had been "the occupation of space." But Chaadaev's account had to be seen as the projected negative of an implied positive picture. Occupied space had now to be colonized with values; implanted with the warmth of a splendid teleology—to become one with mankind; One Body; the Kingdom of God on Earth.

It is also in his essay on the nineteenth century. Here Mandelstam begins by quoting the fragment, written in slate pencil on a slate board and posthumously discovered, by Gabriel Derzhavin, Russia's greatest poet of the eighteenth century and a man who had served as minister of justice under Catherine II. The River of Time in its flowing sweeps everything away, and into the Abyss of Oblivion it pours Tsardoms, Tsars, People; and should it be that through the sounding of Lyre or Horn, *Something should yet remain*—why, then, Eternity seizes it by the Throat; nor does it escape the Common Fate. There, wrote Mandelstam, expressed in the quaint, personified language of the expired eighteenth century was the lesson of the nineteenth: Relativism. The Absolute was dead, and the world was growing colder. The appalled reaction of Derzhavin had its less obvious counterparts in the sciences, each of which tended to separate itself off into a mere methodology, in utilitarianism, in what Mandelstam called "Buddhism" in both science and art—the creation of artificial, abstract, self-contained, "objective" worlds—meaning positivism in science, theosophy in religion, and a Flaubert-Goncourt kind of realism in art. But the century had, still, the potentiality of its eclecticism: the sense of freedom to choose equally among all the products of time. No friend to what he called "the century of pancomprehensibility, the century of relativism with its monstrous capacity for reincarnation," he saw it nevertheless as providing materials for defense against the monumental "Egyptian and Assyrian" cultures to come:

> In relation to this new age, with its immense cruelty, we are colonizers. To Europeanize and to humanize the twentieth century, to heat it with a theological warmth—that is the task of those who have managed to emerge from the wreckage of the nineteenth century, thrown ashore by the will of the fates on a new historical continent.

Most dramatically, this thrust of the self-proclaimed colonizer appears at the end of what is probably Mandelstam's greatest short essay, "The Word and Culture," just before his declaration that "classical poetry is the poetry of revolution." He elaborates here on the eclecticism of the modern poet.

> It is something quite the opposite of erudition. Contemporary poetry for all its complexity and inner violence is naive. . . . For [the contemporary poet] the entire complexity of the old world is a kind of Pushkinian reed. On it, ideas, scientific systems, political theories are played, in precisely the same way as, during the time of his predecessors, nightingales and roses were played on it.

Then, quite unexpectedly, and without even beginning a new paragraph, comes this extraordinary statement: "They say the cause of revolution is hunger in the interplanetary spaces. We need to sow wheat out there, in the ether."

"Crazy," or "senseless," as in the repeated line of poem number 118:

> We'll meet in Petersburg
> as if we'd buried the sun there,
> and for the first time we'll say
> the blessèd senseless word.

A *iuridovyi* always was a little cracked. He speaks the word as it occurs to him; he speaks in tongues—glossolalia—and the word is blessed precisely because it is free from the expected logic of the occasion, from the Reality Principle.

The whole poem hinges on "as if" (*slovno*) a notion inseparable in the Russian from "the word" itself (*slovo*). "Burying the sun" means to go on a binge, a celebration, especially in summertime Saint Petersburg where the sun shines all night. But not in November, when it has to be a celebration "as if,"

> In the black velvet of Soviet night,
> in the velvet of universal emptiness,
> women's eyes sing on, belovèd eyes, blessèd
>   women,
> immortal flowers bloom on.

Women, their eyes, flowers, and singing are all blessed, like the word—blessed by their fullness of physical being, blessed by their exemption from the logic of the situation.

The theater, the opera, is part of the celebration, a warming of the hands, away from the boredom, the cold and the dark. It pursues a drama different from the angry singing of the motorcar in the darkness outside. It permits a certain imaginary defiance:

> I need no night pass,
> I'm not afraid of sentries . . .

Nothing could have been more "as if " than that. It was 1920, and everyone needed a pass, and Mandelstam was frightened stiff of the sentries, especially the sailors in leather jackets.

"Blessèd" words; as the gods are blessed in Homer, because they are immortal. "Blessèd" words, as in poem number 86, **"Solòminka,"** where a euphonious list of mysterious ladies is reeled off: Lenore, Solòminka, Ligeia, Seraphita.

Lenore is of Buerger's Romantic ballad, and of Poe's "Raven"; Ligeia, of Poe's gruesome story, who comes back to life under strange circumstances; Seraphita belongs to a Swedenborgian tale of Balzac's; Solòminka is the diminutive of the Russian word for "straw" (*soloma*), but also the Russian diminutive form of Salomè, who not only danced for the head of John the Baptist but provided a name to a Georgian beauty with whom Mandelstam was in love. The names have their own historical-literary associations and their own meanings; they have also their physical qualities, their "sound" qualities, which are part of their ambience and their living, immortal nature.

Mandelstam compared the physical nature of the word to a paper lantern with a candle inside. Sometimes the candle inside was the meaning and the paper and frame were the sound structure; and sometimes the paper and frame were the meaning and the candle was the sound.

The word was a Psyche, or soul, and immortal. The word was not its object-meaning, or even the sum of its object-meanings, though sometimes it could be felt "hovering over its object like a soul over the recently deceased body of the beloved." The word was a Psyche and could choose its own meaning. Nevertheless, the meanings it had chosen were there, sealed into its image—the word had a history; and conscious meaning could not, without impoverishment, simply be thrown overboard, as Khlebnikov and the Futurists attempted to do.

Not only did the word have *a* history, but for Russia it was history. For when Chaadaev had declared that Russia had no history, he had overlooked language. Russia's history was in its language. And the nature of its language was Hellenic—not in the sense that it derived from the Greek, but in that it "preserved the gift of free incarnation."

The capacity of the Russian word-Psyche to choose its body freely—the "Saint George's Day" of language!—this was the secret basis of kinship with the Greek. And it was based on freedom from the usages of State and Church—from "the King's English," the Royal Society Dictionaries and their attempts to unify, to standardize, to *mechanize* the patterns of meaning. There had been of course the Byzantine monks—they were, Mandelstam wrote, medieval Russia's equivalent of the intelligentsia—and the clerks of Ivan IV's chancery. But the results of their work had been shaky; they had created no sense of communality, no family sense of kindred. Russia had not even an Acropolis. And it was in the seminar of philology rather than in the large formal lecture of political science that the communality created by Russian history was to be discovered.

While it was the constant effort of the priest, the administrator, and the *intelligent* to reduce the word to its ready-made meaning, to its object-meaning, its "mechanical" or "translators'" meaning, it was the poet who kissed it awake and transformed the frog into a prince, the sleeping beauty into a living girl.

> What distinguishes poetry from mechanical speech is that it rouses us and shakes us awake in the middle of a word. Then the word turns out to be far longer than we thought, and we remember that to speak means to be forever on the road ["Talking about Dante"].

To speak, speech—for Mandelstam the impulse to poetry, its "command." The basic metaphor here is *movement*, motion, as in the question Mandelstam poses as to "how many sandals Alighieri wore out in the course of his poetic work, wandering about on the goat paths of Italy?" Or in the need for physical motion manifest in his own response to the presence of poetry. "Restlessness was the first sign," Nadezhda Iakovlevna writes, "that he was working on something, and the second was the moving of his lips." Physical motion and the shape and poise of the body to accommodate that motion is a theme that runs throughout Mandelstam—the movement of the poet's lips, the syllogism of Dante's step on the goat paths of Italy, the complex pattern of a horse's hooves on the cobblestones of provincial Russia (**"Whoever Finds a Horseshoe,"** poem no. 136). For him inspiration began as a buzzing, jangling, humming sound, in which he had to distinguish the words, a concentration that induced motion, sometimes strained and, viewed from the outside, grotesque and anguished.

> His head was twisted around so that his chin almost touched his shoulder; he was twirling his walking stick with one hand and resting the other on one of the stone steps to keep his balance. . . . When he was "composing" he always had a great need of movement. He either paced the room (unfortunately we never had very much space for this) or he kept going outside to walk the streets. The day I came across him sitting on the steps, he had just stopped to rest, tired of walking around.

This, a man old before his time, toothless, eyelids painfully inflamed, with an improperly mended broken arm, suffering from angina pectoris. . . .

"The quality of poetry," Mandelstam himself wrote,

> is determined by the rapidity and decisiveness with which it instills its command, its plan of action, into the instrumentless, dictionary, purely qualitative nature of word formation. One has to run across the whole width of the river, jammed with mobile Chinese junks sailing in various directions. This is how the meaning of poetic speech is created. Its route cannot be reconstructed by interrogating the boatmen: they will not tell how and why we were leaping from junk to junk.

The whirring, humming, buzz, the tangled movement of inspiration, the strain and physical anguish of bodily adaptation. . . . But, as Nadezhda Iakovlevna writes,

> the process of composing verse also involves the *recollection* of something that has never before been said, and the search for lost words is an attempt to *remember* what is still to be brought into being ("I have forgotten the word I wished to say, like a blind swallow it will return to the abode of shadows").

The poetic need for surprise, astonishment, wonder, is a notion essential to Mandelstam, as is the rather Augustinian conception of "re-membering" or "re-collecting."

Indeed, the Logos of the Book of John is very much intertwined with Mandelstam's conception of the word, and for that matter so is Christianity in general. Yet he resists the institutionalization of language through the Church as well as through the State or the Party or the Intelligentsia.

> The speed at which language develops is incommensurable with the development of life itself. Any attempt to adapt language mechanically to the needs of life is doomed to failure before it begins.

Hellenism, the Word, Christianity: all three, closely linked.

Hellenism means the humanization of the cosmos, sowing wheat in the interplanetary ether to allay the hunger in space.

> Hellenism—that is the conscious encirclement of man with the utensil [*utvar'*]; instead of impersonal objects, the transformation of these objects into the utensil, the humanization of the surrounding world, heating it with the most delicate teleological warmth. Hellenism—that is a system in the Bergsonian sense of the word, like a sheaf of phenomena freed of temporal dependence, coordinated in an inner liaison through the human I.

"Christianity," writes Mandelstam, "is the Hellenization of death." Except for the brilliant Russian essay by George Ivask entitled "The Christian Poetry of Mandelstam," it is a subject that critics have spent more energy evading than confronting. Even Nadezhda Iakovlevna—though her husband's Christianity is mentioned in passing from time to time in her splendid book, and though she would not seem to have been unsympathetic to it—tends to avoid the issue. Mandelstam himself is extraordinarily reticent about it, and concerning his conversion there is none of the drama and pageantry surrounding that of, say, Pasternak. It is difficult to note at which point in his life he became a convert. In "The Hum of Time," he writes of "the Judaic chaos" of his family background, the incomprehensibility of the books at the bottom of his parents' shelf and his own incapacity to learn Hebrew. But it is clearly a buzzing, humming chaos, next to the *"silentium"* from which life springs. His first overtly Christian poem, dedicated to Kartashev (no. 100) consists entirely of Jewish imagery. There are earlier references to "a thin cross" (no. 19), to the historical and esthetic eloquence of Christianity (nos. 38, 39, 43, 46, etcetera) and a poem that deals directly with a powerful (if still somewhat ambivalent) religious experience (no. 30). Still, there is no doubt that Ivask is right, and Mandelstam, in his festive, sacrificial manner, resembling Jacob Boehme, thought of Christianity as at once a joyful game that Christ had freed man to play with God and a Road to Calvary: Mandelstam is the most Christian of modern poets.

Even his early ambivalent but passionate involvement with the Revolution is permeated with Christianity, "for every cultivated man is a Christian now," he wrote. And more strikingly:

> an heroic era has opened in the life of the word. The word is flesh and bread. It shares the fate of bread and flesh: suffering. People are hungry. The state is even hungrier. But there is something hungrier yet: time.

> Time wants to devour the state. The threat sounds like that trumpet-voice scratched by Derzhavin on his slate board. Whoever will lift high the word and show it to time, as the priest the Eucharist, will be a second Redeemer. There is nothing hungrier than the contemporary state, and a hungry state is more terrifying than a hungry man. Compassion for the state which denies the word—that is the social path and the great deed [*podvig*] facing the contemporary poet.

Mandelstam called himself a *raznochinets,* that curious Russian word; plural, *raznochintsy.* In poem number 260, Burton Raffel translates it as "middle-class intellectuals," but no single phrase is altogether adequate. It means literally, "people of different ranks," and it was first used in legal documents in the eighteenth century to indicate people outside the established castes—not nobles or merchants or priests or artisans, though possibly their fathers had been—and later, it came to have the connotation, "educated commoners," or "classless intellectuals." In the 1860s, the educated elite was laced with *raznochintsy,* who, new to the universities and the learned professions, new to science and literature, provided a somewhat raw tone and style for the intelligentsia, a style markedly different from that of the "esthetic" and aristocratic 1840s, whose representatives tended to think of the men of the 1860s with nervous distaste, because though comrades in the cause, they "smelled of crushed bugs."

"A *raznochinets,"* writes Mandelstam in his autobiography, "has no biography other than the books he has read."

And he proceeds with a masterful portrait of his family and of himself by way of the family bookcase: the unintelligible and horizontally piled Hebrew books of his father on the bottom shelf, that compressed "Judaic chaos," which he resists and resents but which yet presses upward with its black-and-yellow insistence, its exotic and creative intensity. The next shelf belongs to Schiller and the German Romantics, whom Mandelstam's father read when, sent to a Berlin Yeshiva at the age of fourteen, he broke with home by reading them instead of Talmud and Torah. His father's voice, with its "languagelessness," its lost and touching "no-tongue," fills the room. Neither German nor Russian, and having broken with Hebrew and Yiddish; a struggling leather-merchant, affluent enough to maintain an apartment in Saint Petersburg, a summer place in Pavlovsk, to send his son to the fashionable Tenishev School (ten years later Vladimir Nabokov went there) and to send him abroad for three years, once to Paris and once to Heidelberg; but insecure, unestablished, literally "outside the Pale." And then there is his mother's shelf: the impressive Isakov edition of Pushkin, and beside it, symbol of the intelligentsia psyche of the 1880s, that apotheosis of mediocre secular martyrdom, the poet Nadson. Mandelstam's mother spoke a clear, distinct Russian—with an impoverished vocabulary, but unmistakably *hers,* for unlike the tongue-tied father, she was "intelligentsia" from Vilno.

Mandelstam's relations with his family were not easy, and to those unfamiliar with the drama of Jewish family life (a drama since exhausted to the point of banality in the context of American literature) seemingly grotesque and bizarre. It is unlikely that a *raznochinets* would be more at ease in the bosom of his family than in the bosom of society, for every family is a government in its own way, but he is not necessarily a Nechaev. Mandelstam's relationship to his family was sometimes, as he himself put it, "Terrible, terrible. . . ." That did not mean it was not close.

At a certain age, Karl Kautsky's Marxism colored the cosmos for Mandelstam as vividly as Tiutchev's poetry.

> I perceived the entire world as an economy, a human economy—and the shuttles of English domestic industry that had fallen silent a hundred years ago sounded once more in the ringing autumn air! Yes, I heard with the sharpness of ears caught by the sound of a distant threshing machine in the field the burgeoning and increase, not of the barley in its ear, not of the northern apple, but of the world, the capitalist world, that was ripening in order to fall!

He loved many things that were not to the taste of the ascetic Nadson-worshipping intelligentsia: beautiful women, wine, chocolates, opera, church architecture. Still, he knew a *raznochinets* when he saw one, and he saw one not only in the mediocre, grim-faced Nadson, but in Francois Villon ("Brother Francois!") and above all in Dante, whose apotheosis in the capuche with the aquiline profile had led too many people astray.

> Dante is a poor man . . . an internal *raznochinets* of an ancient Roman line [like Pushkin's Evgeny in "The

Caricature of Mandelstam.

Bronze Horseman"]. . . . He does not know how to act, what to say, how to make a bow. . . . The inner anxiety and the heavy, troubled awkwardness which attend every step of the unselfconfident man . . . who does not know what application to make of his inner experience or how to objectify it in etiquette, the tortured and outcast man. . . . If Dante were to be sent out alone without his *dolce padre,* without Virgil, a scandal would inevitably erupt. . . . The gaucheries averted by Virgil systematically correct and straighten the course of the poem . . . an awkwardness overcome with torturous difficulty. . . . The shade that frightens old women and children was itself afraid, and Alighieri underwent fever and chills all the way from marvelous fits of self-esteem to feelings of utter worthlessness.

And even in Nadson he saw, or perhaps better, "heard," *something*—the pathos of his mother's generation in the hum of time, and he acknowledged a kind of relationship to a poet whom the "esthetes" of the Symbolist generation turned away from in contempt.

The Symbolists either fled everyday reality, like De l'Isle-Adam's hero, Axel, who thought living was something the servants could do for him, or regarded it with horror, like Blok in his brief, simple, powerful poem that begins: "Night. A street. A street-lamp. A drugstore." In contrast to the exaltation of Symbolist esthetics, Mandel-

stam and to a somewhat lesser degree his Acmeist colleagues were, as Nadezhda Iakovlevna put it, "of the earth, earthy. . . ." He celebrated the "thing" as *utvar'*—the humanized utensil—earth, stone, as building material, even the dead weight of which tended to predispose it to be used in building ("Heaviness and Tenderness, sisters . . ." in no. 108). "M. never talked of 'creating' things," Nadezhda Iakovlevna writes, "only of 'building' them."

This feeling of "being the same as everyone else" ("though perhaps not quite as well-made as others . . ."), this sense, "natural for any poet, of a common bond with the street, with ordinary people," never left Mandelstam and was very different from the feeling of a professor or a man of letters.

> Poetry is quite different: the poet is linked only with readers sent his way by Providence and he does not have to be superior to his age, or to the people he lives among. ["On the Interlocutor"]

The Symbolists were "teachers" with a cultural mission, but Mandelstam colonized with his own body. He had no aspiration to be part of a priesthood, an aristocracy; and no inclination, as so many of his generation, who, reacting against "bourgeois democracy" and the First World War tended toward a mystique of the strong and authoritarian personality. Mandelstam, who preferred Christianity to Judaism, because he felt the Trinity provided some shelter from the overwhelming force of a unitarian and totalitarian God, considered himself "a pedestrian," walking with peasants. And the fact that he felt he spoke *with* men rather than *for* them, gave him the poet's sense of confidence, of being right. He knew what he heard. In Voronezh, where he was sent for the political crime of writing a sardonic poem about Stalin, this frail, stricken, hungry, sick man walked with a posture that made the street urchins think he was a general.

Mandelstam favored the Revolution—"but without the death penalty." His encounters with the Socialist Revolutionary adventurer-assassin Bliumkin have been told several times and have assumed a legendary quality. The hero of Mandelstam's one piece of prose fiction, Parnok, vainly attempts to save someone from a revolutionary lynch mob, as Mandelstam tried to save Bliumkin's intended victim. But it was not so much the violence to the Revolution that repelled him—and certainly not its assault upon private property—but rather the tendency within it for the Party, and the intelligentsia dazzled by the Party, to constitute itself a power over language and therefore over the truth.

> Social differences and class antagonisms pale before the division, now, into friends and enemies of the word. Sheep and goats, really. I sense the almost physically unclean goat-spirit emanating from the enemies of the word. . . .

Although the *topoi* of his poems, the commonplaces, the epithets, were often classical, they were at the same time pastoral and everyday. Sheep and shepherds, weaving, the spinning wheel, baking, sailing, plowing, beekeeping, building, woodcutting, well dipping—workmen's motifs. True, he could see in the "aristocratic" game of tennis a parable of love and war (no. 51); but so could he in "democratic" football sense the presence of Judith and Holofernes (no. 167). Attacked again and again for his nonexistent allegiance to the Old Regime, he responded defiantly:

> I drink to soldiers' star-flowers, to everything I was
>   blamed for:
> to lush furcoats, to asthma, to Petersburg days and
>   their bile,
> to pine-trees' music, to petrol in Elysian Fields,
>   . . . . .
> I drink: to which? I still don't know, wine
> from the Pope's cellars, or a lovely Asti
>   spumante . . .
>
>   [No. 233]

"Soldiers' star-flowers" is a euphemism for "officers' epaulettes," which were abolished by the Revolution (only to be restored later by Stalin)—it was the sort of thing Mandelstam the man of the Old Regime was supposed to favor. The accusation of "lush furcoats" was a recurrent motif in the accusations against him; "asthma" meant the "decadent" Proust, whose great novel he admired—in other words, all the "forbidden delights." Yet the poem ends with an equation between "Chateauneuf du Pape," the most aristocratic of wines, and "asti spumante," the poor man's champagne.

In 1924, Mandelstam, already hounded and persecuted, contrasted the "obedient" typewriter of writers courting the regime, trying to play to the tune of the stripped-down Soviet sonata, to his own loyalty to "a marvelous oath to the fourth estate":

> Who else can you kill? Who else make famous?
> What kind of lies will you invent?
> There's the typewriter: quick, rip out a key—
> There's a fishbone in there . . .
>   . . . . .
> But the typewriter's plain sonatina—that's only
> the shadow of those mighty ones and all their
>   mighty music.
>
>   [No. 140]

Between these two poems, the latter written in 1924, the former in 1931, lay a long period of grim poetic silence, during which Mandelstam, harassed and persecuted, failed to hear the hum of poetic inspiration. The "block" was broken by a trip to Armenia, arranged by Mandelstam's "protector," Nikolai Bukharin, himself to fall victim some years later to Stalin's terror. On his return from Armenia, Mandelstam wrote a marvelous, therapeutic rhetorical sketch clearly unpublishable at the time, which he called "Fourth Prose," in part because he saw this vehement fragment as a rebellious fourth estate of words, a *Pugachevshchina* that had risen up inside him to overthrow discretion and restraint, a Luciferian *non serviam:* "I divide all the works of world literature into those written with and without permission. The first are trash, the second—stolen air."

From that day, until the day of his final arrest in 1937, he wrote steadily.

The hum of time. He saw it, felt its pressure, smelled it, above all he *heard* it. As Victor Terras has put it [in his "The Time Philosophy of Osip Mandel'shtam," in *Slavonic and East European Review* 48, July, 1969], he had "'absolute pitch' for time." *Shum vremeni*—"the *hum* of time"—as he called his autobiography; the golden fleece spun out on the wheel and the hum that fills the room even when the wheel is still. In a phrase, a line, a strophe, a paragraph, an aphorism, he could characterize a century, an epoch, a cultural milieu. Thus, the eighteenth century, in his essay on André Chenier: "like a dried-out lake; no depth, no moisture; what was submerged, now all surface." At the center of his concern was the dying nineteenth century, the century of relativism and tolerance, which had nevertheless summoned up a monstrous and barbaric successor, the new Assyrian-Egyptian age. He was fond of the image (gleaned from Pushkin's "Feast in Time of Plague") of the banquet in a dying city. He evokes it at the end of his autobiography, and immediately after that the shade of a nineteenth-century figure with whom he felt a close kinship, the aristocratic esthete Konstantin Leontiev, who had died the year Mandelstam was born.

> If I had a vision of . . . Leontiev yelling for a cabby
> on that snow-covered street . . . it was only because he
> of all Russian writers is most given to handling time
> in lumps. He feels centuries as he feels the weather,
> and he shouts at them. . . . Looking back at the entire
> nineteenth century of Russian culture—shattered,
> finished, unrepeatable, which no one must repeat, which
> no one dares repeat—I wish to hail the century as one
> would hail settled weather, and I see in it the unity
> lent it by the measureless cold which welded decades
> together into one day, one night, one profound winter,
> within which the terrible State glowed, like a stove,
> with ice. And in this wintry period of Russian history,
> literature taken at large, strikes me as something
> *patrician* [italics mine], which puts me [i.e., a
> *raznochinets*] out of countenance: with trembling I lift
> the film of wax paper over the winter cap of the writer.
> No one is to blame in this and there is nothing to be
> ashamed of. A beast must not be ashamed of its furry
> hide. Night furred him. Literature is a beast. The
> furriers—night and winter.

That palpability is not nineteenth-century time; it is its own thing, its own system of relevancies, not the straightforward linear march of progress, the ineluctable, constant surge that wears everything down, even the cliffs of Dover, that frightened Derzhavin and the Tennyson of "In Memoriam," not the time that is measured in the spacial terms of clock faces and calendars; it is Bergsonian, twentieth-century time; time as *durée*; time as a system of inner connections.

But it does not merely toss down, into the abyss, peoples, tsars, and tsardoms. It is a creative element: or rather it is the background against which creation takes place. In the famous "Slate Ode" (no. 137), Derzhavin's gloomy poem immediately sets up a dialogue with Lermontov's "star speaking with star," and the stars themselves become a projection of the writing scratched on slate—a projection of man's creativity in time. The flow of the river of time does not merely corrode—in corroding, it shapes. Flint is the pupil, water the teacher. And if there is a destructive, masculine time; there is by its side the feminine creatrix.

If a man is true to his humanity, he is enriched by time:

> All voyage long the heavy sea-waves boomed,
> and then, leaving his ship, all sea-worn, canvas-
>   stretched,
> Odysseus came home, full of space and time.
>
> [No. 92]

It is almost as though he had been woven by the waiting Penelope.

Under attack by his fellow writers, some of them already close to speaking in an "official" tone, Mandelstam, accused of being out of step with his epoch, a child of the past, found a curious if partly ironical identity in the "dying time." In the series of poems, among his very greatest, beginning with number 130, in which time as a "regal shepherd's helper" coaxes an unsuspected freshness out of stale bread, to the rekindling of fire in the eyes of dying time in number 141, he is the "stepson" of "my lord and master time" (*vek-vlastelin*), his eyelids are inflamed as are those of the patrician past, now dying, whose eyes are apples—apples that come from the mocking revolutionary song about the bourgeois: *"Akh, ty iáblochka, kuda kátish'sia?"* ("Ah, little apple, where are you rolling now?") In number 135, the poet grieves over disjuncture, rupture, discontinuity, and "my time" (*our* time, the age) becomes a dying beast with its backbone broken:

> You stare behind you with a senseless
> smile, cruel, weak,
> like a wounded animal
> staring back at his paw-tracks.

In number 227, under greater pressure still, the age becomes an incompetent wolfhound that doesn't know a sheep from a wolf and attacks the lamb it was meant to guard.

As a boy, Mandelstam used to attend concerts at the huge glass-domed railroad station in Pavlovsk, that zany triumph and juncture of nineteenth-century art and technology, where, as he wrote, "the change of conductors seemed to me a change of dynasties." The world of the timetable had infected literature:

> The railroad has changed the whole course, the whole structure, the whole rhythm of our prose. It has delivered it over to the senseless muttering of the French *moujik* out of *Anna Karenina.* Railroad prose, like the woman's purse of that ominous *moujik,* is full of the coupler's tools, delirious particles, grappling-iron prepositions.

Mandelstam wanted Russian prose off that track. "Destroy your manuscript," he advised,

> but save whatever you have inscribed in the margin out of boredom, out of helplessness, and, as it were, in a dream. These secondary and *involuntary* [italics mine] creations of your fantasy will not be lost in the world but will take their places behind shadowy music stands, like third violins at the Marinsky Theatre, and out of gratitude to their author strike up the overture to *Lenore* or the *Egmont* of Beethoven.

Prose, liberated, would assume the condition of music. But in the poem called **"Concert at a Railway Station,"** number 125, there is an elegy—echoing Lermontov as in the **"Slate Ode,"** and also Tiutchev—a grieving for the entire age. The "roses rotting in hot-houses," suggest, among other things, the *rosalia,* or Roman spring festival for the dead. Among the farewells of his **Tristia,** farewell to the dying time grieves lyrically.

Mandelstam disliked timetable time, and would have no clocks in the meager apartments he and his wife inhabited before their exile to Voronezh, where of course they had no apartment. But for a long time, hounded by the threat of arrest, ironically, they would spend much time in railroad station waiting rooms, where the police would not think of looking for them (no. 224).

At a time when other writers out of timid conformity would have nothing to do with him, Mandelstam—especially during his stay in Armenia—became acquainted with a young biologist, and through him with a number of life scientists. He became fascinated with evolutionary theory and was convinced that literary criticism should take biological science as a model. Perhaps his previous reading of Spengler and Bergson had prepared him a little for that. But his "absolute pitch" for time held him here, too, in good stead, and although his approach to Darwin, Lamarck, Linnaeus, Passy, is that of a poet and he conceives their work poetically, his essay "Around Naturalists" is a most remarkable venture.

Lamarck particularly fascinated him. He saw in Darwin's great predecessor a figure of classic dimension, who combined the eighteenth-century personifying moralism of a La Fontaine with the tragic sense and cosmic scope of a Shakespeare. He found the Darwinian view of "evolution" (a word Mandelstam disliked) sympathetically "Dickensian"—that is to say, playful and optimistic—but he preferred Lamarck's "tragic" view. "What Lamarck feels is precisely the *gaps* in nature." For Lamarck, the environment is not a mere "surrounding," but a *call,* a summons; and there are creatures who respond, yet fail the call. In his great poem **"Lamarck"** (no. 254), Mandelstam takes us *down* the ladder of evolution into the muteness, the strained and straining silence of nature.

The emergence of a new species, in Lamarck's view as interpreted by Mandelstam, is not a question of progress or evolution—it is a break-through, a new creation. It is something like the creation of a poem as described in the passage from "Talking about Dante" quoted earlier in this essay. It is a product of choice, or of a pattern of choices, something like the poet hopping among the "mobile Chinese junks," or something like the chess master about to make an inspired move.

As much interested in geologic as in biologic time, Mandelstam (who came to geologic theory by way of the fifth chapter of Novalis' *Heinrich von Ofterdingen*) believed that,

> a stone is a kind of diary of the weather, a meteorological concentrate as it were. A stone is nothing but weather excluded from atmospheric space and put away in functional space. . . . Meteorology is more basic than mineralogy: it encompasses it, washes over it, it ages and gives meaning to it. [It] is not only the past, it is also the future: there is periodicity in it.

In this sense, Mandelstam believed, "A mineralogical collection is a most excellent organic commentary to Dante."

For what is basic to Dante's poem, according to Mandelstam, is not its rootedness in the scholastic philosophy of Dante's time, but its synchronism, its quality, *like that of a stone,* of an "Aladdin's lamp penetrating into the geologic murk of future times." And Dante's basic metaphor—defined metaphorically by Mandelstam—"designates the standing-still of time."

> Its root is not in the little word "how," but in the word "when." His *quando* sounds like *come*. Ovid's rumbling is closer to him than the French eloquence of Virgil. . . . If the halls of the Hermitage should suddenly go mad, if the paintings of all schools and masters should suddenly break loose from the nails, should fuse, intermingle, and fill the air of the rooms with futuristic howling and colors in violent agitations, the result then would be something like Dante's *Comedy* ["Talking about Dante"].

Mandelstam credits Dante not only with the most extraordinary metaphors of weaving (dear to Mandelstam himself) but with having anticipated the modern polyphonic orchestra, counterpoint and dissonance included: "he was forced to resort to a glossolalia of facts, to a synchronism of events, names, and traditions separated by centuries, *precisely because he heard the hum of time* [italics mine]."

The sense of time that rises above time—like gothic architecture, like the needle point of the Admiralty tower pointing like a mast at the sky, like the Greek word, like that point in the performance of the Eucharist when time comes to a stop:

> It takes the world in its hands, like a simple apple.
> . . . . .
> And like eternal noon the Eucharist endures—
> All partake, are blessed, play, sing . . .
>
> [No. 117]

Similarly, in the poet's own life, the poet's first awareness of himself as distinctively a poet:

> My breath, my warmth has leaned
> against the glass windows of eternity,
>
> And the glass is printed with a design
> no one can know, suddenly.
>
> Let this moment trickle uselessly down:
> that lovely design is fixed forever.
>
> [No. 8]

In this sense, he is at once "no man's contemporary" (no. 141), and unprootedly "a contemporary . . . a citizen of the Mosseamstress Era . . ." (no. 260). Perhaps the most complex, if not the most affirmative, expression of the poet's social role as a link with eternity, as the ritual of the Eucharist is a link with eternity, as in the extraordinary poem, **"Whoever Finds a Horseshoe"** (no. 136).

> We see a forest and say:
> there's a sea-going wood . . .

But the pine tree does not live on in the mast, nor does the spark-strewing run of the horse live on in the horseshoe hanging over the door, which has become a fetish, which has been reduced to mechanical meaning—"good luck"—but which does not hold the flow of the horse's motion over the cobblestones. It is the poet who provides this vital link with the past, the poet who brings the trees to life from the mast, the horse in motion from the horseshoe. Society, without the poet, repeats the last real poet it had:

> Human lips with nothing left to say
> keep the shape of the last word spoken,
> and arms keep the feeling of weight
> though the jug splashed half empty, carrying it
>   home.
>
> [No. 136]

The poet, like a gold coin—legal tender to be exchanged for a living past—is cut down

> . . . like a clipped coin
> and I am no longer sufficient unto myself.
>
> [No. 136]

For all the pastoral *topoi* and metaphors of his usage, Mandelstam is preeminently an urban poet, a poet of the human *polis,* a *political* poet. He is as aware as any of the "Wasteland" aspect of the modern city—the "desolation and glass" of Petersburg. Unlike T. S. Eliot, however, who sees

> Falling towers
> Jerusalem Athens Alexandria
> Vienna London
> Unreal

he sees the "granaries of faith" (no. 124), the latency of stone which cries out to be built:

Mighty Notre Dame, the more I study
your monster's ribs, the more
I think: someday I'll build beauty
out of an evil mass, I will, I too.

                                                    [No. 39]

He sees the thrust of the Admiralty Tower, which itself
reminds him of a ship's mast, and he writes:

Four elements united, rule us, are friendly,
but free man made the fifth.
This chaste-constructed ark: isn't the
superiority of space denied?

                                                    [No. 48]

For the great writers of classic Russian literature, Saint
Petersburg, "the most intentional city in the world," as
Dostoevsky called it, had been a place of illusion and
hallucination, madness, schizophrenia, the dissociation
of personality, in which the dream of reason had produced monsters. It was so, too, for Andrei Biely, whose
modernist novel, *Petersburg,* had made inventive use of
the literary myth of Saint Petersburg, the "abstract" and
"unreal" city. For Mandelstam, however, the city was
"*deeper* than delirium" (no. 45) and included the two-
hundred years of European culture that had come to
Russia by way of "Peter's creation" (no. 45), culture that
he valued not because it was European, but because he
felt it was the only link with the eternal that man could
grasp. Petersburg, like Acmeism, the literary movement
that was born, grew, and died there, was a longing for
world culture.

Attending services at the Uspensky Cathedral in the Moscow Kremlin in 1916 with Marina Tsvetaeva, with whom
he was then in love, Mandelstam could write:

And this tender Cathedral is in Moscow, but is
    Florence.
And Moscow's five-domed cathedrals,
Russian-souled, Italian-souled,
make me think of Eos, Goddess of Dawn,
but with a Russian name, and wearing a fur-coat.

                                                    [No. 84]

But on the whole, Moscow was hostile to him, and he
disliked it. It smelled of the murdered Tsarevich (Dmitry,
said to have been murdered on orders from Boris Godunov) and of the pseudo-Dmitry, who also for reasons of
state and after he had killed Boris was murdered, too. He
disliked the messianic doctrine of Moscow as "the third
Rome," and he shuddered at the new Assyrian-Egyptian
age he felt gathering there. His friend and hero Chaadaev,
as he well remembered, had headed his letters from Moscow, "Necropolis."

Moscow had been known as a city of wood, and in his
later poems Mandelstam associated wood with huge buck-
ets the Mongol khans used to lower disobedient Russian
princes into wells as punishment; with execution blocks
and ax handles for beheading. For him, Asia was far more
strongly *there* than Rome or Florence.

For Petropolis—lovingly Mandelstam bestows its Greek
name—the city of stone, there is a different feeling. Not
that stone is better than wood. Both are material. Both are
there to be fashioned. Both aspire. But Petropolis has the
shape of a boat, of an ark, ready to take off in an argo-
nauts' voyage against space; it is launched into the universe. Mandelstam's feeling is complex. Few of his Petersburg poems are without irony, and in his autobiographical prose the irony predominates. Even the image of the
ark manages to suggest as well the ship image from Biely's
Peterburg—the ship, that is, of the damned soul of the
Flying Dutchman. And in 1916, Mandelstam, addressing
the sea goddess, stone-helmeted Athena, for the first time
associates Petropolis with dying, and with Proserpina,
goddess of the earth and queen of the dead (no. 89). Petersburg has become "transparent"—that is to say phan-
tasmal; belonging already to the kingdom of the dead. So,
Petersburg, too, is a Necropolis. And in a poem of 1918,
Mandelstam addresses a now "transparent" star:

At that terrible height a monstrous ship
spreads huge wings, and flies
Oh green star, your ruined and beautiful
brother, Petropolis, is dying.

                                                    [No. 101]

It is the city's lodestar, its "guiding" or "brother" star—
the projection of its hopes and aspirations, precisely the
wheat sown by the city in the ether of space.

Behind Petropolis are Greece and Rome. The dome of
Saint Peter's, which is compared to a swallow's nest—
and if we take the full elucidation of the myth of Procne
the self-sacrificing, the giver-over of self, and Mandelstam's idea of the swallow as word-soul, we begin to see
the meaning of this great "nest"—the freedom in space
of Kazan Cathedral, designed by a Russian serf who had
lived in Rome: these are among the felt presences. And
one might add the classic shawl slipping from the shoulders of Akhmatova, as in a play by Euripides or Racine.
Unlike any other Russian writer he stresses in dealing
with Petropolis, not its *artifice,* but its human aspiration
to burst bonds, to shake free of dead weight, to unload,
to soar.

Nature is Rome, too, is reflected, now, in Rome.
We see its secular power
in transparent air, like a light-blue circus,
in the forum of fields, in the colonnade of groves.

                                                    [No. 65]

The city is thus *like* nature, and *not* "unnatural."

As for the pathetic impermanence of these seemingly
mighty structures, the death and decay of imperial centers,
of aspirations laid in the dust, Mandelstam makes quite
clear what "Rome" means to him:

It's not Rome, as a city, that lasts forever,
but man's place in the universe.
Kings try to take it,
priests use it as an argument for war,

and without it houses, and altars,
are contemptible rubble, pitiful, wretched.

[No. 66]

In Mandelstam's only fictive story, *The Egyptian Stamp*, which may be taken to mark the end of Russian realism, as Gogol's "Overcoat" which it so much resembles, marked its beginning, the lamblike, sacrificial hero fails, though he tries hard, to prevent a lynching:

> Petersburg had declared itself Nero and was as loathesome as if it were eating a soup of crushed flies. Nevertheless, he telephoned from a pharmacy, telephoned the police, telephoned the government, the state, which had vanished, sleeping like a carp. He might with equal success have telephoned Proserpine or Persephone, who had not yet had a telephone installed.

It is in the telephoning that Rome lives, not in the "innumerable swarm of human locusts" that have by now destroyed their victim in the fish-well boat on the blackened banks of the Fontanka Canal.

Mandelstam, who was fond of birds, identified himself particularly with the goldfinch—perhaps because it had associations with the town of Voronezh, with Kol'tsov, nineteenth-century lyricist, who had lived there and written of goldfinches, because the bird was an indomitable dandy and held its head high and sang through all adversity. In Russia, boys are fond of birds and often catch them and keep them in cages. One such goldfinch provided Mandelstam with a series of poems.

More and more, he worked in "series," preserving draft versions, allowing associations to proliferate, keeping as it were, in Clarence Brown's phrase, the full "phonic shadow." In Mandelstam's extraordinarily self-revealing essay, "Talking about Dante," he wrote: "Draft versions are never destroyed." For the critic, the alert reader, "in order to arrive at the target one has to accept and take account of the wind blowing in a difference direction." It was, he wrote, like "tacking in a sailboat."

Mandelstam also made distinctions between himself and the goldfinch: "'They cannot stop me moving about,'" he told Nadezhda Iakovlevna, "'I have just been on a secret trip to the Crimea.'" And he said about the changing of the seasons: "'This is also a journey . . . and they can't take it away from us.'"

But the noose was tightening. In Voronezh, the Mandelstams were completely isolated. Mandelstam's health was failing—his heart bad, his eyesight dim, his poorly mended arm aching. Perhaps, if he wrote a poem "to order," as so many of his friends had done, an ode to Stalin, his fortunes might be mended. Or if not his, Nadezhda Iakovlevna's. What Akhmatova had called "the relatively vegetarian," or early, period of repression was over, and the Great Purge was in full swing. The radio was full of the most fulsome rhetoric, praising Stalin. On 16 January 1937, just before he resolved to write an ode to Stalin—as a

kind of transition from the goldfinch cycle to the Stalin cycle—he wrote this poem:

> And what do we do with these crushed plains,
> the drawling hunger of this miracle?
> Anyway, that openness we see
> in them we see for ourselves, falling into sleep, we
> see—
> and the question keeps growing—where are they
> going? where are they from?—
> And isn't he crawling slowly along them,
> Him, the one we cry out at in our sleep—
> Him, the Judas of the future?

[No. 350]

The Russian text says, literally, "the Judas of peoples to come." "That openness" is not merely the flatness of the "crushed plains"—the vastness of steppe and sky beyond the Voronezh hills—but the historical and cultural "openness" of Eurasia ("where are they going? where are they from?") which along with the vast spaces and possibilities of the American continent comes as close in terms of historical space and historical experience to the metaphysical sense of what Heidegger in his essay on Rilke called "the Open" as the nonmetaphysical imagination can grasp. It is across the horizon of this openness that Judas crawls. And there can be little doubt as to his historical identity. And it is now not "that openness we see . . . [as we are] falling into sleep," but rather "the one we cry out at . . . Him. . . ." Two days later, Mandelstam wrote

> No comparisons: everyone alive is incomparable.
> With sweet fright
> I'd agree with the steppe's smooth equality, and
> the sky's circle was like a sickness.
>
> I'd turn to the servant-air
> waiting for news, for something,
> and get ready to leave, and I'd drift down an arc
> of journeys that never begin.
>
> Wherever I've got more sky—I'll wander there,
> yes—
> but this bright boredom won't let me leave
> these young Voronezh hills, won't let me go
> to those universal hills—there, clear, distinct, over
> in Tuscany.

[No. 352]

At first glance, the statement that "everyone alive is incomparable" seems like a good Acmeist affirmation. "Equality" refers not only to the flatness of the steppe, but to revolutionary aspirations, distinguishing them from the gradated hierarchies of feudal Europe. "The sky's circle" is confining, like a sickness; yet the poet "agrees"; he might inwardly, in spite of his fear, assent. His getting ready to leave, and his drifting "down the arc of journeys" is, of course, in imagination. Where he'd go would be where horizons were broader. The view from the Florentine hills would be immeasurably broader than that from "these young Voronezh hills"—*because* they are universal, they have universal human significance, they have culturally and historically acquired universality. Mandelstam's nostalgia is not for a physical landscape but for a view of cultural breadth; scope. But he is held down, imprisoned, by the force—not force of gravity (heaviness and tenderness are still sisters; to have weight means to cry out to be built) but the force of the figure looming on the horizon— "the Judas of peoples to come," who will betray the building.

And so, the Mandelstam who in 1921 was ready to greet the revolution in the manner of Hoelderlin greeting the return of the gods—

> our blood, our music, our political sense—all this will find its continuation in the tender being of a new nature, a nature-psyche. In this kingdom of the spirit without man every tree will be a dryad and every phenomenon will speak of its own metamorphosis—.

that Mandelstam in 1937 felt something like a shadow pass obliquely across his grave: "And what's mine has picked itself / up and gone . . ." (no. 346). In several poems he wrote of "Precious world-yeast" (i.e., poetry) and the grim shadow passing obliquely across a grave. Clarence Brown and Nadezhda Iakovlevna have both described the "phonic shadow" of Stalin as it fell over the last poems in the *Second Voronezh Notebook*—the syllables that echoed *"os"* as in *osa* ("wasp") and *os'* ("axle")— central to the only thing both Mandelstam and Stalin had in common, their first name, Joseph, of which both *Osip* and *Iosif* are variants. Among these poems are some of Mandelstam's best. Meanwhile, notebook and pencil lay on the table. Mandelstam rarely used them except at the *end* of the process of composition; and he had in the past felt somewhat sardonic toward Pasternak who complained of needing at least the space and peace and quiet of a writing desk in order to compose; Mandelstam, on the contrary, composed in his head, pacing his room or the streets, his body tense and his lips moving; in his poetry, "moving lips" and not pad and paper were the symbol of poetic composition. "But for the sake of the **'Ode'** he changed all his habits, and while he was writing it we had to eat on the very edge of the table, or even on the window sill."

"'Now, look at Aseyev,'" he said to Nadezhda Iakovlevna, "'he's a real craftsman, he would just dash it off without a moment's thought.'"

Finally, he wrote the **"Ode."** It did not help him, though it may have lightened the lot of Nadezhda Iakovlevna and provided her with the opportunity to save many of the poems. The **"Ode"** itself has not survived. "'It was an illness,'" Mandelstam later said to Akhmatova.

One of the poems that emerged from the Stalin matrix was a vision of himself as Prometheus, which he rejected: "No, never again—tragedies don't come back . . ." (no. 356). Or, if they do, it is as farce; or at the very least as proletarian: "Those lips lead me down into the essence / of Aeschylus the wood-loader, of Sophocles the wood-cutter . . ." (no. 356). One recalls that although

he never read James Joyce, he anticipated *Ulysses* if not altogether *Finnegans Wake*.

"'Why is it that when I think of *him*,'" he asked Nadezhda Iakovlevna—she repeats the question in her chapter on the Stalin Ode—"I see heads, mounds of heads? . . . What is he doing with all those heads?'"

It was the Tatar conquerors of Russia who piled pyramids of heads outside the cities as landmarks to the folly of opposition to their rule. It was part of the Muscovite history from which Mandelstam had shrunk, and from which he had turned briefly to tragic, brief Petropolis. And yet—

> Hillocks of human heads into the horizon,
> and I am diminished—they won't notice me,
> but I'll come back, resurrected in tender books and
> children's games, saying: See? The sun is shining.
>   [No. 341]

Perhaps he will come back.

Robert Alter   (essay date 1974)

SOURCE: "Mandelstam's Witness," in *Commentary*, Vol. 57, No. 6, June, 1974, pp. 69-79.

[*Alter is an American educator and critic. In the following essay, he discusses the influence of Mandelstam's Jewish origins on his poetry.*]

> "I am easy in my mind now," Akhmatova said to me in the sixties. "We have seen how durable poetry is."
>   —Nadezhda Mandelstam, *Hope Against Hope*

> The people need poetry that will be
>   their own secret
> to keep them awake forever,
> and bathe them in the bright-haired wave
> of its breathing.
>   —Osip Mandelstam, *Voronezh Notebooks*

There is something oddly legendary about the posthumous career of Osip Mandelstam, as though he had died not in a Soviet concentration camp in 1938, with a death certificate issued in due form by the totalitarian bureaucracy, but in some shadowy recess of medieval mystery. He is just now beginning to be recognized in the West as one of the major 20th-century poets; many of those who can read him in the original regard him as the greatest Russian poet since Pushkin; but he has achieved this prominence only through an uncanny resurrection after Stalin's attempt to bury his poetic legacy together with him. His poetry has survived largely through the efforts of his extraordinary wife, Nadezhda, much of it actually in an "oral tradition," held fast, line by unpublishable line, in her tenacious memory and in that of a few loyal friends. There is a much more varied oral tradition about Mandelstam's life and death, a good deal of it contradictory, and one of

---

On Mandelstam's creative process:

In 1932 I was coming home one day from the offices of the newspaper *For a Communist Education* on Nikitski Street. At that time we were living on Tverskoi Boulevard. On my way I saw M. sitting on the front steps of a shabby house. His head was twisted around so that his chin almost touched his shoulder; he was twirling his walking stick with one hand and resting the other on one of the stone steps to keep his balance. The moment he saw me, he jumped up and we walked along together.

When he was "composing" he always had a great need of movement. He either paced the room (unfortunately we never had very much space for this) or he kept going outside to walk the streets. The day I came across him sitting on the steps, he had just stopped to rest, tired of walking around. He was then working on the second part of his "Verses About Russian Poetry." For M. poetry and walking were closely connected. In his "Conversation About Dante" he asks how many pairs of shoes Alighieri must have worn out while writing the *Divine Comedy*. The same theme occurs in his poems about Tiflis, of which he says that they "remember the worn splendor" of a visiting poet's shoes. This is not just about his poverty—the soles of his shoes were always worn—but about poetry, too.

I only once saw M. composing verse without moving around. This was in Kiev at my parents' home, where we spent Christmas in 1923; he sat motionless by the iron stove for several days, occasionally asking me or my sister, Anna, to write down the lines of his **"January 1, 1924."** The other time was in Voronezh at a period when he was terribly exhausted by his work and had lain down to rest. But a poem was still buzzing in his head and he could not rid himself of it—it was the one about the singer with the deep voice at the end of the *Second Voronezh Notebook.*

Nadezhda Mandelstam, in her Hope Against Hope: A Memoir, *Collins & Harvill Press, 1971.*

Mme. Mandelstam's functions as a memoirist has been to sift these sundry accounts, trying to separate fact from fabrication.

Toward the end of the first of her two large volumes of memoirs, *Hope Against Hope*—it is a book that will surely remain one of the great texts on the nature of totalitarianism—she attempts to penetrate the curtain that fell between her and her husband when he was taken off for the second and last time, on the night of May 1, 1938, by agents of the NKVD. Over the years she spent exiled in the remote Eastern regions of the USSR, and later when she was permitted to reside again in Moscow after 1964, various survivors of the Great Terror came to see her with what they presented as eyewitness testimonies of her husband's last days in the transports and the camps. These she checks against one another and against what she herself knew of her husband's condition and habits with the shrewd skepticism of an experienced criminal lawyer. Among the stories to which she seems to grant full cre-

dence is one told her by a certain physicist, who chooses to remain anonymous, and who claims to have been in the Vladivostok transit camp at the same time as Mandelstam. One night in the camp, the physicist—Mme. Mandelstam designates him "L."—was invited by a non-political, that is, criminal, prisoner to climb up to a loft with him where, with a whole gang of criminals, L. might listen to some poetry. In the candlelit loft L. made out a barrel on top of which were laid out an open can of food and white bread, unimaginable delicacies in the prison world where no meal was more than a cup of watery soup. "Sitting with the criminals was a man with a gray stubble of beard, wearing a yellow leather coat. He was reciting verse which L. recognized. It was Mandelstam. The criminals offered him bread and the canned stuff, and he calmly helped himself and ate. . . . He was listened to in complete silence and sometimes asked to repeat a poem."

Whether or not the incident actually occurred as reported, the very existence of the story and its acceptance by the poet's widow should suggest that poetry retains an intensity of meaning and value in Russian culture far surpassing any role it now plays in the West. (Could one imagine a story told about Yeats, Valéry, or Wallace Stevens fascinating a rough audience of criminal compatriots, enjoying their protection?) Even should it prove quite faithful to fact, the anecdote has the quality of legend in projecting into a vividly dramatized form a sensed inner truth of the poet's character and the aspirations of his work—like the old story about Judah Halevi, the great medieval Hebrew poet, who was imagined to have been trampled to death by an Arab horseman after finally arriving at the gates of Jerusalem and reciting his "Ode to Zion." The stubble-bearded bard performing to convicts for sustenance in the candlelit loft is the same Mandelstam who from his youth cherished the idea that people would always be good to him because of his gift for poetry. He was not, however, by any means a naive man, and this seemingly childish belief was, as we shall see, rooted in a deeply meditated set of ideas on the nature of poetry and its ontological, spiritual, and political implications.

Osip Mandelstam was born in Warsaw in 1891, the son of a prosperous Jewish leather merchant. When he was still quite small, the family moved to Petersburg, a fact worth noting in its historical context, since Jews were not then permitted to reside in the city, which means that Emil Mandelstam had managed to obtain for himself the status of "privileged Jew." In 1904 Osip was sent to the prestigious Tenishev Commercial School in Petersburg—a decade later one of its students would be Vladimir Nabokov—where he received a thorough classical education (classical antiquity was to pervade his verse) and, extracurricularly, a good dose of Social-Revolutionary Marxism (this he would outgrow). After graduating from the Tenishev School in 1907, Mandelstam traveled in Western Europe, spending some time in Paris and Heidelberg, studying Old French literature, and quite consciously preparing himself for the vocation of poetry he already felt he was destined to fulfill. In 1911 for a while he undertook studies in Romance and Germanic philology at Petersburg University, and in order to escape the university's anti-Jewish *numerus clausus,* he converted to Lutheranism. The conversion, according to his widow, was strictly *pro forma,* but the uncertain evolution of Mandelstam's relation to Christianity is a question to which I shall return.

In 1912, Mandelstam became associated with an important group of younger poets who called themselves Acmeists, and who were rebelling against the Symbolist school which had provided the leading emphasis in Russian poetry for more than a decade. The Acmeists, as Clarence Brown characterizes them in his admirable critical study of Mandelstam [titled *Mandelstam*], were remarkably close in aims and sensibility to the Anglo-American Imagists of the same period—with even a common literary genealogy by way of Théophile Gautier and the French Parnassians. Against the Symbolists' mystical pursuit through poetic language of a hazy beckoning Beyond, the Acmeists cultivated qualities of clarity and hardness in their verse, sought to create out of the tactile and visual concreteness of things here and now a new chaste poetry of classical precision. Mandelstam's first volume of verse appeared in 1913 with the appropriately Acmeist title, **Stone.** Even in translation, one can see that Mandelstam, scarcely out of adolescence, was an astonishingly poised poet. Here, for example, is a poem in his early Acmeist manner, sharply visual, polished to a smooth hardness in its tactile and kinesthetic unity, and explicitly affirming the serene control of the artist. Mandelstam was eighteen when he wrote it.

On the pale blue enamel
conceivable in April
the birches raised their branches
and vespered imperceptibly.

The fragile netting froze
the pattern fine and small
like the design on porcelain
plates—precisely drawn
when the courteous artist limns it
on the firmament of glass,
conscious of his passing power,
unmindful of sad death.

Stone would be followed by only two other volumes of verse in Mandelstam's lifetime, **Tristia,** published in 1922, and, in 1928, **Poems,** which incorporated both the previous volumes and added to them twenty new poems, written between 1921 and 1925. Mandelstam had rapidly moved beyond the Acmeist manner to a more difficult, personal, meditative, and complicated associational style. At the same time, by 1922, after directly witnessing the horrors of the Civil War and the first improvised stages of the Bolshevik terror, he had come to see the full dire implications of the Revolution for everything he truly valued. His sense of estrangement from the new totalitarian Russia led to a five-year period of silence as a poet in the later 20's. By 1929, when it was clear that Mandelstam would not and could not march to party directives in his poetry, he became *persona non grata,* and his verse was no longer publishable, not really because it was counterrevolutionary but because it insisted on a realm of

imagination utterly beyond revolutionary jurisdiction. After achieving a sense of inner release in 1929 by lashing back in an essay, "Fourth Prose," at the Soviet literary hacks who had subjected him to a campaign of vilification, Mandelstam began again to write poetry freely, dictating, as always, to his wife, who hid the precious notebooks from the secret police as the couple moved back and forth across Russia. He was arrested for the first time in Moscow in 1934, after an informer had conveyed to the Cheka the text of his withering poetic lampoon of Stalin. Though his interrogation in the Lubianka, the dreaded Moscow central prison, induced a psychotic episode after his release, he got off "easily" with a sentence of exile to the Urals, and the extraordinary flow of creative activity that had begun in 1930 continued more or less unbroken until his final arrest. The death certificate given to his brother in 1940 lists the date of death as December 27, 1938, the cause: "heart failure."

A good part of the subsequent Mandelstam story has taken place on the other side of the world. In 1955, a carefully annotated two-volume edition of Mandelstam's collected works in Russian was published in New York by two distinguished émigré scholars, Gleb Struve and Boris Filippov; between 1964 and 1971 this was to be reissued in an expanded three-volume edition. Once the collected works appeared in New York, Nadezhda Mandelstam tells us, she felt she could breathe easy for the first time in seventeen years, knowing that the great trust that had been her principal reason for going on alone through such bleakness was now fulfilled: her husband's surviving poetry would be passed on to posterity. By the later 60's, as cultural policy in the USSR again became more repressive after the brief illusory interlude of the Thaw, a new underground literature, or *samizdat,* of forbidden works circulated in typescript, began to flourish, and Mandelstam was soon a cult figure in this world of clandestine Russian letters. His widow's first volume of memoirs was also intently read in *samizdat,* while its publication abroad in 1970, followed now by the appearance here of a second volume, makes the poet's exemplary stance against the despotism of the revolutionary regime a matter of unforgettable public record for Western readers. A qualified, ambiguous, "rehabilitation" of Mandelstam was granted after Khrushchev's anti-Stalin speech at the Twentieth Party Congress in 1956, but the publication of a volume of his selected poems, first announced in 1959, was somehow delayed until 1974. . . .

Did Mandelstam's Jewish origins have anything to do with the nature of his imaginative work, with the stance toward reality that he ultimately assumed? Was he a vestigial Jew, merely an ex-Jew, or a Jew somehow productively conscious of his Jewishness? The second possibility was never open to him, and I think one can say, with only a little schematic simplification, that in the course of his maturation he moved perceptibly from the first position to the third, from a vestigial Jewish identity to one that was integrated into his imaginative life.

To begin with, as the gifted son with literary aspirations of Russified bourgeois parents, being a Jew must have seemed more a hindrance than anything else, an obstacle to entering into the fullness of Russian culture. Mandelstam's lack of compunction about going through the forms of conversion in order to be admitted into Petersburg University is not really surprising. In the autobiographical chapters he composed in 1925 under the title, *The Noise of Time,* the Jewish aspects of his parents' home constitute a moribund realm of obsolescent rituals and traditional objects in tatters and shreds. On the bookshelves of his "enlightened" father, unread Hebrew volumes lay gathering dust a shelf below Goethe and Schiller, and two shelves below his mother's Pushkin and Lermontov. His father, like many comfortable Jewish burghers of the period, hired a Hebrew tutor for the boy, but the language with its "spiky script" remained alien, impenetrable, and the child vividly sensed that this, too, was an empty charade when he saw his young Hebrew nationalist tutor hide his Jewish pride upon going out into the street.

On a visit to his grandparents in Riga, Mandelstam recalls his grandfather placing a black and yellow cloth over his shoulders and making him mumble some uncomprehended Hebrew words. The memory looks suspiciously like a compound of actual recollection and projected fantasy, since there is no traditional practice of placing a *talit* over a child in this way except in synagogue on the festival of Simchat Torah; but the distortion is revealing, for it betrays a sense of being swathed, entangled, in the musty vestitures of a moribund Judaism. The slightly puzzling yellow of the cloth must be that dull brownish-yellow hue that the wool of an old prayer shawl characteristically assumes. In the private symbology of his poetry and prose, Mandelstam would repeatedly use yellow and black as the emblematic colors of Judaism, often reinforcing through them a sense of Judaism as belonging to an inverted netherworld, apart from the multicolored pageantry of Russian reality. In a poem written in 1916, he thinks of himself born into that ancestral world illumined by a black sun: "At Jerusalem's gate / a black sun has risen. / The yellow one frightens me more."

The paradoxical complement to the images of Jewishness as decay and perhaps interment is his reiterated vision of it, again in *The Noise of Time,* as a realm of formless origins: "All the elegant mirage of Petersburg [evoked in the preceding paragraphs] was merely a dream, a brilliant covering thrown over the abyss, while round about there sprawled the chaos of Judaism—not a motherland, not a house, not a hearth, but precisely a chaos, the unknown womb world whence I had issued, which I feared, about which I made vague conjectures and fled, always fled." The flight from the unknown womb world invites psychological conjecture, especially since Mandelstam oddly fancied his marriage to a Jewish woman as an ultimately incestuous union, an idea he stressed in a 1920 poem where Nadezhda figures as the biblical Leah who in turn—the refraction of sources is typical of Mandelstam—blends with Lot's daughters.

For the younger Mandelstam, in other words, to become preeminently Russian, and beyond that, European, was to define oneself by joining with what was patently other,

and so to escape the threat of a primal merging with one's origins. Clarence Brown aptly observes that the implicit opposite to "Judiac chaos" was Christian order, and it is Christianity not as a corpus of belief but primarily as an aesthetic idea, the embodiment of an elaborated order, that attracts this poet devoted to the creation of architectural coherence in language. The allure of order was compounded by a sense of Christianity as a sphere of serious spirituality that stood in contrast to the jejune worldly rationalism of his parents' post-traditional Jewish home. For a while he entertained the notion of the church as the necessary foundation for society, but, his widow informs us, by the 1920's he had completely dropped this idea.

What is behind the younger Mandelstam's theorizing about the need for Christianity is a distinctive Russian version of a familiar modern pattern: the writer of Jewish origins who is impelled at least in part to deny or denigrate his Jewishness in order to participate fully in the literary culture of his country. On the crudest level, but also the one most universally shared, the phenomenon is perceptible in the feeling of so many literary people in this predicament that there is something *unseemly* about being a Jew, something that goes against the very nature of cultivated letters; and the young Mandelstam in fact appears to be troubled by feelings of this sort. Such a sense of malaise, or inferiority, may be no different for a writer than for anyone else suffering from the anxieties of belonging to a cultural minority, but what complicates the situation of the imaginative writer is the profound way in which any national literature constitutes an enormously nuanced, self-allusive system intimately linked with a particular history and a particular set of traditions. For someone from a minority, in other words, to enter into the system and create from within it involves a difficult process of assimilation in depth, what becomes in many a hyper-acculturation.

The Christian character of so much European literature of course poses special problems for the Jewish writer embarked on the adventure of assimilation. In the West, where the Christian aspect of literary culture has tended to be somewhat diffuse or merely residual over the last two centuries, it was usually sufficient for a writer of Jewish origins to make himself into a reasonable facsimile of his counterparts in the majority culture in regard to matters of style, taste, intellectual reference, but not of creed: in America, for example, one could compose a substantial list of such self-consciously acculturated poets, critics, novelists. In Russia, as far as an outsider can judge, the case seems to have been somewhat different, at least until quite recently. The two giants of the 19th-century Russian novel were of course deeply serious Christians. The turn-of-the-century Russian intellectual scene was marked by a reawakened interest in Christian mysticism; and the Symbolists, who were Mandelstam's first models as poets even though he was to break with their poetic procedures, were profoundly involved in Christian religious ideas—in pointed contrast to most of the French Symbolists, from whom they were supposed to have derived.

Russia, then, becomes an instructive extreme instance of the problematics of literary assimilation, offering in our century a literature with strong bonds to Christianity and at the same time a literature where, as nowhere else, Jews achieve the highest artistic eminence. The identification of Russian things with Christian belief is, I suspect, more potent for someone who is primarily a writer of poetry than it is for a writer of prose. Pasternak, who was also born a Jew and with whom Mandelstam maintained a guarded friendship, enthusiastically embraced Christianity, and his conversion surely had some connection with his highly conscious aspiration to attain a place of honor in Russian poetry. Babel, on the other hand, the great short story writer whom Mandelstam also knew and admired, was not tempted by Christianity as such, though in dealing in his fiction with moral character operating in the medium of history, his tendency to hyper-acculturation took the form of an oscillating fascination with the alien Cossack ethos of virility and violence.

Perhaps the apogee of Mandelstam's romance with Christianity is a 1915 essay, "Pushkin and Scriabin," of which only fragments have survived. From the passages Clarence Brown incorporates in his critical study, one can readily observe the strained intermarriage between Mandelstam's personal conception of art and his tendency at that early point in his career to identify art with Christianity. Since redemption and sacrifice have already been effected by Christ, Mandelstam argues, these qualities have no place in art, which is thus left to be absolutely free, to constitute its own sphere of joyous playfulness. It is uniquely through Christianity, then, that art becomes a realm of spontaneous freedom. The rather abstract ingenuity of the argument, of course, has nothing whatever to do with the historical facts of Christianity and the nature of art under the Christian dispensation. The notion of art as play and freedom is something Mandelstam would cling to always, for which he would eventually die, but by the 20's he disavowed "Pushkin and Scriabin" as his aesthetic credo—at least partly, one can assume, because of its programmatic insistence on the Christian component of art.

It is revealing that Mandelstam's fullest, most original statement on the nature of poetry, "Talking About Dante" (1933), manages to discuss the author of *The Divine Comedy* for some 16,000 words without once considering him as a Christian poet. Dante's poem is described as a vast "stereometric body," a many-hued wonder of "crystallographic" form, the supreme realized example of the infinite transformability of poetic material, but it is never spoken of as a statement of Christian faith, a poetic unity made possible through the systematic coherence of classical Christian theology. By this point in his life Mandelstam was sure of the idea of lucid order as a product of humanistic culture, and he no longer needed to associate that idea with Christianity. He had a deeply abiding sense of being heir to a Judeo-Christian tradition, but, as Mme. Mandelstam observes in *Hope Abandoned,* he linked that tradition with the Hellenic one as part of a general Mediterranean heritage of civilizing values; and I think the inference is clear that he came to see Christianity and Judaism alike as bodies of humanistic achievement, not of theological imperatives. Having shifted to that perspective, he was able to adopt a more affirmative attitude toward his own Jewishness, which could now be seen with less ambivalence not as a hindrance but as a valuable, historically authenticated point of departure for profound participation in an overarching European culture.

"As a little bit of musk fills an entire house," Mandelstam noted memorably in *The Noise of Time,* "so the least influence of Judaism overflows all of one's life." In context, the implications of the statement are more ambiguous than might appear, for what immediately follows is that description of the Judaism of his childhood as a moribund world, so the clinging pungency might, by inference, be an odor of decay. The younger Mandelstam indeed exhibits an element of uneasiness about his Jewish origins: in the pre-Revolutionary days in Petersburg, he never invited anyone to his family home, rarely mentioned his parents in conversation, and impatiently disclaimed kinship with another Mandelstam whose path he had crossed. He also, however, resisted the suggestion that he adopt a Russian last name, as many Jewish writers had done, so even at the beginning his vague embarrassment was balanced in part by some residual Jewish pride. The simile of the little bit of musk tends to have greater validity, with more positive implications, for the later Mandelstam, though one must be very careful not to pounce on the aphorism and use its authority to insist on a "Jewish key" to Mandelstam's achievement. Perhaps the essential point to stress here is not the debatable issue of the assertion's objective validity but simply that it had a certain psychological validity for Mandelstam. That is, he came to associate some of his most basic values and imaginative allegiances with his Jewishness, whatever may have been the actual channels through which he came to them. If Judaism had threatened the poet as an unknown womb world, it could also on occasion provide him an organizing myth for his own experience.

Ineluctably, Mandelstam was almost everywhere perceived as a Jew in the world of Russian poetry which his achievement rapidly dominated. At the very outset, after having been taken briefly under the protection of the older Symbolist poet, Zinaida Gippius, he was tagged "Zinaida's Jew-boy," perhaps with a degree of playfulness but certainly not without an element of wry hostility. The attacks on him that began in the later 20's were often laced with anti-Semitism, and that has been true even posthumously, with certain Russian nativists recently referring to him as a "Jewish cancer" on the body of Russian poetry. The mature Mandelstam, especially in the last decade of his life, tended more and more to respond to this repeated imputation of his being a Jewish outsider by insisting on his Jewishness as a major source of his poetic vision, as his distinctive avenue of entrance into the higher European civilization. He took an avid interest in whatever he encountered of Jewish culture, his widow comments in connection with his friendship and enthusiasm for the prominent Yiddish actor and director, Mikhoels (later murdered by Stalin). As the Stalinist barbarism deepened, he appears to have identified imaginatively with historical Jewish suffering as an inspiriting model for confronting his own dire situation. Particularly revealing in this respect is the story with which he turned aside the inquiry of a GPU commandant in Voronezh in 1935 when he was challenged about his current occupation. Deprived of regular employment, he replied, he was devoting himself to the study in Spanish of the work of a certain Jewish poet who had spent years in the dungeons of the Inquisition, every day mentally composing a sonnet, released only to be imprisoned again and put in chains—whereupon he continued to compose sonnets.

Osip Mandelstam did not believe either in Judaism or Christianity: he believed in poetry.

—*Robert Alter*

Altogether, the idea of historical continuity assumed progressively greater central importance for Mandelstam, and his belonging to the preeminently history-harried, history-laden people became in this connection a dynamic element of consciousness. "His conviction," we are told in *Hope Against Hope,* "that culture, like grace, is bestowed by a process of continuity led M. to see the Mediterranean as the 'holy land.'" The Mediterranean sacred soil included for him Greece and Italy as well as Palestine, and, by a loose personal association of climate and geography, the Crimea and the Caucasus, where he traveled with his wife and wrote some of his most glowing poetry. Mme. Mandelstam herself puzzles over this professed affinity for Mediterranean culture, suggesting that it makes no particular sense for a Russian boy raised in Petersburg to imagine he had a biological bond with the Mediterranean world simply because of his Jewish parentage. The point, of course, is not that such an identification with Mediterranean values need be actually grounded in facts of heredity, only that it establish itself as a potent fact of consciousness for the poet. Though Mandelstam was an intensely Russian poet—some of his poems are so dense with allusions to earlier Russian poetry and history as to be impenetrable in any translation—he urgently needed an imaginative bridge out of his time and place, and his awareness of himself as a Jew gave him a sense of inner distance, a feeling of privileged at-homeness in the broad continuum of cultural values that went back three millennia and that was now threatened by the revolutionary reign of bureaucratized brutality. His widow's comment in *Hope Abandoned* on the presence of Jewish themes in his poetry makes perfect sense in the light of this general orientation: such poems were "not numerous—but always deeply significant."

By the end of the 1920's, the "Judaic chaos" always to be fled had given way to a sense of Jewishness as an ancient aristocratic lineage. At the beginning of "Fourth Prose" Mandelstam reflects with satirical tartness on the assimilated bourgeois Jews of Petersburg, "descended from rabbis of patrician blood," who ended up seeking the waters of salvation at Turgenevian and Lermontovian spas. Later in "Fourth Prose," he makes a special point of assuming

the stance of a Jew against the revenging pack of party-prodded hacks (Soviet "writerdom") that wanted to destroy him: "I insist that writerdom, as it has developed in Europe and above all in Russia, is incompatible with the honorable title of Jew, of which I am proud. My blood, burdened with its inheritance from sheep breeders, patriarchs, and kings, rebels against the shifty gypsyishness of the writing tribe."

Two years later, in 1931, he would explore the identification with an ancient Jewish king as a key symbol of his own poetic power in "**Canzone,**" one of the remarkable poems in his mature style of permutated allusions. "**Canzone**" offers a view out across the Armenian landscape as an optical emblem of poetic vision. Armenia, the land of Ararat, and, as Mandelstam called it elsewhere, a "younger sister of Judea," merges with biblical Zion, and the sharp-eyed poet, enriched with "the Psalmist's legacy to a seer," imagines himself peering through "exquisite Zeiss / binoculars, King David's precious gift" (translation by Max Hayward in *Hope Abandoned*). These visionary lenses give a precise definition to details of the landscape, a primary intensity to color in a world where everything has ominously faded. Thus the "Mediterranean" poet, recollecting a recently visited Armenia as he writes in Moscow, dreams of fulfilling his ancient vocation by leaving the northern regions "to steep in vision destiny's finale/and say *selah* to the Chief of the Jews/for his crimson caress."

Mme. Mandelstam devotes several intriguing paragraphs to that peculiar crimson caress, connecting it with Rembrandt's painting, *The Prodigal Son,* that hangs in the Hermitage in Leningrad, in which the figure of the forgiving father is bathed in a reddish aura from his mantle. The Russian color-word, *malinovy,* we are informed in a note by Max Hayward, derives from *malina,* raspberry, and carries connotations of richness, mellowness, warmth. For our purposes, what is most important is the association of crimson with royalty in the figure of the poet-king of ancient Israel, and the fact that by identifying a rich intensity of color with the Jewish heritage Mandelstam was precisely reversing his earlier version of Judaism as faded yellow and stark black over against the polychromatic splendor of the Russian world. Instead of a chaos of origins, the Jewish past had become a vividly imaged myth of origins.

Let us keep ultimate distinctions clear. Osip Mandelstam did not believe either in Judaism or Christianity: he believed in poetry. For a time, he was inclined to associate poetry with Christianity because of his notions of Christian order and of the apparent spiritual seriousness of Christianity. Eventually, he emphasized instead the crucial historical consciousness made available to him as a poet by the fact of his being a Jew, and perhaps the Jewish stress was a more congenial one now precisely because it involved not belief but a sense of participation in a long cultural tradition. In a 1912 manifesto, "The Morning of Acmeism" (a full translation appears in Brown's critical study), Mandelstam talks about the way "a poet raises a phenomenon to its tenth power," producing a "monstrously condensed reality." And that reality, he goes on to say, "is the word as such."

As time went on, Mandelstam would enrich and complicate his conception of the reality generated by the word as such, but two decades later, in his remarkable essay on Dante, it is a conception to which he still remains faithful. Poetry, he announces at the beginning of the essay, is neither part of nature nor, in any ordinary sense of the term, an imitation of nature; "but it is something that, with astonishing independence, settles down in a new extra-spatial field of action, not so much narrating nature as acting it out by means of its instruments, which are called images." These images, of course, are cast in language, and so dynamically interact with one another in a poem in regard to their linguistic and phonetic properties as well as their visual ones. In this way Mandelstam arrives at the view that within the independent, extra-spatial field of its operation, poetic material is not referential but generated by the poem's restless exploration of its own patterns, image begetting image through the complicating reinforcements of multiple association and sound. Poetry is of course made out of human experience in this world, but it achieves its "monstrously condensed reality" through its freedom to follow its own uncannily non-discursive, asyntactical logic of images and sounds.

This doctrine of language and reality has little to do either with Judaism or Christianity, or, for that matter, with any "Judeo-Christian tradition," though the Jewish notion of inexhaustible revelation through words and their exegesis may be more congenial to such an aesthetic than the Christian idea of the Logos, the single incarnate Word. What the doctrine does reflect is Mandelstam's personal relation to the Old Testament and the New, to the corpus of Homer, Ovid, Dante, Villon, Pushkin, as luminous patterns of language. Once he could imagine for himself a connection with Judaism not through the remembered mustiness of his grandfather's house but through words— those of a Spanish poet or of the Psalmist, those of the biblical narrator telling the story of his namesake Joseph— he was free to conceive himself as a Jewish poet, custodian of Mediterranean crimsons and blues and golds in the bleakness of a northern landscape and a harsh time. Homer could as easily have been the imagined source of his legacy as David, and, indeed, there are rich and abundant allusions to Homer in his verse, but it was more natural for him to fashion his personal myth of the poetic vocation out of Psalmist and Levite because of his pressing consciousness of himself as a Jew.

The inner freedom of poetry to "condense" reality was in Mandelstam's view absolutely indispensable to civilized existence—the people needed it as they needed air, bread, and light, he would write in a late poem, "to keep them awake forever"—and it was just this freedom that a totalitarian regime could not tolerate in the least degree. Mandelstam's decision to write the "Stalin Epigram" in 1934 and to read it to a group of friends was a necessary one for him, even with the knowledge that it would probably mean his death. As his wife justly notes in *Hope Abandoned*, he needed an act of defiance like that, and like

"Fourth Prose" before it, "to smash the glass cage in which he was imprisoned and regain his freedom" in order to preserve his own life-sustaining poetic voice. "You cannot write poetry in a glass cage," Mme. Mandelstam concludes, "—there is no air." There is compelling logic in his representation of Stalin in the fatal poem as a kind of mythic antitype to poetry, the implacable issuer of "words like measures of weight" which kill, who arrogates all language to his own homicidal purposes and surrounds himself with fawning retainers that can only grunt and squeal like beasts.

One senses in the magnificent poetry of the so-called Voronezh Notebooks, the poems Mandelstam wrote in his exile in the Don region, 1935-37, a paradoxical quality in the midst of terror that Walter Benjamin once attributed to Kafka—a radiant serenity. It is a quality, I think, that derives in great part from the ultimate faith Mandelstam placed in the abiding validity, the indispensability, of the poetic enterprise, which he was now living out, writing out, to its utmost consequences. To be sure, he was not entirely free of chill premonitions about his own imminent fate and, equally, that of mankind. There are poems, therefore, that touch an ominous note of intimated apocalypse, like the one in which he watches lines of prisoners crossing "the plains' beaten weight" and wonders whether crawling across these expanses is "the one whose name we shriek in our sleep—/the Judas of nations unborn." What is remarkable is that the apocalyptic vision should be given such a secondary emphasis in the Voronezh Notebooks. Mandelstam's poetic celebration of the here and now was never more intense, more sensuously alive, than in these poems. His private Mediterranean myth provides one imaginative source for this celebration, surfacing here and there in the explicit imagery of Cretan pottery, Greek flutes, the Italy of Dante, the yea-saying sea, and, repeatedly, the display of Mediterranean blue. More immediately, the actual Voronezh landscape is present in all its multiplex, poignant particularity—green trees "exploding" out of the muddy spring earth wreathed in milky fog, the ice-clogged canals of a jagged winter scene, a master colorist's version of Deep Saddle-Bow Mountain in yellows and reds, "raspberry and pure gold." It is easy enough to accept on the evidence of the poems alone Nadezhda Mandelstam's assertion that during the Voronezh period the couple were happy as puppies, draining every lived moment to the fullest.

The joyous intensity with which Mandelstam effects these condensations of reality as a *Dichter der irdischen Welt*— a phrase coined by Erich Auerbach to characterize Dante's acute poetic focus on the earthly realm—is perfectly complemented by the utter conviction and dignity of the poems in which the poet quietly, unaffectedly defies his persecutors.

> You took away all the oceans and all the room.
> You gave me my shoe-size in earth with bars
>   around it.
> Where did it get you? Nowhere.
> You left me my lips, and they shape words,
>   even in silence.

In the supreme imaginative clarity of these last poems, Mandelstam stands beyond ethnic origin or credal affiliations as a luminous witness for poetry itself—not its martyr but its exemplary practitioner, demonstrating the vivifying freshness of the poet's transformational play with language even under the impending darkness of the final terror. History and the literary tradition kept running through his head as he crystallized the present moment in his verse, and he may well have thought of his bond with the people that through two millennia had been left only its words, its moving lips, by its oppressors, yet with that had achieved much, and had persisted. In the engulfing cataclysm of his own era, Mandelstam could reflect on the stubborn durability of the whole broad multilingual literary tradition that had come down to him somehow unbroken through all its historical vicissitudes; and so, with the confidence of a master in his perfected craft, he could hope at the end that his poetry, too, would survive the murderous new order determined to extirpate it and all it stood for.

> Mounds of human heads are wandering into the
>   distance.
> I dwindle among them. Nobody sees me. But in books
> much loved, and in children's games I shall rise
> from the dead to say the sun is shining.

Joseph Brodsky   (essay date 1977)

SOURCE: "The Child of Civilization," in *Less Than One: Selected Essays,* Farrar, Straus and Giroux, 1986, pp. 123-44.

[*Brodsky was a Russian poet and critic who emigrated from the Soviet Union in 1972 and became an American citizen in 1977. His work has been well-received by English and American critics, many of whom once called him the greatest living poet. In the following essay, originally published as the introduction to* Fifty Poems *by Osip Mandelstam,* he explores the uniquely Russian characteristics of Mandelstam's work.]

For some odd reason, the expression "death of a poet" always sounds somewhat more concrete than "life of a poet." Perhaps this is because both "life" and "poet," as words, are almost synonymous in their positive vagueness. Whereas "death"—even as a word—is about as definite as a poet's own production, i.e., a poem, the main feature of which is its last line. Whatever a work of art consists of, it runs to the finale which makes for its form and denies resurrection. After the last line of a poem nothing follows except literary criticism. So when we read a poet, we participate in his or his works' death. In the case of Mandelstam, we participate in both.

A work of art is always meant to outlast its maker. Paraphrasing the philosopher, one could say that writing poetry, too, is an exercise in dying. But apart from pure linguistic necessity, what makes one write is not so much a concern for one's perishable flesh as the urge to spare certain things of one's world—of one's personal civilization—one's own non-semantic continuum. Art is not a better, but an alternative existence; it is not an attempt to escape reality but the opposite, an attempt to animate it. It is a spirit seeking flesh but finding words. In the case of Mandelstam, the words happened to be those of the Russian language.

For a spirit, perhaps, there is no better accommodation: Russian is a very inflected language. What this means is that the noun could easily be found sitting at the very end of the sentence, and that the ending of this noun (or adjective, or verb) varies according to gender, number, and case. All this provides any given verbalization with the stereoscopic quality of the perception itself, and (sometimes) sharpens and develops the latter. The best illustration of this is Mandelstam's handling of one of the main themes of his poetry, the theme of time.

There is nothing odder than to apply an analytic device to a synthetic phenomenon; for instance, to write in English about a Russian poet. Yet in dealing with Mandelstam it wouldn't be much easier to apply such a device in Russian either. Poetry is the supreme result of the entire language, and to analyze it is but to diffuse the focus. It is all the more true of Mandelstam, who is an extremely lonely figure in the context of Russian poetry, and it is precisely the density of his focus that accounts for his isolation. Literary criticism is sensible only when the critic operates on the same plane of both psychological and linguistic regard. The way it looks now, Mandelstam is bound for a criticism coming strictly "from below" in either language.

The inferiority of analysis starts with the very notion of theme, be it a theme of time, love, or death. Poetry is, first of all, an art of references, allusions, linguistic and figurative parallels. There is an immense gulf between *Homo sapiens* and *Homo scribens,* because for the writer the notion of theme appears as a result of combining the above techniques and devices, if it appears at all. Writing is literally an existential process; it uses thinking for its own ends, it consumes notions, themes, and the like, not vice versa. What dictates a poem is the language, and this is the voice of the language, which we know under the nicknames of Muse or Inspiration. It is better, then, to speak not about the theme of time in Mandelstam's poetry, but about the presence of time itself, both as an entity and as a theme, if only because time has its seat within a poem anyway, and it is a caesura.

It is because we know this full well that Mandelstam, unlike Goethe, never exclaims "O moment, stay! Thou art so very fair!" but merely tries to extend his caesura. What is more, he does it not so much because of this moment's particular fairness or lack of fairness; his concern (and subsequently his technique) is quite different. It was the sense of an oversaturated existence that the young Mandelstam was trying to convey in his first two collections, and he chose the portrayal of overloaded time as his medium. Using all the phonetic and allusory power of words themselves, Mandelstam's verse in that period expresses the slowing-down, viscous sensation of time's passage. Since he succeeds (as he always does), the effect is that the reader realizes that the words, even their letters—vowels especially—are almost palpable vessels of time.

On the other hand, his is not at all that search for bygone days with its obsessive gropings to recapture and to reconsider the past. Mandelstam seldom looks backward in a poem; he is all in the present—in this moment, which he makes continue, linger beyond its own natural limit. The past, whether personal or historical, has been taken care of by the words' own etymology. But however un-Proustian his treatment of time is, the density of his verse is somewhat akin to the great Frenchman's prose. In a way, it is the same total warfare, the same frontal attack—but in this case, an attack on the present, and with resources of a different nature. It is extremely important to note, for instance, that in almost every case when Mandelstam happens to deal with this theme of time, he resorts to a rather heavily caesuraed verse which echoes the hexameter either in its beat or in its content. It is usually an iambic pentameter lapsing into alexandrine verse, and there is always a paraphrase or a direct reference to either of Homer's epics. As a rule, this kind of poem is set somewhere by the sea, in late summer, which directly or indirectly evokes the ancient Greek background. This is partly because of Russian poetry's traditional regard for the Crimea and the Black Sea as the only available approximation of the Greek world, of which these places—Taurida and Pontus Euxinus—used to be the outskirts. Take, for instance, poems like **"The stream of the golden honey was pouring so slow . . . ," "Insomnia. Homer. Tautly swelling sails . . . ,"** and **"There are orioles in woods and lasting length of vowels,"** where there are these lines:

> . . . Yet nature once a year
> Is bathed in lengthiness as in Homeric meters.
> Like a caesura that day yawns . . .

The importance of this Greek echo is manifold. It might seem to be a purely technical issue, but the point is that the alexandrine verse is the nearest kin to hexameter, if only in terms of using a caesura. Speaking of relatives, the mother of all Muses was Mnemosyne, the Muse of Memory, and a poem (be it a short one or an epic) must be memorized in order to survive. Hexameter was a remarkable mnemonic device, if only because of being so cumbersome and different from the colloquial speech of any audience, Homer's included. So by referring to this vehicle of memory within another one—i.e., within his alexandrine verse—Mandelstam, along with producing an almost physical sensation of time's tunnel, creates the effect of a play within a play, of a caesura within a caesura, of a pause within a pause. Which is, after all, a form of time, if not its meaning: if time does not get stopped by that, it at least gets focused.

Not that Mandelstam does this consciously, deliberately. Or that this is his main purpose while writing a poem. He does it offhandedly, in subordinate clauses, while writing (often about something else), *never* by writing to make this point. His is not topical poetry. Russian poetry on the whole is not very topical. Its basic technique is one of beating around the bush, approaching the theme from various angles. The clear-cut treatment of the subject matter, which is so characteristic of poetry in English, usually gets exercised within this or that line, and then a poet moves on to something else; it seldom makes for an entire poem. Topics and concepts, regardless of their importance, are but material, like words, and they are always there. Language has names for all of them, and the poet is the one who masters language.

> **Mandelstam worked in Russian poetry for thirty years, and what he did will last as long as the Russian language exists. It will certainly outlast the present and any subsequent regime in that country, because of both its lyricism and its profundity.**
>
> **—*Joseph Brodsky***

Greece was always there, so was Rome, and so were the biblical Judea and Christianity. The cornerstones of our civilization, they are treated by Mandelstam's poetry in approximately the same way time itself would treat them: as a unity—and in their unity. To pronounce Mandelstam an adept at either ideology (and especially at the latter) is not only to miniaturize him but also to distort his historical perspective, or rather his historical landscape. Thematically, Mandelstam's poetry repeats the development of our civilization: it flows north, but the parallel streams in this current mingle with each other from the very beginning. Toward the twenties, the Roman themes gradually overtake the Greek and biblical references, largely because of the poet's growing identification with the archetypal predicament of "a poet versus an empire." Still, what created this kind of attitude, apart from the purely political aspects of the situation in Russia at the time, was Mandelstam's own estimate of his work's relation to the rest of contemporary literature, as well as to the moral climate and the intellectual concerns of the rest of the nation. It was the moral and the mental degradation of the latter which were suggesting this imperial scope. And yet it was only a thematic overtaking, never a takeover. Even in *Tristia,* the most Roman poem, where the author clearly quotes from the exiled Ovid, one can trace a certain Hesiodic patriarchal note, implying that the whole enterprise was being viewed through a somewhat Greek prism.

Tristia

I've mastered the great craft of separation
amidst the bare unbraided pleas of night,
those lingerings while oxen chew their ration,

the watchful town's last eyelid's shutting tight.
And I revere that midnight rooster's descant
when shouldering the wayfarer's sack of wrong
eyes stained with tears were peering at the distance
and women's wailings were the Muses' song.

Who is to tell when hearing "separation"
what kind of parting this may resonate,
foreshadowed by a rooster's exclamation
as candles twist the temple's colonnade;
why at the dawn of some new life, new era
when oxen chew their ration in the stall
that wakeful rooster, a new life's towncrier,
flaps its torn wings atop the city wall.

And I adore the worsted yarn's behavior:
the shuttle bustles and the spindle hums;
look how young Delia, barefooted, braver
than down of swans, glides straight into your arms!
Oh, our life's lamentable coarse fabric,
how poor the language of our joy indeed.
What happened once, becomes a worn-out matrix.
Yet, recognition is intensely sweet!

So be it thus: a small translucent figure
spreads like a squirrel pelt across a clean
clay plate; a girl bends over it, her eager
gaze scrutinizes what the wax may mean.
To ponder Erebus, that's not for our acumen.
To women, wax is as to men steel's shine.
Our lot is drawn only in war; to women
it's given to meet death while they divine.

(Translated by Joseph Brodsky)

Later, in the thirties, during what is known as the Voronezh period, when all those themes—including Rome and Christianity—yielded to the "theme" of bare existential horror and a terrifying spiritual acceleration, the pattern of interplay, of interdependence between those realms, becomes even more obvious and dense.

It is not that Mandelstam was a "civilized" poet; he was rather a poet for and of civilization. Once, on being asked to define Acmeism—the literary movement to which he belonged—he answered: "nostalgia for a world culture." This notion of a world culture is distinctly Russian. Because of its location (neither East nor West) and its imperfect history, Russia has always suffered from a sense of cultural inferiority, at least toward the West. Out of this inferiority grew the ideal of a certain cultural unity "out there" and a subsequent intellectual voracity toward anything coming from that direction. This is, in a way, a Russian version of Hellenicism, and Mandelstam's remark about Pushkin's "Hellenistic paleness" was not an idle one.

The mediastinum of this Russian Hellenicism was St. Petersburg. Perhaps the best emblem for Mandelstam's attitude toward this so-called world culture could be that strictly classical portico of the St. Petersburg Admiralty decorated with reliefs of trumpeting angels and topped with a golden spire bearing a silhouette of a clipper at its

tip. In order to understand his poetry better, the English-speaking reader perhaps ought to realize that Mandelstam was a Jew who was living in the capital of Imperial Russia, whose dominant religion was Orthodoxy, whose political structure was inherently Byzantine, and whose alphabet had been devised by two Greek monks. Historically speaking, this organic blend was most strongly felt in Petersburg, which became Mandelstam's "familiar as tears" eschatological niche for the rest of his not-that-long life.

It was long enough, however, to immortalize this place, and if his poetry was sometimes called "Petersburgian," there is more than one reason to consider this definition both accurate and complimentary. Accurate because, apart from being the administrative capital of the empire, Petersburg was also the spiritual center of it, and in the beginning of the century the strands of that current were merging there the way they do in Mandelstam's poems. Complimentary because both the poet and the city profited in meaning by their confrontation. If the West was Athens, Petersburg in the teens of this century was Alexandria. This "window on Europe," as Petersburg was called by some gentle souls of the Enlightenment, this "most invented city," as it was defined later by Dostoevsky, lying at the latitude of Vancouver, in the mouth of a river as wide as the Hudson between Manhattan and New Jersey, was and is beautiful with that kind of beauty which happens to be caused by madness—or which tries to conceal this madness. Classicism never had so much room, and the Italian architects who kept being invited by successive Russian monarchs understood this all too well. The giant, infinite, vertical rafts of white columns from the façades of the embankments' palaces belonging to the Czar, his family, the aristocracy, embassies, and the *nouveaux riches* are carried by the reflecting river down to the Baltic. On the main avenue of the empire—Nevsky Prospect—there are churches of all creeds. The endless, wide streets are filled with cabriolets, newly introduced automobiles, idle, well-dressed crowds, first-class boutiques, confectioneries, etc. Immensely wide squares with mounted statues of previous rulers and triumphal columns taller than Nelson's. Lots of publishing houses, magazines, newspapers, political parties (more than in contemporary America), theaters, restaurants, gypsies. All this is surrounded by the brick Birnam Wood of the factories' smoking chimneys and covered by the damp, gray, widespread blanket of the Northern Hemisphere's sky. One war is lost, another—a world war—is impending, and you are a little Jewish boy with a heart full of Russian iambic pentameters.

In this giant-scale embodiment of perfect order, iambic beat is as natural as cobblestones, Petersburg is a cradle of Russian poetry and, what is more, of its prosody. The idea of a noble structure, regardless of the quality of the content (sometimes precisely *against* its quality, which creates a terrific sense of disparity—indicating not so much the author's but the verse's own evaluation of the described phenomenon), is utterly local. The whole thing started a century ago, and Mandelstam's usage of strict meters in his first book, **Stone,** is clearly reminiscent of Pushkin, and of his pleiad. And yet, again, it is not a result

Mandelstam, 1936.

so groundless that graduate students, military cadets, and clerks felt tempted, and by the turn of the century the genre was compromised to the point of verbal inflation, somewhat like the situation with free verse in America today. Then, surely, devaluation as reaction came, bearing the names of Futurism, Constructivism, Imagism, and so forth. Still, these were isms fighting isms, devices fighting devices. Only two poets, Mandelstam and Tsvetaeva, came up with a qualitatively new content, and their fate reflected in its dreadful way the degree of their spiritual autonomy.

In poetry, as anywhere else, spiritual superiority is always disputed at the physical level. One cannot help thinking it was precisely the rift with the Symbolists (not entirely without anti-Semitic overtones) which contained the germs of Mandelstam's future. I am not referring so much to Georgi Ivanov's sneering at Mandelstam's poem in 1917, which was then echoed by the official ostracism of the thirties, as to Mandelstam's growing separation from any form of mass production, especially linguistic and psychological. The result was an effect in which the clearer a voice gets, the more dissonant it sounds. No choir likes it, and the aesthetic isolation acquires physical dimensions. When a man creates a world of his own, he becomes a foreign body against which all laws are aimed: gravity, compression, rejection, annihilation.

Mandelstam's world was big enough to invite all of these. I don't think that, had Russia chosen a different historical path, his fate would have been that much different. His world was too autonomous to merge. Besides, Russia went the way she did, and for Mandelstam, whose poetic development was rapid by itself, that direction could bring only one thing—a terrifying acceleration. This acceleration affected, first of all, the character of his verse. Its sublime, meditative, caesuraed flow changed into a swift, abrupt, pattering movement. His became a poetry of high velocity and exposed nerves, sometimes cryptic, with numerous leaps over the self-evident with somewhat abbreviated syntax. And yet in this way it became more a song than ever before, not a bardlike but a birdlike song, with its sharp, unpredictable turns and pitches, something like a goldfinch tremolo.

And like that bird, he became a target for all kinds of stones generously hurled at him by his motherland. It is not that Mandelstam opposed the political changes taking place in Russia. His sense of measure and his irony were enough to acknowledge the epic quality of the whole undertaking. Besides, he was a paganistically buoyant person, and, on the other hand, whining intonations were completely usurped by the Symbolist movement. Also, since the beginning of the century, the air was full of loose talk about a redivision of the world, so that when the Revolution came, almost everyone took what had occurred for what was desired. Mandelstam's was perhaps the only sober response to the events which shook the world and made so many thoughtful heads dizzy:

> Well, let us try the cumbersome, the awkward,
> The screeching turning of the wheel . . .
>   (from **"The Twilight of Freedom"**)

of some conscious choice, nor is it a sign of Mandelstam's style being predetermined by the preceding or contemporary processes in Russian poetry.

The presence of an echo is the primal trait of any good acoustics, and Mandelstam merely made a great cupola for his predecessors. The most distinct voices underneath it belong to Derzhavin, Baratynsky, and Batyushkov. To a great extent, however, he was acting very much on his own in spite of any existing idiom—especially the contemporary one. He simply had too much to say to worry about his stylistic uniqueness. But this overloaded quality of his otherwise regular verse was what made him unique.

Ostensibly, his poems did not look so different from the work of the Symbolists, who were dominating the literary scene: he was using fairly regular rhymes, a standard stanzaic design, and the length of his poems was quite ordinary—from sixteen to twenty-four lines. But by using these humble means of transportation he was taking his reader much farther than any of those cozy-because-vague metaphysicists who called themselves Russian Symbolists. As a movement, Symbolism was surely the last great one (and not only in Russia); yet poetry is an extremely individualistic art, it resents isms. The poetic production of Symbolism was as voluminous and seraphic as the enrollment and postulates of this movement were. This soaring upward was

But the stones were already flying, and so was the bird. Their mutual trajectories are fully recorded in the memoirs of the poet's widow, and they took two volumes. These books are not only a guide to his verse, though they are that too. But any poet, no matter how much he writes, expresses in his verse, physically or statistically speaking, at most one-tenth of his life's reality. The rest is normally shrouded in darkness; if any testimony by contemporaries survives, it contains gaping voids, not to mention the differing angles of vision that distort the object.

The memoirs of Osip Mandelstam's widow take care precisely of that, of those nine-tenths. They illuminate the darkness, fill in the voids, eliminate the distortion. The net result is close to a resurrection, except that everything that killed the man, outlived him, and continues to exist and gain popularity is also reincarnated, reenacted in these pages. Because of the material's lethal power, the poet's widow re-creates these elements with the care used in defusing a bomb. Because of this precision and because of the fact that through his verse, by the acts of his life, and by the quality of his death somebody called forth great prose, one would instantly understand—even without knowing a single line by Mandelstam—that it is indeed a great poet being recalled in these pages: because of the quantity and energy of the evil directed against him.

Still, it is important to note that Mandelstam's attitude toward a new historical situation wasn't at all that of outright hostility. On the whole he regarded it as just a harsher form of existential reality, as a qualitatively new challenge. Ever since the Romantics we have had this notion of a poet throwing down the glove to his tyrant. Now if there ever was such a time at all, this sort of action is utter nonsense today: tyrants do not make themselves available for such a tête-à-tête any longer. The distance between us and our masters can be reduced only by the latter, which seldom happens. A poet gets into trouble because of his linguistic, and, by implication, his psychological superiority, rather than because of his politics. A song is a form of linguistic disobedience, and its sound casts a doubt on a lot more than a concrete political system: it questions the entire existential order. And the number of its adversaries grows proportionally.

It would be a simplification to think that it was the poem against Stalin which brought about Mandelstam's doom. This poem, for all its destructive power, was just a byproduct of Mandelstam's treatment of the theme of this not-so-new era. For that matter, there's a much more devastating line in the poem called **"Ariosto"** written earlier the same year (1933): "Power is repulsive as are the barber's fingers . . ." There were plenty of others, too. And yet I think that by themselves these mug-slapping comments wouldn't invite the law of annihilation. The iron broom that was walking across Russia could have missed him if he were merely a political poet or a lyrical poet spilling here and there into politics. After all, he got his warning and he could have learned from that as many others did. Yet he didn't because his instinct for self-preservation had long since yielded to his aesthetics. It was the immense intensity of lyricism in Mandelstam's

poetry which set him apart from his contemporaries and made him an orphan of his epoch, "homeless on an all-union scale." For lyricism is the ethics of language and the superiority of this lyricism to anything that could be achieved within human interplay, of whatever denomination, is what makes for a work of art and lets it survive. That is why the iron broom, whose purpose was the spiritual castration of the entire populace, couldn't have missed him.

> The English-speaking world has yet to hear Mandelstam's nervous, high-pitched, pure voice shot through with love, terror, memory, culture, faith—a voice trembling, perhaps, like a match burning in a high wind, yet utterly inextinguishable.
>
> *—Joseph Brodsky*

It was a case of pure polarization. Song is, after all, restructured time, toward which mute space is inherently hostile. The first has been represented by Mandelstam; the second chose the state as its weapon. There is a certain terrifying logic in the location of that concentration camp where Osip Mandelstam died in 1938: near Vladivostok, in the very bowels of the state-owned space. This is about as far as one can get from Petersburg inside Russia. And here is how high one can get in poetry in terms of lyricism (the poem is in memory of a woman, Olga Vaksel, who reportedly died in Sweden, and was written while Mandelstam was living in Voronezh, where he was transferred from his previous place of exile near the Ural Mountains after having a nervous breakdown). Just four lines:

. . . And stiff swallows of round eyebrows (a)
flew (b) from the grave to me
to tell me they've rested enough in their (a)
cold Stockholm bed (b).

Imagine a four-foot amphibrach with alternating (*a b a b*) rhyme.

This strophe is an apotheosis of restructuring time. For one thing, language is itself a product of the past. The return of these stiff swallows implies both the recurrent character of their presence and of the simile itself, either as an intimate thought or as a spoken phrase. Also, "flew . . . to me" suggests spring, returning seasons. "To tell me they've rested enough," too, suggests past: past imperfect because not attended. And then the last line makes a full circle because the adjective "Stockholm" exposes the hidden allusion to Hans Christian Andersen's children's story about the wounded swallow wintering in the mole's hole, then recovering and flying home. Every schoolboy in Russia knows this story. The conscious process of remembering turns out to be strongly rooted in the subconscious memory and creates a sensation of sorrow so piercing, it's as if this is not a suffering man we hear but the very voice of his wounded psyche. This kind of voice surely clashes with everything, even with its medium's—i.e., poet's—life. It is like Odysseus tying himself to a mast against the call of his soul; this—and not only the fact that Mandelstam is married—is why he is so elliptical here.

He worked in Russian poetry for thirty years, and what he did will last as long as the Russian language exists. It will certainly outlast the present and any subsequent regime in that country, because of both its lyricism and its profundity. Quite frankly, I don't know anything in the poetry of the world comparable to the revelatory quality of these four lines from his **"Verses on the Unknown Soldier,"** written just a year prior to his death:

> An Arabian mess and a muddle,
> The light of speeds honed into a beam—
> And with its slanted soles,
> A ray balances on my retina . . .

There is almost no grammar here but it is not a modernistic device, it is a result of an incredible psychic acceleration, which at other times was responsible for the breakthroughs of Job and Jeremiah. This honing of speeds is as much a self-portrait as an incredible insight into astrophysics. What he heard at his back "hurrying near" wasn't any "wingèd chariot" but his "wolf-hound century," and he ran till there was space. When space ended, he hit time.

Which is to say, us. This pronoun stands not only for his Russian- but also for his English-speaking readers. Perhaps more than anyone in this century, he was a poet of civilization: he contributed to what had inspired him. One may even argue that he became a part of it long before he met death. Of course he was a Russian, but not any more so than Giotto was an Italian. Civilization is the sum total of different cultures animated by a common spiritual numerator, and its main vehicle—speaking both metaphorically and literally—is translation. The wandering of a Greek portico into the latitude of the tundra is a translation.

His life, as well as his death, was a result of this civilization. With a poet, one's ethical posture, indeed one's very temperament, is determined and shaped by one's aesthetics. This is what accounts for poets finding themselves invariably at odds with the social reality, and their death rate indicates the distance which that reality puts between itself and civilization. So does the quality of translation.

A child of a civilization based on the principles of order and sacrifice, Mandelstam incarnated both; and it is only fair to expect from his translators at least a semblance of parity. The rigors involved in producing an echo, formidable though they may seem, are in themselves an homage to that nostalgia for the world culture which drove and fashioned the original. The formal aspects of Mandelstam's verse are not the product of some backward poetics but, in effect, columns of the aforesaid portico. To remove them is not only to reduce one's own "architecture" to

heaps of rubble and shacks: it is to lie about what the poet has lived and died for.

Translation is a search for an equivalent, not for a substitute. It requires stylistic, if not psychological, congeniality. For instance, the stylistic idiom that could be used in translating Mandelstam is that of the late Yeats (with whom he has much in common thematically as well). The trouble of course is that a person who can master such an idiom—if such a person exists—will no doubt prefer to write his own verse anyway and not rack his brains over translation (which doesn't pay that well besides). But apart from technical skills and even psychological congeniality, the most crucial thing that a translator of Mandelstam should possess or else develop is a like-minded sentiment for civilization.

Mandelstam is a formal poet in the highest sense of the word. For him, a poem begins with a sound, with "a sonorous molded shape of form," as he himself called it. The absence of this notion reduces even the most accurate rendition of his imagery to a stimulating read. "I alone in Russia work from the voice, while all round the unmitigated muck scribbles," says Mandelstam of himself in his "Fourth Prose." This is said with the fury and dignity of a poet who realized that the source of his creativity conditioned its method.

It would be futile and unreasonable to expect a translator to follow suit: the voice one works from and by is bound to be unique. Yet the timbre, pitch, and pace reflected in the verse's meter are approachable. It should be remembered that verse meters in themselves are kinds of spiritual magnitudes for which nothing can be substituted. They cannot be replaced even by each other, let alone by free verse. Differences in meters are differences in breath and in heartbeat. Differences in rhyming pattern are those of brain functions. The cavalier treatment of either is at best a sacrilege, at worst a mutilation or a murder. In any case, it is a crime of the mind, for which its perpetrator—especially if he is not caught—pays with the pace of his intellectual degradation. As for the readers, they buy a lie.

Yet the rigors involved in producing a decent echo are too high. They excessively shackle individuality. Calls for the use of an "instrument of poetry in our own time" are too strident. And translators rush to find substitutes. This happens primarily because such translators are themselves usually poets, and their own individuality is dearest of all to them. Their conception of individuality simply precludes the possibility of sacrifice, which is the primary feature of mature individuality (and also the primary requirement of any—even a technical—translation). The net result is that a poem of Mandelstam's, both visually and in its texture, resembles some witless Neruda piece or one from Urdu or Swahili. If it survives, this is due to the oddity of its imagery, or of its intensity, acquiring in the eyes of the reader a certain ethnographic significance. "I don't see why Mandelstam is considered a great poet," said the late W. H. Auden. "The translations that I've seen don't convince me of it."

Small wonder. In the available versions, one encounters an absolutely impersonal product, a sort of common denominator of modern verbal art. If they were simply bad translations, that wouldn't be so bad. For bad translations, precisely because of their badness, stimulate the reader's imagination and provoke a desire to break through or abstract oneself from the text: they spur one's intuition. In the cases at hand this possibility is practically ruled out: these versions bear the imprint of self-assured, insufferable stylistic provincialism; and the only optimistic remark one can make regarding them is that such low-quality art is an unquestionable sign of a culture extremely distant from decadence.

Russian poetry on the whole, and Mandelstam in particular, does not deserve to be treated as a poor relation. The language and its literature, especially its poetry, are the best things that that country has. Yet it is not concern for Mandelstam's or Russia's prestige that makes one shudder at what has been done to his lines in English: it is rather a sense of plundering the English-language culture, of degrading its own criteria, of dodging the spiritual challenge. "O.K.," a young American poet or reader of poetry may conclude after perusing these volumes, "the same thing goes on over there in Russia." But what goes on over there is not at all the same thing. Apart from her metaphors, Russian poetry has set an example of moral purity and firmness, which to no small degree has been reflected in the preservation of so-called classical forms without any damage to content. Herein lies her distinction from her Western sisters, though in no way does one presume to judge whom this distinction favors most. However, it is a distinction, and if only for purely ethnographic reasons, that quality ought to be preserved in translation and not forced into some common mold.

A poem is the result of a certain necessity: it is inevitable, and so is its form. "Necessity," as the poet's widow Nadezhda Mandelstam says in her "Mozart and Salieri" (which is a must for everyone interested in the psychology of creativity), "is not a compulsion and is not the curse of determinism, but is a link between times, if the torch inherited from forebears has not been trampled." Necessities of course cannot be echoed; but a translator's disregard for forms which are illumined and hallowed by time is nothing but stamping out that torch. The only good thing about the theories put forth to justify this practice is that their authors get paid for stating their views in print.

As though it is aware of the fragility and treachery of man's faculties and senses, a poem aims at human memory. To that end, it employs a form which is essentially a mnemonic device allowing one's brain to retain a world—and simplifying the task of retaining it—when the rest of one's frame gives up. Memory usually is the last to go, as if it were trying to keep a record of the going itself. A poem thus may be the last thing to leave one's drooling lips. Nobody expects a native English speaker to mumble at that moment verses of a Russian poet. But if he mumbles something by Auden or Yeats or Frost he will be closer to Mandelstam's originals than current translators are.

In other words, the English-speaking world has yet to hear this nervous, high-pitched, pure voice shot through with love, terror, memory, culture, faith—a voice trembling, perhaps, like a match burning in a high wind, yet utterly inextinguishable. The voice that stays behind when its owner is gone. He was, one is tempted to say, a modern Orpheus: sent to hell, he never returned, while his widow dodged across one-sixth of the earth's surface, clutching the saucepan with his songs rolled up inside, memorizing them by night in the event they were found by Furies with a search warrant. These are our metamorphoses, our myths.

David McDuff   (essay date 1980)

SOURCE: "Teleological Warmth," in *Poetry Review,* Vol. LXX, Nos. 1-2, September, 1980, pp. 48-53.

[*In the following essay, McDuff considers the role of religion in Mandelstam's poetry, contending that "the essential point to grasp about Mandelstam is that he was a profoundly Christian poet."*]

The upsurge of interest which of recent years has manifested itself in the West towards the poetry and the personality of Osip Mandelstam is without doubt to be welcomed. Through the translations of his work and of the two large volumes of memoirs by his widow, Nadezhda Yakovlevna, Western readers have had the chance to glimpse something of the central significance of this poet to an understanding of the dire historical and cultural situation in which we find ourselves. That it has been no more than a glimpse is due to various factors, not the least of which is the traditional tendency of the English—and the Americans—to regard the Soviet Union as a far-flung, mysterious region where human beings, although superficially akin to themselves, act according to certain special and historically determined laws which are considered to be all right for 'them', but inapplicable to 'us'. The old cliché of 'oriental inscrutability' has rendered most of Russian literature and thought opaque to Western readers, even though the works themselves are available in translation. Yet, as the poet Joseph Brodsky has pointed out [in his *Beyond Consolation,* 1974]: 'Russian affairs are not only Russian affairs. Russia should not be viewed as a distant land; she is very close, even too close. The more indifferent the attitude toward her menacing lesson, the closer she is.' The translations of Mandelstam's work which have appeared have assisted towards a breaking-down of these barriers. For the first time it would seem that Western readers have had some insight into the reality of the culture and society of the Soviet Union. Nadezhda Yakovlevna's memoirs have provided a guide to her husband's work—no detached critical assessment this, but a truly existential account of life and art in the face of tyranny. For the Western reader, prepared by Solzhenitsyn's exposure of the Soviet Union as a vast concentration camp, the case of Mandelstam appears to strike a deep chord of sympathy, as no similar case has done in the past. The reasons for this may be many. But one of the principal factors may have been Mandelstam's Jewishness, and the realisation that what happened to him—his persecution and subsequent death in a concentration camp—under a socialist régime differed in no important respects from what happened to other Jews under Hitler.

One of the signs by which the twentieth century has made its presence known has been the numbing of the human response to brutality and destruction. It is doubtful if the advent of the concentration camps, the horrors and miseries of the world wars could have taken place were it not for the growth of a peculiar disability, variously described as 'anomie', the 'absurd', and 'alienation'. In the first chapter of the second volume of her memoirs, Mme Mandelstam describes the way in which she herself experienced this 'loss of identity', trying only to 'shed the burden of time'. Other people she knew reacted to the horror and barbarity they witnessed around them by 'waiting', so that they could 'restore order', i.e. carry out further repressions. Mandelstam's poetry is a living example of what it means to remain sane in a world where all values have been overthrown, and it is for this reason that I believe his poetry has 'caught' in the West, where loss of identity and a sense of 'absurdity' is experienced by many as a condition of daily life. The reasons for this Western predicament lie in the same secularisation of experience, the divorce of humanism from Christianity, which lay at the roots of the Russian revolution and which characterised its aftermath.

The essential point to grasp about Mandelstam is that he was a profoundly Christian poet. His faith in the values of Christian civilisation came to him very early, and was probably in part the result of the years he spent as a young student between 1907 and 1910 in Paris, Heidelberg and elsewhere in Western Europe. From the very beginning the Christian faith was inextricably linked for him with its artistic and architectural expression, the cultural heritage of Western Europe. In 1909 we find him writing to the Symbolist poet Vyacheslav Ivanov and questioning the latter's assertion that 'a man reflects on the truth of Catholicism when he steps under the vaults of Notre Dame and doesn't become a Catholic simply by virtue of being under those vaults'—for Mandelstam the reality of Christian art was the reality of Christian faith, into which one could walk as simply and as comfortably as one might enter a room. The poetry of Dante, of Ariosto, Tasso, medieval French art and verse, the whole flowering of European art from the Renaissance to the Enlightenment was for Mandelstam not an object of study or a cultural tradition to be revered—it was the enactment, straightforward and human, of the Christian notion of the personality as the highest value. The assertion of Mme Mandelstam that 'we have to learn to understand all over again that every individual human life is a symbol of a certain day in history' was the tenet that informed Mandelstam's vision of life and art. For him the 'particular', whether it was a poem, a painting, a sculpture or a human being was a revelation of the 'general'—the will of God.

This focusing on and familiarity with the particular was what characterised Mandelstam's poetry throughout its development. His earliest poems are filled with flashes of acutely observed and felt detail:

Fragments of red wine
and sunny May weather—
and, breaking a thin biscuit,
the whiteness of the slenderest fingers.

. . . and if in icy diamonds
the frost of eternity streams,
here there is the quivering of dragonflies,
quick-living, blue-eyed.

There is an innocence and spontaneity about many of these early poems which is the expression of a joy in creation. Creation is revealed as being specially intended for humans, a gift to them from God. Whether it is nature or art, 'the evening of the wood' or Hagia Sophia, creation is a bounty for which to be thankful, as are the senses with which creation is perceived:

I have the present of a body—what should I do
    with it
so unique it is and so much mine?

For the quiet joy of breathing and of being alive
tell me, whom have I to thank?

I am the gardener and the flower,
in the dungeon of the world I am not alone.

'The dungeon of the world' makes itself known very early in Mandelstam's poetry, however, and a sense of 'emptiness', an obscure dread and negativity haunt the bright and sharply-cut edges of this vision of nature and culture. A prophetic knowledge of doom lies at the heart of the poems, and as the Russian revolution draws closer the note of suffering and despair grows louder, until by 1918, with the shattering of the Christian world in Russia, the poet can write:

Let us celebrate, my brothers, freedom's twilight,
the great twilight year.
Into the seething waters of night
a heavy wood of snares is lowered.
You are arising into dead years
O sun, my judges, people
                              (**"The Twilight of Freedom"**)

The consciousness of the death of a civilisation makes Mandelstam's poems urgent and vivid, particularly since for him it is not a question of the destruction of some abstract ideal, but of the physical world as it is represented to him by his senses. The death of Christianity involves the disruption of the human psyche and of the senses—Mandelstam's poems, with their rapid switches of imagery and jangling phonemes tell us what it feels like when the self, the personality, are threatened with annihilation:

It is only by the voice that we will tell
what was scrabbling, struggling there,
and the coarse slate we will point
there, where the voice points.
I break the night, the burning chalk
for the firm copying of the moment.

I change noise into the singing of arrows,
I change form into angry chatter.
                                                ("Slate-Pencil Ode")

The later poems demonstrate to an increasing extent a similar disruption of reality, and an accompanying interference of 'psycho-babble'. Yet incoherence is never reached, mainly because Mandelstam does not give way to the temptation to write 'free verse'—his poems, however convoluted and strained, are always written with a due regard for the conventions of rhyme and metre, and even the **'Lines about the Unknown Soldier'**, the **"Ode to Stalin"** that is a terrifying witness to the poet's persecution by a Godless tyranny, have a classical musicality of diction and a measured form.

For some of the reasons given above, much has been made of Mandelstam's 'obscurity', of the 'difficulty' of his work. Yet instead of feeling intimidated by the language of Mandelstam's poems we would do better to take seriously something he was fond of repeating, namely that 'poetic speech is infinitely more raw, infinitely more unpolished, than so-called conversational speech'. Mandelstam's familiarity with the world of objects also extended to the realm of language. His poems reflect a truly vernacular discourse, not the 'lingo' of most human conversation, but an expression in linguistic terms of the 'domestic Hellenism' which Mandelstam learned from the poet Innokenty Annensky (also Akhmatova's 'teacher') and which he described in his essay 'On the Nature of the World' as 'the conscious surrounding of man by utensils instead of by indifferent objects, the humanisation of the surrounding world, the warming of it with the most subtle teleological warmth. Hellenism is every stove by which a man sits and treasures its warmth as his own personal warmth'.

Domestic language and imagery abound in Mandelstam's poetry. It is for this reason, perhaps, that readers such as Donald Davie have seen in Mandelstam a defender of 'private life' in a 'public' world [*Trying to Explain*, 1980]. Yet it would be more accurate to say that Mandelstam is describing in his poems the *destruction* of private life, which becomes impossible with the divorce of humanism from Christianity. The interference that makes Mandelstam's poems at times so strange and rich in ambiguity is the voice of the public, the 'social' the 'revolutionary' which will not tolerate the existence of those who represent the 'old' values. Mandelstam was destroyed by the revolution, and with him the sense of time that is inherent to our appreciation and understanding of the cultural and spiritual past. When memory has gone, all things become possible. To destroy the Christian past in the name of 'social justice' is no better than to destroy it in the name of the 'master race'. That sense of outrage, of broken values and dislocated inner time is what makes Mandelstam's poetry what it is, gives it its strength and feeling of 'rightness'.

Donald Davie has reacted to Mandelstam's poetry in a way that seems to be typical of a certain kind of Western response to the Russian poet's work. It may not be out of place, therefore, to devote the end of this short essay to a consideration of what Davie considers to be the most important feature of Mandelstam (and other twentieth-century Russian poets), and of what may in the end really account for Mandelstam's present popularity, although it is a conception, I fear, that is misguided. Davie refers several times in his recent interviews and essays to the fact that in the Soviet Union the poet's words count for much, to the extent that poets there have been made to suffer for what they have written. Davie complains about the scant attention that is paid to poets in the West, particularly in England. He does not see 'why a poet in a poem should be absolved from the duty which we lay on ourselves and on others in other walks of life, of meaning what he says, of saying things which he will stand by. Once we accept that a poet is absolved from that duty which bears on the rest of us, then what is left for poetry except to be a curious entrancing murmur in the background? Again I think of the martyrs and heroes of poetry in our time, the Russian poets particularly. To take that view of poetry is surely to insult the memory of the Akhmatovas and Mandelstams and Pasternaks.'

There is only one way to answer Davie, and others like him, and that is to tell him that in our kind of society, where the marriage of Christianity and humanism has long ceased to exist, the 'duty' to which he refers can have no place in poetry. It is many years now since poetry in the West was anything other than a 'curious entrancing murmur', and for that we should be thankful. Instead of longing for a tyranny to resist, Davie would be much better employed in guarding against the enemy that would soon find another kind of 'duty' for him, the enemy that killed Mandelstam.

Jane Gary Harris   (essay date 1988)

SOURCE: "Voronezh Notebooks," in *Osip Mandelstam*, Twayne Publishers, 1988, pp. 121-45.

[*Harris is an American educator and critic with a special interest in Russian literature. In the following excerpt from her critical study of Mandelstam, she analyzes thematic and stylistic aspects of the* Voronezh Notebooks.]

I am in the heart of the age—the way is unclear
And time distances the goal . . .
                                        (no. 332, 14 December 1936)

People need light and blue air,
They need bread and the snows of Elbrus. . . .
People need poetry secretly their own
To keep them awake forever . . .
To bathe them in its breath.
                                        (no. 355, 19 January 1937)

Mandelstam's arrest and interrogation, his mental anguish and suicide attempt, his exile and the intervention on his behalf of such major figures as Bukharin and Pasternak, followed by the subsequent "miracle"—Stalin's commutation of his sentence to "isolate but preserve," three years of exile in the southern Russian city of Voronezh rather than execution—left their mark on the poet's consciousness and profoundly affected his poetic voice. The shocking events of his private life, however, seem to have strengthened rather than diminished his self-image by reaffirming his faith in the vital role of the poet and poetry. New themes emerge, including, above all, faith in the power and joy of poetry as well as a somewhat mystical adherence to the idea of sharing in the destiny of the common man. Older themes continue in new forms—for example, the imminence of death. Mandelstam's last year in exile testifies to his renewed understanding of poetry as meeting a basic human need—"People need poetry . . . to keep them awake forever"—and discloses his profound sense of his own role as witness on the battlefield of human destiny (**"Verses on the Unknown Soldier"**).

Lydia Ginzburg's remark [in her "The Poetics of Mandelstam"] that "Mandelstam's poetry always has its source at the point where fear of life and love of life meet" is an extraordinarily apt summation of the "impulses" behind the complex texts we know as the *Voronezh Notebooks*. Such "impulses," to use Mandelstam's own terminology from "Conversation about Dante," not only inspired his most powerful verse, but generated the dense and seemingly obtuse quality of the later poetry. Intimate personal reflections ("I am in the heart of the age—the way is unclear") refer directly to that crossroads "where fear of life and love of life meet," for it is there that the poet-speaker's personal-psychological self confronts the experience of his sociopolitical and metaphysical being. Indeed, in the *Voronezh Notebooks* Mandelstam's role as "intermediary" intensified tenfold as "personal experience" literally became his "sole authority and source of conviction."

Oddly enough, the years of Voronezh exile proved even more prolific than the Moscow years. The collections of this period include the *First Voronezh Notebook* (April-July, 1935); the *Second Voronezh Notebook* (December 1936-February 1937), followed almost immediately by the *Third Voronezh Notebook* (March-May 1937).

While the poetry of the *First Notebook* often expresses the poet-speaker's passion for the simple joys of human existence, consciousness of his reprieve as an unexpected gift of life may have simultaneously stimulated ambivalent feelings of guilt as well as some subconscious drive to pay for that gift. Such feelings may have led to the year and a half of silence preceding the *Second Notebook* and to the self-conscious decision to write an **"Ode to Stalin"** in which his own destiny is mystically linked to that of his tormentor through the phonosemantic "axis" (*os'*) of their given names—"Osip" is a form of Stalin's name, "Joseph." The *Third Voronezh Notebook,* which contains extremes of Mandelstam's ecstatic and tragic vision, culminates in his ultimate farewell to mankind: **"Verses on the Unknown Soldier."**

The poem most frequently cited as having caused Mandelstam's arrest—the **"Stalin Epigram"**—was one of several satirical poems written toward the end of 1933. It was read, according to Nadezhda Yakovlevna, "to a number of people—eleven all told, including me, our brothers and Akhmatova. . . . Apart from the eleven named at the interrogation, seven or eight other people, including Shklovsky and Pasternak, had heard the poem. . . ." One of them was obviously an informer: . . . .

> Our lives no longer feel ground under them.
> At ten paces you can't hear our words.
>
> But whenever there's a snatch of talk
> it turns to the Kremlin mountaineer,
> the ten thick worms his fingers,
> his words like measures of weight,
>
> the huge laughing cockroaches on his top lip,
> the glitter of his boot-rims.
>
> Ringed with a scum of chicken-necked bosses
> he toys with the tributes of half-men.
>
> One whistles, another meows, a third snivels.
> He pokes out his finger and he alone goes boom.
>
> He forges decrees in a line like horseshoes,
> One for the groin, one the forehead, temple, eye.
>
> He rolls the executions on his tongue like berries.
> He wishes he could hug them like big friends from
>   home.
>
> (no. 286, November 1933; translated by
>   Brown and Merwin)

The **"Epigram"** contains the most explicit expression of Mandelstam's moral hostility toward the political cynicism of the age implied in his Moscow cycle, and in particular in the **"Wolf"** poem of 1931 which included the lines:

> The wolfhound age springs at my shoulders
> though I'm no wolf by blood.
> Better to be stuffed up a sleeve like a fleece cap
> in a fur coat from the steppes of Siberia,
>
> and so not see the snivelling, nor the sickly smears,
> nor the bloody bones on the wheel,
> so all night the blue foxes would still gleam
> for me as they did in the first times.
>
> Lead me into the night by the Yenesei
> where the pine touches the star.
> I'm no wolf by blood,
> and only my own kind will kill me.
>
> (no. 227, 17-28 March 1931; translated by
>   Brown and Merwin)

Although the **"Wolf"** poem clearly charges that men have abandoned moral values, it falls short of being a full-blown attack on the system or on Stalin. By 1933, however, Mandelstam's explicit anti-Soviet statements in **"The Apartment is Silent as Paper"** and the anti-Stalin **"Epigram"** were apparently enough to cause his arrest. Moreover, the political climate changed radically. Dissent was no longer merely challenged in the media. In 1929 Bukharin could intervene with the literary establishment over the trumped up "plagiarism" charges against Mandelstam and extricate him from the "Eulenspiegel Affair," but in 1934 he had to appeal to Stalin himself. By 1938, no one remained to help.

During the 1930s, the poet's life became his primary lyric material, as distinct from the monuments of human culture he apostrophized so magnificently in the early volumes, or the more abstruse, man-centered meditations on time, conscience, the poet and the age dominating *1921-1925.* However, the intense irony, even self-mockery of the *Moscow Notebooks* was somewhat toned down in the *Voronezh Notebooks,* although the general tonality established in the Moscow years remained.

Both the *Moscow Notebooks* and *Voronezh Notebooks* contain direct, impetuous, and poignant utterances. Exuberant exclamations of delight in the unexpected, in the joys of being alive coexist with frightening visions of the present and future; intimate revelations of the poet's need for warmth and beauty in this world are accompanied by firm declarations of fortitude and courage; oracular, prophetic, and mystical intimations of the future challenge Soviet reality and time itself. The seeming immediacy of shared involvement and the illusion of direct, intimate, and colloquial conversation temper the distance of unambiguous self-confidence, the aesthetic ambiguity of the meditative thinker, and the outrage of the polemicist. The voice of the persona as friend, companion, lover, and, above all, eyewitness, rejoices, rages, fears, despairs, reflects, testifies, judges, and prophesies. The poetry of the 1930s, then, alternates Mandelstam's inimitable spirit of love and defiance with his tragic vision—prescience of his own death, the death of world culture, and the death of humankind. While thematically and metaphorically the *Moscow Notebooks* and *Voronezh Notebooks* continue to record the signs in the universe signaling that all is not lost and the imperatives of the human soul that cannot be denied, structurally they are defined by a verbal texture richer and denser than that of any previous Russian poet. A limpid precision, sharpness of focus, and a vivid, dynamic inner mobility grace the lyrics of maturity with an elegant grandeur rarely encountered in twentieth-century verse.

"Black Earth" ("Chernozem"), the poem which opens the *Voronezh Notebooks,* was written in April 1935. It is a hymn in praise of the rich black earth of the Voronezh region. It is significant that this poem develops two major themes and fields of imagery from the 1920s and 1930s. On the one hand, the theme of the earth as the raw material and renewable source of poetic creation (the motif of "ploughed earth" from *Tristia* and the essay "Word and Culture") is blended with the motifs and imagery of the inexorable "book-like earth" of the Armenian cycle. While these self-reminiscences emphasize the earth as the ultimate source of the creative process, Mandelstam goes one step further in **"Black Earth"** and the "Black Earth" cycle by inscribing the poet himself into his image of the earth.

Nevertheless, it is the subtle introduction of the second major theme—through the seemingly superficial analogy between the Voronezh hills and horses' withers in stanza 1—that actually makes possible the inscription of the poet, or rather his poetic imperative, into the image of the earth. In **"Black Earth,"** the association of the earth—the rolling steppes—with horses' withers suggests self-reminiscence to the poet's imperative—the "verb on horseback"—depicted in *Journey to Armenia.* This theme, although merely suggested here, is more fully developed two years later in no. 365, **"I sing when my throat is moist . . ."** (**"Poiu kogda gortan' syra . . . ,"** 8 February 1937).

> So esteemed, so richly black, all in peak condition,
> All in the little withers, all clean air and grooming,
> All crumbly, all forming a chorus—
> Moist clods of my earth and freedom!
>
> In the days of early ploughing—black verging on blue,
> Its inner work establishes itself unarmed—
> A thousand hills of ploughed-up words—
> It seems something's not surrounding our environs!
>
> All the same the earth's a blunder and a butt—
> You can't plead with it, or fall at its feet:
> Like a decaying flute it alerts your hearing,
> Like a matutinal clarinet it nips your ear like frost.
>
> How pleasing the thick rich layers on the ploughshare,
> How the steppe is silent in April's turning of the soil . . .
> Well, hello there, black-earth, be brave, open your eyes—
> There's black-eloquent silence in your work.
>   (no. 299, April 1935)

Stylistically, both the imagery and unusual diction of **"Black Earth"** develop tendencies initiated in the Armenian and Moscow cycles. Although untypical of early Mandelstam, the conjunction of numerous neologisms with obsolete and colloquial expressions adds an original philological texture to the physical imagery of the later poetry, making translation extremely difficult. For instance, by reiterating the word *vsia* (all, whole, fully, totally) five times, the first stanza emphasizes the unity of the poet-speaker's view over the rolling hills of rich black earth spread out before him like well-groomed horses' withers; indeed, he seems to contemplate the way the earth's contours resemble the bare back of the horse he might ride. Simultaneously, this vision of unity and fullness is contrasted to its "crumbling" units, its "moist clods," praised equally for "crumbling" and for "forming a chorus." What is more, the apostrophized "moist clods" are highly personalized through the personal pronominal adjective, *"my,"* applied to "earth and freedom." Thus, something more than a hymn to the landscape is suggested.

Indeed, the elevated tone of the introductory adjectives—neologisms signifying rhetoric of extreme praise—"most thoroughly esteemed" (*pereuvazhena*) and "most thoroughly or richly black" (*perecherna*), but also possibly suggesting "overly esteemed" and "overly black" in a context of excessive repetition—implies that Mandelstam's hymn may be ambivalent. This possibility is further underscored in the powerful last line by the oxymoronic neologism—"black-eloquent silence in the work" ("*chernorechivoe molchanie v rabote*")—that substitutes for the expected "eloquent" or even "grandiloquent" (*krasnorechivoe*). Substitution of the root "cherno-" (black/hard/heavy) for "krasno-" (red/beautiful), of course, refers back to the black earth's capacity for poetic creation expressed in the "thousand hills of ploughed up words." However, it may also be read as contrasting the "hard work" (*chernaia rabota*) accomplished by the earth, by the peasant's labor, and by the poet, to gratuitous Soviet rhetoric (*krasnorechie*).

Furthermore, stanza 2, which describes spring ploughing, defines the earth's "work" as "unarmed," for, as the archaic verb (*zizhdit'sia*) suggests, that work is in, or of, or created by, the earth, and as such is self-sufficient. It is represented by another neologism—a "thousand hills of ploughed-up words/speech" (*tysiachekholmiia molvy*)—and hence requires no extra protection. The neologisms—*pereuvazhena, perecherna, tysiachekholmiia molvy,* and *provorot,* and the oxymoronic *chernorechivoe molchanie*—may thus be read as the realization of the earth's work—the "thousand hills of words . . . ,"—while the archaic verb to build, create, found (*zizhdit'sia*) emphasizes the historical and metaphysical ontology of the creative process. The "black earth," apostrophized in the poem's last lines, is transmuted into the "black-eloquent silence" of poetry, the mysterious internal creative process that here implies a solemn rejection of official Soviet grandiloquence (*krasnorechie*).

The other fundamental characteristic of the earth—its implacable, inexorable nature—is suggested in stanzas 3 and 4 in conjunction with the poet's gradual inscription of himself into his medium. Conversational idiom and direct dialogue establish an immediate bond between the poet and the earth.

In no. 312, **"Stanzas,"** an autobiographical cycle of eight poems recapitulating the poet's life in the 1930s, the final "Stanza" sums up the speaker's state of mind and projects his future as intimately linked with the earth. The poet defines his voice by claiming the earth itself will be his "weapon," and thus illuminates two major attributes of the earth—its "unarmed" and its inexorable nature.

> And after I get my breath back, in my voice
> The earth will resound—my final weapon—
> The dry moistness of the black earth.
>   (no. 312, no. 8, May-June 1935)

In **"Black Earth"** Mandelstam associates the steadfast nature of the earth with the eternal creative process. He first introduces highly colloquial diction in stanza 3, using words such as *prorukha* and *obukh* (a blunder and a butt) and the phrase *"Kak v nogi ei ne bukhai"* (You can't plead with it, or fall at its feet) to indicate the inexorable power of the earth. He then compares it to musical instru-

ments that irritate rather than soothe the ear, that "alert your hearing." This stanza recalls "To some winter is arrack," in which the poet's ear is alerted by the "cruel imperatives of the stars."

Finally, in the concluding stanza the speaker addresses the earth directly, recalling the self-reflexive dialogue in *Journey to Armenia* where the poet first began to recognize his imperative: the "feeling for the fullness of life characteristic of the Armenian people . . . kept repeating to me: now stay awake, don't fear your own age, don't be coy." In this poem, his greetings to the earth are simultaneously self-exhortation: "Well, hello there, black earth, be brave, keep your eyes open / There's black-eloquent silence in [your] work." An analogy between the poet and the dual nature of the earth is thus drawn. Like the earth the poet both preserves and creates, and like the earth the poet's imperative is demanding and implacable.

Mandelstam's paean, then, is directed toward the organic creative process inscribed in the cyclical silent work of the earth readying itself for "April's turning of the soil" ("*aprel'skii provorot*"), which in turn is associated with the aesthetic and metaphysical impulses to creation implied in the traditional imagery of spring, growth, and resurrection, as well as in philosophical, indeed political, images of freedom, expressed as: "Moist clods of *my* earth and freedom." In addition, Mandelstam's poetic imperative so forcefully depicted in *1921-1925* in his adherence to "the stars" and reiterated in *Journey to Armenia* through the "verb on horseback," is subtly inscribed here in the earth through the imagery of horses' withers and grooming expressed in stanza 1: "all in peak condition, / All in the little withers, all clean air and grooming" ("*vse v khole, khol*khi, prizor"), and phonically associated with "freedom" ("*volia*") in stanza 1 and the "thousand hills of words" ("tysiache*khol*miia mol*v*y") in stanza 2. This hymn to the "black earth and its black-eloquent silence" must thus be read as a reaffirmation of his poetic imperative, his aesthetic principle of unity and synthesis, preservation and promise, as well as an assertion of poetic freedom, a statement of defiance before time and the age.

Baines has shown that **"Black Earth"** was the master poem of a cycle (nos. 300-307) in which the poet's ambivalent vision associated the motif of the earth with self-affirmation or promise on the one hand, but emphasized the theme of death on the other.

Poem no. 305, **"I must live, though I've already died twice"** (**"Ia dolzhen zhit', khotia ia dvazhdy umer"**) begins with an affirmation of the poet's autobiographical imperative to continue living and writing poetry. It affirms life by reiterating the imagery of the "silent" steppe and its motifs of renewal and faith in the creative process.

On the other hand, in no. 306, **"Yes, I am lying in the earth, moving my lips"** (**"Da, ia lezhu v zemle . . ."**), a self-reflexive epitaph, the speaker's posthumous voice predicts immortality for his verse, if not for himself: "But what I am about to say *will be learned* by every schoolboy." This poem blends the theme of the poet's imperative with the Acmeist ideal of the poet's role as teacher of mankind from "On the Nature of the Word."

In contrast to the thematics of affirmation, the *First Voronezh Notebook* also contains anguished appeals for release (no. 301, **"Let me go, Voronezh . . ."** [**"Pusti menia, Voronezh . . ."**]), images of death as terrifyingly real and imminent (no. 304, **"I live in a proper kitchen garden"** [**"Ia zhivu na vazhnykh ogorodakh"**]), and even a mystical nightmare recollecting the horrors of Mandelstam's five-day Calvary, his exile journey to Cherdyn (no. 313, **"The Day was Five-headed"** [**"Den' stoial na piati golovakh,"** April-June 1935]).

"Let me go, Voronezh" is a kind of exorcism,—a single quatrain through which the poet attempts to divine his fate by conjuring up insidious puns on the name Voronezh: *voron* (raven), *nozh* (knife). The verbs are especially keen: *uronish', provoronish', vyronish', vernesh'* (you will drop, waste, let drop, return).

"The Day was Five-headed," also verges on mystical exorcism, for its theme of madness provides the speaker's only hope of escape. Madness allows the poet-speaker to envision himself as the semi-mythical hero, Chapaev, who, in the concluding stanza, "dies, and jumps on his horse." This self-reminiscence recalls, indeed enacts, Mandelstam's Armenian imperative. Madness also reemerges as a positive theme in no. 380, **"Maybe this is the beginning of madness"** (**"Mozhet byt' eto tochka bezumiia"**) from the last *Voronezh Notebook*.

By July 1935 another significant motif appears in conjunction with the theme of death: the poet's tragic vision of shared identity with the nameless masses, common soldiers suffering an aerial death. However, this is fully developed only two years later in Mandelstam's last major poetic cycle, **"Verses on the Unknown Soldier,"** wherein he attempts an "answer" to the unanswerable question concluding no. 320, **"Not like a floury white butterfly"** (**"Ne muchnistoi babochkoiu beloi"**). Here, the poet-speaker juxtaposes his personal desire for a meaningful, poetic death with the loss of individual identity in the mass procession into oblivion:

. . . I want this thinking body
To be turned into a street, a nation—
This vertebral, charred body,
Conscious of its own length.

Comrades—the latest recruits—marched
To work in the hardened sky,
The infantry passed silently
Exclamations of rifles on their shoulders.

And thousands of guns aimed at the air—
Were they hazel eyes or blue—
They marched in confusion—people, people, people—
Who will continue on for them?

(no. 320, July 1935)

This apocalyptic vision was followed by silence until December 1936, when the *Second Voronezh Notebook* began to take shape. At least in part stimulated by contradictory feelings of apprehension and defiance as well as guilt and remorse with respect to Stalin, two major themes dominate this *Notebook*: the joy of creation and the haunting image of Stalin.

Poem no. 342, **"Birth of a Smile"** (**"Rozhdenie ulybki"**), the second poem of the *Second Notebook,* continues the imagery and thematics of creation presented in **"The Octets,"** namely, the poet's joy in the presence of the phenomenon of creation; the metaphorical association of poetic creation and the metaphysical realm; and the motifs of intuition, spontaneity, and teleology so essential to the poet's capacity to recognize, and hence realize, the miracle of creation. Most important, perhaps, in **"Birth of a Smile,"** as in **"The Octets,"** the poetic process itself demonstrates teleological design. The poet's vision of the origins of poetic creation depicted through the organic, scientific, poetic, and teleological unfolding of the miracle of creation, along with his faith in cosmic unity and continuity bearing the promise of the future, are realized once again in the image of "the child," here expressed in the metonymical "smile" and in the emergence of the lost continent of Atlantis as it "strikes the eyes.". . . .

When a child begins to smile,
Parted lips reveal sorrow and sweetness,
The corners of his smile, unlaughing,
Recede into the ocean's anarchy.

Feeling so inexplicably fine,
The corners of his mouth play in the glory—
And a rainbow seam is already being stitched
Into the eternal cognition of the real.

The continent on its paws rears up from the deep—
The helix of the mouth looms up, approaches—
One moment of Atlantis strikes your eyes:
Realization of the real in the miracles of the
    universe.

Space has lost its color and taste
The continent has risen, spine and arc,
The helix snail crawls out, the smile bursts forth,
As their two ends are tied by a rainbow
And the moment of Atlantis strikes both eyes.

(no. 342, 9 December 1936-11 January 1937)

Furthermore, like Mandelstam's hymn to "the black earth," his paean to "the child's smile," is gradually metamorphosed into praise of the miracle of creation. His metaphysical vision of the birth of Atlantis is realized through an intricate combination of linguistic and semantic elements—simple diction of sentimental emotion interacts with physical and metaphysical terminology.

For example, the theme of unity and continuity between the physical and metaphysical worlds is expressed, as in most of Mandelstam's later verse, through phonosemantic metamorphoses of organic and poetic images of creation.

Establishing equivalence through phonic relationships as well as through the imagery of the circular form or endless spiral—between the spiral-shaped snail shell or helix/cochlea (*ulit*ka) and the smile (*ulyb*ka), whose corners meet and merge in the metaphysical, in "Ocean's anarchy/chaos"—suggests the possibility of analogy, and hence unity, of even the most antithetical phenomena, reinforcing Mandelstam's view of the synthetic nature and even purpose of the creative process.

The poet-speaker's witnessing of the process of creation in this poem thus testifies to Mandelstam's teleological vision, to the phenomenon of "the realization of the real" ("iavlen'ia iavnogo"), the coming into being of the miracle of life (*v chislo chudes vselen'ia*). Mandelstam's mythopoetic covenant—the idea of eternal cognition or recognition of the real—recalls *Tristia*: "And only the moment of recognition is sweet." It reemerges as affirmation of faith in the promise of "synthesis" defined in his earliest verse, later in "Word and Culture," where the poet-synthesizer is identified with Verlaine, and subsequently in "Conversation about Dante", in his more theoretical pronouncement that the process of "transmutation and hybridization" is the basis of the poetic process.

Almost simultaneously with **"Birth of a Smile,"** Mandelstam composed no. 330, **"Inside a mountain Idles an Idol"** (**"Vnutri gory bezdeistvuet kumir,"** 10-26 December 1936) which both in its malicious tone and in its extremely negative physiological characterization of Stalin recalls the **"Epigram."** Indeed, no. 330 records a nightmare in which the poet-speaker envisions Stalin—the repulsive "idol"—as once also having had a childhood, as once also subject to a covenant, but now reduced to "laboring to remember his own human countenance." Adhering structurally to one of the unique features of Mandelstam's later poetry—the admission of an odd number of lines—this poem resembles **"Birth of a Smile."** The final stanzas each contain an "extra" line, thereby creating extraordinarily powerful conclusions. Compare "And the flash of Atlantis strikes both eyes" with "And he labors to remember his own human countenance."

One more reference to Stalin appears in early 1937. Among other passages desperately crying out for help, Mandelstam wrote the following in a letter to Korney Chukovsky: "There is now only one person in the whole world to whom I can and must turn. . . ."

When Mandelstam finally sat down to compose his **"Ode to Stalin"** on 12 January 1937, both sets of images intersected, bonding with the extraordinary "impulse" behind the conjunction of human, spiritual, and ideological polarities marking the poet's larger theme—the ambiguous relationship between the powerful and the weak, oppressor and victim, tyrant and subject, father and son, even creator and creation—that informs the **"Ode"** and the twenty or so poems of this period motivated by its composition, the **"Ode"** cycle.

In trying to place the **"Ode to Stalin"** in the "ideological and mythological framework of Mandelstam's writings,"

Freidin notes that it was composed as the poet's term of exile was coming to an end, when he was increasingly apprehensive about his future, and thus decided to try to buy his freedom "by paying Stalin in poetic kind." Nevertheless, he perceives the **"Ode"** as much more than "doggerel," even as "a magnificent paean." He interprets it as a masterpiece that allowed the poet to fulfill the artist's role of *imitatio Christi* identified in his early unfinished essay, "Pushkin and Scriabin": "the scenario [Mandelstam] outlined for himself in the **"Ode"** in such gruesome detail (stanza 5) did include, as in the case of Christ, humiliation, suffering and death. And yet, whatever other reasons for the composition of the poem, he clearly sought in it a 'catharsis, redemption,' as he put it [in 'Pushkin and Scriabin'] not through but 'in art': justification of his fate in Christ's likeness and image. . . . As a magic spell it proved to be quite effective."

Equally significant, perhaps, Mandelstam's ultimate reaffirmation of his synthetic principle, his mythopoetic yearning for freedom through the union of opposing principles, may also have influenced his incredible "transmutation and hybridization" of the themes of creation and Stalin, first in the **"Ode,"** and subsequently in the verse it generated. This aesthetic principle may also at least partly explain his introduction of Christian symbolism into the **"Ode"** as the supreme expression of faith in the ideals of unity and continuity. Begun both as an attempt to expiate his own guilt by inscribing himself in the role of the one who takes mankind's guilt unto himself, and ultimately as an attempt to redeem the world through poetic creation, by inscribing himself in the role of savior (the one to be resurrected in order to resurrect mankind), the poet's endeavor to invoke Stalin as father and creator (not tormentor) bound to the poet as Son and Messiah—bearer of truth to posterity (not victim), once again shaped his work into a mystical-poetic exorcism. Indeed, the association of his own attributes with those of his tormentor—the mystical bonding of their given names through the word, "axis" (*os'*)—suggests their shared identity and destiny, offering Mandelstam mystical protection against both moral degradation and oblivion. The **"Ode,"** then, and the cycle of poems generated by it, seem to have refocused his poetic impulses by exorcising Stalin's power over him.

The twenty-four poems comprising the "Ode" cycle, the remainder of the *Second Voronezh Notebook,* cover a broad thematic and tonal spectrum, some emphasizing Mandelstam's allegiance to the age, others his sense of defiance, others being politically neutral. For instance, in the "twin poems" dated 12-18 January, nos. 346-347, **"Precious Yeast of the World"** (**"Drozhzhi mira dorogie"**), and no. 348, **"A little demon in wet fur crept in"** (**"Vlez besenok v mokroi sherstke"**), Mandelstam hints that something "not his own," something "as if from the side," caused all his troubles—something "mocking and knocking [him] off his true axis"—forcing him to substitute the extraneous for his true task. Nadezhda Mandelstam, presenting the canonical view that Mandelstam did not willingly write the **"Ode,"** refers to this cycle as "free poems" and suggests that the **"Ode"** was at cross purposes with his verse.

The major themes of this cycle range from apologetics for the **"Ode"** (no. 348, **"A little demon . . ."**) to the theme of tragedy and martyrdom (no. 364, **"Like Rembrandt, martyr of chiaroscuro"** [**"Kak svetoteni muchenik Rembrandt"**]); from exaltation of humankind (no. 352: **"Do not compare: the living are incomparable"** [**"Ne sravnivai: zhivushchii nesravnim"**]) and love of life (the last stanza of no. 370, **"I'm down in a lion's ditch"** [**"Ia v l'vinyi rov . . ."**]) to reaffirmation of the "people's need" for poetry (no. 355) and reaffirmation of his own poetic imperative (no. 365, **"I sing when my throat is moist"**). This cycle also treats the theme of "reality" as an absolute which along with "breathing" must be acknowledged as worthy of love and poetry, (no. 359, **"I love frosty breath . . . and reality is reality!"** [**"Liubliu moroznoe dykhan'e,"** 24 January 1937]), as well as the other side of "reality," the terrible pain of homelessness and isolation (no. 360, **"Where can I go, now it's January?"** [**"Kuda mne det'sia v etom Ianvare?"**]) with its poignantly evocative, wishful conclusion: "If I could have a real conversation—a reader, an adviser, a doctor! / Someone to talk to on the jagged stairs!" In addition, as Freidin points out, this cycle includes poems maintaining an obsequious attitude toward Stalin, for example, metonyms "pulled out of a propaganda poster" in no. 371 **"Sleep defends my Don drowsiness"** (**"Oboroniaet son moiu donskuiu son'"**), or the image of the poet rushing into the Kremlin to avow his guilt—"my head heavy with guilt"—before the leader in no. 361. Hence, whether they develop, negate, or reinforce its elements, the poems of this cycle are all loosely interconnected through the **"Ode."**

The **"Ode to Stalin"** and the cycle of poems generated by it, seem to have refocused Mandelstam's poetic impulses by exorcising Stalin's power over him.

—*Jane Gary Harris*

Two extraordinary examples, written on the same day, 8 February 1937 and linked through the imagery of "axis," singing, and poetic imperative, are no. 367, **"Armed with the vision of narrow wasps"** (**"Vooruzhennyi zren'em uzkikh os"**), and no. 365, **"I sing when my throat is damp . . ."** (**"Poiu kogda gortan' syra . . ."**).

While in the **"Ode,"** the poet-speaker presents himself as seeking an "axis of likeness" (*skhodstva os'*) with Stalin (stanza 5), and Stalin is presented as having "shifted the world's axis" (stanza 1), in no. 367, the poet-speaker acknowledges the failure of his creative powers—"I do not sing"—as a result of his inability to "hear the earth's axis." Nevertheless, he establishes his faith in the power of poetry through verbal magic or incantation. He yearns for that day in the future when he shall again "hear the earth's axis" (*os' zemnuiu*). By expressing his yearning in the form of a wish-fantasy, the poet recalls not only the magical flight of fancy in no. 202, the wish to "whistle

through life eating nutpie," or the exorcisms of the "Black earth" cycle, but the incantatory dream-fantasy of "Fourth Prose," his would-be journey to Armenia, which when finally realized led to the return of his poetic voice. In no. 367, the poet-speaker's wish to avert "sleep and death," so that "some day" he might again "hear the earth's axis," is but another form of incantation invoking the return of his poetic voice—to "hear" his poetic imperative so as to challenge time through "creative cognition." Indeed, as we have already noted in discussing the Armenian cycle and the *First Voronezh Notebook,* Mandelstam had to "hear" the imperative of "the earth." Vision alone, no matter how penetrating, was inadequate. His yearning to renew his relationship to the earth—to "hear the earth's axis"—is thus tantamount to involing the return of his poetic imperative. . . .

> Armed with the sight of narrow wasps
> Sucking at the earth's axis, the earth's axis,
> I reexperience everything I've had to meet,
> I remember it by heart, and in vain.
>
> I do not draw, nor do I sing,
> Nor move my dark-voiced bow.
> I only make a little hole in life and enjoy
> Envying the powerful cunning wasps.
>
> Oh, if only some day the sting of the air and
> The summer warmth could make me—
> Passing by sleep and death—
> Hear the earth's axis, the earth's axis. . . .
>
> (no. 367, 8 February 1937)

Mandelstam's poetic imperative is also the subject of no. 365, which uses imagery directly recalling the theme of its reaffirmation in *Journey to Armenia.* Mandelstam projects himself into the likeness of the Caucasian horsemen whose proud task it is to honorably and joyously escort betrothed couples through the dangers of the mountains, singing them "sinless" to their wedding. He thus proclaims his song "selfless" and "pure," his "conscience"—free and clear.

Furthermore, in this poem Mandelstam may be asking after the "health" of the entire Black Sea region—Colchis, the legendary land of the Golden Fleece, of his beloved Crimea, Georgia, and Armenia. Indeed, this poem would seem to expand upon his Armenian covenant. Even the phrase "and my head's deaf" (*golova glukha*) is best interpreted by recalling the paragraphs on the origins of language, the development of concepts and of legend in *Journey to Armenia.* The declaration "it is no longer me singing" implies that his imperative has taken over, clarifying the image "my hearing's sheathed in the mountain" and "my head's deaf," for his "song" now comes from within. "Creative cognition" reigns, and the poet's song emerges natural and pure. The couplet introduced between the two lengthier stanzas provides the only justification Mandelstam sought for his verse: hence, no. 365 may serve as his song of redemption:

> I sing when my throat is damp and my soul dry,
> My vision properly moist, and my conscience clear.

Is wine healthy? Are furs?
Or the blood stirring within all that is Colchis?
But my chest grows shy, silent without language:
It's no longer me singing—it's my breath—
My hearing's sheathed in the mountain and my
    head's deaf.

A selfless song is its own praise.
A comfort for friends, pitch for enemies. . . .

A single-eyed song growing out of moss,
A single-voiced gift of hunting life,
Which they sing on horseback and in the heights,
Breathing freely and openly,
Honorably and sternly caring only to transport
The young couple sinless to their wedding.
                    (no. 365, 8 February 1937)

In February-March 1937 Mandelstam began his last, and possibly most complex poetic cycle, no. 362, **"Verses on the Unknown Soldier"** ("Stikhi o neizvestnom soldate"). This dense and lengthy masterpiece, in effect the poet's requiem for mankind, marked the end of the **"Ode"** cycle and the beginning of the *Third Voronezh Notebook*. As the **"Unknown Solder"** evolved over a period of three months, shorter lyrics emerged simultaneously, forming the remainder of that collection. Poems no. 380, **"Maybe this is a sign of madness"** (15 March 1937), and no. 394, **"Toward the Empty Earth . . ."** (4 May 1937), treating the theme of woman's compassion and love as source of immortality, are of particular note.

"Verses on the Unknown Soldier," however, dominates the *Third Notebook*. Its thematics and the lack of a definitive text allow for more than one interpretation. Indeed, it was not until the end of May that at least one definitive text was recorded, but, according to Nadezhda Yakovlevna, Mandelstam took drafts with him to Samatikha, the writers' rest home outside of Moscow, where he was arrested never to return. Hence, an authorized text does not exist.

Although the basic motifs and narrative structure of Mandelstam's cycle are discernible, its imagery is often dependent on subtextual references. Unfortunately, we can attempt only a brief summary here.

The **"Unknown Soldier"** consists of eight parts of unequal lengths, united by a common metrical pattern—anapestic trimeter—and, according to Levin, through analogy with the musical form of the "oratorio." Part 1, fulfilling the function of the exposition, enunciates the poet's major themes: the cosmos, eternal moral testimony, and death. They are expressed through the voice of the poet-speaker, who invokes the "air" as a "witness" (1.1). However, even "judge and witness" are subject to the "watchful stars," whose ultimate judgment (1.2) is linked to their metaphysical power which recalls the poet's adherence to the "cruel imperatives of the stars" in *1921-1925* (no. 127, **"To some winter is arrack"**). The theme of man's inevitable conflict with the divine forces of the universe and the lyrical reiteration of the ultimate questions of life and

death raised here invoke traditions of Russian philosophical or mediative poetry going back at least to Lomonosov's "Meditations" and to Mandelstam's own meditative verse of *1921-1925*.

Not only are the themes of death, war and destruction, and suffering, presented (1.4), but their calamitous continuation, like rain, is forecast (1.3). Nevertheless, while their victim, "the unknown soldier," has already been "put in his grave," the poet-speaker assumes his posthumous voice (1.5-6). The implication that the poet-persona speaks in the voice of the "unknown soldier" (1.5) is made explicit in his assertion that he will give a "strict report for Lermontov" about "how the grave teaches the stoop-shouldered" (1.6), that is, he will challenge Lermontov's sanguine assumptions about cosmic harmony. On the other hand, the statement that the "aerial pit leads him on" establishes the poet's sense of his "right" to speak for mankind, since death, the source of his renewed imperative, inspires him to continue to write poetry in the form of this requiem. The Lermontov subtext is highly significant here, for as Kiril Taranovsky has pointed out [in *Essays on Mandel'shtam*], Mandelstam's premonition of impending cataclysm opposes Lermontov's sense of cosmic harmony as presented in *Demon*.

Through the airy ocean
Without rudder or sail,
Harmonious chorus of luminaries
Calmly float in the mist.

Mandelstam's own self-reminiscences, namely, to *Tristia* and the swallow image recalling the Persephone myth, are also extremely significant. In appeals to the "sickly swallow / Who has forgotten how to fly," Mandelstam's speaker recalls the vicarious anguish of the poet-persona in no. 113, **"I have forgotten the word . . . ,"** as he follows the journey of the "blind swallow" ("the word") down into the underworld. Allusions to *Tristia* universalize his earlier vision of dying Russian culture, associating the poet in this instance not only with the shared destiny of his age, but with the common destiny of mankind. In asking the swallow to be his Muse, to teach him to master "this aerial grave," he invokes not only Russia but the entire universe as the subject of his requiem. Furthermore, the persona's experience of poetic pain as well as poetic rapture in **"I have forgotten the word . . ."** is reintroduced here through the themes of memory and death, always linked in Mandelstam's work with poetry or song. Death is again accompanied by the "night chorus" of **"I have forgotten the word,"** the antithesis of Lermontov's "Harmonious chorus of luminaries."

Thus, Mandelstam's vision of the imminence of death determines the focus of **"Verses on the Unknown Soldier."** The Voice of the poet as "witness," subject only to the "watchful stars," is juxtaposed to, as well as, merged with, the posthumous voice of human destiny—that of the common man, the "unknown soldier," speaking from his "aerial grave" (1.4-5). Death grants the poet the right to speak both "with his age" and "for everyone," eliminating the fear and ambivalence of the earlier collections.

Part 1.

Let *this* air be witness—
His long-range heart—
Omnivorous and active in the dug-outs too—
An ocean, matter minus a window.

How watchful *these* stars:
Why must they watch everything?
In Judgment of judge and witness,
In the ocean, matter minus a window.

The rain, the unfriendly sower,
His nameless manna,
Remembers how a forest of little crosses mark
The ocean or the battle salient.

Cold, sickly people will kill,
Will suffer cold and hunger,
And an *unknown soldier*
Has been put in his famous grave.

Teach me, sickly swallow
Who has forgotten how to fly,
How I am to master this aerial grave
Without rudder or wing?

And for Lermontov, Mikhail,
I shall give you a strict report
How the grave teaches the stooping
And the aerial pit leads him on.
                    (3 March 1937, Voronezh; my italics)

The brief seven lines of part 2 speak of the evil nature of the contemporary world and hence its threat to Mankind. Parts 2, 5, and 6 are as variations on the main themes, while part 7, in reiterating the themes of part 1, acts as a kind of reprise:

Part 2.

Like grapes rustling on the vine
These worlds threaten us,
They hang like stolen towns,
Like golden slips of the tongue, bits of false evidence—
Berries of poisonous cold—
The tents of tensile constellations—
The golden worlds of constellations.

The mystical, mythical, and numerological message of part 3 seems to be an effort to assure eternal memory and hope in the future, after the Apocalypse, through a mystical Coming. The message of prophecy, "I am the new—the world will be illumined by me," offers the Gospel of John to the "reader in posterity":

Part 3.

Through the decimalized ether,
The light of velocities ground into a ray
Begins a number made transparent
By the lucid pain and mol of zeroes.

But beyond the field of fields a new field
Is flying like a triangular crane—
The message flies on a path of light-dust—
And yesterday's battle creates light.

The message flies on path of light-dust—
I'm not Leipzig, not Waterloo,
I'm not the Battle of Nations. *I am the new*—
The world will be illumined by me.

In the depths of his black-marble shell
The spark of Austerlitz has gone out—
The Mediterranean swallow screws up its eyes,
the pestilential sands of Egypt congeal.

Part 4, stanza 1, seems to inscribe the voice of the poet—"the ray is standing on my retina"—into the voice of prophecy expressed in part 3—the bearer of "light" to the new world after the Apocalypse. Part 4, stanza 2, a clear statement of Mandelstam's pacifism in the face of senseless human slaughter, was arranged as the second stanza of the entire poem and sent as a peace offering to *Znamya* on 11 March 1937, in a last abortive effort to get something published.

Part 4, stanza 3, both echoes and enacts the line, "We will die like footsoldiers," Mandelstam's premonition voiced in no. 260, **"Midnight in Moscow,"** and attempts to answer the ultimate question posed in no. 320, **"Not like a floury white butterfly"**: *"Who* will continue on for [the millions marching into death and oblivion]?" The answer offered here is the poet, in the name of the "unknown soldier," the posthumous spokesman for mankind. Hence, parts 3 and 4 continue and develop the themes of part 1:

Part 4.

An Arabian mash, a jumble,
The light of velocities ground into a ray—
And with its scythe-bearing feet
The ray is standing on my retina.

Millions of cannon fodder
Have tramped the path in the emptiness,
Good night, all the best to them,
On behalf of the earthen fortifications.

Incorruptible trench sky,
Sky of great wholesale deaths,
After you—away from you—O totality of sky
I rush with my lips in the darkness.

Past craters, embankments, and screes,
Through which he hazily dawdled,
The dour, pockmarked and servile genius
Of the shattered graves.

Part 5 returns once again to **"Midnight in Moscow,"** repeating the line "We will die like footsoldiers" from the perspective of the "witness," and to **"I have forgotten the word . . . ,"** invoking the "night chorus" to sing for the world's dead and crippled. The poet enters an ironic plea to cease the destruction of the human race that has created an Age of Cripples:

Part 5.

The infantry dies well,
The night chorus sings well
Over Schweik's flattened smile,
And over Don Quixote's bird-like spear
And over the bird's metatarsus.
And the cripple makes friends with man;
Both of them will be found work.
And the family of wooden crutches
Knocks on the outskirts of the age—
Hey, the earth's globe is a comradely union.

Part 6 appears to be a statement of the poet's wonderment at the human condition, a hymn to "creative cognition." The metonymy of the human skull refers not only to Shakespeare—the acme of human creative power—but to Mandelstam's own dream-vision in *Journey to Armenia*: "How I longed to return to the place where human skulls are equally beautiful at work or in the grave." The human skull, as the poet's microcosm of the universe, may thus offer a ray of hope for the future after the apocalypse:

Part 6.

Is it because the skull must develop
Into an entire forehead from temple to temple
That troops cannot help pouring
Into its precious eye-sockets?
The skull develops out of life
Into an entire forehead from temple to temple,
It teases itself with the cleanness of its seams,
It clarifies itself as an understanding cupola,
It froths with thought, it dreams of itself—
Chalice of chalices, fatherland of fatherlands—
Bonnet sewn with a seam of stars—
Cap of happiness—father of Shakespeare.

Part 7, in reiterating the themes of part 1, strengthens the idea of the poet as under a spell, and optimistically questions the stars about divining man's future. Especially interesting is part 7, stanza 2—the poet's rejoicing in the glorious struggle for "subsistence air" associated with "excess." This recalls his defiant declaration in "Fourth Prose" that the basis of genuine—"nonofficial"—art is "stolen air." In that work not only did he find the "doughnut's value resides in the hole," but he praised Brussel's lace for its "major components . . . air, perforations, and truancy." Indeed, part 7 presents what the poet knows, sees, and intuits, as well as what he hopes to divine. As in his earlier collections, he prophesies redemption through art by suggesting the possibility of divining the future and defying "official" formulas:

Part 7.

The clarity of the ash and perspicacity of the sycamore
Rush into their house with a touch of redness,

As if casting a spell semi-consciously
On both skies with their dim fires.

Only what is excess is allied with us,
Before us is not a fall, but a sounding,
And the fight for our *subsistence air*
Is a glory without peer.

And glutting my mind
With semi-conscious existence,
Do I drink this broth without choice,
Do I consume my head under fire!

Has the tare been drawn up
For enchantment in empty space,
So that white stars can race back into their house
With a touch of redness!—

Can you hear, O stepmother of the starry camp,—
O night, what will be now and in the future?

And finally, in part 8, which Levin terms the coda, the poet emerges in the lineup of the dead—among those awaiting resurrection and the overcoming of anonymity. As Ronen points out, the major impulse behind this poem is Mandelstam's "profound effort to overcome the anonymity of 'wholesale death.'" He terms this conclusion a perfect example of what Segal called "ambivalent antithesis," for although Mandelstam prophesies the apocalypse, he also expresses faith in mankind's ultimate moral redemption—a collective resurrection guaranteed by the poetic word and reiterated here in the evocation of immortality: "the aortas [of the dead] are filled with blood," the living poet-speaker "whispers through [his] blood-drained lips." Furthermore, as Levin indicates, the poet-speaker, concretized and individualized, appears in the subjective authorial role as well as in the role of object—as a persona, ordinary and thus central, assuming the role of the one who has found the "unknown soldier's" gift of speech. The poet—identified by Mandelstam's birthdate—is at the very center of the human-cosmic tragedy: "the centuries surround me with fire. . . ." Hence, the universality of this requiem:

Part 8.

Aortas fill with blood
And a quiet whisper resounds through the ranks:
"I was born in ninety-four,
I was born in ninety-four . . ."
And amidst the mob and the mass,
Squeezing my outworn birthdate in my fist,
I whisper through my blood-drained lips:
"I was born the night of the 2nd-3rd
Of January in the ninety-first
Unreliable year, and the centuries
Surround me with fire."
                    (part 8, February-March 1937, Voronezh)

Mandelstam's magnificent farewell poem, no. 394, **"Toward the empty earth"** (**"K pustoi zemle nevol'no pripadaia"**), is no longer about the "unknown soldiers" who marched into death and oblivion, but about those whose "calling" is "To escort the dead and be first / To greet the resurrected," a subtextual reference to the "blessed women" of no. 118, **"We shall gather again in Petersburg / To bury the sun. . . ."** Begun as an impassioned tribute to Natasha Shtempel, who along with Nadezhda Mandelstam miraculously managed to preserve the poet's Voronezh verse, it emerges as a fervent hymn to love, beauty, and immortality. Particularly noteworthy is the way permanence resounds in the echo of footsteps, in the repetition of nouns and verbs of movement and accompaniment, and in the remarkable recreation of the continuity and discontinuity of time past, present, and future. Presence and absence, prescience and loss, promise and sacrifice are ascribed to the reality of the earth, to spring, and to life, as well as to premonitions of promise and resurrection. The second half of this poem—nearly impossible to render in English—reads approximately:

> There are women kin to the damp earth,
> In whose every step reverberates sobbing;
> To escort the dead and be first
> To greet the resurrected is their calling.
> To demand caresses from them is criminal.
> To part with them is beyond endurance.
> An angel—today; a worm in the grave—tomorrow.
> A mere outline—the day after that.
> What had been her step—is unrecognizable.
> Flowers are immortal. Heaven is whole.
> And what will be—is but a promise.
>
> (no. 394, 4 May 1937)

Poetic justice alone can redeem Mandelstam's "sacrifice" to the power, joy, and truth of poetry. The poet's life and work may be perceived as a fulfilment of his poetic prescience: "People need poetry . . . to keep them awake forever." His last will and testament, his final collection containing both his requiem and hymn to humankind, offers as the poet's greatest gift the "promise" of poetic testimony to his "reader in posterity."

FURTHER READING

Biography

Brown, Clarence. *Mandelstam.* Cambridge: Cambridge University Press, 1973, 320 p.
Definitive biography in English.

Criticism

Baines, Jennifer. *Mandelstam: The Later Poetry.* Cambridge: Cambridge University Press, 1976, 253 p.
Attacks the view that Mandelstam's later poems are weaker than his early works.

Birkerts, Sven. "Osip Mandelstam." In *An Artificial Wilderness: Essays on 20th-Century Literature*, pp. 101-20. New York: William Morrow and Company, 1987.
Provides an overview of Mandelstam's literary career.

Brodsky, Joseph. "Beyond Consolation." *The New York Review of Books* XXI, No. 1 (7 February 1974): 13-16.
Analysis of recent English language translations of Mandelstam's poetry.

Brown, Clarence. "Into the Heart of Darkness: Mandelstam's *Ode to Stalin*." *Slavic Review* XXVI, No. 4 (December 1967): 584-604.
Presents an extended discussion of Mandelstam's most controversial poem.

Broyde, Steven. *Osip Mandel'stam and His Age: A Commentary on the Themes of War and Revolution in the Poetry, 1913-1923.* Cambridge: Harvard University Press, 1975, 257 p.
Examines political themes in Mandelstam's verse, in particular focusing on the effect of the Russian Revolution on his work.

Cavanaugh, Claire. *Osip Mandelstam and the Modernist Creation of Tradition.* Princeton: Princeton University Press, 1995, 379 p.
Places Mandelstam's work within the modernist tradition and compares him with several modernist poets.

Coetzee, J. M. "Osip Mandelstam and the Stalin Ode." *Representations* XXXV (Summer 1991): 72-83.
Discusses the sincerity of the Mandelstam's *Ode to Stalin*.

Cohen, Arthur A. *Osip Emilievich Mandelstam.* Ann Arbor: Ardis, 1974, 74 p.
An overview of Mandelstam's literary career.

France, Peter. "Osip Mandelstam." In *Poets of Modern Russia*, pp. 99-131. Cambridge: Cambridge University Press, 1982.
Provides a thematic and stylistic analysis of several of Mandelstam's poems.

Harris, Jane Gary. *Mandelstam.* Boston: Twayne Publishers, 1988, 167 p.
Full-length critical study of Mandelstam's work.

Heaney, Seamus. "Faith, Hope and Poetry." In *Preoccupations: Selected Prose, 1968-1978*, pp. 217-20. New York: Farrar, Straus & Giroux, 1980.
Defends Mandelstam against the charge of aestheticism.

Mihailovich, Vasa D. "Osip Mandelshtam and His Critics." *Papers on Language and Literature* VI, No. 3 (Summer 1970): 323-35.
Surveys critical reaction to Mandelstam, both in Western countries and the Soviet Union.

Rayfield, Donald. "Mandel'shtam's Creative Process—In the Light of His Widow's Memoirs." In *Russian and Slavic Literature*, edited by Richard Freeborn, R. R. Milner-Gulland,

and Charles A. Ward, pp. 387-95. Cambridge, Mass: Slavica Publishers, 1976.

    Discusses Mandelstam's creative process.

Terras, Victor. "Classical Motives in the Poetry of Osip Mandel'stam." *The Slavic and East European Journal* X, No. 3 (1966): 251-54.

    Analyzes classical themes in Mandelstam's poetry.

Additional coverage of Mandelstam's life and career is contained in the following sources published by Gale Research: *Contemporary Authors*, **Vol. 104; and** *Twentieth-Century Literary Criticism*, **Vols. 2, 6.**

Percy Bysshe Shelley
1792-1822

(Also wrote under the pseudonyms Victor and The Hermit of Marlow) English poet, essayist, dramatist, and novelist.

INTRODUCTION

Shelley was a major poet of the English Romantic period. His foremost works, including *The Revolt of Islam, Prometheus Unbound, Adonais,* and *The Triumph of Life,* are recognized as leading expressions of radical thought written during the Romantic age, while his odes and shorter lyrics are considered among the greatest in the English language.

Biographical Information

Born in Horsham, Sussex, Shelley was educated at University College, Oxford. Before the age of twenty he had published two Gothic novels, *Zastrozzi* and *St. Irvyne,* and two collections of verse, *Original Poetry by Victor and Cazire*—written with his sister—and *Posthumous Fragments of Margaret Nicholson,* coauthored with his Oxford friend Thomas Jefferson Hogg. In 1811 Shelley and Hogg were expelled from Oxford for publishing a pamphlet entitled *The Necessity of Atheism,* an event that estranged him from his family and left him without financial means. Later that year he eloped with Harriet Westbrook, a schoolmate of his sister. During the next three years Shelley and Harriet were actively involved in political and social reform in Ireland and Wales, with Shelley writing radical pamphlets in which he set forth his views on liberty, equality, and justice. In 1814 Shelley remarried Harriet in England to ensure the legality of their union and the legitimacy of their children. Weeks later, however, he fell in love with Mary Godwin, the daughter of the radical English philosopher William Godwin and his first wife, the feminist author Mary Wollstonecraft. Shelley and Mary eloped to Europe, accompanied by Mary's stepsister, Jane (Claire) Clairmont. On their return, Shelley entered into a financial agreement with his family that ensured him a regular income. When Harriet declined to join his household as a "sister," he provided for her and their two children, but continued to live with Mary. In 1816 Shelley, Mary, and Claire traveled to Lake Geneva to meet with the poet Lord Byron. Shelley returned to England in the fall, and shortly thereafter Harriet drowned herself in Hyde Park. Shelley then legalized his relationship with Mary and sought custody of his children, but the Westbrook family successfully blocked him in a lengthy lawsuit. Citing his poem *Queen Mab,* in which he denounced established society and religion in favor of free love and atheism, the Westbrooks convinced the court that Shelley was morally unfit for guardianship. In 1818, motivated by ill

health, financial worries, and the fear of losing custody of his and Mary's two children, Shelley relocated his family to Italy. Renewing his friendship with Byron, who was also living in Italy, Shelley became part of a circle of expatriots known as the "Satanic School" because of their defiance of English social and religious conventions and promotion of radical ideas in their works. Shelley and Mary remained in Italy until Shelley's death in a boating accident off the coast of Lerici in 1822.

Major Works

Shelley's first mature work, *Queen Mab,* was printed in 1813, but not distributed due to its inflammatory subject matter. It was not until 1816, with the appearance of *Alastor; or, The Spirit of Solitude, and Other Poems*—a visionary and semi-autobiographical work—that he earned recognition as a serious poet. Shelley's next lengthy work, *Laon and Cythna; or, The Revolution of the Golden City,* is an account of a bloodless revolution led by a brother and sister. It was immediately suppressed by the printer because of its controversial content, and Shelley subsequently revised the work as *The Revolt of Islam,* minimizing its elements of incest and political revolution. In 1819 Shelley wrote two of his most ambitious works, the verse dramas *Prometheus Unbound* and *The Cenci*. In *Prometheus Unbound*—which is usually regarded as his masterpiece—Shelley transformed the Aeschylean myth of Prometheus into an allegory on the origins of evil and the possibility of regenerating nature and humanity through love. *The Cenci* differs markedly from *Prometheus Unbound* in tone and setting. Shelley based this tragedy on the history of a sixteenth-century Italian Count who raped his daughter and was in turn murdered by her. Although Shelley hoped for a popular success on the English stage, his controversial treatment of the subject of incest outraged critics, preventing the play from being produced. One of Shelley's best-known works, *Adonais: An Elegy on the Death of John Keats,* was written in 1821 as a tribute to Shelley's contemporary, Keats. In the same year, Shelley wrote *Epipsychidion,* in which he chronicled his search for ideal beauty through his relationships with women. Shelley's last work, *The Triumph of Life,* was left unfinished at his death. Despite its fragmentary state, many critics consider *The Triumph of Life* a potential masterpiece and evidence of a pessimistic shift in Shelley's thought. In addition to his long poems and verse dramas, Shelley wrote numerous short lyrics that have proved to be among his most popular works, among them "Hymn to Intellectual Beauty," "Ode to the West Wind," and "Ode to the Skylark."

Critical Reception

The history of Shelley's critical reputation has been characterized by radical shifts. During his lifetime his work was frequently censured because of his atheism and unorthodox philosophy, as well as widespread rumors about his personal life. Those few critics who voiced their admiration of his talents were ironically responsible for further inhibiting his success by causing him to be associated in the public mind with the despised "Cockney School" of poets belittled by John Gibson Lockhart and others in *Blackwood's Magazine.* Nevertheless, Shelley was known and admired by many of his contemporaries, including Byron, Keats, William Wordsworth, Samuel Taylor Coleridge, and Robert Southey. Critics in the late nineteenth century for the most part ignored Shelley's radical politics, celebrating instead the spiritual and aesthetic qualities of his poetry. In the Victorian age he was highly regarded as the poet of ideal love, and the Victorian notion of the poet as a sensitive, misunderstood genius was modeled largely after Shelley. His works, however, again fell into disfavor around the turn of the century. Many critics objected to his seemingly vague imagery, nebulous philosophy, careless technique, and, most of all, his apparent intellectual and emotional immaturity. In the late 1930s Shelley's reputation began to revive as scholars came to recognize the complexity of his philosophy. Modern commentators have generally focused on his imagery, use of language, and technical achievements, in addition to his exploration of the political and social phenomena of his time.

PRINCIPAL WORKS

Poetry

Original Poetry by Victor and Cazire [as Victor, with Elizabeth Shelley] 1810
Posthumous Fragments of Margaret Nicholson [with Thomas Jefferson Hogg] 1810
Queen Mab 1813
Alastor; or, The Spirit of Solitude, and Other Poems 1816
"Hymn to Intellectual Beauty" 1817; published in periodical *The Examiner*
Laon and Cythna; or, The Revolution of the Golden City: A Vision of the Nineteenth Century 1818; also published in revised form as *The Revolt of Islam,* 1818
The Cenci (verse drama) 1819
Rosalind and Helen: A Modern Eclogue, with Other Poems 1819
Prometheus Unbound, with Other Poems (verse drama and poetry) 1820
Adonais: An Elegy on the Death of John Keats 1821
Epipsychidion 1821
Hellas (verse drama) 1822
"Julian and Maddalo" 1824; published in *Posthumous Poems of Percy Bysshe Shelley*
Posthumous Poems of Percy Bysshe Shelley (poetry and verse drama) 1824
The Triumph of Life 1824; published in *Posthumous Poems of Percy Bysshe Shelley*
"The Witch of Atlas" 1824; published in *Posthumous Poems of Percy Bysshe Shelley*
The Masque of Anarchy 1832
The Works of Percy Bysshe Shelley (poetry, verse dramas, and essays) 1847
The Complete Works of Percy Bysshe Shelley. 10 vols. (poetry, verse dramas, essays, and translations) 1924-1930
The Complete Poetical Works of Percy Bysshe Shelley. 2 vols. to date. 1972-

Other Major Works

Zastrozzi (novel) 1810
The Necessity of Atheism (essay) 1811
St. Irvyne; or, The Rosicrucian (novel) 1811
An Address to the Irish People (essay) 1812
A Declaration of Rights (essay) 1812
A Refutation of Deism (dialogue) 1814
An Address to the People on the Death of Princess Charlotte [as The Hermit of Marlow] (essay) 1817
A Proposal for Putting Reform to the Vote [as The Hermit of Marlow] (essay) 1817
A Defence of Poetry (essay) 1840; published in *Essays, Letters from Abroad, Translations, and Fragments by Percy Bysshe Shelley*
Essays, Letters from Abroad, Translations, and Fragments by Percy Bysshe Shelley. 2 vols. (essays, letters, translations, and prose) 1840
The Letters. 2 vols. (letters) 1964

CRITICISM

J. C. Shairp   (essay date 1879)

SOURCE: "Shelley as a Lyric Poet," in *Fraser's Magazine*, Vol. 20, July, 1879, pp. 38-53.

[*In the following essay, originally presented as a lecture at the theater of the Museum at Oxford, Shairp comments on Shelley's lyrics, which he considers intensely personal in nature.*]

The effort to enter into the meaning of Shelley's poetry is not altogether a painless one. Some may ask, Why should it be painful? Cannot you enjoy his poems merely in an æsthetic way, take the marvel of their aërial movement and the magic of their melody, without scrutinising too closely their meaning or moral import? This, I suppose, most of my hearers could do for themselves, without any comment of mine. Such a mere surface, dilettante way of treating the subject would be useless in itself, and altogether unworthy of this place. All true literature, all genuine poetry, is the direct outcome, the condensed essence, of actual life and thought. Lyric poetry for the most part is—Shelley's especially was—the vivid expression of personal experience. It is only as poetry is founded on reality that it has any solid value; otherwise it is worthless. Before, then, attempting to understand Shelley's lyrics I must ask what was the reality out of which they came—that is, what manner of man Shelley was, what were his ruling views of life, along what lines did his thoughts move?

Those who knew Shelley best speak of the sweetness and refinement of his nature, of his lofty disinterestedness, his unworldliness. They even speak of something like heroic self-forgetfulness. These things we can in sort believe, for there are in his writings many traits that look like those qualities. And yet one receives with some decided reserve the high eulogies of his friends; for we feel that these were not generally men whose moral estimates of things we would entirely accept, and his life contained things that seem strangely at variance with such qualities as they attribute to him. When Byron speaks of his purity of mind we cannot but doubt whether Byron was a good judge of purity. We must, moreover, on the evidence of Shelley's own works demur; for there runs through his poems a painful taint of supersubtilised impurity, of aweless shamelessness, which we never can believe came from a mind truly pure. A penetrating taint it is, which has evilly affected many of the higher minds who admire him, in a way which Byron's own more commonplace licentiousness never could have done.

One of his biographers has said that in no man was the moral sense ever more completely developed than in Shelley, in none was the perception of right and wrong more acute. I rather think that the late Mr. [Walter] Bagehot was nearer the mark when he asserted that in Shelley the conscience never had been revealed—that he was almost entirely without conscience. Moral susceptibilities and

impulses, keen and refined, he had. He was inspired with an enthusiasm of humanity after a kind; hated to see pain in others, and would willingly relieve it; hated oppression, and stormed against it, but then he regarded all rule and authority as oppression. He felt for the poor and the suffering, and tried to help them, and willingly would have shared with all men the vision of good which he sought for himself. But these passionate impulses are something very different from conscience. Conscience first reveals itself when we become aware of the strife between a lower and a higher nature within us—a law of the flesh warring against the law of the mind. And it is out of this experience that moral religion is born, the higher law rather leading up and linking us to One whom that law represents. As Canon Mozely has said, 'it is an introspection on which all religion is built—man going into himself and seeing the struggle within him; and thence getting self-knowledge, and thence the knowledge of God.' Of this double nature, this inward strife between flesh and spirit, Shelley knew nothing. He was altogether a child of impulse—of impulse, one, total, all-absorbing. And the impulse that came to him he followed whithersoever it went, without questioning either himself or it. . . . But this peculiarity, which made him so little fitted to guide either his own life or that of others, tended, on the other hand, very powerfully to make him pre-eminently a lyric poet. How it fitted him for this we shall presently see. But abandonment to impulse, however much it may contribute to lyrical inspiration, is a poor guide to conduct; and a poet's conduct in life, of whatever kind it be, quickly reacts on his poetry. It was so with Shelley.

It is painful to recall the unhappy incidents, but we cannot understand his poetry if we forget them. 'Strongly moralised,' Mr. Symonds tells us, his boyhood was; but of a strange—I might say, an unhuman—type the morality must have been which allowed some of the chief acts of his life. His father was no doubt a commonplace and worldly-minded squire, wholly unsympathetic with his dreamy son; but this cannot justify the son's unfilial and irreverent conduct towards his parent, going so far as to curse him for the amusement of coarse Eton companions. Nobility of nature he may have had, but it was such nobility as allowed him, in order to hurl defiance at authority, to start atheist at Eton, and to do the same more boldly at Oxford, with what result you know. It allowed him to engage the heart of a simple and artless girl, who entrusted her life in his keeping, and then after two or three years to abandon her and her child—for no better reason, it would seem, than that she cared too little for her baby, and had an unpleasant sister, who was an offence to Shelley. It allowed him first to insult the religious sense of his fellow men by preaching the wildest atheism, then in the poem ***Laon and Cythna***, which he intended to be his gospel for the world, to outrage the deepest instincts of our nature by introducing a most horrible and unnatural incident. A moral taint there is in this, which has left its trail in many of his after poems. The furies of the sad tragedy of Harriet Westbrook haunted him till the close, and drew forth some strains of weird agony; but even in these there is no manly repentance, no self-reproach that is true and human-hearted. After his second marriage he never repeated the former offence, but many a strain in his later poems, as in *Epipsychidion,* and in his latest lyrics, proves that constancy of affection was not in him, nor reckoned by him among the virtues. Idolators of Shelley will, I know, reply, 'You judge Shelley by the conventional morality of the present day, and, judging him by this standard, of course you harshly condemn him. But it was against these very conventions which you call morality that Shelley's whole life was a protest. He was the prophet of something truer or better than this.' To this I answer that Shelley's revolt was not against the conventional morality of his own time, but against the fundamental morality of all time. Had he merely cried out against the stifling political atmosphere and the dry, dead orthodoxy of the Regency and the reign of George IV., and longed for some ampler air, freer and more life-giving, one could well have understood him, even sympathised with him. But he rebelled not against the limitations and corruptions of his own day, but against the moral verities which two thousand years have made good, and which have been tested and approved not only by eighteen Christian centuries, but no less by the wisdom of Virgil and Cicero, of Aristotle and Sophocles. Shelley may be the prophet of a new morality, but it is one which never can be realised till moral law has been obliterated from the universe and conscience from the heart of man.

A nature which was capable of the things I have alluded to, whatever other traits of nobility it may have had, must have been traversed by some strange deep flaw, marred by some radical inward defect. In some of his gifts and impulses he was more,—in other things essential to goodness, he was far less,—than other men; a fully developed man he certainly was not. I am inclined to believe that, for all his noble impulses and aims, he was in some way deficient in rational and moral sanity. Many of you will remember Hazlitt's somewhat cynical description of him. Yet, to judge by his writings, it looks like truth. He had 'a fire in his eye, a fever in his blood, a maggot in his brain, a hectic flutter in his speech, which mark out the philosophic fanatic. He is sanguine-complexioned and shrill-voiced.' This is just the outward appearance we could fancy for his inward temperament. What was that temperament?

He was entirely a child of impulse, lived and longed for high-strung, intense emotion—simple, all-absorbing, all-penetrating emotion, going straight on in one direction to its object, hating and resenting whatever opposed its progress thitherward. The object which he longed for was some abstract intellectualised spirit of beauty and loveliness, which should thrill his spirit continually with delicious shocks of emotion.

This yearning, panting desire is expressed by him in a thousand forms and figures throughout his poetry. Again and again the refrain recurs—

> I pant for the music which is Divine,
>   My heart in its thirst is a dying flower;
> Pour forth the sound like enchanted wine,
>   Loosen the notes in a silver shower;
> Like a herbless plain for the gentle rain

I gasp, I faint, till they wake again.

> Let me drink the spirit of that sweet sound;
>   More, O more! I am thirsting yet;
> It loosens the serpent which care has bound
>   Upon my heart, to stifle it;
> The dissolving strain, through every vein,
> Passes into my heart and brain.

He sought not mere sensuous enjoyment, like Keats, but keen intellectual and emotional delight—the mental thrill, the glow of soul, the 'tingling of the nerves,' that accompany transcendental rapture. His hungry craving was for intellectual beauty, and the delight it yields; if not that, then for horror, anything to thrill the nerves, though it should curdle the blood and make the flesh creep. Sometimes for a moment this perfect abstract loveliness would seem to have embodied itself in some creature of flesh and blood; but only for a moment would the sight soothe him—the sympathy would cease, the glow of heart would die down—and he would pass on in the hot, insatiable pursuit of new rapture. 'There is no rest for us,' says the great preacher, 'save in quietness, confidence, and affection.' This was not what Shelley sought, but something very different from this.

The pursuit of abstract ideal beauty was one form which his hungry, insatiable desire took. Another passion that possessed him was the longing to pierce to the very heart the mystery of existence. It has been said that before an insoluble mystery, clearly seen to be insoluble, the soul bows down and is at rest, as before an ascertained truth. Shelley knew nothing of this. Before nothing would his soul bow down. Every veil, however sacred, he would rend, pierce the inner shrine of being, and force it to give up its secret. There is in him a profane audacity, an utter awelessness. . . . Reverence was to him another word for hated superstition. Nothing was to him inviolate. All the natural reserves he would break down. Heavenward, he would pierce to the heart of the universe and lay it bare; manward, he would annihilate all the precincts of personality. Every soul should be free to mingle with any other, as so many raindrops do. In his own words,

> The fountains of our deepest life shall be
> Confused in passion's golden purity.

However fine the language in which such feelings may clothe themselves, in truth they are wholly vile; there is no horror of shamelessness which they may not generate. Yet this is what comes of the unbridled desire for 'tingling pulses,' quivering, panting, fainting sensibility, which Shelley everywhere makes the supreme happiness. It issues in awelessness, irreverence, and what some one has called 'moral nudity.'

These two impulses, both combined with another passion, he had—the passion for reforming the world. He had a real, benevolent desire to impart to all men the peculiar good he sought for himself—a life of free, unimpeded impulse, of passionate, unobstructed desire. Liberty, Equality, Fraternity—these of course; but something far beyond these—absolute Perfection, as he conceived it, he believed to be within every man's reach. Attainable, if only all the growths of history could be swept away, all authority and government, all religion, all law, custom, nationality, everything that limits and restrains, and if every man were left open to the uncontrolled expansion of himself and his impulses. The end of this process of making a clean sweep of all that is, and beginning afresh, would be that family, social ranks, government, worship, would disappear, and then man would be king over himself, and wise, gentle, just, and good. Such was his temperament, the original emotional basis of Shelley's nature; such, too, some of the chief aims towards which this temperament impelled him. And certainly these aims do make one think of the 'maggot in his brain.' But a temperament of this kind, whatever aims it turned to, was eminently and essentially lyrical. Those thrills of soul, those tingling nerves, those rapturous glows of feeling, are the very substance out of which high lyrics are woven.

The insatiable craving to pierce the mystery, of course, drove Shelley to philosophy for instruments to pierce it with. During his brief life he was a follower of three distinct schools of thought. At first he began with the philosophy of the senses, was a materialist, adopting Lucretius as his master and holding that atoms are the only realities, with perhaps a pervading life of nature to mould them—that from atoms all things come, to atoms return. Yet even over this dreary creed, without spirit, immortality, or God, he shouted a jubilant 'Eureka,' as though it were some new glad tidings.

From this he passed into the school of Hume—got rid of matter, the dull clods of earth, denied both matter and mind, and held that these were nothing but impressions, with no substance behind them. This was liker Shelley's cast of mind than materialism. Not only dull clods of matter, but personality, the 'I' and the 'thou,' were by this creed eliminated, and that exactly suited Shelley's way of thought. It gave him a phantom world.

From Hume he went on to Plato, and in him found still more congenial nutriment. The solid, fixed entities—matter and mind—he could still deny, while he was led on to believe in eternal archetypes behind all phenomena, as the only realities. These Platonic ideas attracted his abstract intellect and imagination, and are often alluded to in his later poems, as in *Adonais*. Out of this philosophy it is probable that he got the only object of worship which he ever acknowledged, the Spirit of Beauty. Plato's idea of beauty changed into a spirit, but without will, without morality, in his own words:—

> That Light whose smile kindles the universe,
> That Beauty in which all things work and move,
> That Benediction which the eclipsing curse
> Of birth can quench not, that sustaining Love
> Which, through the web of being blindly wove
> By man and beast and earth and air and sea,
> Burns bright or dim, as each are mirrors of
> The fire for which all thirst.

To the moral and religious truths which are the backbone of Plato's thought he never attained. Shelley's thought never had any backbone. Each of these successively adopted philosophies entered into and coloured the successive stages of Shelley's poetry; but through them all his intellect and imagination remained unchanged.

What was the nature of that intellect? It was wholly akin and adapted to the temperament I have described as his. Impatient of solid substances, inaccessible to many kinds of truth, inappreciative of solid, concrete facts, it was quick and subtle to seize the evanescent hues of things, the delicate aromas which are too fine for ordinary perceptions. His intellect waited on his temperament, and, so to speak, did its will—caught up one by one the warm emotions as they were flung off, and worked them up into the most exquisite abstractions. The rush of throbbing pulsations supplied the materials for his keen-edged thought to work on, and these it did mould into the rarest, most beautiful shapes. This his mind was busy doing all his life long. The real world, existence as it is to other minds, he recoiled from—shrank from the dull, gross earth which we see around us—nor less from the unseen world of Righteous Law and Will which we apprehend above us. The solid earth he did not care for. Heaven—a moral heaven—there was that in him which would not believe in. So, as Mr. Hutton has said, his mind made for itself a dwelling-place midway between the two, equally remote from both, some interstellar region, some cold, clear place—

> Pinnacled dim in the intense inane—

which he peopled with ideal shapes and abstractions, wonderful or weird, beautiful or fantastic, all woven out of his own dreaming phantasy.

This was the world in which he was at home; he was not at home with any reality known to other men. No real human characters appear in his poetry; his own pulsations, desires, aspirations, supplied the place of these. Hardly any actual human feeling is in them; only some phase of evanescent emotion, or the shadow of it, is seized—not even the flower of human feeling, but the bloom of the flower or the dream of the bloom. A real landscape he has seldom described, only his own impression of it, or some momentary gleam, some tender light, that has fleeted vanishingly over earth and sea he has caught. Nature he used mainly to cull from it some of its most delicate tints, some faint hues of the dawn or the sunset clouds, to weave in and colour the web of his abstract dream. So entirely at home is he in this abstract shadowy world of his own making, that when he would describe common visible things he does so by likening them to those phantoms of the brain, as though with these last alone he was familiar. Virgil likens the ghosts by the banks of Styx to falling leaves—

> Quam multa in silvis auctumni frigore primo
> Lapsa cadunt folia.

Shelley likens falling leaves to ghosts. Before the wind the dead leaves, he says—

> Are driven, like ghosts from an enchanter fleeing.

Others have compared thought to a breeze. With Shelley the breeze is like thought; the pilot spirit of the blast, he says—

> Wakens the leaves and waves, ere it hath past,
>   To such brief unison as on the brain
> One tone which never can recur has cast
>   One accent, never to return again.

We see thus that nature as it actually exists has little place in Shelley's poetry. And man, as he really is, may be said to have no place at all.

Neither is the world of moral or spiritual truth there—not the living laws by which the world is governed—no presence of a Sovereign Will, no all-wise Personality, behind the fleeting shows of time. The abstract world which his imagination dwelt in is a cold, weird, unearthly, inhuman place, peopled with shapes which we may wonder at, but cannot love. When we first encounter these we are fain to exclaim, Earth we know, and Heaven we know, but who and what are ye? Ye belong neither to things human nor to things divine. After a very brief sojourn in Shelley's ideal world, with its pale abstractions, most men are ready to say with another poet, after a voyage among the stars—

> Then back to earth, the dear green earth;
> Whole ages though I here should roam,
> The world for my remarks and me
> Would not a whit the better be:
>   I've left my heart at home.

In that dear green earth, and the men who have lived or still live on it, in their human hopes and fears, in their faiths and aspirations, lies the truest field for the highest imagination to work in. That I believe to be the haunt and main region for the songs of the greatest poets. The real is the true world for a great poet, but it was not Shelley's world.

Yet Shelley, while the imaginative mood was on him, felt this ideal world of his as real as most men feel the solid earth, and through the pallid lips of its phantom people and dim abstractions he pours as warm a flood of emotion as ever poet did through the rosiest lips and brightest eyes of earth-born creatures. Not more real to Burns were his bonny Jean and his Highland Mary, than to Shelley were the visions of Asia and Panthea, and the Lady of the Sensitive Plant, while he gazed on them. And when his affections did light, not on these abstractions, but on creatures of flesh and blood, yet so penetrated was his thought with his own idealism, that he lifted them up from earth into that rarefied atmosphere, and described them in the same style of imagery and language as that with which he clothes the phantasms of his mind. Thus it will be seen that it was a narrow and limited tract over which Shelley's imagination ranged—that it took little or no note of reality, and that boundless as was its fertility and power of resource within its own chosen circle, yet the widest realm of mere brain creation must be thin and small compared with existing reality both in the seen and the unseen worlds.

We can now see the reason why Shelley's long poems are such absolute failures, his short lyrics so strangely succeed. Mere thrills of soul were weak as connecting bonds for long poems. Distilled essences and personified qualities were poor material out of which to build up great works. These things could give neither unity, nor motive power, nor human interest to long poems. Hence the incoherence which all but a few devoted admirers find in Shelley's long poems, despite their grand passages and their splendid imagery. In fact, if the long poems were to be broken up and thrown into a heap, and the lyric portions riddled out of them and preserved, the world would lose nothing, and would get rid of not a little offensive stuff. An exception to this judgment is generally made in favour of the *Cenci*: but that tragedy turns on an incident so repulsive that, notwithstanding its acknowledged power, it can hardly give pleasure to any healthy mind.

On the other hand, single thrills of rapture, which are such insufficient stuff to make long poems out of, supply the very inspiration for the true lyric. It is this predominance of emotion, so unhappy to himself, which made Shelley the lyrist that he was. When he sings his lyric strains, whatever is most unpleasant in him is softened down, if it does not wholly disappear. Whatever is most unique and excellent in him comes out at its best—his eye for abstract beauty, the subtlety of his thought, the rush of his eager pursuing desire, the splendour of his imagery, the delicate rhythm, the matchless music. These lyrics are gales of melody blown from a far-off region, that looks fair in the distance. Perhaps those enjoy them most who do not inquire too closely what is the nature of that land, or know too exactly the theories and views of life of which these songs are the effluence; for if we come too near we might find that there was poison in the air. Many a one has read those lyrics and felt their fascination without thought of the unhappy experience out of which they have come. They understood 'a beauty in the words, but not the words.' I doubt whether any one after very early youth, any one who has known the realities of life, can continue to take Shelley's best songs to heart, as he can those of Shakespeare or the best of Burns. For, however we may continue to wonder at the genius that is in them, no healthy mind will find in them the expression of its truest and best thoughts. Other lyric poets, it has been said, sing of what they feel. Shelley in his lyrics sings of what he wants to feel. The thrills of desire, the gushes of emotion, are all straining after something seen afar but unattained, something distant or future; or they are passionate despair, utter despondency for something hopelessly gone. Yet it must be owned that those bursts of passionate desire after ideal beauty set our pulses a-throbbing with a strange vibration even when we do not really sympathise with them. Even his desolate wails make those seem for a moment to share his despair who do not really share it. Such is the charm of his impassioned eloquence and the witchery of his music.

Let us turn now to look at some of his lyrics in detail. The earliest of them, those of 1814, were written while Shelley was under the depressing spell of materialistic belief, and at the time when he was abandoning poor Harriet Westbrook. For a time he lived under the spell of that ghastly faith, hugging it, yet hating it; and its progeny are seen in the lyrics of that time, such as **'Death,' 'Mutability,' 'Lines in a Country Churchyard.'** These have a cold, clammy feel. They are full of 'wormy horrors,' as though the poet were one

> who had made his bed
> In charnels and on coffins, where black Death
> Keeps record of the trophies won from Life,

as though by dwelling amid these things he had hoped to force some lone ghost

> to render up the tale
> Of what we are.

And what does it all come to?—what is the lesson he reads there?—

> Lift not the painted veil which those who live
>   Call life. . . . Behind lurk Fear
> And Hope, twin destinies, who ever weave
>   Their shadows o'er the chasm, sightless and drear.

That is all that the belief in mere matter taught Shelley, or ever will teach anyone.

As he passed on, the clayey, clammy sensation is less present. Even Hume's impressions are better than mere dust, and the Platonic ideas are better than Hume's impressions. When he came under the influence of Plato his doctrine of ideas, as eternal existences and the only realities, exercised over Shelley the charm it always has had for imaginative minds; and it furnished him with a form under which he figured to himself his favourite belief in the Spirit of Love and Beauty as the animating spirit of the universe—that for which the human soul pants. It is the passion for this ideal which leads Alastor through his long wanderings to die at last in the Caucasian wilderness without attaining it. It is this which he apostrophises in the **'Hymn to Intellectual Beauty,'** as the power which consecrates all it shines on, as the awful loveliness to which he looks to free this world from its dark slavery. It is this vision which reappears in its highest form in ***Prometheus Unbound,*** the greatest and most attractive of all Shelley's longer poems. That drama is from beginning to end a great lyrical poem, or I should rather say a congeries of lyrics, in which perhaps more than anywhere else Shelley's lyrical power has reached its highest flight. The whole poem is exalted by a grand pervading idea, one which in its truest and deepest form is the grandest we can conceive—the idea of the ultimate renovation of man and the world. And although the powers and processes and personified abstractions which Shelley invoked to effect this end are ludicrously inadequate, as irrational as it would be to try to build a solid house out of shadows and moonbeams, yet the end in view does impart to the poem something of its own elevation. Prometheus, the representative of suffering and struggling humanity, is to be redeemed and perfected by union with Asia, who is the ideal of beauty, the light of life, the spirit of love. To this spirit Shelley looked to rid the world of all its evil and bring in

the diviner day. The lyric poetry, which is exquisite throughout, perhaps culminates in the well-known exquisite song in which Panthea, one of the nymphs, hails her sister Asia, as

> Life of Life! thy lips enkindle
>   With their love the breath between them;
> And thy smiles, before they dwindle,
>   Make the cold air fire; then screen them
> In those looks, where whoso gazes
> Faints, entangled in their mazes.
>
> Child of Light! thy limbs are burning
>   Through the vest which seems to hide them;
> As the radiant lines of morning
>   Through the clouds, ere they divide them;
> And this atmosphere divinest
> Shrouds thee wheresoe'er thou shinest.
>
> Lamp of Earth! where'er thou movest
>   The dim shapes are clad with brightness,
> And the souls of whom thou lovest
>   Walk upon the winds with lightness,
> Till they fail, as I am failing,
> Dizzy, lost, yet unbewailing.

The reply of Asia to this song is hardly less exquisite. Everyone here will remember it:—

> My soul is an enchanted boat,
>   Which, like a sleeping swan, doth float
> Upon the silver waves of thy sweet singing;
>   And thine doth like an angel sit
>   Beside the helm, conducting it,
> Whilst all the winds with melody are ringing;
>   It seems to float ever, for ever,
>   Upon the many-winding river,
>   Between mountains, woods, abysses,
>   A paradise of wildernesses!
> Till, like one in slumber bound,
> Borne to the ocean, I float down, around
> Into a sea profound of ever-spreading sound.
>   Meanwhile thy spirit lifts its pinions
>   In music's most serene dominions,
> Catching the winds that fan that happy heaven.
>   And we sail on, away, afar
>   Without a course, without a star,
> But, by the instinct of sweet music driven;
>   Till through Elysian garden islets
>   By thee, most beautiful of pilots,
>   Where never mortal pinnace glided,
>   The boat of my desire is guided:
> Realms where the air we breathe is love,
> Which in the winds on the waves doth move,
> Harmonising this earth with what we feel above.

In these two lyrics you have Shelley at his highest perfection. Exquisitely beautiful as they are, they are, however, beautiful as the mirage is beautiful, and as unsubstantial. There is nothing in the reality of things answering to Asia. She is not human, she is not divine. There is nothing moral in her—no will, no power to subdue evil; only an exquisite essence, a melting loveliness. There is in her no law, no righteousness; something to enervate, nothing to brace the soul. After her you long for one bracing look on the stern, severe countenance of Duty, of whom another poet sang—

>   Stern lawgiver! yet thou dost wear
>   The Godhead's most benignant grace;
>   Nor know I anything so fair
>   As is the smile upon thy face;
>   Flowers laugh before thee in their beds,
>   And fragrance in thy footing treads;
>   Thou dost preserve the stars from wrong,
>   And the most ancient heavens through thee are fresh
>   and strong.

Perfect as is the workmanship of those lyrics in *Prometheus* and many another, their excellence is lessened by the material out of which they are woven being fantastic, not substantial, truth. Few of them lay hold of real sentiments which are catholic to humanity. They do not deal with permanent emotions which belong to all men and are for all time, but appeal rather to minds in a particular stage of culture, and that not a healthy stage. They are not of such stuff as life is made of. They will not interest all healthy and truthful minds in all stages of culture and in all ages. To do this, however, is, I believe, a note of the highest style of lyric poem.

Another thing to be observed is, that while the imagery of Shelley's lyrics is so splendid and the music of their language so magical, both of these are at that point of over-bloom which is on the verge of decay. The imagery, for all its splendour, is too ornate, too redundant, too much overlays the thought, which has not strength enough to uphold such a weight. Then, as to the music of the words, wonderful as it is, all but exclusive admirers of Shelley must have felt at times as if the sound runs away with the sense. In some of the *Prometheus* lyrics the poet, according to Mr. [J. A.] Symonds, seems to have 'realised the miracle of making words, detached from meaning, the substance of a new ethereal music.' This is, to say the least, a dangerous miracle to practise. Even Shelley, over-borne by the power of melodious words, would at times seem to approach perilously near the borders of the unintelligible, not to say the nonsensical. What it comes to, when adopted as a style, has been seen plainly enough in some of Shelley's chief followers in our own day. Cloyed with overloaded imagery, and satiated almost to sickening with alliterative music, we turn for reinvigoration to poetry that is severe even to baldness.

The *Prometheus Unbound* was written in Italy, and during his four Italian years Shelley's lyric stream flowed on unremittingly, and enriched England's poetry with many lyrics unrivalled in their kind, and evoked from its language a new power. These lyrics are on the whole his best poetic work. To go over them in detail would be impossible, besides being needless. Perhaps his year most prolific in lyrics was 1820, just two years before his death. Among the products of this year were, the *Sensitive Plant*, more than half lyrical, the '**Cloud**,' the '**Skylark**,' '**Love's**

Philosophy,' '**Arethusa**,' '**Hymns of Pan and Apollo**,' all in his best manner, with many besides these. About the lyrics of this time two things are noticeable: more of them are about things of nature than heretofore, and there are several on Greek subjects.

Of all modern attempts to reinstate Greek subjects I know nothing equal to these, except perhaps one or two of the Laureate's happiest efforts. They take the Greek forms and mythologies, and fill them with modern thought and spirit. And perhaps this is the only way to make Greek subjects real and interesting to us; for if we want the very Greek spirit we had better go to the originals and not to any reproductions.

You remember how he makes Pan sing—

>   From the forests and highlands
>   We come, we come;
>   From the river-girt islands,
>   Where loud waves are dumb,
>   Listening to my sweet pipings.
>
>   . . . . .
>
>   Liquid Peneus was flowing,
>   And all dark Tempe lay
>   In Pelion's shadow, outgrowing
>   The light of the dying day,
>   Speeded with my sweet pipings.
>   The Sileni, and Sylvans, and Fauns,
>   And the nymphs of the woods and waves,
>   To the edge of the moist river-lawns,
>   And the brink of the dewy caves,
>   And all that did then attend or follow,
>   Were silent with love, as you now, Apollo,
>   With envy of my sweet pipings.
>   I sang of the dancing stars,
>   I sang of the dædal Earth,
>   And of Heaven, and the giant wars,
>   And Love, and Death, and Birth,
>   And then I changed my pipings—
>   Singing how down the vale of Menalus
>   I pursued a maiden and clasped a weed.
>   Gods and men, we are all deluded thus!
>   It breaks in our bosom, and then we bleed:
>   All wept, as I think both ye now would,
>   If envy or age had not frozen your blood,
>   At the sorrow of my sweet pipings.

Of the lyrics on natural objects the two supreme ones are the '**Ode to the West Wind**' and the '**Skylark**.' Of this last nothing need be said. Artistically and poetically it is unique, has a place of its own in poetry; yet may I be allowed to express a misgiving about it which I have long felt, and others may feel too? For all its beauty, perhaps one would rather not recall it when hearing the skylark's song in the fields on a bright spring morning. The poem is not in tune with the bird's song and the feelings it does and ought to awaken. The rapture with which the strain springs up at first dies down before the close into Shelley's ever-haunting morbidity. Who wishes, when hearing the real skylark, to be told that

> We look before and after,
>   And pine for what is not:
> Our sincerest laughter
>   With some pain is fraught?

If personal feeling is to be inwrought into the living powers of nature, let it be such feeling as is in keeping with the object, appropriate to the theme in hand.

Such is that personal invocation with which Shelley closes his grand **'Ode to the West Wind,'** written the previous year, 1819—

> Make me thy lyre, even as the forest is:
>   What if my leaves are fallen like its own!
> The tumult of thy mighty harmonies
>
> Will take from both a deep autumnal tone,
>   Sweet though in sadness. Be thou, spirit fierce,
> My spirit! be thou me, impetuous one!
>
> Drive my dead thoughts over the universe
>   Like withered leaves, to quicken a new birth;
> And, by the incantation of this verse,
>
> Scatter, as from an unextinguished hearth
>   Ashes and sparks, my words among mankind!
> Be through my lips to unawakened earth
>
> The trumpet of a prophecy! O Wind,
> If Winter comes, can Spring be far behind?

This ode ends with some vigour, some hope; but that is not usual with Shelley. Everyone must have noticed how almost habitually his intensest lyrics—those which have started with the fullest swing of rapture—die down before they close into a wail of despair. It is as though, when the strong gush of emotion had spent itself, there was no more behind, nothing to fall back upon, but blank emptiness and desolation. It is this that makes Shelley's poetry so unspeakably sad—sad with a hopeless sorrow that is like none other. You feel as though he were a wanderer who has lost his way hopelessly in the wilderness of a blank universe. His cry is, as Mr. Carlyle long since said, like 'the infinite inarticulate wailing of forsaken infants.' In the wail of his desolation there are many tones—some wild and weird, some defiant, some full of despondent pathos.

The lines written in **'Dejection,'** on the Bay of Naples, in 1818, are perhaps the most touching of all his wails: the words are so sweet they seem, by their very sweetness, to lighten the load of heart-loneliness:—

> I see the Deep's untrampled floor
>   With green and purple seaweeds strown;
> I see the waves upon the shore,
>   Like light dissolved in star-showers, thrown:
> I sit upon the sands alone;
>   The lightning of the noon-tide ocean

> Is flashing round me, and a tone
>   Arises from its measured motion.
> How sweet! did any heart now share in my emotion.
>
> Alas! I have nor hope, nor health,
>   Nor peace within, nor calm around,
> Nor that content, surpassing wealth,
>   The sage in meditation found.
>
>   . . . . .
>
> Yet now despair itself is mild,
>   Even as the winds and waters are;
> I would lie down like a tired child,
>   And weep away this life of care
> Which I have borne, and yet must bear,
>   Till death like sleep might steal on me,
> And I might feel in the warm air
>   My cheek grow cold, and hear the sea
> Breathe o'er my dying brain its last monotony.

Who that reads these sighing lines but must feel for the heart that breathed them! Yet how can we be surprised that he should have felt so desolate? Every heart needs some real stay. And a heart so sensitive, a spirit so finely touched, as Shelley's needs, far more than unsympathetic and narrow natures, a refuge amid the storms of life. But he knew of none. His universe was a homeless one, had no centre of repose. His universal essence of love, diffused throughout it, contained nothing substantial—no will that could control and support his own. While a soul owns no law, is without awe, lives wholly by impulse, what rest, what central peace, is possible for it? When the ardours of emotion have died down, what remains for it but weakness, exhaustion, despair? The feeling of his weakness woke in Shelley no contriteness or brokenness of spirit, no self-abasement, no reverence. Nature was to him really the whole, and he saw in it nothing but 'a revelation of death, a sepulchral picture, generation after generation disappearing and being heard of and seen no more.' He rejected utterly that other 'consolatory revelation which tells us that we are spiritual beings, and have a spiritual source of life,' and strength, above and beyond the material system. Such a belief, or rather no belief, as his can engender only infinite sadness, infinite despair. And this is the deep undertone of all Shelley's poetry.

I have dwelt on his lyrics because they contain little of the offensive and nothing of the revolting which here and there obtrudes itself in the longer poems. And one may speak of these lyrics without agitating too deeply questions which at present I would rather avoid. Yet even the lyrics bear some impress of the source whence they come. Beautiful though they be, they are like those fine pearls which, we are told, are the products of disease in the parent shell. All Shelley's poetry is, as it were, a gale blown from a richly gifted but unwholesome land; and the taint, though not so perceptible in the lyrics, still hangs more or less over many of the finest. Besides this defect, they are very limited in their range of influence. They cannot reach the hearts of all men. They fascinate only some of the educated, and that probably only while they are young. The time comes when these pass out of that peculiar sphere of thought and find little interest in such poetry. Probably the rare exquisiteness of their workmanship will always preserve Shelley's lyrics, even after the world has lost, as we may hope it will lose, sympathy with their substance. But better, stronger, more vital far are those lyrics which lay hold on the permanent, unchanging emotions of man—those emotions which all healthy natures have felt and always will feel, and which no new stage of thought or civilisation can ever bury out of sight.

Anna Swanick   (essay date 1892)

SOURCE: "Percy Bysshe Shelley," in *Poets: The Interpreters of Their Age*, George Bell & Sons, 1892, pp. 300-11.

[*In the following excerpt, Swanick discusses Shelley's concern with social reform as reflected in his verse.*]

Possessed by a spirit of implacable hostility to oppression and intolerance, under all their manifestations, Shelley, like Byron, may be regarded, under one aspect of his genius, as representing the destructive temper of the Revolution. Both believed in the ultimate triumph of [French] Democracy. Byron has recorded his conviction that "There will be bloodshed like water, and tears like mist, but that the people will conquer in the end"; nevertheless, while holding this opinion theoretically, he does not appear to have been cheered by any vision of a brighter future;—with him the spirit of revolt is predominant.

Shelley, on the contrary, having adopted, with passionate earnestness, the underlying principles of the Revolution, especially that of universal brotherhood, and cherishing unswerving faith in the coming Millennium, proclaimed, through the medium of impassioned verse, the final regeneration of mankind through righteousness, patient endurance, gentleness and love. This faith in the ultimate triumph of Right over Wrong, of Truth over Error, and of Love over Hatred, became one of the ruling and inspiring passions of his life, and hence he may perhaps be not inaptly characterized as the poet of aspiration and of hope.

These ideas being out of harmony with the reactionary spirit of the time which, in its recoil from the excesses of the Revolution, manifested a tendency to selfish and apathetic indifference to the higher interests of humanity, Shelley's poems, in which they were embodied, met with no immediate acceptance. Eventually, however they have doubtless been instrumental, with other agencies, in rekindling that enthusiasm of humanity (an expression originating with him) which, at the outbreak of the Revolution, had fired the nobler spirits of the age, and which, under the form of helpful beneficence, forms so striking a feature of the latter half of the nineteenth century.

Thus, in the fulness of time, has been realized his own fervent prayer, embodied in his magnificent "**Ode to the West Wind.**"

> Make me thy lyre, even as the forest is;
> What if my leaves are falling like its own!
> The tumult of thy mighty harmonics
>
> Will take from both a deep autumnal tone,
> Sweet though in sadness. Be thou, spirit fierce,
> My spirit! Be thou me, impetuous one!
>
> Drive my dead thoughts over the universe
> Like withered leaves to quicken a new birth!
> And, by the incantation of this verse,
>
> Scatter, as from an unextinguished hearth,
> Ashes and sparks, my words among mankind!
> Be through my lips to unawakened earth
>
> The trumpet of a prophecy! O, Wind,
> If winter comes, can Spring be far behind?

"This poem," it has been truly said, "is the clarion-cry of hope in the presence of tumultuous ruin and inevitable decay."

The poetry of Shelley, like that of Byron, strikingly illustrates his individuality; accordingly there are two memorable moments of his early life recorded in his verse which, to quote the words of his latest biographer, "were the consecration of his boyhood."

The story of the first occurs in the Dedication, prefixed to the *Revolt of Islam*, and records how, with the recognition of the prevalence in life of tyranny and wrong, came his high resolve to dedicate himself to the cause of Liberty, and to do unflinching battle with her deadly foes.

This passage "strikes the key-note of the predominating sentiment of Shelley throughout his whole life,—his sympathy with the oppressed!"

"The inspiration of this memorable moment was to elevate and purify Shelley's moral being;—it was hardly less essential that he should dedicate his imagination to the spirit of beauty; this also was accomplished; we read the record of this second spiritual crisis in the '**Hymn to Intellectual Beauty.**'"

> Sudden thy shadow fell on me—
> I shrieked and clasped my hands in ecstasy!
> I vowed that I would dedicate my powers
> To thee and thine; have I not kept my vow?

These two moments may be regarded as introducing Shelley into two distinct spheres of emotion, his enthusiasm of humanity and his love of ideal beauty. These two master-passions, under the influence of one or other of which he habitually lived and worked, formed two independent sources of inspiration, giving birth to two series of poems, the one embodying his aspirations for humanity, and the other reflecting his personal emotions, which were always coloured by his passionate feeling for the Beautiful.

How fervent was Shelley's sympathy with human progress,

and how devoted and disinterested was his determination to lose no opportunity of forwarding the cause he had so much at heart, appears from his visit to Ireland in 1812.

Cherishing the conviction, as stated by himself, that the failure of the French Revolution might be traced to the want of a previous moral movement, fitting the people for the possession of freedom, he came to Ireland not as a public agitator, but as a preacher of morality.

Accordingly, in his Addresses to the Irish nation, he advocates the great principle that political Reform must be based, not upon expediency, but upon virtue and wisdom. In the excited state of public feeling, however, these elevated views, set forth with impassioned eloquence, met with little response; and the young visionary, saddened by the spectacle of squalid misery which met him in the streets of Dublin, and recognizing that he must be content to labour for the future, bade farewell to Ireland, after a sojourn there of seven weeks.

Among the poems of Shelley wherein he appears as the philanthropist fired with zeal for the regeneration of mankind, attention must be called to **Queen Mab,** his first important work, written when he was eighteen, issued privately in 1813, and published surreptitiously in 1821.

Against the publication of this juvenile poem he earnestly protested, on the ground "that he could unreservedly condemn its intemperate spirit, and acknowledge its crudity, in all that concerns moral and political speculation, as well as in the subtler discriminations of metaphysical and religious doctrine."

Notwithstanding this disclaimer on the part of its author, great interest attaches to this early production, not only as illustrating in an eminent degree the more striking characteristics of his genius, his wonderful imaginative power, and his passionate love of visionary beauty, but also as exhibiting what may be regarded as the actuating principles of his life, namely, his intense sympathy with human progress and his faith in human perfectibility; it illustrates also the bitter hatred fostered by his unhappy experience at school and at college, with which, at that time, he regarded all traditional beliefs, and established institutions, the source, as he imagined, of the misery which everywhere prevailed, and against which, with the precipitate rashness and the fearless audacity of youth, he proclaimed irreconcilable war.

With reference to this poem, I may, in justice to Shelley, quote the following words of Robert Browning: "There are growing pains, accompanied by temporary distortion, of the soul also." "Nor will men persist in confounding any more than God confounds, with genuine infidelity and an atheism of the heart, those passionate, impatient struggles of a boy towards distant truth and love, made in the dark."

The Revolt of Islam, while embodying Shelley's profoundest convictions, social, ethical, and political, is also interesting as revealing, through the character of Laon (the idealized portrait of himself), the hopes and aspirations with which in previous years he had entered upon his Irish campaign; notwithstanding the ill-success which had attended that expedition, he cherished unswerving faith in the principles which then actuated him, and the triumph of which he regarded as essential to the redemption of humanity.

Deeply impressed by the misery which prevailed in England at the close of the war, and indignant at the reactionary policy of the government, he felt that, through the medium of impassioned verse, he had a message to deliver, involving the happiness not only of England, but of Mankind.

It was in this spirit that, amid the solitudes of Marlow, *The Revolt of Islam* was composed. With what unremitting ardour he devoted himself to his self-imposed task may be imagined when he speaks of the poem as "that which grew, as it were, from 'the agony and bloody sweat' of intellectual travail." In the preface which accompanied the poem, he states that it was undertaken "in the view of kindling within the bosoms of his readers a virtuous enthusiasm for those doctrines of liberty and justice, that faith and hope in something good, which neither violence, nor misrepresentation, nor prejudice can ever totally extinguish among mankind."

"It was his desire," to quote the words of his biographer, "to present the true ideal of revolution—a national movement based on moral principle, inspired by a passion of justice and a passion of charity, unstained by blood, unclouded by turbulence, and using material force only as the tranquil putting forth, in act, of spiritual powers."

Among the regenerating principles embodied in this poem, one to which Shelley attached supreme importance is the equality of the sexes.

> Never will peace and human nature meet,
> Till free and equal man and woman greet
> Domestic peace.

"Can man be free if woman be a slave?" Accordingly, a prominent part in the work of redemption is assigned to Cythna, the heroine. Together with his hatred of oppression and intolerance, this poem reveals also his faith in the contagion of goodness, in the power of noble sentiments, when embodied in thrilling words, to quell the evil passions in the human heart, and to awaken its latent sympathies with the Right and True; hence his belief in the possibility of a bloodless revolution.

It must, however, be confessed that, notwithstanding the nobleness of its dominant ideas, notwithstanding its thrilling incidents, the music of its verse, and the splendour of its descriptions, among which that of the conflict between the eagle and the serpent, in the first canto, and of the wonderful cloud-scape at the beginning of the eleventh canto, are truly magnificent—the poem as a whole is unsatisfactory. The characters are too visionary and the incidents too remote from actual experience to awaken the sympathy and to sustain the interest of the reader.

"The central motive of *Laon and Cythna*," it has been truly said, "is surrounded by so radiant a photosphere of imagery and eloquence that it is difficult to fix our gaze upon it, blinded as we are by the excess of splendour."

Among the poems embodying Shelley's "passion for reforming mankind," the highest rank must unquestionably be assigned to his master-work, *Prometheus Unbound.* Prometheus, in Shelley's drama, is the idealized representative of Humanity, under its noblest aspect of heroic self-sacrifice. Jupiter is the incarnation of selfishness and oppression, under their various manifestations, including unjust legislation and other social evils, which impede the progress and development of the human race, and to which he attributed, in great measure, the wretchedness and misery which everywhere prevailed. Accordingly, with his fall, a new era is inaugurated, in which gentleness, virtue, wisdom, endurance, and undying hope shall prevail, and wherein, under their guidance, men shall attain to the perfection for which they were designed, and become like their glorious prototype,

> Good, great and joyous, beautiful and free.

The universe is represented as sympathizing with the emancipation of humanity. "The world, in which the action is supposed to move, rings with spirit voices; and what these spirits sing is melody more purged of mortal dross than any other poet's ear has caught, while listening to his own heart's song or to the rhythms of the world."

While thus embodying in immortal verse, his belief in the regeneration and perfectibility of man, Shelley was one of the first to recognize the importance of intellectual and spiritual agencies in accomplishing the emancipation and elevation of the masses. Accordingly, in his *Masque of Anarchy,* in reply to the question, What art thou, Freedom? he replies:

> Science and Poetry and Thought
> Are thy lamps; they make the lot
> Of the dwellers in a cot
> So serene they curse it not.

> Spirit, Patience, Gentleness,
> All that can adorn and bless
> Art thou; let deeds, not words express
> Thy exceeding loveliness.

Literary criticism being foreign to my purpose, and having already alluded to the serious blemishes by which the beauty of some portions of Shelley's poetry is marred, I shall not pursue the subject; nor shall I call attention to those painful aspects of his private life which the admirers of his genius cannot but deplore, and which may doubtless be in some measure attributed to the false notions respecting the relations of the sexes which characterized the ethical school to which he had attached himself. Having, moreover, dwelt at some length upon his longer poems, giving expression to his burning hopes for the regenera-

tion of mankind, I must pass over, with only a cursory notice, the numerous productions which represent other phases of his genius. Among these *The Cenci,* reflecting in its revolting subject the enduring antagonism between Good and Evil, embodied also in his *Prometheus Unbound,* bears witness to his power as a dramatist.

In *Alastor, or the Spirit of Solitude,* a poem "permeated by the personality of Shelley," he represents the universe as imbued with that spirit of ideal beauty, the vision of which had, in his boyhood, formed so memorable an epoch. In this noteworthy poem he portrays the enthusiastic lover of this visionary beauty, haunted for ever by the loveliness which, gleaming through material objects, ever eludes its votary, and who, yearning to assuage the thirst for sympathy, awakened by his own passionate dream, traverses the world in pursuit of his ideal, and failing to realize it, passes away, aimless and hopeless.

The underlying idea of the poem, which has been characterized as describing "the Nemesis of solitary souls," is thus expressed by his biographer: "Shelley, in *Alastor,* would rebuke the seeker for beauty and the seeker for truth, however high-minded, who attempts to exist without human sympathy, and he would rebuke the ever unsatisfied idealist in his own heart."

Very beautiful are the **"Lines written among the Euganean Hills"**; *The Sensitive Plant*; *Epipsychidion*; *Adonais,* and many other of Shelley's master-works; in my judgment, however, the palm must be accorded to his wonderful lyrics; his exquisite lines **"To a Skylark," "To Night,"** his **"Ode to the West Wind," "The Cloud,"** The Last Chorus of *Hellas,* and many others, which, for ethereal music and poetic fire, are unsurpassed in the wide range of English literature.

Thus, for all time, to the genuine lover of poetry, Shelley's master-works will be objects of enthusiastic admiration, while to the philanthropist he will be dear, in that, in a selfish and reactionary age, he cherished unswerving faith in the ultimate triumph of freedom, justice, truth and love, and with a prophet's fervour proclaimed the future reign of righteousness and peace.

His vision of a happier social state, based upon human brotherhood, and to be brought about by the gradual operation of moral causes, more especially through the sovereign and all-conquering agency of love; a vision embodied in magnificent poetry may perhaps be regarded as Shelley's chief contribution to the cause of human progress.

Arthur Symons   (essay date 1907)

SOURCE: "Shelley," in *The Atlantic Monthly,* Vol. 100, No. 3, September, 1907, pp. 347-56.

[Symons was a critic, poet, dramatist, short story writer, and editor who first gained notoriety in the 1890s as an English decadent. Eventually, he established himself as one of the most important critics of the modern era. Sy-

mons provided his English contemporaries with an appropriate vocabulary with which to define the aesthetic of symbolism in his book The Symbolist Movement in Literature *(1899); furthermore, he laid the foundation for much of modern poetic theory by discerning the importance of the symbol as a vehicle by which a "hitherto unknown reality was suddenly revealed." In the following essay, Symons provides an overview of the philosophy behind Shelley's verse.*]

"I have the vanity to write only for poetical minds," Shelley said to Trelawny, "and must be satisfied with few readers." "I am, and I desire to be, nothing," he wrote to Leigh Hunt, while urging him to "assume a station in modern literature which the universal voice of my contemporaries forbids me either to stoop or to aspire to." Yet he said also, "Nothing is more difficult and unwelcome than to write without a confidence of finding readers"; and, "It is impossible to compose except under the strong excitement of an assurance of finding sympathy in what you write." Of the books which he published during his lifetime, some were published without his name, some were suppressed at the very moment of publication. Only *The Cenci* went into a second edition. Without readers, he was without due recognition from the poets of his time. Byron was jealous, if we may believe Trelawny, but neither Keats nor Wordsworth nor Leigh Hunt nor Southey nor Landor seems ever to have considered him seriously as a rival. We must go to the enthusiastic unimportant Wilson, to find an adequate word of praise; for to Wilson "Mr. Shelley was a poet, almost in the very highest sense of that mysterious word." The general public hated him without reading him, and even his death did not raise him from oblivion. But Time has been on his side, and to-day the general reader, if you mention the word poet to him, thinks of Shelley.

It is only by reading contemporary writings and opinions in published letters of the time,—such as Southey's when he writes to Shelley, that the manner in which his powers for poetry "have been employed is such as to prevent me from feeling any desire to see more of productions so monstrous in their kind, and pernicious in their tendency,"—that we can, with a great effort, realize the aspect under which Shelley appeared to the people of his time. What seems to us abnormal in its innocence was to them abnormal in guilt; they imagined a revolution behind every invocation to liberty, and saw [William] Godwin charioted in the clouds of *Prometheus Unbound*. They saw nothing else there, and Shelley himself had moments when he thought that his mission was a prophet's rather than a poet's. All this, which would mean so little to-day, kept Shelley at that time from ever having an audience as a poet. England still feared thought, and still looked upon poetry as worth fearing.

No poet has defined his intentions in poetry more carefully than Shelley. "It is the business of the poet," he said, in the preface to *The Revolt of Islam,* "to communicate to others the pleasure and the enthusiasm arising out of those images and feelings in the vivid presence of which, within his own mind, consists at once his inspiration and his

reward." But, he says further, "I would only awaken the feelings, so that the reader should see the beauty of true virtue, and be incited to those enquiries which have led to my moral and political creed, and that of some of the subtlest intellects in the world." In the preface to *Prometheus Unbound* he says, "Didactic poetry is my abhorrence; nothing can be equally well expressed in prose that is not tedious and supererogatory in vein. My purpose has hitherto been simply to familiarize the highly refined imagination of the more select classes of poetical readers with beautiful idealisms of moral excellence." Writing to Godwin, he says, acutely, "My power consists in sympathy, and that part of the imagination which relates to sentiment and contemplation. . . . I am formed . . . to apprehend minute and remote distinctions of feeling, whether relative to external nature or the living beings which surround us, and to communicate the conceptions which result from considering either the moral or the material universe as a whole." And we are told by Mrs. Shelley that "he said that he deliberated at one time whether he should dedicate himself to poetry or metaphysics."

Shelley was born to be a poet, and his "passion for reforming the world," as well as what he fancied to be his turn for metaphysics, were both part of a temperament and intelligence perhaps more perfectly fitted for the actual production of poetry than those of any other poet. All his life Shelley was a dreamer; never a visionary. We imagine him, like his Asia on the pinnacle, saying,

> my brain
> Grows dizzy: see'st thou shapes within the
> mist?

The mist, to Shelley, was part of what he saw; he never saw anything, in life or art, except through a mist. Blake lived in a continual state of vision, Shelley in a continual state of hallucination. What Blake saw was what Shelley wanted to see; Blake never dreamed, but Shelley never wakened out of that shadow of a dream which was his life.

His poetry is indeed made out of his life; but what was his life to Shelley? The least visible part of his dreams. As the Fourth Spirit sings in *Prometheus Unbound,*—

> Nor seeks nor finds he mortal blisses,
> But feeds on the aërial kisses
> Of shapes that haunt thought's wilderness.

He lived with ardor among ideas, aspirations, and passions in which there was something at once irresponsible and abstract. He followed every impulse, without choice or restraint, with the abandonment of a leaf in the wind. "O lift me as a wave, a leaf, a cloud!" was his prayer to the west wind and to every influence. Circumstances meant so little to him that he was unconscious of the cruelty of change to sentiment, and thus of the extent of his cruelty to women. He aimed at moral perfection, but was really of a perfect æsthetic selfishness. He was full of pity and generosity, and desired the liberation and uplifting of humanity; but humanity was less real to him than his own witch of Atlas. He only touched human action and passion closely in a single one of his works; and he said of *The Cenci,* "I don't think much of it. My object was to see how I could succeed in describing passions I have never felt."

To Shelley the word love meant sympathy, and that word, in that sense, contains his whole life and creed. Is this not why he could say,—

> True love in this differs from gold and clay,
> That to divide is not to take away?

It is a love which is almost sexless, the love of an enthusiastic youth, or of his own hermaphrodite. He was so much of a sentimentalist that he could conceive of incest without repugnance, and be so innocently attracted by so many things which, to one more normally sexual, would have indicated perversity. Shelley is not perverse, but he is fascinated by every problem of evil, which draws him to contemplate it with a child's inquiring wonder of horror. No poet ever handled foulness and horror with such clean hands or so continually. The early novels are filled with tortures, the early poems profess to be the ravings of a hanged madwoman; *Alastor* dwells lingeringly on death, *Queen Mab* and *The Revolt of Islam* on blood and martyrdom; madness is the centre of **"Julian and Maddalo,"** and a dungeon of *Rosalind and Helen;* the first act of *Prometheus* celebrates an unearthly agony, and *The Cenci* is a mart and slaughter-house of souls and bodies; while a comic satire is made up wholly out of the imagery of the swine-trough. Shelley could touch pitch and be undefiled; he writes nobly of every horror; but what is curious is that he should so persistently seek his beauty in such blackness. That a law or tradition existed was enough for him to question it. He does so in the name of abstract liberty, but curiosity was part of his impulse. A new Adam in Eden, the serpent would have tempted him before Eve. He wanted to "root out the infamy" of every prohibition, and would have tasted the forbidden fruit without hunger.

> Shelley was born to be a poet, and his "passion for reforming the world," as well as what he fancied to be his turn for metaphysics, were both part of a temperament and intelligence perhaps more perfectly fitted for the actual production of poetry than those of any other poet.
>
> —*Arthur Symons*

And Shelley was the same from the beginning. In the notes to *Queen Mab* he lays down with immense seriousness the rules on which his life was really to be founded. "Constancy has nothing virtuous in itself," he tells us, "independently of the pleasure it confers, and partakes of the temporizing spirit of vice in proportion as it endures tamely moral defects of magnitude in the object of its indiscreet

choice." Again: "the connection of the sexes is so long sacred as it contributes to the comfort of both parties, and is naturally dissolved when its evils are greater than its benefits." This doctrine of "the comfort of both parties" was what Shelley always intended to carry out, and he probably supposed that it was always the fault of the "other party" when he failed to do so. Grave charges have been brought against him for his cruelty to women, and in particular to Harriet; and it is impossible to forgive him, as a reasonable man, for his abandonment of Harriet. But he was never at any time a reasonable man, and there was never a time when he was not under one form or another of hallucination. It was not that he was carried away irresistibly by a gross passion, it was that he had abandoned himself like a medium to a spiritual influence. A certain selfishness is the inevitable result of every absorption; and Shelley, in every new rapture, was dizzy with it, whether he listened to the skylark in the sky or to the voice of Mary calling to him from the next room. In life, as in poetry, he was the slave of every impulse, but a slave so faultlessly obedient that he mastered every impulse in achieving it, so that his life, which seems casual, was really what he chose to make it, and followed the logic of his being.

Shelley had intuition rather than instinct, and was moved by a sympathy of the affections rather than by passion. His way of falling into and out of love is a sign that his emotions were rapid and on the surface, not that they were deep or permanent. The scent or music of love came to him like a flower's or bird's speech; it went to his head, it did not seize on the heart in his body. It must have filled him with astonishment when Harriet drowned herself, and he could never have really understood that it was his fault. He lived the life of one of those unattached plants which float in water; he had no roots in the earth, and he did not see why anyone should take root there. His love for women seems never to have been sensuous, or at least to have been mostly a matter of sympathies and affinities; if other things followed, it seemed to him natural that they should, and he encouraged them with a kind of unconsciousness. Emilia Viviani, for whom he wrote the sacred love-song of the *Epipsychidion,* would have embarrassed him, I doubt not, if she had answered his invocation practically. He would have done his best for her, and, at the same time, for Mary.

Epipsychidion celebrates love with an icy ecstasy which is the very life-blood of Shelley's soul; there are moments, at the beginning and end, when its sympathy with love passes into the actual possession. But for the most part it is a declaration, not an affirmation; its love is sisterly, and can be divided; it says for once, exultingly and luxuriously and purely, the deepest thing that Shelley had to say, lets out the secret of his feminine or twy-fold soul, and is the epitaph of that Antigone with whom "some of us have in a prior existence been in love." Its only passion is for that intellectual beauty to which it is his greater hymn, and, with Emilia Viviani, he confessed to have been the Ixion of a cloud. "I think," he said in a letter, "one is always in love with something or other; the error, and I confess it is not easy for spirits cased in flesh and blood to avoid it, consists in seeking in a mortal image the likeness of what is, perhaps, eternal." In the poem he has done more than he meant to do, for it is the eternal beauty that it images for us, and no mortal lineaments. Just because it is without personal passion, because it is the worship of a shadow for a shadow, it has come to be this thing fearfully and wonderfully made, into which the mystical passion of Crashaw and the passionate casuistry of Donne seem to have passed as into a crucible:—

> Thou art the wine whose drunkenness is all
> We can desire, O Love!

and the draught is an elixir for all lovers.

That part of himself which Shelley did not put into *Epipsychidion* he put into *Adonais*. In that pageantry of sorrow, in which all temporal things mourn for the poet, and accept the consolation of eternity, there is more of personal confession, more of personal foreboding, than of grief for Keats, who is no less a cloud to him than Emilia Viviani, and whom indeed we know he did not in any sense properly appreciate, at his actual value. The subtlest beauty comes into it when he speaks of himself, "a pardlike spirit beautiful and swift," with that curious self-sympathy which remains not less abstract than his splendid and consoling Pantheism, which shows by figures a real faith in the truth and permanence of beauty. Shelley says of it and justly, "it is a highly wrought piece of art, and perhaps better, in point of composition, than anything I have written." The art is conscious, and recreates *Lycidas* with entire originality; but the vessel of ancient form carries a freshly lighted flame.

Shelley, when he died, left unfinished a splendid fragment, *The Triumph of Life* which, inspired by Petrarch, as *Adonais* was inspired by Milton, shows the deeper influence of Dante. It ends with an interrogation, that interrogation which he had always asked of life and was about to ask of death. He had wanted to die, that he might "solve the great mystery." His last poem comes to us with no solution, but breaks off as if he died before he could finish telling the secret which he was in the act of apprehending.

II

There are two kinds of imagination, that which embodies and that which disembodies. Shelley's is that which disembodies, filling mortal things with unearthly essences or veiling them with unearthly raiment. Wordsworth's imagination embodies, concentrating spirit into man, and nature into a wild flower. Shelley is never more himself than in the fantasy of **"The Witch of Atlas,"** which he wrote in three days, and which is a song in seventy-eight stanzas. It is a glittering cobweb, hung on the horns of the moon's crescent, and left to swing in the wind there. What Fletcher would have shown and withdrawn in a single glimpse of magic, Shelley calls up in a vast wizard landscape which he sets steadily before us. He is the enchanter, but he never mistakes the images which he calls up for realities. They are images to him, and there is always

between him and them the thin circle of the ring. In *Prometheus Unbound,* where he has made a mythology of his own by working on the stable foundation of a great myth of antiquity, his drama is a cloudy procession of phantoms, seen in a divine hallucination by a poet whose mind hovered always in that world

> where do inhabit
> The shadows of all forms that think and live
> Till death unite them, and they part no more;
> Dreams and the light imaginings of men,
> And all that faith creates or love desires,
> Terrible, strange, sublime and beauteous
> shapes.

The shapes hover, pause, and pass on unflagging wings. They are not symbols, they are not embodiments of powers and passions; they are shining or shadowy images of life and death, time and eternity; they are much more immaterial than judgment or mercy, than love or liberty; they are phantoms, "wrapped in sweet sounds as in bright veils," who pass, murmuring "intelligible words and music wild"; but their music comes from somewhere across the moon or under the sea, and their words are without human passion. The liberty which comes to Prometheus is a liberty to dream forever with Asia in a cave; the love which sets free the earth is, like the music, extralunar; this new paradise is a heaven made only for one who is, like Shelley,

> the Spirit of wind
> With lightning eyes, and eager breath, and
> feet
> Disturbing not the drifted snow.

The imagination which built this splendid palace out of clouds, of sunset and sunrise, out of air, water, and fire, has unbodied the human likeness in every element, and made the spirit of the earth itself only a melodious voice, "the delicate spirit" of an eternal cloud, "guiding the earth through heaven." When the "universal sound like wings" is heard, and Demogorgon affirms the final triumph of good, it is to an earth dying like a drop of dew and to a moon shaken like a leaf. And we are left "dizzy as with delight," to rise, like Panthea,

> as from a bath of sparkling water,
> A bath of azure light, among dark rocks,
> Out of the stream of sound.

It was among these forms of imagination,—

> Desires and adorations,
> Winged Persuasions and veiled Destinies,
> Splendours, and Glooms, and glimmering Incarnations
> Of hopes and fears, and twilight Phantasies,—

as he sees them in *Adonais,* that Shelley most loved to walk; but when we come to what Browning calls "the unrivalled *Cenci,"* we are in another atmosphere, and in this atmosphere, not his own, he walks with equal certainty. In the preface to *The Cenci* Shelley defines in a perfect image the quality of dramatic imagination. "Imagination," he says, "is as the immortal God which should assume flesh for the redemption of mortal passion." And, in the dedication, he distinguishes it from his earlier works, "visions which impersonate my own apprehensions of the beautiful and the just." *The Cenci* is the greatest play written in English since *The Duchess of Malfy*, but, in the work of Shelley, it is an episode, an aside, or, as he puts it in his curious phrase, "a work of art." **"Julian and Maddalo"** is not less a work of art, and, for Shelley, an exception. In **"Julian and Maddalo"** and in the *Letter to Maria Gisburne* he has solved the problem of the poem which shall be conventional speech and yet pure poetry. It is astonishing to think that **"Julian and Maddalo"** was written within a year of *Rosalind and Helen*. The one is Byron and water, but the other is Byron and fire. It has set the pattern of the modern poem, and it was probably more difficult for him to do than to write **Prometheus Unbound**. He went straight on from the one to the other, and was probably unconscious quite how much he had done. Was it that a subject, within his personal interests and yet of deep significance, came to him from his visit to Byron at Venice, his study of Byron's mind there, which, as we know, possessed, seemed to overweigh, him? Shelley required no impetus, but he required weight. Just as the subject of **Prometheus Unbound,** an existing myth into which he could read the symbol of his own faith, gave him that definite unshifting substance which he required, and could not invent, so, no doubt, this actual substance in **"Julian and Maddalo"** and the haunting historic substance of *The Cenci* possessed him, drawing him down out of the air, and imprisoning him among human fortunes. There is no doctrine and no fantasy in either, but imagination speaking human speech.

And yet, as Browning has pointed out, though **Prometheus, Epipsychidion,** and the lyrics are "the less organized matter," the "radiant elemental foam and solution" of Shelley's genius, it is precisely in these, and not in any of the more human works, that we must look for the real Shelley. In them it is he himself who is speaking, in that "voice which is contagion to the world." The others he made, supremely well; but these he was.

What he made he made so well because he was so complete a man of letters, in a sense in which no other of his contemporaries was. Wordsworth, when he turned aside from his path, wandered helplessly astray. Byron was so helplessly himself that when he wrote plays he wrote them precisely in the manner which Shelley rightly protested that he himself had not: "under a thin veil converting names and actions into cold impersonations of his own mind." But Shelley could make no such mistake in form. It may be doubted whether the drama of real life would ever have become his natural medium; but, having set himself to write such a drama, he accepted the laws or limitations of the form to the extent of saying, "I have avoided with great care, in writing this play, the introduction of what is commonly called mere poetry." In so doing he produced a masterpiece, but knew himself too well to repeat it.

And he does not less adequately whatever he touches. Shelley had no genius for fun or caricature, but in **Swellfoot the Tyrant,** in **Peter Bell the Third,** he develops a satirical joke with exquisite literary skill. Their main value is to show how well he could do the things for which he had no aptitude. **The Mask of Anarchy** is scarcely more important as a whole, though more poignant in detail. It was done for an occasion, and remains, not as an utterance, but for its temper of poetic eloquence. Even **Hellas,** which he called "a mere improvise," and which was written out of a sudden political enthusiasm, is remembered, not for its "figures of indistinct and visionary delineation," but for its "flowery and starry" choruses. Yet not one of the four was written for the sake of writing a piece of literature; each contains a condemnation, a dogma, or a doctrine.

To Shelley doctrine was a part of poetry; but then, to him doctrine was itself the voice of ecstasy. He was in love not only with love, but with wisdom; and as he wished everyone to be good and happy, he was full of magics and panaceas, Demogorgons or Godwins, which would rejuvenate or redeem the world. There was always something either spiritual or moral in his idea of beauty; he never conceived of æsthetics as a thing apart from ethics; and even in his descriptions he is so anxious to give us the feeling before the details, that the details are as likely as not to go out in a rosy mist.

There are pictures in Shelley which remind us of Turner's. Pure light breaks into all its colors and floods the world, which may be earth or sea or sky, but is, above all, rapture of color. He has few twilights but many dawns; and he loves autumn for its wild breath and broken colors. Fire he plays with, but air and water are his elements; thoughts of drowning are in all his work, always with a sense of strange luxury. He has, more than any poet, Turner's atmosphere; yet seems rarely, like Turner, to paint for atmosphere. It is part of his habitual hallucination; it comes to him with his vision or message, clothing it.

He loved liberty and justice with an impersonal passion, and would have been a martyr for many ideals which were no more to him than the substance itself of enthusiasm. He went about the world, desiring universal sympathy, to suffer delicious and poignant thrills of the soul, and to be at once sad and happy. In his feeling for nature he has the same vague affection and indistinguishing embrace as in his feeling for humanity; the daisy, which was the eye of day to Chaucer, is not visible as a speck in Shelley's wide landscapes; and though in one of his subtlest poems he has noticed "the slow soft toads out of damp corners creep," he is not minutely observant of whatever is not in some way strange or unusual. Even his significant phrase about "the worm beneath the sod" is only meant as a figure of the brain. His chief nature poem, **"The Skylark,"** loses the bird in the air, and only realizes a voice, an "unbodied joy"; and *The Sensitive Plant* is a fairy, and the radiant illustration of "a modest creed."

III

In a minute study of the details of Shelley's philosophy, Mr. Yeats has reminded us, "in ancient times, it seems to me that Blake, who for all his protest was glad to be alive, and ever spoke of his gladness, would have worshipped in some chapel of the Sun, and that Keats, who accepted life gladly, though 'with a delicious, diligent indolence,' would have worshipped in some chapel of the Moon, but that Shelley, who hated life because he sought 'more in life than any understood,' would have wandered, lost in a ceaseless reverie, in some chapel of the Star of infinite desire." Is not Shelley's whole philosophy contained in that one line, "the desire of the moth for the star"? He desired impossible things, and his whole theory of a re-organization of the world, in which anarchy was to be a spiritual deliverer, was a dream of that golden age which all mythologies put in the past. It was not the Christian's dream of heaven, nor the Buddhist's of Nirvana, but a poetical conception of a perfected world, in which innocence was lawless, and liberty selfless and love boundless, and in which all was order and beauty, as in a lovely song or stanza, or the musical answering of line and line in drama. He wrote himself down an atheist, and Browning thinks that in heart he was always really a Christian, so unlimited were his ideals, so imaginary his paradises. When Shelley thought he was planning the reform of the world, he was making literature, and this is shown partly by the fact that no theory or outcry or enthusiasm is ever strong enough to breathe through the form which carries it like a light in a crystal.

The spirit of Shelley will indeed always be a light to every seeker after the things that are outside the world. He found nothing, he did not even name a new star. There is little actual wisdom in his pages, and his beauty is not always a very vital kind of truth. He is a bird on the sea, a sea-bird, a winged diver, swift and exquisite in flight, an inhabitant of land, water, and sky; and to watch him is to be filled with joy, to forget all mean and trivial things, to share a rapture. Shelley teaches us nothing, leads us nowhere, but cries and flies round us like a sea-bird.

Shelley is the only poet who is really vague, and he gets some of his music out of that quality of the air. Poetry, to him, was an instinctive utterance of delight, and it recorded his lightest or deepest mood with equal sensitiveness. He is an unconscious creator of joy, and the mood most frequent with him is the joy of sadness. His poetry, more than that of any poet, is the poetry of the soul, and nothing in his poetry reminds us that he had a body at all, except as a nerve sensitive to light, color, music, and perfume. His happiness is

> To nurse the image of unfelt caresses
> Till dim imagination just possesses
> The half-created shadow,

and to come no nearer to reality. Poetry was his atmosphere, he drew his breath in it as in his native element. Because he is the one perfect illustration of the poetic nature, as that nature is generally conceived, he has some-

times been wrongly taken to be the greatest of poets. His greatness may be questioned, not his authenticity.

Shelley could not write unpoetically. Wordsworth, who is not more possessed than Shelley with ideas of instruction, moral reformation, and the like, drops constantly out of poetry into prose; Shelley never does. Not only verse but poetry came to him so naturally that he could not keep it out, and the least fragment he wrote has poetry in it. Compare him, not only with Wordsworth, but with Keats, Coleridge, Byron, Landor, with every poet of his period, and you will find that while others may excel him in almost every separate poetical quality, none comes near him in this constant level of general poetical excellence.

Is it an excellence or an acquirement? No doubt it was partly technique, the technique of the born executant. It is too often forgotten that technique, like talent, must be born, not made, if it is to do great work. Shelley could not help writing well, whatever he wrote; he was born to write. He was the one perfectly equipped man of letters of his circle, and he added that accomplishment to his genius as a poet. There was nothing he could not do with verse as a form, and his translations from Greek, from Spanish, or from German, are not less sensitive to the forms which he adapted. He had a sound and wide literary culture, and, with curious lack of knowledge, a generalized appreciation of art. He wrote a *Defence of Poetry* which goes far beyond Sidney's and is the most just and noble eulogy of poetry that exists. His letters have grace and facility, and when Matthew Arnold made his foolish joke about his prose being better than his verse (which is as untrue as to say that Milton's prose was better than his verse), he was no doubt rightly conscious that Shelley might have expressed in prose much of the actual contents of his poetry. What would have been lost is the rarest part of it, in its creation of imaginative beauty. It is that rare part, that atmosphere which belongs to a region beyond technique, which, more certainly than even his technique, was what never left him, what made it impossible for him to write unpoetically.

No poetry is more sincere than Shelley's, because his style is a radiant drapery clinging closely to the body which it covers. What he has to express may have little value or coherence, but it is the very breath of his being, or, it may be, the smoke of that breath. He says rightly, in one of his earliest prefaces, that he has imitated no one, "designing that even if what I have produced be worthless, it should still be properly my own." There is no poet, ancient or modern, whom he did not study; but, after the first boyish bewitchment by what was odd in Southey's *Thalaba,* and a casual influence here and there, soon shaken off, whatever came to him was transformed by his inner energy, and became his own. Every poem, whatever else it is, is a personal expression of feeling. There is no egoism of the passionate sort, Catullus's or Villon's; his own passions are almost impersonal to him, they turn to a poem in the mere act of giving voice to themselves. It is his sincerity that so often makes him superficial. Shelley is youth. Great ideas or deep emotions did not come to him, but warm ideas and eager emotions, and he put them straight into verse. You cannot imagine him elaborating a mood, carving it, as Keats does, on the marble flanks of his Grecian urn.

Shelley is the most spontaneous of poets, and one of the most careless among those who, unlike Byron, are artists. He sings naturally, without hesitation, liquidly, not always flawlessly. There is something in him above and below literature, something aside from it, a divine personal accident. His technique, in lyrics, is not to be compared with Coleridge's, but where Keats speaks he sings.

The blank verse of Shelley, at its best in *Prometheus Unbound,* has none of the sweetly broken music of Shakespeare or of the organ harmonies of Milton. It is a music of aërial eloquence, as if sounded by

> The small, clear, silver lute of the young
>   spirit
> That sits i' the morning star.

There is in it a thrilling music, rarer in liquid sound than that of any other poet, and chastened by all the severity that can clothe a spirit of fire and air, an Ariel loosed from Prospero. Can syllables turn to more delicate sound and perfume than in such lines as these:—

> When swift from the white Scythian wilder-
>   ness
> A wind swept forth wrinkling the Earth with
>   frost:
> I looked and all the blossoms were blown
>   down.

If words can breathe, can they breathe a purer breath than in these strange and simple lines in which every consonant and every vowel have obeyed some learned spell unconscious of its witchcraft? Horror puts on all the daintiness of beauty, losing none of its own essence, as when we read how

> foodless toads
> Within voluptuous chambers panting crawled.

And out of this "music of lyres and flutes" there rises a symphony of many instruments, a choral symphony, after which no other music sounds for a time musical. Nor is it only for its music—

> Clear, silver, icy, keen, awakening tones
> Which pierce the sense and live within the
>   soul—

that this blank verse has its power over us. It has an illumined gravity, a shining crystal clearness, a luminous motion, with, in its ample tide, an "ocean-like enchantment of strong sound," and a measure and order as of the paces of the boundless and cadenced sea.

But it is, after all, for his lyrics that Shelley is best remembered, and it is perhaps in them that he is at his best. He wrote no good lyrical verse, except a few stanzas, before the age of twenty-three, when he wrote the song beginning, "The cold earth slept below," in which we find, but for a certain concentration, all the poetic and artistic qualities of "A widow bird sat mourning on a bough," which belongs to the last year of his life. In the summer of the year 1816, he wrote the **"Hymn to Intellectual Beauty,"** and had nothing more to learn. In a letter to Keats he said, "in poetry I have sought to avoid system and mannerism," and in the lyrical work written during the six remaining years of his life there will be found a greater variety, a more easily and continually inventive genius, than in the lyrical work of any other English poet. This faculty which came to him without warning, like an awakening, never flags, and it is only for personal, not for artistic reasons, that it ever exercises itself without a continual enchantment. There are, among these supreme lyrics, which no one but Shelley could have either conceived or written, others, here and there, in which the sentimentalist which was in Shelley the man improvises in verse as Thomas Moore would have improvised if he could. He could not; but to compare with his best lyrics a lyric of Shelley's such as, "The keen stars were twinkling," is to realize how narrow, as well as how impassable, is the gulf between what is not, and what just is, poetry. In the clamorous splendor of the odes there is sometimes rhetoric as well as poetry, but is it more than the tumult and overflow of that poetry? For spiritual energy the **"Ode to the West Wind,"** for untamable choric rapture the **"Hymn to Pan,"** for soft brilliance of color and radiant light the **"Lines written among the Euganean Hills,"** are not less incomparable than the rarest of the songs (such songs as **"To-Night,"** or **"The golden gates of sleep unbar,"** or **"When the lamp is shattered,"** or **"Swiftly walk over the western wave"**), in which the spirit of Fletcher seems returned to earth with a new magic from beyond the moon. And all this work, achieved by a craftsman as if for its own sake, will be found, if read chronologically, with its many fragments, to be in reality a sort of occasional diary. If ever a poet expressed himself fully in his verse, it was Shelley. There is nothing in his life which you will not find written somewhere in it, if only as "the ghost of a forgotten form of sleep." In this diary of lyrics he has noted down whatever most moved him, in a vivid record of the trace of every thrill or excitement, on nerves, or sense, or soul. From the stanzas, **"To Constantia singing,"** to the stanzas, **"With a guitar, to Jane,"** every woman who moved him will have her place in it; and everything that has moved him when, as he said in the preface to *The Revolt of Islam,* "I have sailed down mighty rivers, and seen the sun rise and set, and the stars come forth whilst I have sailed night and day down a rapid stream among mountains." This, no doubt, is his way of referring to the first and second travels abroad with Mary, and to the summer when he sailed up the Thames to its source,—the time of his awakening. And in all this, made day by day out of the very substance of its hours, there will not be a single poem in which the occasion will disturb or overpower the poetical impulse, in which the lyrical cry will be personal at the expense of the music. Or, if there is one such poem, it is that most intimate one which begins: "The serpent is shut out of Paradise." Is there, in this faultless capacity, this in-

On the inspiration Shelley drew from nature:

Such was [Shelley's] love for nature, that every page of his poetry is associated in the minds of his friends with the loveliest scenes of the countries which he inhabited. In early life he visited the most beautiful parts of this country and Ireland. Afterwards the Alps of Switzerland became his inspirers. *Prometheus Unbound* was written among the deserted and flower-grown ruins of Rome; and when he made his home under the Pisan hills, their roofless recesses harboured him as he composed **"The Witch of Atlas,"** *Adonais*, and *Hellas*. In the wild but beautiful Bay of Spezia, the winds and waves which he loved became his playmates. His days were chiefly spent on the water; the management of his boat, its alterations and improvements, were his principal occupation. At night, when the unclouded moon shone on the calm sea, he often went alone in his little shallop to the rocky caves that bordered it, and sitting beneath their shelter wrote *The Triumph of Life*, the last of his productions. The beauty but strangeness of this lonely place, the refined pleasure which he felt in the companionship of a few selected friends, our entire sequestration from the rest of the world, all contributed to render this period of his life one of continued enjoyment. I am convinced that the two months we passed there were the happiest which he had ever known: his health even rapidly improved, and he was never better than when I last saw him, full of spirits and joy, embark for Leghorn, that he might there welcome Leigh Hunt to Italy. I was to have accompanied him, but illness confined me to my room, and thus put the seal on my misfortune. His vessel bore out of sight with a favourable wind, and I remained awaiting his return by the breakers of that sea which was about to engulf him.

Mary Shelley, in her "Preface to the Volume of Posthumous Poems," in The Poetical Works of Percy Bysshe Shelley, *Little, Brown and Company, 1862.*

evitable transposition of feeling into form, something lacking, some absent savor? Is there, in this evocation of the ghost of every thrill, the essence of life itself?

A. C. Bradley   (essay date 1908)

SOURCE: "Shelley's View of Poetry: A Lecture," in *The Albany Review*, Vol. 11, February, 1908, pp. 511-30.

[*In the following essay, which was originally presented as a lecture, Bradley comments on Shelley's adherence in his work to the poetics he set out in his essay* Defence of Poetry.]

The ideas of Wordsworth and of Coleridge about poetry have often been discussed and are familiar. Those of Shelley are much less so, and in his eloquent exposition of them there is a radiance which almost conceals them from many readers. I wish, at the cost of all the radiance,

to try to see them and show them rather more distinctly. Even if they had little value for the theory of poetry, they would still have much as material for that theory, since they allow us to see something of a poet's experience in conceiving and composing. And, in addition, they throw light on some of the chief characteristics of Shelley's own poetry.

His poems in their turn form one of the sources from which his ideas on poetry are to be gathered. We have also some remarks in his letters and in prose pieces not devoted to this subject. We have the prefaces to those of his works which he himself published. And lastly, we have the *Defence of Poetry*. This essay was written in reply to an attack on the poetry of the time by Shelley's friend Peacock,—not a favourable specimen of Peacock's writing. The *Defence*, we can see, was hurriedly composed, and it remains a fragment, being only the first of three projected parts. It contains a good deal of historical matter, highly interesting but too extensive to be considered here. Being polemical, it no doubt exaggerates such of Shelley's views as collided with those of his antagonist. But, besides being the only full expression of these views, it is the most mature, for it was written little more than a year before his death. It appears to owe very little either to Wordsworth's Prefaces or to Coleridge's *Biographia Literaria,* but there are a few reminiscences of Sidney's *Apology,* which Shelley had read just before he wrote his own *Defence;* and it shows, like much of his mature poetry, how deeply he was influenced by the more imaginative dialogues of Plato.

I

Any one familiar with the manner in which Shelley in his verse habitually represents the world could guess at his general view of poetry. The world to him is a melancholy place, a "dim vast vale of tears," illuminated in flashes by the light of a hidden but glorious power. Nor is this power, as that favourite metaphor would imply, wholly outside the world. It works within it as a soul contending with obstruction and striving to penetrate and transform the whole mass. And though the fulness of its glory is concealed, its nature is known in outline. It is the realised perfection of everything good and beautiful on earth; or, in other words, all such goodness and beauty is its partial manifestation. "All," I say: for the splendour of nature, the love of lovers, all affections and virtues, every good action and just law, the wisdom of philosophy, the creations of art, the truths deformed by superstitious religion, are equally operations or appearances of this hidden power. It is of the first importance for the understanding of Shelley to realise how strong in him is the sense and conviction of this unity in life: it is one of his Platonic traits. The Intellectual Beauty of his **"Hymn"** is absolutely the same thing as the Liberty of his **"Ode,"** the Great Spirit of Love that he invokes to bring freedom to Naples, the One which in *Adonaïs* he contrasts with the Many, the Spirit of Nature of *Queen Mab,* and the Vision of *Alastor* and *Epipsychidion*. The skylark of the famous stanzas is free from our sorrows, not because it is below them, but because, as an embodiment of that perfection, it knows the rapture of love without its satiety, and understands death as we cannot. The voice of the mountain, if a whole nation could hear it with the poet's ear, would "repeal large codes of fraud and woe"; it is the same voice as the reformer's and the martyr's. And in the far-off day when the "plastic stress" of this power has overcome the last resistance and is all in all, outward nature, which now suffers with man, will be redeemed with him, and man, in becoming politically free, will become also the perfect lover. Evidently, then, poetry, as the world now is, must be one of the voices of this power, or one tone of its voice. To use the language so dear to Shelley, it is the revelation of those eternal ideas which lie behind the many-coloured, ever-shifting veil that we call reality or life. Or rather, it is one such revelation among many.

When we turn to the *Defence of Poetry* we meet substantially the same view. There is indeed a certain change; for Shelley is now philosophising and writing prose. Thus we hear nothing at first of that perfect power at the heart of things, and Shelley begins by considering poetry as a creation rather than a revelation. But we soon find that this creation is no mere fancy; it represents "those forms which are common to universal nature and existence," and "a poem is the very image of life expressed in its eternal truth." We notice, further, that the more voluntary and conscious work of invention and execution is regarded as quite subordinate in the creative process. It is a process in which the mind, obedient to an influence which it does not understand and cannot control, is driven to produce images of perfection which rather form themselves in it than are formed by it. The greatest stress is laid on this influence or inspiration; and in the end we learn that the origin of the whole process lies in certain exceptional moments when visitations of thought and feeling, elevating and delightful beyond all expression, but always arising unforeseen and departing unbidden, reach the soul; that these are, as it were, the interpenetration of a diviner nature through our own; and that the province of the poet is to arrest these apparitions, to veil them in language, to colour every other form he touches with their evanescent hues, and so to "redeem from decay the visitations of the divinity in man."

Even more decided is the emphasis laid on the unity of all the forms in which the ideal appears. Indeed, throughout a large part of the essay, that "Poetry" which Shelley is defending is something very much wider than poetry in the usual sense. He is attacking the notion that poetry and its influence steadily decline as civilisation advances, and

Shelley's last home, Casa Magni, on the Bay of San Terenzo, near Lerici.

that they are giving place, and ought to give place, to reasoning and the pursuit of utility. And he maintains, on the contrary, that imagination was, is, and always will be, the prime source of everything that has intrinsic value in life. Reasoning, he declares, cannot create, it can only operate upon the products of imagination; and, further, the predominance of mere reasoning and mere utility has become in great part an evil; for while it has deluged us with material goods and moral truths, we distribute the goods iniquitously and fail to apply the truths, because, for want of imagination, we have not sympathy in our hearts and do not feel what we know. In defending poetry, therefore, he means to defend not merely literature in verse, but whatever prose writing is allied to it in substance and form; all the other fine arts; and, in addition, all actions, inventions, institutions, and even ideas and moral dispositions, which imagination brings into being in its effort to satisfy the longing for perfection. Painters and musicians are poets. Plato and Bacon, even Herodotus and Livy, were poets, however large may be the part of their works which is not poetry. So were the men who invented the arts of life, constructed laws for tribes or cities, disclosed, as sages or founders of religion, the excellence of justice and love. And every one, Shelley would say, who, perceiving the beauty of an imagined virtue or deed, translates the image into a fact, is so far a poet. For all these things come from imagination.

Shelley's exposition of this, which is probably the most original part of his theory, is not very clear; but, if I understand his meaning, that which he takes to happen in all these cases might be thus described. The imagination—that is to say, the soul imagining—has before it, or feels within it, something which, answering perfectly to the soul's nature, fills it with delight and a desire to realise what delights it. This something, for want of a better name, we may call an idea, though it is *not* a fully conscious idea. The reason why these ideas thus delight the imagining soul is that they are, in fact, images or forebodings of its own perfection—of itself become perfect, in one aspect or another. These aspects are as various as the elements and forms of its own inner life and outward existence; and so the idea may be that of the perfect harmony of will and feeling (a virtue), or of the perfect union of soul with soul (love), or of the perfect order of certain social relations or forces (a law or institution), or of the perfect adjustment of intellectual elements (a truth); and so on. The formation and expression of any such idea is thus the work of Poetry in the widest sense; while at the same time (as we must add, to complete Shelley's thought) any such idea is a gleam or apparition of the perfect Intellectual Beauty.

I choose this particular title of the hidden power in order to point out (what the reader is left to observe for himself) that the imaginative idea is always regarded by Shelley as beautiful. It is an end in itself, not a mere means; it is immediately attractive; and it has the formal characters of beauty. For, as will have been noticed in the instances given, it is always the image of an order, or harmony, or unity in variety, of the elements concerned. Shelley sometimes even speaks of their "rhythm." For example, he uses this word in reference to an action; and I quote the pas-

sage because, though it occurs at some distance from the exposition of his main view, it illustrates it well. He is saying that the true poetry of Rome, unlike that of Greece, did not fully express itself in poems. "The true poetry of Rome lived in its institutions: for whatever of beautiful, true and majestic they contained, could have sprung only from the faculty which creates the order in which they consist. The life of Camillus; the death of Regulus; the expectation of the senators, in their god-like state, of the victorious Gauls; the refusal of the Republic to make peace with Hannibal after the battle of Cannæ"—these he describes as "a rhythm and order in the shows of life," an order not arranged with a view to utility or outward result, but due to the imagination, which, "beholding the beauty of this order, created it out of itself according to its own idea."

II

If this, then, is the nature of Poetry in the widest sense, how does the poet, in the special sense, differ from other unusually creative souls? Not essentially in the inspiration and general substance of his poetry, but in the kind of expression he gives to them. In so far as he is a poet, his medium of expression, of course, is not virtue, or action, or law; poetry is one of the arts. And again, it differs from the rest, because its particular vehicle is language. We have now to see, therefore, what Shelley has to say of the form of poetry, and especially of poetic language.

First, he claims for language the highest place among the vehicles of artistic expression, on the ground that it is the most direct and also the most plastic. It is itself produced by imagination instead of being simply encountered by it, and it has no relation except to imagination; whereas any more material medium has a nature of its own, and relations to other things in the material world, and this nature and these relations intervene between the artist's conception and his expression of it in the medium. It is to the superiority of its vehicle that Shelley attributes the greater fame which poetry has always enjoyed as compared with other arts. He forgets (if I may interpose a word of criticism) that the media of the other arts have, on their side, certain advantages over language, and that these perhaps counterbalance the inferiority which he notices. He would also have found it difficult to show that language, on its physical side, is any more a product of imagination than stone or pigments. And his idea that the medium in the other arts is an obstacle intervening between conception and expression is, to say the least, one-sided. A sculptor, painter, or musician, would probably reply that it is only the qualities of his medium that enable him to express at all; that what he expresses is inseparable from the vehicle of expression; and that he has no conceptions which are not from the beginning sculpturesque, pictorial, or musical. It is true, no doubt, that the medium is an obstacle as well as a medium; but this is also true of language.

But to resume. Language, Shelley goes on to say, receives in poetry a peculiar form. As it represents in its meaning a perfection which is always an order, harmony, or rhythm, so it itself, as so much sound, *is* an order, harmony, or rhythm. It is measured language, which is not the proper vehicle for the mere recital of facts or for mere reasoning. For Shelley, however, this measured language is not of necessity metrical. The order or measure may remain at the stage which it reaches in beautiful prose, like that of Plato, the melody of whose language, Shelley declares, is the most intense it is possible to conceive. It may again advance to metre; and metrical form, according to Shelley, is convenient, popular, and preferable, especially in poetry containing much action. But he will not have any new great poet tied down to it. It is not essential, while measure is absolutely so. For it is no mere accident of poetry that its language is measured, nor does a delight in this measure mean little. As sensitiveness to the order of the relations of sounds is always connected with sensitiveness to the order of the relations of thoughts, so also the harmony of the words is scarcely less indispensable than their meaning to the communication of the influence of poetry. "Hence," says Shelley, "the vanity of translation: it were as wise to cast a violet into a crucible that you might discover the formal principle of its colour and odour, as seek to transfuse from one language into another the creations of a poet." Strong words to come from the translator of the *Hymn to Mercury* and of Agathon's speech in the *Symposium*! And is not all that Shelley says of the difference between measured and unrhythmical language applicable, at least in some degree, to the difference between metrical and merely measured language? Could he really have supposed that metre is no more than a "convenience," which contributes nothing of any account to the influence of poetry? But I will not criticise. Let me rather point out how surprising, at first sight, and how significant, is Shelley's insistence on the importance of measure or rhythm. No one could assert more absolutely than he the identity of the general substance of poetry with that of moral life and action, of the other arts, and of the higher kinds of philosophy. And yet it would be difficult to go beyond the emphasis of his statement that the formal element (as he understood it) is indispensable to the effect of poetry.

Shelley, however, nowhere considers this element more at length. He has no discussions, like those of Wordsworth and Coleridge, on diction. He never says, with Keats, that he looks on fine phrases like a lover. We hear of his deep-drawn sigh of satisfaction as he finished reading a passage of Homer, but not of his shouting his delight as he ramped through the meadows of Spenser, at some marvellous flower. When in his letters he refers to any poem he is reading he scarcely ever mentions particular lines or expressions, and we have no evidence that, like Coleridge and Keats, he was a curious student of metrical effects or the relations of vowel-sounds. I doubt if all this is wholly accidental. Poetry was to him so essentially an effusion of aspiration, love and worship, that we can imagine his feeling it almost an impiety to break up its unity even for purposes of study, and to give a separate attention to its means of utterance. And what he does say on the subject confirms this impression. In the first place, as I have mentioned, he lays great stress on inspiration; and his statements, if exaggerated and misleading, must reflect in some measure his own experience. No poem, however

inspired, is, he declares, more than a feeble shadow of the original conception; for when composition begins, inspiration is already on the decline. And so in a letter he speaks of the detail of execution destroying all wild and beautiful visions. Still, inspiration, if it declines, does not depart; and he appeals to the greatest poets of his day whether it is not an error to assert that the finest passages of poetry are produced by labour and study. These have their place only in the parts which form a connection between the inspired passages, and he speaks with contempt of the fifty-six various readings of the first line of the *Orlando Furioso*. He seems to exaggerate on this matter because in the *Defence* his foe is cold reason and calculation. In other places he writes more truly of the original conception as being obscure as well as intense; from which it would seem to follow that the feeble shadow, if darker, is at least more distinct than the original. He forgets, too, what is certainly the fact, that the poet in reshaping and revising is able to reawaken in some degree the inspiration of the first impulse. And we know from himself that his greatest works cost him a severe labour not confined to the execution, while his manuscripts show plenty of various readings, if never so many as fifty-six in one line.

Still, what he says is highly characteristic of his own practice in composition. He allowed the rush of his ideas to have its way, without pausing to complete a troublesome line or find a word that did not come; and the next day (if ever) he filled up the gaps and smoothed the ragged edges. And the result answers to his theory. Keats was right in telling him that he might be more of an artist. His language, indeed, unlike Wordsworth's or Byron's, is always that of a poet; we never hear his mere speaking voice; but he is frequently diffuse and obscure, and even in fine passages his constructions are sometimes trailing and amorphous. The glowing metal rushes into the mould so vehemently that it overleaps the bounds and fails to find its way into all the little crevices. But no poetry is more manifestly inspired, and even when it is plainly imperfect it is sometimes so inspired that it is impossible to wish it changed. It has the rapture of the mystic, and that is too rare to lose. Tennyson quaintly said of the hymn **"Life of Life"**: "He seems to go up into the air and burst." It is true: and, if we are to speak of poems as fireworks, I would not compare **"Life of Life"** with a great set piece of Homer or Shakespeare which illumines the whole sky; but, all the same, there is no more thrilling sight than the heavenward rush of a rocket, and it bursts at a height no other fire can reach.

In addition to his praise of inspiration Shelley has some scattered remarks on another point which show the same spirit. He could not bear in poetic style any approach to artifice, or any sign that the writer had a theory or system of style. He thought Keats's earlier poems faulty in this respect, and there is probably a reference to Wordsworth in the following sentence from the Preface to the **Revolt of Islam**: "Nor have I permitted any system relating to mere words to divert the attention of the reader, from whatever interest I may have succeeded in creating, to my own ingenuity in contriving,—to disgust him according to the rules of criticism. I have simply clothed my thoughts in what appeared to me the most obvious and appropriate language. A person familiar with nature, and with the most celebrated productions of the human mind, can scarcely err in following the instinct, with respect to selection of language, produced by that familiarity." His own poetic style certainly corresponds with his intention. It cannot give the kind of pleasure afforded by what may be called without disparagement a learned and artful style, such as Virgil's or Milton's; but, like the best writing of Shakespeare and Goethe, it is, with all its individuality, almost entirely free from mannerism and the other vices of self-consciousness, and appears to flow so directly from the thought that one is ashamed to admire it for itself. This is equally so whether the appropriate style is impassioned and highly figurative or simple and even plain. It is indeed in the latter case that Shelley wins his greatest, because most difficult, triumph. In the dialogue part of **"Julian and Maddalo"** he has succeeded remarkably in keeping the style quite close to that of familiar though serious conversation, while making it nevertheless unmistakably poetic. And the *Cenci* is an example of a success less complete only because the problem was even harder. The ideal of the style of tragic drama in the nineteenth or twentieth century should surely be, not to reproduce with modifications the style of Shakespeare, but to do what Shakespeare did—to idealise, without transforming, the language of contemporary speech. Shelley in the *Cenci* seems to me to have come nearest to this ideal.

III

So much for general exposition. If now we consider more closely what Shelley says of the substance of poetry, a question at once arises. He may seem to think of poetry solely as the direct expression of perfection in some form, and accordingly to think of its effect as simply joy or delighted aspiration. Much of his own poetry, too, is such an expression; and we understand when we find him saying that Homer embodied the ideal perfection of his age in human character, and unveiled in Achilles, Hector, and Ulysses "the truth and beauty of friendship, patriotism, and persevering devotion to an object." But poetry, it is obvious, is not wholly, perhaps not even mainly, of this kind. What is to be said, on Shelley's theory, of his own melancholy lyrics, those "sweetest songs" that "tell of saddest thought"? What of satire, or the epic of conflict and war, or of tragic exhibitions of violent and destructive passion? Does not his theory reflect the weakness of his own practice, his tendency to portray a thin and abstract ideal instead of interpreting the concrete detail of nature and life; and ought we not to oppose to it a theory which would consider poetry simply as a representation of fact?

To this last question I should answer No. Shelley's theory, rightly understood, will take in, I think, everything really poetic. And to a considerable extent he himself shows the way to meet these doubts. He did not mean that the *immediate* subject of poetry must be perfection in some form. The poet, he says, can colour with the hues of the ideal everything he touches. If so, he may write of absolutely anything so long as he *can* so colour it, and nothing would be excluded from his province except such things, if such

exist, in which no positive relation to the ideal, however indirect, can be shown or intimated. Thus, to take the instance of Shelley's melancholy lyrics, clearly the lament which arises from loss of the ideal, and mourns the evanescence of its visitations or the desolation of its absence, is indirectly an expression *of* the ideal; and so on. Shelley's theory is the simplest song of unhappy love or the simplest dirge. Further, he himself observes that, though the joy of poetry is often unalloyed, yet the pleasure of the "highest portions of our being is frequently connected with the pain of the inferior," that "the pleasure that is in sorrow is sweeter than the pleasure of pleasure itself," and that not sorrow only, but "terror, anguish, despair itself, are often the chosen expressions of an approximation to the highest good." That, then, which appeals poetically to such painful emotions will again be an indirect portrayal of the ideal; and it is clear, I think, that this was how Shelley in the *Defence* regarded heroic and tragic poetry, whether narrative or dramatic, with its manifestly imperfect characters and its exhibition of conflict and wild passion. He had, it is true, another and an unsatisfactory way of explaining the presence of these things in poetry; and I will refer to this in a moment. But he tells us that the Athenian tragedies represent the highest idealisms (his name for ideals) of passion and of power (not merely of virtue); and that in them we behold ourselves, "under a thin disguise of circumstance, stripped of all but that ideal perfection and energy which every one feels to be the internal type of all that he loves, admires, and would become." He writes of Milton's Satan in somewhat the same strain. The Shakespearean tragedy from which he most often quotes is one in which evil holds the stage, *Macbeth*; and he was inclined to think *King Lear,* which certainly is no direct portrait of perfection, the greatest drama in the world. Lastly, in the Preface to his own *Cenci* he truly says that the story is fearful and monstrous, but that "the poetry which exists in these tempestuous sufferings and crimes," if duly brought out, "mitigates the pain of the contemplation of moral deformity": so that he regards Count Cenci himself as a *poetic* character, and therefore as in *some* sense an expression of the ideal. He does not further explain his meaning. Perhaps it was that the perfection which poetry is to exhibit includes, together with those qualities which win our immediate and entire approval, others which are capable of becoming the instruments of evil. For these, the energy, power and passion of the soul, though they may be perverted, are in themselves elements of perfection; and so, even in their perversion or their combination with moral deformity, they retain their value, they are not simply ugly or horrible, but appeal through emotions predominantly painful to the same love of the ideal which is directly satisfied by pictures of goodness and beauty. Now to these various considerations we shall wish to add others; but if we bear these in mind, I believe we shall find Shelley's theory wide enough, and must hold that the substance of poetry is never *mere* fact, but is always ideal, though its method of representation is sometimes more direct, sometimes more indirect.

Nevertheless, he does not seem to have made his view quite clear to himself, or to hold to it consistently. We are left with the impression, not merely that he personally preferred the direct method (as he was, of course, entitled to do), but that his use of it shows a certain weakness, and also that even in theory he unconsciously tends to regard it as the primary and proper method, and to admit only by a reluctant after-thought the representation of imperfection. Let me point out some signs of this. He considered his own *Cenci* as a poem inferior in kind to his other main works, even as a sort of accommodation to the public. With all his modesty he knew what to think of the neglected *Prometheus* and *Adonaïs,* but there is no sign that he, any more than the world, was aware that the character of Cenci was a creation without a parallel in our poetry since the seventeenth century. His enthusiasm for some second-rate and third-rate Italian paintings, and his failure to understand Michael Angelo, seem to show the same tendency. He could not enjoy comedy: it seemed to him simply cruel: he did not perceive that to show the absurdity of the imperfect is to glorify the perfect. And, as I mentioned just now, he wavers in his view of the representation of heroic and tragic imperfection. We find in the Preface to *Prometheus Unbound* the strange notion that Prometheus is a more poetic character than Milton's Satan, because he is free from Satan's imperfections, which are said to interfere with the interest. And in the *Defence* a similar error appears. Achilles, Hector, Ulysses, though they exhibit ideal virtues, are, he admits, imperfect. Why, then, did Homer make them so? Because, he seems to reply, Homer's contemporaries regarded their vices (e.g. revengefulness and deceitfulness) as virtues. Homer accordingly had to conceal in the costume of these vices the unspotted beauty that he himself imagined; and, like Homer, "few poets of the highest class have chosen to exhibit the beauty of their conceptions in its naked truth and splendour." Now, this idea, to say nothing of its grotesque improbability in reference to Homer, and its probable baselessness in reference to most other poets, is quite inconsistent with that truer view of heroic and tragic character which was explained just now. It is an example of Shelley's tendency to abstract idealism or spurious Platonism. He is haunted by the fancy that if he could only get at the One, the eternal Idea, in complete aloofness from the Many, from life with all its change, decay, struggle, sorrow and evil, he would have reached the true object of poetry: as if the whole finite world were a mere mistake or illusion, the sheer opposite of the infinite One, and in no way or degree its manifestation. Life, he says—

> Life, like a dome of many-coloured glass,
> Stains the white radiance of eternity;

but the other side, the fact that the many colours *are* the white light broken, he tends to forget, by no means always, but in one, and that not the least inspired, of his moods. This is the source of that thinness and shallowness of which his view of the world and of history is justly accused, a view in which all imperfect being is apt to figure as absolutely gratuitous, and everything and everybody as pure white or pitch black. Hence also his ideals of good, whether as a character or as a mode of life, resting as they do on abstraction from the mass of real existence, tend to lack body and individuality; and indeed, if the existence of the many is a mere calamity, clearly the

next best thing to their disappearance is that they should all be exactly alike, and have as little character as possible. But we must remember that Shelley's strength and weakness are closely allied, and it may be that the very abstractness of his ideal was a condition of that quivering intensity of aspiration towards it in which Shelley's poetry is unequalled. We must not go for this to Homer and Shakespeare and Goethe; and if we go for it to Dante, we shall find, indeed, a mind far vaster than Shelley's, but that very dualism of which we complain in him, and the description of a heaven which, equally with Shelley's regenerated earth, is no place for mere mortality. In any case, as we have seen, although the weakness in his poetical practice occasionally appears also as a defect in his poetical theory, it is no necessary part of that theory.

IV

I pass to his views on a last point. If the business of poetry is somehow to express ideal perfection, it may seem to follow that the poet should embody in his poems his beliefs about this perfection and the way to approach it, and should thus have a moral purpose and aim to be a teacher. And in regard to Shelley this conclusion seems the more natural because his own poetry allows us to see clearly some of his beliefs about morality and moral progress. Yet alike in his Prefaces and in the *Defence* he takes up most decidedly the position that the poet ought neither to affect a moral aim nor to express his own conceptions of right and wrong. "Didactic poetry," he declares, "is my abhorrence: nothing can be equally well expressed in prose that is not tedious and supererogatory in verse." "There was little danger," he tells us, "that Homer or any of the eternal poets" should make a mistake in this matter; but "those in whom the poetical faculty, though great, is less intense, as Euripides, Lucan, Tasso, Spenser, have frequently affected a moral aim, and the effect of their poetry is diminished in exact proportion to the degree in which they compel us to advert to this purpose." These statements may appeal to us, but are they consistent with Shelley's main views of poetry? To answer this question we must observe what exactly it is that he means to condemn.

Shelley was one of the few persons who can literally be said to *love* their kind. He held most strongly, too, that poetry does benefit men, and benefits them morally. The moral purpose, then, to which he objects cannot well be a poet's general purpose of doing moral as well as other good through his poetry—such a purpose, I mean, as he may cherish when he contemplates his life and his life's work. And, indeed, it seems obvious that nobody with any humanity or any sense can object to that, except through some intellectual confusion. Nor does Shelley mean, I think, to condemn even the writing of a particular poem with a view to a particular moral or practical effect; certainly, at least, if this was his meaning he was condemning some of his own poetry. Again, he cannot be referring to the portrayal of moral ideals, for that he regarded as one of the main functions of poetry; and in the very place where he says that didactic poetry is his abhorrence he also says, by way of contrast, that he has tried to familiarise the minds of his readers with beautiful idealisms of moral excellence. It appears, therefore, that what he is really attacking is the attempt to give, in the strict sense, moral *instruction,* to communicate doctrines, to offer argumentative statements of opinion on right and wrong, and more especially, I think, on controversial questions of the day. An example would be Wordsworth's discourse on education at the end of the *Excursion,* a discourse of which Shelley, we know, had a very low opinion. In short, his enemy is not the purpose of producing a moral effect, it is the appeal made for this purpose to the reasoning intellect. In effect he says to the poet: By all means aim at bettering men; you are a man, and are bound to do so; but you are also a poet, and therefore your proper way of doing so is not by reasoning and preaching. His idea is of a piece with his general championship of imagination, and it is quite consistent with his main view of poetry.

What, then, are the *grounds* of this position? They are not clearly set out, but we can trace several, and they are all solid. Reasoning on moral subjects, moral philosophy, was by no means "tedious" to Shelley; it seldom is to real poets. He loved it, and (outside his *Defence*) he rated its value very high. But he thought it tedious and out of place in poetry, because it can be equally well expressed in "unmeasured" language—much better expressed, one may venture to add. You invent an art in order to effect by it a particular purpose which nothing else can effect as well. How foolish, then, to use this art for a purpose better served by something else! I know no answer to this argument, and its application is far wider than that given to it by Shelley. Secondly, Shelley remarks that a poet's own conceptions on moral subjects are usually those of his place and time, while the matter of his poem ought to be eternal, or, as we say, of permanent and universal interest. This, again, seems true, and has a wide application; and it holds good even when the poet, like Shelley himself, is in rebellion against orthodox moral opinion; for his heterodox opinions will equally show the marks of his place and time, and constitute a perishable element in his work. Doubtless no poetry can be without a perishable element; but that poetry has least of it which interprets life least through the medium of systematic and doctrinal ideas. The veil which time and place have hung between Homer and Shakespeare and the general reader of to-day is almost transparent, while even a poetry so intense as that of Dante and Milton is impeded in its passage to him by systems which may be unfamiliar, and, if familiar, may be distasteful.

Lastly—and this is Shelley's central argument—as poetry itself is due to imaginative inspiration and not to reasoning, so its true moral effect is produced through imagination and not through doctrine. Imagination is, for Shelley, "the great instrument of moral good." The "secret of morals is love." It is not "for want of admirable doctrines that men hate and despise and censure and deceive and subjugate one another": it is for want of love. And love is "a going out of our own nature, and an identification of ourselves with the beautiful which exists in thought, action or person not our own." "A man," therefore, "to be greatly good must imagine intensely and comprehensive-

ly." And poetry ministers to moral good, the effect, by acting on its cause, imagination. It strengthens imagination as exercise strengthens a limb, and so it indirectly promotes morality. It also fills the imagination with beautiful impersonations of all that we should wish to be. But moral reasoning does not act upon the cause, it only analyses the effect. And the poet has no right to be content to analyse what he ought indirectly to create. Here, again, in his eagerness, Shelley cuts his antitheses too clean, but the defect is easily made good, and the main argument is sound.

Limits of time will compel me to be guilty of the same fault in adding a consideration which is in the spirit of Shelley's. The chief moral effect claimed for poetry by Shelley is exerted, primarily, by imagination on the emotions; but there is another, exerted primarily through imagination on the understanding. Poetry is largely an interpretation of life; and, considering what life is, that must mean a moral interpretation. This, to have poetic value, must satisfy imagination; but we value it also (and, let me add, we value it *as poetry* the more) because it gives us knowledge, a wider comprehension, a new insight into ourselves and the world. Now, it may be held—and this view answers to a very general feeling among lovers of poetry now—that the most deep and original moral interpretation is not likely to be that which most shows a moral purpose or is most governed by reflective beliefs and opinions, and that as a rule we learn most from those who do not try to teach us, and whose opinions may even remain unknown to us: so that there is this weighty objection to the appearance of such purpose and opinions, that it tends to defeat its own intention. And the reason that I wish to suggest is this, that always we get most from the *genius* in a man of genius and not from the rest of him. Now, although poets often have unusual powers of reflective thought, the specific genius of a poet does not lie there, but in imagination. Therefore his deepest and most original interpretation is likely to come by the way of imagination. And the specific way of imagination is not to clothe in imagery consciously held ideas; it is to produce half-consciously a matter from which, when produced, the reader may extract ideas. Poetry (I must exaggerate to be clear), psychologically considered, is not the *expression* of ideas or of a view of life: it is their discovery or creation, or rather both discovery and creation in one. The interpretation contained in *Hamlet* or *King Lear* was not brought ready-made to the old stories. What was brought to them was the huge substance of Shakespeare's imagination, in which all his experience and thought was latent; and this, dwelling and working on the stories with nothing but a dramatic purpose, and kindling into heat and motion, gradually discovered or created in them a meaning and a mass of truth about life, which was brought to birth by the process of composition, but never preceded it in the shape of ideas, and probably never, even after it, took that shape to the poet's mind. And *this* is the interpretation which we find inexhaustibly instructive, because Shakespeare's *genius* is in it. On the other hand, however much from curiosity and personal feeling towards him we may wish to know his opinions and beliefs about morals or religion or his own poems or Queen Elizabeth, we have not really any reason to suppose that their value would prove extraordinary. And so, to apply this generally, the opinions, reasonings and beliefs of poets are seldom of the same quality as their purely imaginative product. Occasionally, as with Goethe, they are not far off it; but sometimes they are intense without being profound, and more eccentric than original; and often they are very sane and sound, but not very different from those of wise men without genius. And therefore poetry is not the place for them. For we want in poetry a moral interpretation, but not the interpretation we have already. As a rule the genuine artist's quarrel with "morality" in art is not really with morality, it is with a stereotyped or narrow morality; and when he refuses in his art to consider things from what he calls the moral point of view, his reasons are usually wrong, but his instinct is right.

Poetry itself confirms on the whole this contention, though doubtless in these last centuries a great poet's work will usually reveal more of conscious reflection than once it did. Homer and Shakespeare show no moral aim and no system of opinion. Milton was far from justifying the ways of God to men by the argumentation he put into divine and angelic lips; his truer moral insight is in the creations of his genius, e.g. the character of Satan or the picture of the glorious humanity of Adam and Eve. Goethe himself could never have told the world what he was going to express in the first part of *Faust*: the poem told *him,* and it is one of the world's greatest. He knew too well what he was going to express in the second part, and with all its wisdom and beauty it is scarcely a great poem. Wordsworth's original message was delivered, not when he was a Godwinian semi-atheist nor when he had subsided upon orthodoxy, but when his imagination, with a few hints from Coleridge, was creating a kind of natural religion; and this religion itself is more profoundly expressed in his descriptions of his experience than in his attempts to formulate it. The moral virtue of Tennyson is in poems like "Ulysses" and parts of "In Memoriam" where sorrow and the consciousness of a deathless affection or an unquenchable desire for experience forced an utterance; but he succeeded only partially when in the *Idylls* he tried to found a great poem on explicit ideas about the soul and the ravages wrought in it by lawless passion, because these ideas, however sound, were no product of his genius; and so the moral virtue of Shelley's poetry lay, not in his doctrines about the past and future of man, but in an intuition, which was the substance of his soul, of the unique value of love. In the end, for him, the truest name of that perfection called Intellectual Beauty, Liberty, Spirit of Nature, is Love. Whatever in the world has any worth is an expression of Love. Love sometimes talks. Love talking musically is Poetry.

L. Winstanley   (essay date 1913)

SOURCE: "Platonism in Shelley," in *Essays and Studies by Members of the English Association,* Vol. 4, 1913, pp. 72-100.

[*In the following excerpt, Winstanley discusses the Platonic elements in Shelley's works.*]

Shelley was by nature one of the most studious of all English poets; from his Oxford days onwards Greek was his favourite reading and for Plato he had a natural affinity of mind. Hogg says of him:

> It is no exaggeration to affirm that, out of the twenty-four hours, he frequently read sixteen. . . . Few were aware of the extent and still fewer of the profundity of his reading; in his short life and without ostentation he had in truth read more Greek than many an aged pedant. . . . A pocket edition of Plato, of Plutarch, of Euripides, without interpretation or notes . . . was his ordinary companion, and he read the text straightforward for hours.

Shelley's intellectual attitude and development can be best understood if we remember that he found his sustenance mainly in two types of authors; in the Materialist writers who prepared the way for the French Revolution—D'Alembert, Helvétius, Voltaire, Cabanis, &c.,—and in the Greek tragedians and Plato.

There is, of course, an enormous difference between the scientific agnosticism of the eighteenth century and the idealism of Plato; in his youth Shelley does not seem to have been able to choose between the two systems; in *Queen Mab,* for instance, Voltairean scepticism and Platonic idealism lie side by side in curious incongruity, and Shelley seems unaware of the extreme self-contradictions involved in his thought. As he advances in life, however, he becomes more and more a Platonist; in the revised version of *Queen Mab* entitled **'The Daemon of the World'**, the thought is purely Platonic, and scientific materialism, always alien to his true temper, became by degrees impossible to him; in the year of his death he wrote: 'The doctrines of the French and material philosophy are as false as they are pernicious.'

None the less, in certain respects, Shelley's revolutionary theories and his Platonism were not at all antagonistic: it should not be forgotten that the thinkers who brought about the French Revolution, indeed the very members of the *Tiers État* themselves, found their inspiration very largely in the institutions of Greece and Rome, were always quoting classical authors, even those but little known to-day, and followed or tried to follow Greek and Roman ideals of society, while the French Revolution itself was the most striking attempt ever recorded in history to re-model a great and important state on a philosophic basis; the French Revolution might almost have been defined as an attempt to turn from a feudal constitution of society to a classical one. The very thoroughness with which the process of reconstruction was attempted suggests to us such schemes as that of Plato's *Republic,* which hardly differed from existing Hellenic states (i.e. Sparta) more than the new France, desired and partly achieved by the revolutionaries, differed from the France of the preceding centuries.

Modern critics are often alienated from Shelley by what appears to them the wildness of his social and ethical speculations, but they should remember that, in the poet's era, speculations no less remarkable had been made the very foundation of vast social experiments. Again, many readers are exasperated by Shelley's daring departures from accepted conventions on the subject of sex, and are inclined in consequence to accuse him of being, in all such matters, mentally morbid and unsound. They do not remember that Shelley is the disciple of the thinker who was, above all others, most daring in such speculations; Shelley's innovations, excepting only in *The Revolt of Islam,* are unimportant compared with the audacity of the *Republic* and the *Symposium.* Plato, indeed, is remarkable among philosophers for his union of moral and ethical fineness with extreme daring in moral speculation, and this union is just as characteristic of the disciple Shelley as it is of the master.

We may perhaps divide the ideas which Shelley borrows from Plato into four main groups: (1) General religious and philosophical ideas; (2) Cosmic speculations; (3) Social and political ideas; (4) The theory of love.

In dealing with the first group it becomes at once evident that Shelley's religious system is, speaking generally, rather Greek and Platonic than Christian or Biblical. Shelley was one of those to whom the Hebraic ideal appears naturally repugnant, his antipathy to it being as innate as Milton's sympathy. He disliked narrow-mindedness and exclusiveness, he disliked all kinds of formalism, he had the Greek detestation of priestcraft, severity of all kinds he abhorred and severity in morals appeared to him a contradiction in terms; the Jehovah of the Bible he not merely repudiates as an object of worship, he goes much further, and takes Jehovah as a supreme example of the worst type of moral evil. In *Queen Mab* he says of the temple at Jerusalem, in language whose anger has robbed it of all semblance of poetry:

> There an inhuman and uncultured race
> Howled hideous praises to their Demon-God;
> . . . . . their victorious arms
> Left not a soul to breathe. Oh! they were fiends:
> But what was he who taught them that the God
> Of nature and benevolence hath given
> A special sanction to the trade of blood?
> His name and theirs are fading, and the tales,
> Of this barbarian nation, which imposture
> Recites till terror credits, are pursuing
>   Itself into forgetfulness.

In *Prometheus Unbound* Jupiter symbolizes all these religions of fear and terror which, originally given power by the mind of man (Prometheus) now tyrannize over and torture it, and the faith of the Bible is eminent among them; it is probably that

> Dark yet mighty faith, a power as wide
> As is the world it wasted.

Shelley had no more sympathy with modern Hebraism than with ancient Hebraism. He loved Milton, since Milton was a Republican and a daring speculator in morals, but he declares [in *Defence of Poetry*]: 'Milton's Devil as a moral being is as far superior to his God as one who perseveres in some purpose which he has conceived to be excellent in spite of adversity and torture, is to one who in the cold security of undoubted triumph inflicts the most horrible revenge upon his enemy, not from any mistaken notion of inducing him to repent of a perseverance in enmity, but with the alleged design of exasperating him to deserve new torments.'

Nor was this all! Shelley not only disliked Hebraism but— a much more serious loss—he was bitterly opposed to Christianity. There may have been nothing of the ancient Hebrew in his temperament, but there was certainly a great deal of the Christian, for he has many affinities even with St. Francis. But the school of thinkers whom Shelley so greatly admired—those of the Voltairean tradition—were opposed, quite inevitably, to historical Christianity. 'Let us not forget', says Lord Morley, 'that what Catholicism was accomplishing in France in the first half of the eighteenth century, was really not anything less momentous than the slow strangling of French civilization.' Their motto of *'Écrasez l'infâme'* was, under the circumstances, unescapable. Shelley inherited from them this abhorrence: historical Christianity is to him always detestable. In *Prometheus Unbound* he carefully distinguishes between the character of Christ, the most nobly beautiful that has ever appeared upon earth, and the horrible superstition which has perverted his teaching into one of the worst agents of evil.

> One came forth of gentle worth
> Smiling on the sanguine earth;
> His words outlived him, like swift poison
> Withering up truth, peace, and pity,
> . . . Hark that outcry of despair!
> 'Tis his mild and gentle ghost
> Wailing for the faith he kindled.

It was in this sense no doubt—because he hated established religions—that Shelley called himself an atheist, but the whole structure of his mind was essentially religious. His religion was, however, Platonic both in its excellences and in what some might term its defects. Shelley like Plato believes in a supreme Power; it is beyond and above the world but also within, at once immanent and transcendent; it works from within the world, struggling with the obstructions of matter, transforming matter and moulding it to Its will. Like Plato, Shelley is vividly conscious of the unity of the world and of all life, and the underlying spirit, though it reveals itself in many forms, is everywhere and essentially the same. Plato contemplates it sometimes as the One in distinction to the many, sometimes as the supreme Good rising above all lesser goods, sometimes as the supreme Wisdom, sometimes as the supreme Beauty above all lesser beauties. Shelley too celebrates this spirit in many different ways. With him also it is the One in contradistinction to the many:

> The One remains, the many change and pass.
> [*Adonais.*]

It is immanent in the world and yet transcendent; it is that Power

Which wields the world with never-wearied Love
Sustains it from beneath and kindles it above.

In the very language of the *Symposium* Shelley describes it as the forming and formative spirit which compels matter to its will:

> . . . the one Spirit's plastic stress
> Sweeps through the dull dense world, compelling there
> All new successions to the forms they wear;
> Torturing th' unwilling dross that checks its flight
> To its own likeness, as each mass may bear;
> And bursting in its beauty and its might
> From trees and beasts and men into the Heaven's light.

It is the supreme Love above all other loves, which is represented (again in the language of the *Symposium*) as being excellent only in proportion as they reflect it:

> . . . that sustaining Love
> Which through the web of being blindly wove
> By man and beast and earth and air and sea,
> Burns bright or dim, as each are mirrors of
> The fire for which all thirst.

It is also (as in the *Phaedrus*) the supreme Wisdom.

> Wisdom! thy irresistible children rise
> To hail thee, and the elements they chain
> And their own will to swell the glory of thy train.
> O Spirit vast and deep as Night and Heaven!
> Mother and soul of all to which is given
> The light of life, the loveliness of being.
>   **[*Revolt of Islam*]**

As is the case with Plato, Shelley's conception of the Supreme is much less anthropomorphic and personal than the God of the Bible. Another point of importance is that both Plato and Shelley lay hold of the idea of Deity largely from the aesthetic side. The God of the Bible is preeminently a moral ruler, a just and stern judge. Plato, loving as few men have ever loved the glorious beauty of the visible world, admires most in the Creator the element of beauty; in the *Symposium* the supreme vision, the highest good, is represented as the culminating point of an ascent through different stages of aesthetic perception. . . .

[Shelley's] favourite method of approach to the supreme Power is the aesthetic one; it is the Intellectual Beauty of his early '**Hymn**':

> Sudden thy shadow fell on me;
> I shrieked, and clasped my hands in ecstasy!
> I vowed that I would dedicate my powers
> To thee and thine—have I not kept the vow?

Again in *Epipsychidion* he speaks of Emily's beauty as being

> in that Beauty furled

Which penetrates and clasps and fills the world.

In *Adonais* it is

> That beauty in which all things work and move.

Again it should be noted that, as with Plato, Shelley's God is only doubtfully omnipotent; Plato does not appear to solve to his own satisfaction the problem of evil; faced with the dilemma that either 'He is not good or not omnipotent', Plato decides for the latter half of the dilemma and limits his Deity's omnipotence. In his later works, at least, he speaks as if there were a powerful spirit of evil interfering with the Supreme and marring its work. In the *Timaeus* the God of goodness has not merely helpers and subordinates but mighty opponents. In the *Laws* the beneficent principle of the world is matched against an evil principle which possesses contrary powers. In the *Statesman* we find it asserted that the evil principle at times prevails, and periods of universal disorder are said to alternate with orderly periods in which the divine goodness reigns without limitation or check. Plato even speaks occasionally as if matter were itself evil and responded with difficulty to the formative influence of the primal power.

Now in all this Shelley follows him. In **The Revolt of Islam** the whole poem illustrates the conflict between the powers of good and those of evil, symbolized by the fight between the eagle and the snake, the eagle being emblematic of evil and the snake of good. When Laon passes to heaven he stands

> Before the immortal Senate, and the seat
> Of that star-shining spirit . . .
> The better Genius of the world's estate.

Moreover, in the same poem, the spirit of evil triumphs for a time—one of Plato's periods of disorder—since it has been aided by man, who has lent it power:

> Well might men loathe their life . . .
> For they all pined in bondage; body and soul,
> Tyrant and slave, victim and torturer, bent
> Before one Power, to which supreme controul
> Over their will by their own weapons lent,
> Made all its many names omnipotent.

This same conception—of the power for good struggling against and almost overcome by the power for evil—appears in **Prometheus Unbound**. Thus in the speech of Asia:

> How glorious art thou, Earth! And if thou be
> The shadow of some spirit lovelier still,
> Though evil stain its work and it should be
> Like its creation, weak yet beautiful.

In both poems the forces of evil not only predominate but predominate so far that, by the mass of mankind, they are worshipped as deities. In **Prometheus Unbound** (as in Plato's *Statesman*) the universe after a time purifies itself from this evil, and the divine goodness reigns without limitation or check.

The Greek legend of a preceding Golden Age—a reign of Saturn—is taken by Shelley as referring to a previous period of order before disorder began:

> There was the Heaven and Earth at first
> And light and love.

The period of 'disorder' succeeds and then the spirit of good once more becomes clearly and plainly predominant. Asia (typifying love) grows more and more beautiful. Panthea says to her:

> I scarce endure
> The radiance of thy beauty. Some good change
> Is working in the elements which suffer
> Thy presence thus unveiled.

The whole of the fourth Act is a celebration of this new reign of joy in man and nature. As the Spirits sing,

> We come from the mind
> Of human kind
> Which was late so dusk and obscene and blind,
> Now 'tis an ocean
> Of clear emotion,
> A heaven of serene and mighty motion.

And the Semichorus sings of—

> The Spirits which build a new earth and sea
> And a heaven where yet heaven could never be.

Plato's idea of alternating periods of order and disorder is also utilized by Shelley in the great chorus of Hellas:

> The world's great age begins anew,
>   The golden years return.

Just as Shelley is Platonic in his view of the Supreme so also he is Platonic in his conception of the soul and of the world to which the soul inherently belongs. Plato gives, of course, many different points of view. In some dialogues (*Apology*) he appears doubtful of the immortality of the soul, in others (*Phaedo*) he is practically certain of immortality but not quite clear as to the method or manner; in others again (*Meno* and *Phaedrus*) he develops his famous theories concerning the pre-existence of the soul and its reincarnation. In the *Phaedrus* he explains that the soul comes many times upon earth; in the intervals between its various lives it dwells in a heaven-world and, returning to the body, brings back with it prenatal memories.

Shelley, like his master, fluctuates in his belief concerning immortality; but he is, on the whole, much less assured and confident than Plato; he never seems to attain to the serene certainty of the *Meno* and *Phaedrus*. Both Plato and Shelley take what is essentially a spiritual view of the heaven-world; it represents to them a temper of mind, a condition of soul; only the pure can attain to the highest heaven, because only the pure have sufficient affinity with it; its very scenery is mind-stuff and soul-stuff; for this reason it is, as contrasted with the earth, an abode of greater reality; it is not so much another sphere, another world, as the true essence and real being of this; the soul having attained the heaven-world, is delivered from the darkness and 'errors' of the body; it beholds things as they really and essentially are and not the mere reflections of them which are all that we, in this world of matter, can ever hope to attain. . . .

> All men do not easily recall the things of the other world; they may have seen them for a short time only, or they may have been unfortunate when they fell to earth, and may have lost the memory of the holy things which they saw there through some evil and corrupting association.

> The colourless and formless and intangible essence and only reality dwells encircled by true knowledge in this home, visible to the mind alone who is lord of the soul . . . knowledge absolute in existence absolute. [*Phaedrus*]

We find this conception in scores of passages in Shelley:

> The painted veil which those who live call life.
>   [**Prometheus Unbound**]

> Life, like a dome of many-coloured glass,
> Stains the white radiance of eternity
> Until death tramples it to fragments. [**Adonais**]

> Peace, peace, he is not dead, he doth not sleep,
>   He hath awakened from the dream of life—
> 'Tis we, who lost in stormy visions, keep
>   With phantoms an unprofitable strife. [**Adonais**]

Plato is always conscious of the life of the body as being, in comparison with the life of the soul, a mere darkness; in the unforgettable allegory of the Cave in the *Republic* he likens the whole race of men to beings imprisoned in a cave, weighted with chains, who have never beheld any true realities but only the shadows of such realities thrown vaguely upon a wall.

This allegory haunted Shelley; he wrote a poem (unfinished) upon the subject:

> A portal as of shadowy adamant
> Stands yawning on the highway of the life
> Which we all tread, a cavern huge and great.

In the **Triumph of Life** he says—

> Figures ever new
> Rise on the bubble, paint them as you may;
> We have but thrown as those before us threw
> Our shadows on it as it passed away.

Again, in **Hellas** he speaks of a joy which

> Burst, like morning on dream, or like Heaven on

death
Through the walls of our prison.

And again he speaks of himself as a sprite—

Imprisoned for no fault of his
In a body like a grave. ['**With a Guitar**']

Plato's idea of pre-existence is a fairly frequent one in Shelley:

O too late
Beloved! O too soon adored by me!
For in the fields of immortality
    My spirit should at first have worshipped thine.
                [*Epipsychidion*]

Or

                    They seem
Like echoes of an ante-natal dream.

Sometimes Shelley refers only to pre-existence in a heaven-world (*Epipsychidion*), sometimes to re-incarnation or the succession of births and deaths:

They are still immortal
    Who, through birth's orient portal,
And death's dark chasm hurrying to and fro,
    Clothe their unceasing flight
    In the brief dust and light
Gathered around their chariots as they go. [*Hellas*]

Or again (in *Prince Athanase*):—

Memories of an ante-natal life
Made this, where now he dwelt, a penal hell.

The same conception is used to shed an unearthly light over the dreadful character of Cenci:

I do not feel as if I were a man
But like a fiend appointed to chastise
The offences of some unremembered world.

Sometimes he trifles with it delicately:

Your guardian spirit, Ariel, who
From life to life, must still pursue
Your happiness. ['**With a Guitar**']

Both Plato and Shelley admit into their heaven-world, as one of its chief delights, intercourse with the souls of the great dead. In the *Apology* Socrates inquires 'What would not a man give if he might converse with Orpheus and Musaeus and Hesiod and Homer?'

So in *Adonais* Shelley represents his dead poet as meeting with the souls of those who also were gifted and unfortunate and perished young:

Sidney, as he fought
And as he fell and as he lived and loved

Sublimely mild, a Spirit without spot,
Arose; and Lucan by his death approved!

And in *The Revolt of Islam* the hero and heroine are welcomed by the noble dead:

Beneath, there sate on many a sapphire throne,
The Great, who had departed from mankind.

Both Plato and Shelley, though their view of heaven is essentially a spiritual one, do at times express it by means of popular myths, such as the one given in the *Gorgias* or (in the *Republic*) the wonderful vision of Er the Armenian. Shelley gives an Elysium in the close of *The Revolt of Islam,* The consideration of Plato's heaven leads us to what is his chief characteristic as a thinker: the extraordinary tenacity with which he lays hold upon the world of mind; to him the world of sense, vividly as he apprehends it, is always less real, less emphatically existent than the supersensuous world; it always appears as if to him 'mind-stuff' were the essential material of the universe. The common man feels as if the objects of sense were the realities and all mental things 'abstractions'; to Plato the things of the mind are the only true realities, and matter is, in comparison, 'the dream and the shade'. No one has apprehended the splendour of the outer world more fully than he, but, nevertheless, he regarded it in all its magnificent variety, as being only a dull copy of certain divine ideas which, in their eternal beauty, could be seen and realized only with the eyes of the soul. He dwells, by preference, amid abstractions: they are for him a world in themselves—brighter, more vivid, more beautiful and, above all, more *real* than the world of so-called reality.

Now Shelley exactly resembles Plato in this: the supersensuous world is always more real to him than the one of which he can with bodily fingers lay hold; this is the cause of that extreme 'tenuity' which so many of his critics have blamed in his poetry. It is noticeable that he does not, like most poets, illustrate mental processes by physical parallels, but the reverse. As he says himself in the preface to *Prometheus Unbound*: 'The imagery which I have employed will be found, in many instances, to have been drawn from the operations of the human mind or from those external actions by which they are expressed.'

In *Hellas* he describes 'thought' as the most enduring thing upon earth:

Greece and her foundations are
Built below the tide of war,
Based on the crystalline sea
Of thought and its eternity.

            Earth and ocean,
Space, and the isles of life or light that gem
The sapphire floods of interstellar air
            . . . . this Whole
Of suns and worlds and men and beasts and
    flowers,
. . . Is but a vision . . .
Thought is its cradle and its grave.

And again:

> Thought
> Alone, and its quick elements, Will, Passion,
> Reason, Imagination, cannot die;
> They are. . . .
> The stuff whence mutability can weave
> All that it hath dominion o'er.

Before passing to Plato's theories concerning ethics and man in society it may be as well to pause for a moment over his cosmic speculations; these, to modern readers, seem mainly curiosities, but they are worthy of note as they had a considerable influence upon Shelley.

In the *Timaeus* Plato teaches that the entire universe is the self-evolution of an absolute intelligence; thinking in accordance with the laws of its own perfection, it creates and animates the universe. All parts of this universe are inspired by their own intelligences: the sun is the visible embodiment of the supreme spirit; the planets are all divine or are under the guidance of divine spirits; Plato speaks of the 'souls' of the seven planets; the Earth also is a divine being.

Shelley has embodied all these conceptions in his poetry. In the **'Hymn to Apollo'** he shows a truly Greek and Platonic feeling for the sun as the chief source to the universe, not of light and of force only but also of intelligence:

> . . . the Moon's globe
> And the pure stars in their eternal bowers
> Are cinctured with my power as with a robe.
> I am the eye with which the Universe
> Beholds itself and knows itself divine.

Prometheus Unbound is full of Platonic imagery concerning the soul of the Earth and the souls of the planets. The Earth takes a real part in the action of the drama; as is the case with Plato, Shelley is not quite clear whether the Earth herself is living or whether she is inspired by a spirit.

Thus, in the first Act, it is the Earth herself who lives and converses:

> . . . I am the Earth,
> Thy mother. . . .

She speaks of joy as running through all her 'stony veins' at the birth of Prometheus, and of her whole existence becoming poisoned by anger when Jupiter tortures him. As in the *Timaeus,* all those various existences which are contained in the Earth are only the transformations of the same soul of the world acting upon the same matter. In the fourth Act, however, the Earth is considered in its cosmic aspect, as not being in itself alive but inspired by a planetary spirit. Ione says:

> On its head there burns
> A light like a green star, whose emerald beams

> Are twined with its fair hair! how, as it moves
> The splendour drops in flakes upon the grass,
> Knowest thou it?

and Panthea replies:

> It is the delicate spirit
> That guides the earth through heaven. From afar
> The populous constellations call that light
> The loveliest of the planets.

In the fourth act of **Prometheus Unbound,** Shelley, in the most magical way, blends his Platonism with the ideas of modern astronomy. In the *Timaeus* the law of gravitation is explained by Plato as being not only an attraction of lesser bodies to greater, but as having a magnetic power. Shelley avails himself of this idea: the Moon and the Earth he represents as living spirits, and the force of gravity which binds them together as the magnetic attraction of their love; the moon circles ever around the earth:

> Gazing, an insatiate bride,
> On thy form from every side.

In the same way as Plato in the *Timaeus,* Shelley represents the universe as being a congeries of intelligences of all grades

> who have homes,
> From man's high mind even to the central stone
> Of sullen lead; from Heaven's star-fretted domes
> To the dull weed some sea-worm battens on.

With regard to man's nature and general position in society, Shelley again shows certain resemblances to Plato. Plato's most scientific division of man's nature is the triple one of the *Republic*: into the rational and appetitive souls and the body. More usually, however, Plato speaks as if man were a dualism; like most men of strong passions, he is keenly conscious of the 'war in his members'; the famous allegory in the *Phaedrus* of the dark horse and the white horse, the one struggling against the other, represents a mood which is predominant in him. He would have found it difficult to say with Browning's *Rabbi*:

> Nor soul helps flesh now more than flesh helps
>   soul.

Shelley, also, is conscious of a similar dualism. In his **Prometheus Unbound** it forms positively the leading idea: Prometheus is the soul of man, his mind, noble and suffering; in Jupiter is exemplified the baser side of man, his lusts and concupiscence, his errors of mind and his sins of body. Prometheus—the intellect—has originally given power to Jupiter—the ancient religions, harsh superstitions and cruel faiths which, thus enthroned, have countenanced all lusts, persecutions and abominations, and tortured the nobler part of man; this nobler part endures in desolate protest unyielding and therefore finally triumphant. The action of **Prometheus Unbound** is essentially a mental action which explains why so many people fail to understand it as action at all, and why to Shelley it seems all-sufficient; Jupiter, it has been pointed out, does not really resist, when his hour has struck he sinks and falls; but, according to Shelley's thought, there has been, in reality, a long conflict—the good principle has struggled for ages against the evil one—and the passing away of Jupiter marks, in fact, the passing of an obsession from man's mind. The condition of man's soul at the beginning of the drama is like that of the 'unjust man' as described in the *Republic*, where all the lower principles are predominant.

We have pointed out that Plato's view of the supreme Being is a more 'aesthetic' one than that taken by the Christian religion; in the same way his view of morals is largely aesthetic, in the *Republic* he explains how virtue is a harmony and vice a disharmony of the soul, and how disgrace and dishonour attach to a character in which the lower principles predominate. This aesthetic view of virtue is quite consistent with the greatest nobility of ethic ideal; thus in the *Gorgias* Plato makes Socrates maintain that the unjust man, however triumphant, is less happy than the just, that it is better to suffer the cruellest injustice rather than to injure others. Socrates affirms that the wrong-doer is punished by his own soul which becomes wretched; he suffers from an ever-increasing accumulation of misery and sin.

So in Shelley's **Prometheus** the Furies are represented as utterly miserable, while Prometheus amid his tortures can still pity them:

I weigh not what ye do, but what ye suffer,
Being evil. Cruel was the power which called
You, or aught else so wretched, into light.

Plato thinks the possession of arbitrary power the most corrupting influence to which the soul of man can possibly be subject: he has all the usual Greek hatred of the tyrant but intensified to the utmost degree; in the *Republic* he gives a frightful picture of the soul of the tyrant:

He is the natural enemy of all who are high-minded, are valiant, who are wise or wealthy; he enslaves his fellow-citizens, and is surrounded with a body-guard of the abject. The tyrant is drunken, lustful and passionate; his desires are like young ravens crying aloud for food: he will destroy even his parents to gratify his lust: he will commit the foulest murder and eat forbidden food, or be guilty of any other horrid act. His rabble are thieves, burglars, and cut-purses; tyrants will associate only with their own flatterers and tools, and are never the friends of anybody; they are treacherous and unjust; they are the very type of the worst men who have ever appeared upon earth and, just as they are the wickedest, so also they are the most miserable; a city which is enslaved by a tyrant is in the most miserable condition, full of fear, lamentation and pain. The tyrant grows worse and worse from possessing power—more jealous, more faithless, and more impious; supremely miserable, he makes every one else miserable also.

This appalling picture of the tyrant is repeatedly copied by Shelley. In **The Revolt of Islam** the whole land is a desolation because governed by tyrants:—

Tyrants dwelt side by side,
. . . all vied
In evil, slave and despot; fear with lust
Strange fellowship through mutual hate had tied.

For they all pined in bondage; body and soul,
Tyrant and slave, victim and torturer, bent
Before one Power, to which supreme control
Over their will by their own weakness lent,
Made all its many names omnipotent.

or again:

The tyrant's guards resistance yet maintain,
Fearless, and fierce, and hard as beasts of blood,
They stand a speck amid the peopled plain;
Carnage and ruin have been made their food
From infancy—ill has become their good.

He describes the king:

the King, with gathered brow, and lips
Wreathed by long scorn, did inly sneer and frown
With hue like that when some great painter dips
His pencil in the gloom of earthquake and eclipse.

The tyrant is also full of treachery, and, even after he has sworn peace with the rebels, he betrays them and prevails upon his fellow tyrants to dispatch him soldiers:

. . . from the utmost realms of earth, came pouring
The banded slaves whom every despot sent
At that throned traitor's summons.

Jupiter again, among his other meanings, is a type of the tyrant, and the tortures he inflicts upon his noble victim are the natural result of his 'ill tyranny'.

Such is the tyrant's recompense; 'tis just!
He who is evil can receive no good,
And for a world bestowed, or a friend lost,
He can feel hate, fear, shame; not gratitude.

A picture of the tyrant more terrifying still because more human and more carefully studied is Count Cenci; arbitrary power corrupts him until his whole nature becomes a wild longing to torture those who should be most dear to him, to corrupt and ruin them and destroy their souls, and, as with Plato's tyrant, his unnatural hate is combined also with unnatural lust. Shelley has often been accused of exaggerating in his picture of Count Cenci, but to both Plato and Shelley it seemed impossible to exaggerate the wickedness of the man ruined by despotic power. A similar picture occurs in Hellas. Mahmud is another hideous type of the tyrant, his soul full of hate and lust and fear.

Plato was far beyond his time in the position he assigned to women: in the *Republic* he makes the wives of his guardians fully the equals of their husbands, sharing with them in all their pursuits, even in battle. So in *The Revolt of Islam* Cythna is fully the mate of Laon; she shares with him in his ideals of freedom; she also suffers imprisonment; she preaches revolution, she helps to inspire the nation, and finally when he, claiming the masculine privilege of sheltering her, has consented to death, she comes to share his fate. In depicting her, Shelley probably remembers also the warlike heroines of *The Faerie Queene.*

In the *Republic* Plato explains that philosophers make the best rulers of a state. Plato's conception of a philosopher was, however, essentially unlike our modern idea which suggests a professor or even a pedant; in Plato a 'philosopher' means a man of intellectual pursuits, a student, a thinker, almost certainly a lover and, very probably, a person of physical beauty.

Plato himself had been such a practical philosopher; he also had tried to assist in the government of a state, had fallen under the displeasure of a tyrant and, for a time, lost his liberty.

The 'philosopher' in Plato's sense is Shelley's ideal hero. Lionel, in **'Rosalind and Helen,'** is one example: he has wealth and lineage, but is filled with the passion for liberty and inspired by love; he has a rich gift of eloquence and can sway men; he pleads against the oppressor and can move even 'the unpersuaded tyrant' to kindness.

The hero of *Prince Athanase* is similar; he was 'philosophy's accepted guest'. He is hated by the crowd but beloved by his friends; he and his teacher 'Zonoras' discourse together in the Platonic fashion; they read Plato's dialogues—the *Symposium* especially—and from them derive their inspiration. Laon is yet another example: like Plato's ideal philosopher he is 'the spectator of all time and all existence; he has the noblest gifts of nature and makes the highest use of them; . . . he does not fear death or think much of human life' [*Republic,* Book IX]. No ambition entices Laon, but he is compelled into action by the necessities of his country; he meets death with composure and tranquillity.

Shelley's general conception of society, so far as he develops one, is essentially Greek: it consists of a voluntary rule over voluntary subjects. The men who are exalted into rulers in Shelley's poems are always carried into power by the compulsion of circumstances and not by their own choice.

We may turn now to our last division of Platonic influence: the theory of love. Plato's distinctive teachings on this subject have depended mainly upon two circumstances: his philosophy of beauty and the extraordinarily high position which he ascribes to love as an inspiration in human life. Moreover, Plato blends his theory of love with his general metaphysics: he considers it not merely as something peculiar to man or to man and animals, but as a cosmic principle of the greatest nobility and power, involving man, as it were, incidentally. Of course Plato, with his myriad-mindedness, gives on this, as on so many other subjects, more than one point of view, but his most

significant ideas can all be found in Shelley.

In the *Phaedrus* Socrates explains why beauty has such an enormous power over men; it is because they have previously beheld it in the heaven-world and, since sight is the keenest of the bodily senses, they are more powerfully stirred by beauty than by anything else: beholding it they are rapt beyond themselves and henceforward consumed with exalted desire. Such a vision is described many times in Shelley. In *Alastor* the hero receives the revelation of an ideal beauty, like nothing upon earth; henceforth he pursues it through the world and perishes in the vain effort to attain it.

Again, in *The Revolt of Islam* Laon describes Cythna:

> she did seem
> Beside me, gathering beauty as she grew,
> Like the bright shade of some immortal dream,
> Which walks, when tempest sleeps, the wave of
>   life's dark stream.

In the *Symposium* Phaedrus explains that love is the source of the greatest benefits for both the lover and the beloved since they encourage each other in the practice of virtue; love implants the sense of honour and dishonour, and therefore impels to all noble deeds. Phaedrus points out that it inspired the heroes of the past—Orpheus, Achilles, Alkestis. So Shelley makes love an inspiration in his heroes. In *Rosalind and Helen* it exalts to noble deeds: Shelley says of his hero Lionel:

> For love and life in him were twins,
> Born at one birth.

Again, in *The Revolt of Islam* it is the chief inspiration of both Laon and Cythna; without it they would fail under the multitude of their sufferings.

In the *Symposium* Aristophanes dwells on the supreme need for union experienced by lovers; he puts it in a burlesque form, but its essential meaning is sincere enough— they desire a union so absolute that it becomes identity. So in *The Revolt of Islam*:

> What is the strong control
> Which leads the heart that dizzy steep to climb,
> Where far over the world those vapours roll
> Which blend two restless frames in one reposing
>   soul?

Or in *Epipsychidion*:

> One hope within two wills, one will beneath
> Two overshadowing minds, one life, one death,
> One Heaven, one Hell, one immortality,
> And one annihilation.

Again, in the *Symposium* love is treated by Socrates (quoting Diotima) as being an introduction to the highest wisdom: the lover proceeds by grades and stages until he achieves the supreme vision which includes in itself all wisdom and all knowledge.

So in *The Revolt of Islam*:

> In me communion with this purest being
> Kindled intenser zeal and made me wise
> In knowledge, which in hers mine own mind seeing,
> Left in the human world few mysteries.

This supreme vision is described again, and with great eloquence, in *Prometheus Unbound*. Asia typifies the ideal love of Plato: she is a revelation of supreme beauty, she lights and kindles the world, and the final bliss of Prometheus consists in his union with her:

> Love, like the atmosphere
> Of the sun's fire, filling the living world,
> Burst from thee and illumined earth and heaven
> And the deep ocean and the sunless caves
> And all that dwells within them:

and the kindling power of her presence is described in the song:

> Life of Life! thy lips enkindle
> With their love the breath between them.

> Lamp of Earth! where'er thou movest
> Its dim shapes are clad with brightness.

Shelley has been blamed for making his Titan a lover, and doubtless with justice; but we can only say that he substitutes a Platonic ideal for the sterner and grander conception of Aeschylus.

In the *Symposium* Eryximachus explains that love is a principle which extends through all nature; it rules over all things, divine as well as human. The course of the seasons is full of it; when evil love prevails the course of the seasons is disturbed, but when the true love prevails the course of the seasons brings to men, animals, and vegetables health and plenty.

This kind of cosmic love is described in *Prometheus Unbound*, where it pervades all the elements, extending from the greatest of things to the least. *The Sensitive Plant*, again, is a poem full of Platonic ideas: a cosmic love is evident in all parts of nature, and individualizes itself in the individual flowers:

> the Naiad-like lily of the vale;
> Whom youth makes so fair and passion so pale.

The lady herself is more beautiful in mind even than in body, and her lovely body is really the creation of her mind:

> Which, dilating, had moulded her mien and motion,
> Like a sea-flower unfolded beneath the ocean.

She serves, as it were, as the soul of the garden, and, when she perishes, its beauty and its romance decay. The Sensitive Plant itself is a type of the Platonic inspiration:

> It loves, even like Love, its deep heart is full,
> It desires what it has not, the beautiful.

In 'The Witch of Atlas' there is a certain amount of Platonism; the witch herself is of a beauty so resplendent that, beside it, everything else seems shadowy:

> For she was beautiful—her beauty made
> The bright world dim, and everything beside
> Seemed like the fleeting image of a shade.

There is also the suggestion that love tempers opposites:

> Then by strange art she kneaded fire and snow
> Together, tempering the repugnant mass
> With liquid love—all things together grow
> Through which the harmony of love can pass.

In *Epipsychidion*, however, we have Shelley's fullest expression of the Platonic theory of love: large portions of the poem are almost a paraphrase of the *Phaedrus*. Emilia is a winged soul soaring over the darkness of earth: she is an incarnation of a brighter beauty descending from a lovelier and more wonderful world:

> Veiling beneath that radiant form of Woman
> All that is insupportable in thee
> Of light and love and immortality.

In the *Phaedrus* beauty is described as the only one of the ideas which has a perfectly clear and distinct image upon earth; so Emily is the

> Veiled glory of this lampless universe.

She is the mirror which reflects most brightly the glory of the unseen world. The beauty of her mind is far greater than the beauty of her body, which is only its dim reflection; she is an image of the eternal beauty. She and the poet are like notes of music—formed for each other, though dissimilar. She raises the desires of the beholder to the vision of the supreme beauty; the beholder, exalted, is borne above himself and lifted to a higher world. The poet anticipates the ecstatic union of souls:

> Till, like two meteors of expanding flame,
> Those spheres instinct with it become the same,
> Touch, mingle, are transfigured; ever still
> Burning, yet ever inconsumable.

Towards the close of his life Shelley's mind, ever growing and developing, arrived at the conclusion that the great master who had taught him so much and whom he so loved was, notwithstanding all his glories, too much at the mercy of his own erotic impulses; he says in *The Triumph of Life*:

> The star that ruled his doom was far too fair,
> And life, where long that flower of Heaven grew
>   not,

Conquered that heart by love, which gold or pain
Or age or sloth or slavery could subdue not.

Shelley was one of those men who are, by temperament, born Platonists, and it may be surmised that, had he never read a line of Greek or even heard of Plato, except by indirect tradition only, his work would still show a certain number of affinities. Natural resemblance and close study, taken together, have resulted in saturating his whole work with Platonic thought; the above essay has aimed at giving the main outlines of this Platonic influence, but there is still a considerable amount of detail which cannot, in the space here available, be fully discussed.

George Santayana   (essay date 1926)

SOURCE: "Shelley: Or the Poetic Value of Revolutionary Principles," in *Winds of Doctrine: Studies in Contemporary Opinion,* Charles Scribner's Sons, 1926, pp. 155-85.

[*Santayana was a Spanish-born philosopher, poet, novelist, and literary critic. His earliest published works were the poems of* Sonnets, and Other Verses *(1894). Although Santayana is regarded as no more than a fair poet, his facility with language is one of the distinguishing features of his later philosophical works. Written in an elegant, non-technical prose, Santayana's major philosophical work of his early career is the five-volume* Life of Reason *(1905-06). These volumes reflect their author's materialist viewpoint applied to such areas as society, religion, art, and science, and, along with* Scepticism and Animal Faith *(1923) and the four-volume* Realms of Being *(1927-40), put forth the view that while reason undermines belief in anything, an irrational animal faith suggests the existence of a "realm of essences" which leads to the human search for knowledge. Late in his life Santayana stated that "reason and ideals arise in doing something that at bottom there is no reason for doing." "Chaos," he wrote earlier, "is perhaps at the bottom of everything." In the following excerpt, Santayana provides an overview of the major philosophical tenets that inform Shelley's poetry.*]

It is possible to advocate anarchy in criticism as in politics, and there is perhaps nothing coercive to urge against a man who maintains that any work of art is good enough, intrinsically and incommensurably, if it pleased anybody at any time for any reason. In practice, however, the ideal of anarchy is unstable. Irrefutable by argument, it is readily overcome by nature. It melts away before the dogmatic operation of the anarchist's own will, as soon as he allows himself the least creative endeavour. In spite of the infinite variety of what is merely possible, human nature and will have a somewhat definite constitution, and only what is harmonious with their actual constitution can long maintain itself in the moral world. Hence it is a safe principle in the criticism of art that technical proficiency, and brilliancy of fancy or execution, cannot avail to establish a great reputation. They may dazzle for a moment, but they cannot absolve an artist from the need of having an impor-

tant subject-matter and a sane humanity.

If this principle is accepted, however, it might seem that certain artists, and perhaps the greatest, might not fare well at our hands. How would Shelley, for instance, stand such a test? Every one knows the judgment passed on Shelley by Matthew Arnold, a critic who evidently relied on this principle, even if he preferred to speak only in the name of his personal tact and literary experience. Shelley, Matthew Arnold said, was "a beautiful and ineffectual angel, beating his wings in a luminous void in vain." In consequence he declared that Shelley was not a classic, especially as his private circle had had an unsavoury morality, to be expressed only by the French word *sale,* and as moreover Shelley himself occasionally showed a distressing want of the sense of humour, which could only be called *bête.* These strictures, if a bit incoherent, are separately remarkably just. They unmask essential weaknesses not only in Shelley, but in all revolutionary people. The life of reason is a heritage and exists only through tradition. Half of it is an art, an adjustment to an alien reality, which only a long experience can teach: and even the other half, the inward inspiration and ideal of reason, must be also a common inheritance in the race, if people are to work together or so much as to understand one another. Now the misfortune of revolutionists is that they are disinherited, and their folly is that they wish to be disinherited even more than they are. Hence, in the midst of their passionate and even heroic idealisms, there is commonly a strange poverty in their minds, many an ugly turn in their lives, and an ostentatious vileness in their manners. They wish to be the leaders of mankind, but they are wretched representatives of humanity. In the concert of nature it is hard to keep in tune with oneself if one is out of tune with everything.

We should not then be yielding to any private bias, but simply noting the conditions under which art may exist and may be appreciated, if we accepted the classical principle of criticism and asserted that substance, sanity, and even a sort of pervasive wisdom are requisite for supreme works of art. On the other hand—who can honestly doubt it?—the rebels and individualists are the men of direct insight and vital hope. The poetry of Shelley in particular is typically poetical. It is poetry divinely inspired; and Shelley himself is perhaps no more ineffectual or more lacking in humour than an angel properly should be. Nor is his greatness all a matter of æsthetic abstraction and wild music. It is a fact of capital importance in the development of human genius that the great revolution in Christendom against Christianity, a revolution that began with the Renaissance and is not yet completed, should have found angels to herald it, no less than that other revolution did which began at Bethlehem; and that among these new angels there should have been one so winsome, pure, and rapturous as Shelley. How shall we reconcile these conflicting impressions? Shall we force ourselves to call the genius of Shelley second rate because it was revolutionary, and shall we attribute all enthusiasm for him to literary affectation or political prejudice? Or shall we rather abandon the orthodox principle that an important subject-matter and a sane spirit are essential to great works? Or shall we look for a different issue out of our perplexity, by asking if the analysis and comprehension are not perhaps at fault which declare that these things are not present in Shelley's poetry? This last is the direction in which I conceive the truth to lie. A little consideration will show us that Shelley really has a great subject-matter—what ought to be; and that he has a real humanity—though it is humanity in the seed, humanity in its internal principle, rather than in those deformed expressions of it which can flourish in the world.

Shelley seems hardly to have been brought up; he grew up in the nursery among his young sisters, at school among the rude boys, without any affectionate guidance, without imbibing any religious or social tradition. If he received any formal training or correction, he instantly rejected it inwardly, set it down as unjust and absurd, and turned instead to sailing paper boats, to reading romances or to writing them, or to watching with delight the magic of chemical experiments. Thus the mind of Shelley was thoroughly disinherited; but not, like the minds of most revolutionists, by accident and through the niggardliness of fortune, for few revolutionists would be such if they were heirs to a baronetcy. Shelley's mind disinherited itself out of allegiance to itself, because it was too sensitive and too highly endowed for the world into which it had descended. It rejected ordinary education, because it was incapable of assimilating it. Education is suitable to those few animals whose faculties are not completely innate, animals that, like most men, may be perfected by experience because they are born with various imperfect alternative instincts rooted equally in their system. But most animals, and a few men, are not of this sort. They cannot be educated, because they are born complete. Full of predeterminate intuitions, they are without intelligence, which is the power of seeing things as they are. Endowed with a specific, unshakable faith, they are impervious to experience: and as they burst the womb they bring ready-made with them their final and only possible system of philosophy.

Shelley was one of these spokesmen of the *a priori*, one of these nurslings of the womb, like a bee or a butterfly; a dogmatic, inspired, perfect, and incorrigible creature. He was innocent and cruel, swift and wayward, illuminated and blind. Being a finished child of nature, not a joint product, like most of us, of nature, history, and society, he abounded miraculously in his own clear sense, but was obtuse to the droll, miscellaneous lessons of fortune. The cannonade of hard, inexplicable facts that knocks into most of us what little wisdom we have left Shelley dazed and sore, perhaps, but uninstructed. When the storm was over, he began chirping again his own natural note. If the world continued to confine and obsess him, he hated the world, and gasped for freedom. Being incapable of understanding reality, he revelled in creating world after world in idea. For his nature was not merely pre-determined and obdurate, it was also sensitive, vehement, and fertile. With the soul of a bird, he had the senses of a man-child; the instinct of the butterfly was united in him with the instinct of the brooding fowl and of the pelican. This winged spirit had a heart. It darted swiftly on its appointed course, neither expecting nor understanding opposition; but when it met

opposition it did not merely flutter and collapse; it was inwardly outraged, it protested proudly against fate, it cried aloud for liberty and justice.

The consequence was that Shelley, having a nature preformed but at the same time tender, passionate, and moral, was exposed to early and continual suffering. When the world violated the ideal which lay so clear before his eyes, that violation filled him with horror. If to the irrepressible gushing of life from within we add the suffering and horror that continually checked it, we shall have in hand, I think, the chief elements of his genius.

Love of the ideal, passionate apprehension of what ought to be, has for its necessary counterpart condemnation of the actual, wherever the actual does not conform to that ideal. The spontaneous soul, the soul of the child, is naturally revolutionary; and when the revolution fails, the soul of the youth becomes naturally pessimistic. All moral life and moral judgment have this deeply romantic character; they venture to assert a private ideal in the face of an intractable and omnipotent world. Some moralists begin by feeling the attraction of untasted and ideal perfection. These, like Plato, excel in elevation, and they are apt to despise rather than to reform the world. Other moralists begin by a revolt against the actual, at some point where they find the actual particularly galling. These excel in sincerity; their purblind conscience is urgent, and they are reformers in intent and sometimes even in action. But the ideals they frame are fragmentary and shallow, often mere provisional vague watchwords, like liberty, equality, and fraternity; they possess no positive visions or plans for moral life as a whole, like Plato's *Republic*. The utopian or visionary moralists are often rather dazed by this wicked world; being well-intentioned but impotent, they often take comfort in fancying that the ideal they pine for is already actually embodied on earth, or is about to be embodied on earth in a decade or two, or at least is embodied eternally in a sphere immediately above the earth, to which we shall presently climb, and be happy for ever.

Lovers of the ideal who thus hastily believe in its reality are called idealists, and Shelley was an idealist in almost every sense of that hard-used word. He early became an idealist after Berkeley's fashion, in that he discredited the existence of matter and embraced a psychological or (as it was called) intellectual system of the universe. In his drama **Hellas** he puts this view with evident approval into the mouth of Ahasuerus:

> This whole
> Of suns and worlds and men and beasts and
>   flowers,
> With all the silent or tempestuous workings
> By which they have been, are, or cease to be,
> Is but a vision;—all that it inherits
> Are motes of a sick eye, bubbles and dreams.
> Thought is its cradle and its grave; nor less
> The future and the past are idle shadows
> Of thought's eternal flight—they have no being:
> Nought is but that which feels itself to be.

But Shelley was even more deeply and constantly an idealist after the manner of Plato; for he regarded the good as a magnet (inexplicably not working for the moment) that draws all life and motion after it; and he looked on the types and ideals of things as on eternal realities that subsist, beautiful and untarnished, when the glimmerings that reveal them to our senses have died away. From the infinite potentialities of beauty in the abstract, articulate mind draws certain bright forms—the Platonic ideas—"the gathered rays which are reality," as Shelley called them: and it is the light of these ideals cast on objects of sense that lends to these objects some degree of reality and value, making out of them "lovely apparitions, dim at first, then radiant . . . the progeny immortal of painting, sculpture, and rapt poesy."

The only kind of idealism that Shelley had nothing to do with is the kind that prevails in some universities, that Hegelian idealism which teaches that perfect good is a vicious abstraction, and maintains that all the evil that has been, is, and ever shall be is indispensable to make the universe as good as it possibly could be. In this form, idealism is simply contempt for all ideals, and a hearty adoration of things as they are; and as such it appeals mightily to the powers that be, in church and in state; but in that capacity it would have been as hateful to Shelley as the powers that be always were, and as the philosophy was that flattered them. For his moral feeling was based on suffering and horror at what is actual, no less than on love of a visioned good. His conscience was, to a most unusual degree, at once elevated and sincere. It was inspired in equal measure by prophecy and by indignation. He was carried away in turn by enthusiasm for what his ethereal and fertile fancy pictured as possible, and by detestation of the reality forced upon him instead. Hence that extraordinary moral fervour which is the soul of his poetry. His imagination is no playful undirected kaleidoscope; the images, often so tenuous and metaphysical, that crowd upon him, are all sparks thrown off at white heat, embodiments of a fervent, definite, unswerving inspiration. If we think that the **"Cloud"** or the **"West Wind"** or the **"Witch of the Atlas"** are mere fireworks, poetic dust, a sort of *bataille des fleurs* in which we are pelted by a shower of images—we have not understood the passion that overflows in them, as any long-nursed passion may, in any of us, suddenly overflow in an unwonted profusion of words. This is a point at which Francis Thompson's understanding of Shelley, generally so perfect, seems to me to go astray. The universe, Thompson tells us, was Shelley's box of toys. "He gets between the feet of the horses of the sun. He stands in the lap of patient Nature, and twines her loosened tresses after a hundred wilful fashions, to see how she will look nicest in his song." This last is not, I think, Shelley's motive; it is not the truth about the spring of his genius. He undoubtedly shatters the world to bits, but only to build it nearer to the heart's desire, only to make out of its coloured fragments some more Elysian home for love, or some more dazzling symbol for that infinite beauty which is the need—the profound, aching, imperative need—of the human soul. This recreative impulse of the poet's is not wilful, as Thompson calls it: it is moral. Like the *Sensitive Plant*

It loves even like Love,—its deep heart is full;
It desires what it has not, the beautiful.

The question for Shelley is not at all what will look nicest in his song; that is the preoccupation of mincing rhymesters, whose well is soon dry. Shelley's abundance has a more generous source; it springs from his passion for picturing what would be best, not in the picture, but in the world. Hence, when he feels he has pictured or divined it, he can exclaim:

The joy, the triumph, the delight, the madness,
The boundless, overflowing, bursting gladness,
The vaporous exultation, not to be confined!
Ha! Ha! the animation of delight,
Which wraps me like an atmosphere of light,
And bears me as a cloud is borne by its own wind!

To match this gift of bodying forth the ideal Shelley had his vehement sense of wrong; and as he seized upon and recast all images of beauty, to make them more perfectly beautiful, so, to vent his infinite horror of evil, he seized on all the worst images of crime or torture that he could find, and recast them so as to reach the quintessence of distilled badness. His pictures of war, famine, lust, and cruelty are, or seem, forced, although perhaps, as in the *Cenci,* he might urge that he had historical warrant for his descriptions, far better historical warrant, no doubt, than the beauty and happiness actually to be found in the world could give him for his **"Skylark"**, his *Epipsychidion,* or his *Prometheus*. But to exaggerate good is to vivify, to enhance our sense of moral coherence and beautiful naturalness; it is to render things more graceful, intelligible, and congenial to the spirit which they ought to serve. To aggravate evil, on the contrary, is to darken counsel—already dark enough—and the want of truth to nature in this pessimistic sort of exaggeration is not compensated for by any advantage. The violence and, to my feeling, the wantonness of these invectives—for they are invectives in intention and in effect—may have seemed justified to Shelley by his political purpose. He was thirsting to destroy kings, priests, soldiers, parents, and heads of colleges—to destroy them, I mean, in their official capacity; and the exhibition of their vileness in all its diabolical purity might serve to remove scruples in the half-hearted. We, whom the nineteenth century has left so tender to historical rights and historical beauties, may wonder that a poet, an impassioned lover of the beautiful, could have been such a leveller, and such a vandal in his theoretical destructiveness. But here the legacy of the eighteenth century was speaking in Shelley, as that of the nineteenth is speaking in us: and moreover, in his own person, the very fertility of imagination could be a cause of blindness to the past and its contingent sanctities. Shelley was not left standing aghast, like a Philistine, before the threatened destruction of all traditional order. He had, and knew he had, the seeds of a far lovelier order in his own soul; there he found the plan or memory of a perfect commonwealth of nature ready to rise at once on the ruins of this sad world, and to make regret for it impossible.

So much for what I take to be the double foundation of

Shelley's genius, a vivid love of ideal good on the one hand, and on the other, what is complementary to that vivid love, much suffering and horror at the touch of actual evils. On this double foundation he based an opinion which had the greatest influence on his poetry, not merely on the subject-matter of it, but also on the exuberance and urgency of emotion which suffuses it. This opinion was that all that caused suffering and horror in the world could be readily destroyed: it was the belief in perfectibility.

An animal that has rigid instincts and an *a priori* mind is probably very imperfectly adapted to the world he comes into: his organs cannot be moulded by experience and use; unless they are fitted by some miraculous pre-established harmony, or by natural selection, to things as they are, they will never be reconciled with them, and an eternal war will ensue between what the animal needs, loves, and can understand and what the outer reality offers. So long as such a creature lives—and his life will be difficult and short—events will continually disconcert and puzzle him; everything will seem to him unaccountable, inexplicable, unnatural. He will not be able to conceive the real order and connection of things sympathetically, by assimilating his habits of thought to their habits of evolution. His faculties being innate and unadaptable will not allow him to correct his presumptions and axioms; he will never be able to make nature the standard of naturalness. What contradicts his private impulses will seem to him to contradict reason, beauty, and necessity. In this paradoxical situation he will probably take refuge in the conviction that what he finds to exist is an illusion, or at least not a fair sample of reality. Being so perverse, absurd, and repugnant, the given state of things must be, he will say, only accidental and temporary. He will be sure that his own *a priori* imagination is the mirror of all the eternal proprieties, and that as his mind can move only in one predetermined way, things cannot be prevented from moving in that same way save by some strange violence done to their nature. It would be easy, therefore, to set everything right again: nay, everything must be on the point of righting itself spontaneously. Wrong, of its very essence, must be in unstable equilibrium. The conflict between what such a man feels ought to exist and what he finds actually existing must, he will feel sure, end by a speedy revolution in things, and by the removal of all scandals; that it should end by the speedy removal of his own person, or by such a revolution in his demands as might reconcile him to existence, will never occur to him; or, if the thought occurs to him, it will seem too horrible to be true.

Such a creature cannot adapt himself to things by education, and consequently he cannot adapt things to himself by industry. His choice lies absolutely between victory and martyrdom. But at the very moment of martyrdom, martyrs, as is well known, usually feel assured of victory. The *a priori* spirit will therefore be always a prophet of victory, so long as it subsists at all. The vision of a better world at hand absorbed the Israelites in exile, St. John the Baptist in the desert, and Christ on the cross. The martyred spirit always says to the world it leaves, "This day thou shalt be with me in paradise."

In just this way, Shelley believed in perfectibility. In his latest poems—in *Hellas*, in *Adonais*—he was perhaps a little inclined to remove the scene of perfectibility to a metaphysical region, as the Christian church soon removed it to the other world. Indeed, an earth really made perfect is hardly distinguishable from a posthumous heaven: so profoundly must everything in it be changed, and so angel-like must every one in it become. Shelley's earthly paradise, as described in *Prometheus* and in *Epipsychidion*, is too festival-like, too much of a mere culmination, not to be fugitive: it cries aloud to be translated into a changeless and metaphysical heaven, which to Shelley's mind could be nothing but the realm of Platonic ideas, where "life, like a dome of many-coloured glass," no longer "stains the white radiance of eternity." But the age had been an age of revolution and, in spite of disappointments, retained its faith in revolution; and the young Shelley was not satisfied with a paradise removed to the intangible realms of poetry or of religion; he hoped, like the old Hebrews, for a paradise on earth. His notion was that eloquence could change the heart of man, and that love, kindled there by the force of reason and of example, would transform society. He believed, Mrs. Shelley tells us, "that mankind had only to will that there should be no evil, and there would be none." And she adds: "That man could be so perfectionised as to be able to expel evil from his own nature, and from the greater part of creation, was the cardinal point of his system." This cosmic extension of the conversion of men reminds one of the cosmic extension of the Fall conceived by St. Augustine; and in the *Prometheus* Shelley has allowed his fancy, half in symbol, half in glorious physical hyperbole, to carry the warm contagion of love into the very bowels of the earth, and even the moon, by reflection, to catch the light of love, and be alive again.

Shelley, we may safely say, did not understand the real constitution of nature. It was hidden from him by a cloud, all woven of shifting rainbows and bright tears. Only his emotional haste made it possible for him to entertain such opinions as he did entertain; or rather, it was inevitable that the mechanism of nature, as it is in its depths, should remain in his pictures only the shadowiest of backgrounds. His poetry is accordingly a part of the poetry of illusion; the poetry of truth, if we have the courage to hope for such a thing, is reserved for far different and yet unborn poets. But it is only fair to Shelley to remember that the moral being of mankind is as yet in its childhood; all poets play with images not understood; they touch on emotions sharply, at random, as in a dream; they suffer each successive vision, each poignant sentiment, to evaporate into nothing, or to leave behind only a heart vaguely softened and fatigued, a gentle languor, or a tearful hope. Every modern school of poets, once out of fashion, proves itself to have been sadly romantic and sentimental. None has done better than to spangle a confused sensuous pageant with some sparks of truth, or to give it some symbolic relation to moral experience. And this Shelley has done as well as anybody: all other poets also have been poets of illusion. The distinction of Shelley is that his illusions are so wonderfully fine, subtle, and palpitating; that they betray passions and mental habits so singularly generous and pure. And why? Because he did not believe in the necessity of what is vulgar, and did not pay that demoralising respect to it, under the title of fact or of custom, which it exacts from most of us. The past seemed to him no valid precedent, the present no final instance. As he believed in the imminence of an overturn that should make all things new, he was not checked by any divided allegiance, by any sense that he was straying into the vapid or fanciful, when he created what he justly calls "Beautiful idealisms of moral excellence."

That is what his poems are fundamentally—the **"Skylark,"** and the **"Witch of the Atlas,"** and the *Sensitive Plant* no less than the grander pieces. He infused into his gossamer world the strength of his heroic conscience. He felt that what his imagination pictured was a true symbol of what human experience should and might pass into. Otherwise he would have been aware of playing with idle images; his poetry would have been mere millinery and his politics mere business; he would have been a worldling in art and in morals. The clear fire, the sustained breath, the fervent accent of his poetry are due to his faith in his philosophy. As Mrs. Shelley expressed it, he "had no care for any of his poems that did not emanate from the depths of his mind, and develop some high and abstruse truth." Had his poetry not dealt with what was supreme in his own eyes, and dearest to his heart, it could never have been the exquisite and entrancing poetry that it is. It would not have had an adequate subject-matter, as, in spite of Matthew Arnold, I think it had; for nothing can be empty that contains such a soul. An angel cannot be ineffectual if the standard of efficiency is moral; he is what all other things bring about, when they are effectual. And a void that is alive with the beating of luminous wings, and of a luminous heart, is quite sufficiently peopled. Shelley's mind was angelic not merely in its purity and fervour, but also in its moral authority, in its prophetic strain. What was conscience in his generation was life in him.

The mind of man is not merely a sensorium. His intelligence is not merely an instrument for adaptation. There is a germ within, a nucleus of force and organisation, which can be unfolded, under favourable circumstances, into a perfection inwardly determined. Man's constitution is a fountain from which to draw an infinity of gushing music, not representing anything external, yet not unmeaning on that account, since it represents the capacities and passions latent in him from the beginning. These potentialities, however, are no oracles of truth. Being innate they are arbitrary; being *a priori* they are subjective; but they are good principles for fiction, for poetry, for morals, for religion. They are principles for the true expression of man, but not for the true description of the universe. When they are taken for the latter, fiction becomes deception, poetry illusion, morals fanaticism, and religion bad science. The orgy of delusion into which we are then plunged comes from supposing the *a priori* to be capable of controlling the actual, and the innate to be a standard for the true. That rich and definite endowment which might have made the distinction of the poet, then makes the narrowness of the philosopher. So Shelley, with a sort of tyranny of which he does not suspect the possible cruelty, would impose his ideal of love and equality upon all creatures;

he would make enthusiasts of clowns and doves of vultures. In him, as in many people, too intense a need of loving excludes the capacity for intelligent sympathy. His feeling cannot accommodate itself to the inequalities of human nature: his good will is a geyser, and will not consent to grow cool, and to water the flat and vulgar reaches of life. Shelley is blind to the excellences of what he despises, as he is blind to the impossibility of realising what he wants. His sympathies are narrow as his politics are visionary, so that there is a certain moral incompetence in his moral intensity. Yet his abstraction from half of life, or from nine-tenths of it, was perhaps necessary if silence and space were to be won in his mind for its own upwelling, ecstatic harmonies. The world we have always with us, but such spirits we have not always. And the spirit has fire enough within to make a second stellar universe.

An instance of Shelley's moral incompetence in moral intensity is to be found in his view of selfishness and evil. From the point of view of pure spirit, selfishness is quite absurd. As a contemporary of ours has put it: "It is so evident that it is better to secure a greater good for A than a lesser good for B that it is hard to find any still more evident principle by which to prove this. And if A happens to be some one else, and B to be myself, that cannot affect the question." It is very foolish not to love your neighbour as yourself, since his good is no less good than yours. Convince people of this—and who can resist such perfect logic?—and *presto* all property in things has disappeared, all jealousy in love, and all rivalry in honour. How happy and secure every one will suddenly be, and how much richer than in our mean, blind, competitive society! The single word love—and we have just seen that love is a logical necessity—offers an easy and final solution to all moral and political problems. Shelley cannot imagine why this solution is not accepted, and why logic does not produce love. He can only wonder and grieve that it does not; and since selfishness and ill-will seem to him quite gratuitous, his ire is aroused; he thinks them unnatural and monstrous. He could not in the least understand evil, even when he did it himself; all villainy seemed to him wanton, all lust frigid, all hatred insane. All was an abomination alike that was not the lovely spirit of love.

Now this is a very unintelligent view of evil; and if Shelley had had time to read Spinoza—an author with whom he would have found himself largely in sympathy—he might have learned that nothing is evil in itself, and that what is evil in things is not due to any accident in creation, nor to groundless malice in man. Evil is an inevitable aspect which things put on when they are struggling to preserve themselves in the same habitat, in which there is not room or matter enough for them to prosper equally side by side. Under these circumstances the partial success of any creature—say, the cancer-microbe—is an evil from the point of view of those other creatures—say, men— to whom that success is a defeat. Shelley sometimes half perceived this inevitable tragedy. So he says of the fair lady in the *Sensitive Plant*:

> All killing insects and gnawing worms,

And things of obscene and unlovely forms,
She bore in a basket of Indian woof,
Into the rough woods far aloof—
In a basket of grasses and wild flowers full,
The freshest her gentle hands could pull
For the poor banished insects, whose intent,
Although they did ill, was innocent.

Now it is all very well to ask cancer-microbes to be reasonable, and go feed on oak-leaves, if the oak-leaves do not object; oak-leaves might be poison for them, and in any case cancer-microbes cannot listen to reason; they must go on propagating where they are, unless they are quickly and utterly exterminated. And fundamentally men are subject to the same fatality exactly; they cannot listen to reason unless they are reasonable; and it is unreasonable to expect that, being animals, they should be reasonable exclusively. Imagination is indeed at work in them, and makes them capable of sacrificing themselves for any idea that appeals to them, for their children, perhaps, or for their religion. But they are not more capable of sacrificing themselves to what does not interest them than the cancer-microbes are of sacrificing themselves to men.

When Shelley marvels at the perversity of the world, he shows his ignorance of the world. The illusion he suffers from is constitutional, and such as larks and sensitive plants are possibly subject to in their way: what he is marvelling at is really that anything should exist at all not a creature of his own moral disposition. Consequently the more he misunderstands the world and bids it change its nature, the more he expresses his own nature: so that all is not vanity in his illusion, nor night in his blindness. The poet sees most clearly what his ideal is; he suffers no illusion in the expression of his own soul. His political utopias, his belief in the power of love, and his cryingly subjective and inconstant way of judging people are one side of the picture; the other is his lyrical power, wealth, and ecstasy. If he had understood universal nature, he would not have so glorified in his own. And his own nature was worth glorifying; it was, I think, the purest, tenderest, richest, most rational nature ever poured forth in verse. I have not read in any language such a full expression of the unadulterated instincts of the mind. The world of Shelley is that which the vital monad within many of us—I will not say within all, for who shall set bounds to the variations of human nature?—the world which the vital monad within many of us, I say, would gladly live in if it could have its way.

Matthew Arnold said that Shelley was not quite sane; and certainly he was not quite sane, if we place sanity in justness of external perception, adaptation to matter, and docility to the facts; but his lack of sanity was not due to any internal corruption; it was not even an internal eccentricity. He was like a child, like a Platonic soul just fallen from the Empyrean; and the child may be dazed, credulous, and fanciful; but he is not mad. On the contrary, his earnest playfulness, the constant distraction of his attention from observation to daydreams, is the sign of an inward order and fecundity appropriate to his age. If children did not see visions, good men would have nothing to

work for. It is the soul of observant persons, like Matthew Arnold, that is apt not to be quite sane and whole inwardly, but somewhat warped by familiarity with the perversities of real things, and forced to misrepresent its true ideal, like a tree bent by too prevalent a wind. Half the fertility of such a soul is lost, and the other half is denaturalised. No doubt, in its sturdy deformity, the practical mind is an instructive and not unpleasing object, an excellent, if somewhat pathetic, expression of the climate in which it is condemned to grow, and of its dogged clinging to an ingrate soil; but it is a wretched expression of its innate possibilities. Shelley, on the contrary, is like a palm-tree in the desert or a star in the sky; he is perfect in the midst of the void. His obtuseness to things dynamic—to the material order—leaves his whole mind free to develop things æsthetic after their own kind; his abstraction permits purity, his playfulness makes room for creative freedom, his ethereal quality is only humanity having its way.

We perhaps do ourselves an injustice when we think that the heart of us is sordid; what is sordid is rather the situation that cramps or stifles the heart. In itself our generative principle is surely no less fertile and generous than the generative principle of crystals or flowers. As it can produce a more complex body, it is capable of producing a more complex mind; and the beauty and life of this mind, like that of the body, is all predetermined in the seed. Circumstances may suffer the organism to develop, or prevent it from doing so; they cannot change its plan without making it ugly and deformed. What Shelley's mind draws from the outside, its fund of images, is like what the germ of the body draws from the outside, its food—a mass of mere materials to transform and reorganise. With these images Shelley constructs a world determined by his native genius, as the seed organises out of its food a predetermined system of nerves and muscles. Shelley's poetry shows us the perfect but naked body of human happiness. What clothes circumstances may compel most of us to add may be a necessary concession to climate, to custom, or to shame; they can hardly add a new vitality or any beauty comparable to that which they hide.

When the soul, as in Shelley's case, is all goodness, and when the world seems all illegitimacy and obstruction, we need not wonder that *freedom* should be regarded as a panacea. Even if freedom had not been the idol of Shelley's times, he would have made an idol of it for himself. "I never could discern in him," says his friend Hogg, "any more than two principles. The first was a strong, irrepressible love of liberty. . . . The second was an equally ardent love of toleration . . . and . . . an intense abhorrence of persecution." We all fancy nowadays that we believe in liberty and abhor persecution; but the liberty we approve of is usually only a variation in social compulsions, to make them less galling to our latest sentiments than the old compulsions would be if we retained them. Liberty of the press and liberty to vote do not greatly help us in living after our own mind, which is, I suppose, the only positive sort of liberty. From the point of view of a poet, there can be little essential freedom so long as he is forbidden to live with the people he likes, and compelled to live with the people he does not like.

This, to Shelley, seemed the most galling of tyrannies; and free love was, to his feeling, the essence and test of freedom. Love must be spontaneous to be a spiritual bond in the beginning and it must remain spontaneous if it is to remain spiritual. To be bound by one's past is as great a tyranny to pure spirit as to be bound by the sin of Adam, or by the laws of Artaxerxes; and those of us who do not believe in the possibility of free love ought to declare frankly that we do not, at bottom, believe in the possibility of freedom.

> I never was attached to that great sect
> Whose doctrine is that each one should select,
> Out of the crowd, a mistress or a friend
> And all the rest, though fair and wise, commend
> To cold oblivion; though it is the code
> Of modern morals, and the beaten road
> Which those poor slaves with weary footsteps tread
> Who travel to their home among the dead
> By the broad highway of the world, and so
> With one chained friend, perhaps a jealous foe,
> The dreariest and the longest journey go.
> True love in this differs from gold and clay,
> That to divide is not to take away.
> Love is like understanding that grows bright
> Gazing on many truths. . . . Narrow
> The heart that loves, the brain that contemplates,
> The life that wears, the spirit that creates
> One object and one form, and builds thereby
> A sepulchre for its eternity!

The difficulties in reducing this charming theory of love to practice are well exemplified in Shelley's own life. He ran away with his first wife not because she inspired any uncontrollable passion, but because she declared she was a victim of domestic oppression and threw herself upon him for protection. Nevertheless, when he discovered that his best friend was making love to her, in spite of his free-love principles, he was very seriously annoyed. When he presently abandoned her, feeling a spiritual affinity in another direction, she drowned herself in the Serpentine: and his second wife needed all her natural sweetness and all her inherited philosophy to reconcile her to the waves of Platonic enthusiasm for other ladies which periodically swept the too sensitive heart of her husband. Free love would not, then, secure freedom from complications; it would not remove the present occasion for jealousy, reproaches, tragedies, and the dragging of a lengthening chain. Freedom of spirit cannot be translated into freedom of action; you may amend laws, and customs, and social entanglements, but you will still have them; for this world is a lumbering mechanism and not, like love, a plastic dream. Wisdom is very old and therefore often ironical, and it has long taught that it is well for those who would live in the spirit to keep as clear as possible of the world: and that marriage, especially a free-love marriage, is a snare for poets. Let them endure to love freely, hopelessly, and infinitely, after the manner of Plato and Dante, and even of Goethe, when Goethe really loved: that exquisite sacrifice will improve their verse, and it will not kill them. Let them follow in the traces of Shelley when he wrote in his youth: "I have been most of the night pacing a church-yard. I must now engage in scenes of strong interest. . . . I expect to gratify some of this insatiable feeling in poetry. . . . I slept with a loaded pistol and some poison last night, but did not die." Happy man if he had been able to add, "And did not marry!"

Last among the elements of Shelley's thought I may perhaps mention his atheism. Shelley called himself an atheist in his youth; his biographers and critics usually say that he was, or that he became, a pantheist. He was an atheist in the sense that he denied the orthodox conception of a deity who is a voluntary creator, a legislator, and a judge; but his aversion to Christianity was not founded on any sympathetic or imaginative knowledge of it; and a man who preferred the *Paradiso* of Dante to almost any other poem, and preferred it to the popular *Inferno* itself, could evidently be attracted by Christian ideas and sentiment the moment they were presented to him as expressions of moral truth rather than as gratuitous dogmas. A pantheist he was in the sense that he felt how fluid and vital this whole world is; but he seems to have had no tendency to conceive any conscious plan or logical necessity connecting the different parts of the whole; so that rather than a pantheist he might be called a panpsychist; especially as he did not subordinate morally the individual to the cosmos. He did not surrender the authority of moral ideals in the face of physical necessity, which is properly the essence of pantheism. He did the exact opposite; so much so that the chief characteristic of his philosophy is its Promethean spirit. He maintained that the basis of moral authority was internal, diffused among all individuals; that it was the natural love of the beautiful and the good wherever it might spring, and however fate might oppose it.

> To suffer . . .
> To forgive . . .
> To defy Power . . .
> To love and bear; to hope, till hope creates
> From its own wreck the thing it contemplates;
> Neither to change, nor falter, nor repent;
> This . . . is to be
> Good, great and joyous, beautiful and free.

Shelley was also removed from any ordinary atheism by his truly speculative sense for eternity. He was a thorough Platonist. All metaphysics perhaps is poetry, but Platonic metaphysics is good poetry, and to this class Shelley's belongs. For instance:

> The pure spirit shall flow
> Back to the burning fountain whence it came,
> A portion of the eternal, which must glow
> Through time and change, unquenchably the same.
> Peace, peace! he is not dead, he doth not sleep!
> He hath awakened from the dream of life.
> 'Tis we who, lost in stormy visions, keep
> With phantoms an unprofitable strife.
>
> He is made one with Nature. There is heard
> His voice in all her music, from the moan
> Of thunder, to the song of night's sweet bird.
> He is a portion of the loveliness

Which once he made more lovely.

The splendours of the firmament of time
May be eclipsed, but are extinguished not:
Like stars to their appointed height they climb,
And death is a low mist which cannot blot
The brightness it may veil. When lofty thought
Lifts a young heart above its mortal lair,
    . . . the dead live there.

Atheism or pantheism of this stamp cannot be taxed with being gross or materialistic; the trouble is rather that it is too hazy in its sublimity. The poet has not perceived the natural relation between facts and ideals so clearly or correctly as he has felt the moral relation between them. But his allegiance to the intuition which defies, for the sake of felt excellence, every form of idolatry or cowardice wearing the mask of religion—this allegiance is itself the purest religion; and it is capable of inspiring the sweetest and most absolute poetry. In daring to lay bare the truths of fate, the poet creates for himself the subtlest and most heroic harmonies; and he is comforted for the illusions he has lost by being made incapable of desiring them.

We have seen that Shelley, being unteachable, could never put together any just idea of the world: he merely collected images and emotions, and out of them made worlds of his own. His poetry accordingly does not well express history, nor human character, nor the constitution of nature. What he unrolls before us instead is, in a sense, fantastic; it is a series of landscapes, passions, and cataclysms such as never were on earth, and never will be. If you are seriously interested only in what belongs to earth you will not be seriously interested in Shelley. Literature, according to Matthew Arnold, should be criticism of life, and Shelley did not criticise life; so that his poetry had no solidity. But is life, we may ask, the same thing as the circumstances of life on earth? Is the spirit of life, that marks and judges those circumstances, itself nothing? Music is surely no description of the circumstances of life; yet it is relevant to life unmistakably, for it stimulates by means of a torrent of abstract movements and images the formal and emotional possibilities of living which lie in the spirit. By so doing music becomes a part of life, a congruous addition, a parallel life, as it were, to the vulgar one. I see no reason, in the analogies of the natural world, for supposing that the circumstances of human life are the only circumstances in which the spirit of life can disport itself. Even on this planet, there are sea-animals and air-animals, ephemeral beings and self-centred beings, as well as persons who can grow as old as Matthew Arnold, and be as fond as he was of classifying other people. And beyond this planet, and in the interstices of what our limited senses can perceive, there are probably many forms of life not criticised in any of the books which Matthew Arnold said we should read in order to know the best that has been thought and said in the world. The future, too, even among men, may contain, as Shelley puts it, many "arts, though unimagined, yet to be." The divination of poets cannot, of course, be expected to reveal any of these hidden regions as they actually exist or will exist; but

what would be the advantage of revealing them? It could only be what the advantage of criticising human life would be also, to improve subsequent life indirectly by turning it towards attainable goods, and is it not as important a thing to improve life directly and in the present, if one has the gift, by enriching rather than criticising it? Besides, there is need of fixing the ideal by which criticism is to be guided. If you have no image of happiness or beauty or perfect goodness before you, how are you to judge what portions of life are important, and what rendering of them is appropriate?

Being a singer inwardly inspired, Shelley could picture the ideal goals of life, the ultimate joys of experience, better than a discursive critic or observer could have done. The circumstances of life are only the bases or instruments of life: the fruition of life is not in retrospect, not in description of the instruments, but in expression of the spirit itself, to which those instruments may prove useful; as music is not a criticism of violins, but a playing upon them. This expression need not resemble its ground. Experience is diversified by colours that are not produced by colours, sounds that are not conditioned by sounds, names that are not symbols for other names, fixed ideal objects that stand for ever-changing material processes. The mind is fundamentally lyrical, inventive, redundant. Its visions are its own offspring, hatched in the warmth of some favourable cosmic gale. The ambient weather may vary, and these visions be scattered; but the ideal world they pictured may some day be revealed again to some other poet similarly inspired; the possibility of restoring it, or something like it, is perpetual. It is precisely because Shelley's sense for things is so fluid, so illusive, that it opens to us emotionally what is a serious scientific probability; namely, that human life is not all life, nor the landscape of earth the only admired landscape in the universe; that the ancients who believed in gods and spirits were nearer the virtual truth (however anthropomorphically they may have expressed themselves) than any philosophy or religion that makes human affairs the centre and aim of the world. Such moral imagination is to be gained by sinking into oneself, rather than by observing remote happenings, because it is at its heart, not at its fingertips, that the human soul touches matter, and is akin to whatever other centres of life may people the infinite.

For this reason the masters of spontaneity, the prophets, the inspired poets, the saints, the mystics, the musicians are welcome and most appealing companions. In their simplicity and abstraction from the world they come very near the heart. They say little and help much. They do not picture life, but have life, and give it. So we may say, I think, of Shelley's magic universe what he said of Greece; if it

            Must be
A wreck, yet shall its fragments re-assemble,
And build themselves again impregnably
        In a diviner clime,
To Amphionic music, on some cape sublime
Which frowns above the idle foam of time.

"Frowns," says Shelley rhetorically, as if he thought that

something timeless, something merely ideal, could be for-midable, or could threaten existing things with any but an ideal defeat. Tremendous error! Eternal possibilities may indeed beckon; they may attract those who instinctively pursue them as a star may guide those who wish to reach the place over which it happens to shine. But an eternal possibility has no material power. It is only one of an infinity of other things equally possible intrinsically, yet most of them quite unrealisable in this world of blood and mire. The realm of eternal essences rains down no Jovian thunderbolts, but only a ghostly Uranian calm. There is no frown there; rather, a passive and universal welcome to any who may have in them the will and the power to climb. Whether any one has the will depends on his material constitution, and whether he has the power depends on the firm texture of that constitution and on circum-stances happening to be favourable to its operation. Oth-erwise what the rebel or the visionary hails as his ideal will be no picture of his destiny or of that of the world. It will be, and will always remain, merely a picture of his heart. This picture, indestructible in its ideal essence, will mirror also the hearts of those who may share, or may have shared, the nature of the poet who drew it. So purely ideal and so deeply human are the visions of Shelley. So truly does he deserve the epitaph which a clear-sighted friend wrote upon his tomb: *cor cordium,* the heart of hearts.

William Butler Yeats   (essay date 1933)

SOURCE: "Prometheus Unbound," in *The Spectator,* Vol. 150, No. 5464, March 17, 1933, pp. 366-67.

[*Yeats was an Irish poet, playwright, and essayist of the late nineteenth and early twentieth centuries. The leading figure of the Irish Renaissance, Yeats was also an active critic of his contemporaries' work. His critical essays appeared initially in the* Dial *magazine and were collect-ed posthumously in* Essays and Introductions *(1961). Commentators observe that Yeats judged the works of others according to his own poetic values of sincerity, passion, and vital imagination. In the following essay, Yeats provides a personal account of the influence of Shelley's work.*]

When I was a young man I wrote two essays calling Shel-ley's dominant symbol the Morning Star, his poetry the poetry of desire. I had meant to explain *Prometheus Unbound,* but some passing difficulty turned me from a task that began to seem impossible. What does Shelley mean by Demo-gorgon? It lives in the centre of the earth, the sphere of Parmenides, perhaps, in a darkness that sends forth "rays of gloom" as "light from the meridian sun"; it names itself "eternity." When it has succeeded Jupiter, "the supreme of living things," as he did Saturn, when he and it have gone to lie "henceforth in darkness," Prometheus is set free, nature purified. Shelley the polit-ical revolutionary expected miracle, the Kingdom of God in the twinkling of an eye like some Christian of the first

century. He had accepted Berkeley's philosophy as ex-pounded in Sir William Drummond's *Academical Ques-tions.* The ultimate reality is not thought, for thought can-not create, but "can only perceive"; the created world is a stream of images in the human mind, the stream and cav-ern of his symbolism; this stream is Time. Eternity is the abyss which receives and creates. Sometimes the soul is a boat, and in this boat Asia sails against the current from age to youth, from youth to infancy, and so to the pre-natal condition "Peopled by shapes too bright to see." In the fourth act this condition, man's first happiness and his last, sings its ecstatic song; and yet although the first and last it is always near at hand, "Tir n'an og is not far from any of you," as a country-woman said to me:

That garden sweet, that lady fair,
And all sweet shapes and odours there,
In truth, have never passed away;
'Tis we; 'tis ours are changed; not they.

Why then does Demo-gorgon, whose task is beneficent, who lies in wait behind "The mighty portal . . . whence the oracular vapour is hurled up which lonely men drink wandering in their youth," bear so terrible a shape, and not to the eyes of Jupiter, external necessity, alone, but to those of Asia, who is identical with the Venus-Urania of the *Athanais.* Why is Shelley terrified of the Last Day like a Victorian child? It was not terrible to Blake, "For the cherub with the flaming sword is hereby commanded to leave his guard at the Tree of Life; and when he does the whole creation will be consumed and appear infinite and holy, whereas it now appears finite and corrupt."

Demo-gorgon made his plot incoherent, its interpretation impossible, it was thrust there by that something which again and again forced him to balance the object of desire conceived as miraculous and superhuman, with nightmare. Shelley told his friends of attempts upon his life or his liberty, elaborating details between delusion and deceit, believed himself infected with elephantiasis because he had sat opposite a fat woman in an omnibus, encountered terrifying apparitions, one a woman with eyes in her breasts; nor did his friendships escape obsession, his admired Eliz-abeth Hutchinson became "the brown demon . . . an artful, superficial, ugly, hermaphroditical beast of a woman"; nor was *Prometheus* the only nightmare-ridden work; there is nothing in *Swell-foot the Tyrant* but the cold rhetoric of obsession; *The Cenci* for all its magnificent construction is made unendurable upon the stage by an artificial char-acter, the scapegoat of his unconscious hatred. When some-body asked Aubrey Beardsley towards the end of his life why he secreted indecencies in odd corners of his designs, more than once necessitating the destruction of a plate, he answered "Something compels me to sacrifice to Priapus." Shelley, whose art is allied to that of the Salome drawings where sex is sublimated to an unearthly receptivity, though more ardent and positive, imagined under a like compul-sion whatever seemed dark, destructive, indefinite. Blake, though he had his brown demons, kept his freedom in essentials; he had encountered with what seemed his phys-ical eyes but one nightmare "sealy, speckled, very awful" and thought such could visit but seldom imaginative men.

Shelley was not a mystic, his system of thought was constructed by his logical faculty to satisfy desire, not a symbolical revelation received after the suspension of all desire. He could neither say with Dante "Thy will is my peace," nor with Finn in the Irish story "the best music is what happens."

There is a form of mediation which permits an image or symbol to generate itself, and the images and symbols so generated build themselves up into coherent structures often beautiful and startling. When a young man I made an exhaustive study of this condition in myself and in others, choosing as a rule for the initiatory symbol a name or form associated with a Cabbalistic Sephiroth, or with one of the five traditional elements. Sometimes, though not in my own case, trance intervened and the structure attained a seeming physical solidity, this however seldom happened and was considered undesirable. Almost always, after some days or weeks of mediation, a form emerged in sleep or amid the ordinary affairs of life to show or speak some significant message, or at some moment a strange hidden will controlled the unconscious movements of the body. If the experimentalist had an impassioned purpose, some propaganda, let us say, and no critical sense, he might become obsessed by images, voices, that had, it seemed, for their sole object to guard his purpose or to express its contrary and threaten it. The mystic, upon the other hand, is in no such danger, he so lives whether in east or west whether he be Ramakrishna or Boehme, as to dedicate his initiatory image, and its generated images, not to his own but the Divine Purpose, and after certain years attains the Saints' miraculous life. There have been others unfitted for such a life by nature or station, who could yet dedicate their actions and acquire what William Morris has called lucky eyes; "all that he does unwitting he does well." There is much curious evidence to show that the Divine Purpose so invoked descends into the mind at moments of inspiration, not as spiritual life alone but as what seems a physical brightness. Perhaps everybody that pursues that life for however short a time, even, as it were, but touches it, experiences now and again during sleep bright coherent dreams where something is shown or spoken that grows in meaning with the passage of time. Blake spoke of this "Stronger and better light," called its source "the human form divine," Shelley's "harmonious soul of many a soul," or, as we might say, the Divine Purpose. The stationary, joyous energy of certain among his figures, "Christ Blessing" for instance, or of his own life when we regard it as a whole as contrasted with the sadness and disquiet of Shelley's, suggests radiating light. We understand why the first Christian painters encircled certain heads with light. Because this source or purpose is always an action, never a system of thought, its man can attend, as Shelley could not, to the whole drama of life, simplicities, banalities, intoxications, even lie upon his left side and eat dung, set free "from a multitude of opinions."

It was as a mystic that Blake wrote "Sweet joy befall thee," "Soft deceit and idleness," "The Holy Word walks among the ancient trees." Shelley's art shows that he was an unconverted man though certainly a visionary, what people call a "psychic"; his landscapes are vaporised and generalized by his purpose, his spirits have not the separated existence even of those that in "Manfred" curse and yet have "sweet and melancholy" voices. He was the tyrant of his own being, nor was it in all likelihood a part of the plan that it should find freedom, seeing that he worked as did Keats and Marlowe, uncorrecting and unhesitating, as though he knew the shortness of his life. That life, and all lives, would be unintelligible to me did I not think of them as an exfoliation prolonged from life to life; he sang of something beginning.

When I was in my early twenties Shelley was much talked about, London had its important "Shelley Society," *The Cenci* had been performed and forbidden, provincial sketching clubs displayed pictures by young women of the burning of Shelley's body. The orthodox religion, as our mothers had taught it, was no longer credible, those who could not substitute Connoisseurship, or some humanitarian or scientific pursuit found a substitute in Shelley. He had shared our curiosities, our political problems, our conviction that despite all experience to the contrary, love is enough; and unlike Blake, isolated by an arbitrary symbolism, he seemed to sum up all that was metaphysical in English poetry. When in middle life I looked back I found that he and not Blake, whom I had studied more and with more approval, had shaped my life, and when I thought of the tumultuous and often tragic lives of friends or acquaintance I attributed to his direct or indirect influence their Jacobin frenzies, their brown demons.

Another study of that time, less general, more confined to exceptional men, was that of Balzac as a social philosopher. When I was thirteen or fourteen I heard somebody say that he changed men's lives, nor can I think it a coincidence that an epoch founded in such thought as Shelley's ended with an art of solidity and complexity. Me at any rate he saved from the pursuit of a beauty that seeming at once absolute and external requires, to strike a balance, hatred as absolute. Yet Balzac is no complete solution for that can be found in religion alone. One of the sensations of my childhood was a description of a now lost design of Nettleship's, God creating Evil, a vast terrifying face, a woman and a tiger rising from the forehead. Why did it seem so blasphemous and so profound? It was many years before I understood that we must not demand even the welfare of the human race, nor traffic with divinity in our prayers. Divinity moves outside our antinomies, it may be our lot to worship in terror: "Did He who made the lamb make thee?"

F. R. Leavis   (essay date 1935)

SOURCE: "Revaluations (VIII): Shelley," in *Scrutiny*, Vol. 4, No. 2, September, 1935, pp. 150-80.

[Leavis was an influential twentieth-century English critic. His methodology combined close textual criticism with predominantly moral and social concerns; however, Leavis was not interested in the individual writer per se, but rather with the usefulness of his or her art in the scheme

of civilization. In the following essay, Leavis discusses several notable critical attacks on Shelley's style.]

If Shelley had not received some distinguished attention in recent years (and he has been differed over by the most eminent critics) there might, perhaps, have seemed little point in attempting a restatement of the essential critical observations—the essential observations, that is, in the reading and appreciation of Shelley's poetry. For they would seem to be obvious enough. Yet it is only one incitement out of many when a critic of peculiar authority, contemplating the common change from being 'intoxicated by Shelley's poetry at the age of fifteen' to finding it now 'almost unreadable,' invokes for explanation the nature of Shelley's 'ideas' and, in reference to them, that much-canvassed question of the day, 'the question of belief or disbelief':

> It is not so much that thirty years ago I was able to read Shelley under an illusion which experience has dissipated, as that because the question of belief or disbelief did not arise I was in a much better position to enjoy the poetry. I can only regret that Shelley did not live to put his poetic gifts, which were certainly of the first order, at the service of more tenable beliefs—which need not have been, for my purposes, beliefs more acceptable to me. [G. Santayana, "Shelley, Or the Poetic Value of Revolutionary Principles," *Winds of Doctrine,* 1936]

This is, of course, a personal statement; but perhaps if one insists on the more obvious terms of literary criticism—more strictly critical terms—in which such a change might be explained, and suggests that the terms actually used might be found unfortunate in their effect, the impertinence will not be unpardonable. It does, in short, seem worth endeavoring to make finally plain that, when one dissents from persons who, sympathizing with Shelley's revolutionary doctrines and with his idealistic ardours and fervour—with his 'beliefs,' exalt him as a poet, it is strictly the 'poetry' one is criticizing. There would also appear to be some reason for insisting that in finding Shelley almost unreadable one need not be committing oneself to a fashionably limited taste—an inability to appreciate unfashionable kinds of excellence or to understand a use of words that is unlike Hopkins's or Donne's.

It will be well to start, in fact, by examining the working of Shelley's poetry—his characteristic modes of expression—as exemplified in one of his best poems.

> Thou on whose stream, mid the steep sky's commotion,
> Loose clouds like earth's decaying leaves are shed,
> Shook from the tangled boughs of Heaven and Ocean,
>
> Angels of rain and lightning: there are spread
> On the blue surface of thine äery surge,
> Like the bright hair uplifted from the head
> Of some fierce Maenad, even from the dim verge
> Of the horizon to the zenith's height,

> The locks of the approaching storm.

The sweeping movement of the verse, with the accompanying pungency, is so potent that, as many can testify, it is possible to have been for years familiar with the Ode—to know it by heart—without asking the obvious questions. In what respects are the 'loose clouds' like 'decaying leaves'? The correspondence is certainly not in shape, colour or way of moving. It is only the vague general sense of windy tumult that associates the clouds and the leaves; and, accordingly, the appropriateness of the metaphor 'stream' in the first line is not that it suggests a surface on which, like leaves, the clouds might be 'shed,' but that it contributes to the general 'streaming' effect in which the inappropriateness of 'shed' passes unnoticed. What, again, are those 'tangled boughs of Heaven and Ocean'? They stand for nothing that Shelley could have pointed to in the scene before him; the 'boughs,' it is plain, have grown out of the 'leaves' in the previous line, and we are not to ask what the tree is. Nor are we to scrutinize closely the 'stream' metaphor as developed: that 'blue surface' must be the concave of the sky, an oddly smooth surface for a 'surge'—if we consider a moment. But in this poetic surge, while we let ourselves be swept along, there is no considering, the image doesn't challenge any inconvenient degree of realization, and the oddness is lost. Then again, in what ways does the approach of a storm ('loose clouds like earth's decaying leaves,' 'like ghosts from an enchanter fleeing') suggest streaming hair? The appropriateness of the Maenad, clearly, lies in the pervasive suggestion of frenzied onset, and we are not to ask whether her bright hair is to be seen as streaming out in front of her (as, there is no need to assure ourselves, it might be doing if she were running before a still swifter gale: in the kind of reading that got so far as proposing to itself this particular reassurance no general satisfaction could be exacted from Shelley's imagery).

Here, clearly, in these peculiarities of imagery and sense, peculiarities analysable locally in the mode of expression, we have the manifestation of essential characteristics—the Shelleyan characteristics as envisaged by the criticism that works on a philosophical plane and makes judgments of a moral order. In the growth of those 'tangled boughs' out of the leaves, exemplifying as it does a general tendency of the images to forget the status of the metaphor or simile that introduced them and to assume an autonomy and a right to propagate, so that we lose in confused generations and perspectives the perception or thought that was the ostensible *raison d'être* of imagery, we have a recognized essential trait of Shelley's: his weak grasp upon the actual. This weakness, of course, commonly has more or less creditable accounts given of it—idealism, Platonism and so on; and even as unsentimental a judge as Mr. Santayana correlates Shelley's inability to learn from experience with his having been born a 'nature preformed,' a 'spokesman of the *a priori*,' 'a dogmatic, inspired, perfect and incorrigible creature.' It seems to me that Mr. Santayana's essay, admirable as it is, rates the poetry too high. But for the moment it will be enough to recall limitations that are hardly disputed: Shelley was not gifted for drama or narrative. Having said this, I realize that I had forgotten the conventional standing of *The Cenci*; but controversy may be postponed: it is at any rate universally agreed that (to shift tactfully to positive terms) Shelley's genius was 'essentially lyrical.'

This predicate would, in common use, imply a special emotional intensity—a vague gloss, but it is difficult to go further without slipping into terms that are immediately primitive and limiting. Thus there is certainly a sense in which Shelley's poetry is peculiarly emotional, and when we try to define this sense we find ourselves invoking an absence of something. The point may be best made, perhaps, by recalling the observation noted above, that one may have been long familiar with the **'Ode to the West Wind'** without ever having asked the obvious questions; questions that propose themselves at the first critical inspection. This poetry induces—depends for its success on inducing—a kind of attention that doesn't bring the critical intelligence into play: the imagery feels right, the associations work appropriately, if (as it takes conscious resistance not to do) one accepts the immediate feeling and doesn't slow down to think.

Shelley himself can hardly have asked the questions. Not that he didn't expend a great deal of critical labour upon his verse. 'He composed rapidly and attained to perfection by intensive correction. He would sometimes write down a phrase with alterations and rejections time after time until it came within a measure of satisfying him. Words are frequently substituted for others and lines interpolated.' The **'Ode to the West Wind'** itself, as is shown in the repository of fragments the preface to which supplies these observations, profited by the process described, which must be allowed to have been in some sense critical. But the critical part of Shelley's creative labour was a matter of getting the verse to feel right, and feeling, for Shelley as a poet, had—as the insistent concern for 'rightness,' the typical final product being what it is, serves to emphasize—little to do with thinking (though Shelley was in some ways a very intelligent man).

We have here, if not sufficient justification for the predicate 'essentially lyrical,' certainly a large part of the reason for Shelley's being found essentially poetical by the succeeding age. He counted, in fact, for a great deal in what came to be the prevailing idea of 'the poetical'. . . . The Romantic conceptions of genius and inspiration developed (the French Revolution and its ideological background must, of course, be taken into account) in reaction against the Augustan insistence on the social and the rational. When Wordsworth says that 'all good poetry is the spontaneous overflow of powerful feelings' he is of his period, though the intended force of this dictum, the force it has in its context and in relation to Wordsworth's own practice, is very different from that given it when Shelley assents, or when it is assimilated to Byron's 'poetry is the lava of the imagination, whose eruption prevents an earthquake.' But Byron was for the young Tennyson (and the Ruskin parents) the poet, and Shelley (Browning's 'Suntreader') was the idol of the undergraduate Tennyson and his fellow Apostles, and, since the poetry of 'the age of Wordsworth' became canonical, the assent given to Words-

worth's dictum has commonly been Shelleyan.

The force of Shelley's insistence on spontaneity is simple and unequivocal. It will be enough to recall a representative passage or two from the *Defence of Poetry*:

> for the mind in creation is as a fading coal, which some invisible influence, like an inconstant wind, awakes to transitory brightness; this power arises from within, like the colour of a flower which fades and changes as it is developed, and the conscious portions of our nature are unpropped either of its approach or its departure.

'Inspiration' is not something to be tested, clarified, defined and developed in composition,

> but when composition begins, inspiration is already on the decline, and the most glorious poetry that has ever been communicated to the world is probably a feeble shadow of the original conceptions of the poet . . . The toil and delay recommended by critics can be justly interpreted to mean no more than a careful observation of the inspired moments, and an artificial convening of the spaces between their suggestions, by the intertexture of conventional expressions; a necessity only imposed by the limitedness of the poetical faculty itself . . .

The 'poetical faculty,' we are left no room for doubting, can, of its very nature, have nothing to do with any discipline, and can be associated with conscious effort only mechanically and externally, and when Shelley says that Poetry

> is not subject to the control of the active powers of the mind, and that its birth and recurrence have no necessary connexion with consciousness or will

he is not saying merely that the 'active powers of the mind' are insufficient in themselves for creation—that poetry cannot be written merely by taking thought. The effect of Shelley's eloquence is to hand poetry over to a sensibility that has no more dealings with intelligence than it can help; to a 'poetic faculty' that, for its duly responsive vibrating (though the poet must reverently make his pen as sensitive an instrument as possible to 'observe'— in the scientific sense—the vibrations), demands that active intelligence shall be, as it were, switched off.

Shelley, of course, had ideas and ideals; he wrote philosophical essays, and it need not be irrelevant to refer, in discussing his poetry, to Plato, Godwin and other thinkers. But there is nothing grasped in the poetry—no object offered for contemplation, no realized presence to persuade or move us by what it is. Dr. A. C. Bradley, remarking that 'Shelley's ideals of good, whether as a character or as a mode of life, resting as they do on abstraction from the mass of real existence, tend to lack body and individuality,' adds: 'But we must remember that Shelley's strength and weakness are closely allied, and it may be that the very abstractness of his ideal was a condition of that quivering intensity of aspiration towards it in which his poetry is unequalled.' That is the best that can be respectably said. Actually, that 'quivering intensity,' offered in itself apart from any substance, offered instead of any object, is what, though it may make Shelley intoxicating at fifteen makes him almost unreadable, except in very small quantities of his best, to the mature. Even when he is in his own way unmistakably a distinguished poet, as in *Prometheus Unbound,* it is impossible to go on reading him at any length with pleasure; the elusive imagery, the high-pitched emotions, the tone and movement, the ardours, ecstasies and despairs, are too much the same all through. The effect is of vanity and emptiness (Arnold was right) as well as monotony.

The force of the judgment that feeling in Shelley's poetry is divorced from thought needs examining further. Any suspicion that Donne is the implied criterion will, perhaps, be finally averted if for the illuminating contrast we go to Wordsworth. Wordsworth is another 'Romantic' poet; he too is undramatic; and he too invites the criticism (Arnold, his devoted admirer, made it) that he lacks variety. 'Thought' will hardly be found an assertive presence in his best poetry; in so far as the term suggests an overtly active energy it is decidedly inappropriate. 'Emotion,' his own word, is the word most readers would insist on, though they would probably judge Wordsworth's emotion to be less lyrical than Shelley's. The essential difference, however—and it is a very important one—seems, for present purposes, more relevantly stated in the terms I used in discussing Wordsworth's 'recollection in tranquillity.' The process covered by this phrase was one of emotional discipline, critical exploration of experience, pondered valuation and maturing reflection. As a result of it an organization is engaged in Wordsworth's poetry, and the activity and standards of critical intelligence are implicit.

An associated difference was noted in the sureness with which Wordsworth grasps the world of common perception. The illustration suggested was 'The Simplon Pass' in comparison with Shelley's **'Mont Blanc.'** The element of Wordsworth in **'Mont Blanc'** (it is perceptible in these opening lines) serves only to enhance the contrast:

> The everlasting universe of things
> Flows through the mind, and rolls its rapid waves,
> Now dark—now glittering—now reflecting gloom—
> Now lending splendour, where from secret springs
> The source of human thought its tribute brings
> Of waters,—with a sound but half its own,
> Such as a feeble brook will oft assume
> In the wild woods, among the mountains lone,
> Where waterfalls around it leap for ever,
> Where woods and winds contend, and a vast river
> Over its rocks ceaselessly bursts and raves.

The metaphorical and the actual, the real and the imagined, the inner and the outer, could hardly be more unsortably and indistinguishably confused. The setting, of course, provides special excuse for bewildered confusion; but Shelley takes eager advantage of the excuse and the confusion is characteristic—what might be found unusual in **'Mont Blanc'** is a certain compelling vividness. In any case, Wordsworth himself is explicitly offering a sense of sublime bewilderment, similarly inspired:

> Black drizzling crags that spake by the wayside
> As if a voice were in them, the sick sight
> And giddy prospect of the raving stream,
> The unfettered clouds and region of the heavens,
> Tumult and peace, the darkness and the light—
> Were all like workings of one mind, the features
> Of the same face . . .

He is, of course, recollecting in tranquillity; but the collectedness of those twenty lines (as against Shelley's one hundred and forty) does not belong merely to the record; it was present (or at least the movement towards it was) in the experience, as those images, 'one mind,' 'the same face'—epitomizing, as they do, the contrast with Shelley's ecstatic dissipation—may fairly be taken to testify.

This comparison does not aim immediately at a judgment of relative value. **'Mont Blanc'** is very interesting as well as idiosyncratic, and is not obviously the product of the less rare gift. There are, nevertheless, critical judgments to be made—judgments concerning the emotional quality of Wordsworth's poetry and of Shelley's: something more than mere description of idiosyncrasy is in view. What should have come out in the comparison that started as a note on Wordsworth's grasp of the outer world is the unobtrusiveness with which that 'outer' turns into 'inner': the antithesis, clearly, is not altogether, for present purposes, a simple one to apply. What is characteristic of Wordsworth is to grasp surely (which, in the nature of the case, must be delicately and subtly) what he offers, whether this appears as belonging to the outer world—the world as perceived, or to inner experience. He seems always to be presenting an object (wherever this may belong) and the emotion seems to derive from what is presented. The point is very obviously and impressively exemplified in 'A slumber did my spirit seal,' which shows Wordsworth at his supreme height. Here (compare it with the **'Ode to the West Wind,'** where we have Shelley's genius at its best; or, if something more obviously comparable is required, with Tennyson's 'Break, break, break') there is no emotional comment—nothing 'emotional' in phrasing, movement or tone; the facts seem to be presented barely, and the emotional force to be generated by them in the reader's mind when he has taken them in—generated by the two juxtaposed stanzas, in the contrast between the situations or states they represent.

Shelley, at his best and worst, offers the emotion in itself, unattached, in the void. 'In itself,' 'for itself'—it is an easy shift to the pejorative implications of 'for its own sake'; just as, for a poet with the habit of sensibility and expression described, it was an easy shift to deserving them. For Shelley is obnoxious to the pejorative implications of 'habit': being inspired was, for him, too apt to mean surrendering to a kind of hypnotic rote of favourite images, associations and words. 'Inspiration,' there not being an organization for it to engage (as in Wordsworth, whose sameness is of a different order from Shelley's, there was) had only poetical habits to fall back on. We have them in their most innocent aspect in those favourite words: *radiant, aërial, odorous, daedal, faint, sweet, bright, wingèd, -inwoven,* and the rest of the fondled vocabulary that any reader of Shelley could go on enumerating. They manifest themselves as decidedly deplorable in **'The Cloud'** and **'To a Skylark,'** which illustrate the dangers of fostering the kind of inspiration that works only when critical intelligence is switched off. These poems may be not unfairly described as the products of switching poetry on. There has been in recent years some controversy about particular points in **'To a Skylark,'** and there are a score or more points inviting adverse criticism. But this need hardly be offered; it is, or should be, so plain that the poem is a mere tumbled out spate ('spontaneous overflow') of poeticalities, the place of each one of which Shelley could have filled with another without the least difficulty and without making any essential difference. They are held together by the pervasive 'lyrical emotion,' and that this should be capable of holding them together is comment enough on the nature of its strength.

Cheaper surrenders to inspiration may easily be found in the collected Shelley; there are, for instance, gross indulgences in the basest Regency album taste. But criticism of Shelley has something more important to deal with than mere bad poetry; or, rather, there are badnesses inviting the criticism that involves moral judgments. It must have already appeared (it has virtually been said) that surrendering to inspiration cannot, for a poet of Shelley's emotional habits, have been very distinguishable from surrendering to temptation. The point comes out in an element of the favoured vocabulary not exemplified above: *charnel, corpse, phantom, liberticide, aghast, ghastly* and so on. The wrong approach to emotion, the approach from the wrong side or end (so to speak), is apparent here; Shelley would clearly have done well not to have indulged these habits and these likings: the viciousness and corruption are immediately recognizable. But viciousness and corruption do not less attend upon likings for tender ('I love Love'), sympathetic, exalted and ecstatic emotions, and may be especially expected to do so in a mind as little able to hold an object in front of it as Shelley's was.

The transition from the lighter concerns of literary criticism to the diagnosis of radical disabilities and perversions, such as call for moral comment, may be conveniently illustrated from a favourite anthology-piece, **'When the lamp is shattered'**:

> When the lamp is shattered
> The light in the dust lies dead—
> When the cloud is scattered
> The rainbow's glory is shed.
> When the lute is broken,
> Sweet tones are remembered not;
> When the lips have spoken,
> Loved accents are soon forgot.
>
> As music and splendour
> Survive not the lamp and the lute,
> The heart's echoes render
> No song when the spirit is mute:—
> No song but sad dirges,
> Like the wind through a ruined cell,
> Or the mournful surges

> That ring the dead seaman's knell.
>
> When hearts have once mingled
> Love first leaves the well-built nest;
> The weak one is singled
> To endure what it once possessed.
> O Love! who bewailest
> The frailty of all things here,
> Why choose you the frailest
> For your cradle, your home, and your bier?
>
> Its passions will rock thee
> As the storms rock the ravens on high;
> Bright reason will mock thee,
> Like the sun from a wintry sky.
> From thy nest every rafter
> Will rot, and thine eagle home
> Leave thee naked to laughter,
> When leaves fall and cold winds come.

The first two stanzas call for no very close attention— to say so, indeed, is to make the main criticism, seeing that they offer a show of insistent argument. However, reading with an unsolicited closeness, one may stop at the second line and ask whether the effect got with 'lies dead' is legitimate. Certainly, the emotional purpose of the poem is served, but the emotional purpose that went on being served in that way would be suspect. Leaving the question in suspense, perhaps, one passes to 'shed'; 'shed' as tears, petals and coats are shed, or as light is shed? The latter would be a rather more respectable use of the word in connection with a rainbow's glory, but the context indicates the former. Only in the vaguest and slackest state of mind—of imagination and thought—could one so describe the fading of a rainbow; but for the right reader 'shed' sounds right, the alliteration with 'shattered' combining with the verse-movement to produce a kind of inevitability. And, of course, suggesting tears and the last rose of summer, it suits with the general emotional effect. The nature of this is by now so unmistakable that the complete nullity of the clinching 'so,' when it arrives—of the two lines that justify the ten preparatory lines of analogy— seems hardly worth stopping to note:

> The heart's echoes render
> No song when the spirit is mute.

Nor is it surprising that there should turn out to be a song after all, and a pretty powerful one—for those who like that sort of thing; the 'sad dirges,' the 'ruined cell,' the 'mournful surges' and the 'dead seaman's knell' being immediately recognizable as currency values. Those who take pleasure in recognizing and accepting them are not at the same time exacting about sense.

The critical interest up to this point has been to see Shelley, himself (when inspired) so unexacting about sense, giving himself so completely to sentimental banalities. With the next stanza it is much the same, though the emotional clichés take on a grosser unction and the required abeyance of thought (and imagination) becomes more remarkable. In what form are we to imagine Love leaving the well-built nest? For readers who get so far as asking, there can be no acceptable answer. It would be unpoetically literal to suggest that, since the weak one is singled, the truant must be the mate, and, besides, it would raise unnecessary difficulties. Perhaps the mate, the strong one, is what the weak one, deserted by Love, whose alliance made possession once possible, now has to endure? But the suggestion is frivolous; the sense is plain enough—enough, that is, for those who respond to the sentiment. Sufficient recognition of the sense depends neither on thinking, nor on realization of the metaphors, but on response to the sentimental commonplaces: it is only when intelligence and imagination insist on intruding that difficulties arise. So plain is this that there would be no point in contemplating the metaphorical complexity that would develop if we could take the tropes seriously and tried to realize Love making of the weak one, whom it (if we evade the problem of sex) leaves behind in the well-built nest, a cradle, a home and a bier.

The last stanza brings a notable change; it alone in the poem has any distinction, and its personal quality, characteristically Shelleyan, stands out against the sentimental conventionality of the rest. The result is to compel a more radical judgment on the poem than has yet been made. In 'Its passions will rock thee' the 'passions' must be those of Love, so that it can no longer be Love that is being apostrophized. Who, then, is 'thee'? The 'frailest'—the 'weak one'—it would appear. But any notion one may have had that the 'weak one,' as the conventional sentiments imply, is the woman must be abandoned: the 'eagle home,' to which the 'well-built nest' so incongruously turns, is the Poet's. The familiar timbre, the desolate intensity (note particularly the use of 'bright' in 'bright reason'), puts it beyond doubt that Shelley is, characteristically, addressing himself—the 'pardlike Spirit beautiful and swift,' the 'Love in desolation masked,' the 'Power girt round with weakness.'

Characteristically: that is, Shelley's characteristic pathos is self-regarding, directed upon an idealized self in the way suggested by the tags just quoted. This is patently so in some of his best poetry; for instance, in the **'Ode to the West Wind.'** Even there, perhaps, one may find something too like an element of luxury in the poignancy (at any rate, one's limiting criticism of the **'Ode'** would move towards such a judgment); and that in general there must be dangers and weakness attending upon such a habit will hardly be denied. The poem just examined shows how gross may be, in Shelley, the corruptions that are incident. He can make self-pity a luxury at such a level that the conventional pathos of album poeticizing, not excluding the banalities about (it is plainly so in the third stanza) the sad lot of woman, can come in to gratify the appetite.

The abeyance of thought exhibited by the first three stanzas now takes on a more sinister aspect. The switching-off of intelligence that is necessary if the sentiments of the third stanza are to be accepted has now to be invoked in explanation of a graver matter—Shelley's ability to accept the grosser, the truly corrupt, gratifications that have just been indicated. The antipathy of his sensibility to any play

of the critical mind, the uncongeniality of intelligence to inspiration, these clearly go in Shelley, not merely with a capacity for momentary self-deceptions and insincerties, but with a radical lack of self-knowledge. He could say of Wordsworth, implying the opposite of himself, that

> he never could
> Fancy another situation
> From which to dart his contemplation
> Than that wherein he stood.

But, for all his altruistic fervours and his fancied capacity for projecting his sympathies, Shelley is habitually—it is no new observation—his own hero: Alastor, Laon, The Sensitive Plant

> (It loves, even like Love, its deep heart is full,
> It desires what it has not, the Beautiful)

and Prometheus. It is characteristic that he should say to the West Wind,

> A heavy weight of hours has chained and bowed
> One too like thee: tameless, and swift, and proud,

and conclude:

> Be thou, Spirit fierce,
> My spirit! Be thou me, impetuous one!

About the love of such a nature there is likely at the best to be a certain innocent selfishness. And it is with fervour that Shelley says, as he is always saying implicitly, 'I love Love.' Mr. Santayana acutely observes: 'In him, as in many people, too intense a need of loving excludes the capacity for intelligent sympathy.' Perhaps love generally has less in it of intelligent sympathy than the lover supposes, and is less determined by the object of love; but Shelley, we have seen, was, while on the one hand conscious of ardent altruism, on the other peculiarly weak in his hold on objects—peculiarly unable to realize them as existing in their own natures and their own right. His need of loving (in a sense that was not, perhaps, in the full focus of Mr. Santayana's intention) comes out in the erotic element that, as already remarked in these pages, the texture of the poetry pervasively exhibits. There is hardly any need to illustrate here the tender, caressing, voluptuous effects and suggestions of the favourite vocabulary and imagery. The consequences of the need, or 'love,' of loving, combined, as it was, with a notable lack of self-knowledge and a capacity for ecstatic idealizing, are classically extant in *Epipsychidion*.

The love of loathing is, naturally, less conscious than the love of Love. It may fairly be said to involve a love of Hate, if not of hating: justification enough for putting it this way is provided by *The Cenci,* which exhibits a perverse luxury of insistence, not merely upon horror, but upon malignity. This work, of course, is commonly held to require noting as, in the general account of Shelley, a remarkable exception: his genius may be essentially lyrical, but he can, transcending limitations, write great drama. This estimate of *The Cenci* is certainly a remarkable instance of *vis inertiae*—of the power of conventional valuation to perpetuate itself, once established. For it takes no great discernment to see that *The Cenci* is very bad and that its badness is characteristic. Shelley, as usual, is the hero—here the heroine; his relation to Beatrice is of the same order as his relation to Alastor and Prometheus, and the usual vices should not be found more acceptable because of the show of drama.

Nor is this show the less significantly bad because Shelley doesn't know where it comes from—how he is contriving it. He says in his *Preface* that an idea suggested by Calderon is 'the only plagiarism which I have intentionally committed in the whole piece.' Actually, not only is the 'whole piece' Shakespearean in inspiration (how peculiarly dubious an affair inspiration was apt to be for Shelley we have seen); it is full of particular echoes of Shakespeare—echoes protracted, confused and woolly; plagiarisms, that is, of the worst kind. This Shakespeareanizing, general and particular, is—and not the less so for its unconsciousness—quite damning. It means that Shelley's drama and tragedy do not grow out of any realized theme; there is nothing grasped at the core of the piece. Instead there is Beatrice-Shelley, in whose martyrdom the Count acts Jove—with more than Jovian gusto:

> I do not feels as if I were a man,
> But like a fiend appointed to chastise
> The offences of some unremembered world.
> My blood is running up and down my veins;
> A fearful pleasure makes it prick and tingle:
> I feel a giddy sickness of strange awe;
> My heart is beating with an expectation
> Of horrid joy.

The pathos is of corresponding corruptness. The habits that enable Shelley to be unconscious about this kind of indulgence enable him at the same time to turn it into tragic drama by virtue of an unconscious effort to be Shakespeare.

There are, of course, touches of Webster: Beatrice in the trial scene is commonly recognized to have borrowed an effect or two from the White Devil. But the Shakespearean promptings are everywhere, in some places almost ludicrously assorted, obvious and thick. For instance, Act III Sc. ii starts (stage direction: 'Thunder and the sound of a storm') by being at line two obviously Lear. At line eight Othello comes in and carries on for ten lines; and he reasserts himself at line fifty. At line seventy-eight we get an effect from *Macbeth* to be followed by many more in the next act, during which, after much borrowed suspense, the Count's murder is consummated.

The quality of the dramatic poetry and the relation between Shelley and Shakespeare must, for reasons of space, be represented—the example is a fair one—by a single brief passage (Act V Sc. iv 1. 48):

>   O
> My God! Can it be possible I have
> To die so suddenly? So young to go

> Under the obscure, cold, rotting, wormy ground!
> To be nailed down into a narrow place;
> To see no more sweet sunshine; hear no more
> Blithe voice of living thing; muse not again
> Upon familiar thoughts, sad, yet thus lost—
> How fearful! to be nothing! Or to be . . .
> What? Oh, where am I? Let me go not mad!
> Sweet Heaven, forgive weak thoughts! If there
>   should be
> No God, no Heaven, no Earth in the void world;
> The wide, gray, lampless, deep, unpeopled world!

This patently recalls Claudio's speech in *Measure for Measure* (Act III Sc. i):

> Ay, but to die, and go we know not where;
> To lie in cold obstruction and to rot;
> This sensible warm motion to become
> A kneaded clod; and the delighted spirit
> To bathe in fiery floods, or to reside
> In thrilling region of thick-ribbed ice;
> To be imprisoned in the viewless winds,
> And blown with restless violence round about
> The pendent world; or to be worse than worst
> Of those that lawless and incertain thoughts
> Imagine howling:—'tis too horrible!
> The weariest and most loathed worldly life
> That age, ache, penury, and imprisonment
> Can lay on nature is a paradise
> To what we fear of death.

The juxtaposition is enough to expose the vague, generalizing externality of Shelley's rendering. Claudio's words spring from a vividly realized particular situation; from the imagined experience of a given mind in a given critical moment that is felt from the inside—that is lived—with sharp concrete particularly. Claudio's 'Ay, but to die . . .' is not insistently and voluminously emotional like Beatrice's ('wildly')

>   O
> My God! Can it be possible . . .

but it is incomparably more intense. That 'cold obstruction' is not abstract; it gives rather the essence of the situation in which Claudio shrinkingly imagines himself—the sense of the warm body (given by 'cold') struggling ('obstruction' takes an appropriate effort to pronounce) in vain with the suffocating earth. Sentience, warmth and motion, the essentials of being alive as epitomized in the next line, recoil from death, realized brutally in the concrete (the 'clod' is a vehement protest, as 'clay,' which 'kneaded' nevertheless brings appropriately in, would not have been). Sentience, in the 'delighted spirit,' plunges, not into the delightful coolness suggested by 'bathe,' but into the dreadful opposite, and warmth and motion shudder away from the icy prison ('reside' is analogous in working to 'bathe'). The shudder is there in 'thrilling,' which also—such alliteration as that of 'thrilling region' and 'thick-ribbed' is not accidental in a Shakespearean passage of this quality—gives the sharp reverberating report of the ice as, in the intense cold, it is forced up into ridges or ribs (at which, owing to the cracks, the thickness of the ice can be seen).

But there is no need to go on. The point has been sufficiently enforced that, though this vivid concreteness of realization lodged the passage in Shelley's mind, to become at the due moment 'inspiration,' the passage inspired is nothing but wordy emotional generality. It does not grasp and present anything, but merely makes large gestures towards the kind of effect deemed appropriate. We are told emphatically what the emotion is that we are to feel; emphasis and insistence serving instead of realization and advertising its default. The intrusion of the tag from Lear brings out the vague generality of that unconscious set at being Shakespeare which Shelley took for dramatic inspiration.

Inspection of *The Cenci,* then, confirms all the worst in the account of Shelley. Further confirmation would not need much seeking; but, returning to the fact of his genius, it is pleasanter, and more profitable, to recall what may be said by way of explaining how he should have been capable of the worst. His upbringing was against him. As Mr. Santayana says: 'Shelley seems hardly to have been brought up; he grew up in the nursery among his young sisters, at school among the rude boys, without any affectionate guidance, without imbibing any religious or social tradition.' Driven in on himself, he nourished the inner life of adolescence on the trashy fantasies and cheap excitements of the Terror school. The phase of serious tradition in which, in incipient maturity, he began to practise poetry was, in a subtler way, as unfavourable: Shelley needed no encouragement to cultivate spontaneity of emotion and poetical abeyance of thought. Then the state of the world at the time must, in its effect on a spirit of Shelley's sensitive humanity and idealizing bent, be allowed to account for a great deal—as the sonnet, '**England in 1819,**' so curiously intimates:

> An old, mad, blind, despised, and dying king,—
> Princes, the dregs of their dull race, who flow
> Through public scorn,—mud from a muddy
>   spring,—
> Rulers who neither see, nor feel, nor know,
> But leech-like to their fainting country cling,
> Till they drop, blind in blood, without a blow,—
> A people starved and stabbed in the untilled field,—
> An army, which liberticide and prey
> Makes as a two-edged sword to all who wield,—
> Golden and sanguine laws which tempt and slay;
> Religion Christless, Godless—a book sealed;
> A Senate,—Time's worst statute unrepealed,—
> Are graves, from which a glorious Phantom may
> Burst, to illumine our tempestuous day.

The contrast between the unusual strength (for Shelley) of the main body of the sonnet and the pathetic weakness of the final couplet is eloquent. Contemplation of the actual world being unendurable, Shelley devotes himself to the glorious Phantom that may (an oddly ironical stress results from the rime position) work a sudden miraculous change but is in any case as vague as Demogorgon and as

unrelated to actuality—to which Shelley's Evil is correspondingly unrelated.

The strength of the sonnet, though unusual in kind for Shelley, is not of remarkably distinguished quality in itself; the kindred strength of *The Mask of Anarchy* is. Of this poem Professor Elton says [in *Survey of English Literature, 1780-1830,* Vol. II]: 'There is a likeness in it to Blake's [gift] which has often been noticed; the same kind of anvil-stroke, and the same use of an awkward simplicity for the purposes of epigram.' The likeness to Blake is certainly there—much more of a likeness than would have seemed possible from the characteristic work. It lies, not in any assumed broadsheet naïveté or crudity such as the account cited might perhaps suggest, but in a rare emotional intensity and force, deriving from a clear, disinterested and mature vision.

> When one fled past, a maniac mind,
> And her name was Hope, she said:
> But she looked more like Despair,
> And she cried out in the air:
>
> 'My father Time is weak and gray
> With waiting for a better day;
> See how idiot-like he stands,
> Fumbling with his palsied hands!
>
> He has had child after child,
> And the dust of death is piled
> Over every one but me—
> Misery, oh, Misery!'
>
> Then she lay down in the street,
> Right before the horses' feet,
> Expecting, with a patient eye,
> Murder, Fraud, and Anarchy.

These stanzas do not represent all the virtue of the poem, but they show its unusual purity and strength. In spite of 'Murder, Fraud and Anarchy,' there is nothing of the usual Shelleyan emotionalism—no suspicion of indulgence, insistence, corrupt will or improper approach. The emotion seems to inhere in the vision communicated, the situation grasped: Shelley sees what is in front of him too clearly, and with too pure a pity and indignation, to have any regard for his emotions as such; the emotional value of what is presented asserts itself, or rather, does not need asserting. Had he used and developed his genius in the spirit of *The Mask of Anarchy* he would have been a much greater, and a much more readable, poet.

But *The Mask of Anarchy* is little more than a marginal throw-off, and gets perhaps too much stress in even so brief a distinguishing mention as this. The poetry in which Shelley's genius manifests itself characteristically, and for which he has his place in the English tradition, is much more closely related to his weaknesses. It would be perverse to end without recognizing that he achieved memorable things in modes of experience that were peculiarly congenial to the European mind in that phase of its history, and are of permanent interest. The sensibility expressed in the **'Ode to the West Wind'** is much more disablingly limited than current valuation allows, but the consummate expression is rightly treasured. The Shelleyan confusion appears, perhaps, at its most poignant in *The Triumph of Life,* the late unfinished poem. This poem has been paralleled with the revised *Hyperion,* and it is certainly related by more than the *terza rima* to Dante. There is in it a profounder note of disenchantment than before, a new kind of desolation, and, in its questioning, a new and profoundly serious concern for reality:

> . . . their might
> Could not repress the mystery within,
> And for the morn of truth they feigned, deep night
>
> Caught them ere evening . . .
>
> For in the battle Life and they did wage,
> She remained conqueror . . .
>
> 'Whence camest thou? and whither goest thou?
> How did thy course begin?' I said, 'and why?
>
> Mine eyes are sick of this perpetual flow
> Of people, and my heart sick of one sad thought—
> Speak!'
>
> as one between desire and shame

Why T. S. Eliot found Shelley "repellent":

The ideas of Shelley seem to me always to be ideas of adolescence—as there is every reason why they should be. And an enthusiasm for Shelley seems to me also to be an affair of adolescence: for most of us, Shelley has marked an intense period before maturity, but for how many does Shelley remain the companion of age? I confess that I never open the volume of his poems simply because I want to read poetry, but only with some special reason for reference. I find his ideas repellent; and the difficulty of separating Shelley from his ideas and beliefs is still greater than with Wordsworth. And the biographical interest which Shelley has always excited makes it difficult to read the poetry without remembering the man: and the man was humourless, pedantic, self-centred, and sometimes almost a blackguard. Except for an occasional flash of shrewd sense, when he is speaking of someone else and not concerned with his own affairs or with fine writing, his letters are insufferably dull. He makes an astonishing contrast with the attractive Keats. On the other hand, I admit that Wordsworth does not present a very pleasing personality either; yet I not only enjoy his poetry as I cannot enjoy Shelley's, but I enjoy it more than when I first read it. I can only fumble (abating my prejudices as best I can) for reasons why Shelley's abuse of poetry does me more violence than Wordsworth's.

T. S. Eliot, in his "Shelley and Keats," in The Use of Poetry and the Use of Criticism, *Faber and Faber Limited, 1955.*

> Suspended, I said—If, as it doth seem,
> Thou comest from the realm without a name
>
> Into this valley of perpetual dream,
> Show whence I came and where I am, and why—
> Pass not away upon the passing stream.

But in spite of the earnest struggle to grasp something real, the sincere revulsion from personal dreams and fantasies, the poem itself is a drifting phantasmagoria—bewildering and bewildered. Vision opens into vision, dream unfolds within dream, and the visionary perspectives, like those of the imagery in the passage of **'Mont Blanc,'** shift elusively and are lost; and the failure to place the various phases or levels of visionary drift with reference to any grasped reality is the more significant because of the palpable effort. Nevertheless, the *Triumph of Life* is among the few things one can still read and go back to in Shelley when he has become, generally, 'almost unreadable.'

Shelley's part in the later notion of 'the poetical' has been sufficiently indicated. His handling of the medium assimilates him readily, as an influence, to the Spenserian-Miltonic line running through *Hyperion* to Tennyson. Milton is patently present in *Alastor,* the earliest truly Shelleyan poem; and *Adonais*—

> Afar the melancholy thunder moaned,
> Pale Ocean in unquiet slumber lay

—relates him as obviously to *Hyperion* as to *Lycidas.* Indeed, to compare the verse of *Hyperion,* where the Miltonic Grand Style is transmuted by the Spenserianizing Keats, with that of *Adonais* is to bring out the essential relation between the organ resonances of *Paradise Lost* and the pastoral melodizing of *Lycidas.* Mellifluous mourning in *Adonais* is a more fervent luxury than in *Lycidas,* and more declamatory ('Life like a dome of many-coloured glass'—the famous imagery is happily conscious of being impressive, but the impressiveness is for the spellbound, for those sharing the simple happiness of intoxication); and it is, in the voluptuous self-absorption with which the medium enjoys itself, rather nearer to Tennyson.

But, as was virtually said in the discussion of imagery from the **'Ode to the West Wind,'** the Victorian poet with whom Shelley has some peculiar affinities is Swinburne.

Joseph Warren Beach   (essay date 1936)

SOURCE: "Shelley's Naturalism," in *The Concept of Nature in Nineteenth-Century English Poetry,* The Macmillan Publishing Company, 1936, pp. 209-41.

[Beach was an American critic and educator who specialized in American literature and English literature of the Romantic and Victorian eras. In the following excerpt, he examines Shelley's naturalism and the widespread fascination with nature during the Romantic period.]

The word nature is much less frequent in Shelley than in Wordsworth. This is partly owing to the fact that he does not attempt, like Wordsworth, to trace the influence of natural objects in the development of his imagination. It is partly owing to the poetic quality which led him, in his mature work, to employ symbolism in places where Wordsworth used an abstract term. The entire scenery of *Alastor* symbolizes that nature which, to the over-sensitive soul of the poet, furnishes a refuge from the cruelty and misunderstanding of the world, but which in the long run proves his undoing. For Shelley brings to poetry a subtler spirit, a more complicated feeling; he sounds, in this poem, a strong note of romantic irony, and suggests that nature, whom he loves so fanatically as "mother of this unfathomable world," may be a fatal companion for a poet. In later poems—as well as in the earlier *Queen Mab*—nature is shown in a less dubious light. In **"Mont Blanc"** the sublime mountain symbolizes—

> . . . the secret strength of things
> Which governs thought, and to the infinite dome
> Of Heaven is as a law . . .

The west wind, in the famous **"Ode,"** symbolizes the variegated power of natural phenomena and nature's promise of a world reborn to a spirit desolated by the wintry bleakness of the present. In **"The Cloud"** is symbolized the essential oneness of nature amid her manifold changes of form. In the ode **"To a Skylark"** is symbolized the gladness of natural creatures who are free from the "hate, and pride, and fear" which sadden and cloud the spirit of man. In *Prometheus Unbound* there is no need for specific reference to abstract nature since she is represented by one of the leading characters in the allegory; and the physical operations of nature are visibly presented in the masque by Earth and Moon and Ocean and other personifications.

The natural scenery of Shelley has a quality very different from Wordsworth's. It is less realistic, less familiar. It is an imaginative composite of features taken from nature and put together in a pattern suitable to the poet's thought and mood. For this reason Shelley is often felt to be less a poet of nature than Wordsworth; he does not follow nature so faithfully, but compels her to ends of his own. In a sense, however, he is more of a nature-poet. For he readily passes beyond the visible shows of nature to the larger cosmic operations in which she manifests her power and direction. His view is less confined to the surface of the earth where man dwells, more free to follow the movements of cloud and tide and lightning; he visits the secret caves of the earth and circles the orbits of the planets. He is more prone to dwell on the forces and processes—electricity, gravity, light, heat, chemical force, vegetation—by which nature is constituted an entity for scientist and mathematician. The sensuous appeal is as rich and constant in Shelley as in Wordsworth; but it is on a different level of experience, less familiar, and calling for a greater stretch of imagination. In the esthetic synthesis of universal nature with individual "beauteous forms," the element of scientific theory is greater and more constant, though Shelley's symbolism often requires a gloss. And in

a larger proportion of cases, the word nature with him obviously refers to the philosophical abstraction.

THE ORDER OF NATURE

It may be considered unfortunate that the word nature is most frequently used, and the philosophy of nature most sharply defined, in an early and markedly inferior poem— *Queen Mab*—in which Shelley's imagination is thin and conventional, his language bald and feeble, and the "esthetic synthesis" most imperfectly brought about. But for all its crudeness, this poem does include many important elements—some of them abiding elements—in Shelley's philosophy of nature; in many ways it is a preliminary sketch for what he did so magnificently half a dozen years later in *Prometheus Unbound*. And perhaps we should be grateful that Shelley has left a document in which his ideas are so simply exposed to the simplest apprehension.

There are many references in *Queen Mab* to the laws of nature as conceived by science. Or rather the reference is to nature's *law,* as conceived by eighteenth-century materialists, with their penchant for generalizing and simplification, and their frequent confusion of two distinct meanings of the word. The heavenly bodies fulfill immutably "eternal nature's law." Nature can be relied on better than the Christian hell to deal out punishment to wrongdoers.

> And all-sufficing nature can chastise
> Those who transgress her law. . . .

One of the "laws" of nature for Shelley at this period was for men to eat no animal food. The flesh of the lamb which man devoured, "still avenging nature's broken law,"

> Kindled all putrid humours in his frame,
> All evil passions, and all vain belief. . . .

Nature had evidently established vegetarianism as her "law."

Shelley is often felt to be less a poet of nature than Wordsworth; he does not follow nature so faithfully, but compels her to ends of his own. In a sense, however, he is more of a nature-poet. For he readily passes beyond the visible shows of nature to the larger cosmic operations in which she manifests her power and direction.

—Joseph Warren Beach

It will be seen that Shelley carries even farther than Wordsworth the concept of nature as a norm of conduct for human beings. The justice of man is but a feeble reflection—nay, often, perversion—of the justice of nature. Yet Shelley holds, with Rousseau and to some degree with Wordsworth, that the justice of nature may be found, if man will look candidly, in his own heart.

> Spirit of Nature! no.
> The pure diffusion of thy essence throbs
>   Alike in every human heart.
>   Thou, aye, erectest there
> Thy throne of power unappealable;
>   Thou art the judge beneath whose nod
>   Man's brief and frail authority
>   Is powerless as the wind
>   That passeth idly by.
> Thine the tribunal which surpasseth
>   The show of human justice
>   As God surpasses man.

The poet Shelley does not tell us by what signs one may recognize the decrees of nature; but throughout the entire period of his writing he takes for granted that he can recognize them. In *The Revolt of Islam* he declares it to be—

> . . . Nature's law divine that those
>   Who grow together cannot choose but love,
> If faith or custom do not interpose . . .

In *The Cenci* the son of the Count considers that his father's crimes have freed him from the filial obligations which nature imposed upon him.

> "He has cast Nature off, which was his shield,
> And Nature casts him off, who is her shame."

The Lord Chancellor who refused to Shelley the custody of his own children has overthrown "Nature's landmarks." In *Prometheus Unbound* Shelley regards Truth, Liberty and Love as "Nature's sacred watchwords."

The operations of the universe in its entirety are an expression of "Nature's unchanging harmony." It is not by the decrees of nature that man is vicious and miserable. The youthful Shelley states more crudely than Rousseau, more crudely even than Godwin, the doctrine that it is false institutions that have corrupted the natural goodness of man.

> . . . Nature!—no!
> Kings, priests, and statesmen blast the human flower
> Even in its tender bud.

Nature is the eternal, the changeless element in the universe. But it is inherent in her law to bring about the regeneration of a corrupt and ailing world. The fairy guide and prophet in *Queen Mab* assures the spirit of Ianthe that humanity will not be forever slavish and bloody.

> Now, to the scene I show, in silence turn,
> And read the blood-stained charter of all woe,
> Which nature soon, with recreating hand,
> Will blot in mercy from the book of earth.

This work of regeneration will be brought about by man whenever he consents to be reunited with nature and work in concert with her law.

> How sweet a scene will earth become!
> Of purest spirits, a pure dwelling-place,
> Symphonious with the planetary spheres;
> When man, with changeless nature coalescing,
> Will undertake regeneration's work. . . .

This bald and jejune statement in *Queen Mab* is of the utmost importance for the interpretation of Shelley's refined symbolism in *Prometheus Unbound*. For the central allegory of that poem has to do with the regeneration of the world which is to come about when man (Prometheus) "coalesces" with changeless nature (Asia). It is true that Asia stands for much more than mere nature as conceived in *Queen Mab*. She obviously stands for Love as well, and love conceived in a comprehensive platonic fashion. So that she may be said to represent, like Prometheus himself, one of the elements essential to an ideal humanity. But she is also associated in Shelley's allegory with the benevolent order of nature, from which it is possible for man to be temporarily divorced, but with which he must be reunited in order to secure his happiness and restore the world to its perfection.

The history of Shelley's naturalism is roughly parallel to that of Wordsworth's. Naturalism was at first even more dominant in Shelley's view; and it gradually tended to yield, as in Wordsworth, to a more mystical philosophy, made necessary largely by the difficult problems concerned with the nature and origin of the human spirit.

Shelley's naturalism was, in the beginning, of a much more extreme type than Wordsworth's. Wordsworth started with a sort of pantheism, derived mainly from current English poetry. Shelley started with a sort of atheism derived perhaps from current French philosophy. It is known that Shelley had been at an early age a diligent reader of Helvétius, d'Holbach, Condorcet, and Volney, as well as of the English Godwin; and from some or all of these he may have derived the view of nature expressed with so much definiteness—so much baldness and prosiness indeed—in *Queen Mab*.

In this poem the Fairy, who corresponds roughly to the didactic phantom of Volney's *Ruines,* conveys the Spirit of the girl Ianthe in his magic car into the midst of the astronomical heaven, which with its rolling and innumerable systems seems the most fitting temple for the "Spirit of Nature," though "not the lightest leaf that quivers to the passing breeze is less instinct with" this spirit. It is clear that Shelley, like other poets of his day, was most deeply impressed, among the operations of nature, with those which came within the compass of Newton's synthesis. But he too was eager to extend the conception of immutable law beyond physics and astronomy into the realm of human life and morality. The Fairy and the Spirit enter a Hall of Spells—a place of instruction, in which the secrets of the future are to be revealed. Then approaching the parapet which separates the palace from the heavenly abysses—

> There, far as the remotest line
> That bounds imagination's flight,
>   Countless and unending orbs
> In mazy motion intermingled,
> Yet still fulfilled immutably
>   Eternal nature's law.
>   Above, below, around
>   The circling systems formed
>   A wilderness of harmony;
>   Each with undeviating aim,
> In eloquent silence, through the depths of space
>   Pursued its wondrous way.
>
>   . . . . .
>
>   The Fairy pointed to the earth.
>   The spirit's intellectual eye
>   Its kindred beings recognized.
> The thronging thousands, to a passing view,
>   Seemed like an anthill's citizens.
>   How wonderful! that even
> The passions, prejudices, interests,
> That sway the meanest being, the weak touch
>   That moves the finest nerve,
>   And in one human brain
> Causes the faintest thought, becomes a link
>   In the great chain of nature.

NECESSARIANISM

The great chain of nature is a commonplace of eighteenth-century philosophy. The phrase occurs in d'Holbach, for one, a writer from whom Shelley quotes extensively in the notes to **Queen Mab**. D'Holbach was bent on showing that man is himself the work of nature, subject to her laws, unable to extricate himself from their web, unable even to conceive getting clear from the cycle of natural law. In the first chapter of his *Système de la Nature,* d'Holbach points out what an error it is to try to distinguish between man as physical and man as a moral being. "Moral man is nothing but this physical being considered from a certain point of view," etc. In a later chapter d'Holbach makes out that the moral activity of man is identical in essence with the physical activity of matter.

> La conservation est donc le but commun vers lequel toutes les energies, les forces, les facultés des êtres semblent continuellement dirigées. Les Physiciens ont nommé cette tendance ou direction, *gravitation sur soi;* Newton l'appelle *force d'inertie;* les Moralistes l'ont appellée dans l'homme *amour de soi;* qui n'est que la tendance à se conserver, le désir du bonheur, l'amour du bien-être et du plaisir, la promptitude à saisir tout ce qui paroît favorable à son être, et l'aversion marquées pour tour ce qui le trouble ou le menace; sentimens primitifs et communs de tous les êtres de l'espèce humain, que toutes leurs facultés s'efforcent de satisfaire, que toutes leurs passions, leurs volontés, leurs actions ont continuellement pour object et pour fin. Cette *gravitation sur soi* est donc une

disposition nécessaire dans l'homme et dans tous les êtres, qui par des moyens divers, tendent à persévérer dans l'existence qu'ils ont reçue, tant que rien ne dérange l'ordre de leur machine ou sa tendance primitive.

A variant of this mechanical account of man's motivation is found in Volney's *Ruines,* which is known to have had a strong influence on several of Shelley's poems, and from which he quotes in the notes to **Queen Mab**. In Volney's fifth chapter, the wise phantom instructs the author that there is no use in man's referring his ills to fate, or to any obscure agents or mysterious causes.

> Que l'homme connaisse ces lois! *qu'il comprenne la nature des êtres qui l'environnent, et sa propre nature,* et il connaîtra les moteurs de sa destinée; il saura quelles sont les causes de ses maux, et quelles peuvent en être les remèdes. Quand la *puissance secrète* qui *anime l'univers* forma le globe que l'homme habite, elle imprima aux êtres qui le compose des *propriétés essentielles* qui devinrent la *règle* de leurs mouvemens individuels, le lien de leurs rapports réciproques, la cause de l'harmonie de l'ensemble; par-là, elle établit un ordre régulier de causes et d'effects, de principes et de conséquences, lequel, *sous une apparence de basard,* gouverne l'univers et maintient l'équilibre du monde: ainsi, elle attribua au feu le mouvement de l'activité. . . . elle ordonna à la flamme de monter, à la pierre de descendre, à la plante de végéter; à l'homme, *voulant l'exposer au choc* de tant d'êtres divers, et cependant *préserver sa vie fragile,* elle lui donna la faculté *de sentir.* Par cette faculté, toute action nuisible à son existence lui porta une sensation de *mal* et de *douleur;* et toute action favorable, une sensation de *plaisir* et de *bien-être.* Par ces sensations, l'homme, tantôt détourné de ce qui blesse ses sens, et tantôt entrainé vers ce qui les flatte, a été *nécessité d'aimer* et *de conserver sa vie.* Ainsi, *l'amour de soi, le désir du bien-être, l'aversion de la douleur,* ont été les *lois essentielles et primordiales imposés à l'homme par la NATURE même;* les lois que la puissance ordonnatrice quelconque a établies pour le gouverner, et qui, semblables à celles *du mouvement dans le monde physique,* sont devenues le principe simple et fécond de *tout ce qui s'est passé dans le monde moral . . .*

So Volney and d'Holbach bring in together two famous eighteenth-century doctrines—the doctrine of self-interest and that of necessity in the moral world. The doctrine of self-interest is particularly strong with the French writers, and is, I believe, logically essential to this way of explaining human motives. But it was repudiated or modified by Godwin and other English writers of this school; it plays no appreciable part, so far as I know, in the philosophy of Shelley; and therefore I will not pursue it further.

The doctrine of necessity is common to all these writers, French and English, including men so influential with the poets as Hartley, Godwin and Priestley. It is stated compactly by d'Holbach in the following terms:

> La nécessité est la liaison infaillible et constant des causes avec leurs effects. Le feu brule nécessairement les matières combustibles qui sont placée dans la sphère de son action. L'homme désire nécessairement ce qui

est, ou ce qui paroît, utile à son bien-être. La nature dans tous ces phénomènes agit nécessairement d'après l'essence qui lui est propre; tous les êtres qu'elle renferme, agissent nécessairement d'après leurs essences particulières; c'est par le mouvement que tout a des rapports avec ses parties et celles-ci avec le tout; c'est ainsi que tout est lié dans l'univers; il n'est lui-même qu'une chaîne immense de causes et d'effects, qui sans cesse découlent les unes des autres.

With this one may compare the first sentence from Shelley's long note on Necessity: "He who asserts the doctrine of Necessity means that, contemplating the events which compose the moral and material universe, he beholds only an immense and uninterrupted chain of causes and effects, no one of which could occupy any other place than it does occupy, or act in any other place than it does act."

This doctrine of necessity, working in the material and moral worlds, is stated in most uncompromising accents by Shelley in **Queen Mab**. Necessity is there simply another name for the "Universal Spirit" or the "Spirit of Nature,"

> A spirit of activity and life,
> That knows no term, cessation, or decay.

It is "wide diffused" through the "infinite orbs of mingling light"; it guides the whirlwind, works through disease and health,

> Rolls round the eternal universe, and shakes
> Its undecaying battlements, presides,
> Apportioning with irresistible law
> The place each spring of its machine shall fill.

In a storm at sea, while to the eye of the mariner,

> All seems unlinked contingency and chance:
> No atom of this turbulence fulfils
> A vague and unnecessitated task,
> And acts but as it must and ought to act.
> Even the minutest molecule of light
> That in an April sunbeam's fleeting glow
> Fulfils its destined though invisible work,
> The universal Spirit guides; nor less,
> When merciless ambition, or mad zeal,
> Has led two hosts of dupes to battlefield,
> That, blind, they there may dig each other's graves,
> And call the sad work glory, does it rule
> All passions: not a thought, a will, an act,
> No working of the tyrant's moody mind,
> Nor one misgiving of the slaves who boast
> Their servitude, to hide the shame they feel,
> Nor the events enchaining every will
> That from the depths of unrecorded time
> Have drawn all-influencing virtue, pass
> Unrecognized, or unforeseen by thee,
> Soul of the Universe! eternal spring
> Of life and death. . . . etc.
> Spirit of Nature! all-sufficing Power,
> Necessity! thou mother of the world.

To this passage Shelley appended two notes. The first is a citation from d'Holbach, in which the principle of necessity is illustrated by examples taken from the physical and the moral worlds. These examples correspond to those given by Shelley, and doubtless represent the "source" of the entire passage in **Queen Mab**. The first example is that of a storm, in which not a single molecule of dust or water was placed by chance, but "chaque molécule agit précisément comme elle doit agir, et ne peut agir autrement qu'elle ne fait." The second example follows:

> Dans les convulsions terribles qui agitent quelque-fois les sociétés politiques, et qui produisent souvent le renversement d'un empire, il n'y a pas une seule action, une seule parole, une seule pensée, une seule volonté, une seule passion dans les agens qui concourent à la révolution comme destructeurs ou comme victimes, qui ne soit nécessaire, qui n'agisse comme elle doit agir, qui n'opère infailliblement les effets qu'elle doit opérer, suivant la place qu'occupent ces agens dans ce tourbillon moral. Cela paroîtriot évident pour une intelligence qui sera en état de saisir et d'apprécier toutes les actions et réactions des esprits et des corps de ceux qui contribuent à cette révolution.

The second and very long note of Shelley is an exposition of the philosophy of necessity, with an attempt to reconcile it with the action of the will and to indicate how it affects religious beliefs and the attitude towards good and evil. While there are some parts of this discussion that resemble views of d'Holbach, it may have been inspired by Priestley, Godwin or other popular English writers.

The word necessity ceases to be prominent in the finer poetry of Shelley's later years. And in the evolution of Shelley's thought, the deterministic implications tend to fade out of the idea of necessity even when the word is used. In **Prometheus Unbound** much stress is laid on the will as a determining factor in the moral world. As Shelley becomes confirmed in his faith that existence is spiritual in essence, it is no longer possible to conceive of necessity in materialistic terms. The paramount force in the universe is "eternal Love," the sole power not subject to "Fate, Occasion, Chance, and Change." This is the statement of the oracular Demogorgon, himself a refined symbol of Necessity. The Necessity he symbolizes takes on the character of Destiny as conceived by the Greek tragedians. It takes on, too, a platonic cast; for Demogorgon defines himself as Eternity. What he ushers in is "eternal Love," another platonic conception. The process of the world is, in **Prometheus,** clearly conducted by moral forces; and the entire myth is more or less associated with the platonic doctrine of the One and the Many. The perfected state of man on earth which is ushered in by Demogorgon's destruction of Jupiter is associated with the timeless eternal state from which man has been separated by the conditions of mortality. The journey of Asia to the cave of Demogorgon is symbolic of the return of the soul, through the perturbations of mortal existence, back to the unconditioned state of pre-existence.

But the synthesis of Shelley's naturalism and his platonism is anything but perfectly accomplished. And in **Prometheus** we still find lingering traces of the earlier necessarian concept. There is one significant passage in particular—a passage left unexplained, so far as I know, by the commentators—which can best be understood in the light of this concept.

It is in the second scene of the second act. Asia and Panthea have been summoned by dreams to the cave of Demogorgon. They are passing through a dense and flowering forest, through which sounds the voluptuous music of amorous nightingales. The passage I am about to quote suggests that this forest of exquisite odorous flowers and birdsongs symbolizes the life of the senses and desire, the natural human life through which we make our way into the infinitude of the spirit. And then comes the passage in which it is stated clearly enough that the very desires of sense which we follow, or think we follow, of our own will, are but the impulsions of necessity driving us on to our destiny.

> There those enchanted eddies play
>   Of echoes, music-tongued, which draw,
>   By Demogorgon's mighty law,
>   With melting rapture, or sweet awe,
> All spirits on that secret way;
>   As inland boats are driven to Ocean
> Down streams made strong with mountain-thaw:
>   And first there comes a gentle sound
>   To those in talk or slumber bound,
>   And wakes the destined soft emotion,—
> Attracts, impels them; those who saw
>   Say from the breathing earth behind
>   There streams a plume-uplifting wind
> Which drives them on their path, while they
>   Believe their own swift wings and feet
> The sweet desires within obey . . .

Necessity, then, or nature, employs man's very desire for pleasure as the means of drawing or driving him on the path she wishes him to follow. This is the poetical way of expressing the hopeful utilitarian doctrine common to d'Holbach, Condorcet and Volney, to Hartley, Godwin, Erasmus Darwin and Bentham, that men become social and moral beings through the natural working of their desire to avoid pain and secure pleasure. They all believed more or less fervently in the necessary betterment of mankind by the pursuance of this natural law. Perhaps the neatest statement is that of Volney:

> Cette amélioration devient un effect nécessaire des lois de la nature; car, par *la loi de la sensibilité,* l'homme tend aussi invinciblement à se rendre heureux, que *le feu à monter,* que la pierre à graviter, que l'eau *à se niveler.* Son obstacle est son *ignorance,* qui l'égare dans les moyens, qui le trompe sur les effects et les causes. A force d'expérience il s'éclairera; à force d'erreurs il se redressera; il deviendra sage et bon, *parce qu'il est de son intérêt de l'être.* . . .

Shelley may well have supposed that, in *Prometheus,* he had succeeded in reconciling the necessarian doctrine with the platonic concept of "eternal Love" as the moving power. To the critical reader the joining of the two conceptions appears imperfect. . . .

NECESSITY, ATHEISM, AND THE ANIMATING PRINCIPLE

The conception of necessity as the law of nature carries with it, for Shelley, as for many of the French philosophers, the corollary of atheism. Necessity is an "all-sufficing" Power because it rules out the notion of arbitrary and capricious interference, of anything which would confuse or interrupt the working of natural law. With Shelley the intellectual and the moral arguments for atheism were perhaps equally powerful. In *Queen Mab,* as in *The Revolt of Islam,* there are numerous references, in the tone of Volney, to the wars, the crime, the tyranny, and various other evils associated with religion and caused by it. But the intellectual reasons are equally strong, and are introduced in close connection with the moral ones. In *Queen Mab* the Spirit of Ianthe relates how her mother had taken her when an infant to see the burning of an atheist, and how when the child wept over the cruel scene her mother had comforted her.

> Weep not, child! cried my mother, for that man
> Has said, There is no God.

Whereupon the Fairy confirms this declaration of faith by reference to the testimony of Nature.

>   There is no God!
> Nature confirms the faith his death-groan sealed:
> Let heaven and earth, let man's revolting race,
> His ceaseless generations tell their tale;
> Let every part depending on the chain
> That links it to the whole, point to the hand
> That grasps its term! let every seed that falls
> In silent eloquence unfold its store
> Of argument: infinity within,
> Infinity without, belie creation;
> The exterminable spirit it contains
> Is nature's only God; but human pride
> Is skilful to invent most serious names
> To hide its ignorance.

Thus Shelley has made a curious reversal of the argument Coleridge uses to demonstrate the need for assuming a spirit beyond nature. Since each cause in the sequence is itself caused, reasons Coleridge, nothing in nature can be regarded as more than a link in a chain. "The moment we assume an origin in nature, a true *beginning,* an actual first—that moment we rise *above* nature, and are compelled to assume a *supernatural power.*" Just so! reasons Shelley. But to assume a supernatural power is to assume something inconceivable. We cannot conceive of a hand grasping the chain at its beginning. All that we know is the chain of causes extending backward and forward *ad infinitum.* We cannot conceive of a link in the chain which was not itself caused; hence we cannot conceive creation. Men invent gods in their own evil image. But the only divinity in nature is "the exterminable spirit it contains." As Shelley expresses the matter in the note appended to this passage, taking his cue from Hume's famous exposition:

> The only idea which we can form of causation is derivable from the constant conjunction of objects, and the consequent inference of one from the other. In a case where two propositions are diametrically opposite, the mind believes that which is least incomprehensible;— it is easier to suppose that the universe has existed from all eternity, than to conceive a being beyond its limits capable of creating it; if the mind sinks beneath the weight of one, is it an alleviation to increase the intolerability of the burthen?
>
> . . . . .
>
> There certainly is a generative power which is effected by certain instruments: we cannot prove that it is inherent in these instruments; nor is the contrary hypothesis capable of demonstration: we admit that the generative power is incomprehensible; but to suppose that the same cause is produced by an eternal, omniscient, omnipotent being, leaves the cause in the same obscurity, but renders it more incomprehensible.

The great interest of Shelley's argument in our discussion is that the idea of God is ruled out as being inconsistent with the idea of nature.

Similar reasoning Shelley puts in the mouth of Cythna in *The Revolt of Islam*. She is arguing against the peoples' vain notion of "some Power" that "builds for man in solitude."

> What is that Power? Ye mock yourselves, and give
>   A human heart to what ye cannot know:
> As if the cause of life could think and live!
>   'Twere as if man's own works should feel, and show
>   The hopes and fears and thoughts from which they flow,
> And he be like to them!

We who think and live, Shelley argues, are by that very fact finite and limited, subject to the law of necessity. The cause of life itself must be outside all such limitations; it cannot therefore be a thinking and knowing creature; it cannot be what men call God. Shelley prefers to call it necessity.

In substituting the words Nature or Necessity for God, Shelley wished to emphasize his deterministic conception of the universe, especially strong in the earlier years of his writing, and to get rid of the theological connotations of the word God. He could not of course, any more than other nature poets, get rid of the notion of an active principle working in nature. For this active principle he has a variety of terms, such as "the universal Spirit" and the "spirit of activity and life." More frequent in the later poems is some variant of the word power. Thus in *The Revolt of Islam* we read:

> . . . we know not whence we live,
> Or why, or how, or what mute Power may give
> Their being to each plant and star and beast,
>   Or even these thoughts.

In the **"Hymn to Intellectual Beauty,"**

> The awful shadow of some unseen Power
>   Floats tho' unseen among us.

In this more platonic conception the active principle of the universe is represented in the terms of "intellectual Beauty," but it is the same universal Spirit of which Shelley speaks in *Queen Mab*. And there is the same insistence that this unseen power is not the God of theology, but remains the mysterious force which animates nature and is to be interpreted only in terms of nature. Shelley speaks of his efforts as a youth to get an answer to the riddle in religious terms, and states categorically that no response is ever given to such vain questions.

> No voice from some sublimer world has ever
>   To sage or poet these responses given—
>   Therefore the names of Demon, Ghost, and Heaven,
> Remain the records of their vain endeavor . . .

In the same year with the **"Hymn to Intellectual Beauty"** he has another phrasing of the concept of the active principle as power. In his **"Mont Blanc,"** he takes the snow capped mountain as a symbol of that principle, or force, whatever it may be, that animates the universe of material and spiritual beings.

>   The secret strength of things
> Which governs thought, and to the infinite dome
> Of heaven is as a law, inhabits thee!

Whether or not he is here echoing Volney, he is using the exact phrase which occurs in the passage quoted above, "*la puissance secrète qui anime l'univers.*" Note that Volney repeats the phrase, with a variation, in the same passage: "les lois que la puissance ordonnatrice quelconque a établies pour le gouverner" (the laws which the legislative power, whatever it is, established to govern man). Shelley is particularly fond of using the word Strength (or Power) with the word "secret" or some equivalent, suggesting that the animating principle of the universe is mysterious and unsoundable. By Demogorgon's mighty law, the echoes draw "all spirits on that secret way." We do not know "what mute Power" may give their being to the various creatures of nature. It is "the awful shadow of some unseen Power" that floats among us. In *The Revolt of Islam* Cythna speaks of—

> Necessity, whose sightless strength for ever
>   Evil with evil, good with good, must wind
> In bands of union which no power may sever.

In *Alastor* the poet thus addresses nature:

> Mother of this unfathomable world!
> Favour my solemn song, for I have loved
> Thee ever, and thee only; I have watched

Thy shadow, and the darkness of thy steps,
And my heart ever gazes on the depths
Of thy deep mysteries.

It is curious how often these expressions, which have so strong a flavor of the mysteries of religion, occur in passages where Shelley, like Volney, was most expressly repudiating the religious interpretation. They are the nature-poet's substitute for the mysteries of religion. This is a not infrequent phenomenon. We have found it in the early poems of Wordsworth, and we shall find it in Emerson and Swinburne. At times, there is a startling resemblance between the phrasing of the nature-poet and the religious poet. Such is the passage in *Adonais,* so strongly reminiscent of Coleridge:

> . . . he doth bear
His part, while the one Spirit's plastic stress
Sweeps through the dull, dense world, compelling
   there
All new successions to the forms they wear. . . .

But here, of course, the nature-poet has pretty much given way to the mystic platonist. Only there remains the word "compelling" to remind one of the lingering notion of Necessity. . . .

The culmination of Shelley's naturalism is *Prometheus Unbound,* and this in spite of the mystical platonism with which it is there associated. A profoundly naturalistic tendency is shown both in the particular scientific theories which are made so prominent and in the general philosophical doctrine of the poem. This doctrine is obviously naturalistic, in the manner of d'Holbach, Condorcet and Godwin, in its sharp contrast with orthodox Christian philosophy. The faith in human perfectibility upon this planet takes the place of the Christian doctrine of the fall of man and the whole scheme of redemption. An earthly millennium takes the place of the Christian heaven. The operation of destiny—mythical form of necessity—in bringing about this earthly millennium, takes the place of divine providence and the atonement. In the person of Prometheus, man wins his salvation by the exercise of his own will (under the dominion of necessity) and by the exertion of his own intellectual and moral faculties, which have been not so much helped as hindered hitherto by supernatural power. In a certain sense Prometheus takes the place of Christ as the savior of man; but it is to be observed that he is man himself acting as his own savior.

In all interpretations of the poem, beginning with Mrs. Shelley's, Prometheus has been assumed to be a representation of humanity, or of some aspect of man—his mind or genius. Even Leigh Hunt's interpretation, expressed in the romantic idiom of the time, is but a variation on this. Prometheus, according to Hunt, is "a personification of the Benevolent Principle, subjected for a time to the Phantasm of Jupiter." This Benevolent Principle constitutes, for Godwin, one of the most essential characteristics of humanity, and one which is destined to be of the utmost importance in bringing about the reign of justice and reason.

But while Prometheus is represented as working out his own salvation without supernatural aid, it is to be noted that, at the beginning of the poem, chained to his rock, he has been long separated from his beloved Asia, living in exile in her Indian vale, and that his release from torture and the blessed transformation of the world are coincident with his reunion with Asia. One chief clue to the meaning of the poem lies in the correct interpretation of this symbolic Asia. She has been variously interpreted as Nature, as "the spirit of divine beauty and love," as "the Idea of Beauty . . . the spirit of Nature . . . Love and Beauty." And these multiple interpretations have been given authority by Mrs. Shelley's original interpretation of her as symbolizing "Venus and Nature." An examination of the poem makes it clear that Asia stands for all these related abstractions.

The association of beauty and love was familiar enough to Shelley in Plato and the neoplatonists, as well as in simple classical mythology. The association of Venus with nature was familiar to him in the opening lines of Lucretius, whom he read as a boy at Eton. Here Shelley had found the invocation to the goddess as "increase-giving Venus, who beneath the gliding signs of heaven fillest with thy presence the ship-carrying sea, the corn-bearing lands, since through thee every kind of living things is conceived, rises up and beholds the light of the sun." And almost immediately afterward he read that "nature gives birth to all things and increase and nourishment." Abstract nature and the mythical goddess of love he found associated in these terms:

> Since thou then art sole mistress of the nature of things and without thee nothing rises up into the divine borders of light, nothing grows to be glad or lovely, fain would I have thee for a helpmate in writing the verses which I essay to pen on the nature of things . . .

The spiritual significance of the identification of Asia with Venus (goddess of love and beauty) has been widely, though a trifle vaguely, appreciated from the beginning. Christian commentators have been glad to expound Shelley's doctrine that humanity is to be saved by love. But the poem has waited more than a hundred years for an interpreter who should make clear and definite the significance of her identification with nature. Professor Carl Grabo, in *A Newton among Poets* and *"Prometheus Unbound": an Interpretation* has shown how much of the most exquisite and elusive imagery of *Prometheus* and other poems of Shelley was suggested by the writings of contemporary scientists, and how many of the leading ideas of *Prometheus* are derived from the observations and theories of men like Newton, Davy, Beccaria, and Erasmus Darwin. And most important of all is the light he throws by this means on the symbolic significance of Asia.

Mr. Grabo shows that Shelley was deeply indebted to the scientific speculations of Erasmus Darwin in the poetry and notes of *The Botanic Garden* and *The Temple of Nature,* and perhaps also in his *Zoönomia.* And he makes it seem highly probable that Shelley's account of the "uprise" of Asia from the sea is to be read in the light of Darwin's similar account of the emergence of Dione (Aphrodite) in *The Botanic Garden,* and his interpretation of this incident in the notes to *The Botanic Garden* and the text of *The Temple of Nature.* In the second act of *Prometheus* Panthea, addressing her sister Asia, recalls the circumstances of her first appearance.

> The Nereids tell
> That on the day when the clear hyaline
> Was cloven at thine uprise, and thou didst stand
> Within a veinèd shell, which floated on
> Over the calm floor of the crystal sea,
> Among the Aegean isles, and by the shores
> Which bear thy name,—love, like the atmosphere
> Of the sun's fire filling the living world,
> Burst from thee, and illumined earth and heaven
> And the deep ocean and the sunless caves
> And all that dwells within them; till grief cast
> Eclipse upon the soul from which it came.

The corresponding passage in *The Botanic Garden* I give only in part.

> So young DIONE nursed beneath the waves,
> And rock'd by Nereids in their coral caves,
> Charm'd the blue sisterhood with playful wiles,
> Lisp'd her sweet tones, and tried her tender smiles.
> Then on her beryl throne by Tritons borne,
> Bright rose the Goddess like the Star of morn;
> When with soft fires the milky dawn he leads,
> And wakes to light and love the laughing meads . . .

Darwin has the following footnote on this passage:

> There is an ancient gem representing Venus rising out of the ocean supported by two Tritons. . . . It is probable that this beautiful allegory was originally an hieroglyphic picture (before the invention of letters) descriptive of the formation of the earth from the ocean, which seems to have been the opinion of the most ancient philosophers.

In *The Temple of Nature* Darwin definitely associates this mythological incident with his theory of the evolution of organic life—which took its origin in the ocean and made its first great advances in the mud of the seashore.

> ORGANIC LIFE beneath the shoreless waves
> Was born and nurs'd in Ocean's pearly caves;
> First forms minute, unseen by spheric glass,
> Move on the mud, or pierce the watery mass;
> These, as successive generations bloom,
> New powers acquire, and larger limbs assume;
> Whence countless groups of vegetation spring,
> And breathing realms of fin, and feet, and wing.

Darwin goes on to recount the evolution of oak, whale, lion, eagle, and man; he dwells on the evidence of shell and coral, on the emergence of islands and continents; on the emigration of animals from the sea; on the natural history of "musquito," diodons, beavers, remora. Then he comes to the hieroglyphic representation of all this evolution in Egypt's rude designs.

> —So erst, as Egypt's rude designs explain,
> Rose young DIONE from the shoreless main;
> Type of organic Nature! source of bliss!
> Emerging Beauty from the vast abyss!
> Sublime on Chaos borne, the Goddess stood,
> And smiled enchantment on the troubled flood;
> The warring elements to peace restored,
> And young reflection wondered and adored.

The prose comment is partly as follows:

> The Egyptian figure of Venus rising from the sea seems to have represented the Beauty of organic Nature; which the philosophers of that country, the magi, appear to have discovered to have been elevated by earth-quake from the primeval ocean.

The more specifically evolutionary features of Darwin's theory—his views on the origin of species—do not appear in Shelley so far as I have observed. But it seems almost certain that he does mean his Asia to stand—among other things—as "type of organic Nature," and perhaps, in one aspect, as type of the earth in particular. She typifies in nature the same beneficent and increase-giving forces as the classical Venus. And the blessed state of man follows, in Shelley's myth, on his re-alliance with the beneficent forces of nature from which he has been shut off by the evil spells of Jupiter. Asia typifies much more than natural love, to be sure, including in her range of meanings all that Plato includes in his Uranian Venus, with whom Shelley was so well acquainted. But the significant thing for our present study is that she should represent, along with the spiritual ideal of the Uranian Venus, the forces of the physical universe.

That she does represent physical nature Mr. Grabo makes much more likely by showing the relation which she bears in the poem to the Spirit of the Earth. By citations too numerous to be detailed here Mr. Grabo shows that the Spirit of the Earth is closely associated with, or typifies, the operations of atmospheric electricity as they were understood by Beccaria and other writers of the time. And this Spirit of the Earth has a particularly intimate relation to Asia, whom it calls mother, though its actual parentage is unknown. It has been wont to come—

> Each leisure hour to drink the liquid light
> Out of her eyes, for which it said it thirsted
> As one bit by a dipsas . . .

Mr. Grabo interprets plausibly as follows: "The atmospheric electricity derives from, renews itself from, the earth." In this phase of the allegory, then, Asia represents the earth as the source of atmospheric electricity. And, as Mr. Grabo makes probable by several citations, Shelley is identifying love on its physical side with electricity; and not merely that, but with energy, and with the spirit of animation in organic life. In associating electricity with the spirit of animation, Shelley was in line with the speculations of Beccaria and other scientists of the time; even Davy, though he "was cautious in ascribing an electrical character to the spirit of animation," yet "believed the subject to be worthy investigation."

As for Shelley's associating the spiritual operations of love with the material operations of electricity, Mr. Grabo has made this seem plausible by showing that Darwin advanced a theory of matter which identifies it with energy, the units of matter being "no more than radiant points of force." We have seen in an earlier chapter that such a concept was held by Priestley; and it was taken into account as possibly correct by Davy in his speculations. Grabo cites from Shelley's *Refutation of Deism,* a similar interpretation of matter as "immaterial."

> Matter, such as we behold it, is not inert. It is infinitely active and subtile. Light, electricity and magnetism are fluids not surpassed by thought itself in tenuity and activity: like thought they are sometimes the cause and sometimes the effect of motion; and, distinct as they are from every other class of substances, with which we are acquainted, seem to possess equal claims with thought to the unmeaning distinction of immateriality.

It is by reference to such a concept of matter, in which electricity plays a dominant rôle, that Mr. Grabo explains the puzzling description of the Spirit of the Earth in the fourth act of *Prometheus,* in which it is represented by—

> Ten thousand orbs involving and involved,
> Purple and azure, white, green and golden,
> Sphere within sphere . . . etc.

Readers will differ as to the demonstrative character of Mr. Grabo's argument; and many will prefer to leave this extraordinary passage as a mere tissue of fanciful invention on Shelley's part. But the more one studies Shelley, the more one realizes that very little in his poetry is purely fanciful, but that some subtle intellectual concept underlies his most curious metaphors. Without Mr. Grabo's interpretation much of the fourth act of *Prometheus* remains a rather wearisome riot of uncontrolled fancy. He has brought an imposing array of contemporary scientific lore to his interpretation. I believe we must give him the benefit of the doubt, and assume with him that nearly everything in Shelley's account of the Spirit of the Earth in Act IV conforms to his conception of it as an electrical force.

It would take too long to list the scientific theories—astronomical, geological, meteorological—to which, on Grabo's showing, Shelley has given embodiment in *Prometheus Unbound* and to indicate how they are related in his allegory to the moral regeneration of the world which is the theme of the poem. One does not feel certain how far we should assume in his doctrine an *identification* of moral and physical phenomena, or an assertion of the *interdependence* of the two series. Perhaps we are to regard them as merely analogous or parallel. But there are some instances in which they appear to be more than that. In his notes on *Queen Mab,* Shelley expresses the view that the

obliquity of the earth's axis—

> . . . will gradually diminish until the equator coincides with the ecliptic; the nights and days will then become more equal on the earth throughout the year, and probably the seasons also. There is no great extravagance in presuming that the progress of the perpendicularity of the poles may be as rapid as the progress of the intellect; or that there should be a perfect identity between the moral and physical improvement of the human species.

The result of this progress in perpendicularity will be a better climate and accordingly improved mentality for man. In this case the moral phenomena would seem to be a consequence of the physical.

A similar view seems to be expressed in *Prometheus,* but with the terms reversed.

> In *Prometheus Unbound* earth and moon, after the liberation of Prometheus, became warm and habitable. Shelley depicts them as reliving their youth, his scientific authority being, presumably, Darwin, who believed that at one stage in the earth's history the climate was equable from pole to pole and there were no violent storms, a recollection of which time, lingering in the memory of the race, was the origin of the legend of the Garden of Eden.

In this case the physical improvement seems to be represented as following upon the moral. Again, Grabo shows that Shelley associates the destructive phenomena of electricity with Jupiter and his reign of hate, while under the reign of Prometheus, electricity turns good, and lightning is man's slave; that, further, the noxious gases (like nitrous oxide) turn sweet and wholesome in the millennial régime. In Act III there are several passages describing the transformation of the material world which follows on the release of Prometheus and Asia's sounding of her horn. The Spirit of the Earth describes how, at this magic signal, "all things had put their evil nature off." And Earth herself describes to Prometheus how, at the touch of his lips, the spirit of reviving life penetrated her mass, and—

> . . . Henceforth the many children fair
> Folded in my sustaining arms; all plants,
> All creeping forms, and insects rainbow-winged,
> And birds, and beasts, and fish, and human shapes,
> Which drew disease and pain from my wan bosom,
> Draining the poison of despair, shall take
> And interchange sweet nutriment; to me
> Shall they become like sister antelopes . . . etc.

We are perhaps in danger of sometimes taking too literally the physical phenomena by means of which Shelley wished to symbolize a spiritual event—of assuming a factual connection where he wished to suggest a poetical analogy. Thus we may be inclined to read into his thought a transcendental or superstitious meaning which was not intended. But it does seem not unlikely that Shelley believed in something like an occult sympathy between the material and moral worlds. Such a view certainly seems implied in the note to *Queen Mab* cited in the next to the last paragraph. Such an occult sympathy between the material world and the human soul was held to exist by Henrik Steffens, the German geologist and disciple of Schelling. There are traces of this conception in Wordsworth. How far literally it was held by Shelley in writing *Prometheus* it is hard to determine. But certainly he was greatly confirmed and heartened in his perfectibilist philosophy by numerous facts and hypotheses derived from contemporary science, which, if they do not literally *explain* the operations of the spirit, strikingly parallel and illustrate them. In the same way, later enthusiasts found in evolution an encouragement of their faith in human progress and illumination. The paradox of Shelley's case is that he should have summoned science to support a transcendental view of the natural order so little in harmony with the "modesty of nature," the strict sobriety of scientific method. . . .

[Some] brief reference should be made to several features of the poem discussed in this [essay] on which some light may be thrown by the "neoplatonic" speculations of Paracelsus. Miss Elizabeth Pierce Ebeling, in a manuscript thesis deposited in the University of Minnesota library, has made it seem not improbable that Shelley was acquainted with Paracelsus, and that he drew from him many suggestions for the cosmology of *Prometheus*. Among the doctrines of Paracelsus which have their counterpart in the poem is that of the guiding spirits (archeus) of the several heavenly bodies. The Spirit of the Earth in Shelley is, according to Miss Ebeling, such an archeus; and the various other living spirits which appear in the poem are likewise provided for in the system of Paracelsus.

> Another leading idea of Paracelsus is that of the Evestrum, a sort of attendant spirit born with everything, uniting the created being with the eternal. It is the business of the Evestrum to regulate sleep, to reason, and to prefigure future events.
>
> . . . . .
>
> There are two kinds of Evestrum, mortal and immortal. The mortal Evestrum is "like a shadow on the wall. The shadow grows and originates with the body, and remains with it up to its ultimate matter. . . . Everything, animate and inanimate, sensible and insensible, has conjoined with it an Evestrum, just as everything casts a shadow." The eternal Evestra, on the other hand, are not born with individuals, have no beginning and no end. They consist of the Evestrum of comets, the Evestrum of impressions, and the Evestrum of miracles. . . . These Evestra . . . are the means by which celestial things operate, and "Gods by their Evestrum alone have wrought miracles."

Miss Ebeling makes it seem very probable that Demogorgon has much of the character of a "prophetic Evestrum."

Again, as Miss Ebeling points out, the action of the Macrocosm, or universe, in the system of Paracelsus, resembles that of the Microcosm, man; and this is in accordance with the transformation that comes over the physical universe with the spiritual liberation of Prometheus. So that the notion of an occult sympathy between the material

universe and the human spirit may have had its original suggestion at the time when as a boy Shelley "pored over the reveries of Albertus Magnus and Paracelsus."

It can hardly be supposed that in *Prometheus Unbound* Shelley took seriously, as philosophical truth, the "reveries" of a Renaissance astrologer and mystic. The spirits and Evestra of the poem are to be regarded in much the same light as the supernatural machinery of "The Rape of the Lock"—having in mind, to be sure, the deeper seriousness of Shelley's imagination and his faculty for reading a genuine moral significance into imagery drawn from the realms of myth and fancy. The mystical machinery of *Prometheus* does not cancel the naturalism of the poem, but rather serves to give it wings. Behind the machinery, it is true, there do lurk certain metaphysical assumptions, largely of "platonic" origin, which it is difficult to reconcile with the naturalistic point of view. . . .

What is significant for us in the present discussion is that this romantic poet should have sought so earnestly to ground his views in the findings and the spirit of science. In the general action of the poem, certainly, his stress is laid on naturalistic rather than supernatural views of human destiny.

The fall of Jupiter signifies the liberation of man's mind from religious superstition, from ignorance and fear, as well as from political and ecclesiastical tyranny. Jupiter, as I conceive him, is a figure of comprehensive, if negative, significance. He is a kind of Everlasting No. He stands for the force of inertia in human affairs and the heart of man. He is much less substantially real a being than Prometheus or Asia, about as real as "error" in Christian Science philosophy. He is something which man allows himself to think and suffer, the rule of which is limited by man's sufferance, and which is destined to give way before the rule of man's intelligence and will. He stands for all that hampers the progress of civilization. And his downfall coincides with the union of Prometheus and Asia— signifying not merely humanity's espousal of love (in its ideal platonic sense), but also, it now seems likely, man's alliance with nature as explored and interpreted by science.

Frederick L. Jones   (essay date 1946)

SOURCE: "The Inconsistency of Shelley's *Alastor*," in *ELH*, Vol. 13, No. 4, December, 1946, pp. 291-98.

[*In the following essay, Jones attributes the contradictions in Shelley's* Alastor *to a shift in his philosophy.*]

The logical inconsistency of *Alastor* has been the subject of analysis and of some debate, but thus far there has been no satisfactory explanation of how and why Shelley produced the inconsistency and then defended it in an even more inconsistent preface. If the problem can be solved, it is worth the trouble, for on its solution depends not only an understanding of the poem itself but of related passages in later poems.

The poem is inconsistent in that the early part of it represents the Poet as meriting punishment (presumably an early death), while the last lines praise him without qualification as the highest conceivable type. Because the Poet has lived in "self-centered seclusion" while eagerly and happily pursuing knowledge, "sweet human love" is offended by his disregard of humanity, and, to punish him, sends to him a vision of a veilèd maid, whom he instantly desires so ardently that his life is soon brought to an end by his ceaseless but hopeless search for her. Though in the concluding lines Shelley might be expected to drive his lesson home, and to reveal how the Poet deserved his doom, he does quite the opposite. He laments in a high strain that "The child of grace and genius" should die while "many worms And beasts and men live on." The Poet is "some surpassing Spirit" whose loss "is a woe 'too deep for tears'." This praise is not in itself an inconsistency. The inconsistency lies in the fact that the praise is in no way qualified to make evident the avowed purpose of the poem, which is that even a "surpassing spirit" like the Poet, who loves truth and beautiful idealisms, will be punished if he fails to share the trials common to humanity. This purpose, stated in the following lines, is not supported by any other part of the poem:

> The spirit of sweet human love has sent
> A vision to the sleep of him who spurned
> Her choicest gifts.

An explanation of the origin of the inconsistency is, I believe, discoverable if we follow Shelley, in so far as that is necessary for the purpose, through the composition of the poem, the finding of a title, and the writing of a preface.

Before an explanation is possible, however, it is necessary to recall that when Shelley wrote *Alastor,* he (1) was under the strong influence of Wordsworth, (2) was definitely committed to the empirical philosophy of Locke and Hume, and (3) had recently suffered from bad health, which had made him think that his own life might soon be terminated. These points are too well known to require proof. But it does need to be pointed out that shortly after the publication of *Queen Mab,* Shelley's point of view shifted rapidly, mainly as a result of his reading Wordsworth's poetry and Sir William Drummond's *Academical Questions*. When he wrote *Alastor,* his mind was balancing the mystic philosophy of Wordsworth and the "ideal" or "intellectual philosophy" of Drummond, the central doctrine of which was that the senses are the only sources of knowledge and that in consequence all we can know is our own sensations and the ideas derived from their combinations. This was a doctrine which Shelley had long and fully accepted from Locke. Its strict logical application had led him to the necessity for atheism. But under the influence of Drummond's "ideal philosophy," which opposed the prevalent materialistic philosophy, Shelley had found a new and inspiring application of his favorite philosophical doctrine. Wordsworth, too, had given him inspiration and philosophical hope. But Wordsworth had nothing to do with Locke's system of ideas, or the concept that we can know nothing except our own ideas. His doctrine did in-

deed place the highest value on the senses, but he regarded them as a means of direct communication with spiritual reality.

It is my belief that the inconsistency of *Alastor* is the result of Shelley's failure to combine ideas derived from Wordsworth and Drummond. His fragmentary essay *On Life,* which evidently was written soon after *Alastor,* indicates that he had succeeded in reconciling the two influences. The essay contains his most emphatic statements of approval of both. In accord with Drummond he says: "I confess that I am one of those who am [*sic*] unable to refuse my assent to the conclusions of those philosophers who assert that nothing exists but as it is perceived." In accord with Wordsworth, he speaks of man as "a being of high aspirations . . . disclaiming alliance with transcience and decay; incapable of imagining to himself annihilation"; and elaborates on the vivid spiritual impressions of early childhood.—With these facts as a background, it will, I think, be easier to understand *Alastor.*

When Shelley began the composition of *Alastor,* his purpose was to illustrate the fatal consequences of living a self-centered life which shuts one off from the common suffering of mankind, even though the self-centered person should dwell in a world of beautiful idealisms. Though

Mary Shelley, circa 1814.

Shelley, as Newman White suggests, may have been impressed with the evil effects of isolation as expounded in Godwin's *Fleetwood* and illustrated in Sydney Owenson's *The Missionary,* it is more likely that the immediate source of the idea which stimulated his poem was Wordsworth's *Elegiac Stanzas* (*Peele Castle*). The lesson which Wordsworth teaches in that poem is remarkably similar to that which Shelley evidently intended to illustrate in ***Alastor.*** Wordsworth tells how he had lived in a world of beautiful ideas, giving no heed to the harsh realities of human life until a "deep distress" humanized his soul. Though suffering, he finds comfort in the thought that he had been shocked out of a self-centered life. It is, he thinks, better to share the sorrows common to humanity, than to be happy while living in selfish isolation and feeding only on pleasant and beautiful thoughts. The protagonist of ***Alastor*** is, like Wordsworth, a Poet who has lived in a lovely dream world without regard for the thoughts or feelings of his fellow men.

After a Wordsworthian appeal to Nature for aid, Shelley begins his story about the Poet who brought destruction upon himself by living in "self-centered seclusion." This idea would naturally have a strong appeal for one so ardently devoted to reform as was Shelley. Having chosen to write about a poet, it was inevitable that he should write about himself. His recent ill health and expectation of an early grave had caused him to brood over his own fate, and his failure to arouse humanity to strike off the shackles of political, social, and religious tyranny had contributed to his melancholy state of mind. It was a mistake, however, for Shelley to write about himself—about "His cold fireside and alienated home" of early 1814, and his passionate pursuit of knowledge—for he was so carried away with sympathy for his own idealized portrait that he found it impossible to find fault with his Poet. He did, however, remember his original purpose long enough to insert in the right place (immediately after the Poet was fatally ensnared by the vision) three lines to explain the vision, to the effect that it was sent by "The spirit of sweet human love" to punish "him who [had] spurned Her choicest gifts."

The vision itself is probably Shelley's second major mistake in so far as consistency is concerned. He probably meant only to create a woman so lovely that she would, as representing the essence of human love, inspire an instantaneous and consuming passion. But Shelley did more than this. He created a woman who (1) represented his ideal of a wife for himself, and who (2), as he conducted the Poet through his hopeless search for her, came gradually to represent, not the essence of human love at all, but truth and beauty. Instead, therefore, of being an instrument of punishment, the vision became a representation of the highest aspirations and attainments of humanity, which it was a crime *not* to pursue. What else can lines 681-86 mean?

> Oh, that the dream
> Of dark magician in his visioned cave,
> Raking the cinders of a crucible
> For life and power, even when his feeble hand

> Shakes in its last decay, were the true law
> Of this so lovely world!

This was exactly the principle the Poet had followed. In other words, the veilèd maid was created for one purpose but, because Shelley fell in love with her, was used for quite a different purpose. She was created as the agent of an "avenging spirit," but was used as a symbol of truth and beauty.

This shift in the significance of the vision is due, I think, to an unconscious transfer from Wordsworth to Locke and Drummond when Shelley created the veilèd maid. The maid whom he probably meant to create was to be the (Wordsworthian) instrument of offended "sweet human love" (a personification), and as such was meant to be only a woman so lovely as to inspire a hopeless passion. The maid whom he actually created was produced according to Shelley's favorite doctrine from Locke, that all knowledge is derived from the senses, and that we can know only ideas or combinations of ideas. The veilèd maid is therefore an ideal combination of all the loveliest and truest elements in the Poet's vast knowledge. As such, she was (quite unintentionally in the poem, I think) both "an intelligence similar to" the Poet, and an ideal representation of truth and beauty. In short, Shelley meant to create "an avenging spirit," but created instead a symbol of the highest and best, not only in humanity, but also in the intellectual and spiritual realm.

When Shelley had finished his poem, he was at a loss for a title. He consulted his friend Peacock, who, judging more from Shelley's explanation of the meaning of the poem than from the poem itself, suggested the Greek word "Alastor," which means an "evil genius" or avenging spirit. Shelley liked the word, both for its sound and for its aptness for expressing the idea which he had intended to illustrate but had failed to make clear. The sub-title, "The Spirit of Solitude," also suggests the main idea of the poem in that it was the self-chosen isolation of the Poet that supposedly brought the avenging spirit into operation. Moreover, the sub-title expresses the dominant impression of the poem.

Still clinging to the notion that he had shown how the Poet had sinned and had brought destruction upon himself, Shelley wrote a preface in which he intended to make his purpose more perspicuous, but which actually represents a further and later development of his thoughts, and contains elements which are not in the poem itself.

In the Preface Shelley says: The Poet "drinks deep of the fountains of knowledge and is still insatiate. The magnificence and beauty of the external world sinks profoundly into the frame of his conceptions . . . So long as it is possible for his desires to point towards objects thus infinite and unmeasured, he is joyous and tranquil and self-possessed. But the period arrives when these objects cease to suffice. His mind is at length suddenly awakened and thirsts for intercourse with an intelligence similar to itself." The last sentence contains two ideas which are not in the poem: (1) that the Poet's mind was "awakened," and (2) that it thirsted "for intercourse with an intelligence similar to itself." To be "awakened" is to realize that one has not known something before. The Poet had not the least idea that he had neglected anything important; he knew only that he was hopelessly in love with the vision. In the poem there is no hint of any kind that the vision was intended to be "an intelligence similar to" the Poet, though she was such in that "Knowledge and truth and virtue were her theme, And lofty hopes of divine liberty, Thoughts the most dear to him, and poesy, Herself a poet."

In the Preface, Shelley continues: The Poet

> images to himself the Being whom he loves. Conversant with speculations of the sublimest and most perfect natures, the vision in which he embodies his own imaginations unites all of wonderful or wise or beautiful, which the poet, the philosopher or the lover could depicture. The intellectual faculties, the imaginations, the functions of sense have their respective requisitions on the sympathy of corresponding powers in other human beings. The Poet is represented as uniting these requisitions and attaching them to a single image.

Not one thing in the passage just quoted is in the poem. The Poet does not image to himself anything; he does not unite in a single image all that he had learned of the wonderful, wise, and beautiful. The vision was sent to him by offended "sweet human love" as a mode of punishment. In the last lines of the poem Shelley does evidently regard the vision as a symbol of all truth and beauty, but, as has already been pointed out, this is at odds with the stated purpose of the vision.

In the Preface, Shelley states further that the Poet "seeks in vain for a prototype of his conception." This also is not borne out by the poem. The Poet does not seek a prototype, but the vision itself. Indeed, he is no more interested in mortal women who, "taught By nature, would interpret half the woe That wasted him," than he was in the Arab maiden who, before the vision came, brought him food and dared not "for deep awe To speak her love."

In the last paragraph Shelley repeats even more emphatically the same inconsistency observable in the poem. Briefly it is stated that "The Poet's self-centered seclusion was avenged by the furies of an irresistible passion pursuing him to speedy ruin." Shelley then immediately launches upon an ardent laudation of the Poet and a denunciation of "those meaner spirits that dare to abjure its ["that Power"'s, or as in the poem, "sweet human love"'s] dominion. Their destiny is more abject and inglorious as their delinquency is more contemptible and pernicious." These "keep aloof from sympathies with their kind, rejoicing neither in human joy nor mourning with human grief . . . They are morally dead." Again Shelley finds himself incapable of pointing his moral. In the poem, for his offense the Poet is brought by "sweet human love" to "speedy ruin"; while in the Preface "those unforeseeing multitudes who constitute . . . the lasting misery and loneliness of the world" are permitted to reach "old age [and] a miserable grave." This surely is strange justice. The concluding quotation from Wordsworth to the effect that

> The good die first,
> And those whose hearts are dry as summer dust
> Burn to the socket!

is apt enough at this stage of the argument, but it lends no support to the avowed moral, either of the poem or of the Preface.

The poem and the Preface are obviously inconsistent, both separately and conjointly. In the poem the basis of the trouble is probably Shelley's unintentional shift from his Wordsworthian point of view to his older and stronger view that "nothing exists but as it is perceived,"—that is, to Locke's empirical theory of ideas. In the Preface the case is quite the opposite. Shelley begins with the theory that the vision was the result of the Poet's own combination of ideas, and then tries to reconcile with that the Wordsworthian opinion that one should not live apart from the common experiences of humanity, even though he might live in a lovely dream world of his own making. *Alastor* is inconsistent mainly because Shelley's philosophy was in a state of rapid transition. Before he had finished his poem, his thought had changed. And before he had written the Preface, it had changed again; mainly, however, as a development of the implications in the last lines of the poem.

Bennett Weaver   (essay date 1949)

SOURCE: "'Prometheus Bound' and 'Prometheus Unbound,'" in *PMLA*, Vol. 64, No. 1, March, 1949, pp. 115-33.

[*In the following essay, Weaver compares* Prometheus Unbound *with its Greek predecessor,* Prometheus Bound, *by Aeschylus.*]

Shelley's *Prometheus Unbound* in many ways might be considered the most significant and characteristic of his works. Yet in this drama the poet himself has pointed out his indebtedness to the *Prometheus Bound* of Æschylus. Able scholars, in turn, have examined the relationship between the English and the Greek plays. Over half a century ago Vera D. Scudder published her study, and in 1908 Richard Ackermann brought out his critical commentary. Among others, W. J. Alexander and A. M. D. Hughes, in editing their selections from the poems of Shelley, noted the parallels between his work and that of Æschylus. In more recent times, Carl Grabo has gone beyond the study of Greek-English parallels, and Newman Ivey White in the notable twenty-second chapter of his *Shelley* has enriched our understanding of *Prometheus Unbound*. Still one may hope by concentrating on the problem to give fuller meaning to the action of the mind of Æschylus upon that of Shelley as together they face tyranny and pain.

It is in his Preface to the drama that Shelley comments on his choice of the Greek myth. His first sentence is significant. "The Greek tragic writers, in selecting as their subject any portion of their national history or mythology, employed in their treatment of it a certain arbitrary discretion." What discretion, then, does the English poet presume to employ? He is precise in his statement. "The *Prometheus Bound* of Æschylus supposed the reconciliation of Jupiter with his victim as the price of the disclosure of danger threatened to his empire by the consummation of his marriage with Thetis. . . . I was averse from a catastrophe so feeble as that of reconciling the Champion with the Oppressor of mankind." Prometheus is, as it were, "the type of the highest perfection of moral and intellectual nature, impelled by the purest and the truest motives to the best and noblest ends." And what was Shelley's purpose in writing **Prometheus Unbound**? "My purpose has hitherto been simply to familiarize the highly refined imagination of the more select classes of poetical readers with beautiful idealisms of moral excellence"; and thus, through bringing the imaginations of men into close relationship with the admirable, to indulge "what a Scotch philosopher characteristically terms, 'a passion for reforming the world.'"

Since we must pay particular attention to the point, let us return to the "arbitrary discretion" Shelley exercised in selecting from the Greek myth such matter as he wished to use. He was accurate in saying that "the Agamemnon story," for instance, "was exhibited on the Athenian theatre with as many variations as dramas." He had before him similar variations in *The Libation Bearers* of Æschylus and the *Electra* of Sophocles. He would, then, at his own discretion select such materials as he wanted and introduce such variations as suited his purpose. At the very time that he states his claim to the general body of material used by Æschylus, he insists upon his right to treat that material after his own manner. It would seem, then, that Shelley is telling us it is in the variations and not in the general material which he shares with Æschylus that we shall find evidences of his peculiar genius. And he is at pains to make clear his main difference with the Athenian dramatist: he will carry through the marriage of Jupiter with Thetis, he will not allow his Champion to compound with the Oppressor, he will destroy the tyrant and sustain "the moral interest of the fable." In other words, Shelley turns directly to the work of Æschylus, not only admitting his obligation to the elder poet but particularly distinguishing between his purpose and that which the Greek may have had in mind. We are not, then, engaged merely in the study of influences when we try to make clear the relation between Æschylus and Shelley; but, rather, we study the similarities in order to separate from them the essential dissimilarities. Of course, in mentioning all that is involved when one writer either rejects or accepts another, we cannot hope to be utterly accurate. We realize that in the very act of rejecting material a man may reveal the nature of his genius—as, indeed, Shelley did in repudiating the compromise of Æschylus.

We shall, then, confine ourselves to examining the main materials of the two plays as they are related in setting, action, character, and story. We shall look at significant scenes and any special devices employed in them. We shall scrutinize certain ideas which give expressional similarity to various phrases—things that translate through.

Upon reading Shelley's play, one is impressed by a certain substantiality about Act I. That which gives a firmer quality to the act is, I think, the Greek material which is used there. A collation of the two plays will reveal that cross-references in large number run from the *Prometheus Bound* to the first act of the English play. Whereas I find in Shelley's closing act no certain reference to the Greek drama, and only one reference in the third act, and very few outside the Asia-Demogorgon scene in the second act, a casual reader could not but note the massive ways in which the first act of **Prometheus Unbound** is locked into the work of Æschylus. Simply, and to begin with, the two plays are joined by the use of the same scene. Strength, opening *Prometheus Bound,* says:

> Lo! to a plain, earth's boundary remote,
> We now are come,—the tract as Skythian known,
> A desert inaccessible: and now,
> Hephæstos, it is thine to do the hests
> The Father gave thee, to these lofty crags
> To bind this crafty trickster fast in chains.
>
> [*P.B.,* 1-6]

Hephæstos underscores these lines:

> Yet my courage fails
> To bind a God of mine own kin by force
> To this bare rock where tempests wildly sweep.
> [*P.B.,* 16-18]

Against his will he fetters the Titan "to this lone height" where he shall be scorched "in the hot blaze of the sun" and chilled by frost in the "starry-mantled night." "On this rock of little ease"—a phrase repeated again and again—not knowing sleep, Prometheus shall evermore groan and wail. Strength interrupts the sympathetic words of Hephæstos with the sharp command: "Nail him to the rocks." These lines, together with the stage properties available to him, were all that the Greek needed to make clear the immediate scene.

Yet we must observe that it is not in the spirit of Æschylus to leave the scene set only on his limited stage. He is to present a drama dealing with a struggle between immortal gods. As soon, therefore, as he leaves the rather ordinary minds of Hephæstos and Strength, through which he can dress the stage scene admirably, he presents, not to the fleshly eye, but to the eye of the imagination, the very "firmament of God" which over-spreads the theatre. Working through the sublime intelligence of Prometheus he can do what he had no thought of attempting with a blacksmith and a bully. Let us watch this language carefully, for Shelley is very close to it. This is an example of "the sublime majesty of Æschylus" which "filled him with wonder and delight":

> Thou firmament of God, and swift-winged winds,
> Ye springs of rivers, and of ocean waves
> That smile innumerous! Mother of us all,
> O Earth, and Sun's all-seeing eye, behold,
> I pray, what I, a God, from Gods endure.
> Behold in what foul case

I for ten thousand years
Shall struggle in my woe
In these unseemly chains. . . .
Woe, woe! The present and oncoming pang
I wail, as I search out
The place and hour when end of all these ills
Shall dawn on me at last . . . . . .
. . . . but I needs must bear
My destiny.   [*P.B.*, 97-115]

Even so Shelley's hero for "Three thousand years of sleep-unsheltered hours" has gazed upon the "bright and rolling worlds" of the firmament. Even so he cries out:

Nailed to this wall
          of eagle-baffling mountain,
Black, wintry, dead, unmeasured; without herb,
Insect, or beast, or shape or sound of life.
Ah me! alas, pain, pain ever, for ever!

No change, no pause, no hope! Yet I endure.
I ask the Earth, have not the mountains felt?
I ask you Heaven, the all-beholding Sun,
Has it not seen? The Sea, in storm or calm,
Heaven's ever-changing Shadow, spread below,
Have its deaf waves not herd my agony?   [I, 20-29]

Among "The wingless, crawling hours" he knows there is one hour which shall mark the end of his ills. With "all-enduring will" he accepts his destiny.

In heightening the effect of the setting both poets depend upon the play of the elements. In Æschylus the "tempests wildly sweep" about the Titan. "Fiercest winds," swift and stormy, buffet him. He is, indeed, their "wretched plaything." About Shelley's hero there throng the howling "genii of the storm, urging the rage of whirlwind." The "swift Whirlwinds" are his companions. At the time of his impaling, "strange tempest" vexed the sea; and the hounds that later come to torture him are "tempest-walking."

As Æschylus develops his scene he threatens to set the thunders of Jove within the tempests and to hurl the lightning down. Too hardy, the outraged sufferer taunts Hermes:

Let then the blazing levin-flash be hurled;
With white-winged snow-storm and with the earth-
     born thunders
Let Him disturb and trouble all that is.
                                     [*P.B.*, 1079-81]

Hermes replies:

With thunder and the levin's blazing flash
The Father this ravine of rocks shall crush,
And shall thy carcase hide.   [*P.B.*, 1105-07]

Justifying Hermes' warning, the storm breaks. "Wildly conflicting blasts" blend "sky with sea."

Since Æschylus builds his whole drama so as to sustain a tempestuous conclusion, he has an advantage over Shelley

in creating effects of elemental grandeur. The English poet must compress his scene and has much to do besides stirring up Jovian thunders. Yet Earth remembers that when the "almighty Tyrant" with "his thunder chained" Prometheus to the crags that

          the sea
Was lifted by strange tempest, and new fire
From earthquake-rifted mountains of bright snow
Shook its portentous hair beneath Heaven's frown;
Lighting and Inundation vexed the plains.
                                     [I, 165-169]

The Voice from the Mountains recalls the fear with which "o'er the Earthquake's couch we stood," and the Voice from the Whirlwinds asserts that before the cruel act of Zeus had roused the Titan's hate, no "thunder / Nor . . . volcano's flaming fountains" had ever made them mute. But at that dread hour they had

Hung mute and moveless o'er yon hushed abyss,
As thunder, louder than [their] own, made rock
The orbèd world!   [I, 67-69]

"Thunderblots had parched" the waters of the Springs, and they had known the bitterness of blood; but the curse of Prometheus, more awful than thunder, had left them "stagnant with wrinkling frost." As the hero of *Prometheus Bound* at the close of the play hangs feeling "the earth shake to and fro," even so the hero of **Prometheus Unbound** at the beginning of the play cries out against "the Earthquake fiends" who are charged

To wrench the rivets from my quivering wounds
When the rocks split and close again behind.
                                     [I, 38-40]

And finally, just before the fiends are called up against Prometheus, lightning and thunder stun the stage:

White fire
Has cloven to the roots yon huge snow-loaded
     cedar;
How fearfully God's thunder howls behind!
                                     [I, 432-437]

Just as fire and snow are brought together in these lines, so "alternating frost and fire" are used by both poets to heighten the suffering of Prometheus. As we have seen, Hephæstos bemoans his having to fetter his kinsman

          to this lone height,
Where thou shalt know nor voice nor face of man,
But scorching in the hot blaze of the sun,
Shalt lose thy skin's fair beauty. Thou shalt long
For starry-mantled night to hide day's sheen,
For sun to melt the rime of early dawn. [*P.B.*, 24-29]

Let the "white-winged snow" be hurled upon me, cries the defiant Titan. Shelley remembers these lines. His hero, speaking to Mercury, as Æschylus' hero has spoken to Hermes, says:

I gave all
He has; and in return he chains me here
Years, ages, night and day: whether the Sun
Split my parched skin, or in the moony night
The crystal-wingèd snow cling round my hair.

                                   [I, 381-385]

In his opening soliloquy he had said:

The crawling glaciers pierce me with the spears
Of their moon-freezing crystals, the bright chains
Eat with their burning cold into my bones.

                                   [I, 31-33]

And when earlier he had cursed Jupiter, he had defied the
god in these words:

And let alternate frost and fire
Eat into me, and be thine ire
Lightning, and cutting hail.   [I, 268-270]

It might seem that Shelley's Titan suffers more acutely
from cold than from heat, as I suspect the poet himself
did. The whirlwinds "afflict [him] with keen hail." However, Shelley keeps the contrast which Æschylus has set
up, heat being a thing of day and chill a thing of night:

And yet to me welcome is day and night,
Whether one breaks the hoar frost of the morn,
Or starry, dim, and slow the other climbs
The leaden-coloured east.   [I, 44-47]

If one thinks of action as something visibly done upon a
stage, there is a wide difference between the *Prometheus
Bound* and the **Prometheus Unbound**. This difference is
attributable to two things. First, Æschylus gives over the
opening ninety-six lines of his play to the business of
chaining and impaling the Titan. Shelley begins his play
"three thousand years" later, merely referring to the action
as having taken place. Second, once the Greek has fettered Prometheus, there is little more that the author can
do except, in a conventional way, bring in the Chorus and
Okeanos and Io and Hermes in turn. In other words, despite the use of some mechanism which, for 173 lines,
suspends the Chorus in a "swiftly rushing car," and which
brings Okeanos on in "a car drawn by a winged gryphon,"
Æschylus cannot keep his play from becoming static. He
may, and he does, suggest potential or contingent action
of a vivid kind, but the deed done upon the stage is beyond him. Shelley, however, in unbinding the Titan and in
shifting his scene gains in action. There is much more
going on in his play than in the Greek's. His *Dramatis
Personæ* number nineteen as against seven in the cast of
Æschylus. And, particularly, he presents the torture by the
Furies, the destruction of Jupiter, and the release of Prometheus, which things were impossible to his predecessor.

As one studies the two dramas in point of action, however, one cannot forget that Æschylus wrote for production
upon the stage whereas Shelley wrote "simply to familiarize the highly refined imagination . . . with beautiful idealisms." For ninety-six lines the Athenian audience is treated to some rough and realistic action. Hephæstos, Strength,
and Force hale Prometheus on in chains. Hephæstos is an
explicit and hard-working actor. His hands are full of
chains, bolts, rivets, nails, handcuffs, one huge adamantine wedge, and at least one great hammer. No doubt all
these properties add to the realism of the part and, together with his colorful and sympathetic nature, make him
attractive to the people. Yet Hephæstos, at first, in his pity
for his kin, merely talks of bonds and bare rocks and
fetters of bronze. It is Strength, a loud and brutal fellow,
who drives Hephæstos into action. By his constant bel-
lowing of directions he calls attention to what his comrade
is doing and what things he is using. "Fix the chains on
him," he shouts. "With all thy might strike with thine
hammer; nail him to the rocks. Strike harder, rivit." "Lo!"
Hephæstos says, "this arm is fixed inextricably." Strength
ruthlessly continues: "Now rivet thou this other fast. Drive
the stern jaw of the adamant wedge right through his chest.
Cast thy breast-chains round his ribs. With thy full power
fix the galling fetters." Hephæstos bids Strength, "Go below
and rivet both his legs." This done, he says, "His limbs
are bound in chains." So, with no small amount of action
and clatter, they leave the Titan fixed in the "rare handiwork" from which he cannot free himself.

All this action, as I have said, Shelley assumes to have
taken place before his play opens. His dramatic interest is
not in the binding but in the unbinding of Prometheus. He
does, however, use most of the properties which the Greek
used, and by a psychic reaching back he creates an illusion of action. His protagonist is nailed to the wall of
rock; he is chained in "adamantine chains." He is
"Prometheus, the chained Titan"; and he cries out that
Zeus "chains me here" and that "the bright chains eat into
my bones." More ghastly still, when the mountains quake,
they "wrench the rivets from my quivering wounds."
Nowhere else in all of his work, except once in the **"Cy-
clops,"** does Shelley use the word "rivet." In all, we are
given a strong feeling for the "scorn, and chains" with
which the cruel Tyrant has loaded the sufferer.

In making the action clear, however, Æschylus, according
to his need, is not only more reiterative than is Shelley, he
is also much closer to physical horror. The stomach of the
Athenian who at Salamis helped to fill the sea "with wrecks
and carcasses" is less queasy than is the "refined imagination" of the Englishman. When Strength bids Hephæstos
"drive the stern jaw of the adamant wedge right through
his chest," Hephæstos may groan with remorse, yet the act
remains harsh beyond any need Shelley has. Furthermore,
since these things are past for him, the poet could not, had
he willed, admit them into his primary scene with the
peculiar directness which action could give to them.

When Shelley declared himself "averse from . . . reconciling the Champion with the Oppressor of mankind," he
marked an essential distinction in character which he
wished to make between his protagonist and that of the
Greek. Together with the Titan of Æschylus, with Job and
Satan and Tasso, his Prometheus should suffer the oppression of tyranny. But there should be in him no important
sense of outrage, no "taints of ambition, envy, revenge,

and a desire for personal aggrandizement," no boasting followed by compromise. Obviously the character of the sufferer upon Caucasus is to be tempered by the spirit of the sufferer upon Golgotha, infinitely irreconcilable to tyranny. The crucifixion scene alone is sufficient to make the point; and if it does not, the closing lines of Demogorgon do. When Shelley writes, "The only *imaginary* being resembling in any degree Prometheus, is Satan," he does not exclude that *historical* Being whom Prometheus resembles. When Shelley presents the final test of his hero as the viewing of the crucifixion, and when his response is not, "Let this cup pass from me," but "Pour forth the cup of pain," there can be little doubt what character he has in mind. "A pillow of thorns" may be spread for Prometheus; yet, he says

> I would fain
> Be what it is my destiny to be,
> The saviour and the strength of suffering man.
>
> [I, 815-817]

When we study the characters in the two dramas, we observe, first, that the Greek Prometheus rebels against tyranny. When Æschylus' hero declares himself "the foe of Zeus," adding that he hates "all the gods," Shelley's hero addresses Jupiter as "thy foe, eyeless in hate." With "looks of firm defiance, and calm hate," he cries, "all-prevailing foe! I curse thee." That which adds to the bitterness of Prometheus, alike in the *Prometheus Bound* and the **Prometheus Unbound,** is the thankless treachery of Zeus, his inexorable cruelty, and his contemptible weakness. The Greek Titan complains acidly that he took his side with Zeus, and by his counsels made secure the power of the graceless God. Then he adds: "See here the friend of Zeus, / Who helped to seat Him. Thus . . . the mighty ruler of the Gods repays me." The English Titan also "clothed him with . . . dominion." "I gave thee power," he says. Then, while the "thought-executing ministers" of Zeus work woe in the world he cries: "I gave all He has," and see how He "requites me. Such is the tyrant's recompense."

In the midst of the curse which Prometheus had formerly placed upon Jupiter, he spoke these fateful words: "O'er all things but thyself I gave thee power, / And my own *will*." And hence, after "three thousand years" of pain, he cries, "yet I endure." He holds his "all-enduring will" against the haughty tyranny of Zeus. "Enduring thus, the retributive hour" he becomes known even to the Furies as "the Invincible, / The stern of thought" who "yet defies the deepest power of Hell."

Alike in the Greek and the English drama, that which gives significance to the will of Prometheus is pain. He is, above all else, in his own thought and in the opinion of others, *the* sufferer. In *Prometheus Bound* he cries: "I suffer ills . . . woes / Dreadful to suffer." As Job turned upon his tormenting friends, so the Titan turns upon the chorus:

> 'Tis a light thing for one who has his foot
> Beyond the reach of evil to exhort
> And counsel him who suffers.   [*P.B.,* 293-295]

Yet he asks for "sympathy / With him who suffers now." When Okeanos—a perfect Zophar—enters protesting his pity, Prometheus chides him:

> Let be. What boots it? Thou then too art come
> To gaze upon my sufferings.   [*P.B.,* 330-331]

Io, in turn, and much more genuinely, asks: "Why, poor Prometheus, sufferest thou this pain?" And his response to her is this: "I have but now mine own woes ceased to wail."

Shelley, although using such words as *pain* and *suffering* less often than does Æschylus, places unmistakable stress upon the idea. When his Titan curses Jupiter it is "a sufferer's curse" which he hurls upon the god. When the Phantasm of Jupiter is forced to appear, he recognizes Prometheus only as "proud sufferer." And when Mercury comes leading in the furies he pauses to address his victim: "Awful Sufferer!" The essential change that we may sense in the English play is the tempering of the nature of the suffering with vicarious warmth: Shelley's Titan would be not only the foe of Zeus but the saviour of man.

To draw into some patterned statement the many and various references to the pain of Prometheus, either in the Greek or the English drama, would be a large task. Plumptre, in his translation of Æschylus, uses nearly sixty such references, and Shelley close to forty. Yet there remains a very great emphasis upon the general idea of pain; and the problem, I belive, is more than one of numerical comparison. At least in the translation we are using, the *Prometheus Bound* has not only more references to pain but, following the original, a larger variety of words suggesting pain. Some few of these are fairly sharp and kinetic; many of them are general. There are *pangs,* there is *writhing,* and there are *groans* and *wailings.* There are *outrages, penalties, maltreatments,* and *calamities.* But for the most part there are *punishments* and *ills, pain* and *woe* and *misery,* dreary and sad *fate, griefs* and *wrongs.* The effect of the use of all of these terms is to fill the imagination with the concept of suffering.

I believe, however, that when one first reads these two plays one feels in Shelley's work a greater shock and charge of pain than in that of Æschylus. The terms alone which the English poet uses probably cannot account for this feeling, should it be experienced. Among these terms the word *pain* itself is used thirteen times—over one-third of the allotment. *Torture* follows, appearing ten times. *Grief, agony,* and *misery* come next in the list. We find the word *pangs* used twice, and *woe* but once, in the expression "woe-illumined mind." Almost all of these words are general. But there is this difference: they are often used in figures of speech, a circumstance which gives them vividness and impact. Prometheus is linked "to some wheel of pain"; he drinks "the cup of pain"; the furies who attack him "are the ministers of pain"; pain is his "element." Then, too, his agony is a "crawling" thing; and with sudden directness we see the fiends torture him even after he has been afflicted "with keen hail" and after the glaciers have pierced him with their spears and the Earthquake-fiends have wrenched the rivets from his "quivering wounds."

It may be, also, that we feel the pain of the English Prometheus more sharply than that of the Greek because Shelley has contrived to simplify it and focus our responses to it. For the Greek Titan there are two sources of pain: the actual impaling and chaining, and the outrage, the "foul shame" which has been wrought upon him. Of this second source of pain Shelley makes little use. Further, the Greek is punished mainly for giving fire to men and for being lofty. The matter of haughtiness is so greatly developed in Athenian drama as to seem almost peculiar to it. Shelley, although he allows Mercury to say to Prometheus, "Let the will kneel within thy haughty heart," prefers to concentrate upon the theme of the stealing of the fire. Then, too, whereas in the play of Æschylus there is a notable amount of comment by other actors upon the pain of Prometheus, in Shelley's work a great deal of comment is made by the Titan himself. At all three of these points Shelley has gained a greater unity than he found in the Greek play.

Yet, as we study (in the character of Prometheus) the power to endure pain regardless of why the pain is endured, we are impressed by the fundamental similarities of the Greek and the English portrayal. As we have seen in our discussion of the setting, the general conditions under which Prometheus suffers are as similar in the two plays as they well could be. Obviously the English author wishes to avail himself of the Greek tradition to the limit of his need. Further, each stresses the length of time of the suffering: Æschylus,—ten thousand years, a "space of time full long"; Shelley,—three thousand years, "into Eternity." "Has thy pain no end?" queries the Chorus. "Pain, pain ever, forever!" answers the English Titan. Each author makes sure that in his hero there shall be no suggestion of yielding to misery. Let Hermes threaten that "the wingèd hound of Zeus" shall "glut himself upon thy liver dark," Prometheus is unmoved except to deeper wrath. Let "Heaven's wingèd hound" tear up the heart of the English Titan, he is unmoved except to pity Jupiter. Though Æschylus' protagonist "should wither here on these high towering crags," he will not yield. Though Shelley's hero hang "withering in destined pain" upon "this wall of eagle-baffling mountain," he will not yield. In the grander aspects of their characters, the Greek and the English Prometheus resemble each other.

All the agony of the Æschylean Prometheus was brought upon him by his "stealing what belongs to the Gods," the "choicest prize" of Zeus, "the bright glory of fire that all arts spring from," and giving it to men. "I snatched the hidden spring of stolen fire," he boasts. Because of my act, "men the flaming fire possess," and with it, god-like power. "Many an art they'll learn from it. . . . All arts of mortals from Prometheus spring. . . . I gave them fire." I am "Prometheus who gave fire to men." Æschylus is at no end of pains to emphasize and to explain this matter, knowing either that his listeners are fond of the story and therefore like to hear it repeated, or doubting that they are

sufficiently instructed and for dramatic reasons must be more thoroughly informed. Having avoided the old Hesiodic version, he must make sure that the account he is using is understood. In all that he writes, although he makes clear the Titan's compassion for men, his emphasis is upon the point that the filching of the fire is an act of rebellion against Zeus. It is the breaking of the decree of the god, not the kindness done to men, which sets Zeus and the Titan at deadly odds.

Shelley, on the other hand, although he accepts the basic fact of the theft, continues to minimize the Titan's rebellion and to accent his pity for man. Indeed, when Prometheus addresses the Earth, we catch the suggestion of vicarious suffering.

> Mother, thy sons and thou
> Scorn him, without whose all-enduring will
> Beneath the fierce omnipotence of Jove,
> Both they and thou had vanished . . .
>   Know ye not me,
> The Titan? He who made his agony
> The barrier to your else all-conquering foe?
>   . . . me alone, who checked . . .
> The falsehood and the force of him who reigns?
>   [I, 113-127]

This distinction made, however, it is illuminating to compare what the Greek Prometheus says of his daring beneficence and what Asia, in turn, says in glorious defense of her lover. Prometheus speaks.

> My heart is worn,
> Self-contemplating, as I see myself
> Thus outraged. . . .
>   But those woes of men,
> List ye to them,—how they, before as babes,
> By me were *roused to reason, taught to think;* . . .
> For first, though seeing, all in vain they saw,
> And hearing, heard not rightly. But, like forms
> Of phantom-dreams, throughout their life's whole
>   length
> They muddled all at random; did not know
> Houses of brick that catch the sunlight's warmth,
> Nor yet the work of carpentry. *They dwelt*
> *In hollowed holes,* like swarms of tiny ants,
> *In sunless depths of caverns;* and they had
> No certain signs of winter, nor of spring
> Flower-laden, nor of summer with her fruits;
> But without counsel fared their whole life long,
> Until I showed *the rising of the stars,*
> *And settings* hard to recognize. And I
> Found Number for them, chief device of all,
> *Groupings of letters,* Memory's handmaid that,
> And mother of the Muses. . . .
> Nor was it any one but I that found
> *Sea-crossing, canvas-wingèd cars* of ships: . . .
> And this the chief: *if any one fell ill,*
> There was no help for him, nor healing food
> Nor unguent, nor yet potion; but for want
> Of *drugs* they wasted, till I showed to them
> The blendings of all *mild medicaments,*

Wherewith they ward the attacks of *sickness
    sore.* . . .
And *'neath the earth the hidden boons* for men,
Bronze, *iron,* silver, *gold,* who else could say
That he, ere I did, found them? . . .
All arts of mortals from Prometheus spring.
                                    [*P.B.,* 474-544]

Now if we read the speech of Asia, remembering these
italicized words, we shall see not only the open likeness
of the whole but many particular similarities. Shelley may
have felt that for Prometheus to have delivered these
matters in his own person would have set up too close a
parallel to the older play. Or, he may have sensed the
dramatic fitness of Asia's pouring them into her protest in
favor of the being she loved. Obviously, the delivery of so
much detail by the Titan himself in the first act, following
line 409, would have slowed the scene and overweighted
the part. However these things may be, we watch for the
similarities, which are patent. It goes without remark that
certain dissimilarities are eliminated from this comparison, such as Æschylus' references to subjugating animals
and to divination through dreams and through observing
the flight of birds and examining their inward parts. Asia
speaks.

Then Prometheus
Gave wisdom, which is strength, to Jupiter,
And with this law alone, 'Let man be free,'
Clothed him with the dominion of wide Heaven.
To know nor faith, nor love, nor law; to be
Omnipotent but friendless is to reign;
And Jove now reigned; for on the race of man
First famine, and then toil, and then *disease.* . . .
Fell; and the unseasonable *seasons* drove . . .
Their shelterless, pale tribes to *mountain caves;* . . .
Prometheus saw, and waked the legioned hopes . . .
And *he tamed fire* which, like some beast of prey,
Most terrible, but lovely, played beneath
The frown of man; and tortured to his will
Iron and *gold* . . .
Hidden beneath the mountains and the waves.
He gave man speech, and speech created thought,
Which is the measure of the universe;
And *Science* struck the thrones of earth and heaven,
Which shook, but fell not; and the harmonious mind
Poured itself forth in *all-prophetic song;*
And music lifted up the listening spirit . . .
And human hands first mimicked and then
    mocked . . .
The human form, till marble grew divine . . .
He told *the hidden power of herbs and springs,*
And Disease drank and slept. Death grew like sleep.
He taught *the implicated orbits woven
Of the wide-wandering stars;* and how the sun
Changes his lair. . . .
He taught to rule, as life directs the limbs,
The tempest-wingèd chariots of the Ocean . . .
Such, the alleviations of his state,
Prometheus gave to man.
                                    [IV, iv, 43-99]

The changes which for his own purposes Shelley wrought
in the portrayal of Prometheus will, I trust, become more
clear as we go on with our study. But in a simple way we
can see what primary and essential characteristics he took
from Æschylus. There was forethought, a penetrant intelligence. There was will locked in necessity, availing itself
of the laws of fate. There were suffering, and the immense, enduring power to suffer. There was compassion
for men. Out of this compassion came rebellion against
the tyrannic cruelty of Zeus. At this point the two poets
begin to draw apart, Æschylus going on to the compromise which tradition demanded that his Titan make, Shelley going on to eschew all reconciliation of his "Champion with the Oppressor of mankind." Drawn by another
tradition, the English poet must subdue the Greek haughtiness of Prometheus and develop in him that pity which
leaves Zeus to his own nature, and to the self-destruction
which that nature requires.

In the play of Æschylus, Zeus does not appear in person.
We have to judge him by what he has done and by what
others say of him. He is in the very fact of his kingship
fiercely assertive, one who cannot brook the will of another. He can more readily permit those disasters which
flow from his imperious nature to destroy others than he
can tolerate any ease on their part which suggests independence of him. His treatment of his defeated foes reveals the essential ruthlessness of his mind. Upon Atlas
he has piled the weight of earth and heaven. The mighty
Typhon he has left "a helpless, powerless carcase," "his
strength all thunder-shattered." No friend he has and no
need of friends: his is sovereignty, utter, unaccountable
might. Hephæstos remarks upon his inexorable obdurance,
his intemperate harshness. The Chorus holds him insatiate with power, outrageous and wanton in the punishment of his foes, iron hearted, "made of rock."
Prometheus, as we have seen, knows him as graceless,
insulting, diseased with sovereignty, suspicious, "all ways
cruel." But, says the Titan, who glimpses the bully beneath the king, "When he is crushed . . . He'll hasten
unto me / For friendship."

This characterization, which for a tyrant is highly sufficient,
Shelley uses. Jupiter's basic acts in overthrowing Cronos
and in savagely torturing his foes, the English poet accepts.
Cruelty he fixes as the main characteristic of the god. He
concentrates almost a whole life's hatred of tyranny in fashioning this cruel king. And he observes, as Æschylus had
done before him, that "to be Omnipotent but friendless is to
reign." Nor does he miss the Greek's sure perception of the
bully in Zeus. When Jupiter is crushed, he does in Shelley's
play just what Æschylus said he would: he cries out to
Demogorgon, "Oh, / That thou wouldst make mine enemy
my judge!" If Æschylus allows him to take with Io the
pleasant privilege of a god, Shelley will depict the beastly
ravishment of Thetis in order that, just before his fall, we
may see the highest act of tyranny convulsed in the blindest
egotism begetting out of itself its own doom. For Æschylus
this fine impiousness would have been impossible. In Shelley's hands the tyrant is in a sterner grip than formerly he
was. Once having seized him, Shelley will never release
him until he destroys him utterly.

The tyranny of heaven none may retain
Or reassume, or hold, succeeding thee.
                                                [III, i, 57-58]

Another stock character which both dramatists use is Hermes-Mercury. In the older play he is fully typed. He is the messenger of Zeus, young, and by the nature of his office contemptible. In a blunt way he demands to know the secret kept by the Titan, only to be greeted with ironic scorn. Says Prometheus:

I for my part, be sure, would never change
My evil state for that thy bondslave's lot.
                                                [*P.B.*, 1053-54]

The conversation that follows is made up of typical Greek repartee, quick, evasive, sharp, insulting. Hermes retorts upon Prometheus—"it is meet the insulter to insult"—calls him a self-willed, brain-stricken fool, and warns him, as Belial might, of the probability of more dreadful woes:

Yet thou art stiff . . .
Look to it, if thou disobey my words,
How great a storm and triple wave of ills,
Not to be 'scaped, shall come on thee; . . .
And having traversed space of time full long,
Thou shalt come back to light, and then his hound,
The wingèd hound of Zeus, the ravening eagle,
Shall greedily make banquet of thy flesh.
                                                [*P.B.*, 1099-1112]

In this language we may recognize the charge of haughtiness brought against Prometheus by Mercury (I, 274, 387), the thought of the "slow years in torture" (I, 422), and Shelley's vision of "Heaven's wingèd hound" (I, 34) with ravening beak. Further, Hermes' reference to the Titan as frenzied, brain-stricken, "with no slight madness plagued," must have interested "mad Shelley" who, remembering Tasso, perhaps, sang of "great sages bound in madness" (I, 768).

On the whole, the Mercury of the later play is more complex than the young Hermes of the earlier work. He comes, of course, with the same commission: "There is a secret known to thee" (I, 371). That secret he would learn. He conjures Prometheus: "Let the will kneel within thy haughty heart" (I, 378). As did Hermes, he bids Prometheus consider the "space of time full long" in which he may suffer:

Yet pause, and plunge
Into Eternity, where recorded time . . .
Seems but a point, and the reluctant mind
Flags wearily . . .
Perchance it has not numbered the slow years
Which thou must spend in torture, unreprieved?
                                                [I, 416-423]

Then, too, as did Hermes, he must suffer himself to be called a "self-despising slave." But interestingly one of his main characteristics, however tainted, seems to be drawn from Hephæstos. The fire worker recognizes his kinsman as "wise in counsel." Mercury salutes him: "Wise art thou, firm and good." Further, Hephæstos is greatly disturbed by what he has to do, and sincerely protests his reluctance. His handicraft is now intolerable to him. His heart fails him. Under the savage urgings of Strength, he expresses repugnance. He cries out: "Ah me! Prometheus, for thy woes I groan." Whether sincerely or not, Mercury speaks in the same vein.

Awful Sufferer!
To thee unwilling, most unwillingly
I come, by the great Father's will driven down, . . .
Alas! I pity thee, and hate myself. . . .
Most heavily remorse hangs at my heart!
                                                [I, 352-356, 436]

In a work by Shelley it may be expected that even so despicable a creature as Mercury should respond to the goodness of the Titan, but how little he really understands Prometheus is suggested by the leering line:

If thou might'st dwell among the Gods the while
Lapped in voluptuous joy?
                                                [I, 425-426]

Here, of course, Mercury is subtly metamorphosed into Satan tempting Jesus. In all, he is a fit master for the hounds which follow him.

The characters of Okeanos and of Ocean seem unlike. Okeanos is a friendly ancient, as full of proverbs as of age. Like Zophar, or like any old man, he yearns to give advice: "I wish to give thee / My best advice." He means to intercede with Zeus, and deems that Zeus will grant his petition. But Prometheus knows that Okeanos protests too much, that he is indulging himself in fancied bravery. He therefore warns the hoary babbler—"Keep out of harm's way"—and Okeanos patters off at a great rate: "Thou urgest me who am in act to haste."

Shelley can use neither Okeanos nor his proverbs. The Greeks would like him well, just as the Elizabethans must have enjoyed Polonius. But Shelley's Titan is not one to be advised. At the moment of his last agony, which is also the moment of his triumph, he needs no counselor. The English drama, however, does require structurally that something be interposed between the fall of Jupiter and the freeing of Prometheus. These two scenes are too great to juxtapose; they must have psychic space between them. To meet this necessity, Shelley presents Ocean and Apollo. The scene is one of his most characteristic, a lyric gem archly cut and faceted with blue shadows and white fire. But this Ocean is Shelley's own creature, and his voice is Shelley's. Having questioned the fall of Jupiter as though it were an event too joyous to believe, he in turn hymns the diviner day. And then, with words that haunt those who have walked the sands of Via Reggio, he goes: "The loud deep calls me home. Peace, monster; I come now. Farewell."

The Oceanides of Æschylus, after the Greek convention, are presented as a Chorus. No individuals among them are brought forward as are Ione, Panthea, and Asia. Yet one must think that the Chorus made some impress upon the three Oceanides.

Nay, fear thou nought: in Iove
  All our array of wings
  In eager race hath come
To this high peak.

[*P.B.,* 142-145]

This love for Prometheus is the love which we find in the younger Nymphs and, although peculiarly developed, in Asia herself. The fear which stirs the inmost soul of the Chorus is much the same as the fear which shakes Ione and Panthea. What marks the emotion is the rich strain of pity which runs through it. Moved by the woes of the Titan, the Chorus is "wounded to the heart." Just so Ione is wounded as the fiends torture the Titan; and Panthea says:

Let us not tempt worse fear
By looking forth: those groans are grief enough.

[I, 592-593]

Perhaps it is going too far to wonder whether or not, in the characterizing of his Nymphs, Shelley drew upon the kindly and piteous quality of Io's nature. The Io-Prometheus scene lay farther from his purpose than any other. But the four lines of Hercules—"Thus doth strength / To wisdom minister like a slave"—recall the part of Strength in *Prometheus Bound.* However, we come out at last beyond the *dramatis personæ* of the older play among the special characterizations which are not so much different as new. Again, by seeing clearly just what Shelley required and took from Æschylus, we are the better able to see what of his own he added to Æschylus. It would be a dull and insensitive reading which concluded that the characters which are not in *Prometheus Bound* but which are in **Prometheus Unbound** are strange and incongruous. We need not conclude that Demogorgon, the Phantom of Jupiter, Earth, Apollo, the Fauns and the Furies and the many Spirits stand off curiously apart from the creatures of Æschylus' drama. That would be merely to say that Shelley did not have the artistic power to merge his work with that of the Greek. Yet, with the possible exception of Apollo, these characters which Shelley brought to associate with those of Æschylus, are largely mystic and lyric embodiments of ideas. And, with the exception of Apollo, Demogorgon, and Earth, the Shelleyan characters lead the drama toward song. Rather importantly, I think, it is they who suggest the grand transmutation of the character of Prometheus into something approaching the character of the Galilean.

In dealing with the *dramatis personæ* we have of necessity anticipated somewhat the matter of the story. Up to the wedding of Zeus with Thetis, Shelley takes over the myth which Æschylus had used. The point at which he departs from Æschylus is inevitably the point at which the Greek prepares to reconcile "the Champion with the Oppressor of mankind." Since this reconciliation is to be brought about through the Titan's revealing to Zeus the danger latent in the god's proposed marriage with Thetis, it is upon the matter of the wedding that we must fix our attention.

The basic difference, then, between the Greek myth and Shelley's adaptation of it is that in the one Prometheus does "unsay his high language" and trade his secret for his freedom, whereas in the other he does not. Obviously, in Athens, Zeus still reigns, and Æschylus has no desire and no permission to dethrone him. With equal obviousness, in England, Tyranny still reigns, and Shelley has every determination, permission or no permission, to destroy Tyranny. But the difference, in effect, of the two plays is not so great as might be expected. That which creates an impression of similarity between them is Æschylus' skillful treatment of the vital issues as contingent. Through the use of contingency the Greek gains and holds much of the effect of noble and triumphant rebellion on the part of the Titan. Shelley, on the other hand, can go straight to work, pitting the will and the mercy of Prometheus against the will and the tyranny of Zeus. In forthright drama he can achieve for his hero the expected triumph over his villain. When he sets "the period of Jove's power" and says that "it must come," it does come. When he says that the secret known to Prometheus is fatal, it is fatal. When he speaks of the dread marvel, the "prodigy irresistible," he admits no quasi-futurity of the contingent. When he gives Jupiter to say: "Now have I begotten a strange wonder," lo! the "detested prodigy" is already upon him to destroy him. Shelley makes promise and fulfillment meet.

Our story began with the cry of the Titan: "Pain, pain ever, for ever!" It ends with the cry of Jupiter: "I sink / Down, ever, for ever, down." The full circle is drawn. All is complete. We began with intelligence chained, with tyranny regnant. We end with tyranny destroyed, with intelligence and love united and ready to work their eternal wonder in the world. It seems natural now that Shelley, having gained the victory so near to his purpose, should stay further action. He has indeed passed the "far goal of Time" and has come into eternity. There plot and deed alike are grotesque. Song only is fitting. And Shelley, with his genius in full release, sings Act IV, the great "hymn of rejoicing." At the close he lifts Demogorgon out of his dark nature and gives him to chant of "a diviner day." Here Shelley goes beyond the dramatic purpose of the majestic Greek whose drama had, as Mary Shelley says, "Filled him with wonder and delight." He leaves the Acropolis for Golgotha. From that craggy hill another Poet has sought to fold over the world his healing wings. And it is at last the victory of love and creative hope which Shelley sings.

Surely in what may be his most significant and characteristic work Shelley owes a great debt to Æschylus. That debt he acknowledges, and we should sum it accurately. For it is largely when we come to know what he owes to the Greek that we may take up the essential task of scholarship: to essay the worth of his own genius.

Judith S. Chernaik   **(essay date 1968)**

SOURCE: "The Figure of the Poet in Shelley," in *ELH,* Vol. 35, No. 4, December, 1968, pp. 566-90.

On Shelley's detractors:

Few poets have suffered more than Shelley from the modern dislike of the Romantics. It is natural that this should be so. His poetry is, to an unusual degree, entangled in political thought, and in a kind of political thought now generally unpopular. His belief in the natural perfectibility of man justly strikes the Christian reader as foolishness; while, on the other hand, the sort of perfection he has in view is too ideal for dialectical materialists. His writings are too generous for our cynics; his life is too loose for our 'humanist' censors. Almost every recent movement of thought in one way or another serves to discredit him. From some points of view, this reaction cannot be regarded as wholly unfortunate. There is much in Shelley's poetry that has been praised to excess; much even that deserves no praise at all. In his metre, with all its sweetness, there is much ignoble fluidity, much of mere jingle. His use of language is such that he seldom attains for long to the highest qualities of distinction, and often sinks to a facility and commonplace almost Byronic. He is not a *safe* poet; you cannot open his works to refute one of his enemies with any sense of confidence.

> *C. S. Lewis, in his "Shelley, Dryden, and Mr. Eliot," in* Rehabilitations and Other Essays, *Oxford University Press, 1939.*

[*Chernaik is an American-born English author and educator. In the following essay, she discusses the autobiographical and symbolic importance of the recurring poet figure in Shelley's verse.*]

If there is a single image which draws together the most problematic aspects of Shelley's art, it is the recurrent figure of the frail Poet, pale of hue and weak of limb, consecrated to his youthful vision of Beauty but incapable of realizing or recreating it, driven at last to death by unassuageable desire for he knows not what. His literary associations vary from poem to poem, but the unsympathetic reader (and most readers at the present time fall into this camp), noting the resemblances between the fictional heroes of *Alastor* and *The Revolt of Islam,* and the "idealized" self-portraits of *Adonais* and *Epipsychidion,* inevitably takes each appearance of the Poet to be inflated autobiography, the romantic self-projection of a poet whose actual frailty is only too well established by contemporary accounts of his susceptibility to fainting fits, nervous seizures, visions and hallucinations.

One influential school of criticism applies to the figure of the poet terms like "shrill," "hysterical," "self-pitying," "immature." Behind these terms lies the assumption that there is no "objective correlative" for the emotionalism of the poet's cry, "I fall upon the thorns of life! I bleed!", no sense of life or reality behind the rhetoric. The most persuasive arguments against the charges of hysteria and self-indulgence have urged that it is a mistake to identify a lyric protagonist as the voice of the poet, or to read a prayer, elegy, or ode, which has its rhetoric in part determined by tradition, as primarily confessional.

As is often the case when a theory persists both in popular mythology and among sophisticated readers, there is some justification for the reading of the portraits as self-dramatization. The critical events of Shelley's life furnish the substance not only of the self-portraits but of the fictional narratives. His abortive attempts to liberate the surprised peasantry of Ireland and Wales are reconstituted in the heroic struggles of Laon and Lionel; his unhappy marriage to Harriet and his difficult relationship with Mary provide the outlines of the self-portrait in *Epipsychidion*; and his physical suffering, his persecution by the law, his exile abroad, his lack of audience, are traced in several of the portraits, most memorably in *Adonais*. It is tempting to see autobiography not only in the commitment to social justice but in the persistent theme of yearning for the unattainable, the irresistible pull of Eros or Thanatos:

> The desire of the moth for the star,
> Of the night for the morrow,
> The devotion to something afar
>   From the sphere of our sorrow.
>   (*To*———"One word is too often
>   profaned")

Still, the presence of autobiographical elements does not in itself mark Shelley's poetry as unusually self-regarding or immature. His precedent for allegorizing personal experience Shelley took from Dante and Milton; the peculiar authority he attributed to his own thought and its history and process suggests the example of those he considered the "extraordinary intellects of the new age," especially Wordsworth. Indeed, the figure of the Poet is significant not only because it dominates several of Shelley's major works, but because it exemplifies that complex relationship between the personal and the traditional which is at the heart of his poetry, the recasting of subjective experience in terms suggested by the greatest of poetic and philosophical traditions. But the figure of the poet participates as well in the ambitious symbolism which characterizes all of Shelley's poetry.

That poetry has the prodigality and ardor of genius; it is passionate, dazzlingly metaphorical, "intense and comprehensive" in its representation of emotions and ideas. Its motive is "to comprehend the meaning of the visible and invisible world"; its formulations attempt to mediate between what Shelley called "beautiful idealisms of moral excellence"—beauty, love, freedom, justice—and the real experience of world, life, and time. The figure of the poet is clearly part of Shelley's grand design. It is meant to be read as *serious* in the sense in which not only Shelley but Henry James and Matthew Arnold apply that term to art and to the artist's rendering of human life as significant choice between good and evil. If the serious Romantic artist has no prior commitment to a received dogma or system of morality, then poetry becomes a surrogate for religion, an independent and self-sustaining way of asserting or discovering value. When dogma and morality are no longer viable, the center of interest shifts to the seeking mind, embodied for late Romantic writers in the image of the artist, or the novice at life, the youthful hero or heroine, whose impressions of the surface are his only means of penetrating the mystery at the heart of things; embodied for Shelley in the image of the Poet, whose education is similarly rendered in terms of his own naive motive, and the world which resists and ultimately denies his vision.

The resemblances between Shelley's first presentation of the visionary, doomed Poet of *Alastor,* and his later incarnations, have been generally recognized. The unpromising plot of *Alastor,* compounded of Platonic myth and biographical fact, with gleanings from Scott, Wordsworth, and popular romantic fiction, clearly haunted Shelley's imagination, and became a vehicle for his repeated attempts to define the poet's relationship to the world he lives in and the vision he serves. The spiritual history of the Poet is reworked in the unfinished *Prince Athanase,* and its significant events are incorporated in the history of later heroes, both the Laon and Cythna of *The Revolt of Islam* and the Lionel of *Rosalind and Helen.* The **"Hymn to Intellectual Beauty"** provides an autobiographical analogue to the fiction of *Alastor,* turning, like *Alastor,* on the poet's subjection to a vision of truth. The self-portrait of the **"Hymn"** is elaborated in the prefatory stanzas of *The Revolt of Islam* and in *Epipsychidion;* it appears allusively in the **"Ode to the West Wind"** and is dramatized in the figure of the mourning poet described in *Adonais.* What I propose to do in the following summary is to isolate those elements of the poet's history which seem to me to reveal Shelley's basic design.

The Poet of *Alastor* is idealized as a "lovely" youth gifted above all others, possessed of the traditional virtues of the prince, "gentle and brave and generous." There is a suggestion of a heroic ideal in each portrait, though the terms which describe the hero vary. Thus Prince Athanase, like the Poet of *Alastor,* has a Spenserian cast:

> He had a gentle yet aspiring mind;
> Just, innocent, with varied learning fed;
> Fearless he was, and scorning all disguise . . .
> Liberal he was of soul, and frank of heart. . . .
> (Prince Athanase)

In the **"Ode to the West Wind,"** the poet describes himself in his youth as "tameless and swift and proud," terms which suggest the strength and freedom of a natural force; in *Adonais* the frail Form, who represents Shelley, is described in similar terms as a "pardlike spirit, beautiful and swift."

The young Poet of *Alastor* is educated "by solemn vision, and bright silver dream," by nature, philosophy, and the "sacred past." Education, the growth of the poet's mind, includes both passive and active processes, not only the receiving of impressions and the study of books, but the active seeking of experience; thus Shelley describes his

own studies and travels, in the *Preface* to *The Revolt of Islam,* as "an education peculiarly fitted for a Poet." The Poet of *Alastor,* like the poet-author, wanders abroad in search of "Nature's most secret steps" (*Alastor*); the poet's travels reappear in *Epipsychidion* as "visioned wanderings" undertaken "in the clear golden prime of my youth's dawn" (*Epipsychidion*).

Suddenly a Vision appears, which forms a turning point in the youth's spiritual history; his earlier education is a preparation for it, his adult life is determined by its appearance and its loss. The vision is variously defined in the poems, as truth, "intellectual beauty," that which gives meaning to life, or, more obscurely, as a thirst for love, a vacancy of spirit, an awakening to absence. In *Alastor* the vision comes upon the Poet as he sleeps, in the form of a veiled maiden, the "spirit of sweet human love"; her voice is "like the voice of his own soul"; her theme is "Knowledge and truth and virtue" (*Alastor.*) The vision of the **"Hymn to Intellectual Beauty"** descends upon the poet "like the truth of nature"; the Being who appears to the poet in *Epipsychidion* is "robed in such exceeding glory / That I behold her not . . . Her spirit was the harmony of truth" (*Epipsychidion*).

The reality of a vision, by definition subjective, is attested to by the "ecstasy" which admits it. The poet of the **"Hymn to Intellectual Beauty"** describes his visionary seizure: "I shrieked, and clasped my hands in ecstasy"; the Poet of *Alastor,* experiences the ecstasy of sexual union with the veiled maiden (*Alastor*). But the vision dissolves; the spirit vanishes, and the moment of ecstasy is followed by a trial of despair, as the poet, awakened to a cold reality, pursues in vain his lost vision of perfection. In *Alastor* the Poet flees back through time and civilization to the primeval source of being, where he discovers not life or love, but death. Prince Athanase, blasted in his promise by a mysterious ailment, wanders from land to land, weakened by grief. In several of the more personal lyrics, as in these two "allegories," the nature of the poet's despair identifies the vision as love, the failure of which is responsible for the poet's loss of vital powers and his physical decline.

The dedicatory stanzas of *The Revolt of Islam* present as poetic autobiography a sequence of events similar to the fictional narrative of *Alastor.* The poet describes his youthful study of nature and the past, his preparation for a heroic task; he recounts the visionary hour in which his poetic mission is revealed to him.

> I do remember well the hour which burst
> My spirit's sleep. A fresh May-dawn it was,
> When I walked forth upon the glittering grass,
> And wept, I knew not why . . .
> ("To Mary," The Revolt of Islam)

But he suffers a sudden deflection of purpose with the appearance of love, or more specifically, with the desire for love, "a sense of loneliness, a thirst," which comes upon his mind, even as the vision of the veiled maiden descends upon the Poet of *Alastor.* Thereafter he seeks in vain, until his meeting with Mary, for one who answers the thirst of his soul.

> Alas, that love should be a blight and snare
>   To those who seek all sympathies in one!
> Such once I sought in vain; then black despair,
>   The shadow of a starless night, was thrown
>   Over the world in which I moved alone:—
> Yet never found I one not false to me,
>   Hard hearts, and cold, like weights of icy stone
> Which crushed and withered mine, that could not
> be
> Aught but a lifeless clod, until revived by thee.
>   (**"To Mary,"** *The Revolt of Islam*)

As in **Alastor** and **Prince Athanase,** the time of solitude is imaged as a wandering in the wilderness. The poet's despair is described in analogy to the death of winter, the hardening and freezing of the land; as the land dies when its source of life is removed, so the spirit dies when it is not nourished by love. The suggestion is that the spirit, once it has been awakened (or given life) by a vision of truth, requires continuing relationship with a human embodiment of that truth.

In the self-portrait of **Epipsychidion** the revival of love is delusive; Mary's light illumines but does not warm. But the sequence of events follows the pattern of the dedicatory stanzas of *The Revolt of Islam*: the appearance of the Vision, creation and creator of the poet's thought, its unaccountable withdrawal, the black night of despair which follows, the poet's search for a human shape of his ideal, his betrayal by false lovers and subsequent spiritual "death," the revival of life brought about by true love. The poet's pursuit of his lost vision imitates Dante's pursuit of Beatrice, once glimpsed and ever sought afterwards, and the vision itself has the multiple forms of Dante's love; it is a star towards which the spirit soars, a God who can only be reached by crossing the grave, a veiled Divinity of thought and poetry, a "soul out of my soul," and also a love in human form.

> I questioned every tongueless wind that flew
> Over my tower of mourning, if it knew
> Whither 'twas fled, this soul out of my soul . . .
> But neither prayer nor verse could dissipate
> The night which closed on her; nor uncreate
> That world within this Chaos, mine and me,
> Of which she was the veiled Divinity,
> The world I say of thoughts that worshipped her:
> And therefore I went forth, with hope and fear
> And every gentle passion sick to death,
> Feeding my course with expectation's breath,
> Into the wintry forest of our life;
> And struggling through its error with vain strife,
> And stumbling in my weakness and my haste,
> And half bewildered by new forms, I passed,
> Seeking among those untaught foresters
> If I could find one form resembling hers,
> In which she might have masked herself from me.
>   (*Epipsychidion*)

The "wilderness" image of the earlier poems becomes in

Epipsychidion the Dantesque "obscure forest," the "wintry forest of our life," the "wintry wilderness of thorns." And the suggestions of struggle and "vain strife" intimate that this time is not only a quest but an ordeal, a trial, as of the soul in its pilgrimage through life. There is a temporary relief of pain as Mary appears, a mirror image of the poet's lost visionary love. But Mary's love, cold and chaste at best, is withdrawn, and the poet succumbs to despair. His new suffering is rendered in heightened allegory which has the explicit function of concealment, made necessary by the personal tragedy which precipitates the eclipse of love, the death of the Shelleys' two young children. Conventional metaphor is abandoned, as insufficiently opaque or as inadequate to the emotion, and the poet is portrayed not as a wanderer in the wilderness, or a mariner on a storm-tossed sea (as in **"Lines Written among the Euganean Hills"**), but as that storm-tossed sea itself, as an earth, a world, shaken by natural catastrophe.

> What storms then shook the ocean of my sleep,
> Blotting that Moon, whose pale and waning lips
> Then shrank as in the sickness of eclipse;—
> And how my soul was as a lampless sea,
> And who was then its Tempest; and when She,
> The Planet of that hour, was quenched, what frost
> Crept o'er those waters, till from coast to coast
> The moving billows of my being fell
> Into a death of ice, immovable;—
> And then—what earthquakes made it gape and split,
> The white Moon smiling all the while on it,
> These words conceal:—If not, each word would be
> The key of staunchless tears. Weep not for me!
>   (*Epipsychidion*)

The "death of ice" imaged in these lines is related to the imagery of a withered earth in the Dedication to *The Revolt of Islam*: as in the earlier passage, the physical analogy asserts the dependence of the poet's creative powers upon love, as the natural creation is dependent upon heat and light. But the suffering expressed has a new intensity, suggestive of the cosmic suffering of a Lear, and justified by the tragic perception which in Shelley's last poems seems to suffuse and darken his idealism, his awareness that life is indeed at the mercy of death, love at the mercy of life.

The final turn of the allegory restores the natural order; Emily appears, the poet's "long night" ends, and life is miraculously reborn with love. The poet prays to Mary and Emily, Moon and Sun to the poet's "passive Earth," to govern his "sphere of being" in harmony and love:

> Twin Spheres of light who rule this passive Earth,
> This world of love, this *me;* and into birth
> Awaken all its fruits and flowers, and dart
> Magnetic might into its central heart;
> And lift its billows and its mists, and guide
> By everlasting laws, each wind and tide
> To its fit cloud, and its appointed cave . . .
> So ye, bright regents, with alternate sway
> Govern my sphere of being night and day!
>   (*Epipsychidion*)

The prayer to the "bright regents" for governance is similar to the poet's prayer in the **"Ode to the West Wind"** for strength; as the creative powers of the failing prophet require extraordinary inspiration, the violence of storm, the solitary human being requires to be part of a harmonious social order, to respond like others to the pull of love in social relationship.

In his despair the poet is represented as frail, weak, powerless. But his failing power must be seen against the initial portrayal of the poet in his youth as fearless, strong, capable of "visioned wanderings." It is only after the vision seizes hold of his imagination that he loses his strength, and becomes "a Power / Girt round with weakness." Images of a physical wearing away occur in each version of the time of despair. In *Alastor* the Poet's embrace of Death is anticipated in his physical decline:

> And now his limbs were lean; his scattered hair
> Sered by the autumn of strange suffering
> Sung dirges in the wnd; his listless hand
> Hung like dead bone within its withered skin . . .
>
> *(Alastor)*

The Poet is a "spectral form"; his eyes are "wild" with a "strange light." In the dedicatory stanzas to *The Revolt of Islam,* the poet laments his weakness, presumably a reference to actual physical illness, even as he prays for strength to serve as a prophet:

> I would fain
> Reply in hope—but I am worn away,
> And Death and Love are yet contending for their
>   prey.
>
> **("To Mary,"** *The Revolt of Islam*)

The most dramatic representation of the poet's physical weakness is the description of the mourning poet in *Adonais.* The sequence of images, similar to those used for the same purpose in the **"Ode to the West Wind,"** suggest original or potential strength even as they assert actual failure:

> A Love in desolation masked;—a Power
> Girt round with weakness;—it can scarce uplift
> The weight of the superincumbent hour;
> It is a dying lamp, a falling shower,
> A breaking billow:—even whilst we speak
> Is it not broken?
>
> *(Adonais)*

The phrases suggest the exhausted final movement of a process which began in strength, but has run the course of its given or self-generated power.

The poet's loss of strength, though it is imaged in physical terms, is clearly mental and spiritual, like the torments of Prometheus. In both *Adonais* and *Epipsychidion* the image of the hunted deer is used to describe the weakness and extremity of the poet. But the "raging hounds" which pursue him are his own thoughts:

> now he fled astray
> With feeble steps o'er the world's wilderness,
> And his own thoughts, along that rugged way,
> Pursued, like raging hounds, their father and their
>   prey.
>
> *(Adonais)*

> Then, as a hunted deer that could not flee,
> I turned upon my thoughts, and stood at bay,
> Wounded and weak and panting . . .
>
> *(Epipsychidion)*

The image in both poems dramatizes the compulsive nature of the poet's flight; he is not only drawn in pursuit of his vision but is himself pursued, and the furies which pursue him are internal as well as external, self-generated, like the vision itself.

The poet's spiritual history reaches its climax in a sudden reversal, a triumph over despair, as the dying youth undergoes a final apotheosis. In *Alastor,* the Poet discovers a "little shallop . . . floating near the shore," which he is inspired to embark in. Beckoned on by "the light that shone within his soul," he voyages through a varied symbolic topography of tempest-torn sea and wintry river, through a dark cavern and over a raging whirlpool, to a calm dell deep in the forest, where he at last submits himself to Death. Each of the major poems ends with some version of this voyage, this true ending and consummation, whether of love or death. The effect in *Adonais* and *Epipsychidion* is of a sudden widening and lifting, an imaginative transcendence of life. In *Epipsychidion,* as in *Alastor,* a boat materializes, and the poet in imagination embarks.

> Emily,
> A ship is floating in the harbour now,
> A wind is hovering o'er the mountain's brow;
> There is a path on the sea's azure floor,
> No keel has ever ploughed that path before . . .
> The merry mariners are bold and free:
> Say, my heart's sister, wilt thou sail with me?
> Our bark is as an albatross, whose nest
> Is a far Eden of the purple East;
> And we between her wings will sit, while Night,
> And Day, and Storm, and Calm, pursue their flight,
> Our ministers, along the boundless Sea,
> Treading each other's heels, unheededly.
>
> *(Epipsychidion)*

The voyage in *Epipsychidion* reads like an inspired transfiguration of the voyagings of the "little shallop" of *Alastor,* mediated through several other flights, the "divine canoe" which transports Laon and Cythna to the "Temple of the Spirit," the departure of Prometheus and Asia "beyond the peak / Of Bacchic Nysa, Maenad-haunted mountain" to the "simple dwelling" where they may live restored to love and happiness.

Adonais also ends with an imagined voyage:

> The breath whose might I have invoked in song

Descends on me; my spirit's bark is driven,
Far from the shore, far from the trembling throng
Whose sails were never to the tempest given;
The massy earth and spherèd skies are riven!
I am borne darkly, fearfully, afar;
Whilst, burning through the inmost veil of Heaven,
The soul of Adonais, like a star,
Beacons from the abode where the Eternal are.

(Adonais)

The elements of the more extensively developed voyages are all present in these lines: the "spirit's bark," the sails given to the tempest, the spirits which beckon the poet on, the setting apart of the poet from all other men, his triumph over physical impossibility, his far goal beyond the limits of the known world, of time and mortality. Though the relationship between physical and spiritual reality, between image and object, is different in each poem, the voyage is always a voyage of the spirit, the imagination, a giving of the self to the storm, a return to the source.

It can be seen, I think, even from this sketchy account, that the resemblances among the major poems are sufficient to justify the reader's sense that there is but a single figure of the Poet with several variations. I would like to suggest several complementary approaches to a reading of this figure in the hope of illuminating its dramatic and symbolic character, and its relationship to Shelley's theory of poetry.

It may be useful to note first the care with which the several portraits are rendered dramatic, and given an objective form which challenges simple identification with the author. *Alastor* introduces its subject in the manner of Wordsworthian storytelling: "There was a Poet . . ." The *Preface*, furthermore, presents the Poet as an example of a wilful isolation which the author, presumably, deplores. *Epipsychidion* is presented in the elaborate "Advertisement" as the work of an "unfortunate" young man who died at Florence while preparing for the voyage described at the end of the poem. The fiction suggests a second voice, a second view of the hero, with the effect of framing and distancing the subject. In both *Alastor* and *Adonais* the martyred poet, one singular both in his extraordinary gifts and in the severity of his fate, is described through the eyes of another poet, who speaks in his own person, and appears to be rather more representative than the poet he mourns. The dedicatory stanzas of *The Revolt of Islam,* serve a similar function; the idealized account of Shelley's history and his love for Mary frames the poem of Laon and Cythna, the two young martyrs to political idealism, who stand in relation to each other and to the world very much as Shelley and Mary do. As in *Alastor* and *Adonais,* there is a double perspective, that of the romantic fable, heroic, tragic, and exemplary, and that of the poet, human and of the world, who meditates upon it. Similarly, despite the inevitable identification of the mourning poet in *Adonais* with Shelley, the language suggests that he is distinct from the elegist of the poem, who applies the same impersonal description to him that he does to the other mourners:

he, as I guess,
Had gazed on Nature's naked loveliness . . .

It is not until the final line of his presentation—"oh! that it should be so!" that the sudden breaking through of emotion suggests that the elegist is lamenting his own fate.

The framing devices, then, even when they are false clues, are plain obstacles to a reading which identifies the Poet with Shelley. But even where there is a single voice, as in the shorter lyrics, the tone is heightened to suggest that the poet is assuming a literary role as elegist or bard, prophet or dreamer. The effect is to generalize his spiritual history, making it subservient to his function as poet, as vessel for divine inspiration, intermediary between the corrupt world and its source. The propriety of tone is part of a general stylization of the portraits; the elements of the poet's history and the metaphors which describe it are peculiarly appropriate to the context, determined by the "mission" of the poet or by the occasion which summons him forth. Thus the visionary ecstasy of the Poet in the **"Hymn to Intellectual Beauty,"** the "beating heart and streaming eyes" which give evidence of his commitment, are metaphors for the initiation of a novice to the service of his Divinity, or the Spirit which represents it; they are part of the poem's attempt to substitute "Intellectual Beauty"—the "truth of nature"—for the "poisoned names" of orthodox religion, the "frail spells" of traditional worship. The poet prays not for salvation but for "calm" for his "onward life"; his vow is not to fear God and obey his commandments, but "to fear himself, and love all human kind." The controlling effect of metaphor—a metaphor inseparable from the natural and symbolic occasion of the poem—is most striking in the **"Ode to the West Wind,"** where the self-portrait is a matter of only a few lines:

If even
I were as in my boyhood, and could be
The comrade of thy wanderings over Heaven,
As then, when to outstrip thy skiey speed
Scarce seemed a vision; I would ne'er have striven

As thus with thee in prayer in my sore need.
Oh, lift me as a wave, a leaf, a cloud!
I fall upon the thorns of life! I bleed!

A heavy weight of hours has chained and bowed
One too like thee: tameless, and swift, and proud.

The characterization of the poet in youth is drawn from analogy with the Wind, which is free, swift, and tameless; his "strife" is a striving with the Wind, as with an angel of God; and the central line, suggestive of the "wilderness" imagery in all the portraits—"I fall upon the thorns of life! I bleed!"—is a direct response to the prayer which immediately precedes it, and which summarizes the natural action of the Wind upon all of nature except man. Thus the despair of the verb, *I fall,* appears to be suggested by the prayer, *Oh, lift me,* as the "thorns of life" appear to be suggested by the image of leaf and seed.

The portrait which readers have found most difficult to

The Cremation of Shelley's Body *(1869), by Louis-Edouard Fournier and Jean-Léon Gérôme. In this romanticized painting Byron, Leigh Hunt, and Edward John Trelawny stand beside the funeral pyre while Mary Shelley (who did not attend her husband's cremation) kneels behind them.*

accept, and into which they have read the most direct expression of self-pity—the portrait of the "frail Form" in *Adonais*—is similarly governed by its context and occasion. The example of earlier pastoral elegies, especially Milton's *Lycidas,* suggests the procession of a "gentle band" of mountain shepherds come to mourn their fallen comrade, "their garlands sere, their magic mantles rent"; their songs are their poems, which are now turned to grief, their flocks "quick Dreams," fed by the "living streams" of the spirit. Shelley's typically expansive use of tradition suggests the additional figures of the Pilgrim, the sweet lyrist from the "wilds of Ierne," and the "frail Form," a dying singer of songs. The description of the "frail Form, who, of course, represents Shelley, incorporates the related images of a solitary wanderer, a Bacchic celebrant (hence a poet-priest), a swift hunter transformed into the hunter's prey, a "Stranger" identifiable only by the ensanguined mark which links him to the hunter Cain, most grievous of sinners, or to the greatest of shepherds and poet-teachers, Christ. As the "Stranger" weeps his own fate in that of the martyred poet, so the facts of Keats' life suggest other details, the physical illness, the neglect and hostility of the world, and the fact that Keats died abroad, as Shelley himself lived in exile.

Each poem, then, has its own distancing effects, its own artistic rationale. But the persistence of a single pattern— the account of the idealized youth, the vision that comes

upon him, his search to recover it, his final voyage to an imagined Elysium—suggests a larger meaning to which the several disguises of the Poet, the changing autobiographical details, are contributory. This meaning would seem to lie in the suggestiveness of the narrative as a myth or allegory dramatizing the nature of the creative imagination, both its inherent power to change and recreate the world, and its mortal dependence upon love, or relationship with that which lies outside itself. As Shelley rewrote Aeschylus and Dante, so he incorporated in his history of the poet elements of the greatest of earlier classical and Biblical myths of power and dependency, vision and its loss. The Platonic analogues have often been noted; thus the Vision of the **"Hymn to Intellectual Beauty"** and the awakening described in *The Revolt of Islam* suggest the Vision of supreme beauty described by Diotima in the *Symposium.* And the loss of the golden strength, the "visioned wanderings" of youth, the conception of mature life as a progress towards death, a blind stumbling and search, suggest the Platonic myth of recollection. But the outlines of the Poet's history, from his early happiness and strength, his free communion with nature and divinity, to his wandering in the world's wilderness, and his final transcendence of despair, suggest most directly the analogy of the myth of Genesis and parallel classical myths of the Golden Age. Youth's "golden prime" is a time prior to knowledge, love, experience. The mind is described as "sleeping," "vacant," "passive"; it has not yet been awakened, illuminated, "created." And the black night of the soul which follows the Vision suggests the loss of Eden following upon some necessary but fatal knowledge, and exile to a "wilderness of thorns," a fallen world of time and death. As the spirit is awakened to knowledge, so the "mortal passions" of the human being are released, and he becomes as a deer hunted by the "raging hounds" of his own thought. There is no Temptation in Shelley's narrative; he consistently attacked the doctrine that man's fall follows from his disobedience. But there are repeated suggestions of an error, whether it is defined, as in the *Preface* to *Alastor,* as the attempt to exist without human sympathy, or as the mistake of seeking to find in mortal form that which is immortal. And there are repeated hints of a curse, lying either upon the youth who has dared too much, or upon the life which it is the lot of all men to endure.

The "fallen state," after all, is indisputable; mortality, time, passion, are facts of reality. Poetry, like religion, gives meaning to reality by conjecturing a before and after, by naming the present a "fall" from the past. The myth Shelley substitutes for the orthodox fall reflects his sense that the condition of human life must be conceived in terms of loss if it is to be tolerable. It is the nature of the human being to err, he suggests, in seeking to remedy its loss. Yet the single imperative for the imagination is recovery of that Absolute—whether knowledge, love, or beauty—which its own desire asserts to be the necessary source and sustaining power of life. He uses related imagery in *Epipsychidion* when he speaks of those

> to whom this world of life
> Is as a garden ravaged, and whose strife
> Tills for the promise of a later birth
> The wilderness of this Elysian earth.
>
> (*Epipsychidion*)

The poet is one of these—not the poet who goes astray, like the hero of *Alastor,* but the poet who laments him, and whose "strife" is the poem which he utters.

The "promise of a later birth" insists on the primacy of hope and the significance of poetry, the power of the imagination to recover what it divines of the original or potential beauty of the world. Even where it is apparently denied by the narrative, this is the motive behind the spiritual autobiographies in the poems, as it is the informing principle of the "**Ode to the West Wind.**" A similar figure is used in *A Defence of Poetry* to describe the function of poetry as mediator between the human and divine:

> Poetry redeems from decay the visitations of the divinity
> in man. . . . Poetry defeats the curse which binds us to
> be subjected to the accident of surrounding impressions.

In the context of Shelley's general discussion of poetry, the religious metaphor, which displaces redemptive power from an omnipotent deity to the human imagination, is unobtrusive. But Shelley's theory of poetry confirms what we read in the poems: that Shelley's perspective is not that of the visionary or the divinely inspired prophet, but of the faltering human being whose visionary glimpses are fleeting and evanescent, who looks "before and after," whose most precious faculty (and only hope of "salvation" or "redemption"), his poetic imagination, is a delicate plant which requires assiduous care and love. The sojourn in the wilderness, the time of strife, of pain and suffering, is the image for life in the world, for man's condition as a state of longing for what he does not possess and can scarcely apprehend. And the central human interest is, quite properly, not the "fearless youth" in his "golden prime," but the lost soul struggling in the wilderness, the "frail Form," the weakest of hearts, identified in *Epipsychidion* with the poet-lover who alone of men is granted a vision of the eternal, and in *Adonais* both with the suffering Christ and with Cain, the greatest of sinners, a "fugitive and vagabond in the earth," whose punishment is "greater than he can bear."

I would suggest that the poet's history and his final apotheosis should be understood in relation to Shelley's conception of the imagination as the sole agent of "redemption" (in the only sense in which Shelley uses that term), the sole hope of defeating the curse which binds us to ourselves. The poet's struggle can be considered a dramatic representation of the familiar doctrine of the *Defence of Poetry:*

> The great secret of morals is love; or a going out of
> our own nature, and an identification of ourselves
> with the beautiful which exists in thought, action, or
> person, not our own. A man, to be greatly good, must
> imagine intensely and comprehensively, he must put
> himself in the place of another and of many others;
> the pains and pleasures of his species must become
> his own. The great instrument of moral good is the
> imagination . . .

As Laon and Prometheus represent the conscious effort of the human spirit "to be greatly good," the figure of the poet in flight from himself, in restless pursuit of his lost vision, dramatizes the extreme effort of the imagination, imprisoned in its own nature, the frail self, to identify "with the beautiful which exists in thought, action, or person, not our own." It is in this light that we should read the impulse towards identification with the ideal; in the "**Ode to the West Wind,**" the poet praying to be one with that "Spirit fierce"; in *Epipsychidion,* the poet seeking union with the beloved; in *Adonais* the elegist putting himself "in the place of another and of many others," as he bears in his person the "pains . . . of his species," even to Cain's and Christ's, weeps in another's fate his own, and at last seeks identification with the departed poet he mourns. The portrait of the Poet, so often regarded as self-indulgence on Shelley's part, is actually an attempt to render dramatically the imaginative process which is the only escape from self. The great defence Shelley makes of poetry is that it counters egoism, the surrender to ourselves and our time; for both creator and reader it involves an identification with the "other," hence self-forgetfulness. For a non-believer, one who cannot see beyond the language of the poem itself to the sacred or absolute truth which it claims to embody, this stretching of the imagination must still serve as the definitive value of art.

The relationship between imaginative sympathy and moral good is most explicit in the **"Ode to the West Wind,"** where the prayer of the poet for identification with the Wind—"Be thou, Spirit fierce, my spirit! Be thou me, impetuous one!"—is the condition for his social mission, to "quicken a new birth," to prophesy a Spring to follow the Winter of destruction and desolation. But in what sense can we relate the spiritual travail of the poet in *Adonais* or *Epipsychidion* to a "moral good"? The two great lyrics are not even implicitly revolutionary or political; neither asserts the possibility of hope in the world. One hesitates to take as exemplary the poet's lucid and terrible axiom in *Adonais*: "Die, If thou wouldst be with that which thou dost seek!"; this version of the Biblical "die that ye may live" is very different from the poet's prophecy in the **"Ode to the West Wind,"** which insists that the living world itself can be reborn. The "moral good," if it is to be found in the poem, lies not in the advice but in the process which leads to it, the imaginative effort to identify with the martyred poet. What the poet demonstrates in the last stanzas of *Adonais* is the step-by-step process which Shelley describes elsewhere as an awakening and enlarging of the "circumference of the imagination" to possibilities which the familiar world resists, that "going out of our own nature" which is the converse of egoism. The pessimism of the ending is secondary to its imaginative transcendence of physical reality, of time and decay and cold mortality, all that Shelley means by "the shadow of our night." The mourning poet is bid to exercise his imagination, his "spirit's light," in preparation for a final revelation:

> Clasp with thy panting soul the pendulous Earth;
> As from a centre, dart thy spirit's light
> Beyond all worlds, until its spacious might
> Satiate the void circumference: then shrink
> Even to a point within our day and night . . .

These difficult lines affirm the power of spirit over space and time, its independence from the laws of mass and motion; they anticipate the "consolation" of the elegy, that poetry alone is immortal; they prepare the poet for the actual exercise of his power to move "beyond all worlds" and "satiate" the void, as in the final stanza of the poem the imagination effects in the physical world the miracle it desires. The image of the spirit darting its light "beyond all worlds" constitutes a remarkable spatial equivalent of that imaginative expansion of sympathies which is at the heart of Shelley's theory of poetry and morals.

If we read the allegorical dimensions of the poet's history in the terms sketched above, the temptation is to minimize the difficulties which readers find in the portraits, and which have to do mainly, I think, with the rhetoric of despair and ecstasy. Why is the poet in his despair identified with such extreme suffering? Alternately he is identified with Christ—one who suffers for all men—or with figures like Cain, Actaeon, a "Stranger"—one whose suffering is a mark of his exile from human community, his separateness from men, one cursed by God. He is not

merely weak but "of hearts the weakest." Clearly these references are not biographical but symbolic, and should be related not to Shelley's personal suffering but to the suffering of such figures as Byron's Manfred and Cain, or Shelley's own Prometheus, who stand apart from the "trembling throng" as having dared all, or refused obedience to whatever reigns. Dramatically the extreme suffering and weakness of the Poet is the precondition of the final triumph of the spirit's light, the imagination freed by love, as it is fettered by hate. The effect is to suggest that liberation is not only willed but miraculous. But what the reader misses in the drama is the act of willed rebellion, comparable to man's eating of the apple, or Faust's bargain with the devil, or Prometheus' cursing of Jupiter. The Poet, unlike Prometheus, seems to be essentially passive. The vision, whether blessing or curse, comes upon him unsought, his "quest" consists of drifting and wandering, being laid asleep; redemption appears miraculously on his path, his final act is one of submission to his destiny. He is compared to a stricken deer, a bleeding God; he is a "passive Earth" who prays to be "governed" by Sun and Moon. The most memorable lines in the poems are a dramatic rendering of his subjection and weakness: "I fall upon the thorns of life! I bleed!" "I pant, I sink, I tremble, I expire!"

It seems to me that we should read the theme of the poet's passiveness in relation to the doctrine with which it is paired—that it lies in man's will, and only in his will, to be what he envisions. This is the doctrine which Julian propounds against Maddalo's dark fatalism. Julian, of course, speaks for Shelley, Maddalo for Byron:

> it is our will
> That thus enchains us to permitted ill—
> We might be otherwise—we might be all
> We dream of happy, high, majestical.
> Where is the love, beauty, and truth we seek
> But in our mind? And if we were not weak
> Should we be less in deed than in desire?
> **("Julian and Maddalo")**

And it is the doctrine which *Prometheus Unbound* exemplies: both good and evil lie in man's will; guilt and pain exist because man's will "made or suffered them." We are weak, as Julian asserts, and it is his sense of human infirmity that Shelley renders in the history of the Poet. But the ethical imperatives remain the same for weak or strong:

> To suffer woes which Hope thinks infinite;
> To forgive wrongs darker than death or night;
> To defy Power, which seems omnipotent;
> To love, and bear; to hope till Hope creates
> From its own wreck the thing it contemplates . . .
> (*Prometheus Unbound*)

In the history of the poet the ethical imperatives are embodied most clearly in the proud flights of his youth, the vows he makes to be "wise and just, and free and mild." But they can be discerned as well in his seeking after his vison, his blind stumbling. His "black night" is terrible because it is a removal from the possibility of ethical action, a freezing of the will and the imagination. Yet his struggle and strife represent the effort of his imagination against the impendiments of life and the weak self, and his final flight, whether a giving of himself to Death or an imagined flight with Love and the beloved to a "sinless Eden," is a triumph of his imagination to be what it dreams, if not in the real then in the imagined world.

The connections between Shelley's prose and his poetry have often been demonstrated, of course. But the differences between a prose statement of an idea and the poetic rendering of it are especially significant in Shelley's work, and indeed mark him off radically from a poet like Blake, to whom he is in so many ways comparable. In general, ideas which are presented tentatively, with qualifications, in the prose, are rendered absolute and categorical in the poetry; negatives are rendered positively; logic and analogy, proposing relationship, yield to metaphor or myth, asserting identity. Shelley's "Notes" to **Hellas** demonstrate his sophisticated awareness of the nature of poetic "truth," and they suggest why it is possible for one reader to consider him a religious poet, another reader to consider him a rationalist. In his poetry Shelley adopts the prophetic convention, in which truth is revealed to one singled out as mediator between the divine and the human; the convention assumes the absolute nature of the truth so revealed, and the independent existence of divinity. But in his prose Shelley consistently recognizes the subjective limitations on knowledge, and "truth" is relative, speculative, conjectural. The faculty of prophecy is one which bards "possess or feign"; the visions of Isaiah and Virgil were a product not of divine visitation but of their "ardent spirits" "overleaping the actual reign of evil"; the *desire* for immortality is the "strongest and the only presumption" for its existence. With regard to ultimate questions, apart from our desire, apart from the imaginative projections of human desire in myth and legend, "all men are equally ignorant." Or, in the positive, poetic, and religious statement of a prose agnosticism: "The deep truth is imageless" (**Prometheus Unbound**).

The positive expressions both of prophetic hope and prophetic despair in the poems have their rational, qualified, prose counterparts. He wrote to Mrs. Gisborne, "Let us believe in a kind of optimism, in which we are our own gods. . . . because Hope, as Coleridge says, is a solemn duty, which we owe alike to ourselves and to the world." But the pragmatic counsel of a good friend has little place in a prophetic poetry in which faith is not assumed, but granted from above, its object is not intuited but revealed, and disaster is not be prudently avoided but rather to be welcomed as Apocalypse.

It seems to me that the poetic rendering of the figure of the poet as passive, dependent, weak, may be similarly understood in terms of the difference between prose and poetry. Shelley consistently defines the imagination as a combination of active and passive faculties, both in his prose and his poetry. The mind receives data from the external world, but colors what it receives with its own light. Man is, like the lyre, an instrument responsive to impressions. "But there is a principle within the human

being . . . which acts otherwise than in the lyre, and produces not melody alone, but harmony, by an internal adjustment of the sounds or emotions thus excited." The complicated analogy of the mind to the valley of the Arve in **"Mont Blanc"** explores the relationship of mind to an external and perhaps transcendent reality; in the opening stanza the active power of the mind is as a "feeble brook" to the river of impressions which course through it, but the final lines of the poem suggest that the external world may in fact be dependent if not for its existence then for its meaning and value on the mind which perceives it. Passiveness of mind is valued by Shelley, as by Wordsworth and Keats; the term as Shelley uses it suggests not merely the origin of mental experience in passive sensation but the poetic faculty of profound and unconscious receptiveness to reality—that "wise passiveness" which receives more of the world, more of truth, than sensory perception can admit to consciousness. The faculty depends, as it does for Wordsworth, on a prior intuition of "influences" which can be felt if the poet is attuned to them, and it includes the possibility of visionary experience, trance, visitations of divinity. But the passiveness of the poet merely prepares him for the creative act. Shelley insists as strongly as Coleridge and Wordsworth do that the imagination is essentially active, essentially creative; it "creates anew the universe"; it raises the poet above other men to the level of a god.

How shall we relate a theory of the imagination which insists upon its creativity, its power to shape and inform and give value to life, with a symbolic rendering of the Poet as passive, dependent, subject to a Vision which can neither be summoned nor recalled, submissive to the Powers which call him to his destiny? Insofar as the history of the poet is allegorical of the poetic imagination, I would suggest that the terms of the narrative are a paradoxical dramatization of the prose doctrine which they seem to contradict. For the Powers to whom the poet submits, upon whom he depends, are originally extensions of his own active powers of mind. The vision is a "soul out of my soul"; the voyage is imagined, a function of the "spirit's light" darting beyond all worlds. The difference between saying "The poet images to himself the being whom he loves," and "The Being whom he loves appears to him," is not substantive but rhetorical. But the implications of the second statement substitute passive receptiveness for active creation on the part of the Poet, and at the same time they attribute to the Vision an independent reality which the first statement leaves questionable. The prose version is unarguable; the poetic version depends for its "truth" on its emotional conviction and rhetorical persuasiveness; it is the substitution of myth for doctrine.

Shelley's poetic genius lay in his openness to experience and to ideas, his restless, educated eclecticism; this is why his poetry, while it is consistent in its themes, is unsystematic, and cannot be reduced to formulas of symbol or doctrine. But there is always a double perception in his poetry, though the emphasis changes and the formulations vary. As he enters into the limitless aspiration of the spirit, so he recognizes and laments the frailty of the body to which the spirit is bound. His rhetoric may be that of the mystic or visionary with eyes turned to the other world, but his perspective is essentially that of the rational artist pondering the human condition. The emotional power of his poetry has its source in his recognition of the imperatives binding upon the human being powerless to fulfil them, and dependent for what power he has on others of similar frailty. Yet his poetry consistently asserts the power of the imagination to transcend the limitations of sense and language. It is an effort to assert hope against his own full knowledge of the grounds for despair, in fictions which deny orthodox belief in a creator and a benevolent providence, but describe the human substitutes for these, self-generated, purely conceptual, in images and rhetoric derived from religious experience, vision and its loss, despair and its transcendence.

FURTHER READING

Bibliography

Cameron, Kenneth Neill, and Reiman, Donald H., eds. *Shelley and His Circle, 1773-1822.* 8 vols. to date. Cambridge, Mass.: Harvard University Press, 1961-.

   Provides bibliographical and critical material on Shelley, Mary Shelley, Byron, Hunt, and Peacock.

Dunbar, Clement. *A Bibliography of Shelley Studies: 1823-1950.* Garland Reference Library of the Humanities, vol. 32. New York: Garland Publishing, 1976, 320 p.

   A guide to Shelley studies dating from his death to 1950.

Keats-Shelley Journal. New York: Keats-Shelley Association of America, 1952-.

   An annual publication devoted to studies on Keats, Shelley, Byron, and their circles. A detailed bibliography is included in the periodical.

Biography

Blunden, Edmund. *Shelley: A Life Story.* London: Collins, 1946, 320 p.

   A popular biography.

Carey, Gillian. *Shelley.* Literature in Perspective, edited by Kenneth Grose. London: Evans Brothers, 1975, 160 p.

   An introductory survey of Shelley's life and works.

Hogg, Thomas Jefferson. *The Life of Percy Bysshe Shelley.* London: London Library, 1906, 585 p.

   A controversial biography of Shelley originally published in 1858. Hogg has been criticized for altering his sources and for maliciously misrepresenting Shelley; nonetheless, his work had an important influence on the poet's reputation.

Peacock, Thomas Love. *Peacock's Memoirs of Shelley, with Shelley's Letters to Peacock,* edited by H. F. B. Brett-Smith.

London: Henry Frowde, 1909, 219 p.

   An early memoir of Shelley first published between 1858 and 1962. Peacock sought to rectify misrepresentations in accounts by Hogg (see entry above), Trelawny (see entry below), and others.

Reiman, Donald H. *Percy Bysshe Shelley.* Twayne's English Authors Series, edited by Sylvia E. Bowman, vol. 81. New York: Twayne Publishers, 1969, 188 p.

   A general introduction to Shelley's life and works.

Trelawny, E. J. *Recollections of the Last Days of Shelley and Byron.* London: Edward Moxon, 1958, 304 p.

   A lively narrative of Trelawny's friendship with the poets in Italy.

White, Newman Ivey. *Shelley.* 2 vols. New York: Alfred A. Knopf, 1940.

   Considered the definitive biography.

Criticism

Abbey, Lloyd. *Destroyer and Preserver: Shelley's Poetic Skepticism.* Lincoln: University of Nebraska Press, 1979, 171 p.

   Seeks to demonstrate the skepticism of Shelley's philosophy.

Allott, Miriam, ed. *Essays on Shelley.* Totowa, N.J.: Barnes & Noble Books, 1982, 282 p.

   Contains discussions of both individual works and such general topics as Shelley's critical reputation and his Gothicism.

Allsup, James O. *The Magic Circle: A Study of Shelley's Concept of Love.* National University Publications, Literary Criticism Series, edited by John E. Becker. Port Washington, N.Y.: Kennikat Press, 1976, 115 p.

   Discovers a combination of Christian and platonic ideas in Shelley's writings on love.

Barcus, James E., ed. *Shelley: The Critical Heritage.* The Critical Heritage Series, edited by B. C. Southam. London: Routledge & Kegan Paul, 1975, 432 p.

   Reprints early critical assessments of Shelley's work.

Barnard, Ellsworth. *Shelley's Religion.* Minneapolis: University of Minnesota Press, 1937, 320 p.

   An extended exploration of Shelley's religious beliefs.

Barrell, Joseph. *Shelley and the Thought of His Time: A Study in the History of Ideas.* 1947. Reprint. Hamden, Conn.: Archon Books, 1967, 207 p.

   Examines the extent to which Shelley's life and works reflected early nineteenth-century philosophical trends.

Bloom, Harold. *Shelley's Mythmaking.* Yale Studies in English, edited by Benjamin Christie Nangle, vol. 141. New Haven: Yale University Press, 1959, 279 p.

   Considers Shelley as primarily a mythopoeic poet.

————, et al. *Deconstruction and Criticism*. New York: Seabury Press, A Continuum Book, 1979, 256 p.
> Includes two important essays on Shelley, Paul de Man's "Shelley Disfigured" and J. Hillis Miller's "The Critic as Host."

Brown, Nathaniel. *Sexuality and Feminism in Shelley*. Cambridge, Mass.: Harvard University Press, 1979, 298 p.
> Presents Shelley as a proponent of sexual equality whose writings anticipate modern attitudes toward sexuality.

Cameron, Kenneth Neill. *Shelley: The Golden Years*. Cambridge, Mass.: Harvard University Press, 1974, 669 p.
> An acclaimed two-part account of Shelley's intellectual development and writings covering the period from 1809 to 1822.

Campbell, Olwen Ward. *Shelley and the Unromantics*. New York: Charles Scribner's Sons, 1924, 307 p.
> One of the first studies of Shelley's personality and thought based primarily on his letters and other writings.

Cronin, Richard. *Shelley's Poetic Thoughts*. London: Macmillan Press, 1981, 263 p.
> A highly regarded discussion of Shelley's use of language and poetic forms.

Crook, Nora, and Guiton, Derek. *Shelley's Venomed Melody*. Cambridge: Cambridge University Press, 1986, 273 p.
> A study of Shelley's concern with disease, particularly syphilis, and his own state of health.

Curran, Stuart. *Shelley's Annus Mirabilis: The Maturing of an Epic Vision*. San Marino, Calif.: Huntington Library, 1975, 255 p.
> Focuses on the poems Shelley wrote in 1819 and 1820, emphasizing his use of myth.

Dawson, P. M. S. *The Unacknowledged Legislator: Shelley and Politics*. Oxford: Clarendon Press, 1980, 312 p.
> Examines Shelley's political interests and attitudes in their historical context.

Grabo, Carl. *"Prometheus Unbound": An Interpretation*. Chapel Hill: University of North Carolina Press, 1935, 205 p.
> An interpretive study of Shelley's imagery in *Prometheus Unbound* focusing on his revolutionary social philosophy, neoplatonism, and interest in scientific experimentation.

————. *The Magic Plant: The Growth of Shelley's Thought*. Chapel Hill: University of North Carolina Press, 1936, 450 p.
> Examines Shelley's ideology as manifested in his writings. This study helped influence the revival of interest in Shelley's works in the twentieth century.

Keats-Shelley Journal. New York: Keats-Shelley Association of America, 1952-.
> An annual publication devoted to studies on Keats, Shelley, Byron, and their circles. A detailed bibliography is included in the periodical.

King-Hele, Desmond. *Shelley: His Thought and Work*. 3d. ed. London: Macmillan Press, 1984, 383 p.
> An appreciative general introduction to Shelley's poetry with emphasis on his interest in the sciences. King-Hele includes an annotated bibliography of books on Shelley published since 1970.

Kurtz, Benjamin P. *The Pursuit of Death: A Study of Shelley's Poetry*. New York: Oxford University Press, 1933, 339 p.
> A controversial study of Shelley's preoccupation with death.

McNiece, Gerald. *Shelley and the Revolutionary Idea*. Cambridge, Mass.: Harvard University Press, 1969, 303 p.
> A close examination of Shelley's revolutionary ideology in the context of the French Revolution and the philosophies of British radicals.

Norman, Sylva. *Flight of the Skylark: The Development of Shelley's Reputation*. Norman: University of Oklahoma Press, 1954, 304 p.
> Chronicles the development of Shelley's posthumous reputation, emphasizing the role his family and friends played in shaping it.

Pulos, C. E. *The Deep Truth: A Study of Shelley's Scepticism*. Lincoln: University of Nebraska Press, 1954, 124 p.
> A respected survey of Shelley's intellectual development.

Reiman, Donald H. *Shelley's "The Triumph of Life"; A Critical Study Based on a Text Newly Edited from the Bodleian Manuscript*. Illinois Studies in Language and Literature, vol. 55. Urbana: University of Illinois Press, 1965, 272 p.
> A detailed examination of the text and imagery of Shelley's last work.

Ridenour, George M., ed. *Shelley: A Collection of Critical Essays*. Twentieth Century Views, edited by Maynard Mack. Englewood Cliffs, N.J.: Prentice-Hall, 1965, 182 p.
> Reprints essays by such distinguished critics as Humphry House, Carlos Baker, Earl R. Wasserman, G. M. Matthews, G. Wilson Knight, and Harold Bloom.

Rieger, James. *The Mutiny Within: The Heresies of Percy Bysshe Shelley*. New York: George Braziller, 1967, 283 p.
> Discusses Shelley's deviations from the accepted theological doctrines and sociopolitical thought of his time.

Rogers, Neville. *Shelley at Work: A Critical Inquiry*. Oxford: Clarendon Press, 1956, 356 p.
> A study of Shelley's thought and work based on an examination of his rough-draft notebooks.

Schulze, Earl J. *Shelley's Theory of Poetry: A Reappraisal*. Studies in English Literature, Vol XIII. The Hague: Mouton & Co., 1966, 237 p.
> Considered an important study of Shelley's poetics. Schulze's central concern is Shelley's exalted conception of poetry.

Scrivener, Michael Henry. *Radical Shelley: The Philosophical Anarchism and Utopian Thought of Percy Bysshe Shelley.* Princeton, N.J.: Princeton University Press, 1982, 354 p.

An assessment of Shelley's philosophical and political thought.

Wasserman, Earl R. *Shelley: A Critical Reading.* Baltimore: Johns Hopkins Press, 1971, 507 p.

A highly respected study of Shelley's major poems.

Weaver, Bennett. *Toward the Understanding of Shelley.* 1932. Reprint. New York: Octagon Books, 1966, 258 p.

Investigates Shelley's familiarity with the Bible and analyzes his works in the context of biblical prophetic tradition.

Wright, John W. *Shelley's Myth of Metaphor.* Athens: University of Georgia Press, 1970, 79 p.

Discusses the modernity of Shelley's poetics.

Young, Art. *Shelley and Nonviolence.* Studies in English Literature, vol. CIII. The Hague: Mouton, 1975, 172 p.

Attempts to define Shelley's philosophy of nonviolence through a study of his writings.

Additional coverage of Shelley's life and career is contained in the following sources published by Gale Research: *Concise Dictionary of British Literary Biography*, 1789-1832; *DISCovering Authors*; *Dictionary of Literary Biography*, Vols. 96, 110; *Nineteenth Century Literature Criticism*, Vol. 18; and *World Literature Criticism*.

May Swenson
1919-1989

American poet, author of children's books, translator, dramatist, and critic.

INTRODUCTION

Respected for her colorful and perceptive observations of natural phenomena and human and animal behavior, Swenson playfully experimented with poetic language, verse form, and sound, making extensive use of such devices as metaphor, alliteration, assonance, and dissonance. Critics often compare Swenson's poetic style with those of Marianne Moore, Elizabeth Bishop, and e.e. cummings; like Moore and Bishop, Swenson used richly evocative language and exacting detail in descriptions of the complexities of nature, and, like cummings, she displayed a penchant for wordplay. Swenson's poems are typically related in an objective, detached voice that approaches everyday human concerns, scientific topics, and nature with a sense of curiosity and wonder. Dennis Sampson described Swenson as "mischievous, inquisitive in the extreme, totally given over to the task of witnessing the physical world."

Biographical Information

Swenson was born in Logan, Utah. Her parents had emigrated from Sweden to join the Mormon church, and Swenson was raised in that faith. After receiving a degree in English from Utah State University in 1939, she became a newspaper reporter in Salt Lake City. Swenson soon moved to New York City, where she wrote poetry while working as a stenographer. By 1952 her poems had appeared in *The New Yorker*, *Poetry*, *Saturday Review,* and other distinguished journals. Her first collection, *Another Animal*, appeared in 1954 as part of the *Poets of Today* series published by Scribner's. Swenson received a Rockefeller Fellowship in 1955, allowing her to work on her second collection, *A Cage of Spines*, published in 1958. While she was an editor at New Directions publishers from 1959 to 1966, her poetry continued to garner her grants and awards. An Amy Lowell Travelling Scholarship allowed her to travel to Europe in 1961, and several of her most highly praised poems are descriptions of landscapes and monuments she observed on this trip. Though she maintained a home in or near New York City for the rest of her life, Swenson was poet-in-residence at several universities, and read and lectured widely. She died in 1989.

Major Works

Many of the poems in Swenson's first three volumes, *Another Animal, A Cage of Spines*, and *To Mix with Time*,

are carefully structured in sound patterns. Critics praised her verbal ingenuity, clear images, and skillful use of internal rhyme, all of which contribute a fresh perspective on human and animal characteristics, death, sexuality, and the art of poetry. Sven Birkerts commented upon Swenson's early work: "The complexities of animal life and natural form are eagerly seized upon, while the intricacies of the social order and the human emotions are not so much overlooked as proscribed. It is as if the greater part of Swenson's psychic endowment has been channeled into the sense organs, which then become capable of the most precise registrations." Swenson examined the world of nature and science in *Half Sun Half Sleep* and *Iconographs*. The latter title is the word Swenson used to describe typographically distinctive pieces, including her "shape poems," which are rendered in visual form and syntactical structures associated with the subjects being discussed. For example, the poem "Stone Gullets" is divided into three sections by vertically curving lines, providing a visual image to accompany words that describe the ebb and flow of water in a rocky seascape.

Visual and aural elements of language are prominent concerns in *New and Selected Things Taking Place* and *In*

Other Words, which collect many poems originally published in periodicals, including Swenson's frequent contributions to *The New Yorker* magazine. The subject matter of these poems ranges from such ordinary activities as going to the dentist to contemplations of animals, trees, and landscapes. Swenson's continuing interest in science is reflected in poems about an eclipse and the passing of Halley's comet; the five-part "Shuttles" discusses the launches of spaceships and concludes with ruminations on the Challenger shuttle disaster of 1986.

Only about half of Swenson's poems were published in her lifetime, and her reputation has continued to grow with the publication of two posthumous collections, *The Love Poems of May Swenson* in 1991 and *Nature* in 1994. Though most of the poems in the former volume first appeared in other collections, the thematic grouping revealed an erotic vein in Swenson's work that previously had not been fully appreciated. *Similarly, Nature* collects poems from earlier volumes as well as poems never seen before, and emphasizes Swenson's lifelong poetic mission of observing and describing the natural world.

Critical Reception

While several critics have stated that Swenson adopted a more self-conscious voice in her later work that lessened the exuberance of her experiments with poetic form and language, and others comment on the lack of emotion and social consciousness throughout her writings, she is generally praised for her technical abilities and explorations of the challenges and possibilities of language. Mary Jo Salter commented: "Swenson provides comedy in two senses: marrying her words off in one happy ending after another, she makes us laugh as she does so. But whether she writes in jest or earnest, she belongs to that rare company of poets who convert the arbitrary correspondences among the sounds of words into what seems a preexisting order."

PRINCIPAL WORKS

Poetry

Another Animal 1954
A Cage of Spines 1958
To Mix with Time: New and Selected Poems 1963
*Half Sun Half Sleep 1967
Iconographs 1970
New and Selected Things Taking Place 1978
In Other Words 1987
The Love Poems of May Swenson 1991
Nature: Poems Old and New 1994

**Includes new poems and Swenson's translations of six Swedish poets.

Other Major Works

Poems to Solve (poems for children) 1966
The Floor (play) 1967; published in journal *First Stage*
More Poems to Solve (poems for children) 1971
Windows & Stones: Selected Poems by Tomas Transtromer [with Leif Sjoberg] (translations) 1972
American Sports Poems (poems for children) 1988
The Complete Poems to Solve (poems for children) 1993

CRITICISM

John Berryman (essay date 1956)

SOURCE: "The Long Way to MacDiarmid," in *Poetry*, Vol. LXXXVIII, No. 1, April, 1956, pp. 52-61.

[*Berryman is considered one of the most important modern American poets. His work developed from objective, classically controlled poetry into an esoteric, eclectic, and highly emotional expression of his personal vision. In the following review of* Another Animal, *Berryman finds some of Swenson's verse undistinguished but also cites indications of promise.*]

[Swenson's ***Another Animal*** appears in a volume of the series *Poets of Today* with *Poems and Translations* by Harry Duncan and *Samurai and Serpent Poems* by Murray Noss.] Swenson . . . is described on the jacket as having come from Utah "to New York City where she holds an active job." One looks to the next sentence to hear what this may be. No: "Her poems have appeared" etc. It is hard to know whether to be pleased that she holds an active job, or sorry, for an inactive job is surely better for a poet. The difficulties in communication with which modern poetry is charged have reached the jackets. The energy of her verse-making, though, suggests that the job can hardly be too active for her; her first selection is as long as Harry Duncan's and Murray Noss's together, and franker, and more experimental, and vervier. She splits her eighty pages into four sections. With the first and the fourth let us dispense, as she might have done; although the first, which consists of descriptive poems, contains one good description, a fair pastiche of Miss Moore (**"Sketch for a Landscape"** and **"Horse and Swan Feeding"** these are), and the least dramatic account of a lion's private parts that I have seen for some time. Nor is this an exceptional passage, and one hesitates to attribute it to the influence of her general master, Cummings, because other young poets have been doing the same sort of thing—I suppose, to prove that they are not squeamish, for no real use is made of these passages which import perfectly valid but obviously difficult material. A poet is to prove that he is not squeamish, as a poet (his private attitude being nothing), by being absolutely responsible for his material and its psychological or spiritual employment, while technically he is absolutely independent of both; flourishes will not do at all; Baudelaire is our best locus here for both success and failure, unless the reader can call up a better one, and I concede that Rochester at his level gives a sharper black-and-white. The details of pain and humiliation fall under all this along with the various obscene areas; and the subject is of importance, not so much because of Joyce's celebrated admirable, nervous, limited, and driven explorations, as for other reasons: first, the broad squeamishness of American writers as Americans, and second, the supreme exception, in the greatest poem yet written *on* this continent, "Song of Myself."

Miss Swenson shows that she is probably not squeamish in the love-poems of her second section and in the poems about death in her third section. There are some chat-poems, like those James Laughlin used to write (maybe he still does), such as **"The Key to Everything"**; and sometimes she lets the last line do the work (pages 132, 145). Both these bad kinds of poems are pleasant. But she uses both Cummings's cursory and organ styles (**"Evolution"**, **"Why We Die"**; **"Organelle"**, **"To Confirm a Thing"**) and these poems are her best; besides, she writes about her own death as if she had it in mind. It will be interesting to see what she does next. Miss Adrienne Cecile Rich is more accomplished, of course, so far, but I don't know that anyone else is. It is not the least of Miss Swenson's signs that she is livelier at sonal organization over a paragraph or passage than in a phrase or line, though she can make a line ("Yield to the wizard's piercing kiss"). She probably does not revise enough. Who does?

On Swenson's poetic skill:

Nobody writes poetry quite like May Swenson anymore. She is a genuine anomaly: mischievous, inquisitive in the extreme, and totally given over to the task of witnessing the physical world. . . .

Never solemn or self-indulgent, eschewing the big finale, Swenson is intent on noticing everything around her while preferring herself to remain in the wings. Sometimes she subjugates the self to such an extent that it may seem on the verge of disappearing altogether from the poem. But her language is so sensuous and her eye so exacting, one instead comes away from her writing feeling one has been in the presence of a mind as comprehensive as Darwin's, as chimerical as Herbert's or Dickinson's, as felicitous as Donne's.

Dennis Sampson, in a review of In Other Words, *in* The Hudson Review, *Summer, 1988.*

Nat Hentoff   (essay date 1958)

SOURCE: "Spines and Other Worlds," in *The Village Voice,* Vol. IV, No. 2, November 5, 1958, p. 12.

[*Hentoff is an American novelist and critic. His nonfic-*

tion and young adult fiction reflect his passions for jazz, literature, and civil rights. In the following excerpt, he offers a favorable review of A Cage of Spines.]

In *A Cage of Spines* May Swenson continues to indicate she's a poet with an eye that cuts into essences and an ear for song, although the melodies are still rather constricted. It is as if one were listening to an intensely sensitive flutist (and a flutist certainly can be moving) with the cello solos still to come. I mean further that she does not yet—with some exceptions—plunge into the joy and pain of being with Roethke's wholeness of naked song. But perhaps she doesn't want to, and it is usually bootless to compare one artist with another too hortatorily. I feel simply that she can, and probably will, open up more.

What is in the volume is worth having—and buying. The end, for example, of **"The Wave The Flame The Cloud and The Leopard Speak to The Mind."** The Leopard says:

> Go the circle of my cage
> I own nothing but my rage
>   the black and white of the savage
>   This singleness you may assuage

There is the so affectionately understanding a portrait of **"R. F. at Bread Loaf His Hand Against a Tree"**; the gentle but sadly clear humor of **"A Two-Part Pearable"**; the capacity to bring living things into her poems still alive, as in these lines from **"The Tide at Long Point"**:

> The pipers and the terns skate over
> tweaking the air with their talk

and there is from **"Sunday in the Country"**: *Sky, deep and accusing in its blue, scrapes my conscience like a nail,* while from **"Spring Uncovered"**: *Two mallards ride, are sunny baskets; they bear ripe light.*

Miss Swenson bears light, and I hope in the poems ahead she will bare even more of herself, for she is worth knowing—for a long time.

Winfield Townley Scott   (essay date 1959)

SOURCE: "Has Anyone Seen a Trend?," in *The Saturday Review,* New York, Vol. XLII, No. 1, January 3, 1959, pp. 12-14, 32.

[*A New England poet in the tradition of Robert Frost, Scott was a conventional lyricist who favored a straightforward, uncluttered style in his many biographical and story poems. In the following excerpt, he praises Swenson's talent but chastises her excessive cleverness in* A Cage of Spines.]

May Swenson is a young poet who first came to book in a *Poets of Today* volume. Now she has a new collection all by herself, *A Cage of Spines*. She is a devilishly clever technician, and the book fairly buzzes with variety. What a show-off! For much that she does is variety for its own sake, not functional (as in Cummings). Tricks, as in the unreadable poem on Frost, can kill a poem with self-consciousness. Mere stunts in poetry are basically frivolous. And we are all wearied of ladies who can't write exactly like Marianne Moore but try over and over for her exactitudes in descriptions of birds and animals. And yet there are admirable poems in this book when Miss Swenson just quiets down: poems such as **"Her Management"** and **"A Haunted House"** and the charming **"The Centaur,"** and many passages of intensely lively, beautifully managed concentrations. Only a fine poet can do this:

> I see the pigeons print
> a loop in air and, all
> their wings reversing, fall
> with silver undertint
> like poplar leaves, their seams
> in the wind blown.

That's an ear. The real thing. The thing you have or don't. The thing that cannot be taught or learned. And I trust Miss Swenson unlearns her gamey ways and relies on her genuine individuality.

May Swenson is one of the most distinguished poets writing. With an uncanny ear, a sense of line directed by an inner energy and a way with language that is ever a discovery, she stands almost alone as a poet who has triumphed over the continuing skepticism among her colleagues toward their own craft.

Harriet Zinnes, in "No Matter What the Icons Say," in **The Nation,** *February 28, 1972.*

Barbara Gibbs   (essay date 1959)

SOURCE: In a review of *A Cage of Spines*, in *Poetry*, Vol. 94, No. 3, June, 1959, pp. 190-94.

[*Gibbs was an American poet. In this excerpt, she attempts to define the poetry of* A Cage of Spines. *Gibbs concludes her observations with a wish that Swenson would attempt more ambitious poetry.*]

[How], on the basis of the poems in *A Cage of Spines,* would I, as a particular critic—not speaking at all for Miss Swenson, but putting myself as nearly as possible in the poems' posture—describe the view of poetry herein represented? Several questions that I might ask myself occur to me: (1) Does the poem have a subject, other than itself? (2) If it has such a recognizable subject, then in what

relation to same does the poem stand (setting to jewel, pattern to thread, identity, *jeu d'esprit* to occasion, or some other that I cannot now think of)? (3) Or, another way of inquiring about what may well be the same thing, how seriously does the poem take, or commit itself to, its subject? Then (4) What is its language like, not in its personal and particular flavor, but as regards formality or lack thereof, crispness or sloppiness, tightness or looseness—these being the lines of division today? These four will do to start, and I may as well begin by saying that the answer to number one (*does the poem have a subject other than itself?*) will be yes in all cases here under consideration, so that question number one may be eliminated from further discussion. As for number two (*if it has such a recognizable subject, then in what relation to same does the poem stand?*), for *A Cage of Spines* I would answer that the figure of "pattern to thread" comes closest, since the subjects are most often clusters of observation about a single conceit, like fire/lion, or hand/starfish, and the poem is finished when all the small conceits adhering to the central one have been stated. Thus there is no decoration of the subject, but neither is there complete identity between poem and subject, as it is quite easy to imagine there having been one less small conceit in the cluster. This, I believe, points the answer to number three (*how seriously does the poem take, or commit itself to, its subject?*): neither frivolously, nor yet with utter seriousness of commitment, but rather as though one were to play an exquisite game for the sake of the game, and either because of some code of manners, or through fear of the passion's becoming self-destructive, keep oneself partly aloof. In other words, poetry is either an exercise in which manners are important, or else it is a dangerous exercise, And question number four (*what is its language like?*): this is, of course, the hardest to answer, since language must be used to describe language, but I'll do my best. It is *not* a rhetorically heightened language—rather on the plain side, likewise as to vocabulary. It *is* fairly tightly worked as to sound, with rhyme and assonance occurring subtly, irregularly, and often. It is a language without waste—or to avoid the pejorative word—without slack, taken up to the full by its subject. Now, I will make one, perhaps unjustifiable, assumption, namely that a connection exists between a poet's critical position and/or taste, and the poems he writes, and acting on this assumption—with the proviso that it may be wrong—I will hazard these remarks about what Miss Swenson might consider a good poem: it will have a subject, it will not have a merely decorative relation to that subject, it will take its subject seriously, perhaps with a limitation of good manners, and its language will be plain, well-wrought, close-fitting, and addressed to the ear in some fashion. . . .

I would say of *A Cage of Spines* that, just as it chooses its own tradition by the laws of self and idiosyncrasy, it submits to a self-imposed limitation, that of the surface, or mere existence, of things. This can be a prison, and I think in some of her poems one has a sense of too little ventured, while in the book as a whole the riddles and the miraculously apt descriptions tend to cancel one another, in effect. You begin to see, by the end of the book, that if Miss Swenson can do it once—and she certainly can—

then there's nothing to prevent her doing it over and over *ad infinitum.* A somewhat depressing thought. Even granting, as I do, that since she is a gifted poet in this way, each time she does it, it is a new creation, full of marvelous and sparking revelations. I should probably not have brought up this point at all, were it not for the fact that in a few poems it is gainsaid and something entirely different happens and one is suddenly face to face with an emotion rather than a jubilant play of sense. Poems in which this happens are, for me, **"Frontispiece," "The Tide at Long Point," "The Even Sea,"** and some others. I wish there were more like these (not fewer of the others). Why should someone of Miss Swenson's gifts settle for less than the whole business of poetry? Let her be less cautious, I say, less nice. A more hazardous game and chance of greater winnings, as well as greater losses.

Anthony Hecht   (essay date 1963)

SOURCE: In a review of *To Mix with Time,* in *The New York Review of Books,* Vol. I, No. 2, 1963, pp. 33-4.

[*Hecht is an American poet who is known for the elegant style, traditional form, and deep sense of tragedy that characterize his work. The recipient of numerous literary awards, he won a Pulitzer Prize in 1967 for* The Hard Hours. *In the following excerpt from a review of* To Mix with Time, *Hecht offers an enthusiastic endorsement of Swenson's ability.*]

One way of indicating the distinction and quality of May Swenson's poetry is to say that she deserves to be compared to Elizabeth Bishop. And indeed there are things in [*To Mix with Time*], which contains new poems together with selections from two previous volumes, that sound a note of indebtedness. Miss Swenson's **"The Totem,"** for example, about the Empire State Building, may vaguely remind the reader of Miss Bishop's "The Monument." But if there are points of kinship, the differences are still important; and May Swenson has an idiom and voice of her own, both more playful and baroque than Miss Bishop's.

In this ample volume of 183 pages, Miss Swenson exhibits several different kinds of poems. There is a small and excellent group of what are frankly called "riddle poems" in which objects like an egg or a butterfly are ingeniously described at a metaphoric remove. There is a group that entertains metaphysical questions, like: does the eye create visible reality? There are poems scattered throughout the book, but particularly there is a small group about De Chirico paintings, in which Miss Swenson is having fun, like Apollinaire, in the arrangement of a design of words on a page.

So it is hard to characterize her in a simple formula, but if you will allow for the gross simplifications of a book review, I shall make the attempt by saying that she seems to see the world around her with delight and with a cal-

culated naiveté that reminds one of the paintings of Le Douanier Rousseau: there is the same hard clarity of outline, the same freshness and joy, the vivid coloring and innocent awe. There is, in short, magic. As she says herself in one poem, "So innocent this scene, I feel I see it / with a deer's eye." She is able to bring this eye to contemplate a vast variety of objects and events. There is, for example, an extraordinary group of poems written during travel abroad on an Amy Lowell Scholarship which are handsome justifications of the award. One is about a bullfight; others concern a view from the window of a *pensione* in Florence, St. Mark's Cathedral in Venice, the Pantheon in Rome. But if I had room here to quote even a respectable fraction of a long poem called **"Instead of the Camargue"** about a graveyard in France I should leave you in no doubt of Miss Swenson's skill and brilliance.

And it is by no means only the foreign and exotic that charms her. She has a group of poems in which her deer's eye contemplates with equal freshness and delight a variety of aspects of New York City. A woman who feeds pigeons on the steps of the Public Library; the lobby of the Museum of Modern Art; a roller-coaster; Trinity Churchyard. There is even one suggesting that the uglier aspects of New York, seen at a certain distance and in a certain light, can seem beautiful:

> From an airplane, all
> that rigid splatter of the Bronx
> becomes organic, logical
> as web or beehive. Chunks
> of decayed cars in junkyards,
> garbage scows (nimble roaches
> on the Harlem), herds of stalled
> manure-yellow boxes . . .

All these details are assimilated into something lovely. And there is a poem which says that in New York City snow is like poetry; it is beautiful and useless; it gets in the way of the efficient pursuit of our practical lives; it arrests us from action. There is a whole aesthetic doctrine here.

Given all these riches and variety, I am at a loss to know what to quote to show her at something like her best, and have hit, not quite at random, on the first stanza of **"One Morning in New Hampshire."**

> We go to gather berries of rain
> (sharp to the eye as ripe to the tongue)
> that cluster the woods, and, low down
> between the rough-furrowed pine
> trunks, melons of sunlight. Morning, young,
> carries a harvest in its horn:
> colors, shapes, odors, tones
> (various as senses are keen).
> High in the grape-transparent fan
> of boughs are cones
> of crystal that were wooden brown.

X. J. Kennedy   (essay date 1964)

SOURCE: "Underestimations," in *Poetry,* Vol. CIII, No. 5, February, 1964, pp. 330-33.

[Recognized as a national authority on poetry, Kennedy is well respected as a poet for adults as well as children. His verse is written in traditional metric patterns and acknowledged for its amusing and incisive qualities. In the following review, Kennedy praises To Mix with Time.*]*

For once it is easy to agree with a jacket blurb, this by Robert Lowell, who declares that May Swenson's poems "should be hung with permanent fresh paint signs." In her vision Miss Swenson has become again as a child, but a highly sophisticated child who knows her way around both the Piazza San Marco and the New York subway system. Who but she would see the Statue of Liberty's torch as a tip of asparagus? The exactness of eye recalls that of Marianne Moore or Elizabeth Bishop, but Miss Swenson is not to be filed among imitators. (Why, incidentally, do our best woman poets look at things closer-up than our best men do?) Often she strikes out past familiar forms, yet always comes upon new ones. Many—**"The Fountains of Aix,"** the skyscraper-shaped **"The Totem"**—aren't mere experiment. They work. And if Miss Swenson obviously cares about how a poem looks on the page, she cares how it listens, too. In **"The Word 'Beautiful,'"** for instance, the subject is metamorphosed to a

> Long, glossy caterpillar
> with softest feet
> of audible and inaudible vowels;

while in **"Spring Uncovered"**—in a statement that sounds so voluptuous you'd think it would be taxed—"a grackle, fat as burgundy, / gurgles on a limb." A passage too purple for words, I thought at first; then realized that Miss Swenson employs sound here not just for its own sake, but for the sake of all the size, shape, color, balance, and throatiness that grackle and winebottle have in common.

Static rather than dramatic, oftener concerned with places and animals than with persons, Miss Swenson's work might be misread at a glance to seem slighter than it is. From such titles as **"Fireflies"** or **"Sunday in the Country,"** you might expect the kind of poem used in fashion magazines to keep the perfume ads apart; but though, indeed, some of her poems have been so used, there isn't anything trivial about May Swenson. If anyone thinks her work lightweight, let him read the poems so titled; or ponder **"The Wish To Escape into Inner Space," "How To Be Old," "The Contraption"** (a poem about a roller-coaster ride, perhaps also about living and dying); or **"Death, Great Smoothener"**; or **"Question,"** with its soft beginning,

> Body my house
> my horse my hound

> what will I do
> when you are fallen

—the whole of which poem lands with the impact of a blockbuster. There are forty-nine new poems in *To Mix with Time,* plus the gist of two earlier collections. May Swenson often goes deep, seriously deep; but she also persuades, as no other recent poet I can think of, that gaiety still is possible.

A harsh assessment of Swenson:

May Swenson begins and ends in mannerism. She is forever tinkering, taking apart a cat, a watch, a poem. Without evident embarrassment she can tell us (in **"The Watch"**) that the watchmaker ". . . leaned like an ogre over my / naked watch. With critical pincers he / poked and stirred. He / lifted out little private things with a magnet too tiny for me / to watch almost. 'Watch out!' I / almost said . . .'" I'm not just sure what kind of good fun this is. She is endlessly feeling things and relentlessly fashionable about what there is to grab. . . .

For May Swenson things exist so that poems can be written about them, and if most things have been discovered there's always **"A Basin of Eggs"**; "Their cheeks touching, / their cheeks being / their bellies, their / bellies being undimpled, / dimples of dark being." I suppose so, but why couldn't they have been left alone just to lie there as boring old eggs, instead of taking their place in a hyped-up poetic universe? May Swenson has nothing to say, and her many ways of saying it drove me to exasperation.

William H. Pritchard, in a review of Half Sum Half Sleep, *in* The Hudson Review, *Summer, 1967.*

Richard Howard   (essay date 1966)

SOURCE: "May Swenson," in *Tri-Quarterly,* No. 7, Fall, 1966, pp. 119-31.

[Howard is an American poet, critic, and translator who won a Pulitzer Prize in 1970 for his poetry collection Untitled Subjects *(1969). In the following essay, he traces the poetic style evinced in Swenson's verse, finding it magical and incantatory.]*

When May Swenson, speaking in her thaumaturgical fashion of poetry, says that "attention to the silence in between is the amulet that makes it work," we are reminded, while on other occasions in her work we are reassured, that there is a kind of poetry, as there used to be a kind of love, which dares not speak its name. Indeed, it was in the latter's heyday (1891, when Mallarmé thanked Oscar Wilde for *The Picture of Dorian Gray,* "one of the only books that can move me, for its commotion proceeds from an essential reverie, and from the strangest silences of the soul"), that the former's program was devised, by the thanker: "to *name* an object is to suppress three-quarters of our pleasure in the poem, a pleasure which consists in gradually divining . . . ; to *suggest,* that is the ideal. That is making perfect use of the kind of mystery which constitutes the symbol." Of course, there is a complementary impulse to *identify* in this reluctance to call a spade a spade; it is an impulse implicit in the very paradox supported by the word *identification,* which we use both to select an object in all its singularity, and to dissolve that "identical" object into its likeness with another. The refusal, or the reluctance, to *name* in order that she may the more truly *identify* is what we notice first about May Swenson's poetry—though she does not proceed so strictly with the enterprise as Mallarmé, for whom the designation of a flower enforced its absence from any bouquet. When Miss Swenson says:

        beautiful   each   Shape
                                to see
        wonderful   each   Thing
                                to name

she means the kind of ascertaining of Existence Hölderlin meant when he said that poetry was a naming of the Gods—and for such an appeal (such an appellation), the ordinary labels do not suffice. Miss Swenson would not be so extreme about her magic as the symbolists, but she is plainly aware of the numbing power of proper names; as the story of Rumpelstiltskin demonstrates, there is an awful mastery in knowing what a being is called, and in so calling him—indeed such mastery suggests, to May Swenson at least, a corresponding lack of attention to the quality of being itself; a failure, by the wielding of nomination's "mace petrific," to encounter, to espouse form as it *becomes* what it is.

It is an old kind of poetry, then, that this poet resumes in her quest for "my face in the rock, my name on the wildest tree," a poetry that goes back to Orpheus, probably, and moves forward through Blake and Emily Dickinson, whom May Swenson specifically echoes, I think, in her eagerness to see Being wherever she looks:

        Any Object before the Eye
        can fill the space can occupy
        the supple frame of eternity
        my Hand before me such
        tangents reaches into Much
        root and twig extremes can touch
        any Hour can be the all
        expanding like a cunning Ball
        to a Vast from very small
        any Single becomes the More
        multiples sprout from alpha's core
        from Vase of legend vessels of lore . . .

It is the poetry which comes into existence whenever the need is felt (as by Valéry most recently, most magisterially) to *charm,* to *enchant,* to *bind by spells* an existence otherwise apprehended as inaccessibly other. For as Valéry says of Orpheus, it was only by his songs that trees knew the full horror of dancing. Similarly, in May Swenson's kennings, their method "a parliament of overlappings" and their goal "an assuaging singleness," we find that the hand

in her lap, the cat on the sill, the cloud in the sky become, before we have a chance to adjust our sights and to enslave our other senses as well to what we *know,* fables of unlabelled Being:

        For each path leads both out and in
        I come while going   No to and from
        There is only here   And here
        is as well as there   Wherever
        I am led I move within the care
        of the season
        hidden in the creases of her skirts
        of green or brown or beaded red
        And when they are white
        I am not lost   I am not lost then
        only covered for the night

Evidently, Miss Swenson's effort has been to discover runes, the conjurations by which she can not only apostrophize the hand, the cat and the cloud in their innominate otherness, but by which she can, in some essential and relieving way, *become them,* leave her own impinging selfhood in the paralyzed region where names are assigned, and assume instead the energies of natural process.

From the first—in 1954, the first of Scribners' *Poets of Today* series included *her* first collection, the significantly titled *Another Animal*—May Swenson has practiced, in riddles, chants, hex-signs and a whole panoply of invented *sortilege* unwonted in Western poetry since the Witch of Endor brought up Samuel, the way not only of summoning Being into her grasp, but of getting herself out of that grasp and into alien shapes, into those emblems of power most often identified with the sexual:

        . . . on this ball   oh to Endure
             half dark   like the stone
             half light   sufficient
        i walk Upright   to itself alone
        i lie Prone
        within the night   or Reincarnate
                                         like the tree
            the longing   be born each spring
           that i know   to greenery
        is in the Stone also
             it must be   or like the lion
        the same that rises   without law
            in the Tree   to roam the Wild
           the longing   on velvet paw . . .
        in the Lion's call
        speaks for all

Consider the array of instruments in this fragment of the first poem from that first book, **"Evolution"**: the incantatory use of rhyme; the rhythms of the spell; the typography that lines up the first column to stand not only pat but put, as it were, against the outer verticality of the second column, so that the poem on the page articulates, by the space it leaves as by the form it takes, a regular *passage* through which the forces can move to their completion; the lower-casing of the first-person pronoun, and the capitalization of the three Entities addressed, then their relegation to lower-case too, and the assumption of capital status by the two crucial verbs, "Reincarnate" and "Endure," and by the hypostatized adjective "Wild"; the irregular little stanzas content to exhibit, in loving complacency, a single word as an entire line; the rejection of punctuation as an unnecessary artifice in this organum of being. Evidently, this poet is engaged, and more than engaged, is elated, by the responsibilities of form. In subsequent poems in *Another Animal,* as in her other books, Miss Swenson exhibits a very determined attitude toward *contrivance*; aware, I suppose, of the danger inherent in her own siren-songs, with their obsessive reliance on the devices of incantation, she is more than eager to cast off the blasphemies of **"Satanic Form"**:

> Things metallic or glass
> frozen twisted flattened
> stretched to agonized bubbles
> bricks beams receptacles vehicles
> forced through fire hatched to unwilling form

—and to assume in their place the "blessed" and organic avatars it is her art to invoke, not so much to counterfeit as to conjure:

> flower and stone not cursed with symmetry
> cloud and shadow not doomed to shape and fixity
> the intricate body of man without rivet or nail . . .
> O love the juice in the green stem growing

Contraption, like naming, is seen as the wrong version of experience. The paradox of the riddling poet is that she must identify without naming, make without artifice, "a model of time, a map of space." Miss Swenson is engaged in the Higher Fabrication, that *poesis* which is the true baptism; when she fails to devise charms that capture Being in their toils, she becomes, like Dickinson, again, merely charming; the appeal is no more, at times, than appealing, when it needed to be a summons:

> I live by magic
> A little bag in my chest held a whirling stone
> so hot it was past burning
> so radiant it was blinding
> When the moon rose worn and broken
> her face like a coin endlessly exchanged
> in the hands of the sea
> her ray fell upon the doors which opened
> and I walked in the living wood . . .

Throughout this book, as the title itself suggests, and in the course of the collections to come, May Swenson has found a figure which allows her to escape the difficulties of both nomination and mechanism; it is the figure of the centaur, which cannot be merely named for it is imaginary, and which cannot be merely artificial for it is alive. She begins, in the title poem:

> Another animal imagine moving
> in his rippling hide
> down the track of the centaur . . .

the shaped verses undulate down the page in a first presentment of "dappled animals with hooves and human knees"; in **"To Confirm a Thing,"** the figure is moralized a little:

> In the equal Night where oracular beasts
>   the planets depose
> and our Selves assume their orbits . . .
>
> My thighs made marble-hard
>   uncouple only to the Archer
> with his diametrical bow
>   who prances in the South
> himself a part of his horse . . .
>
> Then let me by these signs
>   maintain my magnitude
> as the candid Centaur his dynasty upholds
>   And in the Ecliptic Year
> our sweet rebellions
>   shall not be occulted but remain
> coronals in heaven's Wheel.

And finally, in **"Question,"** the same figure, which has become perhaps too cosmic, too "mechanical" in its astronomic implications, is returned to its erotic energies, the self addressed in that animal form where, by a certain incantation, Miss Swenson best finds her being in its highest range:

> Body my house
> my horse my hound
> what will I do
> when you are fallen
> Where will I sleep
> How will I ride
> What will I hunt
> Where can I go
> without my mount
> all eager and quick . . .

In 1958, Rinehart published May Swenson's second book, *A Cage of Spines,* garlanded with praise by Elizabeth Bishop, Richard Wilbur and Robert Lowell, among others; of these, only Howard Moss seems taken with the notion that in Swenson's "world," Being is illuminated so that "whatever she describes is not only more itself but more than itself." The strategies and devices, the shamanism and sorcery this poet deploys have become, in this larger, luminous collection, more elaborate, more convinced, and deserve further attention; their accommodation of the mystery that only when a thing is apprehended as something else can it be known as itself is fierce and full in *A Cage of Spines.* But we must note, first, an interesting development, from implication to statement, of the Centaur theme, the projection of energies and erotics into animal form, so that the poet may ask, "to what beast's intent / are we the fodder and nourishment?" The new note sounded occurs at the very start of the book, in a poem explicit enough to be called **"The Centaur."** For the first time, Swenson evokes life—her life—in the chatty, novelistic mode previously judged "too effusive in design for our analyses":

> The summer that I was ten—
> Can it be there was only one
> summer that I was ten? It must
> have been a long one then—

Looking down the prospect of her imagination, the poet reports how she would ride her willow branch all morning:

> I was the horse and the rider,
> and the leather I slapped to his rump
> spanked my own behind . . .

and come inside, after an exhausting morning's riding (and being ridden):

> *Where have you been?* said my mother.
> *Been riding,* I said from the sink,
> and filled me a glass of water . . .
> *Go tie back your hair,* said my mother,
> and *why is your mouth all green?*
> *Rob Roy, he pulled some clover*
> *as we crossed the field,* I told her.

Here not by incantation but an exactitude in narrative, Miss Swenson gets across the doubleness in being she strives for throughout. It is a method she will resume in the book after this one, but the rest of *A Cage of Spines* is dedicated to the means of witchcraft. By riddles and charms, the poet aspires to a more resonant being than the life grudgingly acknowledged in her own body:

> . . . I would be inheritor
> of the lamb's way and the deer's,
> my thrust take from the ground
>   I tread or lie on. In thighs of trees,
> in recumbent stones, in the loins
>   of beasts is found
> that line my own nakedness carried.
>   Here, in an Eden of the mind,
> I would remain among my kind,
>   to lake and hill, to tree and beast married.

Not only the shaped poems, the compulsive rhymes and puns ("what seams is only art"), the riddles and agnominations ("the shape of this box keels me oval / Heels feel its bottom / Nape knocks its top"—from the conundrum about eggs), but the discovery of secret messages hidden within ordinary speech, as Being is concealed by Labels, excite Miss Swenson to poems of an almost frantic hermeticism: in two homages to writers, she extends her method to a kind of esoteric dalliance. First in **"Frontispiece,"** which appears to describe a picture of Virginia Woolf in terms of the circumstances that led her to suicide, we realize from an odd, ominous resonance the lines have, that not only the names of the writer herself ("your chaste-fierce name") but the titles of her books have been braided into their verse; thus the "frontispiece" is a compendium of names indeed, only disguised, worked

back into the texture of Being and used not as nominations but proof:

> The waves carve your hearse and tomb
> and toll your voyage out again again.

The second poem of dedication is even more curious, for in it not merely names, but all words are susceptible of disintegration into their secret content; what we are offered is ostensibly a description of Frost (**"R. F., His Hand against a Tree"**) but the account is continually breaking down as Miss Swenson discovers, like Nabokov (whose English is so often a matter of perpetual inside jokes), that she can say more about her subject by letting the language speak for itself, merely doing a little pruning and spacing to let the sense in:

> Lots of trees in the fo
>   rest but this one's an O
> a K that's plan
> ted hims elf and nob
> oddy has k nots of that hand
> some polish or the knarl
> edge of ear th or the obs
> tiny ate servation his blueyes
> make or the tr easures his sent
> ient t humb les find.

These are, as she calls them, "glyphs of a daring alphabet" indeed, and "hide what they depend on." There are other diableries in this book likely to exasperate as well as to exalt; chiefly a poem called **"Parade of Painters"** in which 36 painters are "assigned" first a characteristic color, then a texture ("Manet porcelain, Matisse thistles," etc.), then a shape. Then the whole thing is assembled in a litany of 36 lines which reads something like a dada catalogue, save that Swenson has shown us her method and its underlying logic: we cannot fault it, but we may fail to be charmed by the procession, as it passes, of painter, shape, texture and color:

> . . . Delacroix mouth viscera iris
> Degas witchmoth birch clay
> Pissaro dhow privet marble
> Suerat hourglass linen poplar
> Dufy glove pearl azure
> Rouault mummy serge blood . . .

Much more characteristic of Swenson's excellence, I think, is **"News from the Cabin"**, in which all her impulses congregate joyously around a less arbitrary theme: visits from four creatures, none named but all identified by the characteristic textures, rhythms, and vocabulary we should associate with a woodpecker, a squirrel, a jay and a snake, if we were to *become* them by the power of our *recital* (rather like the interludes young Arthur experiences, in T. H. White's books, as he serves his apprenticeship to fish, hawks, even hedgehogs in order to learn how to be a man). Consider the sound of this from **"Hairy"**:

> Cried *peek!* Beaked it—chiselled the drupe.
> His nostril I saw, slit in a slate whistle,

White-black dominoes clicked in his wings.
Bunched beneath the dangle he heckled with holes,
    bellysack soft, eye a brad, a red-flecked
    mallet his ball-peen head, his neck its haft.

and the movement of the end of **"Scurry"**:

    Sat put, pert, neat, in his suit and his seat, for a minute,
        a frown between snub ears, bulb-eyed head
        toward me sideways, chewed.
    Rocked, squeaked. Stored the stone in his cheek.
        Finished, fell to all fours, a little roan couch;
        flurried paws loped him off, prone-bodied,
        tail turned torch, sail, scarf.

In these extraordinary poems, animal life is invoked, is actually *acquired* for the conjurer's purposes (extended energy, a generalized erotic awareness) by the haptic qualities of language itself, even more than by the riddling process so programmatically set up in the other pieces. The generosity, the abundance of Swenson's means may allow her, on the one hand, to speak somewhat sentimentally in **"East River"** of Brooklyn seen across the water as "a shelf of old shoes, needing repair, but clean knots of smoke are being tied and untied", and thereby we see, though both are patronized, Brooklyn *and* the shoes; but in **"News from the Cabin",** on the other, she also commands, as in the last section, "Supple", an utterance whose imagery is assimilated without condescension to its very movement, a diction so wedded to appearances that the speaker "leaves the spot" enriched with an access of being, an increment which comes only when life has been enchanted to its own understanding:

    I followed that elastic: loose
        unicolored knot, a noose he made as if unconscious.
    Until my shadow touched him; half his curd
        shuddered, the rest lay chill.
    I stirred: the ribbon raised a loop;
        its end stretched, then cringed like an udder;
        a bifid tongue, his only rapid, whirred
        in the vent; vertical pupils lit his hood.
    That part, a groping finger, hinged, stayed upright.
    Indicated what? That I stood
        in his light? I left the spot.

In 1963, Scribner's selected a large group of poems from Miss Swenson's first two volumes and to them added some fifty new poems, under the general title *To Mix With Time,* a phrase which in its own context reiterates her project: "One must work a magic to mix with time / in order to become old." Here the very compression, the proliferation *inward* of the new abacadabras seem to have enabled the poet to be elsewhere quite explicit about her undertaking:

                . . . There unraveled
    from a file in my mind a magic notion
    I, too, used to play with: from chosen words a potion
    could be wrung; pickings of them, eaten, could make
                you fly, walk

on water, be somebody else, do or undo anything, go
    back
or forward on belts of time . . .

It is good to have it spelled out, for there are here many poems of a specifically esoteric quality, whose organization on the page, as in the ear, suggests the location of a mystery in Being which the poet would attain to only by a ritual, a litany of participles and lattices of space:

. . . There is a	Swaddled Thing
There is a	*Swaddled Thing*
There is a	Rocking Box
There is a	*Covered Box*
The	Unwrapping
the	Ripening
Then the	Loosening
the	Spoiling
The	Stiffening
then the	Wrapping
The	Softening
but the long long	Drying
The	Wrapping
the	Wrapping
the	Straightening
and	Wrapping
The rigid	Rolling
the gilded	Wrapping
The	Wrapping
and	Rewrapping
and careful	Thinning
The	Drying
but the	Wrapping
and	Fattening
There is the worm	Coiled
and the straw	Straightened
There is the	Plank
and the glaucous	Bundle
the paper	Skull
and the charred	Hair
the linen	Lip
and the leather	Eyelid
There is a	Person
of flesh that is *a rocking*	*Box*
There is a	Box
of wood that is *a painted*	*Person*

To which the poet, her own exegete, adds this "Note from a diary: I remembered Giotto's fresco, 'Birth of the Virgin' in a cloister in Florence: the 'Mother of God' was a swaddled infant held upright, like a board or plaque, by her nurse . . . and I remembered a mummy in the Vatican Museum in Rome: in her sarcophagus shaped and painted like herself, an Egyptian girl 20,000 years old lay unwrapped to the waist." The notation, in the poem, of identities between the infant and the mummy, and the enactment of vital, or mortal differences that reaches the climax of the last four lines with their paradoxical reversals, dramatizes the kind of formal extremes May Swenson is ready to risk. "The idea," she says in **"Out of my Head,"** one of the first poems in this book, "is to make a vehicle out of it." To employ, that is, the spell in order to be taken somewhere; or as she says in another place, and in her most orphic cadences:

> we weave asleep
> a body
> and awake unravel
> the same veins
> we travel

The unravelling of those travelled veins is undertaken, of course, in other ways besides such necromantic ones. There is a group of poems, in *To Mix with Time,* written in France, Italy and Spain and concerned with the reporting of surfaces, not the casting of spells. As in the earlier **"Centaur,"** the poet appears sufficiently possessed of her identity to feel no need of commanding her surround by voodoo. She can trust her sensibility, in these new old places, to do its work, and oblige the *genius loci* to give up its own ghost:

> Gondola-slim
> above the bridge, a new moon held a dim
> circle of charcoal between its points.
> Bats played in the greenish air,
> their wing-joints
> soft as moths against the bone-gray palazzi where
> not a window was alight . . .

These are secular poems, then, rarely moralized or magicked, but left to speak for themselves, in the descriptive mode of Elizabeth Bishop, though there are exceptions, occurring (as we might expect) in the case of the **"Fountains of Aix,"** where the word "water" is disjoined fifteen times from the lines and made to slide down the side of a stanza:

> . . . A goddess is driving a chariot through water.
> her reins and whips are tight white water.
> Bronze hooves of horses wrangle with   water . . .
> Faces with mossy lips unlocked
> always uttering water.
> Water
> wearing their features blank,
> their ears deaf, their eyes mad
> or patient or blind or astonished at   water
> always uttered out of their mouths . . .

and again in a poem about death, **"The Alyscamps at Arles,"** in which the words "bodies," "bones," "died," "stones" and "flesh" are isolated in a central column, set off like tombs in each line, and recurring some two dozen times. Europe, we take it, is sacred ground, and the mere fact of treading it is enough, almost, for Miss Swenson's genius to speak low to her. The conjugation, in this book, of a temporal response to earth and a runic riddling of it is indeed "to mix with time"; there is a relaxation of need,

somehow, as if the poet had come to find things enthralling enough in themselves:

> in any random, sprawling, decomposing thing
> is the charming string
> of its history—and what it will be next . . .

Like **"Evolution,"** her first poem in her first book, her last one here, **"The Exchange,"** recapitulates her enterprise— to get out of herself and into those larger, warmer energies of earth, and to do so by liturgical means ("Words? Let their / mutations work / toward the escape / of object into the nearest next / shape, motion, assembly, temporal context"):

> Populous and mixed is mind.
> Earth take thought,
> my mouth be moss . . .
>
> Wind be motion,
> birds be passion,
> water invite me to your bed.

"Things Taking Place" was the working title Swenson had originally used for *To Mix With Time*, and its suggestion of a larger interest in a secular world where events occur, where life "happens," and a lessening concern with the cosmic energies of "mere" Being is even more applicable to the poet's latest work, to be published as a book called *Half Sun Half Sleep*. Here as the title suggests, once again, the balance between sacred and profane, ritual and report, is carefully tended:

> The tug of the void
> the will of the world
> together . . .

These new poems are neither so exuberant in their hocus pocus ("One must be a cloud to occupy a house of cloud . . . refusing the fixture of a solid soul," Swenson sighs ruefully), nor so explicit in exploring "the such of the sea's dark mind"; they are no longer the poems of a small furry animal ("the page my acre") nor of a demiurge ("They founded the sun. / When the sun found them / it undertook its path and aim . . . / The air first heard itself / called glory in their lungs."); they are the witty, resigned poems of a woman "hunting clarities of Being," asking "When will I grope my / way clear of the entrails of intellect?"; a woman eager still to manipulate the phenomenal world by magic, but so possessed, now, of the means of her identity that the ritual, spellbinding, litaneutical elements of her art, have grown consistent with her temporal, conditioned, suffering experience and seem—to pay her the highest compliment she could care to receive—no more than natural.

May Swenson   (essay date 1966)

SOURCE: "The Experience of Poetry in a Scientific Age," in *Poets on Poetry,* edited by Howard Nemerov, Basic Books, Inc., Publishers, 1966, pp. 147-59.

[*In the following excerpt, Swenson discusses poetry as an art and compares poetry to science.*]

What is the experience of poetry? Choosing to analyze this experience for myself after an engrossment of many years, I see it based in a craving to get through the curtains of things as they *appear,* to things as they *are,* and then into the larger, wilder space of things as they *are becoming.* This ambition involves a paradox: an instinctive belief in the senses as exquisite tools for this investigation and, at the same time, a suspicion about their crudeness. They may furnish easy deceptions or partial distortions:

> Hold a dandelion and look at the sun.
> Two spheres are side by side.
> Each has a yellow ruff.
>
> Eye, you tell a lie,
> that Near is Large, that Far is Small.
> There must be other deceits. . . .

W. B. Yeats called poetry "the thinking of the body" and said: "It bids us touch and taste and hear and see the world, and shrinks from . . . every abstract thing, from all that is of the brain only—from all that is not a fountain jetting from the entire hopes, memories, and sensations of the body." But sometimes one gets the inkling that there are extrasenses as yet nameless, within the apperceptive system, if only one could differentiate them and identify their organs.

Not to be fully aroused to the potentialities of one's senses means to walk the flat ground of appearances, to take given designations for granted, to accept without a second look the name or category of a thing for the thing itself. On that ground all feelings and notions are borrowed, are secondhand. The poetic experience, by contrast, is one of constant curiosity, skepticism, and testing—astonishment, disillusionment, renewed discovery, reillumination. It amounts to a virtual compulsion to probe with the senses into the complex actuality of all things, outside and inside the self, and to determine relationships between them.

Aroused to the potentialities and delights of the senses and the evaluating intellect and using them daily, the poet, however, comes eventually to their limits and notices that their findings are not enough—often fall short of yielding the total, all-comprehensive pattern that he seeks. A complete and *firm* apprehension of the Whole tantalizingly eludes him—although he receives mirages of it now and then which he projects into his work. He is not so separate from every man as not to be fooled by tricks of perspective, seduced by the obvious, or bogged down in old and comfortable myths.

The limitations of our minds and sensorial equipment partly stem from the brevity of our physical lives. Stendhal somewhere says that man is like a fly born in the summer morning and dead by afternoon. How can he understand the word "night"? If he were allowed five more hours he would see and understand what night is. But unlike the fly, man is sorely conscious of the vastness of the unknown beyond his consciousness. The poet, tracing the edge of a great shadow whose outline shifts and varies, proving there is an invisible moving source of light behind, hopes (naively, in view of his ephemerality) to reach and touch the foot of that solid whatever-it-is that casts the shadow. If sometimes it seems he does touch it, it is only to be faced with a more distant, even less accessible mystery. Because all is movement—expansion or contraction, rotation or revolution—all is breathing change.

May Swenson is something of a philosopher, though her point of view is not mystical but analytical and detached. She takes a refreshing delight in the metaphysically absurd and is, in particular, a mistress of the poetic conceit. Writing of surfaces, of things, of ideas, she prefers to observe them rather than explore more obscure layers of their meaning.

Anne Stevenson, in "With Head and Heart," in The New York Times Book Review, *February 11, 1979.*

The experience of poetry is to suppose that there is a moon of the psyche, let us say, whose illuminated half is familiar to our ordinary eye, but which has another hemisphere which is dark; and that poetry can discover this *other side,* that its thrust can take us toward it. Poetry is used to make maps of that globe, which to the "naked eye" appears disk-like and one-dimensional, seems to "rise" and "set" rather than to orbit; which remains distant and merely a "dead" object until, in the vehicle of poetry and with the speed of poetic light, we approach it. It then enlarges and reveals its surprising topography, becomes a world. And *passing around* it, our senses undergo dilation; there is a transformation of perception by means of this realization of *the round.*

Miniature as we are in the gigantic body of the cosmos, we have somehow an inbuilt craving to get our pincers of perception around the whole of it, to incorporate infinitude and set up comprehensible models of it within our little minds. Poetry tries to do this in its fashion. Science tries it more demonstrably. The impulses of the scientist and the poet, it seems to me, are parallel, although their instruments, methods, and effects are quite divergent. Contrasts between science and poetry are easily illustrated by such apparent opposites as: Objective/Subjective, Reason/Intuition, Fact/Essence—or let me boldly say: Material/Spiritual. However, a point of contiguity between them is that poet and scientist both use *language* to communicate their findings.

The scientific investigator works as one of a team, as a rule. He works with formulae or with objective facts which are classified and reported as nakedly as possible so as to convey, in each instance, a single, specific, unambiguous meaning. The poet works alone, handling concrete sensual particulars, as well as their invisible and intangible essences, with the tools of intuitive perception; he then presents his discoveries wrapped in metaphor, metrical patterns, and often multifarious symbols. The scientist has an actual moon under observation—one he soon hopes to have under manipulation—although no robot or human explorer has yet succeeded in getting to it. "Until one does," I read in *The Saturday Review,* "scientists cannot tell whether the lunar surface is packed hard, porous, or buried deep in dust." And, "because of fuel limitations of the rockets that will orbit the moon and lower a ferryboat to the lunar surface, moon landings must be held within 5 degrees north and south of the moon's equator and within 45 degrees east and west of the moon's central meridian. Within this narrow zone of safety, flat lands must be found to receive the spaceships from earth."

My moon is not in the sky, but within my psyche. More or less subliminal, it orbits within the psyche of every man, a symbol both of the always-known and the never-to-be-known. I do not try to land on that moon. To do so would be to choose lunacy. But in 1958 I wrote a poem called **"Landing on the Moon,"** [*To Mix with Time*], that outlines, in its first three stanzas, a capsule history of the moon's psychic pull on man from primitive times to the present. The two concluding stanzas speculate as to whether it is well for man to succumb, literally, to that hypnotism and let himself be drawn up onto the moon:

Landing on the Moon

When in the mask of night there shone that cut,
we were riddled. A probe reached down
and stroked some nerve in us,
the glint of a wizard's eye, of silver,
slanted out of the mask of the unknown—
pit of riddles, the scratch-marked sky.

When, albino bowl on cloth of jet,
it spilled its virile rays,
our eyes enlarged, our blood reared with the waves.
We craved its secret, but unreachable
it held away from us, chilly and frail.
Distance kept it magnate. Enigma made it white.

When we learned to read it with our rod,
reflected light revealed
a lead mirror, a bruised shield
seamed with scars and shadow-soiled.
A half-faced sycophant, its glitter borrowed,
rode around our throne.

On the moon there shines earth light
as moonlight shines upon the earth . . .
If on its obsidian we set our weightless foot,
and sniff no wind, and lick no rain
and feel no gauze between us and the Fire,
will we trot its grassless skull, sick for the homelike
     shade?

Naked to the earth-beam we will be,
who have arrived to map an apparition,
who walk upon the forehead of a myth.
Can flesh rub with symbol? If our ball
be iron, and not light, our earliest wish
eclipses. Dare we land upon a dream?

Psychologically, then physically, what will happen to man made to mount the moon—the moon being his first wobbling step in a march to the stars? To either extinction or mutation? In an eon or two, will he have *become* a rocket and a robot combined? Maybe. Yet, whether it is well for him or not, I think man will probably colonize the moon, eventually infiltrate the solar system, and go beyond. It may be his destiny. But he may have to pay for it with a transformation amounting to an evolutionary replacement of his species by some other creature-thing, *Homo mechanicus.*

I confess to being envious, in a way, of the astronaut. Though only in my imagination, where I can make him a hero and a lone adventurer. What an array of absolutely new sensations is handed him, like a Christmas paintbox; what an incomparable toy, his capsule with its console of magic dials, gauges, buttons, and signal lights; and what a knight in shining plastic he is in his silver suit. To escape the earth-ball, its tug, and one's own heaviness! To dare the great vacuum and, weightless, be tossed—a moon oneself—around the great roulette wheel with the planets! But, in actuality, could I bear that claustrophobia in a steel womb, attached to that formidable placenta by a synthetic umbilical, dependent on a mechanical nipple for my breath of air?

In Space there is so little space. And who but a preconditioned, tranquilized, denerved, desensualized, automatically responding "test-subject" could stand for long that swaddling as in a rigid iron lung? Not only freedom of movement and of action, but freedom to think an aberrant thought or do an individual impulsive deed must be forfeited, it seems to me. Hooked to the indispensable members of his team by the paraphernalia of intercommunication, the astronaut, I imagine, must learn to forget what solitude, what privacy tastes like. His very heartbeat becomes public, his body and brain an encephalograph, a fluoroscope, a radio, a video screen. First trained to become a piece of equipment; next, perhaps born so. (Sometimes I long to remember my life as a cephalopod under the sea, and cannot.)

But let me go back to a consideration of the poetic method and its effects, compared to the scientific.

For the poet, Self is a universe, and he is embarked on a conquest of Inner Space. From the outside, in this accelerated age, our consciousness is being bombarded with the effects of rapid change and upheaval. It's as if we could *see* the earth shift and change while we walk on it. Familiar Space and Time have hooked together and we have Spacetime. Matter has split into uncountable explosive bits and become Energy. On the one hand—and virtually with the same engine—man prepares to fly to the stars, while on the other he seems intent on annihilating himself along with his sole perch in the universe. There is the temptation sometimes to stuff up the "doors of perception" and regress to that long-ago world that was flat—that was static and secure, since it rested immovably on the back of a turtle! Because the poet's precreative condition must be an emptiness, a solitude, a stillness close to inertia. It is a condition of alert passivity, with blankness behind and before him, while he is centered within the present moment, expectant only of the vividness to come, slowly or suddenly, with the combustion of sensations and impressions gathered and stored beforehand from his active life.

The method is the opposite of analytic industry spurred by communal effort (teamwork) proceeding according to prearranged outline, operating upon the material from the outside. Rather than grasping it a piece at a time, construction-wise, the poet seats himself *within* his subject, at its axis, so that, equidistant from all points of its circumference, he can apprehend its potential form as an immediate whole. This is the organic technique, allowing the growth from within, from the initial seeds of attention, until, as Rilke put it: "All space becomes a fruit around those kernels." I speak here of poetry in its conception; obviously there is an industrious and conscious work of building to be done before the body of a poem is complete.

Science and poetry are alike, or allied, it seems to me, in their largest and main target—to investigate any and all phenomena of existence beyond the flat surface of appearances. The products, as well as the methods of these two processes are very different—not in their relative value—but in the particular uses that they have for their "consumers." Each has a separate role and concern toward the expansion of human consciousness and experience. Poetry has a psychic use. Along with the other arts it is a depository for, and a dispenser of, such psychic realizations as wonder, beauty, surprise, joy, awe, revelation—as well as fear, disgust, perplexity, anxiety, pain, despair. It provides an input and an outlet for all the complex, powerful, fleeting grains and rays of sensation in the human organism. It is a quickener of experience, and it renews the archetypes and icons necessary to the human spirit, by means of which personality is nurtured and formed.

"The world is poetical intrinsically," Aldous Huxley has written, "and what it means is simply itself. Its significance is the enormous mystery of its existence and of our awareness of its existence." Who or what are we? Why are we? And what are we becoming? What is the relationship between man and the universe? Those are questions that ached in the mind of the first poet. They can be said to have created the first poet and to be first source of the art of poetry. Does the fact of our consciousness, unique and seemingly miraculous among all of nature's creatures, *a priori* indicate a superconsciousness shaping and manipulating the cosmos?

How is it that *with* our minds we can explore our own minds? And can we develop a technique to explore Mind—that aspect of the universe we might postulate exists in addition to its mere structural organization? Maybe such a Mind is not yet in existence, but in process; maybe our nervous systems and cortexes are early evidence of its future evolution. As Huxley reports in *Literature and Science,* psychologists know a great deal, but as yet they "have no recognized hypothesis to account for the apparent interaction of mind and matter in a simple act of consciousness." Nor is there even a firm hypothesis to explain the operation of memory. But atomic physics (the most exact of the sciences) is uncovering a factual foundation for many intuitions of existentialist poets and philosophers. According to a statement by physicist Werner Heisenberg, cited by Huxley [in *Literature and Science*], for the first time in the history of the planet man approaches a willingness to admit that he is alone with himself "without a partner and without an adversary." This I believe to be an intuitive hunch, not only of the poet or philosopher, but of every thinking man when in moments of extremity he is forced face-to-face with his own soul. Huxley puts it that "man is in process of becoming his own Providence, his own Cataclysm, his own Saviour, and his own invading horde of Martians." And he adds: "In the realm of pure science the same discovery—that he is alone with himself—awaits him as he progressively refines his analysis of matter." Modern science, according to Heisenberg,

> shows us that we can no longer regard the building blocks of matter, which were considered originally to be the ultimate objective reality, as being things-in-themselves . . . Knowledge of atoms and their movements in themselves—that is to say, *independent of our observation*—is no longer the aim of research; rather we now find ourselves from the very start in the midst of a dialogue between nature and man, a dialogue of which science is only one part, so much so that the conventional division of the world into subject and object, into inner world and outer world, into body and soul, is no longer applicable and raises difficulties. For the sciences of nature, the subject matter of research is no longer nature in itself, but nature subjected to human questioning, and to this extent man, once again, meets only with himself.

From reflection on a statement such as this, one can almost reach the spooky conclusion that all that we conceive as objective and under examination of our sensorial and intellectual equipment, is really subjective and a projection of our own heads! How far significant or how far absurd, I still wonder, is this poem, called **"The Universe,"** that I wrote in 1961:

The Universe

What
is it about,
the universe,
the universe
about
us stretching out? We within our brains within it think
we must unspin the laws that spin it. We think
why because
we think

```
                     because.
                     Because
                              we think
                              we think
                              the universe
                          about
                       us.
                              But does it think
                              the universe?
                 Then what
                     about?
                     About
              us? If not, must there be cause
                              in the universe?
              Must it have laws? And what
                              if the universe
                       is *not about*
                    us? Then what?
                              What
                          is it about
                       and what
                              about
                                   *us?*
```

In 1665 or thereabouts, the American poet Edward Taylor wrote a remarkable poem trying to penetrate into the origin of the universe. A portion of it reads as follows:

Infinity, when all things it beheld,
In Nothing, and of Nothing all did build,
Upon what Base was fixt the Lath, wherein
He turn'd this Globe, and riggalld it so trim?
Who blew the Bellows of his Furnace Vast?
Or held the Mould wherein the world was Cast?
Who laid its Corner Stone? Or whose Command?
Where stand the Pillars upon which it stands?
Who Lac'de and Fillitted the earth so fine,
With Rivers like Green Ribbons Smaragdine?
Who made the Sea's its selvedge, and its locks
Like a Quilt Ball within a Silver Box?
Who Spread its Canopy? Or Curtains Spun?
Who in this Bowling Alley bowld the Sun?
. . . . .
Who? who did this, or who is he? Why, know
It's Onely Might Almighty this did doe.

It's interesting that Edward Taylor should have made Infinity, that great abstraction, the protagonist of his poem—even though he refers to it as "he"—and his expression "It's Onely Might Almighty this did doe" (i.e., Energy) sounds like an intuition prefiguring a finding of modern science rather than reflecting (as he no doubt consciously intended) a God-centered metaphysics of the seventeenth century.

The poet's universe had better be centered within the present; it had better not install itself (and stall itself) in anachronisms either conceptual or expressionistic. Because the poet, I believe, should be in the vanguard of his time. He can, in his unique way, be a synthesizer and synchronizer of the many components and elements of a great new pattern emergent in the investigations of biologists,

psychologists, anthropologists, astronomers, physicists, *et al.* The poet's material has always been nature—human and otherwise—all objects and aspects of our outer environment as well as the "climate of the soul" and the "theater of the emotions." The poet is the great antispecialist. Still possible in our overorganized, compartmentalized culture and still needed is the work and the *play* of the artist. As a free-floating agent, medium, and conduit—a kind of "divining rod"—he may pass anywhere—over, into, around, or *through* the multifold fabric of experience and present the results of his singular discoveries and delights to fellow-searchers, fellow-beholders.

The *play* of the artist is psychologically very important. As the philosopher Huizinga in *Homo Ludens* has written:

. . . in acknowledging play you acknowledge mind, for whatever else play is, it is not matter. Even in the animal world it bursts the bounds of the physically existent. From the point of view of a world wholly determined by the operation of blind forces, play would be altogether superfluous. Play only becomes possible, thinkable, and understandable when an influx of mind breaks down the absolute determinism of the cosmos.

I said earlier that a point of contiguity between the poet and the scientist is that both employ *language* to communicate what they find. At this point there is also a crucial departure, for language is not only a tool in poetry, it is its very being. In a poem, subject is not presented by means of language but language is the thing presented with the aid of subject. Being merely instrumental, a scientific exposition can be restated in various ways without a loss of end-effect; when new facts render its message obsolete, such expositions are replaced and forgotten. But tamper with, or reconstruct the tissue of a poem and you deal death to its cells and molecules. The poet reaches for a vision of reality that is whole, seamless, and undivided; if he succeeds in that, his product need not suffer obsolescence. True art combines the properties of change *and* endurance.

What is it in poetry, beyond subject, beyond *what* is being said, that is given? The management of language for the poem must be such as to capture and fix the essence of the immediate experience—the sensation, illumination, *extra dimension*—that the poet felt when the impulse for the poem (the emotion or psychic mental discovery that engendered it) fell upon him. It must be such that the receiver of the poem recapitulates, as it were physically, the same illumination because it relates to, or fuses with, a vision within himself, dormant and dark until the moment the beam of the poem strikes into him. In the handling of his material, which is language, metaphor is to the poet what the equation is to the mathematician.

In one of his essays on art, published as long ago as 1919, Ezra Pound said:

We might come to believe that the thing that matters in art is a sort of energy, something more or less like electricity or radioactivity, a force transfusing, welding, and unifying . . . The thing that counts is Good Writing. And good writing is perfect control. It is quite easy to control a thing that has in it no energy—provided that it be not too heavy and that you do not wish to make it *move* . . .

Discussing the origins of language, Pound said:

> The whole thing is an evolution. In the beginning simple words were enough: Food; water; fire. Both prose and poetry are but an extension of language. Man desires to communicate with his fellows. And he desires an ever increasingly complicated communication. Gesture serves up to a point. Symbols may serve. But when you desire something not present to the eye or when you desire to communicate ideas, you must have recourse to speech. Gradually you wish to communicate something less bare and ambiguous than *ideas.* You wish to communicate an idea *and* its modifications, an idea *and* a crowd of its effects, atmospheres, contradictions . . .

> Words and their sense must be such as fit the emotion. Or, from the other side, ideas, or fragments of ideas, the emotion *and* concomitant emotions, must be in harmony, they must form an organism . . .

> Poetry is a centaur. The thinking word-arranging, clarifying faculty must move and leap with the energizing, sentient, musical faculties.

At one time, wishing to clarify to myself the distinction between poetry and other modes of expression, I put down these notes:

> Poetry doesn't tell; it shows. Prose tells.
> Poetry is not philosophy; poetry makes things be, right now.
> Not an idea, but a happening.
> It is not music, but it sounds while showing.
> It is mobile; it is a thing taking place—active, interactive, in a place.
> It is not thought; it has to do with senses and muscles.
> It is not dancing, but it moves while it remains.

. . . And it is not science. But the experience of poetry is animated with the insatiable curiosity of science. The universe, inside and out, is properly its laboratory. More plain than ever before is the potent fact that we are human particles in a culture of living change. We must either master the Great Whirl or become victims of it. Science is unavoidably reshaping our environment and in the future will prominently influence the next development of individual man and his species. Art, more intimately, deals with and forms the emotional and spiritual climate of our experience. Poetry can help man to stay human.

Peter Davison   (essay date 1968)

SOURCE: "New Poetry: The Generation of the Twenties," in *The Atlantic Monthly,* Vol. 221, No. 2, February, 1968, pp. 141-42.

[*Early associated with the confessional school of poetry, Davison is an American poet whose first collection of verse,* The Breaking of the Day *(1964), won the Yale Series of Younger Poets Award. In the following excerpt, he finds* Half Sun Half Sleep *less successful than Swenson's previous verse collections.*]

May Swenson, with Marianne Moore and Elizabeth Bishop, is one of the most meticulous poets writing today. In *Half Sun Half Sleep* she extends even further the formal cunning and sensuous resilience that characterized her selected poems, *To Mix With Time*. Her new work (apart from some expert translations from the Swedish) falls into three categories: observation of natural objects, games played with word transformation, and poems in shapes (always a favorite device of Miss Swenson's). The eye and the hand are as cunning as ever, but the emotional freedom of the poems seems sometimes to have been cramped by the very elaboration of technique. The reader is too often made aware of being in the presence of the *mot juste,* as in this opening of a poem about a carrousel: "Under a round roof the flying / horses, held by their heels to the disk of the / floor, move to spurts from a pillar of / music. . . ." Though the garments are still beautiful, something deliberate and self-conscious has begun to stiffen the joints of Miss Swenson's poems. Too few of them are at liberty to fulfill Robert Frost's famous dictum: "Like a piece of ice on a hot stove the poem must ride on its own melting . . . a meaning that once unfolded by surprise as it went." Let us hope that in her next collection she may recover some of the freedom of her earlier poems, when technique was only the servant of her imagination.

Ann Stanford   (essay date 1969)

SOURCE: "May Swenson: The Art of Perceiving," in *The Southern Review,* Louisiana State University, Vol. V, Winter, 1969, pp. 58-75.

[*Stanford was an American poet, educator, and critic. In this essay, she discusses the roles of observation and description in Swenson's poetry.*]

May Swenson is the poet of the perceptible. No writer employs with greater care the organs of sense to apprehend and record the surfaces of the world. She is the exemplar of that first canon of the poet—*Behold!*

From the time her poetry began appearing in the early 1950s in such places as *New Directions in Prose and Poetry, Discovery,* the *New Yorker,* and *Poetry,* Miss Swenson's work in its concentration on the sensible has been very much her own. The preoccupation with perception dominates the poetry of her successive volumes—*Another Animal* (1954), *A Cage of Spines* (1958), *To Mix with Time: New and Selected Poems* (1963), *Poems to Solve* (1966), and *Half Sun Half Sleep* (1967). One can name, however, if not influences, at any rate some poets whose work runs parallel to hers. Her development of visual detail has some relationship to the accurate reporting of Marianne Moore. It is sometimes close to that other remarkable declarer of what is there, Elizabeth Bishop. Her interest in nature, its small creatures and their large implications, is reminiscent of Emily Dickinson. In form, her work may have had some relationship to the experiments of E. E. Cummings, though it has always been a distant one, her experiments having gone farther into the visual and less into the verbal than his.

In a recent essay in *Tri-Quarterly,* Richard Howard has traced through Miss Swenson's several books the thaumaturgical qualities of her work—her desire to cast spells and to escape into enchantment, her refusal to name lest this interfere with identifying. Certainly this is an essential aspect of Miss Swenson's poetry. But for all the casting of spells, there is another quality, noted also by Mr. Howard, without which the enchantment could not exist; that is the ground on which the enchantment is laid, the universe which is assumed—in Miss Swenson's case, the perceptible-to-the-senses.

It is as an observer that May Swenson has become best known. Such a comment as Robert Lowell's "Miss Swenson's quick-eyed poems should be hung with permanent fresh paint signs," represents a common reaction. Miss Swenson achieves this freshness by a good eye enlivened by imagination. But however imaginative, her poetry is continually tied to accuracy of sight, to truth to the literal and concrete. This is so even when the truth is conveyed by metaphor or in a spirit of aesthetic play. From the beginning, Miss Swenson has demonstrated an unusual ability to set down accurate and detailed observations. The opening lines of the early poem **"Green Red Brown and White"** furnish an example:

> Bit an apple on its red
> side   Smelled like snow
> Between white halves broken open
> brown winks slept in sockets of green
>
> Stroked a birch white as a thigh
> scar-flecked smooth as the neck
> of a horse   On mossy pallets green
> the pines dropped down
> their perfect carvings brown

This kind of reproduction of the immediate view becomes the main burden of many poems. Sometimes what she sees astonishes by its inclusiveness—for instance, **"Notes Made in the Piazza San Marco"**:

> The winged lion on top of that column
> (his paws have been patched, he appears to wear
>   boots)
> is bronze but has a white eye—
> his tail sails out long . . . Could it help him fly?
>
> On the other column St. Theodore
> standing on an alligator,
> he and it as white as salt,
> wears an iron halo and an iron sword.

> San Marco is crusty and curly with many crowns,
> or is it a growth of golden thrones?
> The five domes
> covered, it looks like, with stiff crinkly parachute
>   silk
>
> have gold balls on twigs on turnip-tips,
> sharp turrets in between with metal flags that
>   cannot wave.

The poem is fourteen stanzas of such details.

The careful looking that we find in the "Notes" is often not rendered so directly. Instead of focusing on the easily apparent, Miss Swenson is apt to choose an unusual angle. For that matter, even the carvings of the Piazza San Marco seem caught in the enlarging lenses of binoculars. **"Water Picture"** is an exact description, but everything there is upside down, for it is seen in the water. In other poems, she takes other places for view—from low, **"When You Lie Down, the Sea Stands Up"**; from high, **"Flying Home from Utah," "11th Floor, West 4th Street"**; from close up to a small object, **"The Surface"**; through the lashes or with half-closed eyes, **"While Sitting in the Tuileries and Facing the Slanting Sun."**

Writing the poem from an unusual center point is one means by which May Swenson adds heretofore unseen qualities to objects. Sometimes the result is a new sense of the order of material in space or time. Miss Swenson admits the desire to restructure in a poem which reveals part of her poetic rationale:

> Distance
> and a certain light
> makes anything artistic—
> it doesn't matter what.
>
> From an airplane, all
> that rigid splatter of the Bronx
> becomes organic, logical
> as web or beehive. . . .
>
> Rubbish becomes engaging shape—
> you only have to get a bead on it,
> the right light filling the corridor
> of your view—a gob of spit
> under a microscope, fastidious
> in structure as a crystal. No contortion
>
> without intention, and nothing ugly.
> In any random, sprawling, decomposing thing
> is the charming string
> of its history—and what it will be next.

The same rationale—adding the unperceived to what is customarily seen—governs her many riddling poems. An early example is **"Shadow-Maker"**:

> After a season
> apparently sterile he
> displays his achievements

Scale upon layered scale
frieze upon frieze of animate
pointed perfect spine-bright

   notes are they?
gestures for a dance?
glyphs of a daring alphabet?
   Innumerable intimations
   on one theme
   A primal color haunts the whole design

The refusal to name is part of the play of the poem, but it is also a response to the need to render the world in a new way. The above passage illustrates her use of direct, close observation which alternates with metaphor as means of revealing, not only in the riddling poems but in many of the others. Both ways of observing result in descriptions that are true to the perceptible state of the object before the eyes.

One recurring metaphor, the comparison of the human body to landscape, illustrates the kinds of tasks she lays upon analogy. An early poem, **"Sketch for a Landscape,"** describes the human face in terms of landscape. The result is a surrealistic combination:

a clearing her forehead Brisk
wilderness of hair
retreats from the smooth dancing ground
now savage drums are silent In caves
of shade twin jaguars couch
flicking their tails in restless dream Awake
they leap in unison Asleep they sink
like embers Sloping swards her cheekbones
graduate to a natural throne Two lambs
her nostrils curled back to back Follow
the shallow hollow to her lip-points
stung blossoms or bruised fruits Her
lower lip an opulent orchard Her spiral smile
a sweet oasis both hot and cool

soft in center swollen a bole of moss
hiding white stones and a moist spring
where lives a snake so beautiful and shy His
undulant hole is kept a slippery secret A cleft
between the cliff-edge and her mouth we drop
to the shouldered foothills down the neck's
obelisk and rest In the valley's scoop
velvet meadowland

"A Lake Scene" includes the reverse metaphor, though not so developed:

   I think of the smoothest thing:
the inside of a young thigh,
   or the line of a torso when, supine,
the pectoral sheathe crosses the armpit
   to the outflung arm;
at the juncture of lake and hills, that zone,
   the lowest hill in weavings
of fainter others overlaid,
   is a pelvis in shadow.

"Sketch for a Landscape" is a remarkable tour-de-force. **"A Lake Scene"** employs the body-landscape metaphor in a more casual way as an aid in the immediate rendering, just as one would employ simile. Metaphor plays a larger part in the riddling poems and others where mystery is created by description through analogy, and the likeness that the subject of the poem has to other entities becomes an essential part of its own definition.

"At First, At Last" moves through a succession of possibilities. It appears to be a description of passing over land described as sea, or vice-versa, before it lights upon its ultimate subject, the act of love or, as its original suggests, **"A Diagram of Life."**

At first the dips are shallow,
the peaks ever higher.
Until at last the peaks

are lower.
The valleys deepen.
It is a wave

that mounts and recoils.
Coming then to shadows
on the slopes,

rifts in the concaves,
what is there to do
but lie open-eyed and love

the wave? . . .

Similarly, **"The Little Rapids"** begins with what seems to be a description of a mountain stream:

Over its cliff
splashes the
little rapids,
a braid of glossy
motion in perpetual
flow and toss

But the second stanza reveals that the poet is speaking of the blood stream, and the poem ends:

Ravine of my body,
red, incredulous
with autumn,
from here curt death
will hurl me delirious
into the gorge.

In this poem and in **"Sketch for a Landscape"** the face or bloodstream and the landscape are jointly described in terms that will apply to either.

A slightly different transformation, the physical joining of two distinct creatures, takes place in such poems as **"The Centaur"** and **"Horse and Swan Feeding."** In the latter, the horse's neck and head become those of a swan, and the swan too changes:

Her kingly neck on her male
   imperturbable white steed-like body
   rides stately away

In **"The Centaur"** the body of the child and the willow branch she rides merge into one.

Yet even where bodies merge—girl and willow branch, swan and horse, face and landscape—in Miss Swenson's poetry, they do not blend into each other in the way that they do in Wordsworth, where the "plots of cottage ground, the orchard-tufts". . ."lose themselves mid groves and copses." Her merging of forms is the sleight-of-hand of the magician. Though for a moment two things appear to have the same qualities, the poem preserves the integrity of each of the objects:

My head and my neck were mine,

yet they were shaped like a horse.
My hair flopped to the side
like the mane of a horse in the wind.

My forelock swung in my eyes,
my neck arched and I snorted. . . .

I was the horse and the rider,
and the leather I slapped to his rump

spanked my own behind.
Doubled, my two hoofs beat
a gallop along the bank,

the wind twanged in my mane,
my mouth squared to the bit.
And yet I sat on my steed

quiet, negligent riding,
my toes standing the stirrups,
my thighs hugging his ribs.

In the Swenson poems, the poet is aware that the reader knows that things are separate and that it is only for the moment that they are one. There is a holding on to the demonstrably real in the most daring of Miss Swenson's flights:

            If I could get
     out   of my
    head   and
    into   the
  world . . .
            O.K., let's say I'm
     out   and
      in   the
   round free
  word . . .
    Back   there's the tight aluminum sphere
            I jumped
     out   of, slammed the door like an icebox.
            A clean landscape
  around   me, an inch or two of "snow"—
            rock-dust from those

  peaks
    in   the distance. No colder here,
          even if it is wider. Very few things
  around   —just the
  peaks.   It'll take weeks to reach them.
          Of course I came here in my
   head.
          I'll be taking it
  back.
          The idea is to make a vehicle
   out   of it.

We have noted Miss Swenson's skillful use of observation and creation of fresh effects by her changes in the angle of vision and her holding back of the realization of what her poem is about until a new perception of it has been established. One of her ways of doing this might be called "reversal." In **"Water Picture,"** where everything is shown in reflection, nature has done the poet's work of turning things into a new perspective. In other poems, Miss Swenson herself turns something into its opposite. In **"The Even Sea,"** waves are described as cattle, creatures of the land. In **"To the Shore,"** the train for a few lines seems already on the sea:

        We are seated
  In a glass tube, that bullet-headed, cleaves
  the scene, tossing a froth of fields and trees
  and billowing land alongside.

In **"Waiting for IT,"** the poet's cat is waiting for something he knows has already happened:

My cat jumps to the window sill
and sits there still as a jug.
He's waiting for me, but I cannot be
coming, for I am in the room.

His snout, a gloomy V of patience,
pokes out into the sun.
The funnels of his ears expect
to be poured full of my footsteps.

It, the electric moment, a sweet
mouse, will appear; at his gray
eye's edge I'll be coming home
if he sits on the window-ledge.

As in the cat poem, Miss Swenson often adds to a familiar scene relations not ordinarily thought of. A statue in the park (**"Fountain Piece"**) takes on a new dimension with the addition of what has been there all the time, now set into a web of relationships heretofore unperceived.

  A bird
    is perched
      upon a wing

    The wing
   is stone
  The bird
is real

A drapery
  falls about this form
    The form is stone
      The dress is rain

    The pigeon preens his own
  and does not know
he sits upon a wing

        The angel does not feel
        a relative among her large
        feathers stretch
      and take his span
    in charge
    and leave her there
  with her cold
  wings that cannot fold
while his fan
in air.

The fountain raining
  wets the stone
    but does not know it dresses
      an angel in its tresses

    Her stone cheek smiles
  and does not care
that real tears
flow there

The relationships are drawn in the most directly realistic way, and the denial of the pathetic fallacy itself becomes part of the poem. Again, in **"Sunday in the Country"** the poet keeps the actual in mind even when she sets up an analogy. The poem develops the common Romantic concept of the outdoors as a place to worship. The effect is created by a series of comparison words, in which the metaphor is taken literally, rather than by an attempt to make the scene look like a church: "A cricket's creed intoned to the attentive wood . . . The sun's incessant blessing . . . Angels climb through my lashes . . . Long grass, silky as a monk's beard." As so often in the poems, the metaphoric play, having run its course, comes to rest again in the non-magical world from which it first sprang. The spell of sun and light—the Romantic fiction—is denied:

  Until, at the tabernacle's back, a blurt
  guffaw is heard. An atheistic stranger calls
  a shocking word. That wakes the insurrection!
  Wind starts in the wood, and strips the pompous
  cassocks from the pines. A black and
  impudent Voltairean crow has spoiled
  the sacrament. And I can rise and go.

The wit and sense of play demonstrated here, together with accurate observation (we always know Miss Swenson has been there), give poem after poem the freshness of discovery. Sometimes the play, the making of metaphor for the fun of it, predominates. In **"To the Statue,"** people embarking to visit the Statue of Liberty are so close together they are

    stuck up tight as asparagus stalks
inside the red rails (ribbons tying the bunch.)

Returning

      They've been to the Statue.
  She has no face from here, but just a fist.
  (The flame is carved like an asparagus tip.)

Though she revels in the world of objects and is concerned with surfaces, Miss Swenson is also aware of depths and changes. Her poems have many possibilities for interpretation on levels beyond the literal. In the introduction to *Another Animal,* John Hall Wheelock gave an elaborate summary of the levels in **"The Greater Whiteness,"** and many of her other poems contain materials for such analysis. Some, like **"The Primitive,"** are clearly symbolic, while remaining true to the literal. Starting with the line "I walk a path that a mountain crosses," the poem seems to present a primitive point of view, but the reader immediately wonders "who is the primitive?" All the comments of the poem apply to walking up any mountain, but they have to do also with the special mountain which this is. Is it the mountain on the other side of which is death? The primitive does not know. The poem ends with a series of questions and speculations, some contradictory, all of them subjects of a separate inquiry in relation to its symbolic structure. But the symbolism in this and other poems, like May Swenson's magic, grows most often out of a tangible phenomenon, like the path and the mountain, where the poet has an observably solid base.

Miss Swenson's involvement with the perceptibly solid is further seen in her placement of the poem on the page. Lines and spaces are carefully arranged in patterns appropriate to the subject. Some words are given typographical emphasis by being set off and repeated. Even punctuation and capitalization—or the lack of them—are arranged for visual effect.

There are several variants of the shaped poem. The shape may be that of the object involved as in **"Out of the Sea, Early"** where the poem is round to represent the rising sun. Or there may be an uneven margin which undulates or steps back and forth to give the poem a shape of a black figure against a white background as in **"Fountain Piece."** The margin may be placed at the right side of the page instead of the left. Or two columns of narrow stanzas may be placed on the page, their center margins straight.

Other poems use alphabetical devices or whole words which occur in a repeated pattern in a line, emphasized by the spacing of the line. **"Cause & Effect"** is such a poem, and two versions published several years apart indicate the sort of process by which the poem is shaped. The first stanza of the original version reads:

  Am I the bullet,
  Or the target,
  or the hand
  that holds the gun,
  or the whisper

in the brain
saying: *Aim, Fire?*

As revised, the article *the* occupies a central strip throughout the thirty-seven lines of the poem:

```
    Am  I    the   bullet,
        or   the   target,
        or   the   hand
that holds   the   gun?
        Or   the   whisper
        in   the   brain saying Aim, Fire?
```

Whether the change improves this particular poem by placing the emphasis of each line on an unimportant word is a question. It does make the poem more rememberable ("That is the poem with the *thes* down the center!"). The lines of type and space down the center of the poem may be seen as representing the path of the bullet, lines of sight, or lines of force, especially since it first took this new form in a collection of poems written about the assassination of President Kennedy. Moreover, the presentation here adds one more interesting typographical experiment to a body of work in which we have come to look for unusual graphic presentation. (In this case more unusual than ever because the printer has let several lines in the left column slip down so that they do not go with the proper lines on the right—one danger in unorthodox typography.)

"The Engagement" is an even more complicated experiment:

```
When snow       cross
     a wing     to where
  is folded     I flow
over everything in the rainbow

when night      seek me
      a net     in the rock
    dips us     break
  in forget     that lock

when blue       meet me
    my eye      in the wheel
 leaks into     your thread
     a sky      I'll feel

and floss       I'll come
your skin       to where you sink
is what the     in the tiger's
spiders spin    blink

when stone      and catch you
our veins       in the fish
are parted      with my strenuous
   chains       wish

when prism      Find me
     sun        in the flake
  bends us      I will
one from one    wake
```

Here the first stanza on the left and the last on the right are connected by the words "snow" and "flake." The "net" of stanza two is related to "fish" in the next to last stanza. Three and ten are related by "eye" and "blink" and so on. It is as if invisible wires are connecting the two sides of the poem in a careful criss-cross pattern.

This linking of the parts of the poem, the care in its visual physical arrangement, is not related to form alone. It reflects the careful observation, the respect for the whole range of the senses, that goes into the language and concepts that Miss Swenson presents. Her poems are not limited to linear time; they are patterns in space as well. The shaped poem represents the poet's response to the aesthetic need for structure, a need met in other poets by the formal stanza or the syllabic or metric line. The enclosing of the poem within spatial boundaries rather than auditory-rhythmic limits is especially appropriate to the perceptual qualities of Miss Swenson's art.

It is in keeping with her emphasis on perception that in her search for the wonders of the world, Miss Swenson pays little heed to particular specimens of the humanity which surrounds her. The city is a place of buildings, rivers, people en masse. They come in groups, mostly, to be seen objectively. **"At the Museum of Modern Art"** offers a good view of them:

In this arena the exhibits are free and have all
the surprises of art—besides something extra:
sensory restlessness, the play of alternation,
expectation in an incessant spray

thrown from heads, hands, the tendons of ankles.
The shifts and strollings of feet
engender compositions on the shining tiles,
and glide together and pose gambits,

gestures of design, that scatter, rearrange,
trickle into lines, and turn clicking through a wicket
into rooms where caged colors blotch the walls.

And few of her poems explore interior landscapes or the web of invisible ties by which people are bound one to another. There is a relationship here to the writers of the Naturalistic school, who looked at the world as a laboratory and recorded what they saw. The characters she identifies have been the subjects for the Naturalists as well—the old **"Pigeon Woman,"** the drunkard on the sidewalk, the office worker and the elevator man. Even the relationships of love are described in physical terms, as in **"Swimmers"**:

Tossed
by the muscular sea,
we are lost,
and glad to be lost
in troughs of rough

love.

Or in **"August Night"**:

> Shadow like a liquid lies
>   in your body's hollows
> In your eyes garnet stars
>   shift their facets with your breath
> The August night is Nubian
>   something green mixed with the dark
> a powder for your skin that tints
>   the implications of your bones
> with copper light
>   an aura round your knees your navel
> a little pool with pulsing tide

The objectivity of the last poem may be seen by comparing it with another poem in which the shadows assume importance:

> Sliced by blind rifts
> between, my eyeballs
> hurt from long looking
> at the bone-looking
> skin-thin bins
> as yet uncracked,
> and from yearning to exact
>
> the fact of being
> from white-bellied berries'
> oblongs of light.
> I feel how their cheeks
> might grate like
> bearings but for
> buffers of my seeing
> pads of shadow's bruise-
> blue chinks between!

The basin of eggs and the lover's body are both rendered by the presence of shadows. The difference between the poems, both of which describe the subjects visually, is the language chosen, with its sound—in the one case soft and sonorous, in the other, brittle and thin—the overtones of the words, and the length and complexity of the lines. The poet, though she renders objects as they are, is never cold. She declares a feeling along with the description.

Another example of the tendency to render major subjects in physical terms is the poem **"Night Practice"** where the poet practices breathing:

>   I will push out
> a mountain, suck in a valley, deeper than the shout
> YOU MUST DIE, harder, heavier, sharper, a mountain than
> the truth YOU MUST DIE. I will remember.

And death is rendered physically and metaphorically in one of her best poems, the description of the bloody details of an actual bull-fight (**"Death Invited"**):

> Death is dragged from the ring,
> a clumsy hide,
> a finished thing—

back to his pen.
The gate swings shut.

The gate swings wide.
Here comes trotting, snorting death
let loose again.

"Let us prepare to get beyond the organic" says Miss Swenson in *To Mix With Time*:

> for surely there is something else
>   to which it is an impediment an opaque pod
>   What if it is sight that blinds
>   hearing that deafens
>   touch that makes us numb?

But the poem proposes no way of getting beyond the organic other than what seems to be death—"Let us eat nothing but darkness" or the one already refuted in **"Out of My Head."** Though she may for a moment try to imagine what escape feels like, Miss Swenson's art is firmly rooted in the sensible.

In her first book, she had this to say about the poet's work: "The contemporary poet must reconcile these two opposite truths: that all the tributaries of human aspiration in art have apparently already been explored by others before him—and, equally true, that the territory he prepares to invade is virgin, containing heretofore undisclosed treasures which he must unearth—which only he can discover and interpret, by virtue of his own instrument, since this is unique, impossible of duplication, and as inherent in him as his fingerprints."

The territory that May Swenson has invaded and penetrated more deeply than other moderns is that of the perceptible. Except for an occasional flight into the abstract, she has remained at her essential task, that of showing us what we too might have perceived had we been gifted with such unusual sensibility and delight. The ultimate justification of the concentration on the exploration of this territory is best set forth by the poet herself:

> any Object before the Eye
> can fill the space can occupy
> the supple frame of eternity
>
> my Hand before me such
> tangents teaches into Much
> root and twig extremes can touch
>
> any Hour can be the all
> expanding like a cunning Ball
> to a Vast from very small
>
> skull and loin the twin-shaped Cup
> store the glittering grainery up
> for all the sandy stars to sup
>
> any Single becomes the More
> multiples sprout from alpha's core
> from Vase of legend vessels of lore

to this pupil dark and wild
where lives the portrait of a Child
let me then be reconciled

germ of the first Intent to be
i am and must be seen to see
then every New descends from me

uncoiling into Motion i
start a massive panoply
the anamolecular atoms fly

and spread through ether like a foam
appropriating all the Dome
of absoluteness for my home

Given such a credo, the poem can go far. But it begins with the object before the eye. And in May Swenson's poetry, with that object as talisman, the world is recurrently made anew.

Nancy Sullvian   (essay date 1971)

SOURCE: "Iconodule and Iconoclast," in *Poetry,* Vol. CXIX, No. 2, November, 1971, pp. 107-09.

[*Sullivan is an American educator, critic, and poet. In the following excerpt, she praises* Iconographs: *"These poems combine ecstasy with exactness, and speak the truth in truthful language."*]

Iconographs has deliberate visual appeal. Certain poems have "typed shapes and frames invented for this collection", as May Swenson tells us in a note appended to the book. Later in that note she admits, "I have not meant the poems to depend upon, or depend from, their shapes or their frames; these were thought of only after the whole language structure and behavior was complete in each instance. What the poems say or show, their way of doing it with *language,* is the main thing."

These poems say or show a lot. The variety in the book is wide and rare, and because I am not used to a strong vein of overt passion in May Swenson's poems, I was particularly taken with a series of love poems: **"Feel Me," "A Trellis for R.," "Wednesday at the Waldorf,"** and **"The Year of the Double Spring."** The subjects of these poems are persons rather than the bird, the flower, or stunning artifact so often used as levers in her poems.

"Feel me to do right," is what her father said on his deathbed, the deathbed in the poem called **"Feel Me",** a beautiful, strong poem ending,

          "what can we do?   Are you all
                right?" While   the wall opens
           and the blue night pours   through. "What
     can we do? We want to do what's   right."
"Lie down with me, and hold me, tight. Touch   me. Be
          with me. Feel with me. *Feel* me, to do right."

The delicacy of **"A Trellis for R.,"** the witty exuberance of **"Wednesday at the Waldorf"** excite as does the deep truth of **"The Year of the Double Spring,"** a poem acknowledging the eventual loss of the lover:

   Stay with me, A.D. Don't blow. Scout out that bed. Go find

tennis instead of squash mates, surfboarders, volley ball boys
   to play with. I know you will, before long—maybe among the
     lifeguards—
big, cool-coned, straight-hipped, stander-on-one-finger, strong.

There are numerous other very fine poems in this collection; no clinkers, no duds. These poems combine ecstasy with exactness, and speak the truth in truthful language. May Swenson is an established, rather than an establishment, poet.

Alicia Ostriker   (essay date 1978)

SOURCE: "May Swenson and the Shapes of Speculation," in *The American Poetry Review,* Vol. 7, No. 2, March-April, 1978, pp. 35-8.

[*A feminist critic and poet, Ostriker has published numerous studies on the relationship between gender and literature. In the following excerpt, she discusses the feminist power of Swenson's poetry, particularly the poems in* Iconographs.]

Most humanists show very little curiosity about the physical world outside the self, and usually a positive antipathy to the mental processes we call scientific. This was not always the case. Although Western literature has only one *De Rerum Naturam,* persons of letters were once expected to take all knowledge as their province, and to interpret scientific understanding as part of a unified vision of the world. Despite the expanding post-Renaissance hostility between science and art, even as late as the nineteenth century, Blake was defining the implications of Newtonian mechanics for the human imagination, and apparently anticipating aspects of post-Newtonian physics, as he anticipated so much else. Shelley was thrilled by discoveries in electricity and magnetism. Tennyson registered the seismic shock of *The Origin of Species.* When William Carlos Williams in *Paterson* makes Madame Curie's discovery of radium a major metaphor for all artistic discovery, he bridges the supposed "two cultures" completely. Science will not go away because poets ignore it, and in fact we ignore any great human enterprise at our peril. Yet few poets presently venture beyond dread or annoyance toward the works and ways of physics, chemistry, biology, and fewer bring back more than a gimcrack souvenir or two. The Bomb and a fuzzy idea of Relativity were popular awhile ago. Moon-landings and Ecology have recently cornered the market.

May Swenson, born in Utah in 1919, New Yorker by adoption since 1949, has written six well-received books of poems beginning with *Another Animal* in 1954. She is known as a nature poet, "one of the few good poets who write good poems about nature . . . not just comparing it to states of mind or society," as Elizabeth Bishop has remarked. You can easily cull a bestiary from her work, which would include geese, turtles, an owl and its prey, a bee and a rose, frogs, fireflies, cats and caterpillars, landscapes and cityscapes, and always with a wondering, curious eye, an intense concern about the structure and texture of her subject, an extraordinary tactility. "The pines, aggressive as erect tails of cats," begins a poem on **"The Forest."** A poem called **"Spring Uncovered"** begins, "Gone the scab of ice that kept it snug, / the lake is naked," and ends where "a grackle, fat as burgundy, / gurgles on a limb" with "bottle-glossy feathers." She watches things over long periods, and tracks her metaphors through itineraries of implications, with pleasure.

But beyond the naturalist's patient observation lies something else. What critics have called Swenson's "calculated naivete" or her ability to become "a child, but a highly sophisticated child," is actually that child-like ability to envision something freshly, to ask incessant questions and always be prepared for unexpected answers—required of the creative scientist. "What things really are we would like to know," she murmurs, and what else is the motive of the speculative intellect? Swenson's poetry asks as many questions as a four-year-old, and she wants to know not only how things are made and what they resemble, but where they are going and how we fit in. The opening poem of *To Mix With Time* unblushingly titles itself **"The Universe."** *Iconographs* has poems on, for example, the response of a snail to tide, the rotation of a mobile, electronic sound, anti-matter, a telephoto of Earth taken from Orbiter 5, the history of astronomy, man as mammal and (maybe) anima, and the declaration that "THE DNA MOLECULE / is The Nude Descending a Staircase / a circular one." In **"Let Us Prepare,"** the poet seriously considers the possibility of evolution "beyond the oganic," although in a poem about flight—from the thistle seed to flying mammals to Lindbergh to John Glenn—she begins and concludes that "earth will not let go our foot"; thus demonstrating that she can, as a good scientist should, speculate on both sides of a given hypothesis. **"Almanac"** takes note that between the rising and setting of a "moon"— a bruise on her fingernail:

> an unmanned airship
> dived 200 miles to the hem of space, and
> vanished. At the place of Pharaoh Cheops'
> tomb (my full moon floating yellow)
> a boat for ferrying souls to the sun
> was disclosed in a room sealed 5000·years.

> Reaching whiteness, this moon-speck waned
> while an April rained. Across the street
> a vine crept over brick up 14 feet. And
> Einstein (who said there is no hitching
> post in the universe) at 77 turned ghost.

Process and connection concern her in the deepest ways:

> The stone is milked to feed the tree;
> the log is killed when the flame is hungry.
> To arise in the other's body?

But curiosity is a habit of mind at all times. In **"Welcome Aboard the Turbojet Electra"**:

> Why do they say 31,000 feet? Why
> not yards or miles? Why four
> cigarettes and no match?

If this is not typical woman's poetry, Swenson is not a typical woman. All poetry by women just now is potentially interesting for the same reasons that all black poetry is potentially interesting: it may guide us where we've never been. As Carolyn Kizer has wittily observed, women writers "are the custodians of the world's best-kept secret; / Merely the private lives of one-half of humanity." While Swenson does not write on feminist themes most of the time, she does so occasionally, with electrifying results. I will look at one of these poems below. Most often, she blends, she balances. Science, technology, the mental life of observation, speculation: she has invaded these traditionally "masculine" territories. Yet her consistent intimacy with her world, which contains no trace of the archetypal "masculine" will to conquer or control it, seems archetypally "feminine." So does the way she lets herself be precise yet tentative and vulnerable about her observations where a comparable male poet, perhaps driven by the need to overcome alienation, might be pretentious (Snyder?), pedantic (Olsen?), nervous (Ammons? James Wright?) or agonized (Kinnell?); and her affinity for the small-scale object, like Emily Dickinson's, also reads like a feminine characteristic.

No one today is more deft and lucky in discovering a poem than May Swenson. Her work often appears to be proceeding calmly, just descriptive and accurate; but then suddenly it opens into something that looms beyond the material, something that impends and implies.

William Stafford, in "A Five-Book Shelf," in Poetry, *Vol. CXI, No. 3, December, 1967.*

Readers of contemporary American women's poetry will have noticed the extraordinary richness with which it dwells on the flesh, the body, to a degree unduplicated in most men's poetry. (Check your nearest anthology if you doubt this.) To Swenson, everything in the world speaks bodylanguage: a tree has a toenail, spring grass grows "out of each pore . . . itching," a snowplow sucks "celestial clods into its turning neck." The same poet asks, "Body my house / my horse my hound / what will I do / when you are fallen," and concludes a poem on the senses, "in the legs' lair, / carnivora of Touch." If anatomy is destiny, Swenson is at home (and humorous) with that, knowing we share that fate, finding no discrepancy whatever between what some would call a woman's body and a man's mind.

But poetic originality shows itself most obviously through an original form, some shape of a poem that we have not seen, some refreshing play of syntax, a new way words have been thrown in the air and fallen together, been lain one next to the other. Exploratory poetry invites—demands?—exploratory forms. When entering new territory, form can become quite palpably "an extension of content," a ship's prow, an arm reaching, a dog's nose sniffing the air.

Swenson has always had an individual style, though bearing traces here and there of Cummings, Marianne Moore, and especially Emily Dickinson. She has always been committed to formal experimentation, and she has often played with the shapes of poems. I would like to dwell here on one book, *Iconographs,* in which the composition of shaped poems has become systematic, in order to show how, apart from producing some beautiful things to look at, the method extends an observer's eyebeam to a new dimension.

Iconographs consists of 46 poems, each of which plays a typographical game. Each has been given a unique shape or frame. Verticals, angles and curves, quirky spacings and capitalizations have all been used. The intention, Swenson suggests in a note, has been "to cause an instant object-to-eye encounter with each poem even before it is read word-for-word. To have simultaneity as well as sequence. To make an existence in space, as well as time, for the poem." The title, she further remarks, can imply:

icon "a symbol hardly distinguished from the object symbolized"

icono- from the Greek eikonos meaning "image" or "likeness"

graph "diagram" or "system of connections or interrelations"

-graph from the Greek graphe meaning "carve". . . "indicating the instrument as well as the written product of the instrument."

But such descriptions scarcely prepare us for the power of the opening poem, **"Bleeding"**:

Stop bleeding   said the knife.
I would if I could said the cut.
Stop bleeding   you make me messy with this blood.
I'm sorry said the cut.
Stop or   I will sink in farther said the knife.
Don't   said the cut.
The   knife did not say it couldn't help it but
it   sank in farther.
If   only you didn't bleed said the knife I wouldn't
have   to do this.
I know   said the cut I bleed too easily I hate
that I   can't help it I wish I were a knife like
you and   didn't have to bleed.
Well   meanwhile stop bleeding will you said the knife.
Yes you   are a mess and sinking in deeper said the cut I
will have   to stop.

Have you   stopped by now said the knife.
I've almost   stopped I think.
Why must you   bleed in the first place said the knife.
For the same   reason maybe that you must do what you
must do said   the cut.
I can't stand   bleeding said the knife and sank in farther.
I hate it too said   the cut I know it isn't you it's
me you're lucky to be   a knife you ought to be glad about that.
Too many cuts around   said the knife they're
messy I don't know how   they stand themselves.
They don't said the cut.
You're bleeding again
No I've stopped said the cut see you are coming out now the
blood is drying it will rub off you'll be shiny again and clean.
If only cuts wouldn't bleed   so much said the knife coming
out a little.
But then knives might become   dull said the cut.
Aren't you still bleeding a   little said the knife.
I hope not said the cut.
I feel you are just a little.
Maybe just a little but I can   stop now.
I feel a little wetness still   said the knife sinking in a
little but then coming out a   little.
Just a little maybe just enough   said the cut.
That's enough now stop now do   you feel better now said the knife.
I feel I have to bleed to   feel I   think said the cut.
I don't I don't have to   feel said   the knife drying now
becoming shiny.

It would be difficult, among feminist documents, to find a stronger statement about the connection between *bleeding* and *feeling,* which in our culture are both believed to be natural to women, and a bit disgusting, and certainly threatening, while a dry superiority to feeling is a major sign of desirable masculinity. And Swenson's methods are purely poetic: the low-key "said" throughout the dialogue indicating a habitual everyday encounter; the obsessively locked-in repeating of the key terms "bleeding," "bleed," "cut" and "blood;" the sound-pattern intensifying "bleed," "easily," "meanwhile;" The sound-effect of "messy" and "wetness" opposed to the hard sounds of "knife," "drying," "shiny." What the cut "feels," of course, is self-loathing. it agrees with the knife, accepts the values implicit in the terms "messy" versus "shiny." It hates its own messiness, wishes it were a knife. And of course it feels empathy for the knife, which the knife of course does not reciprocate. Yet beyond language, the most frightening thing in the poem is that visible slash down the page, that speaks, that takes the breath away.

Why, when the knife complains of messiness, cannot the cut cry out, "I am bleeding and messy because you are cutting me, you bastard," instead of saying "I'm sorry?" Must we ourselves identify feeling with bleeding? Is the knife unable to feel, or merely unwilling? The poem does not tell. We notice only that at its conclusion, after the back-and-forth, after the pauses, the ragged streak which lacerates the text has begun to branch out.

By its sharply enclosed form, **"Bleeding"** epitomizes vast quantities of writing by and about women, from the masochist thrills of *The Story of O* and its ilk, to the sexual-political anguish of Marge Piercy or Robin Morgan, as well as the large and dreary intermediate terrain of poems and novels about crude and boorish male lovers. Yet—a most important further value—it makes no explicit mention of sex or of sexual roles. It does not exclude the possibility that men may be "cuts" (indeed, it recalls Shylock's moving "If you cut me, do I not bleed" and his cringing masochistic roles throughout *The Merchant of Venice*) and that women may be "knives." Not persons or personalities, but a universal form of sickness has been explored here, has been stated as pattern, as coolly rendered as if the subject were the relation between a microbe and its host.

At an opposite extreme from this sort of pattern-finding, a poem called **"Feel Me"** takes a single induplicable event in the poet's life, and focuses on its most unique or "accidental" element. The mystery is the meaning of a father's deathbed words:

Feel Me

"Feel   me to do right," our father said
on his   death bed. We did not quite
know—   in fact, not at all—what he meant.
    His last   whisper was spent as through a slot in a wall.
He left us   a key, but how did it
fit? "Feel   me
    to do   right." Did it mean

that, though he   died, he would be felt
    through some   aperture, or by some unseen instrument
our dad just then   had come
    to know? So,   to do right always, we need but feel his
        spirit? Or   was it merely
    his apology for   dying? "Feel that I
    do right in not   trying, as you insist, to stay

        on your   side. There is the wide
    gateway and the   splendid tower,
and you implore me to wait   here, with the worms!"
    Had he defined his   terms, and could we discriminate
        among his motives,   we might
have found out how to "do   right" before we died—supposing
        he felt he   suddenly knew

        what dying   was.
        "You do wrong   because you do not feel
as I do now" was maybe the sense. "Feel me, and emulate
        my state, for I am   becoming less dense—
    I am feeling right, for   the first
time." And then the vessel burst, and   we were kneeling
            around an   emptiness.

        We cannot   feel our
        father now. His power   courses through us, yes,
    but he—
            the chest and cheek,   the foot and palm,
            the mouth of oracle—   is calm. And we still
    seek
                his meaning. "Feel me," he said,
            and emphasized that   word.
            Should we have heard   it as a plea

for a caress—   A constant caress,
since flesh to flesh was all   that we could do right
if we would bless him? The   dying must feel
        the pressure   of that
    question—lying flat,   turning cold
    from brow to heel—   the hot
        cowards there   above

    protesting their love,   and saying
        "What can we do?   Are you all
            right?" While   the wall opens
        and the blue night pours   through "What
    can we do? We want to do what's   right."
"Lie down with me, and hold me, tight. Touch   me. Be
        with me. Feel with me. Feel me,   to do right."

Williams suggested, as a formula for the poetic process, "in the particular to discover the universal." This poem stands as a major enactment of that idea. It is particularly touching that the naturalist's habits of patient attention, and the scientific imperative of hypothesizing as many explanations as possible for any mystery, ready to accept each, yet fixing on none, have been applied so perfectly to the depths of the human condition.

Much of the power here, as well as the intelligence, derives from a cross-cut play of rhyming sounds and assonances, either reinforcing or counterpointing meaning. The first stanza alone has "right" and "not quite," "said" and "bed," "all" and "wall," "key" and "me," and finally "how did it / fit?" Later come "dying" and "trying," "worms" and the deflating "terms," "sense" and "dense," "emulate" and "state," the pathos of "first" followed by "burst," "feeling" and "kneeling," "palm" and ironic "calm." In the penultimate stanza the poet repeats "caress," reinforces it with "flesh," "bless," "pressure," then creates the shocking contrast, in sound and sense, of "hot / cowards," and ends with the "all-wall" rhyme from the poem's opening, now fearsomely resonant, and the "do-blue-through" rhymes, and at last the "night," "tight," and final "right." These sound-links lace the poem into a tight unity even while its subject is the loss of unity. They also add a slight tone of levity to the dominant tone of intense attention and devotion—an intensifying device like the jokes in Ginsberg's *Howl*.

"Bleeding" and **"Feel Me"** have in common, technically, a white line cutting the text. This happens often in *Iconographs,* and I will not belabor the possibility that "inner space" may be available as actual substance to a woman poet. The point is that in both poems, space is substantial. It stands in the verbal rhythm for hesitation, a gap the voice must leap in every line. It slows the tempo, enforces stillness, makes room for meditation. Visually it "means" separation, as if, between the knife and the cut, between the living and the dying, between experience and the ability to comprehend experience, falls this white shadow. Emotionally, the space expresses that sadness, appropriately wordless, which we feel in the face of all disunity we wish to heal but—so far, so ill—recognize we cannot.

In Swenson's more typical vein of natural observation and wonderment, but still intimately concerned with relationships and connections, here is a lovely piece:

```
                    F
                    i
                    r
                    e
                  Island

            The Milky Way
              above, the milky
              waves beside,
            when the sand is night
            the sea is galaxy.
           The unseparate stars
          mark a twining coast
          with phosphorescent
         surf
         in the black sky's trough.
       Perhaps we walk on black
     star ash, and watch
  the milks of light foam forward, swish and spill
       while other watchers, out
         walking in their white
          great
            swerve,
            gather
             our
             low
              spark,
               our little Way
                the dark
                  glitter
                    in
                      their
                        s
                        i
                        g
                        h
                        t
```

A trail of stars, a shoreline, the silhouette of a flying bird, the idea of a reflection. Yet notice that the reflection, the symmetry, is not exact, as the poem thins out toward its close, just as a reflection in moving water can only sketchily duplicate its object, and just as our position in the galaxy makes it impossible for us to imagine "other watchers" as substantial as ourselves. The absoluteness of presence versus distance (which is in Einsteinian rather than Newtonian physics) has entered this poem's form. **"Fire Island"** also finely illustrates the fact that the shapes in *Iconographs* are commonly agreeable to look at, but never because of a mechanical symmetry. Order shapes these poems, but so do pinches of disorder and randomness. If one margin of a poem forms a straight line or a simple curve, another is ragged. If sentences are simple, line-breaks cut their syntax unexpectedly. Where rhyme occurs it does so irregularly, or if the rhyme and meter are regular, then the pattern imposed breaks up and disguises them. In other words, Swenson has taken care to make her poems by the same principles—mixing Law and Chance—

which we believe nature itself employs to make all of its objects, from DNA molecules to clusters of galaxies.

The second half of *Iconographs*, located as the poet has become located on Long Island, contains eleven poems taking place around water, some describing scenes, some exploring the action of water on objects—a boat, a bottle, a stick. One states a rule for water, and more:

How Everything Happens (Based on a study of the Wave)

```
                                    happen.
                                  to
                               up
                            stacking
                          is
                      something
When nothing is happening
When it happens
              something
                        pulls
                          back
                            not
                              to
                                happen.
When                    has happened.
     pulling back      stacking up
             happens
          has happened              stacks up.
When it            something      nothing
                   pulls back while
Then nothing is happening.
                       happens.
                         and
                    forward
                 pushes
               up
        something
Then
```

"To generalize is to be an idiot," says William Blake. To generalize about "everything" takes some temerity. Still, the sight of this extraordinary poem may persuade us first that it offers an authentic picture of the activity of waves, and then that this interdependence of impulses, "to happen" and "not to happen," with the quiescence and stasis between, defines organic as well as inorganic motion—defines the growth of plants, animals, humans, the flux of human creativity (Swenson has said this poem happened after a period of writer's block), the surges and withdrawals of anyone's emotional and intellectual life. Even the motions of history: revolution, counter-revolution, revolution.

Visually exciting where it depicts the strong positive and negative forces, visually dull (though the dynamic of the whole depends on that dull still point) where it depicts stasis, the poem seems to flash our desires on its screen like an x-ray. My apologies to Swenson in case she did not mean all this, but my gratitude anyway. Situated in a little historical trough, as we Americans at present are, perhaps melancholy about our incapacity to "stack up" to anything, we may find this a heartening and promising poem. For once, a credible upbeat ending!

Some final points about the method of *Iconographs*. If all poetry approaches metaphor insofar as it creates verbal equivalents for non-verbal experience, then consciously shaped poetry is a sort of P²—poetry raised by one power. First the experience or perception, then the text necessary to state the experience and all its implications truly, then a visual shape related to both. Swenson distinguishes her method of composition from that of concrete poetry by insisting that the text of each poem comes first, and can be considered complete and self-sufficient before the shapes are found. Shape then becomes a metaphor, enriching language as language enriches experience. But where concrete poems typically, and deliberately, have no interest separable from the visual, the technique in *Iconographs* maintains distinctions. Perhaps we should call it an art of simile rather than metaphor. Word and picture do not fuse, any more than the special sensation offered by our ear and eye can ever become one sensation, or any more than the external world we behold and the internal world which beholds it can ever become one. Connection exists instead of identity, tantalizing and delighting.

Form in the history of poetry always comes back, more or less consciously, to an imitation of form in the natural world, prior to all art, which all art celebrates. To a surprising degree, we may relate changing assumptions about artistic form to changing conceptions of natural form, variously interpreted in various ages. The fluidity of Elizabethan song relates directly to a literal belief in the harmonious music of the spheres. Eighteenth century English poetry was rigid because the eighteenth century idea of natural law was exclusively mechanical. When the Romantics decided that Nature equaled spontaneity, Coleridge said poetic form had to be organic, like a tree, not like a machine. Keats wanted verse with the "full-throated ease" of a nightingale. Shelley wanted it "unpremeditated" like the skylark's song, or like the West Wind, or like the spontaneous utterances of a wind-harp.

The formal fragmentation of "free verse" necessarily reflects not only social and political incoherence, but a failure of the belief that nature offers us models of significant form. This reduction begins perhaps with the theory of evolution, and seems to accelerate with the advances of modern physical science, as relativity, quantum mechanics and astrophysics make us seem intolerably tiny and hopeless, in a universe intolerably vast and absurd. "Yet for all this," as Hopkins once wrote, "Nature is never spent"; and Olson asked that the poem "take its place alongside the things of nature." In the sense which I have been trying to suggest, poetry has traditionally done what Olson requires, but needs to be recalled periodically to this understanding of itself—hence the validity of reminders such as Olson's. We may at this moment be coming around to a rediscovery, and a finer perception, of natural laws and natural freedoms, and our position within them.

Swenson does not theorize on the subject, but her work shows some ways to express our relation to the natural world as we comprehend it. The shapes in *Iconographs* are shapes of speculation, balanced between the patterned and the random—for so we presently guess Nature to be—and attempting to capture both the ways we fit into the world and the ways we cannot fit. They are playful, quirky, eccentric, and imply that these are qualities intrinsic to the world as well as ourselves. But Swenson is modest as well as mentally fearless, and will not let us pretend that our model-building is more than that. As she says in an earlier poem, humans have a permanently paradoxical relation to earth, and by extension to all nature:

> We, who through her textures move,
> we specks upon her glass,
> who try to place, relate and name
> all things within her mass.

Michael Heller   (essay date 1988)

SOURCE: "Owls, Monkeys and Spiders in Space," in *The New York Times Book Review*, June 12, 1988, p. 15.

[*An American poet, educator, and critic, Heller has published a study entitled* Conviction's Net of Branches: Essays on the Objectivist Poets and Poetry *(1984). In the following excerpt from a review of* In Other Words, *he calls attention to the combination of wordplay and seriousness in Swenson's poetry.*]

In Other Words is anything but reticent. May Swenson concatenates elegant structures which, like the flora in her poem **"In Florida,"** bloom into "extravagant blushes." It is no surprise that she is one of our best writers of poetry for young readers; her poems make use of dizzying repetitions and rhythms and wear the bright polychromes of play blocks. Yet this is not childlike poetry; the hard, sharp edges are nearly always vaguely menacing. Like the lurid green plastic shrubbery in shopping malls, the veneer of the poems seems to tell us more about ourselves than we like to know. Ms. Swenson can turn the simple, guiltless act of picking strawberries into an indictment of civilization:

> My hands are murder-red. Many a plump head
> drops on the heap in the basket. Or, ripe
> to bursting, they might be hearts, matching
> the blackbird's wing-fleck. Gripped to a reed
> he shrieks his ko-ka-ree in the next field.
> He's left his peck in some juicy cheeks, when
> at first blush and mostly white, they showed
> streaks of sweetness to the marauder.

With a few transposed syllables, she can send up nursery rhymes ghoulishly:

> He difted for drays
> till a hassgropper flying happened to spot
> the boolish feast all debraggled and wet,
> covered with snears and tot.

In **"The Cross Spider,"** one of several poems on the space program, Ms. Swenson has a spider on a space flight as part of a scientific experiment. The poem would seem to limn out her own cautionary metaphysics, but not without an entertaining pun or two:

> "Act as if no center exists,"
> Arabella advised herself. Thus inverted
> was deformed the labyrinth of grammar.
> Angles melted, circles unravelled, ladders
> lost their rungs. . . .
>
> Falling began the crazy web.
> Dizziness completed it. A half-made, half-mad
> asymmetric unnameable jumble, the New
> Became the Wen. On Witch it sit wirligiggly.

Our attempts to understand such large conceptual models as the universe, nature or reality are, from Ms. Swenson's perspective, slightly askew. Her mock-epic **"Banyan,"** a work of poetry and prose, suggests that the problem with our understanding is not lack of knowledge but our insistent anthropomorphizing. **"Banyan,"** the tale of a monkey's relationship to a cockatoo named Blondi, is just one of these comic insistences, with parodies of Pound, Eliot and Milton thrown in. Almost a character, with a mind of its own, is the immense banyan tree, curling its thick growth around lampposts and telephone poles where it meets and blends with the city. The monkey and Blondi wander among the branches, having adventures and reciting philosophical-sounding sentences: "Learn of the green world what can be thy place," says the monkey, and Blondi replies: "The true way goes over a rope which is not stretched at any great height but just above the ground." As Ms. Swenson's favorite themes imply, only love, friendship and perhaps the play of language can assuage the existential vertigo of having to "act as if no center exists."

Michael Collier   (essay date 1991)

SOURCE: "Poetic Voices," in *Partisan Review,* Vol. LVII, No. 3, Summer, 1991, pp. 565-69.

[*Collier is an American poet, educator, and critic. In the following excerpt, he admires the outlook expressed in* In Other Words.]

The familiar voice in May Swenson's *In Other Words: New Poems* speaks with a naturalist's love for the variety and particularity of the world. In poems that take great delight in discovering the shapes and associations hidden in the natural world, Swenson pays homage to Marianne Moore and Elizabeth Bishop, yet her poems are quirkier, more playful and more celebratory than her two precursors. In **"Three White Vases,"** Swenson suggests that the act of making a metaphor precedes the act of description so that the three white egrets she sees "On a lonely, reedy patch / of sand" are first vases, "each differently shaped." By such perceptions Swenson leads us from the surprises inherent in the world back to the world itself. In an elegy

for Elizabeth Bishop, Swenson writes, "A life is little as a dropped feather. Or split shell / tossed ashore, lost under sand. . . . But vision lives! / Vision, potent, regenerative, lives in bodies of words." May Swenson's "bodies" are not metaphorical or symbolic but corporeal, shaped and formed in our mouths as we speak. These bodies make the vision which provides continuity to the human world. Swenson continues her elegy for Bishop, ". . . vision multiplies / is magnified in the bodies of words. / Not vanished, your vision lives from eye to eye, / your words from lip to lip perpetuated."

Although May Swenson often writes about nature and geographies, she is not a poet of place. Instead she is a steadfast and faithful visitor who masks her restlessness with a clear-eyed optimism and curiosity. As a result she searches with patience for ". . . the scene beyond the apron of the eye / about to shift," as she writes in **"From a Daybook."** Sometimes we may feel that a poem has missed this subtle 'shift.' When this happens Swenson's poems can be too purely descriptive. But even when this occurs, as it does in **"Teddy Bears"** and **"Shuttles,"** the writing is always full of exuberance as the poet looks for ways to praise and enjoy the world.

In a section of the book titled "Comics," Swenson plays with the shape of stanzas (one of her long-standing trademarks), mimics songs and advertisements, and includes a parody of a *New Yorker* poem. Her humor and wit are not limited to parody and comedy however. In the poem **"Strawberrying,"** from the book's first section, she writes an optimist's reply to Sylvia Plath's "Blackberrying." Her poem ends with an audacious pun, "—I rise / and stretch. I eat one more big ripe lopped / head. Red-handed, I leave the field." This leads us delightfully back to the poem's opening line, "My hands are murder-red."

In Other Words is a spacious book. It is May Swenson's seventh volume of poetry and unfortunately her last. (She died in 1989.) Appearing more than two years ago, it has received scant attention yet it is a book that deserves to be read widely, for it contains a vision of incredible integrity, a vision that "lives in bodies of words."

Edward Hirsch   (essay date 1992)

SOURCE: In a review of *The Love Poems of May Swenson,* in the *New York Times Book Review,* January 19, 1992, pp. 12-13.

[*Hirsch is the author of* Wild Gratitude *(1986), which received The National Book Critics Circle Award for poetry. Below, he lauds* The Love Poems of May Swenson.]

"Listen, there's just one 'Don't,' one 'Keep Off,' / one 'Keep Away From,'" May Swenson advised the graduating class in her 1982 Harvard Phi Beta Kappa Poem, **"Some Quadrangles"**: "*Don't be a clone.*" Whatever you do, she enjoined them, "make *your own* / moves. Go opposite, or upside down, or Odd." As a poet May Swenson, who died in 1989 at the age of 76, certainly took her own advice. She was an American original, and her poems—with their astonishing formal variety, their quirky visual shapes and incantatory rhythms, and their refreshingly odd, insightful observations about the natural world—stand by themselves in the ever-changing landscape of contemporary poetry. No one else could have created them.

The Love Poems of May Swenson is a sexy book. It is also a useful, even necessary addition to the 10 volumes of poems that Swenson published in her life-time. "In love are we made visible," she wrote, and indeed these 55 poems—13 of which are previously unpublished—help make visible an aspect of her work that has been obscure but nonetheless present all along. Rereading her work by the open light of the love poems, tracking the main themes from her first book, *Another Animal* (1954), to the last one published in her lifetime, *In Other Words* (1987), paying particular attention to the emblematic *Iconographs* (1970) and the two volumes of selected poems, *To Mix With Time* (1963) and *New and Selected Things Taking Place* (1978), it becomes increasingly evident that a large number of Swenson's radiant nature poems are also love poems. Her shaped verses, elaborately designed spacing and quasi-mathematical forms are love letters to Creation itself, and she continually invests the physical world (and the verbal world) with Eros, celebrating its mysteries and discovering a ravenous erotic drive in all natural processes and transfigurations. The sexual energy that flows through her work is defined as both human and natural.

There is an injunction in all of Swenson's work to "look closely." She was a riddling Dickinsonian poet of Being whose initiating impulse was to describe, and whose many poems (she published 450 out of the 800 she wrote) celebrate the external world in all its bewildering variety. Swenson owes her greatest poetic debt to Marianne Moore and Elizabeth Bishop, the two writers who most firmly set the formal terms and moral values—studious observation, visual accuracy, verbal clarity—by which she would proceed as a lyric poet. Much as she owes to the descriptive mode, however, these love poems reveal that there is a sexual ebullience and emotional candor that distinguish Swenson from her poetic models.

Swenson's poems are more high-spirited and unruly, emotionally riskier and more exposed. Her finely shaped surfaces may appear to be reticent and cool, but, in fact, these love poems show her to be anything but reserved. They are filled with moral pangs and surges, with passionate and sometimes awkward desires, with sweet embraces and eager declarations, with fiery invitations and witty promises. The poem **"Untitled"** is characteristic:

```
I   will   be   earth   you   be   the   flower
You   have   found   my   root   you   are   the   rain
I   will   be   boat   and   you   the   rower
You   rock   you   toss   me   you   are   the   sea
How   be   steady   earth   that's   now   a   flood
```

```
The   root's   the   oar's   afloat   where's   blown   our   bud
We   will   be   desert   pure   salt   the   seed
Burn   radiant   sex   born   scorpion   need
```

One of the pleasures in reading Swenson's love poems is the way she discovers appropriate sexual metaphors, resonances and overtones almost anywhere at all, but particularly in observed—inspected—nature. The birds and especially the bees have never been so slyly deployed. Thus she calls dark wild honey that her lover brings home "the sweet that burns." She declares, "I'm a flower breathing / bare, laid open to / your bees' warm stare." She speaks of a splendid day in summer when "the honey in our veins burned deep / We are stored with sweetness / Our breasts are golden hives." I know of no other contemporary poet who has spoken more convincingly of being "unloosed, unharnessed, turned back to the wild by love," or who has more boldly described being in the storm-tossed throes of sexual passion. Here was a late-modern poet willing to risk sentimentality in trying to get at one of the oldest and most traditional poetic subjects—the pure and elemental amazements of love.

In the final poem in this volume, **"Equilibrist,"** Swenson speaks of her body as a "sharpened dart / of longing / coming toward you always." The undertow in these poems sets in when that longing is not reciprocated, isolating and unmooring the lover, leaving her free-floating. In Swenson's highly charged physical world, love alone wakens the self and makes its conscious existence possible. Human connection is all. How firmly she asserts: "No one / can be sure / by himself / of his own being." The beloved is a necessary twin, a mirror to make the self possible. This is less explicit than it might be because of Swenson's ambiguous use of pronouns. "He" is always rhetorical (there are no physical beings who are men here), employed in poems structured like parables. The passionate love poems leave gender unspecified. But when this poet looks in the mirror of the beloved the reflection is female.

There is a compelling reverse spin on Cartesianism in many of Swenson's finest lyrics. Instead of Descartes's *cogito,* we get a plaintive call to the beloved. In **"Symmetrical Companion,"** she writes, "Come release me / Without you I do not yet exist." "Because you believe I exist I exist," she assures her lover in the poem **"You Are."** "Am I?" she asks, and then answers her own question: "yes / and never was / until you made me."

Because I dwell in you, her poetic syllogism runs, I know I am. Because you enfold me, *we know* you are. Therefore, she exclaims happily, "It is proven and the universe exists!" The lovers "prove" each other's reality, confirming their own existence, confirming the existence of all things. They also liberate each other from the enclosures of mind, from the isolated cell of the self. Thus, according to the poem **"In Love Made Visible"**:

```
In love are we set free
Objective bone
and flesh no longer insulate us
to ourselves alone
```

We are released
and flow into each other's cup
Our two frail vials pierced
drink each other up

The Love Poems of May Swenson is a culled, declarative, magnificent book. Part of the splendor of these poems comes from the way they turn not only to the beloved but to the natural world—to the teeming, fluid, emerging, unnamed physical world. These affectionate and intimate poems remind us that May Swenson was that rarest of literary creatures in our century, an authentic poet of celebration and praise, an Orpheus fulfilled. As she wrote in **"Evolution,"** the first poem in her first book:

> beautiful each Shape
>   to see
> wonderful each Thing
>   to name

Alfred Corn   (essay date 1993)

SOURCE: A review of *The Love Poems of May Swenson*, in *Poetry*, Vol. CLXI, No. 5, February, 1993, pp. 295-98.

[*A noted contemporary American poet, Corn has received praise for the informal yet controlled style of his verse, which synthesizes traditional and modern elements. In the following review, he finds many poems in* The Love Poems of May Swenson *erotic and memorable.*]

Maybe I had too high expectations for [*The Love Poems of May Swenson*] when it was first announced. A new book by May Swenson is always welcome, and this time normal anticipation was heightened by the possibility that her estate had decided to publish work that shyness or prudence had prevented her from making available during her lifetime. Hopes slipped a notch when the credits page stated that only thirteen of the poems were previously unpublished; five have before now appeared in magazines, but the remaining thirty-seven can be found in earlier volumes of her poetry.

The title isn't quite accurate. For "love" we should substitute "erotic." In a quite good poem called **"Café Tableau,"** the eroticism involved is not even the author's but high-voltage description of the visible attraction between a white woman and a black waiter. Only in the poem **"Year of the Double Spring"** (one of the poems already collected) is the poet's beloved portrayed in non-erotic contexts so as to emerge as specific and individual—one result being that painful currents of feeling are allowed to appear as they inevitably must when love beyond pure eroticism is dealt with realistically. Partly for that reason **"Year of the Double Spring"** is the poem I liked best in the volume:

> I'm thinking of how I leaned on you, you leaning
> in the stone underpass striped with shadows of tracks

and ties, and I said, "Give me a kiss, A.D.,
> even if you are tranquilized," and I'm thinking
>   of the Day of the Kingfisher, the Indigo Day of
>   the Bunting,
>   of the Catfish Night I locked the keys in the car
>   and you tried to jimmy in, but couldn't with a
>   clothes hanger.

We later see A.D. at a juke joint, pretending to "flake out on the bench," still later, "riffling *Playboy*." Perfect accessibility, perfect unity is not being described: this is a believable love.

Here, as in all the other poems in this volume, the beloved is addressed as "you," never as "she." Agreed, second-person address is more intimate than the third-person, and it removes an obstacle (minor or enormous, depending on the reader) that stands in the way of entire identification with the poet. At a time when we are witnessing the emergence of a new lesbian poetry, it is also a lost opportunity—not just at the level of bare fact or politics, either. When the poet composes with a built-in hindrance, other kinds of unconscious hindrances are likely to operate as well. Not every feeling will be within reach, a loss for the poet and for the audience, unless the audience belongs to those (including, alas, Elizabeth Bishop) who "wish they would just keep it to themselves." The sex of the beloved could, of course, be made explicit even in poems addressed to "you," but this happens glancingly in only a couple of instances where the poet mentions, "our breasts." Otherwise we have to "guess," as the jeans ad tells to, peering intently through the gorgeous beaded curtain of this poet's language where we believe we can see two women, and not the nude male-female couple of the pretty cover photograph. No one who did not come of age as a lesbian in the 1940s, though, has the right to judge Swenson's (or Bishop's) choices, so I will shut up.

The women glimpsed in these poems are in any case very fulfilled. To find physical pleasure rendered as ecstatically as this, you'd have to go to the Bible—*The Song of Songs*—or friezes on Hindu temples. It's as though the poet were paraphrasing Whitman, saying, "There's a lot of us and all so luscious."

> In the sun's heart we are ripe
> as fruits ourselves, enjoyed
> by lips of wind our burnished slopes.
> All round us dark, rapt
> bumble-eyes of susans are deployed
> as if to suck our honey-hides. Ants nip,
> tasting us all over
> with tickling pincers. We are a landscape
> to daddy-long-legs, whose ovoid
> hub on stilts climbs us like a lover,
> trying our dazzle, our warm sap.

"One Morning in New Hampshire"

It's true that, reading this and some of the other more rapturous poems, I had to contend with feeling like a third wheel or some irrelevant daddy-long-legs, enjoying borrowed glory. It may also be true that the storehouse of traditional metaphoric terms for sex is pretty quickly used up: sex is like a dip in the ocean, the visit of a honeybee to a flower, it is like daring to eat a peach or being turned into pure gold. Uninterrupted delight produces a strangely solemn effect in any lyric longer than eight lines, which will always need at least a minimal plot beyond the very familiar one of tingle-to-ecstasy.

On the strength of Swenson's poetry:

Few writers who on occasion strongly remind us of others have created so fully recognizable and inimitable a world [as Swenson] A playful spirit for whom writing is a (very exacting) game—as even the titles of *Poems to Solve* and *More Poems to Solve* suggest—she has in her typographical and syntactical ingenuity recalled, and often surpassed, e. e. cummings. Her penchant for scientific subjects, and her scientist's patience for documentation, evoke Marianne Moore and W. H. Auden. More surprisingly, this very modern poet who exuberantly breaks lines, and rules, in unexpected places takes one back to the 17th century—to the far sterner-minded George Herbert—to find another poet so dedicated to fashioning the right form for the fresh occasion each poem presents.

Mary Jo Salter, in "No Other Words," in The New Republic, *March 7, 1988.*

On the other hand, when the comic narrative of a poem like **"Wednesday at the Waldorf"** seems to invite the laughter of an audience in on the joke, almost everyone will cheerfully go along with it:

> Two white whales have been installed at
> the Waldorf. They are tumbling slowly
> above the tables, butting the chandeliers,
> submerging, and taking soft bites
> out of the red-vested waiters in the
> Peacock Room. They are poking *fleurs-de-lys*
> tails into the long pockets on the
> waiters' thighs. They are stealing
> breakfast strawberries from two eccentric
> guests—one, skunk-cabbage green with
> dark peepers—the other, wild rose and
> milkweed, barelegged, in Lafayette loafers.

The buoyant anarchists somehow follow Swenson's two guests up the elevator to their rooms, where, presumably, Lafayette loafers are kicked off before the pair get in bed and allow the no doubt female Mobys to inspire them to still greater heights. This poem has to be added to the growing literature about one of old New York's classic hotels, the best known example up to now Stevens's "Arrival at the Waldorf," for him a hotel "Where the wild poem is a substitute / For the woman one loves or ought to love. . . ."

There are actually an impressive number of other memorable poems in this collection, **"Swimmers," "Early Morn-**

ing: Cape Cod," "Each Day of Summer," "Organs," "The School of Desire,"** and **"Dark Wild Honey,"** for example. But I will conclude by quoting **"Our Forward Shadows,"** which is suggestive in metaphysical as well as physical ways. Swenson seems to sense that she is on the brink of something for which sex is, apart from being fun, also a metaphor, a metaphor we might understand as describing a future tradition Swenson's poetry is helping to found:

> we are dressed
> each in the other's kisses
>
> our shadows reach
> to teach us our parts
>
> the enchanted prelude starts

Forward, shadows!

Sue Russell   (essay date 1994)

SOURCE: "A Mysterious and Lavish Power: How Things Continue to Take Place in the Work of May Swenson," in *The Kenyon Review,* n.s., Vol. XVI, No. 3, Summer, 1994, pp. 128-39.

[*In the following essay, Russell compares Swenson to other women poets such as Marianne Moore, Elizabeth Bishop, and Emily Dickinson and considers Swenson's refusal of the label "lesbian poet."*]

May Swenson, who died in 1989 at the age of seventy-six, was a lover of riddles. She liked to write them as well as to solve them—the harder the better. Like the riddle poems she assembled in two books for young readers, all her poems have the capacity to tease and delight. "A poem is a thing," Swenson tells us in her introduction to one of these collections, *More Poems to Solve* (1972). Often based on intricate mechanisms that are not easily replicated, Swenson's poems seem more to have been constructed than composed. Excerpting them is an extreme disservice, as it limits the reader's perspective of the overall design. The poems often take up space in every direction on the page, asserting their identity quite literally at every turn. Individual poems have the kinetic ability to spill over diagonally into stanzaic receptacles, embody the shape and spirit of paintings by De Chirico, and spin like a top around a still center. Although Swenson was clearly engaged in the experimental enterprise to a degree that would charm any scientist, her poetic experimentation was more a means than an end. A language poet before the phrase was coined, she surely would have disdained the label, for her poems are clearly "about" more than the words themselves.

If, like Dickinson, Swenson "tells it slant," that slantwise logic is as much a part of her identity as any political or aesthetic affiliation. Riddling, like role playing, is made up of art and craft, and the critic or biographer must rise to the challenge. The poem, **"Her Early Work,"** with its overt reference to Elizabeth Bishop's 1933 poem, "A Word with You" anticipates the biographer's task:

Talked to cats and dogs,
to trees, and to strangers.
To one loved, talked through
layers of masks.
To this day we can't know
who was addressed,
or ever undressed.
Because of the wraparounds,
overlaps and gauzes,
kept between words and skin,
we notice nakedness.
Wild and heathen scents
of shame or sin
hovered since childhood,
when the delicious was always
forbidden. "A Word with You"
had to be whispered,
spoken at the zoo,
not to be overheard
by eavesdropping ape or cockatoo.

(In Other Words)

The "eavesdropping ape or cockatoo" is imported directly from Bishop. The sense of "delicious sin" is more typically Swenson. Bishop had a formative impact on Swenson's poetry, as the two met at Yaddo when Swenson was producing her own "early work." That literary kinship implies a verbal give-and-take which stretches the boundaries of time and corporeality. "A Word with You" is, in fact, a very early poem for Bishop. Its completion date of 1933 places it long before the publication of Bishop's first book, *North and South,* in 1946. **"Her Early Work"** is from the last book published in Swenson's lifetime, *In Other Words* (1987). These "early and late" historical markers are bookends for a literary era. Swenson's book title suggests an act of interpretation which translates the whispered "word with you" into her own terms. The fact that Swenson would choose to look back at this particular Bishop poem implies a personal connection, since the poem is seldom mentioned in other critical or biographical sources on Bishop. Of course the Bishop reference is more far-reaching than any one poem. One instance in which Bishop might be said to have "talked to dogs" is in the poem "Pink Dog," which is among her final work, having been published in 1979, the year of Bishop's death (Bishop 190). This particular dog—"naked and pink, without a single hair"—is emblematic of the female condition at its most exposed.

The poem **"Her Early Work"** thus presupposes the sorting and filing of a poetic enterprise that generally happens after death, or that can feel, to the living writer, like death in life. It has the cumulative effect of drawing us back to the body of Swenson's work and to the work of others by whom she was influenced. In addition, the poem anticipates the possibility of Swenson's own literary influence to poets of future generations. Since Bishop is included in this gesture, the circle of influence would also extend to

Bishop's own poetic mentor, Marianne Moore. The critic Sven Birkerts has noted as well the influence of Moore on Swenson's early work in *Another Animal* (1954), citing similarities between Swenson's **"Horse and Swan Feeding"** and Moore's "No Swan So Fine" [Birkerts, in *Parnassus: Poetry in Review,* Vols. 12-13, Nos. 1-2, 1985]. Interestingly, Birkerts makes the point that Swenson seems to have grown beyond the influence of Moore and Bishop to establish an individual voice in her own later work, which for him, includes the new poems in *Things Taking Place* (1978).

All three poets shared a lifelong fascination with animals and their habits. Each in her own way used observations of animals in natural or man-made environments to suggest elements of the human drama. The zoo setting generates mental images of the famous photograph of Marianne Moore in front of the elephant cage or of a young Bishop and an older Moore on their first public outing to the Ringling Brothers Barnum and Bailey circus in 1934.

Another Swenson poem, **"Zambesi and Ranee,"** from her second book, *A Cage of Spines* (1958), describes a lioness and tigress caged together at the Bronx Zoo. An epigraph from the plaque on their cage attests to the fact that the animals had been "'reared together by hand from early infancy'" because their mothers refused to nurse them. The poet's stance as observer outside the cage stirs a sense memory which Swenson brings home in the poem's penultimate stanza: "The life these ladies lead / upon their stage, repeats itself behind the walls / of many city streets."

In **"Her Early Work,"** Swenson makes a broad gesture to include other poems which document "The life these ladies lead." With the title's assumption of the third-person feminine pronoun, Swenson as tour guide points us in the direction of other poets of her own gender who might be said to have "talked through / layers of masks." For contemporary readers, prominent among them would be Muriel Rukeyser, whose epigrammatic proclamation in "The Poem as Mask" became the title of one of the early feminist anthologies, *No More Masks,* a volume in which a selection of Swenson's poems was also included. Venturing further back in time, she might direct us to certain poems by Emily Dickinson, particularly since the lack of historical documentation precludes any irrefutable knowledge of "who was addressed / or ever undressed." Swenson, herself a close reader of Dickinson, raises these very questions in her essay on the poet, "'Big My Secret, But It's Bandaged'" (1984), which takes its title from poem #1737 in Thomas Johnson's edition of Dickinson's *Complete Poems.* In Swenson's poem, **"Daffodildo,"** published posthumously [in *Paris Review,* 127, 1993], the poet makes the ritual gesture of laying a daffodil from the Dickinson homestead beside Emily's headstone and taking another for herself "threaded / through my buttonhole." The flower becomes a receptacle for the poet's essence, "a yellow small decanter / of her perfume, hermit-wild / and without a stopper," suggesting the physical infusion of one poet's language into another. The poem continues with embedded quotations and complex interlocking rhymes which seem to reinforce the implicit transgenerational connection.

All of these voices are reflected in eulogy, as if the poet had dropped down on her own funeral Tom Sawyer-like, heard these words, and recorded them for the inquiring minds of future generations. Although the speaker may seem to be apologizing for a lack of candor in "her early work," there is also a cautionary note to the reader who is apt to get it wrong, to mistake "her" for the eccentric "spinster" poet talking to "cats and dogs." The continued presence of "that damned ape," as Bishop calls him, mandates secrecy. "Wraparounds, / overlaps and gauzes" are a paradoxical attempt at protection against discovery in a most vulnerable state. With or without them, we are left with the nakedness of body on body, the native ritual with its "wild and heathen scents." The gauzy veil is evidence of the sin of Eve. The child, who would run naked in the street, has parents to rein her in. The poem's closing quatrain rhymes "whispered" with "overheard" and "zoo" with "cockatoo," clashing hard consonants with open vowels for sonorous effect. Another rhyme, "taboo," hovers in the white space.

We do not have to look very far or deep to discern the nature of the taboo. While Swenson did not go out of her way to disclose her lesbianism, neither did she go out of her way to hide it. Relatively late in her life, she expressed her pleasure at the possibility of having certain poems understood in their proper context, but she was apparently less happy about the implication of being a "lesbian poet," with "lesbian" as the modifier or defining term. Swenson's poem, **"To Confirm a Thing,"** dated 1957, appeared in Joan Larkin and Elly Bulkin's anthology, *Amazon Poetry,* the first major collection of its kind, which came out in 1975. Swenson accepted the editors' invitation to include a sample of her work and suggested

Swenson upon her graduation from Utah State.

this particular poem, which after its appearance in *To Mix with Time* (1963), according to Swenson, "has never been paid any particular attention that I know of." She notes as well in her reply to Larkin: "To me the statement it makes doesn't seem at all obscure, but perhaps the metaphors constitute a thicker veil than I expected" (letter 2 Sept. 1975).

Elly Bulkin calls attention to the poem **"To Confirm a Thing"** in her introduction to *Lesbian Poetry,* focusing particularly on these lines: "We are Children incorrigible and perverse / who hold their obstinate seats / on heaven's carousel." It is important as well to examine the formal elements which are indicative of Swenson's larger design. The upper case C of children is a characteristic Swenson device. Particularly in her early work, she often used capitalization in a manner which might be equated with Dickinson's use of the dash—to guide the reader in hearing the rhythm as she herself heard it. In addition, and also like Dickinson, she played with the distinction between common and "proper" nouns, sometimes creating her own heretical orthography. In this and in other ways, Swenson proved herself to be a formalist outside of that historically feminine tradition of what Carolyn Kizer has called "toast-and-teasdales." As a poet, Swenson is more architect than sylph, more athlete than Barrett Browningesque invalid. It would be possible to read right through that word "perverse" but for such devices. The collective pronoun, the first "We" in the poem, forces our attention. The father here is not simply a genetic forebear but Zeus himself. On "heaven's carousel," then, the speaker is horse and rider, who "snort[s] at death." Although there are no gender identities clearly revealed in this poem, and words like *gay* or *lesbian* or even *homosexual* seem distant, the weight of the poem's design is balanced on the word "perverse." We are not sure exactly what "thing" the poem "confirms," but the spirit of vigorous rebellion seems almost to suggest the more contemporary usage of "queer."

The correspondence between Larkin and Swenson also provides a revealing illustration of the care Swenson typically devoted to the technical aspects of poetic construction:

> I found no errors in the text on the Galley [*sic*] of my poem. But the typesetter has not followed the arrangement as shown on the manuscript. Note that the righthand margin of the whole poem, on manuscript, is justified—that is, set straight in same way as the left-hand margin is, whereas your typesetter has left it jagged. I enclose a printed copy to help him see how to set. There is one line in the poem that's not indented either to the left or right side, and this determines the width of the poem. I've marked it with Xs. There are 47 *typed* characters in this line (spaces between words included)—and on my Ms. copy you would find that each two lines, as indented, take up the same number of spaces—47—because letters and spaces on typewriter are all of equal width. But, in *print* this is not the case—that's why the setting of this poem is tricky . . . (28 Oct. 1975).

These instructions illustrate an engineer's precision upon the typewriter's possibilities. In this and in other ways,

Swenson seems to be applying the "womanly" skill of typing to arrive at her "manly" poetic blueprint. I imagine that she would have been happy to get her hands dirty in the printshop if it would have helped to assure the accuracy of the final product. The fact that Swenson herself typed the shaped poems which appear in *Iconographs* attests to the artisan-like physicality of her poetic temperament.

Several years after the publication of *Amazon Poetry,* Bulkin and Larkin approached Swenson and the other poets who appeared in this volume for permission to include their work in a more comprehensive anthology, *Lesbian Poetry.* Swenson withdrew her permission, citing the use of the word "lesbian" in the title as problematic for her. She wrote to Larkin: "I have not sent you any poems for inclusion in the proposed anthology—nor would I do so—anymore than I would submit any writing to a book titled, for instance, 'The Heterosexual Women's Poetry Anthology'" (30 July 1980). In a longer letter following Larkin's response to this decision, she explained her reasoning:

> It strikes me as a label placed on a collection simply in order to arouse attention, and I believe it invites misunderstanding. It is not a *subject* that gives merit (or subtracts it) from poetry; the sole criterian [sic] for choosing poems to go into an anthology with that label as title will look as though it was 1. written by Lesbians, 2. about Lesbianism. People attracted to such a title would not, I think, be looking principally for first rate poetry (19 Aug. 1980).

She wrote that she would have been happier with the title "Amazon Poetry II," as she found the title of the earlier anthology to be "suggestive" but "not inviting the charge of being crude."

Swenson's sensitivity to the new book's title, though potentially disappointing to contemporary readers in search of the "gay positive," does make sense in historical context and in the context of her work. The act of naming, as Richard Howard has pointed out [in "Turned Back to the Wild by Love," *Alone with America,* 1969], takes on a significance for Swenson that is, if not conventionally religious, at least pantheistic. The capacity to name a thing is a sign of mythic understanding. On the other hand, as Alicia Ostriker notes [in "May Swenson and the Shapes of Speculation," in *Writing Like a Woman,* 1983], Swenson would not want her readers to be trapped in "the folly of mistaking names for things." Swenson had a seemingly encyclopedic knowledge of the names of exotic birds, flowers, and moons, and she used them frequently in her work to great effect. One poem, **"If I Had Children"** (*In Other Words,* 1987), continues from the "if " clause of the title, "I might name them astrometeorological names: Meridian, a girl. Zenith, a boy. / Eclipse a pretty name for either one." It seems likely that Swenson's image of herself as a "non-breeder" must have brought with it the iconoclastic power to choose from a larger pool of names than those in the conventional baby book. Still, to be categorized, to be collected under a subject heading, must have carried with it a patronizing air. "Amazon" has the metaphorical resonance of the woman warrior, but "lesbian," in spite of

its classical origins, is a demographic instrument, a way of putting people, or women, or poets, in their places. And it seems to have been Swenson's nature to resist any assumption of what now might be called political correctness.

Swenson's treatment of nature:

[May Swenson] is, to my personal taste, one of the most ingenious and delightful younger poets writing today. She has, at any rate, probably the best eye for nature. What does she not see? . . .

Her attention to nature gives May Swenson's poems a directness of gaze that is sometimes lacking when she turns to other, apparently broader subjects. She needs, perhaps, the concreteness of things close at hand in order to see deeply; it is as though language, in her hands, responded naturally only to the actual and palpable. She has a staggering poetic equipment: visual acuity, a sense of form, a fine ear for rhythm and the colloquial. Among her recent poems there are too many with high pretensions, in the shapes of arrows or zigzags or earthquakes, dealing with the Scheme of Things. A series of travel poems—with the exception of one about a bullfight—strikes me as terribly self-conscious, as though someone had been Taking Notes. But even if, in her straining for fresh ways of saying things, this poet's sureness sometimes deserts her, she just cannot go wrong with her nature poems. They are *seen*; the husks and kernels of nature are *there*. And sometimes, at moments of great simplicity, her poems go almost as far in eloquence as poems can. . . .

Peter Davison, in a review of To Mix With Time *in* The Atlantic, *December, 1963.*

Although she seldom wrote explicitly of feminist issues (the poem **"Women"** is an important exception), Swenson, like Elizabeth Bishop, was part of a transitional generation from the older wave of feminism, with its heartfelt insistence on equality. This sympathy is likely to have been enhanced by experience with the male critical establishment. In a 1977 interview with George Starbuck, Elizabeth Bishop notes, "Most of my life I've been lucky about reviews. But at the very end they often say, 'The best poetry by a woman in this decade, or year, or month.' Well, what's that worth?" [Lorrie Goldensohn, *Elizabeth Bishop: The Biography of a Poetry,* 1992]. Even Bishop's close friend Robert Lowell referred to two of her poems as "the best . . . that I know of written *by a woman* [author's italics] in this century" (Goldensohn). It is not surprising that Bishop refused the invitations from women-only anthologies that Swenson accepted. Whether the designation came from a woman editor or a male critic, Bishop was not one to call attention to her gender. Goldensohn points out that it was not until the feminist resurgence of the 1970s that Bishop was able to talk with some degree of openness about her own experience *as a woman,* as the Starbuck interview indicates. Where contemporary feminists express concern over the misrepresentation of female experience through the assumption of universal maleness, Bishop and Swenson are likely to have been concerned with the possibility that segregation by gender would diminish the impact of their artistic contribution. Separate, by this definition, could not possibly be equal. Guilt by association is a related concern.

Swenson and Bishop are also likely to have been influenced by the tenets of formalist criticism, as they achieved recognition in the era of its prominence. In this case it would be natural, and perhaps socially desirable, to see art as gender-free. If the poem is an artifact with objective existence apart from historical or social context, the gender of the poet is extratextual information. Our backward-looking lens may reject this prescriptive stance from the Old Boys of the New Criticism, but it is not possible to dismiss the impact of their work.

On a continuum of belief, however, Swenson was more willing to show some allegiance to feminist causes and perhaps less concerned with what poet Honor Moore has called "male approval desire." In the year before she died, several of her poems were included by permission in Larkin and Morse's *Gay and Lesbian Poetry in Our Time*. It is difficult to speculate about why she accepted the later invitation and not the earlier one, but we can certainly be grateful for the presence of her poems alongside those of Muriel Rukeyser, Audre Lorde, Adrienne Rich, and many of her gay male peers. In one of the two Swenson poems the editors include, **"Poet to Tiger"** (*Things Taking Place,* 1978), the veil seems to be lifted, and she writes with startling openness of the sensual daily interactions between two women. The poetic sleuth will note the presence of the anatomically correct "three-cornered pelt" embedded in this symmetrical stanza:

> You get into the tub holding *The Naked Ape*
>   in your teeth. You wet that blond
>   three-cornered pelt lie back wide
>   chest afloat. You're reading
>   in the rising steam and I'm
>   drinking coffee from your tiger cup.
>   You say you dreamed
>   I had your baby book
>   and it was pink and blue.
>   I pointed to a page and there
>   was your face with a cub grin.

The notion of the "pink and blue" baby book plays tenderly with the subtleties of gender roles in a nontraditional relationship.

"Poet to Tiger," also featured in the posthumously collected *Love Poems* (1991), is one among many poems which communicate the nuances of domestic life in women's long-term partnering with more clarity than perhaps any other poet has done before or since. These are poems in which women not only sleep together, they also buy beds (or talk about doing so), build shelves, and admire each other's handiwork. There are also poems in this collection which document the double lives of working women from those pre-Stonewall years. One small love lyric, **"To F.,"** an early poem published in *The Formalist* but not included in later book-length collections, reflects

the familiar daily experience of not being able to kiss one's lover good-bye. In the absence of that gesture, hands manage to join and speak:

> Your bus will stop at Christopher
> Mine at Abingdon Square
> Your hand . . . "Good luck" and mine "So long"
> The taxi trumpets blare

In addition to these largely undocumented details of domestic life, Swenson's close concentration on observable phenomena activates a level of metaphor in which the natural world radiates with sensuality. The poem **"Little Lion Face"** (*In Other Words,* 1987), excerpted below, is one of many examples of this tender attention:

> Little lion face
> I stooped to pick
> among the mass of thick
> succulent blooms, the twice
>
> streaked flanges of your silk
> sunwheel relaxed in wide
> dilation, I brought inside. Milk
>
> of your shaggy stem
> sticky on my fingers, and
> your barbs hooked to my hand,
> sudden stings from them
>
> were sweet. Now I'm bold
> to touch your swollen neck,
> put careful lips to slick
> petals, snuff up gold
>
> pollen in your navel cup.
> Still fresh before night
> I leave you, dawn's appetite
> to renew our glide and suck . . .

In a reverse of this metaphorical relationship, **"A Trellis for R."** (formerly titled "Blue") functions as a lesbian "Song of Songs," with each of the lover's features appreciated in turn as individual roses in the lattice frame of human touch: "Glinting hairs / shoot back of your ears' Rose / that tongue likes to feel / the maze of . . ." (*Love Poems*). The downward flow of the enjambed lines is openly sexual and distinctly female.

It is easy to see why the poet Mona Van Duyn called this collection "simply . . . the most moving book of love poems I have ever read" (jacket copy). The book lets us fall in love with love, but in this case it is "the love that dares not speak its name" finally given voice. Even the poems that show evidence of the "gauzes and overlays" of "her early work" take on a clarity in this context which is particularly poignant.

In the long run, it would seem more appropriate to focus on what Swenson was willing to make public than on what she wished not to disclose. The oldest child of ten born to Swedish immigrant parents who settled in Utah, she was raised with a rigid set of expectations of how boys and girls should behave. Having grown up in a family of practicing Mormons, it is certainly not surprising that Swenson would show an overactive attention to "delicious sin." The theme of the recalcitrant child is a strong presence throughout her work in poems like **"The Centaur."** Indeed, the word "tomboy" seems to have been created with Swenson in mind. Her boyish, close-cropped hair is a constant on the dust jacket of each new book. This healthy resistance to authority, however, did not stand in the way of her filial loyalty. From the stringencies of her family of origin to the self-made family of women implied in such poems as **"The Beauty of the Head,"** Swenson seems to have negotiated the boundaries of her various worlds with remarkable grace.

Swenson's eight surviving siblings attended her memorial tribute, given in March 1991 by the Academy of American Poets, for whom Swenson had served as chancellor from 1980 until her death in 1989, replacing Elizabeth Bishop in that post. Swenson's sister, Margaret Swenson Woodbury, one of her younger siblings, was among the presenters who offered reminiscences and read selected poems from the body of Swenson's work. Woodbury read the poem **"I Look at My Hand"** (*Iconographs,* 1970), in which the physical inheritance from parents is literally traced down to the fingertips. In another poem, **"Night Visits with the Family"** (*Things Taking Place,* 1978), variant dreams are attributed to a multitude of family members all identified by first name, including May and Margaret.

The collective presence of the family group takes on added significance in the poem **"Feel Me"** (*Iconographs,* 1970), in which, through a combination of apparent autobiography and linguistic analysis, Swenson/the speaker recalls "our father's" last words and puzzles through several possible interpretations:

> "Feel me to do right," our father said on his
> deathbed.
> We did not quite know—in fact, not at all—what he
> meant.
> His last whisper was spent as through a slot on a
> wall.
> He left us a key, but how did it fit? . . .

The microscopic attention to a small syntactic unit here stands in for the larger emotional work of grief, as if to say, in the absence of any clear message, we fix on the little we have. One possible interpretation to which the speaker does not allude is that, instead of (or in addition to) addressing the family members in his presence, the father might be offering a prayer for God's grace. The implicit "you," in this case, would be God. "Feel me to [have done] right" (with my life) would then be the sense of his words. This seemingly intentional misreading reflects a narrowing perspective which sidesteps the extremity of the situation. If the father is talking to someone other than "us," "we" lose the exercise which gives meaning to "our" grief. Given Swenson's background, it seems likely that she assumes an implicit dialogue between "our

father" on his deathbed and "Our Father," the heavenly maker, to whom the earthbound family members are denied access. In another family poem, **"That the Soul May Wax Plump,"** Swenson writes: "Mother's work before she died was self-purification / a regimen of near starvation, to be worthy to go / to Our Father, Whom she confused (or, more aptly, fused) / with our father, in Heaven long since . . ." (*Things Taking Place,* 1978).

The internal dialogue was a useful strategy for Swenson in grappling with the important questions of her own life. In the previously unpublished poem, **"Manyone Flying"** [*Nature*], she returns to a favorite visual format—the symmetrical arrangement of lines built around a narrow column of white space. In this instance, the structure suggests both the visual formation of birds in flight and the verbal precipice over which the speaker is poised. Swenson's notation on this poem tells us that she started it on a plane flight to Utah for a family visit. It is not surprising that this situation would evoke a soliloquy which traces the speaker's role as both loner and member of the flock, perpetually flying from one life to another and wondering at the need for such flight:

> Out on the ragged   edge flying lonely
> Not all alone   not that brave
> or foolish or   self-sufficient
> or self-believing   In the middle

In other poems, Swenson tackles metaphysical questions with an ironic spin that is gently irreverent. Just as **"Feel Me"** begins with a key that does not seem to fit in any known door, an earlier poem, **"The Key to Everything"** (*Another Animal,* 1954), looks at the hopeless task of the eternal seeker for answers. Here, Swenson uses breathless, unpunctuated verse paragraphs to characterize such an individual, "waiting for / the right person the doctor or / the mother or / the person with the name you keep / mumbling in your sleep. . . ." This is the kind of poem one would love to thrust in the face of New Age friends, particularly for the impact of its final lines: ". . . no once you'd / get there you'd / remember and love me / of course I'd / be gone by then I'd / be far away" (*New and Selected*).

The first two poems in *To Mix with Time* (1963) are entitled **"The Universe"** and **"God."** As Alicia Ostriker has pointed out, there may be no other poet with the audacity to use such titles, and it may be the quality Anthony Hecht refers to as "calculated naiveté" [*New York Review of Books,* Vol. 1, No. 2, 1963] which allows Swenson to pull off the gesture. But Swenson is a child here in Blake's sense of wonderment before the infinite. And, like Whitman, her first poetic impulse is to celebrate. Her early short story, "Appearances" (one of two she published in her lifetime), sets up a dialogue between a physician and a visual artist that embodies Swenson's continuing stance. "'After all,'" the story opens in the tired, paternalistic voice of the doctor, "'we are no longer children.'" The artist, that callow youth, responds, "'On the contrary, I believe that we are all still children.'" The artist then refines his position, exalting the role of the senses in coming to terms with "'a mysterious and lavish power veining everything in nature, spilling free and raw from every stone and leaf'" (*New Directions*, 1951).

Peter Pan, both ageless and androgynous, remains the essential archetype, with nature a positive force that cannot be denied. It is that persistent spirit which leads me to resist a reading of Swenson's work and life that belabors the idea of internalized homophobia or self-hatred. Her absolute willingness to confound gender expectations for subject matter, genre, and style far outweighs her apparent ambivalence about being politically "out."

The first Swenson book I purchased was *To Mix with Time,* and this was long before I called myself a lesbian or saw her work collected in *Amazon Poetry*. I remember standing in the bookstore, transfixed by these lines from **"Out of My Head"**:

> If I could get
> out   of my
> head   and
> into   the
> world.
>   What am I saying?
> Out of my
> head? Isn't my
> head
> in   the
> world?

That immediate move to stand the question itself "on its head," the refusal to separate "head" from "world," the enactment of this separation by means of a continental divide of white space—these are qualities that disarmed me then and now. As a teenager with a hyperactive intelligence and a bent toward poetry, I sensed in Swenson's work the possibilities of a future I did not yet have the words to imagine—one in which I could be "in my head" and "in the world" at the same time and in equal measure. This lesson, of course, is the opposite of what parents and teachers had to say to smart girls—that experience was something we had to go out there and "get" if we wanted to fulfill ourselves as women. Swenson's work and life palpably contradict the voice of authority. Somehow, finding out that she was a lesbian simply confirmed what I already knew. Swenson had an innate distrust for the separation of thinking and feeling states. What she recognized, instead, was the seductive energy of words and ideas, the sensual allure of exploration and discovery, the sexiness of a machine's (or a poem's) working parts. It is the word made flesh and the flesh made word—that moment of union protracted in a body of work. For these reasons, Swenson's readers tend to offer an unqualified admiration that is closer to love. We love the poet who brings us closest to our own true nature—who shows us, through her example, what it means to be truly alive.

Grace Schulman (essay date 1994)

SOURCE: "Life's Miracles: The Poetry of May Swen-

son," in *The American Poetry Review*, Vol. 23, No. 5, September-October 1994, pp. 9-13.

[*An American educator, poet, and critic, Schulman has served as the poetry editor of the journal* Nation. *Here, she gives an overview of Swenson's poetry, including her posthumous collections.*]

The voice of May Swenson combines the directness of intimate speech and the urgency of prayer:

> Body my house
> my horse my hound
> what will I do
> when you are fallen
>
> Where will I sleep
> How will I ride
> What will I hunt
>
> Where can I go
> without my mount . . .

The magic of that lament, **"Question,"** from *Another Animal* (1954), is in its contrasts: while the details are specific, the central situation is a mystery that terrifies with each new speculation. Here as elsewhere in her poems, Swenson dwells on the living body with an immediacy that heightens the dread of its loss. Other gestures that recur in Swenson's poetry are the insistent, unanswerable questions, "what will I do," "How will I ride," "What will I hunt," "Where can I go," all of them precise, all ironic, because futile. Here they are enhanced by obsessive rhyme ("house," "horse," "hound," "hunt," "mount"). Their futility is emphasized by the absence of punctuation, and again by its sudden presence, in the final line. They are meditations. Admirable too, is the voice that is neither androgynous nor gendered, but one that encompasses both sexes in its fluid boundaries and essentially human dimension: "What will I hunt," the male speaker's question, modulates here, with no abrupt tonal change, to a woman's query, "With cloud for shift / how will I hide?"

Questions are the wellsprings of May Swenson's art. She inquires about simple things, such as "What is the worm doing / making its hole," and about principles such as "What / is it about, / the universe, / the universe about us stretching out?" or, considering the moon landing, "Dare we land upon a dream?" In her speculations and her close observations, she fulfills Marianne Moore's formula for the working artist: "Curiosity, observation, and a great deal of joy in the thing." In subject matter a poet who, like Donne, takes all of knowledge as her province, she is as comfortable with animals and flowers as she is with anti-matter, electronic sound, and DNA. Some of her chosen forms incorporate questions, such as her ballad, **"The Centaur"**: *"Where have you been?" "Been riding."* Another is the ancient riddle, a form that enables her to concentrate on the object without naming it. **"The Surface,"** for example, has affinities to Dickinson's riddles, and to her wit: "First I saw the surface, / then I saw it flow, / then I saw the underneath," the poet begins, and gradually unravels the answer, the image of an eye. Swenson riddles in a quest to find a higher reality obscured by conventional names, and to fathom what is deepest within the self. By rejecting ready-made definitions—those designations that enlighten—Swenson sees in the dark. She derides the ordinary labeling of things with its consequent reduction of greatness:

> They said there was a   Thing
> that could not   Change
> They could not   Find
> it so they   Named
> it   God . . .
>
>   (**"God"**)

The poet's unnaming allows her to rename, in an effort to see things outside the context of common parlance. Continually the search is for a deeper meaning, the essence of the thing observed. In **"Evolution,"** the first poem of her first book, she exclaims:

> beautiful each Shape
>   to see
> wonderful each Thing
>   to name
>   here a stone
>   there a tree
>   here a river
>   there a Flame . . .

May Swenson was born in 1913 in Logan, Utah, of a Mormon family, and educated at Utah State University. She was a New Yorker from 1936, and lived in Sea Cliff, New York, for twenty-three years before her death in Ocean View, Delaware, in 1989. In her lifetime, she published eleven books over three decades, nine of them poetry collections, from *Another Animal* (1954) to *In Other Words* (1987). Honored as she was during her lifetime, her books included only four hundred and fifty of the nine hundred poems she composed. Since her death, as new poems and new books continue to appear, it becomes apparent not only that her output is larger than readers have supposed, but that her stature is major.

Nature (1994), the newest of the posthumous books, contains some early poems, hitherto unpublished, whose dominant tone is awe: "Remain aghast at life," the poet resolves in **"Earth Your Dancing Place,"** composed as early as 1936:

> Enter each day
> as upon a stage
> lighted and waiting
> for your step . . .

Wonder prevails in **"Manyone Flying"** (1975), another of the poems that appear posthumously in *Nature*. Here, the poet, in the guise of a high-flying bird, considers the divisions between the individual and humanity:

> Out on the edge,
> my maneuverings,   my wings, think

> they are free.   Flock, where do we
> fly? Are we Ones?   Or One, only?
> if only One, not lonely   . . . being Manyone . . .
> but Who   are We? And Why?

The liveliest of the posthumous books, *The Love Poems of May Swenson* (1991), contains poems that illuminate the work as a whole. Here, the poet who continually questions existence finds love at the source of the quest: existence depends on the other. The bridge between self and other is basic to the polarities, found throughout her work, of life and death, wildness and restraint, past and present, sun and moon, stone and flame. Although out of the fifty-five poems, *The Love Poems* contains only thirteen hitherto unpublished, as well as some familiar poems in altered forms, their publication—as well as their arrangement here—reveal the force of that important theme. And as the love poems occupy the full span of her career, having been composed between 1938 and 1987, so does the theme.

Before elaborating on that large concern, I want to comment on the poetry's marvelous erotic power. Heightened sensations recall the Song of Songs: "thy breasts shall be as clusters of the vine" (King James Version 7:8). All the more credible for risking sentimentality without approaching it, Swenson conveys physical intimacies and shares sensual delights, as, for example, the "dark wild honey,"

> Thick transparent amber
> you brought home,
> the sweet that burns.

The poet cries out in passion: "Burn   radiant   sex born   scorpion   need." She writes of joy: "A rain of diamonds virgule in the mind" (**"Love Is"**); of pain: "Now heart, take up your desert; virgule this spring is cursed" (**"Wild Water,"** 1938); and of yearning: "my body is a sharpened dart / of longing / coming toward you always," in **"The Equilibrist,"** composed in the forties. As for her lustiness, I cannot describe it better than did Edward Hirsch, who wrote in a review of *Love Poems*: "The birds, and especially the bees, have never been so slyly deployed."

Vivid, moving, the love poems take in the intricacies of human nature, the natural world, geography, and invention. They are poems of intense love between women, written at a time when that genre was rare in poetry. I say love between women with qualifications, because of the poetry's aesthetic complexity. Swenson's tone embraces the full human drama. Her metaphors often are male, or animal, or flower. Nevertheless, the sexual love she dramatizes so brilliantly is Sapphic. This is subtly and beautifully apparent in the imagery of four poems that did not appear during Swenson's lifetime:

> I exist in your verdant garden
>   . . .
> I unfurled in your rich soil
>
>   (**"You Are"**)

We are released
and flow into each other's cup
Our two frail vials pierced
drink each other up
                    ("**In Love Made Visible,**" 1946)

To feel your breast
rise with my sigh
To hold you mirrored
in my eye

Neither wanting more
Neither asking why
                    ("**Neither Wanting More,**" 1944)

I open to your dew,
beginning in the spring again . . .
                    ("**Annual,**" 1959).

Sexy poems dominate this book, either by shining out in their own light or by illuminating others. In *Love Poems,* many titles are familiar to Swenson's readers, such as "**August Night**" and "**Another Animal.**" Those familiar poems are strengthened by the context of the newly published pieces. For example, "**The School of Desire**" (from *A Cage of Spines,* 1958) is a symphonic reiteration—the theme stated in full force—of the wildness and freedom that are more reflective in the more recently surfaced poems such as "**In Love Made Visible.**" In a biography published in 1993, *The Wonderful Pen of May Swenson,* R. R. Knudson observed, "For May, power was fear pushed back." So, too, many of the love poems, like primitive chants, derive their power from the expression of inner wildness as well as the immense effort to order it. "**The School of Desire**" captures the poet's energies at their strongest:

Unloosed, unharnessed, turned back to the wild by
    love,
the ring you cantered round with forelock curled,
the geometric music of this world
dissolved and, in its place,
alien as snow to tropic tigers, amphitheatric space
you will know the desert's freedom, wind and sun
rough-currying your mane, the plenitude
of strong caresses on your body nude.

And yet, while the poems capture the physical ecstasy of consummated love, they also evoke the elusiveness of a world beyond the physical. In the grand design of an Elizabethan sonneteer, she writes of mutability: desire changes, the moment it is given form, to flame up and die. Love, a reaction against the process of temporal decay, can enable flesh-bound companions at least to intuit spiritual value.

In love are we set free
Objective bone
and flesh no longer insulate us
to ourselves alone . . .

                    ("**In Love Made Visible**")

As I've said, *The Love Poems* highlights Swenson's manner of incessant inquiry. Early and late, her intellectual probing is acompanied by passionate identification with objects, with technology, and, especially, with nature: the lion's yearning, the lamb's way, the deer's eye; recumbent stones, thighs of trees, horses whose colors are "like leaves or stones / or wealthy textures / liquors of light."

On the other hand, when human love is at stake, human sensibility replaces the unity with animals, as in the poem "**Evolution**":

an Evolution strange
two Tongues touch
exchange
a Feast unknown
to stone
or tree or beast . . .

In the love poems, particularly those that appeared recently, the persistent questions of Swenson's world are put aside as the lover lies content without searching for data: "Because I don't know you / I love you," admits the speaker of an early poem. Fulfillment is

To hold you mirrored
in my eye

Neither wanting more
Neither asking why . . .

Although the love poems do not question overtly, they exhibit a more essential phase of the poet's constant quest. Swenson's earliest efforts on any theme probe the reality of being, and the utter dependence of being upon its opposite is dominant here, especially in the early, posthumously-published work: "As you are Sun to me / O I am moon to you," cries the lover in "**Facing.**" "They are like flame and ice / the elemental You and Me," begins "**The Indivisible Incompatibles,**" a poem written in the 1940s. The lovers are "Not twin / but opposite / as my two hands are opposite," according to "**Symmetrical Companion,**" another early poem, from 1948, that has for an ending, "Come release me / Without you I do not yet exist." Even more directly, the lover asserts:

I dwell
in you
and so
I know
I am

no one
can be sure
by himself
of his own being . . .

And, more firmly, "because you believe I exist I exist" ("**You Are**").

Here the passion is metaphorical, though the details are concrete. The lovers of her poems, steamy though they are, represent parts of a divided self. Their union, that blessed state in which opposites are conjoined, reveals essential being. Mooring in one's otherness allays unanswerable queries about life and death. Furthermore, the process of finding a hidden part of the self reveals a remote world beyond the tangible: "In love are we made visible . . . In love are we set free."

The title of her 1967 volume, *Half Sun Half Sleep,* announces that division of what May Swenson once called, "the primitive bipolar suspension in which my poems often begin to form." Her theme of division is conveyed by many of her shaped poems, or those which contain visual as well as textual metaphors.

Actually, the poet's primary effects are her cadences. The impact of her poems lies in their urgent speech and incantatory rhythms, their music of charms, spells, curses, ritual dances. Never does the typography, however intricate, supersede the cadence. As in primitive poetry, word and appearance are fused for a total effect.

As if to demonstrate subtly that the shaped poems have an auditory life of their own, May Swenson chose to read aloud many of her typographical poems in 1976 on a Caedmon recording, which could not, of course, exhibit the visual pattern to her listeners. One of the poems she read was **"The Lightning,"** which she referred to as a pivotal poem in *Half Sun Half Sleep.* Of its typographical device, the visual metaphor, she commented: "As seen on the page, there is a streak of white space that runs diagonally through the body of the poem and this even splits some of the words." The poem celebrates speech, and the white streak creates meditative pauses in lines, indicating the gap between word and event, between experience and its realization in the poem:

The Lightning

The lightning waked me. It slid unde   r
my eyelid. A black book flipped ope   n
to an illuminated page. Then insta   ntly
shut. Words of destiny were being uttered in the distance. If only I could
make them out! . . . Next day, as I lay
in the sun, a symbol for concei ving the
universe was scratched on my e yeball.
But quickly its   point   eclipse d, and
softened, in the scabbard of my brain.
My cat speaks one word: Fo ur vowels
and   a consonant.   He rece ives with the
hairs of his body the wh ispers of the
stars. The kinglet spe aks by flashing
into view a ruby feath er on his head.
He is held by a threa d to the eye of
the sun and cannot fall into error.
Any flower is a per fect ear, or else it
is a thousand lips ...When will I grope
clear of the entr ails of intellect?

Swenson spoke, too, of a poem whose title is, antithetically, **"Untitled,"** commenting on an earlier version she read

on the recording. She described the visual metaphor created by the typographical appearance on the page, noting that "two black crooked lines pass through the text as if to x it out. The bipolar words 'you,' 'me,' are in the center as if entangled where the two black lines cross." Here, the spaces are between words, and they designate a meditative, almost painful effort at speech. "I   w i l l   be   earth   you   be   the   flower . . . ," the poem begins, and the voice rises in passionate intensity as the lovers flail, boat and sea, earth and flood, desert and salt.

Utterance is the theme, too, of **"Fountains of Aix,"** a poem from the 1963 collection, *To Mix With Time.* In it, the word "water" is split fifteen times from its lines, and poured, in effect, down the side of one stanza:

A goddess is driving a chariot through   water.
Her reins and whips are tight white   water.
Bronze hoofs of horses wrangle with   water.

The streak of space separates the fountain's sculptures from the water spouting from their mouths. Here are dolphins and lions and bulls, and "faces with mossy lips unlocked," all uttering water, "their eyes mad / or patient or blind or astonished." She builds a metaphor of the fluidity of utterance, and thence of poetry. Swenson's pauses emphasize her wonder: In **"Fire Island,"** from *Iconographs* (1970), the poet contemplates the miracle of beholding light and dark—milky foam, black sky—of solitude and the group—walkers on the beach and "other watchers"—while the two ends of the narrow island are splayed out in type above and below, creating pauses between the letters of the words "Fire" and "sight."

Typographical pauses appear throughout Swenson's writing career. Some are part of an intricate pattern, as in **"The Fountains of Aix"** and **"The Lightning."** Many occur in poems of two columns, and of those, some are read down the page, some across the page and still others across *and* down. Early and late, those patterned spaces between the words indicate opposites, ironies, reversals, paradoxes, ambiguities. For example, in a poem whose title conveys a moment in time, **"While Sitting in the Tuileries and Facing the Slanting Sun,"** the poet ironically associates, and then divides by space, a swaddled infant in Giotto's fresco, **"Birth of the Virgin,"** and a mummy in the Vatican Museum:

There is a	Person
of flesh that is a *rocking*	Box
There is a	Box
of wood that is a *painted*	Person . . .

In **"Bleeding,"** from *Iconographs,* a space through the center is a jagged, running wound, effecting caesuras of hesitation in a dialogue between the knife and the cut. The force grows along with the grim realization that bleeding is precisely feeling, in this devastating relationship:

I feel I have to bleed to   feel I   think said the cut.
I don't I don't have to   feel said   the knife drying now
becoming shiny.

Like the polarized images found throughout Swenson's work, the contrasts created by her typographical separations have their roots in the love poems. There are the two columns of **"Evolution"** and **"Facing"** (both to be read down the page, rather than across), each indicating another animal, the lover who is an aspect of the self. Like all the love poems, these two praise opposite beings—flame and ice, sun and moon—who move forward to their destiny.

The love poems, with their high energy and "desert freedom," contain, as do the poems of Shakespeare and Sir Philip Sidney, the irony that vitality can emphasize its very opposite, the certainty of life's decline. From early on, May Swenson sings of life in death's shadow, as in **"Question,"** quoted above, and in poems that have the word "Death" in their titles: **"Deaths," "Death Invited," "The Shape of Death."**

Did Swenson suffer great personal loss? Her biographer, R. R. Knudson, writes that the death of a beloved grandfather prompted May, as a child, to question the finality of loss. Then, as a teenager, May questioned Mormonism, and, in fact, normative religions with their conventional notions of God. It seems that later she was deeply saddened by the atrocities of World War II. Young May's lover, the Czech poet, Anca Vrboska, lost her family to the Nazi death camps. While Vrboska wrote of Auschwitz directly, Swenson internalized, objectified, searched, as always, for the essence of death:

> I will lie down in Autumn
> let birds be flying
>
> swept into a hollow
> by the wind
> I'll wait for dying
>
> I will lie inert unseen
> my hair same-colored
> with grass and leaves . . .

("I Will Lie Down")

Later still, in those poems whose titles say "death," Swenson plays on the Elizabethan paradox that tragic implications are perceived in the midst of life's personal, intimate experience. All are poems that embody contrasts, either in their divided shape on the page, or in their imagery, or both. A fascinating early example is **"Death, Great Smoothener"**:

> Death,
> great smoothener,
> maker of order,
> arrester, unraveler, sifter and changer
> death, great hoarder;
> student, stranger, drifter, traveler,
> flyer and nester all caught at your border;
> death,
> great halter;
> blackener and frightener,

> reducer, dissolver,
> seizer and welder of younger with elder,
> waker with sleeper,
> death, great keeper
> of all that must alter;
> death,
> great heightener,
> leaper, evolver,
> greater smoothener,
> great whitener!

The poem's sheer energy cries of life even as it speaks to death. It has the sound of a pagan incantation, with its frightening direct address presented in clusters of heavy stresses. Swenson achieves her falling rhythm here, as in **"Question,"** with reversed iambs, and depicts death in lists of epithets, enforced by rhyme: "order," "hoarder," "border." In contrast to the chant rhythm, the typographical shape on the page is that of an ornate Christian cross. The resonant epithets echo, for me, Caedmon's hymn, the legendary first song of our first English poet, a song of thanksgiving:

Nu sculon herigean	heofonrices weard
metodes meahte	and his modgethanc
weorc wuldorædur	swa he wundra gehwæs
now shall we praise	heaven's keeper
the maker's might	and his mind thought
father of the world	as of all wonder . . .

Poetically, their techniques are alike: to sing of God, Caedmon uses epithets for the Anglo-Saxon warlords, such as ruler, lord, keeper, father, and qualifies them with Christian adjectives such as "almighty" and "eternal." Swenson chants death in life, and engraves a pagan rhythm in a Christian cross.

The poetry of May Swenson celebrates life's miracles even with death in view: the wonder of speech (**"Fountains of Aix"**); the grandeur of God (**"God"**); the radiance of sight (**"Fire Island"**). In each of these three poems, typographical divisions—white streaks down the middle of the text, make for breath-catching pauses that enhance the excited tone. The ambiguities and paradoxes of Swenson's poetry result from the basic contradiction between our illusion of permanence and our underlying certainty of fatality. This contradiction is articulated most explicitly in one of the love poems. **"The Shape of Death,"** a poem printed, in *Iconographs,* with a white streak down the middle of the text:

> What does love look like? We know the shape of death.
> Death is a cloud, immense   and awesome. At first a
> lid is lifted from the   eye of light. There is a
> clap of sound. A white   blossom belches from the
> jaw of fright.

Then, in sharp contrast to those positive assertions about death, love is presented in a series of questions: "What is its / color and its alchemy?" "Can it be   sown and harvested?" The resounding theme of Swenson's poems is there, in her concluding statement. Like life, love, though fatally transient, is "not alien—it is near—our very skin, a sheath   to keep us pure of fear."

Langdon Hammer   (essay date 1995)

SOURCE: "Poetry in Review," in *The Yale Review,* Vol. 83, No. 1, January, 1995, pp. 121-41.

[*In the following excerpt, Hammer extols the lyricism of Swenson's poems in the posthumous collection* Nature.]

May Swenson's *Nature* collects most of the major work of a master poet. The book's full title is *Nature: Poems Old and New,* and all of the poems in it in some way concern Swenson's great, lifelong subject, nature. The new poems include ten published for the first time and nineteen published for the first time in book form, perhaps as many as five of which are important additions to Swenson's achievement. The old poems include much of Swenson's *New and Selected Things Taking Place* (now long out of print), a few poems from *In Other Words* (the final book Swenson published before her death in 1989), and a selection from two posthumous volumes. *Nature* lacks the clarity of a compact "Selected Poems" and the comprehensiveness of a reliable "Collected"—its topical format makes it something different from (and I think something less than) either of those desirable things. But it is the best collection of Swenson's poetry yet published, and that means it is an extremely valuable book.

Swenson's work is so inward, independent, and intense, so intimate and impersonal at once, it has been difficult to place in the field of contemporary poetry. In some ways, Swenson's work poses the same problems as that of Elizabeth Bishop, her close friend and her near contemporary, to whom two poems in *Nature* are addressed, including a movingly simple, insistent, grief-stricken elegy, **"In the Bodies of Words."** Like Bishop, Swenson maintained her distance from the movements and disputes that define American poetry in this century, and like Bishop, Swenson created a lyric poetry so beautiful and deft it could be mistaken for nothing more than that. But in the past decade Bishop has become, well, Elizabeth Bishop, the subject of a growing shelf of scholarly books and perhaps the most prominent American poet of her generation, while Swenson remains politely admired and all but unread. Bishop may very well be the superior poet. But the contrast between the two poets' reputations today is striking because Swenson and Bishop have a great deal in common. It is also striking that Swenson is praised (when she is praised) for her seeing, her charm, and her skill—that is, she is praised in the same terms that Bishop used to be, but that now seem inadequate and condescending to her. They do not serve Swenson much better. If the quality of her seeing distinguishes her, that is because Swenson is a seer, a visionary poet in the romantic tradition. If she is charming, she is also disturbing and strange. And if Swenson is skilled, she uses her skills for profound moral aims.

Swenson's own claims for her work are not conspicuous. Her poetry is remarkably free of literary allusion; its domain really is nature, not culture. One exception is a poem published here for the first time in book form, the brashly, whimsically titled **"Daffodildo,"** in which Swenson describes a visit to the grave of Emily Dickinson. (Dickinson will reappear several times in this essay. If there is one poet to whom twentieth-century women poets are indebted, and in relation to whom they choose to define themselves, it is Dickinson.) Arriving, fittingly, "on the first day of May," Swenson gives the dead poet a daffodil she took from Dickinson's own "lot"; another flower Swenson threads "through my buttonhole" like a suitor. The simple yellow flower links the two women across time: "One gold dildo / I leave from the host / I stole; / the other, holy, / I will keep until / it shrinks to ghost." Swenson's "gold dildo" mocks any claim for the naturally superior endowments of male poets: a daffodil will do as nicely as a penis. (The sexual sense of *dildo* predates its use as a plant name, and seems to be the source for it.) Swenson's short lines, recalling Dickinson's own, reinforce the point: her three- and two-beat verses, sometimes shrinking to one, are the swaying stem of a flower that stands up on its own. Swenson quotes Dickinson and closes with a pledge:

> "Disdaining men,
> and oxygen,"
> your grassy
> breast I kiss
> and make
> this vow, Emily, to "take
> vaster
> attitudes and strut upon my stem."

Kissing nature, Swenson kisses Dickinson, and struts.

Playful as it is, this kiss is a provocative reminder that Swenson was a lesbian poet. For the most part, readers who have discussed Swenson's sexuality treat it in one of two ways: as a special interest she is able to transcend, or as a secret she refers to furtively, in code. Neither of these views is very accurate. I would say that, rather than transcended or encoded, sexuality is multiform in Swenson's work, complexly involved in the poet's relation to nature. Sometimes sexuality and nature are linked by analogy. **"Swimmers"** elaborates a simple conceit: having sex is like swimming in the sea ("Tossed / by the muscular sea, / we are lost, / and glad to be lost / in troughs of rough // love"). More often, Swenson presses the terms of comparison closer together, eroticizing her relation to natural processes and forms until sexual meanings and intensities permeate nature. **"On Handling Some Small Shells from the Windward Islands"** is a beautiful example. This three-page poem is written in compact couplets placed on alternating sides of the page, as if the poet were examining one shell in one hand and another in the other, over and over again:

> Gathered here in a bowl,

>> their ineradicable inks
>> vivid, declarative

under water. Peculiar fossil-
fruits that suck through ribbed

lips and gaping sutures
into secret clefts

the sweet wet with a tame taste.
Vulviform creatures, or

rather, their rocklike
backs with labial bellies.

This poem is a brilliant act of seeing, but it is important that Swenson is *touching* (not just looking at) the objects described. This touching is always also part of how she speaks: Swenson's idiom, here and elsewhere, drops articles and verbs, compressing and clarifying syntax in a way that eliminates inessentials and pulls nature close.

"Feel Me" is the title of Swenson's homely, haunting elegy for her father, based on his enigmatic final words: "Feel me to do right." It is also what the world says to Swenson. At times it can be a terrifying command—as in "Laocoön Dream Recorded in Diary Dated 1943," one of the new poems in *Nature,* although it is one of the oldest. (The date its composition was begun, which Swenson noted for all her poems, is provided in the book's title index.) Here Swenson dreams of being caught up in a many-armed, serpentine embrace: "caressed all ways at once, / I did not care to identify my lover." Indeed, at first, the lover's identity is excitingly vague. But it quickly becomes clear that the poet is clutched by a "gentle murderer whose many-stranded will / never could be severed." Finally, "my head was swallowed, open-eyed. / The dream was done, so there was no escape." It is only when the poet awakens—"open-eyed"—that the voracious world fully claims her. The poems placed on either side of "Laocoön Dream" explore other versions of polymorphous desire. In "Cabala," another new poem, the poet imagines herself into different forms, all of them "dark," until she is substanceless, "a swiftness on the dark." In "A Dream," Swenson recalls a dream in which she becomes a god of the forest: "I wore a mask of skin-thin silver / My hair was frenzied foam stiffened to ice." These magic changes all have a childlike quality; they indulge perverse and fanciful appetites. The greatest moment of such magic in Swenson's work is a well-known poem, "The Centaur." The poet, remembering the summer she was ten years old, comes home from a ride on the stick-horse she cut from a willow tree, when her mother asks her why her mouth is stained green: *Rob Roy, he pulled some clover / as we crossed the field,* I told her."

Swenson's imagination centers on transformations like this: the poet not only witnesses, but is herself drawn out and into, nature's restless metamorphoses. "Now my body flat, / the ground breathes," Swenson writes in "The Exchange": "I'll be the grass." The poem ends with this exhilarating, solemn series of commands: "Wind, be motion. / Birds, be passion. / Water, invite me to your bed." The unmagical, fully natural metamorphosis that the human body undergoes is aging—which was one of Swen-

son's key subjects. *Nature* includes the short, eerie set of instructions called "How to Be Old" as well as, right next to it (tiresomely, the arrangement of poems in *Nature* insists on thematic connections), the funny, chilling, brief meditation, "View to the North." "As you grow older, it gets colder," it begins. The leaves fall and "You see through things" clear to the horizon. But this heightening and clarifying of vision has a cost: "Magnificent! I'll be thinking / while my eyeballs freeze." The point is that no one survives such a vision—no one can stand apart from nature and enjoy the view.

Swenson does not resist death, however; she accepts it—at times she welcomes it—in ecstatic moments of self-dismissal. These moments multiply in the poems about the sea gathered at the end of *Nature,* including "At First, At Last," "The Sea," "Running on the Shore," and "St. Augustine-by-the-Sea." The finest, most frightening example is a new poem, "Staring at the Sea on the Day of the Death of Another":

The long body of the water fills its hollow,
slowly rolls upon its side,
and in the swaddlings of the waves,
their shadowed hollows falling forward with the
    tide,

like folds of Grecian garments molded to cling
around some classic immemorial marble thing,
I see the vanished bodies of friends who have died.

Each form is furled into its hollow,
white in the dark curl,
the sea a mausoleum, with countless shelves,
cradling the prone effigies of our unearthly selves,

some of the hollows empty, long niches in the tide.
One of them is mine
and gliding forward, gaping wide.

Written late in Swenson's life, "Staring at the Sea on the Day of the Death of Another" is comparable in wisdom and dignity to "A Grave" by Marianne Moore and "At Melville's Tomb" by Hart Crane—which is to say, comparable to poems by two of the supreme lyric poets of this century. In this and perhaps a few other poems in *Nature,* Swenson joins that company.

FURTHER READING

Bibliography

Gadomski, Kenneth E. "May Swenson: A Bibliography of Primary and Secondary Sources." *Bulletin of Bibliography* 44, No. 4 (December 1987): 255-80.

  Indexes materials by Swenson, including her essays, interviews, book reviews, sound recordings, manuscripts, and archival materials, in addition to periodicals in which her poems first appeared. Gadomski's bibliography also lists critical commentary about Swenson.

Biography

Gould, Jean. "May Swenson." In *Modern American Women Poets*, pp. 75-96. New York: Dodd, Mead & Company, 1984.
   Discusses Swenson's poetry in the context of her life and friendships, with much anecdotal material.

Knudson, R. R. *The Wonderful Pen of May Swenson*. New York: Macmillan, 1993, 112 p.
   Account of Swenson's life, with special emphasis on her early years. Knudson includes material from Swenson's letters and diaries.

Criticism

Birkerts, Sven. "May Swenson." In *The Electric Life: Essays on Modern Poetry*, pp. 197-215. New York: William Morrow and Company, 1989.
   Perceives a transformation in Swenson's poetry: "Here is a poet who has, with patience and determination, made her way from a detached fascination with otherness to an increasingly subjective recognition of the self as an agent in the chaotic here and now. The inevitable question arises: What do we cherish more, technical excellence or voice? In Swenson's poetry the latter has been achieved to some extent at the price of the former." This essay was originally published in the journal *Parnassus* in 1985.

Dickey, James. "Poetry in the Unraveling." *The New York Times Book Review* (30 October 1966): 42.
   A review of *Poems to Solve*. Dickey praises Swenson's ability to interest children in poetry.

Dickey, William. "Hopes for Explosions." *The Hudson Review* XVI, No. 2 (Summer 1963): 305-15.
   In a review of ten books of poetry, Dickey ranks Swenson's *To Mix with Time* first.

Petitt, Dorothy. "Poem, Students & the Teacher." *English Journal* 55, No. 2 (February 1966): 222-24.
   Describes teaching Swenson's "Cat & the Weather" to young students.

Additional coverage of Swenson's life and career is contained in the following sources published by Gale Research: *Contemporary Authors*, Vols. 5-8 (rev. ed.), 130; *Contemporary Authors New Revision Series*, Vol. 36; *Contemporary Literary Criticism*, Vols. 4, 14, 61; *DISCovering Authors*; *Dictionary of Literary Biography*, Vol. 5; *Major 20th-Century Writers*; and *Something about the Author*, Vol. 15.

Marina (Ivanovna) Tsvetaeva (Efron)
1892-1941

(Also transliterated as Tsvetayeva, Cvetaeva, and Zwetaewa.) Russian poet, essayist, dramatist, critic, and autobiographer.

INTRODUCTION

Tsvetaeva is recognized as one of modern Russia's "poetic quartet," along with Anna Akhmatova, Osip Mandelstam, and Boris Pasternak, who acted as poet-witnesses of the country's changing values in the early decades of the twentieth century. Their lives and art were influenced by one another and by the cataclysmic political and social upheavals occurring in Russia at the time. Tsvetaeva is often likened to her three contemporaries—to Pasternak for an intense love of Moscow, to Akhmatova for shared feminist concerns, and to Mandelstam for tumultuous emotions. Her central interest as a poet was language, and she used a terse, often verbless construction, with an energy described as taut and virile. Her experiments with syntax and rhythm are considered a unique contribution to Russian literature.

Biographical Information

Tsvetaeva grew up in Moscow, a member of an artistic, scholarly, upper-middle-class family. She privately published her first volume of verse, *Vecherny albom (Evening Album)*, in 1910. This collection received unexpected attention when it was reviewed by the prominent critic Max Voloshin and the poets Nikolay Gumilyov and Valery Bryusov, all of whom wrote favorably of Tsvetaeva's work. In 1911 Tsvetaeva was married to Sergei Efron and the following year published a second collection of poetry, *Volshebny fonar (The Magic Lantern)*. During the Russian Civil War, which lasted from 1918 to 1921, Tsvetaeva lived in poverty in Moscow while her husband fought in the Crimea as an officer of the Czarist White Army. Although she wrote prolifically during this time—composing poetry, essays, memoirs, and dramas—the anti-Bolshevik sentiments pervading many of these works prevented their publication. During a famine in 1919 the younger of her two children died of starvation, and in 1922 Tsvetaeva emigrated with her surviving child, Ariadna, to Germany to join Efron after five years of wartime separation. While the Efrons lived in Berlin and Prague, Tsvetaeva began publishing the products of her previous decade's labor; these found critical favor with émigré writers and publishers. Moving to Paris, Tsvetaeva continued her poetic writing in times marked by physical and emotional hardship. She was unable to sustain her early acceptance by other émigré writers because of her marked independence, her emotional intensity, and the political sympathies of her husband, who had become involved with the Communist party. Tsvetaeva refused to adopt the militant anti-Soviet posture of many émigrés. In the late 1930s Tsvetaeva's son entreated her to

follow her husband and daughter who had already returned to Russia. The poet and her son arrived in Moscow in 1939 to an extreme political situation of totalitarian dictatorship. Artists and intellectuals were automatically suspect and Tsvetaeva was especially endangered by the political activities of her husband, who had been arrested and executed. When German troops attacked Moscow in 1941 Tsvetaeva and her son were evacuated to the village of Elabuga in the Tartar Republic. Tsvetaeva, denied the right to publish, was unable to find acceptable work there or in nearby Christopol where a colony of writers had gathered. Three weeks after her evacuation, she took her life.

Major Works

Tsvetaeva's first two volumes of verse, composed almost entirely before she was eighteen years old, are considered works of technical virtuosity, and their occasionally immature themes do not obscure Tsvetaeva's mastery of traditional Russian lyric forms. Departing sharply from her earlier romantic style, *Vyorsty I* marks the beginning of her mature verse. In this collection, which shows a development in rhythmic control and restraint, she experimented with unusual meters and paranomasia, a technique of associating words with the same or similar roots. *Remeslo (Crafts),* the last volume of poetry Tsvetaeva completed before her emigration, is praised for its metrical experiments and effective blending of folk language, archaisms, and Biblical idioms. Although she generally rejected the practices of contemporary poetic schools, Tsvetaeva did share the Russian Symbolists' refined poetic craftsmanship and the passion for clarity and detail practiced by such Acmeist poets as Mandelstam and Akhmatova.

In the early 1920s Tsvetaeva experimented with narrative verse, adapting traditional Russian folktales in *Tsar-devitsa* and *Molodets (The Swain).* Although she continued to write lyrics, her most significant works in the following years were long poems, such as her satire "Krysolov" ("The Pied Piper"). Tsvetaeva developed a new classical style in her verse drama *Ariadna,* and in the volume *Posle Rossii (After Russia),* which Simon Karlinsky has called "the most mature and perfect of her collections," she fused her early romanticism with colloquial diction. While she based her poems predominantly upon personal experience, she also explored with increased detachment such philosophical themes as the nature of time and space. As the 1930s progressed, Tsvetaeva devoted more energy to prose than to poetry. In such memoirs as "Plennyi dukh" ("Captive Spirit") and "Moy Pushkin" ("My Pushkin"), she recorded her impressions of friends and poets. In a prose style characterized by stream-of-consciousness narrative technique and poetic language, Tsvetaeva expressed her views on literary creation and criticism in such essays as "Iskusstvo pri svete sovesti" ("Art in the Light of Conscience") and "Poet o kritike" ("A Poet on Criticism").

Critical Reception

After her initial critical success and popularity, Tsvetaeva was largely neglected because of her experimental style and her refusal to assume either a pro- or anti-Soviet stance. However, her works eventually gained a wide audience in the Soviet Union during the post-Stalinist "thaw" of the 1950s. International scholarly interest in Tsvetaeva increased during the 1960s, leading to a heightened appreciation for her technical inventiveness, emotional force, and thematic range. Recent critics regard her works as among the most innovative and powerful Russian poetry of the twentieth century.

PRINCIPAL WORKS

Poetry

Vecherny albom 1910
Volshebny fonar 1912
Razluka 1922
Stikhi k Bloku 1922
Tsar-devitsa 1922
Vyorsty I 1922

Psikheya 1923
Remeslo 1923
Molodets 1924
Posle Rossii 1928
*Lebediny stan [*The Demesne of the Swans*] 1957
Izbrannye proizvedeniya (poetry, drama, and autobiography) 1965
Selected Poems 1971
Selected Poems of Marina Tsvetaeva 1987

Other Major Works

"Poet o kritike" ["A Poet on Criticism" published in *The Bitter Air of Exile,* 1977] (essay) 1926
Ariadna (drama) 1927
"Iskusstvo pri svete sovesti" ["Art in the Light of Conscience" published in *Modern Russian Poets on Poetry,* 1976] 1936
Proza (letters and memoirs) 1953
Pisma k Anne Teskovoy (letters) 1969
A Captive Spirit: Selected Prose (essays, criticism, literary portraits, and autobiographical sketches) 1980
Art in the Light of Conscience (essays on poetry) 1992

*This work was written in 1917-21.

CRITICISM

Marina Tsvetaeva (essay date 1934)

SOURCE: "Poets with History and Poets without History," in *Art in the Light of Conscience: Eight Essays on Poetry by Marina Tsvetaeva,* translated with Introduction and Notes by Angela Livingstone, Cambridge, Mass.: Harvard University Press, 1992, pp. 136-48.

[*The following is an excerpt from an article that was originally published in a Serbian journal in 1934. Here, Tsvetaeva differentiates the genius of lyric poets from that of other poets. Lyric poets, she argues, do not, like other poets, seek to gain new experience and self-discovery through their work, but rather they delve again and again into the same experiences in hopes of expressing them more eloquently.*]

. . . What is the 'I' of a poet? It is—to all appearances—the human 'I' expressed in poetic speech. But only to appearances, for often poems give us something that had been hidden, obscured, even quite stifled, something the person hadn't known was in him, and would never have recognised had it not been for poetry, the poetic gift. Action of forces which are unknown to the one who acts, and which he only becomes conscious of in the instant of action. An almost complete analogy to dreaming. If it were possible to direct one's own dreams—and for some it is, especially children—the analogy would be complete. That which is hidden and buried in you is revealed and exposed in your poems: this is the poetic 'I', your dream-self.

The 'I' of the poet, in other words, is his soul's devotion to certain dreams, his being visited by certain dreams, the secret source—not of his will, but of his whole nature.

The poet's self is a dream-self and a language-self; it is the 'I' of a dreamer awakened by inspired speech and realised only in that speech.

This is the sum of the poet's personality. This is the law of his idiosyncrasy. This is why poets are all so alike and so unalike. Like, because all without exception have dreams. Unlike, in what dreams they have. Like—in their ability to dream; unlike—in the dreams.

All poets can be divided into poets with development and poets without development. Into poets with history and poets without history. The first could be depicted graphically as an arrow shot into infinity; the second—as a circle.

Above the first (the image of the arrow) stands the law of gradual self-discovery. These poets discover themselves through all the phenomena they meet along their way, at every step and in every new object.

Mine or others', the vital or the superfluous, the accidental and the eternal: everything is for them a touchstone. Of their power, which increases with each new obstacle. Their self-discovery is their coming to self-knowledge through the world, self-knowledge of the soul through the visible world. Their path is the path of experience. As they walk, we physically sense a wind, the air they cleave with their brows. A wind blows from them.

They walk without turning round. Their experience accumulates as if by itself, and piles up somewhere behind, like a load on the back which never makes the back hunch. One doesn't look round at the sack on one's back. The walker knows nothing of his rucksack until the moment he needs it: at the stopping-place. The Goethe of *Götz von Berlichingen* and the Goethe of the *Metamorphosis of Plants* are not acquainted with each other. Goethe put in his sack everything he needed from *himself of that time,* left himself in the wondrous forests of young Germany and of his own youth, and went—onward. Had the mature Goethe met the young Goethe at a crossroads, he might actually have failed to recognise him and might have sought to make his acquaintance. I'm not talking of Goethe the person, but of Goethe the creator, and I take this great example as an especially evident one.

Poets with history (like people with history in general and like history itself) do not even renounce themselves: they simply don't turn round to themselves—no time for it, only onward! Such is the law of movement and of pressing forward.

The Goethe of *Götz,* the Goethe of *Werther,* the Goethe of the *Roman Elegies,* the Goethe of the *Theory of Colours,* and so on—where is he? Everywhere. Nowhere. How many are there? As many as there are strides. Each step was taken by a different person. One set out, another arrived.

He was no more than the tirelessness of the creative will, the muscle that lifted the walker's foot. The same is true of Pushkin. Maybe this is what genius is?

The loneliness of such walkers! People look for a person you yourself would no longer recognise. They fall in love with the one of you whom you have already disavowed. They give their trust to one you have outgrown. From Goethe, until he was eighty-three (the year of his death), people went on demanding *Götz* (Goethe at twenty!). And—a smaller but nearer example—from the [Alexander] Blok of *The Twelve* they still demand 'The Unknown Woman'.

This is what our Russian Goethean, the poet and philosopher Vyacheslav Ivanov, now living in Padua, meant when he wrote his fine lines:

> The one whose name you trumpet
> has taken another name,
> the one you love today
> has already ceased being loved.
>
> ['Lichinu obvetshaloyu']

It isn't a question of age; we all change. The point is that the mature Goethe didn't understand his own youth. Some poets grow young in their old age: Goethe's *Trilogy of Passion* was written by a seventy-year-old! It's a question of one thing replacing another, of opening horizons, of previously concealed spaces. It's a question of the quantity of minutes, of the infinity of tasks, of the immensity of his Columbus-like strengths. And the rucksack on the back (Goethe really did walk about with a bag for collecting stones and minerals) gets heavier and heavier. And the road keeps stretching ahead. And the shadows grow. And you can neither exhaust your strength nor reach the end of the road!

Poets with history are, above all, poets of a theme. We always know what they are writing about. And, if we don't learn where they were going to, we do at least realise, when their journey is completed, that they had always been going somewhere (the existence of a goal). Rarely are they pure lyricists. Too large in size and scope, their own 'I' is too small for them—even the biggest is too small—or they spread it out till nothing is left and it merges with the rim of the horizon (Goethe, Pushkin). The human 'I' becomes the 'I' of a country—a people—a given continent—a century—a millennium—the heavenly vault (Goethe's geological 'I': 'I live in the millennia'). For such a poet a theme is the occasion for a new self, and not necessarily a human one. Their whole earthly path is a sequence of reincarnations, not necessarily into a human being. From a human to a stone, a flower, a constellation. They seem to incarnate in themselves all the days of creation.

Poets with history are, above all, poets of will. I don't mean the will to fulfil, which is taken for granted: no one will doubt that a physically huge bulk like *Faust,* or indeed any poem of a thousand lines, cannot come into being by itself. Eight, sixteen or, rarely, twenty lines may come about by themselves—the lyric tide most often lays fragments at our feet, albeit the most precious ones. I mean the will to choose, the will to have choice. To decide not merely to become another, but—this particular other. To decide to part with oneself. To decide—like the hero in the fairy tale—between right, left and straight on (but, like that same hero, never backward!). Waking up one morning, Pushkin makes a decision: 'Today I shall write Mozart!' This Mozart is his refusal to a multitude of other visions and subjects; it is total choice—that is, a sacrifice. To use contemporary vocabulary, I'd say that the poet with history rejects everything that lies outside his general line—the line of his personality, his gift, his history. The choice is made by his infallible instinct for the most important. And yet, at the end of Pushkin's path, we have the sense that Pushkin could not have done otherwise than create what he did create, could not have written anything he did not write . . . And no one regrets that in Gogol's favour he refused the *Dead Souls* project, something that lay on Gogol's general line. (The poet with history also has a clear view of others—Pushkin had, especially.) The main feature of poets of this sort is the striving towards a goal. A poet without history cannot have a striving towards a goal. He himself doesn't know what the lyric flood will bring him.

Pure lyric poetry has no project. You can't make yourself have a particular dream or feel a particular feeling. Pure lyricism is the sheer condition of going through something, suffering something through, and in the intervals (when the poet is not being summoned by Apollo to holy sacrifice), in the ebbs of inspiration, it is a condition of infinite poverty. The sea has departed, carried everything away, and won't return *before its own time*. A continual, awful hanging in the air, on the word of honour of perfidious inspiration. And suppose one day it lets you go?

Pure lyric poetry is solely the record of our dreams and feelings, along with the entreaty that these dreams and feelings should never run dry . . . To demand more from lyricism . . . But what *more* could be demanded from it?

The lyric poet has nothing to grasp hold of: he has neither the skeleton of a theme nor obligatory hours of work at a desk; no material he can dip into, which he's preoccupied with or even immersed in, at the ebb times: he is wholly suspended on a thread of trust.

Don't expect sacrifices: the pure lyricist sacrifices nothing—he is glad when anything comes at all. Don't expect moral choice from him either—whatever comes, 'bad' or 'good', he is so happy it has come at all that to you (society, morality, God) he won't yield a thing.

The lyric poet is given only the will to fulfil his task, just enough for sorting out the tide's offerings.

Pure lyricism is nothing but the recording of our dreams and sensations. The greater the poet, the purer the record.

A walker and a stylite. For the poet without history is a stylite or—same thing—a sleeper. Whatever may happen around his pillar, whatever the waves of history may create (or destroy), he sees, hears and knows only what is his. (Whatever may be going on around him, he sees only his own dreams.) Sometimes he seems to be really great, like Boris Pasternak, but the small and the great draw us equally irresistibly into the enchanted circle of dream. We too turn into stone.

To exactly the extent that other people's dreams, when they tell us them, are inexpressive and uninfectious, these lyric dreams are irresistible, affecting us more than our own!

> Now beyond the slumbering mountain
> the evening ray has faded.
> In a resounding stream the hot
> spring faintly sparkles . . .
>
> ['Svidanie']

These lines by the young Lermontov are more powerful than all my childhood dreams—and not only childhood, and not only mine.

It could be said of poets without history that their soul and their personality are formed in their mother's womb. They don't need to learn or acquire or fathom anything at all—they know everything from the start. They don't ask about anything—they make manifest. Evidence, experience are nothing to them.

Sometimes the range of their knowledge is very narrow. They don't go beyond it. Sometimes the range of their knowledge is very wide. They never narrow it to oblige experience.

They came into the world not to learn, but to say. To say what they already know: everything they know (if it is a lot) or the only thing they know (if it is just one thing).

They came into the world to make themselves known. Pure lyricists, only-lyricists, don't allow anything alien into themselves, and they have an instinct for this just as poets with history have an instinct for their own general line. The whole empirical world is to them a foreign body. In this sense they have the power to choose, or more exactly, the power to select, or more exactly still, the power to reject. But the rejection is done by the whole of their nature, not by their will alone. And is usually unconscious. In this, as in much, maybe in everything, they are children. Here is how the world is for them: 'That's the wrong way.'—'No, it's the right way! I know! I know better!' What does he know? That any other way is impossible. They are the absolute opposite: I am the world (meaning the human world—society, family, morality, ruling church, science, common-sense, any form of power—human organisation in general, including our much-famed 'progress'). Enter into the poems and the biography too, which are always a single whole.

For poets with history there are no foreign bodies, they are conscious participants in the world. Their 'I' is equal to the world. From the human to the cosmic.

Here lies the distinction between the genius and the lyric genius. There do exist purely lyric geniuses. But we never call them 'geniuses'. The way this kind of genius is closed upon himself, and doomed to himself, is expressed in the adjective 'lyrical'. Just as the boundlessness of the genius, his impersonality even, is expressed by the absence, even impossibility, of any adjective whatever. (Every adjective, since it gives an exact meaning, is limiting.)

The 'I' cannot be a genius. A genius may call itself 'I', dress itself in a certain name, make use of certain earthly tokens. We must not forget that among ancient peoples 'genius' signified quite factually a good higher being, a divinity from above, not the person himself. Goethe was a genius because above him there hovered a genius. This genius distracted and sustained him up to the end of his eighty-third year, up to the last page of *Faust* Part Two. That same genius is shown in his immortal face.

A last, and perhaps the simplest, explanation. Pure lyric poetry lives on feelings. Feelings are always the same. Feelings are not regular or consistent. They are all given to us at once, all the feelings we are ever to experience; like the flames of a torch, they are squeezed into our breast from birth. Feeling (the childhood of a person, a nation, the planet) always starts at a maximum, and in strong people and in poets it remains at that maximum. Feeling doesn't need a cause, it itself is the cause of everything. Feeling doesn't need experience, it knows everything earlier and better. (Every sentiment is also a presentiment.) Someone in whom there is love, loves; someone in whom there is anger, gets angry; and someone in whom there is a sense of hurt, is hurt, from the day he is born. Sensitivity to hurt gives rise to hurt. Feeling doesn't need experience, it knows in advance that it is doomed. There's nothing for feeling to do on the periphery of the visible, it is in the centre, is itself the centre. There's nothing for feeling to seek along any roads, it knows that it will come—will lead—into itself.

An enchanted circle. A dream circle. A magic circle.

Thus once again:

> Thought is an arrow.
> Feeling is a circle.

This is the essence of the purely lyrical sort of poet, the nature of pure lyricism. And if they sometimes seem to develop and change—it is not *they* that develop and change, but only their vocabulary, their linguistic equipment.

Few lyricists are given the right words, their own words, from the start! From helplessness, they often begin with others' words—not their own, but universal ones (and often it's precisely at that stage that they please the majority, which sees in them its own nothingness). Then, when they start talking their own language, sometimes very soon, we think they have changed and grown up. Yet it's not they who have grown, but their language-self, which has reached them in its growth. Not even the greatest musician can express himself on a child's keyboard.

Some children are born with a ready-made soul. No child is born with ready-made speech. (Or just one was—Mozart.) Pure lyricists, too, learn to talk, for the language of poets is the physics of their creativity, their soul's body, and each body has got to develop. The hardest thing of all for a lyric poet is to find his own language, not his own feeling, as he has that from his birth. But there is no pure lyricist who hasn't already conveyed himself in his childhood—his definitive and fated self—announced his whole self in some fairly complete and exhaustive stanza of four or eight lines, one that he will never offer again and that could stand as an epigraph to the whole of his work, a formula for his whole fate. A first stanza, which could also be the last: a pre-life stanza which could also be a pre-death one (inscription on a tombstone).

Such is Lermontov's 'The Sail'. Pure lyric poets, the majority of them, are children of very early development (and of very short life, both as persons and as writers)—or rather of very early insight, with a presentiment of their being doomed to poetry—*Wunderkinder* in the literal sense, having a wide-awake sense of fate, that is to say of themselves.

The poet with history never knows what is going to happen to him. It is his genius that knows this, guiding him and revealing to him only as much as he needs for free movement: a proximate goal, a sense of direction, constantly keeping the main thing hidden round a turning. The pure lyricist always knows that nothing is going to happen to him, that he will have nothing but himself: his own tragic lyric experience.

Take Pushkin who began with his *lycée* verses, and Lermontov who began with 'The Sail'. In Pushkin's first poems we discern nothing of Pushkin whatsoever—only the genius Derzhavin was able to glimpse the future genius in the living face, voice and gesture of the youth. But in the eighteen-year-old Lermontov's 'The Sail' all Lermontov is present, the Lermontov of turbulence, offence, duel, death. The young Pushkin could not have had such a poem as the 'The Sail'—but not because his talent was undeveloped: he was no less gifted than Lermontov. Simply, Pushkin, like every poet with history, and like history itself, began at the beginning—like Goethe too—and then spent all his life *im Werden* ('in becoming') while Lermontov—immediately—'was'. To find himself, Pushkin had to live not one life, but a hundred. While Lermontov, to find himself, had only to be born.

Of our contemporaries I will name three exceptional cases of perfection in the innate lyrical quality: Anna Akhmatova, Osip Mandelstam and Boris Pasternak, poets born already equipped with their own vocabulary and with maximum expressiveness.

When in the first poem of her first book, the young Akhmatova conveys the confusion of love in the lines:

> I drew my left-hand glove
> onto my right hand—
>
> ['Pesnya Poslednei vstrechi']

she conveys at one blow all feminine and all lyric confusion (all the confusion of the empirical!), immortalising with one flourish of the pen that ancient nervous gesture of woman and of poet who at life's great moments forget right and left—not only of glove, but of hand, and of country of the world, suddenly losing all their certainty. Through a patent and even penetrating precision of detail, something bigger than an emotional state is affirmed and symbolised—a whole structure of the mind. (A poet lets go the pen, a woman lets go her lover's hand, and immediately they can't tell the left hand from the right.) In brief, from these two lines of Akhmatova's, a broad, abundant flow of associations comes into being, associations which spread like the circles from a flung pebble. The whole woman, the whole poet is in these two lines; the whole Akhmatova, unique, unrepeatable, inimitable. Before Akhmatova none of us portrayed a gesture like this. And no one did after her. (Of course, Akhmatova is not only this gesture; I'm giving just one of her main characteristics.) 'Again or still?' was what I asked in 1916, about Akhmatova who in 1912 had begun by dipping the same jug into the same sea. Now, seventeen years later, I can see that then, without suspecting it, she had provided the formula for a lyric constant. Listen to the image: it has a depth. Look at its movement: it conveys roundness. The roundness of the dipping gesture, essentially deep. A jug. A sea. Together they constitute volume. Thinking about it today, seventeen years later, I might say: 'the same bucket into the same well', preferring an accurate image to a beautiful one. But the essence of the image would be the same. I offer this as yet another instance of lyric constancy.

I've never heard anyone say, about Akhmatova or Pasternak: 'Same thing over and over again—boring!' Just as you cannot say 'Same thing over and over again—boring!' about the sea, of which Pasternak wrote the following:

> All becomes dull, only you never grow familiar—
> days pass, years pass, thousands and thousands of
>   years . . .
>
> ['The Year 1905']

For, both Akhmatova and Pasternak scoop not from the surface of the sea (the heart), but from its depth (the fathomless). They can't become boring, just as sleep can't be boring—which is always the same, but with always different dreams. Just as dreaming can't be boring.

When you approach something, you need to know what you may expect from it. And you must expect from it its own self, that which constitutes its being. When you approach the sea—and the lyric poet—you are not going for something new, but for the same again; for a repetition, not a continuation. Lyric poetry, like the sea, even when you're discovering it for the first time, is something you invariably re-read; while with a river, which flows past, as with Pushkin, who walks past—if it's on their banks you've been born—you always read *on*. It is the difference between the crossways, lulling, lyrical motion of the sea, and the linear, never-returning movement of a river. The difference between being somewhere and passing by. You love the river because it is always different, and you love the sea because it is always the same. If you desire novelty, settle by a river.

Lyric poetry, like the sea, rouses and calms itself, happens within itself. Not in vain did Heraclitus say: 'Nobody steps twice into the same river', taking, as his symbol of flowing, not the sea which he saw before him every day and knew well, but—a river.

When you go to the sea and to the lyricist, you are not going for the never returning flow of the current, you're going for the ever-returning flow of the waves; not for the unrepeatable moment, not for the intransient, but precisely for the repeatability of the unforeseen in sea and in lyric, for the invariability of changes and exchanges, for the inevitability of your amazement at them.

Renewal! This is where their power over us lies, the might which sustains all worship of the divine, all sorcery, all magic, all invoking, all cursing, all human and non-human unions. Even the dead are summoned three times.

Who will say to the great and the genuine: 'Be different!'

Be!—is our silent prayer.

To the poet with history we say: 'Look further!' To the poet without history: 'Dive deeper!' To the first: 'Further!' To the second: 'More!'

And if some poets seem dull because of their monotony, then this comes from the shallowness and smallness (the drying up) of the image, not from the fact that the image remains the same. (A dried up sea is no longer a sea.) If a poet bores us with monotony, I'll undertake to prove that he is not a great poet, his imagery is not great. If we take a saucer for a sea, that is not its fault.

Lyricism, for all that it is doomed to itself, is itself inexhaustible. (Perhaps the best formula for the lyrical and for the lyric essence is this: being doomed to inexhaustibility!) The more you draw out, the more there remains. This is why it never disappears. This is why we fling ourselves with such avidity on every new lyric poet: maybe he'll succeed in drawing out all that essence which is the soul, thereby slaking our own? It's as if they were all trying to get us drunk on bitter, salty, green sea-water and each time we believe it is drinking-water. And once again it turns out bitter! (We must not forget that the structure of the sea, of the blood, and of lyricism—is one and the same.)

What's true of dull people is true of dull poets: what's dull is not the monotony, but the fact that the thing repeated—though it may be very varied—is insignificant. How murderously identical are the newspapers on the table, with all their various dissonances; how murderously identical are the Parisian women in the streets with all their variety! As if these things—advertisements, newspapers, Parisian women—were not varied, but were all the same. At all the crossroads, in all the shops and trams, at all auctions, in all concert-halls—innumerable, and yet, however many, they all amount to one thing! And this one thing is: everyone!

It is boring when, instead of a human face, you see something worse than a mask: a mould for the mass production of facelessness: paper money with no security in gold! When, instead of a person's own words, no matter how clumsy, you hear someone else's, no matter how brilliant (which, by the way, straightaway lose their brilliance—like the fur on a dead animal). It is boring when you hear from the person you're talking to not his own words, but somebody else's. Moreover, if a repetition has bored you, you can be pretty sure it's a case of someone else's words—words not created, but repeated. For one cannot repeat oneself in words: even the slightest change in the speech means it is not a repetition but a transformation with another essence behind it. Even if one tries to repeat a thought of one's own, already expressed, one will involuntarily do it differently every time; the slightest change and something new is said. Unless one learns it by heart. When a poet is obviously 'repeating himself', it means he has abandoned his creative self and is robbing himself just as if he were robbing someone else.

In calling renewal the pivot of lyricism, I don't mean the renewal of my own or others' dreams and images, I only mean the return of the lyric wave in which the composition of the lyrical is constant.

The wave always returns, and always returns as a different wave.

The same water—a different wave.

What matters is that it is a *wave*.

What matters is that the wave *will return*.

What matters is that it will *always* return *different*.

What matters most of all: however different the returning wave, it will always return as a wave of the *sea*.

What is a wave? Composition and muscle. The same goes for lyric poetry.

Similarity, variation on the same, is not repetition. Similarity is in the nature of things, at the basis of nature itself. In the renewing (the constant developing) of the given forms of trees, not one oak repeats its neighbour, and on one and the same oak not one leaf repeats a preceding one. Similarity in nature: creation of the similar, not of the same; the like, not the identical; new, not old; creation, not repetition.

Each new leaf is the next variation on the eternal theme of the oak. Renewal in nature: infinite variation on a single theme.

Repetition does not happen in nature, it is outside nature, thus outside creativity too. That is the way it is. Only

Tsvetaeva with her husband, Sergei Efron, in 1911.

machines repeat. In 'poets who repeat', the machine of memory, separated from the springs of creativity, has become a mere mechanism. Repetition is the purely mechanical reproduction of something which inevitably turns into someone else's, even when it is one's own. For, if I've learnt my own thought by heart, I repeat it as though it were someone else's, without the participation of anything creative. It may be that only the intonation is creative, is mine, the feeling, that is, with which I utter it and change its form, the linguistic and semantic vicinity in which I place it. But when, for example, I write on a blank page the bare formula I once found: 'Etre vaut mieux qu'avoir' ('it's better to be than to have'), I repeat a formula which doesn't belong to me any more than an algebraic one does. A thing can only be created once.

Self-repetition, that is self-imitation, is a purely external act. Nature, creating its next leaf, does not look at the already created leaves, doesn't look because it has in itself the whole form of the future leaf: it creates out of itself by an inner image and without a model. God created man in his own image and likeness without repeating himself.

In poetry, every self-repetition and self-imitation is, above all, imitation of form. One steals from oneself or from one's neighbour a certain verse-form, certain phrases, certain public figures or even a theme (thus everyone steals rain from Pasternak, for example, but no one loves it except him and no one serves it except him). No one has the power to steal the essence (their own or another's). Essence cannot be imitated. Therefore, all imitative poems are dead. If they're not dead but stir us with live agitation, then they're not an imitation but a transformation. To imitate means to annihilate in every case—it means destroying the thing to see how it is made; stealing from it the secret of its life, and then reinstating everything except the life.

Some poets start with a minimum and end with the maximum, some start with a maximum and end with the minimum (drying up of the creative vein). And some start with a maximum and stay at this maximum right up to their last line—among our contemporaries, Pasternak and Akhmatova, mentioned already. These never gave either more or less, but always stayed at a maximum of self-expression. If for some there is a path of self-discovery, for these there is no path at all. From their birth, they are here. Their childish babble is a sum, not a source.

> The soft careful break
> of a fruit off a tree
> amidst ceaseless music
> of deep forest quietness.

This quatrain by the seventeen-year-old Osip Mandelstam has in it the whole vocabulary and metre of the mature Mandelstam. A formula for himself. What was the first thing to touch the ear of this lyricist? The sound of a falling apple, the acoustic vision of roundness. What signs are there here of a seventeen-year-old? None. What is there here of Mandelstam? Everything. To be precise: this ripeness of the falling fruit. The stanza is that very falling fruit which he depicts. And, just as from the two lines by Akhmatova, there are unusually wide circles of associations. Of round and warm, of round and cold, of August, Augustus (the emperor), the Hesperides, Paris, Eden, Adam (the throat): Mandelstam gives the reader's imagination all this in a single stanza. (Evocative power of lyricists!) Characteristic of the lyrical: in conveying this apple, the poet did not explicitly name it. And, in a sense, he never departed from this apple.

Who can talk of the poetic path of (to take the greatest, most indisputable lyricists) Heine, Byron, Shelley, Verlaine, Lermontov? They have covered the world with their feelings, laments, sighs and visions, drenched it with their tears, set fire to it on all sides with their indignation.

Do we learn from them? No. We suffer for them and because of them.

It is the French proverb, retailored in my Russian style: 'Les heureux n'ont pas d'historie' ['Happy people have no history'].

One exception, a pure lyricist who did have development and history and a path: Alexander Blok. But, having said 'development', I see that I've not only taken the wrong direction but used a word that contradicts Blok's essence and fate. Development presupposes harmony. Can there

be a development which is—catastrophic? And can there be harmony when what we see is a soul being torn completely apart? Here, without playing with words, but making a severe demand on them and answering for them, I assert: Blok, for the duration of his poetic path, was not developing, but was tearing himself apart.

One could say of Blok that he was trying to escape from one himself to another. From one which tormented him. To another which tormented him even more. The peculiarity is this hope of getting away from himself. Thus a mortally wounded man will run wildly from the wound, thus a sick man tosses from land to land, then from room to room, and finally from side to side.

If we see Blok as a poet with history, then it is solely the history of Blok the lyric poet, of lyricism itself, of suffering. If we see Blok as a poet with a path, then the path consists of running in circles away from himself.

Stopping to draw breath.

And entering the house, to meet oneself there once again!

The sole difference is that Blok started running at birth, while others stayed in one place.

Only once did Blok succeed in running away from himself—when he ran onto the cruel road of the Revolution. That was the leap of a dying man from his bed, of a man fleeing from death into the street, which won't notice him, into the crowd, which will trample him. Into Blok's physically collapsing and spiritually undermined personality rushed the elemental force of the Revolution, with its songs and demons—and it crushed that body. Let us not forget that the last word of *The Twelve* is 'Christ', which was one of the first words Blok spoke.

Such were this pure lyric poet's history, development and path.

Angela Livingstone (essay date 1971)

SOURCE: "Marina Tsvetaeva and Russian Poetry," in *Melbourne Slavonic Studies*, Nos. 5-6, 1971, pp. 178-93.

[*Below, Livingstone discusses Tsvetaeva's place within Russian poetry. She points out aspects of Symbolism, Acmeism, and Futurism in Tsvetaeva's verse.*]

I.

Pasternak said that Marina Tsvetaeva achieved just what the Symbolists wanted to achieve and did it better. The early Tsvetaeva was

> exactly what all the other symbolists, taken together, wanted to be and couldn't. Where their literary efforts helplessly thrashed about in a world of thought-up schemes and lifeless archaisms, Tsvetaeva soared

easily above the difficulties of genuine creation, solved its problems effortlessly, with incomparable technical brilliance. ["Three Shadows," in *Autobiographical Sketch,* 1958].

Simon Karlinsky says [in his *Marina Tsvetaeva, her life and work,* 1966] that she did what . . . the Futurists wanted to do, and, again, that she did it better:

> In terms of language and versification, the poetry of **Posle Rossii** is a staggering accomplishment—a synthesis of meaning, word, and verbal music which the Russian Futurist poetry strove for and so rarely achieved to such a degree.

Where then does Marina Tsvetaeva belong in Russian poetry? She never joined any school or movement, nor did she consider herself to be a member of either. She was born in the early 1890s, years in which many other great Russian poets were born. She was already writing poetry during the period dominated by Symbolism (her first volume of verse appeared in print in 1910). She lived and wrote in Russia during the emergence of two very vocal new schools of thought about the nature of poetry—Acmeism and Futurism, both of which came into being in 1909. They introduced poetic methods and philosophies which they saw as overcoming Symbolism. Tsvetaeva was still in Russia in the early post-revolution period when, after the demise of both Symbolism and Acmeism, and despite the brief proliferation of other schools, Futurism went on developing and establishing itself. In much of her work she often expresses passionate admiration for other poets, especially for Blok, the greatest of the Symbolists, and for Vološin, also a Symbolist; for Mandel'štam and Akhmatova, two very great poets who were both, in their early writing years, closely associated with Acmeism; for Mayakovsky, the best-known and most talented of the Russian Futurists; and for Pasternak, who, like herself, belonged to no school.

A new school means a new description of the act of creation and of the nature or status of poetry, self-consciously distinguishing itself from previous descriptions, as well as an intentional concentration upon and development of certain chosen techniques. Tsvetaeva, though she gives a new description of creation, and though she very powerfully develops new techniques, does not consciously classify herself while doing so. I want to show what I think are 'symbolist' and 'futurist' elements in her view of what the poet is, and what poetry means. But first I shall discuss under these two headings some of the qualities and devices of her own verse.

The Symbolist sought to evoke, by a central use of symbol, and the conveying of a powerful *sense* of symbol, some meaning greater than that of the words and phrases of his poem—whether 'the subtlest overtones of things' (Annesky) or the 'sensibly real and the mystical . . . fused in an indissoluble unity' (Volynsky). In brief, it is the way things are more than how they seem. They point to a reality 'more real' than the ordinary one. Acmeist and Futurist both attacked this notion. The former demanded, instead, the lucid evocation of tangible non-mysterious phenomena of this world, stressing that a poem is a verbal *construction;* the latter also insisted, but much more violently and militantly, that the word itself, not its vague connotations and indications, is the object the poet deals with. They demanded too that the poet be not merely this-worldly, but also modern—urban, technological and political.

There seems to be little of the Acmeist in Tsvetaeva. The tangible things of this world scarcely mattered to her. 'Everything I love', she writes (in a letter in 1926), 'from the moment of my love stops being external and . . . loses its "objective" value. For example, I have got from the sea, brought by the flowing tide or left by the ebb, a petrified chestnut—a talisman. It isn't a thing. It's a sign. What of? Well, if only of the ebb and flow of the tide.' Unlike some poets, (among her contemporaries most notably Pasternak) she does not see afresh the physical world, hardly cares about Nature; things come into her poetry only as signs and similes. Her bitterest complaint of her lover is that he rejects her as if she were a 'thing':

> To throw away, like a thing,
> Me, who didn't respect
>
> A single thing in this
> Inflated world of things!

II.

The programme and the paraphernalia of Symbolism are utterly lacking in her work. But when we see in the Russian Symbolists' poetry and in their statements about poetry that they communicate, through a careful verbal 'music' and deliberate beauty, finely perceived states of mind, and, more, an elusive something else which is often expressed as the presence of the divine in, or seen through the earthly, then we shall find something of this in Tsvetaeva's earlier verse. There are the simple radiant cosmic images of Romantic and Symbolist poetry—sun, moon, snowstorm, angel, hell, or there is the selecting of the beautiful as subject-matter—the burning domes of Moscow churches, the eyelashes of a charming minstrel. There is, too, the mainly smooth-flowing melodious line and lulling repetition of stressed vowels in a verse that is made (unlike much of her later, more rugged verse) of entire sentences in which the syntax is relatively inconspicuous so that sounds, feelings, hints and evocations may dominate:

> We dressed every morning in
> fine Chinese silk, and we would
> sing our paradisal songs at
> the fire of the robbers' camp.
>
> I shall lead you as a guest from
>   another
> country into the Chapel of the
>   Inadvertent Joy

where pure gold domes will be-
    gin to shine
for you, and sleepless bells will
    will start thundering . . .

Many of her *Poems about Moscow,* the cycle *Insomnia,* poems addressed to Mandel'štam, and a cycle of *Poems to Blok* are melodious and evocative in these ways.

A typically Symbolist feature, moreover, is the adoption of an attitude of adoration. This is found in many of Tsvetaeva's poems of the early period. She adores particularly persons rather than the world, or the other world, or God. She expresses her love or admiration as worship and deifies the person. 'Divine boy' she calls Mandel'štam in one poem and is never afraid of being as outspoken as this. She uses the language of prayer—'Zaxodi—grjadi . . .' (Drop in—be manifest . . .). This is not just a hyperbolic trick; nor is it an exaggerated piece of flattery which would suggest no more than itself and make one think at most about the strength of the poet's emotions. Throughout the *Poems to Blok*—whom she often deifies, or sees as a priest, the ecclesiastical language is used with a rigour and firmness that prune it of excess, and make one think rather of the nature of admiration and the nature of genius. In writing of her admiration for men who were poets she is writing about poetry itself, about the inhering of that other, 'divine', element in human beings. These poems always centre upon a person. They are not philosophical, but express rather the 'divinity' in terms of how Tsvetaeva feels about it. They are, however, just as much the assertion of something 'more', but perhaps expressed with a deliberate bluntness and vigour, neglecting the delicate but worn-out effects of Symbolism. They move away from the earth, not because of any spiritual longing, but rather as if they were leaping away from it with both feet.

In a short poem in 1916 Tsvetaeva confesses that she loves people more than she loves God, but people as *angels.* 'God' is humanised—he is 'bent from worry' and he 'smiles'—but the angels are angels, 'with radiant bodies', 'with vast wings'. The divine element is transferred—without becoming less divine—from 'God' to 'angels'.

which is why I weep
so much
because more than God
I love his fair angels.

From the early Tsvetaeva one hears the shout: 'I know the truth—give up all other truths!' In her later work we find both the repeated declaration that she is not writing for those who cannot understand and the brilliant analysis of 'rightness' as the poet's central experience.

—Angela Livingstone

It is easy enough to point out such similarities, less easy to demonstrate too that peculiar sweep and force one senses in her early poems, that sense of the poet herself walking fast through them.

Most theories of poetry speak of getting back to what is real and genuine. The Symbolist too wanted to lift the veil of familiarity and ordinariness from the world and reveal its pristine strangeness or divinity (similarly, the Futurist wanted to tear all the masks and pretences from everyone (—his 'sryvanie masok'). Perhaps the special quality of Tsvetaeva's poetry derives from the way she does this instinctively and unprogrammatically, and as if there never *were* a veil or mask. Characteristic of all her work is this: the declaring and exhibiting of immediate feeling in all its undisguised detail. The unleashed, point-blank, absolutely unintimidated quality of her poetry is perhaps what makes it her own and unlike either of those schools through which she marches like a walker with rucksack and climbing stick who, though he breathes the air and climate of the lands he is tramping through, keeps his eyes fixed on his road.

III.

"My Sister Life"!—The first thing I did, when I'd borne it all, from the first blow to the last, was spread my arms out wide, so that all the joints cracked. I fell under it as under a downpour.

This was Marina Tsvetaeva's reaction in 1922 to the first volume of verse by Pasternak that she read. The sentence tells us much about her attitude of worship and praise. Worship involves action, reaction, movement and the opening of one's self—'spread my arms out wide'. It also shows her method: the disturbing effect of the sentence comes from the last phrase: 'so that all the joints cracked'. How much more familiar this sentence would have been, how much easier to absorb, had that phrase been left out. She conjoins in one conception not only the emotion with the physical action—its sign and silent language—but also with the more precise details of the action, which, though they do emphasise its wholeness and abandon, are really irrelevant. 'So that all the joints cracked'—this is not just physical—the spreading of arms was already that—but it is uncomfortably detailed, and this is not the absurd detail which another poet might have included in order to debunk the emotion. Yet, why is the emotion not debunked by the cracking of joints? Because of that fearless entirety of body and soul that Tsvetaeva believes in, and because it is an example of telling the truth, not about feeling in a material world but about *her* feeling in *her* body. She is instinctively unconcerned by what we traditionalist readers are looking for.

The attitude of worship is far from being typical of Futurist writing, and it is by no means Tsvetaeva's only attitude. Just as she readily, wholeheartedly, glorifies, so she readily attacks and vilifies—especially the bourgeois philistine, that complacent 'reader of newspapers' in the Paris train, or the stuporous suburb-dweller on the hills of Prague. Her friend and critic, Ivask summed her up as the 'poet of eulogy and slander' ('Poet xvaly i xuly'). And just as clearly she expresses her complete certainty about her own knowledge and gift. Is she arrogant, over self-assured? Among the miseries and disasters of her life, the lack of recognition and her being repudiated by so many people, the poet's inner certainty of rightness stands up—strangely like a column in a falling building. Every poet must have this certainty, which becomes a theme instead of an impulse or implication felt only in particular circumstances, for example, in the poetically permissive atmosphere of Futurism, in an epoch of violence and noise where one has to shout to be heard, in an age where the poet is misunderstood, even rejected by most people. Her *speaking* of the assurance of genius shows the influence of the age, while her *feeling* it is something ageless. Mandel'štam [in his essay *Morning of Acmeism,* 1913] virtually defines the poet as the one who is sure he is right. From Tsvetaeva we hear something like that quite unreasonably convincing claim of D. H. Lawrence (in a letter about matters which are otherwise irrelevant here): 'You tell me I am wrong . . . I am not wrong.' For instance, comparing the poet's creating with the child's playing, she addresses the grown-up (the critic with moral objections): 'By bringing in your conscience you will confuse ours (a creative one). "That isn't the way to play" (you say). But yes, that *is* the way to play.' From the early Tsvetaeva one hears the shout: 'I know the truth—give up all other truths!' In her later work we find both the repeated declaration that she is not writing for those who cannot understand and the brilliant analysis of 'rightness' as the poet's central experience. She compares the writer to the dreaming sleeper:

> A series of doors, behind one of them someone—something (more often terrible) is waiting. The doors are identical. Not this one—not this one—not this one—that one. Who told me? No-one. I recognise the one I need by all the unrecognised ones (the right one by all the wrong ones). And so it is with words. Not this one—not this one—not this one—that one. By the obviousness of the wrong I recognise the right. Native to every sleeper and writer is the blow of recognition . . .

IV.

The 'blow of recognition'. The language of violence and of action is characteristic, and this reminds us of Mayakovsky. In one of her letters to Anna Tesková Tsvetaeva writes that she hates the ocean because it takes away her freedom: to engage with it she has to swim—to become horizontal; she prefers the vertical engagement with mountains; and she hates love because it makes her passive—'waiting to see what it will do for you',—preferring the perpendicular of friendship. Elsewhere she expresses a boundless admiration for Pasternak who 'will never wait for death: much too impatient and eager—he'll throw himself into it head-first, chest-first . . .'; and she writes of creation: 'We throw ourselves under the scourge, like leaves . . . under the rain . . . Sheer joy in the blow as such . . .' Of poems she writes: 'I don't trust poems that pour forth; ones that tear forth, yes!' This dynamism is felt in the rhythms of her poetry. Andrej Bely spoke of her

'unconquerable rhythms'; Vladimir Orlov, editor of the Soviet edition of her poems, says that in these you are kept 'incessantly to attention' by the rhythm, and he describes her with words she used of Mayakovsy: 'The physical heartbeat—the blows of the heart—of a horse that has stood still too long, or of a man who is tied up.'

Rhythm is the most assertive and noticeable element in Tsvetaeva's poetry altogether, and she is particularly original and skilful in finding ways of basing poems upon the rhythms of physical or emotional 'reality' (or in precisely evoking those realities through the invention of suggestive rhythms). This she does with more realistic exactness and consistency than Mayakovsky, despite his theory about it. In the essay *How to Make Verse* (1926) Mayakovsky demanded that the rhythms of poetry should be produced by the actual rhythms of life, and, describing the sources of one of his long poems (*To Sergej Esenin*) he mentioned the rhythms of walking along streets and of riding on trams, getting on and off them. Yet the relation between those 'real' rhythms and the rhythms of that poem has to be expounded and is nothing like so direct as that between some of Tsvetaeva's poetic metres and the rhythms of the movement or feeling that is her poem's subject.

Much of Tsvetaeva's originality lies in this combining of something undisguisedly, extraordinarily simple and basic—the shouting or sobbing throat itself, the very stamping feet of her life—with an intellectual sharpness, with poetic conceits, with literary-technical complexity. She has in common with Futurism the element of violence, the shout about herself, self-assurance as a theme and an attitude—hatred of the conservative and philistine mass.

In all this, she is especially like Mayakovsky; but she is unlike him in that she did not 'tread upon the throat of her song' and her emotional range is far wider than his. She remains lyrical, personal, sensitive, private and scornful of those who limit their sensibility to what they conceive to be 'modern' (she says, in another context 'He is of the twentieth century, but I am before all centuries').

V.

Between Tsvetaeva's poetic techniques and those of Futurism there are many more affinities. Karlinsky says that after 1916 she 'entered the language-conscious area of the Russian literary tradition'. Now Tsvetaeva differs from the Futurist experimenters in that, like Pasternak, she preserves strict traditional stanza forms (generally quatrains) and rhyme schemes. Her metres are often highly original and complex, but they are almost always contained in a very regular pattern. Indeed, the regularity or rigidity of the pattern, contrasting with the oddness of the metres, becomes so conspicuous as to seem a novelty.

Another new device, belonging more to the category of rhythmic than of verbal inventiveness, but having the same effect of novelty and strength and of focus upon both the physicality of the word and the inalienability of its meaning, is the emphatic isolation of the monosyllable. Russian is given to polysyllabic words while English abounds in monosyllables—the bane of English translators from a complexly inflected language. But the English monosyllables are, in the main, articles, prepositions, conjunctions and various particles, which in Russian tend to be either represented by longer words or, more often, omitted altogether. Where Russian does have one-syllable words, these are more usually nouns or parts of verbs, which seem to gain a quite inimitable strength from being in a naturally polysyllabic context and *not* being drained of their originality by a surrounding of unemphasised grammatical monosyllables. Here is an example from lyric 2 of *Poem of the End* which goes, in the original, (with a word-for-word version—in which words joined by hyphens represent a single word in the Russian):

> Burning? Thus again-from-the-start
> Life?—The-simplicity of-poems!
> House, this means: out-of house
> Into the-night.

There are several ways in which monosyllables are highlighted in Tsvetaeva's verse; the exploiting of this natural feature of Russian is one of them. Another is the repetitive placing of such words at the beginning and end of lines. This is most noticeable in an early poem, the remarkable third lyric in the *Insomnia* cycle. Not only does every line end with a monosyllable, but the latter rhymes four times, i.e., there is only one rhyme to each quatrain. Moreover, in almost every case this monosyllable is separated by a dash from its line (which, scanned a little differently, could be complete without it). Here are the first two stanzas, with the English translation which has, as far as possible, preserved this oddity:

> In my enormous city it is night.
>
> As from my sleeping house I go out
>
> And people think perhaps I'm a
>   daughter or wife
> But in my mind is one thought only
>   —night.
>
> The July wind now sweeps a way
>   for me
> From somewhere, some window
>   music though faint
> The wind can blow until the dawn
>   too
> In through the fine walls of the
>   breast rib-cage.

One more device used by Tsvetaeva for the isolating of the monosyllable is the use of an extraordinary hyphen to divide a word into its component syllables—each of them stressed. In lyric 8 (*Poem of the End*) it has essentially a rhythmic-imitative purpose. In lyric 10 there is something similar, but it is there for a semantic purpose. Tsvetaeva separates the first syllable (the prefix) of the

word (meaning 'separation') by a dash from the rest of the word, so that the word, with the variants of it used in the poem, graphically represents its own meaning: 'Rasstaemsja; ras-stavanie . . .' (The effect is not metrical as the word does not acquire two stresses.)

VI.

Two devices remain to be discussed: ellipsis and the basing of a poem upon one dominant syntactic pattern. In her later poems Tsvetaeva uses an elliptical style more and more frequently. An example is the opening lyric of *Poem of the End*. The subject is the beginning of a last meeting with her lover:

> Sky of-bad omens:
> Rust and tin.
> Waited at the-usual place.
> Time: six.
>
> This kiss without sound:
> Lips' paralysis.
> Thus to-empresses the-hand,
> To-dead-people—thus . . .

The effect here is different from that produced in the poem by Fet starting, 'Šopot. Robkoe dyxanie. / Treli solov'ja. (Whispering. Timid breathing. / Trills of the nightingale . . .)', with which it is comparable for its omission of parts of speech. Fet's poem is famous for a skilful creating of atmosphere without the use of verbs, and the reader does not specially notice their absence. He may even check with surprise afterwards to find there are no verbs. When, as in this case, Tsvetaeva omits verbs almost altogether, or, as very often, she omits the small auxiliary words, she makes their omission as perceptible as possible. Their absence jolts and increases the oddness and vigour of the rhythm. What is the connection between 'rust' and 'sky'? Who 'waited'? The time of day is told as if by telegram. 'Kiss' is omitted from 'thus the hand of empresses'; and so is 'hand' from the last line with its meaning of 'Thus one kisses dead people's hands'.

The pruning away of particles from the imagery is accompanied by the parallel device of a sharp reduction of environment: 'Sky', unspecified 'rust and tin', 'empresses' (or rather, more generally, 'grand ladies'), 'the dead'. The 'furniture' of the poem is existential; emotions are as fiercely laid bare among the sharply selected *words,* as rhythmic stresses are.

VII.

Tsvetaeva is most original of all in her syntax. Sometimes, in the fundamentally elliptical poems (like the one quoted above), verbs are omitted, so that there is no clear syntax at all. More often, syntactic forms are not only fully present, but there is an intensification of the normal, if poetically compressed, syntactic unit intensified by an extravagantly unvarying repetition of it. Very often this is done in phrases dominated by the instrumental case (a noun case in Russian—rendered not only by 'through' or 'by' or 'by means of' but also, or alternatively, by 'like' or 'as'). A simple example is lyric 2 of *Poem of the End*. After the first two lines,

> A gipsy brotherhood,
> That's what it's led to!

there come six lines, forming a single unit, in which the poet talks of what she sees has happened to the word 'house' (or 'home') now that she has to part with her lover. The irony of the last word in the preceding lyric: 'home'—for they have no home—recalling these images of lyric 2; and it is characteristically an obvious, not specially subtle irony:

> Thunder onto the-head,
> Sword drawn,
> All the-horrors
> Of-words which we-expect
> House collapsing—

'thunder', 'sword', 'horrors', 'house' are all in the instrumental case, so we ask what is the word that will be likened to or identified with these things; and when we read the last line:

> The-word: house.

we are surprised by the least expected of all words, for it has just been said to be like, or to *be,* 'a house collapsing'.

Karlinsky has discussed Tsvetaeva's 'maximal exploitation of the expressive possibilities of two oblique cases, the instrumental and the dative', finding that she uses the instrumental 'with a frequency that seems to exceed its average occurrence in Russian', that she shows a 'definite preference for prepositions and verbs that govern the instrumental' and that she often gives us a set of nouns in an 'energetic-sounding instrumental case', to which no verbs are supplied and the meaning of which is never made clear, or perhaps much later in the poem. . . . I want to draw attention to something not mentioned by Karlinsky, to the fact that almost all the lyrics in *Poem of the End* are based, each one, upon an extraordinary repetition of a single syntactic form. Lyric 3 may be quoted here as an example of this. The following is a word-for-word translation of the first four stanzas of the poem. They are not divided up (a double stroke indicates the end of each quatrain, a single one the end of a line) because I want to emphasise only the varied repeating of the unvaried syntactic unit within the whole statement of the emotion. This repetition itself and its distribution is, and before one deliberately considers its meaning, enthralling at first reading:

> . . . To the water / I hold, as to a solid thickness / Gardens of Semiramis / hanging—so there you are! / / To this water—it's a steel strip / of mortuary colour /— I hold, as to the sheet of music / The singer (holds), (as to) the edge of a wall / / A blind man (holds) . . . Won't you give it back? / No? If I bow down, will you hear? / To the all-quencher of thirsts / I hold, as to the edge of a roof / / the lunatic (holds) . . . But the shiver is not from the river / I was born a naiad! / To hold to the river as to a hand / When your beloved is beside (you) . . .

And there are instances of this device that, far more than merely enthralling and beautiful, will, when looked at closely, show us how the delighted play with syntax, the sheer controlled dance of grammar, belongs at the very heart of the poet's creation; *poetry itself* is revealed in the brilliant syntax of Tsvetaeva.

VIII.

Tsvetaeva shares with all the major poets of her time an intense concern with the origin of poetry, or with the nature of inspiration. Many poets have made this, implicitly or explicitly, the subject of their poems. Tsvetaeva wrote about it mainly in her works of prose, the remarkable essays on her own life, on literature, and on poets she knew, written in the years of her emigration.

For the Symbolist the source of poetry lay in a dimension of reality other than and higher than this ordinary one; on a divine or ideal or supernatural level, 'more real' than the everyday level. The poet, transported by a more than individual, more than earthly ecstasy, participated in a higher truth. He received it, and, in imperfect form, communicated it to others. In the years after his properly Symbolist period Blok modified the otherworldliness of such a notion of the origin of poetry, and developed a concept of 'music' that had less to do with the transcendental realm than with the dynamic essence of history, culture and things happening in the world. But he still saw the experience of inspiration as a kind of reception, something immense, rationally unfathomable, and taking place outside ourselves. In our best moments we listen to it, become one with it and discover symbols for it.

> "There are . . . two times, two spaces; one is that of history, that of the calendar, the other is incalculable, musical . . . we live in the second kind only when we give ourselves to the wave of music issuing from the world orchestra . . .'

The Acmeist, in opposition to this notion, saw the poet as a craftsman who, like a sculptor or architect, or—if we make an analogy with music—like Bach setting up the logical frameworks of his fugues and constructing his order of words. The words were as real as bricks; they referred to ordinary tangible realities and the work was ultimately logical, rational, coherent, explicit, unmysterious; they asserted existence against non-existence as (in Mandel'štam's image) a church steeple asserts physical presence against space, cutting into and assaulting the void of the sky.

The Futurist too insisted that the word itself was the reality rather than some higher than verbal sphere of which it could become an imperfect reflector or to which it could point. He insisted that poetry had to be about, and related to not merely everyday things but up-to-date ones. As for the origin of poetry there was no such thing as inspiration; it was, on the contrary, entirely a matter of work. This idea was most consistently developed by Mayakovsky in his essay "How to make Verse" (1926) and in a number of poems, notably "Conversation with the Inspector of Taxes" (1926), where he defends the poet as a worker no different from other workers, labouring away with language as others do with steel and iron, producing rhymes with the difficulty of sodium extraction. The rhythms of a poem come from the ordinary rhythms of physical activity; its words are those of the verbal stock accumulated by the poet in his everyday observations; its themes are prescribed for him by palpable social and political necessities.

What seems the essential distinction here is this: where for the Romantic or Symbolist, poetry comes from 'outside', and is *received* by the poet, the Acmeist and the Futurist, in their different ways, both denied any 'outside', any other reality than 'this' one and insisted that poetry is *made* by us, *inside* the world and *of* the world.

To some extent Tsvetaeva shares the Symbolist experience. The thing that makes poetry, happens, for her, outside the poet. Yet, her formulation of this experience is quite un-symbolist, and, in fact, very much in the language and tone of the Futurist. The loudness and violence with which the latter affirms this world and himself in it is, in the case of Tsvetaeva, joined to a quasi-religious conception of inspiration, in a way that may be unique.

I am talking, of course, of her formulation of that experience. The experience itself is not new. What is interesting is the way different poets, for all sorts of (usually discoverable) reasons, choose to emphasise different aspects of their creative experience (an emphasis much easier to analyse in their statements about poetry than in their poems).

Tsvetaeva's formulation is also different from that of Pasternak, whose view may be roughly summed up as differing from the Symbolists', in that, where they say 'inspiration' comes from outside and we must receive it, he says it happens outside and we must *copy* it:

> Reality arises in a kind of new category. This category seems to us to be its own condition, not ours . . . We try to name it. The result is art . . . Focussed upon a reality that has been displaced by feeling art is a record of the displacement. It copies it from nature . . . Art is realistic by virtue of the fact that it did not itself invent metaphor but found it in nature and faithfully reproduced it.

Tsvetaeva, now, says something like this: inspiration comes from 'outside' but the poet *resists* it. What is her notion of 'resistance'? In *Art in the Light of Conscience* she writes:

> Genius: the highest degree of subjectedness to inspiration—one; control of this inspiration—two. The highest degree of mental disjunction and the highest—of collectedness. The highest—of passivity, and the highest—of activity.

> To let oneself be annihilated right down to some kind of a last atom; from the survival (the resistance) of which will grow up—a world.

> For in this, this, this atom of resistance (resistivity) lies the whole of mankind's chance of genius. Without

it there is no genius—there is the crushed man, who (it is the same man!) strains the walls not only of Bedlams and Charentons, but also of the most prosperous dwellings.

> There is no genius without will, but still more is there none, still less is there any, without inspiration. Will is that unit to the countless milliards of inspiration thanks to which alone they are milliards (they realise their milliardness) and without which they are zeros—that is, bubbles above the drowner. But will without inspiration—in creation—is simply a stake. An oaken one. Such a poet would do better to go for a soldier.

The fundamental structure of the *experience* Tsvetaeva refers to here is not so very different from Vjačeslav Ivanov's Dionysian-Apollonian diagram of the ascent of the poet to the place of mystical communion with the World-Soul, to which, he says, 'many go up' but from which 'few come down',—i.e. few make a work of art of that knowledge. Tsvetaeva seems to believe that many may be annihilated but few (she implies) possess the 'atom of resistance', which is the only thing that *counts*.

In the same essay, a little later on,—after saying that art does not teach anything, for 'all the lessons which we draw from art *we* put into it', she adds:

> Art is a series of answers to which there are no questions. All art is the sole givenness of the answer . . . All *our* art is in our being able (managing in time) to put to each answer, before it should evaporate, our *own* question. This outgalloping of you with answers is what inspiration is. And how often it is a blank page.

If the Symbolist waits for revelation, accepts the vision when it comes, falls back into the boredom of the everyday when it passes, while the Futurist, far from waiting for, or passively recognising anything, actively asserts *himself* in the labour of *making* verse, then Tsvetaeva is like both in her combination of revelation and self-assertion, of overwhelming vision and the ego's resistance to it.

The interesting thing is that, again unlike those poets with whom in some ways she has so much in common, Tsvetaeva is not concerned to make any metaphysical statement about reality. Ivanov states that the poet ascends *into another realm,* or, that *on another level* he becomes one with the universal mind. Pasternak says that *reality* 'arises in a new category', gets into a new 'displaced' condition where all is—'objectively'—symbolical. These views, though exact accounts of states of mind, are expressed as accounts of the world (which is not to belittle them: they are, after all, about states of mind of a kind that can hardly be distinguished from kinds of reality, or they are about the very awareness—not always available—that states of mind are *real*). Tsvetaeva, however, does not resort to philosophy. By sticking to the *experience* she indubitably knows, she is able to describe to the full the inner dynamic of her inspiration. She does not decide what is real, what is unreal or what is more real. By the same token, she is unlike those Futurists who decided that 'this world', or the social world, is real, while somehow what is subjective is not, or is less so. They found too that 'life' was more real, or more valid than 'art', as Mayakovsky implicitly does in his Sergej Esenin poem: 'First we must change the world, and *then* sing it'.

Tsvetaeva's "Parenthesis about poet and child":

The poet is often compared to the child, for their innocence only. I would compare them for their irresponsibility only. Irresponsibility in everything except play.

When you enter this playing with your human (moral) and man-made (social) laws, you only disturb the game and perhaps bring it to an end.

By bringing your conscience into it, you will confuse our (creative) conscience. 'That isn't the way to play.' Yes, it *is* the way to play.

Either the playing should be forbidden altogether (children's by us, ours by God), or it shouldn't be interfered with.

What to you is 'play' is to us the one thing that is serious.

We shall not even die more seriously.

Marina Tsvetaeva, "Art in the Light of Conscience," in Art in the Light of Conscience: Eight Essays on Poetry by Marina Tsvetaeva, *translated by Angela Livingstone, Harvard University Press, 1992.*

A final comment: both Symbolist and Futurist rejected the idea of poetry as an individual activity: the Symbolist believed he escaped the bonds of individuality and communed with the universal consciousness, the world-soul. The Futurist, or at least Mayakovsky, wanted to see his poems as written not by himself alone, but by the whole mass of the people (the title of his poem, *150 Million,* purports to be the number of its authors, and the poem was left unfinished for everyone else to continue). But Tsvetaeva, despite her idea about annihilation, constantly stresses that her art is individual and personal, that it is her own, and is herself. 'Why out of all those who walk along the streets of Moscow is it just me that it comes upon . . . ?'

David McDuff (essay date 1982)

SOURCE: "Poet of Sacrifice," in *The New York Review of Books,* Vol. XXIX, No. 6, April 15, 1982, pp. 6, 8-9.

[*In this review of* Selected Poems of Marina Tsvetayeva, *McDuff surveys Tsvetaeva's life and works and reviews Elaine Feinstein's translations into English of select poems by Tsvetaeva.*]

"Der Weg von der Innigkeit zur Grösse geht durch das Opfer" ("The way from intense inwardness to greatness

leads through sacrifice" [translated by Michael Hamburger, in *An Unofficial Rilke,* 1981]). These words of the essayist Rudolf Kassner form the epigraph to Rainer Maria Rilke's fateful poem "Wendung" (Turning Point) of 1914, in which the poet acknowledged that his shortcomings, his inability to love and to form lasting personal relationships were the source and sustenance of his life's work:

> Werk des Gesichts ist getan,
> tue nun Herz-Werk
> an den Bildern in dir, jenen gefang-
>   enen; denn du
> überwältigtest sie: aber nun kennst
>   du sie nicht.
> Siehe, innerer Mann, dein inneres
>   Mädchen,
> dieses errungene aus
> tausend Naturen, dieses
> erst nur errungene, nie
> noch geliebte Geschöpf.

> (Work of seeing is done,
> now practice heart-work
> upon those images captive within
>   you; for you
> overpowered them only: but now
>   do not know them.
> Look, inward man, look at your in-
>   ward maiden,
> her the laboriously won
> from a thousand natures, at her the
> being till now only
> won, never yet loved.)

At the time he wrote these lines, Rilke believed himself to be utterly alone. With Kassner's help, he had come to see himself as "the consummation of that marvelous Narcissus-like lyricism that began in England with Keats." He did not know that even then, far away in Russia, he had a kindred spirit, a poet who with justification could be described as an "inward maiden" in search of an "inward man." It is tempting to speculate on the course Rilke's poetry might have taken if he had known of Marina Tsvetayeva's existence in 1914. He was to become aware of her only some ten years later, shortly before his death, when he corresponded with her and wrote a remarkable elegy to her. Yet, in a sense, we do not need to speculate: that other, trans-Rilkean poetry was written for him by the *"inneres Mädchen,"* Tsvetayeva herself. This is a mystery that will never be fully explained, and certainly not by literary critics, commentators, or biographers.

Marina Ivanovna Tsvetayeva was born in Moscow on December 26, 1892. Her father, who came from a poor family, was a well-known philologist and art critic, a professor at Moscow University who also founded the Moscow Museum of Fine Arts (now known as the Pushkin Museum of Visual Arts). He died when Marina Tsvetayeva was twenty-one. Her mother came of Russified Polish-German stock: she was a musician, a pupil of Rubinstein. She died early, when her daughter was only fourteen. Tsvetayeva always maintained that her mother had been a leading influence on her: "Music, nature, poetry, Germany. . . . One against all. Heroica."

Tsvetayeva spent most of her childhood and youth in Moscow and nearby Tarusa, but she also traveled with her family to Italy, Switzerland, Germany, and France. These sojourns abroad were in part made necessary by her mother's tuberculosis. During them, Tsvetayeva was educated at Swiss and German boarding schools. She began to write poetry when she was six, not only in Russian, but also in French and German. Her first book of poems was published in 1910, when she was eighteen, a fairly large volume entitled *Vecherniy albom* (*An Evening Album*). The book was quite widely reviewed, and it attracted favorable attention from such influential and demanding poet-critics as Valery Bryusov, Nikolay Gumilyov, and Maksimilian Voloshin. Tsvetayeva's early poetry shows the marks of her reading: there are poems about Napoleon, whom she worshiped, about Edmond de Rostand, about the romantic painter Mariya Bashkirtseva. It also contains clear evidence that she read Pushkin and Goethe.

From its earliest beginnings, Tsvetayeva's poetry had a startling concision and vividness of emotional effect. Much of the greatness of Rilke's poetry lies in the unity of poetic form and the experience he writes about. A similar unity can be found in Marina Tsvetayeva's work; but while Rilke's poems often seem to reach without restraint beyond the immediately personal toward myth, Tsvetayeva's seem more firmly rooted in the personal, emotional, psychological, physical existence of the poet herself. They take their origins in the lived life of the poet—but they move beyond toward the sacrifice of that life. "Here I am," she declares, and we have instantly the sense that her words are her flesh and blood:

> My poems, written down so soon in
>   life, so early
> I did not know I was a poet yet,
> Were torn from me like droplets
>   from a fountain,
> A rocket's sparking jet.
>
> Poems stormed from me, invading,
>   like some minor devils,
> The sanctuary where sleep and incense twine,
> Their themes made up of youth
>   and death, my poems,
> My always unread lines.
>
> Thrown carelessly about the dusty
>   shelves of bookshops,
> Untouched, then, now, by any
>   reader's thumb,
> My poems, stored deep like wines
>   of precious vintage,
> I know their time will come.
>
>   [Critic's translation]

Tsvetayeva wrote these prophetic lines when she was twenty-one, and their rhythmic assurance and formal discipline are already—so early in her career—the hallmark of her passionate and self-sacrificing art.

Kassner writes [in "Erinnerungen an Rilke," *Buch der Erinnerung,* 1954] that Rilke did not want sacrifice: "He certainly wanted the sacrifice of the Old Testament (the fruits of the field, a lamb or whatever things are dear to human beings), but not that of the New." It is likewise doubtful that Tsvetayeva, if she could have foreseen the path her life was to take, would have willingly gone toward the terrors that awaited her.

In her memoirs, Nadezhda Mandelstam says that she knew of no fate more terrible than that of Marina Tsvetayeva. From a hopeful beginning in the literary Moscow of the pre-1914 and war years, during which time she found and married her husband Sergey Efron and befriended the young Osip Mandelstam, Tsvetayeva's life fell further and further under the shadow of ominous political events. After the Bolshevik takeover, Efron escaped to the south of Russia and joined the White Army. Tsvetayeva was trapped in Moscow with her two young daughters. She did not see Efron from 1917 until 1922, and did not even know whether he was alive or not. During the Moscow famine of the immediate postrevolutionary period Tsvetayeva's younger daughter died in the orphanage in which her mother had been forced to leave her. Tsvetayeva and her elder daughter Ariadna lived a life of the most abject poverty, begging (or even stealing) from neighbors, seldom warm, seldom fed. "'I won't leave you.' Only God can say such a thing—or a peasant with milk in Moscow in the winter of 1918," reads one of Tsvetayeva's diary notes.

Tsvetayeva's poetry of the immediate postrevolutionary time is stark, denuded of ornament, directly personal, and yet also addressed to the age and its evil. For her, the White Guards were the "Gordian knot / Of Russian valour," the "black nails / in the ribs of the Antichrist." Soviet literary critics like to claim that Tsvetayeva "neither accepted nor understood" the Bolshevik revolution. The truth is, however, that while she did not accept the revolution—how can one accept murder and mass extermination?—she understood it only too well, and was appalled and deeply, personally repelled by what she saw and experienced:

> Freedom—a drunken whore sprawling
> In a power-maddened soldier's arms.

Barbara Heldt (essay date 1982)

SOURCE: "Two Poems by Marina Tsvetayeva from 'Posle Rossii,'" in *Modern Language Review,* Vol. 77, No. 3, July, 1982, pp. 679-87.

[*In the following excerpt, Heldt offers an analysis of "Rasshchelina" ("The Crevasse") and "Popytka revnosti" ("An Attempt at Jealousy"), exploring the "specifically female frame of reference in these poems."*]

> Power is only Pain—
> Stranded, thro' Discipline, . . .
>
>   Emily Dickinson, *c.* 1861

'Rasshchelina' ('The Crevasse') and 'Popytka revnosti' ('An Attempt at Jealousy') exemplify a kind of poetry at which the great twentieth-century writer Marina Tsvetayeva excelled—the highly disciplined and crafted poetic response to a painful emotion of love irretrievably ended, culminating in the restoration, though partial or transmuted, of the speaker's self. The strategies that open an impasse and reform an absence into a presence, a split into a unity, have a specifically female frame of reference in these poems. The controlling voice is that of a woman who selects images that often have specifically female bodily and mythic significance.

Both these poems, dated 17 June 1923 and 19 November 1924 respectively, appear in the 'Second Notebook' of Tsvetayeva's most outstanding collection of lyric poetry, *Posle Rossii* (*After Russia*). It contains poems written during the years 1922-25, but was published only in 1928. Although the two poems are addressed to different men, the addressee in both cases matters less than the speaker. Both poems proceed from a painful sensation of loss and take an attitude that refuses to settle for less (or for loss). The poems echo and expand upon the words of Montaigne chosen by Tsvetayeva as the epigraph to the 'Second Notebook' (and used again as an epigraph to the essay 'Poet o kritike' ['Poet on Critic']) in 1926: 'J'en ay assez de peu. . . . J'en ay assez d'un. J'en ay assez de pas un.' It is precisely the forcefulness of the poetic attitude taken to reverse an emotional finality imposed by a man upon a woman that unifies these two poems, each of which in other ways echoes certain of its near and distant neighbours in the collection.

Crevasse

How this incident ended
Neither friendship nor love can learn.
With each day you respond more dully,
With each day you fall through more deeply.

So, [you are] no longer upset by anything,
—Only a tree shifts its branches—
[You have fallen] into any icy crevasse—
Into [my] chest that was *so* smashed against you!

From the treasury of simulacra
Here's a riddle for you at random:
In me as in a crystal coffin you
Sleep, in me as in a deep wound you

Sleep,—tight is the icy cut!
Ice is jealous of its dead men:
Ring—armour—seal—and girdle . . .
Beyond return and beyond recall.

In vain you curse Helen, widows!
[It is] not the flame of red Helen's
Troy! [It is] the icy crevasse's
Blue, at the depths of which you are resting . . .

[I] having coupled with you like Etna
With Empedocles . . . Sleep, dreamer!
And tell the servants that it's futile:
The chest will not give up its dead men.

'Rasshchelina' (meaning crevice, or crevasse) begins with a flat statement of an ending and asserts the impossibility of further knowledge, in an impersonal manner. The chest stands metonymically for the 'I' in the poem, and a glacial crevasse is the poem's central metaphor for this (wounded) part of the body. Distance and disappearance, in time/space, usually conceived of as lateral and outward, are transferred by the poem to the vertical plane, a thrust downward (into the crevasse) and inward (into the chest). The addressee has become literally 'unmoved', frozen; by contrast, a tree moves slightly. The chest, still impersonal at the end of the second quatrain, has been hurt, and pain is expressed by the italicized *so* and by the exclamation mark. In the third quatrain the tone shifts, as the speaker fully assumes the role of defining the situation; she poses a riddle from the storehouse of similes at her command (her power is implied both by her ability to select from many images and by her ability to speak in images at all). The riddle states the I/you relationship two ways: you sleep in me as in a crystal coffin/a deep wound. The first simile reverses the well-known fairy-tale image of Snow White. As we remember, the Prince wishes to possess the beauty in her glass coffin even though he believes her to be dead. Preserved in ice or crystal, the beloved has become an object. The second image, the deep wound, the icy cut, both overlaps and contrasts with the deathly serenity of the first. Line 14 summarizes the theme of possession (by the personification of ice, making jealousy impersonal). It also contains a threat: the ice will not let go. The next line is a catalogue of the personal effects of a dead knight, as if a funeral were taking place. These are the last means of identifying him, metonymic remains of his person. The ring, coat of mail, seal, and girdle are all round (or made of ring-shaped parts); all hold or seal in. The absence is now stated positively, for the speaker has shifted the loss into her own self, where no one else can find it. In the last two quatrains, two other myths are reversed by the speaker. Helen of Troy is not to blame for the Trojan War. It is not the flame of war, but the blue of glacial ice, its opposite in temperature but its twin in intensity, that the emotion is compared to. Finally, Empedocles's legendary death-leap into Etna is rephrased with Etna (female and geological, like the glacier, but hot—the passion before it turned to iciness) being the active force of union. The indicative 'you sleep' becomes an imperative 'sleep!' as the speaker gains total control of the situation, telling those close to the addressee that they search in vain. The final line of the poem imposes a finality of possession in the speaker's own terms: the chest will not give up its dead men. The plural signifies a general rule. The future tense appears for the first time (an earlier variant had 'to the end of ages' in line 10; but a future finality is more effective at the end). Like *Poema kontsa*, 'Rasshchelina' begins with the beginning of the end and finishes with the end of the end, with its literal incorporation (into the corpus of poetry and the physical body of the poet).

Thus the theme of physical loss of a lover/friend made into eternal, spiritual (metaphorically physical) possession is reinforced by a triple feminist reversal of the conven-

Portrait of Tsvetaeva by Magda Nakhman, 1913.

tional myths which tell us: (1) a woman, Snow-White, is made into a dead object for all eyes; (2) a woman, Helen of Troy, wreaks destruction; and (3) a man, Empedocles, takes an active plunge into physical annihilation and immortal glory. The poem, like so many of Tsvetayeva's lyrics, is built upon paradox. The heat of passion becomes the ice of possession. The direct association is made on the level of imagery: the juxtaposition of geological images of ice/crystal and flame/volcano. The speaker's loss of the lover/friend has paradoxically shifted into its opposite: *she* will never lose *him*.

Imagery of the geological crevice keeps yielding place throughout the poem to its anatomical 'literal' explanation. In bodily terms, the imagery is sexual and a reversal of a birth process. He sleeps in her (like a baby), but he will never be born; the pain of his breaking into a crack in her body results in his total absorption by her. The word *propast'*—to fall through, to be lost—becomes a pun, similar to the womb/tomb pun of English poetry.

Having metonymically located pain in one part of her body, the speaker is free to name it. The effect of this poem is that of a horrible deadening of pain intensified to the point at which it is transmuted into the power of possession. But the poem remains static at that point: I possess you (but you are dead); I will not release you (but you are my pain).

The sound structure of the poem activates the intersecting semantic fields at every level. '**Rasshchelina**' is constructed of parallels either strophic or versicular. In fact, only six of the poem's twenty-four lines contain no parallels. These parallels lend an incantational dignity to the lines,

and they also recall certain other poetic genres: a negative simile (it is not one thing; it is another), the Slavic folk epic; the repetition of the verb 'to sleep', a lullaby. On the lexical level, words shift their meaning within a single stanza ('tak' in the second stanza is italicized to indicate a new meaning). The words move slightly higher than in ordinary speech (words like *ogn'* or *koye* are archaic/poetic), so that when the word 'grud'' is used, it tends to connote 'breast' or 'heart' while still keeping its anatomical literalness.

The poem's elliptical syntax, characteristic of Tsvetayeva, here provides verbal mimicry of the glacial gap / chest / wound imagery. Every quatrain but the third (the riddle-posing one) contains a negative statement: the crevasse is empty space. Verbs are omitted altogether or else pulled apart from their subject by an intervening metaphor ('you in me as in a crystal coffin / Sleep'). Enjambements span separate lines in the third and fifth stanzas and jump stanzas, from the third to the fourth. Grammatical disjunctures reflect the unbridged death / life, fire / ice, absence / presence oppositions which inform the poem.

The omissions (the entire poem begins with an omitted explanation) force the reader to concentrate on the words that are present. These are bound together in a dense texture of sound. The poem has a basically anaphoric quality with pairings between lines 1/5, 2/18, 3/4, 5/7, 7/8, 8/24, 11/12, and 12/13, the anaphora occasionally extending well into the line. Such highly resonant ends and beginnings are typical of Tsvetayeva's verse line in general; in this poem, words in mid-position also contain repetitions of sound and grammar: the *ch* in the first line, the velars throughout the third stanza, the stressed *a*'s in the fourth, the *Usni/skazhi* parallel in the last. The syntactic parallels are tightly reinforced by a phonetic organization, the most fundamental structural unit of which becomes neither the stanza nor the line nor even the word, but rather the phoneme. For example, when we examine the end-rhymes (ABAB, alternating with all feminine endings), we notice that in some instances they are both pre- and post-vocalically rich (*prorez'/poyas; snovidets/ne vydast*). In the first quatrain, all four end-rhymes (*sluchay/druzhbe/glushe/glubzhe*) have an *ú* preceded by a liquid sonant and followed by a sibilant. The alliterative *p*'s of line 15 underline similarities more obviously.

Not just end-rhymes but entire lines have a tightly organized phonemic structure. The basic logaoedic line $(xx\acute{x}xx\acute{x}xx\acute{x})$ predominates overwhelmingly (its metrical scheme is fulfilled by word-stress in almost every line) and there is abundant hypermetrical stressing in the opening, often on monosyllabic words set off from the rest of the line by punctuation. [In the *Oxford Slavonic Papers*, 1979] G. S. Smith has described the basic line by the formula 2-2-1́, the numerals expressing intervening syllables, the dash the ictus and the accented dash the constantly stressed ictus. Smith has identified this particular line as 'clearly the most numerous metre (657 lines, 26.9% of all logaoedic lines) among Tsvetayeva's logaoedic structures'.

The extreme richness and variety of distribution of the

sound pattern support the multi-levelled paradox of the theme. In our second poem, some of the same devices (anaphora, enjambement) are used more repetitively, as constants, while the imagery (which has been a constant in the first poem) fluctuates more extremely.

An Attempt at Jealousy

How's your life with the other one—
Easier?—A stroke of the oar!—
Like the coastline
Does it take long for the memory to recede

Of me, a floating island
(In the sky—not on the waters!)
Souls, souls! you should be sisters,
Never lovers—you!

How's your life with an *ordinary*
Woman? *Without* deities?
Now that you've dethroned your Queen
(Having stepped down yourself).

How's your life—do you fuss—
Do you shiver? How do you feel when you get up?
How do you deal with the tax
Of deathless vulgarity, poor man?

'Convulsions and irregular heartbeat—
I've had enough! I'll rent my own place.
How's your life with anyone—
My own chosen one!

More compatible and more palatable
The food? If it palls—don't complain . . .
How's your life with an imitation—
You who have trampled upon Sinai!

How's your life with a local
Stranger? Point-blank—do you love her?
Or does shame, like Zeus' reins,
Lash at your forehead?

How's your life—your health—
How've you been? Are you managing to sing?
How do you deal with the ulcer
Of deathless conscience, poor man?

How's your life with goods
From the market? Is the price steep?
After Carrara marble
How's your life with plaster

Dust? (From a solid block was hewn
A god—and smashed to bits!)
How's your life with one of a hundred-thousand—
You, who have known Lilith!

Are you sated with the newest thing
From the market? Having cooled to magic,
How's your life with an earthly
Woman, without a sixth

Sense?
Well, let's hear it: are you happy?
No? In a shallow, bottomless pit—
How's your life, my darling? Harder than,
Just like, mine with another man?

The speaker of **'Rasshchelina'** may be seen to gain, at the poem's end, 'a Quartz contentment, like a stone'—to use Emily Dickinson's teasingly redundant image for frozen pain. Our second poem, **'Popytka revnosti'**, also takes place *after* the event has occurred, beginning and ending in an inexplicable present. But here the speaker attempts to redefine the situation, giving a hyperbolic explanation to a rather banal turn of events. She reverses 'You have left me for another woman and I'm miserable' into '*You* are miserable with her and here's a reminder of who *I* am!'. Tsvetayeva accomplishes this *tour de force* by the magic of ritual vituperation. She shows her skill by saying the same thing in numerous ways (much like a medieval sermon). The poem keeps leading off with the same rhetorical question ('How's your life?') posed eleven times in twelve stanzas, all but the second one. We—and he—get no relief, presumably because she has none. Jealousy *is* a rhetorical question, getting and needing no answer; it supplies its own.

This poem, too, begins with a movement away (laterally rather than downward): the stroke of the oars followed by a two-beat line suggesting a slow pull, a three-beat line, and finally three four-beat lines as the pace quickens. The poem's metre is as regular as its returning refrain; trochaic tetrameter, the first and fourth ictus always stressed, the fourth line of all stanzas but three omitting the stress on the third ictus, the masculine endings of the second and fourth lines reinforcing the question or exclamation marks they frequently end with, and delivering a double punch with the stressed first syllable of the next line.

Reflexive verbs and adjective/noun combinations in the instrumental (both similes and accompaniments) also dominate the poem; the only direct object accusative, by way of contrast, occurs in the two lines spoken by the departing lover, 'I will rent a house'. These words, uttered as a quote by the speaker, have the mocking irony of words flung up a stairway being thrown back down. They are also simple in comparison with her baroque circumlocutions, and they reinforce the idea that maybe this simple man belongs with a 'simple woman' rather than with the speaker.

Given the essential sameness of its stanzaic structure, the poem is a marvel of variety. The hyperbolic language, once begun, must maintain its pitch and even appear to be stepping it up. Tsvetayeva accomplishes this feat by piling metaphor upon metaphor and by varying the breaks in line and stanza that form the boundary between two questions (although there is a tendency for the second line in each quatrain to have the greatest number of such breaks, even these are varied). The first and last lines of the poem link up with their final words (*s drugoyu/s drugim*) underlining the circular reasoning of the questions.

Part of the variety within the tight framework stems from the formal structure of address (the use of the formal pronoun *vy*, the reflexive verbs and high-toned Church Slavonic lexicon) combined with a colloquial prying into extremely intimate moments of life. This creates an element of humorous backlash important to the total effect of the poem. Hyperbole is commonly used humorously. The speaker calls herself a Queen, Carrara marble, Lilith (according to Rabbinical tradition, the first wife of Adam, the mother of evil spirits, who preferred to have one hundred of her demon children die each day rather than return to him). Tsvetayeva, in her letters, identified herself with Lilith, as opposed to wifely other women, Eves. The other woman is simple, earthly, vulgar, largely defined by hyperbolic contrast to herself. The man is ironically pitied, sarcastically and blasphemously called 'my chosen one' (in the context of other Biblical references, the implication is that the speaker is God); but at the end, when he is called simply '*milyy*', dear, the tone shifts suddenly from the metaphorical plane to the 'real' one. He is still loved; she is living with another man and still loving him. Our desire to laugh along with the speaker as she redefines the all-too-definable is suddenly broken with a return to the original feeling, love.

Tsvetaeva compares poetic significance with poetic greatness:

A significant poet is what anyone—any significant poet—can be. To be a significant poet it is enough to have a poetic gift of significance. To be a great poet, even the most significant gift is too small—he needs an equivalent gift of personality—of mind, soul and will—and the aspiration of the whole personality towards a definite aim; that is, its organization. But a lofty poet is something that even a quite insignificant poet, bearer of the most modest gift, can be—like, say, Alfred de Vigny—by the power of his inner worth alone winning our recognition as a poet. In that case the gift was just big enough. A little less and he'd only have been a hero (which is immeasurably more).

Marina Tsvetaeva, "Art in the Light of Conscience," in Art in the Light of Conscience: Eight Essays on Poetry by Marina Tsvetaeva, *translated by Angela Livingstone, Harvard University Press, 1992.*

How can the title be explained? First of all, this is an attempt at jealousy by someone who fails at the end: the other woman does not really exist for her; only the man does. Secondly, the 'attempt' can be seen as an *exercise de style*; much like Wallace Stevens's 'Thirteen Ways of Looking at a Blackbird', it demonstrates the poet's skill in saying the same thing in different ways, expressing the simultaneous as sequential. The speaker can even change metaphor in mid-stream when she redefines the floating island as being in the sky. Nothing verbal is technically impossible to her.

The rhetoric of vituperative jealousy has famous precedents in the history of the art: Catullus and Shakespeare come readily to mind. But a deliberately crude and blasphemous female lyric voice, exulting in its own sense of freedom in being unladylike, is not to be found until the twentieth century, although certainly women of intellect and emotion have always written in 'good' language of the constraints placed upon them. Tsvetayeva's poetry still gets the uneasy reaction that a woman does not *say* these things, and that it is masochism to flaunt one's pain poetically. But, like Sylvia Plath in her great poem 'Daddy', or Adrienne Rich in 'Diving into the Wreck', Tsvetayeva gives us poetic models for female experience that can often take different bodily, mythic, and verbal shape from the male poetic models which we have too often assumed to be universal.

Peter France (essay date 1982)

SOURCE: "Marina Tsvetaeva," in *Poets of Modern Russia*, Cambridge University Press, 1982, pp. 132-58.

[*In the following excerpt, France examines subjects, themes, and literary techniques in Tsvetaeva's poetry.*]

> To tell you everything . . . But no, all cramped
> In rows and rhymes . . . Wider the heart!
> For a catastrophe so great I fear
> All Shakespeare and Racine are not enough.
>
> 'All wept, and if the blood is aching . . .
> All wept, and if the roses conceal snakes . . .'
> But Phaedra had only one Hippolytus,
> And Ariadne wept for one Theseus.
>
> Excruciation! Without shores or limits!
> Yes, I lose track of figures and declare
> That when I lose you, I lose everyone
> Who *never was* in any time or anywhere!
>
> What can I hope—when riddled through and
>   through
> With you the whole air has grown one with me!
> When my every bone to me is like a Naxos!
> When the blood under my skin is like the Styx!
>
> In vain! It is in me! Everywhere! I close
> My eyes: it is dateless, bottomless.
> The calendar lies . . .
>   As your name is—the Break,
> So I am not Ariadne . . .
>   —I am Loss.
>
> Oh through what seas and towns shall I
> Search for you? (The unseeing for the unseen!)
> I trust my farewells to the telegraph wires
> And, pressed against the telegraph pole—I weep.

This is the second poem in a group entitled **'Wires' ('Provoda')** and written in March 1923. Marina Tsvetaeva's lyric poems are very often addressed by an 'I' to a 'you'. Sometimes these are personae from the store of European culture—Ophelia to Hamlet, Eurydice to Orpheus—but usually we must take the speaker to be the poet herself. This raises problems of information. Often it is possible to find out from other sources such as memoirs or letters the identity of the person addressed and other circumstances which enable one to place the poem. Sometimes too an outside source will clarify an allusion that would otherwise remain mysterious. Beyond this, I doubt whether there is any real need for such scene-setting.

In the present poem, it is certainly interesting to know that the 'you' (here in the initimate second-person singular) was Boris Pasternak, and that the poem was written from Czechoslovakia, where Tsvetaeva had been living for several months in self-chosen exile from Russia. When she left her homeland in May 1922, neither she nor Pasternak had published a great deal, but in the same year both came to the attention of a wider public, and of each other, with important books of poetry. Pasternak (who remained in Russia) was greatly impressed by Tsvetaeva's collection **Milestones (Vyorsty)** while she (in Berlin and Prague) greeted his *My Sister Life* with a rapturous article. So began a correspondence between two poets who felt themselves to be equals in strength.

Tsvetaeva's poem of loss and separation is addressed therefore to a man she had met mainly through poems and letters. Thence, I take it, the declaration in the third stanza that in losing him she is losing all who never were—all the unrealized possibilities of her native land. It is helpful too to know that when she writes 'Your name is the Break', the word *razryv* (break or separation), while it brings in a notion which haunts much of her poetry, is also the title of a memorable cycle of poems included in Pasternak's collection *Themes and Variations,* which had been published a couple of months before this poem was written. All this is worth knowing, but I do not believe it should materially affect our reading any more than such knowledge as we may have about the supposed recipients of love poems by Shakespeare, Ronsard or Pushkin. For all their allusiveness, most of Marina Tsvetaeva's poems can stand on their own without biographical commentary.

In line 4 of this poem, the names of two great tragic poets are used to suggest the size of the poet's misfortune. It is one of Tsvetaeva's habits to see her life in terms of great men and women of history and literature. In earlier collections these emblematic figures include Russian folk heroes such as Stenka Razin and the Pretender Dimitry as well as heroes and heroines of Western Europe—Manon Lescaut, Casanova and many others. In **After Russia (Posle Rossii),** the collection from which the present poem is taken, she tends more often to go back to the Old Testament, Shakespeare and classical antiquity. There are several poems on Hamlet and others on Saul, David, Absalom and Solomon, but probably the dominant images are those from ancient Greece, Achilles and Helen, Orpheus and Eurydice, Phaedra and Hippolytus, Theseus and Ariadne. The last two pairs, with their rejected heroines and their Racinian echoes, provide the subjects of two verse plays of the 1920s. In this poem, the most important figure is Ariadne, abandoned by Theseus on the island of Naxos. But Tsvetaeva goes beyond simple identification; she is more than Ariadne, she is loss itself. And as in

Blok's 'Steps of the Commendatore', the grand legendary images contrast sharply with a real world (of telegraph poles and wires) which is evoked in poem after poem of this collection.

The most striking features of this poem—and in this it is characteristic of its author's mature work—are the broken, elliptical form and the exclamatory eloquence. The first stanza, for instance, moves from the unfinished sentences which mime inexpressible emotion to a full-blooded affirmation which has something of the magniloquence of Mayakovsky's great love poems. Both the second and fourth lines end with exclamation marks, and there are many more of these in the rest of the poem. The exclamation mark seems to be more freely used in Russian poetry than in English, where it tends to give an impression of falsity or naive self-indulgence. Such criticisms are sometimes made of Tsvetaeva too, occasionally coupled (at least in conversation) with a rather disagreeable condescension for the 'hysterical woman' or 'schoolgirl'. Certainly the direct or heightened expression of personal emotion is more characteristic of her poetry than detachment or impersonality.

If the third and fourth lines are direct and emphatic, the first two lines are elliptical—but not obscure. It is easy to complete the first sentence, and 'all cramped into rows and rhymes' must be taken to qualify some noun such as 'emotions'. These are like the ellipses of conversation, where the unfinished sentence is no obstacle to communication. The same is true, I think, of the apparent quotations of lines 5 and 6. I do not know the source of these (perhaps they are of Tsvetaeva's own invention), and both lines are left hanging, but they can be read as objections to the previous lines—a voice, speaking with the wisdom of the ages, tells the poet that her experience is nothing new in a world of tears, and this provokes the retort of lines 7 and 8, which will be amplified in the next three stanzas. Her loss is far more than the loss of one person; it is the loss of a whole world which has become flesh of her flesh.

Partly because of its inflected nature, the Russian language allows meaning to be conveyed in fewer words than in English. There are no articles, pronouns are often not needed, and the verbless sentence is quite common. Tsvetaeva uses these resources to the utmost, creating jagged abrupt sentences, full of dashes and breaks. Thus the third and fourth lines of the fourth stanza could have been run on smoothly in a single sentence, but they are separated by exclamation marks and the instrumental case allows the verbs ('is' or 'resembles') to be understood, not expressed. In the fifth stanza there is a sequence of brief exclamations and only one main verb, and in the final stanza the whole meaning of the two echoing words *nezrimogo—nezryachey* ('the unseeing for the unseen') has to be deduced from the endings. All this makes reading more difficult than a smoother style, and such appears to have been Tsvetaeva's intention—she did not want to make things too easy. In any case its expressive force is undeniable.

It has often been thought that verbal ingenuity is out of place in the poetry of emotion, that it suggests a striving for effect or an inappropriate playfulness. It is one of Tsvetaeva's qualities—and in this as in much else she is close to Mayakovsky—that her work on language is closely bound up with the expression of feeling. It is as if strong feeling, far from decanting the language, searches out new and unsuspected complexities and possibilities. Most obvious of these is the coupling of words similar in sound, but apparently unrelated in meaning—thus *dna* and *dnya* in line 18, the genitive case respectively of words meaning 'bottom' and 'day'. Or else there can be an etymological relationship which is lost in ordinary speech; this is the case with the central pair *provody* (seeing-off) and *provoda* (wires), where the same root gives birth to words that suggest separation and reunion in one line: 'Ya provody vveryayu provodam'. Together with this homonymic play, there are effects such as the accumulation of similar sounds in lines 15 and 16 *(Naksosom, kost', krov', kozhey, stiksom)*, intensified in this case by the sort of chiasmic construction which is made easier by the flexibility of Russian word order.

These and other features of the writing—the metaphors, the clash of formal metre and rhythmical intonation—remind one of the poems of the person to whom these lines are addressed. Indeed one might think Tsvetaeva was doing homage by imitation if it were not for the presence of these elements in her poems long before 1923. Similarly, while this is a poem of exile, it did not need the circumstances of 1923 to produce such notes in her writing. It is true that the experience of separation from Russia and the miseries of emigration provoked some of her finest poetry; the German epigraph to the cycle **'Wires'** reads in translation: 'The wave of the heart would not foam up in such beauty and become spirit, if it were not for the resistance of that old, silent rock, fate.' Even so, much that is in ***After Russia*** is anticipated much earlier.

In 1932, in an essay entitled 'The Poet and Time', Tsvetaeva wrote that 'every poet is essentially an émigré, even in Russia'. This is an ancient view, which was given a new lease of life in the Romantic movement; one finds it in its pure form in Baudelaire's 'The Albatross'. Mayakovsky gave a Futurist colouring to it, addressing his poems insultingly to a 'you' of complacent bourgeois. Something similar is to be found in this early poem of Marina Tsvetaeva:

> You, who pass me by and go on
> To not mine and dubious charms,—
> If only you knew what fire,
> How much life, poured out in vain,
>
> And how much heroic ardour
> On a passing shade, on a sigh . . .
> How this vain outpouring of powder
> Has reduced my heart to ash.
>
> Oh trains that rush into the night,
> Carrying off the station's dreams . . .
> Yet I know that even then,
> If you knew—you would not really know

> Why in endless cigarette smoke
> My speech is hard and sharp,—
> How much dark and menacing grief
> There is in my fair-haired head.

Tsvetaeva was twenty when she wrote these lines—she had already been writing poems for some years. In another poem of the same month she imagined herself speaking to a future sympathizer from the grave; the early work is full of the awareness of impending death and the desire to live as fully as possible. Here she speaks from a gloomy corner to a generalized and alien 'you', not perhaps the fat philistines of Mayakovsky, but still the sort of people who cannot understand the passionate poet. Passion appears as an outpouring and above all a fire (*pyl, ogon', porokh*) which brings devastation. But all this ardour is out of place in an ordinary world, where it can only be wasted on a 'shade' and a 'sigh'. In Tsvetaeva's poems the speaker, a generous force of life, loves more than she is loved; she can find no one to answer the strength of her passion. So here, self-consumed like Phaedra, she is driven back on herself, into an aggressive cigarette-smoking reserve that contrasts sharply with the stock image of the sweet fair-haired girl.

Like the first poem discussed in this chapter, though in a less impressive way, these early verses pose the basic problem which faces the reader of Tsvetaeva: how is one to react to the constant projection of the poet's personality into images which often strike one as all too familiar, however true they may be to the experience of many people? There is in her poems a propensity to work in myths—or at worst clichés—of human behaviour, and this can become unbearable at times. On the other hand, these 'myths' correspond to a desire to heighten the experience of life, to find a place for energy and daring. Overflowing with a powerful imaginative impulse, and often in very difficult material conditions in her later life, Tsvetaeva persisted in this call to transcend or transfigure the world. At times, particularly in the early poems, the result is childish or embarrassing, but then, as one reads on and as the poet's mastery grows, her poetry comes to shame the complacent reader. The poet becomes a goad.

A number of legendary figures are evoked in the youthful poems, heroes, princes and warriors such as Napoleon and his son. She even briefly saw Kerensky as Napoleon in 1917. But it is probably her fellow-poets who provided the most lasting images of power and daring. From 1916 on, she addressed groups of poems to Mandelstam (a 'young Derzhavin' and a 'young eagle'), to Pasternak ('my equal in strength'), to Mayakovsky (a 'toiling archangel') and to Akhmatova ('muse of weeping, most beautiful of the muses'.) All of these are transfigured in Tsvetaeva's gaze, but none so much as Blok, who was of course of an older generation (though only about twelve years older, be it said) and represented for her a saintly ideal of poetry. He was a 'knight without reproach'. There is a cycle of sixteen **'Poems to Blok'**, half of them written in 1916, the others shortly before or after his death in 1921. The first group contains this one:

> For the beat—a den,
> For the traveller—a road,
> For the dead—a hearse.
> For each—his own.
>
> For the woman—cunning,
> For the tsar—ruling,
> For me—praising
> Thy name.

Eight lines, sixteen words. Tsvetaeva is close to the silence of adoration. I doubt if Blok, who knew himself only too well, would have approved of this hero-worship, but Tsvetaeva is addressing the poet rather than the man, and she perceived in him—rightly—a call to absolute values. The first line here echoes Matthew 8:20: 'The foxes have holes, and the birds of the air have nests, but the Son of Man hath not where to lay his head.' So Blok is associated with Jesus—and Tsvetaeva perhaps with Mary Magdalene. The poem, like many of hers, is made up on the litany principle (repetition of the same form with varying words), and verblessness is carried to an extreme. The rhymes and the rhythm tie the poem into a tight unity, but here again there are variations within repetition; the number of syllables changes, the two shortest lines are kept to the end, the seventh line runs straight into the eighth, and the final line is without the dash which divides and slows down all the rest. The vocabulary is simple and old, though not actually archaic; its effect is to reduce the complexity of life to a series of characteristic acts or attributes, the most obvious possible, as if there were an immutable grand order in which tsars always rule (this in 1916) and women, like Delilah, are always cunning.

One of the impulses in Tsvetaeva's poems, whether political or personal, is towards a fixed world of this kind, the world of duty, peace and transcendence, like that of Blok's Beautiful Lady. But Blok was also the poet of wild passion and the gipsy song, and in Tsvetaeva too, though not in the **'Poems to Blok',** the element of wild movement, dance and passion is rarely absent for long. In her very early poem **'Prayer'**, written at the age of seventeen, she had prayed for an intensity of life which would include fighting like an Amazon, reading the stars in a black tower and setting out 'with the soul of a gipsy on a bandit raid'. The warrior, the rebel, the bandit and the gipsy reappear in many of her poems, the gipsy for instance in a cycle of three poems called **'Fortune-Telling'** (**'Gadan'e'**), written between the February and October revolutions in May 1917—a month after the birth of her second daughter:

> She looked in my eyes,
> Dully menacing.
> Somewhere a thunderclap answered.
> —Ah, my young lady!
> Let me tell you
> Your fortune in years to come.

> Blue clouds have gathered into a funnel.
> Somewhere it thunders—they thunder.
> Into my child the fortune-teller
> Has plunged her somnolent gaze.

> 'What can you tell us?'
> —Everything true.
> 'Too late for me,
> Too early for her.'

> —Oh, hold your tongue, my beauty.
> Why say in advance 'I don't believe it.'—
> And the fan of cards spread wide
> In a black—all in silver—hand.

> —Bold in your speech,
> Simple in your ways,
> You live generously,
> Hoarding no beauty.
> An evil man will drown you, alas,
> In a spoonful of water.

> Soon in the night an unexpected journey.
> Life-line short,
> Short in fortune.
> Cross my palm with gold.—

> And with a stroke of thunder appears
> Black upon black—the ace.

The self-image is by now familiar, that of the ill-fated, passionate, generous heroine, very much mindful of death. The reader's attention is perhaps caught above all by the striking language of the poem. As in the poem to Blok, lines tend to begin on a stressed syllable; some characteristic stress patterns are:

$$/ \ \breve{}\breve{}\ /$$
$$/ \ \breve{}\breve{}\ / \ \breve{}$$
$$/ \ \breve{}\breve{}\ / \ \breve{}\ / \ \breve{}\breve{}\ /$$

The first of these is the fundamental one; it is called the choriamb and is much used in Tsvetaeva's mature verse. The second can be seen as an extension of the first and the third is a doubling up of the second. In all cases the result is a line where one half pulls hard against the other and the stressed syllables stand out with considerable force. Add to this the shortness of most of the lines, the tendency to separate lines by commas, full stops or exclamation marks and the breaks introduced even into short lines by the use of dashes, and the result is an abrupt and powerful rhythm which reinforces the impact of the poem's subject, the confrontation between fortune-teller and mother and child, and the clashing colours, the silver of rings, gold of money and bright cards against the darkness of skin, thunderclouds and the ace (of spades?).

Unlike the poems discussed so far in this chapter, this is not a message from the poet to a supposed hearer or reader, but a dialogue. It anticipates the very successful rendering of conversation in some of Tsvetaeva's longer poems. The talk here is not framed with much explanatory scene-setting, and as in many ballads such introductory formulae as 'she said' are omitted. The essential elements (eyes, cards, thunder) are rapidly evoked at the beginning, in the middle and again at the end; otherwise the poem is staccato talk, mostly the talk of the fortune-teller.

With the gipsy's words we see a different linguistic element in Tsvetaeva's poetry. The poems to Blok are couched in a simple but distinctly poetic language, with biblical echoes. In **'Fortune-Telling'** there is an attempt to represent popular speech. According to an expert who heard the poem soon after it was written, it was a very successful attempt—the use of the word *liniya* for instance was exactly that of the gipsy palmist. This version of popular language has the same concise vigour as one finds in Tsvetaeva's more 'literary' register. The two styles set one another off admirably: thus in this poem the final lines come across with added force after the gipsy's speech. In the years that followed, Tsvetaeva continued to exploit this vein and to draw, like so many of her contemporaries, on the language of popular literature and song, from the modern city romance to the ancient oral poetry of the countryside. Her long verse poems *The Tsar-Maiden (Tsar'-Devitsa)* and *The Champion (Molodets)* are ambitious attempts to harness old stories, old forms and old language to the poet's own personal concerns.

In spite of her love of popular language and culture and her sympathy for such folk heroes as the rebel Stenka Razin, Marina Tsvetaeva committed herself to the White cause after the October Revolution. Being the person she was, she did so with as great a zeal as Mayakovsky on the other side; she became the (unacknowledged) bard of the Counter-Revolution. Her husband, Sergey Efron, joined the White Army, and she composed a series of poems, later published (though not, of course, in the Soviet Union) under the title *The Swans' Encampment (Lebedinyy stan)*, in which she praised the nobility of those who had died for the anti-revolutionary cause. They are swans, white and pure, against the ravens; they are also compared to the warriors of Prince Igor's army fighting against the Tatars, or to the heroes who died fighting against the French Revolution.

There is no doubt about Tsvetaeva's position at this time, but equally there is no doubt that her heart went out above all to the gallant loser, the victim, whether it was the Tsar or Stenka Razin. Hers is not what is usually called a political stance. In one poem she declares that she has only two enemies, 'the hunger of the hungry and the fullness of the full', and in another, mourning the dead of the Civil War, she writes:

> He was white, now he is red:
> Blood has reddened him.
> He was red, now he is white:
> Death has whitened him.

In the hungry year of 1918, when she had a hard time simply staying alive in Moscow, Tsvetaeva wrote this poem, which was later included in *The Swans' Encampment*:

> In my figure there's an officer's straightness,
> In my ribs, an officer's honour.
> I'll take any pain without protest:
> In me there's a soldier's endurance!
>
> As if once with rifle-butt and steel
> My step had been straightened out.
> Not in vain, not in vain my Circassian waist
> And my tightly drawn leather belt.
>
> But when Reveille sounds—dear God!—
> I could storm the gates of heaven!
> These shoulders, it seems, were made wide
> To carry a soldier's pack.
>
> Who knows—perhaps over my cradle
> Some crazy veteran sang . . .
> And something lives on from that day:
> I take my aim at the word!
>
> And over the RSFSR
> My heart gnashes—fed or unfed—
> As if I too was an officer
> In those fatal October days.

Read in the context of *The Swans' Encampment,* this is clearly a 'White' poem. The RSFSR of the last stanza is the newly created Russian Soviet Federal Socialist Republic; by using the word *skrezheshchet* (usually used of gnashing the teeth, but here associated with the heart), Tsvetaeva is defiantly refusing the new power, even at the cost of starvation. The regular beat is almost that of a marching song; this is Tsvetaeva the drummer of the Counter-Revolution (as Mayakovsky was the drummer of the Revolution). Only in the last line do the grammatical forms show that the speaker is a woman. Most of the poem could be spoken by a man, and Tsvetaeva, who in many other poems rejects the quiet lot of the docile woman, is here identifying herself with the heroic White officers whom she praised and mourned in other poems. The fourth stanza shows that for her the act of writing is associated with battle; as a writer in revolutionary Moscow she can show the same nobility, patience and daring as those who died fighting.

And indeed Marina Tsvetaeva was a daring spirit. She left a lovely account of a 'Poetesses' Evening' in Moscow in 1921 at which she turned up among the other well-dressed lady poets wearing an old coat, a belt of the White Army, and over her shoulder an officer's leather bag. Out of a feeling of duty, she read a series of poems in memory of the victims of the Revolution, even poems with lines such as 'Hurrah! For the Tsar! Hurrah!'. She was energetically applauded. The political meaning of her poems passed over the heads of her audience. So too with the poem above; in a note of 1938 Tsvetaeva records that 'in Moscow this poem was called **"Verses about a Red Officer"** and over a period of eighteen months I read it at every poetry reading to unfailingly loud applause on the unfailing demand of the students'.

Tsvetaeva is an extremely candid poet, quite possibly the most candid in the history of Russian poetry. She makes no secret of anything, least of all of her aesthetic and philosophical credos, which are scattered about her verse and prose with the frequency of a first person singular pronoun.

—*Joseph Brodsky, "Footnote to a Poem,"* *in his* **Less Than One: Selected Essays, 1986**.

No doubt this misreading was due in part to the circumstances of transmission, it is easier to misunderstand an oral message. But I think it also stems from something in the poem itself. The hymn to military qualities and the march-like rhythm could appeal to Red audiences as much as to Whites. The idea of storming the gates of heaven sounds more revolutionary than counter-revolutionary, and even the more precise message of the last stanza might still be open to a double reading. The October days had been fatal to combatants on both sides, and the heart might 'gnash' either at the success of the RSFSR or at the troubles it was encountering.

Indeed, writing about this poem in her 1932 essay 'The Poet and Time', Tsvetaeva declared that the audiences had been right in their misunderstanding:

> There is something in poetry which is more important than its meaning—the way it sounds. The soldiers in Moscow in 1920 were not wrong; this poem is in its essence more concerned with the Red officer (and even the Red soldier) than with the White, who would not have accepted it, who (between 1922 and 1932) *did not accept it*.

And she goes on to say how at one such meeting, someone said to her: 'In spite of everything you are a revolutionary poet. You have our rhythm.'

Of course there was a big difference between a revolutionary poet and what Tsvetaeva called a 'bard of the Revolution'. The two only coincided in Mayakovsky, for whom she continued to proclaim her admiration against all the criticism of émigré circles. What she meant by 'revolutionary poet' was the poet who feels and expresses the time, this being for Russia a time of revolution. 'Whether you accept or avoid or reject the Revolution, it is already in you.'

This article of 1932 was written at a time when her poetry was generally rejected by the Russian community in Paris, where she was living, and when her defence of Mayakovsky had turned many away from her. It is not surpris-

ing that it is full of nostalgia for what she imagined to be a more vital relationship between poet, language and public in her native country: 'In Russia, as in the steppe, as at sea, there is space to speak from, space to speak into. If only speaking were allowed . . . Here there is a certain Russia, there there is all of Russia.' Ten years earlier the desire to escape had been stronger and her revulsion for the new Russia greater. Repudiation of the Revolution is combined with the influence of popular culture and language in a striking little cycle composed in September 1921 and entitled **'A Captive of the Khan'** (**'Khansky polon'**). This is the third poem in the group of four:

> Your tracks are untried,
> Matted your forelock.
> Loosestrife and touch-me-not
> Crunch under hoof.
>
> An untrampled road,
> A reckless fire.—
> Oh, Mother Russia,
> A steed unshod!
>
> Your calico unsold,
> Your axeman armless.
> A poor empty trough
> In the hall—and a hook.
>
> I'll stuff myself with bark,—
> That's nothing new now!
> Oh, Mother Russia,
> Enchanted steed!
>
> You must leap to the saddle!
> Once up, don't complain!
> There is only one rider
> To fit you: Mamay!
>
> Slant-eyed foulness,
> Palm of a thief . . .
> —Ah, Mother Russia,
> Remorseless steed!

The fundamental image is a traditional one; Russia, to whom the poem is mostly addressed, is a runaway horse, charging wildly into dangerous, uncharted country. The only possible rider (the Bolsheviks) is seen in the frightening figure of Mamay, a Tatar chief. The theme of the Revolution as a barbaric Asiatic eruption was common enough at this time, and Tsvetaeva had already alluded in **The Swans' Encampment** to the old Russian poems and legends of struggle against the Tatar Horde. What is most interesting here is the poetic form.

In **'Fortune-Telling'** there was an attempt to suggest popular speech in the dialogue with a gipsy, but it was framed in the poetic speech of a narrator. In this poem, on the other hand, the speaker is not identified, except in the title of the cycle. The poet's longing to escape from Russia reaches us through the voice of someone who is a prisoner in the camp of the Khan, and this voice speaks a language which is archaic, popular, abrupt and often obscure. The very word for 'captivity' (*polon*) in the title is an archaism which has long disappeared from normal speech, and several of the words used in the poem are almost equally old and rare. In the first stanza, for instance, the words *sledok* (track) and *nepytan* (untried) are unusual derivations from familiar roots. The two plant-names in line 4 of the original (line 3 of the translation) are old country words which evoke a world of popular belief; the former (*razryv*) was supposed to have the power of breaking locks, while the second (*plakun*) was said to make witches weep. More than this, *razryv* is the word for separation which Tsvetaeva later connects with Pasternak in **'Wires'**, and *plakun* immediately suggests the verb *plakat'* (to weep). A lot is done in two words.

There is much that sounds like popular speech. *Okh, Rodina-Rus'* ('Oh Mother Russia') is a refrain echoing the language of folk song, and there are also colloquial words such as *neputyovyy* (reckless) and *nazhrus'* ('I'll stuff myself'), popular forms of words such as *non'* (for *nyne* meaning 'now'), and the use of *da* to mean 'and'. In the fourth stanza (and elsewhere) there is a marked contrast between the coarse speech ('I'll stuff myself with bark') and the loftily poetic (because somewhat archaic) 'enchanted steed'—and then a return to the syntax of ordinary speech in the first two lines of stanza 5.

As so often, the syntax is elliptical and verbless. If the rhythm of the 'poem about the Red officer' was a march, here we have a gallop; the short lines each have two stressed syllables, separated by two unstressed, and the poem jerks and pounds on from line to line and rhyme to rhyme in a violent movement. Again one is reminded of what Tsvetaeva wrote about the rhythm of the time, the rhythm of revolution. This is a declaration of hate for the new order—as in the violent expression of racial loathing in the last stanza—but the rhythm seems to me to carry a feeling of excitement. Tsvetaeva was consciously putting herself on the opposite side from Blok, but her poem has something of the same ambiguity as *The Twelve* in its depiction of an elemental force. The wild, unshod, enchanted and remorseless steed (*kon'*, a poetic word *par excellence*) could not be totally alien to her; only a year earlier she had written a long poem entitled **'On a Red Steed'**, in which the fiery, red horse represents inspiration, a violent muse.

'A Captive of the Khan' was first published in a collection entitled *Craft (Remeslo)*. In some ways this volume marks a break with Tsvetaeva's earlier writing; the new work is more innovatory, more at odds with the conventional norms of poetry. In this poem one sees archaic and popular language, short lines, jagged rhythms and a tendency to the unexplained and the obscure. This new 'craft' of verse is developed still further in her later writing, particularly in the collection entitled *After Russia* (1928), which met with considerable hostility in émigré literary circles.

Obscurity certainly is a problem. In this poem, for instance, apart from the use of unfamiliar words, there is the difficulty of relating the exclamations of lines 17 and 18 to what precedes and follows. It is possible that obscurity

is a way of getting past the censor—for all its violent abuse, this poem was published in the Soviet Union. But caution was never one of Tsvetaeva's failings, and the difficulty of her later work is rather to be seen as a deliberately high threshold to discourage the lazy philistine. She is not going to make concessions to the sort of readability she later mocked in a virulent satirical piece called **'Newspaper Readers'** (**'Chitateli gazet'**). Her poems make the reader work; the captivating rhythms and strange teasing language are a promise that the work will be rewarded—and indeed, sometimes after many readings, the reward usually comes.

'A Captive of the Khan' is—among other things—an exercise in invective, the violent self-defence of an isolated and suffering person. This vein is one that becomes increasingly important in Tsvetaeva's writing in the 1920s and 1930s. The targets of her abuse are the same as those of Mayakovsky, the smug philistine, the world of unaspiring comfort, but she also goes further than Mayakovsky and sets herself against the modern, industrial world. In opposition to this alien world, she maintains a strong sense of her own rightness and of the demands of the absolute. Above all, there is the constant need for a life of emotional intensity and self-giving, which leads her to project her life and passion through figures such as Phaedra and Ophelia and to see in those she loved more than they could possibly give. Thus, in 1921, she wrote a cycle of poems entitled **'Adolescent'** (**'Otrok'**) and addressed to a young poet. The first poem is one of breathless, extravagant eloquence:

> Emptinesses of adolescent eyes! Abysses
> Into azure. Azure—however black!
> Playthings for an unparalleled battle,
> Gift-treasure-houses of storms.
>
> Mirror-like! They have neither ripple nor depths.
> The universe holds its course in them.
> Azure! Azure! Desert-like clangour,—
> Book-warehouses of emptiness!
>
> Abysses of adolescent eyes! Arches!
> Waterhole of scorched souls.
> Oases!—That all may gulp and sip
> And choke themselves on emptiness.
>
> I drink—cannot drink enough. Sighs—gasps,
> And subterranean roar of rumbling blood.
> So by night, troubling the sleep of David,
> Came the choking gulps of King Saul.

A comparison of this poem with **'A Captive of the Khan'**, which was written just one month later, shows the range of Tsvetaeva's writing. She always speaks from her own personal situation, but in many voices. This is a poem in the high Romantic tradition, an incantation in which the vocabulary is elevated and in places archaic, culminating in a scene from the Old Testament. Like Baudelaire's 'La Chevelure' it starts from a physical feature (here, the young man's eyes) and expands by a series of images. In the first three stanzas the basic structure is simply an accumulation of exclamatory metaphors. The last of these (again reminiscent of Baudelaire: 'Tes yeux sont la citerne où boivent mes ennuis') leads in the last stanza from an evocation of the man's eyes to the poet herself, gazing at him as the troubled Saul gazed at the young David (I Samuel 16:23).

It is above all a poem of thirst—thirst being a fundamental impulse in Tsvetaeva's poetry, as indeed it is in Mayakovsky's. One of her earliest surviving poems begins with the words 'I thirst for a miracle', and this need for a renewed source of life never leaves her. It is expressed in a number of poems of the 1920s, as here, in the image of an older woman, burning or burnt-out, addressing a beautiful and inaccessible youth—Phaedra to Hippolytus, the Sibyl to a young man. **'Adolescent'** does not express the passion of a Phaedra, but there is the same desire for a refreshing presence. It is noteworthy that the eyes are figured as empty spaces; the youth is less a living human being than a way of access to a higher plane, the 'azure' and the universe. In other words, as in so much love poetry, the other person is desired as a means of escape and transcendence, or at least as an oasis in the desert.

Given the extremity of Tsvetaeva's demands on others, it is not surprising that life and other people failed to live up to them. Some of her best poetry comes from the pain of failed love and separation. The best of all is probably her long poem of 1924, the *Poem of the End (Poema kontsa)*. This is made of fourteen separate sections, which together tell most movingly of the end of a love affair. Like almost all of Tsvetaeva's mature work, this poem is elliptical and sometimes hard to 'explain' in detail, but its overall structure is clear and strong. We follow the two lovers as they meet, walk through Prague, talk, weep and finally separate. Some idea of the quality of the poem may be had from this short extract, the third section, which shows the two speakers walking along an embankment and preparing for the final explanation:

> And—the embankment. To water
> I cling as to a dense slab.
> Semiramis's hanging gardens
> Of Babylon—so this is you!
>
> To water—a steely band
> The colour of a corpse—
> I cling as to her music
> A singer—or to a wall's edge
>
> A blind man . . . You won't give back?
> No? If I stoop—will you hear?
> To the quencher of all thirst
> I cling, as to a roof's edge
>
> A lunatic . . .
> But not from the river
> My trembling—a Nayad born!
> I cling to the river like a hand
> When the man you love is close

> And faithful . . .
> The dead are faithful.
> Yes, but not to all in the cell . . .
> Death on my left, and on my right—
> You. My right side seems dead.
>
> A sheaf of transfixing light.
> A laugh like a tambourine.
> 'You and I need to . . .'
> (Shudder.)
> . . . 'Are we going to be brave?'

It will be seen that the force of this passage comes from a mixture of compression and expansiveness. The narrative line is kept to a verbless minimum, as in the opening words and the final stanza, where the arrival at a café door is announced in two rapid notations. The dialogue at the end, as throughout the poem, is given in staccato form, with no indication of the speaker and only a brief 'stage direction' in brackets. But if the outward scene is all brief brush-strokes and broken dialogue, the representation of the woman's thoughts and feelings is expansive and eloquent. It seeks to convey half-conscious levels of experience, largely by rhythm and a series of metaphors and similes. The shift from one image to another is often unexpected and unaccountable (for instance the introduction of the hanging gardens), since the poem expresses a state of wordless confusion and panic. Particularly striking is the repeated use of the verb 'to cling to' (*derzhat'sya*); as is often the case in Tsvetaeva's poetry, the actual verb is sometimes omitted and has to be deduced from the syntax. The woman clings to the water as a sort of protection; with her name of Marina, she liked to think of herself as a child or spirit of water. Water is also the quencher of all thirst, like the oases of the young man's eyes in **'Adolescent'**, and at the same time it is connected with death, not only by the colour evoked in the second stanza, but as a possible refuge from life in stanza 5.

Even more than these images, the rhythm of the lines impresses itself on the reader. As in **'Adolescent'**, the fundamental metre is iambic, but for most of the poem this is set in violent opposition to an impassioned non-metrical rhythm. The use of long words such as *naberezhnaya* (embankment), *Semiramidina* (of Semiramis) and *vseutolitel'nitsa* (universal quencher) reduces the number of stresses, and the regularity of the line is further broken by dashes (perhaps Tsvetaeva's favourite punctuation) and by constant *enjambement* in the first four stanzas. As a result, while the underlying metre can still be sensed as a regular movement towards an inevitable end, the immediate effect is one of an exclamatory, headlong movement, that of the desire to escape. Only in the last two stanzas is the movement halted, first by the awareness of the lover's unyielding presence—the word 'you' is given special prominence—and then by the harsh and relatively regular end-stopped lines which take one brutally away from the thirst-quenching water to the hateful world of ordinary human society. And this is the signal for a quite different rhythm. The next section of the poem will be a satirical ballad of the commercial and amorous vulgarity of a Prague café, which is followed in its turn by a tense piece of conversation leading up to the words 'Let us part then'. In its varied but inexorable movement from beginning to end, this poem is both moving and wonderfully inventive; Tsvetaeva shows once again, as Donne had done long before in England, that what a prejudiced reader might call verbal virtuosity can cast a vivid light on the inner world and become a renewed source of emotion.

Tsvetaeva had little use for the ordinary world of gossip, business and newspapers which she satirizes in the Prague café ballad just mentioned. Neither could she find lasting satisfaction in devotion to a cause (as the struggle of the White Army was followed by the less heroic reality of emigration) or in love (which seemed doomed to disillusionment and collapse). In all the poems I have discussed so far she has been seen as a poet of human society, of love, hate, contempt or devotion. As one reads her, however, one becomes aware of a desire for a different sort of reality. In places, particularly in the early poems, she adopts a provocatively anti-religious pose, but there are many other times when she expresses what can only be called religious aspirations, whether in ecstatic poems about the churches of Moscow or in a more general thirst for an undefined absolute. The natural world does not play a very large part in her early collections, but in the poems of the 1920s, trees come to the fore as a refuge from the heated, wearing world of human worries. In *After Russia* there is a very fine cycle simply called **'Trees' ('Derev'ya')**, of which this is the second poem (it was written in September 1922):

When my angry soul has drunk
Its fill of injury,
When seven times it has renounced
The struggle with demons—

Not those flung down to the abyss
In a hail of fire:
But the petty basenesses of every day
And human inertia,—

Trees! Then I come to you! To hide
From the market's roar!
Your outflingings skyward seem
To breathe forth the heart!

God-defying oak! Striding
With all your roots to battle!
My future-gazing willow trees!
Maidenly birches!

Elm—vehement Absalom,
In torture upreared
Pine—and you, psalm of my lips,
Mountain-ash bitterness . . .

To you! Into the live-splashing quicksilver
Of leaves—even though falling!
To stretch out my arms for the first time!
To scatter manuscripts!

Swarms of green light and shade . . .
As if splashing into my hands . . .
Bare-headed ones of mine,
My tremulous ones!

It is perhaps unnecessary to say much about this beautiful invocation. As a poem of celebration it is more readily comprehensible than many other poems of this period; there is no need here for the reader to know anything of the poet's life. Once again Tsvetaeva alludes to the Old Testament, not only Absalom, but the fall of the angels in the opening stanzas. And generally, as in much of the poetry of the 1920s, the language tends towards the archaic. To take two examples, the word *semizhdy* (seven times) belongs to Church Slavonic rather than to modern Russian and the invented compound adjective *zhivopleshchushchiy* (live-splashing) recalls the archaic coinages of Russia's eighteenth-century poets, who in their turn were striving to create a Homeric style. Throughout this poem, in fact, the language is markedly 'poetic', with none of the colloquialisms which Tsvetaeva liked to use elsewhere. In writing of trees she escapes into an ancient sylvan world.

Many formal features of the poem are worthy of note, but I have already discussed such questions at some length in this chapter. Above all it is a poem of *sound*. Thus, after the vigorous upsurging sounds and images of stanzas 4 and 5, there is a beautiful shimmering effect of liquid leaves, full of palatalized consonants and sibilants:

K vam! V zhivopleshchushchuyu rtut'
Listvy—pust' rushashcheysya!

Here and throughout the poem Tsvetaeva writes with the sort of evocative magic that one finds also in Khlebnikov. It is a poetry of enchantment, beyond good and evil.

The idea that poetry—or art—is essentially amoral is in fact expressed—in somewhat Nietzschean terms—in a brilliant essay written by Marina Tsvetaeva in the 1930s, 'Art in the Light of Conscience'. Poetry is defined as a force of nature, something that happens to the poet, something as elemental as the plague. The genius is the one who is most open to this onrush and most able to make something of it—Nietzsche's combination of the Dionysian and the Apollonian. But unlike Nietzsche, Tsvetaeva does not conclude from this that art is *above* morality or that it can replace religion. For her as for Blok the artist is a demonic rather than a holy figure. To the imagined objection that 'the priest serves God in his way, you in your way', she replies: 'Blasphemy . . . When I write of the Tatars in the open spaces I am serving no God except the wind . . . All my poems on Russian subjects are elemental, and therefore sinful. One must be clear what forces are in play. When will we stop taking strength for truth and enchantment for holiness?'

So while she expresses in the most powerful terms the irresponsible nature of poetry, based as it is on a 'necessary atrophy of conscience', Tsvetaeva does not use this as an alibi, but faces the old Russian demand for morality and usefulness, the demand expressed in exemplary form by Tolstoy, the perfect artist who preferred truth and goodness to art. Often, though not always, the law of art will be opposed to the moral law, and in the end the moral sphere matters more: 'To be a human being is more important because it is more necessary. The doctor and priest are more necessary than the poet because they and not we stand by the death-bed.' And yet, knowing and admitting this, she ends her essay with the declaration: 'I would not change my work for any other. Knowing more, I do less, and therefore I shall not be forgiven. Only from such as me will a reckoning be demanded at the last judgement of conscience. But if there is a last judgement of the word, there I am innocent.'

For all its myth-making, this is a wonderfully clear-sighted essay. Tsvetaeva may exaggerate the 'sinfulness' of the poet, but she gives full weight to the paradoxical importance of this sinful art. It is worth noticing too that even though she presents the poet as one who 'receives' his poem—in a state akin to sleep—she stresses the will and the labour that are needed to transform this gift into a poem. In another essay, 'The Poet and Criticism', she insists that poetry is a craft (*Craft*, it will be remembered, is the title she gave to one of her major collections), and for all her doubts about the moral worth of this labour, Tsvetaeva lived a life of poetic dedication, writing through the most difficult personal experiences, and maintaining through everything the integrity and independence of the writer. It seems right then to finish this [essay] with a short, simple but rich poem which connects the craft of poetry both with tears and passion and with trees and the earth. It was written in 1933 and included in a cycle called **'Desk'** (**'Stol'**):

> My faithful writing desk!
> Thanks that you have remained,
> While giving a tree to me
> To become a desk, a tree!
>
> With the youthful play of leaves
> Over eyes, with the living bark,
> With the *living* resin tears,
> With roots deep down in earth!

Sibelan Forrester   (essay date 1992)

SOURCE: "Bells and Cupolas: The Formative Role of the Female Body in Marina Tsvetaeva's Poetry," in *Slavic Review,* Vol. 51, No. 2, Summer, 1992, pp. 232-46.

[*In the following excerpt, Forrester explores the relationship between the female body and Moscow architecture, particularly the church, in Tsvetaeva's poetry.*]

Like many other Russian women writers, Marina Tsvetaeva did not merely include women's language and physical experience in her poetry; they were central to her concern with poetry and poetic creation. These elements of her work have in recent years evoked an interest from women readers and feminist scholars of Russian literature which

is reflected in the number of studies devoted to aspects of her work. Antonina Gove discusses the presence and chronological development of female roles in Tsvetaeva's poetry ["The Feminine Stereotype and Beyond: Role Conflict and Resolution in the Poetics of Marina Tsvetaeva," *Slavic Review,* Vol. 36, 1977]; Anya Kroth illustrates the importance of gender and specifically androgyny in Tsvetaeva's construction of a dichotomous world-view ["Androgyny as an Exemplary Feature of Marina Tsvetaeva's Dichotomous Poetic Vision," *Slavic Review,* Vol. 38, 1979]. Barbara Heldt's landmark study of women in Russian literature, *Terrible Perfection,* devotes several pages to Tsvetaeva as an autobiographer and a woman poet liberated from the "split selves" of her predecessors [*Terrible Perfection: Women and Russian Literature,* 1987]. In her recent book *Death in Quotation Marks,* Svetlana Boym examines how Tsvetaeva's self-mythologization as a poet involves "killing the poetess," that female dilettante stereotyped in Russian culture ["The Death of the Poetess," *Death in Quotation Marks: Cultural Myths of the Modern Poet,* 1991]. These and other studies discuss the poet's multifaceted treatment of female physicality and sexuality in poetry that explores the complex links between culture and physical experience, and that significantly expands the Russian tradition. Tsvetaeva worked within the stereotypes of Russian and western European culture to locate and test their effects on women and experiment with their constructs of gender. Women's language leads to a wide variety of consequences in her poetry, from traditional to subversive, from empowering to tragic.

The use of grammatically marked "female" language by Russian poets, male or female, has yet to be systematically studied, but the existence of unambiguously feminine linguistic markers might be seen as providing an identifiable "women's" language and hence the possibility of textual expression of the female body. Indeed, French literary theorist Hélène Cixous claims in a provocative reading that Tsvetaeva herself is a practitioner of *écriture féminine,* a process whereby the female body inscribes itself as text ["Difficult Joys," *The Body and Text: Hélène Cixous, Reading and Teaching,* 1990]. Cixous interprets parts of Tsvetaeva's autobiographic prose as metaphorical recovery of the female body; much of Tsvetaeva's poetry similarly investigates the sublimation of female physicality in Russian culture and religion. In poems devoted to the architecture of Moscow, Tsvetaeva re-realizes the female body: she revives the church by the presence of a woman's body and language while at the same time the church's status and aesthetic value lend value to the poet's words.

Tsvetaeva depicted a connection between Moscow and women in the early poem **"Domiki staroi Moskvy"** (**"Houses of Old Moscow"**) published in 1912 in *Volshebnyi fonar' (The Magic Lantern)* and that association continued into her poetry of the revolutionary and civil war period when she compared the city to female historical figures. As Simon Karlinsky points out, the city of Moscow is "a central unifying leitmotif" in Tsvetaeva's 1916 collection, *Versty (vypusk I) (Versts [number I]).* In it she locates herself amid the city's historic figures and poetic geography and outlines for herself, a little-known 24-year-old poet, a place among established Petersburg poets, including the foremost woman poet of her age, Anna Akhmatova. Tsvetaeva described her concern with Petersburg and its traditions in her 1936 prose memoir, "Nezdeshnii vecher" ("An Otherworldly Evening"), which details a visit to Petrograd at the end of 1915 and its influence on her writing of 1916. Much has been made of her use of the commonplaces that distinguish Moscow from St. Petersburg, many of them springing from oppositions based on gender. When she met Mikhail Kuzmin and other Petersburg poets, Tsvetaeva felt marked by her Moscow speech and reacted by speaking with increasingly Muscovite mannerisms: "Leniu fizicheski chisto dolzhen razdrazhat' moi moskovskii go-vor:—spasibo—ladno—takoe, kotoroe on neizmenno ot-mechaet:—Nastoiashchaia moskvichka!—chtó menia uzhe nachinaet zlit' i uzhe zastavliaet ètu moskovskost'—usilivat', tak chto s Lenei, gladkogolovym, tochnym, tochenym—ia, v'iushchaiasia v skobku, so svoim 'push-che' i 'gushche'—nemnozhko vrode moskovskogo iam-shchika" (Lenya must be purely physically irritated by my Moscow speech: "spasibo," "ladno," the sort of thing he invariably notes: "a real Moscow woman!" This starts to get me angry and forces me to intensify my Moscow-ness, so that with Lenya [smooth-headed, exact, chiseled], I [curving into a parenthesis] with my "pushche" and "gushche" am a little like a Moscow coachman). Tsvetaeva recited poems in order to represent Moscow to "ves' Peterburg" (all of Petersburg) and included Akhmatova with the male poets mentioned in "An Otherworldly Evening" in that monolithic masculine "ves' Peterburg" to stress the feminine gender of "odna Moskva" (Moscow alone).

Of course, Tsvetaeva was born and raised in Moscow and so might have been expected to make poetic use of the city's associations in Russian history and culture. The same origin, however, did not prevent many other poets from joining Petersburg literary movements. Tsvetaeva's selection of "backward," patriarchal Moscow as an element of her poetic identity suggests that its many "feminine" associations provided her with language and possibilities that Petersburg did not: among other things, a historical and architectural background that is "female." Even the Moscow Kremlin, grammatically masculine and symbol of patriarchal authority in Muscovite Russia, was transformed by Tsvetaeva's focus on the "feminine" churches at its heart and by its geographical and poetic proximity to the (doubly-feminine) Moskvareka (Moscow River). A close reading of poems from 1916 shows that Tsvetaeva rejected denigration of Moscow as a poetic and historical back-water as she elaborated instead her own version of her native city and its traditions. Moscow thus assumes equal status with St. Petersburg and Tsvetaeva claimed equality with the best-known poets from that city.

Moscow's "female" church architecture determines elements of the poet's identities in three poems which I will discuss here. The poems, **"Kanun Blagoveshchen'ia"** ("Annunciation Eve"), **"U tonkoi provoloki nad volnoi ovsov"** ("The slender wire above the sea of oats") and

"Zakinuv golovu i opustiv glaza" (**"Lifting my fore-head and lowering my eyes"**), set up a relationship of physical body to textual body through bells and cupolas. As Jane Taubman points out in her article "Tsvetaeva and Akhmatova: Two Female Voices in a Poetic Quartet" [*Russian Literature Triquarterly,* Vol. 9, 1974], the bells and cupolas that recur in Tsvetaeva's poetry from 1916 to 1918 are not only real and evocative elements of the Moscow landscape but are also "enclosing spaces" with revealing Freudian significance. The church is, of course, an extremely resonant symbol of Russian culture which more or less links Russian Christianity with the rest of Christian and especially western European culture. Joanna Hubbs points out in her recent book, *Mother Russia, The Feminine Myth in Russian Culture,* that Christian churches in Russia are traditionally built and described in structural equivalence to the female body. Female elements in religion contribute to Tsvetaeva's definition of her being as a poet and her use of the discourse of religion underlines her reverence for poetry.

"Annunciation Eve," dated March 24-25, the eve and the day of that holiday, marks one of the first appearances in Tsvetaeva's poetry of Moscow's church architecture and gives a detailed description of architectural features that she would later abbreviate. The Immaculate Conception has been an image of great power for women writers, linking as it does womb and word; in Tsvetaeva's poetry it proves to be a crucial metaphor for the poetic process. The time (the Eve of the Annunciation) and place (the Cathedral of the Annunciation) coincide in a numinous location in the heart (or womb) of Moscow. This long poem has a looser rhyme scheme than Tsvetaeva usually favored and is unified by its sound texture; it also explores a disharmony between writing and motherhood absent in many other poems which she wrote at the time. She first describes the cathedral with moon and star above it (recalling Constantinople), beggars on the porch with repulsive voices, lamps and chandelier, saints with faces black from insomnia and icy windows in the cupola. While the worshipers pass a candle from hand to hand, the speaker herself prays to "Solntse-Materi" (the Sun-Mother), asking that she protect her daughter and keep her from her mother's "slovesnoi pyshnosti" (verbal luxuriance) so that the little girl will not also become "khishchnitsei, / Chernoknizhnitsei" (a bird of prey, / A practitioner of black magic). Once the service ends, people go their various ways but the speaker merrily shoves them aside "kak volny valkie" (like unsteady waves) and runs to the Moscow River to watch the ice breaking.

Though the male clergy and male saints are tacitly present in this poem, Tsvetaeva's speaker describes women: the beggar-women in the porch at the beginning of the poem, the old women who pause to cross themselves at its end and the speaker herself. Inside the church, at the center of the poem, is a gendered space seen as female, underscored here by its dedication not only to the Mother of God but also to the conception of her child, which highlights Mary's womb and her role as a vessel. Her perfection is defined by a lack (of sin, here: sexual relations with a man) and by maternal devotion. She displays the traditional patriarchal construct of woman as space rather than voice. Unless sublimated into architecture, female anatomy is intrinsically sinful (except in the case of Mary) while language, the vehicle of male intellect and poetic/religious tradition, is elevated and spiritual. The Word that Mary bears is not her own, but rather God the Father's; furthermore, the Word incarnate is male. Mary bore a son but, like her own mother, Tsvetaeva in 1916 had only a female child. Girl-children might be potential bearers of the Word but in any but the most heretical Christian sects they can never *be* the Word.

Mary is mute and passive, just like Tsvetaeva's presentation of one of Russian culture's most notorious women, Pushkin's wife Natal'ia Goncharova, whose emptiness drove Pushkin to try to fill it. Stephanie Sandler's article, "Embodied Words: Gender in Cvetaeva's Reading of Puškin," points out that Tsvetaeva emphasized Natal'ia Nikolaevna's wordlessness: "Once again, the woman's silence merits Cvetaeva's implicit criticism, as well as the reiteration that the wordless beauty is a blank space, a nobody" [in the *Slavic and East European Journal,* Vol. 34, No. 2, Summer 1990]. Mary also recalls the Sibyl in Tsvetaeva's poems of 1922 and 1923: the Sibyl is invaded by Apollo and he reduces her body to a cave, womb or resonating space for the Voice that she bears. These myths of Mary and the Sibyl connect womb, breast, mouth and head, all of which are also united in the church's arrangement of space. The two types of female physicality exemplified by Mary and the Sibyl and inhabited by male language differ only in Tsvetaeva's attitude towards them depending on their expression in her culture. Mary's "Word" is not her own but Tsvetaeva's quotation of Ovid's Sibyl stresses possession of voice over that of body: "Moi zhily issiaknut, moi kosti vysokhnut, no *golos, golos—* ostavit mne Sud'ba!" (My veins shall run dry, my bones shall wither, but Fate shall leave me my *voice,* my *voice!*)

The narrator of **"Annunciation Eve"** is a woman who uses her voice and combines word and womb differently from Mary, a mere recipient of the Word and of the narrator's prayer. The speaker addresses neither God the Father nor God the Son (nor her husband, unless he can be understood as the angel who has flown from her), rather, she asks Mary, who shares the experience of motherhood, to protect her daughter. At the same time, the narrator distances herself from Mary since her prayer is the conception of her *own* word. The purpose of her prayer, besides sharing the joy of the holiday, might be that her daughter too be free to choose between church and poetry. In the end, the narrator flees outside to the spring thaw, leaving Mary inside the church where nothing seems to thaw or change.

It is significant as well that the narrator does not once do what I have already done several times: refer to *Bogoroditsa* (Bearer of God) as "Mary." Instead she adheres to the Orthodox tradition wherein Mary is identified by the titles "Bogoroditsa" or "Bogomater'" (God's mother) which describe Mary in terms of motherhood, as if she is not a person in her own right. The ambiguous phrase "Mater'— materi" (Mother—to a mother) evokes Tsvetaeva's mother, also named Marina, who died when the poet was a

Tsvetaeva, 1941.

child. This hidden equivalence adds undertones to the poet's relationship with the woman whom she addresses: the poet's mother and the Virgin are conflated into a single figure who has abandoned the narrator.

Motherhood is celebrated in the Orthodox liturgy for the Annunciation, part of which is echoed in the poem. Worshipers re-enact Mary's conception by enlivening the church-womb with words—a magical liturgical language— and fire—candles that illuminate and warm the virgin's icy womb. The word becomes fire that sparks conception: at the end of the poem, the ice on the Moscow river is breaking on this holy day near the equinox and the approach of spring and sunlight. The church itself is a womb: worshipers are in the position of children of the Mother of God and like the narrator are "born" out of the church at the end of the service. The narrator's exit is likened explicitly to the birth-like violence of the thaw of the Moscow river: she shoves her way out "like unsteady waves" to watch the ice break (freeing water and language) and takes with her the poem she conceived while in church.

Although the center of the poem echoes church liturgy, the narrator's relationship to the church is highly ambiguous. She admires the splendid lights but juxtaposes Mary's icon to the "disgusting voices" of beggar-women in the porch and sees the faces of the saints "shining with black insomnia." The poem also has a strong pagan or heretical subtext: the speaker's first glimpse of the moon above the church reminds her of Holy Sophia, the main cathedral of Byzantine Orthodoxy converted to a mosque; the moon recalls the Islamic moon abbreviated in the base of the Orthodox cross, the symbol of Russian conquest of the Tatars. These religious symbols contain their own negation and hint at mutability. Mary is addressed as "Sun-Mother," a locution from the pagan, pre-Christian stratum of Russian folk religion which reflects her amenability to reinterpretation by those who do not adhere to church dogma.

If Mary is the narrator's "Mother," the narrator cannot be the Word: besides her gender, her sin of "verbal luxuriance" makes her "a bird of prey" and "a [female] practitioner of black magic." The "black book" (chernaia kniga) of the poet-witch is *not* the Bible, a book of someone else's words to read and repeat. To recite or write one's own words, for a woman at least, is subversive if not sinful and here it clearly leads the narrator away from her child. It is not conceiving and writing a poem that is antithetical to child-bearing (since the speaker has done both) but, rather, choosing to be a poet, devoting all one's capacities to the production of one's own words rather than to reproduction of children.

Tsvetaeva's narrator not only does not imitate Mary but in this and many later poems her narrators reject repetition of established Orthodox doctrine. This poem itself is preceded and followed by poems that celebrate a folk *razgul* (debauch) chosen in defiance of inevitable patriarchal condemnation and punishment. In later poetry Tsvetaeva turned to the Greek myth of the Sibyl whom she both equated with and differentiated from the Virgin: while Mary gazes at her Son in silent adoration or suffers at His death, the Sibyl speaks words that her listeners must strive to hear and interpret and she is associated with poetry rather than with motherhood. With this shift, the poet gained not only the status of an oracle but a persona who was able to give birth to words repeatedly. Tsvetaeva's poems from 1916 also search for alternative deities: her narrator lights a large candle to Dmitrii and Marina, as if to icons and addresses Blok and Akhmatova in fulsomely religious language. The Virgin herself can assume alternative identities as a folk *Bogoroditsa-Troeruchitsa* (Three-armed Mother of God) or as part of someone else's poetic mythology (e.g. Akhmatova holding her son or Blok's last love).

In her prose reminiscences, Tsvetaeva retrospectively stressed the importance of Anna Akhmatova for her poetic development. The tenth poem in the 1916 cycle **"Stikhi k Akhmatovoi"** (**"Poems to Akhmatova"**), **"U tonkoi provoloki nad volnoi ovsov"** (**"The slender wire above the sea of oats"**) elaborates Akhmatova's influence on other women writing poetry at the time. . . .

(The slender wire above the sea of oats / Today has a voice—like a thousand voices! / And the coach bells driving past—holy, holy, holy— / Don't they speak, Lord, in the same voice. / I stand and listen and rub an ear of grain apart, / And the voice closes me in like a dark cupola. / / It's not these swimming willow branches / I touch devoutly—but your hand. / For all who languorously praise your approach,— / You are an earthly woman, but to me— a heavenly cross! / Nights I bow in prayer to you alone,— / And all the icons look out with *your* eyes!) Repetition of the word *golos* (voice) four times in the first six lines of the poem underlines its significance in Tsvetaeva's poetic philosophy. Here it is not the narrator's own voice but the objects around her that express Akhmatova's fame and, finally, Akhmatova's own voice. Religious imagery (particularly "holy, holy, holy") recalls the 1916 cycle of poems addressed to Blok as well as the rest of this cycle: such religious and liturgical vocabulary emphasizes poetry's significance in the narrator's life and in the world. The icons here, all looking with Akhmatova's eyes, grant Akhmatova semi-divine status. They are not only objects of prayer and worship but also windows into heaven; the worshiper's prayer, in effect, obliges Akhmatova to notice her.

More important than the icons for the purposes of this analysis is the "dark cupola" which encloses the speaker: both the voices that praise Akhmatova and Akhmatova's own voice place the narrator inside a church as a possibly unwilling worshiper. The union of voice and cupola recalls Blok's "Devushka pela v tserkovnom khore" ("A girl was singing in the church choir") with its ambiguous combination of artistic beauty and final despair. If the voice can go no farther than the cupola, it might as well die there. The narrator has been listening and rubbing apart an ear of grain, as if undoing her own poetic labor (the ripe ear perhaps equivalent to the completed poem). Akhmatova's voice and reputation put the speaker back in the womb where she can neither see nor move. There she also presumably grows and matures; her voice resonates and strengthens as she emerges from this imposed poetic daughterhood: the grain is free to be reborn from the earth's darkness. Although Tsvetaeva's daughter asserted that Akhmatova and Tsvetaeva were *sisters* in poetry, this poem suggests instead that their relationship was like that of mother and daughter. In another poem from the same cycle, Tsvetaeva imagines herself in the position of an heir beside Akhmatova's dead body; in yet another she equates Akhmatova with a heretical Virgin Mary, intimating the same connotations of womb and word discussed above. This implication is strengthened by comparison with the last poem she wrote to Sof'ia Parnok, **"V ony dni, ty mne byla kak mat'"** (**"In those days you were like a mother to me"**), also from 1916.

At the same time, Tsvetaeva's insistence in this cycle on naming, a prerogative she jealously reserves for mothers, allows her in turn to reverse roles, to mother and to assume power over Akhmatova. If a woman's possible relationships to a man include bearing the man's child as well as mothering him (an alternative Tsvetaeva frequently exploits), relations with other women, including Akhmatova, might entail becoming simultaneously poetic mother and daughter. The ambiguous nature of such a relationship is embodied by Akhmatova's presence in the poem: she is illuminated (an icon lit by a lamp, a heavenly cross that is both guide and burden) but also shadowed (like the dark interior of a cupola whose outside may shine with gold but whose inside provides no guide for the narrator). The ambiguity as to who is mother and who is daughter emphasizes the poet's agency in forming her own textual body: she is free to choose her own ancestors, to *become* someone else's poetic lover or child. The relationship takes place within a linguistic world that she herself takes part in creating.

The narrator's relationship with God, the saints and angels emerges in terms of church architecture in **"Zakinuv golovu i opustiv glaza" ("Lifting my forehead and lowering my eyes")**, written in 1918, the third poem in Part II of *Versty (vypusk II) (Versts [number II])*. Part II of this collection is commonly seen as a shift in focus from the flesh to the soul and its relationship with the body; in this poem too the body is a bearer of spiritual meaning. . . .

(Lifting my forehead and lowering my eyes, / I stand—before the visage of the Lord and all the saints. / Today is my holiday, today is—Judgment. / The assembly of youthful angels is embarrassed to tears. / The righteous are dispassionate. Only Thou, / On a throne-cloud, lookest as a friend would. / What thou wishest—ask. Thou art kind and old, / And thou wilt understand that with this kind of Kremlin bell / In my breast—it's impossible to lie. / And thou wilt understand how passionately, day and night, / Providence and Arbitrariness struggled / In the breast that moves—millstones. / Thus, as a mortal woman,—my gaze is lowered, / Thus, as a wrathful angel—my forehead is lifted, / On Annunciation day, at the Royal Gates, / Before thy face—look!—I stand. / And my voice, after abandoning my breast like a dove / moves in a circle in the red-golden cupola.) The assonantal texture of the poem (for example in line 11, "Bo-*ro-lis'* Pro-m*ysel* i Pro-*iz-vol*") and the absence of a regular rhyme scheme suggest the complexity of the equations it draws; rhymes and alliterations turn up unexpectedly both within lines and in final positions. The stressed ("masculine") line endings place extra emphasis on final words and syllables.

The narrator's physical presence is established by several details: her head is lifted while her eyes look down, and her breast or chest (*grud'*) is the emphasized final word in three lines. Direction simultaneously upward and downward reflects the narrator's dual nature of mortal woman and wrathful angel, a being who is both gendered and ungendered. The loss of gender at the scene of judgment is maintained by the absence of any grammatical indications of the speaker's gender until the penultimate stanza; as Anya Kroth points out, angels are beings who transcend gender. (In the Russian tradition, however, this transcendance is usually expressed through masculine names and forms.) The duality grows stronger when the woman is explicitly labeled as one who shall die whereas an angel is immortal and partakes of divinity. The Russian tradition has always retained the ambiguous, dually sensual and

religious connotations of the word *strast'* (passion) but here the passion associated with the speaker is denied to the Righteous, perhaps privileging the woman's body over those of "holy" men.

What appears at first reading to be merely duality is multiplied by the complexity of associations and by the vertical convergence, typical of Tsvetaeva's poetics, in which heaven and hell, God and devil are separated by no more than a breath. Even the angelic nature of the speaker is not simple: the angel is facing God rather than standing with him, a prideful posture that might suggest Lucifer. Two lines in the poem end with *"stoiu"* (I stand) set off by dashes from the rest of the line; the effect is one of a narrator frozen in space, her stance a challenge, as if she will wait there until judgment is forthcoming.

Facing the speaker are God, the angels and the Righteous, as depicted in icons on the Russian church's iconostasis. The Church Slavic preposition in the phrase *"Pred likom"* (before the visage) and the capitalization of *"Sud"* (Judgment) underline the gravity of the narrator's position: this is not merely a pictorial version of theology but the Last Judgment itself. *"Lik"* (visage) refers to the ineffable quality of the icon but also identifies it as merely an image, a symbol of the God provided by her culture and religion. The narrator's position at the royal gates (which divide the main space of the church, accessible to the mass of worshippers, from the inner sanctum) echoes that of a soul seeking admission to paradise, as in the epigraph to Tsvetaeva's *Versts* (*number I*), "Ptitsy raiskie poiut, / V rai voiti nam ne daiut" (Birds of paradise sing, / They do not let us enter paradise). God himself, however, looks at the speaker as a friend would and, after its first appearance, the informal pronoun *Ty* (Thou) is no longer capitalized. The speaker grows less formal and more intimate with God as the poem progresses: by the first line of the last stanza, this increasing intimacy incorporates God's presence in the space that the poem creates and the solemn "Before the visage" of the first stanza gives way to the everyday forms *"Pered litsom tvoim"* (In front of thy face) in the sixth stanza. Unlike many poems in which the reader may assume the role of addressee, the impossibility of assuming God's role at the Last Judgment renders the reader a mere spectator to the poem and reminds us that the poet, however much she may value our attention and admiration, is concerned primarily with other questions.

The Last Judgment for the poet occurs on "[her] holiday," the Annunciation, two years after the date of **"Annunciation Eve."** Another earlier poem, **"V den' Blagoveshchen'ia" ("On Annunciation Day")**, refers to the day as *"prazdnik moi"* (my holiday) as does this one and shows the narrator freeing tame birds in accord with the folk tradition of the holiday. The Annunciation illuminates Tsvetaeva's activity as a woman poet, a woman who bears the Word. She is to be judged both as a mortal being of the female gender and as a poet, if indeed the two can be separated while they are united in the same person. While **"Annunciation Eve"** treats the eve of the holiday, in **"Lifting my fore-**

head and lowering my eyes" the narrator is to be judged on the day itself: her deeds (or poems) are complete and immutable, no longer open to advice or command but only to explanation and justification.

The teleology of the Last Judgment is emphasized by Tsvetaeva's use of capitalization which follows the standard usage of her time in most of the poem but highlights the words *"Promysel"* and *"Proizvol."* Their significance as "Providence" and "Arbitrariness" may perhaps also be translated as "Cosmos" and "Chaos"; capitalization calls attention to their identical prefix *pro-,* meaning "going through" or "passing." Thus the two categories that struggle within her breast achieve a directedness quite appropriate to the final event of a life in linear time. At the same time, this directedness is opposed to the cyclic action of the millstones in the speaker's breast, a circling which is repeated in the end by the freed voice in the cupola.

The image of millstones harks back to the grain that the narrator rubs in **"The slender wire above the sea of oats"** as well as to other poems from the revolutionary period in which Tsvetaeva equates poetry with agricultural processes. Grinding grain is hard labor, the fate of human beings cast out of Paradise. Nonetheless, grain ground into flour results in the bread that becomes flesh or Flesh, a transsubstantiation that ties labor directly to inspiration. Work and inspiration, perhaps in parallel to "Providence" and "Arbitrariness," inhabit the speaker's breast and generate her poetry.

The last stanza of **"Lifting my forehead and lowering my eyes"** differs from the others in that the first line, which continues the syntax of the preceding stanza, is separated graphically from the following two lines. The physical separation on the page mirrors the flight of the narrator's voice as it leaves her body and circles high above her head, following the acoustics of the church's interior. Her voice moves like a dove (the first syllables *gol*-os and *gol*-ub' recall *kol*-okol of the third stanza) which is also located in the speaker's breast. This dove is the symbol of the Annunciation, the Holy Spirit and the bird that is traditionally to be freed on the holiday. The cupola where it circles is neither icy nor dark, as in the earlier poems, but bright red-gold: the narrator has emerged from night and daughterhood into the day when she will be judged as a mature poet. The inspiration of the day is simultaneous with the birth of the words which emerge from her body and take flight as a separate being.

The narrator's voice has left her at the moment which will presumably seal her fate forever and this offers several possible readings. Perhaps, just as the dove has risen above the iconostasis, the speaker may rise above the judgment represented by the church's iconography. Without her voice and its spiritually redeeming qualities, though, she may be found wanting. The dove circling above may convey that the cyclic and timeless nature of poetry exempts it from the linear model of human life: the voice remains after the speaker has been judged and has passed on to heaven or hell. The ever-present subtext of Blok's "A girl was sing-

ing in the church choir" reminds us that the bird, flying or not, is still within the cupola rather than free in the sky.

The result of the judgment which the speaker anticipates is up in the air. Possibilities range from the most joyful (to be assumed, body and soul, into heaven since, like Mary, the speaker has borne the Word) to the most sinister (to be cast down as a wrathful angel, Lucifer, who was often linked in Christian tradition to the female sex). What can be said with certainty is that the poet, as both woman and angel, both body and voice, is a microcosm of the earth capable of containing any number of apparently contradictory elements. Tsvetaeva explores the implications of her gender here not by including the male (equally-gendered) alternative but by ascribing to herself traits of an angel who transcends gender. She is perpetually at a point where opposites contact and interact with one another in a tension that produces the holy bread of her poetry.

The cupola and iconostasis in this poem convey a complex interplay of church and female body: the architecture peculiar to Moscow and Muscovite Russia is internalized by a poem in which Moscow itself is no longer celebrated. The narrator's breast holds millstones and a Kremlin bell and, like the *Tsar'-kolokol* which once housed a small chapel, it is itself a church. The Moscow church contains the narrator's body which is itself a church and which also contains the church of her breast. With its depictions of divine beings and its history, a church is a microcosm of the world; its cupola above (golden here, in other cases dark blue with golden stars) represents the sky or heaven. The narrator's voice, then, has reached heaven like a dove that will intercede for her. At the same time, the resonant cupola is a womb, so that the voice's ascent mirrors the descent of the dove—the Holy Spirit—at the Annunciation.

This poem and the others that I have discussed treat the Russian church as a body and the woman poet's body as a church (not necessarily an orthodox one!), allowing female experience to move from the periphery of Russian culture to the center. For all its repression or diabolization of the "feminine" elements that do not fit patriarchal definitions of acceptable womanhood, the church still houses its liturgy within architectural forms which are both beautiful and "female" and which offer the woman poet a paradigm for poetic creation that is deeply problematic but also very fertile. The "tower of the symbolists," readable as an attempt to move away from earthly reality and closer to the Absolute, is transformed in Tsvetaeva's poems to resemble a bell tower that links earth to heaven but belongs to neither. This explains why the poet in her **"Poèt—izdaleka zavodit rech' . . ."** (**"The poet acquires speech from afar . . ."**) might swing off the bell tower: ringing bells is what poets always do. Tsvetaeva expressed the urge to plunge downward or fly upward rather than continue the tension that made human life so difficult for her, even though it provided the disharmonies of gender, physicality and spirituality, etc. as bases for her poetry.

The narrators of these poems are neither mortal nor divine, neither totally mother nor totally poet. Each assumes a medial place that is typical both of Tsvetaeva's poetics and of sacrificial roles in mythology: suspended from a high place, wise beings and victims assume a location between heaven and earth. A woman is both bearer, the Marian or Sibylline vessel of life and the word, and potential martyr, a broken body whose soul has flown like the narrator's voice in the third poem examined here. The numinous moment of childbirth, especially in Tsvetaeva's era, often involved both possibilities. A complex relationship of body and soul or spirit emerges from an analysis of the place of female physicality in Tsvetaeva's poetics. Final judgment of poetic activity remains suspended, however, since it is not clear whether creating new beings through language amounts to praiseworthy imitation of God or damnable competition.

Michael Makin   (essay date 1993)

SOURCE: "The Late Poetry," in *Marina Tsvetaeva: Poetics of Appropriation,* Oxford at the Clarendon Press, 1993, pp. 295-323.

[*In the following excerpt, Makin discusses Tsvetaeva's poetic output in her later years, particularly her transition from writing lyrics to long poems or* poemy.]

The distinguishing features of the late Tsvetaeva are clearest of all in her lyric poetry. From 1907 to 1925 she completed over 1,000 lyrics. In her last sixteen years she is known to have written fewer than 100: an average of roughly six poems a year. There were, of course, more or less prolific years in both the first and the second halves of her career, but the first half saw the completion of seven major collections, the second the completion of fewer lyrics than are contained in *Remeslo* alone, a collection composed in just over twelve months. The reasons for this dramatic decline in her lyric output are far from clear. Tsvetaeva frequently spoke of her isolation in emigration and the hostility of literary journals. Following these remarks, some scholars have explained the decline as a consequence of her move to prose, which she wrote because it was more acceptable to the journals. Others point to her increased interest in other genres: the verse play and the narrative poem. Undoubtedly, there is some truth in both explanations: she did write more prose after 1925 than before, and her tendency to narrative, evident throughout her poetry, was now directly expressed in her long, non-lyric works. But it should be remembered that she had previously been able to write prolifically in many different genres, as the vast output of lyrics, plays, *poemy,* and prose in the late 1910s and early 1920s proves. Moreover, it is hard to believe that the editorial policies of journals had any influence over her, for, of all the forms of poetry, long narrative works were the least welcome in *émigré* journals, yet these were precisely the works to which Tsvetaeva devoted enormous time and energy in the late 1920s. The material hardship to which Tsvetaeva herself referred is also cited by some writers as an explanation for the lyric decline. Again, it is hard to deny the influence of her straitened circumstances on her writing, but it should be recalled that some of her most productive years were in Moscow after the Revolution, when she lived in great poverty (and wrote without any immediate prospect of publication).

An examination of the poetry itself is at least as informative as other possible approaches, and is of particular interest to the student of Tsvetaeva's use of literary sources. The break of 1926 is strongly marked in her lyrics: whereas the majority of her poems from 1907 until 1925 are organized in *etapnye sborniki,* uniting many or all of the lyrics of a given period, the poetry of the late Tsvetaeva is discrete: after *Posle Rossii* she did not compose another collection. Moreover, within the *etapnye sborniki,* and even in the uncollected poetry of 1916-26, lyrics form long, loosely associated narrative sequences in which, as has been shown, a poem is often followed by its opposite in theme, reference, or style, or by a poem which develops one aspect of the preceding work. The narrative pull expressed in the organization of the collections and sequences is restricted in the late lyrics to a series of cycles, containing associated poems, such as the cycles in memory of Mayakovsky and of Voloshin, the poems to Pushkin and to Shteiger. With the abandonment of complex narrative patterns comes a new style: simpler, more openly rhetorical, less dependent on the complex linguistic distortion which characterizes the lyrics of *Remeslo* and *Posle Rossii.* Poems with repeated and simple refrains, and emphatic, unequivocal statement are far more common; the enigmatic fragments encountered frequently in the earlier poetry are proportionately rarer. The occasion and contents of poems are more often announced in titles: **'Stikhi k Pushkinu' ('Poems to Pushkin'), 'Ici-haut. Pamyati Maksimiliana Voloshina' ('Ici-haut. To the Memory of Maksimilian Voloshin'),** for example. In other words, there is a consistent development towards the direct and relatively undemanding: the baroque flourishes of the early 1920s are replaced with a simpler rhetoric. The emergence of prominent rhetorical patterns in *Posle Rossii* has already been noted; the simplification of this rhetoric in the later lyrics may be seen not only as another stage in the poet's development, but also perhaps as an expression of the influence of the apparently larger number of major public readings which she gave after moving to Paris: her later lyrics reveal a style more suited to public, stage performance. Writing to A. A. Polyakov, one of the editors of the newspaper *Poslednie novosti,* Tsvetaeva accompanies her complaints about unsympathetic journals with the remark that *u menya net vozmozhnosti obshchat'sya s russkim chitatelem inache, chem ustno* ('I have no opportunity to address the *Russian* reader, except orally'; emphasis Tsvetaeva's) ['Tsvetaeva v pis'makh: Iz Bakhmetevskogo arkhiva Kolumbiiskogo universiteta', ed. J. Malmstad, *Literaturnoe obazrenie,* 1990, no. 7 (letter of 29 March 1935)]. Questionable though this assertion may be, it emphasizes the importance of her public readings. It also suggests that Tsvetaeva felt considerable linguistic isolation—a circumstance which will be explored below.

By the 1930s Tsvetaeva's lyrics had been pared down: little remained of the earlier complexities of reference and language, and the hidden narratives associated with the intense lyric production of the early 1920s. As has been shown, the poetry of that period was remarkable for its literary saturation: sources from the Bible to *Slovo o polku Igoreve,* from the story of Ariadne to that of Hamlet are prominent in the lyrics of **Remelso** and **Posle Rossii.** The late lyrics continue to show some interest in literary topics: the addresses of many are poets (Pushkin, Tsvetaeva's contemporaries Gronsky and Shteiger, for example) and literary references are still made—for example, to Wolfe's poem 'The Burial of Sir John Moore at Corunna' in the first two lines of the sixth of the **'Stikhi k Pushkinu',** or to Dostoevsky's *Brat'ya Karamazovy (The Brothers Karamazov)* in the eighth of the March **'Stikhi k Chekhii'** (**'Poems to Bohemia'**). Echoes of Derzhavin, one of Tsvetaeva's favourite poets, have been suggested in **'Razgovor s geniem'** (**'Conversation with my Inspiration'**) and the second poem of the cycle **'Nadgrobie', 'Naprasno glazom, kak gvozdem'** (**'Epitaph', 'In vain with eye as with a nail'**) (3: 138-9; 3: 182). **'Dvukh stanov ne boets, a—esli gost' sluchainyi—'** (**'Not a fighter for two positions, but—if I'm a casual guest—'**), a polemical poem of 1935, opens with a distortion of the first line of a poem by A. K. Tolstoy. As will be seen, one of her very last poems offers the most significant examples of advertised rewriting in her late period. However, not one of the lyrics written after 1925 can be said to be in total a rewriting of a literary source, such as are so many of the poems in her prolific period. This strongly suggests, as has been maintained throughout, an association between the production of her intense and difficult poetry and her use of literary sources—perhaps a causal association. Abandoning such sources—consciously or not—was part of a move away from complexity in form, reference, and theme, which also entailed a considerable decline in output.

The story of the late narrative poetry is rather different. As has been seen, by 1926 Tsvetaeva had completed the only *poemy* of over 1,000 lines which she ever published: *Tsar'-Devitsa, Molodets,* and *Krysolov.* These, like *Pereulochki,* are based on literary sources. In Prague she had written two shorter *poemy* (**'Poema gory'** and **'Poema kontsa'**) not based on literary sources and much shorter than the **'poemy-skazki'** and *Krysolov.* These shorter works can be described as a mixture of the realistic and the discursive. Between 1926 and 1928 she wrote six more *poemy* which belong to the same group as **'Poema gory'** and **'Poema kontsa.'** They are all based on realistic, non-literary themes, although the treatment of these themes is often abstract, and they are not without literary reference. These works are: **'S morya'** (**'From the Seaside'**), a verse-letter addressed to Pasternak, and sent from the seaside; **'Lestnitsa'** (**'Staircase'**), a satirical description of the life of and on a gloomy staircase in an apartment house; **'Popytka komnaty'** (**'An Attempt at a Room'**), an attempt to create the physical space of a room in verse; **'Novogodnee'** (**'For New Year'**), a New Year's letter addressed to the newly deceased Rilke, and sent from this world to the next, where the addressee now resides; **'Poema vozdukha'** (**'Poem of the Air'**), written at the time of Lindbergh's flight across the Atlantic, and describing in rather abstract terms the climb through the various levels of the atmo-

sphere; **'Krasnyi bychok'** (**'The Red Steer'**), describing a nightmare of pursuit by a red steer. An unfinished *poema* of 1926, in which Tsvetaeva reflected on recent Russian history, on the phenomenon of emigration, and on her fate as an *émigrée,* should also be mentioned. After this period of intense activity on short *poemy* she wrote two more works belonging to the same group: **'Avtobus'** (**'The Omnibus'**) (1934-6), describing a bus trip into the French countryside, and the narrator's conversation with her companion; **'Pevitsa'** (**'The Singer'**) (1935), describing the enchantment felt by two people hearing a neighbour's voice through the thin walls of their apartment. Neither work was published in her lifetime, and the latter is unfinished. As with the lyrics, a pattern of intense activity and prolific production is followed by a decline in output; as with the lyrics, this is accompanied by a move away from complexity towards simple, direct narration: **'Poema vozdukha'** and **'Popytka komnaty,'** written at the height of her interest in the genre, are the most complex of the short *poemy,* and are followed by the much easier **'Krasnyi bychok,' 'Avtobus,'** and **'Pevitsa'.** These short *poemy* differ from the lyrics, and from every other poetic genre in which Tsvetaeva worked, in that none of them is based on a literary source. This confirms the impression given by the lyrics that after 1925 she was seeking a new manner, free of literary saturation and more direct. On the other hand, the concept of rewriting an inherited text in the wider sense is still applicable: **'S morya'** and **'Novogodnee'** both take the familiar inherited (and, as so often in Tsvetaeva's work, archaic) 'text' of the literary epistle, the former providing a defence for the poet's method in so doing, when the narrator writes of herself as picking up the bits and pieces left on the shore by the sea:

Just the sand, between fingers, runny.
Wait now: the fragments of some sort of stanza:
'Underground shrine of fame'.
All right. You'll write the rest.

In other words, a fragment of poetry is found (inherited) by one poet (the narrator) and passed on to another poet (the addressee, Pasternak) for him to complete. Thus, the action of the sea provides a metaphor for the use of literary material observed throughout Tsvetaeva's poetry (as it did in the lyric 'Tak plyli—golova i lira' in **Remeslo**).

All of the shorter *poemy* which form this group take a familiar situation or scene and rewrite it, employing much of the linguistic distortion and narrative discontinuity first used in the treatment of literary material. Brodsky in his essay on **'Novogodnee'** correctly emphasizes that *Deistvitel'nost' dlya nee—vsegda otpravnaya tochka, a ne tochka opory ili tsel' puteshestviya* ('Reality for her is always a starting-point, and not the fulcrum or end of the journey'), but the novelty of these *poemy* is in the presence of reality (and not literature) even as a starting-point ['Ob odnom stikhotvorenii (Vmesto predisloviya)' (introductory essay to *Stikhotvoreniya i poemy*)].

The case of the longer *poemy* is more curious. The first three long *poemy* which Tsvetaeva completed are among her finest works, were well received, even if only by her most sensitive readers, and were dependent on the use of a familiar literary source. Yet, despite the success of *Tsar'-Devitsa, Molodets,* and *Krysolov,* after 1925 she attempted to abandon literature as the starting-point for her long *poemy* too. First, in 1928, she returned to *Egorushka.* She wrote the fifth canto, **'Sokolinaya slobodka'** (**'Falcon City'**), and further plans. **'Sokolinaya slobodka'** is less marked by imitations of folkloric narrative and style than the earlier cantos. It is more concise and more self-conscious, reading in places rather like parts of *Krysolov.* The main action—the hero's several acts of magical craftsmanship—resolves what had been opposites in her earlier poetry: art as craft and art as magic. None the less, as will be recalled, she again abandoned the work without completing it. Although she cannot have been satisfied with *Egorushka,* she continued to experiment with long narrative poems and abandoned literary sources altogether. Her last two long *poemy* were **'Perekop'** and the so-called **'Poema o tsarskoi sem'e'** (**'Poem about the Imperial Family'**); of the latter only fragments are extant. They too suggest that she was trying to find a new manner and a new range of themes. Both are historical works, using written but not strictly literary sources, still less a single source or a unified body of sources. For **'Perekop,'** describing the final stand of the White Army under Wrangel at the Crimean isthmus of Perekop in 1920, the principal source was the unpublished diary of her husband, Sergei Efron, who participated in the campaign. For **'Poema o tsarskoi sem'e'** the sources are described by the editors of *Sochineniya* as a *bol'shoe kolichestvo istoricheskikh materialov* ('a large collection of historical materials'). Thus, neither poem takes and rewrites a familiar source which can provide a clear basic structure. Both *poemy* are the products of an attempt to write realistic and, at the same time, epic works, describing events of the recent past. They both were, despite their 'White' themes and sympathies, totally inconsonant with the demands of the *émigré* press, and not least with the political tendency of the liberal *Volya Rossii,* the only journal at all likely to publish long narrative poetry by Tsvetaeva. That she should devote so much time to such obviously 'unwanted' works is clear evidence that, despite her own complaints about editors, editorial policy had little influence on her writing, and that appealing to an audience, and even earning a living, were not of paramount concern to her, although all these factors may well have influenced her ability to construct a necessary 'imaginary' or 'ideal' audience. Indeed, those to whom she read these *poemy* offered her as little encouragement as the representatives of the literary 'establishment'. Only one listener was able to exercise any influence by voicing an adverse opinion: Sergei Efron, who, no longer sympathetic to the cause which he had once served, seems to have prevented her from writing the last part of **'Perekop,'** which was to have been a description of the Whites after their counter-attack, with which **'Perekop'** now ends. Thus far it is a finished work, however. As Tsvetaeva herself said, *Zakonchila, no i ne zakonchila* ('I completed it, without completing it'). Indeed, that it ends with victory, not defeat, provides a 'rewriting' of familiar events typical for Tsvetaeva, and comparable to the revisions to sources evident in the endings of *Tsar'-Devitsa, Pereulochki,* and *Molodets.* Of course, it

is impossible to tell how the work would have looked if the poet had written what she called the 'last Perekop'—the final rout (4: 320). She worked on it from August 1928 to May 1929, and returned to it in 1939, when she produced a fair copy, accompanied by a number of explanatory notes, which she sent for safe keeping to a Slavist in Switzerland, judging that **'Perekop'** was unsuitable for transport to the Soviet Union. This fair copy is now in the Basle archive. **'Perekop'** was finally published in 1967, in the New York almanac *Vozdushnye puti.* **'Perekop'** was published in the Soviet Union in 1990. The fate of **'Poema o tsarskoi sem'e'** is similar, although most accounts suggest that it was finished. It described the last months of the Russian imperial family, with digressions on the history of Siberia, apropos of their imprisonment there. Only one canto was published, first in *Volya Rossii* in 1931, under the title **'Sibir''.** The rest of the *poema* has been lost, except for fragments published by Korkina.

'Perekop' and **'Sibir''** are revealing about the change in Tsvetaeva's narrative poetry. Like the late lyrics, they lack both the density and the intensity of their predecessors. The abandoning of literary sources is accompanied by the development of a style which is more uniform and far more penetrable than the most difficult parts of *Krysolov* or *Molodets*: in particular, there is less metrical and linguistic diversity. But the abandoning of literary sources also produces a narrative which (paradoxically) is too disjunctive and incoherent: the unifying structure provided by a single source is lost. Whereas the earlier works relied upon the disruption of a familiar inherited narrative and plot, usually recognized by the reader (that is, relied upon the establishment of tension between disjunction and coherence), **'Perekop'** declines into episodic *longueurs,* and, to judge from **'Sibir'',** the same was probably true of **'Poema o tsarskoi sem'e.'** Furthermore, the move towards historical realism causes problems: the speech of historical characters, especially from the recent past, cannot be presented in the same way as the speech of the fantastic characters of *Tsar'-Devitsa, Molodets,* or *Krysolov.* This is well illustrated in the passage of **'Perekop'** describing the address of the *polkovnik sed* ('colonel, hair-of-grey') (itself an uncomfortable term for a commander addressing a modern army) to his troops before the decisive attack:

> But—the second essence's,
> The material and worldly speech—
> Interrupts the spiritual father's—
> Speech of our father the commander,
> Colonel, hair-of-grey:
>
> —Fate of all the fatherland,
> That—is ours! Of millions
> Who are not-red, not-green,
> That is ours! Of generations
> Is in su—ccess in conflict!
>
> You commanders of battalions
> Draw up your battalions!
> And prepare yourselves for the
> Du—ties of the conflict!

But first to the strike in battle—
Are hearts. They make ears ring out!
In whispers the commands
Are issued, and battalions
Are moving.—Silence.—Leaving,
You?!—What?—It cannot be!—*Aye-aye*
Cap'n. Firecracker—
Upwards. One! Now two sir! No end
To 'em. It is your palette,
Hell! Sudden—not in ears—in chest—
Sound;—Barbed wire's cut throu—ou—
ough! Barbed wire's cut barbed wire's cut
Through! Not to have been here—
Is not to have lived.

Till when the whole sky was
Alight, and we still *did*
Not blink an eye, to the stars—so bright,
That—'lights or are you shedding tears?'

Oh, youthful-commander-bright-light-Markov-the
bold—did you not survive to this?!

(emphasis Tsvetaeva's)

The familiar devices—the division of words (*V u—
dache . . .*), the combination of several words into com-
pounds with hyphens (*Ekh, mlad-komandir-svet-Markov-
/kvnat . . .*), the punning (*Do miga, kogda vse nebo /
Migalo . . .*)—fit very uncomfortably into a poem which
claims to be telling the story of Perekop as it actually
happened. Moreover, the absence of *literary* conflict
between source and version—in part motivating such
effects elsewhere—leads, conversely, to rather unsatisfactory prominence for other literary elements: the set-
piece pre-battle speech and the folkloric language have
neither the energy nor the playfulness of earlier *poemy*.
Tsvetaeva herself seems to have been dissatisfied. When
she produced the fair copy to send to Switzerland she
included in her extensive explanatory notes appended to
the *poema* (a unique example in her work of such an
apparatus) an apologetic comment on her *beznadezhnaya
neizlechimaya voennaya slepost'* ('hopeless, incurable
military blindness') (4: 326). Of the poem about the imperial family she wrote equally harshly: *Istorik poeta—
zagnal* ('the historian drove out the poet'). These last
two long *poemy* are an attempt to develop a new artistic
manner: realistic, historical, without literary saturation.
The failure of this attempt helps to explain why there were
no successors to them.

The case of the verse plays is different again. As has
been shown, the two classical plays were a successful
and novel development of the form used with far less
success in the early plays. None the less, after completing the second play of the planned trilogy (*Fedra*) in
1927, she abandoned her plans for the third, *Elena*. One
reason for this may be that, although the classical plays,
unlike the two late long *poemy*, are successful developments of an earlier form, their success is dependent on a
complex and highly literary model, and on the very evident use of literary sources. This was alien to the gener-

al development of her original work towards greater clarity
and simplicity, and away from the literary saturation which
had characterized her work in the early 1920s.

By the early 1930s her output in all kinds of verse had
declined enormously. She continued to write lyrics, but at
a much reduced rate. After *Fedra* there were no more
plays. The short *poemy* of the late 1920s had only two,
unsatisfactory, successors after 1930 ('**Avtobus**' and '**Pevitsa**'). She worked on '**Poema o tsarskoi sem'e**,' the
last of her long *poemy*, in the 1930s, but it, like '**Perekop**'
and *Egorushka,* was not a success.

There can be no doubt that her life in emigration was
difficult, and that the lack of an enthusiastic readership
played its part in this decline. But it has generally been
ignored that the decline coincides with an attempt to simplify her poetry, and to find new and more accessible
forms: indeed, her work in each genre follows a similar
pattern of development concluding with a reduction in
output. There are consecutive and partially overlapping
periods of intense activity in each genre as follows: in
lyric poetry from about 1914 to about 1924 (relatively
few poems for *Posle Rossii* being composed in her last
months in Prague); in verse plays from 1918 to 1927; in
poemy from 1920 to 1930 (though with work on '**Poema
o tsarskoi sem'e**' into the mid-1930s). This shows that
the division made at 1925 is no more than a rough guide,
not, as at least one scholar has suggested, a dramatic and
critical break. On the other hand, by the end of 1925
Tsvetaeva had accomplished most of her major work in
each of these genres: only one homogeneous group of
works (the short *poemy*) belongs principally to the period
after her move to Paris. Associated with this general decline in output is the abandonment of literary sources,
used so frequently up to this date. This seems to have
been part of an attempt to simplify and make more realistic her previously difficult, elusive, and allusive poetry—an attempt which also leads to the writing of far less
poetry in general. After '**Poema o tsarskoi sem'e**' Tsvetaeva wrote only lyrics, and at a much reduced rate, many
of them in response to particular events which had affected her deeply, such as the deaths of her erstwhile admirer
Gronsky ('**Nadgrobie**') or the German occupation of
Czechoslovakia ('**Stikhi k Chekhii**').

In the 1930s she worked in another verse genre which
should be considered here, especially since it has received
little scholarly attention: the translation. Although her translations are not as significant as her original work, they
clearly played an increasingly important part in her writing, and helped to maintain her literary activity and live-
liness after her lyric and other outputs had declined. That
they were part of an overall development in her career is
strongly suggested by the fact that she also turned to prose
translation and to writing her own prose in another language. The verse translations, themselves rewritings of the
inherited texts of the originals, are important proof that
she remained active as a poet to the end of her life. . . .

Tsvetaeva, in her verse translations, rewrites the originals,
producing versions which are new when compared to the

source, and to other treatments of similar sources (that is, other verse translations into French). Thus, the transformation of inherited material, a dominant feature of much of her work until the late 1920s, is present, if covert, in her work in the 1930s. Its presence as a guiding principle of her translations justifies considering them as part of her poetic output, and shows the poet looking once again for a new form of expression. Her work in French helped to fill the gap left by the decline in her output of original poetry: it shows that working with inherited material still stimulated her originality as a poet (and suggests that abandoning literary sources may have contributed to the decline in her lyrics and *poemy*). It also suggests that she was becoming increasingly unhappy with Russian as a poetic medium. She can hardly have expected to create a new literary career for herself as a French poet—and considerations of that kind hardly ever influenced her. The work in French must have answered a different need. Perhaps it expresses her alienation from her native tongue, after years without the constant contact with all sorts of spoken Russian, popular as well as educated, which she had enjoyed between the Revolution and her emigration, and which had proved a major stimulus to her work. There can be no doubt that the linguistic isolation of the *émigré* poet is acute, especially when the poet is working with a language which is far from the classical literary medium.

Tsvetaeva's isolation in Paris grew throughout the 1930s. Her husband and daughter became Soviet sympathizers, and were active in pro-Soviet organizations. Ariadna returned to the Soviet Union on 15 March 1937. Sergei Efron fled to the Soviet Union after it became known that he had been involved in the murder of the Soviet defector Ignatii Reiss in September 1937. After this, Tsvetaeva's isolation was complete. On 12 June 1939 she left France for the Soviet Union, accompanied by her son, Georgii. Shortly after her return both Ariadna and Sergei were arrested: Ariadna was sent to the camps; he was to be shot, apparently in August 1941. Tsvetaeva struggled on alone, avoided by most of her former friends, who were fearful of the consequences of associating with a former *émigrée* whose relatives had been arrested. When war broke out in June 1941 she joined the evacuation of writers. With her son she found accommodation in the small town of Elabuga in the Tatar Autonomous Republic. On 31 August, ten days after her arrival in Elabuga, she committed suicide. She is buried in an unmarked grave in the town cemetery.

Beyond these brutally bare facts lie complex issues disputed by biographers and memoirists, but irrelevant here. However, it is important to state that those who claim that Tsvetaeva was inactive as a poet in these last two years are mistaken. It is now known that she wrote original poems in the Soviet Union. It was once claimed that, on her return to the Soviet Union, her *otkaz ot stikhov byl printsipial'no izbrannoi pozitsiei* ('refusal to write verse was a position chosen on principle'), but clearer evidence of such a position is the fact that, after her return to the Soviet Union, Tsvetaeva did not write any *udarnye stikhi* (effectively, 'hack verse'), such as her **'Stikhi k synu'** (**'Poems to my Son'**) or **'Chelyuskintsy'** (**'The Crew of the *Chelyuskin*'**) (written in Paris in the 1930s). The pro-Soviet attitude of those works was an outrage to *émigré* opinion, whereas such poems would have helped her in Moscow. Instead, she omitted all pro-Soviet poetry from the so-called *sbornik sorokovogo goda* ('1940 Selected Works'), commissioned by the publishing house Sovetskii pisatel', on which she worked with complete seriousness, although in the full knowledge that its chances of passing beyond a damning 'in-house' review were very small. Not surprisingly, her attempt to 'show willing' (a very provocative, but also very professional attempt) failed and the selection duly received precisely the sort of condemnation which she had anticipated. This selection not only further demonstrates Tsvetaeva's continued interest in her poetry, but also shows her continuing to rewrite inherited texts, in this case her own, for many of the early poems which she included in the new *sbornik* were rewritten as they were prepared for a publication which she knew would never take place.

In preparation for her departure for the Soviet Union Tsvetaeva had carefully worked through her archive. Posthumous publications based on that archive show that her work included the emendation, clarification, and, especially, simplification of her earlier poetry. The titles which she added to many of the more enigmatic poems in the *sbornik* are thus a continuation of this practice, itself part of the general development of her poetics in the late period. Just as her poetry of the twenties frequently alludes to and 'corrects' (often by complication and rendering more 'poetic') her earlier work, so her editing of the late 1930s reveals the same self-conscious preoccupation with revision and rewriting. It continues the dialogue within herself, or, rather, between various lyric selves (and thus might be compared with Pasternak's notorious later remaking of his early verse).

Tsvetaeva continued her work as a translator after her return to the Soviet Union, now translating mostly into Russian (although sometimes into French). Unlike her work in Paris, these translations were commissioned, and she was paid for them. Obviously, the choice of poems to translate was not hers: it includes a fair number of *udarnye stikhi* from other Slavonic languages, and three narrative poems by the Georgian Vazha Pshavela, all works selected for political purposes. In the case of these last (stylized nineteenth-century appropriations of folkloric motifs) not only was the choice of poems to translate imposed upon her, but also the metre: the trochaic tetrameter so familiar from earlier literary versions of folklore in Russian.

None the less, there can be no doubt that she treated these translations entirely seriously, and that in working on them she remained active as a poet. Her translations of Lorca, Baudelaire, Vazha Pshavela, and English and German folk songs and ballads are of particular interest. Tsybulevskii, in his extensive treatments of her translations of Vazha Pshavela, *Gogotur i Apshina* ('Gogotur and Apshina'), *Eteri,* and *Ranenyi bars* ('The Wounded Puma'), proves that, as was the case with her French versions of Pushkin, her translations of Pshavela are idiosyncratic rewritings of the originals, in which the most Tsvetaevan motifs are given emphasis, and a new version of the source is produced.

This brief survey of the late Tsvetaeva has shown, firstly, that the decline in output of lyrics and narrative poems is associated with the abandoning of literary sources, and, secondly, that when Tsvetaeva took up translating in the 1930s she worked on the originals in the same way as she had earlier done on the literary sources of her own works. This further confirms that the rewriting of inherited texts underlies not only her treatment of literary sources, but also much of her work in general, as has also been illustrated by the examination of the short *poemy* of the late 1920s, none of which is based upon a literary source, but all of which can be seen as rewritings of familiar inherited 'texts'.

It is therefore appropriate that her last known lyric, **'Vse povtoryayu pervyi stikh'** (**'I keep repeating the first line'**), dated 6 March 1941, begins with the appropriation and manipulation of part of another literary text. The appropriated text is the opening of a poem ('Stol nakryt na shesterykh' ('Table set for six')) by Arsenii Tarkovskii, to whom Tsvetaeva was close in that last year, and who addressed a number of poems to her after her death. The clarity with which the appropriation is announced (as befits the late period) is belied by the fact that the 'first line' of Tarkovskii's poem has itself been altered:

> Vse povtoryayu pervyi stikh
> I vse perepravlyayu slovo:
> —'Ya stol nakryl na shesterykh . . .'
> Ty odnogo zabyl—sed'mogo.

> I keep repeating the first line
> And keep on altering one word:
> —'I've set the table for six people . . .'
> There's one whom you forgot—the seventh.

The seventh (seven is one of Tsvetaeva's favourite numbers, it will be recalled, and the number of strings on the gypsy guitar) is, of course, the speaker, whose isolation is ironically marked by the poem.

Although **'Vse povtoryayu pervyi stikh'** does not rewrite Tarkovskii's poem in the manner of the rewritings examined throughout this study, merely elaborating on one line, it clearly and self-consciously 'corrects' 'Stol nakryt na shesterykh'. Friction with the 'alien discourse' of another text has remained a vital stimulus to the very end of Tsvetaeva's poetic career. And the implications of this marked (and 'impossible') correction, given the acute literary (as well as personal) isolation of Tsvetaeva in her last two years, make this lyric a very eloquent final work.

The rewriting of inherited material dominates Tsvetaeva's entire career. It enabled her to produce some of her finest work in lyric, narrative, and dramatic poetry. But it is more than literary 'technique' or tool: it renders visible the processes of poetry—not only creation by the poet, but also the creative functions of literary systems; the remaking involved in reading as well as writing and the proximity of these two acts; the appropriation and rewriting of non-literary 'texts'; and the play between tradition and innovation, upon all of which the poetic text depends for its recognition as poetry. Tsvetaeva's poetry, in which these features seem especially dramatic, cannot but be constantly rewritten.

FURTHER READING

Bibliography

Proffer, Carl R. "Marina Tsvetaeva." In *Modern Russian Poets on Poetry,* p. 20. Ann Arbor: Ardis, 1976.
    Selected critical bibliography including translations.

Biography

Feiler, Lily. *Marina Tsvetaeva: The Double Beat of Heaven and Hell.* Durham: Duke University Press, 1994, 299 p.
    Study of Tsvetaeva's life and work.

Feinstein, Elaine. *A Captive Lion: The Life of Marina Tsvetayeva.* London: Century Hutchinson, 1987, 289 p.
    Biography of Tsvetaeva by one of the major translators of her poetry.

Proffer, Ellendea. *Tsvetaeva: A Pictorial Biography,* translated by J. Marin King. Ann Arbor: Ardis, 1980, 138 p.
    Bilingual text of letters, poems, and prose along with black and white photo reproductions of Tsvetaeva, her family, and her contemporaries.

Criticism

Brodsky, Joseph. "Footnote to a Poem." In *Less Than One: Selected Essays,* translated by Barry Rubin, pp. 195-267. New York: Farrar, Straus, Giroux, 1986.
    A discussion of the confessional nature of "Novogodnee," a poem Tsvetaeva wrote on the occasion of Rainer Maria Rilke's death.

Feinstein, Elaine. "Poetry and Conscience: Russian Women Poets of the Twentieth Century." In *Women Writing and Writing About Women,* edited by Mary Jacobus, pp. 133-58. Totowa, N.J.: Barnes & Noble Books, 1979.
    Compares and contrasts the lives and poetry of Tsvetaeva, Anna Akhmatova, Margarita Aliger, Yunna Moritz, and Bella Akhmadulina.

Hasty, Olga Peters. "*Poèma* vs. Cycle in Cvetaeva's Definintion of Lyric Verse." *Slavic and East European Journal* 32, No. 3 (Fall 1988): 390-98.
    A close and analytical interpretation of Tsvetaeva's lyric poetry versus her long poems.

Ivina, Zhanna. "With the Grandeur of Homer and the Purity of Sappho. . . ." In *Women and Russia: Feminist Writing from the Soviet Union*, edited by Tatyana Mamonova with Sarah Matilsky, translated by Rebecca Park and Catherine A. Fitzpatrick, pp. 155-63. Boston: Beacon Press, 1984.

> Examines the poetry of Tsvetaeva and Walt Whitman, maintaining that "both are brilliant articulators of a cosmic consciousness, of the intuitive thought of poetic insight."

Karlinsky, Simon. *Marina Tsvetaeva: The Woman, her World, and her Poetry*. Cambridge: Cambridge University Press, 1985, 289 p.

> One of the most authoritative and critically comprehensive examinations of Tsvetaeva's major works.

Mirsky, D. S. "Marina Tsvetaeva." In *The Bitter Air of Exile: Russian Writers in the West, 1922-1972*, edited by Simon Karlinsky and Alfred Appel, Jr., pp. 88-93. Berkeley and Los Angeles: University of California Press, 1977.

> Review of Tsvetaeva's verse tale "The Swain" which originally appeared in 1926.

Pasternak, Boris; Tsvetayeva, Marina; and Rilke, Rainer Maria. *Letters: Summer 1926*, edited by Yevgeny Pasternak, Yelena Pasternak, and Konstantin M. Azadovsky, translated by Margaret Wettlin and Walter Arndt. San Diego: Harcourt Brace Jovanovich, 1985, 251 p.

> Translations of the letters exchanged by these three poets in the summer of 1926 and commentary by the editors.

Pierpont, Claudia Roth. "The Rage of Aphrodite." In *The New Yorker* LXIX, No. 49 (7 February 1994): 90-8.

> Stylistic overview of Tsvetaeva's work. Pierpont also examines Tsvetaeva's literary reputation in Russia and the United States, noting particularly that it is difficult to translate the power and linguistic complexity of her poems into English.

Pilling, John. "Life and the Poet: Marina Tsvetaeva." *PN Review* 8, No. 1 (1981): 28-31.

> Examines Tsvetaeva's philosophical ideas as related through her poetry and provides critical commentary by Tsvetaeva's peers.

Schweitzer, Viktoria. *Tsvetaeva*, edited by Angela Livingstone, translated by Robert Chandler and H. T. Willetts. New York: HarperCollins, 1993, 413 p.

> Traces Tsvetaeva's history with critical examination of poetry written during different periods of her life.

Sontag, Susan. "A Poet's Prose." *Times Literary Supplement* No. 4197 (9 September 1983): 953.

> Cites Tsvetaeva's prose as an example of "poet's prose," defined in the essay as "a particular kind of prose: impatient, ardent, elliptical prose, usually in the first person, often using discontinuous or broken forms, that is mainly written by poets." Sontag concludes that "there is the same quality of emotional soaring in [Tsvetaeva's] prose as in her poetry: no modern writer takes one as close to an experience of sublimity."

Additional coverage of Tsvetaeva's life and career is contained in the following sources published by Gale Research: *Contemporary Authors*, Vols. 104, 128; *Major 20th-Century Writers*; and *Twentieth-Century Literary Criticism*, Vols. 7, 35.

Judith Wright
1915–

Australian poet, essayist, historical novelist, and critic.

INTRODUCTION

One of Australia's most celebrated female poets, Wright has garnered critical acclaim for concise, traditional verse in which she demonstrates an intellectual awareness of European and American literary traditions and vividly evokes the landscapes and lifestyles of Australia. Although some critics fault her later poems for lyrical abstraction, vague mysticism, and opinionated political observations, Wright has been widely praised for her treatment of such themes as humanity's tenuous perception of time and reality, the struggle of the poet to attain permanence and security, and the need to overcome transience through love. For Wright, poetry "is a means of regaining faith in man" as well as "a way of finding a difficult balance" between internal and external reality.

Biographical Information

Critics often attribute Wright's interest in Australian landscape to her childhood at "Wallamumbi," her family's sheep ranch in New South Wales. After spending her early years there, she left home at age thirteen, when she was sent to boarding school. From there she went on to study at the University of Sydney and later traveled through Europe with friends. Upon her return to Australia, she worked at various jobs before returning to Wallamumbi to help her father run the station during World War II. It was then that Wright reconnected with the land of her childhood, and found the poetic voice that informs much of her verse. While working as a clerk at the University of Queensland in Brisbane in the 1940s, Wright began to publish her poems in such literary magazines as *Meanjin* and *Southerly*. Many of these works were included in her first published collection *The Moving Image* in 1946. Wright married Jack McKinney, a philosophy writer, and the couple raised one child, Meredith. The poems about love and childbirth in Wright's book *Woman to Man* were drawn directly from her own experience, and her personal and public life have remained an important part of her poetry. She has been active in promoting the rights of Australia's Aborigines and conservation of the environment and has used these issues as topics for her verse. She also wrote children's stories and poems during her daughter's childhood, then stopped when Meredith was grown. Following her husband's death in 1966, Wright expanded her political involvement and became active in debates over the teaching and uses of poetry, in addition to environ-

mental and social issues. After living in the state of Queensland for many years, she now resides in New South Wales, Australia, near Braidwood.

Major Works

In her first collection of verse, *The Moving Image*, Wright uses lucid, graceful lyrics to evoke a mythic dimension in her subjects. In the process, she conveys a vivid sense of the landscape and history of the New England region of Australia. Her second volume, *Woman to Man*, is a celebration of womanhood, offering insights into such topics as conception, pregnancy, and childbirth. Often regarded as Wright's most profound work, critics have found *Woman to Man* notable for its striking imagery and focus on love and chaos. Wright's next two collections moved away from personal and anecdotal material toward more metaphysical and universal subject matter. *The Gateway* shows the influence of William Blake and T. S. Eliot in its consideration of love, creation, and eternity. The title poem of *The Two Fires* explores two opposing infernos—one that metaphorically represents the love from which humanity originated and one that is the man-made atomic fire that might extinguish love. Amidst such solemn works, Wright also produced *Birds* in 1963, a collection of poems that comments on the characteristics of Australia's winged wildlife. She returned to metaphysical issues in many of her poems written in the mid-1960s, with *The Other Half* addressing the mystic relationship between the conscious and unconscious mind. Of a more worldly nature are the new works in *Collected Poems, 1942-1970,* several of which attempt to reconcile Wright's private and public roles as a poet. Likewise, *Alive: Poems, 1971-1972* also deals with temporal matters as Wright contrasts the natural beauty of her Queensland home with urban ruin, using this comparison to comment on the destruction of the Australian wilderness. In the 1977 collection *Fourth Quarter and Other Poems,* Wright interweaves childhood reminiscences with observations on old age, but also addresses contemporary political and sociological issues. The book also demonstrates Wright's abilities as a free verse poet, and employs a more relaxed tone than some of her other works. After a lengthy break from publishing poetry collections, Wright's *Phantom Dwelling* appeared in 1985. In this volume, she brings new light to bear on the themes that dominate so much of her poetry, particularly man's relationship with nature and death. The book also demonstrates Wright's continuing experimentation with a more relaxed, often ironic, poetic style.

Critical Reception

With few exceptions, critical response to Judith Wright's first two collections of poetry has been overwhelmingly positive. Employing a traditional lyric style, Wright was lauded for her fresh treatment of the subject matter in both volumes. Appraising *The Moving Image,* Vincent Buckley argued that "Judith Wright surpasses all other Australian poets in the extent to which she . . . reveals the contours of Australia as a place, an atmosphere, a separate being." Similar praise was echoed by other critics as *The Moving Image* established Wright as one of Australia's major poets. Her second volume, *Woman to Man,* was credited with giving a uniquely female perspective to poems dealing with love, creation, and the universe. Elizabeth Vassilief contended that in this collection Wright exhibits the "the ability to re-create the meanings of common words with every new usage; to refresh, deepen and invigorate the language. . . . And in this power I think she has no equal among Australian poets." The collections published since *Woman to Man* have split critics into two general camps. Many contend that her increasingly metaphysical focus, coupled with forays into rather literal protest poetry, diluted her ability to distill universal and poetic images from common events. Her departure from the more traditional style of her early verse has also been scorned by some observers. Others, however, have characterized her excursions into politics and mysticism, and her stylistic experiments with free verse, as the explorations of a serious poet, who, not content to rest on her laurels, continues to redefine herself and her subject matter as she matures.

PRINCIPAL WORKS

Poetry

The Moving Image 1946
Woman to Man 1949
The Gateway 1953
The Two Fires 1955
Birds 1962
Five Senses: Selected Poems 1963; revised edition 1972
Judith Wright (selected poems) 1963
City Sunrise 1964
The Other Half 1966
Collected Poems, 1942-1970 1971
Alive: Poems 1971-1972 1973
Fourth Quarter, and Other Poems 1976
The Double Tree: Selected Poems 1942-76 1978
Phantom Dwelling 1985

Other Major Works

King of Dingoes (juvenilia) 1958
The Generations of Men (fictional biography) 1959
The Day the Mountains Played (juvenilia) 1960
Range the Mountains High (juvenilia) 1962; revised edition 1971
Charles Harpur (biography and criticism) 1963; revised edition 1977
Country Towns (juvenilia) 1963
Preoccupations in Australian Poetry (criticism) 1965
The Nature of Love (short stories) 1966
The River and the Road (juvenilia) 1966; revised edition 1971
Henry Lawson (criticism) 1967
Because I Was Invited (essays) 1975
The Coral Battleground (nonfiction) 1977
The Cry for the Dead (fictional biography) 1981
We Call for a Treaty (nonfiction) 1985

CRITICISM

Philip Lindsay (essay date 1950)

SOURCE: "Poetry in Australasia: Judith Wright," in *Poetry Review,* Vol. XLI, No. 4, July-August 1950, pp. 207-11.

[*In this essay concerning Wright's* Woman to Man, *Lindsay asserts that Wright is the first woman poet to speak of love with a truly female voice.*]

Of Judith Wright's poetry it might well be said that she is the only woman who has kissed and told. Other women have sung of love, but apart from Sappho—and she, after all, was a man in female skin—none have written honestly and without shame of their desires. Usually we find that women poets were sexually inexperienced ladies, transmuting their desires into religious or metaphysical ecstasies, as with Emily Brontë and Christina Rossetti, or, like Emily Dickenson, they have had to invent a lover on whom they could pour the passion of their starved hearts. The last thing I wish is to start a discussion on this question, and, of course, exceptions can be found, but it remains broadly true that sexual repression has commonly been the inspiration of women's art. When I was an art-student, I was surprised to notice how many girls showing genuine promise abandoned their work once they were married. It was as though a hitherto unsatisfied yearning had found completion and the substitute of painting was no longer needed. This is often true also of poetry. Elizabeth Barrett certainly continued to write after her marriage but she might as well never have married for all the revelation it brought into her work and she never unveiled the secrets of her womanly delight in love, save abstractly.

This, Judith Wright has done for us, the Sphinx answering the cry of man down the ages: "What is love to you?" when he holds his beloved in his arms. To explain what I mean, it were best that I quote the title poem of her latest collection, **"Woman to Man"**:

> The eyeless labourer in the night,
> the selfless, shapeless seed I hold,
> builds for its resurrection day—
> silent and swift and deep from sight
> foresees the unimagined light.
>
> This is no child with a child's face;
> this has no name to name it by:
> yet you and I have known it well.
> This is our hunter and our chase,
> the third who lay in our embrace.
>
> This is the strength that your arm knows,
> the arc of flesh that is my breast,
> the precise crystals of our eyes.
> This is the blood's wild tree that grows
> the intricate and folded rose.
>
> This is the maker and the made;
> this is the question and reply;
> the blind head butting at the dark,
> the blaze of light along the blade.
> Oh hold me, for I am afraid.

By stressing this vital aspect of Miss Wright's poetry, I am liable to throw into darkness her other great qualities and the subtle beauty of her vision which sees with pity yet delight the colours of the world and its sounds and its unhappy people. There is haunting music in many of her lines which remain to sing in one's memory:

> While past the camp fire's crimson ring
> the star-struck darkness cupped him round,
> and centuries of cattlebells
> rang with their sweet uneasy sound.

Always her vision is a woman's vision whether she wonders on the miracle of a conch-shell or on the need for pain "that knifes us in blind alleys," on children or trees, on gardens, flowers or lonely spinsters lacking love, on the half-mad bullocky with his camp-fire in the bush, on the sick soldier Man-jack home from the war, on the dead snake and the ants that "drink at his hollow eye," on country-dances and the terrifying bush-fire, on the trapped dingo or the surfer or the half-caste girl, or whether she merrily laughs with a **"Song in a Wine-Bar"**?

> Toss up your spinning silver,
> wild boy, my sailor.
> We'll dance till Time is done
> who are hot with Time's fever.
> Among the tilting buildings
> gay boy, wild lover,
> we will go on dancing
> till our dancing day is over.
>
> Toss up your shining money,
> wild boy, my sailor,
> like a Saturday fountain,
> like a holiday river.
>
> Fill the lit street full
> of wine as hot as a lover;
> and we will go on dancing
> till Saturday night is over.

Such light-hearted gaiety is, however, rare in Miss Wright's work. Her feelings are too profound for such drunken moods to last, and continually she returns to contemplate that wonderful sensuous world of her own heart and to glory in her body that can contain her child. But as with all true lovers, her love embraces the world and rejects disgust. Even the sight of the **"Metho Drinker"** stirs in her, not horror or even pity; she who is rich with love must see even this castaway as a lover:

> Under the death of winter's leave she lies
> who cried to Nothing and the terrible night
> to be his home and bread. "O take from me
> the weight and waterfall of ceaseless Time
> that batters down my weakness; the knives of light
> whose thrust I cannot turn; the cruelty
> of human eyes that dare not touch nor pity."
> Under the worn leaves of the winter city
> safe in the house of Nothing now he lies.
>
> His white and burning girl, his woman of fire,
> creeps to his heart and sets a candle there
> to melt away the flesh that hides the bone,
> to eat the nerve that tethers him in Time.
> He will lie warm until the bone is bare
> and on a dead dark moon he wakes alone.
> It was for Death he took her; death is but this
> and yet he is uneasy under her kiss
> and winces from that acid of her desire.

Here, as in all her poems, no matter what the subject, one senses her intense femininity. Impossible, one feels, would it be for any man to have written this. Take her portrait of **"The Bull"**:

In the olive darkness of the sally-trees
silently moved the air from night to day.
The summer-grass was thick with honey-daisies
where he, a curled god, a red Jupiter,
heavy with power among his women lay.
But summer's bubble-sound of sweet creek-water
dwindles and is silent; the seeding grasses
grow harsh, and wind and frost in the black sallies
roughens the sleek-haired slopes. Seek him out, then,
the angry god betrayed, whose godhead passes,

and down the hillsides drive him from his mob.
What enemy steals his strength—what rival steals
his mastered cows? His thunders powerless,
the red storm of his body shrunk with fear,
runs the great bull, the dogs upon his heels.

I have quoted largely, for quotations are essential if you would appreciate my claim for Miss Wright as being the first woman honestly to unbare her lover's heart in verse; and I wish I could quote poem after poem. Wherever I dip into her books, lines demand my repeating them; but I dare not continue lest I overspill my space. At her best— and it is far from often that she falls below the high standard she has set herself—her poetry has in it fire and joy and, sometimes, terror. Also—and in this she is unique— she offers the open cup of love to any of us unafraid to look into the naked heart that is both the possessed and the possessing, that is both courageous and timid, both demanding and submissive, of a woman above the cowardly evasions of so many of her sex, one honest and proud of her strong womanhood that can excite and satisfy love. Humbly, I offer thanks and salute her courage.

R. F. Brissenden   (essay date 1953)

SOURCE: "The Poetry of Judith Wright," in *Meanjin*, Vol. XII, No. 3, September, 1953, pp. 255-67.

[*Here, Brissenden examines Wright's first three volumes of poetry. The critic praises many aspects of the poet's work, but worries that the metaphysical ponderings in the third volume,* The Gateway, *denote a shift in Wright's focus, "away from the personal, the particular and the dramatic towards the abstract and the impersonal."*]

When Judith Wright's first book, **The Moving Image,** appeared it was greeted by the critics with enthusiasm, one writer going so far as to declare that its publication was 'the most important poetic event of 1946'. Another claimed that 'no book of poems has received such an enthusiastic reception here since O'Dowd's *The Bush*.' Since then she has brought out two more collections of verse: **Woman to Man** and **The Gateway**. The growth of her reputation has kept pace with her output of poetry: it would be quite safe to say that she is now widely regarded as one of our leading poets; and there are some who would even support Mr. H. M. Green in placing her 'among the principal poets writing in English today' [*Modern Australian Poetry,* 1952].

There can be no doubt that her work stands well out from the great mass of Australian poetry—indeed from much of the poetry which fills the pages of literary journals in England and America. Two things in particular lift her poems above the common ruck: their consistently careful and polished technique, and the demand which they make to be considered not just as single poems but as members of a unified body of work.

Judith Wright is first of all a craftsman. She is at her best in her shorter poems, and in the finest of these her mastery of form is always sure and unobtrusive: images and ideas that are often complex are brought together into a controlled and lucid unity in which everything contributes to the central theme; there is nothing superfluous, nothing wanting; the surface texture has that clarity and simplicity which can result only from a mature discipline; and the whole poem has that radiance which comes when each image shines not only with its own light, but also with the light shed on it by every other image in the poem.

This is true also of her work as a whole. The impression which any individual poem makes is deepened and intensified if one has a knowledge of the rest of her poetry: certain themes appear again and again in her poems, and there are certain human problems with which she seems to be constantly pre-occupied. These themes and problems are, moreover, related to one another—the comprehension of one helps to illuminate all the rest. It becomes obvious, once one is familiar with the main body of her work, that Judith Wright is a poetic thinker, someone with a coherent view of life, a view of life which is not only stated but also initially conceived in poetic terms. The problems with which she is concerned are seen through the eyes of a poet; even more significantly, poetry itself is seen to be an important part of their solution.

> There can be no doubt that her work stands well out from the great mass of Australian poetry—indeed from much of the poetry which fills the pages of literary journals in England and America.
>
> —R. F. Brissenden

There is nothing unique about the problems with which she is most deeply concerned—they are those which have engaged the minds of most serious writers for the past fifty years or so: the problems of discovering, in an age of cultural disintegration and confusion, some significant pattern or purpose in life; the problems of merely existing which are presented by an age in which for so many people, as William Faulkner has remarked [in *The Stockholm Address*], 'There are no longer problems of the spirit. There is only one question: when will I be blown up?'

It has become something of a cliché to say that we live in an age of transition—a label which could be attached to almost any historical period. There are times however in which an unusually large number of things are all changing at the same time, and in which the process of change itself is not only extended but also vastly accelerated. Such is the character of our own age. Social institutions, moral values, the pictures which people have of man in relation to the universe and to other men—things in which the rate of change can usually be measured in terms of generations or even centuries—are today altering within the span of a single life-time. And the literature and philosophy of our age are haunted by the themes of time and change: it is no mere accident of titling which links together such seemingly unrelated works as *The Time Machine, A la Recherche du Temps Perdu, The Lost Childhood, Space, Time and Deity, Essay on Memory, Five Bells* and **The Moving Image**. 'The cancer of time,' says Henry Miller, 'is eating us away.' No other civilization has ever been so obsessed with time as our own.

The 'moving image' of Judith Wright's first book is Time—Time conceived in an absolute sense as the very process of change itself, the flux of things, which carries us inexorably forward into the future; the shifting and impermanent world through which, according to Plato, we glimpse dimly those truths which are eternal and unchanging. Looked at in this way, Time becomes the enemy which brings us, as individuals, out of the paradise of childhood into the world of maturity in which 'the clock begins to race,' and

> We are caught in the endless circle of time and star
> that never chime with the blood.

It becomes history, the rising tide of events which has brought us to our present crisis in which

> Promise and legend fail us and lose power.
> Words are rubbed smooth and faceless as old coins
> and any story is only word upon word.
> Each of us, solitary on his tower,
> speaks and dares not listen to what he has said
> for fear it lose all meaning as it is heard.

Judith Wright is not alone, even among Australian poets, in her pre-occupation with time. Time is both the theme and the inspiration of 'Five Bells' and 'Essay on Memory'; and Slessor and FitzGerald are as keenly aware as she of the tragic inevitability of change and death. In Judith Wright's poetry, however, the consciousness of time is accompanied by a feeling for history and tradition which is something new in Australian poetry. Slessor and FitzGerald tend to raise their voices, to pose with a somewhat self-consciously romantic air when they present us with their Captain Cooks or their bony hands of memory—these, after all, are History with a capital H.

The past is obviously just as fertile a source of inspiration to Judith Wright as it is to these poets—New England, where her family has lived for more than one generation, lies in the background of much of her poetry: 'part of my blood's country' she calls it in 'South of My Days'.

> I know it dark against the stars, the high
>   lean country
> full of old stories that still go walking
>   in my sleep.

But it is a background and a past which are perfectly assimilated: as a result her poetry is free alike from the bitter nostalgia of Hope and McAuley; from the strident nationalism which still lingers (in an inverted form) in the romanticism of Slessor, FitzGerald and D. Stewart; and from the pseudo-mysticism of the Jindyworobaks. (She has, by the way, inscribed the epitaph of this last group in a small poem called **'Bora Ring'**.

> The song is gone; the dance
> is secret with the dancers in the earth,
> the ritual useless, and the tribal story
> lost in an alien tale.)

This balanced, easy and completely unaffected acceptance of Australia—both the land and its people—has, perhaps, its own defects; but it seems to me to be one of the most important of Judith Wright's qualities as a poet. No matter what criticism may be levelled at her, she can never (save for an odd phrase or two) be called immature or provincial. She is neither 'ashamed' of being an Australian, nor irrationally proud of the fact: she merely accepts the Australian landscape and the Australian people as inevitable and natural features of the milieu in which she lives and writes.

That she should be able to do this is a mark not only of her own maturity but also of the maturity of Australian poetry in general. She is not the only modern Australian whose work reveals this unselfconscious acceptance of Australia; but she is, I believe, the first in whose poetry it has been present from the very beginning. In years to come Judith Wright will almost certainly be regarded as the typical poet of the 'forties: the decade in which Australian poetry came of age and learned to forget that it was adolescent and antipodean.

Together with this awareness of history and tradition there is apparent in her work what I can only describe as a sense of society: a sense at once of the fundamental community of common humanity to which we all belong, and of the artificial barriers of race, religion and politics which grow up within this community, and which blind our eyes to its existence. The concluding lines from **'Nigger's Leap: New England,'** illustrate very clearly her awareness of the inevitability of history and her feeling for the ways in which men are linked together and divided against each other. She is speaking of the aborigines:

> Did we not know their blood channelled our rivers,
> and the black dust our crops ate was their dust?
> O all men are one man at last. We should have known
> the night that tided up the cliffs and hid them
> had the same question on its tongue for us.
> And there lie that were ourselves writ strange.

Never from earth again the coolamon
of thin black children dancing like the shadows
of saplings in the wind. Night lips the harsh
scarp of the tableland and cools its granite.
Night floods us suddenly as history
that has sunk many islands in its good time.

The touch of the true poet is evident in almost every line
of **'Nigger's Leap'**. One overlooks the trite flatness of
'writ strange' in admiration of the sure and subtle integra-
tion of image and theme, the exact and evocative use of
words: 'lips' and 'cools' for instance function perfectly at
every level—in the sensitive precision with which they
suggest the actual approach of evening; in the way which
they strike an unobtrusive harmony with the central sea-
metaphor of the poem; and most of all in their faint but
distinct overtone of imminent menace. 'Lips' suggests not
only the sound and movement of the rising tide, but also
that 'dark throat' of the sea which has engulfed 'many
islands in its good time'.

The sea—Time—Society—the natural processes of birth,
decay and death: they are all forces in the face of which
the individual can be lonely and powerless; and Miss
Wright produces her best work when she presents such a
situation—when she suggests through a dramatic, particular incident the general feelings and ideas which the
contemplation of woman, man and time has aroused in
her. **'Nigger's Leap'** has for its subject two dramatic
incidents—the suicide of the aboriginal, years ago, and
the approach of dusk on this particular night—that 'fall
of evening (which) is the rebirth of knowing'. **'The Company of Lovers'**, a relatively simple poem, gains its
power not only from the honesty with which its theme is
presented, but also from its note of urgent immediacy.
And it is on a similar note that she concludes **'Woman
to Man'**—a poem so fine that it deserves to be quoted
in full.

> The eyeless labourer in the night,
> the selfless, shapeless seed I hold,
> builds for its resurrection day—
> silent and swift and deep from sight
> foresees the unimagined light.
>
> This is no child with a child's face;
> this has no name to name it by:
> yet you and I have known it well.
> This is our hunter and our chase,
> the third who lay in our embrace.
>
> This is the strength that your arm knows,
> the arc of flesh that is my breast,
> the precise crystals of our eyes.
> This is the blood's wild tree that grows
> the intricate and folded rose.
>
> This is the maker and the made;
> this is the question and reply;
> the blind head butting at the dark,
> the blaze of light along the blade.
> Oh hold me, for I am afraid.

The tone of the first two stanzas is metaphysical: it is
brought about by the way in which rather abstract concepts and restrained but deeply felt emotions are blended
and fused; and the poem as a whole is notable for the
precision with which its paradoxes are stated and the
delicate balance in which they are held. Its force and
beauty, however, are focused and intensified by the naked
simplicity and directness of the last line: the situation is
suddenly made dramatic and individual—one woman
speaking to one man at a particular time and place.

It is this ability to invest typical human situations with a
dramatic significance that gives the best of Miss Wright's
poetry its power. In her earlier work this ability often
finds its expression in lyrical portraits of individual people—poems such as **'Bullocky'**, **'The Hawthorn Hedge'**,
'Brother and Sisters', and others. And even when she
ceases to portray individuals and cuts through to that fundamental world in which 'all men are one man', the basic
human situation is still often presented dramatically—

> Yet where the circle was joined
> the desperate chase began;
> where love in love dissolved
> sprang up the woman and man.
>
> ('Eden')

There is nothing static about Judith Wright's poetry—her
world is one of continual movement, change and development. And although she is always conscious of the inevitability of death, she is just as keenly aware of the inevitability of birth: she knows that change does not necessarily involve decay: she sees time not only as a destructive but also as a regenerative force. It is because her
vision has this breadth that her work never reflects what
is merely a sentimental pessimism. 'Those who are given
to grief know grief only', she writes in **'Letter to a
Friend'**.

> It is because of the joy in my heart
> that I am your fit mourner.

And the source of much of her inspiration lies in the effort
to comprehend in one vision the antinomies of birth and
death; growth and decay; love and loneliness; union and
isolation. In her best work this effort results in a tension
of ideas and an intensity of feeling which remind one of
Yeats. The finest poems in **Woman to Man** and **The
Gateway** have the genuine metaphysical note; and they
are, moreover, expressed with a disciplined clarity that is
not common enough in modern poetry.

One can never resolve the paradoxes of death-in-life and
life-in-death by explaining them away. By a conscious
acceptance of them and their mystery, however, the difficulties they present can, in a way, be transcended. But the
achievement of a single vision in which these things can
be held is no passive thing: the note in much of Miss
Wright's later poetry, is not one of mere acceptance but
one of triumph and affirmation:

Darkness where I find my sight,
shadowless and burning night,
here where death and life are met
is the fire of being set.
                         ('**Midnight**')

And in the poem which gives her latest volume, *The Gateway*, its title, the affirmation becomes even more explicit.

In the depth of nothing
I met my home.

All ended there,
yet all began.
All sank in dissolution
yet rose renewed.

This note of affirmation sounds most strongly in poems such as '**Woman to Man**', '**Woman to Child**' and (from *The Gateway*) '**The Promised One**'; poems in which the mystical vision of 'the depth of nothing' is given weight and substance by some positive human action: a word or gesture of love. It is only through love that the threats and terrors of existence can be overcome: for love is at once unifying and creative. By bringing people together it destroys loneliness, isolation, intolerance and hatred; and through what it creates—peaceful communities as well as children—it defeats death and drives out fear. It is her passionate apprehension of this which gives to the best of Judith Wright's poetry its individuality and beauty. The love poetry in *Woman to Man* and *The Gateway* is unique in its combination of intellectual strength with feminine feeling. Only a woman could write poetry like this, and no other woman has done it in quite this way.

Poems such as these can obviously arise only out of deeply felt personal experience; but the strength of these poems probably comes as much from the poet's realization of the necessity of love for the happiness of other people—both as individuals and as members of a society—as it does from her awareness of her own feelings. She is conscious both of the misery of loneliness and of the danger to humanity of the fear and intolerance which loneliness can breed. Love is the solution: and since Judith Wright is a poet, she sees language—the word—as one of the most vital expressions of love, in the intimate, personal sense and in the general, social sense. As she has said in a recent article, it is only through language that the private world of one individual—'the flux of personal and relative experience'—can be made intelligible both to himself and to other individuals. 'Language is . . . a crystallization of our experience in common; it is the final achievement of men as builders of a picture of their world' ['The Writer and the Crisis' *Language*, April-May, 1952].

The various themes and problems which, as I have been suggesting, dominate the work of this poet, are not of course always all present in a single poem. But one is never completely unconscious of them: they form a background, a poetic world into which each individual poem can be fitted. And there are some poems which seem to present a focused and concentrated picture of this whole world—in which all its various aspects are gathered together into one pattern. Perhaps the best example of this sort of thing is '**The Bones Speak**', with its dominant image of the 'untenanted hollow of this cave' into which 'man with his woman fled from woman and man'.

And the rock fell, and we dissolved in night
and walked the ceaseless maze of emptiness
hollow-socketed, alone, alone;
her once sweet flesh impersonal as stone,
for love is lost in terror, child of sight.

Yet from this universe of vagrancy
always I hear the river underground,
the ceaseless liquid voices of the river
run through these bones that here lie loose together,
a quiver, a whispering, a promise of sound.

The river whose waters move toward the day
the river that wears down our night of stone—
I hear its voice of fall and flood deny
the reign of silence and the realm of bone;
its mining fingers work for this cave's ruin.

The fundamental symbols in this poem—the cave, the bones, the river with 'its voice of fall and flood' which at the same time carries in that voice a 'promise of sound', a hope of rebirth and regeneration—carry the basic and archetypal religious associations which they have borne for generations: but they are brought together into a fresh and individual design, the expected echoes are given a new timbre by our memory of other poems in which love and the word have been set against loneliness and silence.

There is nothing particularly novel in the themes or the images which symbolise them in a poem such as this—if there were it would perhaps not be so effective. But in this, and other poems, Miss Wright's interpretation of these themes is modern, unselfconsciously Australian, and often original.

Despite the individuality of her style, however, one becomes aware after a while of certain literary echoes—faint but inescapable. Mad Tom and Blind Jimmy Delaney are Yeatsian fools from the twenty-eighth phase, and not, I think, particularly successful ones. Mad Tom especially is a rather muddled rhetorician; and in '**The Blind Man**', as in Miss Wright's other attempts at a long poem, such as '**The Moving Image**' and '**The Flood**', the movement of thought and the control of form tend to become hesitant and confused. Once she leaves the confines of the small lyric, or single dramatic statement, a dangerous tendency to philosophise appears—a tendency to talk about ideas and feelings rather than to crystallise them into images. The faint flap of the aged eagle's wings can be heard occasionally too, in the dry air of New England—

I would resolve my mind upon this faith
finding a meaning in annihilation.
Since blood has been your gift, let me accept it,
remembering that for spring's resurrection

some sacrifice was always necessary.
Osiris, Christ; your flesh broken like bread . . .

And there is obviously a certain similarity between Judith Wright's views on time, man and poetry and those of T. S. Eliot, to whom the purification of the dialect of the tribe is a sacred duty, and who can pronounce the discovery of a new verse form as the most important thing that can happen to a nation. The *Four Quartets* stand somewhere in the background of even such a fine poem as 'Niggers Leap: New England'; and the shadow of Canterbury Cathedral lies over the deliberately flat and understated imagery of lines like these—

> The labourer thinks and spits and looks aside;
> the young girls laugh and look frightened;
> the fat man with pale eyes passes on the rumour
> although he does not believe it.

The echoes are not always so obvious as this; and although it is clear that she has been influenced both by the theory and the practice of Eliot, I do not suggest that either her poetry or the structure of thought behind it is in any important way derivative. Literary influences are after all inevitable and, for those with independent personalities and strong literary digestions, usually beneficial. Superficially at any rate there are few echoes in Judith Wright's later poetry.

The way in which her poetry has developed, however, parallels in a disturbing fashion the pattern of development which can be seen in the poetry of Eliot. The general tone of *The Gateway* is noticeably different from the tone of the earlier books—especially *The Moving Image*. One can see that her poetry is moving away from the personal, the particular and the dramatic towards the abstract and the impersonal: a movement sanctioned if not inspired by the example set in the *Four Quartets*. The poetic aridity which blights certain passages in the *Four Quartets* is not immediately obvious, however, because of that superb rhythmical control which gives to even the most desiccated of Eliot's utterances the strength and life of vigorous speech. But it is in just this aspect of poetic technique that Miss Wright is at her weakest—the 'free verse' of 'The Flood', 'Letter to a Friend', 'The Gateway', and other of her later poems is slack and nerveless.

Far more obvious than the Eliot influence in *The Gateway* is the influence—again in a diffuse and fairly well-assimilated way—of Blake. Instead of finding eternity in the acts of woman and man, Miss Wright seems to be seeking it in the grain of sand. Flowers, trees, seeds, birds and insects are beginning to displace men and women as the subjects of her poems; and instead of using the cyclic processes of life which these things exemplify to throw light on the problems and questions of human existence, she does just the opposite. Woman and man seem to be no more significant than the cicadas or the cedar trees: in fact it is not even life but the *process* of life which seems to be engaging more and more of her attention.

Although there are some fine poems in *The Gateway,* and, as always, the standard of poetic craftsmanship is remarkably high, one misses the depth and passion which make the best poems of *Woman to Man* so outstanding. This slackening of tension, and the emphasis on speculation rather than symbolic statement, are due perhaps to the fact that she has lost some of the philosophical certainty on which her ealier work was based. Judith Wright is after all a remarkably honest poet, and one cannot blame her for trying to work out her difficulties in her poetry. The results however do not seem to me to be always satisfactory. In particular the attempt to create some sort of private mythology, as in poems like 'Legend', 'Nursery Rhyme for a Seventh Son', 'Fairytale'—and some earlier poems—are flat, disappointing, and obviously artificial.

This is not to say that *The Gateway* is an unrewarding book. Occasionally she achieves the authentic simplicity she is seeking—

> Lion, let your desert eyes
> turn on me.
> Look beyond my flesh and see
> that in it which never dies.

And some of the love poems—'Song', 'All Things Conspire'—take us back to the world of *Woman to Man*. In general, however, the poems in *The Gateway* lack that directness and intensity which distinguish the best of her earlier work. It is interesting in this respect to compare 'Dark Gift', the first poem in *The Gateway,* with 'Woman to Man', the poem which opens the previous collection:

> The flower begins in the dark
> where life is not.
> Death has a word to speak
> and the flower begins.
>
> How small, how closely bound
> in nothing's net
> the word waits in the ground
> for the cloak earth spins.
>
> The root goes down in the night
> and from night's mud
> the unmade, the inchoate
> starts to take shape and rise.
>
> The blind, the upward hand
> clenches its bud.
> What message does death send
> from the grave where he lies?
>
> Open, green hand, and give
> the dark gift you hold.
>
> Oh wild mysterious gold!
> Oh act of passionate love!

The same sort of symbolism is being used in 'Dark Gift' as was used in 'Woman to Man', only in this later poem the symbols are themselves the subject of the poem: they are not being used to illuminate a human situation but for their own sake. As a result there is a slight forcing of the emotion: the 'pathetic fallacy', instead of intensifying the feeling in the poem draws attention to itself: the last two lines,

Oh wild mysterious gold!
Oh act of passionate love!

form a neat climax, but it is weakened by the fact that the poet has had to describe the feelings which, in the earlier poem, were implicit. There is no need for any overt statement of the emotion in **'Woman to Man'**: the poem is self-contained: it suggests its own mystery and passion.

Judith Wright's attempts at creating her own allegory and mythology are not always unsuccessful. Some of them—such as **'The Forest Path'** and **'The Lost Man'**—though rather highly pitched, do succeed in creating their own atmosphere. **'The Traveller and the Angel'** I find particularly interesting. It tells how, in the strength of his youth, the traveller sets out on his journey. At the ford he meets the first of his tasks: the angel with whom he must wrestle to test his strength.

Marvellously and matched like lovers
we fought there by the ford,
till, every truth elicited,
I, unsurpassably weary,

felt with that weariness
darkness increase on my sight,
and felt the angel failing
in his glorious strength.

Altering, dissolving, vanishing,
he slipped through my fingers,
till when I groped for the death-blow,
I groped and could not find him.

But his voice on the air
pierced the depths of my heart.
"I was your strength; our battle
leaves you doubly strong.

"Now the way is open
and you must rise and find it—
the way to the next ford
where waits the second angel."

But weak with loss and fear
I lie still by the ford.
Now that the angel is gone
I am a man, and weary.

Return, angel, return.
I fear the journey.

Is it too much, I wonder, to see in this poem a parable of the poet's own poetic development? It seems obvious, at least, that Judith Wright herself feels that she has reached the end of one phase of her growth as a poet and thinker—and also that she is not quite certain where she is going next. 'Go easy with me, old man', she says in one poem; 'I am helping to clear a track to unknown water.'

At the risk of appearing unkind, I would suggest that unless she discovers the water she is seeking her work may not develop any further. One can only hope that she finds her new source of inspiration—and that when she does she can translate it into new and more vital poetry. Unless she can do this it seems to me that her work stands in real danger of becoming repetitive and stagnant.

It would be a lasting pity if this were to happen. Even if it should, however, it could not take away from the excellence of what she has already achieved: a body of poetry more coherent and self consistent than that produced by any contemporary Australian poet; and a few poems which are fit to stand with the best that have appeared in England and America during the last ten or fifteen years.

Robert Ian Scott (essay date 1956)

SOURCE: "Judith Wright's World-View," in *Southerly*, Vol. 17, No. 4, 1956, pp. 189-95.

[*In the following essay, Scott places the philosophical underpinnings of the poet's work within the context of a Platonic worldview, noting her dual views of nature: on one hand it represents the immediate world and worldly concerns, while on the other it symbolizes an unchanging cosmos that is sensed unconsciously and idealized as Eden.*]

Most of the 155 poems in Judith Wright's four books make manifest love and birth and death, which are abstract ideas having in themselves no single form, in terms of such concrete particulars as lovers, old people, little children and Australian landscapes. These subjects, love and birth and death, are shown as all inter-related and aspects of time, and as provoking questions we continue to ask, but never finally answer, about what and why we and life and time are.

Our philosophies are formed in part by what we read, and the epigraphs of Judith Wright's books suggest what world-view her poems present. The epigraph of her first book, *The Moving Image* (1946), is from Plato's cosmography, the *Timaeus*: "Time is a moving image of eternity". Plato based his philosophy on, among other things, the ideas of three earlier Greek thinkers, Pythagoras, Herakleitos and Parmenides. Pythagoras (or his followers) held that our souls and consciousnesses are identical, are immortal, and pass through many cycles of birth and death in different bodies until they gain their goal, some unchanging eden, out of time, and for which all life and time and this earth itself are but a drab prelude. Such poems as **"The Bones Speak"** and **"Fire at Murdering Hut"** are Pythagorean in that Judith Wright speaks in them in terms of other consciousnesses than her own, showing us what bones and fire presumably might feel in order to show us what bones and fire (and we) are. In such poems as **"Woman to Man"**, **"The Cedars"**, **"Transformations"** and **"Landscapes"**, she concerns herself with the cyclic transformations which love and birth and death effect within the seasons of our lives and of the years. This is the Herakleitean world in time.

According to Herakleitos, everything changes but change itself. Parmenides claimed that reality does not change; what changes is only illusion. Judith Wright's poems report Herakleitean sense-data, and, in seeking some Parmenidean constancy in it, or cause for it, articulate this sense-data and give it a meaningful coherency. Plato, combining the views of Parmenides, Herakleitos and Pythagoras, wrote that this earth in time is but a changing (and thus an imperfect) replica of an eternal reality. This is a complex world-view, and Judith Wright's poems present various aspects of it.

In her first book, *The Moving Image,* Judith Wright is concerned more with this earth and with time than with eternity—with the moving image we experience directly and not with any reality which we may guess at or posit beyond earthly experience. Accordingly, in the poem **"Northern River"**, she speaks of time as

> the sea that encompasses
> all sorrow and all delight,
> and holds the memories
> of every stream and river.

This is to say that all lives end in time and die, and so we must enjoy what present pleasures and what memories we have while we can; and must love, now, even while death begins to trap and end us, as in **"The Company of Lovers"**. Some of these lives—and what, in time, they came to—are the subjects of **"Remittance Man"**, **"Bullocky"**, **"Brother and Sisters"**, **"The Hawthorn Hedge"**, **"Bora Ring"** and **"Soldier's Farm"** in this first book, and of many poems in the three later books.

Judith Wright explores memories of her childhood on the granite New England tableland around Armidale, New South Wales (where she was born in 1915), in these poems and in **"South of My Days"**:

> South of my days' circle, part of my blood's country,
> rises that tableland, high delicate outline
> of bony slopes wincing under the winter,
> low trees blue-leaved and olive, outcropping granite—
> clean, lean, hungry country. The creek's leaf-silenced,
> willow-choked, the slope a tangle of medlar and crab-
> apple
> branching over and under, blotched with a green lichen;
> and the old cottage lurches in for shelter.
>
> O cold the black-frost night. The walls draw in to the
> warmth
> and the old roof cracks its joints; the slung kettle
> hisses a leak on the fire. Hardly to be believed that
> summer
> will turn up again some day in a wave of rambler roses,

thrust its hot face in here to tell another yarn—
a story old Dan can spin into a blanket against the
winter.
Seventy years of stories he clutches round his bones.
Seventy summers are hived in him like old honey.

Droving that year, Charleville to the Hunter,
nineteen-one it was, and the drought beginning;
sixty head left at the McIntyre, the mud round them
hardened like iron; and the yellow boy died
in the sulky ahead with the gear, but the horse went on,
stopped at the Sandy Camp and waited in the evening.
It was the flies we seen first, swarming like bees.
Came to the Hunter, three hundred head of a thousand—
cruel to keep them alive—and the river was dust.
Or mustering up in the Bogongs in the autumn
when the blizzards came early. Brought them down;
we brought them down, what aren't there yet.

Or driving for Cobb's on the run up from Tamworth—
Thunderbolt at the top of Hungry Hill,
and I gave him a wink. I wouldn't wait long, Fred,
not if I was you; the troopers are just behind,
coming for that job at the Hillgrove. He went like a luny,
him on his big black horse. Oh, they slide and they
vanish
as he shuffles the years like a pack of conjuror's cards.
True or not, it's all the same; and the frost on the roof
cracks like a whip, and the back-log breaks into ash.
Wake, old man. This is winter, and the yarns are over.
No one is listening. South of my days' circle
I know it dark against the stars, the high lean country
full of old stories that still go walking in my sleep.

Such poems as these and **"Nigger's Leap: New England"** and **"For New England"** attempt, as Wordsworth put it, in his preface to the second edition of his *Lyrical Ballads,*

> to choose incidents and situations from common life, and to relate or describe them, throughout, as far as was possible in a selection of language really used by men, and at the same time to throw over them a certain colouring of imagination, whereby ordinary things should be presented to the mind in an unusual aspect; and further, and above all, to make these incidents and situations interesting, by tracing in them, truly though not ostentatiously, the primary laws of our nature . . .

This is to explore both a mental and a geographical environment. What is shown to us, both in these shorter poems and in the longer title-poem in the first book, is what is seen and has been seen, within the limits set by one life, in one locality. Here the poet attempts simply to see and to show us what does exist within these limits—the "high lean country" and the "old stories that still go walking in my sleep"—rather than to suggest that some eternal reality, some cause imagined to exist beyond these limits, causes and explains everything, us included.

In the poem **"Waiting"**, in *The Moving Image,* what ails us is that we are caught in earth and time, rather than in some eden to shelter us from the effects of time and earth: death, pain and disillusionment. Eden is linked with love more frequently and more explicitly in the second book, *Woman to Man* (1949), the epigraph of which is

> Love was the most ancient of all the gods, and existed before everything else, except Chaos, which is held coeval therewith. . . . The summary or collective law of nature, or the principle of love, impressed by God upon the original particles of all things, so as to make them attack each other and come together, by the repetition and multiplication whereof all variety in the universe is produced, can scarcely find full admittance in the thoughts of man, though some faint notion may be had thereof. [Francis Bacon, *The Wisdom of the Ancients*]

This has a Lucretian ring, but there is, in this second book, little of Lucretius' scepticism of bitterness. Love is shown as creating life and as giving to an otherwise chaotic world some meaning and coherence, as in, for instance, **"Woman to Child"**:

> You who were darkness warmed my flesh
> where out of darkness rose the seed.
> Then all a world I made in me;
> all the world you hear and see
> hung upon my dreaming blood.
>
> There moved the multitudinous stars,
> and coloured birds and fishes moved.
> There swam the sliding continents.
> All time lay rolled in me, and sense,
> and love that knew not its beloved.
>
> O node and focus of the world;
> I hold you deep within that well
> you shall escape and not escape—
> that mirrors still your sleeping shape;
> that nurtures still your crescent cell.
> I wither and you break from me;
> yet though you dance in living light
> I am the earth, I am the root,
> I am the stem that fed the fruit,
> the link that joins you to the night.

Yet love may be mistaken, and end us, as in **"Metho Drinker"**:

> Under the death of winter's leaves he lies
> who cried to Nothing and the terrible night
> to be his home and bread. "O take from me
> the weight and waterfall of ceaseless Time
> that batters down my weakness; the knives of light
> whose thrust I cannot turn; the cruelty
> of human eyes that dare not touch nor pity."
> Under the worn leaves of the winter city
> safe in the house of Nothing now he lies.
> His white and burning girl, his woman of fire,

> creeps to his heart and sets a candle there
> to melt away the flesh that hides the bone,
> to eat the nerve that tethers him in Time.
> He will lie warm until the bone is bare
> and on a dead dark moon he wakes alone.
> It was for Death he took her; death is but this
> and yet he is uneasy under her kiss
> and winces from that acid of her desire.

There is a duality, apparently, in all things, or in the way we see them. We desire life, consciousness, at times, and sleep or death or forgetfulness at other times, and may think eden or alcohol the only way we can resolve our conflicting desires. Or we may be sadly sure that there are no edens, or none that we can reach, while alive or after death. But it is eden, as cause of this earth and time, and our refuge, the result and goal of love, that is the coherency sought in the third book, *The Gateway* (1953), as its epigraph indicates:

> Thou perceivest the Flowers put forth their precious
>   Odours;
> And none can tell from how small a centre comes
>   such sweet,
> Forgetting that within that centre Eternity expands
>   Its ever-during doors . . .
>   [William Blake, *Milton*]

Love is less earthly here, and is our way to this central eden. In the poem **"Eden"**, Judith Wright argues that it is only there, out of time, that we can reconcile our warring desires and make whole our divided souls. In **"The Orange Tree"**, eden is that "single perfect world of gold / no storm can undo nor death deny", where we will not feel what she calls the "pangs of life". In **"Botanical Gardens"**, we must endure our earthly lives while dreams of eden torment us. All these things are true enough emotionally to move us, and yet may cloy, may raise more doubts than they settle: time and pain and this earth are all real things, felt now, by us, here, and eden is, for us here, only a word, a dream, and nothing more.

In her poem **"Unknown Water"**, Judith Wright would apparently agree, when she says that truth is a kind of life, or an answer made more by actions than by words to those questions life thrusts at us. Words fail; reasons fail; whatever we believe is tested against our senses, against the Herakleitean flux of our earthly experience in time (which seems to change all things), as perhaps she recognizes in her choice of an epigraph for her fourth book, *The Two Fires* (1955):

> This world, which is the same for all, no one of gods or men has made; but it was ever, is now, and ever shall be an ever-living Fire, with measures of its kindling, and measures going out. [Herakleitos, fragment 20, *Early Greek Philosophy*]

And this nominalist view is expressed in **"Gum-Trees Stripping"** in the fourth book:

Say the need's born within the tree,
and waits a trigger set for light;
say sap is tidal like the sea,
and rises with the solstice-heat—
but wisdom shells the words away
to watch this fountain slowed in air
where sun joins earth—to watch the place
at which these silent rituals are.

Words are not meanings for a tree.
So it is truer not to say,
"These rags look like humility,
or this year's wreck of last year's love,
or wounds ripped by the summer's claw."
If it is possible to be wise
here, wisdom lies outside the word
in the earlier answer of the eyes.

Wisdom can see the red, the rose,
the stained and sculptured curve of grey,
the charcoal scars of fire, and see
around that living tower of tree
the hermit tatters of old bark
split down and strip to end the season;
and can be quiet and not look
for reasons past the edge of reason.

These two quite different views—one, to ignore this world, to seek some eden, and the other, to take this changing earth as our only reality, if no refuge—these two views expressed in these poems reflect the essential duality of any Platonic world-view. Philosophers generally try to explain all eventualities by, and to resolve them within, some single self-coherent plan, and so Plato tried to combine within his one world-view both Herakleitean concrete particulars (such as gum-trees) and some central abstract Parmenidean reality as cause and explanation of everything. Poets generally try to articulate not whole world-orders, but, instead, to crystallize moments of emotional perception, and to make them clear and significant to every man. Judith Wright expresses her concern with saying precisely what it is she senses, and for relating that sense-data to some central general meaning, in her poem **"For Precision"**, in which she says she wants to

    . . pin with one irremediable stroke—
what?—the escaping wavering wandering light,
the blur, the brilliance; forming into one chord
what's separate and distracted; making the vague hard—
catching the wraith—speaking with a pure voice,
and that the gull's sole note like a steel nail
that driven through cloud, sky, and irrelevant seas,
joins all, gives all a meaning, makes all whole.

She writes almost as if any intense, exact perception is a way towards the centre, explaining all things, is an act of love, and a way to stop or to put off time. Her poems attempt to articulate such perception, and in doing so to present some part of the complex Platonic world-view. In this fourth book, the poems **"Storm"**, **"Gum-Trees Stripping"** and **"West Wind"** concern the Herakleitean flux of earthly things, and **"Landscapes"** and **"Wildflower Plain"**

note how cyclic death brings on rebirth. This is one half-world, and she asks after the other in such poems as **"Silence"** and **"Song"** in *The Two Fires*:

O where does the dancer dance—
the invisible centre spin—
whose bright periphery holds
the world we wander in?

For it is he we seek—
the source and death of desire;
we blind as blundering moths
around that heart of fire.

Caught between birth and death
we stand alone in the dark
to watch the blazing wheel
on which the earth is a spark,

crying, Where does the dancer dance—
the terrible centre spin,
whose flower will open at last
to let the wanderer in?

Judith Wright attempts to express each half-world in terms of the other. She states the duality of her Platonic world-view in such phrases as

Not till life halved, and parted
one from the other,
did time begin, and knowledge

(from **"In Praise of Marriages"**) and as (in **"Return"**)

. . . unity becomes duality,
and action scars perfection like a pin.

The mind in contemplation sought its peace—
that round and calm horizon's purity—
which, known one instant, must subsist always.
But life breaks in again, time does not cease;
that calm lies quiet under storms of days.

These poems attempt to catch, to crystallize, what we feel and what we see, and to say why, and what it means. Where her poems fail, it is generally either because the end-emotion in them is only stated, and not a result of the poem, or because what is shown to us is not at once concrete or lastingly meaningful. Then, the direct statement fails to convince, the metaphor falls apart or is not formed, and neither metaphor nor statement is related to what we feel and sense and know, and so they do not involve us emotionally.

Judith Wright has moved from exploring her childhood environment and memories to attempts to articulate and explain her world in terms of love and of eden. This is to present, first, what she has known of Herakleitean earth and time, and then to seek the Parmenidean explanation, the eternal reality, of which earth and time are but moving images. These are the two halves of the one world-view her poems present, all of which was always implicit in the epigraph of the first book. This world-view may not be entirely convincing, and there are no final answers in it, or in any other world-view, but Judith Wright has put some statements most cogently and coherently where we can expect no answers but life and death themselves.

William Fleming (essay date 1958)

SOURCE: "Keeping the Home Fires Burning: Australian Poetry, Judith Wright," *Shenandoah,* Vol. IX, No. 3, Summer, 1958, pp. 33-9.

[*In the following essay, Fleming takes issue with the generally warm response Australian critics have given Wright's poetry. He methodically attacks both the "content" and the "form" of Wright's works, and decries what he terms her "paucity of imagination."*]

Some verse is made to be sung, some intoned, some declaimed, some spoken—and some mumbled. Judith Wright's belongs to the last category. Compare this

> Fra bank to bank, fra wood to wood I rin,
> Ourhailit with my feeble fantasie
> Lik til a leaf that fallis from a tree
> Or til a reed ourblowin with the wind
> > Mark Alexander Boyd (1563-1601), *Sonet*

with this

> Sanctuary, the sign said. Sanctuary
> trees, not houses; flat skins pinned to the road
> of possum and native cat; and here the old tree stood
> for how many thousand years? that old gnome—tree
> some axe-new boy cut down. Sanctuary, it sad:
> but only the road has meaning here. It leads
> into the world's cities like a long fuse laid.
> > Judith Wright, **"Sanctuary"**

It is necessary to be thus unhandsome at the outset because it has become universal practice for Australian critics to write of Judith Wright's verse no more responsibly than does the writer of the dust-jacket blurb of . . . *The Two Fires*: "It is safe to predict that many of them [referring to the verses of an earlier book], by their inspired fusion of passion, intellect, and artistry, will live in the literature of the English-speaking world." Similarly, Kenneth Slessor's "Five Bells" has in this continent been described on at least one occasion as superior to T. S. Eliot's "The Waste Land."

In view of which things it seems advisable in the present examination not to beat about the bush.

The poetry of *The Two Fires* is poetry made of certain classifiable ingredients: of epithets—

> Nothing is so bare as truth—
> that lean geometry of thought
> > **"The Man Beneath the Tree"**

of apostrophes—

> Oh, Passionate gazer, oh enraptured hearer,
> oh eager climber, perhaps you climb too late.
> > **"Dialogue"**

and, especially, of appositions—

> . . . making the vague hard—
> catching the wraith—speaking with a pure voice,
> and that the gull's sole note like a steel nail
> that driven through cloud, sky, and irrelevant seas,
> joins all, gives all a meaning, makes all whole.
> > **"For Precision"**

> . . . Stone—
> stone our mother locks in, tongueless, without feeling,
> our far blind brothers, future, and past who had no luck
> and never was born.
> > **"Landscapes"**

—all of which are rhetorical devices for simulating *fervor; which is a different thing from poetry.*

Quite probably it is this quality of *fervor* which accounts for the high prestige in Australia of Judith Wright's work. As Yeats remarked, "They don't like poetry; they like something else, but they like to think they like poetry."

Other detracting characteristics of Judith Wright's work, of which critics to date have been equally oblivious, would be abstractionism (notice how characters like Old Gustav, Mr. Ferritt, the Prospector, are generalized *before* being realized), a didacticism that generally blows up in bathos—

> Yet it is time that holds,
> somewhere although not now,
> the peal of trumpets for us; time that bears,
> made fertile even by those tears,
> even by this darkness, even by this loss,
> incredible redemptions—hours that grow,
> as trees grow fruit, in a blind holiness,
> the truths unknown, the loves unloved by us.
> > **"The Harp and the King"**

and a high frequency of appearance of the off-key adjective (gonfalon of the contemporary band-wagon)—

> The solitary mountain is as tall as grief
> > **"Mount Mary"**

> This is what I can neither bear nor heal
> for you—that the fierce various street,
> the country tower of tree and bell of bird,
> are blown aside a little by the venomous wind
> that twitches at the curtain over hell . . .
> > **"Two Generations"**

On the other hand, to be fair, what Judith Wright seems to have her eye on, through these "incidentals," is a registering of sudden "illuminations" (whatever that may mean); as thus:

> Hunger and force his beauty made
> and turned a bird to a knife-blade.
>   **"Black-shouldered Kite"**

> Root, limb, and leaf unfold
> out of the seed, and these rejoice
> till the tree dreams it has a voice
> to join four truths in one great world of gold.
>   **"The Wattle-tree"**

I suppose it may be possible to compose in this fashion useful *poetry* even though the *verse* be inferior (*e.g.* Keats?), but it is an unsatisfying and unlikely accomplishment. Prosody, after all, is what essentially distinguishes verse from prose; and the prosody of **The Two Fires,** as manifested in recurrent vocal awkwardnesses such as "like a long fuse laid," "makes all whole," "which, known one instant, must subsist always." "No Mother's Day present planned," is unlovely.

Having isolated a few, but quite damaging, points in the matter of "form," it remains to consider the more tricky matter of "content."

It is first necessary, however, to clarify this distinction—important, in general use, but little understood—of "form" and "content." "Content," to start with the essential matter first, is that part (qualitative part, say aspect) of a poem which is translatable *without loss* into other words—whether arranged in verse, prose, or a foreign language; as melody may be played without loss on any instrument, or be sung, or whistled: as design may be executed without loss in pencil, in water color, or oil—so "content." It is the basic, first received part of a poem, that on which it is constructed, called *inscape* by Hopkins, *phanopoeia* by Pound (understood as the play of images on the imaginative eye), *plot* by Aristotle—also *form* (in the technical sense as distinct from its meaning in the looser usage). When this "content," "inscape," "phanopoeia," "form" is slight, as it well may be, there must be considerable melodic or verbal interest to compensate (as in the Elizabethan songs). On the other hand, excellence in *plot* can cover all manner of defects in *technique* (*e.g.* though Villon and Corbiere may have nowhere near the technical resource of Laforgue, say, they are nevertheless the better poets).

Rather than contrasting "content" and "form," then, it is better to contrast "plot" and "technique"—better still to make use of the poet's terminology, "phanopoeia," "melopoeia" and "logopoiea," subdividing "technique" into two. Thus:

> phanopoeia: the conception, the idea, "what it says" *together with* "the way of putting it";

> melopeia: the music—sound, rhythm, metre, rhyme;

> logopoeia: the implication—what's implied by the words and by the words and by the sound, in toto—the relation which all the parts bear to each other and to the whole *and* to all the other poems, writing, expressions, etc., that may be expected to be known to the cultivated reader whether as tradition or as current clichéd usage.

Let us now apply these distinctions to Judith Wright's work: the "melopoeia" has been shown to be crude; the "logopoeia" she makes use of is the non-sophisticated type, the blurred, non-rational "heavy-going" kind of association which means everything or nothing, not being precise. Now for the "phanopoeia." For convenience let us subdivide this into two parts, (1) "what it says" (the literal side), and (2) "how it puts it" (the imaginative side—previously called Wit).

In regard first to the literal side, "what it says," it may be useful to keep in mind that some writers are interested in the life of the mind (*i.e.* the advancement and promotion of useful, communicable knowledge), while some are not. The "content" of those who are not, though possibly interesting as a curiosity, must necessarily be considerably less significant than that of those who are. Though deadly serious in most of her poems (as one wanting to have it both ways), Judith Wright does not evidence in her work any noteworthy such interest. Indeed, it can be categorically asserted, harshly perhaps but necessarily, that her quasi-biological musings along pre-Socratic lines of speculation (One / Many / All / Time) have added nothing to the quantum of human knowledge.

As thus for instance: in **"At Cooloolah,"** as frequently elsewhere, Judith Wright broaches the time-honored theme of the "rootlessness" of European peoples in the Australian aboriginal's land—in such incredibly incompetent lines as

> Those dark-skinned people who once named Cooloolah
> knew that no land is lost or won by wars
> for earth is spirit: the invader's feet will tangle
> in nets there and his blood be thinned by fears.

I should imagine that a genuinely satisfactory mental accommodation to a strange landscape and climate would consist in distinguishing its features and aspects, and in naming them accordingly. Which process immediately *separates* one from most of those who dance corroborees: *they* are the ones whose "blood is thinned by fears." Judith Wright appears to exhort us in much of her work to go *back* to the mental attitude of people who dance corroborees—that is, to some variety of Animism.

Now Animism in one form or another seems currently to be the "philosophy" most favored in verse, particularly in the official critical circles—possibly because "thought" along such lines does not impinge seriously on matters ethical or political. Hence perhaps another reason for the high standard of Judith Wright's work. . . . But for the life of me I cannot fathom how people to whom the whole heritage of Western civilization is available as a birthright must go hankering after barbarisms and darkness—on cultural manifestations, at any rate, far less rational *and less spiritual* than ours (specialists naturally excepted).

In conclusion, I should like to set in juxtaposition for the reader's meditation two disconnected stanzas from Judith Wright's **"The Man Beneath the Tree"** and two from William Carlos Williams' "The Fool's Song." In this case we are pointing up the paucity of the *imaginative* side, "how it puts it," of her "content" / "phanopoeia"; but the sound and associative values of the two exhibits may also be profitably compared. The comparison should illustrate how it is no truly kind service to the local product irresponsibly to inflate its importance.

Nothing is so far as truth;
nothing is so plain to see.
Look where light has married earth
through the green leaves on the tree.

Oh, love and truth and I should meet,
sighed the man beneath the tree;
but where should our acquaintance be?
Between your hat and the soles of your feet,
sang the bird on the top of the tree.

. . . . .

I tried to put a bird in a cage.
    O fool that I was!
  For the bird was Truth.
Sing merrily, Truth: I tried to put
    Truth in a cage!

And when I had the bird in the cage,
    O fool that I am!
  Why, it broke my pretty cage.
Sing merrily, Truth; I tried to put
    Truth in a cage!

G. A. Wilkes (essay date 1965)

SOURCE: "The Later Poetry of Judith Wright," in *Southerly*, Vol. 25, No. 3, 1965, pp. 163-71.

[*Here, Wilkes defends Wright's third and fourth volumes of poetry,* The Gateway *and* The Two Fires, *contending that the two collections represent an expansion in Wright's poetry, an attempt "to reach beyond the immediate experience, to probe its significance." Additionally, Wilkes examines the significance of two later collections,* Birds *and* Five Senses, *in Wright's body of work.*]

The Recognition so quickly won by Judith Wright's early work, in *The Moving Image* (1946) and *Woman to Man* (1949), has proved strangely prejudicial to her later verse. *The Moving Image* was a volume in which sense perceptions were held and explored, the titles of the poems read-

ing like a series of talismans—**"Trapped Dingo"**, **"Bullocky"**, **"The Surfer"**, **"Nigger's Leap: New England"**—and their impact coming from the sheer individuality of perception:

South of my days' circle, part of my blood's country,
rises that tableland, high delicate outline
of bony slopes wincing under the winter;
low trees blue-leaved and olive; outcropping granite—
clean, lean, hungry country.

The same immediacy and vitality was felt in the lyrical poetry of her second book, in the set of love poems on the woman, the man and the unborn child—"the third who lay in our embrace".

The collections that followed, *The Gateway* (1953) and *The Two Fires* (1955), were received with less enthusiasm, if not with positive misgivings at the "increasing impersonality" of Judith Wright's work, its movement towards the general and the abstract. To the reader who valued *The Moving Image* and *Woman to Man, The Gateway* could well seem like a collection of the poems rejected from those earlier books. Criticism of the later verse in general has been influenced by an assumption that Judith Wright was still trying to write the kind of poetry she had written before, but was now failing in the attempt. I should argue, to the contrary, that in *The Gateway* and *The Two Fires* she is attempting poetry of another kind.

> **Judith Wright's earlier poetry had been established in one world, the finite world available to the senses, and had drawn its strength from the clarity and vitality of her sense perceptions. The effort of the later poetry is to reach beyond that world into regions unexplored before.**
>
> *—G. A. Wilkes*

It had been clear in *The Moving Image* itself that Judith Wright was not content merely to write poems of observation, however acute and sensitive: there had been a constant effort to reach beyond the immediate experience, to probe its significance. This effort was felt in the strained endings of **"The Surfer"** and **"Bullocky"**, and in the forcing of the Homeric parallel in **"Trapped Dingo"**; it was felt also in the title-poem in the attempt at a large philosophical pronouncement on Time, as "a moving image of eternity". *Woman to Man,* interpreted in the light of its epigraph, upheld love ("the summary or collective law of nature . . . imposed by God upon the original particles of all things") as a counter to the destructiveness of Time, a force of renewal and regeneration. The tendencies pursued in the later verse are tendencies present from the beginning, but they confront Judith Wright with dilemmas that compel a departure from her earlier manner.

The surface change—the one repeatedly noted—is that the world as perceived, hitherto the main source of her poetic inspiration, ceases to dominate her field of vision. Instead it offers now a starting-point for reflection, as in **"Phaius Orchid"**; or a symbolic situation to be explored, as in **"The Pool and the Star"**; or it is translated from literal reality into a sphere of imagination and dream, as in **"Lion"**. A poem like **"The Cycads"** in *Woman to Man* already indicates the change. The trees are seen as enduring through the centuries, surviving generation after generation of other forms of life:

> Only the antique cycads sullenly
> keep the old bargain life has long since broken:
> and, cursed by age, through each chill century
> they watch the shrunken moon, but never die,
>
> for time forgets the promise he once made,
> and change forgets that they are left alone.
> Among the complicated birds and flowers
> they seem a generation carved in stone

but the cycads are not here "observed" as they would have been in *The Moving Image*. The reader could not learn from the poem that cycads are palm-like, or discover much else of their physical appearance as Macrozamia. The cycads figure only as part of the reverie of the poet, as a symbol of time itself:

> Leaning together, down those gulfs they stare
> over whose darkness dance the brilliant birds
> that cry in air one moment, and are gone;
> and with their countless suns the years spin on.
>
> Take their cold seed and set it in the mind,
> and its slow root will lengthen deep and deep
> till, following, you cling on the last ledge
> over the unthinkable, unfathomed edge
> beyond which man remembers only sleep.

From *The Gateway* onward, individual poems gain from their relationship to one another, and to the total movement of which they are part. It is significant that the epigraph to *The Gateway* is taken from Blake (while a later poem is addressed to Traherne), and that of the Australian poets whom Judith Wright has studied, she has written most perceptively of John Shaw Neilson. It is not so much that her poetry is losing its grasp on the actual world; it is rather that the instinct she possessed from the outset, to press towards the underlying significance of a given experience, is becoming more searching and insistent. A possible access to Judith Wright's later verse lies through the concept of the "two lives", to which she herself referred in discussing the poetry of Chris Brennan. He gave his own formulation of it in his lectures on symbolism in 1904 [published in *Preoccupations in Australian Poetry*, 1965]:

> There are, as most of us keenly feel, two lives: that lies in the brightness of truth, this stumbles in error; that is radiant with love and beauty, this is vexed with its own littleness and meanness; that is unfettered, lying

beyond good and evil, this is caught in the quagmire . . . Poetry, mediating between the two, necessarily enters into the conflict . . . its part is both to exasperate and reconcile that war.

Judith Wright's earlier poetry had been established in one world, the finite world available to the senses, and had drawn its strength from the clarity and vitality of her sense perceptions. The effort of the later poetry is to reach beyond that world—an effort that is always arduous and most often frustrated, but that leads Judith Wright into regions unexplored before. In *The Gateway* and *The Two Fires* the contingent world has become both an earnest of the ideal world and a denial of it, at times a prison and at times a means of release.

Thematically the most instructive of these later poems is **"The Gateway"** itself, which takes up the conception of the journey developed also in **"The Lost Man"** and **"The Traveller and the Angel"**. Through the gateway lies the land where the contingent world falls away and the self is the "sole reality"; the way leads on until the path itself vanishes and the self is dissolved in turn—then from nothingness, it is remade:

> To say that I recall that time,
> that country,
> would be a lie; time was not,
> and I nowhere.
> Yet two things remain—
> one was the last surrender,
> the other the last peace.
> In the depths of nothing
> I found my home.
>
> All ended there,
> yet all began.
> All sank in dissolution
> and rose renewed.

This is the only poem in which the transition from the one world to the other is completed, and then only at the level of descriptive statement. The other poems in *The Gateway* remain fixed in the world of time, where the only renewal offered is a rebirth into the natural cycle, as presented so painfully in **"The Cicadas"**:

> Terrible is the pressure of light into the heart.
> The womb is withered and cracked, the birth is begun,
> and shuddering and groaning to break that iron grasp
> the new is delivered as the old is torn apart . . .

Spring, bringing new life, is resented in **"The Cedars"** as confirming the bondage to the processes of time:

> Spring, returner, knocker at the iron gates,
> why should you return? None wish to live again . . .
>
> For it is anguish to be reborn and reborn:
> at every return of the overmastering season
> to shed our lives in pain, to waken into the cold . . .

The natural world is seen here as a prison, mocking efforts to escape from it. At other times, in its obedience to its own law, it possesses a harmony and rightness that by contrast prove a torment to the divided self. This is an idea touched on in **"The Flame Tree"**

> How to live, I said, as the flame-tree lives?
> To know what the flame-tree knows—to be
> prodigal of my life as that wild tree
> and wear my passion so?

and developed in **"Birds"**:

> Whatever the bird does is right for the bird to do—
> cruel kestrel dividing in his hunger the sky,
> thrush in the trembling dew beginning to sing,
> parrot clinging and quarrelling and veiling his queer
>   eye—
> all these are as birds are and good for birds to do.
> But I am torn and beleaguered by my own people.
> The blood that feeds my heart is the blood they
>   gave me,
> and my heart is the house where they gather and
>   fight for dominion—
> all different, all with a wish and a will to save me,
> to turn me into the ways of other people.

At other moments again, the world is seen with the particularity characteristic of *The Moving Image,* but with the difference that its beauty now symbolises the plight of existence subject to time. For whom does the phaius orchid flower? For the lizards and the ants merely, in a purposeless splendour?

> Out of the brackish sand
> see the phaius orchid build
> her intricate moonlight tower
> that rusts away in flower.
>
> For whose eyes—for whose eyes
> does this blind being weave
> sand's poverty, water's sour,
> the white and black of the hour
>
> into the image I hold
> and cannot understand?
> Is it for the ants, the bees,
> the lizard outside his cave,
>
> or is it to garland time—
> eternity's cold tool
> that severs with its blade
> the gift as soon as made?

These later poems betray an increasing consciousness of dualities that refuse to be resolved into singleness—the duality of life in time and life beyond it, of disorder and harmony, of flesh and spirit, of reason and unreason. This motif persists in *The Two Fires* (1955), perhaps giving more identity to the collection than its declared theme, mankind threatened by the atomic bomb. There is a recurring sense of the poet trying to scrutinise her own mental

processes (**"Flesh"**), being baffled in a conscious search for what should come effortlessly (**"The Man Beneath the Tree"**), or finding in the outside world (**"Nameless Flower"**, **"Gum-trees Stripping"**) modes of existence whose simplicity and completeness humble the ego. Although a poem like **"The Man Beneath the Tree"** so strongly recalls Shaw Neilson, this is not to suggest that Judith Wright is a mystic—though perhaps she might wish that she were. From the time of *Woman to Man* at least, she has been especially concerned with the role of the poet, the poet as "The Maker"—

> All things that glow and move,
> all things that change and pass,
> I gather their delight
> as in a burning-glass;
>
> all things I focus in
> the crystal of my sense.
> I give them breath and life
> and set them free in the dance

and in *The Two Fires* the emphasis falls more strongly on the poet's power to impose coherence on the disorder of the world. In **"For Precision"**, his role is defined in a way that would put an end to the sense of duality haunting Judith Wright's work:

> pin with one irremediable stroke—
> what?—the escaping wavering wandering light,
> the blur, the brilliance; forming into one chord
> what's separate and distracted; making the vague
>   hard
> catching the wraith—speaking with a pure voice,
> and that the gull's sole note like a steel nail
> that driven through cloud, sky, and irrelevant seas,
> joins all, gives all a meaning, makes all whole.

In "forming into one chord / what's separate and distracted", the poet may establish a moment of harmony, transcend—if only for an instant—the world of flux and the sense of the divided self. The enigmatic piece **"The Cup"** fixes on silence as a state or quality that is likewise isolated from the conflict; **"Song"** presents the dance as another symbol of transcendence, recalling Yeats.

Yet the poem that concludes *The Two Fires* reproduces most painfully the dilemma that all Judith Wright's later verse has sought to escape. **"The Harp and the King"** insists on the captivity of human life in time. The old king is frightened and despairing, calling the harp to comfort him as he feels "night and the soul's terror coming on":

> The world's a traitor to the self-betrayed;
> but once I thought there was a truth in time,
> while now my terror is eternity.
> So do not take me outside time.
> Make me believe in my mortality,
> since that is all I have, the old king said.

The harp replies that time offers "aching drought" and resurgent fertility, suffering and failure followed by "incredible redemptions"—and yet is finally comfortless, unless it be transcended:

> This is the praise of time, the harp cried out—
> that we betray all truths that we possess.
> Time strips the soul and leaves it comfortless
> and sends it thirsty through a bone-white drought.
> Time's subtler treacheries teach us to betray.
> What else could drive us on our way?
> Wounded we cross the desert's emptiness
> and must be false to what would make us whole.
> For only change and distance shape for us
> some new tremendous symbol for the soul.

While the theoretical scheme of the poem asserts the possibility of transcendence or release, this is eclipsed in the stronger feeling of compulsive bondage to time.

After *The Two Fires* there was an interval of seven years before Judith Wright published another collection. On its appearance, *Birds* (1962) seemed something of an interlude in her career. The delicacy of perception in **"Dotterel"** and **"Parrots"** would seem like a return to the mode of *The Moving Image,* except that this is a talent she has had always at command, like the gift for the "character" poem seen from **"Remittance Man"** to **"Old House"** to **"Bachelor Uncle"**. At the same time a poem like **"Eggs and Nestlings"** reveals that the cruel contrast of the "two lives" can make itself felt even here:

> The moss-rose and the palings made
> a solemn and a waiting shade
> where eagerly the mother pressed
> a sheltering curve into her nest.
>
> Her tranced eye, her softened stare,
> warned me when I saw her there,
> and perfect as the grey nest's round,
> three fail and powdered eggs I found.
>
> My mother called me there one day.
> Beneath the nest the eggshells lay,
> and in it throbbed the triple greed
> of one incessant angry need.
>
> Those yellow gapes, those starveling cries,
> how they disquieted my eyes!—
> the shapeless furies come to be
> from shape's most pure serenity.

Birds was followed in 1963 by *Five Senses,* Judith Wright's choice from all her previously published work, with the addition of the new series **"The Forest"**. The sense of continuing search is stressed in the poem of this title: although over the years the strangeness of the forest has been subdued into the named and known, still

> My search is further.
> There's still to name and know
> beyond the flowers I gather
> that one that does not wither—
> the truth from which they grow.

Many of the poems assembled in **"The Forest"** were first published in the 1950's, and this series does not so much advance the search as confer a symmetry on it. There is even a suggestion that it is becoming stylised, as poems like **"Interplay"**, **"The Lake"**, **"Double Image"** and **"Vision"** seem to rely on a depersonalised introspection, an oracular manner, and references to love as an absolute. The originality of Judith Wright's talent is not in question, as **"For My Daughter"** is enough to show, or a more recent poem like **"Typists in the Phoenix Building"** (*Quadrant* 26, 1963) which she has chosen not to include. The poems she has included in **"The Forest"** contribute to the unity of *Five Senses,* as a determination of her work up to 1963. The title itself is significant, as drawn from a poem published seven years earlier, and perhaps defining the aspiration behind her verse since that time. **"Five Senses"** describes the effort to win "shape's most pure serenity" from an incoherent and imperfect world, through the creative activity of the poet:

> Now my five senses
> gather into a meaning
> all acts, all presences;
> and as a lily gathers
> the elements together,
> in me this dark and shining,
> that stillness and that moving,
> these shapes that spring from nothing,
> become a rhythm that dances,
> a pure design

while the poet's activity in turn is guided by something beyond his knowing, so that the poem at once embodies the union of his creative mind and the world outside it, and yet forms a reality transcending them both:

> While I'm in my five senses
> they send me spinning
> all sounds and silences,
> all shape and colour
> as thread for that weaver,
> whose web within me growing
> follows beyond my knowing
> some pattern sprung from nothing—
> a rhythm that dances
> and is not mine.

At such moments—and poems as early as **"Wonga Vine"** are their record—the "two lives" become one.

John K. Ewers (essay date 1968)

SOURCE: "The Genius of Judith Wright," in *Westerly,* No. 1, March, 1968, pp. 42-51.

[*Using his review of* The Other Half *(1966) as an occasion to write a retrospective of Wright's career, Ewers traces her development from regionalist to universalist, and concludes that she is a mystic with a poetic voice.*]

Before attempting to come to terms with Judith Wright's latest volume, *The Other Half,* I propose, first to take a brief sampling of what critics and reviewers had to say about her earlier work as it appeared, and then to examine it in more detail as a whole. This will enable us to establish her poetic background, to mark some common factors to be found in all her poetry and the differences that emerge from time to time.

Much credit is due to C. B. Christesen, editor of *Meanjin* in which a number of her poems had already appeared, for publishing her first book, *The Moving Image* (1946). This brought nothing but praise from the critics. Professor S. Musgrove said [in *Southerly* 8, No. 3 (1947)]: "This book confirms what we have for some time suspected from Judith Wright's periodical pieces, that she is the only poet among the younger Australians who can challenge the stature of R. D. FitzGerald." Nan McDonald, herself a poet, wrote: "After wading through many books of verse where only a faint glimmer of poetry haunts the bog of words, the reader can ask nothing better than to be dealt the old familiar blow that says, beyond all shadow of doubt, 'This is poetry'. Judith Wright's first book, *The Moving Image,* does that." *Woman to Man* (1949) was no less enthusiastically received. By the time H. M. Green had published the second edition of his anthology, *Modern Australian Poetry,* in 1952, he was prepared on the evidence of these two volumes alone to place her "among the principal poets writing in English today". Still confining himself to these two books, Green amplified this further in his *A History of Australian Literature,* Vol. 2, 1923-1950: "A couple of lines that certainly and several whole poems that probably belong to world literature; half a dozen poems that are among the best of their kind in the present day: it is an amazing production for a woman of thirty-five, and it fixes Judith Wright's position, alongside those of FitzGerald and Slessor, among the first of living poets, in Australia or elsewhere."

There was less enthusiasm for the third volume, *The Gateway* (1953). Elyne Mitchell [in *Southerly* 16, No. 1 (1955)] regretted that the language and the imagery were "similar to those recording the spiritual journeys of other poets", and T. Inglis Moore [in *Meanjin* 17, No. 3 (1958)] found "a relaxing of the high tension, a recurring sense of uncertainty, a feeling that the poet has stopped on her path to look around, unsure of her way". About the fourth volume, *The Two Fires* (1955) the critics themselves were divided. Someone writing in *Southerly,* No. 2, 1956, with the initials of J. T. declared that many poems "lend colour to a suspicion that the author is forcing her art". He even went so far as to suggest that "half-baked critics or importunate publishers may have hurried this fine poet into putting out a fourth book before she was ready to do so". But Robert D. FitzGerald (who is certainly no "half-baked critic") after commenting on the changing direction shown in this new volume, said "the earlier impressions return of poetry that has almost everything we could ask of it", adding later that "one is continuously conscious of a power of vision beyond the ordinary sight of mankind" [*Meanjin* 15, No. 2 (1956)]. In the final chapter of his History already referred to—a chapter bringing the record up to 1960—H. M. Green amended his previously expressed opinion that Judith Wright was "essentially lyrist rather than intellectual". This he said, no longer held, for her third and fourth books showed her "moving inward, less often making her vision concrete and lyrical with pictures and lovely images and more often realizing some inner experience". He conceded that this showed "her poetic attitude is not static, an important thing for a writer who has already made so high a place for herself".

Judith Wright's fifth volume was *Birds* (1962). F. H. Mares in *The Australian Book Review* [Vol. 2, No. 6] said: "These are beautifully wrought small poems: I had hoped for a great deal more, and I fear a withdrawal here." There is a tendency, it seems, for the contemporary reviewer to anticipate what the writer may do next and to be disappointed when his own anticipation is not fulfilled. It was timely therefore that these five volumes should be followed by two selections, each made by the poet herself, so that we could get the flavour of her work as a whole up to that point. The first of these was in Angus & Robertson's Australian Poets series and appeared in 1963, to be followed by a rather fuller selection, *Five Senses,* in 1964. Both contained some poems under the heading of "The Forest" not previously published in book form, of which more will be said presently.

This then was the position as far as some critics and reviewers saw it up to the publication of her latest volume of new work, *The Other Half*. It was clear that all were agreed that Judith Wright was a poet of considerable statute, but not all were prepared to concede that her genius had not sometimes faltered in her six published volumes (seven, if we count "The Forest" poems which occur for the first time in the two volumes of selections).

I have now spent some weeks reading at leisure Judith Wright's entire published poems in an attempt to distil from them some unifying essence. When met again after many years, a number of poems in her early volumes assumed, for me, the classic quality of memorableness. What I wish to convey by this is that apparently these poems had at earlier readings entered into my subconscious to a degree I had not realized. Others familiar with this author's work, attempting a similar exercise in re-acquaintance, would no doubt share this experience and be prepared to name further poems which produced a similar effect on them. Among those which came to me in the re-reading with the force and familiarity of old and well-tried companions were **"Nigger's Leap: New England"**, **"Bullocky"** and **"South of my Days"** from the first volume, **"Woman to Man"**, **"Woman's Song"**, **"Woman to Child"** and **"Lost Child"** from the second, **"Birds"** and **"Old House"** from the third, and the title poem from the fourth. There were others where the impact of familiarity was also present but to a lesser degree. This is a very subjective approach and mere memorableness for any individual is not necessarily a virtue. When it is coupled with the undoubted quality which such poems possess and when it is shared with a great number of other readers—as I believe is true of Judith Wright's work—it means a great deal.

One of the strongest impressions I received was the relationship much of her work bears to the time it was written. This can be a disadvantage; it can make for ephemeral work if the poet is too closely a victim of her time. But Judith Wright manages to transcend the ephemeral where many a lesser poet has been engulfed by it. This is well illustrated by the mood of most of the poems in *The Moving Image*. This was published in 1946, but all the poems except one are grouped under the heading: Poems, 1940-1944; that is, they were written during World War II. The title poem is undated, but it *could* be regarded as a war-poem with its overtones of destruction, although it is much more than that in its full implications.

World War II was a time when Australia's survival as a nation in the Pacific received its first full challenge and this evoked a great deal of inward-looking. We might not last long, the time seemed to say. What are we? How far have we come? The year before the outbreak of war had seen the announcement of the Jindyworobak manifesto by Rex Ingamells who gathered around him a group of nationalistic poets whose talents (many of them limited) drew also upon this inward-looking fostered by the threat to survival. Writers in this group over-stressed background and local colour, and aroused a good deal of hostility in certain quarters. Judith Wright was never close to the movement, but when asked by its founder to contribute to a review of its achievements at the end of 10 years she offered a comment that was untouched by the rancour that coloured the criticisms of many others.

> "The Russian, the English, the Norwegian writer can concentrate his attention on the social or psychological problem in hand; his background is already filled in, taken for granted" she wrote in an article called *Perspective* [in *Jindyworobak Review* (1948)]. "But the Australian background, important as it is to the Australian psychology, has never thus been assimilated. So a kind of split in the writer's consciousness is often manifest; he cannot solve his immediate problem, he cannot keep attention concentrated on his foreground, while his background keeps intruding. Perhaps this duality, this unsolved problem, is partly the cause of the gaps in Australian literature, and the curious lack of writers with anything like a 'body of work' to their credit. Only the single-minded with a track of their own to follow, or the genuinely great writer, can by-pass that boulder in the road. (Henry Handel Richardson managed it in the Mahony trilogy, Slessor and FitzGerald managed it, though neither of them can be called prolific writers; Hugh McCrae and his circle managed it by simply detaching themselves completely from the ground and flying over it, but nevertheless their work as a whole was seriously weakened by the evasion.)

> "It seems to me that the Jindy movement was essentially an effort to get the problem into perspective. I don't necessarily mean that the Jindy writers themselves have done that, but rather that in the ensuing argument the issues found some kind of clarification; and in fact the work of the outstanding Jindy writers has to some extent already broken the problem down. To emphasize our regionalism instead of trying to elude it—this has had a value in itself, and it has performed the further function of leading to a reaction against itself. That is to say, that having found out what happens when one tries to treat the problem as an end in itself, it is now possible to apply the knowledge. The regional, the national outlook *has* a value, and no doubt some writers do their best work within such a closed circuit. But there are other jobs to do; and Jindyworobak has probably contributed something towards finding the means to do them. It may be that because of the Jindy movement, *even those most fiercely opposed or most indifferent to it know themselves a little better.*"

The italics at the end are mine. Whether, in fact, Judith Wright herself was opposed or indifferent to the Jindyworobak attitude is not clear, but her poetry in this first volume stands in sharp contrast to that of the bulk of Jindyworobak verse in that, while sometimes saying the same thing, it says it from much greater depth. Reg Ingamells had written in *his* first book of verse published ten years earlier:

> Where now uninterrupted sun
>   Is shrivelling the sheaves,
> Black children leap and laugh and run
>   Beneath a sky of leaves;
> And where the farmer thrashes wheat
>   With steel machinery,
> Go glimmerings of their little feet,
>   If we could only see.

It's a pleasant enough concept and here put forward probably for the first time, but it is shallow and poetically not distinguished. Judith Wright in **"Nigger's Leap: New England"** puts a similar thought into much richer language:

> Did we not know their blood channelled our rivers,
> and the black dust our crops ate was their dust?

She follows this with an extension of thought to the oneness of man, an extension, it may be added, which seldom if ever entered into the verse of the Jindyworobaks:

> O all men are one man at last. We should have known
> the night that tided up the cliffs and hid them
> had the same question on its tongue for us.
> And there they lie that were ourselves writ strange.

Her main preoccupation in this first volume is with what we have grown out of; it derives from the inward-looking that was part of the time in which she was writing. It occurs over and over again. In **"Country Town"** she says:

> This is no longer the landscape that they knew,
> the sad green enemy country of their exile,
> those branded men whose songs were of rebellion.
>   . . . . .

This is a landscape that the town creeps over;
a landscape safe with bitumen and banks.
The hostile hills are netted in with fences
and the roads lead to houses and the pictures.
Thunderbolt was killed by Constable Walker
long ago; the bones are buried, the story printed.
And yet in the night of the sleeping town, the voices:
This is not ours, not ours the flowering tree.
What is it we have lost and left behind?

Where the Jindyworobaks were accusing early settlers of despoiling the countryside, thundering imprecations about "the rape of the land", Judith Wright was enquiring into the sources from which she herself had sprung. The poem concludes with a call to

Remember Thunderbolt, buried under the
   air-raid trenches.
Remember the bearded men singing of exile.
Remember the shepherds under their strange stars.

That this call for remembrance is, for her, very personal is shown in many places and nowhere better than in **"South of my Days"** which begins:

South of my days' circle, part of my blood's
   country,
rises the tableland, high delicate outline
of bony slopes wincing under the winter,
low trees blue-leaved and olive, outcropping
   granite—
clean, lean, hungry country. . . .

and ends:

South of my days' circle
I know it against the stars, the high lean country
full of old stories that still go walking in my sleep.

If there has been despoilment, this seems to imply, then we are all touched with some guilt and out of the original hate-love relationship between our forebears and this alien earth has come the fulfilment of love.

Her poem, **"Bullocky"**, expressed in a ballad-like form she was not often to use again, became at once a favourite anthology piece. The first three stanzas suffice to show its mood:

Beside his heavy-shouldered team,
thirsty with drought and chilled with rain,
he weathered all the striding years
till they ran widdershins in his brain:

Till the long solitary tracks
etched deeper with each lurching load
were populous before his eyes,
and fiends and angels used his road.

All the long straining journey grew
a mad apocalyptic dream,
and he old Moses, and the slaves
his suffering and stubborn team.

This is landscape poetry, but it is a landscape with people. In **"South of my Days"** there was old Dan:

Seventy years of stories he clutches round his bones.
Seventy summers are hived in him like old honey.

In **"Brother and Sisters"** there are Millie, Lucy and John struggling against time and lack of fulfilment on a no-good farm:

The road turned out to be a cul-de-sac;
stopped like a lost intention at the gate
and never crossed the mountains to the coast.
But they stayed on.

"Half-caste Girl" is pure Jindyworobak, but written with much deeper insight:

Little Josie buried under the bright moon
is tired of being dead, death lasts too long.
She would like to push death aside, and
      stand on the hill
and beat with a waddy on the bright moon
      like a gong.

Across the hills, the hills that belong to no people
and so to none are foreign,
once she climbed high to find the native cherry;
the lithe darkhearted lubra
who in her beads like blood
dressed delicately for love
moves her long hands among the strings of the wind,
singing the songs of women,
the songs of love and dying.

Most of the poetry in *The Moving Image* is essentially regional; its appeal could be largely to those who, however vicariously, have shared the emotions which regionalism of any sort calls up. We are reminded of her words in the Jindyworobak review: "The regional, the national outlook *has* a value, and no doubt some writers do their best work within such a closed circuit. But there are other jobs to do." Judith Wright worked magnificently within that closed circuit, but did not confine herself to it. Even in this early volume **"The Company of Lovers"** entirely forsakes regionalism. It does, however, remain a poem of its time, the time of a world at war:

We meet and part now over all the world;
we, the lost company,
take hands together in the night, forget
the night in our brief happiness, silently.
We, who sought many things, throw all away
for this one thing, one only,

remembering that in the narrow grave
we shall be lonely.

Death marshals up his armies round us now.
Their footsteps crowd too near.
Lock your warm hands above the chilling heart
and for a time I live without my fear.
Grope in the night to find me and embrace
for the dark preludes of the drums begin,
and round us, round the company of lovers,
death draws his cordons in.

This poem serves to introduce us to the prevailing mood of her second volume, **Woman to Man**. Love is a recurring theme in these and later poems. At first it begins as the love between man and woman; later it takes on a more transcendental quality—love, the moving force of all life. Just as the landscape poems, wherever they occur in the flow of her poetry, are peopled with personal memories or derivations, so her love poems have a deeply personal quality. It is doubtful whether any aspect of what she says in the title-poem of this volume has ever been better said and a great deal would be lost were it not quoted in full:

The eyeless labourer in the night,
the selfless, shapeless seed I hold,
builds for its resurrection day—
silent and swift and deep from sight
foresees the unimagined light.

This is no child with a child's face;
this has no name to name it by:
yet you and I have known it well.
This is our hunter and our chase,
the third who lay in our embrace.

This is the strength that your arm knows,
the arc of flesh that is my breast,
the precise crystals of our eyes.
This is the blood's wild tree that grows
the intricate and folded rose.

This is the maker and the made;
this is the question and reply;
the blind head butting in the dark,
the blaze of light along the blade.
Oh hold me, for I am afraid.

The two poems which follow this, **"Woman's Song"** and **"Woman to Child"**, and another later in the book, **"The Unborn"**, are complementary pieces. They serve to establish the fact that the physical "love" of which she writes here, distinct from the more transcendental "love" to be found in many other poems, is always that of the woman. It is the love for the child she is to bear; it is never the passionate love that men feel and write of, never the pursuit and the capture. Nor is it romantic love which is the subject of many poems, most of them by

men and some by women aping men. In this respect her attitude towards love is similar to that of Mary Gilmore, although its expression is usually more intense, more poetic. There are other similarities between these two women poets, notably an emotional drawing from the well of the past, an awareness of the significance in our history of the displaced people, the aborigines (although here Mary Gilmore's poetry is far more emotive) and a strong sense of common humanity. But there are sharp differences, too. Both are feminine, but Mary Gilmore is sometimes also feminist, a characteristic never to be found in Judith Wright's work or her personal attitudes. Nor does she espouse causes or champion the underdog. And nothing could be more out of character than to imagine Miss Wright rushing off to join a socialist colony in Paraguay or anywhere else!

Many poems in this second volume make reference to children: **"Child in Wattle Tree"**, **"The Child"**, **"The World and the Child"**, **"Night and the Child"**. All these are to some degree the result of an intense awareness of the impingement of age upon youth, part of the duality which is stressed in many other ways in other poems: light and dark, real and unreal, life and death. In **"Lost Child"**, a section of the closing sequence of poems in this book, she gives a hint of the metaphysical realms she is to explore more frequently and at considerable depth in later volumes:

Is the boy lost? Then I know where he is gone.
He has gone climbing the terrible crags of the Sun.

The searchers go through the green valley, shouting his
    name;
the dogs are moaning on the hill for the scent of his
    track;
but the men will all be hoarse and the dogs lame
before the Hamilton's boy is found or comes back.
Through the smouldering ice of the moon he is stumbling
    alone.
I shall rise from my dark and follow where he is gone.

I heard from my bed his bugle breath go by
and the drum of his heart in the measure of an old song.
I shall travel into silence, and in that fierce country
When we meet he will know he has been away too long.
They are looking for him now in the vine-scrub over the
    hill,
but I think he is alone in a place that I know well.

Is the boy lost? Then I know where he is gone.
He is climbing to Paradise up a river of stars and stone.

It may have been because the contemporary critics expected some blending of the regionalism of her first volume and the various interpretations of love that coloured her second that they paused uncertainly before the third. Its significance seems to be crystallized in four lines from the title-poem, which is placed right at the very end of the book:

In the land of oblivion
among the black-mouthed ghosts,

I knew my Self
the sole reality.

Henceforth and in many different ways, the poet is to embark upon a voyage of discovery in Self, a Self that is not merely of this time but in all time. There are hints of a growing wonder at the miracle of life and of the life-giving force, love. This is the theme of the opening poem, **"Dark Gift"**, in which the poet marvels at the growth of a flower that "begins in the dark where life is not" until with the calyx folded she cries:

Open, green hand, and give
the dark gift you hold.

Oh wild mysterious gold!
Oh act of passionate love!

There is also a growing preoccupation here with the receding of youth, with the approach of age, although she is still only in her late thirties. Often she re-states with no less force and vision the regionalism of the best poems in *The Moving Image*. Thus we have **"Eroded Hills"**, **"Drought"**, **"Unknown Water"**, **"The Ancestors"** and most memorably **"Old House"**, which begins:

Where now outside the weary house the pepperina,
that great broken tree, gropes with its blind hands
and sings a moment in the magpie's voice, there he
    stood once,
that redhaired man my great-great-grand-father,
his long face amiable as an animal's,
and thought of vines and horses.
He moved in that mindless country like a red ant,
running tireless in the summer heat among the trees—
the nameless trees, the sleeping soil, the original
    river—
and said that the eastern slope would do for a
    vineyard.

It was no doubt the diversity of subjects dealt with in this third volume which aroused some misgivings in the minds of contemporary critics, which caused T. Inglis Moore to feel that "the poet has stopped on her path to look around, unsure of her way". But one cannot share Elyne Mitchell's regret that often her language and imagery were "similar to those recording the spiritual journeys of other poets". What different language or imagery could possibly be desirable for **"Birds"**, one of her most profound poems?

Whatever the bird is, is perfect for the bird.
Weapon kestrel hard as a blade's curve,
thrush round as a mother or a full drop of water
fruit-green parrot wise in his shrieking swerve—
all are what bird is and do not reach beyond bird.

Must we deny the validity of "weapon kestrel", "blade's curve", "round as a mother or a full drop of water?" One wonders whether this poem arose out of the fragmentary thought in R. D. FitzGerald's *Essay on Memory*: that sometimes one sees "the bird's flight as the bird". Judith Wright is here emphasizing the apparent simplicity of motives guiding the lives of the "cruel kestrel", the "thrush in the trembling dew beginning to sing", the "parrot clinging and quarrelling and veiling his queer eye". This is contrasted with the complexity of human motives:

But I am torn and beleaguered by my own people.
The blood that feeds my heart is the blood they
    gave me
and my heart is the house where they gather and
    fight for dominion—
all different, all with a wish and a will to save me,
to turn me into the ways of other people.

The poem concludes with a yearning to

. . . . melt the past, the present and the future in one
and find the words that lie behind all these languages.
Then I could fuse my passions into one clear stone
and be simple to myself as the bird is to the bird.

If the imagery lacks the sharp Australianism that characterized her more regional poetry, it is because she has moved out of regionalism into the universal. Her future work is to move more and more in that direction, yet in a subtle way its universal aspects are involved in the regional. Thus in her fourth book, *The Two Fires,* we have **"The Wattle Tree"** with its opening lines:

The tree knows four truths—
earth, water, air, and fire of the sun.
The tree holds four truths in one.
Root, limb and leaf unfold
out of the seed, and these rejoice
till the tree dreams it has a voice
to join four truths in one great word of gold.

It could be any tree—oak, elm, cedar or what you will. But it is a wattle tree; the last line tells us that. Here, too, is emerging a theme that is to recur more and more frequently in her work—the kinship with nature, yet an apartness, a separateness from it. Under the bark of a "Scribbly-gum" she finds:

. . . . . . the written track
of a life I could not read.

However, *The Two Fires* is once again a book arising out of its time. The poet is very personally concerned with the threat of man's destruction through the possible use of the atom bomb. The title-poem shows this concern in a magnificent poetic conception of the earth born out of fire and returning to fire:

My father rock, do you forget the kingdom of the fire?
The aeons grind you into bread—

into the soil that feeds the living and transforms the
    dead;
and have we eaten in the heart of the yellow wheat
the sullen unforgetting seed of fire?

And now set free by the climate of man's hate,
that seed sets time ablaze.
The leaves of fallen years, the forest of living days,
have caught like matchwood. Look, the whole world
    burns.
The ancient kingdom of the fire returns.
And the world, that flower that housed the bridegroom
    and the bride,
burns on the breast of night.
The world's denied.

Other poems like **"The Precipice"**, **"West Wind"**, **"Two
Generations"**, and **"Searchlight Practice"** also develop
this concept. They contain lines that stamp her as a poet
of the highest possible artistry and sensitivity, lines that
cause the reader to pause and marvel when he comes upon
them. Has the dilemma of our times ever been better stated than in these from **"West Wind"**?

for to love in a time of hate and to live in a time
    of death
is lonely and dangerous as the last leaf on the tree
and wrenches the stem of the blood and twists the
    words from truth.

Her kinship with nature persists in the much slighter poems of her fifth volume, **Birds,** which were written for her
teenage daughter and are therefore less adult in their approach, but are not quite, as Max Harris has said [in *The
Literature of Australia,* ed. by Geoffrey Dutton, 1964],
merely the work of a poet who is "keeping her hand in".
A lesser poet would have written a very different set of
verses for a teenage daughter! Here are some delightful
vignettes which, apart from their poetic quality, can only
have come from one who has lived close to nature and
who has drawn some of her strength from it. Whether it be
"that old clever Noah's Ark, the well turned, well-carved
pelican with his wise comic eye" or the magpies who "walk
with hands in pockets, left and right" and whose song
thanks "God with every note" or the chattering Apostle
Birds ("How they talked about us!")—there is a great deal
of shrewd observation here and more than that, a quality
of mystic interpretation which, if the single audience for
which they were meant were extended to others of that
age, might well awaken an interest in those aspects of the
Australian environment which have so moved and influenced the poet herself.

Those who are unfamiliar with the poetry of Judith Wright
could not do better than make an approach to her work
through **Five Senses** published in 1964 in Angus & Robertson's Sirius paperback series. Here are most of her
truly memorable poems and it is interesting to note that,
as if to challenge some of the contemporary critics, she

has chosen heavily from **The Gateway** and **The Two
Fires**—the third and fourth volumes which caused some
concern at the time because of their apparent departure
from what had come to be accepted as typical of this
writer. It is particularly interesting because it contains
twenty-eight poems hitherto unpublished, under the collective title of "The Forest." These take us a step further
along the very personal road of Judith Wright's poetry.
They are distinguished by the same certainly of language
and techniques we have come to expect. The title-poem
of this series, although there are many excellent and
diverse poems here, seems to me to crystallize simply
and unpretentiously the nature of her quest. I quote it in
full:

When first I knew this forest
its flowers were strange.
Their different forms and faces
changed with the seasons' change—

white violets smudged with purple,
the wild-ginger spray,
ground-orchids small and single
haunted my day.

the thick-fleshed Murray-lily,
flame-tree's bright blood,
and where the creek runs shallow,
the cunjevoi's green hood.

When first I knew this forest,
time was to spend,
and time's renewing harvest
could never reach an end.

Now that its vines and flowers
are named and known,
like long-fulfilled desires
those first strange joys are gone.

My search is further.
There's still to name and know
beyond the flowers I gather
that one that does not wither—
the truth from which they grow.

It is a remarkable poem, less complex than many she has
written, yet summarizing, I would suggest, her whole poetic
endeavour. The vines and flowers, the familiar things of
life whether of nature or of man, *are named and known.*
From time to time she will return to them, but not merely
to identify or describe. Henceforth the search is further: to
"the truth from which they grow". In this single poem we
see her moving, as the whole of her poetic work has moved,
from the regional to the universal.

And now, at last, having attempted to distil the essence of her writing, let us now look at her latest collection, *The Other Half* (1966). The concluding piece, **"Turning Fifty"**, reminds us that the poet is now no longer young, no longer the "woman of thirty-five" whose work, on the evidence of two published volumes, H. M. Green found "amazing". At fifty she reviews the times through which she has lived:

> Though we've polluted
> even this air I breathe
> and spoiled green earth;

> though, granted life or death,
> death's what we're choosing,
> and though these years we live
> scar flesh and mind,

> still, as the sun comes up,
> bearing my birthday,
> having met time and love
> I raise my cup—

> dark, bitter, neutral, clean,
> sober as morning—
> to all I've seen and known—
> to this new sun.

Poems written to celebrate one's own birthday are seldom memorable and this is no exception. It is nevertheless impressive in its homely sincerity. This is a coffee cup she is raising, not a convivial glass, and it is clear that she is still possessed by the doubts and fears which were the main theme of *The Two Fires*. So much profound writing, so much word magic and control, so much that has been accepted as the best of contemporary Australian poetry—all this stems from a woman, now turned fifty, greeting "the new sun" with courage undimmed and, as one knows from what she has already produced, equipped while strength remains with her to continue her quest of ultimate truth.

The themes she has chosen for this latest volume are varied, but there is this recurring note of age, accompanied by a somewhat wistful note of the inevitability of change that age brings. Among the poems in *The Forest* series was one, **"For My Daughter"**, which reviewed the problem of the woman who is also a mother, her child grown up and going her separate way:

> My body gave you then
> what was ordained to give,
> and did not need my will.
> But now we learn to live
> apart, what must I do?

"The Curtain", describing the homecoming of a grown child, continues this thought:

> So grown you looked, in the same unaltered room,
> so much of your childhood you were already
>   forgetting,
> while I remembered. Yet in the unforgetting dream
> you will come here all your life for renewal and
>   meeting.

> It was your breath, so softly rising and falling,
> that kept me silent. With your lids like buds
>   unbroken
> you watched on their curtain of your life, a stream
>   of shadows moving.
> When I touched your shoulder, I too had a little
>   dreamed and woken.

It may be said that Judith Wright, however deeply she feels, however much she is moved by the transience of life or the eternal quest for its underlying truths, will never and can never be dogmatic in her statement. A brief poem, **"Wishes"**, gives her answers to the questions: What do I wish to be? What do I wish to do? To the first she replies, "I wish to be wise". To the second, "I wish to love". The final couplet admits the contradiction:

> To love and to be wise?
> Down, fool, and lower your eyes.

There are several remarkable poems in this volume. The title-poem is yet another attempt to bring about some reconciliation of opposites which we have noted before. This time the opposites are "the self that night undrowns when I'm asleep" and "my daylight self," the subconscious and the conscious. She brings them tentatively together again in a final couplet:

> So we may meet at last, and meeting bless,
> And turn into one truth in singleness.

We should perhaps have noted earlier this recurring practice of summing up in a couplet the ideas that the poem has been exploring. In this she is not uniformly successful. There are times when one feels that in her desire to round off a poem as neatly as possible she has yielded a little to rhetoric, a little to emotion. In this couplet I have quoted, one may well wonder whether these two opposites can be reconciled in singleness.

The outstanding poems in *The Other Half* are **"To Hafiz of Shiraz"**, **"Naked Girl and Mirror"** and the New Guinea sequence, **"The Finding of the Moon"**. I name these three because of certain intrinsic differences about them, but would not suggest that any others in the volume fall short of the high standard of thought and expression that characterize all Judith Wright's verse. She is, it seems, too fine an artist ever to write a bad poem; if some reach greater heights than others it is because initially they are aimed at greater heights.

"To Hafiz and Shiraz" is prefaced by the statement "the rose has come into the garden, from Nothingness to Being", which reminds us somewhat of an earlier poem, **"Dark Gift"**. Its philosophical theme is the inevitability of fruition, so that it is no longer "any poem" that might follow her pen, but the certainty that in poetry, as in living:

> Every path and life leads one way only,
> out of continual miracle, through creation's fable,
> over and over repeated, but never yet understood,
> as every word leads back to the blinding original
>   Word.

"Naked Girl and Mirror" must take its place amongst Judith Wright's finest poems. It is a reflective essay on the problem facing an adolescent girl whose body once served only the elemental needs of childhood, but is now awakening to the fuller needs of maturity and love. This she sees at first as a betrayal and is afraid. She longs to return to what she was but finally realizes that she cannot do this, although she still hopes to retain something of her original self:

> Let me go—let me be gone
> You are half of some other who may never come.
> Why should I tend you? You are not my own;
> you seek that other—he will be your home
> Yet I pity your eyes in the mirror, misted with tears;
> I lean to your kiss. I must serve you: I will obey.
> Some day we may love. I may miss your going, some
>   day,
> though I shall always resent your dumb and fruitful
>   years.
> Your lovers shall learn better, and bitterly too,
> if their arrogance dares to think I am part of you.

In the New Guinea sequence, **"The Finding of the Moon"**, she captures to an extraordinary degree the atmosphere of a tribal village in which a young man, Aruako, turns his back Endymion-like on sensual love in his pursuit of the Moon. It is notable that Miss Wright should depart from her familiar Australian background and that she should with her own poetic vision so successfully enter into this new world. There are some poems here with a quaintly domestic atmosphere that perhaps do not quite do justice to her talents—poems like **"To Another Housewife"**, **"Cleaning Day"** and **"Portrait"**, but others, although comparatively slight like **"The Trap"**, **"A Document"** and **"Snakeskin on a Gate"**, show that she has lost nothing of her technical skill or sensitivity. In short, *The Other Half* is a worthy successor to the volumes that have preceded it. No doubt it will be followed

by others if we are to judge from her supplication in the final stanza of **"Prayer"**:

> And you, who speak in me when I speak well,
> withdraw not now your grace, leave me not dry and
>   cold.
> I have praised you in the pain of love, I would praise
>   you still
> in the slowing of the blood, the time when I grow old.

What then is the real nature of the genius of Judith Wright? Always she has worked within certain specified limits. Most of her poems are quite short. She has never attempted the epic and has touched only incidentally, through the recalled past, on the heroic. Once or twice she has been tempted towards the slightly satirical (**"Eve to her Daughter"** in this latest volume is an example), but not very successfully perhaps because this is not fundamentally part of her nature. In the main she has blended the emotions and the intellect, and throughout has developed technical skills which, in spite of attempts by some critics to find influences of Blake and Yeats and T. S. Eliot, have remained peculiarly her own. Not the least of her skills lies in the felicity of her choice of word and phrase and the ability to say a great deal in very few words. Let any who doubt this compare the examples I have given with the language in most other contemporary volumes of Australian poetry.

We have seen how her first two books caused H. M. Green to classify her as a lyricist and how her next two caused him to amend that classification. We have seen how early critics applauded her regional poetry and how some later ones regretted her partial abandonment of the regional for the universal. Throughout a now considerable number of volumes she has established for herself an identity which does not easily fit into any category, but it is clear that she is fundamentally a mystic, seeking through her own personal experiences to find the true significance in all creation of Love and the Word, which in the last analysis are synonymous. That she gives no final answer is not the least of her virtues, since this carries with her a company of readers prepared to go along with her in her quest. There are also many, no doubt, who are less concerned with the quest, but equally prepared to accompany her because of the unique quality of the poetry which she uses to pursue it.

James McAuley (essay date 1968)

SOURCE: "Some Poems of Judith Wright," in *Australian Literary Studies*, Vol. 3, No. 3, May, 1968, pp. 201-13.

[*McAuley was an Australian poet, critic, and educator who influenced his country's literature through his emphasis on traditional poetic forms and techniques and his*

*opposition to the nationalistic tendencies of some Austra-
lian writers and critics, including those in the "Jindyworobak" movement that championed native Australian
elements in the arts. In the following analysis of several
of Wright's poems, McAuley studies both content and
mechanics to contrast what he considers Wright's better
poetry with her less successful work. He concludes that
Wright's best poems are endowed with a consonance of
form, content, and purpose that the others, while successful on certain levels, lack.]*

I want to consider first of all some of the very good poems in Judith Wright's first two volumes. A few of these
stand out in an order of excellence of their own, though
surrounded by others of considerable interest.

In *The Moving Image* (1946) the poem **'Bullocky'** has
proved most durable in general liking and critical estima-
tion. It is an evocation of the pioneer past of the Hunter
River district. In the first stanza the word 'widdershins'
catches the mind with its unexpected rightness:

> Beside his heavy-shouldered team,
> thirsty with drought and chilled with rain,
> he weathered all the striding years
> till they ran widdershins in his brain:

'widdershins', meaning in the opposite direction or backwards, defines the movement of the rest of the poem, which
is a backwards look into time. The bullocky is seen as
leading the entry of a new people into a new Promised
Land. The identification of the bullocky with Moses is
imputed in stanzas 2 and 3 to the bullocky himself, more
perhaps for dramatic emphasis than as a probability. The
result is a double-image effect. We see the bullocky, but
we see also a symbolic fiction superimposed on or coa-
lescing with the natural scene:

> All the long straining journey grew
> a mad apocalyptic dream,
> and he old Moses, and the slaves
> his suffering and stubborn team.

> Then in his evening camp beneath
> the half-light pillars of the trees
> he filled the steepled cone of night
> with shouted prayers and prophecies.

The latter stanza presents the bullocky at his camp-fire,
but the scene is also wrought to a cathedral-image: the
trees are pillars, the firelight scoops out a steepled cone in
the dark. There is thus the simultaneous presentation of
type and anti-type: a meaningful symbolic pattern is ad-
duced from the past, together with the new reality which
fulfils the pattern in an unexpected way. The effect in the
above stanzas is mainly a visual one: it is not just a stir
of allusions in the words, for a definite picture is created.

In the next stanza the double-image effect is produced in
sound:

> While past the camp fire's crimson ring
> the star-struck darkness cupped him round,
> and centuries of cattlebells
> rang with their sweet uneasy sound.

A delicate play of meanings and associations occurs on
the word 'centuries', meaning hundreds, as well as ages of
time. The bells are actual in the bullocky's time, but they
also ring out of a deep and mysterious past (a 'star-struck
darkness'), because the patterns of the past are being reenacted. It seems right to allow the cathedral image of the
previous stanza to influence the reading, so that the suggestion of sanctuary bells is not excluded, though not
unduly stressed. Perhaps there is also, in the use of the
word 'centuries', a faint sidelong reminiscence of Traherne's use of the word in *Centuries of Meditations*. The
word 'uneasy' in the last line is superbly right, combining
as it does an accurate physical impression with a vague
fleeting suggestion of uncertainty. It is surely permissible
to explicate these subtle subordinate filaments of meaning
or association, so long as it is understood that by bringing
them to the surface in sharp focus we tend to distort their
proper effect: the reader must restore the disturbed balance when he turns from the interpreter's laborious clum-
siness back to the text—with perception nevertheless sharpened, one hopes.

In the last stanza of **'Bullocky'** the double-image effect
reaches its climax and justification. The bullocky lies buried
in the soil as Moses was buried in the Promised Land. The
root of the vine—the reference is to the vineyards of the
Hunter River district—reaches down to grasp the bone:

> O vine grow close upon that bone
> and hold it with your rooted hand.
> The prophet Moses feeds the grape,
> And fruitful is the Promised Land.

Again the effect is sharply visual: the root becomes at the
same time a hand reaching down to *take hold* of the past.
The meaning is that the fruitfulness of the land is rooted
in the lives and work of the pioneers, and it must hold
close to its origins, its tradition, and be nourished by it.

The typology used in the poem, comparing the new settlement to the entry into the Promised Land, has been a
natural and recurring one in colonial literatures. Sometimes it has been required to carry the burden of utopian
hallucinations, staling down to clichés of political rhetoric. But Judith Wright does not embarrass us with the
crackpot portentousness that O'Dowd would have put into
such an analogy. Equally, she did not feel compelled to
make the analogy work with that evasive irony which is a
disfiguring tic in modern poetry. There is an obvious tension between the hallowed grandeur of Moses and the raw

actuality of the bullocky: but the poem accepts this and overcomes it. The bullocky's role is ennobled without being falsified.

The poem's quiet assurance in what it is saying is reflected in its simple firm structure. The iambic tetrameter quatrains, rhyming only in the second and fourth lines, regularly divide, according to their grammatical articulation, into matching halves: two lines plus two lines. Each of these halves tends, moreover, to form a single long line, an octameter with a crease in the middle:

> Then in the evening camp beneath the half-light
>   pillars of the trees
> He filled the steepled cone of night with shouted
>   prayers and prophecies.

Within this metrical framework the poem moves by successive statements, not by argument. The statements are for the most part grammatically co-ordinate, linked by 'and' or an equivalent. There is also a good deal of parallelism, though not too rigidly enforced:

> Grass is across the wagon-tracks,
> and plough strikes bone across the grass,
> and vineyards cover all the slopes
> where the dead teams were used to pass.

Particularly in the later part of the poem, the effect of this organization is responsorial: the second half of the stanza 'answering' the first as in the Ambrosian hymns. There is thus a fundamental constitutive dualism governing the poem in every aspect. [McAuley adds in a footnote: The stanzas also fall naturally into couples, with the exception of stanza 3, which stands on its own. It is devoted to making explicit the analogy underlying the rest of the poem. The additional (superfluous?) character of this stanza, with its slightly officious explanation by slightly strained phrasing ('mad apocalyptic dream' is questionable, and the inversion of 'slaves' and 'team' just a little awkward), seems evident. If I seem to be peering at the structure with niggling pedantry, my excuse is that I want to show how, when Judith Wright is at the height of her inspiration, there is an extraordinary intuitive coherence.]

In the second volume, **Woman to Man** (1949), the title-poem is by common consent the summit of her achievement. I hope that a close and rather technical examination of the poem will illuminate its peculiar rightness.

The grammatical structure of **'Woman to Man'** is the main engine of its expressive power. Phrase is laid by phrase, clause by clause in a continued insistent parallelism. The successive parallel statements are not linked by co-ordinating conjunctions. To use a technical term, the poem proceeds by parataxis. This simplest of all forms of grammatical articulation is the mode of a great deal of poetry. A complex grammar with subordination of clauses as well as varied coordination is natural when the logic is argumentative; but poetry often moves simply by successive strokes, whose relationships the mind supplies without the need of connective words. The first stanza

moves by appositions: the second and fourth lines amplifying the first, and the last line amplifying the third:

> The eyeless labourer in the night,
> The selfless, shapeless seed I hold,
> builds for its resurrection day—
> silent and swift and deep from sight
> foresees the unimagined light.

In the second and third stanzas the parallel clauses and phrases unfold paratactically, except for the third line of stanza 2 which twists the paradox tighter:

> *yet* you and I have known it well.

This rhetorical parallelism is not static, but dynamic and cumulative, moving forward with increasing urgency to the climax in the last stanza, when meditation on the mystery of conception and gestation changes into an anticipation of the moment of birth:

> This is the maker and the made;
> this is the question and reply;
> the blind head butting at the dark,
> the blaze of light along the blade.
> Oh hold me, for I am afraid.

'The blaze of light' symbolizes the first flash of light and consciousness, but first of all refers literally to the knife cutting the cord. The sudden change of feeling and direction in the last line is very effective, as the woman turns from absorption in the inner mystery to utter a direct personal cry to the man.

It is a sign of complete inspiration when the phonic texture of the poem supports the meaning, giving a true registration of feeling and a sense of woven unity. For example, in the first stanza the sound announced in 'eye' recurs significantly, and together with other details creates an incantatory effect, drawing us into the woman's absorption in the mystery. One need hardly point out in the last stanza the reinforcement of the meaning by the heavy insistent alliteration and the management of stress.

Another sign of mastery is the expressive use of 'word-build'—the size, shape, and stress-profile of individual words. Thus in the first two lines there are four emphatic two-syllabled words with the same 'trochaic' profile, set *across* the iambic metrical frame, not coinciding with it:

> The *eyeless labourer* in the night,
> The *selfless shapeless* seed I hold

This has its own absorbed insistency, but it also enables the big word 'resurrection' in the third line to emerge more noticeably:

> builds for its resurrection day.

In stanza 2, monosyllables notably predominate, tending to slow the lines and increase the effect of deliberation.

Stanza 3 continues in the first two lines with monosyllables, and thus ensures that the peaked structure of line 3 stands out:

the *precise crystals* of our eyes.

(The metrical pattern again cuts across the word-build.) Similarly in this stanza the monosyllables of line 4 enable the important epithets in the last line to emerge with full effect:

the *intricate* and *folded* rose.

Judith Wright seems to me to have been at this period of her work a poet who worked intuitively, almost gropingly, towards the expression of a particular sense of the mystery of organic life and process and of human passion. **'Woman to Man'** brings these two things into a single focus. When her intuition succeeds, the formal elements of the poetry follow suit: image, grammar, phonic texture, versification come together and co-operate. The phrasing in **'Woman to Man'** puts some strain on our understanding, but I think it justifies itself. All the references to the unborn child develop one of two ideas. (1) The child is the product of two persons who have become one; by a metaphorical leap, the child *is* these two: the man's strength of body, the passionate tension of the woman's breast, the clarity of the eyes of both, constitute the being of this 'third who lay in our embrace'. (2) The child is not just the effect or result of their union: it is also its 'final cause', teleologically speaking: that is, it is the end to which their love is ordered, the end which also determines the process, unconscious but unerring, of growth in the womb.

I should like to consider two other poems in Judith Wright's second volume, which also seem to me to exhibit the coherence of her art at its best. **'The Bull'** combines a splendid celebration of organic life—in particular of fulfilled sexuality—with a kind of lament and fear. The first stanza presents an image of sensuous magnificence, to which everything contributes:

In the olive darkness of the sally-trees
silently moved the air from night to day.
The summer-grass was thick with honey-daisies
where he, a curled god, a red Jupiter,
heavy with power among his women lay.

Among the expressive felicities of this texture I hope it won't seem too fanciful to draw attention to the word 'olive' in the first line. Its consonants are picked up again in 'si*l*ent*l*y mo*v*ed'; the 'l' sound is then carried forward into 'cur*l*ed god', while the 'v' sound is carried forward into 'hea*v*y with power'—prominent and highly expressive words which make these linkages of sound effective. This may be conscious artifice on the poet's part, or intuitive rightness: the distinction is rather unreal. In regard to meaning, 'olive' begins as a colour-descriptive word, but its latent possibilities of suggestion are, it seems to me, stirred retroactively by the image of the curled god, the red Jupiter. The latent suggestions are of ripeness, fullness, oil, anointment, an athletic body gleaming. Again

one must admit that explicit analysis tends to distort the text by its thick-fingered laboriousness; but the problem is to make the text account for a complex significance and a sensuous effect which are certainly there.

The poem goes on to show us this sovereign power suddenly lose its godlike authority. It is introduced by the obvious but delightful ingenuity of expressive sound-play in the lines:

But summer's bubble-sound of sweet creek-water
dwindles and is silent

where the kinaesthetic element in the use of sounds may also be noted. The bull is driven by dogs, humiliated, unable to cope with these harrying forces of the outer world. I won't stop to comment on the management of sound-quality and rhythm and word-build in these lines; but I want to draw attention to the grammatical and rhetorical structure. Again parataxis prevails, though some of the clauses have a simple co-ordination. Again the rhetoric relies heavily on parallelism in phrase and clause. Monotony is avoided in several ways. For example, one of the statements is cast in the form of a command, and two in the form of a question. Moreover the parallelism does not always coincide with the line-structure:

What enemy steals his strength—what rival steals
his mastered cows?

In such a poem we may ask what is the full meaning, of which the presented subject is the overt surface? Poetry always has human reference. If it deals with the non-human, it does so with some implicit or explicit reference to human concerns. It is noteworthy that the bull is anthropomorphized: he lies heavy with power 'among his women', and the image of the 'curled god, a red Jupiter' is anthropomorphic. Here too there is a visual double-image effect: we see the bull in the field, at the same time as we see him as a god. The total result is a rich emblem of human instinctual potency and fulfilment.

Again we may note that the poem does not move dialectically or argumentatively, as if proving a thesis. And there is no prepared *irony* of the routine contemporary kind. The second part, when the bull is discomfited and humiliated does not react destructively on the values affirmed in the first part. The poem does *not* say: *although* the bull seems a god he is only a creature that can be ignominiously reduced to servitude. The paratactic structure preserves the correct relationship: both of the moments of the bull are true and valid, and we must comprehend both in our grasp of reality.

The other poem in the second volume which I want to commend is perhaps a slighter one. **'The Old Prison'** does not exhibit the brooding sensual power, the concentrated vehemence of **'Woman to Man'** or **'The Bull'**; but it has its own intensity and lyrical expressiveness, and again the various factors combine to form a coherent rightness. I should like to point out especially the intonation: that is, the effect of tune created by the varying pitch of the vowels, especially in the first two stanzas. This is a factor of variable importance in poetry, but here it is of the essence:

> The rows of cells are unroofed,
> a flute for the wind's mouth,
> who comes with a breath of ice
> from the blue caves of the south.
>
> O dark and fierce day:
> the wind like an angry bee
> hunts for the black honey
> in the pits of the hollow sea.

These stanzas give the images which control the poem. The unroofed prison cells suggest a broken deserted hive: but with an inner contrast in the comparison; for this hive was never fruitful, it is sterile, stored with bitterness not sweetness. The other image is that of a flute with holes, through which the wind blows; and again there is a contrast, for this is a stone flute, its music is bitter and desolating, a cry of despair and isolation.

Once more we may note that the grammatical structure of the poem is mainly paratactic, though there is some simple co-ordination by 'and'. Again monotony is avoided by rhetorical means: one statement is turned into a question, another into an O-exclamation. The parallelism and responsorial effect have a cumulative power in the later part:

> Who built and laboured here?
> The wind and the sea say
> —Their cold nest is broken
> and they are blown away.
>
> They did not breed nor love.
> Each in his cell alone
> cried as the wind now cries
> through this flute of stone.

The stanzas do not all, as they do in **'Bullocky'**, break into two matching halves: there is some local asymmetry within the general dualistic balance of the whole.

Many of the poems in the first two volumes seem to me interesting and valuable, but not to attain the order of excellence of those I have been commenting on. If I have succeeded in showing how the very best poems work, I may provide some clues about what happens in poems of a perceptibly lower order of achievement, admirable as some of these may be in their own way.

The well-liked poem **'South of My Days'** in the first volume seems to me to be of a second order of achievement. The poet is in Queensland, thinking back to New England, and summoning up the New England past as **'Bullocky'** did in a different way:

> South of my day's circle, part of my blood's
>   country,
> rises that tableland, high delicate outline
> of bony slopes wincing under the winter. . . .

The poem starts with a well-cadenced memorable rhythm. The phrases are striking, though already with a hint of manufacture and proliferation. Gradually the versification spreads out into that treacherous loopy laxity which has been the snare of many Australian poets since Douglas Stewart showed the way. The line hovers and oscillates uneasily between accentual verse and traditional iambic metre; it prefers the loosening effect of feminine endings—26 out of 40 here—free from the stiffening of rhyme. This kind of verse needs to be constantly galvanized by special devices. The poem rather advertizes its free access to colloquial speech.

> Or mustering up in the Bogongs in the autumn
> when the blizzards came early. Brought them down;
>   we brought them
> down, what aren't there yet. Or driving for Cobb's
>   on the run
> up from Tamworth—Thunderbolt at the top of
>   Hungry Hill,
> and I give him a wink. I wouldn't wait long, Fred,
> not if I was you: the troopers are just behind,
> coming for that job at the Hillgrove. He went like a
>   luny,
> him on his big black horse.

The colloquial phrasing is accommodated, not in strict counterpoint to a metrical pattern, but rather by bending and relaxing the metrical framework.

In its method the poem belongs to the idiom of the forties in Australia. The formula, which is still in use, was fresher then. Again we may note the paratactic structure, with occasional simple coordination ('and', 'or'). Again there is habitual use of rhetorical parallelism. But now the effect of these forms of organization is not cumulative, but simply one thing after another, strung along a thematic thread. This poem lacks the dynamic development of **'Woman to Man'**. Its organization is not much above the level of the shuffled pack of cards to which the old-timer's reminiscences are compared. The theme—the poet's feeling for the New England past—is merely an outline, a hold-all for an assortment of impressions. The poem has to live by the varied momentary attractiveness of its component pieces. The poet is also not fully absorbed in the theme: there remains a touch of self-consciousness, the matey hearty knowingness of the Australian littérateur showing his easy familiarity with outbackery—the very thing that Judith Wright is blessedly free from for the most part.

Another poem that provokes analysis is the attempt in **'Woman to Child'** to repeat the success of **'Woman to Man'**. It is akin in theme, similar in method, so that the difference is instructive. Though by no means a mere failure, it does not reach the height of the other poem, and does not, to my apprehension, have the same coherence.

As one tries to analyze it, one can see that instead of all factors coming together co-operatively, there is a continuous incipient disorganization.

For example in stanzas 1 and 2 the child is apparently already born and is being spoken to. In stanza 3 the child being spoken to seems to be back in the womb, not yet born. In stanza 4 the child is again already born.

But even in the opening lines there is a disturbance of the time perspective:

> You who were darkness warmed my flesh
> where out of darkness rose the seed.

The child is already an embryo in the first line when the seed 'rises' out of the darkness in the second line. Such an objection may seem ridiculously captious in an individual instance; but these imprecisions and dislocations have a cumulative effect. One becomes aware also in the above lines that the poet is under strain to produce phrasing adequate to the sense of mystery intended. The repetition of 'darkness' is a perfunctory expedient rather than a real find. In the rest of the stanza a new symbol is taken up, the child as microcosm. This does not spring out of the first two lines but is a fresh start, and the two parts of the stanza thus created are not successfully integrated. It is significant that the sounds clash: the rhyme-words 'me' and 'see' chime dissonantly against 'seed', and the off-rhyme 'seed' and 'blood' seems not to accord with the tonality of the poem.

In stanza 2, the microcosm idea is amplified by parallel clauses which don't quite do their work. There is a faint Shakesperean echo in the platitudinous 'multitudinous' stars—the connection with 'multitudinous seas' prompting the oceanic images which follow. The third line fills out the stanza by adding a phrase alliterated to give it life, but lacking in precision:

> There *swam* the *sliding* continents.

Motion in respect of what? Surely this is not an early reference to the hypothesis of continental drift? Are the continents 'sliding' through air but also 'swimming' because surrounded by water? In the next two lines the segmented phrasing is not rhythmically strong, and the last line leaves us suspended between three possible meanings:

> and love that knew not its beloved.

I presume that this means that the unborn child did not know whom it would love in the future. But this idea is blurred by other possible interpretations: that the child did not yet know its mother; or that the mother held within herself love for the child she did not yet know. An unresolved triplicity of possible meaning could, of course, be the precise intention of the poet; but there is nothing to suggest that this is so.

By the third stanza the poet has sunk into deeper difficulty. An O-exclamation tries to give the poem a new impulse, producing an infelicitous tricycle of sound, O-o-o, in the first line. The difficulty of seeing the syntax of this stanza, or grasping it when it is read aloud reveals that something is wrong.

> O node and focus of the world;
> I hold you deep within that well
> you shall escape and not escape—
> that mirrors still your sleeping shape;
> that nurtures still your crescent cell.

The child—now an embryo awaiting birth—is 'node and focus of the world' and this 'node and focus' is in a well. The well 'mirrors' (reflects in water? conforms in shape to?) the child's 'sleeping shape'. One has to scratch up tentative meanings, which prove unsatisfactory. Evidently the poet was worried about this intractable stanza, because in the 1963 selection entitled *Five Senses* she attempted a re-punctuation, which created the appearance of new logical connections, but without clarifying the sense or making it move more naturally:

> O node and focus of the world—
> I hold you deep within that well
> you shall escape and not escape—
> that mirrors still your sleeping shape,
> that nurtures still your crescent cell.

Is it now the world that 'mirrors' the sleeping shape and nurtures the crescent cell, as a macro-womb? The poet abandoned this unprofitable 1963 revision in the 1965 Australian Poets selection, which goes back to the original version.

In the last stanza, a partial recovery gets under way, but even here the parataxis and parallelism suddenly get out of hand and set up a thumping burlesque rhythm with an inappropriate House-that-Jack-Built effect:

> I am the earth, I am the root,
> I am the stem that fed the fruit. . . .

I have been pulling rather gracelessly at the fabric of this poem because I think it shows how some failure, however slight, in the poet's intuitive grasp of the theme has spreading ill-effects which ingenuity cannot fully overcome. Meanings, images, syntax, phonic texture, versification do not grow perfectly together; there are hair-line cracks, and bits of patchwork. Nevertheless, we do respond to the imaginative riches of the poem: the possibilities of the theme, the images, the symbolism, *are* actualized to a considerable extent, whether or not I am right in the foregoing analysis of certain defects.

At a certain point, in the career of most poets, the first élan ceases. There is a time of re-assessment: a need to deepen or widen one's range, a change in values or emphasis. The passage from one state to another is often through darkness and bafflement. Sometimes the poetic solution lies precisely in including this experience of defeat within a new victory. This seems to me to happen in some of the fine later poems of Judith Wright, such as **'Phaius Orchid'** and **'The Forest'**, where it is not only a metaphysical search that is expressed but also the sense of being foiled in that search. The best of Judith Wright's later poetry is not an attempt to reproduce the 'primitive' intensity of the earlier successes but represents the emergence of a more critical awareness, and a fuller conscious control. **'For My Daughter'** is a return to the subject-matter of **'Woman to Child'**; it is better articulated, though not as sensuously rich. **'Sports Field'** develops an extended allegory, which is not a mode used earlier. It has a poignancy which is a gift of the experienced heart. In ***The Other Half*** (1966), **'Portrait'** and **'Naked Girl and Mirror'** and **'A Document'** stand for a continuing conquest of personal experience—I must admit that I shy away from some other poems which go on about poetry and being a poet. A close formal analysis of the best of the later work would certainly reveal some continuity with the earlier work, but also some difference in spirit, reflected in change and development in method and organization.

Devindra Kohli (essay date 1971)

SOURCE: "The Crystal Glance of Love: Judith Wright as a Love Poet," in *The Journal of Commonwealth Literature,* Vol. VI, No. 1, June, 1971, pp. 42-52.

[*Here, Kohli contrasts Wright's work with the more overtly sensual poems of Indian poet Kamala Das. Kohli argues that words and communication have a higher value in Judith Wright's poetic vision of love than they do in the poetry of Das, whose emphasis on passion"makes words irrelevant." The critic also maintains that Wright's work depicts love as a source of contentment and completion.*]

Robert Graves describes our age as one of 'lovelessness' and asserts that true poetry comes from 'the state of being in love'. His vision is much more comprehensive and complex than it appears to be for the intensity with which his man-persona *does* homage to the Woman who *is* 'the more important partner in this difficult relationship' has a sense of terror and doom in it—perhaps because it grows out of the landscape of war. It is useful to turn to Judith Wright, whose love poetry, besides being a delicate and truthful communication of Woman to Man, is a distinct and fruitful assimilation of the darkness and light of the Australian landscape. 'The writer', says Judith Wright, 'must be at peace with his landscape before he can turn confidently to its human figures'. It is her strength that she writes poetry which has the physical richness of her landscape and an 'intellectual pride' in the contemplation of the continuity of life. There is a sense of largeness in her lyrical contemplation, a feeling of an open-hearted ease: 'It is because of the joy in my heart / that I am your fit mourner'. This feeling lies behind every gesture she makes:

> We are the white grave-worms of the grave.
> We are the eyeless beginning of the world.
> Oh blind, kind flesh, we are the drinking seed
> that aches and swells towards its flower of love.
> ['**The City Asleep**']

She takes into herself 'all living things that are', and thus 'My days burn with the sun, / my nights with moon and star'. This sense of an open-hearted ease, this receptive calm, as distinct from the constraining tensions of A. D. Hope, is reflected not only in her organic imagery but in the controlled assertiveness of tone, as well as in the traditional rhythms enacting the circular repetition of the organic life:

> Here where I walk was the green world of a child;
> the infinity of day that closed in day,
> the widening spiral turning and returning,
> the same and not the same, that had not end.
> Does the heart know no better than to pray
> that time unwind its coil, the bone unbuild
> till that lost world sit like a fruit in the hand—
> till the felled trees rise upright where they lay
> and leaves and birds spring on them as they stand?
> ['**The Moving Image**']

Her passionate concern with earth and time, and her search for values which can resolve the dichotomy of 'the endless circle of time and star / that never chime with the blood', lead her to the realization of the power of love. Love is a true metaphor for her feminine interaction with life, for it turns upon the strength of a mother-child relationship. In **'Power'**, she summons the power of Love as 'awful voice', and then taking heart replies: '. . . even to rejoice / calling myself your child'. Or sometimes she personifies Love, and like a mother affirms its power and beauty, again, as in **'The Moving Image'**:

> I am the maker. I have made both time and fear,
> knowing that to yield to either is to be dead.
> All that is real is to live, to desire, to be,
> till I say to the child I was, 'It is this; it is her.
> In the doomed cell I have found love's whole
>   eternity.'

Unlike Kamala Das, the Indian poet, who notwithstanding the rich traditions available within her own national culture, turns to the intensity of love as the human affirmative, Judith Wright celebrates such an affirmative as a meaningful inter-relationship with the landscape. This is refreshingly valid in the absence of the alternative of a native tradition. Caught between her Australian identity and the identity deriving from the use of English, she attempts to revive 'the song [that] is gone'; 'the dance / [that is] secret with the dancers in the earth' manifests itself in terms of the most traditional of themes, love. The search for 'the hunter [who] is gone' fructifies in 'ordinary love' which offers to Judith Wright 'the solitudes of poetry', and also a sense of personal identity. Whether it is an organic kinship with the landscape:

> All the hills' gathered waters feed my seas
> who am the swimmer and the mountain-river;
> and the long slopes' concurrence is my flesh
> who am the gazer and the land I stare on;
> and dogwood blooms within my winter blood,
> and orchards fruit in me and need no season.
> ['**For New England**']

Or, in the narrower sense, with the lover and the child:

This is no child with a child's face;
this has no name to name it by;
yet you and I have known it well.
This is our hunter and our chase,
the third who lay in our embrace.

['Woman to Man']

Whether it is pain or joy, it is 'blood's red thread' which unites all her perceptions and gives them a sense of organic completeness. There is almost always a frank recognition of the incompleteness of the woman, for she can speak for the woman:

The heart can blaze with candour
as though it housed a star;
but this my midnight splendour
is not my own to wear:
it lights by what you are.

['Five Senses']

This obsessive presence of the image of light shows why, despite the tonal directness of Judith Wright, her love poems modulate more into the intellectual than the sensuous. And it is the intellectual meditativeness which enables her to bring multiple levels of relationship to bear on the 'You and I'. 'You', which lights the passion of her heart, is both the world and the lover. It is also the child who is 'the maker and the made'. 'Blood's red thread . . . binds us fast in history.' She makes the world, but she is also made by it. She is the creator of the child, but she is incomplete without the man who brings the seed. But then it is the love for the unknown, 'the third who lay in our embrace', which unites the lovers and is

. . . the strength that your arm knows,
the arc of flesh that is my breast,
the precise crystals of our eyes.
That is the blood's wild tree that grows
the intricate and folded rose.

['Woman to Man']

Man, woman, and the child are the sap, the earth and the tree, and are united by 'blood's red thread' into an organic entity, like Yeats's image of the dancer or the chestnut-tree.

The power of the poems in *Woman to Man,* and of those like **'Ishtar'** from the later volume, lies in the frankness and truthfulness with which Judith Wright celebrates the glory of childbirth. Thus Philip Lindsay [in *Poetry Review* XLI, No. 4 (July-August 1950)] is led to write ecstatically:

Of Judith Wright's poetry it might well be said that she is the *only* woman who has kissed and told. Other women have sung of love, but apart from Sappho— and she, after all, was a man in female skin—none have written honestly and without shame of their desires.

He pronounces Judith Wright 'as being the first woman honestly to unbare her lover's heart in verse', in contrast to Emily Bronte, Emily Dickinson, and Christina Rossetti, whose love poetry is inspired by 'sexual repression' and 'starved hearts' rather than sexual fulfilment. Without undermining these three poets, who, it might well be argued, wrote better poetry, Judith Wright can be compared with Kamala Das whose central theme is love, and whose spontaneity and uninhibited treatment of a woman's passions are unique, because, apart from their poetic merit, they are written against the background of a culture different from, and more conservative than, Judith Wright's. Kamala Das concentrates more particularly on sexual love, and her woman-persona, far from being repressed, speaks with a sense of confessional urgency which should make Lindsay qualify his opinion on Judith Wright:

We came together like two suns meeting, and each
Raging to burn the other out. He said you are
A forest-conflagration and I, poor forest,
Must burn. But lay on me, light and white as
    embers
Over inert fires, Burn on, elemental
Fire, warm the coal streams of his eternal flesh till
At last, they boiling flow, so turbulent with life.

['The Conflagration']

Both are at their best when they write short poems, though Judith Wright's range and skills are greater. Mrs Das has published only two volumes of poems. And although in the second, there is a noticeable falling-off, the admirable concentration on the feminine point of view, the burning introversion with sexual love never falters, even when, as in 'Composition' and 'The Looking Glass', the tone is patronizing and indulgent and the expression not too happy:

. . . Gift him all,
Gift him what makes you woman, the scent of
Long hair, the musk of sweat between the breasts,
The warm shock of menstrual blood, and all your
Endless female hungers.

['The Looking Glass']

'Captive' describes her love as 'an empty gift, a gilded empty container' and herself as the captive of 'the womb's blinded hunger, the muted whisper at the core'. The poem is ambiguous in tone, but the theme of sexual love receives greater relevance from the unmistakable whisper at the core of the poem that love's fulfilment lies in containment not in emptiness. This theme of the glory of creation, of childbirth as the fulfilment of love, which is the theme of *Woman to Man,* and is also at the heart of Judith Wright's vision of organic continuity, finds a fine expression in Kamala Das's 'Jaisurya'. In a style which admirably combines the narrative and the meditative, she goes through the whole gamut of feelings preceding and following the birth of a son. Right at the start, she sets the interior mood by describing the outer:

It was again the time of rain and on
Every weeping tree, the lush moss spread like
Eczema, and from beneath the swashy
Earth the fat worms surfaced to explode
Under rain.

The rain is friendly; and by 'sighing, wailing, and roaring' it actually helps the persona briefly to forget her own 'pain'. It is only 'the unloving' who feel pain. And since the persona herself is involved in the loving act of creation, ' . . . the first / Tinge of blood seemed like another dawn / Breaking'. She feels and becomes earth, and finds meaning and fulfilment in love which is not an 'empty container' but is filled with a child:

> Walk into the waiting room, I had cried,
> When once my heart was vacant, fill the
> Emptiness, stranger, fill it with a child.
> Love is not important, that makes the blood
> Carouse, nor the man who brands you with his
> Lust, but is shed as slough at the end of each
> Embrace. Only that matters which forms as
> Toadstool under lightning and rain, the soft
> Stir in womb, the foetus growing, for,
> Only the treasures matter that were washed
> Ashore, not the long blue tides that washed them
> In.

The poem brings together light and darkness, fire and water, to weave a pattern of feeling which holds itself with the joy of creation. When the rain stops and 'the light was gay on our / Casurina leaves, it was early / Afternoon'. Then comes the child itself 'the sun-drenched golden day'. It is characteristic of Kamala Das, so deep is her assimilation of the Indian landscape, that meaningful things happen to her at or around noon time under the virgin whiteness of the sun. The child is a day that is 'Separated from darkness that was mine / And in me'.

This symbolism of light and dark is at the heart of Judith Wright's love poems, especially those dealing with childbirth. In **'Woman's Song'** the woman longs for the birth of the child; she asks it to 'wake in me' for

> The knife of day is bright
> to cut the thread that binds you
> within the flesh of night.

In **'Woman to Child',** the act of separation of the child from the mother is seen not as a disunity but an affirmation of an abiding relationship between the day and night:

> I wither and you break from me;
> yet though you dance in living light
> I am the earth, I am the root,
> I am the stem that fed the fruit,
> the link that joins you to the night.

In **'Conch-Shell'** the poet glorifies this abiding relationship. After the childbirth, the house is washed clean and

> The spiral passage turns upon itself.
> The sweet enclosing curve of pearl
> Shuts in the room that was the cell of birth.

But this is a new beginning for the 'windless shelter housing nothing'. The child who is the 'delicate argument and hieroglyph / of flesh that followed outward from the germ',

is both a culmination of one and a beginning of another argument in organic mystery. In the state of mind following on childbirth, she can 'half-guess' that the creative force 'burns forward still in me against the night':

> And here, half-guess, half-knowledge, I contract
> into a beast's blind orbit, stare deep down
> the cliffs not I have climbed . . .

The Eliotic echo in 'half-guess, half-knowledge' and the Yeatsian cadences in 'beast's blind orbit' and 'stare' have been made fully her own, though these echoes enrich our understanding of Judith Wright's metaphors of 'the house' (for the womb), 'delicate argument' (for the child), the 'puzzle' (for birth)—all intended to give the weight of history to the persona's sense of continuity of the orbit. Like Kamala Das, Judith Wright is rejoicing in the captivity of 'the womb's blinded hunger'. Though both poets are aware of the pain that its absence or the fulfilment involves, neither successfully relates this pain to the paranoia of contemporary history, as, for example, John Berryman does in 'Homage to Mistress Bradstreet', one of the greatest love poems of this century. Berryman's attempt to discover his poetic voice in the voice of Anne Bradstreet, since he cannot do it in the voice of any particular tradition, involves him in a passionate relationship with the woman persona herself. With the help of tortured rhythms and the vocabulary of guilt, suggesting seventeenth-century Calvinism, Berryman dramatizes his personal poetic problem and the need for certitude:

> . . . We are on each other's hands
> who care. Both of our worlds unhanded us. Lie
> stark.

The stanzas which describe the sexual experience and childbirth are perhaps the most lyrical in the poem. It is the woman persona who, retrieved from oblivion, comes alive, and in describing her sexual experience conveys the terror of history:

> faintings black, rigour, chilling, brown
> parching, back, brain burning, the grey pocks
> itch, a mainic stench
> of pustules snapping, pain floods the palm,
> sleepless, or a red shaft with a dreadful start
> rides at the chapel, like a slipping heart.
> My soul strains in one qualm
> ah but *this* is not to save me but to throw me
> down.

It is not only an orgasm but a qualm; and the language of ecstasy is also the language of delirium. Though the relationship is adulterous and hence guilt-ridden, it is not lust. It is the poet's impassioned search for meaning and certitude. What is true of sexual love is also true of the outcome of it. As the persona becomes aware of the 'ingrown months, blessing a swelling trance', the world appears both 'strange and merciful'. And instead of a sense of release, we have in her an uneasy feeling for liberation:

> . . . I love you & hate
> Off with you. Ages! *Useless.* Below my waist

he has me in Hell's vise.
Stalling. He let go. Come back: brace
me somewhere. No. No. Yes! everything down
hardens I press with horrible joy down
my back cracks like wrist
shame I am voiding oh behind it is too late.

The poem culminates in the recharged stillness of

In the rain of pain & departure, still
Love has no body and presides the sun,
and elfs from silence melody. I run.
Hover, utter, still,
a sourcing, whom my lost candle like the firefly loves.

These lines remind us that Berryman's poetic adultery with
Anne Bradstreet reverberates with an ironic sense of certitude in love and in poetry.

**It is Wright's strength that she writes
poetry which has the physical richness of
her landscape and an 'intellectual pride'
in the contemplation of the continuity of
life. There is a sense of largeness in her
lyrical contemplation, a feeling of an
open-hearted ease.**

—Devindra Kohli

Although Judith Wright has written poems about war,
and although her vision encompasses life and death, love
and pain, her faith in existence, in the certitudes of beauty, is unflinching. Her relationship with the external world
has a strong sense of family. So has her relationship with
her lover and child. Graves, whose idea of love is 'non-
domestic' and is dominated by the woman, does not delight in the birth of children; he describes 'love at first
sight' as the misnaming of 'Discovery of twinned helplessness / Against the huge tug of procreation' [*Collected
Poems,* 1965]. In 'Call it a Good Marriage', he suggests,
with some irony, that love can be intense despite a lack of
children:

Call it a good marriage:
More drew these two together
Despite a lack of children,
Than pulled them apart.

It is an intensity which grows out of tension: there is no
'comfortable point-of-rest' in Graves's love relationship.
Judith Wright uses images of marriage to embody her sense
of completeness and 'comfortable point-of-rest'. The sis
ters in the poem of the same title are old and look nostal-
gically back to the days of their youth. They can do so

with a sense of ease, because they have found their fulfilment in marriage and children:

Thinking of their lives apart and the men they married,
thinking of the marriage-bed and the birth of the first
    child,
they look down smiling. 'My life was wide and wild,
and who can know my heart? There in that golden
    jungle
I walk alone', say the old sisters on the veranda.
                                        [*Woman to Man*]

'In Praise of Marriages' glorifies marriage as a means
of knowing 'all possible' of 'this field of power' which
'spreads' out of the marriage of 'the I and the you'. In
Kamala Das there is some sense of union, and in *The
Descendents,* it is, happily, viewed in the framework of a
family. This gives to some of her old themes a new perspective and to her work a sense of progression, despite
the faults of style. One hopes that she will bring to her
words a wider range of associations and the quality of
irradiation.

Although these two woman poets seem to have similar
poetic concerns, they differ in their attitudes to the 'place'
of words in the love-experience. For Kamala Das, the
intensity of passions makes words irrelevant. In 'Spoiling
the Name', she associates name with abstraction:

. . . why should this name, so
Sweet-sounding, enter not all the room
Where I go to meet a man
Who gives me nothing but himself, who
Calls me in his private hours
By no name . . .

Words can be a 'nuisance', a distraction. In 'Substitute'
they are a filling, and suggest discord:

Our bodies after love-making
Turned away, rejecting,
Our words began to sound
Like clatter of swords in fight.

In 'Convicts', words are submerged in the darkness of the
passions, the music of the silence:

. . . We were earth under hot
Sun. There was a burning in our
Veins and the cool mountain nights did
Nothing to lessen heat. When he
And I were one, we were neither
Male nor female. There were no more
Words left, all words, lay imprisoned
In the ageing arms of night.

Kamala Das's preoccupation with the intensity of sexual
love does not bring her to the brink of inarticulation. It is
an unconscious irony perhaps that despite her frequent
gestures of denial of power to words, despite her view
that words are inadequate for love, her own affirmations
of love are striking, eloquent, and concrete.

Judith Wright, on the other hand, believes that 'love takes no pains with words / but is most eloquent'. To love is to communicate and thus to feel divine; and to communicate is to feel creative. Language is an affirmation of the power of love. Words are necessary for interpreting one's passions: 'I cannot know my heart's beauty /—say all the creatures—till you interpret me in god-made words.' In **'Birds'**, the desire to escape into 'the forest of a bird' is an impassioned attempt to 'find the words that lie behind all these languages'. In **'Water'**, the simple perception of the movement of water can stimulate a perception of a profounder process:

> Such sentences, such cadences of speech
> the tonguing water stutters in its race
> as may have set us talking each to each
> before our language found its proper pace.

Concern with the relationship between language and creation is at the heart of **'Camping at Split Rock'**. Each perception is an involvement within a word:

> The finger of age-old water splits the rock
> and makes us room to live: the age-old word
> runs on in language and from obstinate dark
> hollows us room for seeing.

And though 'the birds go by', 'we can name and hold them', for each of them is a 'word' that goes beyond the mortality of the bird. In **'Prayer'**, confronted with the thought of death herself, she prays that she retain love which includes the power 'to see the words', as well as the power to speak words:

> And you, who speak in me when I speak well,
> withdraw not your grace, leave me not dry and cold.
> I have praised you in the pain of love, I would praise
>   you still
> in the slowing of the blood, the time when I grow old.

Judith Wright never gets breathless even when she is at her most intense in **Woman to Man**. In **'To Hafiz of Shiraz'**, she suggests that with the repetition of experience, there is corresponding simplification of words but that repetition and simplification need not mean the loss of intensity, for 'every word leads back to the blinding original Word'; there are no two ways for her, 'the way up and the way down', but one way only.

It is an unconscious irony in Judith Wright, one ventures to say, that she is concerned with words in the sense of a theme in poems which seem, on the whole, inferior to those in **Woman and Man**. The tone of most of these poems is discursive, and although one notices the simplicity of the words one also misses in fact, the blinding light of the original Word. In **Woman to Man,** she does not *seek* to assert explicitly the power of words as she does, for example, in **The Other Half**, because, in the former, language is a mode of feeling and thus the power of words is felt in the power of the experience of love that she undergoes:

> The burning wires of nerves, the crimson way
> from head to heart, the towering tree of blood—
> who travels here must move, not as he would,
> but fed and lit by love alone he may.

William H. Pritchard (essay date 1978)

SOURCE: A review of *The Double Tree,* in *The New York Times Book Review,* November 26, 1978, pp. 62, 64.

[*In this review of Wright's retrospective collection* The Double Tree, *Pritchard notes an increasing flexibility in Wright's poetic tone, comparing her work to that of D. H. Lawrence and W. B. Yeats.*]

Judith Wright is an Australian poet, author of 10 books of verse from which the present selection [*The Double Tree*] has been made. Assuming that American readers need help with work that comes out of an unfamiliar country, she provides an introduction telling us a bit about Australia, of where she was born and brought up (the New England Country of New South Wales), and of her life during World War II and after, her founding of a society for wildlife conservation, her membership on a government committee of inquiry. It is an odd way to introduce one's poems, and in fact although I am unfamiliar enough with dingoes and wagtails, or with "the whipstick scrub on the Thirty-Mile Dry" (these occur in **"Drought Year"**), she surely overestimates the remoteness of her experience and materials. Especially since she writes in a forcefully direct manner, has no interest in obliquities or ambiguities of expression and finds English syntax fully adequate to her concerns.

These concerns are no less than typically human ones—observations about nature and human nature, birds and daughters, growing up and growing old, momentary discoveries that make a difference to the self:

> Walking one lukewarm, lamp-black night I heard,
> a yard from me his harsh rattle of warning,
> and in a landing-net of torch-light saw him
>   crouch—
>
>   . . .
>
> A bird with a broken breast. But what a stare
> he fronted me with!—his look abashed my own.
> He was all eyes, furious, meant to wound.
> And I, who meant to heal, took in my hand
> his depth of down, his air-light delicate bone,
> his heart in the last extreme of pain and fear.

If one thinks of D. H. Lawrence's "Birds, Beasts and Flowers," Judith Wright has the advantage in reality. She is wary about turning birds into symbols, at least until they have been established in their own birdlike identities; while the modest but subtle tone and pace of her lines build confidence in us rather than (as too often with Lawrence) alienating us by their exclamatory hysteria.

Her own voice—and readers of different temperament may not agree—is a high outer seriousness unrelieved, in the poems from the 1940's and 1950's, by inner humor. As with her introduction, her poems do not always avoid solemnity. A list of most-used words from the volume's first half would include "love," "eternity," "life," "star," "blood," "death," "seed," "flesh," "tree," "bird," "dream," "faith" and "night," a diction she shares with Edwin Muir, whom she resembles in other ways. One is also conscious of Yeats in these earlier poems, but Judith Wright was reluctant or unable to dramatize an "I" with much individuality, so that when (in **"Dream"**) she writes "O dying tree, I move beneath your shade," or "I sought upon the hill the crimson rose," the personal engagement feels minimal and the poetry rather conventional.

Somewhere around the mid-1960's her work grew more various, more flexible in tone, willing on occasion to eschew rhyme and exploit lines of irregular length. While not in themselves virtues, these practices may have helped move her in the direction of more pointedly personal reflection.

By the 1970's her poetic presence is a more inclusive one, able to say one thing and mean another, take on a dead metaphor and resucitate it, as in **"Black/White"**:

> This time I shall recover
> from my brief blowtorch fever,
> The sweats of living
> flood me; I wake again,
> pondering the moves of anti and of pro.
> Back into play I go
>
> Had it been pro-biotics they gave me
> would I still live?
> Anti-biotics maybe snub the truth
> cheating the black King's
> move—
> emptily save me,
> a counter-ghost tricked from a rightful death.

Off-rhymes, the witty invention of "pro-biotics" and of "blowtorch" as an adjective contribute to the generally sharp alterness and agility of this verse, which embodies the moves and "play" of its main metaphor:

> But you can play on black squares or on white,
> do without counters even; in theory
> even the dead still influence what we do,
> direct our strategy.
> I'm none too sure exactly why I'm here,
> which side I'm playing for—

Complicating itself, the poem risks confusion, then snaps back to pull itself together, its author unwilling to fall upon the thorns of life for very long:

> But still here's day, here's night,
> the checkerboard of yes and no
> and take and give.

> Again I meet you face to face,
> which in itself is unexpected grace.
> To arms, my waiting opposite—
> we live.

A final, extra line, strong rhymes, a balanced readiness to resume: both serious and humorous, it shows this accomplished poet at her best.

Alur Janakiram (essay date 1981)

SOURCE: "Judith Wright and the Colonial Experience: A Selective Approach," in *The Colonial and the Neo-Colonial Encounters in Commonwealth Literature*, edited by H. H. Anniah Gowda, Prasaranga, University of Mysore, 1983, pp. 173-86.

[*The following essay was delivered as a seminar in 1981. In this analysis, Janakiram examines and applauds Wright's struggle, in both poems and in life, to create a relationship "to be won by love only" between the European settlers of Australia, the Aborigine population and culture, and the land itself. Jankiram maintains that Wright uses this relationship to achieve a true Australian identity, not as an exile or a conqueror, but as a native at peace in her homeland.*]

As Leonie Kramer has noted [in "Judith Wright, Hope, Mcaulcy," *Literary Criterion,* Vol. XV, Nos. 3-4, 1980], Judith Wright, A. D. Hope and James Mcauley form a major trinity, who together with R. D. FitzGerald, Douglas Stewart and David Campbell, "virtually wrote the history of Australian poetry" in the period after the world war II. "Their work represents", according to Kramer, "not so much a renaissance in Australian poetry as a first full flowering, which established poetry as a form able to challenge what had hitherto been the dominance of fiction." Whatever poetry is or may be, it has its springs in the human condition and reflects the personal and social aspirations of a particular milieu that produces it. The history of Australian poetry may be described, briefly, as the history of the white man's encounter with an alien landscape and alien tribes. The story of the white man's colonial adventure in Australia, a short one since it covers just three or four life-times, has been reflected in the Australian verse produced over the years and accounts for its peculiar pre-occupations with the landscape, the bush, the bushrangers and explorer-heroes. The dominance of the Romantic-Symbolist tradition in this poetry, with a greater share going to the Romantic component, can be explained by the fact that Australian poets, in their attempts to come to terms with their exiled consciousness in a "desolate country", found the Romantic mode quite handy for their purposes. As a result, nature or landscape receives much greater attention than the human figures and the images of light and dark, night and day, noises and silences persist frequently even in the poetry of the later period, and more so in the poetry of Judith Wright.

James Mcauley, Judith Wright's distinguished contemporary, has remarked about her poems that many of them "make high claims for themselves by the nature of their themes and language: they play for high stakes" [*A Map of Australian Verse,* 1975].

Her encounter with the natural environment and rural life is devoid of any urban bias; it is largely "meditative intuitive, emotional, with strong metaphysical searching." While a sense of immediacy and reflective intensity, coupled with a remarkable gift for image making, marks her earlier verse of the 40's and 50's, a movement towards the general and the abstract with a tendency to probe the metaphysical significance of experience has been noted by critics as a new development in her later poetry. "The surface change" in her poetry, as C. A. Wilkes puts it [in "The Later Poetry of Judith Wright," *Southerly, A Review of Australian Literature,* Vol. 25, No. 3, 1965], is that the main source of her poetic inspiration in her earlier period is the "finite world" available to the senses, while the effort of the later poetry is to reach beyond that world. However, there are a few themes that recur frequently both in her earlier and later verse; time as the moving image of eternity, the poet as the maker, love creativity and settlement, and the disappearance of the Aboriginal culture.

An effort is made in this paper to close-read a few of her poems dealing with the colonial experience of the white man in Australia particularly themes of colonisation, settlement and dispossession of the Aborigines. About four or five poems have been selected for a close examination for whatever light they may throw on the issue of colonial encounter.

The much anthologised piece, **"Bullocky"**, that appeared first in ***The Moving Image*** (1946), as a familiar recreation of the Australian Dream in terms of the Biblical myth. The white man's colonising ventures in Australia recall the first settlement of the Jews in their Promised Land; the Bullocky man of the frontier days, thus, becomes a kind of "old Moses" and his "stubbourn team", the slaves that were led out of Egypt. Camping under the "half-light pillars of the trees" at night, the Bullocky man

> filled the steeple cone of night
> with shouted prayers and prophecies,

in order to overcome the terror of silence. The last two stanzas evoke the nature of the first colonial encounter with the vast bush and state how the pioneering ventures of the early settlers have transformed a desolate and intractable wild into "the promised Land" of the prophet Moses.

> Grass is across the wagon-tracks,
> and plough strikes bone across the grass,
> and vineyards cover all the slopes
> where the dead teams were used to pass.
> O vine, grow close upon that bone
> and hold it with your rooted hand.
> The prophet Moses feeds the grape,
> and fruitful is the Promised Land.

"Remittance Man", another poem of the same collection, concerns itself like **"Bullocky"**, with the early white settlers. The remittance man was the "freak" who could never settle, who was content to go "tramping the backtracks" in summer haze and "let everything but life slip through his fingers." His easy-going habits led to his dis-inheritance and dismal end which are viewed in a matter-of-fact manner by his prosperous brother, the Squire.

> That harsh biblical country of the scapegoat
> closed its magnificence finally round his bones
> polished by diligent ants. The squire his brother,
> presuming death, signed over the documents, and
> lifting his eyes across the inherited garden
> let a vague pity blur the formal roses.

The well-known piece, **"Nigger's Leap: New England"**, is unique for articulating a sharper sense of guilt, for offering a new perspective about the European adventure that has thrived at the expense of the primitive tribes of the land. Based on a particular incident of European reprisal, in 1844, in New South Wales, the poem recalls how the hapless Niggers, pursued to the top of the "Lipped cliff", "screamed falling in flesh" from those heights "and then were silent". The "bone and skull" lying securely under "the spine of range" and "the enveloping night call" for a "synthesis", for a revaluation of a historical relationship:

> Did we not know their blood channeled our rivers,
> and the black dust our crops ate was their dust?
> O all men are one man at last. We should have
>   known
> the night that tided up the cliffs and hid them
> had the same question on its tongue for us.
> And there they lie that were ourselves writ strange.

The sentiments recorded in these lines are a good example of what J. J. Healy [in "The Absolute and the Image of Man in Australian," *Awakened Conscience,* 1978] has termed as the "we-phenomenon", an expanded consciousness that acknowledges collective responsibility for a particular event of history, that sees the victim as a segment of the self-inflicted wound. Hence the call for "synthesis", for undoing a past injury.

It is interesting to note that Judith Wright's poetic mode of communication in all the poems dealing with the themes of settlement and usurpation is characterised by nature imagery of grass, rock, sea and dust. We have already seen how **"Bullocky"** [states its meaning] in terms of this basic imagery; here again, in [**"Nigger's Leap: New England"**], earth, wind and saplings play their own part in conveying what needs to be conveyed.

> Never from earth again the coolamon,
> or thin black children dancing like the shadows
> of saplings in the wind. . . . . .
> Night floods us suddenly as history,
> that has sunk many islands in its good time.

Similar concerns of shared guilt that colonial encounter has entailed also inform, at a much deeper level, the long poem, **"The Blind Man"**, originally published in the *Woman to Man* series (1949).

The issue of the white man's relationship with the land and its tribes is presented symbolically in the wider perspective of the dance of dust. And the dance of the "pollen-coloured dust" is none other than the eternal dance of birth and death. Jimmy Delaney, the blind man who sings under the Moreton Bay fig, "speaks in the voice of the forgotten dust". And his song carries much authenticity as a faithful narrative of the colonial venture since he himself, "is of that dust three generations made". The account begins with the pioneering efforts of the first generation Horrie Delaney who arrived at the place with his cattle and "shook the dust out of its golden sleep". However, he too had to shuffle across like "another shadow between the earth and the sun", and his adventure has culminated in being one with the tribes below the ground.

> Deeper than the shadows of trees and tribes, deep
> lay the spring that issues in death and birth.
> Horrie Delaney with his dogs and his gun
> came like another shadow between the earth and the
>   sun
> and now with the tribes he is gone down in death.

Then is recounted the venture of the second generation pioneer, Dick Delaney the combo, who cleared the hills and the bush finally for human settlement by dint of his sweat and labour:

> Easily the bush fell and lightly, now it seems
> to us who forget the sweat of Dick Delaney,
> and the humpy and the scalding sunlight and the
>   black
> hate between the white skin and the black.

There is an important suggestion here that the adventure of the white man has both sides to it: the black hate involving the racial tension and the hard labour and sweat of the white man. It may be that both the labour and the hate lie hidden under the "marred earth" and its humble dust. However, whatever the outcome of the metamorphosis that has come over the pioneers, the vanquished tribe and the descendents of both, the dust has been performing its impersonal functions by keeping up the inexorable dance pattern of birth and death, growth and decay, in successive generations:

> Dance upright in the wind, dry-voiced and humble
>   dust
> out of whose breast the great green fig-tree springs,
> and the proud man, and the singer, and the outcast.

Admittedly, the colonial encounter, as presented in this poem, is not a simple tale of "came, saw and conquered"; it has wider ramifications of another kind of dance that the whirligig of time weaves in terms of dust, light and wind. This dance, assuming the pattern of generation, once

sustained the green fig tree, the conqueror-dreamer and the dispossessed tribe. Assuming another form of negation and decay, the same dance has whittled them all into "shadows between the earth and the sun", into golden dust "driven by a restless wind":

> The conqueror who possessed a world alone,
> and he who hammered a world on his heart's stone,
> and last the man whose world splintered in fear
> their shadows lengthen in the light of noon,
> their dust bites deep, driven by a restless wind.

The metaphysical overtones of this long narrative, of a blind singer's version of the Australian colonial experience, become clear and more pronounced as the account reaches its close. The speaker proclaims apocryphally with an assurance that is the outcome of an intent listening to the voices of the dark:

> I repeat the small speech of the worm in the ground,
> and out of the depths of the rock my words are made.
> I have laid my ear to the dust, and the thing it said
> was Silence. Therefore I have made silence speak;
>   I found
> for the night a sound. . . .
> I am the yellow snake with a dark, double tongue,
>   speaking from the dust to the two rulers of the
>   world.

One feels constrained to ask the inevitable question: who are the two rulers of the world, the dreamer-explorer or the dispossessed tribal cherishing his own vanished dream? Clearly, the answer is in favour of the primeval elemental forces of birth and death, rather than the puny man. Perhaps, conquest, dispossession and defeat are altogether non-issues when they are placed in the wider perspective of decay and death, generation and degeneration—a pattern that the golden earth never tires of repeating at whatever level. This seems to be the note on which the blindman's song concludes: (that the "unregarded dust" is the ultimate conqueror).

Another longer piece, **"Seven Songs for a Journey"**, belonging to *The Two Fires* (1955) series of poems, has a bearing on the colonial theme of settlement and adaptation under discussion in this paper. Here again, the core of the experience is presented symbolically through the basic and primary images of nature: this time of cliffs and creeks, moon and bone, sea-tides and mountain rocks. At the outset, the poet offers her song as a humble garland of word and phrase to the ageless rock and water of Carnarvon ranges and Creek. The song at once strikes us with its forceful bumping short rhythms of the Australian bush-ballad:

> Carnarvon Creek
> and cliffs of Carnarvon,
> your tribes are silent;
> I will sing for you—
> each phrase
> the size of a stone—
> a red stone,

a white stone,
a grey,
and a purple;
. . . . . .
each word a sign
to set on your cliffs,
each phrase a stone
to lie in your waters.

All that the poet would ask in exchange from the cliffs are the "white orchard" from her slope and a fish from her waters.

The second section, "Brigalow Country", presents the tribal girl Margery as dancing "awkward as an emu" under the "metal-blue moon", with only the brigalow scrub on the slope and the far-off singing Dingoes to give her company. Her abject condition as a poor dweller of a fringe-community is reflected in her bemoaning song she sings while dancing under the moon. The burden of her lament is that she has neither money nor sympathy and is as unregarded as the brigalow scrub on the slope, a silent companion in distress;

Living lost and lonely
with the tribe of the brigalows,
don't want to stay
but never can go.
Never get no money
for when I go hungry,
never get no kisses
for when I feel sad—
rooted like the brigalows
until I'm dead . . .
And the tribe of the brigalows
drop their shadows
like still black water
and watch her there

The third section addresses itself to Night, a favourite image and preoccupation of Judith Wright. The contours of Night, like the contours of Carnarvon mountain rock, have endured as lasting onlookers on the scene although these contours have been occasionally eroded by the moon's pale creek and the "floods of sunlight" and water. Night here emerges as the emblem of the mysterious dark, the unknowable, that somehow keeps up the phenomenal dance and negates all our dreams, including the "earth"'s:

Night is what remains
when the equation is finished.
Night is the earth's dream
that the sun is dead.
Night is man's dream
that he has invented God—
the dream of before-creation;
the dream of falling.
Night blocks our way, saying
I at least am real.

The 4th section "The Prospector" takes up the theme of settlement and colonial history and the attendant displace-ment and injury they have caused in the bargain. Burdened by the uneasy awareness that she is an intruder on this scene, the poet watches the moon rise in her full splendour

on the range where no bird's speaking
except in the crow's voice—
on the land to be won by love only;

The awareness that the desolate landscape, in order to be one with the inner landscape, requires the mediation of love also includes the other knowledge concerning the aspirations of the old skeletons and bones dreaming on under the bright white moon:

Rise up and walk, old skeleton
But no; lie still.
Let no phase of the moon disturb you,
no heats recall.
Let the bones dream on, the kind dream
that was their last—
dream the mirage's river
has quenched the world's thirst.

It is with such a heavy and burdened heart that the poet realises what her own place is vis-a-vis the landscape and the scene:

Full moon's too bright for sleeping—
too white the sky.
And foreign to this country
restless I lie.
But you, moon, you're no stranger;
You're known here, moon,
drawing your mad hands over
rock, dust and bone.

It is not just the rock, dust, bone and moon that stand out as "witnesses against our lives" and as onlookers of recent history, for they have been "initialled by clumsy knives". But the sea, "anonymous pilgrim", "free of time and space" and history, carries no memory or any mark except the "unshaped bone and the splinter of raft". This is indeed a strange inference, for we know that the sea which has made its own contribution to the discovery and formation of Australian geography and history, cannot be relegated to a background figure as free of time and space. Perhaps, the poet's implication seems to be that the sea bears no concrete traces of human history except that it transforms and cleans whatever it receives from the human side.

At the end of this remarkable song for the human journey under debate, the only witnesses to the human aspirations and achievements that the poet has presented, are the tall Carnarvon cliffs and shallow creeks.—Unlike the sea, the solitary mountain, emerging finally as a "tall", sad "figure in an estranged landscape, drawing her biblical blue cloak across her shoulders," is presented as a mother figure, "virgin and widow", weeping her small pools of tears and with nothing "left for her to dream on". She at least seems to be a participator in human history, if not the neutral sea.

"**At Cooloola**", a short poem, is of a piece with the two long poems discussed here as far as its central preoccupation with the antinomies of antipodean exile is concerned. The operative symbols in this short poem are: the blue crane, the white swan, the clean sand and the drift-wood spear. Oppressed by "arrogant guilt" of usurpation which, as Judith Wright remarks in one of her published lectures, is a sore on the Australian's relationship with the land, she observes in her wanderings near Cooloola how the ancient "blue crane" has been fishing down the centuries with a calm and assurance denied to herself. She is aware that

> He is the certain heir of lake and evening,
> and he will wear their colours till he dies.

The outward scene turns the poet's attention inward, to an examination of her own relationship with the environment:

> I cannot share his calm, who watch his lake
> being unloved by all my eyes delight in
> and made uneasy for an old murder's sake.

The third section of the poem glances backward at the mysterious beckoning which her grandfather received ninety years earlier from a ghostly black warrior. The past incident of crime and racial tension casts its gloom over the poet's present self-critical awareness. White shores of sand, says the poet, do "clear heavenly levels for the crane and swan" but not for her, smarting as she is under the burden of memory:

> I know that we are justified only by love,
> but oppressed by arrogant guilt, have room for none.
> And walking on clean sand among the prints
> of bird and animal, I am challenged by a driftwood
> spear
> thrust from water; and, like my grandfather,
> must quiet a heart accused by its own fear.

The solution to the moral dilemma presented in the poem is the time-honoured one: that any meaningful relationship with the land of one's exile or conquest, and its earlier inhabitants, has to be based on love and understanding, the positives of human existence, rather than fear and hatred that are self-negating. Love, a redeeming experience, forms the basic link in any relationship between man and man, either black or white, or man and nature. And much of Judith Wright's poetry has this insistent theme: that love alone is the "dark gift" that helps man sustain not only his human creativity and identity but his inward peace as well. Perhaps, the opening piece of the *Five Senses,* "**The Company of Lovers**" (1946) provides a clue to the chief direction the metaphysical quest the poet has taken in her later verse:

> we, the lost company,
> take hands together in the night, forget
> the night in our brief happiness, silently.
> We, who sought many things, throw all away
> for this one thing, one only,
> remembering that in the narrow grave
> we shall be lonely.

To sum up, the colonial encounter in Judith Wright's poetry may be said to take the form of a quest for a genuine Australian identity, an identity that has rid itself of an adolescent nostalgia and emotional hankering for its ancestral home and tried to overcome the hampering effects of an exile consciousness. This quest, as in much of Australian poetry, has meant an imaginative effort to integrate the outer landscape, together with its trees and tribes, with a coherent and fulsome inner landscape, something wholly lived with rather than only observed from outside. In other words, the effort has meant a metamorphosis of a shipwrecked state into a situation of being really "at home"— of the kind described in James Mcauley's beautiful little piece, "Terra Australis"

> It is your land of similes: the wattle
> Scatters its pollen on the doubting heart;
> The flowers are wide awake; the air gives ease
> There you come home. . . .
>   [*The Penguin Book of Australian Verse,* 1961]

This attitude towards the land "to be won by love only", as Judith Wright reminds us repeatedly, also partakes of an imaginative concern for the Aboriginals and their ancient culture, of a desire to strike a meaningful relationship with them in place of the earlier one based on "arrogant guilt." It is a measure of Judith Wright's integrity as poet and crusader for certain human values that she has voiced this concern not only in the few poems discussed in this paper but even in her two published lectures: "Aboriginals in Australian Poetry" and "The Voice of the Aboriginals" [published in *Because I was Invited,* 1975].

> **The colonial encounter in Judith Wright's poetry may be said to take the form of a quest for a genuine Australian identity, an identity that has rid itself of an adolescent nostalgia and emotional hankering for its ancestral home and tried to overcome the hampering effects of an exile consciousness.**
>
> *—Alur Janakiram*

The first lecture, delivered in 1971 in Sydney, takes stock of the attitudes in Australian poetry towards the tribal people and goes on to assess the impact of the encounter with a primitive culture on the Australian imagination. A salutary fallout of the Jindiworobak movement, she notes, has been the birth of a rather belated recognition that "the long despised people had a value in themselves" and that their culture, based on complex but close ritualistic links with the land, had something to give to the whites and the wider world. She further notes that "the old attitudes of contempt and silence have been seriously undermined by the increasing publication of studies of Aboriginal culture and the Aboriginal plight." In the second lecture, "The

Voice of the Aboriginals", delivered at East-West Centre in Honululu in 1974, she attempts a critical assessment of the Aboriginal protest and creative writing in English and shows how the process of the liberation of the Australian imagination from its earlier smugness and guilty silences has been further activated by the voices of the Aboriginal writers and thinkers themselves—Kath Walker, Davis, Gilbert, Johnson and the rest. Her genuine concern for the tribal culture deserves to be placed in the context of her wider and shared concern for the welfare of our planet, very much threatened by, what she calls, modern scientism and the predatory economic exploitation of our environment by our overgrown technological civilisation; and this concern is effectively voiced in all her writings on the Conservation Movement of which she herself has been an active campaigner. That her concern for the tribal people has been sincere and large-hearted is self-evident in the estimate she offers of the impact of the Aboriginal writers:

> . . . Voices such as theirs can help to convince us that Aboriginals are capable of weighing their own choices, deciding their own problems and living successfully in their own way, if not in ours. If they are emerging at last, whether to accuse us, to demand a new respect and consideration, or to tell us their own stories, it is certainly none too early. The tragedy might rather be that it is, perhaps, too late.

Shirley Walker (essay date 1991)

SOURCE: "*Alive, Fourth Quarter* and *Phantom Dwelling*," in *Flame and Shadow: A Study of Judith Wright's Poetry,* University of Queensland Press, 1991, pp. 176-205, 210.

[*In this excerpt, Walker argues that Wright's collections* Fourth Quarter *and* Phantom Dwelling *represent a growth in the poet's already estimable talent and vision. Walker contends that in these books Wright brings a variety of new influences and insights to bear on old themes, answering with clarity questions left open by old poems, and finding peace through reconciliation where once she found conflict.*]

The poems of *Fourth Quarter* represent a break-through into a newer and more vigorous poetic world; an expression of that acceptance which [the poem] **"Shadow"** anticipated, but which the poems of *Alive* did not quite achieve. This is one of the most thematically unified of Wright's volumes, for the collection as a whole is a celebration of the feminine principle, of intuition, imagination, love and creativity. The central symbol is the moon in its different phases and various aspects, for the moon controls the ebb and flow of the tide, the mysterious cycles of the feminine, and the "salt blood" of humanity which betrays its marine origin. The sublunary world is the world of physical change and flux, and in these poems Wright reaffirms her earlier commitment to it. Moreover the moon, as muse, inspires the imaginative and creative power of the unconscious which, according to Jung, is

feminine in essence. In these poems the emphasis is upon psychic rather than physical creativity, and the source of psychic power, the unconscious, is symbolised by sleep, dream and water. Water and the sea image the source of and the ebb and flow of creativity. All aspects of creativity, such as the vision of Walter Burley Griffin, the architect of Canberra, are related to this generative compulsion. Subsidiary symbolic motifs such as the owl and the hare (creatures traditionally associated with the moon), the platypus, the whale and the termite queen, are brought into play to amplify the conception, and to expand its reverberations out to the furthest horizons of feeling, intuition, meditation, and vision.

In opposition to creativity Wright sets the concept of rationalism, which is symbolised by the daylight world, the land and the active male principle. There is a significant change in Wright's attitude towards evil which is no longer an inherent human characteristic, but a consequence of rationalistic ways of thought. In **"White Night"** (*Alive*) she posed a question which has been a constant preoccupation throughout her poetry: "Where does it all begin? / If evil has a beginning / it may disclose its meaning." The poems of *Fourth Quarter* provide her answer. Here evil is not condoned, but is placed in perspective as the inevitable consequence of that split in the sensibility, the dissociation of thought and feeling . . . and the denial of human values which this involves. The consequences of rationalism are, once again, taken to their furthest limits. They apply not only to the physical world but to the human mind. The sludge and detritus of modern civilisation has silted up and choked not only the pure streams of the natural world, from Cedar Creek to the Kamo, but the well-springs of the unconscious. Yet nature will not be spoiled, nor will the creative power of the psyche ever be completely suppressed. This is the point of **"Platypus"** where the platypus is both itself and the elusive poetic impulse which is threatened by the ugly consequences of a polluted world and rationalistic thought:

> Platypus, wary paradox,
> ancient of beasts,
> like a strange word rising
> through the waterhole's rocks,
>
> you're gone. That once bright water
> won't hold you now.
> No quicksilver bubble-trail
> in that scummy fetor . . .

Yet when conditions are right ("At midnight and alone / there's a stir in my mind") the streams run clear, and the paradoxical image, half memory and half symbol, rises up through the "scummy fetor" which threatens to block it:

> suddenly my mind
> runs clear and you rise through . . .
> platypus, paradox—
> like the ripples of your wake.

Within this dialectical framework—the creative feminine principle as opposed to the rationalistic will to power—

the keynote of the poetry is acceptance. Wright is no longer interested in philosophical or linguistic rationalisations of inadequacy, for her own shortcomings are freely conceded, placed in perspective, and accepted as simply a reflection of and a parallel to the waning moon and the ebbing tide. The poet accepts her decline, projects herself into the tragi-comic figures of age and sibylline power—the "hag" and "witch" of **"Easter Moon and Owl"**—and defies the moon's advice to "throw it in", for her response to nature is still powerful, still sensuous.

In the **"Interface"** sequence, the dualism of human nature, the "schizophrenic imbalance" which has always disturbed Wright, is seen as a logical consequence of evolution. Having left the mother element, water, the human being is now a creature of both the sea (intuition and emotion) and the land (the intellect). The opposition of unconscious and conscious states is symbolised throughout the volume by sleep (or dream) and waking, sea and land. Mist and sea signify a dimension to which the individual has access only in sleep or the dream-life of the imagination:

> Dreams: waves. Their wind-meandering changes
> reach to the edge of shore, no further.
> Their soft admonishing voices
> sound from a sea where we can swim no longer.
> Now we must wake.

In **"Half-dream"** the poet, like the old boat, is moored to the land by a fraying rope, drawn by the ebb and flow of the water and the moon-road. The poem also suggests the unity of the mind with the creatures of night and water, and the inevitability of the final drift out towards darkness and death. **"Dream"** is far more vigorous than **"Half-dream"**; it suggests that the unconscious expresses the truth of life far more accurately than the waking mind, which deals in comfortable rationalisations. Indeed the individual can have access to truth only in states of dream, intuition and vision, for the evolutionary process has betrayed the human race, "unfinned", to the daytime rational life ashore. Because of its essentially dualistic or amphibian nature, there is no hope for humanity which, according to the poem **"By-pass"**, is now on the highroad which is sweeping it into a world of increasing violence, with the chance for a "U Turn" missed forever. Modern men and women are the products of the age of violent and contending forces which Wright celebrates in **"For the Quaternary Age"**. In this poem, however, Wright not only accepts her dualistic nature, but delights in it:

> I'm still your child,
> adoring this sudden light, the gaps between
> terrors, the glow of cloud-tops, crevices
> of green serenity. Whimpering, half in love,
> I press on the armoured glass to watch you, lean
> to your diverse passages, asking what you mean
> by those mute and merciful designs of pearl.

Part of this acceptance is the acceptance of love. **"Eve Sings"**, a magnificent love lyric, is informed and strengthened by its acceptance of the imperfection of love. The keyword is "human" and its full implications are suggested by the old Edenic symbols: the serpent, the crossed swords, Eden, the tree and a doomed world. Against the full knowledge of guilt, failure and betrayal the poet sets the "greed and joy" of love, for:

> . . . the tree
> drops one last fruit for you and me.
> I gather it for your human hands
> I look into your human eyes.

In **"Eve Scolds"** the implications of being "human" are further developed, for the individual woman, Eve and mother earth are identified and opposed to the active, rapacious male principle, "so entrepreneurial, vulgarly moreish, / plunging on and exploring where there's nothing / left to explore, exhausting the last of our flesh". The two impulses—creative (female) and imperialistic (male)—are clearly incompatible:

> But you and I, at heart, never got on.
> Each of us wants to own—
> You, to own me, but even more, the world;
> I, to own you.

As always the female impulse is to surrender: "I go overboard for you, / here at the world's last edge. / Ravage us still; the very last green's our kiss." The witty colloquialisms—"I go overboard" and "the world's last edge"—suggest that, because of love, the surrender to male domination is inevitable. Acceptance of this breeds detachment and the poem's irony is light and humorous, in keeping with the title.

Age is more difficult to accept, and the narcissistic young woman in the orchard in **"Woman in Orchard"** (Eve again?) who "kneels / to love her body in the pool / and dream herself for ever young" confronts instead her *alter ego,* herself grown old, the witch who "steals / not the flesh but the joy of it". **"Moving South"**, a poem which deals with Wright's move from Mount Tamborine to Braidwood in New South Wales, is more serious and less complex, for moving south, closer to the pole, is a metaphor for divesting oneself of the fleshly extravagance of "summer" existence—an extravagance which is, after all, a cheating enchantment (*Beauté de diable*)—in order to approach the essence of experience; not only the "root's endurance" which the poet has been stressing throughout her work, but also the waiting winter and death.

In *Fourth Quarter* Wright returns to old themes with a new vigour and often in a completely new context, always demonstrating control, detachment and a mastery of her material. In **"The Dark Ones"**, for instance, the Aborigines are identified with the dark and potent contents of the unconscious. They rise up like wraiths to reproach the confidence and assurance of the daylight world:

> In the town on pension day
> mute shadows glide.
> The white talk dies away
> the faces turn aside.

A shudder like breath caught
runs through the town.
Are *they* still here? We thought . . .
Let us alone.

The Aborigines are the shadow side of the self; to deny
them is the same as denying a part of the self:

The night ghosts of a land
only by day possessed
come haunting into the mind
like a shadow cast.

Like the Jungian shadow, the Aborigines must be brought
up into the consciousness and accepted before the shame
and guilt of the white race can be healed. This is a significant and moving poem; quite as powerful as the early
"Bora Ring" and **"Nigger's Leap, New England"**, for it
relates the immediate racial problem to the deepest levels
of the psyche, of feeling and intuition, repressed guilt and
shame which, like the "dark ones" of the poem, is denied
at our own risk.

"Boundaries" returns to the problem of the relationship
between the mind and the world with a new confidence in
the ability of the imagination to "first distinguish, then
forget distinction; / record the many, then rejoin the all".
The imagination is able to see the "whole flow" in the
particular, despite the categories of mind (such as language) which insist upon limit, form and time. The imagination can not only *re*-create the totality from the constituent portion—"I've seen a hat / build under itself a person
long since dead"—but, given a stimulus, can create the
totality for itself:

That lock of wild bronze hair
that Byron cut from a girl's head
sprang under my touch alive with the whole girl.

The important thing here is that the power of the imagination is affirmed in the face of the limitations which language imposes upon it, and **"Boundaries"** is an answer to
that series of poems which deals with epistemological
breakdown resulting from the breakdown of language.

There are in this volume and in *Phantom Dwelling* a number of poems which appear on first sight to be simply
descriptive of nature, examples of that reverence for nature and concern for its uniqueness which the poet has
always advocated. These poems are, however, a new departure for, by imitative form and subtle modulations in
linguistic texture, the poet captures the visual, tactile and
even the kinetic quality of the subject. In this way Wright
avoids, as far as possible, the propensity of language and
symbolism to humanise nature. Instead she attempts, by
imitative form, to capture the individuality of the natural
form and so to preserve its autonomy. For instance the
long and flexible, broken yet springy rhythms of **"The
Eucalypt and the National Character"** effectively imitate the "sprawling and informal; / even dishevelled, disorderly" landscape:

Ready for any catastrophe, every extreme,
she leaves herself plenty of margin. Nothing is stiff,
symmetrical, indispensable. Everything bends
whip-supple, pivoting, loose . . .

In **"Case-moth"**, too, the texture of the language captures
the visual form, the movement and the life-quality of this
particular organism:

Homespun, homewoven pod,
case-moth wears a clever web.
Sloth-grey, slug-slow,
slung safe in a sad-coloured sack,
a twig-camouflaged bedsock,
shifts from leaf to next leaf;
lips life at a bag mouth.

"Swamp Plant" and **"Encounter"** are similarly impressive. At the same time these poems achieve Ponge's "invasion of qualities". **"Case-moth"**, for instance, conveys
the tenacity of life and the cautious subterfuges required
for survival, and suggests that such caution stunts the life
of the moth ("Inside, your wings wither") and, by extension to the human sphere, the life of the imagination. The
termite queen too is seen on a naturalistic level, yet becomes a superb indigenous symbol for the generative feminine principle, in this way tying the poem to the central
theme of the volume:

She is nursery, granary, industry,
army and agriculture.
Her swollen motionless tissues
rule every tentacle.

The predatory echidna symbolises the threat to the dark
generative world of nature and the unconscious by the
daylight forces of philistinism and rationalism. Here the
reservations expressed earlier about the symbolism of some
of the poems of *The Gateway* and later volumes are answered in full, for the indigenous creatures—whale, platypus, termite queen and echidna—are transmuted into resonant symbols, yet their own character is not betrayed.
The balance between inner and outer is exquisite, particularly in the case of the platypus; while the whale, the
water-inhabiting, air-breathing mammal, becomes a wholly appropriate symbol for the dissociated psyche. Throughout *Fourth Quarter* symbolism is a finely integrated structural feature, exemplified not only by the basic symbolic
dualisms which dominate the volume (darkness and light,
water and land, dream and waking), but by the symbolism
of individual poems. Wright's detachment, control and
surer touch are also demonstrated in the tighter structure
of these poems. Verse forms are more regular, and almost
imperceptible patterns of rhyme, half-rhyme and assonance
give a new sense of structure and tension to the poetry.
There is a new vigour too, born of the poet's greater sense
of assurance and control. This confidence is demonstrated
in a number of ways: there is a wide-ranging allusiveness,
a new use of wit and word-play, and an assured use of
colloquialisms, often with a double meaning. "Lover, we've
made, between us, / one hell of a world" (**"Eve Scolds"**),
for instance, is suitably chilling, both in the Edenic con-

text and the context of conservation; while "you may yet grin last" ("**Easter Moon and Owl**") suggests not only the visual form of the moon, but the durability of poetry and the imagination—"He who laughs last laughs longest".

Irony and humour are a feature of this volume, and a number of Wright's serious preoccupations are satirised. In "**At Cedar Creek**", for instance, she seeks a "formula" for poetry in a satiric "schema" which parodies her previous concern with culture, nature, primitivism and myth; the conscious and the unconscious:

> Complex ritual connections
> between Culture and Nature
> are demonstrated by linguistic studies.
> The myths of primitive people
> can reveal codes
> we may interpret . . .

> Religions suppress the decays of time
> and relate the Conscious
> to the Unconscious (collective).
> Metaphorical apprehensions
> of the relations of deities, men and animals
> can be set out in this schema.

"**Creation-Annihilation**" treats the previously sacred creative act with irreverent irony. Creation is no longer the linguistic feat of humanity, but the work of a jubilant and playful God who, with untidy gusto, scatters his "mudscraps and sparks of light" everywhere to the bewilderment of man:

> Motes from his hand's delight
> crowded earth, water, air,
> too small, it seemed, for care;
> too small for Adam's eye
> when all the names began.
> None of the words of man
> reached lower than the Fly.

The importance of Anthony van Leeuwenhoek in the context of this poem and this volume is not only that he discovered minute forms of life such as bacteria, previously un-named and so considered not to exist, but that he established the basic unity on the level of sexual generation of humans, fleas, weevils and other "scraps and huslement[s]" of the Creation—hence Man's insecurity; he is no longer "Favourite Child"! In its wit, sheer energy and virtuosity, this poem is quite different from anything previous to it. Versatility is displayed to a lesser extent in other poems of *Fourth Quarter* such as "Counting in Sevens" which has the surface simplicity of a child's counting rhyme, yet is a moving recapitulation of the poet's emotional life-story. Indeed the whole volume is characterised by vigour, assurance and a mastery of her medium; all of which stem from acceptance and a subsequent liberation from fear.

The publication of *Phantom Dwelling,* nine years after *Fourth Quarter,* is a striking testament to Wright's continuing vitality and poetic skill. The most obvious aspect of this volume is its energy and versatility, and it is not surprising that the dominant imagery is that of fire. At the same time its mood is relaxed, laconic and even playful. The feminine sensuality of the earlier poetry is still there, not only in the attraction to and love of nature, and in the sensuous images in which nature is celebrated, but also in the constant evocation of warmth, red wine and love—all of which have a positive affinity with fire.

Many of its themes are familiar: Wright's obsession with nature, love and language is as strong as ever, but modulated and strengthened by tolerance and detachment, the quality for which she prayed in the much earlier "**Request to a Year**". When love is mentioned, it is either in defiance of the autumnal season of the poems, or in delight at love's recurrence: "Blood slows, thickens, silts—yet when I saw you / once again, what a joy set this pulse jumping" ("**Pressures**"). Wright's obsession with nature is as strong as ever but here, more than in any preceding volume, she concedes the essential "otherness" of nature and the impossibility, as she puts it in "**Rainforest**", of entering the "dream", the world of the creatures. Wright has also come to terms with her family, the pastoral way of life, and her New England heritage. These are treated realistically yet compassionately in "**For a Pastoral Family**". Myth and language are still seen as related human constructs, the powerful and traditional symbolic forms through which humanity creates its visions of reality, and there is more attention to these than in either *Alive* or *Fourth Quarter*. Yet, at the same time, both myth and language are treated in a relaxed and often humorous manner. The local exponent of myth, the poet Christopher Brennan, is given especially tender treatment. The poem "**Brennan**" is not only an elegy for that incongruous and flawed figure, seen as a "black leaf blowing / in a wind of the wrong hemisphere", but also for the loss of all tradition in a world where "History's burning garbage / of myths searches / sends up its smoke-wreath / from the city dump".

In the poems of *Phantom Dwelling* there is a wide and eclectic reference, often to Eastern thought, myth and poetry, and the latter is envied for its brevity and clarity of its images. Where the influence of Eliot's diction and imagery was marked (and often damaging) in a number of the early poems, leading at times to stereotyped wasteland images and prosaic diction, the influence of Eastern poets, as well as the more familiar Wallace Stevens and Yeats, is obvious in this volume. One is reminded of Yeats in particular, not only by a number of direct references, but by the relaxation of tone and diction, and the obvious power and energy which spring in old age from the forgiveness of self and others.

In "**Brevity**", the first poem in "**Notes at Edge**" ("Edge" is Wright's home within the Mongarlowe Wildlife Reserve), Wright seeks a minimalist poetic—one of "honed brevities" and "inclusive silences", of "few words" and "no rhetoric", of the economy and elegance of the haiku. The poems which follow are the equivalent of botanical sketches; they capture with an almost scientific exactitude the appearance, form, shape and behaviour of an organism or a natural feature, subjected to the intent gaze of the solitary poet. She observes and records the hills in summer "where a eucalyptine vapour / dreams up in windless air"; the dead kangaroo-doe, a "slender skeleton / tumbled above the water with her long shanks / cleaned white as moonlight"; the caddis fly, a "small twilight helicopter", and the fox, that "rufous canterer". The poem **"Fox"** in particular is a triumph of aural as well as visual effects as it mimics the sound as well as tracing the path of the fox's escape: "running like a flame. / Against storm-black Budawang / a bushfire bristle of brush. / Under the candlebark trees / a rustle in dry litter." These spare, honed images have the greater impact because of the brevity of the poems; they are "enclosed by silence / as is the thrush's song" (**"Brevity"**).

The most striking innovation in the volume is the sequence **"The Shadow of Fire"**, twelve poems identified as ghazals which indicate the power and variability of Wright's poetic at this time. The extended flexible lines, the unrhymed couplets, the variable and even jaunty rhythm, are perfectly suited to both the sensuality which is characteristic of the ghazal, and the philosophical and metaphysical questioning which has always been a feature of Wright's work. Within these structures she is able to make a laconic comment such as "My generation is dying, after long lives / swung from war to depression to war to fatness" with the matter-of-fact detachment which suits the theme of this poem **"Rockpool"**. Individual couplets have the compression, the clarity and the brilliance of haiku, for instance the lines in **"Memory"** which suggest love in declining years:

> Now only two dragonflies dance on the narrowed
>   water.
> The river's noise in the stones is a sunken song.

Concluding couplets, with their assurance and sense of finality, encapsulate the concerns of the poem. The concluding couplet of **"Rockpool"**, for instance, sums up that conflict between nature and the individual which has been one of Wright's lifelong obsessions:

> the stretching of toothed claws to food, the breeding
> on the ocean's edge. 'Accept it? Gad, madam, you
>   had better.'

and, at the same time, dismiss it in a humorous and decisive way.

Though each poem can stand independently, the sequence read as a whole forms a meditation on life itself from the point of view of serene old age. The first ghazal **"Rockpool"** is concerned with the violence, the conflict, the "devouring and mating", which are the essence of physical life and which are to be observed most clearly in the microcosm of the pool:

> I watch the claws in the rockpool; the scuttle, the
>   crouch—
> green humps, the biggest barnacled, eaten by seaworms.

> In comes the biggest wave, the irresistible
> clean wash and backswirl. Where have the dead gone?

In the context of the relentless flux of nature, and the power and impersonality of the sea which is now the great cleanser as well as obliterator, the question "Where have the dead gone?" seems irrelevant. Wright's acceptance of violence and conflict is not, however, a passive or a flaccid thing; it comes from strength, from a perception of herself as a being of fire, a part of the conflict and energy of the universe ("who wants to be a mere onlooker? Every cell of me / has been pierced through by plunging intergalactic messages", **"Connections"**). There is the recognition that all life—physical, spiritual and emotional—is energy, and that the you and I of the ghazal **"Winter"** are part of it:

> The paths that energy takes on its way to exhaustion
> are not to be forecast. These pathways, you and me,

> followed unguessable routes. But all of us end
> at the same point, like the wood on the fire,

> the wine in the belly. Let's drink to that point—like
>   Hafiz.

The symbolism of the ghazals, that of fire, is appropriate in this context, and fire appears once again in all its volatility. It can be comfortable and domestic (the hearth, the radiator, the torch) or the "fireflies, glow-worms, fungal lights" which indicate the secret life of nature. But it can also be the fire of atomic explosion which signifies the human capacity for violence: "Brighter than a thousand suns'—that blinding glare / circled the world and settled in our bones." This progression is seen in the final ghazal, **"Patterns"**, a meditation upon human evil where Wright returns to the old Herakleitean notion of cosmic balance, of the reconciliation of opposing principles:

> All's fire, said Heraclitus; measures of it
> kindle as others fade. All changes yet all's one.

> We are born of ethereal fire and we return there.
> Understand the Logos; reconcile opposing
>   principles.

> Perhaps the dark itself is the source of meaning,
> the fires of the galaxy its visible destruction . . .

> Impossible to choose between absolutes, ultimates.
> Pure light, pure lightlessness cannot be perceived . . .

Still unable to come completely to terms with the evil symbolised by the strontium bomb—"Well, Greek, we have not found the road to virtue. / I shiver by the fire this winter day."—Wright is still prepared to assert that humanity is born of fire, of the energy and power of the cosmos, yet somehow inexplicably given to, "possessed by", darkness.

> We are all of us born of fire, possessed by
>   darkness.

The note of reconciliation and balance on which the ghazals, and the volume, conclude is also a feature of the earlier three sections—"New Zealand Poems," "Poems 1978-1980" and "Notes at Edge."

A number of the poems accept the impossibility of a complete identification with nature; of entering the consciousness of another form of life. This is the point of **"Rainforest"** from **"Poems 1978-1980,"** an elegant lyric, moving and simple in its diction, imagery and emotional appeal. The poem is concerned with the "otherness" of nature, the way in which nature resists the "dividing eyes" of the human, which "measure, distinguish and are gone", and yet fail to understand the ecological unity and harmony of the rainforest where "all is one and one is all".

The ghazal **"Summer"** is also concerned with the human inability to enter the consciousness of nature. Here the speaker contemplates the ruins of a mining settlement and seeks the "quality" of a place which was once human, which once "drank dark blood . . . heard cries ande running of feet". The essence of the place is not its brief human history, marked now by "a tumble of chimney-stones / shafts near the river", but the efforts of the earth to heal itself, to rid itself of the damage of alien occupation. The business of the earth and its creatures goes on unaware of the human dimension, and unknowable to the human mind:

> I'll never know its inhabitants. Evening torchlight
> catches the moonstone eyes of big wolf-spiders.
>
> All day the jenny-lizard dug hard ground
> watching for shadows of hawk or kookaburra.
>
> At evening, her pearl-eggs hidden, she raked back earth
> over the tunnel, wearing a wide grey smile.
>
> In a burned-out summer, I try to see without words
> as they do. But I live through a web of language.

"Connections", another of the ghazals, treats the inability of the human mind to share the consciousness of nature with an irreverence which is characteristic of this volume: "I can smell the whitebeard heath when it's under my nose, / and that should be enough for someone who isn't a moth."

Despite this recognition of the "otherness" of nature, or perhaps because of it, the poems of this volume celebrate the earth with love; indeed no previous volume has been so concerned with nature for its own diversity, power and beauty, rather than in relation to humanity, or as a personal threat to the individual. The power of nature is now fearlessly acknowledged, in images which glory in its contending forces:

> Deep down, the world-plates struggle
> in strangling quiet on each other.
> Offshore, deliberate breakers hit the coasts.
> **"From the Wellington Museum"**

The progression of the seasons is likewise no longer seen as a mythic analogue for the human condition, but is celebrated for its own beauty and power. Detachment brings a cosmic rather than a human perspective, and in **"Backyard"** autumn is celebrated in an original, startling and completely appropriate image:

> Autumn swings earth round sun
> at the invisible lasso's end,
> turning this latitude south and winterward.

From an ant's eye view, as it were, Wright moves into closer focus to observe, with detached interest, the carrying out of earth's "ancient orders", as the Autumn season enacts the "shorthand" encoded in the seasonal change:

> In last alchemic leaves held to the light,
> in soundless bursts of seed,
> in the tough satin of the spider's case
> and the foam-plastic comb the mantis lays,
> in branched green-copper-scaly spires of dock
> the season's shorthand coils its final code;
> This treeless trampled scrap of earth
> fibrous with rot and weed
> repeats its ancient orders. Use all death
> to feed all life. The lockup of the frost
> will melt, the codes translate with nothing lost.

There is complete assurance here, the assurance of the achieved vision which no longer fears the "ancient orders" of the earth, orders which are to "Use all death / to feed all life".

The compressed accuracy and appeal of the natural images in **"Notes at Edge"** is also a feature of the sequence **"Four Poems from New Zealand,"** which captures the New Zealand landscape with unerring accuracy: a countryside of "Gorse, bracken, blackberries" which "scab over wounded ground"; of sheep which "eat, eat, eat and trot dementedly"; and of the beach at Hokitika:

> A narrow shelf below the southern alps,
> a slate-grey beach scattered with drifted wood
> darkens the sullen jade
> of Tasman's breakers. Blackbacked gulls
> hunt the green turn of waves.

The sequence also captures another reality; that of a colonised nation whose history in many ways parallels that of Australia; the nation, like Wellington, is "built on a fault-line". Images of colonisation are everywhere: in the place-names, the country rituals, the Anglicised tea-shops, and the attitudes, for instance the negal-granite stance" of a "grizzled man, scotch-eyed, grey-overcoated". Despite the poem's acknowledgement of political realities, these images are presented without rancour. But behind the comfortable images of European settlement Wright perceives another reality, the dark spirit of the forest and the alien landscape of New Zealand—"a swoop of mountains, scope of snow / northward and southward. Jags, saw-teeth, blades of light / nobody could inhabit"—and this reality is Maori.

The empathy of the Maori with the land is captured in Wright's image of the Maori genealogies in the Wellington museum:

> Vine-spiralling Maori genealogies,
> carved paths through forests
> inscribed with life-forms, coded histories
> tangled my eyes
> never quite able to meet that paua-stare.

The genealogies, the natural history and the traditions of the Maori are "coded", their essential meaning unavailable to the white observer who is "never quite able to meet that paua-stare". Wright is closest to Maori reality on the deserted beach at Hokitika where she contemplates the solitary figure of a Maori girl: "But for her smile, the beach is bare." The sequence concludes with an image of reconciliation, of the recognition and celebration of all struggle, of "being, itself. Being that's ground by glaciers, seas and time".

Three poems from **"Poems 1978-1980"**—**"Smalltown Dance"**, **"For a Pastoral Family"** and **"Words, Roses, Stars"**—return to familiar themes and demonstrate Wright's continuing skill and versatility. The first of these is an elegant and accomplished poem which explores, as did a number of earlier poems, the metaphysical implications of humble domestic activity. The poem is concerned with the way in which the feminine spirit is enthralled, in bondage to an all too easy and often attractive domesticity. The smalltown dance of the title is that of women folding the sheets in an ancient ritual, and the poem begins with a particularly impressive image, that of the finding of the square-root of the sheet, the pulling on its diagonal to straighten the warp:

> Two women find the square-root of a sheet.
> This is an ancient dance:
> arms wide: together: again: two forward steps:
>   hands meet
> your partner's once and twice.

The mathematical connotations of this image are appropriate to the programmed, ritualised dance of the women. As well, the pulling into shape *against* the warp could be symbolically significant not only for the sheets, but also for the women. The world enclosed by the sheets on washday is a world which is a loving and comforting one for the child: "Simpler than arms, they wrapped and comforted / clean corridors of hiding, roofed with blue." However, although the child has a sense of unlimited possibility symbolised by "that glimpse of unobstructed waiting green", the poem is full of images of female suppression. The image of the clean sheets, those "wallowing white dreamers" of the washday world, can also apply to the feminine psyche: "The sheets that tug / sometimes struggle from the peg, / don't travel far" and dreams must be surrendered to the constriction of the domestic cupboard:

> First pull those wallowing white dreamers down,
> spread arms: then close them. Fold
> those beckoning roads to some impossible world . . .

That white expanse
reduces to a neat
compression fitting in the smallest space
a sheet can pack in on a cupboard shelf.

What is noticeable about the poem is the humorous and relaxed tone; the sustained imagery by which the humble washday provides a symbolic reference for female destiny; the return to imagery of the dance, the pattern of life itself; and the evocation, once again, of the paradisal world of the child in contrast to the ritualised repression of the adult world.

> **What is obvious is the energy with which Wright continues to express her timeless obsessions with nature, love and language. It is as if old age had produced an alchemic change, ridding the poetry of the baser elements, the fear, defensiveness and the dwelling upon philosophical qualifications which inhibited many of the poems of her middle years.**
>
> **—Shirley Walker**

In the sequence **"For a Pastoral Family"** Wright returns to and revalues her New England heritage. With old age and the dropping of all pretence there is no longer a need to distance the pastoral world by romantic nostalgia as in **"South of my Days"**, by castigation as in **"Eroded Hills"**, or by mythologising as in **"Falls Country"**. These earlier poems, fine in themselves, mark stages through which the poet has passed on her way to a human acceptance of all aspects of her heritage. This involves a direct confrontation with the issues of corruption, of self-interest, guilt and evasion on which the pastoral conquest was based and then sustained. The tone varies from ironic, to patronising, to sarcastic as the sequence satirises first of all an "arrogant clan" who were "fairly kind to horses / and to people not too different from ourselves", then the rationalisations of the past, in particular those concerning the massacre and dispersal of the Aborigines: "after all / the previous owners put up little fight, / did not believe in ownership, and so were scarcely human." Her own generation was protected by a "comforting cover of legality" for:

> the really deplorable deeds
> had happened out of our sight, allowing us innocence.
> We were not born, or there was silence kept.

At the same time, despite this clear-sighted satire, the paradisal beauty of the pastoral life, the seasons, and the child's world is recognised. Nostalgia breaks through in **"Kinship"**, which dwells lovingly upon memories of a sheltered childhood, the shared life of the children, Wright's two younger brothers and herself, now "two old men, one older woman", and the ties which persist between them, despite political and other differences:

> Blue early mist in the valley. Apricots
> bowing the orchard trees, flushed red with summer,
> loading bronze-plaqued branches;
> our teeth in those sweet buttock-curves. Remember
> the horses swinging to the yards, the smell
> of cattle, sweat and saddle-leather?
> Blue ranges underlined the sky. In any weather
> it was well, being young and simple,
> letting the horses canter home together.

"Smalltown Dance" and **"Kinship"** are the latest, but perhaps not the final poems, in a series which deals with the paradisal world of the child and contrasts it with the corrupt world of the adult. **"Change"** uses the imagery of the mountain stream (from Yeats) to express the inevitability of corruption: "streams go / through settlement and town / darkened by chemical silt. / Dams hold and slow them down, / trade thickens them like guilt. / All men grow evil with trade / as all roads lead to the city." At the same time, in a gesture of balance and reconciliation which is characteristic of this volume, Wright recognises that the alternative, remaining in the cold purity of the hills, must result in ignorance.

The third of these poems is **"Words, Roses, Stars"**, dedicated to the poet John Bechervaise, and perhaps the most assured of all that series of poems, from the fifties onward, in which Wright deals with the relationship between the world, the human mind and language. **"Words, Roses, Stars"** skilfully accommodates its philosophical complexity, and the subtle progression of its thought, within the lyric form. The address is direct, to "my friend" Bechervaise and to all of us, to "you, and you", who are under instruction as to the simplicity and absolute rightness of philosophical concepts which were once handled in a ponderous and problematic way. The rose itself is a "swirl of atoms", an image which captures the shape and movement and physical composition of the bloom. But the rose is also a human construct, for it is "bodied in a word. / And words are human":

> A rose, my friend, a rose—
> and what's a rose?
> A swirl of atoms bodied in a word.
> And words are human; language comes and goes
> with us, and lives among us. Not absurd
> to think the human spans the Milky Way.

The second stanza recognises the beauty, the appeal and the validity of all three ways of looking at nature, through myth, through science, and through the language in which both myth and science are expressed. Myth is the "gift of life, the endless dream" and science is a visionary search for a "mathematical glory in the sky":

> Baiame bends beside his crystal stream
> shaded beneath his darker cypress-tree
> and gives the gift of life, the endless dream,
> to Koori people, and to you and me.

> Astronomers and physicists compute
> a mathematical glory in the sky.
> But all these calculations, let's admit,
> are filtered through a human brain and eye.

The knowledge that "words are human" is no longer a threat as it was in the earlier **"The Lake"** or **"Nameless Flower"**, for "sight and touch and scent / join in that symbol" and "the word is true, / plucked by a path where human vision went". This is a significant reassertion of the power of vision. While there is a constant recognition in this volume that humans cannot "see without words" (**"Summer"**) and that all vision is "filtered through a human brain and eye" the earlier defensiveness and fear is gone.

Reconciliation and balance are key concepts in these last poems and are expressed in finely balanced images which contain and reconcile opposing states such as old age and love:

> fallen leaves on the current scarcely move
> But the kingfisher flashes upriver still.
>
> **"Dust"**

There are also overt statements of reconciliation like that which concludes *Phantom Dwelling*—"We are all of us born of fire, possessed by darkness"—perhaps the best example with which to conclude this study. There is, however, no real conclusion, for there is as yet no conclusion to Wright's work. What is obvious is the energy with which she continues to express her timeless obsessions with nature, love and language. It is as if old age had produced an alchemic change, ridding the poetry of the baser elements, the fear, defensiveness and the dwelling upon philosophical qualifications which inhibited many of the poems of her middle years. Her declaration, in the ghazal **"Oppositions"**—"I choose fire, not snow"—is more than justified.

FURTHER READING

Bibliography

Walker, Shirley. *Judith Wright.* Melbourne: Oxford University Press, 1981.
> Primary and secondary bibliography extensively covering the years 1925 through 1979, and partially covering 1980. Critical material is subdivided into the following categories: books and theses, general articles, lectures and verse; shorter references; brief notes; and specific review.

Biography

Smith, Graeme Kinross. "Judith Wright 1915-." In *Australia's Writers,* pp. 289-96. Melbourne: Thomas Nelson Australia, 1980.

Biographical consideration of Wright's poems and politics.

Criticism

Bennett, Bruce. "Judith Wright, Moralist." *Westerly,* No. 1 (March 1976): 76-82.
  Examines both Wright's poetry and prose to expose the "unifying principle of love . . . as the basis of a constructive and life-enhancing moral outlook."

————. "Judith Wright: An Ecological Vision." In *International Literature in English: Essays on Major Writers,* edited by Robert L. Ross, pp. 205-21. New York: Garland Publishing, 1991.
  Traces the recurring themes of conservation and ecological responsibility through the entire body of Wright's work.

Brennan, G. A. "The Aborigine in the Works of Judith Wright." Westerly, No. 4 (December 1972): 46-50.
  Considers the attitudes Wright expresses in her writings toward Australia's Aborigines and white European settlers. Brennan concludes that those of Wright's poems that focus on the tragic events of the past do so not with a tone of condemnation toward the pioneers, but with a sincere lament for the passing of the Aboriginal culture.

Buckley, Vincent. "The Poetry of Judith Wright." In *Essays in Poetry: Mainly Australian,* pp. 158-76. Melbourne: Melbourne University Press, 1957.
  Echoes the widely held perception that Wright's *The Gateway,* is an inferior follow-up to her first two collections of poetry, placing at least some of the blame on the overzealous acclaim given to those earlier volumes; nonetheless, Buckley argues that her place in literature is secure.

Dowling, David. "Judith Wright's Delicate Balance." *Australian Literary Studies* 9, No. 4 (October 1980): 488-96.
  Outlines the constant concern with duality and reconciliation of "the basic dichotomies of human existence" that dominates most of Wright's poetry.

Heseltine, H. P. "Wrestling with the Angel: Judith Wright's Poetry in the 1950s." *Southerly: A Review of Australian Literature* 38, No. 2 (June 1978): 163-71.
  Highlights the use of Old Testament imagery in Wright's earlier poems.

Higham Charles. "Judith Wright's Vision." *Quadrant* V, No. 2 (Autumn 1961): 33-41.
  Strives for a fresh look at Wright's first four collections of poetry, asserting as many others do, that Wright's talent is made most evident in her first two collections.

Hope, A. D. *Judith Wright.* Melbourne: Oxford University Press, 1975.
  Overview of Wright's career.

Kramer, Leonie. "Judith Wright, Hope, McAuley." *The Literary Criterion* XV, Nos. 3-4 (1980): 83-92.

Attempts to place Wright, Hope, and McAuley within a modernist framework, while contrasting Wright's lack of "interior conflict" with the despair and "radical disquiet" of the other two poets.

McAuley, James. "Judith Wright." In *A Map of Australian Verse: The Twentieth Century,* pp. 160-77. Melbourne: Oxford University Press, 1975.
  Includes an introduction by McAuley, as well as excerpted commentary from other critics, and several of Wright's poems printed in full.

Mares, F. H. "Judith Wright and Australian Poetry." *Durham University Journal* 19, No. 2 (March 1958): 76-84.
  Compares Wright's use of her Australian background to Dylan Thomas's synthesis of his Welsh experiences.

Moore, T. Inglis. "The Quest of Judith Wright." *Meanjin* 17, No. 3 (Spring 1958): 237-50.
  Analysis of Wright's third book of poems. Moore asserts that the poet's desertion of metaphysical themes for social and personal ones is accompanied by a use of allegories in place of symbols she had earlier utilized.

Scott, W. N. *Focus on Judith Wright.* St. Lucia, Queensland, Australia: University of Queensland Press, 1967.
  Chronicles Wright's life and works through the mid-1960s.

Strauss, Jennifer. "Modulations of High Seriousness: The Later Poetry of Judith Wright." In *STOP LAUGHING! I'M BEING SERIOUS: Three Studies in Seriousness and Wit in Contemporary Australian Poetry,* pp. 1-29. North Queensland, Australia: James Cook University Foundation for Australian Literary Studies, 1990.
  An examination, in particular, of the tone of Wright's poetry.

Sturm, Terry. "Continuity and Development in the Work of Judith Wright." *Southerly: A Review of Australian Literature* 36, No. 2 (June 1976).
  Places Wright's work within the Romantic tradition of the "visionary poetry [of] Blake, Shelley and Yeats."

Tatum, Stephen. "Tradition of the Exile: Judith Wright's Australian 'West.'" In *Women, Women Writers, and the West,* edited by L. L. Lee and Merr Lewis, pp. 233-44. Troy, N.Y.: The Whitston Publishing Company, 1979.
  Contrasts the use of frontier imagery in Wright's poems with non-Australian literary frontier images, particularly of the American West.

Walker, Shirley. "Judith Wright's Linguistic Philosophy—'It's the word that's strange'." *Australian Literary Studies* 8, No. 1 (May 1977): 7-15.
  Explores Wright's use of language, primarily as a symbolic tool to "fuse factual experience and its emotional significance."

Wright, Dorena. "Judith Wright *Brother and Sisters, Old Man, Two Old Men.*" In *Australian Poems in Perspective: A Collection of Poems and Critical Commentaries,* edited by

P. K. Elkin, pp. 141-59. St. Lucia, Queensland, Australia:
University of Queensland Press, 1978.
    Analysis of three of Wright's character poems.

Wright, Judith. "A Statement at Writers' Week." *Overland,*
No. 89 (October 1982): 29-31.
    Assesses the role of the writer as spokesperson for
political and social causes.

Zwicky, Fay. "Another Side of Paradise: A. D. Hope and
Judith Wright." *Southerly* 48, No. 1 (March 1988): 3-21.
    Compares two of Australia's most popular native poets,
centering specifically on their treatments of Eden as
metaphor and attributing their different viewpoints and
styles primarily to their difference in gender.

Interview

Wright, Judith, and Davidson, Jim. An interview. *Meanjin*
41, No. 3 (September 1982): 321-38.
    Discusses the particular aspects of Australian experience
that have influenced her writing, including the verse of
early Australian poets, issues surrounding the Aborigine's
place in modern Australia, and the white's historical
and current impact on Australia's historical and social
landscape. Additionally, Wright touches on the particular
problems she faces as a poet in contemporary Australia.

**Additional coverage of Wright's life and career is contained in the following sources
published by Gale Research:** *Contemporary Authors,* **13-16 (rev. ed.);** *Contemporary Authors
New Revision Series,* **Vol. 31;** *Contemporary Literary Criticism,* **Vols. 11, 53;** *Major 20th-
Century Writers;* **and** *Something about the Author,* **Vol. 14.**

Poetry Criticism
INDEXES

Literary Criticism Series
Cumulative Author Index

Cumulative Nationality Index

Cumulative Title Index

How to Use This Index

The main references

Calvino, Italo
1923-1985.....CLC 5, 8, 11, 22, 33, 39,
73; SSC 3

---

list all author entries in the following Gale Literary Criticism series:

BLC = *Black Literature Criticism*
CLC = *Contemporary Literary Criticism*
CLR = *Children's Literature Review*
CMLC = *Classical and Medieval Literature Criticism*
DA = *DISCovering Authors*
DC = *Drama Criticism*
HLC = *Hispanic Literature Criticism*
LC = *Literature Criticism from 1400 to 1800*
NCLC = *Nineteenth-Century Literature Criticism*
PC = *Poetry Criticism*
SSC = *Short Story Criticism*
TCLC = *Twentieth-Century Literary Criticism*
WLC = *World Literature Criticism, 1500 to the Present*

The cross-references

See also CANR 23; CA 85-88;
obituary CA 116

---

list all author entries in the following Gale biographical and literary sources:

AAYA = *Authors & Artists for Young Adults*
AITN = *Authors in the News*
BEST = *Bestsellers*
BW = *Black Writers*
CA = *Contemporary Authors*
CAAS = *Contemporary Authors Autobiography Series*
CABS = *Contemporary Authors Bibliographical Series*
CANR = *Contemporary Authors New Revision Series*
CAP = *Contemporary Authors Permanent Series*
CDALB = *Concise Dictionary of American Literary Biography*
CDBLB = *Concise Dictionary of British Literary Biography*
DLB = *Dictionary of Literary Biography*
DLBD = *Dictionary of Literary Biography Documentary Series*
DLBY = *Dictionary of Literary Biography Yearbook*
HW = *Hispanic Writers*
JRDA = *Junior DISCovering Authors*
MAICYA = *Major Authors and Illustrators for Children and Young Adults*
MTCW = *Major 20th-Century Writers*
NNAL = *Native North American Literature*
SAAS = *Something about the Author Autobiography Series*
SATA = *Something about the Author*
YABC = *Yesterday's Authors of Books for Children*

Literary Criticism Series
Cumulative Author Index

Alcott, Amos Bronson 1799-1888 .. **NCLC 1**
See also DLB 1

Alcott, Louisa May
1832-1888 .... **NCLC 6; DA; DAB;
DAC; WLC**
See also CDALB 1865-1917; CLR 1, 38;
DAM MST, NOV; DLB 1, 42, 79; JRDA;
MAICYA; YABC 1

Aldanov, M. A.
See Aldanov, Mark (Alexandrovich)

Aldanov, Mark (Alexandrovich)
1886(?)-1957 .... **TCLC 23**
See also CA 118

Aldington, Richard 1892-1962...... **CLC 49**
See also CA 85-88; CANR 45; DLB 20, 36,
100, 149

Aldiss, Brian W(ilson)
1925- .... **CLC 5, 14, 40**
See also CA 5-8R; CAAS 2; CANR 5, 28;
DAM NOV; DLB 14; MTCW; SATA 34

Alegria, Claribel 1924-............ **CLC 75**
See also CA 131; CAAS 15; DAM MULT;
DLB 145; HW

Alegria, Fernando 1918-........... **CLC 57**
See also CA 9-12R; CANR 5, 32; HW

Aleichem, Sholom .... **TCLC 1, 35**
See also Rabinovitch, Sholem

Aleixandre, Vicente 1898-1984 ... **CLC 9, 36**
See also CA 85-88; 114; CANR 26;
DAM POET; DLB 108; HW; MTCW

Alepoudelis, Odysseus
See Elytis, Odysseus

Aleshkovsky, Joseph 1929-
See Aleshkovsky, Yuz
See also CA 121; 128

Aleshkovsky, Yuz .... **CLC 44**
See also Aleshkovsky, Joseph

Alexander, Lloyd (Chudley) 1924- .. **CLC 35**
See also AAYA 1; CA 1-4R; CANR 1, 24,
38; CLR 1, 5; DLB 52; JRDA; MAICYA;
MTCW; SAAS 19; SATA 3, 49, 81

Alfau, Felipe 1902-............... **CLC 66**
See also CA 137

Alger, Horatio, Jr. 1832-1899 ..... **NCLC 8**
See also DLB 42; SATA 16

Algren, Nelson 1909-1981 .... **CLC 4, 10, 33**
See also CA 13-16R; 103; CANR 20;
CDALB 1941-1968; DLB 9; DLBY 81,
82; MTCW

Ali, Ahmed 1910- .... **CLC 69**
See also CA 25-28R; CANR 15, 34

Alighieri, Dante 1265-1321 .... **CMLC 3**

Allan, John B.
See Westlake, Donald E(dwin)

Allen, Edward 1948-.............. **CLC 59**

Allen, Paula Gunn 1939- .... **CLC 84**
See also CA 112; 143; DAM MULT;
NNAL

Allen, Roland
See Ayckbourn, Alan

Allen, Sarah A.
See Hopkins, Pauline Elizabeth

Allen, Woody 1935-........... **CLC 16, 52**
See also AAYA 10; CA 33-36R; CANR 27,
38; DAM POP; DLB 44; MTCW

Allende, Isabel 1942-.... **CLC 39, 57; HLC**
See also CA 125; 130; DAM MULT, NOV;
DLB 145; HW; INT 130; MTCW

Alleyn, Ellen
See Rossetti, Christina (Georgina)

Allingham, Margery (Louise)
1904-1966 .... **CLC 19**
See also CA 5-8R; 25-28R; CANR 4;
DLB 77; MTCW

Allingham, William 1824-1889 ... **NCLC 25**
See also DLB 35

Allison, Dorothy E. 1949- .... **CLC 78**
See also CA 140

Allston, Washington 1779-1843.... **NCLC 2**
See also DLB 1

Almedingen, E. M. .... **CLC 12**
See also Almedingen, Martha Edith von
See also SATA 3

Almedingen, Martha Edith von 1898-1971
See Almedingen, E. M.
See also CA 1-4R; CANR 1

Almqvist, Carl Jonas Love
1793-1866 .... **NCLC 42**

Alonso, Damaso 1898-1990 .... **CLC 14**
See also CA 110; 131; 130; DLB 108; HW

Alov
See Gogol, Nikolai (Vasilyevich)

Alta 1942-...................... **CLC 19**
See also CA 57-60

Alter, Robert B(ernard) 1935-...... **CLC 34**
See also CA 49-52; CANR 1, 47

Alther, Lisa 1944-.............. **CLC 7, 41**
See also CA 65-68; CANR 12, 30; MTCW

Altman, Robert 1925-............. **CLC 16**
See also CA 73-76; CANR 43

Alvarez, A(lfred) 1929-.......... **CLC 5, 13**
See also CA 1-4R; CANR 3, 33; DLB 14,
40

Alvarez, Alejandro Rodriguez 1903-1965
See Casona, Alejandro
See also CA 131; 93-96; HW

Alvaro, Corrado 1896-1956 ...... **TCLC 60**

Amado, Jorge 1912-..... **CLC 13, 40; HLC**
See also CA 77-80; CANR 35;
DAM MULT, NOV; DLB 113; MTCW

Ambler, Eric 1909-............. **CLC 4, 6, 9**
See also CA 9-12R; CANR 7, 38; DLB 77;
MTCW

Amichai, Yehuda 1924- ...... **CLC 9, 22, 57**
See also CA 85-88; CANR 46; MTCW

Amiel, Henri Frederic 1821-1881 .. **NCLC 4**

Amis, Kingsley (William)
1922- ...... **CLC 1, 2, 3, 5, 8, 13, 40, 44;
DA; DAB; DAC**
See also AITN 2; CA 9-12R; CANR 8, 28;
CDBLB 1945-1960; DAM MST, NOV;
DLB 15, 27, 100, 139; INT CANR-8;
MTCW

Amis, Martin (Louis)
1949- .... **CLC 4, 9, 38, 62**
See also BEST 90:3; CA 65-68; CANR 8,
27; DLB 14; INT CANR-27

Ammons, A(rchie) R(andolph)
1926- .... **CLC 2, 3, 5, 8, 9, 25, 57**
See also AITN 1; CA 9-12R; CANR 6, 36;
DAM POET; DLB 5; MTCW

Amo, Tauraatua i
See Adams, Henry (Brooks)

Anand, Mulk Raj 1905-........... **CLC 23**
See also CA 65-68; CANR 32; DAM NOV;
MTCW

Anatol
See Schnitzler, Arthur

Anaya, Rudolfo A(lfonso)
1937- .... **CLC 23; HLC**
See also CA 45-48; CAAS 4; CANR 1, 32;
DAM MULT, NOV; DLB 82; HW 1;
MTCW

Andersen, Hans Christian
1805-1875 .... **NCLC 7; DA; DAB;
DAC; SSC 6; WLC**
See also CLR 6; DAM MST, POP;
MAICYA; YABC 1

Anderson, C. Farley
See Mencken, H(enry) L(ouis); Nathan,
George Jean

Anderson, Jessica (Margaret) Queale
.... **CLC 37**
See also CA 9-12R; CANR 4

Anderson, Jon (Victor) 1940- .... **CLC 9**
See also CA 25-28R; CANR 20;
DAM POET

Anderson, Lindsay (Gordon)
1923-1994 .... **CLC 20**
See also CA 125; 128; 146

Anderson, Maxwell 1888-1959 ..... **TCLC 2**
See also CA 105; DAM DRAM; DLB 7

Anderson, Poul (William) 1926- .... **CLC 15**
See also AAYA 5; CA 1-4R; CAAS 2;
CANR 2, 15, 34; DLB 8; INT CANR-15;
MTCW; SATA-Brief 39

Anderson, Robert (Woodruff)
1917- .... **CLC 23**
See also AITN 1; CA 21-24R; CANR 32;
DAM DRAM; DLB 7

Anderson, Sherwood
1876-1941 .... **TCLC 1, 10, 24; DA;
DAB; DAC; SSC 1; WLC**
See also CA 104; 121; CDALB 1917-1929;
DAM MST, NOV; DLB 4, 9, 86;
DLBD 1; MTCW

Andouard
See Giraudoux, (Hippolyte) Jean

Andrade, Carlos Drummond de ...... **CLC 18**
See also Drummond de Andrade, Carlos

Andrade, Mario de 1893-1945..... **TCLC 43**

Andreae, Johann V. 1586-1654 ...... **LC 32**

Andreas-Salome, Lou 1861-1937... **TCLC 56**
See also DLB 66

Andrewes, Lancelot 1555-1626 .... **LC 5**
See also DLB 151

Andrews, Cicily Fairfield
See West, Rebecca

Andrews, Elton V.
See Pohl, Frederik

Andreyev, Leonid (Nikolaevich)
1871-1919 .... TCLC 3
See also CA 104

Andric, Ivo 1892-1975 .... CLC 8
See also CA 81-84; 57-60; CANR 43;
DLB 147; MTCW

Angelique, Pierre
See Bataille, Georges

Angell, Roger 1920- .... CLC 26
See also CA 57-60; CANR 13, 44

Angelou, Maya
1928- .... CLC 12, 35, 64, 77; BLC; DA;
DAB; DAC
See also AAYA 7; BW 2; CA 65-68;
CANR 19, 42; DAM MST, MULT,
POET, POP; DLB 38; MTCW; SATA 49

Annensky, Innokenty Fyodorovich
1856-1909 .... TCLC 14
See also CA 110

Anon, Charles Robert
See Pessoa, Fernando (Antonio Nogueira)

Anouilh, Jean (Marie Lucien Pierre)
1910-1987 ..... CLC 1, 3, 8, 13, 40, 50
See also CA 17-20R; 123; CANR 32;
DAM DRAM; MTCW

Anthony, Florence
See Ai

Anthony, John
See Ciardi, John (Anthony)

Anthony, Peter
See Shaffer, Anthony (Joshua); Shaffer,
Peter (Levin)

Anthony, Piers 1934- .... CLC 35
See also AAYA 11; CA 21-24R; CANR 28;
DAM POP; DLB 8; MTCW; SATA 84

Antoine, Marc
See Proust, (Valentin-Louis-George-Eugene-)
Marcel

Antoninus, Brother
See Everson, William (Oliver)

Antonioni, Michelangelo 1912- ..... CLC 20
See also CA 73-76; CANR 45

Antschel, Paul 1920-1970
See Celan, Paul
See also CA 85-88; CANR 33; MTCW

Anwar, Chairil 1922-1949 .... TCLC 22
See also CA 121

Apollinaire, Guillaume .. TCLC 3, 8, 51; PC 7
See also Kostrowitzki, Wilhelm Apollinaris
de
See also DAM POET

Appelfeld, Aharon 1932- .... CLC 23, 47
See also CA 112; 133

Apple, Max (Isaac) 1941- .... CLC 9, 33
See also CA 81-84; CANR 19; DLB 130

Appleman, Philip (Dean) 1926- ..... CLC 51
See also CA 13-16R; CAAS 18; CANR 6,
29

Appleton, Lawrence
See Lovecraft, H(oward) P(hillips)

Apteryx
See Eliot, T(homas) S(tearns)

Apuleius, (Lucius Madaurensis)
125(?)-175(?) .... CMLC 1

Aquin, Hubert 1929-1977 .... CLC 15
See also CA 105; DLB 53

Aragon, Louis 1897-1982 .... CLC 3, 22
See also CA 69-72; 108; CANR 28;
DAM NOV, POET; DLB 72; MTCW

Arany, Janos 1817-1882 .... NCLC 34

Arbuthnot, John 1667-1735 .... LC 1
See also DLB 101

Archer, Herbert Winslow
See Mencken, H(enry) L(ouis)

Archer, Jeffrey (Howard) 1940- .... CLC 28
See also AAYA 16; BEST 89:3; CA 77-80;
CANR 22; DAM POP; INT CANR-22

Archer, Jules 1915- .... CLC 12
See also CA 9-12R; CANR 6; SAAS 5;
SATA 4, 85

Archer, Lee
See Ellison, Harlan (Jay)

Arden, John 1930- .... CLC 6, 13, 15
See also CA 13-16R; CAAS 4; CANR 31;
DAM DRAM; DLB 13; MTCW

Arenas, Reinaldo
1943-1990 .... CLC 41; HLC
See also CA 124; 128; 133; DAM MULT;
DLB 145; HW

Arendt, Hannah 1906-1975 .... CLC 66
See also CA 17-20R; 61-64; CANR 26;
MTCW

Aretino, Pietro 1492-1556 .... LC 12

Arghezi, Tudor .... CLC 80
See also Theodorescu, Ion N.

Arguedas, Jose Maria
1911-1969 .... CLC 10, 18
See also CA 89-92; DLB 113; HW

Argueta, Manlio 1936- .... CLC 31
See also CA 131; DLB 145; HW

Ariosto, Ludovico 1474-1533 .... LC 6

Aristides
See Epstein, Joseph

Aristophanes
450B.C.-385B.C. .... CMLC 4; DA;
DAB; DAC; DC 2
See also DAM DRAM, MST

Arlt, Roberto (Godofredo Christophersen)
1900-1942 .... TCLC 29; HLC
See also CA 123; 131; DAM MULT; HW

Armah, Ayi Kwei 1939- .... CLC 5, 33; BLC
See also BW 1; CA 61-64; CANR 21;
DAM MULT, POET; DLB 117; MTCW

Armatrading, Joan 1950- .... CLC 17
See also CA 114

Arnette, Robert
See Silverberg, Robert

**Arnim, Achim von (Ludwig Joachim von
Arnim)** 1781-1831 .... NCLC 5
See also DLB 90

Arnim, Bettina von 1785-1859 .... NCLC 38
See also DLB 90

Arnold, Matthew
1822-1888 ..... NCLC 6, 29; DA; DAB;
DAC; PC 5; WLC
See also CDBLB 1832-1890; DAM MST,
POET; DLB 32, 57

Arnold, Thomas 1795-1842 ...... NCLC 18
See also DLB 55

Arnow, Harriette (Louisa) Simpson
1908-1986 .... CLC 2, 7, 18
See also CA 9-12R; 118; CANR 14; DLB 6;
MTCW; SATA 42; SATA-Obit 47

Arp, Hans
See Arp, Jean

Arp, Jean 1887-1966. .... CLC 5
See also CA 81-84; 25-28R; CANR 42

Arrabal
See Arrabal, Fernando

Arrabal, Fernando 1932- ... CLC 2, 9, 18, 58
See also CA 9-12R; CANR 15

Arrick, Fran .... CLC 30
See also Gaberman, Judie Angell

Artaud, Antonin (Marie Joseph)
1896-1948 .... TCLC 3, 36
See also CA 104; 149; DAM DRAM

Arthur, Ruth M(abel) 1905-1979 .... CLC 12
See also CA 9-12R; 85-88; CANR 4;
SATA 7, 26

Artsybashev, Mikhail (Petrovich)
1878-1927 .... TCLC 31

Arundel, Honor (Morfydd)
1919-1973 .... CLC 17
See also CA 21-22; 41-44R; CAP 2;
CLR 35; SATA 4; SATA-Obit 24

Asch, Sholem 1880-1957 .... TCLC 3
See also CA 105

Ash, Shalom
See Asch, Sholem

Ashbery, John (Lawrence)
1927- ...... CLC 2, 3, 4, 6, 9, 13, 15, 25,
41, 77
See also CA 5-8R; CANR 9, 37;
DAM POET; DLB 5; DLBY 81;
INT CANR-9; MTCW

Ashdown, Clifford
See Freeman, R(ichard) Austin

Ashe, Gordon
See Creasey, John

Ashton-Warner, Sylvia (Constance)
1908-1984 .... CLC 19
See also CA 69-72; 112; CANR 29; MTCW

Asimov, Isaac
1920-1992 ...... CLC 1, 3, 9, 19, 26, 76
See also AAYA 13; BEST 90:2; CA 1-4R;
137; CANR 2, 19, 36; CLR 12;
DAM POP; DLB 8; DLBY 92;
INT CANR-19; JRDA; MAICYA;
MTCW; SATA 1, 26, 74

Astley, Thea (Beatrice May)
1925- .... CLC 41
See also CA 65-68; CANR 11, 43

Aston, James
See White, T(erence) H(anbury)

Bamdad, A.
See Shamlu, Ahmad

Banat, D. R.
See Bradbury, Ray (Douglas)

Bancroft, Laura
See Baum, L(yman) Frank

Banim, John　1798-1842 . . . .　**NCLC 13**
See also DLB 116, 158, 159

Banim, Michael　1796-1874 . . . . . .　**NCLC 13**
See also DLB 158, 159

Banks, Iain
See Banks, Iain M(enzies)

Banks, Iain M(enzies)　1954- . . . .　**CLC 34**
See also CA 123; 128; INT 128

Banks, Lynne Reid . . . .　**CLC 23**
See also Reid Banks, Lynne
See also AAYA 6

Banks, Russell　1940- . . . .　**CLC 37, 72**
See also CA 65-68; CAAS 15; CANR 19;
DLB 130

Banville, John　1945- . . . .　**CLC 46**
See also CA 117; 128; DLB 14; INT 128

Banville, Theodore (Faullain) de
1832-1891 . . . .　**NCLC 9**

Baraka, Amiri
1934- . . . .　**CLC 1, 2, 3, 5, 10, 14, 33;**
BLC; DA; DAC; DC 6; PC 4
See also Jones, LeRoi
See also BW 2; CA 21-24R; CABS 3;
CANR 27, 38; CDALB 1941-1968;
DAM MST, MULT, POET, POP;
DLB 5, 7, 16, 38; DLBD 8; MTCW

Barbauld, Anna Laetitia
1743-1825 . . . .　**NCLC 50**
See also DLB 107, 109, 142, 158

Barbellion, W. N. P. . . . .　**TCLC 24**
See also Cummings, Bruce F(rederick)

Barbera, Jack (Vincent)　1945- . . . . . .　**CLC 44**
See also CA 110; CANR 45

Barbey d'Aurevilly, Jules Amedee
1808-1889 . . . .　**NCLC 1; SSC 17**
See also DLB 119

Barbusse, Henri　1873-1935 . . . .　**TCLC 5**
See also CA 105; DLB 65

Barclay, Bill
See Moorcock, Michael (John)

Barclay, William Ewert
See Moorcock, Michael (John)

Barea, Arturo　1897-1957 . . . .　**TCLC 14**
See also CA 111

Barfoot, Joan　1946- . . . .　**CLC 18**
See also CA 105

Baring, Maurice　1874-1945 . . . .　**TCLC 8**
See also CA 105; DLB 34

Barker, Clive　1952- . . . .　**CLC 52**
See also AAYA 10; BEST 90:3; CA 121;
129; DAM POP; INT 129; MTCW

Barker, George Granville
1913-1991 . . . .　**CLC 8, 48**
See also CA 9-12R; 135; CANR 7, 38;
DAM POET; DLB 20; MTCW

Barker, Harley Granville
See Granville-Barker, Harley
See also DLB 10

Barker, Howard　1946- . . . .　**CLC 37**
See also CA 102; DLB 13

Barker, Pat(ricia)　1943- . . . .　**CLC 32**
See also CA 117; 122; CANR 50; INT 122

Barlow, Joel　1754-1812 . . . .　**NCLC 23**
See also DLB 37

Barnard, Mary (Ethel)　1909- . . . .　**CLC 48**
See also CA 21-22; CAP 2

Barnes, Djuna
1892-1982 . . .　**CLC 3, 4, 8, 11, 29; SSC 3**
See also CA 9-12R; 107; CANR 16; DLB 4,
9, 45; MTCW

Barnes, Julian　1946- . . . .　**CLC 42; DAB**
See also CA 102; CANR 19; DLBY 93

Barnes, Peter　1931- . . . .　**CLC 5, 56**
See also CA 65-68; CAAS 12; CANR 33,
34; DLB 13; MTCW

Baroja (y Nessi), Pio
1872-1956 . . . .　**TCLC 8; HLC**
See also CA 104

Baron, David
See Pinter, Harold

Baron Corvo
See Rolfe, Frederick (William Serafino
Austin Lewis Mary)

Barondess, Sue K(aufman)
1926-1977 . . . .　**CLC 8**
See also Kaufman, Sue
See also CA 1-4R; 69-72; CANR 1

Baron de Teive
See Pessoa, Fernando (Antonio Nogueira)

Barres, Maurice　1862-1923 . . . .　**TCLC 47**
See also DLB 123

Barreto, Afonso Henrique de Lima
See Lima Barreto, Afonso Henrique de

Barrett, (Roger) Syd　1946- . . . .　**CLC 35**

Barrett, William (Christopher)
1913-1992 . . . .　**CLC 27**
See also CA 13-16R; 139; CANR 11;
INT CANR-11

Barrie, J(ames) M(atthew)
1860-1937 . . . .　**TCLC 2; DAB**
See also CA 104; 136; CDBLB 1890-1914;
CLR 16; DAM DRAM; DLB 10, 141,
156; MAICYA; YABC 1

Barrington, Michael
See Moorcock, Michael (John)

Barrol, Grady
See Bograd, Larry

Barry, Mike
See Malzberg, Barry N(athaniel)

Barry, Philip　1896-1949 . . . .　**TCLC 11**
See also CA 109; DLB 7

Bart, Andre Schwarz
See Schwarz-Bart, Andre

Barth, John (Simmons)
1930- . . . . . .　**CLC 1, 2, 3, 5, 7, 9, 10, 14,**
27, 51, 89; SSC 10
See also AITN 1, 2; CA 1-4R; CABS 1;
CANR 5, 23, 49; DAM NOV; DLB 2;
MTCW

Barthelme, Donald
1931-1989 . . . . . .　**CLC 1, 2, 3, 5, 6, 8, 13,**
23, 46, 59; SSC 2
See also CA 21-24R; 129; CANR 20;
DAM NOV; DLB 2; DLBY 80, 89;
MTCW; SATA 7; SATA-Obit 62

Barthelme, Frederick　1943- . . . .　**CLC 36**
See also CA 114; 122; DLBY 85; INT 122

Barthes, Roland (Gerard)
1915-1980 . . . .　**CLC 24, 83**
See also CA 130; 97-100; MTCW

Barzun, Jacques (Martin)　1907- . . . .　**CLC 51**
See also CA 61-64; CANR 22

Bashevis, Isaac
See Singer, Isaac Bashevis

Bashkirtseff, Marie　1859-1884 . . .　**NCLC 27**

Basho
See Matsuo Basho

Bass, Kingsley B., Jr.
See Bullins, Ed

Bass, Rick　1958- . . . .　**CLC 79**
See also CA 126

Bassani, Giorgio　1916- . . . .　**CLC 9**
See also CA 65-68; CANR 33; DLB 128;
MTCW

Bastos, Augusto (Antonio) Roa
See Roa Bastos, Augusto (Antonio)

Bataille, Georges　1897-1962 . . . .　**CLC 29**
See also CA 101; 89-92

Bates, H(erbert) E(rnest)
1905-1974 . . . . . .　**CLC 46; DAB; SSC 10**
See also CA 93-96; 45-48; CANR 34;
DAM POP; MTCW

Bauchart
See Camus, Albert

Baudelaire, Charles
1821-1867 . . . . .　**NCLC 6, 29; DA; DAB;**
DAC; PC 1; SSC 18; WLC
See also DAM MST, POET

Baudrillard, Jean　1929- . . . .　**CLC 60**

Baum, L(yman) Frank　1856-1919 . . .　**TCLC 7**
See also CA 108; 133; CLR 15; DLB 22;
JRDA; MAICYA; MTCW; SATA 18

Baum, Louis F.
See Baum, L(yman) Frank

Baumbach, Jonathan　1933- . . . . . .　**CLC 6, 23**
See also CA 13-16R; CAAS 5; CANR 12;
DLBY 80; INT CANR-12; MTCW

Bausch, Richard (Carl)　1945- . . . . . .　**CLC 51**
See also CA 101; CAAS 14; CANR 43;
DLB 130

Baxter, Charles　1947- . . . .　**CLC 45, 78**
See also CA 57-60; CANR 40; DAM POP;
DLB 130

Baxter, George Owen
See Faust, Frederick (Schiller)

Baxter, James K(eir)　1926-1972 . . . .　**CLC 14**
See also CA 77-80

Baxter, John
See Hunt, E(verette) Howard, (Jr.)

Bayer, Sylvia
See Glassco, John

Baynton, Barbara　1857-1929 . . . . . .　**TCLC 57**

Bennett, George Harold 1930-
See Bennett, Hal
See also BW 1; CA 97-100

Bennett, Hal . . . . **CLC 5**
See also Bennett, George Harold
See also DLB 33

Bennett, Jay 1912- . . . . **CLC 35**
See also AAYA 10; CA 69-72; CANR 11,
42; JRDA; SAAS 4; SATA 41;
SATA-Brief 27

Bennett, Louise (Simone)
1919- . . . . **CLC 28; BLC**
See also BW 2; DAM MULT; DLB 117

Benson, E(dward) F(rederic)
1867-1940 . . . . **TCLC 27**
See also CA 114; DLB 135, 153

Benson, Jackson J. 1930- . . . . **CLC 34**
See also CA 25-28R; DLB 111

Benson, Sally 1900-1972 . . . . **CLC 17**
See also CA 19-20; 37-40R; CAP 1;
SATA 1, 35; SATA-Obit 27

Benson, Stella 1892-1933 . . . . **TCLC 17**
See also CA 117; DLB 36

Bentham, Jeremy 1748-1832 . . . . . **NCLC 38**
See also DLB 107, 158

Bentley, E(dmund) C(lerihew)
1875-1956 . . . . **TCLC 12**
See also CA 108; DLB 70

Bentley, Eric (Russell) 1916- . . . . **CLC 24**
See also CA 5-8R; CANR 6; INT CANR-6

Beranger, Pierre Jean de
1780-1857 . . . . **NCLC 34**

Berendt, John (Lawrence) 1939- . . . . **CLC 86**
See also CA 146

Berger, Colonel
See Malraux, (Georges-)Andre

Berger, John (Peter) 1926- . . . . . . **CLC 2, 19**
See also CA 81-84; DLB 14

Berger, Melvin H. 1927- . . . . **CLC 12**
See also CA 5-8R; CANR 4; CLR 32;
SAAS 2; SATA 5

Berger, Thomas (Louis)
1924- . . . . **CLC 3, 5, 8, 11, 18, 38**
See also CA 1-4R; CANR 5, 28;
DAM NOV; DLB 2; DLBY 80;
INT CANR-28; MTCW

Bergman, (Ernst) Ingmar
1918- . . . . **CLC 16, 72**
See also CA 81-84; CANR 33

Bergson, Henri 1859-1941 . . . . **TCLC 32**

Bergstein, Eleanor 1938- . . . . **CLC 4**
See also CA 53-56; CANR 5

Berkoff, Steven 1937- . . . . **CLC 56**
See also CA 104

Bermant, Chaim (Icyk) 1929- . . . . . . **CLC 40**
See also CA 57-60; CANR 6, 31

Bern, Victoria
See Fisher, M(ary) F(rances) K(ennedy)

Bernanos, (Paul Louis) Georges
1888-1948 . . . . **TCLC 3**
See also CA 104; 130; DLB 72

Bernard, April 1956- . . . . **CLC 59**
See also CA 131

Berne, Victoria
See Fisher, M(ary) F(rances) K(ennedy)

Bernhard, Thomas
1931-1989 . . . . **CLC 3, 32, 61**
See also CA 85-88; 127; CANR 32;
DLB 85, 124; MTCW

Berriault, Gina 1926- . . . . **CLC 54**
See also CA 116; 129; DLB 130

Berrigan, Daniel 1921- . . . . **CLC 4**
See also CA 33-36R; CAAS 1; CANR 11,
43; DLB 5

Berrigan, Edmund Joseph Michael, Jr.
1934-1983
See Berrigan, Ted
See also CA 61-64; 110; CANR 14

Berrigan, Ted . . . . **CLC 37**
See also Berrigan, Edmund Joseph Michael,
Jr.
See also DLB 5

Berry, Charles Edward Anderson 1931-
See Berry, Chuck
See also CA 115

Berry, Chuck . . . . **CLC 17**
See also Berry, Charles Edward Anderson

Berry, Jonas
See Ashbery, John (Lawrence)

Berry, Wendell (Erdman)
1934- . . . . **CLC 4, 6, 8, 27, 46**
See also AITN 1; CA 73-76; CANR 50;
DAM POET; DLB 5, 6

Berryman, John
1914-1972 . . . . . . **CLC 1, 2, 3, 4, 6, 8, 10,
13, 25, 62**
See also CA 13-16; 33-36R; CABS 2;
CANR 35; CAP 1; CDALB 1941-1968,
DAM POET; DLB 48; MTCW

Bertolucci, Bernardo 1940- . . . . **CLC 16**
See also CA 106

Bertrand, Aloysius 1807-1841 . . . . **NCLC 31**

Bertran de Born c. 1140-1215 . . . . . **CMLC 5**

Besant, Annie (Wood) 1847-1933 . . . **TCLC 9**
See also CA 105

Bessie, Alvah 1904-1985 . . . . **CLC 23**
See also CA 5-8R; 116; CANR 2; DLB 26

Bethlen, T. D.
See Silverberg, Robert

Beti, Mongo . . . . **CLC 27; BLC**
See also Biyidi, Alexandre
See also DAM MULT

Betjeman, John
1906-1984 . . . **CLC 2, 6, 10, 34, 43; DAB**
See also CA 9-12R; 112; CANR 33;
CDBLB 1945-1960; DAM MST, POET;
DLB 20; DLBY 84; MTCW

Bettelheim, Bruno 1903-1990 . . . . . . **CLC 79**
See also CA 81-84; 131; CANR 23; MTCW

Betti, Ugo 1892-1953 . . . . **TCLC 5**
See also CA 104

Betts, Doris (Waugh) 1932- . . . . **CLC 3, 6, 28**
See also CA 13-16R; CANR 9; DLBY 82;
INT CANR-9

Bevan, Alistair
See Roberts, Keith (John Kingston)

Bialik, Chaim Nachman
1873-1934 . . . . **TCLC 25**

Bickerstaff, Isaac
See Swift, Jonathan

Bidart, Frank 1939- . . . . **CLC 33**
See also CA 140

Bienek, Horst 1930- . . . . **CLC 7, 11**
See also CA 73-76; DLB 75

Bierce, Ambrose (Gwinett)
1842-1914(?) . . . . **TCLC 1, 7, 44; DA;
DAC; SSC 9; WLC**
See also CA 104; 139; CDALB 1865-1917;
DAM MST; DLB 11, 12, 23, 71, 74

Billings, Josh
See Shaw, Henry Wheeler

Billington, (Lady) Rachel (Mary)
1942- . . . . **CLC 43**
See also AITN 2; CA 33-36R; CANR 44

Binyon, T(imothy) J(ohn) 1936- . . . . **CLC 34**
See also CA 111; CANR 28

Bioy Casares, Adolfo
1914- . . . **CLC 4, 8, 13, 88; HLC; SSC 17**
See also CA 29-32R; CANR 19, 43;
DAM MULT; DLB 113; HW; MTCW

Bird, Cordwainer
See Ellison, Harlan (Jay)

Bird, Robert Montgomery
1806-1854 . . . . **NCLC 1**

Birney, (Alfred) Earle
1904- . . . . **CLC 1, 4, 6, 11; DAC**
See also CA 1-4R; CANR 5, 20;
DAM MST, POET; DLB 88; MTCW

Bishop, Elizabeth
1911-1979 . . . . . . **CLC 1, 4, 9, 13, 15, 32;
DA; DAC; PC 3**
See also CA 5-8R; 89-92; CABS 2;
CANR 26; CDALB 1968-1988;
DAM MST, POET; DLB 5; MTCW;
SATA-Obit 24

Bishop, John 1935- . . . . **CLC 10**
See also CA 105

Bissett, Bill 1939- . . . . **CLC 18; PC 14**
See also CA 69-72; CAAS 19; CANR 15;
DLB 53; MTCW

Bitov, Andrei (Georgievich) 1937- . . . **CLC 57**
See also CA 142

Biyidi, Alexandre 1932-
See Beti, Mongo
See also BW 1; CA 114; 124; MTCW

Bjarme, Brynjolf
See Ibsen, Henrik (Johan)

Bjornson, Bjornstjerne (Martinius)
1832-1910 . . . . **TCLC 7, 37**
See also CA 104

Black, Robert
See Holdstock, Robert P.

Blackburn, Paul 1926-1971 . . . . . . **CLC 9, 43**
See also CA 81-84; 33-36R; CANR 34;
DLB 16; DLBY 81

Black Elk 1863-1950 . . . . **TCLC 33**
See also CA 144; DAM MULT; NNAL

Black Hobart
See Sanders, (James) Ed(ward)

Blacklin, Malcolm
See Chambers, Aidan

Buck, Pearl S(ydenstricker)
1892-1973 .... **CLC 7, 11, 18; DA; DAB; DAC**
See also AITN 1; CA 1-4R; 41-44R; CANR 1, 34; DAM MST, NOV; DLB 9, 102; MTCW; SATA 1, 25

Buckler, Ernest 1908-1984.... **CLC 13; DAC**
See also CA 11-12; 114; CAP 1; DAM MST; DLB 68; SATA 47

Buckley, Vincent (Thomas)
1925-1988 .... **CLC 57**
See also CA 101

Buckley, William F(rank), Jr.
1925- .... **CLC 7, 18, 37**
See also AITN 1; CA 1-4R; CANR 1, 24; DAM POP; DLB 137; DLBY 80; INT CANR-24; MTCW

Buechner, (Carl) Frederick
1926- .... **CLC 2, 4, 6, 9**
See also CA 13-16R; CANR 11, 39; DAM NOV; DLBY 80; INT CANR-11; MTCW

Buell, John (Edward) 1927-........ **CLC 10**
See also CA 1-4R, DLB 53

Buero Vallejo, Antonio 1916- ... **CLC 15, 46**
See also CA 106; CANR 24, 49; HW; MTCW

Bufalino, Gesualdo 1920(?)-........ **CLC 74**

Bugayev, Boris Nikolayevich 1880-1934
See Bely, Andrey
See also CA 104

Bukowski, Charles
1920-1994 .... **CLC 2, 5, 9, 41, 82**
See also CA 17-20R; 144; CANR 40; DAM NOV, POET; DLB 5, 130; MTCW

Bulgakov, Mikhail (Afanas'evich)
1891-1940 .... **TCLC 2, 16; SSC 18**
See also CA 105; DAM DRAM, NOV

Bulgya, Alexander Alexandrovich
1901-1956 .... **TCLC 53**
See also Fadeyev, Alexander
See also CA 117

Bullins, Ed 1935- .. **CLC 1, 5, 7; BLC; DC 6**
See also BW 2; CA 49-52; CAAS 16; CANR 24, 46; DAM DRAM, MULT; DLB 7, 38; MTCW

Bulwer-Lytton, Edward (George Earle Lytton)
1803-1873 .... **NCLC 1, 45**
See also DLB 21

Bunin, Ivan Alexeyevich
1870-1953 .... **TCLC 6; SSC 5**
See also CA 104

Bunting, Basil 1900-1985.... **CLC 10, 39, 47**
See also CA 53-56; 115; CANR 7; DAM POET; DLB 20

Bunuel, Luis 1900-1983 .. **CLC 16, 80; HLC**
See also CA 101; 110; CANR 32; DAM MULT; HW

Bunyan, John
1628-1688 ...... **LC 4; DA; DAB; DAC; WLC**
See also CDBLB 1660-1789; DAM MST; DLB 39

Burckhardt, Jacob (Christoph)
1818-1897 .... **NCLC 49**

Burford, Eleanor
See Hibbert, Eleanor Alice Burford

Burgess, Anthony
. **CLC 1, 2, 4, 5, 8, 10, 13, 15, 22, 40, 62, 81; DAB**
See also Wilson, John (Anthony) Burgess
See also AITN 1; CDBLB 1960 to Present; DLB 14

Burke, Edmund
1729(?)-1797 .... **LC 7; DA; DAB; DAC; WLC**
See also DAM MST; DLB 104

Burke, Kenneth (Duva)
1897-1993 .... **CLC 2, 24**
See also CA 5-8R; 143; CANR 39; DLB 45, 63; MTCW

Burke, Leda
See Garnett, David

Burke, Ralph
See Silverberg, Robert

Burney, Fanny 1752-1840 .... **NCLC 12**
See also DLB 39

Burns, Robert 1759-1796............ **PC 6**
See also CDBLB 1789-1832; DA; DAB; DAC; DAM MST, POET; DLB 109; WLC

Burns, Tex
See L'Amour, Louis (Dearborn)

Burnshaw, Stanley 1906-..... **CLC 3, 13, 44**
See also CA 9-12R; DLB 48

Burr, Anne 1937- .... **CLC 6**
See also CA 25-28R

Burroughs, Edgar Rice
1875-1950 .... **TCLC 2, 32**
See also AAYA 11; CA 104; 132; DAM NOV; DLB 8; MTCW; SATA 41

Burroughs, William S(eward)
1914- .... **CLC 1, 2, 5, 15, 22, 42, 75; DA; DAB; DAC; WLC**
See also AITN 2; CA 9-12R; CANR 20; DAM MST, NOV, POP; DLB 2, 8, 16, 152; DLBY 81; MTCW

Burton, Richard F. 1821-1890.... **NCLC 42**
See also DLB 55

Busch, Frederick 1941- ... **CLC 7, 10, 18, 47**
See also CA 33-36R; CAAS 1; CANR 45; DLB 6

Bush, Ronald 1946- .... **CLC 34**
See also CA 136

Bustos, F(rancisco)
See Borges, Jorge Luis

Bustos Domecq, H(onorio)
See Bioy Casares, Adolfo; Borges, Jorge Luis

Butler, Octavia E(stelle) 1947- ..... **CLC 38**
See also BW 2; CA 73-76; CANR 12, 24, 38; DAM MULT, POP; DLB 33; MTCW; SATA 84

Butler, Robert Olen (Jr.) 1945-..... **CLC 81**
See also CA 112; DAM POP; INT 112

Butler, Samuel 1612-1680 .... **LC 16**
See also DLB 101, 126

Butler, Samuel
1835-1902 ...... **TCLC 1, 33; DA; DAB; DAC; WLC**
See also CA 143; CDBLB 1890-1914; DAM MST, NOV; DLB 18, 57

Butler, Walter C.
See Faust, Frederick (Schiller)

Butor, Michel (Marie Francois)
1926- .... **CLC 1, 3, 8, 11, 15**
See also CA 9-12R; CANR 33; DLB 83; MTCW

Buzo, Alexander (John) 1944-...... **CLC 61**
See also CA 97-100; CANR 17, 39

Buzzati, Dino 1906-1972 .... **CLC 36**
See also CA 33-36R

Byars, Betsy (Cromer) 1928-....... **CLC 35**
See also CA 33-36R; CANR 18, 36; CLR 1, 16; DLB 52; INT CANR-18; JRDA; MAICYA; MTCW; SAAS 1; SATA 4, 46, 80

Byatt, A(ntonia) S(usan Drabble)
1936- .... **CLC 19, 65**
See also CA 13-16R; CANR 13, 33, 50; DAM NOV, POP; DLB 14; MTCW

Byrne, David 1952-............... **CLC 26**
See also CA 127

Byrne, John Keyes 1926-
See Leonard, Hugh
See also CA 102; INT 102

Byron, George Gordon (Noel)
1788-1824 ..... **NCLC 2, 12; DA; DAB; DAC; WLC**
See also CDBLB 1789-1832; DAM MST, POET; DLB 96, 110

C. 3. 3.
See Wilde, Oscar (Fingal O'Flahertie Wills)

Caballero, Fernan 1796-1877 ..... **NCLC 10**

Cabell, James Branch 1879-1958 ... **TCLC 6**
See also CA 105; DLB 9, 78

Cable, George Washington
1844-1925 .... **TCLC 4; SSC 4**
See also CA 104; DLB 12, 74; DLBD 13

Cabral de Melo Neto, Joao 1920-... **CLC 76**
See also DAM MULT

Cabrera Infante, G(uillermo)
1929- .... **CLC 5, 25, 45; HLC**
See also CA 85-88; CANR 29; DAM MULT; DLB 113; HW; MTCW

Cade, Toni
See Bambara, Toni Cade

Cadmus and Harmonia
See Buchan, John

Caedmon fl. 658-680.............. **CMLC 7**
See also DLB 146

Caeiro, Alberto
See Pessoa, Fernando (Antonio Nogueira)

Cage, John (Milton, Jr.) 1912-..... **CLC 41**
See also CA 13-16R; CANR 9; INT CANR-9

Cain, G.
See Cabrera Infante, G(uillermo)

Cain, Guillermo
See Cabrera Infante, G(uillermo)

Cary, (Arthur) Joyce (Lunel)
1888-1957 .... TCLC 1, 29
See also CA 104; CDBLB 1914-1945;
DLB 15, 100

Casanova de Seingalt, Giovanni Jacopo
1725-1798 .... LC 13

Casares, Adolfo Bioy
See Bioy Casares, Adolfo

Casely-Hayford, J(oseph) E(phraim)
1866-1930 .... TCLC 24; BLC
See also BW 2; CA 123; DAM MULT

Casey, John (Dudley) 1939-........ CLC 59
See also BEST 90:2; CA 69-72; CANR 23

Casey, Michael 1947-.............. CLC 2
See also CA 65-68; DLB 5

Casey, Patrick
See Thurman, Wallace (Henry)

Casey, Warren (Peter) 1935-1988 ... CLC 12
See also CA 101; 127; INT 101

Casona, Alejandro................. CLC 49
See also Alvarez, Alejandro Rodriguez

Cassavetes, John 1929-1989........ CLC 20
See also CA 85-88; 127

Cassill, R(onald) V(erlin) 1919-... CLC 4, 23
See also CA 9-12R; CAAS 1; CANR 7, 45;
DLB 6

Cassirer, Ernst 1874-1945 .... TCLC 61

Cassity, (Allen) Turner 1929- .... CLC 6, 42
See also CA 17-20R; CAAS 8; CANR 11;
DLB 105

Castaneda, Carlos 1931(?)-......... CLC 12
See also CA 25-28R; CANR 32; HW;
MTCW

Castedo, Elena 1937- .... CLC 65
See also CA 132

Castedo-Ellerman, Elena
See Castedo, Elena

Castellanos, Rosario
1925-1974 .... CLC 66; HLC
See also CA 131; 53-56; DAM MULT;
DLB 113; HW

Castelvetro, Lodovico 1505-1571..... LC 12

Castiglione, Baldassare 1478-1529 ... LC 12

Castle, Robert
See Hamilton, Edmond

Castro, Guillen de 1569-1631........ LC 19

Castro, Rosalia de 1837-1885 ..... NCLC 3
See also DAM MULT

Cather, Willa
See Cather, Willa Sibert

Cather, Willa Sibert
1873-1947 .... TCLC 1, 11, 31; DA;
DAB; DAC; SSC 2; WLC
See also CA 104; 128; CDALB 1865-1917;
DAM MST, NOV; DLB 9, 54, 78;
DLBD 1; MTCW; SATA 30

Catton, (Charles) Bruce
1899-1978 .... CLC 35
See also AITN 1; CA 5-8R; 81-84;
CANR 7; DLB 17; SATA 2;
SATA-Obit 24

Cauldwell, Frank
See King, Francis (Henry)

Caunitz, William J. 1933- .... CLC 34
See also BEST 89:3; CA 125; 130; INT 130

Causley, Charles (Stanley) 1917-..... CLC 7
See also CA 9-12R; CANR 5, 35; CLR 30;
DLB 27; MTCW; SATA 3, 66

Caute, David 1936-............... CLC 29
See also CA 1-4R; CAAS 4; CANR 1, 33;
DAM NOV; DLB 14

Cavafy, C(onstantine) P(eter)
1863-1933 .... TCLC 2, 7
See also Kavafis, Konstantinos Petrou
See also CA 148; DAM POET

Cavallo, Evelyn
See Spark, Muriel (Sarah)

Cavanna, Betty .... CLC 12
See also Harrison, Elizabeth Cavanna
See also JRDA; MAICYA; SAAS 4;
SATA 1, 30

Cavendish, Margaret Lucas
1623-1673 .... LC 30
See also DLB 131

Caxton, William 1421(?)-1491(?)..... LC 17

Cayrol, Jean 1911-................ CLC 11
See also CA 89-92; DLB 83

Cela, Camilo Jose
1916- .... CLC 4, 13, 59; HLC
See also BEST 90:2; CA 21-24R; CAAS 10;
CANR 21, 32; DAM MULT; DLBY 89;
HW; MTCW

Celan, Paul ...... CLC 10, 19, 53, 82; PC 10
See also Antschel, Paul
See also DLB 69

Celine, Louis-Ferdinand
.... CLC 1, 3, 4, 7, 9, 15, 47
See also Destouches, Louis-Ferdinand
See also DLB 72

Cellini, Benvenuto 1500-1571 .... LC 7

Cendrars, Blaise .... CLC 18
See also Sauser-Hall, Frederic

Cernuda (y Bidon), Luis
1902-1963 .... CLC 54
See also CA 131; 89-92; DAM POET;
DLB 134; HW

Cervantes (Saavedra), Miguel de
1547-1616 .... LC 6, 23; DA; DAB;
DAC; SSC 12; WLC
See also DAM MST, NOV

Cesaire, Aime (Fernand)
1913- .... CLC 19, 32; BLC
See also BW 2; CA 65-68; CANR 24, 43;
DAM MULT, POET; MTCW

Chabon, Michael 1965(?)- .... CLC 55
See also CA 139

Chabrol, Claude 1930- .... CLC 16
See also CA 110

Challans, Mary 1905-1983
See Renault, Mary
See also CA 81-84; 111; SATA 23;
SATA-Obit 36

Challis, George
See Faust, Frederick (Schiller)

Chambers, Aidan 1934- .... CLC 35
See also CA 25-28R; CANR 12, 31; JRDA;
MAICYA; SAAS 12; SATA 1, 69

Chambers, James 1948-
See Cliff, Jimmy
See also CA 124

Chambers, Jessie
See Lawrence, D(avid) H(erbert Richards)

Chambers, Robert W. 1865-1933... TCLC 41

Chandler, Raymond (Thornton)
1888-1959 .... TCLC 1, 7
See also CA 104; 129; CDALB 1929-1941;
DLBD 6; MTCW

Chang, Jung 1952- .... CLC 71
See also CA 142

Channing, William Ellery
1780-1842 .... NCLC 17
See also DLB 1, 59

Chaplin, Charles Spencer
1889-1977 .... CLC 16
See also Chaplin, Charlie
See also CA 81-84; 73-76

Chaplin, Charlie
See Chaplin, Charles Spencer
See also DLB 44

Chapman, George 1559(?)-1634...... LC 22
See also DAM DRAM; DLB 62, 121

Chapman, Graham 1941-1989 ...... CLC 21
See also Monty Python
See also CA 116; 129; CANR 35

Chapman, John Jay 1862-1933 ..... TCLC 7
See also CA 104

Chapman, Walker
See Silverberg, Robert

Chappell, Fred (Davis) 1936-.... CLC 40, 78
See also CA 5-8R; CAAS 4; CANR 8, 33;
DLB 6, 105

Char, Rene(-Emile)
1907-1988 .... CLC 9, 11, 14, 55
See also CA 13-16R; 124; CANR 32;
DAM POET; MTCW

Charby, Jay
See Ellison, Harlan (Jay)

Chardin, Pierre Teilhard de
See Teilhard de Chardin, (Marie Joseph)
Pierre

Charles I 1600-1649............... LC 13

Charyn, Jerome 1937- .... CLC 5, 8, 18
See also CA 5-8R; CAAS 1; CANR 7;
DLBY 83; MTCW

Chase, Mary (Coyle) 1907-1981 ...... DC 1
See also CA 77-80; 105; SATA 17;
SATA-Obit 29

Chase, Mary Ellen 1887-1973 .... CLC 2
See also CA 13-16; 41-44R; CAP 1;
SATA 10

Chase, Nicholas
See Hyde, Anthony

Chateaubriand, Francois Rene de
1768-1848 .... NCLC 3
See also DLB 119

Chatterje, Sarat Chandra 1876-1936(?)
See Chatterji, Saratchandra
See also CA 109

Chatterji, Bankim Chandra
1838-1894 .... NCLC 19

Clarke, Marcus (Andrew Hislop)
1846-1881 .... NCLC 19

Clarke, Shirley 1925-............. CLC 16

Clash, The
See Headon, (Nicky) Topper; Jones, Mick;
Simonon, Paul; Strummer, Joe

Claudel, Paul (Louis Charles Marie)
1868-1955 .... TCLC 2, 10
See also CA 104

Clavell, James (duMaresq)
1925-1994 .... CLC 6, 25, 87
See also CA 25-28R; 146; CANR 26, 48;
DAM NOV, POP; MTCW

Cleaver, (Leroy) Eldridge
1935- .... CLC 30; BLC
See also BW 1; CA 21-24R; CANR 16;
DAM MULT

Cleese, John (Marwood) 1939- ..... CLC 21
See also Monty Python
See also CA 112; 116; CANR 35; MTCW

Cleishbotham, Jebediah
See Scott, Walter

Cleland, John 1710-1789 .... LC 2
See also DLB 39

Clemens, Samuel Langhorne 1835-1910
See Twain, Mark
See also CA 104; 135; CDALB 1865-1917;
DA; DAB; DAC; DAM MST, NOV;
DLB 11, 12, 23, 64, 74; JRDA;
MAICYA; YABC 2

Cleophil
See Congreve, William

Clerihew, E.
See Bentley, E(dmund) C(lerihew)

Clerk, N. W.
See Lewis, C(live) S(taples)

Cliff, Jimmy.................... CLC 21
See also Chambers, James

Clifton, (Thelma) Lucille
1936- .... CLC 19, 66; BLC
See also BW 2; CA 49-52; CANR 2, 24, 42;
CLR 5; DAM MULT, POET; DLB 5, 41;
MAICYA; MTCW; SATA 20, 69

Clinton, Dirk
See Silverberg, Robert

Clough, Arthur Hugh 1819-1861.. NCLC 27
See also DLB 32

Clutha, Janet Paterson Frame 1924-
See Frame, Janet
See also CA 1-4R; CANR 2, 36; MTCW

Clyne, Terence
See Blatty, William Peter

Cobalt, Martin
See Mayne, William (James Carter)

Cobbett, William 1763-1835 ..... NCLC 49
See also DLB 43, 107, 158

Coburn, D(onald) L(ee) 1938- ...... CLC 10
See also CA 89-92

Cocteau, Jean (Maurice Eugene Clement)
1889-1963 .... CLC 1, 8, 15, 16, 43; DA;
DAB; DAC; WLC
See also CA 25-28; CANR 40; CAP 2;
DAM DRAM, MST, NOV; DLB 65;
MTCW

Codrescu, Andrei 1946-........... CLC 46
See also CA 33-36R; CAAS 19; CANR 13,
34; DAM POET

Coe, Max
See Bourne, Randolph S(illiman)

Coe, Tucker
See Westlake, Donald E(dwin)

Coetzee, J(ohn) M(ichael)
1940- .... CLC 23, 33, 66
See also CA 77-80; CANR 41; DAM NOV;
MTCW

Coffey, Brian
See Koontz, Dean R(ay)

Cohan, George M. 1878-1942 ..... TCLC 60

Cohen, Arthur A(llen)
1928-1986 .... CLC 7, 31
See also CA 1-4R; 120; CANR 1, 17, 42;
DLB 28

Cohen, Leonard (Norman)
1934- .... CLC 3, 38; DAC
See also CA 21-24R; CANR 14;
DAM MST; DLB 53; MTCW

Cohen, Matt 1942-.......... CLC 19; DAC
See also CA 61-64; CAAS 18; CANR 40;
DLB 53

Cohen-Solal, Annie 19(?)- .... CLC 50

Colegate, Isabel 1931- .... CLC 36
See also CA 17-20R; CANR 8, 22; DLB 14;
INT CANR-22; MTCW

Coleman, Emmett
See Reed, Ishmael

Coleridge, Samuel Taylor
1772-1834 .... NCLC 9; DA; DAB;
DAC; PC 11; WLC
See also CDBLB 1789-1832; DAM MST,
POET; DLB 93, 107

Coleridge, Sara 1802-1852....... NCLC 31

Coles, Don 1928- .... CLC 46
See also CA 115; CANR 38

Colette, (Sidonie-Gabrielle)
1873-1954 ...... TCLC 1, 5, 16; SSC 10
See also CA 104; 131; DAM NOV; DLB 65;
MTCW

Collett, (Jacobine) Camilla (Wergeland)
1813-1895 .... NCLC 22

Collier, Christopher 1930-......... CLC 30
See also AAYA 13; CA 33-36R; CANR 13,
33; JRDA; MAICYA; SATA 16, 70

Collier, James L(incoln) 1928- ..... CLC 30
See also AAYA 13; CA 9-12R; CANR 4,
33; CLR 3; DAM POP; JRDA;
MAICYA; SAAS 21; SATA 8, 70

Collier, Jeremy 1650-1726.......... LC 6

Collier, John 1901-1980........... SSC 19
See also CA 65-68; 97-100; CANR 10;
DLB 77

Collins, Hunt
See Hunter, Evan

Collins, Linda 1931-.............. CLC 44
See also CA 125

Collins, (William) Wilkie
1824-1889 .... NCLC 1, 18
See also CDBLB 1832-1890; DLB 18, 70,
159

Collins, William 1721-1759 .... LC 4
See also DAM POET; DLB 109

Colman, George
See Glassco, John

Colt, Winchester Remington
See Hubbard, L(afayette) Ron(ald)

Colter, Cyrus 1910- .... CLC 58
See also BW 1; CA 65-68; CANR 10;
DLB 33

Colton, James
See Hansen, Joseph

Colum, Padraic 1881-1972........ CLC 28
See also CA 73-76; 33-36R; CANR 35;
CLR 36; MAICYA; MTCW; SATA 15

Colvin, James
See Moorcock, Michael (John)

Colwin, Laurie (E.)
1944-1992 .... CLC 5, 13, 23, 84
See also CA 89-92; 139; CANR 20, 46;
DLBY 80; MTCW

Comfort, Alex(ander) 1920-........ CLC 7
See also CA 1-4R; CANR 1, 45; DAM POP

Comfort, Montgomery
See Campbell, (John) Ramsey

Compton-Burnett, I(vy)
1884(?)-1969 ...... CLC 1, 3, 10, 15, 34
See also CA 1-4R; 25-28R; CANR 4;
DAM NOV; DLB 36; MTCW

Comstock, Anthony 1844-1915 .... TCLC 13
See also CA 110

Conan Doyle, Arthur
See Doyle, Arthur Conan

Conde, Maryse 1937-............. CLC 52
See also Boucolon, Maryse
See also BW 2; DAM MULT

Condillac, Etienne Bonnot de
1714-1780 .... LC 26

Condon, Richard (Thomas)
1915- .... CLC 4, 6, 8, 10, 45
See also BEST 90:3; CA 1-4R; CAAS 1;
CANR 2, 23; DAM NOV;
INT CANR-23; MTCW

Congreve, William
1670-1729 .... LC 5, 21; DA; DAB;
DAC; DC 2; WLC
See also CDBLB 1660-1789; DAM DRAM,
MST, POET; DLB 39, 84

Connell, Evan S(helby), Jr.
1924- .... CLC 4, 6, 45
See also AAYA 7; CA 1-4R; CAAS 2;
CANR 2, 39; DAM NOV; DLB 2;
DLBY 81; MTCW

Connelly, Marc(us Cook)
1890-1980 .... CLC 7
See also CA 85-88; 102; CANR 30; DLB 7;
DLBY 80; SATA-Obit 25

Connor, Ralph................... TCLC 31
See also Gordon, Charles William
See also DLB 92

Conrad, Joseph
1857-1924 .... TCLC 1, 6, 13, 25, 43, 57;
DA; DAB; DAC; SSC 9; WLC
See also CA 104; 131; CDBLB 1890-1914;
DAM MST, NOV; DLB 10, 34, 98, 156;
MTCW; SATA 27

Conrad, Robert Arnold
See Hart, Moss

Conroy, Pat 1945-............ CLC 30, 74
See also AAYA 8; AITN 1; CA 85-88;
CANR 24; DAM NOV, POP; DLB 6;
MTCW

Constant (de Rebecque), (Henri) Benjamin
1767-1830 .... NCLC 6
See also DLB 119

Conybeare, Charles Augustus
See Eliot, T(homas) S(tearns)

Cook, Michael 1933- .... CLC 58
See also CA 93-96; DLB 53

Cook, Robin 1940- .... CLC 14
See also BEST 90:2; CA 108; 111;
CANR 41; DAM POP; INT 111

Cook, Roy
See Silverberg, Robert

Cooke, Elizabeth 1948- .... CLC 55
See also CA 129

Cooke, John Esten 1830-1886 ..... NCLC 5
See also DLB 3

Cooke, John Estes
See Baum, L(yman) Frank

Cooke, M. E.
See Creasey, John

Cooke, Margaret
See Creasey, John

Cooney, Ray .... CLC 62

Cooper, Douglas 1960-............ CLC 86

Cooper, Henry St. John
See Creasey, John

Cooper, J. California.............. CLC 56
See also AAYA 12; BW 1; CA 125;
DAM MULT

Cooper, James Fenimore
1789-1851 .... NCLC 1, 27
See also CDALB 1640-1865; DLB 3;
SATA 19

Coover, Robert (Lowell)
1932- .. CLC 3, 7, 15, 32, 46, 87; SSC 15
See also CA 45-48; CANR 3, 37;
DAM NOV; DLB 2; DLBY 81; MTCW

Copeland, Stewart (Armstrong)
1952- .... CLC 26

Coppard, A(lfred) E(dgar)
1878-1957 .... TCLC 5; SSC 21
See also CA 114; YABC 1

Coppee, Francois 1842-1908 ...... TCLC 25

Coppola, Francis Ford 1939-....... CLC 16
See also CA 77-80; CANR 40; DLB 44

Corbiere, Tristan 1845-1875 ..... NCLC 43

Corcoran, Barbara 1911-.......... CLC 17
See also AAYA 14; CA 21-24R; CAAS 2;
CANR 11, 28, 48; DLB 52; JRDA;
SAAS 20; SATA 3, 77

Cordelier, Maurice
See Giraudoux, (Hippolyte) Jean

Corelli, Marie 1855-1924........ TCLC 51
See also Mackay, Mary
See also DLB 34, 156

Corman, Cid...................... CLC 9
See also Corman, Sidney
See also CAAS 2; DLB 5

Corman, Sidney 1924-
See Corman, Cid
See also CA 85-88; CANR 44; DAM POET

Cormier, Robert (Edmund)
1925- ..... CLC 12, 30; DA; DAB; DAC
See also AAYA 3; CA 1-4R; CANR 5, 23;
CDALB 1968-1988; CLR 12; DAM MST,
NOV; DLB 52; INT CANR-23; JRDA;
MAICYA; MTCW; SATA 10, 45, 83

Corn, Alfred (DeWitt III) 1943-.... CLC 33
See also CA 104; CANR 44; DLB 120;
DLBY 80

Corneille, Pierre 1606-1684.... LC 28; DAB
See also DAM MST

Cornwell, David (John Moore)
1931- .... CLC 9, 15
See also le Carre, John
See also CA 5-8R; CANR 13, 33;
DAM POP; MTCW

Corso, (Nunzio) Gregory 1930-... CLC 1, 11
See also CA 5-8R; CANR 41; DLB 5, 16;
MTCW

Cortazar, Julio
1914-1984 ...... CLC 2, 3, 5, 10, 13, 15,
                          33, 34; HLC; SSC 7
See also CA 21-24R; CANR 12, 32;
DAM MULT, NOV; DLB 113; HW;
MTCW

CORTES, HERNAN 1484-1547..... LC 31

Corwin, Cecil
See Kornbluth, C(yril) M.

Cosic, Dobrica 1921- .... CLC 14
See also CA 122; 138

Costain, Thomas B(ertram)
1885-1965 .... CLC 30
See also CA 5-8R; 25-28R; DLB 9

Costantini, Humberto
1924(?)-1987 .... CLC 49
See also CA 131; 122; HW

Costello, Elvis 1955-.............. CLC 21

Cotter, Joseph Seamon Sr.
1861-1949 .... TCLC 28; BLC
See also BW 1; CA 124; DAM MULT;
DLB 50

Couch, Arthur Thomas Quiller
See Quiller-Couch, Arthur Thomas

Coulton, James
See Hansen, Joseph

Couperus, Louis (Marie Anne)
1863-1923 .... TCLC 15
See also CA 115

Coupland, Douglas 1961-..... CLC 85; DAC
See also CA 142; DAM POP

Court, Wesli
See Turco, Lewis (Putnam)

Courtenay, Bryce 1933-........... CLC 59
See also CA 138

Courtney, Robert
See Ellison, Harlan (Jay)

Cousteau, Jacques-Yves 1910-...... CLC 30
See also CA 65-68; CANR 15; MTCW;
SATA 38

Coward, Noel (Peirce)
1899-1973 .... CLC 1, 9, 29, 51
See also AITN 1; CA 17-18; 41-44R;
CANR 35; CAP 2; CDBLB 1914-1945;
DAM DRAM; DLB 10; MTCW

Cowley, Malcolm 1898-1989 .... CLC 39
See also CA 5-8R; 128; CANR 3; DLB 4,
48; DLBY 81, 89; MTCW

Cowper, William 1731-1800....... NCLC 8
See also DAM POET; DLB 104, 109

Cox, William Trevor 1928- ... CLC 9, 14, 71
See also Trevor, William
See also CA 9-12R; CANR 4, 37;
DAM NOV; DLB 14; INT CANR-37;
MTCW

Coyne, P. J.
See Masters, Hilary

Cozzens, James Gould
1903-1978 .... CLC 1, 4, 11
See also CA 9-12R; 81-84; CANR 19;
CDALB 1941-1968; DLB 9; DLBD 2;
DLBY 84; MTCW

Crabbe, George 1754-1832 .... NCLC 26
See also DLB 93

Craig, A. A.
See Anderson, Poul (William)

Craik, Dinah Maria (Mulock)
1826-1887 .... NCLC 38
See also DLB 35; MAICYA; SATA 34

Cram, Ralph Adams 1863-1942.... TCLC 45

Crane, (Harold) Hart
1899-1932 .... TCLC 2, 5; DA; DAB;
                        DAC; PC 3; WLC
See also CA 104; 127; CDALB 1917-1929;
DAM MST, POET; DLB 4, 48; MTCW

Crane, R(onald) S(almon)
1886-1967 .... CLC 27
See also CA 85-88; DLB 63

Crane, Stephen (Townley)
1871-1900 .... TCLC 11, 17, 32; DA;
                   DAB; DAC; SSC 7; WLC
See also CA 109; 140; CDALB 1865-1917;
DAM MST, NOV, POET; DLB 12, 54,
78; YABC 2

Crase, Douglas 1944-.............. CLC 58
See also CA 106

Crashaw, Richard 1612(?)-1649...... LC 24
See also DLB 126

Craven, Margaret
1901-1980 .... CLC 17; DAC
See also CA 103

Crawford, F(rancis) Marion
1854-1909 .... TCLC 10
See also CA 107; DLB 71

Crawford, Isabella Valancy
1850-1887 .... NCLC 12
See also DLB 92

Crayon, Geoffrey
See Irving, Washington

Creasey, John 1908-1973.......... CLC 11
See also CA 5-8R; 41-44R; CANR 8;
DLB 77; MTCW

Crebillon, Claude Prosper Jolyot de (fils)
1707-1777 .... LC 28

Credo
See Creasey, John

Creeley, Robert (White)
1926- ..... **CLC 1, 2, 4, 8, 11, 15, 36, 78**
See also CA 1-4R; CAAS 10; CANR 23, 43;
DAM POET; DLB 5, 16; MTCW

Crews, Harry (Eugene)
1935- .... **CLC 6, 23, 49**
See also AITN 1; CA 25-28R; CANR 20;
DLB 6, 143; MTCW

Crichton, (John) Michael
1942- .... **CLC 2, 6, 54, 90**
See also AAYA 10; AITN 2; CA 25-28R;
CANR 13, 40; DAM NOV, POP;
DLBY 81; INT CANR-13; JRDA;
MTCW; SATA 9

Crispin, Edmund .... **CLC 22**
See also Montgomery, (Robert) Bruce
See also DLB 87

Cristofer, Michael 1945(?)- .... **CLC 28**
See also CA 110; DAM DRAM; DLB 7

Croce, Benedetto 1866-1952 ...... **TCLC 37**
See also CA 120

Crockett, David 1786-1836 .... **NCLC 8**
See also DLB 3, 11

Crockett, Davy
See Crockett, David

Crofts, Freeman Wills
1879-1957 .... **TCLC 55**
See also CA 115; DLB 77

Croker, John Wilson 1780-1857 .. **NCLC 10**
See also DLB 110

Crommelynck, Fernand 1885-1970 .. **CLC 75**
See also CA 89-92

Cronin, A(rchibald) J(oseph)
1896-1981 .... **CLC 32**
See also CA 1-4R; 102; CANR 5; SATA 47;
SATA-Obit 25

Cross, Amanda
See Heilbrun, Carolyn G(old)

Crothers, Rachel 1878(?)-1958..... **TCLC 19**
See also CA 113; DLB 7

Croves, Hal
See Traven, B.

Crowfield, Christopher
See Stowe, Harriet (Elizabeth) Beecher

Crowley, Aleister.................... TCLC 7
See also Crowley, Edward Alexander

Crowley, Edward Alexander 1875-1947
See Crowley, Aleister
See also CA 104

Crowley, John 1942-.............. **CLC 57**
See also CA 61-64; CANR 43; DLBY 82;
SATA 65

Crud
See Crumb, R(obert)

Crumarums
See Crumb, R(obert)

Crumb, R(obert) 1943-........... **CLC 17**
See also CA 106

Crumbum
See Crumb, R(obert)

Crumski
See Crumb, R(obert)

Crum the Bum
See Crumb, R(obert)

Crunk
See Crumb, R(obert)

Crustt
See Crumb, R(obert)

Cryer, Gretchen (Kiger) 1935-...... **CLC 21**
See also CA 114; 123

Csath, Geza 1887-1919.......... **TCLC 13**
See also CA 111

Cudlip, David 1933- .... **CLC 34**

Cullen, Countee
1903-1946 ...... **TCLC 4, 37; BLC; DA;
DAC**
See also BW 1; CA 108; 124;
CDALB 1917-1929; DAM MST, MULT,
POET; DLB 4, 48, 51; MTCW; SATA 18

Cum, R.
See Crumb, R(obert)

Cummings, Bruce F(rederick) 1889-1919
See Barbellion, W. N. P.
See also CA 123

Cummings, E(dward) E(stlin)
1894-1962 ...... **CLC 1, 3, 8, 12, 15, 68;
DA; DAB; DAC; PC 5; WLC 2**
See also CA 73-76; CANR 31;
CDALB 1929-1941; DAM MST, POET;
DLB 4, 48; MTCW

Cunha, Euclides (Rodrigues Pimenta) da
1866-1909 .... **TCLC 24**
See also CA 123

Cunningham, E. V.
See Fast, Howard (Melvin)

Cunningham, J(ames) V(incent)
1911-1985 .... **CLC 3, 31**
See also CA 1-4R; 115; CANR 1; DLB 5

Cunningham, Julia (Woolfolk)
1916- .... **CLC 12**
See also CA 9-12R; CANR 4, 19, 36;
JRDA; MAICYA; SAAS 2; SATA 1, 26

Cunningham, Michael 1952- .... **CLC 34**
See also CA 136

Cunninghame Graham, R(obert) B(ontine)
1852-1936 .... **TCLC 19**
See also Graham, R(obert) B(ontine)
Cunninghame
See also CA 119; DLB 98

Currie, Ellen 19(?)-.............. **CLC 44**

Curtin, Philip
See Lowndes, Marie Adelaide (Belloc)

Curtis, Price
See Ellison, Harlan (Jay)

Cutrate, Joe
See Spiegelman, Art

Czaczkes, Shmuel Yosef
See Agnon, S(hmuel) Y(osef Halevi)

Dabrowska, Maria (Szumska)
1889-1965 .... **CLC 15**
See also CA 106

Dabydeen, David 1955- .... **CLC 34**
See also BW 1; CA 125

Dacey, Philip 1939- .... **CLC 51**
See also CA 37-40R; CAAS 17; CANR 14,
32; DLB 105

Dagerman, Stig (Halvard)
1923-1954 .... **TCLC 17**
See also CA 117

Dahl, Roald
1916-1990 ...... **CLC 1, 6, 18, 79; DAB;
DAC**
See also AAYA 15; CA 1-4R; 133;
CANR 6, 32, 37; CLR 1, 7; DAM MST,
NOV, POP; DLB 139; JRDA; MAICYA;
MTCW; SATA 1, 26, 73; SATA-Obit 65

Dahlberg, Edward 1900-1977... **CLC 1, 7, 14**
See also CA 9-12R; 69-72; CANR 31;
DLB 48; MTCW

Dale, Colin...................... TCLC 18
See also Lawrence, T(homas) E(dward)

Dale, George E.
See Asimov, Isaac

Daly, Elizabeth 1878-1967........ **CLC 52**
See also CA 23-24; 25-28R; CAP 2

Daly, Maureen 1921-............. **CLC 17**
See also AAYA 5; CANR 37; JRDA;
MAICYA; SAAS 1; SATA 2

Damas, Leon-Gontran 1912-1978 ... **CLC 84**
See also BW 1; CA 125; 73-76

Dana, Richard Henry Sr.
1787-1879 .... **NCLC 53**

Daniel, Samuel 1562(?)-1619........ **LC 24**
See also DLB 62

Daniels, Brett
See Adler, Renata

Dannay, Frederic 1905-1982 .... **CLC 11**
See also Queen, Ellery
See also CA 1-4R; 107; CANR 1, 39;
DAM POP; DLB 137, MTCW

D'Annunzio, Gabriele
1863-1938 .... **TCLC 6, 40**
See also CA 104

d'Antibes, Germain
See Simenon, Georges (Jacques Christian)

Danvers, Dennis 1947-............ **CLC 70**

Danziger, Paula 1944- .... **CLC 21**
See also AAYA 4; CA 112; 115; CANR 37;
CLR 20; JRDA; MAICYA; SATA 36,
63; SATA-Brief 30

Da Ponte, Lorenzo 1749-1838.... **NCLC 50**

Dario, Ruben 1867-1916 .... **TCLC 4; HLC**
See also CA 131; DAM MULT; HW;
MTCW

Darley, George 1795-1846........ **NCLC 2**
See also DLB 96

Daryush, Elizabeth 1887-1977.... **CLC 6, 19**
See also CA 49-52; CANR 3; DLB 20

Dashwood, Edmee Elizabeth Monica de la
Pasture 1890-1943
See Delafield, E. M.
See also CA 119

Daudet, (Louis Marie) Alphonse
1840-1897 .... **NCLC 1**
See also DLB 123

Daumal, Rene 1908-1944........ **TCLC 14**
See also CA 114

Davenport, Guy (Mattison, Jr.)
1927- .... **CLC 6, 14, 38; SSC 16**
See also CA 33-36R; CANR 23; DLB 130

Davidson, Avram   1923-
See Queen, Ellery
See also CA 101; CANR 26; DLB 8

Davidson, Donald (Grady)
1893-1968 . . . . CLC 2, 13, 19
See also CA 5-8R; 25-28R; CANR 4;
DLB 45

Davidson, Hugh
See Hamilton, Edmond

Davidson, John   1857-1909 . . . . TCLC 24
See also CA 118; DLB 19

Davidson, Sara   1943- . . . . CLC 9
See also CA 81-84; CANR 44

Davie, Donald (Alfred)
1922- . . . . CLC 5, 8, 10, 31
See also CA 1-4R; CAAS 3; CANR 1, 44;
DLB 27; MTCW

Davies, Ray(mond Douglas)   1944- . . CLC 21
See also CA 116; 146

Davies, Rhys   1903-1978 . . . . CLC 23
See also CA 9-12R; 81-84; CANR 4;
DLB 139

Davies, (William) Robertson
1913- . . . . . CLC 2, 7, 13, 25, 42, 75; DA;
DAB; DAC; WLC
See also BEST 89:2; CA 33-36R; CANR 17,
42; DAM MST, NOV, POP; DLB 68;
INT CANR-17; MTCW

Davies, W(illiam) H(enry)
1871-1940 . . . . TCLC 5
See also CA 104; DLB 19

Davies, Walter C.
See Kornbluth, C(yril) M.

Davis, Angela (Yvonne)   1944- . . . . . . CLC 77
See also BW 2; CA 57-60; CANR 10;
DAM MULT

Davis, B. Lynch
See Bioy Casares, Adolfo; Borges, Jorge
Luis

Davis, Gordon
See Hunt, E(verette) Howard, (Jr.)

Davis, Harold Lenoir   1896-1960 . . . . CLC 49
See also CA 89-92; DLB 9

Davis, Rebecca (Blaine) Harding
1831-1910 . . . . TCLC 6
See also CA 104; DLB 74

Davis, Richard Harding
1864-1916 . . . . TCLC 24
See also CA 114; DLB 12, 23, 78, 79;
DLBD 13

Davison, Frank Dalby   1893-1970 . . . CLC 15
See also CA 116

Davison, Lawrence H.
See Lawrence, D(avid) H(erbert Richards)

Davison, Peter (Hubert)   1928- . . . . . CLC 28
See also CA 9-12R; CAAS 4; CANR 3, 43;
DLB 5

Davys, Mary   1674-1732 . . . . LC 1
See also DLB 39

Dawson, Fielding   1930- . . . . CLC 6
See also CA 85-88; DLB 130

Dawson, Peter
See Faust, Frederick (Schiller)

Day, Clarence (Shepard, Jr.)
1874-1935 . . . . TCLC 25
See also CA 108; DLB 11

Day, Thomas   1748-1789 . . . . LC 1
See also DLB 39; YABC 1

Day Lewis, C(ecil)
1904-1972 . . . . CLC 1, 6, 10; PC 11
See also Blake, Nicholas
See also CA 13-16; 33-36R; CANR 34;
CAP 1; DAM POET; DLB 15, 20;
MTCW

Dazai, Osamu . . . . TCLC 11
See also Tsushima, Shuji

de Andrade, Carlos Drummond
See Drummond de Andrade, Carlos

Deane, Norman
See Creasey, John

de Beauvoir, Simone (Lucie Ernestine Marie
Bertrand)
See Beauvoir, Simone (Lucie Ernestine
Marie Bertrand) de

de Brissac, Malcolm
See Dickinson, Peter (Malcolm)

de Chardin, Pierre Teilhard
See Teilhard de Chardin, (Marie Joseph)
Pierre

Dee, John   1527-1608 . . . . LC 20

Deer, Sandra   1940- . . . . CLC 45

De Ferrari, Gabriella   1941- . . . . CLC 65
See also CA 146

Defoe, Daniel
1660(?)-1731 . . . . LC 1; DA; DAB; DAC;
WLC
See also CDBLB 1660-1789; DAM MST,
NOV; DLB 39, 95, 101; JRDA;
MAICYA; SATA 22

de Gourmont, Remy
See Gourmont, Remy de

de Hartog, Jan   1914- . . . . CLC 19
See also CA 1-4R; CANR 1

de Hostos, E. M.
See Hostos (y Bonilla), Eugenio Maria de

de Hostos, Eugenio M.
See Hostos (y Bonilla), Eugenio Maria de

Deighton, Len . . . . CLC 4, 7, 22, 46
See also Deighton, Leonard Cyril
See also AAYA 6; BEST 89:2;
CDBLB 1960 to Present; DLB 87

Deighton, Leonard Cyril   1929-
See Deighton, Len
See also CA 9-12R; CANR 19, 33;
DAM NOV, POP; MTCW

Dekker, Thomas   1572(?)-1632 . . . . . . LC 22
See also CDBLB Before 1660;
DAM DRAM; DLB 62

Delafield, E. M.   1890-1943 . . . . TCLC 61
See also Dashwood, Edmee Elizabeth
Monica de la Pasture
See also DLB 34

de la Mare, Walter (John)
1873-1956 . . . . TCLC 4, 53; DAB; DAC;
SSC 14; WLC
See also CDBLB 1914-1945; CLR 23;
DAM MST, POET; DLB 19, 153;
SATA 16

Delaney, Franey
See O'Hara, John (Henry)

Delaney, Shelagh   1939- . . . . CLC 29
See also CA 17-20R; CANR 30;
CDBLB 1960 to Present; DAM DRAM;
DLB 13; MTCW

Delany, Mary (Granville Pendarves)
1700-1788 . . . . LC 12

Delany, Samuel R(ay, Jr.)
1942- . . . . CLC 8, 14, 38; BLC
See also BW 2; CA 81-84; CANR 27, 43;
DAM MULT; DLB 8, 33; MTCW

De La Ramee, (Marie) Louise   1839-1908
See Ouida
See also SATA 20

de la Roche, Mazo   1879-1961 . . . . . . CLC 14
See also CA 85-88; CANR 30; DLB 68;
SATA 64

Delbanco, Nicholas (Franklin)
1942- . . . . CLC 6, 13
See also CA 17-20R; CAAS 2; CANR 29;
DLB 6

del Castillo, Michel   1933- . . . . CLC 38
See also CA 109

Deledda, Grazia (Cosima)
1875(?)-1936 . . . . TCLC 23
See also CA 123

Delibes, Miguel . . . . CLC 8, 18
See also Delibes Setien, Miguel

Delibes Setien, Miguel   1920-
See Delibes, Miguel
See also CA 45-48; CANR 1, 32; HW;
MTCW

DeLillo, Don
1936- . . . . . CLC 8, 10, 13, 27, 39, 54, 76
See also BEST 89:1; CA 81-84; CANR 21;
DAM NOV, POP; DLB 6; MTCW

de Lisser, H. G.
See De Lisser, Herbert George
See also DLB 117

De Lisser, Herbert George
1878-1944 . . . . TCLC 12
See also de Lisser, H. G.
See also BW 2; CA 109

Deloria, Vine (Victor), Jr.   1933- . . . . CLC 21
See also CA 53-56; CANR 5, 20, 48;
DAM MULT; MTCW; NNAL; SATA 21

Del Vecchio, John M(ichael)
1947- . . . . CLC 29
See also CA 110; DLBD 9

de Man, Paul (Adolph Michel)
1919-1983 . . . . CLC 55
See also CA 128; 111; DLB 67; MTCW

De Marinis, Rick   1934- . . . . CLC 54
See also CA 57-60; CANR 9, 25, 50

Demby, William   1922- . . . . CLC 53; BLC
See also BW 1; CA 81-84; DAM MULT;
DLB 33

Demijohn, Thom
See Disch, Thomas M(ichael)

de Montherlant, Henry (Milon)
See Montherlant, Henry (Milon) de

Demosthenes   384B.C.-322B.C. . . . . CMLC 13

de Natale, Francine
See Malzberg, Barry N(athaniel)

Denby, Edwin (Orr) 1903-1983 . . . . . **CLC 48**
See also CA 138; 110

Denis, Julio
See Cortazar, Julio

Denmark, Harrison
See Zelazny, Roger (Joseph)

Dennis, John 1658-1734 . . . . **LC 11**
See also DLB 101

Dennis, Nigel (Forbes) 1912-1989 . . . . **CLC 8**
See also CA 25-28R; 129; DLB 13, 15;
MTCW

De Palma, Brian (Russell) 1940- . . . . **CLC 20**
See also CA 109

De Quincey, Thomas 1785-1859 . . . **NCLC 4**
See also CDBLB 1789-1832; DLB 110; 144

Deren, Eleanora 1908(?)-1961
See Deren, Maya
See also CA 111

Deren, Maya . . . . **CLC 16**
See also Deren, Eleanora

Derleth, August (William)
1909-1971 . . . . **CLC 31**
See also CA 1-4R; 29-32R; CANR 4;
DLB 9; SATA 5

Der Nister 1884-1950 . . . . **TCLC 56**

de Routisie, Albert
See Aragon, Louis

Derrida, Jacques 1930- . . . . **CLC 24, 87**
See also CA 124; 127

Derry Down Derry
See Lear, Edward

Dersonnes, Jacques
See Simenon, Georges (Jacques Christian)

Desai, Anita 1937- . . . . . . **CLC 19, 37; DAB**
See also CA 81-84; CANR 33; DAM NOV;
MTCW; SATA 63

de Saint-Luc, Jean
See Glassco, John

de Saint Roman, Arnaud
See Aragon, Louis

Descartes, Rene 1596-1650 . . . . **LC 20**

De Sica, Vittorio 1901(?)-1974 . . . . . **CLC 20**
See also CA 117

Desnos, Robert 1900-1945 . . . . **TCLC 22**
See also CA 121

Destouches, Louis-Ferdinand
1894-1961 . . . . **CLC 9, 15**
See also Celine, Louis-Ferdinand
See also CA 85-88; CANR 28; MTCW

Deutsch, Babette 1895-1982 . . . . **CLC 18**
See also CA 1-4R; 108; CANR 4; DLB 45;
SATA 1; SATA-Obit 33

Devenant, William 1606-1649 . . . . . . **LC 13**

Devkota, Laxmiprasad
1909-1959 . . . . **TCLC 23**
See also CA 123

De Voto, Bernard (Augustine)
1897-1955 . . . . **TCLC 29**
See also CA 113; DLB 9

De Vries, Peter
1910-1993 . . . . **CLC 1, 2, 3, 7, 10, 28, 46**
See also CA 17-20R; 142; CANR 41;
DAM NOV; DLB 6; DLBY 82; MTCW

Dexter, Martin
See Faust, Frederick (Schiller)

Dexter, Pete 1943- . . . . **CLC 34, 55**
See also BEST 89:2; CA 127; 131;
DAM POP; INT 131; MTCW

Diamano, Silmang
See Senghor, Leopold Sedar

Diamond, Neil 1941- . . . . **CLC 30**
See also CA 108

Diaz del Castillo, Bernal 1496-1584 . . **LC 31**

di Bassetto, Corno
See Shaw, George Bernard

Dick, Philip K(indred)
1928-1982 . . . . **CLC 10, 30, 72**
See also CA 49-52; 106; CANR 2, 16;
DAM NOV, POP; DLB 8; MTCW

Dickens, Charles (John Huffam)
1812-1870 . . . . . . **NCLC 3, 8, 18, 26, 37,
50; DA; DAB; DAC; SSC 17; WLC**
See also CDBLB 1832-1890; DAM MST,
NOV; DLB 21, 55, 70, 159; JRDA;
MAICYA; SATA 15

Dickey, James (Lafayette)
1923- . . . . **CLC 1, 2, 4, 7, 10, 15, 47**
See also AITN 1, 2; CA 9-12R; CABS 2;
CANR 10, 48; CDALB 1968-1988;
DAM NOV, POET, POP; DLB 5;
DLBD 7; DLBY 82, 93; INT CANR-10;
MTCW

Dickey, William 1928-1994 . . . . . . **CLC 3, 28**
See also CA 9-12R; 145; CANR 24; DLB 5

Dickinson, Charles 1951- . . . . **CLC 49**
See also CA 128

Dickinson, Emily (Elizabeth)
1830-1886 . . . . . . **NCLC 21; DA; DAB;
DAC; PC 1; WLC**
See also CDALB 1865-1917; DAM MST,
POET; DLB 1; SATA 29

Dickinson, Peter (Malcolm)
1927- . . . . **CLC 12, 35**
See also AAYA 9; CA 41-44R; CANR 31;
CLR 29; DLB 87, 161; JRDA; MAICYA;
SATA 5, 62

Dickson, Carr
See Carr, John Dickson

Dickson, Carter
See Carr, John Dickson

Diderot, Denis 1713-1784 . . . . **LC 26**

Didion, Joan 1934- . . . . . **CLC 1, 3, 8, 14, 32**
See also AITN 1; CA 5-8R; CANR 14;
CDALB 1968-1988; DAM NOV; DLB 2;
DLBY 81, 86; MTCW

Dietrich, Robert
See Hunt, E(verette) Howard, (Jr.)

Dillard, Annie 1945- . . . . **CLC 9, 60**
See also AAYA 6; CA 49-52; CANR 3, 43;
DAM NOV; DLBY 80; MTCW;
SATA 10

Dillard, R(ichard) H(enry) W(ilde)
1937- . . . . **CLC 5**
See also CA 21-24R; CAAS 7; CANR 10;
DLB 5

Dillon, Eilis 1920-1994 . . . . **CLC 17**
See also CA 9-12R; 147; CAAS 3; CANR 4,
38; CLR 26; MAICYA; SATA 2, 74;
SATA-Obit 83

Dimont, Penelope
See Mortimer, Penelope (Ruth)

Dinesen, Isak . . . . **CLC 10, 29; SSC 7**
See also Blixen, Karen (Christentze
Dinesen)

Ding Ling . . . . **CLC 68**
See also Chiang Pin-chin

Disch, Thomas M(ichael) 1940- . . . **CLC 7, 36**
See also AAYA 17; CA 21-24R; CAAS 4;
CANR 17, 36; CLR 18; DLB 8;
MAICYA; MTCW; SAAS 15; SATA 54

Disch, Tom
See Disch, Thomas M(ichael)

d'Isly, Georges
See Simenon, Georges (Jacques Christian)

Disraeli, Benjamin 1804-1881 . . **NCLC 2, 39**
See also DLB 21, 55

Ditcum, Steve
See Crumb, R(obert)

Dixon, Paige
See Corcoran, Barbara

Dixon, Stephen 1936- . . . . . **CLC 52; SSC 16**
See also CA 89-92, CANR 17, 40; DLB 130

Dobell, Sydney Thompson
1824-1874 . . . . **NCLC 43**
See also DLB 32

Doblin, Alfred . . . . **TCLC 13**
See also Doeblin, Alfred

Dobrolyubov, Nikolai Alexandrovich
1836-1861 . . . . **NCLC 5**

Dobyns, Stephen 1941- . . . . **CLC 37**
See also CA 45-48; CANR 2, 18

Doctorow, E(dgar) L(aurence)
1931- . . . **CLC 6, 11, 15, 18, 37, 44, 65**
See also AITN 2; BEST 89:3; CA 45-48;
CANR 2, 33; CDALB 1968-1988;
DAM NOV, POP; DLB 2, 28; DLBY 80;
MTCW

Dodgson, Charles Lutwidge 1832-1898
See Carroll, Lewis
See also CLR 2; DA; DAB; DAC;
DAM MST, NOV, POET; MAICYA;
YABC 2

Dodson, Owen (Vincent)
1914-1983 . . . . **CLC 79; BLC**
See also BW 1; CA 65-68; 110; CANR 24;
DAM MULT; DLB 76

Doeblin, Alfred 1878-1957 . . . . **TCLC 13**
See also Doblin, Alfred
See also CA 110; 141; DLB 66

Doerr, Harriet 1910- . . . . **CLC 34**
See also CA 117; 122; CANR 47; INT 122

Domecq, H(onorio) Bustos
See Bioy Casares, Adolfo; Borges, Jorge
Luis

Domini, Rey
See Lorde, Audre (Geraldine)

Dominique
See Proust, (Valentin-Louis-George-Eugene-)
Marcel

Don, A
See Stephen, Leslie

Donaldson, Stephen R. 1947- . . . . **CLC 46**
See also CA 89-92; CANR 13; DAM POP;
INT CANR-13

Donleavy, J(ames) P(atrick)
1926- . . . . CLC 1, 4, 6, 10, 45
See also AITN 2; CA 9-12R; CANR 24, 49;
DLB 6; INT CANR-24; MTCW

Donne, John
1572-1631 . . . . . . LC 10, 24; DA; DAB;
DAC; PC 1
See also CDBLB Before 1660; DAM MST,
POET; DLB 121, 151

Donnell, David   1939(?)- . . . . CLC 34

Donoghue, P. S.
See Hunt, E(verette) Howard, (Jr.)

Donoso (Yanez), Jose
1924- . . . . CLC 4, 8, 11, 32; HLC
See also CA 81-84; CANR 32;
DAM MULT; DLB 113; HW; MTCW

Donovan, John   1928-1992 . . . . CLC 35
See also CA 97-100; 137; CLR 3;
MAICYA; SATA 72; SATA-Brief 29

Don Roberto
See Cunninghame Graham, R(obert)
B(ontine)

Doolittle, Hilda
1886-1961 . . . . . CLC 3, 8, 14, 31, 34, 73;
DA; DAC; PC 5; WLC
See also H. D.
See also CA 97-100; CANR 35; DAM MST,
POET; DLB 4, 45; MTCW

Dorfman, Ariel   1942- . . . . CLC 48, 77; HLC
See also CA 124; 130; DAM MULT; HW;
INT 130

Dorn, Edward (Merton)   1929- . . . CLC 10, 18
See also CA 93-96; CANR 42; DLB 5;
INT 93-96

Dorsan, Luc
See Simenon, Georges (Jacques Christian)

Dorsange, Jean
See Simenon, Georges (Jacques Christian)

Dos Passos, John (Roderigo)
1896-1970 . . . . . . CLC 1, 4, 8, 11, 15, 25,
34, 82; DA; DAB; DAC; WLC
See also CA 1-4R; 29-32R; CANR 3;
CDALB 1929-1941; DAM MST, NOV;
DLB 4, 9; DLBD 1; MTCW

Dossage, Jean
See Simenon, Georges (Jacques Christian)

Dostoevsky, Fedor Mikhailovich
1821-1881 . . . . . NCLC 2, 7, 21, 33, 43;
DA; DAB; DAC; SSC 2; WLC
See also DAM MST, NOV

Doughty, Charles M(ontagu)
1843-1926 . . . . TCLC 27
See also CA 115; DLB 19, 57

Douglas, Ellen . . . . CLC 73
See also Haxton, Josephine Ayres;
Williamson, Ellen Douglas

Douglas, Gavin   1475(?)-1522 . . . . LC 20

Douglas, Keith   1920-1944 . . . . TCLC 40
See also DLB 27

Douglas, Leonard
See Bradbury, Ray (Douglas)

Douglas, Michael
See Crichton, (John) Michael

Douglass, Frederick
1817(?)-1895 . . . . . . NCLC 7; BLC; DA;
DAC; WLC
See also CDALB 1640-1865; DAM MST,
MULT; DLB 1, 43, 50, 79; SATA 29

Dourado, (Waldomiro Freitas) Autran
1926- . . . . CLC 23, 60
See also CA 25-28R; CANR 34

Dourado, Waldomiro Autran
See Dourado, (Waldomiro Freitas) Autran

Dove, Rita (Frances)
1952- . . . . CLC 50, 81; PC 6
See also BW 2; CA 109; CAAS 19;
CANR 27, 42; DAM MULT, POET;
DLB 120

Dowell, Coleman   1925-1985 . . . . CLC 60
See also CA 25-28R; 117; CANR 10;
DLB 130

Dowson, Ernest Christopher
1867-1900 . . . . TCLC 4
See also CA 105; DLB 19, 135

Doyle, A. Conan
See Doyle, Arthur Conan

Doyle, Arthur Conan
1859-1930 . . . . TCLC 7; DA; DAB;
DAC; SSC 12; WLC
See also AAYA 14; CA 104; 122;
CDBLB 1890-1914; DAM MST, NOV;
DLB 18, 70, 156; MTCW; SATA 24

Doyle, Conan
See Doyle, Arthur Conan

Doyle, John
See Graves, Robert (von Ranke)

Doyle, Roddy   1958(?)- . . . . CLC 81
See also AAYA 14; CA 143

Doyle, Sir A. Conan
See Doyle, Arthur Conan

Doyle, Sir Arthur Conan
See Doyle, Arthur Conan

Dr. A
See Asimov, Isaac; Silverstein, Alvin

Drabble, Margaret
1939- . . . . CLC 2, 3, 5, 8, 10, 22, 53;
DAB; DAC
See also CA 13-16R; CANR 18, 35;
CDBLB 1960 to Present; DAM MST,
NOV, POP; DLB 14, 155; MTCW;
SATA 48

Drapier, M. B.
See Swift, Jonathan

Drayham, James
See Mencken, H(enry) L(ouis)

Drayton, Michael   1563-1631 . . . . LC 8

Dreadstone, Carl
See Campbell, (John) Ramsey

Dreiser, Theodore (Herman Albert)
1871-1945 . . . . . . TCLC 10, 18, 35; DA;
DAC; WLC
See also CA 106; 132; CDALB 1865-1917;
DAM MST, NOV; DLB 9, 12, 102, 137;
DLBD 1; MTCW

Drexler, Rosalyn   1926- . . . . CLC 2, 6
See also CA 81-84

Dreyer, Carl Theodor   1889-1968 . . . . CLC 16
See also CA 116

Drieu la Rochelle, Pierre(-Eugene)
1893-1945 . . . . TCLC 21
See also CA 117; DLB 72

Drinkwater, John   1882-1937 . . . . . . TCLC 57
See also CA 109; 149; DLB 10, 19, 149

Drop Shot
See Cable, George Washington

Droste-Hulshoff, Annette Freiin von
1797-1848 . . . . NCLC 3
See also DLB 133

Drummond, Walter
See Silverberg, Robert

Drummond, William Henry
1854-1907 . . . . TCLC 25
See also DLB 92

Drummond de Andrade, Carlos
1902-1987 . . . . CLC 18
See also Andrade, Carlos Drummond de
See also CA 132; 123

Drury, Allen (Stuart)   1918- . . . . CLC 37
See also CA 57-60; CANR 18;
INT CANR-18

Dryden, John
1631-1700 . . . . LC 3, 21; DA; DAB;
DAC; DC 3; WLC
See also CDBLB 1660-1789; DAM DRAM,
MST, POET; DLB 80, 101, 131

Duberman, Martin   1930- . . . . CLC 8
See also CA 1-4R; CANR 2

Dubie, Norman (Evans)   1945- . . . . . . CLC 36
See also CA 69-72; CANR 12; DLB 120

Du Bois, W(illiam) E(dward) B(urghardt)
1868-1963 . . . . . . CLC 1, 2, 13, 64; BLC;
DA; DAC; WLC
See also BW 1; CA 85-88; CANR 34;
CDALB 1865-1917; DAM MST, MULT,
NOV; DLB 47, 50, 91; MTCW; SATA 42

Dubus, Andre   1936- . . . CLC 13, 36; SSC 15
See also CA 21-24R; CANR 17; DLB 130;
INT CANR-17

Duca Minimo
See D'Annunzio, Gabriele

Ducharme, Rejean   1941- . . . . CLC 74
See also DLB 60

Duclos, Charles Pinot   1704-1772 . . . . . LC 1

Dudek, Louis   1918- . . . . CLC 11, 19
See also CA 45-48; CAAS 14; CANR 1;
DLB 88

Duerrenmatt, Friedrich
1921-1990 . . . . . . CLC 1, 4, 8, 11, 15, 43
See also CA 17-20R; CANR 33;
DAM DRAM; DLB 69, 124; MTCW

Duffy, Bruce   (?)- . . . . CLC 50

Duffy, Maureen   1933- . . . . CLC 37
See also CA 25-28R; CANR 33; DLB 14;
MTCW

Dugan, Alan   1923- . . . . CLC 2, 6
See also CA 81-84; DLB 5

du Gard, Roger Martin
See Martin du Gard, Roger

Duhamel, Georges   1884-1966 . . . . CLC 8
See also CA 81-84; 25-28R; CANR 35;
DLB 65; MTCW

Fugard, (Harold) Athol
    1932- .... CLC 5, 9, 14, 25, 40, 80; DC 3
    See also AAYA 17; CA 85-88; CANR 32;
    DAM DRAM; MTCW

Fugard, Sheila   1932- .... CLC 48
    See also CA 125

Fuller, Charles (H., Jr.)
    1939- .... CLC 25; BLC; DC 1
    See also BW 2; CA 108; 112;
    DAM DRAM, MULT; DLB 38;
    INT 112; MTCW

Fuller, John (Leopold)   1937- .... CLC 62
    See also CA 21-24R; CANR 9, 44; DLB 40

Fuller, Margaret .... NCLC 5, 50
    See also Ossoli, Sarah Margaret (Fuller
    marchesa d')

Fuller, Roy (Broadbent)
    1912-1991 .... CLC 4, 28
    See also CA 5-8R; 135; CAAS 10; DLB 15,
    20

Fulton, Alice   1952- .... CLC 52
    See also CA 116

Furphy, Joseph   1843-1912 .... TCLC 25

Fussell, Paul   1924- .... CLC 74
    See also BEST 90:1; CA 17-20R; CANR 8,
    21, 35; INT CANR-21; MTCW

Futabatei, Shimei   1864-1909 ...... TCLC 44

Futrelle, Jacques   1875-1912 ...... TCLC 19
    See also CA 113

Gaboriau, Emile   1835-1873 ...... NCLC 14

Gadda, Carlo Emilio   1893-1973 .... CLC 11
    See also CA 89-92

Gaddis, William
    1922- ..... CLC 1, 3, 6, 8, 10, 19, 43, 86
    See also CA 17-20R; CANR 21, 48; DLB 2;
    MTCW

Gaines, Ernest J(ames)
    1933- .... CLC 3, 11, 18, 86; BLC
    See also AITN 1; BW 2; CA 9-12R;
    CANR 6, 24, 42; CDALB 1968-1988;
    DAM MULT; DLB 2, 33, 152; DLBY 80;
    MTCW

Gaitskill, Mary   1954- .... CLC 69
    See also CA 128

Galdos, Benito Perez
    See Perez Galdos, Benito

Gale, Zona   1874-1938 .... TCLC 7
    See also CA 105; DAM DRAM; DLB 9, 78

Galeano, Eduardo (Hughes)   1940- ... CLC 72
    See also CA 29-32R; CANR 13, 32; HW

Galiano, Juan Valera y Alcala
    See Valera y Alcala-Galiano, Juan

Gallagher, Tess   1943- .... CLC 18, 63; PC 9
    See also CA 106; DAM POET; DLB 120

Gallant, Mavis
    1922- ...... CLC 7, 18, 38; DAC; SSC 5
    See also CA 69-72; CANR 29; DAM MST;
    DLB 53; MTCW

Gallant, Roy A(rthur)   1924- .... CLC 17
    See also CA 5-8R; CANR 4, 29; CLR 30;
    MAICYA; SATA 4, 68

Gallico, Paul (William)   1897-1976 ... CLC 2
    See also AITN 1; CA 5-8R; 69-72;
    CANR 23; DLB 9; MAICYA; SATA 13

Gallup, Ralph
    See Whitemore, Hugh (John)

Galsworthy, John
    1867-1933 ...... TCLC 1, 45; DA; DAB;
                          DAC; WLC 2
    See also CA 104; 141; CDBLB 1890-1914;
    DAM DRAM, MST, NOV; DLB 10, 34,
    98

Galt, John   1779-1839 .... NCLC 1
    See also DLB 99, 116, 159

Galvin, James   1951- .... CLC 38
    See also CA 108; CANR 26

Gamboa, Federico   1864-1939 ...... TCLC 36

Gandhi, M. K.
    See Gandhi, Mohandas Karamchand

Gandhi, Mahatma
    See Gandhi, Mohandas Karamchand

Gandhi, Mohandas Karamchand
    1869-1948 .... TCLC 59
    See also CA 121; 132; DAM MULT;
    MTCW

Gann, Ernest Kellogg   1910-1991 .... CLC 23
    See also AITN 1; CA 1-4R; 136; CANR 1

Garcia, Cristina   1958- .... CLC 76
    See also CA 141

Garcia Lorca, Federico
    1898-1936 ... TCLC 1, 7, 49; DA; DAB;
                    DAC; DC 2; HLC; PC 3; WLC
    See also CA 104; 131; DAM DRAM, MST,
    MULT, POET; DLB 108; HW; MTCW

Garcia Marquez, Gabriel (Jose)
    1928- .... CLC 2, 3, 8, 10, 15, 27, 47, 55,
        68; DA; DAB; DAC; HLC; SSC 8; WLC
    See also AAYA 3; BEST 89:1, 90:4;
    CA 33-36R; CANR 10, 28, 50;
    DAM MST, MULT, NOV, POP;
    DLB 113; HW; MTCW

Gard, Janice
    See Latham, Jean Lee

Gard, Roger Martin du
    See Martin du Gard, Roger

Gardam, Jane   1928- .... CLC 43
    See also CA 49-52; CANR 2, 18, 33;
    CLR 12; DLB 14, 161; MAICYA;
    MTCW; SAAS 9; SATA 39, 76;
    SATA-Brief 28

Gardner, Herb .... CLC 44

Gardner, John (Champlin), Jr.
    1933-1982 ..... CLC 2, 3, 5, 7, 8, 10, 18,
                          28, 34; SSC 7
    See also AITN 1; CA 65-68; 107;
    CANR 33; DAM NOV, POP; DLB 2;
    DLBY 82; MTCW; SATA 40;
    SATA-Obit 31

Gardner, John (Edmund)   1926- ..... CLC 30
    See also CA 103; CANR 15; DAM POP;
    MTCW

Gardner, Noel
    See Kuttner, Henry

Gardons, S. S.
    See Snodgrass, W(illiam) D(e Witt)

Garfield, Leon   1921- .... CLC 12
    See also AAYA 8; CA 17-20R; CANR 38,
    41; CLR 21; DLB 161; JRDA; MAICYA;
    SATA 1, 32, 76

Garland, (Hannibal) Hamlin
    1860-1940 .... TCLC 3; SSC 18
    See also CA 104; DLB 12, 71, 78

Garneau, (Hector de) Saint-Denys
    1912-1943 .... TCLC 13
    See also CA 111; DLB 88

Garner, Alan   1934- .... CLC 17; DAB
    See also CA 73-76; CANR 15; CLR 20;
    DAM POP; DLB 161; MAICYA;
    MTCW; SATA 18, 69

Garner, Hugh   1913-1979 .... CLC 13
    See also CA 69-72; CANR 31; DLB 68

Garnett, David   1892-1981 .... CLC 3
    See also CA 5-8R; 103; CANR 17; DLB 34

Garos, Stephanie
    See Katz, Steve

Garrett, George (Palmer)
    1929- .... CLC 3, 11, 51
    See also CA 1-4R; CAAS 5; CANR 1, 42;
    DLB 2, 5, 130, 152; DLBY 83

Garrick, David   1717-1779 .... LC 15
    See also DAM DRAM; DLB 84

Garrigue, Jean   1914-1972 .... CLC 2, 8
    See also CA 5-8R; 37-40R; CANR 20

Garrison, Frederick
    See Sinclair, Upton (Beall)

Garth, Will
    See Hamilton, Edmond; Kuttner, Henry

Garvey, Marcus (Moziah, Jr.)
    1887-1940 .... TCLC 41; BLC
    See also BW 1; CA 120; 124; DAM MULT

Gary, Romain .... CLC 25
    See also Kacew, Romain
    See also DLB 83

Gascar, Pierre .... CLC 11
    See also Fournier, Pierre

Gascoyne, David (Emery)   1916- .... CLC 45
    See also CA 65-68; CANR 10, 28; DLB 20;
    MTCW

Gaskell, Elizabeth Cleghorn
    1810-1865 .... NCLC 5; DAB
    See also CDBLB 1832-1890; DAM MST;
    DLB 21, 144, 159

Gass, William H(oward)
    1924- ... CLC 1, 2, 8, 11, 15, 39; SSC 12
    See also CA 17-20R; CANR 30; DLB 2;
    MTCW

Gasset, Jose Ortega y
    See Ortega y Gasset, Jose

Gates, Henry Louis, Jr.   1950- ...... CLC 65
    See also BW 2; CA 109; CANR 25;
    DAM MULT; DLB 67

Gautier, Theophile
    1811-1872 .... NCLC 1; SSC 20
    See also DAM POET; DLB 119

Gawsworth, John
    See Bates, H(erbert) E(rnest)

Gaye, Marvin (Penze)   1939-1984 ... CLC 26
    See also CA 112

Gebler, Carlo (Ernest)   1954- .... CLC 39
    See also CA 119; 133

Gee, Maggie (Mary)   1948- .... CLC 57
    See also CA 130

Gee, Maurice (Gough) 1931- .... CLC 29
See also CA 97-100; SATA 46

Gelbart, Larry (Simon) 1923- ... CLC 21, 61
See also CA 73-76; CANR 45

Gelber, Jack 1932- .... CLC 1, 6, 14, 79
See also CA 1-4R; CANR 2; DLB 7

Gellhorn, Martha (Ellis) 1908- .. CLC 14, 60
See also CA 77-80; CANR 44; DLBY 82

Genet, Jean
1910-1986 ... CLC 1, 2, 5, 10, 14, 44, 46
See also CA 13-16R; CANR 18;
DAM DRAM; DLB 72; DLBY 86;
MTCW

Gent, Peter 1942- .... CLC 29
See also AITN 1; CA 89-92; DLBY 82

Gentlewoman in New England, A
See Bradstreet, Anne

Gentlewoman in Those Parts, A
See Bradstreet, Anne

George, Jean Craighead 1919- ...... CLC 35
See also AAYA 8; CA 5-8R; CANR 25;
CLR 1; DLB 52; JRDA; MAICYA;
SATA 2, 68

George, Stefan (Anton)
1868-1933 .... TCLC 2, 14
See also CA 104

Georges, Georges Martin
See Simenon, Georges (Jacques Christian)

Gerhardi, William Alexander
See Gerhardie, William Alexander

Gerhardie, William Alexander
1895-1977 .... CLC 5
See also CA 25-28R; 73-76; CANR 18;
DLB 36

Gerstler, Amy 1956- .... CLC 70
See also CA 146

Gertler, T. .... CLC 34
See also CA 116; 121; INT 121

Ghalib 1797-1869 .... NCLC 39

Ghelderode, Michel de
1898-1962 .... CLC 6, 11
See also CA 85-88; CANR 40;
DAM DRAM

Ghiselin, Brewster 1903- .... CLC 23
See also CA 13-16R; CAAS 10; CANR 13

Ghose, Zulfikar 1935- .... CLC 42
See also CA 65-68

Ghosh, Amitav 1956- .... CLC 44
See also CA 147

Giacosa, Giuseppe 1847-1906 ...... TCLC 7
See also CA 104

Gibb, Lee
See Waterhouse, Keith (Spencer)

Gibbon, Lewis Grassic .... TCLC 4
See also Mitchell, James Leslie

Gibbons, Kaye 1960- .... CLC 50, 88
See also DAM POP

Gibran, Kahlil
1883-1931 .... TCLC 1, 9; PC 9
See also CA 104; DAM POET, POP

Gibson, William
1914- .... CLC 23; DA; DAB; DAC
See also CA 9-12R; CANR 9, 42;
DAM DRAM, MST; DLB 7; SATA 66

Gibson, William (Ford) 1948- ... CLC 39, 63
See also AAYA 12; CA 126; 133;
DAM POP

Gide, Andre (Paul Guillaume)
1869-1951 .... TCLC 5, 12, 36; DA;
DAB; DAC; SSC 13; WLC
See also CA 104; 124; DAM MST, NOV;
DLB 65; MTCW

Gifford, Barry (Colby) 1946- .... CLC 34
See also CA 65-68; CANR 9, 30, 40

Gilbert, W(illiam) S(chwenck)
1836-1911 .... TCLC 3
See also CA 104; DAM DRAM, POET;
SATA 36

Gilbreth, Frank B., Jr. 1911- .... CLC 17
See also CA 9-12R; SATA 2

Gilchrist, Ellen 1935- .. CLC 34, 48; SSC 14
See also CA 113; 116; CANR 41;
DAM POP; DLB 130; MTCW

Giles, Molly 1942- .... CLC 39
See also CA 126

Gill, Patrick
See Creasey, John

Gilliam, Terry (Vance) 1940- .... CLC 21
See also Monty Python
See also CA 108; 113; CANR 35; INT 113

Gillian, Jerry
See Gilliam, Terry (Vance)

Gilliatt, Penelope (Ann Douglass)
1932-1993 .... CLC 2, 10, 13, 53
See also AITN 2; CA 13-16R; 141;
CANR 49; DLB 14

Gilman, Charlotte (Anna) Perkins (Stetson)
1860-1935 .... TCLC 9, 37; SSC 13
See also CA 106

Gilmour, David 1949- .... CLC 35
See also CA 138, 147

Gilpin, William 1724-1804 .... NCLC 30

Gilray, J. D.
See Mencken, H(enry) L(ouis)

Gilroy, Frank D(aniel) 1925- .... CLC 2
See also CA 81-84; CANR 32; DLB 7

Ginsberg, Allen
1926- ...... CLC 1, 2, 3, 4, 6, 13, 36, 69;
DA; DAB; DAC; PC 4; WLC 3
See also AITN 1; CA 1-4R; CANR 2, 41;
CDALB 1941-1968; DAM MST, POET;
DLB 5, 16; MTCW

Ginzburg, Natalia
1916-1991 .... CLC 5, 11, 54, 70
See also CA 85-88; 135; CANR 33; MTCW

Giono, Jean 1895-1970 .... CLC 4, 11
See also CA 45-48; 29-32R; CANR 2, 35;
DLB 72; MTCW

Giovanni, Nikki
1943- ...... CLC 2, 4, 19, 64; BLC; DA;
DAB; DAC
See also AITN 1; BW 2; CA 29-32R;
CAAS 6; CANR 18, 41; CLR 6;
DAM MST, MULT, POET; DLB 5, 41;
INT CANR-18; MAICYA; MTCW;
SATA 24

Giovene, Andrea 1904- .... CLC 7
See also CA 85-88

Gippius, Zinaida (Nikolayevna) 1869-1945
See Hippius, Zinaida
See also CA 106

Giraudoux, (Hippolyte) Jean
1882-1944 .... TCLC 2, 7
See also CA 104; DAM DRAM; DLB 65

Gironella, Jose Maria 1917- .... CLC 11
See also CA 101

Gissing, George (Robert)
1857-1903 .... TCLC 3, 24, 47
See also CA 105; DLB 18, 135

Giurlani, Aldo
See Palazzeschi, Aldo

Gladkov, Fyodor (Vasilyevich)
1883-1958 .... TCLC 27

Glanville, Brian (Lester) 1931- ...... CLC 6
See also CA 5-8R; CAAS 9; CANR 3;
DLB 15, 139; SATA 42

Glasgow, Ellen (Anderson Gholson)
1873(?)-1945 .... TCLC 2, 7
See also CA 104; DLB 9, 12

Glaspell, Susan (Keating)
1882(?)-1948 .... TCLC 55
See also CA 110; DLB 7, 9, 78; YABC 2

Glassco, John 1909-1981 .... CLC 9
See also CA 13-16R; 102; CANR 15;
DLB 68

Glasscock, Amnesia
See Steinbeck, John (Ernst)

Glasser, Ronald J. 1940(?)- .... CLC 37

Glassman, Joyce
See Johnson, Joyce

Glendinning, Victoria 1937- .... CLC 50
See also CA 120; 127; DLB 155

Glissant, Edouard 1928- .... CLC 10, 68
See also DAM MULT

Gloag, Julian 1930- .... CLC 40
See also AITN 1; CA 65-68; CANR 10

Glowacki, Aleksander
See Prus, Boleslaw

Glueck, Louise (Elisabeth)
1943- .... CLC 7, 22, 44, 81
See also CA 33-36R; CANR 40;
DAM POET; DLB 5

Gobineau, Joseph Arthur (Comte) de
1816-1882 .... NCLC 17
See also DLB 123

Godard, Jean-Luc 1930- .... CLC 20
See also CA 93-96

Godden, (Margaret) Rumer 1907- ... CLC 53
See also AAYA 6; CA 5-8R; CANR 4, 27,
36; CLR 20; DLB 161; MAICYA;
SAAS 12; SATA 3, 36

Godoy Alcayaga, Lucila 1889-1957
See Mistral, Gabriela
See also BW 2; CA 104; 131; DAM MULT;
HW; MTCW

Godwin, Gail (Kathleen)
1937- .... CLC 5, 8, 22, 31, 69
See also CA 29-32R; CANR 15, 43;
DAM POP; DLB 6; INT CANR-15;
MTCW

Godwin, William 1756-1836 ...... NCLC 14
See also CDBLB 1789-1832; DLB 39, 104,
142, 158

Goethe, Johann Wolfgang von
1749-1832 . . . . NCLC 4, 22, 34; DA;
DAB; DAC; PC 5; WLC 3
See also DAM DRAM, MST, POET;
DLB 94

Gogarty, Oliver St. John
1878-1957 . . . . TCLC 15
See also CA 109; DLB 15, 19

Gogol, Nikolai (Vasilyevich)
1809-1852 . . . . NCLC 5, 15, 31; DA;
DAB; DAC; DC 1; SSC 4; WLC
See also DAM DRAM, MST

Goines, Donald
1937(?)-1974 . . . . CLC 80; BLC
See also AITN 1; BW 1; CA 124; 114;
DAM MULT, POP; DLB 33

Gold, Herbert 1924- . . . . CLC 4, 7, 14, 42
See also CA 9-12R; CANR 17, 45; DLB 2;
DLBY 81

Goldbarth, Albert 1948- . . . . CLC 5, 38
See also CA 53-56; CANR 6, 40; DLB 120

Goldberg, Anatol 1910-1982 . . . . CLC 34
See also CA 131; 117

Goldemberg, Isaac 1945- . . . . CLC 52
See also CA 69-72; CAAS 12; CANR 11,
32; HW

Golding, William (Gerald)
1911-1993 . . . . CLC 1, 2, 3, 8, 10, 17, 27,
58, 81; DA; DAB; DAC; WLC
See also AAYA 5; CA 5-8R; 141;
CANR 13, 33; CDBLB 1945-1960;
DAM MST, NOV; DLB 15, 100; MTCW

Goldman, Emma 1869-1940 . . . . . . TCLC 13
See also CA 110

Goldman, Francisco 1955- . . . . CLC 76

Goldman, William (W.) 1931- . . . . CLC 1, 48
See also CA 9-12R; CANR 29; DLB 44

Goldmann, Lucien 1913-1970 . . . . . . CLC 24
See also CA 25-28; CAP 2

Goldoni, Carlo 1707-1793 . . . . LC 4
See also DAM DRAM

Goldsberry, Steven 1949- . . . . CLC 34
See also CA 131

Goldsmith, Oliver
1728-1774 . . . . . . LC 2; DA; DAB; DAC;
WLC
See also CDBLB 1660-1789; DAM DRAM,
MST, NOV, POET; DLB 39, 89, 104,
109, 142; SATA 26

Goldsmith, Peter
See Priestley, J(ohn) B(oynton)

Gombrowicz, Witold
1904-1969 . . . . CLC 4, 7, 11, 49
See also CA 19-20; 25-28R; CAP 2;
DAM DRAM

Gomez de la Serna, Ramon
1888-1963 . . . . CLC 9
See also CA 116; HW

Goncharov, Ivan Alexandrovich
1812-1891 . . . . NCLC 1

Goncourt, Edmond (Louis Antoine Huot) de
1822-1896 . . . . NCLC 7
See also DLB 123

Goncourt, Jules (Alfred Huot) de
1830-1870 . . . . NCLC 7
See also DLB 123

Gontier, Fernande 19(?)- . . . . CLC 50

Goodman, Paul 1911-1972 . . . . CLC 1, 2, 4, 7
See also CA 19-20; 37-40R; CANR 34;
CAP 2; DLB 130; MTCW

Gordimer, Nadine
1923- . . . . CLC 3, 5, 7, 10, 18, 33, 51, 70;
DA; DAB; DAC; SSC 17
See also CA 5-8R; CANR 3, 28;
DAM MST, NOV; INT CANR-28;
MTCW

Gordon, Adam Lindsay
1833-1870 . . . . NCLC 21

Gordon, Caroline
1895-1981 . . . CLC 6, 13, 29, 83; SSC 15
See also CA 11-12; 103; CANR 36; CAP 1;
DLB 4, 9, 102; DLBY 81; MTCW

Gordon, Charles William 1860-1937
See Connor, Ralph
See also CA 109

Gordon, Mary (Catherine)
1949- . . . . CLC 13, 22
See also CA 102; CANR 44; DLB 6;
DLBY 81; INT 102; MTCW

Gordon, Sol 1923- . . . . CLC 26
See also CA 53-56; CANR 4; SATA 11

Gordone, Charles 1925- . . . . CLC 1, 4
See also BW 1; CA 93-96; DAM DRAM;
DLB 7; INT 93-96; MTCW

Gorenko, Anna Andreevna
See Akhmatova, Anna

Gorky, Maxim . . . . TCLC 8; DAB; WLC
See also Peshkov, Alexei Maximovich

Goryan, Sirak
See Saroyan, William

Gosse, Edmund (William)
1849-1928 . . . . TCLC 28
See also CA 117; DLB 57, 144

Gotlieb, Phyllis Fay (Bloom)
1926- . . . . CLC 18
See also CA 13-16R; CANR 7; DLB 88

Gottesman, S. D.
See Kornbluth, C(yril) M.; Pohl, Frederik

Gottfried von Strassburg
fl. c. 1210- . . . . CMLC 10
See also DLB 138

Gould, Lois . . . . CLC 4, 10
See also CA 77-80; CANR 29; MTCW

Gourmont, Remy de 1858-1915 . . . . TCLC 17
See also CA 109

Govier, Katherine 1948- . . . . CLC 51
See also CA 101; CANR 18, 40

Goyen, (Charles) William
1915-1983 . . . . CLC 5, 8, 14, 40
See also AITN 2; CA 5-8R; 110; CANR 6;
DLB 2; DLBY 83; INT CANR-6

Goytisolo, Juan
1931- . . . . CLC 5, 10, 23; HLC
See also CA 85-88; CANR 32;
DAM MULT; HW; MTCW

Gozzano, Guido 1883-1916 . . . . PC 10
See also DLB 114

Gozzi, (Conte) Carlo 1720-1806 . . NCLC 23

Grabbe, Christian Dietrich
1801-1836 . . . . NCLC 2
See also DLB 133

Grace, Patricia 1937- . . . . CLC 56

Gracian y Morales, Baltasar
1601-1658 . . . . LC 15

Gracq, Julien . . . . CLC 11, 48
See also Poirier, Louis
See also DLB 83

Grade, Chaim 1910-1982 . . . . CLC 10
See also CA 93-96; 107

Graduate of Oxford, A
See Ruskin, John

Graham, John
See Phillips, David Graham

Graham, Jorie 1951- . . . . CLC 48
See also CA 111; DLB 120

Graham, R(obert) B(ontine) Cunninghame
See Cunninghame Graham, R(obert)
B(ontine)
See also DLB 98, 135

Graham, Robert
See Haldeman, Joe (William)

Graham, Tom
See Lewis, (Harry) Sinclair

Graham, W(illiam) S(ydney)
1918-1986 . . . . CLC 29
See also CA 73-76; 118; DLB 20

Graham, Winston (Mawdsley)
1910- . . . . CLC 23
See also CA 49-52; CANR 2, 22, 45;
DLB 77

Grant, Skeeter
See Spiegelman, Art

Granville-Barker, Harley
1877-1946 . . . . TCLC 2
See also Barker, Harley Granville
See also CA 104; DAM DRAM

Grass, Guenter (Wilhelm)
1927- . . . . . CLC 1, 2, 4, 6, 11, 15, 22, 32,
49, 88; DA; DAB; DAC; WLC
See also CA 13-16R; CANR 20;
DAM MST, NOV; DLB 75, 124; MTCW

Gratton, Thomas
See Hulme, T(homas) E(rnest)

Grau, Shirley Ann
1929- . . . . CLC 4, 9; SSC 15
See also CA 89-92; CANR 22; DLB 2;
INT CANR-22; MTCW

Gravel, Fern
See Hall, James Norman

Graver, Elizabeth 1964- . . . . CLC 70
See also CA 135

Graves, Richard Perceval 1945- . . . . CLC 44
See also CA 65-68; CANR 9, 26

Graves, Robert (von Ranke)
1895-1985 . . . . . . CLC 1, 2, 6, 11, 39, 44,
45; DAB; DAC; PC 6
See also CA 5-8R; 117; CANR 5, 36;
CDBLB 1914-1945; DAM MST, POET;
DLB 20, 100; DLBY 85; MTCW;
SATA 45

Gray, Alasdair (James) 1934- . . . . . . CLC 41
See also CA 126; CANR 47; INT 126;
MTCW

Guillois
See Desnos, Robert

Guiney, Louise Imogen
1861-1920 .... TCLC 41
See also DLB 54

Guiraldes, Ricardo (Guillermo)
1886-1927 .... TCLC 39
See also CA 131; HW; MTCW

Gumilev, Nikolai Stephanovich
1886-1921 .... TCLC 60

Gunn, Bill .... CLC 5
See also Gunn, William Harrison
See also DLB 38

Gunn, Thom(son William)
1929- .... CLC 3, 6, 18, 32, 81
See also CA 17-20R; CANR 9, 33;
CDBLB 1960 to Present; DAM POET;
DLB 27; INT CANR-33; MTCW

Gunn, William Harrison 1934(?)-1989
See Gunn, Bill
See also AITN 1; BW 1; CA 13-16R; 128;
CANR 12, 25

Gunnars, Kristjana 1948-........... CLC 69
See also CA 113; DLB 60

Gurganus, Allan 1947-............. CLC 70
See also BEST 90:1; CA 135; DAM POP

Gurney, A(lbert) R(amsdell), Jr.
1930- .... CLC 32, 50, 54
See also CA 77-80; CANR 32;
DAM DRAM

Gurney, Ivor (Bertie) 1890-1937 ... TCLC 33

Gurney, Peter
See Gurney, A(lbert) R(amsdell), Jr.

Guro, Elena 1877-1913........... TCLC 56

Gustafson, Ralph (Barker) 1909-.... CLC 36
See also CA 21-24R; CANR 8, 45; DLB 88

Gut, Gom
See Simenon, Georges (Jacques Christian)

Guthrie, A(lfred) B(ertram), Jr.
1901-1991 .... CLC 23
See also CA 57-60; 134; CANR 24; DLB 6;
SATA 62; SATA-Obit 67

Guthrie, Isobel
See Grieve, C(hristopher) M(urray)

Guthrie, Woodrow Wilson 1912-1967
See Guthrie, Woody
See also CA 113; 93-96

Guthrie, Woody................... CLC 35
See also Guthrie, Woodrow Wilson

Guy, Rosa (Cuthbert) 1928-........ CLC 26
See also AAYA 4; BW 2; CA 17-20R;
CANR 14, 34; CLR 13; DLB 33; JRDA;
MAICYA; SATA 14, 62

Gwendolyn
See Bennett, (Enoch) Arnold

H. D. .... CLC 3, 8, 14, 31, 34, 73; PC 5
See also Doolittle, Hilda

H. de V.
See Buchan, John

Haavikko, Paavo Juhani
1931- .... CLC 18, 34
See also CA 106

Habbema, Koos
See Heijermans, Herman

Hacker, Marilyn 1942- .... CLC 5, 9, 23, 72
See also CA 77-80; DAM POET; DLB 120

Haggard, H(enry) Rider
1856-1925 .... TCLC 11
See also CA 108; 148; DLB 70, 156;
SATA 16

Hagiwara Sakutaro 1886-1942 .... TCLC 60

Haig, Fenil
See Ford, Ford Madox

Haig-Brown, Roderick (Langmere)
1908-1976 .... CLC 21
See also CA 5-8R; 69-72; CANR 4, 38;
CLR 31; DLB 88; MAICYA; SATA 12

Hailey, Arthur 1920-.............. CLC 5
See also AITN 2; BEST 90:3; CA 1-4R;
CANR 2, 36; DAM NOV, POP; DLB 88;
DLBY 82; MTCW

Hailey, Elizabeth Forsythe 1938-... CLC 40
See also CA 93-96; CAAS 1; CANR 15, 48;
INT CANR-15

Haines, John (Meade) 1924-....... CLC 58
See also CA 17-20R; CANR 13, 34; DLB 5

Hakluyt, Richard 1552-1616........ LC 31

Haldeman, Joe (William) 1943-..... CLC 61
See also CA 53-56; CANR 6; DLB 8;
INT CANR-6

Haley, Alex(ander Murray Palmer)
1921-1992 .... CLC 8, 12, 76; BLC; DA;
                        DAB; DAC
See also BW 2; CA 77-80; 136; DAM MST,
MULT, POP; DLB 38; MTCW

Haliburton, Thomas Chandler
1796-1865 .... NCLC 15
See also DLB 11, 99

Hall, Donald (Andrew, Jr.)
1928- .... CLC 1, 13, 37, 59
See also CA 5-8R; CAAS 7; CANR 2, 44;
DAM POET; DLB 5; SATA 23

Hall, Frederic Sauser
See Sauser-Hall, Frederic

Hall, James
See Kuttner, Henry

Hall, James Norman 1887-1951 ... TCLC 23
See also CA 123; SATA 21

Hall, (Marguerite) Radclyffe
1886(?)-1943 .... TCLC 12
See also CA 110

Hall, Rodney 1935- .... CLC 51
See also CA 109

Halleck, Fitz-Greene 1790-1867 .. NCLC 47
See also DLB 3

Halliday, Michael
See Creasey, John

Halpern, Daniel 1945- .... CLC 14
See also CA 33-36R

Hamburger, Michael (Peter Leopold)
1924- .... CLC 5, 14
See also CA 5-8R; CAAS 4; CANR 2, 47;
DLB 27

Hamill, Pete 1935-............... CLC 10
See also CA 25-28R; CANR 18

Hamilton, Alexander
1755(?)-1804 .... NCLC 49
See also DLB 37

Hamilton, Clive
See Lewis, C(live) S(taples)

Hamilton, Edmond 1904-1977....... CLC 1
See also CA 1-4R; CANR 3; DLB 8

Hamilton, Eugene (Jacob) Lee
See Lee-Hamilton, Eugene (Jacob)

Hamilton, Franklin
See Silverberg, Robert

Hamilton, Gail
See Corcoran, Barbara

Hamilton, Mollie
See Kaye, M(ary) M(argaret)

Hamilton, (Anthony Walter) Patrick
1904-1962 .... CLC 51
See also CA 113; DLB 10

Hamilton, Virginia 1936-.......... CLC 26
See also AAYA 2; BW 2; CA 25-28R;
CANR 20, 37; CLR 1, 11; DAM MULT;
DLB 33, 52; INT CANR-20; JRDA;
MAICYA; MTCW; SATA 4, 56, 79

Hammett, (Samuel) Dashiell
1894-1961 .... CLC 3, 5, 10, 19, 47;
                        SSC 17
See also AITN 1; CA 81-84; CANR 42;
CDALB 1929-1941; DLBD 6; MTCW

Hammon, Jupiter
1711(?)-1800(?) .... NCLC 5; BLC
See also DAM MULT, POET; DLB 31, 50

Hammond, Keith
See Kuttner, Henry

Hamner, Earl (Henry), Jr. 1923- ... CLC 12
See also AITN 2; CA 73-76; DLB 6

Hampton, Christopher (James)
1946- .... CLC 4
See also CA 25-28R; DLB 13; MTCW

Hamsun, Knut............. TCLC 2, 14, 49
See also Pedersen, Knut

Handke, Peter 1942- .. CLC 5, 8, 10, 15, 38
See also CA 77-80; CANR 33;
DAM DRAM, NOV; DLB 85, 124;
MTCW

Hanley, James 1901-1985 ... CLC 3, 5, 8, 13
See also CA 73-76; 117; CANR 36; MTCW

Hannah, Barry 1942-....... CLC 23, 38, 90
See also CA 108; 110; CANR 43; DLB 6;
INT 110; MTCW

Hannon, Ezra
See Hunter, Evan

Hansberry, Lorraine (Vivian)
1930-1965 ...... CLC 17, 62; BLC; DA;
                        DAB; DAC; DC 2
See also BW 1; CA 109; 25-28R; CABS 3;
CDALB 1941-1968; DAM DRAM, MST,
MULT; DLB 7, 38; MTCW

Hansen, Joseph 1923-............. CLC 38
See also CA 29-32R; CAAS 17; CANR 16,
44; INT CANR-16

Hansen, Martin A. 1909-1955..... TCLC 32

Hanson, Kenneth O(stlin) 1922- .... CLC 13
See also CA 53-56; CANR 7

Hardwick, Elizabeth 1916- .... CLC 13
See also CA 5-8R; CANR 3, 32;
DAM NOV; DLB 6; MTCW

Hardy, Thomas
  1840-1928 . . . . . . **TCLC 4, 10, 18, 32, 48,**
  53; DA; DAB; DAC; PC 8; SSC 2; WLC
  See also CA 104; 123; CDBLB 1890-1914;
  DAM MST, NOV, POET; DLB 18, 19,
  135; MTCW

Hare, David 1947- . . . . **CLC 29, 58**
  See also CA 97-100; CANR 39; DLB 13;
  MTCW

Harford, Henry
  See Hudson, W(illiam) H(enry)

Hargrave, Leonie
  See Disch, Thomas M(ichael)

Harjo, Joy 1951- . . . . **CLC 83**
  See also CA 114; CANR 35; DAM MULT;
  DLB 120; NNAL

Harlan, Louis R(udolph) 1922- . . . . . **CLC 34**
  See also CA 21-24R; CANR 25

Harling, Robert 1951(?)- . . . . **CLC 53**
  See also CA 147

Harmon, William (Ruth) 1938- . . . . . **CLC 38**
  See also CA 33-36R; CANR 14, 32, 35;
  SATA 65

Harper, F. E. W.
  See Harper, Frances Ellen Watkins

Harper, Frances E. W.
  See Harper, Frances Ellen Watkins

Harper, Frances E. Watkins
  See Harper, Frances Ellen Watkins

Harper, Frances Ellen
  See Harper, Frances Ellen Watkins

Harper, Frances Ellen Watkins
  1825-1911 . . . . **TCLC 14; BLC**
  See also BW 1; CA 111; 125; DAM MULT,
  POET; DLB 50

Harper, Michael S(teven) 1938- . . **CLC 7, 22**
  See also BW 1; CA 33-36R; CANR 24;
  DLB 41

Harper, Mrs. F. E. W.
  See Harper, Frances Ellen Watkins

Harris, Christie (Lucy) Irwin
  1907- . . . . **CLC 12**
  See also CA 5-8R; CANR 6; DLB 88;
  JRDA; MAICYA; SAAS 10; SATA 6, 74

Harris, Frank 1856(?)-1931 . . . . **TCLC 24**
  See also CA 109; DLB 156

Harris, George Washington
  1814-1869 . . . . **NCLC 23**
  See also DLB 3, 11

Harris, Joel Chandler
  1848-1908 . . . . **TCLC 2; SSC 19**
  See also CA 104; 137; DLB 11, 23, 42, 78,
  91; MAICYA; YABC 1

Harris, John (Wyndham Parkes Lucas)
  Beynon 1903-1969
  See Wyndham, John
  See also CA 102; 89-92

Harris, MacDonald . . . . **CLC 9**
  See also Heiney, Donald (William)

Harris, Mark 1922- . . . . **CLC 19**
  See also CA 5-8R; CAAS 3; CANR 2;
  DLB 2; DLBY 80

Harris, (Theodore) Wilson 1921- . . . . **CLC 25**
  See also BW 2; CA 65-68; CAAS 16;
  CANR 11, 27; DLB 117; MTCW

Harrison, Elizabeth Cavanna 1909-
  See Cavanna, Betty
  See also CA 9-12R; CANR 6, 27

Harrison, Harry (Max) 1925- . . . . . . **CLC 42**
  See also CA 1-4R; CANR 5, 21; DLB 8;
  SATA 4

Harrison, James (Thomas)
  1937- . . . . **CLC 6, 14, 33, 66; SSC 19**
  See also CA 13-16R; CANR 8; DLBY 82;
  INT CANR-8

Harrison, Jim
  See Harrison, James (Thomas)

Harrison, Kathryn 1961- . . . . **CLC 70**
  See also CA 144

Harrison, Tony 1937- . . . . **CLC 43**
  See also CA 65-68; CANR 44; DLB 40;
  MTCW

Harriss, Will(ard Irvin) 1922- . . . . . . **CLC 34**
  See also CA 111

Harson, Sley
  See Ellison, Harlan (Jay)

Hart, Ellis
  See Ellison, Harlan (Jay)

Hart, Josephine 1942(?)- . . . . **CLC 70**
  See also CA 138; DAM POP

Hart, Moss 1904-1961 . . . . **CLC 66**
  See also CA 109; 89-92; DAM DRAM;
  DLB 7

Harte, (Francis) Bret(t)
  1836(?)-1902 . . . . **TCLC 1, 25; DA; DAC;**
  SSC 8; WLC
  See also CA 104; 140; CDALB 1865-1917;
  DAM MST; DLB 12, 64, 74, 79;
  SATA 26

Hartley, L(eslie) P(oles)
  1895-1972 . . . . **CLC 2, 22**
  See also CA 45-48; 37-40R; CANR 33;
  DLB 15, 139; MTCW

Hartman, Geoffrey H. 1929- . . . . **CLC 27**
  See also CA 117; 125; DLB 67

Hartmann von Aue
  c. 1160-c. 1205 . . . . **CMLC 15**
  See also DLB 138

Hartmann von Aue 1170-1210 . . . . **CMLC 15**

Haruf, Kent 1943- . . . . **CLC 34**
  See also CA 149

Harwood, Ronald 1934- . . . . **CLC 32**
  See also CA 1-4R; CANR 4; DAM DRAM,
  MST; DLB 13

Hasek, Jaroslav (Matej Frantisek)
  1883-1923 . . . . **TCLC 4**
  See also CA 104; 129; MTCW

Hass, Robert 1941- . . . . **CLC 18, 39**
  See also CA 111; CANR 30, 50; DLB 105

Hastings, Hudson
  See Kuttner, Henry

Hastings, Selina . . . . **CLC 44**

Hatteras, Amelia
  See Mencken, H(enry) L(ouis)

Hatteras, Owen . . . . **TCLC 18**
  See also Mencken, H(enry) L(ouis); Nathan,
  George Jean

Hauptmann, Gerhart (Johann Robert)
  1862-1946 . . . . **TCLC 4**
  See also CA 104; DAM DRAM; DLB 66,
  118

Havel, Vaclav
  1936- . . . . **CLC 25, 58, 65; DC 6**
  See also CA 104; CANR 36; DAM DRAM;
  MTCW

Haviaras, Stratis . . . . **CLC 33**
  See also Chaviaras, Strates

Hawes, Stephen 1475(?)-1523(?) . . . . . **LC 17**

Hawkes, John (Clendennin Burne, Jr.)
  1925- . . . . . . **CLC 1, 2, 3, 4, 7, 9, 14, 15,**
  27, 49
  See also CA 1-4R; CANR 2, 47; DLB 2, 7;
  DLBY 80; MTCW

Hawking, S. W.
  See Hawking, Stephen W(illiam)

Hawking, Stephen W(illiam)
  1942- . . . . **CLC 63**
  See also AAYA 13; BEST 89:1; CA 126;
  129; CANR 48

Hawthorne, Julian 1846-1934 . . . . . **TCLC 25**

Hawthorne, Nathaniel
  1804-1864 . . . . **NCLC 39; DA; DAB;**
  DAC; SSC 3; WLC
  See also CDALB 1640-1865; DAM MST,
  NOV; DLB 1, 74; YABC 2

Haxton, Josephine Ayres 1921-
  See Douglas, Ellen
  See also CA 115; CANR 41

Hayaseca y Eizaguirre, Jorge
  See Echegaray (y Eizaguirre), Jose (Maria
  Waldo)

Hayashi Fumiko 1904-1951 . . . . **TCLC 27**

Haycraft, Anna
  See Ellis, Alice Thomas
  See also CA 122

Hayden, Robert E(arl)
  1913-1980 . . . . . . **CLC 5, 9, 14, 37; BLC;**
  DA; DAC; PC 6
  See also BW 1; CA 69-72; 97-100; CABS 2;
  CANR 24; CDALB 1941-1968;
  DAM MST, MULT, POET; DLB 5, 76;
  MTCW; SATA 19; SATA-Obit 26

Hayford, J(oseph) E(phraim) Casely
  See Casely-Hayford, J(oseph) E(phraim)

Hayman, Ronald 1932- . . . . **CLC 44**
  See also CA 25-28R; CANR 18, 50;
  DLB 155

Haywood, Eliza (Fowler)
  1693(?)-1756 . . . . **LC 1**

Hazlitt, William 1778-1830 . . . . . . **NCLC 29**
  See also DLB 110, 158

Hazzard, Shirley 1931- . . . . **CLC 18**
  See also CA 9-12R; CANR 4; DLBY 82;
  MTCW

Head, Bessie 1937-1986 . . . **CLC 25, 67; BLC**
  See also BW 2; CA 29-32R; 119; CANR 25;
  DAM MULT; DLB 117; MTCW

Headon, (Nicky) Topper 1956(?)- . . . **CLC 30**

Heaney, Seamus (Justin)
1939- . . . . CLC 5, 7, 14, 25, 37, 74; DAB
See also CA 85-88; CANR 25, 48;
CDBLB 1960 to Present; DAM POET;
DLB 40; MTCW

Hearn, (Patricio) Lafcadio (Tessima Carlos)
1850-1904 . . . . TCLC 9
See also CA 105; DLB 12, 78

Hearne, Vicki 1946- . . . . CLC 56
See also CA 139

Hearon, Shelby 1931- . . . . CLC 63
See also AITN 2; CA 25-28R; CANR 18,
48

Heat-Moon, William Least . . . . CLC 29
See also Trogdon, William (Lewis)
See also AAYA 9

Hebbel, Friedrich 1813-1863 . . . . . NCLC 43
See also DAM DRAM; DLB 129

Hebert, Anne 1916- . . . CLC 4, 13, 29; DAC
See also CA 85-88; DAM MST, POET;
DLB 68; MTCW

Hecht, Anthony (Evan)
1923- . . . . CLC 8, 13, 19
See also CA 9-12R; CANR 6; DAM POET;
DLB 5

Hecht, Ben 1894-1964 . . . . CLC 8
See also CA 85-88; DLB 7, 9, 25, 26, 28, 86

Hedayat, Sadeq 1903-1951 . . . . TCLC 21
See also CA 120

Hegel, Georg Wilhelm Friedrich
1770-1831 . . . . NCLC 46
See also DLB 90

Heidegger, Martin 1889-1976 . . . . . . CLC 24
See also CA 81-84; 65-68; CANR 34;
MTCW

Heidenstam, (Carl Gustaf) Verner von
1859-1940 . . . . TCLC 5
See also CA 104

Heifner, Jack 1946- . . . . CLC 11
See also CA 105; CANR 47

Heijermans, Herman 1864-1924 . . . TCLC 24
See also CA 123

Heilbrun, Carolyn G(old) 1926- . . . . . CLC 25
See also CA 45-48; CANR 1, 28

Heine, Heinrich 1797-1856 . . . . NCLC 4
See also DLB 90

Heinemann, Larry (Curtiss) 1944- . . CLC 50
See also CA 110; CAAS 21; CANR 31;
DLBD 9; INT CANR-31

Heiney, Donald (William) 1921-1993
See Harris, MacDonald
See also CA 1-4R; 142; CANR 3

Heinlein, Robert A(nson)
1907-1988 . . . . . . CLC 1, 3, 8, 14, 26, 55
See also AAYA 17; CA 1-4R; 125;
CANR 1, 20; DAM POP; DLB 8; JRDA;
MAICYA; MTCW; SATA 9, 69;
SATA-Obit 56

Helforth, John
See Doolittle, Hilda

Hellenhofferu, Vojtech Kapristian z
See Hasek, Jaroslav (Matej Frantisek)

Heller, Joseph
1923- . . . . CLC 1, 3, 5, 8, 11, 36, 63; DA;
DAB; DAC; WLC
See also AITN 1; CA 5-8R; CABS 1;
CANR 8, 42; DAM MST, NOV, POP;
DLB 2, 28; DLBY 80; INT CANR-8;
MTCW

Hellman, Lillian (Florence)
1906-1984 . . . . . . CLC 2, 4, 8, 14, 18, 34,
44, 52; DC 1
See also AITN 1, 2; CA 13-16R; 112;
CANR 33; DAM DRAM; DLB 7;
DLBY 84; MTCW

Helprin, Mark 1947- . . . . . CLC 7, 10, 22, 32
See also CA 81-84; CANR 47; DAM NOV,
POP; DLBY 85; MTCW

Helvetius, Claude-Adrien
1715-1771 . . . . LC 26

Helyar, Jane Penelope Josephine 1933-
See Poole, Josephine
See also CA 21-24R; CANR 10, 26;
SATA 82

Hemans, Felicia 1793-1835 . . . . . . NCLC 29
See also DLB 96

Hemingway, Ernest (Miller)
1899-1961 . . . . CLC 1, 3, 6, 8, 10, 13, 19,
30, 34, 39, 41, 44, 50, 61, 80; DA; DAB;
DAC; SSC 1; WLC
See also CA 77-80; CANR 34;
CDALB 1917-1929; DAM MST, NOV;
DLB 4, 9, 102; DLBD 1; DLBY 81, 87;
MTCW

Hempel, Amy 1951- . . . . CLC 39
See also CA 118; 137

Henderson, F. C.
See Mencken, H(enry) L(ouis)

Henderson, Sylvia
See Ashton-Warner, Sylvia (Constance)

Henley, Beth . . . . CLC 23; DC 6
See also Henley, Elizabeth Becker
See also CABS 3; DLBY 86

Henley, Elizabeth Becker 1952-
See Henley, Beth
See also CA 107; CANR 32; DAM DRAM,
MST; MTCW

Henley, William Ernest
1849-1903 . . . . TCLC 8
See also CA 105; DLB 19

Hennissart, Martha
See Lathen, Emma
See also CA 85-88

Henry, O. . . . . TCLC 1, 19; SSC 5; WLC
See also Porter, William Sydney

Henry, Patrick 1736-1799 . . . . LC 25

Henryson, Robert 1430(?)-1506(?). . . . LC 20
See also DLB 146

Henry VIII 1491-1547 . . . . LC 10

Henschke, Alfred
See Klabund

Hentoff, Nat(han Irving) 1925- . . . . . CLC 26
See also AAYA 4; CA 1-4R; CAAS 6;
CANR 5, 25; CLR 1; INT CANR-25;
JRDA; MAICYA; SATA 42, 69;
SATA-Brief 27

Heppenstall, (John) Rayner
1911-1981 . . . . CLC 10
See also CA 1-4R; 103; CANR 29

Herbert, Frank (Patrick)
1920-1986 . . . . . . CLC 12, 23, 35, 44, 85
See also CA 53-56; 118; CANR 5, 43;
DAM POP; DLB 8; INT CANR-5;
MTCW; SATA 9, 37; SATA-Obit 47

Herbert, George
1593-1633 . . . . LC 24; DAB; PC 4
See also CDBLB Before 1660; DAM POET;
DLB 126

Herbert, Zbigniew 1924- . . . . CLC 9, 43
See also CA 89-92; CANR 36;
DAM POET; MTCW

Herbst, Josephine (Frey)
1897-1969 . . . . CLC 34
See also CA 5-8R; 25-28R; DLB 9

Hergesheimer, Joseph
1880-1954 . . . . TCLC 11
See also CA 109; DLB 102, 9

Herlihy, James Leo 1927-1993 . . . . . . CLC 6
See also CA 1-4R; 143; CANR 2

Hermogenes fl. c. 175- . . . . CMLC 6

Hernandez, Jose 1834-1886 . . . . . . NCLC 17

Herodotus c. 484B.C.-429B.C. . . . . CMLC 17

Herrick, Robert
1591-1674 . . . . . LC 13; DA; DAB; DAC;
PC 9
See also DAM MST, POP; DLB 126

Herring, Guilles
See Somerville, Edith

Herriot, James 1916-1995 . . . . CLC 12
See also Wight, James Alfred
See also AAYA 1; CA 148; CANR 40;
DAM POP

Herrmann, Dorothy 1941- . . . . CLC 44
See also CA 107

Herrmann, Taffy
See Herrmann, Dorothy

Hersey, John (Richard)
1914-1993 . . . . CLC 1, 2, 7, 9, 40, 81
See also CA 17-20R; 140; CANR 33;
DAM POP; DLB 6; MTCW; SATA 25;
SATA-Obit 76

Herzen, Aleksandr Ivanovich
1812-1870 . . . . NCLC 10

Herzl, Theodor 1860-1904 . . . . TCLC 36

Herzog, Werner 1942- . . . . CLC 16
See also CA 89-92

Hesiod c. 8th cent. B.C.- . . . . CMLC 5

Hesse, Hermann
1877-1962 . . . . CLC 1, 2, 3, 6, 11, 17, 25,
69; DA; DAB; DAC; SSC 9; WLC
See also CA 17-18; CAP 2; DAM MST,
NOV; DLB 66; MTCW; SATA 50

Hewes, Cady
See De Voto, Bernard (Augustine)

Heyen, William 1940- . . . . CLC 13, 18
See also CA 33-36R; CAAS 9; DLB 5

Heyerdahl, Thor 1914- . . . . CLC 26
See also CA 5-8R; CANR 5, 22; MTCW;
SATA 2, 52

Heym, Georg (Theodor Franz Arthur)
1887-1912 . . . . TCLC 9
See also CA 106

Heym, Stefan 1913- . . . . CLC 41
See also CA 9-12R; CANR 4; DLB 69

Heyse, Paul (Johann Ludwig von)
1830-1914 . . . . TCLC 8
See also CA 104; DLB 129

Heyward, (Edwin) DuBose
1885-1940 . . . . TCLC 59
See also CA 108; DLB 7, 9, 45; SATA 21

Hibbert, Eleanor Alice Burford
1906-1993 . . . . CLC 7
See also BEST 90:4; CA 17-20R; 140;
CANR 9, 28; DAM POP; SATA 2;
SATA-Obit 74

Higgins, George V(incent)
1939- . . . . CLC 4, 7, 10, 18
See also CA 77-80; CAAS 5; CANR 17;
DLB 2; DLBY 81; INT CANR-17;
MTCW

Higginson, Thomas Wentworth
1823-1911 . . . . TCLC 36
See also DLB 1, 64

Highet, Helen
See MacInnes, Helen (Clark)

Highsmith, (Mary) Patricia
1921-1995 . . . . CLC 2, 4, 14, 42
See also CA 1-4R; 147; CANR 1, 20, 48;
DAM NOV, POP; MTCW

Highwater, Jamake (Mamake)
1942(?)- . . . . CLC 12
See also AAYA 7; CA 65-68; CAAS 7;
CANR 10, 34; CLR 17; DLB 52;
DLBY 85; JRDA, MAICYA, SATA 32,
69; SATA-Brief 30

Higuchi, Ichiyo 1872-1896 . . . . . . NCLC 49

Hijuelos, Oscar 1951- . . . . . . CLC 65; HLC
See also BEST 90:1; CA 123; CANR 50;
DAM MULT, POP; DLB 145; HW

Hikmet, Nazim 1902(?)-1963 . . . . . . CLC 40
See also CA 141; 93-96

Hildesheimer, Wolfgang
1916-1991 . . . . CLC 49
See also CA 101; 135; DLB 69, 124

Hill, Geoffrey (William)
1932- . . . . CLC 5, 8, 18, 45
See also CA 81-84; CANR 21;
CDBLB 1960 to Present; DAM POET;
DLB 40; MTCW

Hill, George Roy 1921- . . . . CLC 26
See also CA 110; 122

Hill, John
See Koontz, Dean R(ay)

Hill, Susan (Elizabeth)
1942- . . . . CLC 4; DAB
See also CA 33-36R; CANR 29;
DAM MST, NOV; DLB 14, 139; MTCW

Hillerman, Tony 1925- . . . . CLC 62
See also AAYA 6; BEST 89:1; CA 29-32R;
CANR 21, 42; DAM POP; SATA 6

Hillesum, Etty 1914-1943 . . . . TCLC 49
See also CA 137

Hilliard, Noel (Harvey) 1929- . . . . . . CLC 15
See also CA 9-12R; CANR 7

Hillis, Rick 1956- . . . . CLC 66
See also CA 134

Hilton, James 1900-1954 . . . . TCLC 21
See also CA 108; DLB 34, 77; SATA 34

Himes, Chester (Bomar)
1909-1984 . . . . CLC 2, 4, 7, 18, 58; BLC
See also BW 2; CA 25-28R; 114; CANR 22;
DAM MULT; DLB 2, 76, 143; MTCW

Hinde, Thomas . . . . CLC 6, 11
See also Chitty, Thomas Willes

Hindin, Nathan
See Bloch, Robert (Albert)

Hine, (William) Daryl 1936- . . . . CLC 15
See also CA 1-4R; CAAS 15; CANR 1, 20;
DLB 60

Hinkson, Katharine Tynan
See Tynan, Katharine

Hinton, S(usan) E(loise)
1950- . . . . CLC 30; DA; DAB; DAC
See also AAYA 2; CA 81-84; CANR 32;
CLR 3, 23; DAM MST, NOV; JRDA;
MAICYA; MTCW; SATA 19, 58

Hippius, Zinaida . . . . TCLC 9
See also Gippius, Zinaida (Nikolayevna)

Hiraoka, Kimitake 1925-1970
See Mishima, Yukio
See also CA 97-100; 29-32R; DAM DRAM;
MTCW

Hirsch, E(ric) D(onald), Jr. 1928-. . . CLC 79
See also CA 25-28R; CANR 27; DLB 67;
INT CANR-27; MTCW

Hirsch, Edward 1950- . . . . CLC 31, 50
See also CA 104; CANR 20, 42; DLB 120

Hitchcock, Alfred (Joseph)
1899-1980 . . . . CLC 16
See also CA 97-100; SATA 27;
SATA-Obit 24

Hitler, Adolf 1889-1945 . . . . TCLC 53
See also CA 117; 147

Hoagland, Edward 1932- . . . . CLC 28
See also CA 1-4R; CANR 2, 31; DLB 6;
SATA 51

Hoban, Russell (Conwell) 1925- . . CLC 7, 25
See also CA 5-8R; CANR 23, 37; CLR 3;
DAM NOV; DLB 52; MAICYA;
MTCW; SATA 1, 40, 78

Hobbs, Perry
See Blackmur, R(ichard) P(almer)

Hobson, Laura Z(ametkin)
1900-1986 . . . . CLC 7, 25
See also CA 17-20R; 118; DLB 28;
SATA 52

Hochhuth, Rolf 1931- . . . . CLC 4, 11, 18
See also CA 5-8R; CANR 33;
DAM DRAM; DLB 124; MTCW

Hochman, Sandra 1936- . . . . CLC 3, 8
See also CA 5-8R; DLB 5

Hochwaelder, Fritz 1911-1986 . . . . . . CLC 36
See also CA 29-32R; 120; CANR 42;
DAM DRAM; MTCW

Hochwalder, Fritz
See Hochwaelder, Fritz

Hocking, Mary (Eunice) 1921- . . . . . CLC 13
See also CA 101; CANR 18, 40

Hodgins, Jack 1938-. . . . . CLC 23
See also CA 93-96; DLB 60

Hodgson, William Hope
1877(?)-1918 . . . . TCLC 13
See also CA 111; DLB 70, 153, 156

Hoffman, Alice 1952- . . . . CLC 51
See also CA 77-80; CANR 34; DAM NOV;
MTCW

Hoffman, Daniel (Gerard)
1923- . . . . CLC 6, 13, 23
See also CA 1-4R; CANR 4; DLB 5

Hoffman, Stanley 1944- . . . . CLC 5
See also CA 77-80

Hoffman, William M(oses) 1939- . . . CLC 40
See also CA 57-60; CANR 11

Hoffmann, E(rnst) T(heodor) A(madeus)
1776-1822 . . . . NCLC 2; SSC 13
See also DLB 90; SATA 27

Hofmann, Gert 1931- . . . . CLC 54
See also CA 128

Hofmannsthal, Hugo von
1874-1929 . . . . TCLC 11; DC 4
See also CA 106; DAM DRAM; DLB 81,
118

Hogan, Linda 1947- . . . . CLC 73
See also CA 120; CANR 45; DAM MULT;
NNAL

Hogarth, Charles
See Creasey, John

Hogg, James 1770-1835 . . . . NCLC 4
See also DLB 93, 116, 159

Holbach, Paul Henri Thiry Baron
1723-1789 . . . . LC 14

Holberg, Ludvig 1684-1754 . . . . LC 6

Holden, Ursula 1921- . . . . CLC 18
See also CA 101; CAAS 8; CANR 22

Holderlin, (Johann Christian) Friedrich
1770-1843 . . . . NCLC 16; PC 4

Holdstock, Robert
See Holdstock, Robert P.

Holdstock, Robert P. 1948-. . . . . CLC 39
See also CA 131

Holland, Isabelle 1920- . . . . CLC 21
See also AAYA 11; CA 21-24R; CANR 10,
25, 47; JRDA; MAICYA; SATA 8, 70

Holland, Marcus
See Caldwell, (Janet Miriam) Taylor
(Holland)

Hollander, John 1929- . . . . . . CLC 2, 5, 8, 14
See also CA 1-4R; CANR 1; DLB 5;
SATA 13

Hollander, Paul
See Silverberg, Robert

Holleran, Andrew 1943(?)-. . . . . CLC 38
See also CA 144

Hollinghurst, Alan 1954- . . . . CLC 55
See also CA 114

Hollis, Jim
See Summers, Hollis (Spurgeon, Jr.)

Holmes, John
See Souster, (Holmes) Raymond

Holmes, John Clellon 1926-1988. . . . CLC 56
See also CA 9-12R; 125; CANR 4; DLB 16

Holmes, Oliver Wendell
1809-1894 . . . . **NCLC 14**
See also CDALB 1640-1865; DLB 1;
SATA 34

Holmes, Raymond
See Souster, (Holmes) Raymond

Holt, Victoria
See Hibbert, Eleanor Alice Burford

Holub, Miroslav 1923- . . . . **CLC 4**
See also CA 21-24R; CANR 10

Homer
c. 8th cent. B.C.- . . . . . **CMLC 1, 16; DA;
DAB; DAC**
See also DAM MST, POET

Honig, Edwin 1919- . . . . **CLC 33**
See also CA 5-8R; CAAS 8; CANR 4, 45;
DLB 5

Hood, Hugh (John Blagdon)
1928- . . . . **CLC 15, 28**
See also CA 49-52; CAAS 17; CANR 1, 33;
DLB 53

Hood, Thomas 1799-1845. . . . . **NCLC 16**
See also DLB 96

Hooker, (Peter) Jeremy 1941- . . . . . . **CLC 43**
See also CA 77-80; CANR 22; DLB 40

Hope, A(lec) D(erwent) 1907- . . . . **CLC 3, 51**
See also CA 21-24R; CANR 33; MTCW

Hope, Brian
See Creasey, John

Hope, Christopher (David Tully)
1944- . . . . **CLC 52**
See also CA 106; CANR 47; SATA 62

Hopkins, Gerard Manley
1844-1889 . . . . **NCLC 17; DA; DAB;
DAC; WLC**
See also CDBLB 1890-1914; DAM MST,
POET; DLB 35, 57

Hopkins, John (Richard) 1931- . . . . . . **CLC 4**
See also CA 85-88

Hopkins, Pauline Elizabeth
1859-1930 . . . . **TCLC 28; BLC**
See also BW 2; CA 141; DAM MULT;
DLB 50

Hopkinson, Francis 1737-1791 . . . . . . **LC 25**
See also DLB 31

Hopley-Woolrich, Cornell George 1903-1968
See Woolrich, Cornell
See also CA 13-14; CAP 1

Horatio
See Proust, (Valentin-Louis-George-Eugene-)
Marcel

Horgan, Paul (George Vincent O'Shaughnessy)
1903-1995 . . . . **CLC 9, 53**
See also CA 13-16R; 147; CANR 9, 35;
DAM NOV; DLB 102; DLBY 85;
INT CANR-9; MTCW; SATA 13;
SATA-Obit 84

Horn, Peter
See Kuttner, Henry

Hornem, Horace Esq.
See Byron, George Gordon (Noel)

Hornung, E(rnest) W(illiam)
1866-1921 . . . . **TCLC 59**
See also CA 108; DLB 70

Horovitz, Israel (Arthur) 1939- . . . . . **CLC 56**
See also CA 33-36R; CANR 46;
DAM DRAM; DLB 7

Horvath, Odon von
See Horvath, Oedoen von
See also DLB 85, 124

Horvath, Oedoen von 1901-1938 . . . **TCLC 45**
See also Horvath, Odon von
See also CA 118

Horwitz, Julius 1920-1986 . . . . **CLC 14**
See also CA 9-12R; 119; CANR 12

Hospital, Janette Turner 1942- . . . . . **CLC 42**
See also CA 108; CANR 48

Hostos, E. M. de
See Hostos (y Bonilla), Eugenio Maria de

Hostos, Eugenio M. de
See Hostos (y Bonilla), Eugenio Maria de

Hostos, Eugenio Maria
See Hostos (y Bonilla), Eugenio Maria de

Hostos (y Bonilla), Eugenio Maria de
1839-1903 . . . . **TCLC 24**
See also CA 123; 131; HW

Houdini
See Lovecraft, H(oward) P(hillips)

Hougan, Carolyn 1943- . . . . **CLC 34**
See also CA 139

Household, Geoffrey (Edward West)
1900-1988 . . . . **CLC 11**
See also CA 77-80; 126; DLB 87; SATA 14;
SATA-Obit 59

Housman, A(lfred) E(dward)
1859-1936 . . . . . . **TCLC 1, 10; DA; DAB;
DAC; PC 2**
See also CA 104; 125; DAM MST, POET;
DLB 19; MTCW

Housman, Laurence 1865-1959 . . . . . **TCLC 7**
See also CA 106; DLB 10; SATA 25

Howard, Elizabeth Jane 1923- . . . **CLC 7, 29**
See also CA 5-8R; CANR 8

Howard, Maureen 1930- . . . . . **CLC 5, 14, 46**
See also CA 53-56; CANR 31; DLBY 83;
INT CANR-31; MTCW

Howard, Richard 1929- . . . . . . **CLC 7, 10, 47**
See also AITN 1; CA 85-88; CANR 25;
DLB 5; INT CANR-25

Howard, Robert Ervin 1906-1936 . . . **TCLC 8**
See also CA 105

Howard, Warren F.
See Pohl, Frederik

Howe, Fanny 1940- . . . . **CLC 47**
See also CA 117; SATA-Brief 52

Howe, Irving 1920-1993 . . . . **CLC 85**
See also CA 9-12R; 141; CANR 21, 50;
DLB 67; MTCW

Howe, Julia Ward 1819-1910 . . . . . **TCLC 21**
See also CA 117; DLB 1

Howe, Susan 1937- . . . . **CLC 72**
See also DLB 120

Howe, Tina 1937- . . . . **CLC 48**
See also CA 109

Howell, James 1594(?)-1666 . . . . **LC 13**
See also DLB 151

Howells, W. D.
See Howells, William Dean

Howells, William D.
See Howells, William Dean

Howells, William Dean
1837-1920 . . . . **TCLC 7, 17, 41**
See also CA 104; 134; CDALB 1865-1917;
DLB 12, 64, 74, 79

Howes, Barbara 1914- . . . . **CLC 15**
See also CA 9-12R; CAAS 3; SATA 5

Hrabal, Bohumil 1914- . . . . **CLC 13, 67**
See also CA 106; CAAS 12

Hsun, Lu
See Lu Hsun

Hubbard, L(afayette) Ron(ald)
1911-1986 . . . . **CLC 43**
See also CA 77-80; 118; CANR 22;
DAM POP

Huch, Ricarda (Octavia)
1864-1947 . . . . **TCLC 13**
See also CA 111; DLB 66

Huddle, David 1942- . . . . **CLC 49**
See also CA 57-60; CAAS 20; DLB 130

Hudson, Jeffrey
See Crichton, (John) Michael

Hudson, W(illiam) H(enry)
1841-1922 . . . . **TCLC 29**
See also CA 115; DLB 98, 153; SATA 35

Hueffer, Ford Madox
See Ford, Ford Madox

Hughart, Barry 1934- . . . . **CLC 39**
See also CA 137

Hughes, Colin
See Creasey, John

Hughes, David (John) 1930- . . . . **CLC 48**
See also CA 116; 129; DLB 14

Hughes, (James) Langston
1902-1967 . . . . . **CLC 1, 5, 10, 15, 35, 44;
BLC; DA; DAB; DAC; DC 3; PC 1;
SSC 6; WLC**
See also AAYA 12; BW 1; CA 1-4R;
25-28R; CANR 1, 34; CDALB 1929-1941;
CLR 17; DAM DRAM, MST, MULT,
POET; DLB 4, 7, 48, 51, 86; JRDA;
MAICYA; MTCW; SATA 4, 33

Hughes, Richard (Arthur Warren)
1900-1976 . . . . **CLC 1, 11**
See also CA 5-8R; 65-68; CANR 4;
DAM NOV; DLB 15, 161; MTCW;
SATA 8; SATA-Obit 25

Hughes, Ted
1930- . . . . **CLC 2, 4, 9, 14, 37; DAB;
DAC; PC 7**
See also CA 1-4R; CANR 1, 33; CLR 3;
DLB 40, 161; MAICYA; MTCW;
SATA 49; SATA-Brief 27

Hugo, Richard F(ranklin)
1923-1982 . . . . **CLC 6, 18, 32**
See also CA 49-52; 108; CANR 3;
DAM POET; DLB 5

Hugo, Victor (Marie)
1802-1885 . . . . **NCLC 3, 10, 21; DA;
DAB; DAC; WLC**
See also DAM DRAM, MST, NOV, POET;
DLB 119; SATA 47

Huidobro, Vicente
See Huidobro Fernandez, Vicente Garcia

Huidobro Fernandez, Vicente Garcia
    1893-1948 .... TCLC 31
    See also CA 131; HW

Hulme, Keri 1947- .... CLC 39
    See also CA 125; INT 125

Hulme, T(homas) E(rnest)
    1883-1917 .... TCLC 21
    See also CA 117; DLB 19

Hume, David 1711-1776............ LC 7
    See also DLB 104

Humphrey, William 1924- .... CLC 45
    See also CA 77-80; DLB 6

Humphreys, Emyr Owen 1919-..... CLC 47
    See also CA 5-8R; CANR 3, 24; DLB 15

Humphreys, Josephine 1945-.... CLC 34, 57
    See also CA 121; 127; INT 127

Hungerford, Pixie
    See Brinsmead, H(esba) F(ay)

Hunt, E(verette) Howard, (Jr.)
    1918- .... CLC 3
    See also AITN 1; CA 45-48; CANR 2, 47

Hunt, Kyle
    See Creasey, John

Hunt, (James Henry) Leigh
    1784-1859 .... NCLC 1
    See also DAM POET

Hunt, Marsha 1946-.............. CLC 70
    See also BW 2; CA 143

Hunt, Violet 1866-1942 .... TCLC 53

Hunter, E. Waldo
    See Sturgeon, Theodore (Hamilton)

Hunter, Evan 1926- .... CLC 11, 31
    See also CA 5-8R; CANR 5, 38;
        DAM POP; DLBY 82; INT CANR-5;
        MTCW; SATA 25

Hunter, Kristin (Eggleston) 1931-... CLC 35
    See also AITN 1; BW 1; CA 13-16R;
        CANR 13; CLR 3; DLB 33;
        INT CANR-13; MAICYA; SAAS 10;
        SATA 12

Hunter, Mollie 1922- .... CLC 21
    See also McIlwraith, Maureen Mollie
        Hunter
    See also AAYA 13; CANR 37; CLR 25;
        DLB 161; JRDA; MAICYA; SAAS 7;
        SATA 54

Hunter, Robert (?)-1734............. LC 7

Hurston, Zora Neale
    1903-1960 .... CLC 7, 30, 61; BLC; DA;
                                    DAC; SSC 4
    See also AAYA 15; BW 1; CA 85-88;
        DAM MST, MULT, NOV; DLB 51, 86;
        MTCW

Huston, John (Marcellus)
    1906-1987 .... CLC 20
    See also CA 73-76; 123; CANR 34; DLB 26

Hustvedt, Siri 1955-.............. CLC 76
    See also CA 137

Hutten, Ulrich von 1488-1523....... LC 16

Huxley, Aldous (Leonard)
    1894-1963 ..... CLC 1, 3, 4, 5, 8, 11, 18,
                        35, 79; DA; DAB; DAC; WLC
    See also AAYA 11; CA 85-88; CANR 44;
        CDBLB 1914-1945; DAM MST, NOV;
        DLB 36, 100; MTCW; SATA 63

Huysmans, Charles Marie Georges
    1848-1907
    See Huysmans, Joris-Karl
    See also CA 104

Huysmans, Joris-Karl.............. TCLC 7
    See also Huysmans, Charles Marie Georges
    See also DLB 123

Hwang, David Henry
    1957- .... CLC 55; DC 4
    See also CA 127; 132; DAM DRAM;
        INT 132

Hyde, Anthony 1946-............. CLC 42
    See also CA 136

Hyde, Margaret O(ldroyd) 1917- ... CLC 21
    See also CA 1-4R; CANR 1, 36; CLR 23;
        JRDA; MAICYA; SAAS 8; SATA 1, 42,
        76

Hynes, James 1956(?)-............ CLC 65

Ian, Janis 1951- .... CLC 21
    See also CA 105

Ibanez, Vicente Blasco
    See Blasco Ibanez, Vicente

Ibarguengoitia, Jorge 1928-1983.... CLC 37
    See also CA 124; 113; HW

Ibsen, Henrik (Johan)
    1828-1906 .... TCLC 2, 8, 16, 37, 52;
                        DA; DAB; DAC; DC 2; WLC
    See also CA 104; 141; DAM DRAM, MST

Ibuse Masuji 1898-1993........... CLC 22
    See also CA 127; 141

Ichikawa, Kon 1915-.............. CLC 20
    See also CA 121

Idle, Eric 1943-.................. CLC 21
    See also Monty Python
    See also CA 116; CANR 35

Ignatow, David 1914-...... CLC 4, 7, 14, 40
    See also CA 9-12R; CAAS 3; CANR 31;
        DLB 5

Ihimaera, Witi 1944- .... CLC 46
    See also CA 77-80

Ilf, Ilya........................ TCLC 21
    See also Fainzilberg, Ilya Arnoldovich

Immermann, Karl (Lebrecht)
    1796-1840 .... NCLC 4, 49
    See also DLB 133

Inclan, Ramon (Maria) del Valle
    See Valle-Inclan, Ramon (Maria) del

Infante, G(uillermo) Cabrera
    See Cabrera Infante, G(uillermo)

Ingalls, Rachel (Holmes) 1940-..... CLC 42
    See also CA 123; 127

Ingamells, Rex 1913-1955 .... TCLC 35

Inge, William Motter
    1913-1973 .... CLC 1, 8, 19
    See also CA 9-12R; CDALB 1941-1968;
        DAM DRAM; DLB 7; MTCW

Ingelow, Jean 1820-1897 .... NCLC 39
    See also DLB 35; SATA 33

Ingram, Willis J.
    See Harris, Mark

Innaurato, Albert (F.) 1948(?)- .. CLC 21, 60
    See also CA 115; 122; INT 122

Innes, Michael
    See Stewart, J(ohn) I(nnes) M(ackintosh)

Ionesco, Eugene
    1909-1994 .... CLC 1, 4, 6, 9, 11, 15, 41,
                        86; DA; DAB; DAC; WLC
    See also CA 9-12R; 144; DAM DRAM,
        MST; MTCW; SATA 7; SATA-Obit 79

Iqbal, Muhammad 1873-1938 ..... TCLC 28

Ireland, Patrick
    See O'Doherty, Brian

Iron, Ralph
    See Schreiner, Olive (Emilie Albertina)

Irving, John (Winslow)
    1942- .... CLC 13, 23, 38
    See also AAYA 8; BEST 89:3; CA 25-28R;
        CANR 28; DAM NOV, POP; DLB 6;
        DLBY 82; MTCW

Irving, Washington
    1783-1859 ..... NCLC 2, 19; DA; DAB;
                                SSC 2; WLC
    See also CDALB 1640-1865; DAM MST;
        DLB 3, 11, 30, 59, 73, 74; YABC 2

Irwin, P. K.
    See Page, P(atricia) K(athleen)

Isaacs, Susan 1943- .... CLC 32
    See also BEST 89:1; CA 89-92; CANR 20,
        41; DAM POP; INT CANR-20; MTCW

Isherwood, Christopher (William Bradshaw)
    1904-1986 .... CLC 1, 9, 11, 14, 44
    See also CA 13-16R; 117; CANR 35;
        DAM DRAM, NOV; DLB 15; DLBY 86;
        MTCW

Ishiguro, Kazuo 1954- ...... CLC 27, 56, 59
    See also BEST 90:2; CA 120; CANR 49;
        DAM NOV; MTCW

Ishikawa Takuboku
    1886(?)-1912 .... TCLC 15; PC 10
    See also CA 113; DAM POET

Iskander, Fazil 1929-............. CLC 47
    See also CA 102

Ivan IV 1530-1584 .... LC 17

Ivanov, Vyacheslav Ivanovich
    1866-1949 .... TCLC 33
    See also CA 122

Ivask, Ivar Vidrik 1927-1992....... CLC 14
    See also CA 37-40R; 139; CANR 24

Jackson, Daniel
    See Wingrove, David (John)

Jackson, Jesse 1908-1983 .... CLC 12
    See also BW 1; CA 25-28R; 109; CANR 27;
        CLR 28; MAICYA; SATA 2, 29;
        SATA-Obit 48

Jackson, Laura (Riding) 1901-1991
    See Riding, Laura
    See also CA 65-68; 135; CANR 28; DLB 48

Jackson, Sam
    See Trumbo, Dalton

Jackson, Sara
    See Wingrove, David (John)

Jackson, Shirley
    1919-1965 .... CLC 11, 60, 87; DA;
                        DAC; SSC 9; WLC
    See also AAYA 9; CA 1-4R; 25-28R;
        CANR 4; CDALB 1941-1968;
        DAM MST; DLB 6; SATA 2

Jacob, (Cyprien-)Max 1876-1944 ... TCLC 6
    See also CA 104

Kim
See Simenon, Georges (Jacques Christian)

Kincaid, Jamaica 1949- ... **CLC 43, 68; BLC**
See also AAYA 13; BW 2; CA 125;
CANR 47; DAM MULT, NOV;
DLB 157

King, Francis (Henry) 1923- ..... **CLC 8, 53**
See also CA 1-4R; CANR 1, 33;
DAM NOV; DLB 15, 139; MTCW

King, Martin Luther, Jr.
1929-1968 .... **CLC 83; BLC; DA; DAB;**
DAC
See also BW 2; CA 25-28; CANR 27, 44;
CAP 2; DAM MST, MULT; MTCW;
SATA 14

King, Stephen (Edwin)
1947- ...... **CLC 12, 26, 37, 61; SSC 17**
See also AAYA 1, 17; BEST 90:1;
CA 61-64; CANR 1, 30; DAM NOV,
POP; DLB 143; DLBY 80; JRDA;
MTCW; SATA 9, 55

King, Steve
See King, Stephen (Edwin)

King, Thomas 1943- .... **CLC 89; DAC**
See also CA 144; DAM MULT; NNAL

Kingman, Lee .... **CLC 17**
See also Natti, (Mary) Lee
See also SAAS 3; SATA 1, 67

Kingsley, Charles 1819-1875 ..... **NCLC 35**
See also DLB 21, 32; YABC 2

Kingsley, Sidney 1906-1995 .... **CLC 44**
See also CA 85-88; 147; DLB 7

Kingsolver, Barbara 1955- ...... **CLC 55, 81**
See also AAYA 15; CA 129; 134;
DAM POP; INT 134

Kingston, Maxine (Ting Ting) Hong
1940- .... **CLC 12, 19, 58**
See also AAYA 8; CA 69-72; CANR 13,
38; DAM MULT, NOV; DLBY 80;
INT CANR-13; MTCW; SATA 53

Kinnell, Galway
1927- .... **CLC 1, 2, 3, 5, 13, 29**
See also CA 9-12R; CANR 10, 34; DLB 5;
DLBY 87; INT CANR-34; MTCW

Kinsella, Thomas 1928- .... **CLC 4, 19**
See also CA 17-20R; CANR 15; DLB 27;
MTCW

Kinsella, W(illiam) P(atrick)
1935- .... **CLC 27, 43; DAC**
See also AAYA 7; CA 97-100; CAAS 7;
CANR 21, 35; DAM NOV, POP;
INT CANR-21; MTCW

Kipling, (Joseph) Rudyard
1865-1936 ...... **TCLC 8, 17; DA; DAB;**
DAC; PC 3; SSC 5; WLC
See also CA 105; 120; CANR 33;
CDBLB 1890-1914; CLR 39; DAM MST,
POET; DLB 19, 34, 141, 156; MAICYA;
MTCW; YABC 2

Kirkup, James 1918- .... **CLC 1**
See also CA 1-4R; CAAS 4; CANR 2;
DLB 27; SATA 12

Kirkwood, James 1930(?)-1989 ...... **CLC 9**
See also AITN 2; CA 1-4R; 128; CANR 6,
40

Kirshner, Sidney
See Kingsley, Sidney

Kis, Danilo 1935-1989 .... **CLC 57**
See also CA 109; 118; 129; MTCW

Kivi, Aleksis 1834-1872 .... **NCLC 30**

Kizer, Carolyn (Ashley)
1925- .... **CLC 15, 39, 80**
See also CA 65-68; CAAS 5; CANR 24;
DAM POET; DLB 5

Klabund 1890-1928 .... **TCLC 44**
See also DLB 66

Klappert, Peter 1942- .... **CLC 57**
See also CA 33-36R; DLB 5

Klein, A(braham) M(oses)
1909-1972 .... **CLC 19; DAB; DAC**
See also CA 101; 37-40R; DAM MST;
DLB 68

Klein, Norma 1938-1989 .... **CLC 30**
See also AAYA 2; CA 41-44R; 128;
CANR 15, 37; CLR 2, 19;
INT CANR-15; JRDA; MAICYA;
SAAS 1; SATA 7, 57

Klein, T(heodore) E(ibon) D(onald)
1947- .... **CLC 34**
See also CA 119; CANR 44

Kleist, Heinrich von
1777-1811 .... **NCLC 2, 37**
See also DAM DRAM; DLB 90

Klima, Ivan 1931- .... **CLC 56**
See also CA 25-28R; CANR 17, 50;
DAM NOV

Klimentov, Andrei Platonovich 1899-1951
See Platonov, Andrei
See also CA 108

Klinger, Friedrich Maximilian von
1752-1831 .... **NCLC 1**
See also DLB 94

Klopstock, Friedrich Gottlieb
1724-1803 .... **NCLC 11**
See also DLB 97

Knebel, Fletcher 1911-1993 .... **CLC 14**
See also AITN 1; CA 1-4R; 140; CAAS 3;
CANR 1, 36; SATA 36; SATA-Obit 75

Knickerbocker, Diedrich
See Irving, Washington

Knight, Etheridge
1931-1991 .... **CLC 40; BLC; PC 14**
See also BW 1; CA 21-24R; 133; CANR 23;
DAM POET; DLB 41

Knight, Sarah Kemble 1666-1727 ..... **LC 7**
See also DLB 24

Knister, Raymond 1899-1932 ...... **TCLC 56**
See also DLB 68

Knowles, John
1926- ...... **CLC 1, 4, 10, 26; DA; DAC**
See also AAYA 10; CA 17-20R; CANR 40;
CDALB 1968-1988; DAM MST, NOV;
DLB 6; MTCW; SATA 8

Knox, Calvin M.
See Silverberg, Robert

Knye, Cassandra
See Disch, Thomas M(ichael)

Koch, C(hristopher) J(ohn) 1932- ... **CLC 42**
See also CA 127

Koch, Christopher
See Koch, C(hristopher) J(ohn)

Koch, Kenneth 1925- .... **CLC 5, 8, 44**
See also CA 1-4R; CANR 6, 36;
DAM POET; DLB 5; INT CANR-36;
SATA 65

Kochanowski, Jan 1530-1584 .... **LC 10**

Kock, Charles Paul de
1794-1871 .... **NCLC 16**

Koda Shigeyuki 1867-1947
See Rohan, Koda
See also CA 121

Koestler, Arthur
1905-1983 .... **CLC 1, 3, 6, 8, 15, 33**
See also CA 1-4R; 109; CANR 1, 33;
CDBLB 1945-1960; DLBY 83; MTCW

Kogawa, Joy Nozomi 1935- ... **CLC 78; DAC**
See also CA 101; CANR 19; DAM MST,
MULT

Kohout, Pavel 1928- .... **CLC 13**
See also CA 45-48; CANR 3

Koizumi, Yakumo
See Hearn, (Patricio) Lafcadio (Tessima
Carlos)

Kolmar, Gertrud 1894-1943 ...... **TCLC 40**

Komunyakaa, Yusef 1947- .... **CLC 86**
See also CA 147; DLB 120

Konrad, George
See Konrad, Gyoergy

Konrad, Gyoergy 1933- ...... **CLC 4, 10, 73**
See also CA 85-88

Konwicki, Tadeusz 1926- ..... **CLC 8, 28, 54**
See also CA 101; CAAS 9; CANR 39;
MTCW

Koontz, Dean R(ay) 1945- .... **CLC 78**
See also AAYA 9; BEST 89:3, 90:2;
CA 108; CANR 19, 36; DAM NOV,
POP; MTCW

Kopit, Arthur (Lee) 1937- .... **CLC 1, 18, 33**
See also AITN 1; CA 81-84; CABS 3;
DAM DRAM; DLB 7; MTCW

Kops, Bernard 1926- .... **CLC 4**
See also CA 5-8R; DLB 13

Kornbluth, C(yril) M. 1923-1958 .... **TCLC 8**
See also CA 105; DLB 8

Korolenko, V. G.
See Korolenko, Vladimir Galaktionovich

Korolenko, Vladimir
See Korolenko, Vladimir Galaktionovich

Korolenko, Vladimir G.
See Korolenko, Vladimir Galaktionovich

Korolenko, Vladimir Galaktionovich
1853-1921 .... **TCLC 22**
See also CA 121

Korzybski, Alfred (Habdank Skarbek)
1879-1950 .... **TCLC 61**
See also CA 123

Kosinski, Jerzy (Nikodem)
1933-1991 .... **CLC 1, 2, 3, 6, 10, 15, 53,**
70
See also CA 17-20R; 134; CANR 9, 46;
DAM NOV; DLB 2, DLBY 82; MTCW

Kostelanetz, Richard (Cory) 1940- .. **CLC 28**
See also CA 13-16R; CAAS 8; CANR 38

Lane, Patrick 1939- . . . . CLC 25
See also CA 97-100; DAM POET; DLB 53;
INT 97-100

Lang, Andrew 1844-1912 . . . . TCLC 16
See also CA 114; 137; DLB 98, 141;
MAICYA; SATA 16

Lang, Fritz 1890-1976 . . . . CLC 20
See also CA 77-80; 69-72; CANR 30

Lange, John
See Crichton, (John) Michael

Langer, Elinor 1939- . . . . CLC 34
See also CA 121

Langland, William
1330(?)-1400(?) . . . . . . LC 19; DA; DAB;
DAC
See also DAM MST, POET; DLB 146

Langstaff, Launcelot
See Irving, Washington

Lanier, Sidney 1842-1881 . . . . NCLC 6
See also DAM POET; DLB 64; DLBD 13;
MAICYA; SATA 18

Lanyer, Aemilia 1569-1645 . . . . . . LC 10, 30
See also DLB 121

Lao Tzu . . . . CMLC 7

Lapine, James (Elliot) 1949- . . . . CLC 39
See also CA 123; 130; INT 130

Larbaud, Valery (Nicolas)
1881-1957 . . . . TCLC 9
See also CA 106

Lardner, Ring
See Lardner, Ring(gold) W(ilmer)

Lardner, Ring W., Jr.
See Lardner, Ring(gold) W(ilmer)

Lardner, Ring(gold) W(ilmer)
1885-1933 . . . . TCLC 2, 14
See also CA 104; 131; CDALB 1917-1929;
DLB 11, 25, 86; MTCW

Laredo, Betty
See Codrescu, Andrei

Larkin, Maia
See Wojciechowska, Maia (Teresa)

Larkin, Philip (Arthur)
1922-1985 . . . . CLC 3, 5, 8, 9, 13, 18, 33,
39, 64; DAB
See also CA 5-8R; 117; CANR 24;
CDBLB 1960 to Present; DAM MST,
POET; DLB 27; MTCW

Larra (y Sanchez de Castro), Mariano Jose de
1809-1837 . . . . NCLC 17

Larsen, Eric 1941- . . . . CLC 55
See also CA 132

Larsen, Nella 1891-1964 . . . . . CLC 37; BLC
See also BW 1; CA 125; DAM MULT;
DLB 51

Larson, Charles R(aymond) 1938- . . . CLC 31
See also CA 53-56; CANR 4

Las Casas, Bartolome de 1474-1566 . . LC 31

Lasker-Schueler, Else 1869-1945 . . TCLC 57
See also DLB 66, 124

Latham, Jean Lee 1902- . . . . CLC 12
See also AITN 1; CA 5-8R; CANR 7;
MAICYA; SATA 2, 68

Latham, Mavis
See Clark, Mavis Thorpe

Lathen, Emma . . . . CLC 2
See also Hennissart, Martha; Latsis, Mary
J(ane)

Lathrop, Francis
See Leiber, Fritz (Reuter, Jr.)

Latsis, Mary J(ane)
See Lathen, Emma
See also CA 85-88

Lattimore, Richmond (Alexander)
1906-1984 . . . . CLC 3
See also CA 1-4R; 112; CANR 1

Laughlin, James 1914- . . . . CLC 49
See also CA 21-24R; CAAS 22; CANR 9,
47; DLB 48

Laurence, (Jean) Margaret (Wemyss)
1926-1987 . . . . CLC 3, 6, 13, 50, 62;
DAC; SSC 7
See also CA 5-8R; 121; CANR 33;
DAM MST; DLB 53; MTCW;
SATA-Obit 50

Laurent, Antoine 1952- . . . . CLC 50

Lauscher, Hermann
See Hesse, Hermann

Lautreamont, Comte de
1846-1870 . . . . NCLC 12; SSC 14

Laverty, Donald
See Blish, James (Benjamin)

Lavin, Mary 1912- . . . . CLC 4, 18; SSC 4
See also CA 9-12R; CANR 33; DLB 15;
MTCW

Lavond, Paul Dennis
See Kornbluth, C(yril) M.; Pohl, Frederik

Lawler, Raymond Evenor 1922- . . . . CLC 58
See also CA 103

Lawrence, D(avid) H(erbert Richards)
1885-1930 . . . . TCLC 2, 9, 16, 33, 48, 61;
DA; DAB; DAC; SSC 4, 19; WLC
See also CA 104; 121; CDBLB 1914-1945;
DAM MST, NOV, POET; DLB 10, 19,
36, 98; MTCW

Lawrence, T(homas) E(dward)
1888-1935 . . . . TCLC 18
See also Dale, Colin
See also CA 115

Lawrence of Arabia
See Lawrence, T(homas) E(dward)

Lawson, Henry (Archibald Hertzberg)
1867-1922 . . . . TCLC 27; SSC 18
See also CA 120

Lawton, Dennis
See Faust, Frederick (Schiller)

Laxness, Halldor . . . . CLC 25
See also Gudjonsson, Halldor Kiljan

Layamon fl. c. 1200- . . . . CMLC 10
See also DLB 146

Laye, Camara 1928-1980 . . . CLC 4, 38; BLC
See also BW 1; CA 85-88; 97-100;
CANR 25; DAM MULT; MTCW

Layton, Irving (Peter)
1912- . . . . CLC 2, 15; DAC
See also CA 1-4R; CANR 2, 33, 43;
DAM MST, POET; DLB 88; MTCW

Lazarus, Emma 1849-1887 . . . . NCLC 8

Lazarus, Felix
See Cable, George Washington

Lazarus, Henry
See Slavitt, David R(ytman)

Lea, Joan
See Neufeld, John (Arthur)

Leacock, Stephen (Butler)
1869-1944 . . . . TCLC 2; DAC
See also CA 104; 141; DAM MST; DLB 92

Lear, Edward 1812-1888 . . . . NCLC 3
See also CLR 1; DLB 32; MAICYA;
SATA 18

Lear, Norman (Milton) 1922- . . . . . . CLC 12
See also CA 73-76

Leavis, F(rank) R(aymond)
1895-1978 . . . . CLC 24
See also CA 21-24R; 77-80; CANR 44;
MTCW

Leavitt, David 1961- . . . . CLC 34
See also CA 116; 122; CANR 50;
DAM POP; DLB 130; INT 122

Leblanc, Maurice (Marie Emile)
1864-1941 . . . . TCLC 49
See also CA 110

Lebowitz, Fran(ces Ann)
1951(?)- . . . . CLC 11, 36
See also CA 81-84; CANR 14;
INT CANR-14; MTCW

Lebrecht, Peter
See Tieck, (Johann) Ludwig

le Carre, John . . . . CLC 3, 5, 9, 15, 28
See also Cornwell, David (John Moore)
See also BEST 89:4; CDBLB 1960 to
Present; DLB 87

Le Clezio, J(ean) M(arie) G(ustave)
1940- . . . . CLC 31
See also CA 116; 128; DLB 83

Leconte de Lisle, Charles-Marie-Rene
1818-1894 . . . . NCLC 29

Le Coq, Monsieur
See Simenon, Georges (Jacques Christian)

Leduc, Violette 1907-1972 . . . . CLC 22
See also CA 13-14; 33-36R; CAP 1

Ledwidge, Francis 1887(?)-1917 . . . TCLC 23
See also CA 123; DLB 20

Lee, Andrea 1953- . . . . CLC 36; BLC
See also BW 1; CA 125; DAM MULT

Lee, Andrew
See Auchincloss, Louis (Stanton)

Lee, Don L. . . . . CLC 2
See also Madhubuti, Haki R.

Lee, George W(ashington)
1894-1976 . . . . CLC 52; BLC
See also BW 1; CA 125; DAM MULT;
DLB 51

Lee, (Nelle) Harper
1926- . . . . CLC 12, 60; DA; DAB; DAC;
WLC
See also AAYA 13; CA 13-16R;
CDALB 1941-1968; DAM MST, NOV;
DLB 6; MTCW; SATA 11

Lee, Helen Elaine 1959(?)- . . . . CLC 86
See also CA 148

Lee, Julian
See Latham, Jean Lee

Lee, Larry
See Lee, Lawrence

Author Index

Lewis, Matthew Gregory
    1775-1818 . . . . **NCLC 11**
    See also DLB 39, 158

Lewis, (Harry) Sinclair
    1885-1951 . . . . . **TCLC 4, 13, 23, 39; DA;**
                DAB; DAC; WLC
    See also CA 104; 133; CDALB 1917-1929;
        DAM MST, NOV; DLB 9, 102; DLBD 1;
        MTCW

Lewis, (Percy) Wyndham
    1884(?)-1957 . . . . **TCLC 2, 9**
    See also CA 104; DLB 15

Lewisohn, Ludwig 1883-1955 . . . . . . **TCLC 19**
    See also CA 107; DLB 4, 9, 28, 102

Lezama Lima, Jose 1910-1976 . . . **CLC 4, 10**
    See also CA 77-80; DAM MULT;
        DLB 113; HW

L'Heureux, John (Clarke) 1934- . . . . **CLC 52**
    See also CA 13-16R; CANR 23, 45

Liddell, C. H.
    See Kuttner, Henry

Lie, Jonas (Lauritz Idemil)
    1833-1908(?) . . . . **TCLC 5**
    See also CA 115

Lieber, Joel 1937-1971 . . . . **CLC 6**
    See also CA 73-76; 29-32R

Lieber, Stanley Martin
    See Lee, Stan

Lieberman, Laurence (James)
    1935- . . . . **CLC 4, 36**
    See also CA 17-20R; CANR 8, 36

Lieksman, Anders
    See Haavikko, Paavo Juhani

Li Fei-kan 1904-
    See Pa Chin
    See also CA 105

Lifton, Robert Jay 1926- . . . . **CLC 67**
    See also CA 17-20R; CANR 27;
        INT CANR-27; SATA 66

Lightfoot, Gordon 1938- . . . . **CLC 26**
    See also CA 109

Lightman, Alan P. 1948- . . . . **CLC 81**
    See also CA 141

Ligotti, Thomas (Robert)
    1953- . . . . **CLC 44; SSC 16**
    See also CA 123; CANR 49

Li Ho 791-817 . . . . **PC 13**

Liliencron, (Friedrich Adolf Axel) Detlev von
    1844-1909 . . . . **TCLC 18**
    See also CA 117

Lilly, William 1602-1681 . . . . **LC 27**

Lima, Jose Lezama
    See Lezama Lima, Jose

Lima Barreto, Afonso Henrique de
    1881-1922 . . . . **TCLC 23**
    See also CA 117

Limonov, Edward 1944- . . . . **CLC 67**
    See also CA 137

Lin, Frank
    See Atherton, Gertrude (Franklin Horn)

Lincoln, Abraham 1809-1865 . . . . . **NCLC 18**

Lind, Jakov . . . . **CLC 1, 2, 4, 27, 82**
    See also Landwirth, Heinz
    See also CAAS 4

Lindbergh, Anne (Spencer) Morrow
    1906- . . . . **CLC 82**
    See also CA 17-20R; CANR 16;
        DAM NOV; MTCW; SATA 33

Lindsay, David 1878-1945 . . . . **TCLC 15**
    See also CA 113

Lindsay, (Nicholas) Vachel
    1879-1931 . . . **TCLC 17; DA; DAC; WLC**
    See also CA 114; 135; CDALB 1865-1917;
        DAM MST, POET; DLB 54; SATA 40

Linke-Poot
    See Doeblin, Alfred

Linney, Romulus 1930- . . . . **CLC 51**
    See also CA 1-4R; CANR 40, 44

Linton, Eliza Lynn 1822-1898 . . . . **NCLC 41**
    See also DLB 18

Li Po 701-763 . . . . **CMLC 2**

Lipsius, Justus 1547-1606 . . . . **LC 16**

Lipsyte, Robert (Michael)
    1938- . . . . **CLC 21; DA; DAC**
    See also AAYA 7; CA 17-20R; CANR 8;
        CLR 23; DAM MST, NOV; JRDA;
        MAICYA; SATA 5, 68

Lish, Gordon (Jay) 1934- . . **CLC 45; SSC 18**
    See also CA 113; 117; DLB 130; INT 117

Lispector, Clarice 1925-1977 . . . . . . **CLC 43**
    See also CA 139; 116; DLB 113

Littell, Robert 1935(?)- . . . . **CLC 42**
    See also CA 109; 112

Little, Malcolm 1925-1965
    See Malcolm X
    See also BW 1; CA 125; 111; DA; DAB;
        DAC; DAM MST, MULT; MTCW

Littlewit, Humphrey Gent.
    See Lovecraft, H(oward) P(hillips)

Litwos
    See Sienkiewicz, Henryk (Adam Alexander
        Pius)

Liu E 1857-1909 . . . . **TCLC 15**
    See also CA 115

Lively, Penelope (Margaret)
    1933- . . . . **CLC 32, 50**
    See also CA 41-44R; CANR 29; CLR 7;
        DAM NOV; DLB 14, 161; JRDA;
        MAICYA; MTCW; SATA 7, 60

Livesay, Dorothy (Kathleen)
    1909- . . . . **CLC 4, 15, 79; DAC**
    See also AITN 2; CA 25-28R; CAAS 8;
        CANR 36; DAM MST, POET; DLB 68;
        MTCW

Livy c. 59B.C.-c. 17 . . . . **CMLC 11**

Lizardi, Jose Joaquin Fernandez de
    1776-1827 . . . . **NCLC 30**

Llewellyn, Richard
    See Llewellyn Lloyd, Richard Dafydd
        Vivian
    See also DLB 15

Llewellyn Lloyd, Richard Dafydd Vivian
    1906-1983 . . . . **CLC 7, 80**
    See also Llewellyn, Richard
    See also CA 53-56; 111; CANR 7;
        SATA 11; SATA-Obit 37

Llosa, (Jorge) Mario (Pedro) Vargas
    See Vargas Llosa, (Jorge) Mario (Pedro)

Lloyd Webber, Andrew 1948-
    See Webber, Andrew Lloyd
    See also AAYA 1; CA 116; 149;
        DAM DRAM; SATA 56

Llull, Ramon c. 1235-c. 1316 . . . . . **CMLC 12**

Locke, Alain (Le Roy)
    1886-1954 . . . . **TCLC 43**
    See also BW 1; CA 106; 124; DLB 51

Locke, John 1632-1704 . . . . **LC 7**
    See also DLB 101

Locke-Elliott, Sumner
    See Elliott, Sumner Locke

Lockhart, John Gibson
    1794-1854 . . . . **NCLC 6**
    See also DLB 110, 116, 144

Lodge, David (John) 1935- . . . . **CLC 36**
    See also BEST 90:1; CA 17-20R; CANR 19;
        DAM POP; DLB 14; INT CANR-19;
        MTCW

Loennbohm, Armas Eino Leopold 1878-1926
    See Leino, Eino
    See also CA 123

Loewinsohn, Ron(ald William)
    1937- . . . . **CLC 52**
    See also CA 25-28R

Logan, Jake
    See Smith, Martin Cruz

Logan, John (Burton) 1923-1987 . . . . . **CLC 5**
    See also CA 77-80; 124; CANR 45; DLB 5

Lo Kuan-chung 1330(?)-1400(?) . . . . . . **LC 12**

Lombard, Nap
    See Johnson, Pamela Hansford

London, Jack . . **TCLC 9, 15, 39; SSC 4; WLC**
    See also London, John Griffith
    See also AAYA 13; AITN 2;
        CDALB 1865-1917; DLB 8, 12, 78;
        SATA 18

London, John Griffith 1876-1916
    See London, Jack
    See also CA 110; 119; DA; DAB; DAC;
        DAM MST, NOV; JRDA; MAICYA;
        MTCW

Long, Emmett
    See Leonard, Elmore (John, Jr.)

Longbaugh, Harry
    See Goldman, William (W.)

Longfellow, Henry Wadsworth
    1807-1882 . . . . . **NCLC 2, 45; DA; DAB;**
                                                DAC
    See also CDALB 1640-1865; DAM MST,
        POET; DLB 1, 59; SATA 19

Longley, Michael 1939- . . . . **CLC 29**
    See also CA 102; DLB 40

Longus fl. c. 2nd cent. - . . . . **CMLC 7**

Longway, A. Hugh
    See Lang, Andrew

Lonnrot, Elias 1802-1884 . . . . **NCLC 53**

Lopate, Phillip 1943- . . . . **CLC 29**
    See also CA 97-100; DLBY 80; INT 97-100

Lopez Portillo (y Pacheco), Jose
    1920- . . . . **CLC 46**
    See also CA 129; HW

MacInnes, Colin 1914-1976...... **CLC 4, 23**
See also CA 69-72; 65-68; CANR 21;
DLB 14; MTCW

MacInnes, Helen (Clark)
1907-1985 .... **CLC 27, 39**
See also CA 1-4R; 117; CANR 1, 28;
DAM POP; DLB 87; MTCW; SATA 22;
SATA-Obit 44

Mackay, Mary 1855-1924
See Corelli, Marie
See also CA 118

Mackenzie, Compton (Edward Montague)
1883-1972 .... **CLC 18**
See also CA 21-22; 37-40R; CAP 2;
DLB 34, 100

Mackenzie, Henry 1745-1831 .... **NCLC 41**
See also DLB 39

Mackintosh, Elizabeth 1896(?)-1952
See Tey, Josephine
See also CA 110

MacLaren, James
See Grieve, C(hristopher) M(urray)

Mac Laverty, Bernard 1942-....... **CLC 31**
See also CA 116; 118; CANR 43; INT 118

MacLean, Alistair (Stuart)
1922-1987 .... **CLC 3, 13, 50, 63**
See also CA 57-60; 121; CANR 28;
DAM POP; MTCW; SATA 23;
SATA-Obit 50

Maclean, Norman (Fitzroy)
1902-1990 .... **CLC 78; SSC 13**
See also CA 102; 132; CANR 49;
DAM POP

MacLeish, Archibald
1892-1982 .... **CLC 3, 8, 14, 68**
See also CA 9-12R; 106; CANR 33;
DAM POET; DLB 4, 7, 45; DLBY 82;
MTCW

MacLennan, (John) Hugh
1907-1990 .... **CLC 2, 14; DAC**
See also CA 5-8R; 142; CANR 33;
DAM MST; DLB 68; MTCW

MacLeod, Alistair 1936- ..... **CLC 56; DAC**
See also CA 123; DAM MST; DLB 60

MacNeice, (Frederick) Louis
1907-1963 ...... **CLC 1, 4, 10, 53; DAB**
See also CA 85-88; DAM POET; DLB 10,
20; MTCW

MacNeill, Dand
See Fraser, George MacDonald

Macpherson, James 1736-1796 ...... **LC 29**
See also DLB 109

Macpherson, (Jean) Jay 1931-..... **CLC 14**
See also CA 5-8R; DLB 53

MacShane, Frank 1927-........... **CLC 39**
See also CA 9-12R; CANR 3, 33; DLB 111

Macumber, Mari
See Sandoz, Mari(e Susette)

Madach, Imre 1823-1864........ **NCLC 19**

Madden, (Jerry) David 1933- .... **CLC 5, 15**
See also CA 1-4R; CAAS 3; CANR 4, 45;
DLB 6; MTCW

Maddern, Al(an)
See Ellison, Harlan (Jay)

Madhubuti, Haki R.
1942- .... **CLC 6, 73; BLC; PC 5**
See also Lee, Don L.
See also BW 2; CA 73-76; CANR 24;
DAM MULT, POET; DLB 5, 41;
DLBD 8

Maepenn, Hugh
See Kuttner, Henry

Maepenn, K. H.
See Kuttner, Henry

Maeterlinck, Maurice 1862-1949 ... **TCLC 3**
See also CA 104; 136; DAM DRAM;
SATA 66

Maginn, William 1794-1842....... **NCLC 8**
See also DLB 110, 159

Mahapatra, Jayanta 1928-......... **CLC 33**
See also CA 73-76; CAAS 9; CANR 15, 33;
DAM MULT

Mahfouz, Naguib (Abdel Aziz Al-Sabilgi)
1911(?)-
See Mahfuz, Najib
See also BEST 89:2; CA 128; DAM NOV;
MTCW

Mahfuz, Najib................. CLC 52, 55
See also Mahfouz, Naguib (Abdel Aziz
Al-Sabilgi)
See also DLBY 88

Mahon, Derek 1941-.............. **CLC 27**
See also CA 113; 128; DLB 40

Mailer, Norman
1923- ...... **CLC 1, 2, 3, 4, 5, 8, 11, 14,
28, 39, 74; DA; DAB; DAC**
See also AITN 2; CA 9-12R; CABS 1;
CANR 28; CDALB 1968-1988;
DAM MST, NOV, POP; DLB 2, 16, 28;
DLBD 3; DLBY 80, 83; MTCW

Maillet, Antonine 1929-...... **CLC 54; DAC**
See also CA 115; 120; CANR 46; DLB 60;
INT 120

Mais, Roger 1905-1955 .... **TCLC 8**
See also BW 1; CA 105; 124; DLB 125;
MTCW

Maistre, Joseph de 1753-1821.... **NCLC 37**

Maitland, Sara (Louise) 1950-...... **CLC 49**
See also CA 69-72; CANR 13

Major, Clarence
1936- .... **CLC 3, 19, 48; BLC**
See also BW 2; CA 21-24R; CAAS 6;
CANR 13, 25; DAM MULT; DLB 33

Major, Kevin (Gerald)
1949- .... **CLC 26; DAC**
See also AAYA 16; CA 97-100; CANR 21,
38; CLR 11; DLB 60; INT CANR-21;
JRDA; MAICYA; SATA 32, 82

Maki, James
See Ozu, Yasujiro

Malabaila, Damiano
See Levi, Primo

Malamud, Bernard
1914-1986 ...... **CLC 1, 2, 3, 5, 8, 9, 11,
18, 27, 44, 78, 85; DA; DAB; DAC;
SSC 15; WLC**
See also AAYA 16; CA 5-8R; 118; CABS 1;
CANR 28; CDALB 1941-1968;
DAM MST, NOV, POP; DLB 2, 28, 152;
DLBY 80, 86; MTCW

Malaparte, Curzio 1898-1957 ..... **TCLC 52**

Malcolm, Dan
See Silverberg, Robert

Malcolm X.................. CLC 82; BLC
See also Little, Malcolm

Malherbe, Francois de 1555-1628..... **LC 5**

Mallarme, Stephane
1842-1898 .... **NCLC 4, 41; PC 4**
See also DAM POET

Mallet-Joris, Francoise 1930-...... **CLC 11**
See also CA 65-68; CANR 17; DLB 83

Malley, Ern
See McAuley, James Phillip

Mallowan, Agatha Christie
See Christie, Agatha (Mary Clarissa)

Maloff, Saul 1922-................. **CLC 5**
See also CA 33-36R

Malone, Louis
See MacNeice, (Frederick) Louis

Malone, Michael (Christopher)
1942- .... **CLC 43**
See also CA 77-80; CANR 14, 32

Malory, (Sir) Thomas
1410(?)-1471(?) ...... **LC 11; DA; DAB;
DAC**
See also CDBLB Before 1660; DAM MST;
DLB 146; SATA 59; SATA-Brief 33

Malouf, (George Joseph) David
1934- .... **CLC 28, 86**
See also CA 124; CANR 50

Malraux, (Georges-)Andre
1901-1976 ...... **CLC 1, 4, 9, 13, 15, 57**
See also CA 21-22; 69-72; CANR 34;
CAP 2; DAM NOV; DLB 72; MTCW

Malzberg, Barry N(athaniel) 1939-... **CLC 7**
See also CA 61-64; CAAS 4; CANR 16;
DLB 8

Mamet, David (Alan)
1947- .... **CLC 9, 15, 34, 46; DC 4**
See also AAYA 3; CA 81-84; CABS 3;
CANR 15, 41; DAM DRAM; DLB 7;
MTCW

Mamoulian, Rouben (Zachary)
1897-1987 .... **CLC 16**
See also CA 25-28R; 124

Mandelstam, Osip (Emilievich)
1891(?)-1938(?) ...... **TCLC 2, 6; PC 14**
See also CA 104

Mander, (Mary) Jane 1877-1949... **TCLC 31**

Mandiargues, Andre Pieyre de....... CLC 41
See also Pieyre de Mandiargues, Andre
See also DLB 83

Mandrake, Ethel Belle
See Thurman, Wallace (Henry)

Mangan, James Clarence
1803-1849 .... **NCLC 27**

Maniere, J.-E.
See Giraudoux, (Hippolyte) Jean

Manley, (Mary) Delariviere
1672(?)-1724 .... **LC 1**
See also DLB 39, 80

Mann, Abel
See Creasey, John

Mann, (Luiz) Heinrich 1871-1950... TCLC 9
    See also CA 106; DLB 66

Mann, (Paul) Thomas
    1875-1955 .... TCLC 2, 8, 14, 21, 35, 44,
        60; DA; DAB; DAC; SSC 5; WLC
    See also CA 104; 128; DAM MST, NOV;
        DLB 66; MTCW

Manning, David
    See Faust, Frederick (Schiller)

Manning, Frederic 1887(?)-1935 ... TCLC 25
    See also CA 124

Manning, Olivia 1915-1980 ...... CLC 5, 19
    See also CA 5-8R; 101; CANR 29; MTCW

Mano, D. Keith 1942- .... CLC 2, 10
    See also CA 25-28R; CAAS 6; CANR 26;
        DLB 6

Mansfield, Katherine
    ..... TCLC 2, 8, 39; DAB; SSC 9; WLC
    See also Beauchamp, Kathleen Mansfield

Manso, Peter 1940- .... CLC 39
    See also CA 29-32R; CANR 44

Mantecon, Juan Jimenez
    See Jimenez (Mantecon), Juan Ramon

Manton, Peter
    See Creasey, John

Man Without a Spleen, A
    See Chekhov, Anton (Pavlovich)

Manzoni, Alessandro 1785-1873 .. NCLC 29

Mapu, Abraham (ben Jekutiel)
    1808-1867 .... NCLC 18

Mara, Sally
    See Queneau, Raymond

Marat, Jean Paul 1743-1793 .... LC 10

Marcel, Gabriel Honore
    1889-1973 .... CLC 15
    See also CA 102; 45-48; MTCW

Marchbanks, Samuel
    See Davies, (William) Robertson

Marchi, Giacomo
    See Bassani, Giorgio

Margulies, Donald................. CLC 76

Marie de France c. 12th cent. -.... CMLC 8

Marie de l'Incarnation 1599-1672.... LC 10

Mariner, Scott
    See Pohl, Frederik

Marinetti, Filippo Tommaso
    1876-1944 .... TCLC 10
    See also CA 107; DLB 114

Marivaux, Pierre Carlet de Chamblain de
    1688-1763 .... LC 4

Markandaya, Kamala .... CLC 8, 38
    See also Taylor, Kamala (Purnaiya)

Markfield, Wallace 1926- .... CLC 8
    See also CA 69-72; CAAS 3; DLB 2, 28

Markham, Edwin 1852-1940 ...... TCLC 47
    See also DLB 54

Markham, Robert
    See Amis, Kingsley (William)

Marks, J
    See Highwater, Jamake (Mamake)

Marks-Highwater, J
    See Highwater, Jamake (Mamake)

Markson, David M(errill) 1927- .... CLC 67
    See also CA 49-52; CANR 1

Marley, Bob...................... CLC 17
    See also Marley, Robert Nesta

Marley, Robert Nesta 1945-1981
    See Marley, Bob
    See also CA 107; 103

Marlowe, Christopher
    1564-1593 ..... LC 22; DA; DAB; DAC;
        DC 1; WLC
    See also CDBLB Before 1660;
        DAM DRAM, MST; DLB 62

Marmontel, Jean-Francois
    1723-1799 .... LC 2

Marquand, John P(hillips)
    1893-1960 .... CLC 2, 10
    See also CA 85-88; DLB 9, 102

Marquez, Gabriel (Jose) Garcia
    See Garcia Marquez, Gabriel (Jose)

Marquis, Don(ald Robert Perry)
    1878-1937 .... TCLC 7
    See also CA 104; DLB 11, 25

Marric, J. J.
    See Creasey, John

Marrow, Bernard
    See Moore, Brian

Marryat, Frederick 1792-1848 .... NCLC 3
    See also DLB 21

Marsden, James
    See Creasey, John

Marsh, (Edith) Ngaio
    1899-1982 .... CLC 7, 53
    See also CA 9-12R; CANR 6; DAM POP;
        DLB 77; MTCW

Marshall, Garry 1934- .... CLC 17
    See also AAYA 3; CA 111; SATA 60

Marshall, Paule
    1929- .... CLC 27, 72; BLC; SSC 3
    See also BW 2; CA 77-80; CANR 25;
        DAM MULT; DLB 157; MTCW

Marsten, Richard
    See Hunter, Evan

Martha, Henry
    See Harris, Mark

Martial c. 40-c. 104 .... PC 10

Martin, Ken
    See Hubbard, L(afayette) Ron(ald)

Martin, Richard
    See Creasey, John

Martin, Steve 1945- .... CLC 30
    See also CA 97-100; CANR 30; MTCW

Martin, Valerie 1948- .... CLC 89
    See also BEST 90:2; CA 85-88; CANR 49

Martin, Violet Florence
    1862-1915 .... TCLC 51

Martin, Webber
    See Silverberg, Robert

Martindale, Patrick Victor
    See White, Patrick (Victor Martindale)

Martin du Gard, Roger
    1881-1958 .... TCLC 24
    See also CA 118; DLB 65

Martineau, Harriet 1802-1876.... NCLC 26
    See also DLB 21, 55, 159; YABC 2

Martines, Julia
    See O'Faolain, Julia

Martinez, Jacinto Benavente y
    See Benavente (y Martinez), Jacinto

Martinez Ruiz, Jose 1873-1967
    See Azorin; Ruiz, Jose Martinez
    See also CA 93-96; HW

Martinez Sierra, Gregorio
    1881-1947 .... TCLC 6
    See also CA 115

Martinez Sierra, Maria (de la O'LeJarraga)
    1874-1974 .... TCLC 6
    See also CA 115

Martinsen, Martin
    See Follett, Ken(neth Martin)

Martinson, Harry (Edmund)
    1904-1978 .... CLC 14
    See also CA 77-80; CANR 34

Marut, Ret
    See Traven, B.

Marut, Robert
    See Traven, B.

Marvell, Andrew
    1621-1678 ...... LC 4; DA; DAB; DAC;
        PC 10; WLC
    See also CDBLB 1660-1789; DAM MST,
        POET; DLB 131

Marx, Karl (Heinrich)
    1818-1883 .... NCLC 17
    See also DLB 129

Masaoka Shiki.................... TCLC 18
    See also Masaoka Tsunenori

Masaoka Tsunenori 1867-1902
    See Masaoka Shiki
    See also CA 117

Masefield, John (Edward)
    1878-1967 .... CLC 11, 47
    See also CA 19-20; 25-28R; CANR 33;
        CAP 2; CDBLB 1890-1914; DAM POET;
        DLB 10, 19, 153, 160; MTCW; SATA 19

Maso, Carole 19(?)- .... CLC 44

Mason, Bobbie Ann
    1940- .... CLC 28, 43, 82; SSC 4
    See also AAYA 5; CA 53-56; CANR 11,
        31; DLBY 87; INT CANR-31; MTCW

Mason, Ernst
    See Pohl, Frederik

Mason, Lee W.
    See Malzberg, Barry N(athaniel)

Mason, Nick 1945- .... CLC 35

Mason, Tally
    See Derleth, August (William)

Mass, William
    See Gibson, William

Masters, Edgar Lee
    1868-1950 ...... TCLC 2, 25; DA; DAC;
        PC 1
    See also CA 104; 133; CDALB 1865-1917;
        DAM MST, POET; DLB 54; MTCW

Masters, Hilary 1928- .... CLC 48
    See also CA 25-28R; CANR 13, 47

Mastrosimone, William 19(?)- ...... CLC 36

Mathe, Albert
    See Camus, Albert

Matheson, Richard Burton 1926- ... **CLC 37**
See also CA 97-100; DLB 8, 44; INT 97-100

Mathews, Harry 1930-......... **CLC 6, 52**
See also CA 21-24R; CAAS 6; CANR 18,
40

Mathews, John Joseph 1894-1979... **CLC 84**
See also CA 19-20; 142; CANR 45; CAP 2;
DAM MULT; NNAL

Mathias, Roland (Glyn) 1915-...... **CLC 45**
See also CA 97-100; CANR 19, 41; DLB 27

Matsuo Basho 1644-1694........... **PC 3**
See also DAM POET

Mattheson, Rodney
See Creasey, John

Matthews, Greg 1949-............ **CLC 45**
See also CA 135

Matthews, William 1942-......... **CLC 40**
See also CA 29-32R; CAAS 18; CANR 12;
DLB 5

Matthias, John (Edward) 1941-...... **CLC 9**
See also CA 33-36R

Matthiessen, Peter
1927-........... **CLC 5, 7, 11, 32, 64**
See also AAYA 6; BEST 90:4; CA 9-12R;
CANR 21, 50; DAM NOV; DLB 6;
MTCW; SATA 27

Maturin, Charles Robert
1780(?)-1824 .... **NCLC 6**

Matute (Ausejo), Ana Maria
1925-............... **CLC 11**
See also CA 89-92; MTCW

Maugham, W. S.
See Maugham, W(illiam) Somerset

Maugham, W(illiam) Somerset
1874-1965 ...... **CLC 1, 11, 15, 67; DA;
DAB; DAC; SSC 8; WLC**
See also CA 5-8R; 25-28R; CANR 40;
CDBLB 1914-1945; DAM DRAM, MST,
NOV; DLB 10, 36, 77, 100; MTCW;
SATA 54

Maugham, William Somerset
See Maugham, W(illiam) Somerset

Maupassant, (Henri Rene Albert) Guy de
1850-1893 ..... **NCLC 1, 42; DA; DAB;
DAC; SSC 1; WLC**
See also DAM MST; DLB 123

Maurhut, Richard
See Traven, B.

Mauriac, Claude 1914-............. **CLC 9**
See also CA 89-92; DLB 83

Mauriac, Francois (Charles)
1885-1970.............. **CLC 4, 9, 56**
See also CA 25-28; CAP 2; DLB 65;
MTCW

Mavor, Osborne Henry 1888-1951
See Bridie, James
See also CA 104

Maxwell, William (Keepers, Jr.)
1908-................... **CLC 19**
See also CA 93-96; DLBY 80; INT 93-96

May, Elaine 1932-............... **CLC 16**
See also CA 124; 142; DLB 44

Mayakovski, Vladimir (Vladimirovich)
1893-1930 .... **TCLC 4, 18**
See also CA 104

Mayhew, Henry 1812-1887 ...... **NCLC 31**
See also DLB 18, 55

Mayle, Peter 1939(?)-............. **CLC 89**
See also CA 139

Maynard, Joyce 1953-............ **CLC 23**
See also CA 111; 129

Mayne, William (James Carter)
1928-...................... **CLC 12**
See also CA 9-12R; CANR 37; CLR 25;
JRDA; MAICYA; SAAS 11; SATA 6, 68

Mayo, Jim
See L'Amour, Louis (Dearborn)

Maysles, Albert 1926-............ **CLC 16**
See also CA 29-32R

Maysles, David 1932-............. **CLC 16**

Mazer, Norma Fox 1931- .... **CLC 26**
See also AAYA 5; CA 69-72; CANR 12,
32; CLR 23; JRDA; MAICYA; SAAS 1;
SATA 24, 67

Mazzini, Guiseppe 1805-1872 .... **NCLC 34**

McAuley, James Phillip
1917-1976 .... **CLC 45**
See also CA 97-100

McBain, Ed
See Hunter, Evan

McBrien, William Augustine
1930-...................... **CLC 44**
See also CA 107

McCaffrey, Anne (Inez) 1926-...... **CLC 17**
See also AAYA 6; AITN 2; BEST 89:2;
CA 25-28R; CANR 15, 35; DAM NOV,
POP; DLB 8; JRDA; MAICYA; MTCW;
SAAS 11; SATA 8, 70

McCall, Nathan 1955(?)-.......... **CLC 86**
See also CA 146

McCann, Arthur
See Campbell, John W(ood, Jr.)

McCann, Edson
See Pohl, Frederik

McCarthy, Charles, Jr. 1933-
See McCarthy, Cormac
See also CANR 42; DAM POP

McCarthy, Cormac 1933-..... **CLC 4, 57, 59**
See also McCarthy, Charles, Jr.
See also DLB 6, 143

McCarthy, Mary (Therese)
1912-1989 ... **CLC 1, 3, 5, 14, 24, 39, 59**
See also CA 5-8R; 129; CANR 16, 50;
DLB 2; DLBY 81; INT CANR-16;
MTCW

McCartney, (James) Paul
1942-................... **CLC 12, 35**
See also CA 146

McCauley, Stephen (D.) 1955- ..... **CLC 50**
See also CA 141

McClure, Michael (Thomas)
1932-................... **CLC 6, 10**
See also CA 21-24R; CANR 17, 46;
DLB 16

McCorkle, Jill (Collins) 1958-...... **CLC 51**
See also CA 121; DLBY 87

McCourt, James 1941-............ **CLC 5**
See also CA 57-60

McCoy, Horace (Stanley)
1897-1955 .... **TCLC 28**
See also CA 108; DLB 9

McCrae, John 1872-1918........ **TCLC 12**
See also CA 109; DLB 92

McCreigh, James
See Pohl, Frederik

McCullers, (Lula) Carson (Smith)
1917-1967 .... **CLC 1, 4, 10, 12, 48; DA;
DAB; DAC; SSC 9; WLC**
See also CA 5-8R; 25-28R; CABS 1, 3;
CANR 18; CDALB 1941-1968;
DAM MST, NOV; DLB 2, 7; MTCW;
SATA 27

McCulloch, John Tyler
See Burroughs, Edgar Rice

McCullough, Colleen 1938(?)-...... **CLC 27**
See also CA 81-84; CANR 17, 46;
DAM NOV, POP; MTCW

McDermott, Alice 1953- .... **CLC 90**
See also CA 109; CANR 40

McElroy, Joseph 1930- .... **CLC 5, 47**
See also CA 17-20R

McEwan, Ian (Russell) 1948- ... **CLC 13, 66**
See also BEST 90:4; CA 61-64; CANR 14,
41; DAM NOV; DLB 14; MTCW

McFadden, David 1940-.......... **CLC 48**
See also CA 104; DLB 60; INT 104

McFarland, Dennis 1950- .... **CLC 65**

McGahern, John
1934-.......... **CLC 5, 9, 48; SSC 17**
See also CA 17-20R; CANR 29; DLB 14;
MTCW

McGinley, Patrick (Anthony)
1937-...................... **CLC 41**
See also CA 120; 127; INT 127

McGinley, Phyllis 1905-1978 ...... **CLC 14**
See also CA 9-12R; 77-80; CANR 19;
DLB 11, 48; SATA 2, 44; SATA-Obit 24

McGinniss, Joe 1942-............. **CLC 32**
See also AITN 2; BEST 89:2; CA 25-28R;
CANR 26; INT CANR-26

McGivern, Maureen Daly
See Daly, Maureen

McGrath, Patrick 1950-........... **CLC 55**
See also CA 136

McGrath, Thomas (Matthew)
1916-1990 .... **CLC 28, 59**
See also CA 9-12R; 132; CANR 6, 33;
DAM POET; MTCW; SATA 41;
SATA-Obit 66

McGuane, Thomas (Francis III)
1939- ....CLC 3, 7, 18, 45
See also AITN 2; CA 49-52; CANR 5, 24,
49; DLB 2; DLBY 80; INT CANR-24;
MTCW

McGuckian, Medbh 1950-......... **CLC 48**
See also CA 143; DAM POET; DLB 40

McHale, Tom 1942(?)-1982...... **CLC 3, 5**
See also AITN 1; CA 77-80; 106

McIlvanney, William 1936-...... **CLC 42**
See also CA 25-28R; DLB 14

McIlwraith, Maureen Mollie Hunter
See Hunter, Mollie
See also SATA 2

McInerney, Jay 1955- . . . . CLC 34
See also CA 116; 123; CANR 45;
DAM POP; INT 123

McIntyre, Vonda N(eel) 1948- . . . . . CLC 18
See also CA 81-84; CANR 17, 34; MTCW

McKay, Claude
. . . . TCLC 7, 41; BLC; DAB; PC 2
See also McKay, Festus Claudius
See also DLB 4, 45, 51, 117

McKay, Festus Claudius 1889-1948
See McKay, Claude
See also BW 1; CA 104; 124; DA; DAC;
DAM MST, MULT, NOV, POET;
MTCW; WLC

McKuen, Rod 1933- . . . . CLC 1, 3
See also AITN 1; CA 41-44R; CANR 40

McLoughlin, R. B.
See Mencken, H(enry) L(ouis)

McLuhan, (Herbert) Marshall
1911-1980 . . . . CLC 37, 83
See also CA 9-12R; 102; CANR 12, 34;
DLB 88; INT CANR-12; MTCW

McMillan, Terry (L.) 1951- . . . . . CLC 50, 61
See also BW 2; CA 140; DAM MULT,
NOV, POP

McMurtry, Larry (Jeff)
1936- . . . . CLC 2, 3, 7, 11, 27, 44
See also AAYA 15; AITN 2; BEST 89:2;
CA 5-8R; CANR 19, 43;
CDALB 1968-1988; DAM NOV, POP;
DLB 2, 143; DLBY 80, 87; MTCW

McNally, T. M. 1961- . . . . CLC 82

McNally, Terrence 1939- . . . . . . CLC 4, 7, 41
See also CA 45-48; CANR 2;
DAM DRAM; DLB 7

McNamer, Deirdre 1950- . . . . CLC 70

McNeile, Herman Cyril 1888-1937
See Sapper
See also DLB 77

McNickle, (William) D'Arcy
1904-1977 . . . . CLC 89
See also CA 9-12R; 85-88; CANR 5, 45;
DAM MULT; NNAL; SATA-Obit 22

McPhee, John (Angus) 1931- . . . . . . CLC 36
See also BEST 90:1; CA 65-68; CANR 20,
46; MTCW

McPherson, James Alan
1943- . . . . CLC 19, 77
See also BW 1; CA 25-28R; CAAS 17;
CANR 24; DLB 38; MTCW

McPherson, William (Alexander)
1933- . . . . CLC 34
See also CA 69-72; CANR 28;
INT CANR-28

Mead, Margaret 1901-1978 . . . . CLC 37
See also AITN 1; CA 1-4R; 81-84;
CANR 4; MTCW; SATA-Obit 20

Meaker, Marijane (Agnes) 1927-
See Kerr, M. E.
See also CA 107; CANR 37; INT 107;
JRDA; MAICYA; MTCW; SATA 20, 61

Medoff, Mark (Howard) 1940- . . . CLC 6, 23
See also AITN 1; CA 53-56; CANR 5;
DAM DRAM; DLB 7; INT CANR-5

Medvedev, P. N.
See Bakhtin, Mikhail Mikhailovich

Meged, Aharon
See Megged, Aharon

Meged, Aron
See Megged, Aharon

Megged, Aharon 1920- . . . . CLC 9
See also CA 49-52; CAAS 13; CANR 1

Mehta, Ved (Parkash) 1934- . . . . CLC 37
See also CA 1-4R; CANR 2, 23; MTCW

Melanter
See Blackmore, R(ichard) D(oddridge)

Melikow, Loris
See Hofmannsthal, Hugo von

Melmoth, Sebastian
See Wilde, Oscar (Fingal O'Flahertie Wills)

Meltzer, Milton 1915- . . . . CLC 26
See also AAYA 8; CA 13-16R; CANR 38;
CLR 13; DLB 61; JRDA; MAICYA;
SAAS 1; SATA 1, 50, 80

Melville, Herman
1819-1891 . . . . . NCLC 3, 12, 29, 45, 49;
DA; DAB; DAC; SSC 1, 17; WLC
See also CDALB 1640-1865; DAM MST,
NOV; DLB 3, 74; SATA 59

Menander
c. 342B.C.-c. 292B.C. . . . CMLC 9; DC 3
See also DAM DRAM

Mencken, H(enry) L(ouis)
1880-1956 . . . . TCLC 13
See also CA 105; 125; CDALB 1917-1929;
DLB 11, 29, 63, 137; MTCW

Mercer, David 1928-1980 . . . . CLC 5
See also CA 9-12R; 102; CANR 23;
DAM DRAM; DLB 13; MTCW

Merchant, Paul
See Ellison, Harlan (Jay)

Meredith, George 1828-1909 . . . TCLC 17, 43
See also CA 117; CDBLB 1832-1890;
DAM POET; DLB 18, 35, 57, 159

Meredith, William (Morris)
1919- . . . . CLC 4, 13, 22, 55
See also CA 9-12R; CAAS 14; CANR 6, 40;
DAM POET; DLB 5

Merezhkovsky, Dmitry Sergeyevich
1865-1941 . . . . TCLC 29

Merimee, Prosper
1803-1870 . . . . NCLC 6; SSC 7
See also DLB 119

Merkin, Daphne 1954- . . . . CLC 44
See also CA 123

Merlin, Arthur
See Blish, James (Benjamin)

Merrill, James (Ingram)
1926-1995 . . . . CLC 2, 3, 6, 8, 13, 18, 34
See also CA 13-16R; 147; CANR 10, 49;
DAM POET; DLB 5; DLBY 85;
INT CANR-10; MTCW

Merriman, Alex
See Silverberg, Robert

Merritt, E. B.
See Waddington, Miriam

Merton, Thomas
1915-1968 . . CLC 1, 3, 11, 34, 83; PC 10
See also CA 5-8R; 25-28R; CANR 22;
DLB 48; DLBY 81; MTCW

Merwin, W(illiam) S(tanley)
1927- . . . CLC 1, 2, 3, 5, 8, 13, 18, 45, 88
See also CA 13-16R; CANR 15;
DAM POET; DLB 5; INT CANR-15;
MTCW

Metcalf, John 1938- . . . . CLC 37
See also CA 113; DLB 60

Metcalf, Suzanne
See Baum, L(yman) Frank

Mew, Charlotte (Mary)
1870-1928 . . . . TCLC 8
See also CA 105; DLB 19, 135

Mewshaw, Michael 1943- . . . . CLC 9
See also CA 53-56; CANR 7, 47; DLBY 80

Meyer, June
See Jordan, June

Meyer, Lynn
See Slavitt, David R(ytman)

Meyer-Meyrink, Gustav 1868-1932
See Meyrink, Gustav
See also CA 117

Meyers, Jeffrey 1939- . . . . CLC 39
See also CA 73-76; DLB 111

Meynell, Alice (Christina Gertrude Thompson)
1847-1922 . . . . TCLC 6
See also CA 104; DLB 19, 98

Meyrink, Gustav . . . . TCLC 21
See also Meyer-Meyrink, Gustav
See also DLB 81

Michaels, Leonard
1933- . . . . CLC 6, 25; SSC 16
See also CA 61-64; CANR 21; DLB 130;
MTCW

Michaux, Henri 1899-1984 . . . . . . CLC 8, 19
See also CA 85-88; 114

Michelangelo 1475-1564 . . . . LC 12

Michelet, Jules 1798-1874 . . . . NCLC 31

Michener, James A(lbert)
1907(?)- . . . . CLC 1, 5, 11, 29, 60
See also AITN 1; BEST 90:1; CA 5-8R;
CANR 21, 45; DAM NOV, POP; DLB 6;
MTCW

Mickiewicz, Adam 1798-1855 . . . . . NCLC 3

Middleton, Christopher 1926- . . . . . . CLC 13
See also CA 13-16R; CANR 29; DLB 40

Middleton, Richard (Barham)
1882-1911 . . . . TCLC 56
See also DLB 156

Middleton, Stanley 1919- . . . . CLC 7, 38
See also CA 25-28R; CANR 21, 46;
DLB 14

Middleton, Thomas 1580-1627 . . . . DC 5
See also DAM DRAM, MST; DLB 58

Migueis, Jose Rodrigues 1901- . . . . . CLC 10

Mikszath, Kalman 1847-1910 . . . . . TCLC 31

Miles, Josephine
1911-1985 . . . . CLC 1, 2, 14, 34, 39
See also CA 1-4R; 116; CANR 2;
DAM POET; DLB 48

Militant
See Sandburg, Carl (August)

Mill, John Stuart 1806-1873 . . . . . NCLC 11
See also CDBLB 1832-1890; DLB 55

Millar, Kenneth 1915-1983 .... CLC **14**
    See also Macdonald, Ross
    See also CA 9-12R; 110; CANR 16;
        DAM POP; DLB 2; DLBD 6; DLBY 83;
        MTCW

Millay, E. Vincent
    See Millay, Edna St. Vincent

Millay, Edna St. Vincent
    1892-1950 ..... TCLC **4, 49**; DA; DAB;
                                        DAC; PC **6**
    See also CA 104; 130; CDALB 1917-1929;
        DAM MST, POET; DLB 45; MTCW

Miller, Arthur
    1915- .... CLC **1, 2, 6, 10, 15, 26, 47, 78**;
                DA; DAB; DAC; DC **1**; WLC
    See also AAYA 15; AITN 1; CA 1-4R;
        CABS 3; CANR 2, 30;
        CDALB 1941-1968; DAM DRAM, MST;
        DLB 7; MTCW

Miller, Henry (Valentine)
    1891-1980 .... CLC **1, 2, 4, 9, 14, 43, 84**;
                        DA; DAB; DAC; WLC
    See also CA 9-12R; 97-100; CANR 33;
        CDALB 1929-1941; DAM MST, NOV;
        DLB 4, 9; DLBY 80; MTCW

Miller, Jason 1939(?)- .... CLC **2**
    See also AITN 1; CA 73-76; DLB 7

Miller, Sue 1943- .... CLC **44**
    See also BEST 90:3; CA 139; DAM POP;
        DLB 143

Miller, Walter M(ichael, Jr.)
    1923- .... CLC **4, 30**
    See also CA 85-88; DLB 8

Millett, Kate 1934-............... CLC **67**
    See also AITN 1; CA 73-76; CANR 32;
        MTCW

Millhauser, Steven 1943-....... CLC **21, 54**
    See also CA 110; 111; DLB 2; INT 111

Millin, Sarah Gertrude 1889-1968 .. CLC **49**
    See also CA 102; 93-96

Milne, A(lan) A(lexander)
    1882-1956 .... TCLC **6**; DAB; DAC
    See also CA 104; 133; CLR 1, 26;
        DAM MST; DLB 10, 77, 100, 160;
        MAICYA; MTCW; YABC 1

Milner, Ron(ald) 1938-....... CLC **56**; BLC
    See also AITN 1; BW 1; CA 73-76;
        CANR 24; DAM MULT; DLB 38;
        MTCW

Milosz, Czeslaw
    1911- ... CLC **5, 11, 22, 31, 56, 82**; PC **8**
    See also CA 81-84; CANR 23; DAM MST,
        POET; MTCW

Milton, John
    1608-1674 ...... LC **9**; DA; DAB; DAC;
                                        WLC
    See also CDBLB 1660-1789; DAM MST,
        POET; DLB 131, 151

Min, Anchee 1957-............... CLC **86**
    See also CA 146

Minehaha, Cornelius
    See Wedekind, (Benjamin) Frank(lin)

Miner, Valerie 1947- .... CLC **40**
    See also CA 97-100

Minimo, Duca
    See D'Annunzio, Gabriele

Minot, Susan 1956- .... CLC **44**
    See also CA 134

Minus, Ed 1938-................. CLC **39**

Miranda, Javier
    See Bioy Casares, Adolfo

Mirbeau, Octave 1848-1917....... TCLC **55**
    See also DLB 123

Miro (Ferrer), Gabriel (Francisco Victor)
    1879-1930 ....TCLC **5**
    See also CA 104

Mishima, Yukio
    .... CLC **2, 4, 6, 9, 27**; DC **1**; SSC **4**
    See also Hiraoka, Kimitake

Mistral, Frederic 1830-1914 ...... TCLC **51**
    See also CA 122

Mistral, Gabriela........... TCLC **2**; HLC
    See also Godoy Alcayaga, Lucila

Mistry, Rohinton 1952-...... CLC **71**; DAC
    See also CA 141

Mitchell, Clyde
    See Ellison, Harlan (Jay); Silverberg, Robert

Mitchell, James Leslie 1901-1935
    See Gibbon, Lewis Grassic
    See also CA 104; DLB 15

Mitchell, Joni 1943-............. CLC **12**
    See also CA 112

Mitchell, Margaret (Munnerlyn)
    1900-1949 .... TCLC **11**
    See also CA 109; 125; DAM NOV, POP;
        DLB 9; MTCW

Mitchell, Peggy
    See Mitchell, Margaret (Munnerlyn)

Mitchell, S(ilas) Weir 1829-1914 .. TCLC **36**

Mitchell, W(illiam) O(rmond)
    1914- .... CLC **25**; DAC
    See also CA 77-80; CANR 15, 43;
        DAM MST; DLB 88

Mitford, Mary Russell 1787-1855.. NCLC **4**
    See also DLB 110, 116

Mitford, Nancy 1904-1973......... CLC **44**
    See also CA 9-12R

Miyamoto, Yuriko 1899-1951 ..... TCLC **37**

Mo, Timothy (Peter) 1950(?)-...... CLC **46**
    See also CA 117; MTCW

Modarressi, Taghi (M.) 1931-...... CLC **44**
    See also CA 121; 134; INT 134

Modiano, Patrick (Jean) 1945-..... CLC **18**
    See also CA 85-88; CANR 17, 40; DLB 83

Moerck, Paal
    See Roelvaag, O(le) E(dvart)

Mofolo, Thomas (Mokopu)
    1875(?)-1948 .... TCLC **22**; BLC
    See also CA 121; DAM MULT

Mohr, Nicholasa 1935-...... CLC **12**; HLC
    See also AAYA 8; CA 49-52; CANR 1, 32;
        CLR 22; DAM MULT; DLB 145; HW;
        JRDA; SAAS 8; SATA 8

Mojtabai, A(nn) G(race)
    1938- .... CLC **5, 9, 15, 29**
    See also CA 85-88

Moliere
    1622-1673 ..... LC **28**; DA; DAB; DAC;
                                        WLC
    See also DAM DRAM, MST

Molin, Charles
    See Mayne, William (James Carter)

Molnar, Ferenc 1878-1952........ TCLC **20**
    See also CA 109; DAM DRAM

Momaday, N(avarre) Scott
    1934- ... CLC **2, 19, 85**; DA; DAB; DAC
    See also AAYA 11; CA 25-28R; CANR 14,
        34; DAM MST, MULT, NOV, POP;
        DLB 143; INT CANR-14; MTCW;
        NNAL; SATA 48; SATA-Brief 30

Monette, Paul 1945-1995.......... CLC **82**
    See also CA 139; 147

Monroe, Harriet 1860-1936....... TCLC **12**
    See also CA 109; DLB 54, 91

Monroe, Lyle
    See Heinlein, Robert A(nson)

Montagu, Elizabeth 1917-........ NCLC **7**
    See also CA 9-12R

Montagu, Mary (Pierrepont) Wortley
    1689-1762 .... LC **9**
    See also DLB 95, 101

Montagu, W. H.
    See Coleridge, Samuel Taylor

Montague, John (Patrick)
    1929- .... CLC **13, 46**
    See also CA 9-12R; CANR 9; DLB 40;
        MTCW

Montaigne, Michel (Eyquem) de
    1533-1592 ...... LC **8**; DA; DAB; DAC;
                                        WLC
    See also DAM MST

Montale, Eugenio
    1896-1981 .... CLC **7, 9, 18**; PC **13**
    See also CA 17-20R; 104; CANR 30;
        DLB 114; MTCW

Montesquieu, Charles-Louis de Secondat
    1689-1755 .... LC **7**

Montgomery, (Robert) Bruce 1921-1978
    See Crispin, Edmund
    See also CA 104

Montgomery, L(ucy) M(aud)
    1874-1942 .... TCLC **51**; DAC
    See also AAYA 12; CA 108; 137; CLR 8;
        DAM MST; DLB 92; JRDA; MAICYA;
        YABC 1

Montgomery, Marion H., Jr. 1925- .. CLC **7**
    See also AITN 1; CA 1-4R; CANR 3, 48;
        DLB 6

Montgomery, Max
    See Davenport, Guy (Mattison, Jr.)

Montherlant, Henry (Milon) de
    1896-1972 .... CLC **8, 19**
    See also CA 85-88; 37-40R; DAM DRAM;
        DLB 72; MTCW

Monty Python
    See Chapman, Graham; Cleese, John
        (Marwood); Gilliam, Terry (Vance); Idle,
        Eric; Jones, Terence Graham Parry; Palin,
        Michael (Edward)
    See also AAYA 7

Moodie, Susanna (Strickland)
    1803-1885 .... NCLC **14**
    See also DLB 99

Mooney, Edward 1951-
    See Mooney, Ted
    See also CA 130

O'Donovan, Michael John
1903-1966 . . . . CLC 14
See also O'Connor, Frank
See also CA 93-96

Oe, Kenzaburo
1935- . . . . CLC 10, 36, 86; SSC 20
See also CA 97-100; CANR 36, 50;
DAM NOV; DLBY 94; MTCW

O'Faolain, Julia   1932- . . . . CLC 6, 19, 47
See also CA 81-84; CAAS 2; CANR 12;
DLB 14; MTCW

O'Faolain, Sean
1900-1991 . . . . . . CLC 1, 7, 14, 32, 70;
SSC 13
See also CA 61-64; 134; CANR 12;
DLB 15; MTCW

O'Flaherty, Liam
1896-1984 . . . . CLC 5, 34; SSC 6
See also CA 101; 113; CANR 35; DLB 36;
DLBY 84; MTCW

Ogilvy, Gavin
See Barrie, J(ames) M(atthew)

O'Grady, Standish James
1846-1928 . . . . TCLC 5
See also CA 104

O'Grady, Timothy   1951- . . . . CLC 59
See also CA 138

O'Hara, Frank
1926-1966 . . . . CLC 2, 5, 13, 78
See also CA 9-12R; 25-28R; CANR 33;
DAM POET; DLB 5, 16; MTCW

O'Hara, John (Henry)
1905-1970 . . . . . . CLC 1, 2, 3, 6, 11, 42;
SSC 15
See also CA 5-8R; 25-28R; CANR 31;
CDALB 1929-1941; DAM NOV; DLB 9,
86; DLBD 2; MTCW

O Hehir, Diana   1922- . . . . CLC 41
See also CA 93-96

Okigbo, Christopher (Ifenayichukwu)
1932-1967 . . . . . . CLC 25, 84; BLC; PC 7
See also BW 1; CA 77-80; DAM MULT,
POET; DLB 125; MTCW

Okri, Ben   1959- . . . . CLC 87
See also BW 2; CA 130; 138; DLB 157;
INT 138

Olds, Sharon   1942- . . . . CLC 32, 39, 85
See also CA 101; CANR 18, 41;
DAM POET; DLB 120

Oldstyle, Jonathan
See Irving, Washington

Olesha, Yuri (Karlovich)
1899-1960 . . . . CLC 8
See also CA 85-88

Oliphant, Laurence
1829(?)-1888 . . . . NCLC 47
See also DLB 18

Oliphant, Margaret (Oliphant Wilson)
1828-1897 . . . . NCLC 11
See also DLB 18, 159

Oliver, Mary   1935- . . . . CLC 19, 34
See also CA 21-24R; CANR 9, 43; DLB 5

Olivier, Laurence (Kerr)
1907-1989 . . . . CLC 20
See also CA 111; 129

Olsen, Tillie
1913- . . . . . CLC 4, 13; DA; DAB; DAC;
SSC 11
See also CA 1-4R; CANR 1, 43;
DAM MST; DLB 28; DLBY 80; MTCW

Olson, Charles (John)
1910-1970 . . . . . CLC 1, 2, 5, 6, 9, 11, 29
See also CA 13-16; 25-28R; CABS 2;
CANR 35; CAP 1; DAM POET; DLB 5,
16; MTCW

Olson, Toby   1937- . . . . CLC 28
See also CA 65-68; CANR 9, 31

Olyesha, Yuri
See Olesha, Yuri (Karlovich)

Ondaatje, (Philip) Michael
1943- . . . CLC 14, 29, 51, 76; DAB; DAC
See also CA 77-80; CANR 42; DAM MST;
DLB 60

Oneal, Elizabeth   1934-
See Oneal, Zibby
See also CA 106; CANR 28; MAICYA;
SATA 30, 82

Oneal, Zibby . . . . CLC 30
See also Oneal, Elizabeth
See also AAYA 5; CLR 13; JRDA

O'Neill, Eugene (Gladstone)
1888-1953 . . . . . . TCLC 1, 6, 27, 49; DA;
DAB; DAC; WLC
See also AITN 1; CA 110; 132;
CDALB 1929-1941; DAM DRAM, MST;
DLB 7; MTCW

Onetti, Juan Carlos   1909-1994 . . . CLC 7, 10
See also CA 85-88; 145; CANR 32;
DAM MULT, NOV; DLB 113; HW;
MTCW

O Nuallain, Brian   1911-1966
See O'Brien, Flann
See also CA 21-22; 25-28R; CAP 2

Oppen, George   1908-1984 . . . . CLC 7, 13, 34
See also CA 13-16R; 113; CANR 8; DLB 5

Oppenheim, E(dward) Phillips
1866-1946 . . . . TCLC 45
See also CA 111; DLB 70

Orlovitz, Gil   1918-1973 . . . . CLC 22
See also CA 77-80; 45-48; DLB 2, 5

Orris
See Ingelow, Jean

Ortega y Gasset, Jose
1883-1955 . . . . TCLC 9; HLC
See also CA 106; 130; DAM MULT; HW;
MTCW

Ortese, Anna Maria   1914- . . . . . . CLC 89

Ortiz, Simon J(oseph)   1941- . . . . CLC 45
See also CA 134; DAM MULT, POET;
DLB 120; NNAL

Orton, Joe . . . . CLC 4, 13, 43; DC 3
See also Orton, John Kingsley
See also CDBLB 1960 to Present; DLB 13

Orton, John Kingsley   1933-1967
See Orton, Joe
See also CA 85-88; CANR 35;
DAM DRAM; MTCW

Orwell, George
. . . . . TCLC 2, 6, 15, 31, 51; DAB; WLC
See also Blair, Eric (Arthur)
See also CDBLB 1945-1960; DLB 15, 98

Osborne, David
See Silverberg, Robert

Osborne, George
See Silverberg, Robert

Osborne, John (James)
1929-1994 . . . . . CLC 1, 2, 5, 11, 45; DA;
DAB; DAC; WLC
See also CA 13-16R; 147; CANR 21;
CDBLB 1945-1960; DAM DRAM, MST;
DLB 13; MTCW

Osborne, Lawrence   1958- . . . . CLC 50

Oshima, Nagisa   1932- . . . . CLC 20
See also CA 116; 121

Oskison, John Milton
1874-1947 . . . . TCLC 35
See also CA 144; DAM MULT; NNAL

Ossoli, Sarah Margaret (Fuller marchesa d')
1810-1850
See Fuller, Margaret
See also SATA 25

Ostrovsky, Alexander
1823-1886 . . . . NCLC 30

Otero, Blas de   1916-1979 . . . . CLC 11
See also CA 89-92; DLB 134

Otto, Whitney   1955- . . . . CLC 70
See also CA 140

Ouida . . . . TCLC 43
See also De La Ramee, (Marie) Louise
See also DLB 18, 156

Ousmane, Sembene   1923- . . . . CLC 66; BLC
See also BW 1; CA 117; 125; MTCW

Ovid   43B.C.-18(?) . . . . CMLC 7; PC 2
See also DAM POET

Owen, Hugh
See Faust, Frederick (Schiller)

Owen, Wilfred (Edward Salter)
1893-1918 . . . . . . TCLC 5, 27; DA; DAB;
DAC; WLC
See also CA 104; 141; CDBLB 1914-1945;
DAM MST, POET; DLB 20

Owens, Rochelle   1936- . . . . CLC 8
See also CA 17-20R; CAAS 2; CANR 39

Oz, Amos   1939- . . . CLC 5, 8, 11, 27, 33, 54
See also CA 53-56; CANR 27, 47;
DAM NOV; MTCW

Ozick, Cynthia
1928- . . . . CLC 3, 7, 28, 62; SSC 15
See also BEST 90:1; CA 17-20R; CANR 23;
DAM NOV, POP; DLB 28, 152;
DLBY 82; INT CANR-23; MTCW

Ozu, Yasujiro   1903-1963 . . . . CLC 16
See also CA 112

Pacheco, C.
See Pessoa, Fernando (Antonio Nogueira)

Pa Chin . . . . CLC 18
See also Li Fei-kan

Pack, Robert   1929- . . . . CLC 13
See also CA 1-4R; CANR 3, 44; DLB 5

Padgett, Lewis
See Kuttner, Henry

Padilla (Lorenzo), Heberto   1932- . . . CLC 38
See also AITN 1; CA 123; 131; HW

Page, Jimmy   1944- . . . . CLC 12

Page, Louise 1955-............... CLC 40
See also CA 140

Page, P(atricia) K(athleen)
1916-......... **CLC 7, 18; DAC; PC 12**
See also CA 53-56; CANR 4, 22;
DAM MST; DLB 68; MTCW

Paget, Violet 1856-1935
See Lee, Vernon
See also CA 104

Paget-Lowe, Henry
See Lovecraft, H(oward) P(hillips)

Paglia, Camille (Anna) 1947-....... CLC 68
See also CA 140

Paige, Richard
See Koontz, Dean R(ay)

Pakenham, Antonia
See Fraser, (Lady) Antonia (Pakenham)

Palamas, Kostes 1859-1943 .... TCLC 5
See also CA 105

Palazzeschi, Aldo 1885-1974....... CLC 11
See also CA 89-92; 53-56; DLB 114

Paley, Grace 1922-.... **CLC 4, 6, 37; SSC 8**
See also CA 25-28R; CANR 13, 46;
DAM POP; DLB 28; INT CANR-13;
MTCW

Palin, Michael (Edward) 1943-..... CLC 21
See also Monty Python
See also CA 107; CANR 35; SATA 67

Palliser, Charles 1947-............ CLC 65
See also CA 136

Palma, Ricardo 1833-1919........ TCLC 29

Pancake, Breece Dexter 1952-1979
See Pancake, Breece D'J
See also CA 123; 109

Pancake, Breece D'J............... CLC 29
See also Pancake, Breece Dexter
See also DLB 130

Panko, Rudy
See Gogol, Nikolai (Vasilyevich)

Papadiamantis, Alexandros
1851-1911 .... TCLC 29

Papadiamantopoulos, Johannes 1856-1910
See Moreas, Jean
See also CA 117

Papini, Giovanni 1881-1956....... TCLC 22
See also CA 121

Paracelsus 1493-1541.............. LC 14

Parasol, Peter
See Stevens, Wallace

Parfenie, Maria
See Codrescu, Andrei

Parini, Jay (Lee) 1948- .... CLC 54
See also CA 97-100; CAAS 16; CANR 32

Park, Jordan
See Kornbluth, C(yril) M.; Pohl, Frederik

Parker, Bert
See Ellison, Harlan (Jay)

Parker, Dorothy (Rothschild)
1893-1967 .... **CLC 15, 68; SSC 2**
See also CA 19-20; 25-28R; CAP 2;
DAM POET; DLB 11, 45, 86; MTCW

Parker, Robert B(rown) 1932-...... CLC 27
See also BEST 89:4; CA 49-52; CANR 1,
26; DAM NOV, POP; INT CANR-26;
MTCW

Parkin, Frank 1940-.............. CLC 43
See also CA 147

Parkman, Francis, Jr.
1823-1893 .... NCLC 12
See also DLB 1, 30

Parks, Gordon (Alexander Buchanan)
1912-................ **CLC 1, 16; BLC**
See also AITN 2; BW 2; CA 41-44R;
CANR 26; DAM MULT; DLB 33;
SATA 8

Parnell, Thomas 1679-1718.......... LC 3
See also DLB 94

Parra, Nicanor 1914-........ **CLC 2; HLC**
See also CA 85-88; CANR 32;
DAM MULT; HW; MTCW

Parrish, Mary Frances
See Fisher, M(ary) F(rances) K(ennedy)

Parson
See Coleridge, Samuel Taylor

Parson Lot
See Kingsley, Charles

Partridge, Anthony
See Oppenheim, E(dward) Phillips

Pascoli, Giovanni 1855-1912...... TCLC 45

Pasolini, Pier Paolo
1922-1975 .... CLC 20, 37
See also CA 93-96; 61-64; DLB 128;
MTCW

Pasquini
See Silone, Ignazio

Pastan, Linda (Olenik) 1932- ...... CLC 27
See also CA 61-64; CANR 18, 40;
DAM POET; DLB 5

Pasternak, Boris (Leonidovich)
1890-1960 ...... **CLC 7, 10, 18, 63; DA;**
DAB; DAC; PC 6; WLC
See also CA 127; 116; DAM MST, NOV,
POET; MTCW

Patchen, Kenneth 1911-1972... **CLC 1, 2, 18**
See also CA 1-4R; 33-36R; CANR 3, 35;
DAM POET; DLB 16, 48; MTCW

Pater, Walter (Horatio)
1839-1894 .... NCLC 7
See also CDBLB 1832-1890; DLB 57, 156

Paterson, A(ndrew) B(arton)
1864-1941 .... TCLC 32

Paterson, Katherine (Womeldorf)
1932-.................... CLC 12, 30
See also AAYA 1; CA 21-24R; CANR 28;
CLR 7; DLB 52; JRDA; MAICYA;
MTCW; SATA 13, 53

Patmore, Coventry Kersey Dighton
1823-1896 .... NCLC 9
See also DLB 35, 98

Paton, Alan (Stewart)
1903-1988 ...... **CLC 4, 10, 25, 55; DA;**
DAB; DAC; WLC
See also CA 13-16; 125; CANR 22; CAP 1;
DAM MST, NOV; MTCW; SATA 11;
SATA-Obit 56

Paton Walsh, Gillian 1937-
See Walsh, Jill Paton
See also CANR 38; JRDA; MAICYA;
SAAS 3; SATA 4, 72

Paulding, James Kirke 1778-1860.. NCLC 2
See also DLB 3, 59, 74

Paulin, Thomas Neilson 1949-
See Paulin, Tom
See also CA 123; 128

Paulin, Tom...................... CLC 37
See also Paulin, Thomas Neilson
See also DLB 40

Paustovsky, Konstantin (Georgievich)
1892-1968 .... CLC 40
See also CA 93-96; 25-28R

Pavese, Cesare
1908-1950 ..... **TCLC 3; PC 13; SSC 19**
See also CA 104; DLB 128

Pavic, Milorad 1929-............. CLC 60
See also CA 136

Payne, Alan
See Jakes, John (William)

Paz, Gil
See Lugones, Leopoldo

Paz, Octavio
1914-....... **CLC 3, 4, 6, 10, 19, 51, 65;**
DA; DAB; DAC; HLC; PC 1; WLC
See also CA 73-76; CANR 32; DAM MST,
MULT, POET; DLBY 90; HW; MTCW

Peacock, Molly 1947-............. CLC 60
See also CA 103; CAAS 21; DLB 120

Peacock, Thomas Love
1785-1866 .... NCLC 22
See also DLB 96, 116

Peake, Mervyn 1911-1968....... CLC 7, 54
See also CA 5-8R; 25-28R; CANR 3;
DLB 15, 160; MTCW; SATA 23

Pearce, Philippa .... CLC 21
See also Christie, (Ann) Philippa
See also CLR 9; DLB 161; MAICYA;
SATA 1, 67

Pearl, Eric
See Elman, Richard

Pearson, T(homas) R(eid) 1956- .... CLC 39
See also CA 120; 130; INT 130

Peck, Dale 1967- .... CLC 81
See also CA 146

Peck, John 1941- .... CLC 3
See also CA 49-52; CANR 3

Peck, Richard (Wayne) 1934-...... CLC 21
See also AAYA 1; CA 85-88; CANR 19,
38; CLR 15; INT CANR-19; JRDA;
MAICYA; SAAS 2; SATA 18, 55

Peck, Robert Newton
1928-.................. **CLC 17; DA; DAC**
See also AAYA 3; CA 81-84; CANR 31;
DAM MST; JRDA; MAICYA; SAAS 1;
SATA 21, 62

Peckinpah, (David) Sam(uel)
1925-1984 .... CLC 20
See also CA 109; 114

Pedersen, Knut 1859-1952
See Hamsun, Knut
See also CA 104; 119; MTCW

Peeslake, Gaffer
See Durrell, Lawrence (George)

Peguy, Charles Pierre
1873-1914 . . . . **TCLC 10**
See also CA 107

Pena, Ramon del Valle y
See Valle-Inclan, Ramon (Maria) del

Pendennis, Arthur Esquir
See Thackeray, William Makepeace

Penn, William 1644-1718 . . . . **LC 25**
See also DLB 24

Pepys, Samuel
1633-1703 . . . . . **LC 11; DA; DAB; DAC;**
WLC
See also CDBLB 1660-1789; DAM MST;
DLB 101

Percy, Walker
1916-1990 . . . . **CLC 2, 3, 6, 8, 14, 18, 47,**
65
See also CA 1-4R; 131; CANR 1, 23;
DAM NOV, POP; DLB 2; DLBY 80, 90;
MTCW

Perec, Georges 1936-1982 . . . . **CLC 56**
See also CA 141; DLB 83

Pereda (y Sanchez de Porrua), Jose Maria de
1833-1906 . . . . **TCLC 16**
See also CA 117

Pereda y Porrua, Jose Maria de
See Pereda (y Sanchez de Porrua), Jose
Maria de

Peregoy, George Weems
See Mencken, H(enry) L(ouis)

Perelman, S(idney) J(oseph)
1904-1979 . . . **CLC 3, 5, 9, 15, 23, 44, 49**
See also AITN 1, 2; CA 73-76; 89-92;
CANR 18; DAM DRAM; DLB 11, 44;
MTCW

Peret, Benjamin 1899-1959 . . . . **TCLC 20**
See also CA 117

Peretz, Isaac Loeb 1851(?)-1915 . . . **TCLC 16**
See also CA 109

Peretz, Yitzhok Leibush
See Peretz, Isaac Loeb

Perez Galdos, Benito 1843-1920 . . . **TCLC 27**
See also CA 125; HW

Perrault, Charles 1628-1703 . . . . **LC 2**
See also MAICYA; SATA 25

Perry, Brighton
See Sherwood, Robert E(mmet)

Perse, St.-John . . . . **CLC 4, 11, 46**
See also Leger, (Marie-Rene Auguste) Alexis
Saint-Leger

Perutz, Leo 1882-1957 . . . . **TCLC 60**
See also DLB 81

Peseenz, Tulio F.
See Lopez y Fuentes, Gregorio

Pesetsky, Bette 1932- . . . . **CLC 28**
See also CA 133; DLB 130

Peshkov, Alexei Maximovich 1868-1936
See Gorky, Maxim
See also CA 105; 141; DA; DAC;
DAM DRAM, MST, NOV

Pessoa, Fernando (Antonio Nogueira)
1888-1935 . . . . **TCLC 27; HLC**
See also CA 125

Peterkin, Julia Mood 1880-1961 . . . . **CLC 31**
See also CA 102; DLB 9

Peters, Joan K. 1945- . . . . **CLC 39**

Peters, Robert L(ouis) 1924- . . . . **CLC 7**
See also CA 13-16R; CAAS 8; DLB 105

Petofi, Sandor 1823-1849 . . . . **NCLC 21**

Petrakis, Harry Mark 1923- . . . . **CLC 3**
See also CA 9-12R; CANR 4, 30

Petrarch 1304-1374 . . . . **PC 8**
See also DAM POET

Petrov, Evgeny . . . . **TCLC 21**
See also Kataev, Evgeny Petrovich

Petry, Ann (Lane) 1908- . . . . . . **CLC 1, 7, 18**
See also BW 1; CA 5-8R; CAAS 6;
CANR 4, 46; CLR 12; DLB 76; JRDA;
MAICYA; MTCW; SATA 5

Petursson, Halligrimur 1614-1674 . . . . **LC 8**

Philips, Katherine 1632-1664 . . . . **LC 30**
See also DLB 131

Philipson, Morris H. 1926- . . . . **CLC 53**
See also CA 1-4R; CANR 4

Phillips, David Graham
1867-1911 . . . . **TCLC 44**
See also CA 108; DLB 9, 12

Phillips, Jack
See Sandburg, Carl (August)

Phillips, Jayne Anne
1952- . . . . **CLC 15, 33; SSC 16**
See also CA 101; CANR 24, 50; DLBY 80;
INT CANR-24; MTCW

Phillips, Richard
See Dick, Philip K(indred)

Phillips, Robert (Schaeffer) 1938- . . . **CLC 28**
See also CA 17-20R; CAAS 13; CANR 8;
DLB 105

Phillips, Ward
See Lovecraft, H(oward) P(hillips)

Piccolo, Lucio 1901-1969 . . . . **CLC 13**
See also CA 97-100; DLB 114

Pickthall, Marjorie L(owry) C(hristie)
1883-1922 . . . . **TCLC 21**
See also CA 107; DLB 92

Pico della Mirandola, Giovanni
1463-1494 . . . . **LC 15**

Piercy, Marge
1936- . . . . **CLC 3, 6, 14, 18, 27, 62**
See also CA 21-24R; CAAS 1; CANR 13,
43; DLB 120; MTCW

Piers, Robert
See Anthony, Piers

Pleyre de Mandiargues, Andre 1909-1991
See Mandiargues, Andre Pieyre de
See also CA 103; 136; CANR 22

Pilnyak, Boris . . . . **TCLC 23**
See also Vogau, Boris Andreyevich

Pincherle, Alberto 1907-1990 . . . **CLC 11, 18**
See also Moravia, Alberto
See also CA 25-28R; 132; CANR 33;
DAM NOV; MTCW

Pinckney, Darryl 1953- . . . . **CLC 76**
See also BW 2; CA 143

Pindar 518B.C.-446B.C. . . . . **CMLC 12**

Pineda, Cecile 1942- . . . . **CLC 39**
See also CA 118

Pinero, Arthur Wing 1855-1934 . . . **TCLC 32**
See also CA 110; DAM DRAM; DLB 10

Pinero, Miguel (Antonio Gomez)
1946-1988 . . . . **CLC 4, 55**
See also CA 61-64; 125; CANR 29; HW

Pinget, Robert 1919- . . . . **CLC 7, 13, 37**
See also CA 85-88; DLB 83

Pink Floyd
See Barrett, (Roger) Syd; Gilmour, David;
Mason, Nick; Waters, Roger; Wright,
Rick

Pinkney, Edward 1802-1828 . . . . . **NCLC 31**

Pinkwater, Daniel Manus 1941- . . . . **CLC 35**
See also Pinkwater, Manus
See also AAYA 1; CA 29-32R; CANR 12,
38; CLR 4; JRDA; MAICYA; SAAS 3;
SATA 46, 76

Pinkwater, Manus
See Pinkwater, Daniel Manus
See also SATA 8

Pinsky, Robert 1940- . . . . **CLC 9, 19, 38**
See also CA 29-32R; CAAS 4;
DAM POET; DLBY 82

Pinta, Harold
See Pinter, Harold

Pinter, Harold
1930- . . . . . **CLC 1, 3, 6, 9, 11, 15, 27, 58,**
73; DA; DAB; DAC; WLC
See also CA 5-8R; CANR 33; CDBLB 1960
to Present; DAM DRAM, MST; DLB 13;
MTCW

Pirandello, Luigi
1867-1936 . . . . . . **TCLC 4, 29; DA; DAB;**
DAC; DC 5; WLC
See also CA 104; DAM DRAM, MST

Pirsig, Robert M(aynard)
1928- . . . . **CLC 4, 6, 73**
See also CA 53-56; CANR 42; DAM POP;
MTCW; SATA 39

Pisarev, Dmitry Ivanovich
1840-1868 . . . . **NCLC 25**

Pix, Mary (Griffith) 1666-1709 . . . . **LC 8**
See also DLB 80

Pixerecourt, Guilbert de
1773-1844 . . . . **NCLC 39**

Plaidy, Jean
See Hibbert, Eleanor Alice Burford

Planche, James Robinson
1796-1880 . . . . **NCLC 42**

Plant, Robert 1948- . . . . **CLC 12**

Plante, David (Robert)
1940- . . . . **CLC 7, 23, 38**
See also CA 37-40R; CANR 12, 36;
DAM NOV; DLBY 83; INT CANR-12;
MTCW

Plath, Sylvia
1932-1963 . . . . . **CLC 1, 2, 3, 5, 9, 11, 14,**
17, 50, 51, 62; DA; DAB; DAC; PC 1;
WLC
See also AAYA 13; CA 19-20; CANR 34;
CAP 2; CDALB 1941-1968; DAM MST,
POET; DLB 5, 6, 152; MTCW

Pritchard, William H(arrison)
1932- . . . . **CLC 34**
See also CA 65-68; CANR 23; DLB 111

Pritchett, V(ictor) S(awdon)
1900- . . . . **CLC 5, 13, 15, 41; SSC 14**
See also CA 61-64; CANR 31; DAM NOV;
DLB 15, 139; MTCW

Private 19022
See Manning, Frederic

Probst, Mark 1925- . . . . **CLC 59**
See also CA 130

Prokosch, Frederic 1908-1989 . . . . **CLC 4, 48**
See also CA 73-76; 128; DLB 48

Prophet, The
See Dreiser, Theodore (Herman Albert)

Prose, Francine 1947- . . . . **CLC 45**
See also CA 109; 112; CANR 46

Proudhon
See Cunha, Euclides (Rodrigues Pimenta) da

Proulx, E. Annie 1935- . . . . **CLC 81**

Proust, (Valentin-Louis-George-Eugene-)
Marcel
1871-1922 . . . . **TCLC 7, 13, 33; DA;**
DAB; DAC; WLC
See also CA 104; 120; DAM MST, NOV;
DLB 65; MTCW

Prowler, Harley
See Masters, Edgar Lee

Prus, Boleslaw 1845-1912 . . . . **TCLC 48**

Pryor, Richard (Franklin Lenox Thomas)
1940- . . . . **CLC 26**
See also CA 122

Przybyszewski, Stanislaw
1868-1927 . . . . **TCLC 36**
See also DLB 66

Pteleon
See Grieve, C(hristopher) M(urray)
See also DAM POET

Puckett, Lute
See Masters, Edgar Lee

Puig, Manuel
1932-1990 . . . **CLC 3, 5, 10, 28, 65; HLC**
See also CA 45-48; CANR 2, 32;
DAM MULT; DLB 113; HW; MTCW

Purdy, Al(fred Wellington)
1918- . . . . **CLC 3, 6, 14, 50; DAC**
See also CA 81-84; CAAS 17; CANR 42;
DAM MST, POET; DLB 88

Purdy, James (Amos)
1923- . . . . **CLC 2, 4, 10, 28, 52**
See also CA 33-36R; CAAS 1; CANR 19;
DLB 2; INT CANR-19; MTCW

Pure, Simon
See Swinnerton, Frank Arthur

Pushkin, Alexander (Sergeyevich)
1799-1837 . . . . . **NCLC 3, 27; DA; DAB;**
DAC; PC 10; WLC
See also DAM DRAM, MST, POET;
SATA 61

P'u Sung-ling 1640-1715 . . . . **LC 3**

Putnam, Arthur Lee
See Alger, Horatio, Jr.

Puzo, Mario 1920- . . . . **CLC 1, 2, 6, 36**
See also CA 65-68; CANR 4, 42;
DAM NOV, POP; DLB 6; MTCW

Pym, Barbara (Mary Crampton)
1913-1980 . . . . **CLC 13, 19, 37**
See also CA 13-14; 97-100; CANR 13, 34;
CAP 1; DLB 14; DLBY 87; MTCW

Pynchon, Thomas (Ruggles, Jr.)
1937- . . . . . **CLC 2, 3, 6, 9, 11, 18, 33, 62,**
72; DA; DAB; DAC; SSC 14; WLC
See also BEST 90:2; CA 17-20R; CANR 22,
46; DAM MST, NOV, POP; DLB 2;
MTCW

Qian Zhongshu
See Ch'ien Chung-shu

Qroll
See Dagerman, Stig (Halvard)

Quarrington, Paul (Lewis) 1953- . . . . **CLC 65**
See also CA 129

Quasimodo, Salvatore 1901-1968 . . . **CLC 10**
See also CA 13-16; 25-28R; CAP 1;
DLB 114; MTCW

Queen, Ellery . . . . **CLC 3, 11**
See also Dannay, Frederic; Davidson,
Avram; Lee, Manfred B(ennington);
Sturgeon, Theodore (Hamilton); Vance,
John Holbrook

Queen, Ellery, Jr.
See Dannay, Frederic; Lee, Manfred
B(ennington)

Queneau, Raymond
1903-1976 . . . . **CLC 2, 5, 10, 42**
See also CA 77-80; 69-72; CANR 32;
DLB 72; MTCW

Quevedo, Francisco de 1580-1645 . . . . **LC 23**

Quiller-Couch, Arthur Thomas
1863-1944 . . . . **TCLC 53**
See also CA 118; DLB 135, 153

Quin, Ann (Marie) 1936-1973 . . . . **CLC 6**
See also CA 9-12R; 45-48; DLB 14

Quinn, Martin
See Smith, Martin Cruz

Quinn, Simon
See Smith, Martin Cruz

Quiroga, Horacio (Sylvestre)
1878-1937 . . . . **TCLC 20; HLC**
See also CA 117; 131; DAM MULT; HW;
MTCW

Quoirez, Francoise 1935- . . . . **CLC 9**
See also Sagan, Francoise
See also CA 49-52; CANR 6, 39; MTCW

Raabe, Wilhelm 1831-1910 . . . . **TCLC 45**
See also DLB 129

Rabe, David (William) 1940- . . . **CLC 4, 8, 33**
See also CA 85-88; CABS 3; DAM DRAM;
DLB 7

Rabelais, Francois
1483-1553 . . . . . . **LC 5; DA; DAB; DAC;**
WLC
See also DAM MST

Rabinovitch, Sholem 1859-1916
See Aleichem, Sholom
See also CA 104

Racine, Jean 1639-1699 . . . . . . **LC 28; DAB**
See also DAM MST

Radcliffe, Ann (Ward) 1764-1823 . . **NCLC 6**
See also DLB 39

Radiguet, Raymond 1903-1923 . . . . **TCLC 29**
See also DLB 65

Radnoti, Miklos 1909-1944 . . . . **TCLC 16**
See also CA 118

Rado, James 1939- . . . . **CLC 17**
See also CA 105

Radvanyi, Netty 1900-1983
See Seghers, Anna
See also CA 85-88; 110

Rae, Ben
See Griffiths, Trevor

Raeburn, John (Hay) 1941- . . . . **CLC 34**
See also CA 57-60

Ragni, Gerome 1942-1991 . . . . **CLC 17**
See also CA 105; 134

Rahv, Philip 1908-1973 . . . . **CLC 24**
See also Greenberg, Ivan
See also DLB 137

Raine, Craig 1944- . . . . **CLC 32**
See also CA 108; CANR 29; DLB 40

Raine, Kathleen (Jessie) 1908- . . . **CLC 7, 45**
See also CA 85-88; CANR 46; DLB 20;
MTCW

Rainis, Janis 1865-1929 . . . . **TCLC 29**

Rakosi, Carl . . . . **CLC 47**
See also Rawley, Callman
See also CAAS 5

Raleigh, Richard
See Lovecraft, H(oward) P(hillips)

Raleigh, Sir Walter 1554(?)-1618 . . . . **LC 31**
See also CDBLB Before 1660

Rallentando, H. P.
See Sayers, Dorothy L(eigh)

Ramal, Walter
See de la Mare, Walter (John)

Ramon, Juan
See Jimenez (Mantecon), Juan Ramon

Ramos, Graciliano 1892-1953 . . . . . **TCLC 32**

Rampersad, Arnold 1941- . . . . **CLC 44**
See also BW 2; CA 127; 133; DLB 111;
INT 133

Rampling, Anne
See Rice, Anne

Ramsay, Allan 1684(?)-1758 . . . . **LC 29**
See also DLB 95

Ramuz, Charles-Ferdinand
1878-1947 . . . . **TCLC 33**

Rand, Ayn
1905-1982 . . . . . . **CLC 3, 30, 44, 79; DA;**
DAC; WLC
See also AAYA 10; CA 13-16R; 105;
CANR 27; DAM MST, NOV, POP;
MTCW

Randall, Dudley (Felker)
1914- . . . . **CLC 1; BLC**
See also BW 1; CA 25-28R; CANR 23;
DAM MULT; DLB 41

Randall, Robert
See Silverberg, Robert

Ranger, Ken
See Creasey, John

Ransom, John Crowe
1888-1974 . . . . **CLC 2, 4, 5, 11, 24**
See also CA 5-8R; 49-52; CANR 6, 34;
DAM POET; DLB 45, 63; MTCW

Rao, Raja 1909- . . . . **CLC 25, 56**
See also CA 73-76; DAM NOV; MTCW

Raphael, Frederic (Michael)
1931- . . . . **CLC 2, 14**
See also CA 1-4R; CANR 1; DLB 14

Ratcliffe, James P.
See Mencken, H(enry) L(ouis)

Rathbone, Julian 1935- . . . . **CLC 41**
See also CA 101; CANR 34

Rattigan, Terence (Mervyn)
1911-1977 . . . . **CLC 7**
See also CA 85-88; 73-76;
CDBLB 1945-1960; DAM DRAM;
DLB 13; MTCW

Ratushinskaya, Irina 1954- . . . . **CLC 54**
See also CA 129

Raven, Simon (Arthur Noel)
1927- . . . . **CLC 14**
See also CA 81-84

Rawley, Callman 1903-
See Rakosi, Carl
See also CA 21-24R; CANR 12, 32

Rawlings, Marjorie Kinnan
1896-1953 . . . . **TCLC 4**
See also CA 104; 137; DLB 9, 22, 102;
JRDA; MAICYA; YABC 1

Ray, Satyajit 1921-1992 . . . . **CLC 16, 76**
See also CA 114; 137; DAM MULT

Read, Herbert Edward 1893-1968 . . . . **CLC 4**
See also CA 85-88; 25-28R; DLB 20, 149

Read, Piers Paul 1941- . . . . . . **CLC 4, 10, 25**
See also CA 21-24R; CANR 38; DLB 14;
SATA 21

Reade, Charles 1814-1884 . . . . **NCLC 2**
See also DLB 21

Reade, Hamish
See Gray, Simon (James Holliday)

Reading, Peter 1946- . . . . **CLC 47**
See also CA 103; CANR 46; DLB 40

Reaney, James 1926- . . . . **CLC 13; DAC**
See also CA 41-44R; CAAS 15; CANR 42;
DAM MST; DLB 68; SATA 43

Rebreanu, Liviu 1885-1944 . . . . **TCLC 28**

Rechy, John (Francisco)
1934- . . . . **CLC 1, 7, 14, 18; HLC**
See also CA 5-8R; CAAS 4; CANR 6, 32;
DAM MULT; DLB 122; DLBY 82; HW;
INT CANR-6

Redcam, Tom 1870-1933 . . . . **TCLC 25**

Reddin, Keith . . . . **CLC 67**

Redgrove, Peter (William)
1932- . . . . **CLC 6, 41**
See also CA 1-4R; CANR 3, 39; DLB 40

Redmon, Anne . . . . **CLC 22**
See also Nightingale, Anne Redmon
See also DLBY 86

Reed, Eliot
See Ambler, Eric

Reed, Ishmael
1938- . . . **CLC 2, 3, 5, 6, 13, 32, 60; BLC**
See also BW 2; CA 21-24R; CANR 25, 48;
DAM MULT; DLB 2, 5, 33; DLBD 8;
MTCW

Reed, John (Silas) 1887-1920 . . . . . . **TCLC 9**
See also CA 106

Reed, Lou . . . . **CLC 21**
See also Firbank, Louis

Reeve, Clara 1729-1807 . . . . **NCLC 19**
See also DLB 39

Reich, Wilhelm 1897-1957 . . . . **TCLC 57**

Reid, Christopher (John) 1949- . . . . . **CLC 33**
See also CA 140; DLB 40

Reid, Desmond
See Moorcock, Michael (John)

Reid Banks, Lynne 1929-
See Banks, Lynne Reid
See also CA 1-4R; CANR 6, 22, 38;
CLR 24; JRDA; MAICYA; SATA 22, 75

Reilly, William K.
See Creasey, John

Reiner, Max
See Caldwell, (Janet Miriam) Taylor
(Holland)

Reis, Ricardo
See Pessoa, Fernando (Antonio Nogueira)

Remarque, Erich Maria
1898-1970 . . . . **CLC 21; DA; DAB; DAC**
See also CA 77-80; 29-32R; DAM MST,
NOV; DLB 56; MTCW

Remizov, A.
See Remizov, Aleksei (Mikhailovich)

Remizov, A. M.
See Remizov, Aleksei (Mikhailovich)

Remizov, Aleksei (Mikhailovich)
1877-1957 . . . . **TCLC 27**
See also CA 125; 133

Renan, Joseph Ernest
1823-1892 . . . . **NCLC 26**

Renard, Jules 1864-1910 . . . . **TCLC 17**
See also CA 117

Renault, Mary . . . . **CLC 3, 11, 17**
See also Challans, Mary
See also DLBY 83

Rendell, Ruth (Barbara) 1930- . . **CLC 28, 48**
See also Vine, Barbara
See also CA 109; CANR 32; DAM POP;
DLB 87; INT CANR-32; MTCW

Renoir, Jean 1894-1979 . . . . **CLC 20**
See also CA 129; 85-88

Resnais, Alain 1922- . . . . **CLC 16**

Reverdy, Pierre 1889-1960 . . . . **CLC 53**
See also CA 97-100; 89-92

Rexroth, Kenneth
1905-1982 . . . . . . **CLC 1, 2, 6, 11, 22, 49**
See also CA 5-8R; 107; CANR 14, 34;
CDALB 1941-1968; DAM POET;
DLB 16, 48; DLBY 82; INT CANR-14;
MTCW

Reyes, Alfonso 1889-1959 . . . . **TCLC 33**
See also CA 131; HW

Reyes y Basoalto, Ricardo Eliecer Neftali
See Neruda, Pablo

Reymont, Wladyslaw (Stanislaw)
1868(?)-1925 . . . . **TCLC 5**
See also CA 104

Reynolds, Jonathan 1942- . . . . **CLC 6, 38**
See also CA 65-68; CANR 28

Reynolds, Joshua 1723-1792 . . . . **LC 15**
See also DLB 104

Reynolds, Michael Shane 1937- . . . . **CLC 44**
See also CA 65-68; CANR 9

Reznikoff, Charles 1894-1976 . . . . **CLC 9**
See also CA 33-36; 61-64; CAP 2; DLB 28,
45

Rezzori (d'Arezzo), Gregor von
1914- . . . . **CLC 25**
See also CA 122; 136

Rhine, Richard
See Silverstein, Alvin

Rhodes, Eugene Manlove
1869-1934 . . . . **TCLC 53**

R'hoone
See Balzac, Honore de

Rhys, Jean
1890(?)-1979 . . . . **CLC 2, 4, 6, 14, 19, 51;**
SSC 21
See also CA 25-28R; 85-88; CANR 35;
CDBLB 1945-1960; DAM NOV; DLB 36,
117; MTCW

Ribeiro, Darcy 1922- . . . . **CLC 34**
See also CA 33-36R

Ribeiro, Joao Ubaldo (Osorio Pimentel)
1941- . . . . **CLC 10, 67**
See also CA 81-84

Ribman, Ronald (Burt) 1932- . . . . **CLC 7**
See also CA 21-24R; CANR 46

Ricci, Nino 1959- . . . . **CLC 70**
See also CA 137

Rice, Anne 1941- . . . . **CLC 41**
See also AAYA 9; BEST 89:2; CA 65-68;
CANR 12, 36; DAM POP

Rice, Elmer (Leopold)
1892-1967 . . . . **CLC 7, 49**
See also CA 21-22; 25-28R; CAP 2;
DAM DRAM; DLB 4, 7; MTCW

Rice, Tim(othy Miles Bindon)
1944- . . . . **CLC 21**
See also CA 103; CANR 46

Rich, Adrienne (Cecile)
1929- . . . . **CLC 3, 6, 7, 11, 18, 36, 73, 76;**
PC 5
See also CA 9-12R; CANR 20;
DAM POET; DLB 5, 67; MTCW

Rich, Barbara
See Graves, Robert (von Ranke)

Rich, Robert
See Trumbo, Dalton

Richard, Keith . . . . **CLC 17**
See also Richards, Keith

Richards, David Adams
1950- . . . . **CLC 59; DAC**
See also CA 93-96; DLB 53

Richards, I(vor) A(rmstrong)
1893-1979 . . . . **CLC 14, 24**
See also CA 41-44R; 89-92; CANR 34;
DLB 27

Richards, Keith 1943-
See Richard, Keith
See also CA 107

Richardson, Anne
See Roiphe, Anne (Richardson)

Richardson, Dorothy Miller
1873-1957 .... TCLC 3
See also CA 104; DLB 36

Richardson, Ethel Florence (Lindesay)
1870-1946
See Richardson, Henry Handel
See also CA 105

Richardson, Henry Handel. .... TCLC 4
See also Richardson, Ethel Florence
(Lindesay)

Richardson, Samuel
1689-1761 ...... LC 1; DA; DAB; DAC;
WLC
See also CDBLB 1660-1789; DAM MST,
NOV; DLB 39

Richler, Mordecai
1931- .... CLC 3, 5, 9, 13, 18, 46, 70;
DAC
See also AITN 1; CA 65-68; CANR 31;
CLR 17; DAM MST, NOV; DLB 53;
MAICYA; MTCW; SATA 44;
SATA-Brief 27

Richter, Conrad (Michael)
1890-1968 .... CLC 30
See also CA 5-8R; 25-28R; CANR 23;
DLB 9; MTCW; SATA 3

Ricostranza, Tom
See Ellis, Trey

Riddell, J. H. 1832-1906 .... TCLC 40

Riding, Laura. .... CLC 3, 7
See also Jackson, Laura (Riding)

Riefenstahl, Berta Helene Amalia 1902-
See Riefenstahl, Leni
See also CA 108

Riefenstahl, Leni. .... CLC 16
See also Riefenstahl, Berta Helene Amalia

Riffe, Ernest
See Bergman, (Ernst) Ingmar

Riggs, (Rolla) Lynn 1899-1954 .... TCLC 56
See also CA 144; DAM MULT; NNAL

Riley, James Whitcomb
1849-1916 .... TCLC 51
See also CA 118; 137; DAM POET;
MAICYA; SATA 17

Riley, Tex
See Creasey, John

Rilke, Rainer Maria
1875-1926 .... TCLC 1, 6, 19; PC 2
See also CA 104; 132; DAM POET;
DLB 81; MTCW

Rimbaud, (Jean Nicolas) Arthur
1854-1891 ..... NCLC 4, 35; DA; DAB;
DAC; PC 3; WLC
See also DAM MST, POET

Rinehart, Mary Roberts
1876-1958 .... TCLC 52
See also CA 108

Ringmaster, The
See Mencken, H(enry) L(ouis)

Ringwood, Gwen(dolyn Margaret) Pharis
1910-1984 .... CLC 48
See also CA 148; 112; DLB 88

Rio, Michel 19(?)- .... CLC 43

Ritsos, Giannes
See Ritsos, Yannis

Ritsos, Yannis 1909-1990..... CLC 6, 13, 31
See also CA 77-80; 133; CANR 39; MTCW

Ritter, Erika 1948(?)- .... CLC 52

Rivera, Jose Eustasio 1889-1928... TCLC 35
See also HW

Rivers, Conrad Kent 1933-1968...... CLC 1
See also BW 1; CA 85-88; DLB 41

Rivers, Elfrida
See Bradley, Marion Zimmer

Riverside, John
See Heinlein, Robert A(nson)

Rizal, Jose 1861-1896.......... NCLC 27

Roa Bastos, Augusto (Antonio)
1917- .... CLC 45; HLC
See also CA 131; DAM MULT; DLB 113;
HW

Robbe-Grillet, Alain
1922- ...... CLC 1, 2, 4, 6, 8, 10, 14, 43
See also CA 9-12R; CANR 33; DLB 83;
MTCW

Robbins, Harold 1916-............. CLC 5
See also CA 73-76; CANR 26; DAM NOV;
MTCW

Robbins, Thomas Eugene 1936-
See Robbins, Tom
See also CA 81-84; CANR 29; DAM NOV,
POP; MTCW

Robbins, Tom. .... CLC 9, 32, 64
See also Robbins, Thomas Eugene
See also BEST 90:3; DLBY 80

Robbins, Trina 1938- .... CLC 21
See also CA 128

Roberts, Charles G(eorge) D(ouglas)
1860-1943 .... TCLC 8
See also CA 105; CLR 33; DLB 92;
SATA-Brief 29

Roberts, Kate 1891-1985 .... CLC 15
See also CA 107; 116

Roberts, Keith (John Kingston)
1935- .... CLC 14
See also CA 25-28R; CANR 46

Roberts, Kenneth (Lewis)
1885-1957 .... TCLC 23
See also CA 109; DLB 9

Roberts, Michele (B.) 1949-........ CLC 48
See also CA 115

Robertson, Ellis
See Ellison, Harlan (Jay); Silverberg, Robert

Robertson, Thomas William
1829-1871 .... NCLC 35
See also DAM DRAM

Robinson, Edwin Arlington
1869-1935 .... TCLC 5; DA; DAC; PC 1
See also CA 104; 133; CDALB 1865-1917;
DAM MST, POET; DLB 54; MTCW

Robinson, Henry Crabb
1775-1867 .... NCLC 15
See also DLB 107

Robinson, Jill 1936-.............. CLC 10
See also CA 102; INT 102

Robinson, Kim Stanley 1952-...... CLC 34
See also CA 126

Robinson, Lloyd
See Silverberg, Robert

Robinson, Marilynne 1944-........ CLC 25
See also CA 116

Robinson, Smokey. .... CLC 21
See also Robinson, William, Jr.

Robinson, William, Jr. 1940-
See Robinson, Smokey
See also CA 116

Robison, Mary 1949-.............. CLC 42
See also CA 113; 116; DLB 130; INT 116

Rod, Edouard 1857-1910 .... TCLC 52

Roddenberry, Eugene Wesley 1921-1991
See Roddenberry, Gene
See also CA 110; 135; CANR 37; SATA 45;
SATA-Obit 69

Roddenberry, Gene .... CLC 17
See also Roddenberry, Eugene Wesley
See also AAYA 5; SATA-Obit 69

Rodgers, Mary 1931-.............. CLC 12
See also CA 49-52; CANR 8; CLR 20;
INT CANR-8; JRDA; MAICYA;
SATA 8

Rodgers, W(illiam) R(obert)
1909-1969 .... CLC 7
See also CA 85-88; DLB 20

Rodman, Eric
See Silverberg, Robert

Rodman, Howard 1920(?)-1985..... CLC 65
See also CA 118

Rodman, Maia
See Wojciechowska, Maia (Teresa)

Rodriguez, Claudio 1934.......... CLC 10
See also DLB 134

Roelvaag, O(le) E(dvart)
1876-1931 .... TCLC 17
See also CA 117; DLB 9

Roethke, Theodore (Huebner)
1908-1963 ...... CLC 1, 3, 8, 11, 19, 46
See also CA 81-84; CABS 2;
CDALB 1941-1968; DAM POET; DLB 5;
MTCW

Rogers, Thomas Hunton 1927-..... CLC 57
See also CA 89-92; INT 89-92

Rogers, Will(iam Penn Adair)
1879-1935 .... TCLC 8
See also CA 105; 144; DAM MULT;
DLB 11; NNAL

Rogin, Gilbert 1929-.............. CLC 18
See also CA 65-68; CANR 15

Rohan, Koda .... TCLC 22
See also Koda Shigeyuki

Rohmer, Eric. .... CLC 16
See also Scherer, Jean-Marie Maurice

Rohmer, Sax .... TCLC 28
See also Ward, Arthur Henry Sarsfield
See also DLB 70

Saba, Umberto   1883-1957 . . . . **TCLC 33**
See also CA 144; DLB 114

Sabatini, Rafael   1875-1950 . . . . **TCLC 47**

Sabato, Ernesto (R.)
1911- . . . . **CLC 10, 23; HLC**
See also CA 97-100; CANR 32;
DAM MULT; DLB 145; HW; MTCW

Sacastru, Martin
See Bioy Casares, Adolfo

Sacher-Masoch, Leopold von
1836(?)-1895 . . . . **NCLC 31**

Sachs, Marilyn (Stickle)   1927- . . . . . **CLC 35**
See also AAYA 2; CA 17-20R; CANR 13,
47; CLR 2; JRDA; MAICYA; SAAS 2;
SATA 3, 68

Sachs, Nelly   1891-1970 . . . . **CLC 14**
See also CA 17-18; 25-28R; CAP 2

Sackler, Howard (Oliver)
1929-1982 . . . . **CLC 14**
See also CA 61-64; 108; CANR 30; DLB 7

Sacks, Oliver (Wolf)   1933- . . . . **CLC 67**
See also CA 53-56; CANR 28, 50;
INT CANR-28; MTCW

Sade, Donatien Alphonse Francois Comte
1740-1814 . . . . **NCLC 47**

Sadoff, Ira   1945- . . . . **CLC 9**
See also CA 53-56; CANR 5, 21; DLB 120

Saetone
See Camus, Albert

Safire, William   1929- . . . . **CLC 10**
See also CA 17-20R; CANR 31

Sagan, Carl (Edward)   1934- . . . . **CLC 30**
See also AAYA 2; CA 25-28R; CANR 11,
36; MTCW; SATA 58

Sagan, Francoise . . . . **CLC 3, 6, 9, 17, 36**
See also Quoirez, Francoise
See also DLB 83

Sahgal, Nayantara (Pandit)   1927- . . . **CLC 41**
See also CA 9-12R; CANR 11

Saint, H(arry) F.   1941- . . . . **CLC 50**
See also CA 127

St. Aubin de Teran, Lisa   1953-
See Teran, Lisa St. Aubin de
See also CA 118; 126; INT 126

Sainte-Beuve, Charles Augustin
1804-1869 . . . . **NCLC 5**

Saint-Exupery, Antoine (Jean Baptiste Marie
Roger) de
1900-1944 . . . . **TCLC 2, 56; WLC**
See also CA 108; 132; CLR 10; DAM NOV;
DLB 72; MAICYA; MTCW; SATA 20

St. John, David
See Hunt, E(verette) Howard, (Jr.)

Saint-John Perse
See Leger, (Marie-Rene Auguste) Alexis
Saint-Leger

Saintsbury, George (Edward Bateman)
1845-1933 . . . . **TCLC 31**
See also DLB 57, 149

Sait Faik . . . . **TCLC 23**
See also Abasiyanik, Sait Faik

Saki . . . . **TCLC 3; SSC 12**
See also Munro, H(ector) H(ugh)

Sala, George Augustus . . . . **NCLC 46**

Salama, Hannu   1936- . . . . **CLC 18**

Salamanca, J(ack) R(ichard)
1922- . . . . **CLC 4, 15**
See also CA 25-28R

Sale, J. Kirkpatrick
See Sale, Kirkpatrick

Sale, Kirkpatrick   1937- . . . . **CLC 68**
See also CA 13-16R; CANR 10

Salinas, Luis Omar   1937- . . . **CLC 90; HLC**
See also CA 131; DAM MULT; DLB 82;
HW

Salinas (y Serrano), Pedro
1891(?)-1951 . . . . **TCLC 17**
See also CA 117; DLB 134

Salinger, J(erome) D(avid)
1919- . . . . . . **CLC 1, 3, 8, 12, 55, 56; DA;
DAB; DAC; SSC 2; WLC**
See also AAYA 2; CA 5-8R; CANR 39;
CDALB 1941-1968; CLR 18; DAM MST,
NOV, POP; DLB 2, 102; MAICYA;
MTCW; SATA 67

Salisbury, John
See Caute, David

Salter, James   1925- . . . . **CLC 7, 52, 59**
See also CA 73-76; DLB 130

Saltus, Edgar (Everton)
1855-1921 . . . . **TCLC 8**
See also CA 105

Saltykov, Mikhail Evgrafovich
1826-1889 . . . . **NCLC 16**

Samarakis, Antonis   1919- . . . . **CLC 5**
See also CA 25-28R; CAAS 16; CANR 36

Sanchez, Florencio   1875-1910 . . . . . **TCLC 37**
See also HW

Sanchez, Luis Rafael   1936- . . . . **CLC 23**
See also CA 128; DLB 145; HW

Sanchez, Sonia   1934- . . . **CLC 5; BLC; PC 9**
See also BW 2; CA 33-36R; CANR 24, 49;
CLR 18; DAM MULT; DLB 41;
DLBD 8; MAICYA; MTCW; SATA 22

Sand, George
1804-1876 . . . . . **NCLC 2, 42; DA; DAB;
DAC; WLC**
See also DAM MST, NOV; DLB 119

Sandburg, Carl (August)
1878-1967 . . . . **CLC 1, 4, 10, 15, 35; DA;
DAB; DAC; PC 2; WLC**
See also CA 5-8R; 25-28R; CANR 35;
CDALB 1865-1917; DAM MST, POET;
DLB 17, 54; MAICYA; MTCW; SATA 8

Sandburg, Charles
See Sandburg, Carl (August)

Sandburg, Charles A.
See Sandburg, Carl (August)

Sanders, (James) Ed(ward)   1939- . . . **CLC 53**
See also CA 13-16R; CAAS 21; CANR 13,
44; DLB 16

Sanders, Lawrence   1920- . . . . **CLC 41**
See also BEST 89:4; CA 81-84; CANR 33;
DAM POP; MTCW

Sanders, Noah
See Blount, Roy (Alton), Jr.

Sanders, Winston P.
See Anderson, Poul (William)

Sandoz, Mari(e Susette)
1896-1966 . . . . **CLC 28**
See also CA 1-4R; 25-28R; CANR 17;
DLB 9; MTCW; SATA 5

Saner, Reg(inald Anthony)   1931- . . . . **CLC 9**
See also CA 65-68

Sannazaro, Jacopo   1456(?)-1530 . . . . . . **LC 8**

Sansom, William
1912-1976 . . . . **CLC 2, 6; SSC 21**
See also CA 5-8R; 65-68; CANR 42;
DAM NOV; DLB 139; MTCW

Santayana, George   1863-1952 . . . . . **TCLC 40**
See also CA 115; DLB 54, 71; DLBD 13

Santiago, Danny . . . . **CLC 33**
See also James, Daniel (Lewis)
See also DLB 122

Santmyer, Helen Hoover
1895-1986 . . . . **CLC 33**
See also CA 1-4R; 118; CANR 15, 33;
DLBY 84; MTCW

Santos, Bienvenido N(uqui)   1911- . . . **CLC 22**
See also CA 101; CANR 19, 46;
DAM MULT

Sapper . . . . **TCLC 44**
See also McNeile, Herman Cyril

Sappho   fl. 6th cent. B.C.- . . . . . **CMLC 3; PC 5**
See also DAM POET

Sarduy, Severo   1937-1993 . . . . **CLC 6**
See also CA 89-92; 142; DLB 113; HW

Sargeson, Frank   1903-1982 . . . . **CLC 31**
See also CA 25-28R; 106; CANR 38

Sarmiento, Felix Ruben Garcia
See Dario, Ruben

Saroyan, William
1908-1981 . . . . . **CLC 1, 8, 10, 29, 34, 56;
DA; DAB; DAC; SSC 21; WLC**
See also CA 5-8R; 103; CANR 30;
DAM DRAM, MST, NOV; DLB 7, 9, 86;
DLBY 81; MTCW; SATA 23;
SATA-Obit 24

Sarraute, Nathalie
1900- . . . . **CLC 1, 2, 4, 8, 10, 31, 80**
See also CA 9-12R; CANR 23; DLB 83;
MTCW

Sarton, (Eleanor) May
1912- . . . . **CLC 4, 14, 49**
See also CA 1-4R; CANR 1, 34;
DAM POET; DLB 48; DLBY 81;
INT CANR-34; MTCW; SATA 36

Sartre, Jean-Paul
1905-1980 . . . . **CLC 1, 4, 7, 9, 13, 18, 24,
44, 50, 52; DA; DAB; DAC; DC 3; WLC**
See also CA 9-12R; 97-100; CANR 21;
DAM DRAM, MST, NOV; DLB 72;
MTCW

Sassoon, Siegfried (Lorraine)
1886-1967 . . . . **CLC 36; DAB; PC 12**
See also CA 104; 25-28R; CANR 36;
DAM MST, NOV, POET; DLB 20;
MTCW

Satterfield, Charles
See Pohl, Frederik

Saul, John (W. III)   1942- . . . . **CLC 46**
See also AAYA 10; BEST 90:4; CA 81-84;
CANR 16, 40; DAM NOV, POP

Seelye, John 1931- . . . . CLC 7

Seferiades, Giorgos Stylianou 1900-1971
See Seferis, George
See also CA 5-8R; 33-36R; CANR 5, 36;
MTCW

Seferis, George . . . . CLC 5, 11
See also Seferiades, Giorgos Stylianou

Segal, Erich (Wolf) 1937- . . . . CLC 3, 10
See also BEST 89:1; CA 25-28R; CANR 20,
36; DAM POP; DLBY 86;
INT CANR-20; MTCW

Seger, Bob 1945- . . . . CLC 35

Seghers, Anna . . . . CLC 7
See also Radvanyi, Netty
See also DLB 69

Seidel, Frederick (Lewis) 1936- . . . . . CLC 18
See also CA 13-16R; CANR 8; DLBY 84

Seifert, Jaroslav 1901-1986 . . . . . CLC 34, 44
See also CA 127; MTCW

Sei Shonagon c. 966-1017(?) . . . . . . CMLC 6

Selby, Hubert, Jr.
1928- . . . . CLC 1, 2, 4, 8; SSC 20
See also CA 13-16R; CANR 33; DLB 2

Selzer, Richard 1928- . . . . CLC 74
See also CA 65-68; CANR 14

Sembene, Ousmane
See Ousmane, Sembene

Senancour, Etienne Pivert de
1770-1846 . . . . NCLC 16
See also DLB 119

Sender, Ramon (Jose)
1902-1982 . . . . CLC 8; HLC
See also CA 5-8R; 105; CANR 8;
DAM MULT; HW; MTCW

Seneca, Lucius Annaeus
4B.C.-65 . . . . CMLC 6; DC 5
See also DAM DRAM

Senghor, Leopold Sedar
1906- . . . . CLC 54; BLC
See also BW 2; CA 116; 125; CANR 47;
DAM MULT, POET; MTCW

Serling, (Edward) Rod(man)
1924-1975 . . . . CLC 30
See also AAYA 14; AITN 1; CA 65-68;
57-60; DLB 26

Serna, Ramon Gomez de la
See Gomez de la Serna, Ramon

Serpieres
See Guillevic, (Eugene)

Service, Robert
See Service, Robert W(illiam)
See also DAB; DLB 92

Service, Robert W(illiam)
1874(?)-1958 . . . . . . TCLC 15; DA; DAC;
WLC
See also Service, Robert
See also CA 115; 140; DAM MST, POET;
SATA 20

Seth, Vikram 1952- . . . . CLC 43, 90
See also CA 121; 127; CANR 50;
DAM MULT; DLB 120; INT 127

Seton, Cynthia Propper
1926-1982 . . . . CLC 27
See also CA 5-8R; 108; CANR 7

Seton, Ernest (Evan) Thompson
1860-1946 . . . . TCLC 31
See also CA 109; DLB 92; DLBD 13;
JRDA; SATA 18

Seton-Thompson, Ernest
See Seton, Ernest (Evan) Thompson

Settle, Mary Lee 1918- . . . . CLC 19, 61
See also CA 89-92; CAAS 1; CANR 44;
DLB 6; INT 89-92

Seuphor, Michel
See Arp, Jean

**Sevigne, Marie (de Rabutin-Chantal) Marquise
de** 1626-1696 . . . . LC 11

Sexton, Anne (Harvey)
1928-1974 . . . . CLC 2, 4, 6, 8, 10, 15, 53;
DA; DAB; DAC; PC 2; WLC
See also CA 1-4R; 53-56; CABS 2;
CANR 3, 36; CDALB 1941-1968;
DAM MST, POET; DLB 5; MTCW;
SATA 10

Shaara, Michael (Joseph, Jr.)
1929-1988 . . . . CLC 15
See also AITN 1; CA 102; 125; DAM POP;
DLBY 83

Shackleton, C. C.
See Aldiss, Brian W(ilson)

Shacochis, Bob . . . . CLC 39
See also Shacochis, Robert G.

Shacochis, Robert G. 1951-
See Shacochis, Bob
See also CA 119; 124; INT 124

Shaffer, Anthony (Joshua) 1926- . . . . CLC 19
See also CA 110; 116; DAM DRAM;
DLB 13

Shaffer, Peter (Levin)
1926- . . . . . . CLC 5, 14, 18, 37, 60; DAB
See also CA 25-28R; CANR 25, 47;
CDBLB 1960 to Present; DAM DRAM,
MST; DLB 13; MTCW

Shakey, Bernard
See Young, Neil

Shalamov, Varlam (Tikhonovich)
1907(?)-1982 . . . . CLC 18
See also CA 129; 105

Shamlu, Ahmad 1925- . . . . CLC 10

Shammas, Anton 1951- . . . . CLC 55

Shange, Ntozake
1948- . . . . CLC 8, 25, 38, 74; BLC; DC 3
See also AAYA 9; BW 2; CA 85-88;
CABS 3; CANR 27, 48; DAM DRAM,
MULT; DLB 38; MTCW

Shanley, John Patrick 1950- . . . . CLC 75
See also CA 128; 133

Shapcott, Thomas W(illiam) 1935- . . CLC 38
See also CA 69-72; CANR 49

Shapiro, Jane . . . . CLC 76

Shapiro, Karl (Jay) 1913- . . CLC 4, 8, 15, 53
See also CA 1-4R; CAAS 6; CANR 1, 36;
DLB 48; MTCW

Sharp, William 1855-1905 . . . . TCLC 39
See also DLB 156

Sharpe, Thomas Ridley 1928-
See Sharpe, Tom
See also CA 114; 122; INT 122

Sharpe, Tom . . . . CLC 36
See also Sharpe, Thomas Ridley
See also DLB 14

Shaw, Bernard . . . . TCLC 45
See also Shaw, George Bernard
See also BW 1

Shaw, G. Bernard
See Shaw, George Bernard

Shaw, George Bernard
1856-1950 . . . TCLC 3, 9, 21; DA; DAB;
DAC; WLC
See also Shaw, Bernard
See also CA 104; 128; CDBLB 1914-1945;
DAM DRAM, MST; DLB 10, 57;
MTCW

Shaw, Henry Wheeler
1818-1885 . . . . NCLC 15
See also DLB 11

Shaw, Irwin 1913-1984 . . . . . . CLC 7, 23, 34
See also AITN 1; CA 13-16R; 112;
CANR 21; CDALB 1941-1968;
DAM DRAM, POP; DLB 6, 102;
DLBY 84; MTCW

Shaw, Robert 1927-1978 . . . . CLC 5
See also AITN 1; CA 1-4R; 81-84;
CANR 4; DLB 13, 14

Shaw, T. E.
See Lawrence, T(homas) E(dward)

Shawn, Wallace 1943- . . . . CLC 41
See also CA 112

Shea, Lisa 1953- . . . . CLC 86
See also CA 147

Sheed, Wilfrid (John Joseph)
1930- . . . . CLC 2, 4, 10, 53
See also CA 65-68; CANR 30; DLB 6;
MTCW

Sheldon, Alice Hastings Bradley
1915(?)-1987
See Tiptree, James, Jr.
See also CA 108; 122; CANR 34; INT 108;
MTCW

Sheldon, John
See Bloch, Robert (Albert)

Shelley, Mary Wollstonecraft (Godwin)
1797-1851 . . . . NCLC 14; DA; DAB;
DAC; WLC
See also CDBLB 1789-1832; DAM MST,
NOV; DLB 110, 116, 159; SATA 29

Shelley, Percy Bysshe
1792-1822 . . . . NCLC 18; DA; DAB;
DAC; PC 14; WLC
See also CDBLB 1789-1832; DAM MST,
POET; DLB 96, 110, 158

Shepard, Jim 1956- . . . . CLC 36
See also CA 137

Shepard, Lucius 1947- . . . . CLC 34
See also CA 128; 141

Shepard, Sam
1943- . . . . CLC 4, 6, 17, 34, 41, 44; DC 5
See also AAYA 1; CA 69-72; CABS 3;
CANR 22; DAM DRAM; DLB 7;
MTCW

Shepherd, Michael
See Ludlum, Robert

Singh, Khushwant 1915-.......... **CLC 11**
See also CA 9-12R; CAAS 9; CANR 6

Sinjohn, John
See Galsworthy, John

Sinyavsky, Andrei (Donatevich)
1925-....................... **CLC 8**
See also CA 85-88

Sirin, V.
See Nabokov, Vladimir (Vladimirovich)

Sissman, L(ouis) E(dward)
1928-1976 .... **CLC 9, 18**
See also CA 21-24R; 65-68; CANR 13;
DLB 5

Sisson, C(harles) H(ubert) 1914-..... **CLC 8**
See also CA 1-4R; CAAS 3; CANR 3, 48;
DLB 27

Sitwell, Dame Edith
1887-1964 .... **CLC 2, 9, 67; PC 3**
See also CA 9-12R; CANR 35;
CDBLB 1945-1960; DAM POET;
DLB 20; MTCW

Sjoewall, Maj 1935-............... **CLC 7**
See also CA 65-68

Sjowall, Maj
See Sjoewall, Maj

Skelton, Robin 1925-............. **CLC 13**
See also AITN 2; CA 5-8R; CAAS 5;
CANR 28; DLB 27, 53

Skolimowski, Jerzy 1938-......... **CLC 20**
See also CA 128

Skram, Amalie (Bertha)
1847-1905 .... **TCLC 25**

Skvorecky, Josef (Vaclav)
1924- .... **CLC 15, 39, 69; DAC**
See also CA 61-64; CAAS 1; CANR 10, 34;
DAM NOV; MTCW

Slade, Bernard................. **CLC 11, 46**
See also Newbound, Bernard Slade
See also CAAS 9; DLB 53

Slaughter, Carolyn 1946-.......... **CLC 56**
See also CA 85-88

Slaughter, Frank G(ill) 1908- ...... **CLC 29**
See also AITN 2; CA 5-8R; CANR 5;
INT CANR-5

Slavitt, David R(ytman) 1935-.... **CLC 5, 14**
See also CA 21-24R; CAAS 3; CANR 41;
DLB 5, 6

Slesinger, Tess 1905-1945 .... **TCLC 10**
See also CA 107; DLB 102

Slessor, Kenneth 1901-1971........ **CLC 14**
See also CA 102; 89-92

Slowacki, Juliusz 1809-1849 ..... **NCLC 15**

Smart, Christopher
1722-1771 .... **LC 3; PC 13**
See also DAM POET; DLB 109

Smart, Elizabeth 1913-1986....... **CLC 54**
See also CA 81-84; 118; DLB 88

Smiley, Jane (Graves) 1949- .... **CLC 53, 76**
See also CA 104; CANR 30, 50;
DAM POP; INT CANR-30

Smith, A(rthur) J(ames) M(arshall)
1902-1980 .... **CLC 15; DAC**
See also CA 1-4R; 102; CANR 4; DLB 88

Smith, Anna Deavere 1950-........ **CLC 86**
See also CA 133

Smith, Betty (Wehner) 1896-1972... **CLC 19**
See also CA 5-8R; 33-36R; DLBY 82;
SATA 6

Smith, Charlotte (Turner)
1749-1806 .... **NCLC 23**
See also DLB 39, 109

Smith, Clark Ashton 1893-1961 .... **CLC 43**
See also CA 143

Smith, Dave.................. **CLC 22, 42**
See also Smith, David (Jeddie)
See also CAAS 7; DLB 5

Smith, David (Jeddie) 1942-
See Smith, Dave
See also CA 49-52; CANR 1; DAM POET

Smith, Florence Margaret 1902-1971
See Smith, Stevie
See also CA 17-18; 29-32R; CANR 35;
CAP 2; DAM POET; MTCW

Smith, Iain Crichton 1928- .... **CLC 64**
See also CA 21-24R; DLB 40, 139

Smith, John 1580(?)-1631 .... **LC 9**

Smith, Johnston
See Crane, Stephen (Townley)

Smith, Joseph, Jr. 1805-1844 .... **NCLC 53**

Smith, Lee 1944-.............. **CLC 25, 73**
See also CA 114; 119; CANR 46; DLB 143;
DLBY 83; INT 119

Smith, Martin
See Smith, Martin Cruz

Smith, Martin Cruz 1942-......... **CLC 25**
See also BEST 89:4, CA 85-88, CANR 6,
23, 43; DAM MULT, POP;
INT CANR-23; NNAL

Smith, Mary-Ann Tirone 1944-..... **CLC 39**
See also CA 118; 136

Smith, Patti 1946- .... **CLC 12**
See also CA 93-96

Smith, Pauline (Urmson)
1882-1959 .... **TCLC 25**

Smith, Rosamond
See Oates, Joyce Carol

Smith, Sheila Kaye
See Kaye-Smith, Sheila

Smith, Stevie ...... **CLC 3, 8, 25, 44; PC 12**
See also Smith, Florence Margaret
See also DLB 20

Smith, Wilbur (Addison) 1933-..... **CLC 33**
See also CA 13-16R; CANR 7, 46; MTCW

Smith, William Jay 1918- .... **CLC 6**
See also CA 5-8R; CANR 44; DLB 5;
MAICYA; SATA 2, 68

Smith, Woodrow Wilson
See Kuttner, Henry

Smolenskin, Peretz 1842-1885.... **NCLC 30**

Smollett, Tobias (George) 1721-1771 .. **LC 2**
See also CDBLB 1660-1789; DLB 39, 104

Snodgrass, W(illiam) D(e Witt)
1926- .... **CLC 2, 6, 10, 18, 68**
See also CA 1-4R; CANR 6, 36;
DAM POET; DLB 5; MTCW

Snow, C(harles) P(ercy)
1905-1980 .... **CLC 1, 4, 6, 9, 13, 19**
See also CA 5-8R; 101; CANR 28;
CDBLB 1945-1960; DAM NOV; DLB 15,
77; MTCW

Snow, Frances Compton
See Adams, Henry (Brooks)

Snyder, Gary (Sherman)
1930- .... **CLC 1, 2, 5, 9, 32**
See also CA 17-20R; CANR 30;
DAM POET; DLB 5, 16

Snyder, Zilpha Keatley 1927- ...... **CLC 17**
See also AAYA 15; CA 9-12R; CANR 38;
CLR 31; JRDA; MAICYA; SAAS 2;
SATA 1, 28, 75

Soares, Bernardo
See Pessoa, Fernando (Antonio Nogueira)

Sobh, A.
See Shamlu, Ahmad

Sobol, Joshua..................... **CLC 60**

Soderberg, Hjalmar 1869-1941 .... **TCLC 39**

Sodergran, Edith (Irene)
See Soedergran, Edith (Irene)

Soedergran, Edith (Irene)
1892-1923 .... **TCLC 31**

Softly, Edgar
See Lovecraft, H(oward) P(hillips)

Softly, Edward
See Lovecraft, H(oward) P(hillips)

Sokolov, Raymond 1941-.......... **CLC 7**
See also CA 85-88

Solo, Jay
See Ellison, Harlan (Jay)

Sologub, Fyodor .... **TCLC 9**
See also Teternikov, Fyodor Kuzmich

Solomons, Ikey Esquir
See Thackeray, William Makepeace

Solomos, Dionysios 1798-1857 ... **NCLC 15**

Solwoska, Mara
See French, Marilyn

Solzhenitsyn, Aleksandr I(sayevich)
1918- ...... **CLC 1, 2, 4, 7, 9, 10, 18, 26,
34, 78; DA; DAB; DAC; WLC**
See also AITN 1; CA 69-72; CANR 40;
DAM MST, NOV; MTCW

Somers, Jane
See Lessing, Doris (May)

Somerville, Edith 1858-1949 ...... **TCLC 51**
See also DLB 135

Somerville & Ross
See Martin, Violet Florence; Somerville,
Edith

Sommer, Scott 1951- .... **CLC 25**
See also CA 106

Sondheim, Stephen (Joshua)
1930- .... **CLC 30, 39**
See also AAYA 11; CA 103; CANR 47;
DAM DRAM

Sontag, Susan 1933-... **CLC 1, 2, 10, 13, 31**
See also CA 17-20R; CANR 25;
DAM POP; DLB 2, 67; MTCW

Sophocles
496(?)B.C.-406(?)B.C..... **CMLC 2; DA; DAB; DAC; DC 1**
See also DAM DRAM, MST

Sordello   1189-1269............. **CMLC 15**

Sorel, Julia
See Drexler, Rosalyn

Sorrentino, Gilbert
1929-............ **CLC 3, 7, 14, 22, 40**
See also CA 77-80; CANR 14, 33; DLB 5; DLBY 80; INT CANR-14

Soto, Gary   1952-........ **CLC 32, 80; HLC**
See also AAYA 10; CA 119; 125; CANR 50; CLR 38; DAM MULT; DLB 82; HW; INT 125; JRDA; SATA 80

Soupault, Philippe   1897-1990 ...... **CLC 68**
See also CA 116; 147; 131

Souster, (Holmes) Raymond
1921-.............. **CLC 5, 14; DAC**
See also CA 13-16R; CAAS 14; CANR 13, 29; DAM POET; DLB 88; SATA 63

Southern, Terry   1926-............. **CLC 7**
See also CA 1-4R; CANR 1; DLB 2

Southey, Robert   1774-1843 .... **NCLC 8**
See also DLB 93, 107, 142; SATA 54

Southworth, Emma Dorothy Eliza Nevitte
1819-1899 .... **NCLC 26**

Souza, Ernest
See Scott, Evelyn

Soyinka, Wole
1934-....... **CLC 3, 5, 14, 36, 44; BLC; DA; DAB; DAC; DC 2; WLC**
See also BW 2; CA 13-16R; CANR 27, 39; DAM DRAM, MST, MULT; DLB 125; MTCW

Spackman, W(illiam) M(ode)
1905-1990 .... **CLC 46**
See also CA 81-84; 132

Spacks, Barry   1931-.............. **CLC 14**
See also CA 29-32R; CANR 33; DLB 105

Spanidou, Irini   1946-............. **CLC 44**

Spark, Muriel (Sarah)
1918-........ **CLC 2, 3, 5, 8, 13, 18, 40; DAB; DAC; SSC 10**
See also CA 5-8R; CANR 12, 36; CDBLB 1945-1960; DAM MST, NOV; DLB 15, 139; INT CANR-12; MTCW

Spaulding, Douglas
See Bradbury, Ray (Douglas)

Spaulding, Leonard
See Bradbury, Ray (Douglas)

Spence, J. A. D.
See Eliot, T(homas) S(tearns)

Spencer, Elizabeth   1921-.......... **CLC 22**
See also CA 13-16R; CANR 32; DLB 6; MTCW; SATA 14

Spencer, Leonard G.
See Silverberg, Robert

Spencer, Scott   1945-.............. **CLC 30**
See also CA 113; DLBY 86

Spender, Stephen (Harold)
1909-............. **CLC 1, 2, 5, 10, 41**
See also CA 9-12R; CANR 31; CDBLB 1945-1960; DAM POET; DLB 20; MTCW

Spengler, Oswald (Arnold Gottfried)
1880-1936 .... **TCLC 25**
See also CA 118

Spenser, Edmund
1552(?)-1599 .... **LC 5; DA; DAB; DAC; PC 8; WLC**
See also CDBLB Before 1660; DAM MST, POET

Spicer, Jack   1925-1965 ...... **CLC 8, 18, 72**
See also CA 85-88; DAM POET; DLB 5, 16

Spiegelman, Art   1948-............ **CLC 76**
See also AAYA 10; CA 125; CANR 41

Spielberg, Peter   1929-............ **CLC 6**
See also CA 5-8R; CANR 4, 48; DLBY 81

Spielberg, Steven   1947-........... **CLC 20**
See also AAYA 8; CA 77-80; CANR 32; SATA 32

Spillane, Frank Morrison   1918-
See Spillane, Mickey
See also CA 25-28R; CANR 28; MTCW; SATA 66

Spillane, Mickey .... **CLC 3, 13**
See also Spillane, Frank Morrison

Spinoza, Benedictus de   1632-1677 .... **LC 9**

Spinrad, Norman (Richard)   1940-... **CLC 46**
See also CA 37-40R; CAAS 19; CANR 20; DLB 8; INT CANR-20

Spitteler, Carl (Friedrich Georg)
1845-1924 .... **TCLC 12**
See also CA 109; DLB 129

Spivack, Kathleen (Romola Drucker)
1938- .... **CLC 6**
See also CA 49-52

Spoto, Donald   1941-.............. **CLC 39**
See also CA 65-68; CANR 11

Springsteen, Bruce (F.)   1949- ...... **CLC 17**
See also CA 111

Spurling, Hilary   1940-............ **CLC 34**
See also CA 104; CANR 25

Spyker, John Howland
See Elman, Richard

Squires, (James) Radcliffe
1917-1993 .... **CLC 51**
See also CA 1-4R; 140; CANR 6, 21

Srivastava, Dhanpat Rai   1880(?)-1936
See Premchand
See also CA 118

Stacy, Donald
See Pohl, Frederik

Stael, Germaine de
See Stael-Holstein, Anne Louise Germaine Necker Baronn
See also DLB 119

Stael-Holstein, Anne Louise Germaine Necker Baronn   1766-1817 .... **NCLC 3**
See also Stael, Germaine de

Stafford, Jean   1915-1979 ... **CLC 4, 7, 19, 68**
See also CA 1-4R; 85-88; CANR 3; DLB 2; MTCW; SATA-Obit 22

Stafford, William (Edgar)
1914-1993 .... **CLC 4, 7, 29**
See also CA 5-8R; 142; CAAS 3; CANR 5, 22; DAM POET; DLB 5; INT CANR-22

Staines, Trevor
See Brunner, John (Kilian Houston)

Stairs, Gordon
See Austin, Mary (Hunter)

Stannard, Martin   1947-.......... **CLC 44**
See also CA 142; DLB 155

Stanton, Maura   1946- .... **CLC 9**
See also CA 89-92; CANR 15; DLB 120

Stanton, Schuyler
See Baum, L(yman) Frank

Stapledon, (William) Olaf
1886-1950 .... **TCLC 22**
See also CA 111; DLB 15

Starbuck, George (Edwin)   1931-.... **CLC 53**
See also CA 21-24R; CANR 23; DAM POET

Stark, Richard
See Westlake, Donald E(dwin)

Staunton, Schuyler
See Baum, L(yman) Frank

Stead, Christina (Ellen)
1902-1983 .... **CLC 2, 5, 8, 32, 80**
See also CA 13-16R; 109; CANR 33, 40; MTCW

Stead, William Thomas
1849-1912 .... **TCLC 48**

Steele, Richard   1672-1729.......... **LC 18**
See also CDBLB 1660-1789; DLB 84, 101

Steele, Timothy (Reid)   1948-....... **CLC 45**
See also CA 93-96; CANR 16, 50; DLB 120

Steffens, (Joseph) Lincoln
1866-1936 .... **TCLC 20**
See also CA 117

Stegner, Wallace (Earle)
1909-1993 .... **CLC 9, 49, 81**
See also AITN 1; BEST 90:3; CA 1-4R; 141; CAAS 9; CANR 1, 21, 46; DAM NOV; DLB 9; DLBY 93; MTCW

Stein, Gertrude
1874-1946 ...... **TCLC 1, 6, 28, 48; DA; DAB; DAC; WLC**
See also CA 104; 132; CDALB 1917-1929; DAM MST, NOV, POET; DLB 4, 54, 86; MTCW

Steinbeck, John (Ernst)
1902-1968 ...... **CLC 1, 5, 9, 13, 21, 34, 45, 75; DA; DAB; DAC; SSC 11; WLC**
See also AAYA 12; CA 1-4R; 25-28R; CANR 1, 35; CDALB 1929-1941; DAM DRAM, MST, NOV; DLB 7, 9; DLBD 2; MTCW; SATA 9

Steinem, Gloria   1934-............. **CLC 63**
See also CA 53-56; CANR 28; MTCW

Steiner, George   1929-............. **CLC 24**
See also CA 73-76; CANR 31; DAM NOV; DLB 67; MTCW; SATA 62

Steiner, K. Leslie
See Delany, Samuel R(ay, Jr.)

Steiner, Rudolf   1861-1925........ **TCLC 13**
See also CA 107

Stendhal
1783-1842 .... **NCLC 23, 46; DA; DAB; DAC; WLC**
See also DAM MST, NOV; DLB 119

Stephen, Leslie   1832-1904....... **TCLC 23**
See also CA 123; DLB 57, 144

Su Chien 1884-1918
See Su Man-shu
See also CA 123

Suckow, Ruth 1892-1960 . . . . **SSC 18**
See also CA 113; DLB 9, 102

Sudermann, Hermann 1857-1928 . . **TCLC 15**
See also CA 107; DLB 118

Sue, Eugene 1804-1857 . . . . **NCLC 1**
See also DLB 119

Sueskind, Patrick 1949- . . . . **CLC 44**
See also Suskind, Patrick

Sukenick, Ronald 1932- . . . . . **CLC 3, 4, 6, 48**
See also CA 25-28R; CAAS 8; CANR 32;
DLBY 81

Suknaski, Andrew 1942- . . . . **CLC 19**
See also CA 101; DLB 53

Sullivan, Vernon
See Vian, Boris

Sully Prudhomme 1839-1907 . . . . . . **TCLC 31**

Su Man-shu . . . . **TCLC 24**
See also Su Chien

Summerforest, Ivy B.
See Kirkup, James

Summers, Andrew James 1942- . . . . . **CLC 26**

Summers, Andy
See Summers, Andrew James

Summers, Hollis (Spurgeon, Jr.)
1916- . . . . **CLC 10**
See also CA 5-8R; CANR 3; DLB 6

Summers, (Alphonsus Joseph-Mary Augustus)
Montague 1880-1948 . . . . **TCLC 16**
See also CA 118

Sumner, Gordon Matthew 1951- . . . . **CLC 26**

Surtees, Robert Smith
1803-1864 . . . . **NCLC 14**
See also DLB 21

Susann, Jacqueline 1921-1974 . . . . **CLC 3**
See also AITN 1; CA 65-68; 53-56; MTCW

Su Shih 1036-1101 . . . . **CMLC 15**

Suskind, Patrick
See Sueskind, Patrick
See also CA 145

Sutcliff, Rosemary
1920-1992 . . . . **CLC 26; DAB; DAC**
See also AAYA 10; CA 5-8R; 139;
CANR 37; CLR 1, 37; DAM MST, POP;
JRDA; MAICYA; SATA 6, 44, 78;
SATA-Obit 73

Sutro, Alfred 1863-1933 . . . . **TCLC 6**
See also CA 105; DLB 10

Sutton, Henry
See Slavitt, David R(ytman)

Svevo, Italo . . . . **TCLC 2, 35**
See also Schmitz, Aron Hector

Swados, Elizabeth (A.) 1951- . . . . **CLC 12**
See also CA 97-100; CANR 49; INT 97-100

Swados, Harvey 1920-1972 . . . . **CLC 5**
See also CA 5-8R; 37-40R; CANR 6;
DLB 2

Swan, Gladys 1934- . . . . **CLC 69**
See also CA 101; CANR 17, 39

Swarthout, Glendon (Fred)
1918-1992 . . . . **CLC 35**
See also CA 1-4R; 139; CANR 1, 47;
SATA 26

Sweet, Sarah C.
See Jewett, (Theodora) Sarah Orne

Swenson, May
1919-1989 . . . . **CLC 4, 14, 61; DA; DAB;**
DAC; PC 14
See also CA 5-8R; 130; CANR 36;
DAM MST, POET; DLB 5; MTCW;
SATA 15

Swift, Augustus
See Lovecraft, H(oward) P(hillips)

Swift, Graham (Colin) 1949- . . . . **CLC 41, 88**
See also CA 117; 122; CANR 46

Swift, Jonathan
1667-1745 . . . . . . **LC 1; DA; DAB; DAC;**
PC 9; WLC
See also CDBLB 1660-1789; DAM MST,
NOV, POET; DLB 39, 95, 101; SATA 19

Swinburne, Algernon Charles
1837-1909 . . . . . . **TCLC 8, 36; DA; DAB;**
DAC; WLC
See also CA 105; 140; CDBLB 1832-1890;
DAM MST, POET; DLB 35, 57

Swinfen, Ann . . . . **CLC 34**

Swinnerton, Frank Arthur
1884-1982 . . . . **CLC 31**
See also CA 108; DLB 34

Swithen, John
See King, Stephen (Edwin)

Sylvia
See Ashton-Warner, Sylvia (Constance)

Symmes, Robert Edward
See Duncan, Robert (Edward)

Symonds, John Addington
1840-1893 . . . . **NCLC 34**
See also DLB 57, 144

Symons, Arthur 1865-1945 . . . . **TCLC 11**
See also CA 107; DLB 19, 57, 149

Symons, Julian (Gustave)
1912-1994 . . . . **CLC 2, 14, 32**
See also CA 49-52; 147; CAAS 3; CANR 3,
33; DLB 87, 155; DLBY 92; MTCW

Synge, (Edmund) J(ohn) M(illington)
1871-1909 . . . . **TCLC 6, 37; DC 2**
See also CA 104; 141; CDBLB 1890-1914;
DAM DRAM; DLB 10, 19

Syruc, J.
See Milosz, Czeslaw

Szirtes, George 1948- . . . . **CLC 46**
See also CA 109; CANR 27

Tabori, George 1914- . . . . **CLC 19**
See also CA 49-52; CANR 4

Tagore, Rabindranath
1861-1941 . . . . **TCLC 3, 53; PC 8**
See also CA 104; 120; DAM DRAM,
POET; MTCW

Taine, Hippolyte Adolphe
1828-1893 . . . . **NCLC 15**

Talese, Gay 1932- . . . . **CLC 37**
See also AITN 1; CA 1-4R; CANR 9;
INT CANR-9; MTCW

Tallent, Elizabeth (Ann) 1954- . . . . . **CLC 45**
See also CA 117; DLB 130

Tally, Ted 1952- . . . . **CLC 42**
See also CA 120; 124; INT 124

Tamayo y Baus, Manuel
1829-1898 . . . . **NCLC 1**

Tammsaare, A(nton) H(ansen)
1878-1940 . . . . **TCLC 27**

Tan, Amy 1952- . . . . **CLC 59**
See also AAYA 9; BEST 89:3; CA 136;
DAM MULT, NOV, POP; SATA 75

Tandem, Felix
See Spitteler, Carl (Friedrich Georg)

Tanizaki, Jun'ichiro
1886-1965 . . . . . . **CLC 8, 14, 28; SSC 21**
See also CA 93-96; 25-28R

Tanner, William
See Amis, Kingsley (William)

Tao Lao
See Storni, Alfonsina

Tarassoff, Lev
See Troyat, Henri

Tarbell, Ida M(inerva)
1857-1944 . . . . **TCLC 40**
See also CA 122; DLB 47

Tarkington, (Newton) Booth
1869-1946 . . . . **TCLC 9**
See also CA 110; 143; DLB 9, 102;
SATA 17

Tarkovsky, Andrei (Arsenyevich)
1932-1986 . . . . **CLC 75**
See also CA 127

Tartt, Donna 1964(?)- . . . . **CLC 76**
See also CA 142

Tasso, Torquato 1544-1595 . . . . **LC 5**

Tate, (John Orley) Allen
1899-1979 . . . . **CLC 2, 4, 6, 9, 11, 14, 24**
See also CA 5-8R; 85-88; CANR 32;
DLB 4, 45, 63; MTCW

Tate, Ellalice
See Hibbert, Eleanor Alice Burford

Tate, James (Vincent) 1943- . . . **CLC 2, 6, 25**
See also CA 21-24R; CANR 29; DLB 5

Tavel, Ronald 1940- . . . . **CLC 6**
See also CA 21-24R; CANR 33

Taylor, C(ecil) P(hilip) 1929-1981 . . . **CLC 27**
See also CA 25-28R; 105; CANR 47

Taylor, Edward
1642(?)-1729 . . . **LC 11; DA; DAB; DAC**
See also DAM MST, POET; DLB 24

Taylor, Eleanor Ross 1920- . . . . **CLC 5**
See also CA 81-84

Taylor, Elizabeth 1912-1975 . . . **CLC 2, 4, 29**
See also CA 13-16R; CANR 9; DLB 139;
MTCW; SATA 13

Taylor, Henry (Splawn) 1942- . . . . . . **CLC 44**
See also CA 33-36R; CAAS 7; CANR 31;
DLB 5

Taylor, Kamala (Purnaiya) 1924-
See Markandaya, Kamala
See also CA 77-80

Tolkien, J(ohn) R(onald) R(euel)
1892-1973 ...... CLC 1, 2, 3, 8, 12, 38;
DA; DAB; DAC; WLC
See also AAYA 10; AITN 1; CA 17-18;
45-48; CANR 36; CAP 2;
CDBLB 1914-1945; DAM MST, NOV,
POP; DLB 15, 160; JRDA; MAICYA;
MTCW; SATA 2, 32; SATA-Obit 24

Toller, Ernst   1893-1939 .... TCLC 10
See also CA 107; DLB 124

Tolson, M. B.
See Tolson, Melvin B(eaunorus)

Tolson, Melvin B(eaunorus)
1898(?)-1966 .... CLC 36; BLC
See also BW 1; CA 124; 89-92;
DAM MULT, POET; DLB 48, 76

Tolstoi, Aleksei Nikolaevich
See Tolstoy, Alexey Nikolaevich

Tolstoy, Alexey Nikolaevich
1882-1945 .... TCLC 18
See also CA 107

Tolstoy, Count Leo
See Tolstoy, Leo (Nikolaevich)

Tolstoy, Leo (Nikolaevich)
1828-1910 ...... TCLC 4, 11, 17, 28, 44;
DA; DAB; DAC; SSC 9; WLC
See also CA 104; 123; DAM MST, NOV;
SATA 26

Tomasi di Lampedusa, Giuseppe   1896-1957
See Lampedusa, Giuseppe (Tomasi) di
See also CA 111

Tomlin, Lily .... CLC 17
See also Tomlin, Mary Jean

Tomlin, Mary Jean   1939(?)-
See Tomlin, Lily
See also CA 117

Tomlinson, (Alfred) Charles
1927- .... CLC 2, 4, 6, 13, 45
See also CA 5-8R; CANR 33; DAM POET;
DLB 40

Tonson, Jacob
See Bennett, (Enoch) Arnold

Toole, John Kennedy
1937-1969 .... CLC 19, 64
See also CA 104; DLBY 81

Toomer, Jean
1894-1967 ...... CLC 1, 4, 13, 22; BLC;
PC 7; SSC 1
See also BW 1; CA 85-88;
CDALB 1917-1929; DAM MULT;
DLB 45, 51; MTCW

Torley, Luke
See Blish, James (Benjamin)

Tornimparte, Alessandra
See Ginzburg, Natalia

Torre, Raoul della
See Mencken, H(enry) L(ouis)

Torrey, E(dwin) Fuller   1937- .... CLC 34
See also CA 119

Torsvan, Ben Traven
See Traven, B.

Torsvan, Benno Traven
See Traven, B.

Torsvan, Berick Traven
See Traven, B.

Torsvan, Berwick Traven
See Traven, B.

Torsvan, Bruno Traven
See Traven, B.

Torsvan, Traven
See Traven, B.

Tournier, Michel (Edouard)
1924- .... CLC 6, 23, 36
See also CA 49-52; CANR 3, 36; DLB 83;
MTCW; SATA 23

Tournimparte, Alessandra
See Ginzburg, Natalia

Towers, Ivar
See Kornbluth, C(yril) M.

Towne, Robert (Burton)   1936(?)- .... CLC 87
See also CA 108; DLB 44

Townsend, Sue   1946- .. CLC 61; DAB; DAC
See also CA 119; 127; INT 127; MTCW;
SATA 55; SATA-Brief 48

Townshend, Peter (Dennis Blandford)
1945- .... CLC 17, 42
See also CA 107

Tozzi, Federigo   1883-1920 .... TCLC 31

Traill, Catharine Parr
1802-1899 .... NCLC 31
See also DLB 99

Trakl, Georg   1887-1914 .... TCLC 5
See also CA 104

Transtroemer, Tomas (Goesta)
1931- .... CLC 52, 65
See also CA 117; 129; CAAS 17;
DAM POET

Transtromer, Tomas Gosta
See Transtroemer, Tomas (Goesta)

Traven, B.   (?)-1969 .... CLC 8, 11
See also CA 19-20; 25-28R; CAP 2; DLB 9,
56; MTCW

Treitel, Jonathan   1959- .... CLC 70

Tremain, Rose   1943- .... CLC 42
See also CA 97-100; CANR 44; DLB 14

Tremblay, Michel   1942- ...... CLC 29; DAC
See also CA 116; 128; DAM MST; DLB 60;
MTCW

Trevanian .... CLC 29
See also Whitaker, Rod(ney)

Trevor, Glen
See Hilton, James

Trevor, William
1928- ..... CLC 7, 9, 14, 25, 71; SSC 21
See also Cox, William Trevor
See also DLB 14, 139

Trifonov, Yuri (Valentinovich)
1925-1981 .... CLC 45
See also CA 126; 103; MTCW

Trilling, Lionel   1905-1975 .... CLC 9, 11, 24
See also CA 9-12R; 61-64; CANR 10;
DLB 28, 63; INT CANR-10; MTCW

Trimball, W. H.
See Mencken, H(enry) L(ouis)

Tristan
See Gomez de la Serna, Ramon

Tristram
See Housman, A(lfred) E(dward)

Trogdon, William (Lewis)   1939-
See Heat-Moon, William Least
See also CA 115; 119; CANR 47; INT 119

Trollope, Anthony
1815-1882 ..... NCLC 6, 33; DA; DAB;
DAC; WLC
See also CDBLB 1832-1890; DAM MST,
NOV; DLB 21, 57, 159; SATA 22

Trollope, Frances   1779-1863 ..... NCLC 30
See also DLB 21

Trotsky, Leon   1879-1940 .... TCLC 22
See also CA 118

Trotter (Cockburn), Catharine
1679-1749 .... LC 8
See also DLB 84

Trout, Kilgore
See Farmer, Philip Jose

Trow, George W. S.   1943- .... CLC 52
See also CA 126

Troyat, Henri   1911- .... CLC 23
See also CA 45-48; CANR 2, 33; MTCW

Trudeau, G(arretson) B(eekman)   1948-
See Trudeau, Garry B.
See also CA 81-84; CANR 31; SATA 35

Trudeau, Garry B. .... CLC 12
See also Trudeau, G(arretson) B(eekman)
See also AAYA 10; AITN 2

Truffaut, Francois   1932-1984 .... CLC 20
See also CA 81-84; 113; CANR 34

Trumbo, Dalton   1905-1976 .... CLC 19
See also CA 21-24R; 69-72; CANR 10;
DLB 26

Trumbull, John   1750-1831 .... NCLC 30
See also DLB 31

Trundlett, Helen B.
See Eliot, T(homas) S(tearns)

Tryon, Thomas   1926-1991 .... CLC 3, 11
See also AITN 1; CA 29-32R; 135;
CANR 32; DAM POP; MTCW

Tryon, Tom
See Tryon, Thomas

Ts'ao Hsueh-ch'in   1715(?)-1763 .... LC 1

Tsushima, Shuji   1909-1948
See Dazai, Osamu
See also CA 107

Tsvetaeva (Efron), Marina (Ivanovna)
1892-1941 .... TCLC 7, 35; PC 14
See also CA 104; 128; MTCW

Tuck, Lily   1938- .... CLC 70
See also CA 139

Tu Fu   712-770 .... PC 9
See also DAM MULT

Tunis, John R(oberts)   1889-1975 ... CLC 12
See also CA 61-64; DLB 22; JRDA;
MAICYA; SATA 37; SATA-Brief 30

Tuohy, Frank .... CLC 37
See also Tuohy, John Francis
See also DLB 14, 139

Tuohy, John Francis   1925-
See Tuohy, Frank
See also CA 5-8R; CANR 3, 47

Turco, Lewis (Putnam)   1934- ... CLC 11, 63
See also CA 13-16R; CAAS 22; CANR 24;
DLBY 84

Walker, Alice (Malsenior)
1944- .... CLC **5, 6, 9, 19, 27, 46, 58;**
BLC; DA; DAB; DAC; SSC **5**
See also AAYA 3; BEST 89:4; BW 2;
CA 37-40R; CANR 9, 27, 49;
CDALB 1968-1988; DAM MST, MULT,
NOV, POET, POP; DLB 6, 33, 143;
INT CANR-27; MTCW; SATA 31

Walker, David Harry 1911-1992.... CLC **14**
See also CA 1-4R; 137; CANR 1; SATA 8;
SATA-Obit 71

Walker, Edward Joseph 1934-
See Walker, Ted
See also CA 21-24R; CANR 12, 28

Walker, George F.
1947- .... CLC **44, 61; DAB; DAC**
See also CA 103; CANR 21, 43;
DAM MST; DLB 60

Walker, Joseph A. 1935- .... CLC **19**
See also BW 1; CA 89-92; CANR 26;
DAM DRAM, MST; DLB 38

Walker, Margaret (Abigail)
1915- .... CLC **1, 6; BLC**
See also BW 2; CA 73-76; CANR 26;
DAM MULT; DLB 76, 152; MTCW

Walker, Ted...................... CLC **13**
See also Walker, Edward Joseph
See also DLB 40

Wallace, David Foster 1962- .... CLC **50**
See also CA 132

Wallace, Dexter
See Masters, Edgar Lee

Wallace, (Richard Horatio) Edgar
1875-1932 .... TCLC **57**
See also CA 115; DLB 70

Wallace, Irving 1916-1990 ...... CLC **7, 13**
See also AITN 1; CA 1-4R; 132; CAAS 1;
CANR 1, 27; DAM NOV, POP;
INT CANR-27; MTCW

Wallant, Edward Lewis
1926-1962 .... CLC **5, 10**
See also CA 1-4R; CANR 22; DLB 2, 28,
143; MTCW

Walley, Byron
See Card, Orson Scott

Walpole, Horace 1717-1797.......... LC **2**
See also DLB 39, 104

Walpole, Hugh (Seymour)
1884-1941 .... TCLC **5**
See also CA 104; DLB 34

Walser, Martin 1927-............. CLC **27**
See also CA 57-60; CANR 8, 46; DLB 75,
124

Walser, Robert
1878-1956 .... TCLC **18; SSC 20**
See also CA 118; DLB 66

Walsh, Jill Paton.................. CLC **35**
See also Paton Walsh, Gillian
See also AAYA 11; CLR 2; DLB 161;
SAAS 3

Walter, Villiam Christian
See Andersen, Hans Christian

Wambaugh, Joseph (Aloysius, Jr.)
1937- .... CLC **3, 18**
See also AITN 1; BEST 89:3; CA 33-36R;
CANR 42; DAM NOV, POP; DLB 6;
DLBY 83; MTCW

Ward, Arthur Henry Sarsfield 1883-1959
See Rohmer, Sax
See also CA 108

Ward, Douglas Turner 1930-....... CLC **19**
See also BW 1; CA 81-84; CANR 27;
DLB 7, 38

Ward, Mary Augusta
See Ward, Mrs. Humphry

Ward, Mrs. Humphry
1851-1920 .... TCLC **55**
See also DLB 18

Ward, Peter
See Faust, Frederick (Schiller)

Warhol, Andy 1928(?)-1987........ CLC **20**
See also AAYA 12; BEST 89:4; CA 89-92;
121; CANR 34

Warner, Francis (Robert le Plastrier)
1937- .... CLC **14**
See also CA 53-56; CANR 11

Warner, Marina 1946-............. CLC **59**
See also CA 65-68; CANR 21

Warner, Rex (Ernest) 1905-1986.... CLC **45**
See also CA 89-92; 119; DLB 15

Warner, Susan (Bogert)
1819-1885 .... NCLC **31**
See also DLB 3, 42

Warner, Sylvia (Constance) Ashton
See Ashton-Warner, Sylvia (Constance)

Warner, Sylvia Townsend
1893-1978 .... CLC **7, 19**
See also CA 61-64; 77-80; CANR 16;
DLB 34, 139; MTCW

Warren, Mercy Otis 1728-1814... NCLC **13**
See also DLB 31

Warren, Robert Penn
1905-1989 .... CLC **1, 4, 6, 8, 10, 13, 18,
39, 53, 59; DA; DAB; DAC; SSC 4; WLC**
See also AITN 1; CA 13-16R; 129;
CANR 10, 47; CDALB 1968-1988;
DAM MST, NOV, POET; DLB 2, 48,
152; DLBY 80, 89; INT CANR-10;
MTCW; SATA 46; SATA-Obit 63

Warshofsky, Isaac
See Singer, Isaac Bashevis

Warton, Thomas 1728-1790......... LC **15**
See also DAM POET; DLB 104, 109

Waruk, Kona
See Harris, (Theodore) Wilson

Warung, Price 1855-1911........ TCLC **45**

Warwick, Jarvis
See Garner, Hugh

Washington, Alex
See Harris, Mark

Washington, Booker T(aliaferro)
1856-1915 .... TCLC **10; BLC**
See also BW 1; CA 114; 125; DAM MULT;
SATA 28

Washington, George 1732-1799...... LC **25**
See also DLB 31

Wassermann, (Karl) Jakob
1873-1934 .... TCLC **6**
See also CA 104; DLB 66

Wasserstein, Wendy
1950- .... CLC **32, 59, 90; DC 4**
See also CA 121; 129; CABS 3;
DAM DRAM; INT 129

Waterhouse, Keith (Spencer)
1929- .... CLC **47**
See also CA 5-8R; CANR 38; DLB 13, 15;
MTCW

Waters, Frank (Joseph) 1902-...... CLC **88**
See also CA 5-8R; CAAS 13; CANR 3, 18;
DLBY 86

Waters, Roger 1944-.............. CLC **35**

Watkins, Frances Ellen
See Harper, Frances Ellen Watkins

Watkins, Gerrold
See Malzberg, Barry N(athaniel)

Watkins, Paul 1964-.............. CLC **55**
See also CA 132

Watkins, Vernon Phillips
1906-1967 .... CLC **43**
See also CA 9-10; 25-28R; CAP 1; DLB 20

Watson, Irving S.
See Mencken, H(enry) L(ouis)

Watson, John H.
See Farmer, Philip Jose

Watson, Richard F.
See Silverberg, Robert

Waugh, Auberon (Alexander) 1939-... CLC **7**
See also CA 45-48; CANR 6, 22; DLB 14

Waugh, Evelyn (Arthur St. John)
1903-1966 ...... CLC **1, 3, 8, 13, 19, 27,
44; DA; DAB; DAC; WLC**
See also CA 85-88; 25-28R; CANR 22;
CDBLB 1914-1945; DAM MST, NOV,
POP; DLB 15; MTCW

Waugh, Harriet 1944- .... CLC **6**
See also CA 85-88; CANR 22

Ways, C. R.
See Blount, Roy (Alton), Jr.

Waystaff, Simon
See Swift, Jonathan

Webb, (Martha) Beatrice (Potter)
1858-1943 .... TCLC **22**
See also Potter, Beatrice
See also CA 117

Webb, Charles (Richard) 1939-...... CLC **7**
See also CA 25-28R

Webb, James H(enry), Jr. 1946-.... CLC **22**
See also CA 81-84

Webb, Mary (Gladys Meredith)
1881-1927 .... TCLC **24**
See also CA 123; DLB 34

Webb, Mrs. Sidney
See Webb, (Martha) Beatrice (Potter)

Webb, Phyllis 1927-.............. CLC **18**
See also CA 104; CANR 23; DLB 53

Webb, Sidney (James)
1859-1947 .... TCLC **22**
See also CA 117

Webber, Andrew Lloyd............. CLC **21**
See also Lloyd Webber, Andrew

Weber, Lenora Mattingly
        1895-1971 .... CLC 12
    See also CA 19-20; 29-32R; CAP 1;
        SATA 2; SATA-Obit 26

Webster, John   1579(?)-1634(?) .... DC 2
    See also CDBLB Before 1660; DA; DAB;
        DAC; DAM DRAM, MST; DLB 58;
        WLC

Webster, Noah   1758-1843 .... NCLC 30

Wedekind, (Benjamin) Frank(lin)
        1864-1918 .... TCLC 7
    See also CA 104; DAM DRAM; DLB 118

Weidman, Jerome   1913-............ CLC 7
    See also AITN 2; CA 1-4R; CANR 1;
        DLB 28

Weil, Simone (Adolphine)
        1909-1943 .... TCLC 23
    See also CA 117

Weinstein, Nathan
    See West, Nathanael

Weinstein, Nathan von Wallenstein
    See West, Nathanael

Weir, Peter (Lindsay)   1944- .... CLC 20
    See also CA 113; 123

Weiss, Peter (Ulrich)
        1916-1982 .... CLC 3, 15, 51
    See also CA 45-48; 106; CANR 3;
        DAM DRAM; DLB 69, 124

Weiss, Theodore (Russell)
        1916- .... CLC 3, 8, 14
    See also CA 9-12R; CAAS 2; CANR 46;
        DLB 5

Welch, (Maurice) Denton
        1915-1948 .... TCLC 22
    See also CA 121; 148

Welch, James   1940-......... CLC 6, 14, 52
    See also CA 85-88; CANR 42;
        DAM MULT, POP; NNAL

Weldon, Fay
        1933-......... CLC 6, 9, 11, 19, 36, 59
    See also CA 21-24R; CANR 16, 46;
        CDBLB 1960 to Present; DAM POP;
        DLB 14; INT CANR-16; MTCW

Wellek, Rene   1903- .... CLC 28
    See also CA 5-8R; CAAS 7; CANR 8;
        DLB 63; INT CANR-8

Weller, Michael   1942-......... CLC 10, 53
    See also CA 85-88

Weller, Paul   1958-............... CLC 26

Wellershoff, Dieter   1925-.......... CLC 46
    See also CA 89-92; CANR 16, 37

Welles, (George) Orson
        1915-1985 .... CLC 20, 80
    See also CA 93-96; 117

Wellman, Mac   1945- .... CLC 65

Wellman, Manly Wade   1903-1986 .. CLC 49
    See also CA 1-4R; 118; CANR 6, 16, 44;
        SATA 6; SATA-Obit 47

Wells, Carolyn   1869(?)-1942 ..... TCLC 35
    See also CA 113; DLB 11

Wells, H(erbert) G(eorge)
        1866-1946 .... TCLC 6, 12, 19; DA;
                        DAB; DAC; SSC 6; WLC
    See also CA 110; 121; CDBLB 1914-1945;
        DAM MST, NOV; DLB 34, 70, 156;
        MTCW; SATA 20

Wells, Rosemary   1943-............ CLC 12
    See also AAYA 13; CA 85-88; CANR 48;
        CLR 16; MAICYA; SAAS 1; SATA 18,
        69

Welty, Eudora
        1909- ...... CLC 1, 2, 5, 14, 22, 33; DA;
                        DAB; DAC; SSC 1; WLC
    See also CA 9-12R; CABS 1; CANR 32;
        CDALB 1941-1968; DAM MST, NOV;
        DLB 2, 102, 143; DLBD 12; DLBY 87;
        MTCW

Wen I-to   1899-1946 .... TCLC 28

Wentworth, Robert
    See Hamilton, Edmond

Werfel, Franz (V.)   1890-1945 ...... TCLC 8
    See also CA 104; DLB 81, 124

Wergeland, Henrik Arnold
        1808-1845 .... NCLC 5

Wersba, Barbara   1932-.......... CLC 30
    See also AAYA 2; CA 29-32R; CANR 16,
        38; CLR 3; DLB 52; JRDA; MAICYA;
        SAAS 2; SATA 1, 58

Wertmueller, Lina   1928- .... CLC 16
    See also CA 97-100; CANR 39

Wescott, Glenway   1901-1987....... CLC 13
    See also CA 13-16R; 121; CANR 23;
        DLB 4, 9, 102

Wesker, Arnold   1932- .. CLC 3, 5, 42; DAB
    See also CA 1-4R; CAAS 7; CANR 1, 33;
        CDBLB 1960 to Present; DAM DRAM;
        DLB 13; MTCW

Wesley, Richard (Errol)   1945-....... CLC 7
    See also BW 1; CA 57-60; CANR 27;
        DLB 38

Wessel, Johan Herman   1742-1785 .... LC 7

West, Anthony (Panther)
        1914-1987 .... CLC 50
    See also CA 45-48; 124; CANR 3, 19;
        DLB 15

West, C. P.
    See Wodehouse, P(elham) G(renville)

West, (Mary) Jessamyn
        1902-1984 .... CLC 7, 17
    See also CA 9-12R; 112; CANR 27; DLB 6;
        DLBY 84; MTCW; SATA-Obit 37

West, Morris L(anglo)   1916-..... CLC 6, 33
    See also CA 5-8R; CANR 24, 49; MTCW

West, Nathanael
        1903-1940 ..... TCLC 1, 14, 44; SSC 16
    See also CA 104; 125; CDALB 1929-1941;
        DLB 4, 9, 28; MTCW

West, Owen
    See Koontz, Dean R(ay)

West, Paul   1930-................ CLC 7, 14
    See also CA 13-16R; CAAS 7; CANR 22;
        DLB 14; INT CANR-22

West, Rebecca   1892-1983 .. CLC 7, 9, 31, 50
    See also CA 5-8R; 109; CANR 19; DLB 36;
        DLBY 83; MTCW

Westall, Robert (Atkinson)
        1929-1993 .... CLC 17
    See also AAYA 12; CA 69-72; 141;
        CANR 18; CLR 13; JRDA; MAICYA;
        SAAS 2; SATA 23, 69; SATA-Obit 75

Westlake, Donald E(dwin)
        1933- .... CLC 7, 33
    See also CA 17-20R; CAAS 13; CANR 16,
        44; DAM POP; INT CANR-16

Westmacott, Mary
    See Christie, Agatha (Mary Clarissa)

Weston, Allen
    See Norton, Andre

Wetcheek, J. L.
    See Feuchtwanger, Lion

Wetering, Janwillem van de
    See van de Wetering, Janwillem

Wetherell, Elizabeth
    See Warner, Susan (Bogert)

Whalen, Philip   1923- .... CLC 6, 29
    See also CA 9-12R; CANR 5, 39; DLB 16

Wharton, Edith (Newbold Jones)
        1862-1937 ...... TCLC 3, 9, 27, 53; DA;
                        DAB; DAC; SSC 6; WLC
    See also CA 104; 132; CDALB 1865-1917;
        DAM MST, NOV; DLB 4, 9, 12, 78;
        DLBD 13; MTCW

Wharton, James
    See Mencken, H(enry) L(ouis)

Wharton, William (a pseudonym)
        .... CLC 18, 37
    See also CA 93-96; DLBY 80; INT 93-96

Wheatley (Peters), Phillis
        1754(?)-1784 .... LC 3; BLC; DA; DAC;
                                        PC 3; WLC
    See also CDALB 1640-1865; DAM MST,
        MULT, POET; DLB 31, 50

Wheelock, John Hall   1886-1978.... CLC 14
    See also CA 13-16R; 77-80; CANR 14;
        DLB 45

White, E(lwyn) B(rooks)
        1899-1985 .... CLC 10, 34, 39
    See also AITN 2; CA 13-16R; 116;
        CANR 16, 37; CLR 1, 21; DAM POP;
        DLB 11, 22; MAICYA; MTCW;
        SATA 2, 29; SATA-Obit 44

White, Edmund (Valentine III)
        1940- .... CLC 27
    See also AAYA 7; CA 45-48; CANR 3, 19,
        36; DAM POP; MTCW

White, Patrick (Victor Martindale)
        1912-1990 .. CLC 3, 4, 5, 7, 9, 18, 65, 69
    See also CA 81-84; 132; CANR 43; MTCW

White, Phyllis Dorothy James   1920-
    See James, P. D.
    See also CA 21-24R; CANR 17, 43;
        DAM POP; MTCW

White, T(erence) H(anbury)
        1906-1964 .... CLC 30
    See also CA 73-76; CANR 37; DLB 160;
        JRDA; MAICYA; SATA 12

White, Terence de Vere
        1912-1994 .... CLC 49
    See also CA 49-52; 145; CANR 3

White, Walter F(rancis)
1893-1955 .... TCLC 15
See also White, Walter
See also BW 1; CA 115; 124; DLB 51

White, William Hale   1831-1913
See Rutherford, Mark
See also CA 121

Whitehead, E(dward) A(nthony)
1933- .... CLC 5
See also CA 65-68

Whitemore, Hugh (John) 1936-..... CLC 37
See also CA 132; INT 132

Whitman, Sarah Helen (Power)
1803-1878 .... NCLC 19
See also DLB 1

Whitman, Walt(er)
1819-1892 ..... NCLC 4, 31; DA; DAB;
DAC; PC 3; WLC
See also CDALB 1640-1865; DAM MST,
POET; DLB 3, 64; SATA 20

Whitney, Phyllis A(yame) 1903-.... CLC 42
See also AITN 2; BEST 90:3; CA 1-4R;
CANR 3, 25, 38; DAM POP; JRDA;
MAICYA; SATA 1, 30

Whittemore, (Edward) Reed (Jr.)
1919- .... CLC 4
See also CA 9-12R; CAAS 8; CANR 4;
DLB 5

Whittier, John Greenleaf
1807-1892 .... NCLC 8
See also CDALB 1640-1865; DAM POET;
DLB 1

Whittlebot, Hernia
See Coward, Noel (Peirce)

Wicker, Thomas Grey   1926
See Wicker, Tom
See also CA 65-68; CANR 21, 46

Wicker, Tom .... CLC 7
See also Wicker, Thomas Grey

Wideman, John Edgar
1941- .... CLC 5, 34, 36, 67; BLC
See also BW 2; CA 85-88; CANR 14, 42;
DAM MULT; DLB 33, 143

Wiebe, Rudy (Henry)
1934- .... CLC 6, 11, 14; DAC
See also CA 37-40R; CANR 42;
DAM MST; DLB 60

Wieland, Christoph Martin
1733-1813 .... NCLC 17
See also DLB 97

Wiene, Robert   1881-1938........ TCLC 56

Wieners, John   1934-............... CLC 7
See also CA 13-16R; DLB 16

Wiesel, Elie(zer)
1928- ...... CLC 3, 5, 11, 37; DA; DAB;
DAC
See also AAYA 7; AITN 1; CA 5-8R;
CAAS 4; CANR 8, 40; DAM MST,
NOV; DLB 83; DLBY 87; INT CANR-8;
MTCW; SATA 56

Wiggins, Marianne 1947-.......... CLC 57
See also BEST 89:3; CA 130

Wight, James Alfred   1916-
See Herriot, James
See also CA 77-80; SATA 55;
SATA-Brief 44

Wilbur, Richard (Purdy)
1921- ... CLC 3, 6, 9, 14, 53; DA; DAB;
DAC
See also CA 1-4R; CABS 2; CANR 2, 29;
DAM MST, POET; DLB 5;
INT CANR-29; MTCW; SATA 9

Wild, Peter   1940-................ CLC 14
See also CA 37-40R; DLB 5

Wilde, Oscar (Fingal O'Flahertie Wills)
1854(?)-1900 .... TCLC 1, 8, 23, 41; DA;
DAB; DAC; SSC 11; WLC
See also CA 104; 119; CDBLB 1890-1914;
DAM DRAM, MST, NOV; DLB 10, 19,
34, 57, 141, 156; SATA 24

Wilder, Billy .... CLC 20
See also Wilder, Samuel
See also DLB 26

Wilder, Samuel   1906-
See Wilder, Billy
See also CA 89-92

Wilder, Thornton (Niven)
1897-1975 ...... CLC 1, 5, 6, 10, 15, 35,
82; DA; DAB; DAC; DC 1; WLC
See also AITN 2; CA 13-16R; 61-64;
CANR 40; DAM DRAM, MST, NOV;
DLB 4, 7, 9; MTCW

Wilding, Michael   1942-.......... CLC 73
See also CA 104; CANR 24, 49

Wiley, Richard   1944-............. CLC 44
See also CA 121; 129

Wilhelm, Kate .... CLC 7
See also Wilhelm, Katie Gertrude
See also CAAS 5; DLB 8; INT CANR-17

Wilhelm, Katie Gertrude   1928-
See Wilhelm, Kate
See also CA 37-40R; CANR 17, 36; MTCW

Wilkins, Mary
See Freeman, Mary Eleanor Wilkins

Willard, Nancy   1936-........... CLC 7, 37
See also CA 89-92; CANR 10, 39; CLR 5;
DLB 5, 52; MAICYA; MTCW;
SATA 37, 71; SATA-Brief 30

Williams, C(harles) K(enneth)
1936- .... CLC 33, 56
See also CA 37-40R; DAM POET; DLB 5

Williams, Charles
See Collier, James L(incoln)

Williams, Charles (Walter Stansby)
1886-1945 .... TCLC 1, 11
See also CA 104; DLB 100, 153

Williams, (George) Emlyn
1905-1987 .... CLC 15
See also CA 104; 123; CANR 36;
DAM DRAM; DLB 10, 77; MTCW

Williams, Hugo   1942-............. CLC 42
See also CA 17-20R; CANR 45; DLB 40

Williams, J. Walker
See Wodehouse, P(elham) G(renville)

Williams, John A(lfred)
1925- .... CLC 5, 13; BLC
See also BW 2; CA 53-56; CAAS 3;
CANR 6, 26; DAM MULT; DLB 2, 33;
INT CANR-6

Williams, Jonathan (Chamberlain)
1929- .... CLC 13
See also CA 9-12R; CAAS 12; CANR 8;
DLB 5

Williams, Joy   1944-.............. CLC 31
See also CA 41-44R; CANR 22, 48

Williams, Norman   1952- .... CLC 39
See also CA 118

Williams, Sherley Anne
1944- .... CLC 89; BLC
See also BW 2; CA 73-76; CANR 25;
DAM MULT, POET; DLB 41;
INT CANR-25; SATA 78

Williams, Shirley
See Williams, Sherley Anne

Williams, Tennessee
1911-1983 ..... CLC 1, 2, 5, 7, 8, 11, 15,
19, 30, 39, 45, 71; DA; DAB; DAC;
DC 4; WLC
See also AITN 1, 2; CA 5-8R; 108;
CABS 3; CANR 31; CDALB 1941-1968;
DAM DRAM, MST; DLB 7; DLBD 4;
DLBY 83; MTCW

Williams, Thomas (Alonzo)
1926-1990 .... CLC 14
See also CA 1-4R; 132; CANR 2

Williams, William C.
See Williams, William Carlos

Williams, William Carlos
1883-1963 .... CLC 1, 2, 5, 9, 13, 22, 42,
67; DA; DAB; DAC; PC 7
See also CA 89-92; CANR 34;
CDALB 1917-1929; DAM MST, POET;
DLB 4, 16, 54, 86; MTCW

Williamson, David (Keith) 1942-.... CLC 56
See also CA 103; CANR 41

Williamson, Ellen Douglas   1905-1984
See Douglas, Ellen
See also CA 17-20R; 114; CANR 39

Williamson, Jack................ CLC 29
See also Williamson, John Stewart
See also CAAS 8; DLB 8

Williamson, John Stewart   1908-
See Williamson, Jack
See also CA 17-20R; CANR 23

Willie, Frederick
See Lovecraft, H(oward) P(hillips)

Willingham, Calder (Baynard, Jr.)
1922-1995 .... CLC 5, 51
See also CA 5-8R; 147; CANR 3; DLB 2,
44; MTCW

Willis, Charles
See Clarke, Arthur C(harles)

Willy
See Colette, (Sidonie-Gabrielle)

Willy, Colette
See Colette, (Sidonie-Gabrielle)

Wilson, A(ndrew) N(orman) 1950- .. CLC 33
See also CA 112; 122; DLB 14, 155

Wilson, Angus (Frank Johnstone)
1913-1991 .. CLC 2, 3, 5, 25, 34; SSC 21
See also CA 5-8R; 134; CANR 21; DLB 15,
139, 155; MTCW

PC Cumulative Nationality Index

PC Cumulative Title Index

Title Index

Title Index

Title Index

Title Index

"Theme and Variations" (Pasternak)   6:251
Themes and Variations (Pasternak)
    See *Temy i variatsi*
"Then I Saw What the Calling Was"
    (Rukeyser)   12:223
"Theodore Dreiser" (Masters)   1:343
"Theodore the Poet" (Masters)   1:345
"Theology" (Dunbar)   5:120, 125, 127
"Theology" (Hughes)   7:123, 159
"Theory of Art" (Baraka)   4:9
"Theory of Evil" (Hayden)   6:194, 196
"Theory of Flight" (Rukeyser)   12:207, 218,
    225
Theory of Flight (Rukeyser)   12:202-03, 206,
    209-10, 226-27, 235-36
"Theory of Maya" (Tagore)
    See "Mayavada"
"ther may have been a tunnel thru which my
    train rolld" (Bissett)   14:34
"There" (Verlaine)   2:416
"There Are Blk/Puritans" (Sanchez)   9:218
"There Are Orioles in Woods and Lasting
    Length of Vowels" (Mandelstam)   14:141
"There Has to Be a Jail for Ladies" (Merton)
    10:341
"There Is Only One of Everything" (Atwood)
    8:23, 28
"There Once Lived a Poor Knight" (Pushkin)
    See "Zhil Na Svete Rytsar' Bednyi"
"There Shines the Moon, at Noon of Night"
    (Bronte)   8:75
"There Should be No Despair" (Bronte)
    8:68-9
"There Was a Child Went Forth" (Whitman)
    3:392, 396, 415
"There Was a Lad Was Born in Kyle" (Burns)
    6:76
"There Was a Poor Knight" (Pushkin)
    See "Zhil Na Svete Rytsar' Bednyi"
"There Was a Saviour" (Thomas)   2:390
Therefore (Mallarme)
    See *Igitur*
"These" (Williams)   7:360, 362-63
"These States: To Miami Presidential
    Convention" (Ginsberg)   4:82
"Theseus and Ariadne" (Graves)   6:136-37,
    144, 146
"Thetis" (H. D.)   5:267-68
"They" (Sassoon)   12:241, 249, 263, 275, 277-
    78, 286
"They Are Not Missed" (Toomer)   7:338-39
"They Are Not Ready" (Madhubuti)   5:338
"They Eat Out" (Atwood)   8:6
"They'd Never Know Me Now" (Masters)
    1:344
"The Thin People" (Plath)   1:388, 406
"Things of August" (Stevens)   6:313
Things Taking Place (Swenson)
    See *New and Selected Things Taking Place*
"Think No More, Lad: Laugh, Be Jolly"
    (Housman)   2:179, 183, 185
"Think of It" (Celan)   10:98
"The Thinker" (Williams)   7:353
"Thinking about El Salvador" (Levertov)
    11:198
"Thinking of Old Tu Fu" (Matsuo Basho)
    3:10
"Third Degree" (Hughes)   1:248
"The Third Dimension" (Levertov)   11:159
"Third Elegy" (Rilke)   2:271
"Third Georgic" (Vergil)   12:361

"Third Hymn to Lenin" (MacDiarmid)
    9:180-81, 197
"Third Psalm" (Sexton)   2:367
The Third Residence (Neruda)
    See *Tercera residencia, 1935-1945*
Third Residence (Neruda)
    See *Tercera residencia, 1935-1945*
"The Third Sermon of the Warpland"
    (Brooks)   7:88-9
"Third Song" (Rilke)   2:273
The Third Symphony (Bely)
    See *Vozvrat: Tretiia simfoniia*
Third Voronezh Notebook (Mandelstam)
    14:149, 152, 155
"The Third World" (Ferlinghetti)   1:186
"Third World Calling" (Ferlinghetti)   1:183
"Thirteen Ways of Looking at a Blackbird"
    (Stevens)   6:293, 326-27
Thirty Poems (Merton)   10:338-39, 350-51
"Thirty Rhymes to Hermit Chang Piao" (Tu
    Fu)   9:326
"This Bread I Break" (Thomas)   2:379, 389
"This Cold Man" (Page)
    See "Now This Cold Man"
"This Compost" (Whitman)   3:410
"This Day" (Levertov)   11:198-99, 201
"This Florida: 1924" (Williams)   7:369
"This Frieze of Birds" (Page)   12:168
"This Is a Photograph of Me" (Atwood)
    8:12, 23
"This is Disgraceful and Abominable" (Smith)
    12:293, 309
"This Is Just to Say" (Williams)   7:363, 399,
    401
"This Is Noon" (Graves)   6:166
"This Is Their Fault" (Forche)   10:142
"This (Let's Remember) day Died Again and"
    (Cummings)   5:107
"This Life" (Dove)   6:108
"This Lime-Tree Bower My Prison"
    (Coleridge)   11:51, 53, 72, 83, 88-9, 97, 104,
    107
"This Near-At-Hand" (Rossetti)   7:276
"This Place Rumord to Have Been Sodom"
    (Duncan)   2:127
"This Side of Truth" (Thomas)   2:390
"This Urn Contains Earth from German
    Concentration Camps" (Lorde)   12:136
"This Was a Poet" (Dickinson)   1:96, 102
"Thistles" (Hughes)   7:121, 137
Thomas and Beulah (Dove)   6:104, 107, 110-
    20, 122
"Thomas at the Wheel" (Dove)   6:111
"Thompson's Lunch Room" (Lowell)   13:79
"Thorkild's Song" (Kipling)   3:183
"The Thorn" (Wordsworth)   4:381, 402, 412,
    416-17, 426, 428
"Thorn Piece" (Lowell)   13:85
"Those Times" (Sexton)   2:362-63, 370
"Those Various Scalpels" (Moore)   4:263-64,
    270
"Those Winter Sundays" (Hayden)   6:194-95
"The Thou" (Montale)
    See "Il tu"
"Thou Famished Grave, I Will Not Fill Thee
    Yet" (Millay)   6:242
"A Thought of Columbus" (Whitman)
    See "A Prayer of Columbus"
"The Thought-Fox" (Hughes)   7:120, 158,
    166, 168-69
"Thoughts about the Christian Doctrine of
    Eternal Hell" (Smith)   12:301, 325, 333

"Thoughts about the Person from Porlock"
    (Smith)   12:293, 330, 350
"Thoughts in 1932" (Sassoon)   12:252
"Thoughts on a Breath" (Ginsberg)   4:76
"Thoughts on His Excellency Major General
    Lee" ("On Major General Lee") (Wheatley)
    3:337
"Thoughts on the Works of Providence" ("On
    the Works of Providence") (Wheatley)
    3:332, 339, 358, 361, 363
"Thousand League Pool" (Tu Fu)   9:333
Thread-Suns (Celan)
    See *Fadensonnen*
"3 A.M. Kitchen: My Father Talking"
    (Gallagher)   9:53
"The Three Captains" (Kipling)   3:157
"The Three Decker" (Kipling)   3:161
"Three Desk Objects" (Atwood)   8:2, 13
"Three Ghosts" (Sandburg)   2:309
"The Three Grayes" (Coleridge)   11:117
"Three Green Windows" (Sexton)   2:363
*Three Hundred and Sixty Degrees of Blackness
    Comin at You* (Sanchez)   9:222
Three Material Cantos (Neruda)
    See *Homenaje a Pablo Neruda de los poetas
    espanoles: Tres cantos materiales*
Three Material Songs (Neruda)
    See *Homenaje a Pablo Neruda de los poetas
    espanoles: Tres cantos materiales*
"Three Meditations" (Levertov)   11:169
"Three Modes of History and Culture"
    (Baraka)   4:16
"Three Movements and a Coda" (Baraka)
    4:9, 19, 24
"Three Nuns" (Rossetti)   7:277
"Three Postcards from the Monastery"
    (Merton)   10:332
"Three Songs" (Crane)   3:106
The Three Taverns (Robinson)   1:465-66, 468
"Three Times in Love" (Graves)   6:172
"Three Travellers Watch a Sunrise" (Stevens)
    6:295
"Three United States Sonnets" (Cummings)
    5:94
"Three White Vases" (Swenson)   14:273
"Threes" (Atwood)   8:21
"Three-year-old" (Tagore)
    See "Tritiya"
Thrones, 96-109 de los cantares (Pound)
    4:337-38, 352, 353, 357
"Through Corralitos under Rolls of Cloud"
    (Rich)   5:401
"Through Nightmare" (Graves)   6:137, 173
"Through the Looking Glass" (Ferlinghetti)
    1:173
"Throughout Our Lands" (Milosz)   8:187,
    194, 214
"Throw Away Thy Rod" ("Discipline")
    (Herbert)   4:103, 121
A Throw of the Dice Never Will Abolish Chance
    (Mallarme)
    See *Un coup de dés jamais n'abolira le
    hasard*
A Throw of the Dice Will Never Abolish Chance
    (Mallarme)
    See *Un coup de dés jamais n'abolira le
    hasard*
"Thrushes" (Hughes)   7:119, 169
"Thrushes" (Sassoon)   12:253
"Thrust and Riposte" (Montale)
    See "Botta e riposte"
"Thunder Can Break" (Okigbo)

ISBN 0-7876-0473-9